Fundamentals of
CORPORATE FINANCE

The McGraw-Hill Education Series in Finance, Insurance, and Real Estate

Financial Management

Block, Hirt, and Danielsen
Foundations of Financial Management
Sixteenth Edition

Brealey, Myers, and Allen
Principles of Corporate Finance
Twelfth Edition

Brealey, Myers, and Allen
Principles of Corporate Finance, Concise
Second Edition

Brealey, Myers, and Marcus
Fundamentals of Corporate Finance
Ninth Edition

Brooks
FinGame Online 5.0

Bruner, Eades, and Schill
Case Studies in Finance: Managing for Corporate Value Creation
Eighth Edition

Cornett, Adair, and Nofsinger
Finance: Applications and Theory
Fourth Edition

Cornett, Adair, and Nofsinger
M: Finance
Fourth Edition

DeMello
Cases in Finance
Third Edition

Grinblatt (editor)
Stephen A. Ross, Mentor: Influence through Generations

Grinblatt and Titman
Financial Markets and Corporate Strategy
Second Edition

Higgins
Analysis for Financial Management
Twelfth Edition

Ross, Westerfield, Jaffe, and Jordan
Corporate Finance
Eleventh Edition

Ross, Westerfield, Jaffe, and Jordan
Corporate Finance: Core Principles and Applications
Fifth Edition

Ross, Westerfield, and Jordan
Essentials of Corporate Finance
Ninth Edition

Ross, Westerfield, and Jordan
Fundamentals of Corporate Finance
Twelfth Edition

Shefrin
Behavioral Corporate Finance: Decisions that Create Value
Second Edition

Investments

Bodie, Kane, and Marcus
Essentials of Investments
Tenth Edition

Bodie, Kane, and Marcus
Investments
Eleventh Edition

Hirt and Block
Fundamentals of Investment Management
Tenth Edition

Jordan, Miller, and Dolvin
Fundamentals of Investments: Valuation and Management
Eighth Edition

Stewart, Piros, and Heisler
Running Money: Professional Portfolio Management
First Edition

Sundaram and Das
Derivatives: Principles and Practice
Second Edition

Financial Institutions and Markets

Rose and Hudgins
Bank Management and Financial Services
Ninth Edition

Rose and Marquis
Financial Institutions and Markets
Eleventh Edition

Saunders and Cornett
Financial Institutions Management: A Risk Management Approach
Ninth Edition

Saunders and Cornett
Financial Markets and Institutions
Seventh Edition

International Finance

Eun and Resnick
International Financial Management
Eighth Edition

Real Estate

Brueggeman and Fisher
Real Estate Finance and Investments
Sixteenth Edition

Ling and Archer
Real Estate Principles: A Value Approach
Fifth Edition

Financial Planning and Insurance

Allen, Melone, Rosenbloom, and Mahoney
Retirement Plans: 401(k)s, IRAs, and Other Deferred Compensation Approaches
Twelfth Edition

Altfest
Personal Financial Planning
Second Edition

Harrington and Niehaus
Risk Management and Insurance
Second Edition

Kapoor, Dlabay, Hughes, and Hart
Focus on Personal Finance: An Active Approach to Help You Achieve Financial Literacy
Sixth Edition

Kapoor, Dlabay, Hughes, and Hart
Personal Finance
Twelfth Edition

Walker and Walker
Personal Finance: Building Your Future
Second Edition

Fundamentals of
CORPORATE FINANCE

Twelfth Edition

Stephen A. Ross

Randolph W. Westerfield
University of Southern California, Emeritus

Bradford D. Jordan
University of Kentucky

Mc
Graw
Hill
Education

FUNDAMENTALS OF CORPORATE FINANCE

Published by McGraw-Hill Education, 2 Penn Plaza, New York, NY 10121. Copyright ©2019 by McGraw-Hill Education. All rights reserved. Printed in the United States of America. No part of this publication may be reproduced or distributed in any form or by any means, or stored in a database or retrieval system, without the prior written consent of McGraw-Hill Education, including, but not limited to, in any network or other electronic storage or transmission, or broadcast for distance learning.

Some ancillaries, including electronic and print components, may not be available to customers outside the United States.

This book is printed on acid-free paper.

1 2 3 4 5 6 7 8 9 LWI 21 20 19 18

ISBN 978-1-260-09190-8

MHID 1-260-09190-2

Cover Image: ©*Jose A. Bernat Bacete/Getty Images*

The Internet addresses listed in the text were accurate at the time of publication. The inclusion of a website does not indicate an endorsement by the authors or McGraw-Hill Education, and McGraw-Hill Education does not guarantee the accuracy of the information presented at these sites.

mheducation.com/highered

To Stephen A. Ross and family

Our great friend, colleague, and coauthor Steve Ross passed away on March 3, 2017, while we were working on this edition of *Fundamentals of Corporate Finance*. Steve's influence on our textbook is seminal, deep, and enduring, and we will miss him greatly. We are confident that on the foundation of Steve's lasting and invaluable contributions, our textbook will continue to reach the highest level of excellence that we all aspire to.

R.W.W.   B.D.J.

STEPHEN A. ROSS

Stephen A. Ross was the Franco Modigliani Professor of Finance and Economics at the Sloan School of Management, Massachusetts Institute of Technology. One of the most widely published authors in finance and economics, Professor Ross was widely recognized for his work in developing the Arbitrage Pricing Theory and his substantial contributions to the discipline through his research in signaling, agency theory, option pricing, and the theory of the term structure of interest rates, among other topics. A past president of the American Finance Association, he also served as an associate editor of several academic and practitioner journals. He was a trustee of CalTech. He died suddenly in March of 2017.

RANDOLPH W. WESTERFIELD

Marshall School of Business, University of Southern California

Randolph W. Westerfield is Dean Emeritus and the Charles B. Thornton Professor in Finance Emeritus of the University of Southern California's Marshall School of Business. Professor Westerfield came to USC from the Wharton School, University of Pennsylvania, where he was the chairman of the finance department and a member of the finance faculty for 20 years. He is a member of the board of trustees of Oaktree Capital mutual funds. His areas of expertise include corporate financial policy, investment management, and stock market price behavior.

BRADFORD D. JORDAN

Gatton College of Business and Economics, University of Kentucky

Bradford D. Jordan is Professor of Finance and holder of the duPont Endowed Chair in Banking and Financial Services at the University of Kentucky. He has a long-standing interest in both applied and theoretical issues in corporate finance and has extensive experience teaching all levels of corporate finance and financial management policy. Professor Jordan has published numerous articles on issues such as cost of capital, capital structure, and the behavior of security prices. He is a past president of the Southern Finance Association, and he is coauthor of *Fundamentals of Investments: Valuation and Management,* 8e, a leading investments text, also published by McGraw-Hill.

When the three of us decided to write a book, we were united by one strongly held principle: Corporate finance should be developed in terms of a few integrated, powerful ideas. We believed that the subject was all too often presented as a collection of loosely related topics, unified primarily by virtue of being bound together in one book, and we thought there must be a better way.

One thing we knew for certain was that we didn't want to write a "me-too" book. So, with a lot of help, we took a hard look at what was truly important and useful. In doing so, we were led to eliminate topics of dubious relevance, downplay purely theoretical issues, and minimize the use of extensive and elaborate calculations to illustrate points that are either intuitively obvious or of limited practical use.

As a result of this process, three basic themes became our central focus in writing *Fundamentals of Corporate Finance:*

AN EMPHASIS ON INTUITION

We always try to separate and explain the principles at work on a commonsense, intuitive level before launching into any specifics. The underlying ideas are discussed first in very general terms and then by way of examples that illustrate in more concrete terms how a financial manager might proceed in a given situation.

A UNIFIED VALUATION APPROACH

We treat net present value (NPV) as the basic concept underlying corporate finance. Many texts stop well short of consistently integrating this important principle. The most basic and important notion, that NPV represents the excess of market value over cost, often is lost in an overly mechanical approach that emphasizes computation at the expense of comprehension. In contrast, every subject we cover is firmly rooted in valuation, and care is taken throughout to explain how particular decisions have valuation effects.

A MANAGERIAL FOCUS

Students shouldn't lose sight of the fact that financial management concerns management. We emphasize the role of the financial manager as decision maker, and we stress the need for managerial input and judgment. We consciously avoid "black box" approaches to finance, and, where appropriate, the approximate, pragmatic nature of financial analysis is made explicit, possible pitfalls are described, and limitations are discussed.

In retrospect, looking back to our 1991 first edition IPO, we had the same hopes and fears as any entrepreneurs. How would we be received in the market? At the time, we had no idea that 26 years later, we would be working on a twelfth edition. We certainly never dreamed that in those years we would work with friends and colleagues from around the world to create country-specific Australian, Canadian, and South African editions, an International edition, Chinese, French, Polish, Portuguese, Thai, Russian, Korean, and Spanish language editions, and an entirely separate book, *Essentials of Corporate Finance,* now in its ninth edition.

Today, as we prepare to once more enter the market, our goal is to stick with the basic principles that have brought us this far. However, based on the enormous amount of feedback we have received from you and your colleagues, we have made this edition and its package even *more flexible* than previous editions. We offer flexibility in coverage, as customized editions of this text can be crafted in any combination through McGraw-Hill's *CREATE* system, and flexibility in pedagogy, by providing a wide variety of features in the book to help students to learn about corporate finance. We also provide flexibility in package options by offering the most extensive collection of teaching, learning, and technology aids of any corporate finance text. Whether you use only the textbook, or the book in conjunction with our other products, we believe you will find a combination with this edition that will meet your current as well as your changing course needs.

Stephen A. Ross
Randolph W. Westerfield
Bradford D. Jordan

THE TAX CUTS AND JOBS ACT (TCJA) IS INCORPORATED THROUGHOUT ROSS FUNDAMENTALS OF CORPORATE FINANCE, 12E.

There are six primary areas of change and will be reflected in the 12th edition:

1. Corporate tax. The new, flat-rate 21 percent corporate rate is discussed and compared to the old progressive system. The new rate is used throughout the text in examples and problems. Entities other than C corporations still face progressive taxation, so the discussion of marginal versus average tax rates remains relevant and is retained.
2. Bonus depreciation. For a limited time, businesses can take a 100 percent depreciation charge the first year for most non-real estate, MACRS-qualified investments. This "bonus depreciation" ends in a few years and MACRS returns, so the MACRS material remains relevant and is retained. The impact of bonus depreciation is illustrated in various problems.
3. Limitations on interest deductions. The amount of interest that may be deducted for tax purposes is limited. Interest that cannot be deducted can be carried forward to future tax years (but not carried back; see next).
4. Carrybacks. Net operating loss (NOL) carrybacks have been eliminated and NOL carryforward deductions are limited in any one tax year.
5. Dividends received tax break. The tax break on dividends received by a corporation has been reduced, meaning that the portion subject to taxation has increased.
6. Repatriation. The distinction between U.S. and non-U.S. profits has been essentially eliminated. All "overseas" assets, both liquid and illiquid, are subject to a one-time "deemed" tax.

With the 12e we've also included coverage of:

- Clawbacks and deferred compensation
- Inversions
- Negative interest rates
- NYSE market operations
- Direct Listings and Cryptocurrency Initial Coin Offerings (ICOs)
- Regulation CF
- Brexit
- Repatriation
- Changes in lease accounting

This book was designed and developed explicitly for a first course in business or corporate finance, for both finance majors and non-majors alike. In terms of background or prerequisites, the book is nearly self-contained, assuming some familiarity with basic algebra and accounting concepts, while still reviewing important accounting principles very early on. The organization of this text has been developed to give instructors the flexibility they need.

The following grid presents, for each chapter, some of the most significant features as well as a few selected chapter highlights of the 12th edition of *Fundamentals*. Of course, in every chapter, opening vignettes, boxed features, in-chapter illustrated examples using real companies, and end-of-chapter material have been thoroughly updated as well.

Chapters	Selected Topics of Interest	Benefits to You
PART 1 Overview of Corporate Finance		
CHAPTER 1 Introduction to Corporate Finance	Goal of the firm and agency problems.	Stresses value creation as the most fundamental aspect of management and describes agency issues that can arise.
	Ethics, financial management, and executive compensation.	Brings in real-world issues concerning conflicts of interest and current controversies surrounding ethical conduct and management pay.
	Sarbanes-Oxley.	Up-to-date discussion of Sarbanes-Oxley and its implications and impact.
	New: Clawbacks and deferred compensation.	Discusses new rules on bonus clawbacks and deferred compensation.
	Minicase: The McGee Cake Company.	Examines the choice of organization form for a small business.
CHAPTER 2 Financial Statements, Taxes, and Cash Flow	Cash flow vs. earnings.	Clearly defines cash flow and spells out the differences between cash flow and earnings.
	Market values vs. book values.	Emphasizes the relevance of market values over book values.
	Brief discussion of average corporate tax rates.	Highlights the variation in corporate tax rates across industries in practice.
	New: Inversions.	Discusses the controversial issue of mergers that are also tax inversions.
	Minicase: Cash Flows and Financial.	Reinforces key cash flow concepts in a small business setting.
	Statements at Sunset Boards, Inc.	

Chapters	Selected Topics of Interest	Benefits to You
PART 2 Financial Statements and Long-Term Financial Planning		
CHAPTER 3 Working with Financial Statements	Expanded DuPont analysis.	Expands the basic DuPont equation to better explore the interrelationships between operating and financial performance.
	DuPont analysis for real companies using data from S&P *Market Insight*.	Analysis shows students how to get and use real-world data, thereby applying key chapter ideas.
	Ratio and financial statement analysis using smaller firm data.	Uses firm data from *RMA* to show students how to actually get and evaluate financial statement benchmarks.
	Understanding financial statements.	Thorough coverage of standardized financial statements and key ratios.
	The enterprise value-EBITDA ratio.	Defines enterprise value (EV) and discusses the widely used EV-EBITDA ratio.
	Minicase: Ratio Analysis at S&S Air, Inc.	Illustrates the use of ratios and some pitfalls in a small business context.
CHAPTER 4 Long-Term Financial Planning and Growth	Expanded discussion of sustainable growth calculations.	Illustrates the importance of financial planning in a small firm.
	Explanation of alternative formulas for sustainable and internal growth rates.	Explanation of growth rate formulas clears up a common misunderstanding about these formulas and the circumstances under which alternative formulas are correct.
	Thorough coverage of sustainable growth as a planning tool.	Provides a vehicle for examining the interrelationships between operations, financing, and growth.
	Long-range financial planning.	Covers the percentage of sales approach to creating pro forma statements.
	Minicase: Planning for Growth at S&S Air.	Discusses the importance of a financial plan and capacity utilization for a small business.
PART 3 Valuation of Future Cash Flows		
CHAPTER 5 Introduction to Valuation: The Time Value of Money	First of two chapters on time value of money.	Relatively short chapter introduces just the basic ideas on time value of money to get students started on this traditionally difficult topic.
CHAPTER 6 Discounted Cash Flow Valuation	Growing annuities and perpetuities.	Covers more advanced time value topics with numerous examples, calculator tips, and Excel spreadsheet exhibits. Contains many real-world examples.
	Second of two chapters on time value of money.	Explores the financial pros and cons of pursuing an MBA degree.
	Minicase: The MBA Decision.	

Chapters	Selected Topics of Interest	Benefits to You
CHAPTER 7 Interest Rates and Bond Valuation	*New:* Negative interest rates.	New chapter opener explores the recent phenomenon of negative interest on government bonds.
	Bond valuation.	Complete coverage of bond valuation and bond features.
	Interest rates.	Discusses real versus nominal rates and the determinants of the term structure.
	"Clean" vs. "dirty" bond prices and accrued interest.	Clears up the pricing of bonds between coupon payment dates and also bond market quoting conventions.
	TRACE system and transparency in the corporate bond market.	Up-to-date discussion of new developments in fixed income with regard to price, volume, and transactions reporting.
	"Make-whole" call provisions.	Up-to-date discussion of a relatively new type of call provision that has become very common.
	Islamic finance.	Provides basics of some important concepts in Islamic finance.
	Minicase: Financing S&S Air's Expansion Plans with a Bond Issue.	Discusses the issues that come up in selling bonds to the public.
CHAPTER 8 Stock Valuation	Stock valuation.	Thorough coverage of constant and non-constant growth models.
	New: NYSE market operations.	Up-to-date description of major stock market operations.
	Valuation using multiples.	Illustrates using PE and price/sales ratios for equity valuation.
	Minicase: Stock Valuation at Ragan, Inc.	Illustrates the difficulties and issues surrounding small business valuation.

PART 4   Capital Budgeting

Chapters	Selected Topics of Interest	Benefits to You
CHAPTER 9 Net Present Value and Other Investment Criteria	First of three chapters on capital budgeting.	Relatively short chapter introduces key ideas on an intuitive level to help students with this traditionally difficult topic.
	NPV, IRR, payback, discounted payback, MIRR, and accounting rate of return.	Consistent, balanced examination of advantages and disadvantages of various criteria.
	Minicase: Bullock Gold Mining.	Explores different capital budgeting techniques with nonstandard cash flows.
CHAPTER 10 Making Capital Investment Decisions	Project cash flow.	Thorough coverage of project cash flows and the relevant numbers for a project analysis.
	Alternative cash flow definitions.	Emphasizes the equivalence of various formulas, thereby removing common misunderstandings.
	Special cases of DCF analysis.	Considers important applications of chapter tools.
	Minicase: Conch Republic Electronics, Part 1.	Analyzes capital budgeting issues and complexities.
CHAPTER 11 Project Analysis and Evaluation	Sources of value.	Stresses the need to understand the economic basis for value creation in a project.
	Scenario and sensitivity "what-if" analyses.	Illustrates how to actually apply and interpret these tools in a project analysis.
	Break-even analysis.	Covers cash, accounting, and financial break-even levels.
	Minicase: Conch Republic Electronics, Part 2.	Illustrates the use of sensitivity analysis in capital budgeting.

Chapters	Selected Topics of Interest	Benefits to You
PART 5 Risk and Return		
CHAPTER 12 Some Lessons from Capital Market History	Expanded discussion of geometric vs. arithmetic returns.	Discusses calculation and interpretation of geometric returns. Clarifies common misconceptions regarding appropriate use of arithmetic vs. geometric average returns.
	Capital market history.	Extensive coverage of historical returns, volatilities, and risk premiums.
	Market efficiency.	Efficient markets hypothesis discussed along with common misconceptions.
	The equity risk premium.	Section discusses the equity premium puzzle and latest international evidence.
	The 2008 experience.	Section on the stock market turmoil of 2008.
	Minicase: A Job at S&S Air.	Discusses selection of investments for a 401(k) plan.
CHAPTER 13 Return, Risk, and the Security Market Line	Diversification and systematic and unsystematic risk.	Illustrates basics of risk and return in a straightforward fashion.
	Beta and the security market line.	Develops the security market line with an intuitive approach that bypasses much of the usual portfolio theory and statistics.
	Minicase: The Beta for Colgate-Palmolive.	Detailed discussion of beta estimation.
PART 6 Cost of Capital and Long-Term Financial Policy		
CHAPTER 14 Cost of Capital	Cost of capital estimation.	Contains a complete, web-based illustration of cost of capital for a real company.
	Geometric vs. arithmetic growth rates.	Both approaches are used in practice. Clears up issues surrounding growth rate estimates.
	Firm valuation.	Develops the free cash flow approach to firm valuation.
	Minicase: Cost of Capital for Swan Motors.	Covers pure play approach to cost of capital estimation.
CHAPTER 15 Raising Capital	Dutch auction IPOs.	Explains uniform price auctions.
	New: Regulation CF.	Explains the new Regulation CF for crowdfunding and provides some examples.
	IPO "quiet periods."	Explains the SEC's quiet period rules.
	Rights vs. warrants.	Clarifies the optionlike nature of rights prior to their expiration dates.
	IPO valuation.	Extensive, up-to-date discussion of IPOs, including the 1999–2000 period.
	Minicase: S&S Air Goes Public.	Covers the key parts of the IPO process for a small firm.
CHAPTER 16 Financial Leverage and Capital Structure Policy	Basics of financial leverage.	Illustrates effect of leverage on risk and return.
	Optimal capital structure.	Describes the basic trade-offs leading to an optimal capital structure.
	Financial distress and bankruptcy.	Briefly surveys the bankruptcy process.
	Minicase: Stephenson Real Estate Recapitalization.	Discusses optimal capital structure for a medium-sized firm.

Chapters	Selected Topics of Interest	Benefits to You
CHAPTER 17 Dividends and Payout Policy	Very recent survey evidence on dividend policy.	New survey results show the most important (and least important) factors considered by financial managers in setting dividend policy.
	Effect of new tax laws.	Discusses implications of new, lower dividend and capital gains rates.
	Dividends and dividend policy.	Describes dividend payments and the factors favoring higher and lower payout policies.
	Optimal payout policy.	Extensive discussion of the latest research and survey evidence on dividend policy, including life-cycle theory.
	Stock repurchases.	Thorough coverage of buybacks as an alternative to cash dividends.
	Minicase: Electronic Timing, Inc.	Describes the dividend/share repurchase issue for a small company.

PART 7 Short-Term Financial Planning and Management

Chapters	Selected Topics of Interest	Benefits to You
CHAPTER 18 Short-Term Finance and Planning	Operating and cash cycles.	Stresses the importance of cash flow timing.
	Short-term financial planning.	Illustrates creation of cash budgets and potential need for financing.
	Purchase order financing.	Brief discussion of PO financing, which is popular with small and medium-sized firms.
	Minicase: Piepkorn Manufacturing Working Capital Management.	Illustrates the construction of a cash budget and short-term financial plan for a small company.
CHAPTER 19 Cash and Liquidity Management	Float management.	Thorough coverage of float management and potential ethical issues.
	Cash collection and disbursement.	Examination of systems used by firms to handle cash inflows and outflows.
	Minicase: Cash Management at Webb Corporation.	Evaluates alternative cash concentration systems for a small firm.
CHAPTER 20 Credit and Inventory Management	Credit management.	Analysis of credit policy and implementation.
	Inventory management.	Brief overview of important inventory concepts.
	Minicase: Credit Policy at Howlett Industries.	Evaluates working capital issues for a small firm.

PART 8 Topics in Corporate Finance

Chapters	Selected Topics of Interest	Benefits to You
CHAPTER 21 International Corporate Finance	Foreign exchange.	Covers essentials of exchange rates and their determination.
	International capital budgeting.	Shows how to adapt basic DCF approach to handle exchange rates.
	Exchange rate and political risk.	Discusses hedging and issues surrounding sovereign risk.
	New: Brexit.	Uses "Brexit" as an illustration of political risk.
	New: Repatriation.	New opener and in-chapter discussion of the immense overseas cash holdings by U.S. corporations.
	Minicase: S&S Air Goes International.	Discusses factors in an international expansion for a small firm.

Chapters	Selected Topics of Interest	Benefits to You
CHAPTER 22 Behavioral Finance: Implications for Financial Management	Behavioral finance.	Unique and innovative coverage of the effects of biases and heuristics on financial management decisions. "In Their Own Words" box by Hersh Shefrin.
	Case against efficient markets.	Presents the behavioral case for market inefficiency and related evidence pro and con.
	Minicase: Your 401(k) Account at S&S Air.	Illustrates the considerations to be taken when selecting investment options.
CHAPTER 23 Enterprise Risk Management	Volatility and risk.	Illustrates need to manage risk and some of the most important types of risk.
	Hedging with forwards, options, and swaps.	Shows how many risks can be managed with financial derivatives.
	Minicase: Chatman Mortgage, Inc.	Analyzes hedging of interest rate risk.
CHAPTER 24 Options and Corporate Finance	Stock options, employee stock options, and real options.	Discusses the basics of these important option types.
	Option-embedded securities.	Describes the different types of options found in corporate securities.
	Minicase: S&S Air's Convertible Bond.	Examines security issuance issues for a small firm.
CHAPTER 25 Option Valuation	Put-call parity and Black-Scholes.	Develops modern option valuation and factors influencing option values.
	Options and corporate finance.	Applies option valuation to a variety of corporate issues, including mergers and capital budgeting.
	Minicase: Exotic Cuisines Employee Stock Options.	Illustrates complexities that arise in valuing employee stock options.
CHAPTER 26 Mergers and Acquisitions	Alternatives to mergers and acquisitions.	Covers strategic alliances and joint ventures and why they are important alternatives.
	Defensive tactics.	Expanded discussion of antitakeover provisions.
	Divestitures and restructurings.	Examines important actions such as equity carve-outs, spins-offs, and split-ups.
	Mergers and acquisitions.	Develops essentials of M&A analysis, including financial, tax, and accounting issues.
	Minicase: The Birdie Golf–Hybrid Golf Merger.	Covers small business valuation for acquisition purposes.
CHAPTER 27 Leasing	*New:* Changes in lease accounting.	Discusses upcoming changes in lease accounting rules and the curtailment of "off-balance-sheet" financing.
	Leases and lease valuation.	Examines essentials of leasing, good and bad reasons for leasing, and NPV of leasing.
	Minicase: The Decision to Lease or Buy at Warf Computers.	Covers lease-or-buy and related issues for a small business.

To meet the varied needs of its intended audience, *Fundamentals of Corporate Finance* is rich in valuable learning tools and support.

CHAPTER-OPENING VIGNETTES

Vignettes drawn from real-world events introduce students to the chapter concepts.

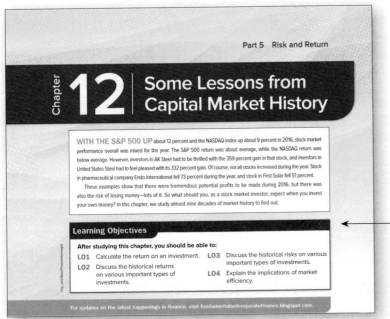

CHAPTER LEARNING OBJECTIVES

This feature maps out the topics and learning goals in every chapter. Each end-of-chapter problem and test bank question is linked to a learning objective, to help you organize your assessment of knowledge and comprehension.

PEDAGOGICAL USE OF COLOR

This learning tool continues to be an important feature of *Fundamentals of Corporate Finance*. In almost every chapter, color plays an extensive, nonschematic, and largely self-evident role. A guide to the functional use of color is on pages xlv–xlvi of this front matter.

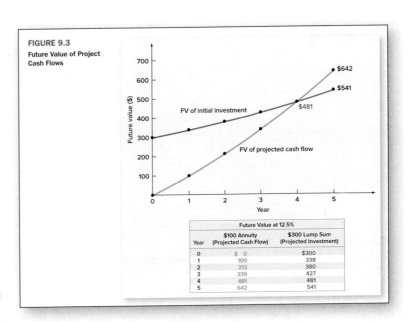

FIGURE 9.3
Future Value of Project Cash Flows

| | Future Value at 12.5% | |
Year	$100 Annuity (Projected Cash Flow)	$300 Lump Sum (Projected Investment)
0	$ 0	$300
1	100	338
2	213	380
3	339	427
4	481	481
5	642	541

IN THEIR OWN WORDS BOXES

This series of boxes features popular articles on key topics in the text written by distinguished scholars and practitioners. Boxes include essays by Merton Miller on capital structure, Fischer Black on dividends, and Roger Ibbotson on capital market history. A complete list of "In Their Own Words" boxes appears on page xliv.

IN THEIR OWN WORDS ...

Robert C. Higgins on Sustainable Growth

Most financial officers know intuitively that it takes money to make money. Rapid sales growth requires increased assets in the form of accounts receivable, inventory, and fixed plant, which, in turn, require money to pay for assets. They also know that if their company does not have the money when needed, it can literally "grow broke." The sustainable growth equation states these intuitive truths explicitly.

Sustainable growth is often used by bankers and other external analysts to assess a company's creditworthiness. They are aided in this exercise by several sophisticated computer software packages that provide detailed analyses of the company's past financial performance, including its annual sustainable growth rate.

Bankers use this information in several ways. Quick comparison of a company's actual growth rate to its sustainable rate tells the banker what issues will be at the top of management's financial agenda. If actual growth consistently exceeds sustainable growth, management's problem will be where to get the cash to finance growth. The banker thus can anticipate interest in loan products. Conversely, if sustainable growth consistently exceeds actual, the banker had best be prepared to talk about investment products, because management's problem will be what to do with all the cash that keeps piling up in the till.

Bankers also find the sustainable growth equation useful for explaining to financially inexperienced small business owners and overly optimistic entrepreneurs that, for the long-run viability of their business, it is necessary to keep growth and profitability in proper balance.

Finally, comparison of actual to sustainable growth rates helps a banker understand why a loan applicant needs money and for how long the need might continue. In one instance, a loan applicant requested $100,000 to pay off several insistent suppliers and promised to repay in a few months when he collected some accounts receivable that were coming due. A sustainable growth analysis revealed that the firm had been growing at four to six times its sustainable growth rate and that this pattern was likely to continue in the foreseeable future. This alerted the banker to the fact that impatient suppliers were only a symptom of the much more fundamental disease of overly rapid growth, and that a $100,000 loan would likely prove to be only the down payment on a much larger, multiyear commitment.

Robert C. Higgins is the Marguerite Reimers Professor of Finance, Emeritus, at the Foster School of Business at the University of Washington. He pioneered the use of sustainable growth as a tool for financial analysis.

A NOTE ABOUT SUSTAINABLE GROWTH RATE CALCULATIONS

Very commonly, the sustainable growth rate is calculated using just the numerator in our expression, ROE × b. This causes some confusion, which we can clear up here. The issue has to do with how ROE is computed. Recall that ROE is calculated as net income divided by total equity. If total equity is taken from an ending balance sheet (as we have done consistently, and is commonly done in practice), then our formula is the right one. However, if total equity is from the beginning of the period, then the simpler formula is the correct one.

WORK THE WEB

As we discussed in this chapter, ratios are an important tool for examining a company's performance. Gathering the necessary financial statements to calculate ratios can be tedious and time-consuming. Fortunately, many sites on the web provide this information for free. One of the best is www.reuters.com. We went there, entered the ticker symbol "HD" (for Home Depot), and then went to the "Financials" page. Here is an abbreviated look at the results:

	Company	Industry	Sector
Quick Ratio (MRQ)	0.42	1.03	1.26
Current Ratio (MRQ)	1.34	1.91	1.58
LT Debt to Equity (MRQ)	397.33	84.80	34.40
Total Debt to Equity (MRQ)	406.99	98.04	64.39
Interest Coverage (TTM)	18.56	14.73	3.63

The website reports the company, industry, and sector ratios. As you can see, Home Depot has lower quick and current ratios than the industry.

Questions
1. Go to www.reuters.com and find the major ratio categories listed on this website. How do the categories differ from the categories listed in this textbook?
2. Go to www.reuters.com and find all the ratios for Home Depot. How does the company compare to the industry for the ratios presented on this website?

WORK THE WEB BOXES

These boxes show students how to research financial issues using the web and then how to use the information they find to make business decisions. Work the Web boxes also include interactive follow-up questions and exercises.

REAL-WORLD EXAMPLES

Actual events are integrated throughout the text, tying chapter concepts to real life through illustration and reinforcing the relevance of the material. Some examples tie into the chapter-opening vignette for added reinforcement.

SPREADSHEET STRATEGIES

This feature introduces students to Excel and shows them how to set up spreadsheets in order to analyze common financial problems—a vital part of every business student's education.

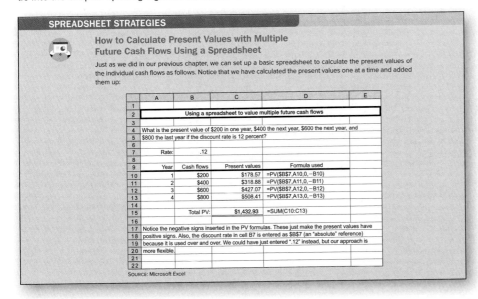

SPREADSHEET STRATEGIES

How to Calculate Present Values with Multiple Future Cash Flows Using a Spreadsheet

Just as we did in our previous chapter, we can set up a basic spreadsheet to calculate the present values of the individual cash flows as follows. Notice that we have calculated the present values one at a time and added them up:

	A	B	C	D	E
1					
2			Using a spreadsheet to value multiple future cash flows		
3					
4	What is the present value of $200 in one year, $400 the next year, $600 the next year, and				
5	$800 the last year if the discount rate is 12 percent?				
6					
7	Rate:	.12			
8					
9	Year	Cash flows	Present values	Formula used	
10	1	$200	$178.57	=PV($B$7,A10,0,−B10)	
11	2	$400	$318.88	=PV($B$7,A11,0,−B11)	
12	3	$600	$427.07	=PV($B$7,A12,0,−B12)	
13	4	$800	$508.41	=PV($B$7,A13,0,−B13)	
14					
15		Total PV:	$1,432.93	=SUM(C10:C13)	
16					
17	Notice the negative signs inserted in the PV formulas. These just make the present values have				
18	positive signs. Also, the discount rate in cell B7 is entered as $B$7 (an "absolute" reference)				
19	because it is used over and over. We could have just entered ".12" instead, but our approach is				
20	more flexible.				
21					
22					

SOURCE: Microsoft Excel

CALCULATOR HINTS

Brief calculator tutorials appear in selected chapters to help students learn or brush up on their financial calculator skills. These complement the Spreadsheet Strategies.

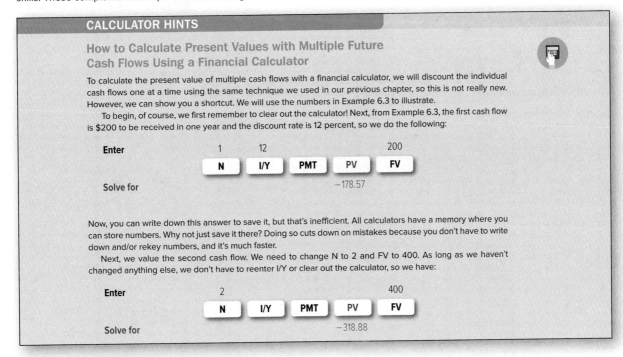

CALCULATOR HINTS

How to Calculate Present Values with Multiple Future Cash Flows Using a Financial Calculator

To calculate the present value of multiple cash flows with a financial calculator, we will discount the individual cash flows one at a time using the same technique we used in our previous chapter, so this is not really new. However, we can show you a shortcut. We will use the numbers in Example 6.3 to illustrate.

To begin, of course, we first remember to clear out the calculator! Next, from Example 6.3, the first cash flow is $200 to be received in one year and the discount rate is 12 percent, so we do the following:

Enter   1   12   200

| N | I/Y | PMT | PV | FV |

Solve for   −178.57

Now, you can write down this answer to save it, but that's inefficient. All calculators have a memory where you can store numbers. Why not just save it there? Doing so cuts down on mistakes because you don't have to write down and/or rekey numbers, and it's much faster.

Next, we value the second cash flow. We need to change N to 2 and FV to 400. As long as we haven't changed anything else, we don't have to reenter I/Y or clear out the calculator, so we have:

Enter   2   400

| N | I/Y | PMT | PV | FV |

Solve for   −318.88

CONCEPT BUILDING

Chapter sections are intentionally kept short to promote a step-by-step, building block approach to learning. Each section is then followed by a series of short concept questions that highlight the key ideas just presented. Students use these questions to make sure they can identify and understand the most important concepts as they read.

Concept Questions

3.3a What are the five groups of ratios? Give two or three examples of each kind.

3.3b Given the total debt ratio, what other two ratios can be computed? Explain how.

3.3c Turnover ratios all have one of two figures as the numerator. What are these two figures? What do these ratios measure? How do you interpret the results?

3.3d Profitability ratios all have the same figure in the numerator. What is it? What do these ratios measure? How do you interpret the results?

SUMMARY TABLES

These tables succinctly restate key principles, results, and equations. They appear whenever it is useful to emphasize and summarize a group of related concepts. For an example, see Chapter 3, page 68.

PV for a perpetuity = *C/r*

For example, an investment offers a perpetual cash flow of $500 every year. The return you require on such an investment is 8 percent. What is the value of this investment? The value of this perpetuity is:

Perpetuity PV = C/r = $500/.08 = $6,250

For future reference, Table 6.2 contains a summary of the annuity and perpetuity basic calculations we have described in this section. By now, you probably think that you'll just use online calculators to handle annuity problems. Before you do, see our nearby *Work the Web* box!

Preferred Stock   **EXAMPLE 6.7**

Preferred stock (or *preference stock*) is an important example of a perpetuity. When a corporation sells preferred stock, the buyer is promised a fixed cash dividend every period (usually every quarter) forever. This dividend must be paid before any dividend can be paid to regular stockholders—hence the term *preferred*.

Suppose the Fellini Co. wants to sell preferred stock at $100 per share. A similar issue of preferred stock already outstanding has a price of $40 per share and offers a dividend of $1 every quarter. What dividend will Fellini have to offer if the preferred stock is going to sell?

LABELED EXAMPLES

Separate numbered and titled examples are extensively integrated into the chapters. These examples provide detailed applications and illustrations of the text material in a step-by-step format. Each example is completely self-contained so students don't have to search for additional information. Based on our classroom testing, these examples are among the most useful learning aids because they provide both detail and explanation.

KEY TERMS

Key Terms are printed in bold type and defined within the text the first time they appear. They also appear in the margins with definitions for easy location and identification by the student.

EXPLANATORY WEB LINKS

These web links are provided in the margins of the text. They are specifically selected to accompany text material and provide students and instructors with a quick way to check for additional information using the Internet.

The SEC has a good overview of the bankruptcy process in its "Online Publications" section at **www.sec.gov**.

1. A petition is filed in a federal court. Corporations may file a voluntary petition, or involuntary petitions may be filed against the corporation by several of its creditors.

2. A trustee-in-bankruptcy is elected by the creditors to take over the assets of the debtor corporation. The trustee will attempt to liquidate the assets.

3. When the assets are liquidated, after payment of the bankruptcy administration costs, the proceeds are distributed among the creditors.

4. If any proceeds remain, after expenses and payments to creditors, they are distributed to the shareholders.

KEY EQUATIONS

Called out in the text, key equations are identified by an equation number. The list in Appendix B shows the key equations by chapter, providing students with a convenient reference.

Based on our examples, we can now write the general expression for the value of a bond. If a bond has (1) a face value of F paid at maturity, (2) a coupon of C paid per period, (3) t periods to maturity, and (4) a yield of r per period, its value is:

$$\text{Bond value} = C \times [1 - 1/(1 + r)^t]/r \quad + \quad F/(1 + r)^t$$

$$\text{Bond value} = \quad \begin{array}{c} \text{Present value} \\ \text{of the coupons} \end{array} \quad + \quad \begin{array}{c} \text{Present value} \\ \text{of the face amount} \end{array}$$

7.1

HIGHLIGHTED CONCEPTS

Throughout the text, important ideas are pulled out and presented in a highlighted box—signaling to students that this material is particularly relevant and critical for their understanding. For examples, Chapter 10, page 313; Chapter 13, page 434.

EXCEL MASTER

Icons in the margin identify concepts and skills covered in our unique, RWJ-created Excel Master program. For more training in Excel functions for finance, and for more practice, log on to McGraw-Hill's *Connect Finance* for *Fundamentals of Corporate Finance* to access the Excel Master files. This pedagogically superior tool will help get your students the practice they need to succeed—and to exceed expectations.

Average Returns: The First Lesson   12.3

As you've probably begun to notice, the history of capital market returns is too complicated to be of much use in its undigested form. We need to begin summarizing all these numbers. Accordingly, we discuss how to go about condensing the detailed data. We start out by calculating average returns.

Excel Master It!
Excel Master coverage online

CALCULATING AVERAGE RETURNS

The obvious way to calculate the average returns on the different investments in Table 12.1 is to add up the yearly returns and divide by 91. The result is the historical average of the individual values.

For example, if you add up the returns for the large-company stocks in Figure 12.5 for the 91 years, you will get about 10.88. The average annual return is 10.88/91 = .120, or 12.0%. You interpret this 12.0 percent just like any other average. If you were to pick a year at random from the 91-year history and you had to guess what the return in that year was, the best guess would be 12.0 percent.

AVERAGE RETURNS: THE HISTORICAL RECORD

Table 12.2 shows the average returns for the investments we have discussed. As shown, in a typical year, the small-company stocks increased in value by 16.6 percent. Notice also how much larger the returns are for stocks, compared to the returns on bonds.

These averages are, of course, nominal because we haven't worried about inflation. Notice that the average inflation rate was 3.0 percent per year over this 91-year span. The nominal return on U.S. Treasury bills was 3.4 percent per year. The average real return on

CHAPTER SUMMARY AND CONCLUSIONS

Every chapter ends with a concise, but thorough, summary of the important ideas—
helping students review the key points and providing closure to the chapter.

CHAPTER REVIEW AND SELF-TEST PROBLEM

2.1 **Cash Flow for Mara Corporation** This problem will give you some practice working with financial statements and figuring cash flow. Based on the following information for Mara Corporation, prepare an income statement for 2018 and balance sheets for 2017 and 2018. Next, following our U.S. Corporation examples in the chapter, calculate cash flow from assets, cash flow to creditors, and cash flow to stockholders for Mara for 2018. Use a 21 percent tax rate throughout. You can check your answers against ours, found in the following section.

	2017	2018
Sales	$4,203	$4,507
Cost of goods sold	2,422	2,633
Depreciation	785	952
Interest	180	196
Dividends	275	352
Current assets	2,205	2,429
Net fixed assets	7,344	7,650
Current liabilities	1,003	1,255
Long-term debt	3,106	2,085

CHAPTER REVIEW AND SELF-TEST PROBLEMS

Appearing after the Summary and Conclusions, each chapter includes a Chapter Review and Self-Test Problem section. These questions and answers allow students to test their abilities in solving key problems related to the chapter content and provide instant reinforcement.

CONCEPTS REVIEW AND CRITICAL THINKING QUESTIONS

This successful end-of-chapter section facilitates your students' knowledge of key principles, as well as their intuitive understanding of the chapter concepts. A number of the questions relate to the chapter-opening vignette—reinforcing student critical thinking skills and the learning of chapter material.

CONCEPTS REVIEW AND CRITICAL THINKING QUESTIONS

1. **Liquidity** [LO1] What does liquidity measure? Explain the trade-off a firm faces between high liquidity and low liquidity levels.
2. **Accounting and Cash Flows** [LO2] Why might the revenue and cost figures shown on a standard income statement not be representative of the actual cash inflows and outflows that occurred during a period?
3. **Book Values versus Market Values** [LO1] In preparing a balance sheet, why do you think standard accounting practice focuses on historical cost rather than market value?
4. **Operating Cash Flow** [LO2] In comparing accounting net income and operating cash flow, name two items you typically find in net income that are not in operating cash flow. Explain what each is and why it is excluded in operating cash flow.
5. **Book Values versus Market Values** [LO1] Under standard accounting rules, it is possible for a company's liabilities to exceed its assets. When this occurs, the owners' equity is negative. Can this happen with market values? Why or why not?
6. **Cash Flow from Assets** [LO4] Suppose a company's cash flow from assets is negative for a particular period. Is this necessarily a good sign or a bad sign?
7. **Operating Cash Flow** [LO4] Suppose a company's operating cash flow has been negative for several years running. Is this necessarily a good sign or a bad sign?
8. **Net Working Capital and Capital Spending** [LO4] Could a company's change in NWC be negative in a given year? (*Hint:* Yes.) Explain how this might come about. What about net capital spending?
9. **Cash Flow to Stockholders and Creditors** [LO4] Could a company's cash flow to stockholders be negative in a given year? (*Hint:* Yes.) Explain how this might come about. What about cash flow to creditors?
10. **Firm Values** [LO1] Referring back to the Boeing example used at the beginning of the chapter, note that we suggested that Boeing's stockholders probably didn't suffer as a result of the reported loss. What do you think was the basis for our conclusion?

END-OF-CHAPTER QUESTIONS AND PROBLEMS

Students learn better when they have plenty of opportunity to practice; therefore, *Fundamentals*, 12e, provides extensive end-of-chapter questions and problems. The end-of-chapter support greatly exceeds typical introductory textbooks. The questions and problems are separated into three learning levels: Basic, Intermediate, and Challenge. Answers to selected end-of-chapter material appear in Appendix C. Also, most problems are available in McGraw-Hill's *Connect*—see page xxiv for details.

QUESTIONS AND PROBLEMS

connect

BASIC
(Questions 1–10)

1. **Building a Balance Sheet** [LO1] Wims, Inc., has current assets of $4,900, net fixed assets of $27,300, current liabilities of $4,100, and long-term debt of $10,200. What is the value of the shareholders' equity account for this firm? How much is net working capital?

2. **Building an Income Statement** [LO1] Griffin's Goat Farm, Inc., has sales of $796,000, costs of $327,000, depreciation expense of $42,000, interest expense of $34,000, and a tax rate of 21 percent. What is the net income for this firm?

3. **Dividends and Retained Earnings** [LO1] Suppose the firm in Problem 2 paid out $95,000 in cash dividends. What is the addition to retained earnings?

4. **Per-Share Earnings and Dividends** [LO1] Suppose the firm in Problem 3 had 80,000 shares of common stock outstanding. What is the earnings per share, or EPS, figure? What is the dividends per share figure?

5. **Calculating OCF** [LO4] Pompeii, Inc., has sales of $46,200, costs of $23,100, depreciation expense of $2,200, and interest expense of $1,700. If the tax rate is 22 percent, what is the operating cash flow, or OCF?

END-OF-CHAPTER CASES

Located at the end of the book's chapters, these minicases focus on real-life company situations that embody important corporate finance topics. Each case presents a new scenario, data, and a dilemma. Several questions at the end of each case require students to analyze and focus on all of the material they learned from each chapter.

MINICASE

Bullock Gold Mining

Seth Bullock, the owner of Bullock Gold Mining, is evaluating a new gold mine in South Dakota. Dan Dority, the company's geologist, has just finished his analysis of the mine site. He has estimated that the mine would be productive for eight years, after which the gold would be completely mined. Dan has taken an estimate of the gold deposits to Alma Garrett, the company's financial officer. Alma has been asked by Seth to perform an analysis of the new mine and present her recommendation on whether the company should open the new mine.

Alma has used the estimates provided by Dan to determine the revenues that could be expected from the mine. She has also projected the expense of opening the mine and the annual operating expenses. If the company opens the mine, it will cost $635 million today, and it will have a cash outflow of $45 million nine years from today in costs associated with closing the mine and reclaiming the area surrounding it. The expected cash flows each year from the mine are shown in the table. Bullock Mining has a required return of 12 percent on all of its gold mines.

Year	Cash Flow
0	−$635,000,000
1	89,000,000
2	105,000,000
3	130,000,000
4	173,000,000
5	205,000,000
6	155,000,000
7	145,000,000
8	122,000,000
9	− 45,000,000

QUESTIONS

1. Construct a spreadsheet to calculate the payback period, internal rate of return, modified internal rate of return, and net present value of the proposed mine.

2. Based on your analysis, should the company open the mine?

3. Bonus question: Most spreadsheets do not have a built-in formula to calculate the payback period. Write a VBA script that calculates the payback period for a project.

WEB EXERCISES (ONLINE ONLY)

For instructors interested in integrating even more online resources and problems into their course, these web activities show students how to learn from the vast amount of financial resources available on the internet. In the 12th edition of *Fundamentals*, these web exercises are available to students and instructors through *Connect*.

Comprehensive Teaching and Learning Package

This edition of *Fundamentals* has several options in terms of the textbook, instructor supplements, student supplements, and multimedia products. Mix and match to create a package that is perfect for your course!

TEXTBOOK

Customize your version of *Fundamentals* 12e through McGraw-Hill's *Create* platform. Teach the chapters you want in the order you want—your rep can show you how!

INSTRUCTOR RESOURCES

Keep all the supplements in one place! Your *Connect* Library contains all the necessary supplements—Teaching Resource Manual, Solutions, Test Bank, Computerized Test Bank, and PowerPoint—all in one easy-to-find, easy-to-use, integrated place: Your *Connect Finance* course.

- **Teaching Resource Manual (TRM)**
  The TRM is a full-service implementation guide designed to support you in the delivery of your curriculum and assist you in integrating Connect.

- **Solutions Manual (SM)**
  Prepared by Brad Jordan, University of Kentucky, and Joe Smolira, Belmont University
  The *Fundamentals* Solutions Manual provides detailed solutions to the extensive end-of-chapter material, including concept review questions, quantitative problems, and cases.

- **Test Bank**
  Prepared by Kay Johnson
  Over 100 questions and problems per chapter! Each chapter includes questions that test the understanding of key terms in the book; questions patterned after learning objectives, concept questions, chapter opening vignettes, boxes, and highlighted phrases; multiple-choice problems patterned after end-of-chapter questions at a variety of skill levels; and essay questions to test problem-solving skills and more advanced understanding of concepts.

- **Computerized Test Bank**
  TestGen is a complete, state-of-the-art test generator and editing application software that allows instructors to quickly and easily select test items from McGraw Hill's test bank content. The instructors can then organize, edit, and customize questions and answers to rapidly generate tests for paper or online administration. Questions can include stylized text, symbols, graphics, and equations that are inserted directly into questions using built-in mathematical templates. TestGen's random generator provides the option to display different text or calculated number values each time questions are used. With both quick-and-simple test creation and flexible and robust editing tools, TestGen is a complete test generator system for today's educators.

- **Excel Simulations**
  Expanded for this edition! With 180 Excel simulation questions now included in Connect, RWJ is the unparalleled leader in offering students the opportunity to practice using the Excel functions they will use throughout their careers in finance.

- **Corporate Finance Videos**
  New for this edition, brief and engaging conceptual videos (and accompanying questions) help students to master the building blocks of the Corporate Finance course.

- **PowerPoint Presentations**

  The PowerPoint slides for the 12th edition have been revised to include a wealth of instructor material, including lecture tips, real-world examples, and international notes. Each presentation also includes slides dedicated entirely to ethics notes that relate to the chapter topics.

STUDENT RESOURCES

Student resources for this edition can be found through the Library tab in your *Connect Finance* course. If you aren't using *Connect*, visit us at http://connect.mheducation.com to learn more, and ask your professor about using it in your course for access to a great group of supplement resources!

- **Excel Resources**

  For those seeking additional practice, students can access Excel template problems and Excel Master, designed by Brad Jordan and Joe Smolira.

- **Narrated Lecture Videos**

  Updated for this edition, the Narrated Lecture videos provide real-world examples accompanied by step-by-step instructions and explanations for solving problems presented in the chapter. The Concept Checks from the text are also integrated into the slides to reinforce the key topics in the chapter. Designed specifically to appeal to the different learning methods of students, the slides provide a visual and audio explanation of topics and problems.

TEACHING SUPPORT

Along with having access to all of the student resource materials through the *Connect* Library tab, you also have password-protected access to the Instructor's Manual, solutions to end-of-chapter problems and cases, Instructor's PowerPoint, Excel Template Solutions, video clips, and video projects and questions.

HOW THE MARKET WORKS

Students receive free access to this web-based portfolio simulation with a hypothetical brokerage account to buy and sell stocks and mutual funds. Students can use the real data found at this site in conjunction with the chapters on investments. They can also compete against students in their class and around the United States to run the most successful portfolio. This site is powered by Stock-Trak, the leading provider of investment simulation services to the academic community.

AVAILABLE FOR PURCHASE & PACKAGING

FinGame Online 5.0

By LeRoy Brooks, John Carroll University

(ISBN 10: 0077219880/ISBN 13: 9780077219888)

Just $15.00 when packaged with this text. In this comprehensive simulation game, students control a hypothetical company over numerous periods of operation. The game is now tied to the text by exercises found on the *Connect* Student Library. As students make major financial and operating decisions for their company, they will develop and enhance their skills in financial management and financial accounting statement analysis.

McGraw-Hill Connect® is a highly reliable, easy-to-use homework and learning management solution that utilizes learning science and award-winning adaptive tools to improve student results.

Homework and Adaptive Learning

- Connect's assignments help students contextualize what they've learned through application, so they can better understand the material and think critically.

- Connect will create a personalized study path customized to individual student needs through SmartBook®.

- SmartBook helps students study more efficiently by delivering an interactive reading experience through adaptive highlighting and review.

Over **7 billion questions** have been answered, making McGraw-Hill Education products more intelligent, reliable, and precise.

Connect's Impact on Retention Rates, Pass Rates, and Average Exam Scores

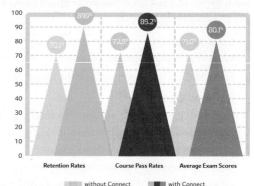

Using **Connect** improves retention rates by **19.8%**, passing rates by **12.7%, and** exam scores by **9.1%.**

73% of instructors who use **Connect** require it; instructor satisfaction **increases** by 28% when **Connect** is required.

Quality Content and Learning Resources

- Connect content is authored by the world's best subject matter experts, and is available to your class through a simple and intuitive interface.

- The Connect eBook makes it easy for students to access their reading material on smartphones and tablets. They can study on the go and don't need Internet access to use the eBook as a reference, with full functionality.

- Multimedia content such as videos, simulations, and games drive student engagement and critical thinking skills.

Robust Analytics and Reporting

- Connect Insight® generates easy-to-read reports on individual students, the class as a whole, and on specific assignments.

- The Connect Insight dashboard delivers data on performance, study behavior, and effort. Instructors can quickly identify students who struggle and focus on material that the class has yet to master.

- Connect automatically grades assignments and quizzes, providing easy-to-read reports on individual and class performance.

©Hero Images/Getty Images

Impact on Final Course Grade Distribution

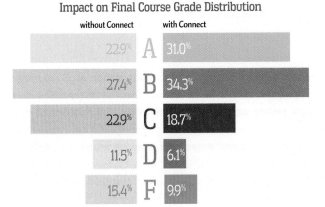

	without Connect	with Connect
A	22.9%	31.0%
B	27.4%	34.3%
C	22.9%	18.7%
D	11.5%	6.1%
F	15.4%	9.9%

More students earn **As** and **Bs** when they use **Connect**.

Trusted Service and Support

- Connect integrates with your LMS to provide single sign-on and automatic syncing of grades. Integration with Blackboard®, D2L®, and Canvas also provides automatic syncing of the course calendar and assignment-level linking.

- Connect offers comprehensive service, support, and training throughout every phase of your implementation.

- If you're looking for some guidance on how to use Connect, or want to learn tips and tricks from super users, you can find tutorials as you work. Our Digital Faculty Consultants and Student Ambassadors offer insight into how to achieve the results you want with Connect.

www.mheducation.com/connect

FINANCIAL ANALYSIS WITH AN ELECTRONIC CALCULATOR, SIXTH EDITION

by Mark A. White, University of Virginia, McIntire School of Commerce
(ISBN 10: 0073217093/ISBN 13: 9780073217093)
The information and procedures in this supplementary text enable students to master the use of financial calculators and develop a working knowledge of financial mathematics and problem solving. Complete instructions are included for solving all major problem types on four popular models: HP 10B and 12C, TI BA II Plus, and TI-84. Hands-on problems with detailed solutions allow students to practice the skills outlined in the text and obtain instant reinforcement. *Financial Analysis with an Electronic Calculator* is a self-contained supplement to the introductory financial management course.

MCGRAW-HILL CUSTOMER CARE CONTACT INFORMATION

At McGraw-Hill, we understand that getting the most from new technology can be challenging. That's why our services don't stop after you purchase our products. You can chat with our Product Specialists 24 hours a day to get product training online. Or you can search our knowledge bank of Frequently Asked Questions on our support website. For Customer Support, call **800-331-5094**, or visit **mpss.mhhe.com**. One of our Technical Support Analysts will be able to assist you in a timely fashion.

Assurance of Learning Ready

Assurance of Learning is an important element of many accreditation standards. *Fundamentals of Corporate Finance*, 12e, is designed specifically to support your assurance of learning initiatives. Each chapter in the book begins with a list of numbered learning objectives that appear throughout the chapter, as well as in the end-of-chapter problems and exercises. Every test bank question is also linked to one of these objectives, in addition to level of difficulty, topic area, Bloom's Taxonomy level, and AACSB skill area. *Connect*, McGraw-Hill's online homework solution, and EZ Test, McGraw-Hill's easy-to-use test bank software, can search the test bank using these and other categories, providing an engine for targeted Assurance of Learning analysis and assessment.

AACSB Statement

McGraw-Hill Education is a proud corporate member of AACSB International. Understanding the importance and value of AACSB Accreditation, *Fundamentals of Corporate Finance*, 12e, has sought to recognize the curricula guidelines detailed in the AACSB standards for business accreditation by connecting selected questions in the test bank to the general knowledge and skill guidelines found in the AACSB standards.

The statements contained in *Fundamentals of Corporate Finance*, 12e, are provided only as a guide for the users of this text. The AACSB leaves content coverage and assessment within the purview of individual schools, the mission of the school, and the faculty. While *Fundamentals of Corporate Finance*, 12e, and the teaching package make no claim of any specific AACSB qualification or evaluation, we have, within the test bank, labeled selected questions according to the eight general knowledge and skills areas.

Acknowledgments

To borrow a phrase, writing an introductory finance textbook is easy—all you do is sit down at a word processor and open a vein. We never would have completed this book without the incredible amount of help and support we received from literally hundreds of our colleagues, students, editors, family members, and friends. We would like to thank, without implicating, all of you.

Clearly, our greatest debt is to our many colleagues (and their students) who, like us, wanted to try an alternative to what they were using and made the decision to change. Needless to say, without this support, we would not be publishing a 12th edition!

A great many of our colleagues read the drafts of our first and subsequent editions. The fact that this book has so little in common with our earliest drafts, along with the many changes and improvements we have made over the years, is a reflection of the value we placed on the many comments and suggestions that we received. To the following reviewers, then, we are grateful for their many contributions:

Ibrahim Affeneh
Jan Ambrose
Mike Anderson
Sung C. Bae
Robert Benecke
Gary Benesh
Scott Besley
Sanjai Bhaghat
Vigdis Boasson
Elizabeth Booth
Denis Boudreaux
Jim Boyd
William Brent
Ray Brooks
Charles C. Brown
Lawrence Byerly
Steve Byers
Steve Caples
Asim Celik
Christina Cella
Mary Chaffin
Fan Chen
Raju Chenna
Barbara J. Childs
Charles M. Cox
Natalya Delcoure
Michael Dorigan
David A. Dumpe
Michael Dunn
Alan Eastman
Adrian C. Edwards

Uchenna Elike
Steve Engel
Angelo V. Esposito
James Estes
Cheri Etling
Thomas H. Eyssell
Dave Fehr
Michael Ferguson
Deborah Ann Ford
Jim Forjan
Micah Frankel
Jennifer R. Frazier
Deborah M. Giarusso
Devra Golbe
A. Steven Graham
Mark Graham
Darryl E. J. Gurley
Wendy D. Habegger
Karen Hallows
David Harraway
John M. Harris, Jr.
R. Stevenson Hawkey
Delvin D. Hawley
Eric Haye
Robert C. Higgins
Karen Hogan
Matthew Hood
Steve Isberg
James Jackson
Pankaj Jain
James M. Johnson

Randy Jorgensen
Daniel Jubinski
Jarl G. Kallberg
Ashok Kapoor
Terry Keasler
Howard Keen
David N. Ketcher
Jim Keys
Kee Kim
Deborah King
Robert Kleinman
Ladd Kochman
Sophie Kong
David Kuipers
Morris A. Lamberson
Qin Lan
Dina Layish
Chun Lee
Adam Y. C. Lei
George Lentz
John Lightstone
Jason Lin
Scott Lowe
Robert Lutz
Qingzhong Ma
Pawan Madhogarhia
Timothy Manuel
David G. Martin
Dubos J. Masson
Mario Mastrandrea
Leslie Mathis

John McDougald
Bob McElreath
Bahlous Mejda
Gordon Melms
Richard R. Mendenhall
Wayne Mikkelson
Lalatendu Misra
Karlyn Mitchell
Sunil Mohanty
Scott Moore
Belinda Mucklow
Barry Mulholland
Frederick H. Mull
Michael J. Murray
Randy Nelson
Oris Odom
Keith Osher
Bulent Parker
Megan Partch
Samuel Penkar
Pamela P. Peterson
Robert Phillips
Greg Pierce
Steve Pilloff
Robert Puelz
George A. Racette
Charu G. Raheja
Narendar V. Rao

Russ Ray
Ron Reiber
Thomas Rietz
Jay R. Ritter
Ricardo J. Rodriguez
Stu Rosenstein
Kenneth Roskelley
Ivan Roten
Philip Russel
Gary Sanger
Travis Sapp
Martha A. Schary
Robert Schwebach
Roger Severns
Michael Sher
Dilip K. Shome
Neil W. Sicherman
Timothy Smaby
Ahmad Sohrabian
Michael F. Spivey
Vic Stanton
Charlene Sullivan
Alice Sun
George S. Swales, Jr.
Lee Swartz
Philip Swensen
Philip Swicegood
Brian Tarrant

Rhonda Tenkku
John G. Thatcher
Harry Thiewes
A. Frank Thompson
Joseph Trefzger
George Turk
Michael R. Vetsuypens
Joe Walker
Jun Wang
James Washam
Alan Weatherford
Gwendolyn Webb
Marsha Weber
Jill Wetmore
Mark White
Susan White
Annie Wong
Colbrin Wright
David J. Wright
Steve B. Wyatt
Tung-Hsiao Yang
Morris Yarmish
Michael Young
Mei Zhang
J. Kenton Zumwalt
Tom Zwirlein

Several of our most respected colleagues contributed original essays for this edition, which are entitled "In Their Own Words," and appear in selected chapters. To these individuals we extend a special thanks:

Edward I. Altman
New York University
Robert C. Higgins
University of Washington
Roger Ibbotson
Yale University, Ibbotson Associates
Erik Lie
University of Iowa
Robert C. Merton
Harvard University,

Massachusetts Institute of Technology
Jay R. Ritter
University of Florida
Richard Roll
California Institute of Technology
Fischer Black
Jeremy Siegel
University of Pennsylvania

Hersh Shefrin
Santa Clara University
Bennett Stewart
Stern Stewart & Co.
Samuel C. Weaver
Lehigh University
Merton H. Miller

We are lucky to have had skilled and experienced instructors developing the supplement material for this edition. We greatly appreciate the contributions of Joe Smolira, Belmont University, who worked closely with us to develop the Solutions Manual, the new and improved

Instructor's Guide, and to create Excel templates for many of the end-of-chapter problems. Thank you also to Kay Johnson for thorough updating, revising, and tagging of every problem in the test bank.

The following proofers did outstanding work on this edition of *Fundamentals:* Emily Bello and Steve Hailey. To them fell the unenviable task of technical proofreading, and in particular, careful checking of each calculation throughout the text and Instructor's Manual.

Finally, in every phase of this project, we have been privileged to have had the complete and unwavering support of a great organization, McGraw-Hill Education. We especially thank the sales group. The suggestions they provide, their professionalism in assisting potential adopters, and the service they provide to current users have been a major factor in our success.

We are deeply grateful to the select group of professionals who served as our development team on this edition: Chuck Synovec, Director; Jennifer Upton, Senior Product Developer; Trina Maurer, Senior Marketing Manager; Matt Diamond, Designer; Jill Eccher, Core Project Manager. Others at McGraw-Hill/Irwin, too numerous to list here, have improved the book in countless ways.

Throughout the development of this edition, we have taken great care to discover and eliminate errors. Our goal is to provide the best textbook available on the subject. To ensure that future editions are error-free, we gladly offer $10 per arithmetic error to the first individual reporting it as a modest token of our appreciation. More than this, we would like to hear from instructors and students alike. Please write and tell us how to make this a better text. Forward your comments to: Dr. Brad Jordan, c/o Editorial—Finance, McGraw-Hill Education, 1333 Burr Ridge Parkway, Burr Ridge, IL 60527.

Stephen A. Ross
Randolph W. Westerfield
Bradford D. Jordan

Brief Contents

xxx

Contents

PART 4 Capital Budgeting

PART 5   Risk and Return

CHAPTER 12

SOME LESSONS FROM CAPITAL MARKET HISTORY *382*

CHAPTER 13

RETURN, RISK, AND THE SECURITY MARKET LINE *420*

CHAPTER 17

DIVIDENDS AND PAYOUT POLICY 574

PART 7　Short-Term Financial Planning and Management

PART 8   Topics in Corporate Finance

CHAPTER 21

INTERNATIONAL CORPORATE FINANCE *711*

CHAPTER 22

BEHAVIORAL FINANCE: IMPLICATIONS FOR FINANCIAL MANAGEMENT *740*

In Their Own Words Boxes

Pedagogical Use of Color

Throughout the 12th edition of *Fundamentals of Corporate Finance,* we make color a functional dimension of the discussion. In almost every chapter, color plays an extensive and largely self-evident role. Color in these chapters alerts students to the relationship between numbers in a discussion and an accompanying table or figure.

CHAPTER 2

Blue: Identifies net capital spending and change in net working capital
Green: Identifies cash flow numbers

CHAPTERS 3 AND 4

Throughout the chapter
Blue: Identifies income statements
Green: Identifies balance sheets (Also see all 23 ratios in Chapter 3)

CHAPTER 7

Section 7.4
Blue: Identifies the implicit interest expense
Green: Identifies the straight-line interest expense

CHAPTER 9

Section 9.5
Blue: Identifies Project A
Green: Identifies Project B

CHAPTER 13

Sections 13.1 and 13.2
Blue: Identifies Stock L
Green: Identifies Stock U

Section 13.7
Blue: Identifies Asset B
Green: Identifies Asset A

CHAPTER 14

Section 14.2
Blue: Identifies dollar and percentage changes in dividends
Green: Identifies dividends

CHAPTER 15

Section 15.9
Blue: Identifies values of shares with and without dilution
Green: Identifies original values of shares

CHAPTER 16

Section 16.2
Blue: Identifies the proposed capital structure
Green: Identifies the current capital structure

Section 16.4
Blue: Identifies Firm L
Green: Identifies Firm U

CHAPTER 18

Section 18.4
Blue: Identifies total cash collections
Green: Identifies total cash disbursements
Bold Black: Identifies the net cash inflows

CHAPTER 19

Section 19.2
Blue: Receipts and deposits
Green: Total float
End-of-chapter Appendix
Blue: Identifies contributing costs
Green: Identifies the opportunity, trading, and total costs

CHAPTER 20

Section 20.8
Blue: Identifies numbers exceeding the cost-minimizing restock quantity
Green: Identifies numbers falling below the cost-minimizing restock quantity
Bold Black: Identifies cost-minimizing quantity

CHAPTER 21

Section 21.5
Blue: Identifies cash flows
Green: Identifies expected exchange rates

CHAPTER 23

Sections 23.2, 23.3, and 23.6
Blue: Identifies the payoff profile

Green: Identifies the risk profile
Magenta: Identifies the hedge position

CHAPTER 24

Section 24.1
Blue: Identifies puts
Green: Identifies calls
Section 24.2
Blue: Identifies stock value
Green: Identifies portfolio value

CHAPTER 26

Sections 26.3 and 26.5 (See Tables 26.1 and 26.2)
Blue: Identifies Firm A and Global Resources
Green: Identifies Firm B and Regional Enterprises
Bold Black: Identifies the merged firm, Firm AB, and the merged identity of Global Resources

CHAPTER 27

Tables 27.2 and 27.3
Blue: Identifies cash flow components
Green: Identifies total cash flow

Introduction to Corporate Finance

THE CONTROL of a corporation typically rests with its shareholders, who receive one vote for each share of stock they own. However, Alphabet (the parent company of Google) and Facebook are two well-known companies with unusual voting rights. Both companies originally had two classes of stock: Class A, with 1 vote per share, and Class B, with 10 votes per share. The B shares were mostly held by the founding shareholders, so the voting structure meant that Mark Zuckerberg (Facebook) and Sergey Brin and Larry Page (Alphabet) retained control of the companies they started.

In 2016, Facebook announced that it would create Class C shares, similar to what Google had done in 2014. The Class C shares would have the same economic benefit as Class A and B shares, but no voting rights. So why would these two companies create shares of stock with different voting rights, and in the case of Class C stock, no voting rights? The answer leads us to the corporate form of organization, corporate goals, and corporate control, all of which we discuss in this chapter.

Learning Objectives

After studying this chapter, you should be able to:

LO1 Define the basic types of financial management decisions and the role of the financial manager.

LO2 Explain the goal of financial management.

LO3 Articulate the financial implications of the different forms of business organization.

LO4 Explain the conflicts of interest that can arise between managers and owners.

©by_adri/iStockPhoto/GettyImages

For updates on the latest happenings in finance, visit fundamentalsofcorporatefinance .blogspot.com.

To begin our study of modern corporate finance and financial management, we need to address two central issues. First, what is corporate finance and what is the role of the financial manager in the corporation? Second, what is the goal of financial management? To describe the financial management environment, we consider the corporate form of organization and discuss some conflicts that can arise within the corporation. We also take a brief look at financial markets in the United States.

1.1 Corporate Finance and the Financial Manager

In this section, we discuss where the financial manager fits in the corporation. We start by defining *corporate finance* and the financial manager's job.

WHAT IS CORPORATE FINANCE?

Imagine that you were to start your own business. No matter what type you started, you would have to answer the following three questions in some form or another:

1. What long-term investments should you take on? That is, what lines of business will you be in and what sorts of buildings, machinery, and equipment will you need?
2. Where will you get the long-term financing to pay for your investment? Will you bring in other owners or will you borrow the money?
3. How will you manage your everyday financial activities such as collecting from customers and paying suppliers?

These are not the only questions by any means, but they are among the most important. Corporate finance, broadly speaking, is the study of ways to answer these three questions. Accordingly, we'll be looking at each of them in the chapters ahead.

THE FINANCIAL MANAGER

A striking feature of large corporations is that the owners (the stockholders) are usually not directly involved in making business decisions, particularly on a day-to-day basis. Instead, the corporation employs managers to represent the owners' interests and make decisions on their behalf. In a large corporation, the financial manager would be in charge of answering the three questions we raised in the preceding section.

The financial management function is usually associated with a top officer of the firm, such as a vice president of finance or some other chief financial officer (CFO). Figure 1.1 is a simplified organizational chart that highlights the finance activity in a large firm. As shown, the vice president of finance coordinates the activities of the treasurer and the controller. The controller's office handles cost and financial accounting, tax payments, and management information systems. The treasurer's office is responsible for managing the firm's cash and credit, its financial planning, and its capital expenditures. These treasury activities are all related to the three general questions raised earlier, and the chapters ahead deal primarily with these issues. Our study thus bears mostly on activities usually associated with the treasurer's office.

For current issues facing CFOs, see **ww2.cfo.com**.

FINANCIAL MANAGEMENT DECISIONS

As the preceding discussion suggests, the financial manager must be concerned with three basic types of questions. We consider these in greater detail next.

capital budgeting
The process of planning and managing a firm's long-term investments.

Capital Budgeting   The first question concerns the firm's long-term investments. The process of planning and managing a firm's long-term investments is called **capital budgeting**. In capital budgeting, the financial manager tries to identify investment opportunities that are worth more to the firm than they cost to acquire. Loosely speaking, this means that the value of the cash flow generated by an asset exceeds the cost of that asset.

The types of investment opportunities that would typically be considered depend in part on the nature of the firm's business. For a large retailer such as Walmart, deciding whether to open another store would be an important capital budgeting decision. Similarly, for a

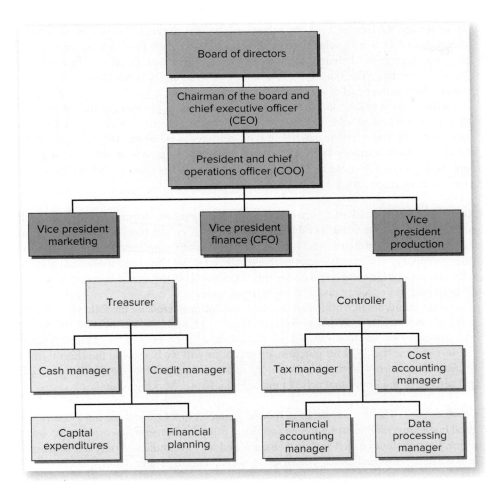

FIGURE 1.1

A Sample Simplified Organizational Chart

software company such as Oracle or Microsoft, the decision to develop and market a new spreadsheet program would be a major capital budgeting decision. Some decisions, such as what type of computer system to purchase, might not depend so much on a particular line of business.

Regardless of the specific nature of an opportunity under consideration, financial managers must be concerned not only with how much cash they expect to receive, but also with when they expect to receive it and how likely they are to receive it. Evaluating the *size, timing,* and *risk* of future cash flows is the essence of capital budgeting. In fact, as we will see in the chapters ahead, whenever we evaluate a business decision, the size, timing, and risk of the cash flows will be by far the most important things we will consider.

Capital Structure   The second question for the financial manager concerns ways in which the firm obtains and manages the long-term financing it needs to support its long-term investments. A firm's **capital structure** (or financial structure) is the specific mixture of long-term debt and equity the firm uses to finance its operations. The financial manager has two concerns in this area. First, how much should the firm borrow? That is, what mixture of debt and equity is best? The mixture chosen will affect both the risk and the value of the firm. Second, what are the least expensive sources of funds for the firm?

capital structure
The mixture of debt and equity maintained by a firm.

If we picture the firm as a pie, then the firm's capital structure determines how that pie is sliced—in other words, what percentage of the firm's cash flow goes to creditors and what percentage goes to shareholders. Firms have a great deal of flexibility in choosing a financial structure. The question of whether one structure is better than any other for a particular firm is the heart of the capital structure issue.

In addition to deciding on the financing mix, the financial manager has to decide exactly how and where to raise the money. The expenses associated with raising long-term financing can be considerable, so different possibilities must be carefully evaluated. Also, corporations borrow money from a variety of lenders in a number of different, and sometimes exotic, ways. Choosing among lenders and among loan types is another job handled by the financial manager.

working capital
A firm's short-term assets and liabilities.

Working Capital Management   The third question concerns **working capital** management. The term *working capital* refers to a firm's short-term assets, such as inventory, and its short-term liabilities, such as money owed to suppliers. Managing the firm's working capital is a day-to-day activity that ensures that the firm has sufficient resources to continue its operations and avoid costly interruptions. This involves a number of activities related to the firm's receipt and disbursement of cash.

Some questions about working capital that must be answered are the following: (1) How much cash and inventory should we keep on hand? (2) Should we sell on credit? If so, what terms will we offer, and to whom will we extend them? (3) How will we obtain any needed short-term financing? Will we purchase on credit, or will we borrow in the short term and pay cash? If we borrow in the short term, how and where should we do it? These are just a small sample of the issues that arise in managing a firm's working capital.

Conclusion   The three areas of corporate financial management we have described—capital budgeting, capital structure, and working capital management—are very broad categories. Each includes a rich variety of topics, and we have indicated only a few questions that arise in the different areas. The chapters ahead contain greater detail.

Concept Questions

1.1a   What is the capital budgeting decision?
1.1b   What do you call the specific mixture of long-term debt and equity that a firm chooses to use?
1.1c   Into what category of financial management does cash management fall?

1.2 Forms of Business Organization

Large firms in the United States, such as Ford and Microsoft, are almost all organized as corporations. We examine the three different legal forms of business organization—sole proprietorship, partnership, and corporation—to see why this is so. Each form has distinct advantages and disadvantages for the life of the business, the ability of the business to raise cash, and taxes. A key observation is that as a firm grows, the advantages of the corporate form may come to outweigh the disadvantages.

SOLE PROPRIETORSHIP

sole proprietorship
A business owned by a single individual.

A **sole proprietorship** is a business owned by one person. This is the simplest type of business to start and is the least regulated form of organization. Depending on where you live, you might be able to start a proprietorship by doing little more than getting a business license and opening your doors. For this reason, there are more proprietorships than any other type of business, and many businesses that later become large corporations start out as small proprietorships.

The owner of a sole proprietorship keeps all the profits. That's the good news. The bad news is that the owner has *unlimited liability* for business debts. This means that creditors can look beyond business assets to the proprietor's personal assets for payment. Similarly, there is no distinction between personal and business income, so all business income is taxed as personal income. However, with the passage of the Tax Cuts and Jobs Act of 2017, up to 20 percent of business income may be exempt from taxation (the specific rules are too complex to cover here).

The life of a sole proprietorship is limited to the owner's life span, and the amount of equity that can be raised is limited to the amount of the proprietor's personal wealth. This limitation often means that the business is unable to exploit new opportunities because of insufficient capital. Ownership of a sole proprietorship may be difficult to transfer because this transfer requires the sale of the entire business to a new owner.

PARTNERSHIP

A **partnership** is similar to a proprietorship except that there are two or more owners (partners). In a *general partnership*, all the partners share in gains or losses, and all have unlimited liability for *all* partnership debts, not just some particular share. The way partnership gains (and losses) are divided is described in the *partnership agreement*. This agreement can be an informal oral agreement, such as "let's start a lawn mowing business," or a lengthy, formal written document.

partnership
A business formed by two or more individuals or entities.

In a *limited partnership*, one or more *general partners* will run the business and have unlimited liability, but there will be one or more *limited partners* who will not actively participate in the business. A limited partner's liability for business debts is limited to the amount that partner contributes to the partnership. This form of organization is common in real estate ventures, for example.

The advantages and disadvantages of a partnership are basically the same as those of a proprietorship. Partnerships based on a relatively informal agreement are easy and inexpensive to form. General partners have unlimited liability for partnership debts, and the partnership terminates when a general partner wishes to sell out or dies. All income is taxed as personal income to the partners, and the amount of equity that can be raised is limited to the partners' combined wealth. As with sole proprietorships, beginning in 2018, up to 20 percent of a partner's income may be exempt depending on various rules spelled out in the Tax Cuts and Jobs Act of 2017. Ownership of a general partnership is not easily transferred because a transfer requires that a new partnership be formed. A limited partner's interest can be sold without dissolving the partnership, but finding a buyer may be difficult.

Because a partner in a general partnership can be held responsible for all partnership debts, having a written agreement is very important. Failure to spell out the rights and duties of the partners frequently leads to misunderstandings later on. Also, if you are a limited partner, you must not become deeply involved in business decisions unless you are willing to assume the obligations of a general partner. The reason is that if things go badly, you may be deemed to be a general partner even though you say you are a limited partner.

Based on our discussion, the primary disadvantages of sole proprietorships and partnerships as forms of business organization are (1) unlimited liability for business debts on the part of the owners, (2) limited life of the business, and (3) difficulty of transferring ownership. These three disadvantages add up to a single, central problem: The ability of such businesses to grow can be seriously limited by an inability to raise cash for investment.

CORPORATION

The **corporation** is the most important form (in terms of size) of business organization in the United States. A corporation is a legal "person," separate and distinct from its owners,

corporation
A business created as a distinct legal entity composed of one or more individuals or entities.

and it has many of the rights, duties, and privileges of an actual person. Corporations can borrow money and own property, sue and be sued, and enter into contracts. A corporation can even be a general partner or a limited partner in a partnership, and a corporation can own stock in another corporation.

Not surprisingly, starting a corporation is somewhat more complicated than starting the other forms of business organization. Forming a corporation involves preparing *articles of incorporation* (or a charter) and a set of *bylaws*. The articles of incorporation must contain a number of things, including the corporation's name, its intended life (which can be forever), its business purpose, and the number of shares that can be issued. This information must normally be supplied to the state in which the firm will be incorporated. For most legal purposes, the corporation is a "resident" of that state.

The bylaws are rules describing how the corporation regulates its existence. For example, the bylaws describe how directors are elected. These bylaws may be a simple statement of a few rules and procedures, or they may be quite extensive for a large corporation. The bylaws may be amended or extended from time to time by the stockholders.

In a large corporation, the stockholders and the managers are usually separate groups. The stockholders elect the board of directors, who then select the managers. Managers are charged with running the corporation's affairs in the stockholders' interests. In principle, stockholders control the corporation because they elect the directors.

As a result of the separation of ownership and management, the corporate form has several advantages. Ownership (represented by shares of stock) can be readily transferred, and the life of the corporation is therefore not limited. The corporation borrows money in its own name. As a result, the stockholders in a corporation have limited liability for corporate debts. The most they can lose is what they have invested.

The relative ease of transferring ownership, the limited liability for business debts, and the unlimited life of the business are why the corporate form is superior for raising cash. If a corporation needs new equity, for example, it can sell new shares of stock and attract new investors. Apple is an example. The company was a pioneer in the personal computer business. As demand for its products exploded, it had to convert to the corporate form of organization to raise the capital needed to fund growth and new product development. The number of owners can be huge; larger corporations have many thousands or even millions of stockholders. For example, in 2017, General Electric Company (better known as GE) had about 440,000 stockholders and about 8.7 billion shares outstanding. In such cases, ownership can change continuously without affecting the continuity of the business.

The corporate form has a significant disadvantage. Because a corporation is a legal person, it must pay taxes. Moreover, money paid out to stockholders in the form of dividends is taxed again as income to those stockholders. This is *double taxation*, meaning that corporate profits are taxed twice: First at the corporate level when they are earned and again at the personal level when they are paid out.[1]

Today, all 50 states have enacted laws allowing for the creation of a relatively new form of business organization, the limited liability company (LLC). The goal of this entity is to operate and be taxed like a partnership but retain limited liability for owners, so an LLC is essentially a hybrid of partnership and corporation. Although states have differing definitions for LLCs, the more important scorekeeper is the Internal Revenue Service (IRS). The IRS will consider an LLC a corporation, thereby subjecting it to double taxation, unless it meets certain specific criteria. In essence, an LLC cannot be too corporation-like, or it will be treated as one by the IRS. LLCs have become common. For example, Goldman, Sachs and Co., one of Wall Street's last remaining partnerships, decided to convert from a private

---

[1]An S corporation is a special type of small corporation that is essentially taxed like a partnership and thus avoids double taxation. In 2017, the maximum number of shareholders in an S corporation was 100.

TABLE 1.1   International Corporations

Company	Country of Origin	Type of Company	
		In Original Language	Translated
Bayerische Motoren Werke (BMW) AG	Germany	Aktiengesellschaft	Corporation
Dornier GmbH	Germany	Gesellschaft mit Beschränkter Haftung	Limited liability company
Rolls-Royce PLC	United Kingdom	Public limited company	Public limited company
Shell UK Ltd.	United Kingdom	Limited	Corporation
Unilever NV	Netherlands	Naamloze Vennootschap	Joint stock company
Fiat SpA	Italy	Società per Azioni	Joint stock company
Volvo AB	Sweden	Aktiebolag	Joint stock company
Peugeot SA	France	Société Anonyme	Joint stock company

partnership to an LLC (it later "went public," becoming a publicly held corporation). Large accounting firms and law firms by the score have converted to LLCs.

As the discussion in this section illustrates, because of their need for outside investors and creditors, the corporate form will generally be the best choice for large firms. We focus on corporations in the chapters ahead because of the importance of the corporate form in the United States and world economies. Also, a few important financial management issues, such as dividend policy, are unique to corporations. However, businesses of all types and sizes need financial management, so the majority of the subjects we discuss bear on any form of business.

A CORPORATION BY ANOTHER NAME . . .

The corporate form of organization has many variations around the world. The exact laws and regulations differ from country to country, of course, but the essential features of public ownership and limited liability remain. These firms are often called *joint stock companies*, *public limited companies*, or *limited liability companies*, depending on the specific nature of the firm and the country of origin.

Table 1.1 gives the names of a few well-known international corporations, their countries of origin, and a translation of the abbreviation that follows the company name.

Concept Questions

1.2a   What are the three forms of business organization?

1.2b   What are the primary advantages and disadvantages of sole proprietorships and partnerships?

1.2c   What is the difference between a general and a limited partnership?

1.2d   Why is the corporate form superior when it comes to raising cash?

The Goal of Financial Management   1.3

Assuming that we restrict ourselves to for-profit businesses, the goal of financial management is to make money or add value for the owners. This goal is a little vague, of course, so we examine some different ways of formulating it to come up with a more precise definition. Such a definition is important because it leads to an objective basis for making and evaluating financial decisions.

POSSIBLE GOALS

If we were to consider possible financial goals, we might come up with some ideas like the following:

Survive.

Avoid financial distress and bankruptcy.

Beat the competition.

Maximize sales or market share.

Minimize costs.

Maximize profits.

Maintain steady earnings growth.

These are only a few of the goals we could list. Furthermore, each of these possibilities presents problems as a goal for the financial manager.

For example, it's easy to increase market share or unit sales: All we have to do is lower our prices or relax our credit terms. Similarly, we can always cut costs simply by doing away with things such as research and development. We can avoid bankruptcy by never borrowing any money or never taking any risks, and so on. It's not clear that any of these actions are in the stockholders' best interests.

Profit maximization would probably be the most commonly cited goal, but even this is not a precise objective. Do we mean profits this year? If so, we should note that actions such as deferring maintenance, letting inventories run down, and taking other short-run cost-cutting measures will tend to increase profits now, but these activities aren't necessarily desirable.

The goal of maximizing profits may refer to some sort of "long-run" or "average" profits, but it's still unclear exactly what this means. First, do we mean something like accounting net income or earnings per share? As we will see in more detail in the next chapter, these accounting numbers may have little to do with what is good or bad for the firm. Second, what do we mean by the long run? As a famous economist once remarked, in the long run, we're all dead! More to the point, this goal doesn't tell us what the appropriate trade-off is between current and future profits.

The goals we've listed here are all different, but they tend to fall into two classes. The first of these relates to profitability. The goals involving sales, market share, and cost control all relate, at least potentially, to different ways of earning or increasing profits. The goals in the second group, involving bankruptcy avoidance, stability, and safety, relate in some way to controlling risk. Unfortunately, these two types of goals are somewhat contradictory. The pursuit of profit normally involves some element of risk, so it isn't really possible to maximize both safety and profit. What we need, therefore, is a goal that encompasses both factors.

THE GOAL OF FINANCIAL MANAGEMENT

The financial manager in a corporation makes decisions for the stockholders of the firm. Given this, instead of listing possible goals for the financial manager, we really need to answer a more fundamental question: From the stockholders' point of view, what is a good financial management decision?

If we assume that stockholders buy stock because they seek to gain financially, then the answer is obvious: Good decisions increase the value of the stock, and poor decisions decrease the value of the stock.

Given our observations, it follows that the financial manager acts in the shareholders' best interests by making decisions that increase the value of the stock. The appropriate goal for the financial manager can thus be stated quite easily:

> **The goal of financial management is to maximize the current value per share of the existing stock.**

The goal of maximizing the value of the stock avoids the problems associated with the different goals we listed earlier. There is no ambiguity in the criterion, and there is no short-run versus long-run issue. We explicitly mean that our goal is to maximize the *current* stock value.

If this goal seems a little strong or one-dimensional to you, keep in mind that the stockholders in a firm are residual owners. By this we mean that they are entitled to only what is left after employees, suppliers, and creditors (and anyone else with a legitimate claim) are paid their due. If any of these groups go unpaid, the stockholders get nothing. So, if the stockholders are winning in the sense that the leftover, residual portion is growing, it must be true that everyone else is winning also.

Because the goal of financial management is to maximize the value of the stock, we need to learn how to identify investments and financing arrangements that favorably impact the value of the stock. This is precisely what we will be studying. In fact, we could have defined *corporate finance* as the study of the relationship between business decisions and the value of the stock in the business.

A MORE GENERAL GOAL

Given our goal as stated in the preceding section (maximize the value of the stock), an obvious question comes up: What is the appropriate goal when the firm has no traded stock? Corporations are certainly not the only type of business; and the stock in many corporations rarely changes hands, so it's difficult to say what the value per share is at any given time.

As long as we are dealing with for-profit businesses, only a slight modification is needed. The total value of the stock in a corporation is simply equal to the value of the owners' equity. Therefore, a more general way of stating our goal is as follows: Maximize the market value of the existing owners' equity.

With this in mind, it doesn't matter whether the business is a proprietorship, a partnership, or a corporation. For each of these, good financial decisions increase the market value of the owners' equity and poor financial decisions decrease it. In fact, although we focus on corporations in the chapters ahead, the principles we develop apply to all forms of business. Many of them even apply to the not-for-profit sector.

Finally, our goal does not imply that the financial manager should take illegal or unethical actions in the hope of increasing the value of the equity in the firm. What we mean is that the financial manager best serves the owners of the business by identifying goods and services that add value to the firm because they are desired and valued in the free marketplace.

SARBANES-OXLEY

In response to corporate scandals at companies such as Enron, WorldCom, Tyco, and Adelphia, Congress enacted the Sarbanes-Oxley Act in 2002. The act, better known as "Sarbox," is intended to protect investors from corporate abuses. For example, one section of Sarbox prohibits personal loans from a company to its officers, such as the ones that were received by WorldCom CEO Bernie Ebbers.

One of the key sections of Sarbox took effect on November 15, 2004. Section 404 requires, among other things, that each company's annual report must have an assessment of the company's internal control structure and financial reporting. An independent auditor must then evaluate and attest to management's assessment of these issues.

Sarbox contains other key requirements. For example, the officers of the corporation must review and sign the annual reports. They must explicitly declare that the annual report does not contain any false statements or material omissions; that the financial statements fairly represent the financial results; and that they are responsible for all internal controls. Finally, the annual report must list any deficiencies in internal controls. In essence, Sarbox makes company management responsible for the accuracy of the company's financial statements.

Because of its extensive reporting requirements, compliance with Sarbox can be very costly, which has led to some unintended results. Since its implementation, hundreds of public firms have chosen to "go dark," meaning that their shares are no longer traded on the major stock exchanges, in which case Sarbox does not apply. Most of these companies stated that their reason was to avoid the cost of compliance. Ironically, in such cases, the law has had the effect of eliminating public disclosure instead of improving it.

For more about
Sarbanes-Oxley, visit
www.soxlaw.com.

Concept Questions

1.3a   What is the goal of financial management?

1.3b   What are some shortcomings of the goal of profit maximization?

1.3c   Can you give a definition of *corporate finance*?

1.4 The Agency Problem and Control of the Corporation

We've seen that the financial manager acts in the best interests of the stockholders by taking actions that increase the value of the stock. However, we've also seen that in large corporations ownership can be spread over a huge number of stockholders. This dispersion of ownership arguably means that management effectively controls the firm. In this case, will management necessarily act in the best interests of the stockholders? Put another way, might management choose to pursue its own goals at the stockholders' expense? In the following pages, we briefly consider some of the arguments relating to this question.

AGENCY RELATIONSHIPS

The relationship between stockholders and management is called an *agency relationship*. Such a relationship exists whenever someone (the principal) hires another (the agent) to represent his or her interests. For example, you might hire someone (an agent) to sell a car you own while you are away at school. In all such relationships, there is a possibility of conflict of interest between the principal and the agent. Such a conflict is called an **agency problem.**

agency problem
The possibility of conflict
of interest between the
stockholders and management
of a firm.

Suppose you hire someone to sell your car and agree to pay that person a flat fee when he or she sells the car. The agent's incentive in this case is to make the sale, not necessarily to get you the best price. If you offer a commission of, say, 10 percent of the sales price instead of a flat fee, then this problem might not exist. This example illustrates that the way in which an agent is compensated is one factor that affects agency problems.

MANAGEMENT GOALS

To see how management and stockholder interests might differ, imagine that the firm is considering a new investment. The new investment is expected to favorably impact the share value, but it is also a relatively risky venture. The owners of the firm will wish to take the investment (because the stock value will rise), but management may not because there is the possibility that things will turn out badly and management jobs will be lost. If management does not take the investment, then the stockholders may lose a valuable opportunity. This is one example of an agency cost.

More generally, the term *agency costs* refers to the costs of the conflict of interest between stockholders and management. These costs can be indirect or direct. An indirect agency cost is a lost opportunity, such as the one we have just described.

Direct agency costs come in two forms. The first type is a corporate expenditure that benefits management but costs the stockholders. Perhaps the purchase of a luxurious and unneeded corporate jet would fall under this heading. The second type of direct agency cost is an expense that arises from the need to monitor management actions. Paying outside auditors to assess the accuracy of financial statement information could be one example.

It is sometimes argued that, left to themselves, managers would tend to maximize the amount of resources over which they have control or, more generally, corporate power or wealth. This goal could lead to an overemphasis on corporate size or growth. For example, cases in which management is accused of overpaying to buy another company just to increase the size of the business or to demonstrate corporate power are not uncommon. Obviously, if overpayment does take place, such a purchase does not benefit the stockholders of the purchasing company.

Our discussion indicates that management may tend to overemphasize organizational survival to protect job security. Also, management may dislike outside interference, so independence and corporate self-sufficiency may be important goals.

DO MANAGERS ACT IN THE STOCKHOLDERS' INTERESTS?

Whether managers will, in fact, act in the best interests of stockholders depends on two factors. First, how closely are management goals aligned with stockholder goals? This question relates, at least in part, to the way managers are compensated. Second, can managers be replaced if they do not pursue stockholder goals? This issue relates to control of the firm. As we will discuss, there are a number of reasons to think that even in the largest firms, management has a significant incentive to act in the interests of stockholders.

Managerial Compensation Management will frequently have a significant economic incentive to increase share value for two reasons. First, managerial compensation, particularly at the top, is usually tied to financial performance in general and often to share value in particular. For example, managers are frequently given the option to buy stock at a bargain price. The more the stock is worth, the more valuable is this option. In fact, options are often used to motivate employees of all types, not just top managers. For example, in late 2016, Alphabet's more than 72,000 employees owned enough options to buy 3.3 million shares in the company. Many other corporations, large and small, have adopted similar policies.

The second incentive managers have relates to job prospects. Better performers within the firm will tend to get promoted. More generally, managers who are successful in pursuing stockholder goals will be in greater demand in the labor market and thus command higher salaries.

In fact, managers who are successful in pursuing stockholder goals can reap enormous rewards. For example, according to Equilar, the best-paid executive in 2016 was Thomas Rutledge, the CEO of Charter Communications, who made about $98 million. By way of comparison, Rutledge made less than performer Katy Perry ($135 million) and way less than boxer Floyd Mayweather ($300 million). Information about executive compensation, along with lots of other information, can be easily found on the web for almost any public company. Our nearby *Work the Web* box shows you how to get started.

WORK THE WEB

The web is a great place to learn more about individual companies, and there are a slew of sites available to help you. Try pointing your web browser to finance.yahoo.com. Once you get there, you should see a link for a "Quote Lookup".

To look up a company, you can use its "ticker symbol" (or just ticker for short), which is a unique one-to five-letter identifier. You can even type the company name into the lookup box and Yahoo Finance will show you the ticker symbol. We typed in "PZZA", which is the ticker for pizza maker Papa John's. Here is a portion of what we found:

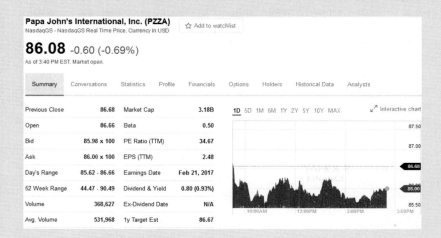

There's a lot of information here and many links for you to explore, so have at it. By the end of the term, we hope it all makes sense to you!

Questions

1. Go to finance.yahoo.com and find the current stock prices for Southwest Airlines (LUV), Harley-Davidson (HOG), and Anheuser-Busch InBev (BUD).
2. Get a quote for American Express (AXP) and follow the "Statistics" link. What information is available on this link? What do mrq, ttm, yoy, and lfy mean?

Business ethics are considered at **www.business-ethics.com**.

While the appropriate level of executive compensation can be debated, bonuses and other payments made to executives who receive payments due to illegal or unethical behavior are a problem. Recently, "clawbacks" and deferred compensation have been introduced to combat such questionable payments. With a clawback, a bonus can be reclaimed by the company for specific reasons, such as fraud. For example, in 2016, former Wells Fargo CEO John Stumpf was forced to forfeit $41 million and former retail banking head Carrie Tolstedt had to give up $19 million due to behavior while the two led the company. Then, in April 2017, Stumpf was forced to return another $28 million and Tolstedt was forced to return an additional $47.3 million. The use of deferred compensation has also increased. Deferred compensation is money paid to an executive several years after it is earned. With a deferred compensation agreement, if circumstances warrant, the payment can be canceled.

Control of the Firm   Control of the firm ultimately rests with stockholders. They elect the board of directors, who in turn hire and fire managers. The fact that stockholders control the corporation was made abundantly clear by Steve Jobs's experience at Apple. Even though he was a founder of the corporation and was largely responsible for its most successful products, there came a time when shareholders, through their elected directors, decided that Apple would be better off without him, so out he went. Of course, he was later rehired and helped turn Apple around with great new products such as the iPod, iPhone, and iPad. Going back to the chapter opener, why would Facebook, specifically Mark Zuckerberg, want to create new shares of stock with no voting rights? The answer is that Zuckerberg had pledged to give away 99 percent of his shares in Facebook during his lifetime. The new C shares he received with no voting rights were to be given to the Chan Zuckerberg Initiative, a philanthropic entity that he created. Therefore, even in giving away these shares, he still retained control of Facebook. In Alphabet's case, Brin and Page had seen their voting power drop to about 56 percent of votes because of the number of Class A shares issued to fund acquisitions and employee stock awards. The new Class C shares were to be used to fund these areas going forward.

An important mechanism by which unhappy stockholders can act to replace existing management is called a *proxy fight*. A proxy is the authority to vote someone else's stock. A proxy fight develops when a group solicits proxies in order to replace the existing board and thereby replace existing managers. For example, in 2016, activist investor Starboard Value LP launched a proxy battle with Yahoo!, arguing that Yahoo! should sell its core business. In response, Yahoo! agreed to a deal that granted four seats on its board of directors to Starboard's nominees—and thus a long proxy fight was defused. Several months later, Yahoo! announced that it would be purchased by Verizon for $4.8 billion, although the acquisition price was reduced by $350 million due to a 2013 e-mail hack experienced by Yahoo! that had not been made public.

Another way that managers can be replaced is by takeover. Firms that are poorly managed are more attractive as acquisitions because a greater profit potential exists. Thus, avoiding a takeover gives management another incentive to act in the stockholders' interests. For example, in 2016, Marriott completed its takeover of Starwood Hotels. Marriott expected to save $250 million per year in operating the combined companies, with much of the savings coming from job cuts in the executive ranks at Starwood. In short, Marriott bought Starwood and fired most of its top executives, eliminating those salaries and saving money.

Conclusion   The available theory and evidence are consistent with the view that stockholders control the firm and that stockholder wealth maximization is the relevant goal of the corporation. Even so, there will undoubtedly be times when management goals are pursued at the expense of the stockholders, at least temporarily.

STAKEHOLDERS

Our discussion thus far implies that management and stockholders are the only parties with an interest in the firm's decisions. This is an oversimplification, of course. Employees, customers, suppliers, and even the government all have a financial interest in the firm.

Taken together, these various groups are called **stakeholders** in the firm. In general, a stakeholder is someone other than a stockholder or creditor who potentially has a claim on the cash flows of the firm. Such groups will also attempt to exert control over the firm, perhaps to the detriment of the owners.

stakeholder
Someone other than a stockholder or creditor who potentially has a claim on the cash flows of the firm.

1.5 Financial Markets and the Corporation

We've seen that the primary advantages of the corporate form of organization are that ownership can be transferred more quickly and easily than with other forms and that money can be raised more readily. Both of these advantages are significantly enhanced by the existence of financial markets, and financial markets play an extremely important role in corporate finance.

CASH FLOWS TO AND FROM THE FIRM

The interplay between the corporation and the financial markets is illustrated in Figure 1.2. The arrows in Figure 1.2 trace the passage of cash from the financial markets to the firm and from the firm back to the financial markets.

Suppose we start with the firm selling shares of stock and borrowing money to raise cash. Cash flows to the firm from the financial markets (A). The firm invests the cash in current and fixed assets (B). These assets generate cash (C), some of which goes to pay corporate taxes (D). After taxes are paid, some of this cash flow is reinvested in the firm (E). The rest goes back to the financial markets as cash paid to creditors and shareholders (F).

FIGURE 1.2

Cash Flows between the Firm and the Financial Markets

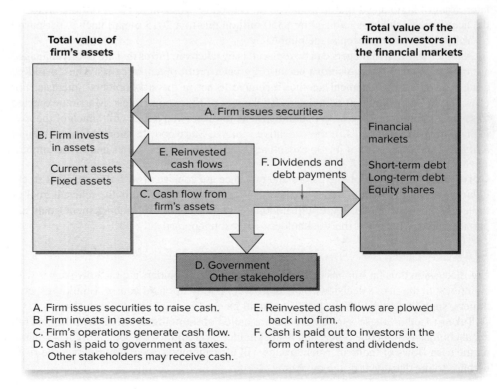

A. Firm issues securities to raise cash.
B. Firm invests in assets.
C. Firm's operations generate cash flow.
D. Cash is paid to government as taxes. Other stakeholders may receive cash.
E. Reinvested cash flows are plowed back into firm.
F. Cash is paid out to investors in the form of interest and dividends.

A financial market, like any market, is just a way of bringing buyers and sellers together. In financial markets, it is debt and equity securities that are bought and sold. Financial markets differ in detail, however. The most important differences concern the types of securities that are traded, how trading is conducted, and who the buyers and sellers are. Some of these differences are discussed next.

PRIMARY VERSUS SECONDARY MARKETS

Financial markets function as both primary and secondary markets for debt and equity securities. The term *primary market* refers to the original sale of securities by governments and corporations. The *secondary markets* are those in which these securities are bought and sold after the original sale. Equities are, of course, issued solely by corporations. Debt securities are issued by both governments and corporations. In the discussion that follows, we focus on corporate securities only.

Primary Markets   In a primary market transaction, the corporation is the seller, and the transaction raises money for the corporation. Corporations engage in two types of primary market transactions: public offerings and private placements. A public offering, as the name suggests, involves selling securities to the general public, whereas a private placement is a negotiated sale involving a specific buyer.

By law, public offerings of debt and equity must be registered with the Securities and Exchange Commission (SEC). Registration requires the firm to disclose a great deal of information before selling any securities. The accounting, legal, and selling costs of public offerings can be considerable.

To learn more about the SEC, visit **www.sec.gov**.

Partly to avoid the various regulatory requirements and the expense of public offerings, debt and equity are often sold privately to large financial institutions such as life insurance companies or mutual funds. Such private placements do not have to be registered with the SEC and do not require the involvement of underwriters (investment banks that specialize in selling securities to the public).

Secondary Markets   A secondary market transaction involves one owner or creditor selling to another. Therefore, the secondary markets provide the means for transferring ownership of corporate securities. Although a corporation is directly involved only in a primary market transaction (when it sells securities to raise cash), the secondary markets are still critical to large corporations. The reason is that investors are much more willing to purchase securities in a primary market transaction when they know that those securities can later be resold if desired.

Dealer versus Auction Markets   There are two kinds of secondary markets: *auction* markets and *dealer* markets. Generally speaking, dealers buy and sell for themselves, at their own risk. A car dealer, for example, buys and sells automobiles. In contrast, brokers and agents match buyers and sellers, but they do not actually own the commodity that is bought or sold. A real estate agent, for example, does not normally buy and sell houses.

Dealer markets in stocks and long-term debt are called *over-the-counter* (OTC) markets. Most trading in debt securities takes place over the counter. The expression *over the counter* refers to days of old when securities were literally bought and sold at counters in offices around the country. Today, a significant fraction of the market for stocks and almost all of the market for long-term debt have no central location; the many dealers are connected electronically.

Auction markets differ from dealer markets in two ways. First, an auction market or exchange has a physical location (like Wall Street). Second, in a dealer market, most of the buying and selling is done by the dealer. The primary purpose of an auction market, on the other hand, is to match those who wish to sell with those who wish to buy. Dealers play a limited role.

Trading in Corporate Securities   The equity shares of most of the large firms in the United States trade in organized auction markets. The largest such market is the New York Stock Exchange (NYSE). There is also a large OTC market for stocks. In 1971, the National Association of Securities Dealers (NASD) made available to dealers and brokers an electronic quotation system called NASDAQ (which originally stood for NASD Automated Quotation system and is pronounced "naz-dak"). NASDAQ-listed companies tend to be smaller and trade less actively. There are exceptions, of course. Both Microsoft and Intel trade OTC, for example. Nonetheless, the total value of NASDAQ stocks is much less than the total value of NYSE stocks.

To learn more about the exchanges, visit **www.nyse.com** and **www.nasdaq.com**.

There are many large and important financial markets outside the United States, of course, and U.S. corporations are increasingly looking to these markets to raise cash. The Tokyo Stock Exchange and the London Stock Exchange (TSE and LSE, respectively) are two well-known examples. The fact that OTC markets have no physical location means that national borders do not present a great barrier, and there is now a huge international OTC debt market. Because of globalization, financial markets have reached the point where trading in many investments never stops; it just travels around the world.

Listing   Stocks that trade on an organized exchange are said to be *listed* on that exchange. To be listed, firms must meet certain minimum criteria concerning, for example, asset size and number of shareholders. These criteria differ from one exchange to another.

The NYSE has the most stringent requirements of the exchanges in the United States. For example, to be listed on the NYSE, a company is expected to have a market value for its publicly held shares of at least $100 million. There are additional minimums on earnings, assets, and number of shares outstanding.

Concept Questions

1.5a   What is a dealer market? How do dealer and auction markets differ?

1.5b   What does *OTC* stand for? What is the large OTC market for stocks called?

1.5c   What is the largest auction market in the United States?

1.6 Summary and Conclusions

This chapter introduced you to some of the basic ideas in corporate finance:

1. Corporate finance has three main areas of concern:
   a. Capital budgeting: What long-term investments should the firm undertake?
   b. Capital structure: Where will the firm get the long-term financing to pay for its investments? In other words, what mixture of debt and equity should the firm use to fund operations?
   c. Working capital management: How should the firm manage its everyday financial activities?

2. The goal of financial management in a for-profit business is to make decisions that increase the value of the stock or, more generally, increase the market value of the equity.

3. The corporate form of organization is superior to other forms when it comes to raising money and transferring ownership interests, but it has the significant disadvantage of double taxation.

4. There is the possibility of conflicts between stockholders and management in a large corporation. We called these conflicts *agency problems* and discussed how they might be controlled and reduced.

5. The advantages of the corporate form are enhanced by the existence of financial markets. Financial markets function as both primary and secondary markets for corporate securities and can be organized as either dealer or auction markets.

Of the topics we've discussed thus far, the most important is the goal of financial management: Maximizing the value of the stock. Throughout the text, we will be analyzing many different financial decisions, but we will always ask the same question: How does the decision under consideration affect the value of the stock?

CONNECT TO FINANCE

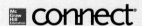 *Connect Finance* offers you plenty of opportunities to practice mastering these concepts. Log on to connect.mheducation.com to learn more. If you like what you see, ask your professor about using *Connect Finance*!

Can you answer the following *Connect* Quiz questions?

Section 1.1   Deciding which fixed assets should be purchased is an example of what type of decision?

Section 1.2   What form of ownership is easiest to transfer?

Section 1.3   What best describes the goal of financial management?

Section 1.4   In a corporation, the primary agency conflict arises between which two parties?

CONCEPTS REVIEW AND CRITICAL THINKING QUESTIONS

1. **The Financial Management Decision Process [LO1]** What are the three types of financial management decisions? For each type of decision, give an example of a business transaction that would be relevant.

2. **Sole Proprietorships and Partnerships [LO3]** What are the four primary disadvantages of the sole proprietorship and partnership forms of business organization? What benefits are there to these types of business organization as opposed to the corporate form?

3. **Corporations [LO3]** What is the primary disadvantage of the corporate form of organization? Name at least two advantages of corporate organization.

4. **Sarbanes-Oxley [LO4]** In response to the Sarbanes-Oxley Act, many small firms in the United States have opted to "go dark" and delist their stock. Why might a company choose this route? What are the costs of "going dark"?

5. **Corporate Finance Organization [LO1]** In a large corporation, what are the two distinct groups that report to the chief financial officer? Which group is the focus of corporate finance?

6. **Goal of Financial Management** [LO2] What goal should always motivate the actions of a firm's financial manager?

7. **Agency Problems** [LO4] Who owns a corporation? Describe the process whereby the owners control the firm's management. What is the main reason that an agency relationship exists in the corporate form of organization? In this context, what kinds of problems can arise?

8. **Primary versus Secondary Markets** [LO3] You've probably noticed coverage in the financial press of an initial public offering (IPO) of a company's securities. Is an IPO a primary market transaction or a secondary market transaction?

9. **Auction versus Dealer Markets** [LO3] What does it mean when we say the New York Stock Exchange is an auction market? How are auction markets different from dealer markets? What kind of market is NASDAQ?

10. **Not-for-Profit Firm Goals** [LO2] Suppose you were the financial manager of a not-for-profit business (a not-for-profit hospital, perhaps). What kinds of goals do you think would be appropriate?

11. **Goal of the Firm** [LO2] Evaluate the following statement: Managers should not focus on the current stock value because doing so will lead to an overemphasis on short-term profits at the expense of long-term profits.

12. **Ethics and Firm Goals** [LO2] Can our goal of maximizing the value of the stock conflict with other goals, such as avoiding unethical or illegal behavior? In particular, do you think subjects like customer and employee safety, the environment, and the general good of society fit in this framework, or are they essentially ignored? Think of some specific scenarios to illustrate your answer.

13. **International Firm Goal** [LO2] Would our goal of maximizing the value of the stock be different if we were thinking about financial management in a foreign country? Why or why not?

14. **Agency Problems** [LO4] Suppose you own stock in a company. The current price per share is $25. Another company has just announced that it wants to buy your company and will pay $35 per share to acquire all the outstanding stock. Your company's management immediately begins fighting off this hostile bid. Is management acting in the shareholders' best interests? Why or why not?

15. **Agency Problems and Corporate Ownership** [LO4] Corporate ownership varies around the world. Historically individuals have owned the majority of shares in public corporations in the United States. In Germany and Japan, however, banks, other large financial institutions, and other companies own most of the stock in public corporations. Do you think agency problems are likely to be more or less severe in Germany and Japan than in the United States? Why? Over the last few decades, large financial institutions such as mutual funds and pension funds have been becoming the dominant owners of stock in the United States, and these institutions are becoming more active in corporate affairs. What are the implications of this trend for agency problems and corporate control?

16. **Executive Compensation** [LO4] Critics have charged that compensation to top managers in the United States is simply too high and should be cut back. For example, focusing on large corporations, Mark Parker, CEO of Nike, earned about $47.6 million in 2016. Are such amounts excessive? In answering, it might be helpful to recognize that superstar athletes such as LeBron James, top entertainers such as Taylor Swift and Dwayne Johnson, and many others at the top of their respective fields earn at least as much, if not a great deal more.

The McGee Cake Company

In early 2013, Doc and Lyn McGee formed the McGee Cake Company. The company produced a full line of cakes, and its specialties included chess cake,* lemon pound cake, and double-iced, double-chocolate cake. The couple formed the company as an outside interest, and both continued to work at their current jobs. Doc did all the baking, and Lyn handled the marketing and distribution. With good product quality and a sound marketing plan, the company grew rapidly. In early 2016, the company was featured in a widely distributed entre-preneurial magazine. Later that year, the company was featured in *Gourmet Desserts*, a leading specialty food magazine. After the article appeared in *Gourmet Desserts*, sales exploded, and the company began receiving orders from all over the world.

Because of the increased sales, Doc left his other job, fol-lowed shortly by Lyn. The company hired additional workers to meet demand. Unfortunately, the fast growth experienced by the company led to cash flow and capacity problems. The com-pany is currently producing as many cakes as possible with

*Chess cake is quite delicious and distinct from cheesecake. The origin of the name is obscure.

the assets it owns, but demand for its cakes is still growing. Further, the company has been approached by a national super-market chain with a proposal to put four of its cakes in all of the chain's stores, and a national restaurant chain has contacted the company about selling McGee cakes in its restaurants. The restaurant would sell the cakes without a brand name.

Doc and Lyn have operated the company as a sole propri-etorship. They have approached you to help manage and direct the company's growth. Specifically, they have asked you to an-swer the following questions.

QUESTIONS

1. What are the advantages and disadvantages of changing the company organization from a sole proprietorship to an LLC?

2. What are the advantages and disadvantages of changing the company organization from a sole proprietorship to a corporation?

3. Ultimately, what action would you recommend the com-pany undertake? Why?

2 | Financial Statements, Taxes, and Cash Flow

IN DECEMBER 2017, the Tax Cuts and Jobs Act was enacted into law beginning in 2018. The new law was a sweeping change to corporate taxes in the U.S. For example, rather than depreciating an asset over time for tax purposes, companies are allowed to depreciate the entire purchase price in the first year. Another change was a limit to the tax deductibility of interest expense. However, possibly the biggest change was the switch from a graduated corporate income tax structure, which ranged from 15 percent to 39 percent, to a flat 21 percent corporate tax rate.

While the change in the corporate tax rate affects net income, there is a more important impact. Because taxes are a key consideration in making investment decisions, the change in the tax rate could lead to a significant change in corporate behavior. Understanding why ultimately leads us to the main subject of this chapter: That all-important substance known as *cash flow*.

Learning Objectives

After studying this chapter, you should be able to:

LO1 Describe the difference between accounting value (or *book value*) and market value.

LO2 Describe the difference between accounting income and cash flow.

LO3 Describe the difference between average and marginal tax rates.

LO4 Determine a firm's cash flow from its financial statements.

For updates on the latest happenings in finance, visit fundamentalsofcorporatefinance.blogspot.com.

In this chapter, we examine financial statements, taxes, and cash flow. Our emphasis is not on preparing financial statements. Instead, we recognize that financial statements are frequently a key source of information for financial decisions, so our goal is to briefly examine such statements and point out some of their more relevant features. We pay special attention to some of the practical details of cash flow.

As you read, pay particular attention to two important differences: (1) the difference between accounting value and market value and (2) the difference between accounting income and cash flow. These distinctions will be important throughout the book.

The Balance Sheet

2.1

Excel Master It!
Excel Master coverage online

The **balance sheet** is a snapshot of the firm. It is a convenient means of organizing and summarizing what a firm owns (its assets), what a firm owes (its liabilities), and the difference between the two (the firm's equity) at a given point in time. Figure 2.1 illustrates how the balance sheet is constructed. As shown, the left side lists the assets of the firm, and the right side lists the liabilities and equity.

balance sheet
Financial statement showing a firm's accounting value on a particular date.

ASSETS: THE LEFT SIDE

Assets are classified as either *current* or *fixed* assets. A fixed asset is one that has a relatively long life. Fixed assets can be either *tangible*, such as a truck or a computer, or *intangible*, such as a trademark or patent. A current asset has a life of less than one year. This means that the asset will convert to cash within 12 months. For example, inventory would normally be purchased and sold within a year and is classified as a current asset. Obviously, cash itself is a current asset. Accounts receivable (money owed to the firm by its customers) are also current assets.

Three excellent sites for company financial information are **finance.yahoo.com**, **finance.google.com**, and **money.cnn.com**.

LIABILITIES AND OWNERS' EQUITY: THE RIGHT SIDE

The firm's liabilities are the first thing listed on the right side of the balance sheet. These are classified as either *current* or *long-term*. Current liabilities, like current assets, have a life of less than one year (meaning they must be paid within the year) and are listed before long-term liabilities. Accounts payable (money the firm owes to its suppliers) are one example of a current liability.

A debt that is not due in the coming year is classified as a long-term liability. A loan that the firm will pay off in five years is one such long-term debt. Firms borrow in the long term from a variety of sources. We will tend to use the terms *bond* and *bondholders* generically to refer to long-term debt and long-term creditors, respectively.

Finally, by definition, the difference between the total value of the assets (current and fixed) and the total value of the liabilities (current and long-term) is the *shareholders' equity*, also called *common equity* or *owners' equity*. This feature of the balance sheet is intended to reflect the fact that, if the firm were to sell all its assets and use the money to pay off its debts, then whatever residual value remained would belong to the shareholders. So, the balance sheet "balances" because the value of the left side always equals the value

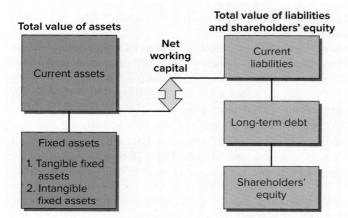

FIGURE 2.1

The Balance Sheet. Left Side: Total Value of Assets. Right Side: Total Value of Liabilities and Shareholders' Equity.

The Balance Sheet

The **balance sheet** is a snapshot of the firm. It is a convenient means of organizing and summarizing what a firm owns (its assets), what a firm owes (its liabilities), and the difference between the two (the firm's equity) at a given point in time. Figure 2.1 illustrates how the balance sheet is constructed. As shown, the left side lists the assets of the firm, and the right side lists the liabilities and equity.

Excel Master It!

Excel Master coverage online

ASSETS: THE LEFT SIDE

Assets are classified as either *current* or *fixed* assets. A fixed asset is one that has a relatively long life. Fixed assets can be either *tangible*, such as a truck or a computer, or *intangible*, such as a trademark or patent. A current asset has a life of less than one year. This means that the asset will convert to cash within 12 months. For example, inventory would normally be purchased and sold within a year and is classified as a current asset. Obviously, cash itself is a current asset. Accounts receivable (money owed to the firm by its customers) are also current assets.

balance sheet
Financial statement showing a firm's accounting value on a particular date.

LIABILITIES AND OWNERS' EQUITY: THE RIGHT SIDE

The firm's liabilities are the first thing listed on the right side of the balance sheet. These are classified as either *current* or *long-term*. Current liabilities, like current assets, have a life of less than one year (meaning they must be paid within the year) and are listed before long-term liabilities. Accounts payable (money the firm owes to its suppliers) are one example of a current liability.

A debt that is not due in the coming year is classified as a long-term liability. A loan that the firm will pay off in five years is one such long-term debt. Firms borrow in the long term from a variety of sources. We will tend to use the terms *bond* and *bondholders* generically to refer to long-term debt and long-term creditors, respectively.

Finally, by definition, the difference between the total value of the assets (current and fixed) and the total value of the liabilities (current and long-term) is the *shareholders' equity*, also called *common equity* or *owners' equity*. This feature of the balance sheet is intended to reflect the fact that, if the firm were to sell all its assets and use the money to pay off its debts, then whatever residual value remained would belong to the shareholders. So, the balance sheet "balances" because the value of the left side always equals the value

Three excellent sites for company financial information are **finance.yahoo.com**, **finance.google.com**, and **money.cnn.com**.

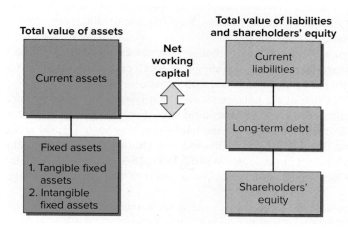

FIGURE 2.1

The Balance Sheet. Left Side: Total Value of Assets. Right Side: Total Value of Liabilities and Shareholders' Equity.

of the right side. That is, the value of the firm's assets is equal to the sum of its liabilities and shareholders' equity:[1]

Assets = Liabilities + Shareholders' equity

2.1

This is the *balance sheet identity*, or equation, and it always holds because shareholders' equity is defined as the difference between assets and liabilities.

NET WORKING CAPITAL

net working capital
Current assets less current liabilities.

As shown in Figure 2.1, the difference between a firm's current assets and its current liabilities is called **net working capital**. Net working capital is positive when current assets exceed current liabilities. Based on the definitions of current assets and current liabilities, this means the cash that will become available over the next 12 months exceeds the cash that must be paid over the same period. For this reason, net working capital is usually positive in a healthy firm.

EXAMPLE 2.1	Building the Balance Sheet

A firm has current assets of $100, net fixed assets of $500, short-term debt of $70, and long-term debt of $200. What does the balance sheet look like? What is shareholders' equity? What is net working capital?

In this case, total assets are $100 + 500 = $600 and total liabilities are $70 + 200 = $270, so shareholders' equity is the difference: $600 − 270 = $330. The balance sheet would look like this:

Assets		Liabilities and Shareholders' Equity	
Current assets	$100	Current liabilities	$ 70
Net fixed assets	500	Long-term debt	200
		Shareholders' equity	330
Total assets	$600	Total liabilities and shareholders' equity	$600

Net working capital is the difference between current assets and current liabilities, or $100 − 70 = $30.

Table 2.1 shows simplified balance sheets for the fictitious U.S. Corporation. The assets on the balance sheet are listed in order of the length of time it takes for them to convert to cash in the normal course of business. Similarly, the liabilities are listed in the order in which they would normally be paid.

The structure of the assets for a particular firm reflects the line of business the firm is in, as well as managerial decisions regarding how much cash and inventory to have on hand, the firm's credit policy, fixed-asset acquisitions, and so on.

The liabilities side of the balance sheet primarily reflects managerial decisions about capital structure and the use of short-term debt. For example, in 2018, total long-term debt for U.S. Corporation was $454 and total equity was $640 + 1,690 = $2,330, so total long-term financing was $454 + 2,330 = $2,784. (Note that, throughout, all figures are in millions of dollars.) Of this amount, $454/$2,784 = 16.31 percent was long-term debt. This percentage reflects capital structure decisions made in the past by the management of U.S.

Disney has a good investor relations site at **thewaltdisneycompany.com /investors**.

---

[1]The terms *owners' equity, shareholders' equity,* and *stockholders' equity* are used interchangeably to refer to the equity in a corporation. The term *net worth* is also used. Variations exist in addition to these.

TABLE 2.1
Balance Sheets

U.S. CORPORATION
2017 and 2018 Balance Sheets
($ in millions)

Assets			Liabilities and Owners' Equity		
	2017	**2018**		**2017**	**2018**
Current assets			Current liabilities		
Cash	$ 104	$ 221	Accounts payable	$ 232	$ 266
Accounts receivable	455	688	Notes payable	196	123
Inventory	553	555	Total	$ 428	$ 389
Total	$1,112	$1,464			
Fixed assets					
Net plant and equipment	$1,644	$1,709	Long-term debt	$ 408	$ 454
			Owners' equity		
			Common stock and paid-in surplus	600	640
			Retained earnings	1,320	1,690
			Total	$1,920	$2,330
Total assets	$2,756	$3,173	Total liabilities and owners' equity	$2,756	$3,173

There are three particularly important things to keep in mind when examining a balance sheet: liquidity, debt versus equity, and market value versus book value.

LIQUIDITY

Liquidity refers to the speed and ease with which an asset can be converted to cash. Gold is a relatively liquid asset; a custom manufacturing facility is not. Liquidity actually has two dimensions: Ease of conversion versus loss of value. Any asset can be converted to cash quickly if we cut the price enough. A highly liquid asset is therefore one that can be quickly sold without significant loss of value. An illiquid asset is one that cannot be quickly converted to cash without a substantial price reduction.

Assets are normally listed on the balance sheet in order of decreasing liquidity, meaning that the most liquid assets are listed first. Current assets are relatively liquid and include cash and assets we expect to convert to cash over the next 12 months. Accounts receivable, for example, represent amounts not yet collected from customers on sales already made. Naturally, we hope these will convert to cash in the near future. Inventory is probably the least liquid of the current assets, at least for many businesses.

Fixed assets are, for the most part, relatively illiquid. These consist of tangible things such as buildings and equipment that don't convert to cash at all in normal business activity (they are, of course, used in the business to generate cash). Intangible assets, such as a trademark, have no physical existence but can be very valuable. Like tangible fixed assets, they won't ordinarily convert to cash and are generally considered illiquid.

Liquidity is valuable. The more liquid a business is, the less likely it is to experience financial distress (that is, difficulty in paying debts or buying needed assets). Unfortunately, liquid assets are generally less profitable to hold. Cash holdings are the most liquid of all investments, but they sometimes earn no return at all—they just sit there. There is therefore a trade-off between the advantages of liquidity and forgone potential profits.

Annual and quarterly financial statements (and lots more) for most public U.S. corporations can be found in the EDGAR database at **www.sec.gov**.

DEBT VERSUS EQUITY

To the extent that a firm borrows money, it usually gives first claim to the firm's cash flow to creditors. Equity holders are entitled to only the residual value, the portion left after creditors are paid. The value of this residual portion is the shareholders' equity in the firm, which is just the value of the firm's assets less the value of the firm's liabilities:

Shareholders' equity = Assets − Liabilities

This is true in an accounting sense because shareholders' equity is defined as this residual portion. More important, it is true in an economic sense: If the firm sells its assets and pays its debts, whatever cash is left belongs to the shareholders.

The use of debt in a firm's capital structure is called *financial leverage*. The more debt a firm has (as a percentage of assets), the greater is its degree of financial leverage. As we discuss in later chapters, debt acts like a lever in the sense that using it can greatly magnify both gains and losses. So, financial leverage increases the potential reward to shareholders, but it also increases the potential for financial distress and business failure.

MARKET VALUE VERSUS BOOK VALUE

Generally Accepted Accounting Principles (GAAP)
The common set of standards and procedures by which audited financial statements are prepared.

The home page for the Financial Accounting Standards Board (FASB) is **www.fasb.org**.

The values shown on the balance sheet for the firm's assets are *book values* and generally are not what the assets are actually worth. Under **Generally Accepted Accounting Principles (GAAP)**, audited financial statements in the United States mostly show assets at *historical cost*. In other words, assets are "carried on the books" at what the firm paid for them, no matter how long ago they were purchased or how much they are worth today.

For current assets, market value and book value might be somewhat similar because current assets are bought and converted into cash over a relatively short span of time. In other circumstances, the two values might differ quite a bit. Moreover, for fixed assets, it would be purely a coincidence if the actual market value of an asset (what the asset could be sold for) were equal to its book value. For example, a railroad might own enormous tracts of land purchased a century or more ago. What the railroad paid for that land could be hundreds or thousands of times less than what the land is worth today. The balance sheet would nonetheless show the historical cost.

The difference between market value and book value is important for understanding the impact of reported gains and losses. For example, from time to time, accounting rule changes take place that lead to reductions in the book value of certain types of assets. However, a change in accounting rules all by itself has no effect on what the assets in question are really worth. Instead, the market value of an asset depends on things like its riskiness and cash flows, neither of which have anything to do with accounting.

The balance sheet is potentially useful to many different parties. A supplier might look at the size of accounts payable to see how promptly the firm pays its bills. A potential creditor would examine the liquidity and degree of financial leverage. Managers within the firm can track things like the amount of cash and the amount of inventory the firm keeps on hand. Uses such as these are discussed in more detail in Chapter 3.

Managers and investors will frequently be interested in knowing the value of the firm. This information is not on the balance sheet. The fact that balance sheet assets are listed at cost means that there is no necessary connection between the total assets shown and the value of the firm. Indeed, many of the most valuable assets a firm might have—good management, a good reputation, talented employees—don't appear on the balance sheet at all.

Similarly, the shareholders' equity figure on the balance sheet and the true value of the stock need not be related. For example, in late 2017, the book value of IBM's equity was about $18 billion, while the market value was $142 billion. At the same time, Alphabet's book value was $139 billion, while the market value was $731 billion.

For financial managers, then, the accounting value of the stock is not an especially important concern; it is the market value that matters. Henceforth, whenever we speak of the value of an asset or the value of the firm, we will normally mean its *market value*. So, for example, when we say the goal of the financial manager is to increase the value of the stock, we mean the market value of the stock.

Market Value versus Book Value — EXAMPLE 2.2

The Klingon Corporation has net fixed assets with a book value of $700 and an appraised market value of about $1,000. Net working capital is $400 on the books, but approximately $600 would be realized if all the current accounts were liquidated. Klingon has $500 in long-term debt, both book value and market value. What is the book value of the equity? What is the market value?

We can construct two simplified balance sheets, one in accounting (book value) terms and one in economic (market value) terms:

KLINGON CORPORATION
Balance Sheets
Market Value versus Book Value

Assets			Liabilities and Shareholders' Equity		
	Book	Market		Book	Market
Net working capital	$ 400	$ 600	Long-term debt	$ 500	$ 500
Net fixed assets	700	1,000	Shareholders' equity	600	1,100
	$1,100	$1,600		$1,100	$1,600

In this example, shareholders' equity is actually worth almost twice as much as what is shown on the books. The distinction between book and market values is important precisely because book values can be so different from true economic value.

Concept Questions

2.1a   What is the balance sheet identity?
2.1b   What is liquidity? Why is it important?
2.1c   What do we mean by financial leverage?
2.1d   Explain the difference between book value and market value. Which is more important to the financial manager? Why?

income statement
Financial statement summarizing a firm's performance over a period of time.

The Income Statement

2.2

The **income statement** measures performance over some period of time, usually a quarter or a year. The income statement equation is:

Revenues − Expenses = Income

If you think of the balance sheet as a snapshot, then you can think of the income statement as a video recording covering the period between before and after pictures. Table 2.2 gives a simplified income statement for U.S. Corporation.

Excel Master It!
Excel Master coverage online

TABLE 2.2

Income Statement

U.S. CORPORATION 2018 Income Statement ($ in millions)		
Net sales		$1,509
Cost of goods sold		750
Depreciation		65
Earnings before interest and taxes		$ 694
Interest paid		70
Taxable income		$ 624
Taxes (21%)		131
Net income		$ 493
Dividends	$123	
Addition to retained earnings	370	

The first thing reported on an income statement would usually be revenue and expenses from the firm's principal operations. Subsequent parts include, among other things, financing expenses such as interest paid. Taxes paid are reported separately. The last item is *net income* (the so-called bottom line). Net income is often expressed on a per-share basis and called *earnings per share* (EPS).

As indicated, U.S. Corporation paid cash dividends of $123. The difference between net income and cash dividends, $370, is the addition to retained earnings for the year. This amount is added to the cumulative retained earnings account on the balance sheet. If you look back at the two balance sheets for U.S. Corporation, you'll see that retained earnings did go up by this amount: $1,320 + 370 = $1,690.

EXAMPLE 2.3	Calculating Earnings and Dividends per Share

Suppose U.S. had 200 million shares outstanding at the end of 2018. Based on the income statement in Table 2.2, what was EPS? What were dividends per share?

From the income statement, we see that U.S. had a net income of $493 million for the year. Total dividends were $123 million. Because 200 million shares were outstanding, we can calculate earnings per share, or EPS, and dividends per share as follows:

$$\text{Earnings per share} = \text{Net income/Total shares outstanding}$$
$$= \$493/200 = \$2.46 \text{ per share}$$
$$\text{Dividends per share} = \text{Total dividends/Total shares outstanding}$$
$$= \$123/200 = \$.615 \text{ per share}$$

When looking at an income statement, the financial manager needs to keep three things in mind: GAAP, cash versus noncash items, and time and costs.

GAAP AND THE INCOME STATEMENT

An income statement prepared using GAAP will show revenue when it accrues. This is not necessarily when the cash comes in. The general rule (the *recognition* or *realization principle*) is to recognize revenue when the earnings process is virtually complete and the value of an exchange of goods or services is known or can be reliably determined. In practice, this principle usually means that revenue is recognized at the time of sale, which need not be the same as the time of collection.

Expenses shown on the income statement are based on the *matching principle*. The basic idea here is to first determine revenues as described previously and then match those revenues with the costs associated with producing them. So, if we manufacture a product and then sell it on credit, the revenue is realized at the time of sale. The production and other costs associated with the sale of that product will likewise be recognized at that time. Once again, the actual cash outflows may have occurred at some different time.

As a result of the way revenues and expenses are realized, the figures shown on the income statement may not be at all representative of the actual cash inflows and outflows that occurred during a particular period.

NONCASH ITEMS

A primary reason that accounting income differs from cash flow is that an income statement contains **noncash items**. The most important of these is *depreciation*. Suppose a firm purchases an asset for $5,000 and pays in cash. Obviously, the firm has a $5,000 cash outflow at the time of purchase. However, instead of deducting the $5,000 as an expense, an accountant might depreciate the asset over a five-year period.

If the depreciation is straight-line and the asset is written down to zero over that period, then $5,000/5 = $1,000 will be deducted each year as an expense.[2] The important thing to recognize is that this $1,000 deduction isn't cash—it's an accounting number. The actual cash outflow occurred when the asset was purchased.

noncash items
Expenses charged against revenues that do not directly affect cash flow, such as depreciation.

The depreciation deduction is another application of the matching principle in accounting. The revenues associated with an asset generally occur over some length of time. So, the accountant seeks to match the expense of purchasing the asset with the benefits produced from owning it.

As we will see, for the financial manager, the actual timing of cash inflows and outflows is critical in coming up with a reasonable estimate of market value. For this reason, we need to learn how to separate the cash flows from the noncash accounting entries. In reality, the difference between cash flow and accounting income can be pretty dramatic. For example, consider the case of U.S. Steel, which reported a net loss of $340 million for the first quarter of 2016. Sounds bad, but U.S. Steel also reported a *positive* cash flow of $113 million, a difference of about $453 million!

TIME AND COSTS

It is often useful to think of the future as having two distinct parts: The short run and the long run. These are not precise time periods. The distinction has to do with whether costs are fixed or variable. In the long run, all business costs are variable. Given sufficient time, assets can be sold, debts can be paid, and so on.

If our time horizon is relatively short, however, some costs are effectively fixed—they must be paid no matter what (property taxes, for example). Other costs, such as wages to laborers and payments to suppliers, are still variable. As a result, even in the short run, the firm can vary its output level by varying expenditures in these areas.

The distinction between fixed and variable costs is important, at times, to the financial manager, but the way costs are reported on the income statement is not a good guide to which costs are which. The reason is that, in practice, accountants tend to classify costs as either product costs or period costs.

---

[2]By *straight-line*, we mean that the depreciation deduction is the same every year. By *written down to zero*, we mean that the asset is assumed to have no value at the end of five years. Depreciation is discussed in more detail in Chapter 10.

WORK THE WEB

The U.S. Securities and Exchange Commission (SEC) requires that most public companies file regular reports, including annual and quarterly financial statements. The SEC has a public site named EDGAR that makes these free reports available at www.sec.gov. We went to "Search EDGAR" and looked up Alphabet:

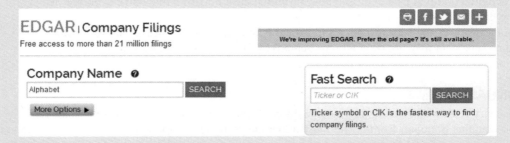

Here is a partial view of what we found:

The two reports we look at the most are the 10-K, which is the annual report filed with the SEC, and the 10-Q. The 10-K includes the list of officers and their salaries, financial statements for the previous fiscal year, and an explanation by the company of the financial results. The 10-Q is a smaller report that includes the financial statements for the quarter.

Questions

1. As you can imagine, electronic filing of documents with the SEC has not been around for very long. Go to www.sec.gov and find the filings for General Electric. What is the date of the oldest 10-K available on the website for General Electric? Look up the 10-K forms for IBM and Apple to see if the year of the first electronic filing is the same for these companies.

2. Go to www.sec.gov and find out when the following forms are used: Form DEF 14A, Form 8-K, and Form 6-K.

Product costs include such things as raw materials, direct labor expense, and manufacturing overhead. These are reported on the income statement as costs of goods sold, but they include both fixed and variable costs. Similarly, *period costs* are incurred during a particular time period and might be reported as selling, general, and administrative expenses. Once again, some of these period costs may be fixed and others may be variable. The company president's salary, for example, is a period cost and is probably fixed, at least in the short run.

The balance sheets and income statement we have been using thus far are hypothetical. Our nearby *Work the Web* box shows how to find actual balance sheets and income statements online for almost any company. Also, with the increasing globalization of business, there is a clear need for accounting standards to become more comparable across countries. Accordingly, in recent years, U.S. accounting standards have become more closely tied to International Financial Reporting Standards (IFRS). In particular, the Financial Accounting Standards Board (FASB), which is in charge of U.S. GAAP policies, and the International Accounting Standards Board, which is in charge of IFRS policies, have been working toward a convergence of policies since 2002. Although GAAP and IFRS have become similar in important ways, as of early 2018, it appears that a full convergence of accounting policies is off the table, at least for now.

For more information about IFRS, check out the website **www.ifrs.org**.

Concept Questions

2.2a   What is the income statement equation?

2.2b   What are the three things to keep in mind when looking at an income statement?

2.2c   Why is accounting income not the same as cash flow? Give two reasons.

Taxes

2.3

Taxes can be one of the largest cash outflows a firm experiences. For example, for the fiscal year 2016, JPMorgan Chase's earnings before taxes were about $34.54 billion. Its tax bill, including all taxes paid worldwide, was a whopping $9.8 billion, or about 28 percent of its pretax earnings. Also for fiscal year 2016, Walmart had a taxable income of $20.50 billion, and the company paid $6.2 billion in taxes—an average tax rate of 30 percent.

Excel Master It!

Excel Master coverage online

The size of a company's tax bill is determined by the tax code, an often amended set of rules. In this section, we examine corporate tax rates and how taxes are calculated. If the various rules of taxation seem a little bizarre or convoluted to you, keep in mind that the tax code is the result of political, not economic, forces. As a result, there is no reason why it has to make economic sense.

CORPORATE TAX RATES

Corporate tax rates in effect for 2017 (but not 2018 and beyond) are shown in Table 2.3. As shown, corporate tax rates rise from 15 percent to 39 percent, but they drop back to 34 percent on income over $335,000. They then rise to 38 percent and subsequently fall to 35 percent.

The tax rate schedule in Table 2.3 was simplified considerably by the Tax Cuts and Jobs Act of 2017. Beginning in 2018, the corporate tax rate is 21 percent, and that rate applies regardless of the level of taxable income.

TABLE 2.3

Corporate Tax Rates for 2017

Taxable Income	Tax Rate
$ 0– 50,000	15%
50,001– 75,000	25
75,001– 100,000	34
100,001– 335,000	39
335,001–10,000,000	34
10,000,001–15,000,000	35
15,000,001–18,333,333	38
18,333,334+	35

AVERAGE VERSUS MARGINAL TAX RATES

average tax rate
Total taxes paid divided by total taxable income.

marginal tax rate
Amount of tax payable on the next dollar earned.

In making financial decisions, it is frequently important to distinguish between average and marginal tax rates. Your **average tax rate** is your tax bill divided by your taxable income— in other words, the percentage of your income that goes to pay taxes. Your **marginal tax rate** is the rate of the extra tax you would pay if you earned one more dollar. The percentage tax rates shown in Table 2.3 are all marginal rates. Put another way, the tax rates in Table 2.3 applied to the part of income in the indicated range only, not all income.

The difference between average and marginal tax rates can best be illustrated with an example. Suppose our corporation had a taxable income of $200,000 in 2017. What was the tax bill? Using Table 2.3, we can figure our tax bill:

```
.15($50,000)              = $ 7,500
.25($75,000 − 50,000)     =   6,250
.34($100,000 − 75,000)    =   8,500
.39($200,000 − 100,000)   =  39,000
                            $61,250
```

The IRS has a great website! Check out **www.irs.gov**.

Our total tax was $61,250.

In our example, what is the average tax rate? We had a taxable income of $200,000 and a tax bill of $61,250, so the average tax rate is $61,250/$200,000 = 30.625 percent. What is the marginal tax rate? If we made one more dollar, the tax on that dollar would be 39 cents, so our marginal rate is 39 percent.

EXAMPLE 2.4   **Deep in the Heart of Taxes**

Algernon, Inc., has a taxable income of $85,000 for 2017. What is its tax bill? What is its average tax rate? Its marginal tax rate? What would these be in 2018 and beyond?

From Table 2.3, we see that the tax rate applied to the first $50,000 is 15 percent; the rate applied to the next $25,000 is 25 percent; and the rate applied after that up to $100,000 is 34 percent. So Algernon must pay .15 × $50,000 + .25 × $25,000 + .34 × ($85,000 − 75,000) = $17,150. The average tax rate is thus $17,150/$85,000 = 20.18 percent. The marginal rate is 34 percent because Algernon's taxes would rise by 34 cents if it had another dollar in taxable income.

In 2018 and beyond, the average rate and the marginal rate are the same, 21 percent. There is no need to do any calculations!

Table 2.4 summarizes some different taxable incomes, marginal tax rates, and average tax rates for corporations. Notice how the average and marginal tax rates come together at 35 percent.

(1) Taxable Income	(2) Marginal Tax Rate	(3) Total Tax	(3)/(1) Average Tax Rate
$ 45,000	15%	$ 6,750	15.00%
70,000	25	12,500	17.86
95,000	34	20,550	21.63
250,000	39	80,750	32.30
1,000,000	34	340,000	34.00
17,500,000	38	6,100,000	34.86
50,000,000	35	17,500,000	35.00
100,000,000	35	35,000,000	35.00

TABLE 2.4

Corporate Taxes and Tax Rates

With a *flat-rate* tax, there is only one tax rate, so the rate is the same for all income levels. The 21 percent corporate tax created by the Tax Cuts and Jobs Act of 2017 is such a tax. In this case, as Example 2.4 illustrates, the marginal tax rate is always the same as the average tax rate. As it stands now, corporate taxation in the United States shifted in 2018 from a modified flat-rate tax, which became a true flat rate for only the highest incomes, to a true flat rate.

Normally the marginal tax rate is relevant for financial decision making. The reason is that any new cash flows will be taxed at that marginal rate. Because financial decisions usually involve new cash flows or changes in existing ones, this rate will tell us the marginal effect of a decision on our tax bill.

We should note that we have simplified the U.S. tax code in our discussions. In reality, the tax code is much more complex and riddled with various tax deductions and loopholes allowed for certain industries. As a result, the average corporate tax rate may be far from 21 percent for many companies. Table 2.5 displays average tax rates for various industries. Note that these rates pre-date the 21 percent flat tax instituted for 2018, but we still expect to see a wide range of average tax rates in 2018 and beyond due to other features of the tax code.

Prior to 2018, with a tax rate of 35 percent for large, profitable companies, the U.S. corporate tax rate was the highest in the world among developed economies. As a result, several companies in recent years have undertaken a controversial reorganization called a *tax inversion*. In a tax inversion, a company transfers ownership of its U.S.-based operations to a corporation domiciled in a foreign country, typically by a merger. This maneuver allows the company to avoid paying taxes in the United States on earnings from outside the United

Industry	Number of Companies	Average Tax Rate
Electric utilities (Eastern U.S.)	24	33.8%
Trucking	33	32.7
Railroad	15	27.4
Securities brokerage	30	20.5
Banking	481	17.5
Medical supplies	264	11.2
Internet	239	5.9
Pharmaceutical	337	5.6
Biotechnology	121	4.5

TABLE 2.5

Average Tax Rates

States. The 2017 reduction in the corporate tax rate to 21 percent puts the United States more-or-less in the middle relative to other developed economies, and a primary reason for the reduction was to eliminate the incentive for tax inversions and other strategies to avoid the U.S. corporate tax.

Before moving on, we should note that the tax rates we have discussed in this section relate to federal taxes only. Overall tax rates can be higher if state, local, and any other taxes are considered.

Concept Questions

2.3a   What is the difference between a marginal and an average tax rate?

2.3b   What was the impact of the Tax Cuts and Jobs Act of 2017 on corporate tax rates?

2.4 Cash Flow

Excel Master It!

Excel Master coverage online

At this point, we are ready to discuss perhaps one of the most important pieces of financial information that can be gleaned from financial statements: Cash flow. By *cash flow*, we mean the difference between the number of dollars that came in and the number of dollars that went out. For example, if you were the owner of a business, you might be very interested in how much cash you actually took out of your business in a given year. How to determine this amount is one of the things we discuss next.

No standard financial statement presents this information in the way that we wish. We will therefore discuss how to calculate cash flow for U.S. Corporation and point out how the result differs from that of standard financial statement calculations. There is a standard financial accounting statement called the *statement of cash flows*, but it is concerned with a somewhat different issue that should not be confused with what is discussed in this section. The accounting statement of cash flows is discussed in Chapter 3.

From the balance sheet identity, we know that the value of a firm's assets is equal to the value of its liabilities plus the value of its equity. Similarly, the cash flow from the firm's assets must equal the sum of the cash flow to creditors and the cash flow to stockholders (or owners):

Cash flow from assets = Cash flow to creditors + Cash flow to stockholders   **2.3**

This is the *cash flow identity*. It says that the cash flow from the firm's assets is equal to the cash flow paid to suppliers of capital to the firm. What it reflects is the fact that a firm generates cash through its various activities, and that cash is either used to pay creditors or paid out to the owners of the firm. We discuss the various things that make up these cash flows next.

CASH FLOW FROM ASSETS

cash flow from assets
The total of cash flow to creditors and cash flow to stockholders, consisting of the following: operating cash flow, capital spending, and change in net working capital.

operating cash flow
Cash generated from a firm's normal business activities.

Cash flow from assets involves three components: operating cash flow, capital spending, and change in net working capital. **Operating cash flow** refers to the cash flow that results from the firm's day-to-day activities of producing and selling. Expenses associated with the firm's financing of its assets are not included because they are not operating expenses.

As we discussed in Chapter 1, some portion of the firm's cash flow is reinvested in the firm. *Capital spending* refers to the net spending on fixed assets (purchases of fixed assets less sales of fixed assets). Finally, *change in net working capital* is measured as the net change in current assets relative to current liabilities for the period being examined and represents the amount spent on net working capital. The three components of cash flow are examined in more detail next.

Operating Cash Flow   To calculate operating cash flow (OCF), we want to calculate revenues minus costs, but we don't want to include depreciation because it's not a cash outflow, and we don't want to include interest because it's a financing expense. We do want to include taxes because taxes are (unfortunately) paid in cash.

If we look at U.S. Corporation's income statement (Table 2.2), we see that earnings before interest and taxes (EBIT) are $694. This is almost what we want because it doesn't include interest paid. However, we need to make two adjustments. First, recall that depreciation is a noncash expense. To get cash flow, we first add back the $65 in depreciation because it wasn't a cash deduction. The other adjustment is to subtract the $131 in taxes because these were paid in cash. The result is operating cash flow:

U.S. CORPORATION 2018 Operating Cash Flow	
Earnings before interest and taxes	$694
+ Depreciation	65
− Taxes	131
Operating cash flow	$628

U.S. Corporation had a 2018 operating cash flow of $628.

Operating cash flow is an important number because it tells us, on a very basic level, whether a firm's cash inflows from its business operations are sufficient to cover its everyday cash outflows. For this reason, a negative operating cash flow is often a sign of trouble.

There is an unpleasant possibility of confusion when we speak of operating cash flow. In accounting practice, operating cash flow is often defined as net income plus depreciation. For U.S. Corporation, this would amount to $493 + 65 = $558.

The accounting definition of operating cash flow differs from ours in one important way: Interest is deducted when net income is computed. Notice that the difference between the $628 operating cash flow we calculated and this $558 is $70, the amount of interest paid for the year. This definition of cash flow thus considers interest paid to be an operating expense. Our definition treats it properly as a financing expense. If there were no interest expense, the two definitions would be the same.

To finish our calculation of cash flow from assets for U.S. Corporation, we need to consider how much of the $628 operating cash flow was reinvested in the firm. We consider spending on fixed assets first.

Capital Spending   Net capital spending is money spent on fixed assets less money received from the sale of fixed assets. At the end of 2017, net fixed assets for U.S. Corporation (Table 2.1) were $1,644. During the year, U.S. wrote off (depreciated) $65 worth of fixed assets on the income statement. So, if the firm didn't purchase any new fixed assets, net fixed assets would have been $1,644 − 65 = $1,579 at year's end. The 2018 balance sheet shows $1,709 in net fixed assets, so U.S. must have spent a total of $1,709 − 1,579 = $130 on fixed assets during the year:

This $130 is the net capital spending for 2018.

Ending net fixed assets	$1,709
− Beginning net fixed assets	1,644
+ Depreciation	65
Net capital spending	$ 130

Could net capital spending be negative? The answer is yes. This would happen if the firm sold more assets than it purchased. The *net* here refers to purchases of fixed assets net of any sales of fixed assets. You will often see capital spending called CAPEX, which is an acronym for capital expenditures. It usually means the same thing.

Change in Net Working Capital   In addition to investing in fixed assets, a firm will also invest in current assets. For example, going back to the balance sheets in Table 2.1, we see that, at the end of 2018, U.S. had current assets of $1,464. At the end of 2017, current assets were $1,112; so, during the year, U.S. invested $1,464 − 1,112 = $352 in current assets.

As the firm changes its investment in current assets, its current liabilities will usually change as well. To determine the change in net working capital, the easiest approach is to take the difference between the beginning and ending net working capital (NWC) figures. Net working capital at the end of 2018 was $1,464 − 389 = $1,075. Similarly, at the end of 2017, net working capital was $1,112 − 428 = $684. Given these figures, we have the following:

Ending NWC	$1,075
− Beginning NWC	684
Change in NWC	$ 391

Net working capital thus increased by $391. Put another way, U.S. Corporation had a net investment of $391 in NWC for the year. This change in NWC is often referred to as the "addition to" NWC.

Conclusion   Given the figures we've come up with, we're ready to calculate cash flow from assets. The total cash flow from assets is given by operating cash flow less the amounts invested in fixed assets and net working capital. So, for U.S. Corporation, we have:

U.S. CORPORATION 2018 Cash Flow from Assets	
Operating cash flow	$628
− Net capital spending	130
− Change in NWC	391
Cash flow from assets	$107

From the cash flow identity given earlier, we know that this $107 cash flow from assets equals the sum of the firm's cash flow to creditors and its cash flow to stockholders. We consider these next.

It wouldn't be at all unusual for a growing corporation to have a negative cash flow. As we see next, a negative cash flow means that the firm raised more money by borrowing and selling stock than it paid out to creditors and stockholders during the year.

free cash flow
Another name for cash flow from assets.

A Note about "Free" Cash Flow   Cash flow from assets sometimes goes by a different name, **free cash flow**. Of course, there is no such thing as "free" cash (we wish!). Instead the name refers to cash that the firm is free to distribute to creditors and stockholders because it is not needed for working capital or fixed asset investments. We will stick with "cash flow from assets" as our label for this important concept because, in practice, there is some variation in exactly how free cash flow is computed; different users calculate it in different ways. Nonetheless, whenever you hear the phrase "free cash flow," you should understand that what is being discussed is cash flow from assets or something quite similar.

CASH FLOW TO CREDITORS AND STOCKHOLDERS

The cash flows to creditors and stockholders represent the net payments to creditors and owners during the year. Their calculation is similar to that of cash flow from assets. **Cash flow to creditors** is interest paid less net new borrowing; **cash flow to stockholders** is dividends paid less net new equity raised.

cash flow to creditors
A firm's interest payments to creditors less net new borrowing.

cash flow to stockholders
Dividends paid out by a firm less net new equity raised.

Cash Flow to Creditors   Looking at the income statement in Table 2.2, we see that U.S. Corporation paid $70 in interest to creditors. From the balance sheets in Table 2.1, we see that long-term debt rose by $454 − 408 = $46. So U.S. Corporation paid out $70 in interest, but it borrowed an additional $46. Thus, net cash flow to creditors is:

U.S. CORPORATION	
2018 Cash Flow to Creditors	
Interest paid	$70
− Net new borrowing	46
Cash flow to creditors	$24

Cash flow to creditors is sometimes called *cash flow to bondholders*; we will use these terms interchangeably.

Cash Flow to Stockholders   From the income statement, we see that dividends paid to stockholders amounted to $123. To get net new equity raised, we need to look at the common stock and paid-in surplus account. This account tells us how much stock the company has sold. During the year, this account rose by $40, so $40 in net new equity was raised. Given this, we have the following:

U.S. CORPORATION	
2018 Cash Flow to Stockholders	
Dividends paid	$123
− Net new equity raised	40
Cash flow to stockholders	$ 83

The cash flow to stockholders for 2018 was $83.

The last thing we need to do is to verify that the cash flow identity holds to be sure we didn't make any mistakes. From the previous section, we know that cash flow from assets is $107. Cash flow to creditors and stockholders is $24 + 83 = $107, so everything checks out. Table 2.6 contains a summary of the various cash flow calculations for future reference.

As our discussion indicates, it is essential that a firm keep an eye on its cash flow. The following serves as an excellent reminder of why doing so is a good idea, unless the firm's owners wish to end up in the "Po' " house:

QUOTH THE BANKER, "WATCH CASH FLOW"

Once upon a midnight dreary as I pondered weak and weary
Over many a quaint and curious volume of accounting lore,
Seeking gimmicks (without scruple) to squeeze through some new tax loophole,
Suddenly I heard a knock upon my door, Only this, and nothing more.

Then I felt a queasy tingling and I heard the cash a-jingling
As a fearsome banker entered whom I'd often seen before.
His face was money-green and in his eyes there could be seen
Dollar-signs that seemed to glitter as he reckoned up the score.
  "Cash flow," the banker said, and nothing more.

TABLE 2.6

Cash Flow Summary

I. The cash flow identity
Cash flow from assets = Cash flow to creditors (bondholders) + Cash flow to stockholders (owners)
II. Cash flow from assets
Cash flow from assets = Operating cash flow – Net capital spending – Change in net working capital (NWC) where: Operating cash flow = Earnings before interest and taxes (EBIT) + Depreciation – Taxes Net capital spending = Ending net fixed assets – Beginning net fixed assets + Depreciation Change in NWC = Ending NWC – Beginning NWC
III. Cash flow to creditors (bondholders)
Cash flow to creditors = Interest paid – Net new borrowing
IV. Cash flow to stockholders (owners)
Cash flow to stockholders = Dividends paid – Net new equity raised

I had always thought it fine to show a jet black bottom line.
But the banker sounded a resounding, "No.
Your receivables are high, mounting upward toward the sky;
Write-offs loom. What matters is cash flow."
    He repeated, "Watch cash flow."

Then I tried to tell the story of our lovely inventory
Which, though large, is full of most delightful stuff.
But the banker saw its growth, and with a mighty oath
He waved his arms and shouted, "Stop! Enough!
    Pay the interest, and don't give me any guff!"

Next I looked for noncash items which could add ad infinitum
To replace the ever-outward flow of cash,
But to keep my statement black I'd held depreciation back,
And my banker said that I'd done something rash.
    He quivered, and his teeth began to gnash.

When I asked him for a loan, he responded, with a groan,
That the interest rate would be just prime plus eight,
And to guarantee my purity he'd insist on some security—
All my assets plus the scalp upon my pate.
    Only this, a standard rate.

Though my bottom line is black, I am flat upon my back,
My cash flows out and customers pay slow.
The growth of my receivables is almost unbelievable:
The result is certain—unremitting woe!
And I hear the banker utter an ominous low mutter,
    "Watch cash flow."

Herbert S. Bailey Jr.

"Quoth the Banker, 'Watch Cash Flow,'" from *Publishers Weekly*, January 13, 1975. ©1975 by *Publishers Weekly*. All rights reserved. Used with permission.

To which we can only add, "Amen."

AN EXAMPLE: CASH FLOWS FOR DOLE COLA

This extended example covers the various cash flow calculations discussed in the chapter. It also illustrates a few variations that may arise.

Operating Cash Flow   During the year, Dole Cola, Inc., had sales and cost of goods sold of $600 and $300, respectively. Depreciation was $150 and interest paid was $30. Taxes were calculated at a straight 21 percent. Dividends were $36. (All figures are in millions of dollars.) What was operating cash flow for Dole? Why is this different from net income?

The easiest thing to do here is to create an income statement. We can then pick up the numbers we need. Dole Cola's income statement is given here:

DOLE COLA 2018 Income Statement	
Net sales	$600
Cost of goods sold	300
Depreciation	150
Earnings before interest and taxes	$150
Interest paid	30
Taxable income	$120
Taxes	25
Net income	$ 95
Dividends	$36
Addition to retained earnings	59

Net income for Dole was $95. We now have all the numbers we need. Referring back to the U.S. Corporation example and Table 2.6, we have this:

DOLE COLA 2018 Operating Cash Flow	
Earnings before interest and taxes	$150
+ Depreciation	150
− Taxes	25
Operating cash flow	$275

As this example illustrates, operating cash flow is not the same as net income because depreciation and interest are subtracted out when net income is calculated. If you recall our earlier discussion, we don't subtract these out in computing operating cash flow because depreciation is not a cash expense and interest paid is a financing expense, not an operating expense.

Net Capital Spending   Suppose beginning net fixed assets were $500 and ending net fixed assets were $750. What was the net capital spending for the year?

From the income statement for Dole, we know that depreciation for the year was $150. Net fixed assets rose by $250. Dole thus spent $250 along with an additional $150, for a total of $400.

Change in NWC and Cash Flow from Assets   Suppose Dole Cola started the year with $2,130 in current assets and $1,620 in current liabilities, and the corresponding ending figures were $2,276 and $1,710. What was the change in NWC during the year? What was cash flow from assets? How does this compare to net income?

Net working capital started out as $2,130 − 1,620 = $510 and ended up at $2,276 − 1,710 = $566. The addition to NWC was $566 − 510 = $56. Putting together all the information for Dole, we have the following:

DOLE COLA	
2018 Cash Flow from Assets	
Operating cash flow	$275
− Net capital spending	400
− Change in NWC	56
Cash flow from assets	−$181

Dole had a cash flow from assets of −$181. Net income was positive at $95. Is the fact that cash flow from assets was negative a cause for alarm? Not necessarily. The cash flow here is negative primarily because of a large investment in fixed assets. If these are good investments, the resulting negative cash flow is not a worry.

Cash Flow to Stockholders and Creditors   We saw that Dole Cola had cash flow from assets of −$181. The fact that this is negative means that Dole raised more money in the form of new debt and equity than it paid out for the year. For example, suppose we know that Dole didn't sell any new equity for the year. What was cash flow to stockholders? To creditors?

Because it didn't raise any new equity, Dole's cash flow to stockholders is equal to the cash dividend paid:

DOLE COLA	
2018 Cash Flow to Stockholders	
Dividends paid	$36
− Net new equity raised	0
Cash flow to stockholders	$36

Now, from the cash flow identity, we know that the total cash paid to creditors and stockholders was −$181. Cash flow to stockholders is $36, so cash flow to creditors must be equal to −$181 − 36 = −$217:

Cash flow to creditors + Cash flow to stockholders = −$181
Cash flow to creditors + $36   = −$181
Cash flow to creditors   = −$217

Because we know that cash flow to creditors is −$217 and interest paid is $30 (from the income statement), we can now determine net new borrowing. Dole must have borrowed $247 during the year to help finance the fixed asset expansion:

DOLE COLA	
2018 Cash Flow to Creditors	
Interest paid	$ 30
− Net new borrowing	− 247
Cash flow to creditors	−$217

Concept Questions

2.4a   What is the cash flow identity? Explain what it says.
2.4b   What are the components of operating cash flow?
2.4c   Why is interest paid not a component of operating cash flow?

Summary and Conclusions   2.5

This chapter has introduced some of the basics of financial statements, taxes, and cash flow:

1. The book values on an accounting balance sheet can be very different from market values. The goal of financial management is to maximize the market value of the stock, not its book value.

2. Net income as it is computed on the income statement is not cash flow. A primary reason is that depreciation, a noncash expense, is deducted when net income is computed.

3. Marginal and average tax rates can be different, and it is the marginal tax rate that is relevant for most financial decisions.

4. The tax rate paid by corporations is a flat tax of 21 percent, although state and local taxes can increase this rate.

5. There is a cash flow identity much like the balance sheet identity. It says that cash flow from assets equals cash flow to creditors and stockholders.

The calculation of cash flow from financial statements isn't difficult. Care must be taken in handling noncash expenses, such as depreciation, and operating costs must not be confused with financing costs. Most of all, it is important not to confuse book values with market values, or accounting income with cash flow.

CONNECT TO FINANCE

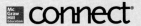 Do you use *Connect Finance* to practice what you learned? If you don't, you should—we can help you master the topics presented in this material. Log on to connect.mheducation.com to learn more!

Can you answer the following *Connect* Quiz questions?

Section 2.1   What types of accounts are the most liquid?
Section 2.2   What is an example of a noncash expense?
Section 2.3   The marginal tax rate is the tax rate that _____.
Section 2.4   Interest expense is treated as what type of cash flow?

CHAPTER REVIEW AND SELF-TEST PROBLEM

2.1   Cash Flow for Mara Corporation This problem will give you some practice working with financial statements and figuring cash flow. Based on the following information for Mara Corporation, prepare an income statement for 2018 and balance sheets for 2017 and 2018. Next, following our U.S. Corporation examples in the chapter, calculate cash flow from assets, cash flow to creditors, and cash flow to stockholders for Mara for 2018. Use a 21 percent tax rate throughout. You can check your answers against ours, found in the following section.

	2017	2018
Sales	$4,203	$4,507
Cost of goods sold	2,422	2,633
Depreciation	785	952
Interest	180	196
Dividends	275	352
Current assets	2,205	2,429
Net fixed assets	7,344	7,650
Current liabilities	1,003	1,255
Long-term debt	3,106	2,085

ANSWER TO CHAPTER REVIEW AND SELF-TEST PROBLEM

2.1   In preparing the balance sheets, remember that shareholders' equity is the residual. With this in mind, Mara's balance sheets are as follows:

MARA CORPORATION 2017 and 2018 Balance Sheets					
	2017	2018		2017	2018
Current assets	$2,205	$ 2,429	Current liabilities	$1,003	$ 1,255
Net fixed assets	7,344	7,650	Long-term debt	3,106	2,085
			Equity	5,440	6,739
Total assets	$9,549	$10,079	Total liabilities and shareholders' equity	$9,549	$10,079

The income statement is straightforward:

MARA CORPORATION 2018 Income Statement	
Sales	$4,507
Cost of goods sold	2,633
Depreciation	952
Earnings before interest and taxes	$ 922
Interest paid	196
Taxable income	$ 726
Taxes (21%)	152
Net income	$ 574
Dividends	$352
Addition to retained earnings	222

Notice that the addition to retained earnings is net income less cash dividends.

We can now pick up the figures we need to get operating cash flow:

MARA CORPORATION 2018 Operating Cash Flow	
Earnings before interest and taxes	$ 922
+ Depreciation	952
− Taxes	152
Operating cash flow	$1,722

Next, we get the net capital spending for the year by looking at the change in fixed assets, remembering to account for depreciation:

Ending net fixed assets	$7,650
− Beginning net fixed assets	7,344
+ Depreciation	952
Net capital spending	$1,258

After calculating beginning and ending NWC, we take the difference to get the change in NWC:

Ending NWC	$1,174
− Beginning NWC	1,202
Change in NWC	−$ 28

We now combine operating cash flow, net capital spending, and the change in net working capital to get the total cash flow from assets:

MARA CORPORATION Cash Flow from Assets	
Operating cash flow	$1,722
− Net capital spending	1,258
− Change in NWC	−28
Cash flow from assets	$ 492

To get cash flow to creditors, notice that long-term borrowing decreased by $1,021 during the year and that interest paid was $196:

MARA CORPORATION 2018 Cash Flow to Creditors	
Interest paid	$ 196
− Net new borrowing	−1,021
Cash flow to creditors	$ 1,217

Finally, dividends paid were $352. To get net new equity raised, we have to do some extra calculating. Total equity was up by $6,739 − 5,440 = $1,299. Of this increase, $222 was from additions to retained earnings, so $1,077 in new equity was raised during the year. Cash flow to stockholders was thus:

MARA CORPORATION 2018 Cash Flow to Stockholders	
Dividends paid	$ 352
− Net new equity raised	1,077
Cash flow to stockholders	−$ 725

As a check, notice that cash flow from assets ($492) equals cash flow to creditors plus cash flow to stockholders ($1,217 − 725 = $492).

CONCEPTS REVIEW AND CRITICAL THINKING QUESTIONS

1. **Liquidity** [LO1] What does liquidity measure? Explain the trade-off a firm faces between high liquidity and low liquidity levels.

2. **Accounting and Cash Flows** [LO2] Why might the revenue and cost figures shown on a standard income statement not be representative of the actual cash inflows and outflows that occurred during a period?

3. **Book Values versus Market Values** [LO1] In preparing a balance sheet, why do you think standard accounting practice focuses on historical cost rather than market value?

4. **Operating Cash Flow** [LO2] In comparing accounting net income and operating cash flow, name two items you typically find in net income that are not in operating cash flow. Explain what each is and why it is excluded in operating cash flow.

5. **Book Values versus Market Values** [LO1] Under standard accounting rules, it is possible for a company's liabilities to exceed its assets. When this occurs, the owners' equity is negative. Can this happen with market values? Why or why not?

6. **Cash Flow from Assets** [LO4] Suppose a company's cash flow from assets is negative for a particular period. Is this necessarily a good sign or a bad sign?

7. **Operating Cash Flow** [LO4] Suppose a company's operating cash flow has been negative for several years running. Is this necessarily a good sign or a bad sign?

8. **Net Working Capital and Capital Spending** [LO4] Could a company's change in NWC be negative in a given year? (*Hint*: Yes.) Explain how this might come about. What about net capital spending?

9. **Cash Flow to Stockholders and Creditors** [LO4] Could a company's cash flow to stockholders be negative in a given year? (*Hint*: Yes.) Explain how this might come about. What about cash flow to creditors?

10. **Firm Values** [LO1] Referring back to the Boeing example used at the beginning of the chapter, note that we suggested that Boeing's stockholders probably didn't suffer as a result of the reported loss. What do you think was the basis for our conclusion?

11. **Enterprise Value** [LO1] A firm's *enterprise value* is equal to the market value of its debt and equity, less the firm's holdings of cash and cash equivalents. This figure is particularly relevant to potential purchasers of the firm. Why?

12. **Earnings Management** [LO2] Companies often try to keep accounting earnings growing at a relatively steady pace, thereby avoiding large swings in earnings from period to period. They also try to meet earnings targets. To do so, they use a variety of tactics. The simplest way is to control the timing of accounting revenues and costs, which all firms can do to at least some extent. For example, if earnings are looking too low this quarter, then some accounting costs can be deferred until next quarter. This practice is called *earnings management*. It is common, and it raises a lot of questions. Why do firms do it? Why are firms even allowed to do it under GAAP? Is it ethical? What are the implications for cash flow and shareholder wealth?

QUESTIONS AND PROBLEMS

1. **Building a Balance Sheet** [LO1] Wims, Inc., has current assets of $4,900, net fixed assets of $27,300, current liabilities of $4,100, and long-term debt of $10,200. What is the value of the shareholders' equity account for this firm? How much is net working capital?

2. **Building an Income Statement** [LO1] Griffin's Goat Farm, Inc., has sales of $796,000, costs of $327,000, depreciation expense of $42,000, interest expense of $34,000, and a tax rate of 21 percent. What is the net income for this firm?

3. **Dividends and Retained Earnings** [LO1] Suppose the firm in Problem 2 paid out $95,000 in cash dividends. What is the addition to retained earnings?

4. **Per-Share Earnings and Dividends** [LO1] Suppose the firm in Problem 3 had 80,000 shares of common stock outstanding. What is the earnings per share, or EPS, figure? What is the dividends per share figure?

5. **Calculating OCF** [LO4] Pompeii, Inc., has sales of $46,200, costs of $23,100, depreciation expense of $2,200, and interest expense of $1,700. If the tax rate is 22 percent, what is the operating cash flow, or OCF?

6. **Calculating Net Capital Spending** [LO4] Logano Driving School's 2017 balance sheet showed net fixed assets of $2.4 million, and the 2018 balance sheet showed net fixed assets of $3.3 million. The company's 2018 income statement showed a depreciation expense of $319,000. What was net capital spending for 2018?

7. **Calculating Additions to NWC** [LO4] The 2017 balance sheet of Dream, Inc., showed current assets of $4,810 and current liabilities of $2,230. The 2018 balance sheet showed current assets of $5,360 and current liabilities of $2,970. What was the company's 2018 change in net working capital, or NWC?

8. **Cash Flow to Creditors** [LO4] The 2017 balance sheet of Kerber's Tennis Shop, Inc., showed long-term debt of $1.87 million, and the 2018 balance sheet showed long-term debt of $2.21 million. The 2018 income statement showed an interest expense of $255,000. What was the firm's cash flow to creditors during 2018?

9. **Cash Flow to Stockholders** [LO4] The 2017 balance sheet of Kerber's Tennis Shop, Inc., showed $650,000 in the common stock account and $3.98 million in the additional paid-in surplus account. The 2018 balance sheet showed $805,000 and $4.2 million in the same two accounts, respectively. If the company paid out $545,000 in cash dividends during 2018, what was the cash flow to stockholders for the year?

BASIC
(Questions 1–10)

10. **Calculating Total Cash Flows** [LO4] Given the information for Kerber's Tennis Shop, Inc., in Problems 8 and 9, suppose you also know that the firm's net capital spending for 2018 was $1,250,000 and that the firm reduced its net working capital investment by $45,000. What was the firm's 2018 operating cash flow, or OCF?

INTERMEDIATE
(Questions 11–19)

11. **Market Values and Book Values** [LO1] Klingon Widgets, Inc., purchased new cloaking machinery three years ago for $6 million. The machinery can be sold to the Romulans today for $5.1 million. Klingon's current balance sheet shows net fixed assets of $3.4 million, current liabilities of $895,000, and net working capital of $235,000. If the current assets and current liabilities were liquidated today, the company would receive a total of $1.15 million cash. What is the book value of Klingon's total assets today? What is the sum of the market value of NWC and the market value of fixed assets?

12. **Calculating Total Cash Flows** [LO4] Square Hammer Corp. shows the following information on its 2018 income statement: Sales = $305,000; Costs = $176,000; Other expenses = $8,900; Depreciation expense = $18,700; Interest expense = $12,900; Taxes = $23,345; Dividends = $19,500. In addition, you're told that the firm issued $6,400 in new equity during 2018 and redeemed $4,900 in outstanding long-term debt.
    a. What is the 2018 operating cash flow?
    b. What is the 2018 cash flow to creditors?
    c. What is the 2018 cash flow to stockholders?
    d. If net fixed assets increased by $46,000 during the year, what was the addition to NWC?

13. **Using Income Statements** [LO1] Given the following information for Bowie Pizza Co., calculate the depreciation expense: Sales = $64,000; Costs = $30,700; Addition to retained earnings = $5,700; Dividends paid = $1,980; Interest expense = $4,400; Tax rate = 22 percent.

14. **Preparing a Balance Sheet** [LO1] Prepare a 2018 balance sheet for Rogers Corp. based on the following information: Cash = $127,000; Patents and copyrights = $660,000; Accounts payable = $210,000; Accounts receivable = $115,000; Tangible net fixed assets = $1,610,000; Inventory = $286,000; Notes payable = $155,000; Accumulated retained earnings = $1,368,000; Long-term debt = $830,000.

15. **Residual Claims** [LO1] Bishop, Inc., is obligated to pay its creditors $7,800 during the year.
    a. What is the market value of the shareholders' equity if assets have a market value of $9,400?
    b. What if assets equal $6,700?

16. **Net Income and OCF** [LO2] During 2018, Raines Umbrella Corp. had sales of $705,000. Cost of goods sold, administrative and selling expenses, and depreciation expenses were $445,000, $95,000, and $140,000, respectively. In addition, the company had an interest expense of $70,000 and a tax rate of 25 percent. (Ignore any tax loss carryforward provisions and assume interest expense is fully deductible.)
    a. What is the company's net income for 2018?
    b. What is its operating cash flow?
    c. Explain your results in (a) and (b).

17. **Accounting Values versus Cash Flows [LO2]** In Problem 16, suppose Raines Umbrella Corp. paid out $102,000 in cash dividends. Is this possible? If net capital spending and net working capital were both zero, and if no new stock was issued during the year, what do you know about the firm's long-term debt account?

18. **Calculating Cash Flows [LO2]** Cardinal Industries had the following operating results for 2018: Sales = $33,106; Cost of goods sold = $23,624; Depreciation expense = $5,877; Interest expense = $2,650; Dividends paid = $1,888. At the beginning of the year, net fixed assets were $19,820, current assets were $6,970, and current liabilities were $3,920. At the end of the year, net fixed assets were $24,394, current assets were $8,612, and current liabilities were $4,575. The tax rate for 2018 was 22 percent.

    a. What is net income for 2018?
    b. What is the operating cash flow for 2018?
    c. What is the cash flow from assets for 2018? Is this possible? Explain.
    d. If no new debt was issued during the year, what is the cash flow to creditors? What is the cash flow to stockholders? Explain and interpret the positive and negative signs of your answers in (a) through (d).

19. **Calculating Cash Flows [LO4]** Consider the following abbreviated financial statements for Parrothead Enterprises:

PARROTHEAD ENTERPRISES 2017 and 2018 Partial Balance Sheets					
Assets			**Liabilities and Owners' Equity**		
	2017	2018		2017	2018
Current assets	$1,206	$1,307	Current liabilities	$ 482	$ 541
Net fixed assets	4,973	5,988	Long-term debt	2,628	2,795

PARROTHEAD ENTERPRISES 2018 Income Statement	
Sales	$15,301
Costs	7,135
Depreciation	1,363
Interest paid	388

    a. What is owners' equity for 2017 and 2018?
    b. What is the change in net working capital for 2018?
    c. In 2018, Parrothead Enterprises purchased $2,496 in new fixed assets. How much in fixed assets did Parrothead Enterprises sell? What is the cash flow from assets for the year? The tax rate is 21 percent.
    d. During 2018, Parrothead Enterprises raised $504 in new long-term debt. How much long-term debt must Parrothead Enterprises have paid off during the year? What is the cash flow to creditors?

20. **Net Fixed Assets and Depreciation [LO4]** On the balance sheet, the net fixed assets (NFA) account is equal to the gross fixed assets (FA) account (which records the acquisition cost of fixed assets) minus the accumulated depreciation (AD) account (which records the total depreciation taken by the firm against its fixed assets). Using the fact that NFA = FA − AD, show that the expression given in the chapter for net capital spending, $NFA_{end} - NFA_{beg} + D$ (where D is the depreciation expense during the year), is equivalent to $FA_{end} - FA_{beg}$.

CHALLENGE
(Questions 20–22)

Use the following information for Taco Swell, Inc., for Problems 21 and 22 (assume the tax rate is 21 percent):

	2017	2018
Sales	$16,549	$18,498
Depreciation	2,376	2,484
Cost of goods sold	5,690	6,731
Other expenses	1,353	1,178
Interest	1,110	1,325
Cash	8,676	9,247
Accounts receivable	11,488	13,482
Short-term notes payable	1,674	1,641
Long-term debt	29,060	35,229
Net fixed assets	72,770	77,610
Accounts payable	6,269	6,640
Inventory	20,424	21,862
Dividends	1,979	2,314

21. **Financial Statements [LO1]** Draw up an income statement and balance sheet for this company for 2017 and 2018.
22. **Calculating Cash Flow [LO4]** For 2018, calculate the cash flow from assets, cash flow to creditors, and cash flow to stockholders.

EXCEL MASTER IT! PROBLEM

Using Excel to find the marginal tax rate can be accomplished using the VLOOKUP function. However, calculating the total tax bill is a little more difficult. Below we have shown a copy of the IRS tax table for an unmarried individual for 2018. Often, tax tables are presented in this format.

If taxable income is over ...	But not over ...	The tax is:
$ 0	$ 9,525	10% of the amount over $0
9,526	38,700	$952.50 plus 15% of the amount over $9,525
38,701	93,700	$5,328.75 plus 25% of the amount over $38,700
93,701	195,450	$19,078.75 plus 28% of the amount over $93,700
195,451	424,950	$47,568.75 plus 33% of the amount over $195,450
424,951	426,700	$123,303.75 plus 35% of the amount over $424,950
426,701		$123,916.25 plus 39.6% of the amount over $426,700

In reading this table, the marginal tax rate for taxable income less than $9,525 is 10 percent. If the taxable income is between $9,525 and $38,700, the tax bill is $952.50 plus the marginal taxes. The marginal taxes are calculated as the taxable income minus $9,525 times the marginal tax rate of 15 percent.

Below, we have the corporate tax table that was applicable 2017 and as shown in Table 2.3.

Taxable income is greater than or equal to...	But less than...	Tax rate
$ 0	$ 50,000	15%
50,001	75,000	25
75,001	100,000	34
100,001	335,000	39
335,001	10,000,000	34
10,000,001	15,000,000	35
15,000,001	18,333,333	38
18,333,334		35

a. Create a tax table in Excel for corporate taxes similar to the individual tax table shown above. Your spreadsheet should then calculate the marginal tax rate, the average tax rate, and the tax bill for any level of taxable income input by a user.
b. For a taxable income of $1,350,000, what is the marginal tax rate?
c. For a taxable income of $1,350,000, what is the total tax bill?
d. For a taxable income of $1,350,000, what is the average tax rate?

MINICASE

Cash Flows and Financial Statements at Sunset Boards, Inc.

Sunset Boards is a small company that manufactures and sells surfboards in Malibu. Tad Marks, the founder of the company, is in charge of the design and sale of the surfboards, but his background is in surfing, not business. As a result, the company's financial records are not well maintained.

The initial investment in Sunset Boards was provided by Tad and his friends and family. Because the initial investment was relatively small, and the company has made surfboards only for its own store, the investors haven't required detailed financial statements from Tad. But thanks to word of mouth among professional surfers, sales have picked up recently, and Tad is considering a major expansion. His plans include opening another surfboard store in Hawaii, as well as supplying his "sticks" (surfer lingo for boards) to other sellers.

Tad's expansion plans require a significant investment, which he plans to finance with a combination of additional funds from outsiders plus some money borrowed from banks. Naturally, the new investors and creditors require more organized and detailed financial statements than Tad has previously prepared. At the urging of his investors, Tad has hired financial analyst Christina Wolfe to evaluate the performance of the company over the past year.

After rooting through old bank statements, sales receipts, tax returns, and other records, Christina has assembled the following information:

	2017	2018
Cost of goods sold	$255,605	$322,742
Cash	36,884	55,725
Depreciation	72,158	81,559
Interest expense	15,687	17,980
Selling and administrative	50,268	65,610
Accounts payable	26,186	44,318
Net fixed assets	318,345	387,855
Sales	501,441	611,224
Accounts receivable	26,136	33,901
Notes payable	29,712	32,441
Long-term debt	160,689	175,340
Inventory	50,318	67,674
New equity	0	19,500

Sunset Boards currently pays out 40 percent of net income as dividends to Tad and the other original investors, and it has a 21 percent tax rate. You are Christina's assistant, and she has asked you to prepare the following:

1. An income statement for 2017 and 2018.
2. A balance sheet for 2017 and 2018.
3. Operating cash flow for each year.
4. Cash flow from assets for 2018.
5. Cash flow to creditors for 2018.
6. Cash flow to stockholders for 2018.

QUESTIONS

1. How would you describe Sunset Boards's cash flows for 2018? Write a brief discussion.

2. In light of your discussion in the previous question, what do you think about Tad's expansion plans?

Working with Financial Statements

3 Chapter

THE PRICE OF A SHARE OF COMMON STOCK in corner pharmacy CVS Health closed at about $82 on January 6, 2017. At that price, CVS had a price-earnings (PE) ratio of 18. That is, investors were willing to pay $18 for every dollar in income earned by CVS. At the same time, investors were willing to pay $55, $34, and $6 for each dollar earned by Adobe Systems, Pfizer, and Ford, respectively. At the other extreme were Blackberry and Twitter. Both had negative earnings for the previous year, yet Blackberry was priced at about $8 per share and Twitter at about $17 per share. Because they had negative earnings, their PE ratios would have been negative, so they were not reported. At the time, the typical stock in the S&P 500 index of large company stocks was trading at a PE of about 16, or about 16 times earnings, as they say on Wall Street.

Price-to-earnings comparisons are examples of the use of financial ratios. As we will see in this chapter, there are a wide variety of financial ratios, all designed to summarize specific aspects of a firm's financial position. In addition to discussing how to analyze financial statements and compute financial ratios, we will have quite a bit to say about who uses this information and why.

Learning Objectives

After studying this chapter, you should be able to:

LO1 Standardize financial statements for comparison purposes.

LO2 Compute and, more importantly, interpret some common ratios.

LO3 Name the determinants of a firm's profitability.

LO4 Explain some of the problems and pitfalls in financial statement analysis.

©by_adrii/iStockPhoto/GettyImages

For updates on the latest happenings in finance, visit fundamentalsofcorporatefinance.blogspot.com.

In Chapter 2, we discussed some of the essential concepts of financial statements and cash flow. Part 2, this chapter and the next, continues where our earlier discussion left off. Our goal here is to expand your understanding of the uses (and abuses) of financial statement information.

Financial statement information will crop up in various places in the remainder of our book. Part 2 is not essential for understanding this material, but it will help give you an overall perspective on the role of financial statement information in corporate finance.

A good working knowledge of financial statements is desirable because such statements, and numbers derived from those statements, are the primary means of communicating financial information both within the firm and outside the firm. In short, much of the language of corporate finance is rooted in the ideas we discuss in this chapter.

Furthermore, as we will see, there are many different ways of using financial statement information and many different types of users. This diversity reflects the fact that financial statement information plays an important part in many types of decisions.

In the best of all worlds, the financial manager has full market value information about all of the firm's assets. This will rarely (if ever) happen. So, the reason we rely on accounting figures for much of our financial information is that we are almost always unable to obtain all (or even part) of the market information we want. The only meaningful yardstick for evaluating business decisions is whether they create economic value (see Chapter 1). However, in many important situations, it will not be possible to make this judgment directly because we can't see the market value effects of decisions.

We recognize that accounting numbers are often pale reflections of economic reality, but they are frequently the best available information. For privately held corporations, not-for-profit businesses, and smaller firms, for example, very little direct market value information exists at all. The accountant's reporting function is crucial in these circumstances.

Clearly, one important goal of the accountant is to report financial information to the user in a form useful for decision making. Ironically, the information frequently does not come to the user in such a form. In other words, financial statements don't come with a user's guide. This chapter and the next are first steps in filling this gap.

3.1 Cash Flow and Financial Statements: A Closer Look

Excel Master It!
Excel Master coverage online

At the most fundamental level, firms do two different things: They generate cash and they spend it. Cash is generated by selling a product, an asset, or a security. Selling a security involves either borrowing or selling an equity interest (shares of stock) in the firm. Cash is spent in paying for materials and labor to produce a product and in purchasing assets. Payments to creditors and owners also require the spending of cash.

In Chapter 2, we saw that the cash activities of a firm could be summarized by a simple identity:

Cash flow from assets = Cash flow to creditors + Cash flow to owners

This cash flow identity summarizes the total cash result of all transactions a firm engages in during the year. In this section, we return to the subject of cash flow by taking a closer look at the cash events during the year that led to these total figures.

SOURCES AND USES OF CASH

sources of cash
A firm's activities that generate cash.

uses of cash
A firm's activities in which cash is spent. Also called *applications of cash*.

Activities that bring in cash are called **sources of cash**. Activities that involve spending cash are called **uses** (or *applications*) **of cash**. What we need to do is to trace the changes in the firm's balance sheet to see how the firm obtained and spent its cash during some period.

To get started, consider the balance sheets for the Prufrock Corporation in Table 3.1. Notice that we have calculated the change in each of the items on the balance sheets.

Looking over the balance sheets for Prufrock, we see that quite a few things changed during the year. For example, Prufrock increased its net fixed assets by $149 and its inventory by $29. (Note that, throughout, all figures are in millions of dollars.) Where did the money come from? To answer this and related questions, we need to first identify those changes that used up cash (uses) and those that brought in cash (sources).

A little common sense is useful here. A firm uses cash by either buying assets or making payments. So, loosely speaking, an increase in an asset account means the firm, on a net basis, bought some assets—a use of cash. If an asset account went down, then on a net basis, the firm sold some assets. This would be a net source. Similarly, if a liability account goes down, then the firm has made a net payment—a use of cash.

TABLE 3.1

PRUFROCK CORPORATION 2017 and 2018 Balance Sheets ($ in millions)			
	2017	2018	Change
Assets			
Current assets			
Cash	$ 84	$ 146	+$ 62
Accounts receivable	165	188	+ 23
Inventory	393	422	+ 29
Total	$ 642	$ 756	+$114
Fixed assets			
Net plant and equipment	$2,731	$2,880	+$149
Total assets	$3,373	$3,636	+$263
Liabilities and Owners' Equity			
Current liabilities			
Accounts payable	$ 312	$ 344	+$ 32
Notes payable	231	196	− 35
Total	$ 543	$ 540	−$ 3
Long-term debt	$ 531	$ 457	−$ 74
Owners' equity			
Common stock and paid-in surplus	$ 500	$ 550	+$ 50
Retained earnings	1,799	2,089	+ 290
Total	$2,299	$2,639	+$340
Total liabilities and owners' equity	$3,373	$3,636	+$263

Given this reasoning, there is a simple, albeit mechanical, definition you may find useful. An increase in a left-side (asset) account or a decrease in a right-side (liability or equity) account is a use of cash. Likewise, a decrease in an asset account or an increase in a liability (or equity) account is a source of cash.

Looking again at Prufrock, we see that inventory rose by $29. This is a net use of cash because Prufrock effectively paid out $29 to increase inventories. Accounts payable rose by $32. This is a source of cash because Prufrock effectively has borrowed an additional $32 payable by the end of the year. Notes payable, on the other hand, went down by $35, so Prufrock effectively paid off $35 worth of short-term debt—a use of cash.

Based on our discussion, we can summarize the sources and uses of cash from the balance sheet as follows:

Company financial information can be found in many places on the web, including **finance.yahoo .com**, **finance.google.com**, and **money.msn.com**.

Sources of cash:	
Increase in accounts payable	$ 32
Increase in common stock	50
Increase in retained earnings	290
Total sources	$372
Uses of cash:	
Increase in accounts receivable	$ 23
Increase in inventory	29
Decrease in notes payable	35
Decrease in long-term debt	74
Net fixed asset acquisitions	149
Total uses	$310
Net addition to cash	$ 62

TABLE 3.2

PRUFROCK CORPORATION 2018 Income Statement ($ in millions)	
Sales	$2,311
Cost of goods sold	1,344
Depreciation	276
Earnings before interest and taxes	$ 691
Interest paid	141
Taxable income	$ 550
Taxes (21%)	116
Net income	$ 435

Dividends	$145	
Addition to retained earnings	290	

The net addition to cash is the difference between sources and uses, and our $62 result here agrees with the $62 change shown on the balance sheet.

This simple statement tells us much of what happened during the year, but it doesn't tell the whole story. For example, the increase in retained earnings is net income (a source of funds) less dividends (a use of funds). It would be more enlightening to have these reported separately so we could see the breakdown. Also, we have considered only net fixed asset acquisitions. Total or gross spending would be more interesting to know.

To further trace the flow of cash through the firm during the year, we need an income statement. For Prufrock, the results for the year are shown in Table 3.2.

Notice here that the $290 addition to retained earnings we calculated from the balance sheet is the difference between the net income of $435 and the dividends of $145.

THE STATEMENT OF CASH FLOWS

statement of cash flows
A firm's financial statement that summarizes its sources and uses of cash over a specified period.

There is some flexibility in summarizing the sources and uses of cash in the form of a financial statement. However it is presented, the result is called the **statement of cash flows**.

We present a particular format for this statement in Table 3.3. The basic idea is to group all the changes into three categories: operating activities, financing activities, and investment activities. The exact form differs in detail from one preparer to the next.

Don't be surprised if you come across different arrangements. The types of information presented will be similar; the exact order can differ. The key thing to remember in this case is that we started out with $84 in cash and ended up with $146, for a net increase of $62. We're trying to see what events led to this change.

Going back to Chapter 2, we note that there is a slight conceptual problem here. Interest paid should really go under financing activities, but unfortunately that's not the way the accounting is handled. The reason, you may recall, is that interest is deducted as an expense when net income is computed. Also, notice that the net purchase of fixed assets was $149. Because Prufrock wrote off $276 worth of assets (the depreciation), it must have actually spent a total of $149 + 276 = $425 on fixed assets.

Once we have this statement, it might seem appropriate to express the change in cash on a per-share basis, much as we did for net income. Ironically, despite the interest we might have in some measure of cash flow per share, standard accounting practice expressly prohibits reporting this information. The reason is that accountants feel that cash flow (or some component of cash flow) is not an alternative to accounting income, so only earnings per share are to be reported.

As shown in Table 3.4, it is sometimes useful to present the same information a bit differently. We will call this the "sources and uses of cash" statement. There is no such

TABLE 3.3

PRUFROCK CORPORATION 2018 Statement of Cash Flows ($ in millions)	
Cash, beginning of year	$ 84
Operating activity	
Net income	$ 435
Plus:	
Depreciation	276
Increase in accounts payable	32
Less:	
Increase in accounts receivable	− 23
Increase in inventory	− 29
Net cash from operating activity	$ 691
Investment activity	
Fixed asset acquisitions	−$ 425
Net cash from investment activity	−$ 425
Financing activity	
Decrease in notes payable	−$ 35
Decrease in long-term debt	− 74
Dividends paid	− 145
Increase in common stock	50
Net cash from financing activity	−$ 204
Net increase in cash	$ 62
Cash, end of year	$ 146

TABLE 3.4

PRUFROCK CORPORATION 2018 Sources and Uses of Cash ($ in millions)	
Cash, beginning of year	$ 84
Sources of cash	
Operations:	
Net income	$435
Depreciation	276
	$711
Working capital:	
Increase in accounts payable	$ 32
Long-term financing:	
Increase in common stock	50
Total sources of cash	$793
Uses of cash	
Working capital:	
Increase in accounts receivable	$ 23
Increase in inventory	29
Decrease in notes payable	35
Long-term financing:	
Decrease in long-term debt	74
Fixed asset acquisitions	425
Dividends paid	145
Total uses of cash	$731
Net addition to cash	$ 62
Cash, end of year	$146

statement in financial accounting, but this arrangement resembles one used many years ago. As we will discuss, this form can come in handy, but we emphasize again that it is not the way this information is normally presented.

Now that we have the various cash pieces in place, we can get a good idea of what happened during the year. Prufrock's major cash outlays were fixed asset acquisitions and cash dividends. It paid for these activities primarily with cash generated from operations.

Prufrock also retired some long-term debt and increased current assets. Finally, current liabilities were not greatly changed, and a relatively small amount of new equity was sold. Altogether, this short sketch captures Prufrock's major sources and uses of cash for the year.

Concept Questions

3.1a   What is a source of cash? Give three examples.

3.1b   What is a use, or application, of cash? Give three examples.

3.2   Standardized Financial Statements

Excel Master It!

Excel Master coverage online

The next thing we might want to do with Prufrock's financial statements is compare them to those of other similar companies. We would immediately have a problem, however. It's almost impossible to directly compare the financial statements for two companies because of differences in size.

For example, Ford and GM are serious rivals in the auto market, but GM is bigger (in terms of market share), so it is difficult to compare them directly. For that matter, it's difficult even to compare financial statements from different points in time for the same company if the company's size has changed. The size problem is compounded if we try to compare GM and, say, Toyota. If Toyota's financial statements are denominated in yen, then we have size *and* currency differences.

To start making comparisons, one obvious thing we might try to do is to somehow standardize the financial statements. One common and useful way of doing this is to work with percentages instead of total dollars. In this section, we describe two different ways of standardizing financial statements along these lines.

COMMON-SIZE STATEMENTS

common-size statement
A standardized financial statement presenting all items in percentage terms. Balance sheet items are shown as a percentage of assets and income statement items as a percentage of sales.

To get started, a useful way of standardizing financial statements is to express each item on the balance sheet as a percentage of assets and to express each item on the income statement as a percentage of sales. The resulting financial statements are called **common-size statements**. We consider these next.

Common-Size Balance Sheets   One way, though not the only way, to construct a common-size balance sheet is to express each item as a percentage of total assets. Prufrock's 2017 and 2018 common-size balance sheets are shown in Table 3.5.

Notice that some of the totals don't check exactly because of rounding. Also notice that the total change has to be zero because the beginning and ending numbers must add up to 100 percent.

In this form, financial statements are relatively easy to read and compare. For example, looking at the two balance sheets for Prufrock, we see that current assets

TABLE 3.5

PRUFROCK CORPORATION 2017 and 2018 Common-Size Balance Sheets			
	2017	2018	Change
Assets			
Current assets			
Cash	2.5%	4.0%	+1.5%
Accounts receivable	4.9	5.2	+ .3
Inventory	11.7	11.6	+ 0
Total	19.0	20.8	+1.8
Fixed assets			
Net plant and equipment	81.0	79.2	−1.8
Total assets	100.0%	100.0%	0
Liabilities and Owners' Equity			
Current liabilities			
Accounts payable	9.2%	9.5%	+ .2%
Notes payable	6.8	5.4	−1.5
Total	16.1	14.9	−1.2
Long-term debt	15.7	12.6	−3.2
Owners' equity			
Common stock and paid-in surplus	14.8	15.1	+ .3
Retained earnings	53.3	57.5	+4.1
Total	68.2	72.6	+4.4
Total liabilities and owners' equity	100.0%	100.0%	0

were 20.8 percent of total assets in 2018, up from 19.0 percent in 2017. Current liabilities declined from 16.1 percent to 14.9 percent of total liabilities and equity over that same time. Similarly, total equity rose from 68.2 percent of total liabilities and equity to 72.6 percent.

Overall, Prufrock's liquidity, as measured by current assets compared to current liabilities, increased over the year. Simultaneously, Prufrock's indebtedness diminished as a percentage of total assets. We might be tempted to conclude that the balance sheet has grown "stronger." We will say more about this later.

Common-Size Income Statements   A useful way of standardizing the income statement is to express each item as a percentage of total sales, as illustrated for Prufrock in Table 3.6.

This income statement tells us what happens to each dollar in sales. For Prufrock, interest expense eats up $.061 out of every sales dollar and taxes take another $.05. When all is said and done, $.188 of each dollar flows through to the bottom line (net income), and that amount is split into $.125 retained in the business and $.063 paid out in dividends.

These percentages are useful in comparisons. For example, a relevant figure is the cost percentage. For Prufrock, $.582 of each $1 in sales goes to pay for goods sold. It would be interesting to compute the same percentage for Prufrock's main competitors to see how Prufrock stacks up in terms of cost control.

TABLE 3.6

PRUFROCK CORPORATION 2018 Common-Size Income Statement	
Sales	100.0%
Cost of goods sold	58.2
Depreciation	11.9
Earnings before interest and taxes	29.9
Interest paid	6.1
Taxable income	23.8
Taxes (21%)	5.0
Net income	18.8%
Dividends	6.3%
Addition to retained earnings	12.5

Common-Size Statements of Cash Flows Although we have not presented it here, it is also possible and useful to prepare a common-size statement of cash flows. Unfortunately, with the current statement of cash flows, there is no obvious denominator such as total assets or total sales. However, if the information is arranged in a way similar to that in Table 3.4, then each item can be expressed as a percentage of total sources (or total uses). The results can then be interpreted as the percentage of total sources of cash supplied or as the percentage of total uses of cash for a particular item.

COMMON-BASE YEAR FINANCIAL STATEMENTS: TREND ANALYSIS

Imagine we were given balance sheets for the last 10 years for some company and we were trying to investigate trends in the firm's pattern of operations. Does the firm use more or less debt? Has the firm grown more or less liquid? A useful way of standardizing financial statements in this case is to choose a base year and then express each item relative to the base amount. We will call the resulting statements **common-base year statements**.

common-base year statement
A standardized financial statement presenting all items relative to a certain base year amount.

For example, from 2017 to 2018, looking at Table 3.1, Prufrock's inventory rose from $393 to $422. If we pick 2017 as our base year, then we would set inventory equal to 1.00 for that year. For the next year, we would calculate inventory relative to the base year as $422/$393 = 1.07. In this case, we could say inventory grew by about 7 percent during the year. If we had multiple years, we would divide the inventory figure for each one by $393. The resulting series is easy to plot, and it is then easy to compare companies. Table 3.7 summarizes these calculations for the asset side of the balance sheet.

COMBINED COMMON-SIZE AND BASE YEAR ANALYSIS

The trend analysis we have been discussing can be combined with the common-size analysis discussed earlier. The reason for doing this is that as total assets grow, most of the other accounts must grow as well. By first forming the common-size statements, we eliminate the effect of this overall growth.

For example, looking at Table 3.7, we see that Prufrock's accounts receivable were $165, or 4.9 percent of total assets, in 2017. In 2018, they had risen to $188, which was 5.2 percent of total assets. If we do our analysis in terms of dollars, then the 2018 figure would be $188/$165 = 1.14, representing a 14 percent increase in receivables. However, if we work with the common-size statements, then the 2018 figure would be 5.2%/4.9% = 1.06. This tells us accounts receivable, as a percentage of total assets, grew by 6 percent. Roughly speaking, what we see is that of the 14 percent total increase, about 8 percent (= 14% − 6%) is attributable to growth in total assets.

TABLE 3.7

	PRUFROCK CORPORATION Summary of Standardized Balance Sheets (Asset Side Only)					
	Assets ($ in millions)		Common-Size Assets		Common-Base Year Assets	Combined Common-Size and Base Year Assets
	2017	2018	2017	2018	2018	2018
Current assets						
Cash	$ 84	$ 146	2.5%	4.0%	1.74	1.61
Accounts receivable	165	188	4.9	5.2	1.14	1.06
Inventory	393	422	11.7	11.6	1.07	1.00
Total current assets	$ 642	$ 756	19.0	20.8	1.18	1.09
Fixed assets						
Net plant and equipment	$2,731	$2,880	81.0	79.2	1.05	.98
Total assets	$3,373	$3,636	100.0%	100.0%	1.08	1.00

NOTE: The common-size numbers are calculated by dividing each item by total assets for that year. For example, the 2017 common-size cash amount is $84/$3,373 = .025, or 2.5%. The common-base year numbers are calculated by dividing each 2018 item by the base year (2017) dollar amount. The common-base year cash is thus $146/$84 = 1.74, representing a 74 percent increase. The combined common-size and base year figures are calculated by dividing each common-size amount by the base year (2017) common-size amount. The cash figure is therefore 4.0%/2.5% = 1.61, representing a 61 percent increase in cash holdings as a percentage of total assets. Columns may not total precisely due to rounding.

Concept Questions

3.2a   Why is it often necessary to standardize financial statements?
3.2b   Name two types of standardized statements and describe how each is formed.

Ratio Analysis

3.3

Excel Master It!

xlsx Excel Master coverage online

Another way of avoiding the problems involved in comparing companies of different sizes is to calculate and compare **financial ratios**. Such ratios are ways of comparing and investigating the relationships between different pieces of financial information. Using ratios eliminates the size problem because the size effectively divides out. We're then left with percentages, multiples, or time periods.

There is a problem in discussing financial ratios. Because a ratio is one number divided by another, and because there are so many accounting numbers out there, we could examine a huge number of possible ratios. Everybody has a favorite. We will restrict ourselves to a representative sampling.

In this section, we only want to introduce you to some commonly used financial ratios. These are not necessarily the ones we think are the best. In fact, some of them may strike you as illogical or not as useful as some alternatives. If they do, don't be concerned. As a financial analyst, you can always decide how to compute your own ratios.

What you do need to worry about is the fact that different people and different sources seldom compute these ratios in exactly the same way, and this leads to much confusion. The specific definitions we use here may or may not be the same as ones you have seen or will see elsewhere. If you are ever using ratios as a tool for analysis, you should be careful to document how you calculate each one. And if you are comparing your numbers to numbers from another source, be sure you know how those numbers have been computed.

financial ratios
Relationships determined from a firm's financial information and used for comparison purposes.

We will defer much of our discussion of how ratios are used and some problems that come up with using them until later in the chapter. For now, for each of the ratios we discuss, we consider several questions:

1. How is it computed?
2. What is it intended to measure, and why might we be interested?
3. What is the unit of measurement?
4. What might a high or low value tell us? How might such values be misleading?
5. How could this measure be improved?

Financial ratios are traditionally grouped into the following categories:

1. Short-term solvency, or liquidity, ratios.
2. Long-term solvency, or financial leverage, ratios.
3. Asset management, or turnover, ratios.
4. Profitability ratios.
5. Market value ratios.

We will consider each of these in turn. In calculating these numbers for Prufrock, we will use the ending balance sheet (2018) figures unless we say otherwise. Also notice that the various ratios are color keyed to indicate which numbers come from the income statement (blue) and which come from the balance sheet (green).

SHORT-TERM SOLVENCY, OR LIQUIDITY, MEASURES

As the name suggests, short-term solvency ratios as a group are intended to provide information about a firm's liquidity, and these ratios are sometimes called *liquidity measures*. The primary concern is the firm's ability to pay its bills over the short run without undue stress. Consequently, these ratios focus on current assets and current liabilities.

For obvious reasons, liquidity ratios are particularly interesting to short-term creditors. Because financial managers work constantly with banks and other short-term lenders, an understanding of these ratios is essential.

One advantage of looking at current assets and liabilities is that their book values and market values are likely to be similar. Often (though not always), these assets and liabilities don't live long enough for the two to get seriously out of step. On the other hand, like any type of near-cash, current assets and liabilities can and do change fairly rapidly, so today's amounts may not be a reliable guide to the future.

Go to **www.reuters.com** to examine comparative ratios for a huge number of companies.

Current Ratio   One of the best known and most widely used ratios is the *current ratio*. As you might guess, the current ratio is defined as follows:

$$\text{Current ratio} = \frac{\text{Current assets}}{\text{Current liabilities}}$$ **3.1**

Here is Prufrock's 2018 current ratio:

$$\text{Current ratio} = \frac{\$756}{\$540} = 1.40 \text{ times}$$

Because current assets and liabilities are, in principle, converted to cash over the following 12 months, the current ratio is a measure of short-term liquidity. The unit of measurement is either dollars or times. So, we could say Prufrock has $1.40 in current assets for every $1 in current liabilities, or we could say Prufrock has its current liabilities covered 1.40 times over.

To a creditor—particularly a short-term creditor such as a supplier—the higher the current ratio, the better. To the firm, a high current ratio indicates liquidity, but it also may indicate an inefficient use of cash and other short-term assets. Absent some extraordinary circumstances, we would expect to see a current ratio of at least 1 because a current ratio of less than 1 would mean that net working capital (current assets less current liabilities) is negative. This would be unusual in a healthy firm, at least for most types of businesses.

The current ratio, like any ratio, is affected by various types of transactions. For example, suppose the firm borrows over the long term to raise money. The short-run effect would be an increase in cash from the issue proceeds and an increase in long-term debt. Current liabilities would not be affected, so the current ratio would rise.

Finally, note that an apparently low current ratio may not be a bad sign for a company with a large reserve of untapped borrowing power.

Current Events   **EXAMPLE 3.1**

Suppose a firm pays off some of its suppliers and short-term creditors. What happens to the current ratio? Suppose a firm buys some inventory. What happens in this case? What happens if a firm sells some merchandise?

The first case is a trick question. What happens is that the current ratio moves away from 1. If it is greater than 1 (the usual case), it will get bigger. But if it is less than 1, it will get smaller. To see this, suppose the firm has $4 in current assets and $2 in current liabilities for a current ratio of 2. If we use $1 in cash to reduce current liabilities, then the new current ratio is ($4 − 1)/($2 − 1) = 3. If we reverse the original situation to $2 in current assets and $4 in current liabilities, then the change will cause the current ratio to fall to 1/3 from 1/2.

The second case is not quite as tricky. Nothing happens to the current ratio because cash goes down while inventory goes up—total current assets are unaffected.

In the third case, the current ratio will usually rise because inventory is normally shown at cost and the sale will normally be at something greater than cost (the difference is the markup). The increase in either cash or receivables is therefore greater than the decrease in inventory. This increases current assets, and the current ratio rises.

The Quick (or Acid-Test) Ratio Inventory is often the least liquid current asset. It's also the one for which the book values are least reliable as measures of market value because the quality of the inventory isn't considered. Some of the inventory may later turn out to be damaged, obsolete, or lost.

More to the point, relatively large inventories are often a sign of short-term trouble. The firm may have overestimated sales and overbought or overproduced as a result. In this case, the firm may have a substantial portion of its liquidity tied up in slow-moving inventory.

To further evaluate liquidity, the *quick*, or *acid-test*, *ratio* is computed just like the current ratio, except inventory is omitted:

$$\text{Quick ratio} = \frac{\text{Current assets} - \text{Inventory}}{\text{Current liabilities}}$$ **3.2**

Notice that using cash to buy inventory does not affect the current ratio, but it reduces the quick ratio. Again, the idea is that inventory is relatively illiquid compared to cash.

For Prufrock, this ratio for 2018 was:

$$\text{Quick ratio} = \frac{\$756 - 422}{\$540} = .62 \text{ times}$$

The quick ratio here tells a somewhat different story than the current ratio because inventory accounts for more than half of Prufrock's current assets. To exaggerate the point, if this inventory consisted of, say, unsold nuclear power plants, then this would be a cause for concern.

To give an example of current versus quick ratios, based on recent financial statements, Walmart and ManpowerGroup had current ratios of .85 and 1.39, respectively. However, Manpower carries no inventory to speak of, whereas Walmart's current assets are virtually all inventory. As a result, Walmart's quick ratio was only .22, whereas ManpowerGroup's was 1.39, the same as its current ratio.

Other Liquidity Ratios   We briefly mention three other measures of liquidity. A very short-term creditor might be interested in the *cash ratio*:

$$\text{Cash ratio} = \frac{\text{Cash}}{\text{Current liabilities}} \qquad \text{[3.3]}$$

You can verify that for 2018 this works out to be .27 times for Prufrock.

Because net working capital, or NWC, is frequently viewed as the amount of short-term liquidity a firm has, we can consider the ratio of *NWC to total assets*:

$$\text{Net working capital to total assets} = \frac{\text{Net working capital}}{\text{Total assets}} \qquad \text{[3.4]}$$

A relatively low value might indicate relatively low levels of liquidity. Here, this ratio works out to be ($756 − 540)/$3,636 = .06 times.

Finally, imagine that Prufrock was facing a strike and cash inflows began to dry up. How long could the business keep running? One answer is given by the *interval measure*:

$$\text{Interval measure} = \frac{\text{Current assets}}{\text{Average daily operating costs}} \qquad \text{[3.5]}$$

Total costs for the year, excluding depreciation and interest, were $1,344. The average daily cost was $1,344/365 = $3.68 per day.[1] The interval measure is thus $756/$3.68 = 205 days. Based on this, Prufrock could hang on for six months or so.[2]

The interval measure (or something similar) is also useful for newly founded or start-up companies that often have little in the way of revenues. For such companies, the interval measure indicates how long the company can operate until it needs another round of financing. The average daily operating cost for start-up companies is often called the *burn rate*, meaning the rate at which cash is burned in the race to become profitable.

LONG-TERM SOLVENCY MEASURES

Long-term solvency ratios are intended to address the firm's long-term ability to meet its obligations, or, more generally, its financial leverage. These are sometimes called *financial leverage ratios* or *leverage ratios*. We consider three commonly used measures and some variations.

Total Debt Ratio   The *total debt ratio* takes into account all debts of all maturities to all creditors. It can be defined in several ways, the easiest of which is this:

$$\begin{aligned}\text{Total debt ratio} &= \frac{\text{Total assets} - \text{Total equity}}{\text{Total assets}} \\ &= \frac{\$3,636 - 2,639}{\$3,636} = .27 \text{ times}\end{aligned} \qquad \text{[3.6]}$$

---

[1]For many of these ratios that involve average daily amounts, a 360-day year is often used in practice. This so-called banker's year has exactly four quarters of 90 days each and was computationally convenient in the days before pocket calculators. We'll use 365 days.

[2]Sometimes depreciation and/or interest is included in calculating average daily costs. Depreciation isn't a cash expense, so its inclusion doesn't make a lot of sense. Interest is a financing cost, so we excluded it by definition (we looked at only operating costs). We could, of course, define a different ratio that included interest expense.

In this case, an analyst might say that Prufrock uses 27 percent debt.[3] Whether this is high or low or whether it even makes any difference depends on whether capital structure matters, a subject we discuss in Part 6.

Prufrock has $.27 in debt for every $1 in assets. Therefore, there is $.73 in equity (= $1 − .27) for every $.27 in debt. With this in mind, we can define two useful variations on the total debt ratio—the *debt-equity ratio* and the *equity multiplier*:

Debt-equity ratio = Total debt/Total equity   **3.7**

$$= \$.27/\$.73 = .38 \text{ times}$$

Equity multiplier = Total assets/Total equity   **3.8**

$$= \$1/\$.73 = 1.38 \text{ times}$$

The fact that the equity multiplier is 1 plus the debt-equity ratio is not a coincidence:

$$\text{Equity multiplier} = \text{Total assets/Total equity} = \$1/\$.73 = 1.38$$
$$= (\text{Total equity} + \text{Total debt})/\text{Total equity}$$
$$= 1 + \text{Debt-equity ratio} = 1.38 \text{ times}$$

The thing to notice here is that given any one of these three ratios, you can immediately calculate the other two; so, they all say exactly the same thing.

A Brief Digression: Total Capitalization versus Total Assets   Frequently, financial analysts are more concerned with a firm's long-term debt than its short-term debt because the short-term debt will be constantly changing. Also, a firm's accounts payable may reflect trade practice more than debt management policy. For these reasons, the *long-term debt ratio* is often calculated as follows:

Ratios used to analyze technology firms can be found at **www.chalfin.com** under the "Publications" link.

Long-term debt ratio = $\dfrac{\text{Long-term debt}}{\text{Long-term debt} + \text{Total equity}}$ **3.9**

$$= \frac{\$457}{\$457 + 2,639} = \frac{\$457}{\$3,096} = .15 \text{ times}$$

The $3,096 in total long-term debt and equity is sometimes called the firm's *total capitalization*, and the financial manager will frequently focus on this quantity rather than on total assets.

To complicate matters, different people (and different books) mean different things by the term *debt ratio*. Some mean a ratio of total debt, some mean a ratio of long-term debt only, and, unfortunately, a substantial number are vague about which one they mean.

This is a source of confusion, so we choose to give two separate names to the two measures. The same problem comes up in discussing the debt-equity ratio. Financial analysts frequently calculate this ratio using only long-term debt.

Times Interest Earned   Another common measure of long-term solvency is the *times interest earned* (TIE) *ratio*. Once again, there are several possible (and common) definitions, but we'll stick with the most traditional:

Times interest earned ratio = $\dfrac{\text{EBIT}}{\text{Interest}}$ **3.10**

$$= \frac{\$691}{\$141} = 4.9 \text{ times}$$

---

[3]Total equity here includes preferred stock (discussed in Chapter 8 and elsewhere), if there is any. An equivalent numerator in this ratio would be Current liabilities + Long-term debt.

As the name suggests, this ratio measures how well a company has its interest obligations covered, and it is often called the *interest coverage ratio*. For Prufrock, the interest bill is covered 4.9 times over.

Cash Coverage   A problem with the TIE ratio is that it is based on EBIT, which is not really a measure of cash available to pay interest. The reason is that depreciation, a noncash expense, has been deducted out. Because interest is definitely a cash outflow (to creditors), one way to define the *cash coverage ratio* is this:

$$\text{Cash coverage ratio} = \frac{\text{EBIT + Depreciation}}{\text{Interest}}$$

$$= \frac{\$691 + 276}{\$141} = \frac{\$967}{\$141} = 6.86 \text{ times}$$

[3.11]

The numerator here, EBIT plus depreciation, is often abbreviated EBITD (earnings before interest, taxes, and depreciation—say "ebbit-dee"). It is a basic measure of the firm's ability to generate cash from operations, and it is frequently used as a measure of cash flow available to meet financial obligations.

A common variation on EBITD is earnings before interest, taxes, depreciation, and amortization (EBITDA—say "ebbit-dah"). Here *amortization* refers to a noncash deduction similar conceptually to depreciation, except it applies to an intangible asset (such as a patent) rather than a tangible asset (such as a machine). Note that the word *amortization* here does not refer to the repayment of debt, a subject we discuss in a later chapter.

ASSET MANAGEMENT, OR TURNOVER, MEASURES

We next turn our attention to the efficiency with which Prufrock uses its assets. The measures in this section are sometimes called *asset utilization ratios*. The specific ratios we discuss can all be interpreted as measures of turnover. What they are intended to describe is how efficiently or intensively a firm uses its assets to generate sales. We first look at two important current assets: inventory and receivables.

Inventory Turnover and Days' Sales in Inventory   During the year, Prufrock had a cost of goods sold of $1,344. Inventory at the end of the year was $422. With these numbers, *inventory turnover* can be calculated as follows:

$$\text{Inventory turnover} = \frac{\text{Cost of goods sold}}{\text{Inventory}}$$

$$= \frac{\$1,344}{\$422} = 3.18 \text{ times}$$

[3.12]

In a sense, Prufrock sold off or turned over the entire inventory 3.18 times.[4] As long as we are not running out of stock and thereby forgoing sales, the higher this ratio is, the more efficiently we are managing inventory.

If we know we turned our inventory over 3.18 times during the year, we can immediately figure out how long it took us to turn it over on average. The result is the average *days' sales in inventory*:

$$\text{Days' sales in inventory} = \frac{365 \text{ days}}{\text{Inventory turnover}}$$

$$= \frac{365 \text{ days}}{3.18} = 115 \text{ days}$$

[3.13]

---

[4]Notice that we used cost of goods sold in the top of this ratio. For some purposes, it might be more useful to use sales instead of costs. For example, if we wanted to know the amount of sales generated per dollar of inventory, we could just replace the cost of goods sold with sales.

This tells us that, roughly speaking, inventory sits 115 days on average before it is sold. Alternatively, assuming we have used the most recent inventory and cost figures, it will take about 115 days to work off our current inventory.

To give an example, in September 2017, the U.S. automobile industry as a whole had a 74-day supply of cars, higher than the 60-day supply considered normal. This figure means that at the then-current rate of sales, it would have taken 62 days to deplete the available supply. Of course, there was significant variation among the auto manufacturers. For example, BMW had only a 40-day supply of inventory, while Mitsubishi's days' sales in inventory was 125 days.

It might make more sense to use the average inventory in calculating turnover. Inventory turnover would then be $1,344/[($393 + 422)/2] = 3.3$ times.[5] It depends on the purpose of the calculation. If we are interested in how long it will take us to sell our current inventory, then using the ending figure (as we did initially) is probably better.

In many of the ratios we discuss in this chapter, average figures could just as well be used. Again, it depends on whether we are worried about the past, in which case averages are appropriate, or the future, in which case ending figures might be better. Also, using ending figures is common in reporting industry averages; so, for comparison purposes, ending figures should be used in such cases. In any event, using ending figures is definitely less work, so we'll continue to use them.

Receivables Turnover and Days' Sales in Receivables   Our inventory measures give some indication of how fast we can sell product. We now look at how fast we collect on those sales. The *receivables turnover* is defined much like inventory turnover:

$$\text{Receivables turnover} = \frac{\text{Sales}}{\text{Accounts receivable}}$$

3.14

$$= \frac{\$2,311}{\$188} = 12.29 \text{ times}$$

Loosely speaking, Prufrock collected its outstanding credit accounts and reloaned the money 12.29 times during the year.[6]

This ratio makes more sense if we convert it to days, so here is the *days' sales in receivables*:

$$\text{Days' sales in receivables} = \frac{365 \text{ days}}{\text{Receivables turnover}}$$

3.15

$$= \frac{365}{12.29} = 30 \text{ days}$$

Therefore, on average, Prufrock collects on its credit sales in 30 days. For obvious reasons, this ratio is frequently called the *average collection period* (ACP).

Note that if we are using the most recent figures, we could also say that we have 30 days' worth of sales currently uncollected. We will learn more about this subject when we study credit policy in a later chapter.

---

[5]Notice that we calculated the average as (Beginning value + Ending value)/2.

[6]Here we have implicitly assumed that all sales are credit sales. If they were not, we would simply use total credit sales in these calculations, not total sales.

Payables Turnover	**EXAMPLE 3.2**

Here is a variation on the receivables collection period. How long, on average, does it take for Prufrock Corporation to pay its bills? To answer, we need to calculate the accounts payable turnover rate using cost of goods sold. We will assume that Prufrock purchases everything on credit.

The cost of goods sold is $1,344, and accounts payable are $344. The turnover is therefore $1,344/$344 = 3.91 times. So, payables turned over about every 365/3.91 = 94 days. On average, then, Prufrock takes 94 days to pay. As a potential creditor, we might take note of this fact.

Asset Turnover Ratios   Moving away from specific accounts like inventory or receivables, we can consider several "big picture" ratios. For example, *NWC turnover* is:

$$\text{NWC turnover} = \frac{\text{Sales}}{\text{NWC}}$$

$$= \frac{\$2,311}{\$756 - 540} = 10.7 \text{ times}$$

3.16

This ratio measures how much "work" we get out of our working capital. Once again, assuming we aren't missing out on sales, a high value is preferred. (Why?)

Similarly, *fixed asset turnover* is:

$$\text{Fixed asset turnover} = \frac{\text{Sales}}{\text{Net fixed assets}}$$

$$= \frac{\$2,311}{\$2,880} = .80 \text{ times}$$

3.17

With this ratio, it probably makes more sense to say that for every dollar in fixed assets, Prufrock generated $.80 in sales.

Our final asset management ratio, *total asset turnover*, comes up quite a bit. We will see it later in this chapter and in the next chapter. As the name suggests, the total asset turnover is:

$$\text{Total asset turnover} = \frac{\text{Sales}}{\text{Total assets}}$$

$$= \frac{\$2,311}{\$3,588} = .64 \text{ times}$$

3.18

In other words, for every dollar in assets, Prufrock generated $.64 in sales.

To give an example of fixed and total asset turnover, based on recent financial statements, Southwest Airlines had a total asset turnover of .85, compared to .74 for IBM. However, the much higher investment in fixed assets in an airline is reflected in Southwest's fixed asset turnover of 1.03, compared to IBM's 1.20.

EXAMPLE 3.3   **More Turnover**

Suppose you find that a particular company generates $.40 in sales for every dollar in total assets. How often does this company turn over its total assets?

The total asset turnover here is .40 times per year. It takes 1/.40 = 2.5 years to turn total assets over completely.

PROFITABILITY MEASURES

The three measures we discuss in this section are probably the best known and most widely used of all financial ratios. In one form or another, they are intended to measure how efficiently a firm uses its assets and manages its operations. The focus in this group is on the bottom line, net income.

Profit Margin   Companies pay a great deal of attention to their *profit margins*:

$$\text{Profit margin} = \frac{\text{Net income}}{\text{Sales}}$$

$$= \frac{\$435}{\$2,311} = .1880, \text{ or } 18.80\%$$

[3.19]

This tells us that Prufrock, in an accounting sense, generates a little less than 19 cents in profit for every dollar in sales.

All other things being equal, a relatively high profit margin is obviously desirable. This situation corresponds to low expense ratios relative to sales. However, we hasten to add that other things are often not equal.

For example, lowering our sales price will usually increase unit volume but will normally cause profit margins to shrink. Total profit (or, more important, operating cash flow) may go up or down; so the fact that margins are smaller isn't necessarily bad. After all, isn't it possible that, as the saying goes, "Our prices are so low that we lose money on everything we sell, but we make it up in volume"?[7]

Return on Assets   *Return on assets* (ROA) is a measure of profit per dollar of assets. It can be defined several ways, but the most common is this:

$$\text{Return on assets} = \frac{\text{Net income}}{\text{Total assets}}$$

$$= \frac{\$435}{\$3,636} = .1195, \text{ or } 11.95\%$$

[3.20]

Return on Equity   *Return on equity* (ROE) is a measure of how the stockholders fared during the year. Because benefiting shareholders is our goal, ROE is, in an accounting sense, the true bottom-line measure of performance. ROE is usually measured as follows:

$$\text{Return on equity} = \frac{\text{Net income}}{\text{Total equity}}$$

$$= \frac{\$435}{\$2,639} = .1646, \text{ or } 16.46\%$$

[3.21]

For every dollar in equity, therefore, Prufrock generated 16.46 cents in profit; but this is correct only in accounting terms.

Because ROA and ROE are such commonly cited numbers, we stress that it is important to remember they are accounting rates of return. For this reason, these measures should properly be called *return on book assets* and *return on book equity*. In fact, ROE is sometimes called *return on net worth*. Whatever it's called, it would be inappropriate to compare the result to, for example, an interest rate observed in the financial markets. We will have more to say about accounting rates of return in later chapters.

The fact that ROE exceeds ROA reflects Prufrock's use of financial leverage. We will examine the relationship between these two measures in more detail shortly.

---

[7]No, it's not.

ROE and ROA	EXAMPLE 3.4

Because ROE and ROA are usually intended to measure performance over a prior period, it makes a certain amount of sense to base them on average equity and average assets, respectively. For Prufrock, how would you calculate these?

We first need to calculate average assets and average equity:

Average assets = ($3,373 + 3,636)/2 = $3,505
Average equity = ($2,299 + 2,639)/2 = $2,469

With these averages, we can recalculate ROA and ROE as follows:

$$\text{ROA} = \frac{\$435}{\$3,505} = .1240, \text{ or } 12.40\%$$

$$\text{ROE} = \frac{\$435}{\$2,469} = .1760, \text{ or } 17.60\%$$

These are slightly higher than our previous calculations because assets and equity grew during the year, so the average values are below the ending values.

MARKET VALUE MEASURES

Our final group of measures is based, in part, on information not necessarily contained in financial statements—the market price per share of stock. Obviously, these measures can be calculated directly only for publicly traded companies.

We assume that Prufrock has 33 million shares outstanding and the stock sold for $88 per share at the end of the year. If we recall that Prufrock's net income was $435 million, we can calculate its earnings per share:

$$\text{EPS} = \frac{\text{Net income}}{\text{Shares outstanding}} = \frac{\$435}{33} = \$13.17$$

Price-Earnings Ratio   The first of our market value measures, the *price-earnings* (PE) *ratio* (or multiple), is defined here:

$$\textbf{PE ratio} = \frac{\textbf{Price per share}}{\textbf{Earnings per share}}$$

$$= \frac{\$88}{\$13.17} = 6.68 \text{ times}$$

3.22

In the vernacular, we would say that Prufrock shares sell for almost seven times earnings, or we might say that Prufrock shares have or "carry" a PE multiple of 6.68.

PE ratios vary substantially across companies, but, in 2017, a typical large company in the United States had a PE in the 15–20 range. This is on the high side by historical standards, but not dramatically so. A low point for PEs was about 5 in 1974. PEs also vary across countries. For example, Japanese PEs have historically been much higher than those of their U.S. counterparts.

Because the PE ratio measures how much investors are willing to pay per dollar of current earnings, higher PEs are often taken to mean the firm has significant prospects for future growth. Of course, if a firm had no or almost no earnings, its PE would probably be quite large; so, as always, care is needed in interpreting this ratio.

Sometimes analysts divide PE ratios by expected future earnings growth rates (after multiplying the growth rate by 100). The result is the PEG ratio. Suppose Prufrock's anticipated growth rate in EPS was 6 percent. Its PEG ratio would then be 6.68/6 = 1.11. The idea behind the PEG ratio is that whether a PE ratio is high or low depends on expected future growth. High PEG ratios suggest that the PE is too high relative to growth, and vice versa.

Price-Sales Ratio   In some cases, companies will have negative earnings for extended periods, so their PE ratios are not very meaningful. A good example is a recent start-up. Such companies usually do have some revenues, so analysts will often look at the *price-sales ratio*:

Price-sales ratio = Price per share/Sales per share

In Prufrock's case, sales were $2,311, so here is the price-sales ratio:

Price-sales ratio = $88/($2,311/33) = $88/$70 = 1.26 times

As with PE ratios, whether a particular price-sales ratio is high or low depends on the industry involved.

Market-to-Book Ratio   A third commonly quoted market value measure is the *market-to-book ratio*:

$$\text{Market-to-book ratio} = \frac{\text{Market value per share}}{\text{Book value per share}}$$

$$= \frac{\$88}{(\$2,639/33)} = \frac{\$88}{\$80.0} = 1.10 \text{ times}$$

Notice that book value per share is total equity (not just common stock) divided by the number of shares outstanding.

Because book value per share is an accounting number, it reflects historical costs. In a loose sense, the market-to-book ratio compares the market value of the firm's investments to their cost. A value less than 1 could mean that the firm has not been successful overall in creating value for its stockholders.

Market-to-book ratios in recent years appear high relative to past values. For example, for the 30 blue-chip companies that make up the widely followed Dow Jones Industrial Average, the historical norm is about 1.7; however, the market-to-book ratio for this group has recently been twice this size.

Another ratio, called *Tobin's Q ratio*, is much like the market-to-book ratio. Tobin's Q is the market value of a firm's assets divided by their replacement cost:

Tobin's Q = Market value of firm's assets/Replacement cost of firm's assets

= Market value of firm's debt and equity/Replacement cost of firm's assets

Notice that we used two equivalent numerators here: the market value of the firm's assets and the market value of its debt and equity.

Conceptually, the Q ratio is superior to the market-to-book ratio because it focuses on what the firm is worth today relative to what it would cost to replace it today. Firms with high Q ratios tend to be those with attractive investment opportunities or significant competitive advantages (or both). In contrast, the market-to-book ratio focuses on historical costs, which are less relevant.

As a practical matter, however, Q ratios are difficult to calculate with accuracy because estimating the replacement cost of a firm's assets is not an easy task. Also, market values for a firm's debt are often unobservable. Book values can be used instead in such cases, but accuracy may suffer.

Enterprise Value-EBITDA Ratio   A company's enterprise value is an estimate of the market value of the company's operating assets. By operating assets, we mean all the assets of the firm except cash. Of course, it's not practical to work with the individual assets of a firm because market values would usually not be available. Instead, we can use the right-hand side of the balance sheet and calculate the enterprise value as:

Enterprise value = Total market value of the stock

+ Book value of all liabilities − Cash

We use the book value for liabilities because we typically can't get the market values, at least not for all of them. However, book value is usually a reasonable approximation for market value when it comes to liabilities, particularly short-term debts. Notice that the sum of the value of the market values of the stock and all liabilities equals the value of the firm's assets from the balance sheet identity. Once we have this number, we subtract the cash to get the enterprise value.

TABLE 3.8 Common Financial Ratios

I. Short-term solvency, or liquidity, ratios		II. Long-term solvency, or financial leverage, ratios	
Current ratio = $\dfrac{\text{Current assets}}{\text{Current liabilities}}$		Total debt ratio = $\dfrac{\text{Total assets} - \text{Total equity}}{\text{Total assets}}$	
Quick ratio = $\dfrac{\text{Current assets} - \text{Inventory}}{\text{Current liabilities}}$		Debt-equity ratio = Total debt/Total equity	
Cash ratio = $\dfrac{\text{Cash}}{\text{Current liabilities}}$		Equity multiplier = Total assets/Total equity	
Net working capital to total assets = $\dfrac{\text{Net working capital}}{\text{Total assets}}$		Long-term debt ratio = $\dfrac{\text{Long-term debt}}{\text{Long-term debt} + \text{Total equity}}$	
Interval measure = $\dfrac{\text{Current assets}}{\text{Average daily operating costs}}$		Times interest earned ratio = $\dfrac{\text{EBIT}}{\text{Interest}}$	
		Cash coverage ratio = $\dfrac{\text{EBIT} + \text{Depreciation}}{\text{Interest}}$	

III. Asset management, or turnover, ratios		IV. Profitability ratios	
Inventory turnover = $\dfrac{\text{Cost of goods sold}}{\text{Inventory}}$		Profit margin = $\dfrac{\text{Net income}}{\text{Sales}}$	
Days' sales in inventory = $\dfrac{365 \text{ days}}{\text{Inventory turnover}}$		Return on assets (ROA) = $\dfrac{\text{Net income}}{\text{Total assets}}$	
Receivables turnover = $\dfrac{\text{Sales}}{\text{Accounts receivable}}$		Return on equity (ROE) = $\dfrac{\text{Net income}}{\text{Total equity}}$	
Days' sales in receivables = $\dfrac{365 \text{ days}}{\text{Receivables turnover}}$		ROE = $\dfrac{\text{Net income}}{\text{Sales}} \times \dfrac{\text{Sales}}{\text{Assets}} \times \dfrac{\text{Assets}^*}{\text{Equity}}$	
NWC turnover = $\dfrac{\text{Sales}}{\text{NWC}}$		**V. Market value ratios**	
Fixed asset turnover = $\dfrac{\text{Sales}}{\text{Net fixed assets}}$		Price-earnings ratio = $\dfrac{\text{Price per share}}{\text{Earnings per share}}$	
Total asset turnover = $\dfrac{\text{Sales}}{\text{Total assets}}$		PEG ratio = $\dfrac{\text{Price-earnings ratio}}{\text{Earnings growth rate (\%)}}$	
		Price-sales ratio = $\dfrac{\text{Price per share}}{\text{Sales per share}}$	
		Market-to-book-ratio = $\dfrac{\text{Market value per share}}{\text{Book value per share}}$	
		Tobin's Q ratio = $\dfrac{\text{Market value of assets}}{\text{Replacement cost of assets}}$	
		Enterprise value-EBITDA ratio = $\dfrac{\text{Enterprise value}}{\text{EBITDA}}$	

*This ROE decomposition is covered in Section 3.4.

Enterprise value is frequently used to calculate the EBITDA ratio (or enterprise multiple):

EBITDA ratio = Enterprise value/EBITDA

3.25

This ratio is similar in spirit to the PE ratio, but it relates the value of all the operating assets (the enterprise value) to a measure of the operating cash flow generated by those assets (EBITDA).

CONCLUSION

This completes our definitions of some common ratios. We could tell you about more of them, but these are enough for now. We'll go on to discuss some ways of using these ratios instead of just how to calculate them. Table 3.8 summarizes the ratios we've discussed.

3.3a   What are the five groups of ratios? Give two or three examples of each kind.

3.3b   Given the total debt ratio, what other two ratios can be computed? Explain how.

3.3c   Turnover ratios all have one of two figures as the numerator. What are these two figures? What do these ratios measure? How do you interpret the results?

3.3d   Profitability ratios all have the same figure in the numerator. What is it? What do these ratios measure? How do you interpret the results?

The DuPont Identity

3.4

Excel Master It!
Excel Master coverage online

As we mentioned in discussing ROA and ROE, the difference between these two profitability measures is a reflection of the use of debt financing, or financial leverage. We illustrate the relationship between these measures in this section by investigating a famous way of decomposing ROE into its component parts.

A CLOSER LOOK AT ROE

To begin, let's recall the definition of ROE:

$$\text{Return on equity} = \frac{\text{Net income}}{\text{Total equity}}$$

If we were so inclined, we could multiply this ratio by Assets/Assets without changing anything:

$$\text{Return on equity} = \frac{\text{Net income}}{\text{Total equity}} = \frac{\text{Net income}}{\text{Total equity}} \times \frac{\text{Assets}}{\text{Assets}}$$

$$= \frac{\text{Net income}}{\text{Assets}} \times \frac{\text{Assets}}{\text{Total equity}}$$

Notice that we have expressed the ROE as the product of two other ratios—ROA and the equity multiplier:

$$\text{ROE} = \text{ROA} \times \text{Equity multiplier} = \text{ROA} \times (1 + \text{Debt-equity ratio})$$

Looking back at Prufrock, for example, we see that the debt-equity ratio was .38 and ROA was 11.95 percent. Our work here implies that Prufrock's ROE, as we previously calculated, is this:

$$\text{ROE} = .1195 \times 1.38 = .1646, \text{ or } 16.46\%$$

The difference between ROE and ROA can be substantial, particularly for certain businesses. For example, in 2016, American Express had an ROA of 3.40 percent, which is fairly typical for financial institutions. However, financial institutions tend to borrow a lot of money and, as a result, have relatively large equity multipliers. For American Express, ROE was about 26.38 percent, implying an equity multiplier of 7.75 times.

We can further decompose ROE by multiplying the top and bottom by total sales:

$$\text{ROE} = \frac{\text{Sales}}{\text{Sales}} \times \frac{\text{Net income}}{\text{Assets}} \times \frac{\text{Assets}}{\text{Total equity}}$$

If we rearrange things a bit, ROE looks like this:

$$\text{ROE} = \underbrace{\frac{\text{Net income}}{\text{Sales}} \times \frac{\text{Sales}}{\text{Assets}}}_{\text{Return on assets}} \times \frac{\text{Assets}}{\text{Total equity}}$$

3.26

= Profit margin × Total asset turnover × Equity multiplier

DuPont identity

Popular expression breaking ROE into three parts: operating efficiency, asset use efficiency, and financial leverage.

What we have now done is to partition ROA into its two component parts, profit margin and total asset turnover. The last expression of the preceding equation is called the **DuPont identity**, after the DuPont Corporation, which popularized its use.

We can check this relationship for Prufrock by noting that the profit margin was 15.71 percent and the total asset turnover was .64:

ROE = Profit margin × Total asset turnover × Equity multiplier

    =   .1880   ×   .64   ×   1.38

    = .1646, or 16.46%

This 16.46 percent ROE is exactly what we had before.

The DuPont identity tells us that ROE is affected by three things:

1. Operating efficiency (as measured by profit margin).
2. Asset use efficiency (as measured by total asset turnover).
3. Financial leverage (as measured by the equity multiplier).

Weakness in either operating or asset use efficiency (or both) will show up in a diminished return on assets, which will translate into a lower ROE.

Considering the DuPont identity, it appears that the ROE could be leveraged up by increasing the amount of debt in the firm. However, notice that increasing debt also increases interest expense, which reduces profit margins, which acts to reduce ROE. So, ROE could go up or down, depending on other variables. More important, the use of debt financing has a number of other effects, and, as we discuss at some length in Part 6, the amount of leverage a firm uses is governed by its capital structure policy.

The decomposition of ROE we've discussed in this section is a convenient way of systematically approaching financial statement analysis. If ROE is unsatisfactory by some measure, then the DuPont identity tells you where to start looking for the reasons.

General Motors provides a good example of how DuPont analysis can be very useful and also illustrates why care must be taken in interpreting ROE values. In 1989, GM had an ROE of 12.1 percent. By 1993, its ROE had improved to 44.1 percent, a dramatic improvement. On closer inspection, however, we find that over the same period GM's profit margin had declined from 3.4 to 1.8 percent, and ROA had declined from 2.4 to 1.3 percent. The decline in ROA was moderated only slightly by an increase in total asset turnover from .71 to .73 over the period.

Given this information, how is it possible for GM's ROE to have climbed so sharply? From our understanding of the DuPont identity, it must be the case that GM's equity multiplier increased substantially. In fact, what happened was that GM's book equity value was almost wiped out overnight in 1992 by changes in the accounting treatment of pension liabilities. If a company's equity value declines sharply, its equity multiplier rises. In GM's case, the multiplier went from 4.95 in 1989 to 33.62 in 1993. In sum, the dramatic "improvement" in GM's ROE was almost entirely due to an accounting change that affected the equity multiplier and didn't really represent an improvement in financial performance at all.

DuPont analysis (and ratio analysis in general) can be used to compare two companies as well. Yahoo! and Alphabet are among the most important Internet companies in the world. We will use them to illustrate how DuPont analysis can be useful in helping to ask the right questions about a firm's financial performance. The DuPont breakdowns for Yahoo! and Alphabet are summarized in Table 3.9.

As shown, in 2015, Yahoo! had an ROE of −15.0 percent, well down from its ROE in 2013 of 10.4 percent. In contrast, in 2015, Alphabet had an ROE of 13.6 percent, about the same as its ROE in 2013 of 14.8 percent. Given this information, how is it possible that

TABLE 3.9

	ROE		Profit margin		Total asset turnover		Equity multiplier
Yahoo!							
2015	−15.0%	=	−87.5%	×	.110	×	1.56
2014	.4	=	3.1	×	.075	×	1.59
2013	10.4	=	29.2	×	.279	×	1.29
Alphabet							
2015	13.6%	=	21.8%	×	.509	×	1.23
2014	13.6	=	21.4	×	.511	×	1.24
2013	14.8	=	21.6	×	.539	×	1.27

Alphabet's ROE could be so much higher during this period of time, and what accounts for the decrease in Yahoo!'s ROE?

On closer inspection of the DuPont breakdown, we see that Yahoo!'s profit margin in 2015 was −87.5 percent, really poor performance. Meanwhile, Alphabet's profit margin was 21.8 percent. While much of the difference in ROE can be explained by the difference in the profit margin, Yahoo! and Alphabet have similar financial leverage. However, it is also important to note that Alphabet has another advantage over Yahoo! in ROE—namely, the much higher asset utilization.

AN EXPANDED DUPONT ANALYSIS

So far, we've seen how the DuPont equation lets us break down ROE into its basic three components: profit margin, total asset turnover, and financial leverage. We now extend this analysis to take a closer look at how key parts of a firm's operations feed into ROE. To get going, we went to finance.yahoo.com and found financial statements for science and technology giant DuPont. What we found is summarized in Table 3.10.

Using the information in Table 3.10, Figure 3.1 shows how we can construct an expanded DuPont analysis for DuPont and present that analysis in chart form. The advantage of the extended DuPont chart is that it lets us examine several ratios at once, thereby getting a better overall picture of a company's performance and also allowing us to determine possible items to improve.

TABLE 3.10

FINANCIAL STATEMENTS FOR DUPONT 12 months ending December 31, 2016 (All numbers are in millions)					
Income Statement		**Balance Sheet**			
Sales	$24,750	Current assets		Current liabilities	
CoGS	14,469	Cash	$ 5,967	Accounts payable	$ 8,468
Gross profit	$10,281	Accounts receivable	4,971	Other	429
SG&A expenses	5,005	Inventory	6,179	Total	$ 8,897
R&D expenses	1,641	Total	$17,117		
EBIT	$ 3,635				
Interest	370	Fixed assets	$22,847	Total long-term debt	$21,069
EBT	$ 3,265				
Taxes	744			Total equity	$ 9,998
Net income	$ 2,521	Total assets	$39,964	Total liabilities and equity	$39,964

FIGURE 3.1   Extended DuPont Chart for DuPont

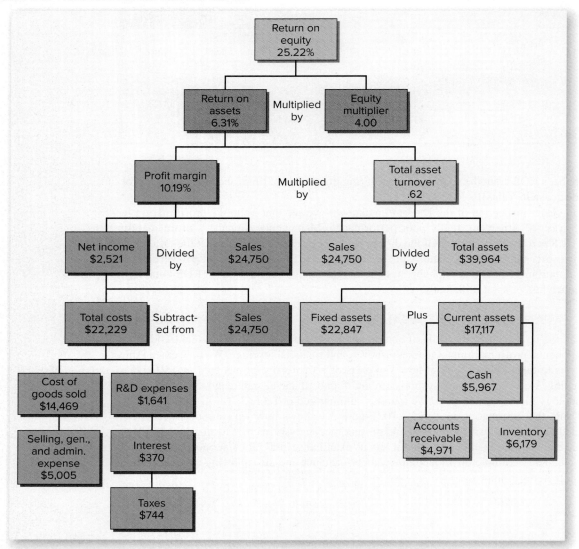

Looking at the left side of our DuPont chart in Figure 3.1, we see items related to profitability. As always, profit margin is calculated as net income divided by sales. But as our chart emphasizes, net income depends on sales and a variety of costs, such as cost of goods sold (CoGS) and selling, general, and administrative expenses (SG&A expense). DuPont can increase its ROE by increasing sales and also by reducing one or more of these costs. In other words, if we want to improve profitability, our chart clearly shows us the areas on which we should focus.

Turning to the right side of Figure 3.1, we have an analysis of the key factors underlying total asset turnover. Thus, for example, we see that reducing inventory holdings through more efficient management reduces current assets, which reduces total assets, which then improves total asset turnover.

Concept Questions

3.4a   Return on assets, or ROA, can be expressed as the product of two ratios. Which two?

3.4b   Return on equity, or ROE, can be expressed as the product of three ratios. Which three?

Using Financial Statement Information

3.5

Excel Master It!
xlsx   Excel Master
coverage online

Our last task in this chapter is to discuss in more detail some practical aspects of financial statement analysis. In particular, we will look at reasons for analyzing financial statements, how to get benchmark information, and some problems that come up in the process.

WHY EVALUATE FINANCIAL STATEMENTS?

As we have discussed, the primary reason for looking at accounting information is that we don't have, and can't reasonably expect to get, market value information. We stress that whenever we have market information, we will use it instead of accounting data. Also, if there is a conflict between accounting and market data, market data should be given precedence.

Financial statement analysis is essentially an application of "management by exception." In many cases, such analysis will boil down to comparing ratios for one business with average or representative ratios. Those ratios that seem to differ the most from the averages are tagged for further study.

Internal Uses   Financial statement information has a variety of uses within a firm. Among the most important of these is performance evaluation. For example, managers are frequently evaluated and compensated on the basis of accounting measures of performance such as profit margin and return on equity. Also, firms with multiple divisions frequently compare the performance of those divisions using financial statement information.

Another important internal use we will explore in the next chapter is planning for the future. As we will see, historical financial statement information is useful for generating projections about the future and for checking the realism of assumptions made in those projections.

External Uses   Financial statements are useful to parties outside the firm, including short-term and long-term creditors and potential investors. For example, we would find such information quite useful in deciding whether to grant credit to a new customer.

We would also use this information to evaluate suppliers, and suppliers would review our statements before deciding to extend credit to us. Large customers use this information to decide if we are likely to be around in the future. Credit-rating agencies rely on financial statements in assessing a firm's overall creditworthiness. The common theme here is that financial statements are a prime source of information about a firm's financial health.

We would also find such information useful in evaluating our main competitors. We might be thinking of launching a new product. A prime concern would be whether the competition would jump in shortly thereafter. In this case, we would be interested in learning about our competitors' financial strength to see if they could afford the necessary development.

Finally, we might be thinking of acquiring another firm. Financial statement information would be essential in identifying potential targets and deciding what to offer.

CHOOSING A BENCHMARK

Given that we want to evaluate a division or a firm based on its financial statements, a basic problem immediately comes up. How do we choose a benchmark, or a standard of comparison? We describe some ways of getting started in this section.

Time Trend Analysis   One standard we could use is history. Suppose we found that the current ratio for a particular firm is 2.4 based on the most recent financial statement information. Looking back over the last 10 years, we might find that this ratio had declined fairly steadily over that period.

Based on this, we might wonder if the liquidity position of the firm has deteriorated. It could be, of course, that the firm has made changes that allow it to more efficiently use its current assets, the nature of the firm's business has changed, or business practices have changed. If we investigate, we might find any of these possible explanations behind the decline. This is an example of what we mean by management by exception—a deteriorating time trend may not be bad, but it does merit investigation.

Peer Group Analysis   The second means of establishing a benchmark is to identify firms similar in the sense that they compete in the same markets, have similar assets, and operate in similar ways. In other words, we need to identify a *peer group*. There are obvious problems with doing this because no two companies are identical. Ultimately, the choice of which companies to use as a basis for comparison is subjective.

One common way of identifying potential peers is based on **Standard Industrial Classification (SIC) codes**. These are four-digit codes established by the U.S. government for statistical reporting. Firms with the same SIC code are frequently assumed to be similar.

The first digit in an SIC code establishes the general type of business. For example, firms engaged in finance, insurance, and real estate have SIC codes beginning with 6. Each additional digit narrows down the industry. So, companies with SIC codes beginning with 60 are mostly banks and banklike businesses; those with codes beginning with 602 are mostly commercial banks; and SIC code 6025 is assigned to national banks that are members of the Federal Reserve system. Table 3.11 lists selected two-digit codes (the first two digits of the four-digit SIC codes) and the industries they represent.

Standard Industrial Classification (SIC) code
A U.S. government code used to classify a firm by its type of business operations.

TABLE 3.11

Selected Two-Digit SIC Codes

Agriculture, Forestry, and Fishing	Transportation, Communication, Electric, Gas, and Sanitary Service
01 Agriculture production—crops	40 Railroad transportation
08 Forestry	45 Transportation by air
09 Fishing, hunting, and trapping	49 Electric, gas, and sanitary services
Mining	**Retail Trade**
10 Metal mining	54 Food stores
12 Bituminous coal and lignite mining	55 Automobile dealers and gas stations
13 Oil and gas extraction	58 Eating and drinking places
Construction	**Finance, Insurance, and Real Estate**
15 Building construction	60 Banking
16 Construction other than building	63 Insurance
17 Construction—special trade contractors	65 Real estate
Manufacturing	**Services**
28 Chemicals and allied products	78 Motion pictures
29 Petroleum refining and related industries	80 Health services
37 Transportation equipment	82 Educational services

SIC codes are far from perfect. For example, suppose you were examining financial statements for Walmart, the largest retailer in the United States. The relevant two-digit SIC code is 53, General Merchandise Stores. In a quick scan of the nearest financial database, you would find about 20 large, publicly owned corporations with a similar SIC code, but you might not be comfortable with some of them. Target would seem to be a reasonable peer, but Neiman Marcus also carries the same industry code. Are Walmart and Neiman Marcus really comparable?

As this example illustrates, it is probably not appropriate to blindly use SIC code-based averages. Instead, analysts often identify a set of primary competitors and then compute a set of averages based on just this group. Also, we may be more concerned with a group of the top firms in an industry, not the average firm. Such a group is called an *aspirant group* because we aspire to be like its members. In this case, a financial statement analysis reveals how far we have to go.

Beginning in 1997, a new industry classification system was initiated. Specifically, the North American Industry Classification System (NAICS, pronounced "nakes") is intended to replace the older SIC codes, and it will eventually. Currently, however, SIC codes are still widely used.

With these caveats about industry codes in mind, we can now take a look at a specific industry. Suppose we are in the wine making business. Table 3.12 contains some condensed common-size financial statements for this industry from the Risk Management Association (RMA, formerly known as Robert Morris Associates), one of many sources of such information. Table 3.13 contains selected ratios from the same source.

Learn more about NAICS at **www.naics.com**.

There is a large amount of information here, most of which is self-explanatory. On the right in Table 3.12, we have current information reported for different groups based on sales. Within each sales group, common-size information is reported. For example, firms with sales in the $10 million to $25 million range have cash and equivalents equal to 2.0 percent of total assets. There are 48 companies in this group, out of 258 in all.

On the left, we have three years' worth of summary historical information for the entire group. For example, operating profit decreased slightly from 11.7 percent of sales to 11.4 percent over that time.

Table 3.13 contains some selected ratios, again reported by sales groups on the right and time period on the left. To see how we might use this information, suppose our firm has a current ratio of 2. Based on these ratios, is this value unusual?

Looking at the current ratio for the overall group for the most recent year (third column from the left in Table 3.13), we see that three numbers are reported. The one in the middle, 2.1, is the median, meaning that half of the 258 firms had current ratios that were lower and half had higher current ratios. The other two numbers are the upper and lower quartiles. So, 25 percent of the firms had a current ratio larger than 4.0 and 25 percent had a current ratio smaller than 1.4. Our value of 2 falls comfortably within these bounds, so it doesn't appear too unusual. This comparison illustrates how knowledge of the range of ratios is important in addition to knowledge of the average. Notice how stable the current ratio has been for the last three years.

More Ratios	**EXAMPLE 3.5**

Take a look at the most recent numbers reported for Cost of Sales/Inventory and EBIT/Interest in Table 3.13. What are the overall median values? What are these ratios?

If you look back at our discussion, you will see that these are the inventory turnover and the times interest earned, or TIE, ratios. The median value for inventory turnover for the entire group is .7 times. So, the days' sales in inventory would be 365/.7 = 521 days, which is the boldfaced number reported. While this is long compared to other industries, this doesn't seem like very long for fine wines. The median for the TIE is 3.7 times. The number in parentheses indicates that the calculation is meaningful for, and therefore based on, only 235 of the 258 companies. In this case, the reason is that only 235 companies paid any significant amount of interest.

TABLE 3.12   Selected Financial Statement Information

Manufacturing—Wineries (NAICS 312130)									
COMPARATIVE HISTORICAL DATA				CURRENT DATA SORTED BY SALES					
			Type of Statement						
38	33	29	Unqualified	1			2	4	22
40	53	41	Reviewed		2		15	15	9
17	15	12	Compiled	1	2	3	3	2	1
24	25	26	Tax Returns	11	6	4	4	1	
100	150	150	Other	24	35	20	18	26	27
4/1/13–3/31/14	4/1/14–3/31/15	4/1/15–3/31/16		31 (4/1–9/30/15)		227 (10/1/15–3/31/16)			
ALL 219	ALL 276	ALL 258	**NUMBER OF STATEMENTS**	0–1MM 37	1–3MM 45	3–5MM 27	5–10MM 42	10–25MM 48	25MM & OVER 59
%	%	%	**Assets**	%	%	%	%	%	%
5.2	5.3	5.0	Cash & Equivalents	6.8	5.0	8.7	5.2	2.0	4.4
8.4	8.1	9.2	Trade Receivables (net)	5.6	7.3	7.5	9.0	11.0	12.3
44.4	47.4	47.3	Inventory	52.0	50.1	49.4	42.6	47.0	44.9
2.4	1.9	1.7	All Other Current	.6	1.6	.7	1.8	1.6	2.8
60.5	62.7	63.1	Total Current	65.0	64.0	66.3	58.6	61.6	64.3
32.0	29.2	29.8	Fixed Assets (net)	28.4	32.6	22.9	36.3	29.4	27.6
3.5	4.0	3.7	Intangibles (net)	4.5	1.5	3.7	3.1	5.0	4.1
4.0	4.1	3.4	All Other Non-current	2.0	2.0	7.1	2.0	3.9	4.0
100.0	100.0	100.0	Total	100.0	100.0	100.0	100.0	100.0	100.0
			Liabilities						
14.1	16.8	15.7	Notes Payable-Short term	17.7	14.3	10.0	12.3	18.8	18.1
2.1	1.8	1.3	Cur. Mat.-L.T.D	.9	1.0	.9	2.0	1.4	1.6
8.8	8.9	8.8	Trade Payables	5.9	9.0	7.2	7.8	12.2	9.3
.2	.2	.2	Income Taxes Payable	.4	.3	.0	.3	.0	.1
6.0	6.0	6.5	All Other Current	7.6	4.8	6.0	4.1	8.7	7.4
31.2	33.8	32.6	Total Current	32.5	29.3	24.1	26.5	41.2	36.5
19.8	17.4	18.5	Long-Term Debt	20.5	17.5	17.8	22.5	17.4	16.6
.4	.3	.4	Deferred Taxes	.0	.0	.2	.7	.7	.4
6.3	6.7	6.6	All Other Non-current	13.5	5.6	7.8	7.5	4.4	3.6
42.2	41.8	41.9	Net Worth	33.5	47.6	50.1	42.8	36.3	42.9
100.0	100.0	100.0	Total Liabilities & Net Worth	100.0	100.0	100.0	100.0	100.0	100.0
			Income Data						
100.0	100.0	100.0	Net Sales	100.0	100.0	100.0	100.0	100.0	100.0
48.9	50.0	49.3	Gross Profit	57.1	54.1	55.8	49.5	45.0	41.0
37.2	37.9	37.9	Operating Expenses	51.4	44.5	39.4	38.2	32.5	27.8
11.7	12.0	11.4	Operating Profit	5.7	9.7	16.4	11.3	12.5	13.3
2.7	2.6	2.6	All Other Expenses (net)	3.4	1.9	1.1	4.3	2.9	2.1
9.0	9.5	8.8	Profit Before Taxes	2.3	7.8	15.3	7.1	9.6	11.2

M = $ thousand; MM = $ million.

Interpretation of Statement Studies Figures: RMA cautions that the studies be regarded only as a general guideline and not as an absolute industry norm. This is due to limited samples within categories, the categorization of companies by their primary Standard Industrial Classification (SIC) number only, and different methods of operations by companies within the same industry. For these reasons, RMA recommends that the figures be used only as general guidelines in addition to other methods of financial analysis.

TABLE 3.13 Selected Ratios

Manufacturing—Wineries (NAICS 312130)									
COMPARATIVE HISTORICAL DATA				CURRENT DATA SORTED BY SALES					
			Type of Statement						
38	33	29	Unqualified	1			2	4	22
40	53	41	Reviewed		2		15	15	9
17	15	12	Compiled	1	2	3	3	2	1
24	25	26	Tax Returns	11	6	4	4	1	
100	150	150	Other	24	35	20	18	26	27
4/1/13–3/31/14 ALL 219	4/1/14–3/31/15 ALL 276	4/1/15–3/31/16 ALL 258	NUMBER OF STATEMENTS	31 (4/1–9/30/15) 0–1MM 37	1–3MM 45	3–5MM 27	227 (10/1/15–3/31/16) 5–10MM 42	10–25MM 48	25MM & OVER 59
			Ratios						
4.0	4.5	4.0	Current	4.1	5.8	5.9	3.8	2.4	3.4
2.1	2.0	2.1		2.7	2.3	3.3	2.3	1.5	1.9
1.4	1.4	1.4		1.4	1.5	1.8	1.8	1.2	1.3
.9	.9	.9	Quick	1.2	1.1	1.9	1.2	.6	.7
.3	.3	.3		.3	.3	.5	.4	.3	.4
.2	.2	.2		.1	.2	.2	.2	.1	.2
16 23.0	15 24.8	15 23.7	Sales/ Receivables	0 UND	7 49.3	11 32.8	16 22.4	21 17.2	28 13.1
30 12.2	34 10.6	31 11.8		10 35.6	28 12.9	20 18.3	29 12.6	37 9.8	41 8.9
51 7.1	52 7.0	52 7.0		46 7.9	50 7.3	39 9.4	57 6.4	56 6.5	59 6.2
261 1.4	332 1.1	304 1.2	Cost of Sales/ Inventory	192 1.9	304 1.2	261 1.4	304 1.2	365 1.0	261 1.4
456 .8	521 .7	521 .7		608 .6	608 .6	608 .6	608 .6	521 .7	365 1.0
730 .5	912 .4	730 .5		912 .4	912 .4	730 .5	730 .5	730 .5	608 .6
25 14.4	26 14.0	21 17.3	Cost of Sales/ Payables	0 UND	10 36.2	21 17.2	23 16.0	36 10.1	23 16.1
55 6.6	59 6.2	51 7.2		48 7.6	53 6.9	35 10.3	47 7.8	69 5.3	51 7.2
101 3.6	122 3.0	107 3.4		166 2.2	146 2.5	70 5.2	122 3.0	122 3.0	76 4.8
1.4	1.3	1.3	Sales/Working Capital	1.2	1.2	1.1	1.3	2.0	1.9
2.7	2.4	2.6		2.0	2.8	2.3	2.1	3.7	2.9
6.6	5.1	5.2		7.8	5.8	4.0	2.8	6.7	6.0
9.7	11.4	14.3	EBIT/Interest	4.5	7.9	31.5	12.3	13.0	19.9
(200) 3.9	(252) 4.7	(235) 3.7		(31) 1.0	(36) 3.6	(25) 9.0	(40) 2.3	(46) 4.1	(57) 5.7
1.4	1.7	1.3		−2.1	1.2	2.1	1.1	1.2	2.8
8.0	9.1	9.5	Net Profit + Depr., Dep,. Amort./Cur. Mat. L/T/D					6.9	17.3
(42) 4.8	(55) 5.0	(45) 5.9						(10) 3.5	(24) 7.7
1.9	2.6	2.6						1.8	4.3
.3	.2	.2	Fixed/Worth	.2	.2	.1	.4	.2	.3
.8	.7	.7		.6	.7	.4	1.0	.8	.8
1.6	1.4	1.5		4.5	1.5	1.1	1.5	1.9	1.3
.6	.6	.6	Debt/Worth	.5	.5	.4	.6	1.2	.8
1.5	1.4	1.4		2.6	1.0	1.2	1.4	2.1	1.1
4.1	3.0	3.9		24.2	2.7	4.3	2.8	4.3	3.2
32.8	33.9	32.7	% Profit Before Taxes/Tangible Net Worth	34.2	25.0	47.0	20.0	42.2	27.9
(194) 14.8	(253) 15.6	(230) 13.6		(29) 5.5	(41) 11.8	(25) 20.5	(38) 7.4	(43) 19.6	(54) 18.3
2.7	3.3	2.7		−8.9	4.6	3.3	.4	3.7	10.2

(continued)

TABLE 3.13 (*continued*)

4/1/13–3/31/14 ALL 219	4/1/14–3/31/15 ALL 276	4/1/15–3/31/16 ALL 258	NUMBER OF STATEMENTS	31 (4/1–9/30/15) 0–1MM 37	1–3MM 45	3–5MM 27	227 (10/1/15–3/31/16) 5–10MM 42	10–25MM 48	25MM & OVER 59
12.0	12.8	12.1	% Profit Before	13.6	9.1	23.9	8.7	13.4	13.1
5.1	5.6	4.8	Taxes/Total	1.4	5.2	7.2	2.7	4.4	7.0
.7	.9	.6	Assets	−5.0	.8	1.5	.2	.8	3.0
7.4	9.5	8.6	Sales/Net	7.3	6.8	13.9	3.9	33.5	9.0
2.5	3.0	2.9	Fixed Assets	5.0	2.3	5.1	1.4	2.1	3.3
1.1	1.1	1.2		2.4	1.5	1.7	.9	1.0	1.4
1.1	1.0	1.1	Sales/Total	1.1	1.1	1.2	1.0	1.1	1.1
.7	.7	.7	Assets	.7	.7	.8	.6	.7	.7
.5	.5	.5		.5	.5	.5	.4	.4	.5
2.4	2.4	2.1	% Depr., Dep.,	3.4	1.6	1.1	2.7	2.3	1.4
(171) 5.2	(214) 5.1	(199) 5.3	Amort./Sales	(22) 5.9	(31) 5.8	(18) 3.9	(35) 7.1	(37) 6.1	(56) 4.0
8.3	8.1	8.4		14.3	8.7	9.6	9.1	9.3	7.1
3.1	2.7	2.6	% Officers',						
(27) 4.3	(35) 4.1	(33) 4.1	Directors',						
7.7	9.5	7.3	Owners' Comp/Sales						
4892971M	8360552M	5519014M	Net Sales ($)	19825M	82307M	103312M	287163M	774866M	4251541M
6963108M	8811913M	8435750M	Total Assets ($)	49293M	161278M	147637M	602723M	1722233M	5752586M

M = $ thousand; MM = $ million.

There are many sources of ratio information in addition to the one we examine here. Our nearby *Work the Web* box shows how to get this information for just about any company, along with some useful benchmarking information. Be sure to look it over and then benchmark your favorite company.

PROBLEMS WITH FINANCIAL STATEMENT ANALYSIS

We close our chapter on financial statements by discussing some additional problems that can arise in using financial statements. In one way or another, the basic problem with financial statement analysis is that there is no underlying theory to help us identify which quantities to look at and to use in establishing benchmarks.

As we discuss in other chapters, there are many cases in which financial theory and economic logic provide guidance in making judgments about value and risk. Little such help exists with financial statements. This is why we can't say which ratios matter the most and what may be considered a high or low value.

One particularly severe problem is that many firms are conglomerates, owning more or less unrelated lines of business. The consolidated financial statements for such firms don't fit any neat industry category. Well-known companies like General Electric (GE) and 3M fall into this category. More generally, the kind of peer group analysis we have been describing works best when the firms are strictly in the same line of business, the industry is competitive, and there is only one way of operating.

Another problem that is becoming increasingly common is that major competitors and natural peer group members in an industry may be scattered around the globe. The automobile industry is an obvious example. The problem here is that financial statements from outside the United States do not necessarily conform at all to generally accepted accounting

Other websites provide different information about a company's ratios. For example, check out **www.marketwatch.com** and **www.morningstar.com**.

WORK THE WEB

As we discussed in this chapter, ratios are an important tool for examining a company's performance. Gathering the necessary financial statements to calculate ratios can be tedious and time-consuming. Fortunately, many sites on the web provide this information for free. One of the best is www.reuters.com. We went there, entered the ticker symbol "HD" (for Home Depot), and then went to the "Financials" page. Here is an abbreviated look at the results:

	Company	industry	sector
Quick Ratio (MRQ)	0.42	1.03	1.26
Current Ratio (MRQ)	1.34	1.91	1.58
LT Debt to Equity (MRQ)	397.33	84.80	34.40
Total Debt to Equity (MRQ)	406.99	98.04	64.39
Interest Coverage (TTM)	18.56	14.73	3.63

The website reports the company, industry, and sector ratios. As you can see, Home Depot has lower quick and current ratios than the industry.

Questions

1. Go to www.reuters.com and find the major ratio categories listed on this website. How do the categories differ from the categories listed in this textbook?
2. Go to www.reuters.com and find all the ratios for Home Depot. How does the company compare to the industry for the ratios presented on this website?

principles (GAAP). The existence of different standards and procedures makes it difficult to compare financial statements across national borders.

Even companies that are clearly in the same line of business may not be comparable. For example, electric utilities engaged primarily in power generation are all classified in the same group (SIC 4911). This group is often thought to be relatively homogeneous. However, most utilities operate as regulated monopolies, so they don't compete much with each other, at least not historically. Many have stockholders, and many are organized as cooperatives with no stockholders. There are several different ways of generating power, ranging from hydroelectric to nuclear, so the operating activities of these utilities can differ quite a bit. Finally, profitability is strongly affected by the regulatory environment, so utilities in different locations can be similar but show different profits.

Several other general problems frequently crop up. First, different firms use different accounting procedures—for inventory, for example. This makes it difficult to compare statements. Second, different firms end their fiscal years at different times. For firms in seasonal businesses (such as a retailer with a large Christmas season), this can lead to difficulties in comparing balance sheets because of fluctuations in accounts during the year. Finally, for any particular firm, unusual or transient events, such as a one-time profit from an asset sale, may affect financial performance. In comparing firms, such events can give misleading signals.

Concept Questions

3.5a   What are some uses for financial statement analysis?

3.5b   Why do we say that financial statement analysis is management by exception?

3.5c   What are SIC codes and how might they be useful?

3.5d   What are some problems that can arise with financial statement analysis?

3.6 Summary and Conclusions

This chapter has discussed aspects of financial statement analysis:

1. *Sources and uses of cash*: We discussed how to identify the ways in which businesses obtain and use cash, and we described how to trace the flow of cash through a business over the course of the year. We briefly looked at the statement of cash flows.

2. *Standardized financial statements*: We explained that differences in size make it difficult to compare financial statements, and we discussed how to form common-size and common-base period statements to make comparisons easier.

3. *Ratio analysis*: Evaluating ratios of accounting numbers is another way of comparing financial statement information. We defined and discussed a number of the most commonly reported and used financial ratios. We also discussed the famous DuPont identity as a way of analyzing financial performance.

4. *Using financial statements*: We described how to establish benchmarks for comparison and discussed some types of information that are available. We then examined potential problems that can arise.

After you have studied this chapter, we hope that you have some perspective on the uses and abuses of financial statements. You should also find that your vocabulary of business and financial terms has grown substantially.

CONNECT TO FINANCE

 For more practice, you should be in Connect Finance. Log on to connect.mheducation.com to get started!

Can you answer the following *Connect* Quiz questions?

Section 3.1   What is an example of a source of cash?

Section 3.2   Pioneer Aviation has total liabilities of $23,800 and total equity of $46,200. Current assets are $8,600. What is the common-size percentage for the current assets?

Section 3.3   What ratio measures the number of days that a firm can operate based on its current assets?

Section 3.4   What is the correct formula for computing the return on equity?

Section 3.5   If you want to identify other firms that have assets and operations that are similar to those of your firm, what should you refer to?

CHAPTER REVIEW AND SELF-TEST PROBLEMS

3.1 **Sources and Uses of Cash** Consider the following balance sheets for the Philippe Corporation. Calculate the changes in the various accounts and, where applicable, identify the change as a source or use of cash. What were the major sources and uses of cash? Did the company become more or less liquid during the year? What happened to cash during the year?

PHILIPPE CORPORATION 2017 and 2018 Balance Sheets ($ in millions)		
	2017	**2018**
Assets		
Current assets		
Cash	$ 210	$ 215
Accounts receivable	355	310
Inventory	507	328
Total	$1,072	$ 853
Fixed assets		
Net plant and equipment	$6,085	$6,527
Total assets	$7,157	$7,380
Liabilities and Owners' Equity		
Current liabilities		
Accounts payable	$ 207	$ 298
Notes payable	1,715	1,427
Total	$1,922	$1,725
Long-term debt	$1,987	$2,308
Owners' equity		
Common stock and paid-in surplus	$1,000	$1,000
Retained earnings	2,248	2,347
Total	$3,248	$3,347
Total liabilities and owners' equity	$7,157	$7,380

3.2 **Common-Size Statements** Here is the most recent income statement for Philippe. Prepare a common-size income statement based on this information. How do you interpret the standardized net income? What percentage of sales goes to cost of goods sold?

PHILIPPE CORPORATION 2018 Income Statement ($ in millions)	
Sales	$4,053
Cost of goods sold	2,816
Depreciation	550
Earnings before interest and taxes	$ 687
Interest paid	502
Taxable income	$ 185
Taxes (21%)	39
Net income	$ 146
Dividends	$47
Addition to retained earnings	99

3.3   Financial Ratios Based on the balance sheets and income statement in the previous two problems, calculate the following ratios for 2018:

Current ratio	_____
Quick ratio	_____
Cash ratio	_____
Inventory turnover	_____
Receivables turnover	_____
Days' sales in inventory	_____
Days' sales in receivables	_____
Total debt ratio	_____
Long-term debt ratio	_____
Times interest earned ratio	_____
Cash coverage ratio	_____

3.4   ROE and the DuPont Identity Calculate the 2018 ROE for the Philippe Corporation and then break down your answer into its component parts using the DuPont identity.

ANSWERS TO CHAPTER REVIEW AND SELF-TEST PROBLEMS

3.1   We've filled in the answers in the following table. Remember, increases in assets and decreases in liabilities indicate that we spent some cash. Decreases in assets and increases in liabilities are ways of getting cash.

Philippe used its cash primarily to purchase fixed assets and to pay off short-term debt. The major sources of cash to do this were additional long-term borrowing, reductions in current assets, and additions to retained earnings.

PHILIPPE CORPORATION 2017 and 2018 Balance Sheets ($ in millions)				
	2017	2018	Change	Source or Use of Cash
Assets				
Current assets				
Cash	$ 210	$ 215	+$ 5	
Accounts receivable	355	310	− 45	Source
Inventory	507	328	− 179	Source
Total	$1,072	$ 853	−$219	
Fixed assets				
Net plant and equipment	$6,085	$6,527	+$442	Use
Total assets	$7,157	$7,380	+$223	
Liabilities and Owners' Equity				
Current liabilities				
Accounts payable	$ 207	$ 298	+$ 91	Source
Notes payable	1,715	1,427	− 288	Use
Total	$1,922	$1,725	−$197	
Long-term debt	$1,987	$2,308	+$321	Source
Owners' equity				
Common stock and paid-in surplus	$1,000	$1,000	+$ 0	—
Retained earnings	2,248	2,347	+ 99	Source
Total	$3,248	$3,347	+$ 99	
Total liabilities and owners' equity	$7,157	$7,380	+$223	

The current ratio went from $1,072/$1,922 = .56 to $853/$1,725 = .49, so the firm's liquidity appears to have declined somewhat. Overall, however, the amount of cash on hand increased by $5.

3.2 We've calculated the common-size income statement here. Remember that we simply divide each item by total sales.

PHILIPPE CORPORATION 2018 Common-Size Income Statement		
Sales		100.0%
Cost of goods sold		69.5
Depreciation		13.6
Earnings before interest and taxes		17.0
Interest paid		12.4
Taxable income		4.6
Taxes (21%)		1.0
Net income		3.6
Dividends	1.2%	
Addition to retained earnings	2.4	

Net income is 3.6 percent of sales. Because this is the percentage of each sales dollar that makes its way to the bottom line, the standardized net income is the firm's profit margin. Cost of goods sold is 69.5 percent of sales.

3.3 We've calculated the following ratios based on the ending figures. If you don't remember a definition, refer back to Table 3.8.

Current ratio	$853/$1,725	= .49 times
Quick ratio	$525/$1,725	= .30 times
Cash ratio	$215/$1,725	= .12 times
Inventory turnover	$2,816/$328	= 8.59 times
Receivables turnover	$4,053/$310	= 13.07 times
Days' sales in inventory	365/8.59	= 42.51 days
Days' sales in receivables	365/13.07	= 27.92 days
Total debt ratio	$4,033/$7,380	= .546, or 54.6%
Long-term debt ratio	$2,308/$5,655	= .408, or 40.8%
Times interest earned ratio	$687/$502	= 1.37 times
Cash coverage ratio	$1,237/$502	= 2.46 times

3.4 The return on equity is the ratio of net income to total equity. For Philippe, this is $146/$3,347 = 4.4 percent, which is not outstanding.

Given the DuPont identity, ROE can be written as follows:

ROE = Profit margin × Total asset turnover × Equity multiplier

$$= \$146/\$4,053 \quad \times \$4,053/\$7,380 \qquad \times \$7,380/\$3,347$$
$$= \quad .036\% \qquad \times \quad .549 \qquad \qquad \times \qquad 2.20$$
$$= \quad .044, \text{ or } 4.4\%$$

Notice that return on assets, ROA, is .036% × .549 = 1.98 percent.

CONCEPTS REVIEW AND CRITICAL THINKING QUESTIONS

1. **Current Ratio** [LO2] What effect would the following actions have on a firm's current ratio? Assume that net working capital is positive.
    a. Inventory is purchased.
    b. A supplier is paid.
    c. A short-term bank loan is repaid.
    d. A long-term debt is paid off early.
    e. A customer pays off a credit account.
    f. Inventory is sold at cost.
    g. Inventory is sold for a profit.

2. **Current Ratio and Quick Ratio** [LO2] In recent years, Dixie Co. has greatly increased its current ratio. At the same time, the quick ratio has fallen. What has happened? Has the liquidity of the company improved?

3. **Current Ratio** [LO2] Explain what it means for a firm to have a current ratio equal to .50. Would the firm be better off if the current ratio were 1.50? What if it were 15.0? Explain your answers.

4. **Financial Ratios** [LO2] Fully explain the kind of information the following financial ratios provide about a firm:
    a. Quick ratio.
    b. Cash ratio.
    c. Total asset turnover.
    d. Equity multiplier.
    e. Long-term debt ratio.
    f. Times interest earned ratio.
    g. Profit margin.
    h. Return on assets.
    i. Return on equity.
    j. Price–earnings ratio.

5. **Standardized Financial Statements** [LO1] What types of information do common-size financial statements reveal about the firm? What is the best use for these common-size statements? What purpose do common-base year statements have? When would you use them?

6. **Peer Group Analysis** [LO2] Explain what peer group analysis is. As a financial manager, how could you use the results of peer group analysis to evaluate the performance of your firm? How is a peer group different from an aspirant group?

7. **DuPont Identity** [LO3] Why is the DuPont identity a valuable tool for analyzing the performance of a firm? Discuss the types of information it reveals compared to ROE considered by itself.

8. **Industry-Specific Ratios** [LO2] Specialized ratios are sometimes used in specific industries. For example, the so-called book-to-bill ratio is closely watched for semiconductor manufacturers. A ratio of .93 indicates that for every $100 worth of chips shipped over some period, only $93 worth of new orders were received. In November 2016, the semiconductor equipment industry's book-to-bill ratio was .96, compared to .91 during the month of October 2016. The book-to-bill ratio reached a recent low of .47 during January 2009 and a recent high of 1.23 during July 2010. What is this ratio intended to measure? Why do you think it is so closely followed?

9. **Industry-Specific Ratios** [LO2] So-called same-store sales are a very important measure for companies as diverse as McDonald's and Sears. As the name suggests, examining same-store sales means comparing revenues from the same stores or restaurants at two different points in time. Why might companies focus on same-store sales rather than total sales?

10. **Industry-Specific Ratios** [LO2] There are many ways of using standardized financial information beyond those discussed in this chapter. The usual goal is to put firms

on an equal footing for comparison purposes. For example, for auto manufacturers, it is common to express sales, costs, and profits on a per-car basis. For each of the following industries, give an example of an actual company and discuss one or more potentially useful means of standardizing financial information:

a. Public utilities.

b. Large retailers.

c. Airlines.

d. Online services.

e. Hospitals.

f. College textbook publishers.

11. **Statement of Cash Flows** [LO4] In recent years, several manufacturing companies have reported the cash flow from the sale of Treasury securities in the cash from operations section of the statement of cash flows. What is the problem with this practice? Is there any situation in which this practice would be acceptable?

12. **Statement of Cash Flows** [LO4] Suppose a company lengthens the time it takes to pay suppliers. How would this affect the statement of cash flows? How sustainable is the change in cash flows from this practice?

QUESTIONS AND PROBLEMS

1. **Calculating Liquidity Ratios** [LO2] SDJ, Inc., has net working capital of $2,170, current liabilities of $4,590, and inventory of $3,860. What is the current ratio? What is the quick ratio?

BASIC
(Questions 1–17)

2. **Calculating Profitability Ratios** [LO2] DTO, Inc., has sales of $16.7 million, total assets of $12.9 million, and total debt of $5.7 million. If the profit margin is 5 percent, what is net income? What is ROA? What is ROE?

3. **Calculating the Average Collection Period** [LO2] Twist Corp. has a current accounts receivable balance of $537,810. Credit sales for the year just ended were $5,473,640. What is the receivables turnover? The days' sales in receivables? How long did it take on average for credit customers to pay off their accounts during the past year?

4. **Calculating Inventory Turnover** [LO2] The King Corporation has ending inventory of $386,735, and cost of goods sold for the year just ended was $4,981,315. What is the inventory turnover? The days' sales in inventory? How long on average did a unit of inventory sit on the shelf before it was sold?

5. **Calculating Leverage Ratios** [LO2] Queen, Inc., has a total debt ratio of .46. What is its debt-equity ratio? What is its equity multiplier?

6. **Calculating Market Value Ratios** [LO2] Makers Corp. had additions to retained earnings for the year just ended of $415,000. The firm paid out $220,000 in cash dividends, and it has ending total equity of $5.6 million. If the company currently has 170,000 shares of common stock outstanding, what are earnings per share? Dividends per share? Book value per share? If the stock currently sells for $65 per share, what is the market-to-book ratio? The price-earnings ratio? If the company had sales of $7.45 million, what is the price-sales ratio?

7. **DuPont Identity** [LO3] If Roten Rooters, Inc., has an equity multiplier of 1.27, total asset turnover of 2.10, and a profit margin of 6.1 percent, what is its ROE?

8. **DuPont Identity** [LO3] Jack Corp. has a profit margin of 6.4 percent, total asset turnover of 1.77, and ROE of 15.84 percent. What is this firm's debt-equity ratio?

9. **Sources and Uses of Cash** [LO1] Based only on the following information for Thrice Corp., did cash go up or down? By how much? Classify each event as a source or use of cash.

Decrease in inventory	$375
Decrease in accounts payable	220
Increase in notes payable	290
Increase in accounts receivable	270

10. **Calculating Average Payables Period** [LO2] Heritage, Inc., had a cost of goods sold of $68,314. At the end of the year, the accounts payable balance was $15,486. How long on average did it take the company to pay off its suppliers during the year? What might a large value for this ratio imply?

11. **Enterprise Value-EBITDA Multiple** [LO2] The market value of the equity of Hudgins, Inc., is $645,000. The balance sheet shows $53,000 in cash and $215,000 in debt, while the income statement has EBIT of $91,000 and a total of $157,000 in depreciation and amortization. What is the enterprise value-EBITDA multiple for this company?

12. **Equity Multiplier and Return on Equity** [LO3] SME Company has a debt-equity ratio of .57. Return on assets is 7.9 percent, and total equity is $620,000. What is the equity multiplier? Return on equity? Net income?

Just Dew It Corporation reports the following balance sheet information for 2017 and 2018. Use this information to work Problems 13 through 17.

JUST DEW IT CORPORATION 2017 and 2018 Balance Sheets					
Assets			**Liabilities and Owners' Equity**		
	2017	2018		2017	2018
Current assets			Current liabilities		
Cash	$ 12,157	$ 14,105	Accounts payable	$ 46,382	$ 49,276
Accounts receivable	29,382	32,815	Notes payable	18,246	19,784
Inventory	54,632	57,204	Total	$ 64,628	$ 69,060
Total	$ 96,171	$104,124			
			Long-term debt	$ 49,000	$ 45,000
			Owners' equity		
			Common stock and		
			paid-in surplus	$ 50,000	$ 50,000
			Retained earnings	299,784	315,894
Net plant and equipment	$367,241	$375,830	Total	$349,784	$365,894
			Total liabilities and		
Total assets	$463,412	$479,954	owners' equity	$463,412	$479,954

13. **Preparing Standardized Financial Statements** [LO1] Prepare the 2017 and 2018 common-size balance sheets for Just Dew It.

14. **Preparing Standardized Financial Statements** [LO1] Prepare the 2018 common-base year balance sheet for Just Dew It.

15. **Preparing Standardized Financial Statements** [LO1] Prepare the 2018 combined common-size, common-base year balance sheet for Just Dew It.

16. **Sources and Uses of Cash** [LO1] For each account on this company's balance sheet, show the change in the account during 2018 and note whether this change was a

source or use of cash. Do your numbers add up and make sense? Explain your answer for total assets as compared to your answer for total liabilities and owners' equity.

17. **Calculating Financial Ratios** [LO2] Based on the balance sheets given for Just Dew It, calculate the following financial ratios for each year:

    a Current ratio.

    b Quick ratio.

    c Cash ratio.

    d NWC to total assets ratio

    e Debt-equity ratio and equity multiplier.

    f Total debt ratio and long-term debt ratio.

18. **Using the DuPont Identity** [LO3] Y3K, Inc., has sales of $6,183, total assets of $2,974, and a debt-equity ratio of .57. If its return on equity is 11 percent, what is its net income?

    INTERMEDIATE
    (Questions 18–30)

19. **Days' Sales in Receivables** [LO2] A company has net income of $196,500, a profit margin of 6.8 percent, and an accounts receivable balance of $119,630. Assuming 65 percent of sales are on credit, what is the company's days' sales in receivables?

20. **Ratios and Fixed Assets** [LO2] The Maurer Company has a long-term debt ratio of .35 and a current ratio of 1.30. Current liabilities are $955, sales are $7,210, profit margin is 8.3 percent, and ROE is 17.5 percent. What is the amount of the firm's net fixed assets?

21. **Profit Margin** [LO4] In response to complaints about high prices, a grocery chain runs the following advertising campaign: "If you pay your child $1.50 to go buy $50 worth of groceries, then your child makes twice as much on the trip as we do." You've collected the following information from the grocery chain's financial statements:

($ in millions)	
Sales	$680
Net income	10.2
Total assets	380
Total debt	270

    Evaluate the grocery chain's claim. What is the basis for the statement? Is this claim misleading? Why or why not?

22. **Return on Equity** [LO2] Firm A and Firm B have debt-total asset ratios of 65 percent and 45 percent, respectively, and returns on total assets of 5 percent and 9 percent, respectively. Which firm has a greater return on equity?

23. **Calculating the Cash Coverage Ratio** [LO2] Pop Evil Inc.'s net income for the most recent year was $16,481. The tax rate was 21 percent. The firm paid $3,681 in total interest expense and deducted $4,385 in depreciation expense. What was the cash coverage ratio for the year?

24. **Cost of Goods Sold** [LO2] Highly Suspect Corp. has current liabilities of $415,000, a quick ratio of .79, inventory turnover of 9.5, and a current ratio of 1.25. What is the cost of goods sold for the company?

25. **Ratios and Foreign Companies** [LO2] Prince Albert Canning PLC had a net loss of £29,157 on sales of £315,650. What was the company's profit margin? Does the fact that these figures are quoted in a foreign currency make any difference? Why? In dollars, sales were $395,183. What was the net loss in dollars?

    Some recent financial statements for Smolira Golf Corp. follow. Use this information to work Problems 26 through 30.

SMOLIRA GOLF CORP. 2017 and 2018 Balance Sheets					
Assets			**Liabilities and Owners' Equity**		
	2017	**2018**		**2017**	**2018**
Current assets			Current liabilities		
Cash	$ 34,385	$ 37,837	Accounts payable	$ 36,722	$ 42,582
Accounts receivable	17,801	27,766	Notes payable	19,008	16,200
Inventory	36,310	42,632	Other	19,864	24,634
Total	$ 88,496	$108,235	Total	$ 75,594	$ 83,416
			Long-term debt	$115,000	$145,000
			Owners' equity		
			Common stock and paid-in surplus	$ 55,000	$ 55,000
Fixed assets			Accumulated retained earnings	307,217	344,452
Net plant and equipment	464,315	519,633	Total	$362,217	$399,452
			Total liabilities and		
Total assets	$552,811	$627,868	owners' equity	$552,811	$627,868

SMOLIRA GOLF CORP. 2018 Income Statement		
Sales		$506,454
Cost of goods sold		359,328
Depreciation		44,463
Earnings before interest and taxes		$102,663
Interest paid		19,683
Taxable income		$ 82,980
Taxes (25%)		20,745
Net income		$ 62,235
Dividends	$25,000	
Retained earnings	37,235	

26. **Calculating Financial Ratios [LO2]** Find the following financial ratios for Smolira Golf Corp. (use year-end figures rather than average values where appropriate):

Short-term solvency ratios:

a. Current ratio.   _____

b. Quick ratio.   _____

c. Cash ratio.   _____

Asset utilization ratios:

d. Total asset turnover.   _____

e. Inventory turnover.   _____

f. Receivables turnover.   _____

Long-term solvency ratios:

g. Total debt ratio.   _____

h. Debt-equity ratio.   _____

   i. Equity multiplier.   _____

   j. Times interest earned ratio.   _____

   k. Cash coverage ratio.   _____

   Profitability ratios:

   l. Profit margin.   _____

   m. Return on assets.   _____

   n. Return on equity.   _____

27.   **DuPont Identity [LO3]** Construct the DuPont identity for Smolira Golf Corp.

28.   **Statement of Cash Flows [LO1]** Prepare the 2018 statement of cash flows for Smolira Golf Corp.

29.   **Market Value Ratios [LO2]** Smolira Golf Corp. has 20,000 shares of common stock outstanding, and the market price for a share of stock at the end of 2018 was $58. What is the price-earnings ratio? What are the dividends per share? What is the market-to-book ratio at the end of 2018? If the company's growth rate is 9 percent, what is the PEG ratio?

30.   **Tobin's Q [LO2]** What is Tobin's Q for Smolira Golf? What assumptions are you making about the book value of debt and the market value of debt? What about the book value of assets and the market value of assets? Are these assumptions realistic? Why or why not?

EXCEL MASTER IT! PROBLEM

The eXtensible Business Reporting Language (XBRL) is the future of financial reporting. XBRL is a computer language that "tags" each item and specifies what that item is. XBRL reporting has also been adopted for use in Australia, Japan, and the United Kingdom. The Securities and Exchange Commission (SEC) requires that U.S. companies submit financial reports to the SEC in XBRL format. XBRL reporting allows investors to quickly download financial statements for analysis.

For this assignment, go to the SEC website at www.sec.gov. Once there, look up the financials for a company. Next to the 10-Q (quarterly) and 10-K (annual) reports, you should notice a link that says "InteractiveData." Click on this link, follow the "Financial Statements" link, and select "View Excel Document." This link will allow you to download all of the financial statements in one Excel document. Download the Excel document and copy into the next worksheet. Use these statements to calculate the ratios on that worksheet. Do you notice any changes in these ratios that might indicate further investigation?

MINICASE

Ratio Analysis at S&S Air, Inc.

Chris Guthrie was recently hired by S&S Air, Inc., to assist the company with its financial planning and to evaluate the company's performance. Chris graduated from college five years ago with a finance degree. He has been employed in the finance department of a *Fortune* 500 company since then.

S&S Air was founded 10 years ago by friends Mark Sexton and Todd Story. The company has manufactured and sold light airplanes over this period, and the company's products have received high reviews for safety and reliability. The company has a niche market in that it sells primarily to individuals who own and fly their own airplanes. The company has two models: the Birdie, which sells for $103,000, and the Eagle, which sells for $178,000.

Although the company manufactures aircraft, its operations are different from commercial aircraft companies. S&S Air builds aircraft to order. By using prefabricated parts, the company can complete the manufacture of an airplane in only five weeks. The company also receives a deposit on each order, as well as another partial payment before the order is complete. In contrast, a commercial airplane may take one and one-half to two years to manufacture once the order is placed.

Mark and Todd have provided the following financial statements. Chris has gathered the industry ratios for the light airplane manufacturing industry.

S&S AIR, INC. 2018 Income Statement	
Sales	$46,298,115
Cost of goods sold	34,536,913
Other expenses	5,870,865
Depreciation	2,074,853
EBIT	$ 3,815,484
Interest	725,098
Taxable income	$ 3,090,386
Taxes (25%)	772,597
Net income	$ 2,317,789
Dividends	$ 705,000
Add to retained earnings	1,612,789

S&S AIR, INC. 2018 Balance Sheet			
Assets		**Liabilities and Equity**	
Current assets		Current liabilities	
Cash	$ 524,963	Accounts payable	$ 1,068,356
Accounts receivable	843,094	Notes payable	2,439,553
Inventory	1,235,161	Total current liabilities	$ 3,507,909
Total current assets	$ 2,603,218		
		Long-term debt	$ 6,300,000
Fixed assets			
Net plant and equipment	$20,381,945	Shareholder equity	
		Common stock	$ 460,000
		Retained earnings	12,717,254
		Total equity	$13,177,254
Total assets	$22,985,163	Total liabilities and equity	$22,985,163

Light Airplane Industry Ratios			
	Lower Quartile	Median	Upper Quartile
Current ratio	.50	1.43	1.89
Quick ratio	.21	.35	.62
Cash ratio	.08	.21	.39
Total asset turnover	.68	.85	1.38
Inventory turnover	4.89	6.15	10.89
Receivables turnover	6.27	9.82	14.11
Total debt ratio	.41	.52	.61
Debt-equity ratio	.68	1.08	1.56
Equity multiplier	1.68	2.08	2.56
Times interest earned	5.18	8.06	9.83
Cash coverage ratio	5.84	9.41	10.27
Profit margin	4.05%	5.10%	7.15%
Return on assets	6.05%	9.53%	13.21%
Return on equity	9.93%	15.14%	19.15%

QUESTIONS

1. Using the financial statements provided for S&S Air, calculate each of the ratios listed in the table for the light aircraft industry.

2. Mark and Todd agree that a ratio analysis can provide a measure of the company's performance. They have chosen Boeing as an aspirant company. Would you choose Boeing as an aspirant company? Why or why not? There are other aircraft manufacturers S&S Air could use as aspirant companies. Discuss whether it is appropriate to use any of the following companies: Bombardier, Embraer, Cirrus Aircraft Corporation, and Cessna Aircraft Company.

3. Compare the performance of S&S Air to the industry. For each ratio, comment on why it might be viewed as positive or negative relative to the industry. Suppose you create an inventory ratio calculated as inventory divided by current liabilities. How do you think S&S Air's ratio would compare to the industry average?

Long-Term Financial Planning and Growth

GROWTH RATES ARE IMPORTANT TOOLS for evaluating a company and, as we will see later, for valuing a company's stock. When thinking about (and calculating) growth rates, a little common sense goes a long way. For example, in 2017, retailing giant Walmart had about 1.156 billion square feet of stores, distribution centers, and so forth. The company expected to increase its square footage by about 4 percent over the next year. This doesn't sound too outrageous, but can Walmart grow its square footage at 4 percent indefinitely?

We'll get into the calculation in our next chapter, but if you assume that Walmart grows at 4 percent per year over the next 291 years, the company will have about 105 trillion square feet of property, which is about the total land mass of the entire United States! In other words, if Walmart keeps growing at 4 percent, the entire country will eventually be one big Walmart. Scary.

Sirius XM Satellite Radio is another example in which common sense comes in handy. The company had total revenues of about $805,000 in 2002 and $4.9 billion in 2016. This represents an annual increase of about 86 percent! How likely do you think it is that the company can continue this growth rate? If this growth continued, the company would have revenues of about $16.01 trillion in just 13 years, which is about the same as the gross domestic product (GDP) of the United States. Obviously, Sirius XM Radio's growth rate will slow substantially in the next several years. So, long-term growth rate estimates must be chosen very carefully. As a rule of thumb, for really long-term growth estimates, you should probably assume that a company will not grow much faster than the economy as a whole, which is about 1 to 3 percent (inflation-adjusted).

Proper management of growth is vital. Thus, this chapter emphasizes the importance of planning for the future and discusses some tools firms use to think about, and manage, growth.

Learning Objectives

After studying this chapter, you should be able to:

LO1 Apply the percentage of sales method.

LO2 Compute the external financing needed to fund a firm's growth.

LO3 Name the determinants of a firm's growth.

LO4 Anticipate some of the problems in planning for growth.

©by_adri/iStockPhoto/GettyImages

For updates on the latest happenings in finance, visit fundamentalsofcorporatefinance.blogspot.com.

A lack of effective long-range planning is a commonly cited reason for financial distress and failure. As we discuss in this chapter, long-range planning is a means of systematically thinking about the future and anticipating possible problems before they arrive. There are no magic mirrors, of course, so the best we can hope for is a logical and organized procedure for exploring the unknown. As one member of GM's board was heard to say, "Planning is a process that at best helps the firm avoid stumbling into the future backward."

Financial planning establishes guidelines for change and growth in a firm. It normally focuses on the big picture. This means it is concerned with the major elements of a firm's financial and investment policies without examining the individual components of those policies in detail.

Our primary goals in this chapter are to discuss financial planning and to illustrate the interrelatedness of the various investment and financing decisions a firm makes. In the chapters ahead, we will examine in much more detail how these decisions are made.

We first describe what is usually meant by *financial planning*. For the most part, we talk about long-term planning. Short-term financial planning is discussed in a later chapter. We examine what the firm can accomplish by developing a long-term financial plan. To do this, we develop a simple but useful long-range planning technique: The percentage of sales approach. We describe how to apply this approach in some simple cases, and we discuss some extensions.

To develop an explicit financial plan, managers must establish certain basic elements of the firm's financial policy:

1. *The firm's needed investment in new assets*: This will arise from the investment opportunities the firm chooses to undertake, and it is the result of the firm's capital budgeting decisions.
2. *The degree of financial leverage the firm chooses to employ*: This will determine the amount of borrowing the firm will use to finance its investments in real assets. This is the firm's capital structure policy.
3. *The amount of cash the firm thinks is necessary and appropriate to pay shareholders*: This is the firm's dividend policy.
4. *The amount of liquidity and working capital the firm needs on an ongoing basis*: This is the firm's net working capital decision.

As we will see, the decisions a firm makes in these four areas will directly affect its future profitability, its need for external financing, and its opportunities for growth.

A key lesson to be learned from this chapter is that a firm's investment and financing policies interact and thus cannot truly be considered in isolation from one another. The types and amounts of assets a firm plans on purchasing must be considered along with the firm's ability to raise the capital necessary to fund those investments. Many business students are aware of the classic three *P*s (or even four *P*s) of marketing. Not to be outdone, financial planners have no fewer than six *P*s: *Proper Prior Planning Prevents Poor Performance*.

Financial planning forces the corporation to think about goals. A goal frequently espoused by corporations is growth, and almost all firms use an explicit, companywide growth rate as a major component of their long-term financial planning. For example, in September 2007, Toyota Motor announced that it planned to sell about 9.8 million vehicles in 2008 and 10.4 million vehicles in 2009, becoming the first auto manufacturer to sell more than 10 million vehicles in a year. Of course, Toyota's plans didn't come to fruition. In 2009, the company sold only 7.2 million cars, and it sold 8.6 million in 2010. In 2013, the company sold 9.98 million cars, almost reaching the goal set four years prior, before selling 10.14 million vehicles in 2014 and 10.15 million vehicles in 2015.

There are direct connections between the growth a company can achieve and its financial policy. In the following sections, we show how financial planning models can be used to better understand how growth is achieved. We also show how such models can be used to establish the limits on possible growth.

What Is Financial Planning?

4.1

Financial planning formulates the way in which financial goals are to be achieved. A financial plan is thus a statement of what is to be done in the future. Many decisions have long lead times, which means they take a long time to implement. In an uncertain world, this requires that decisions be made far in advance of their implementation. If a firm wants to build a factory in 2020, for example, it might have to begin lining up contractors and financing in 2018 or even earlier.

GROWTH AS A FINANCIAL MANAGEMENT GOAL

Because the subject of growth will be discussed in various places in this chapter, we need to start out with an important warning: Growth, by itself, is not an appropriate goal for the financial manager. Clothing retailer J. Peterman Co., whose quirky catalogs were made famous on the TV show *Seinfeld*, learned this lesson the hard way. Despite its strong brand name and years of explosive revenue growth, the company was ultimately forced to file for bankruptcy—the victim of an overly ambitious, growth-oriented expansion plan.

Amazon.com, the big online retailer, is another example. At one time, Amazon's motto seemed to be "growth at any cost." Unfortunately, what really grew rapidly for the company were losses. As a result, Amazon refocused its business, explicitly sacrificing growth in the hope of achieving profitability. The plan seems to be working, as Amazon has become a profitable retailing giant.

As we discussed in Chapter 1, the appropriate goal for a firm is increasing the market value of the owners' equity. Of course, if a firm is successful in doing this, then growth will usually result. Growth may thus be a desirable consequence of good decision making, but it is not an end unto itself. We discuss growth because growth rates are so commonly used in the planning process. As we will see, growth is a convenient means of summarizing various aspects of a firm's financial and investment policies. Also, if we think of growth as growth in the market value of the equity in the firm, then goals of growth and increasing the market value of the equity in the firm are not all that different.

You can find growth rates at **www.reuters.com** and **finance.yahoo.com**.

DIMENSIONS OF FINANCIAL PLANNING

It is often useful for planning purposes to think of the future as having a short run and a long run. The short run, in practice, is usually the coming 12 months. We focus our attention on financial planning over the long run, which is usually taken to be the coming two to five years. This time period is called the **planning horizon**, and it is the first dimension of the planning process that must be established.

In drawing up a financial plan, all of the individual projects and investments the firm will undertake are combined to determine the total needed investment. In effect, the smaller investment proposals of each operational unit are added up, and the sum is treated as one big project. This process is called **aggregation**. The level of aggregation is the second dimension of the planning process that needs to be determined.

Once the planning horizon and level of aggregation are established, a financial plan requires inputs in the form of alternative sets of assumptions about important variables. For example, suppose a company has two separate divisions: One for consumer products and

planning horizon
The long-range time period on which the financial planning process focuses (usually the next two to five years).

aggregation
The process by which smaller investment proposals of each of a firm's operational units are added up and treated as one big project.

one for gas turbine engines. The financial planning process might require each division to prepare three alternative business plans for the next three years:

1. *A worst case*: This plan would require making relatively pessimistic assumptions about the company's products and the state of the economy. This kind of disaster planning would emphasize a division's ability to withstand significant economic adversity, and it would require details concerning cost cutting and even divestiture and liquidation. For example, in 2016, Lenovo announced that it had written off $173 million in smartphone inventory. The company had evidently overestimated the demand for its products.

2. *A normal case*: This plan would require making the most likely assumptions about the company and the economy.

3. *A best case*: Each division would be required to work out a case based on optimistic assumptions. It could involve new products and expansion and then detail the financing needed to fund the expansion. For example, in 2016, Amazon ran out of its Echo hands-free speaker on December 9. The company didn't expect to get any back in stock until at least December 30th, missing much of the Christmas shopping season. The smaller Echo Dot was also sold out and not expected to be back in stock until December 27th. In fact, because of the shortage, Echos were selling on eBay for $399, almost triple the Amazon retail price of $139. Evidently, Amazon underestimated the best case.

In this discussion, business activities are aggregated along divisional lines, and the planning horizon is three years. This type of planning, which considers all possible events, is particularly important for cyclical businesses (businesses with sales that are strongly affected by the overall state of the economy or business cycles).

WHAT CAN PLANNING ACCOMPLISH?

Because a company is likely to spend a lot of time examining the different scenarios that will become the basis for its financial plan, it seems reasonable to ask what the planning process will accomplish.

Examining Interactions   As we discuss in greater detail in the following pages, the financial plan must make explicit the linkages between investment proposals for the different operating activities of the firm and its available financing choices. In other words, if the firm is planning on expanding and undertaking new investments and projects, where will the financing be obtained to pay for this activity?

Exploring Options   The financial plan allows the firm to develop, analyze, and compare many different scenarios in a consistent way. Various investment and financing options can be explored, and their impact on the firm's shareholders can be evaluated. Questions concerning the firm's future lines of business and optimal financing arrangements are addressed. Options such as marketing new products or closing plants might be evaluated.

Avoiding Surprises   Financial planning should identify what may happen to the firm if different events take place. In particular, it should address what actions the firm will take if things go seriously wrong or, more generally, if assumptions made today about the future are seriously in error. As physicist Niels Bohr once observed, "Prediction is very difficult, particularly when it concerns the future."* Thus, one purpose of financial planning is to avoid surprises and develop contingency plans.

---

*Source: Niels Bohr (1885–1962)

For example, when Tesla Motors announced its new Model X in February 2012, the company promised that production would begin in 2013. In 2013, when production had yet to start, Tesla pushed back production until late 2014. A company spokesperson stated that production was being delayed "to allow ourselves to focus on production and enhancements in Model S." Of course, even though production of the Model S had begun on time several years earlier, production of that model was below expectations for at least a year. And Tesla didn't meet its revised goal; the first Model X didn't hit the market until September 2015. Thus, a lack of proper planning can be a problem for even the most high-tech companies.

Ensuring Feasibility and Internal Consistency   Beyond a general goal of creating value, a firm will normally have many specific goals. Such goals might be couched in terms of market share, return on equity, financial leverage, and so on. At times, the linkages between different goals and different aspects of a firm's business are difficult to see. A financial plan makes these linkages explicit, while also imposing a unified structure for reconciling goals and objectives. In other words, financial planning is a way of verifying that the goals and plans made for specific areas of a firm's operations are feasible and internally consistent. Conflicting goals will often exist. To generate a coherent plan, goals and objectives will have to be modified, and priorities will have to be established.

For example, one goal a firm might have is 12 percent growth in unit sales per year. Another goal might be to reduce the firm's total debt ratio from 40 to 20 percent. Are these two goals compatible? Can they be accomplished simultaneously? Maybe yes, maybe no. As we will discuss, financial planning is a way of finding out what is possible—and, by implication, what is not.

Conclusion   Probably the most important result of the planning process is that it forces managers to think about goals and establish priorities. In fact, conventional business wisdom holds that financial plans don't work, but financial planning does. The future is inherently unknown. What we can do is establish the direction in which we want to travel and make some educated guesses about what we will find along the way. If we do a good job, we won't be caught off guard when the future rolls around.

Concept Questions

4.1a   What are the two dimensions of the financial planning process?
4.1b   Why should firms draw up financial plans?

Financial Planning Models: A First Look   4.2

Just as companies differ in size and products, the financial planning process will differ from firm to firm. In this section, we discuss some common elements in financial plans and develop a basic model to illustrate these elements. What follows is a quick overview; later sections will take up the various topics in more detail.

Excel Master It!

xlsx   Excel Master
coverage online

A FINANCIAL PLANNING MODEL: THE INGREDIENTS

Most financial planning models require the user to specify some assumptions about the future. Based on those assumptions, the model generates predicted values for many other variables. Models can vary quite a bit in complexity, but almost all have the elements we discuss next.

Sales Forecast   Almost all financial plans require an externally supplied sales forecast. In our models that follow, for example, the sales forecast will be the "driver," meaning that the user of the planning model will supply this value, and most other values will be calculated based on it. This arrangement is common for many types of business; planning will focus on projected future sales and the assets and financing needed to support those sales.

Frequently, the sales forecast will be given as the growth rate in sales rather than as an explicit sales figure. These two approaches are essentially the same because we can calculate projected sales once we know the growth rate. Perfect sales forecasts are not possible, of course, because sales depend on the uncertain future state of the economy. To help a firm come up with its projections, some businesses specialize in macroeconomic and industry projections.

As we discussed previously, we frequently will be interested in evaluating alternative scenarios, so it isn't necessarily crucial that the sales forecast be accurate. In such cases, our goal is to examine the interplay between investment and financing needs at different possible sales levels, not to pinpoint what we expect to happen.

Pro Forma Statements   A financial plan will have a forecast balance sheet, income statement, and statement of cash flows. These are called *pro forma statements*, or *pro formas* for short. The phrase *pro forma* literally means "as a matter of form." In our case, this means the financial statements are the form we use to summarize the different events projected for the future. At a minimum, a financial planning model will generate these statements based on projections of key items such as sales.

In the planning models we will describe, the pro formas are the output from the financial planning model. The user will supply a sales figure, and the model will generate the resulting income statement and balance sheet.

Asset Requirements   The plan will describe projected capital spending. At a minimum, the projected balance sheet will contain changes in total fixed assets and net working capital. These changes are effectively the firm's total capital budget. Proposed capital spending in different areas must be reconciled with the overall increases contained in the long-range plan.

Financial Requirements   The plan will include a section about the necessary financing arrangements. This part of the plan should discuss dividend policy and debt policy. Sometimes firms will expect to raise cash by selling new shares of stock or by borrowing. In this case, the plan will have to consider what kinds of securities have to be sold and what methods of issuance are most appropriate. These are subjects we consider in Part 6 of our book, where we discuss long-term financing, capital structure, and dividend policy.

The Plug   After the firm has a sales forecast and an estimate of the required spending on assets, some amount of new financing will often be necessary because projected total assets will exceed projected total liabilities and equity. In other words, the balance sheet will no longer balance.

Because new financing may be necessary to cover all of the projected capital spending, a financial "plug" variable must be selected. The plug is the designated source or sources of external financing needed to deal with any shortfall (or surplus) in financing and thereby bring the balance sheet into balance.

For example, a firm with a great number of investment opportunities and limited cash flow may have to raise new equity. Other firms with few growth opportunities and ample cash flow will have a surplus and thus might pay an extra dividend. In the first case, external equity is the plug variable. In the second, the dividend is used.

Economic Assumptions   The plan will have to state explicitly the economic environment in which the firm expects to reside over the life of the plan. Among the more important economic assumptions that will have to be made are the level of interest rates and the firm's tax rate.

A SIMPLE FINANCIAL PLANNING MODEL

We can begin our discussion of long-term planning models with a relatively simple example. The Computerfield Corporation's financial statements from the most recent year are as follows:

COMPUTERFIELD CORPORATION Financial Statements					
Income Statement			**Balance Sheet**		
Sales	$1,000	Assets	$500	Debt	$250
Costs	800			Equity	250
Net income	$ 200	Total	$500	Total	$500

Unless otherwise stated, the financial planners at Computerfield assume that all variables are tied directly to sales and current relationships are optimal. This means that all items will grow at exactly the same rate as sales. This is obviously oversimplified; we use this assumption only to make a point.

Suppose sales increase by 20 percent, rising from $1,000 to $1,200. Planners would then also forecast a 20 percent increase in costs, from $800 to $800 × 1.2 = $960. The pro forma income statement would be:

Pro Forma Income Statement	
Sales	$1,200
Costs	960
Net income	$ 240

The assumption that all variables will grow by 20 percent lets us easily construct the pro forma balance sheet as well:

Pro Forma Balance Sheet			
Assets	$600 (+100)	Debt	$300 (+ 50)
		Equity	300 (+ 50)
Total	$600 (+100)	Total	$600 (+100)

Notice that we have increased every item by 20 percent. The numbers in parentheses are the dollar changes for the different items.

Now we have to reconcile these two pro formas. How, for example, can net income be equal to $240 and equity increase by only $50? The answer is that Computerfield must have paid out the difference of $240 − 50 = $190, possibly as a cash dividend. In this case, dividends are the plug variable.

Suppose Computerfield does not pay out the $190. In this case, the addition to retained earnings is the full $240. Computerfield's equity will grow to $250 (the starting amount) plus $240 (net income), or $490, and debt must be retired to keep total assets equal to $600.

Planware provides insight into cash flow forecasting (**www.planware.org**).

With $600 in total assets and $490 in equity, debt will have to be $600 − 490 = $110. Because we started with $250 in debt, Computerfield will have to retire $250 − 110 = $140 in debt. The resulting pro forma balance sheet would look like this:

Pro Forma Balance Sheet			
Assets	$600 (+100)	Debt	$110 (−140)
		Equity	490 (+240)
Total	$600 (+100)	Total	$600 (+100)

In this case, debt is the plug variable used to balance projected total assets and liabilities.

This example shows the interaction between sales growth and financial policy. As sales increase, so do total assets. This occurs because the firm must invest in net working capital and fixed assets to support higher sales levels. Because assets are growing, total liabilities and equity (the right side of the balance sheet) will grow as well.

The thing to notice from our simple example is that the way the liabilities and owners' equity change depends on the firm's financing policy and its dividend policy. The growth in assets requires that the firm decide on how to finance that growth. This is strictly a managerial decision. Note that in our example, the firm needed no outside funds. This won't usually be the case, so we explore a more detailed situation in the next section.

Concept Questions

4.2a What are the basic components of a financial plan?

4.2b Why is it necessary to designate a plug in a financial planning model?

4.3 The Percentage of Sales Approach

In the previous section, we described a simple planning model in which every item increased at the same rate as sales. This may be a reasonable assumption for some elements. For others, such as long-term borrowing, it probably is not: The amount of long-term borrowing is something set by management, and it does not necessarily relate directly to the level of sales.

In this section, we describe an extended version of our simple model. The basic idea is to separate the income statement and balance sheet accounts into two groups—those that vary directly with sales and those that do not. Given a sales forecast, we will then be able to calculate how much financing the firm will need to support the predicted sales level.

percentage of sales approach

A financial planning method in which accounts are varied depending on a firm's predicted sales level.

The financial planning model we describe next is based on the **percentage of sales approach**. Our goal here is to develop a quick and practical way of generating pro forma statements. We defer discussion of some "bells and whistles" to a later section.

THE INCOME STATEMENT

We start out with the most recent income statement for the Rosengarten Corporation, as shown in Table 4.1. Notice we have still simplified things by including costs, depreciation, and interest in a single cost figure.

Rosengarten has projected a 25 percent increase in sales for the coming year, so we are anticipating sales of $1,000 × 1.25 = $1,250. To generate a pro forma income statement, we assume that total costs will continue to run at $833/$1,000 = .833, or 83.3% of sales. With this assumption, Rosengarten's pro forma income statement is shown in Table 4.2. The effect

ROSENGARTEN CORPORATION Income Statement	
Sales	$1,000
Costs	833
Taxable income	$ 167
Taxes (21%)	35
Net income	$ 132
Dividends	$44
Addition to retained earnings	88

TABLE 4.1

Rosengarten Corporation Income Statement

ROSENGARTEN CORPORATION Pro Forma Income Statement	
Sales (projected)	$1,250
Costs (83.3% of sales)	1,041
Taxable income	$ 209
Taxes (21%)	44
Net income	$ 165

TABLE 4.2

Rosengarten Corporation Pro Forma Income Statement

here of assuming that costs are a constant percentage of sales is to assume that the profit margin is constant. To check this, notice that the profit margin was $132/$1,000 = .132, or 13.2%. In our pro forma, the profit margin is $165/$1,250 = .132, or 13.2%, so it is unchanged.

Next, we need to project the dividend payment. This amount is up to Rosengarten's management. We will assume Rosengarten has a policy of paying out a constant fraction of net income in the form of a cash dividend. For the most recent year, the **dividend payout ratio** was this:

> **dividend payout ratio**
> The amount of cash paid out to shareholders divided by net income.

Dividend payout ratio = Cash dividends/Net income
$$= \$44/\$132 = 1/3$$

We can also calculate the ratio of the addition to retained earnings to net income:

Addition to retained earnings/Net income = $88/$132 = 2/3

This ratio is called the **retention ratio** or **plowback ratio**, and it is equal to 1 minus the dividend payout ratio because everything not paid out is retained. Assuming that the payout ratio is constant, here are the projected dividends and addition to retained earnings:

> **retention ratio**
> The addition to retained earnings divided by net income. Also called the *plowback ratio*.

Projected dividends paid to shareholders = $165 × 1/3 = $ 55
Projected addition to retained earnings = $165 × 2/3 = 110
                                                       $165

THE BALANCE SHEET

To generate a pro forma balance sheet, we start with the most recent statement, as shown in Table 4.3.

On our balance sheet, we assume that some items vary directly with sales and others do not. For items that vary with sales, we express each as a percentage of sales for the year just completed. When an item does not vary directly with sales, we write "n/a" for "not applicable."

TABLE 4.3   Rosengarten Corporation Balance Sheet

ROSENGARTEN CORPORATION Balance Sheet					
Assets			**Liabilities and Owners' Equity**		
	$	**Percentage of Sales**		**$**	**Percentage of Sales**
Current assets			Current liabilities		
Cash	$ 160	16%	Accounts payable	$ 300	30%
Accounts receivable	440	44	Notes payable	100	n/a
Inventory	600	60	Total	$ 400	n/a
Total	$1,200	120	Long-term debt	$ 800	n/a
Fixed assets			Owners' equity		
Net plant and equipment	$1,800	180	Common stock and paid-in surplus	$ 800	n/a
			Retained earnings	1,000	n/a
			Total	$1,800	n/a
Total assets	$3,000	300%	Total liabilities and owners' equity	$3,000	n/a

For example, on the asset side, inventory is equal to 60 percent of sales (= $600/$1,000) for the year just ended. We assume this percentage applies to the coming year, so for each $1 increase in sales, inventory will rise by $.60. More generally, the ratio of total assets to sales for the year just ended is $3,000/$1,000 = 3, or 300%.

This ratio of total assets to sales is sometimes called the **capital intensity ratio**. It tells us the amount of assets needed to generate $1 in sales; so the higher the ratio is, the more capital-intensive is the firm. Notice also that this ratio is the reciprocal of the total asset turnover ratio we defined in the last chapter.

For Rosengarten, assuming that this ratio is constant, it takes $3 in total assets to generate $1 in sales (apparently Rosengarten is in a relatively capital-intensive business). Therefore, if sales are to increase by $100, Rosengarten will have to increase total assets by three times this amount, or $300.

On the liability side of the balance sheet, we show accounts payable varying with sales. The reason is that we expect to place more orders with our suppliers as sales volume increases, so payables will change "spontaneously" with sales. Notes payable, on the other hand, represent short-term debt such as bank borrowing. This item will not vary unless we take specific actions to change the amount, so we mark it as "n/a."

Similarly, we use "n/a" for long-term debt because it won't automatically change with sales. The same is true for common stock and paid-in surplus. The last item on the right side, retained earnings, will vary with sales, but it won't be a simple percentage of sales. Instead, we will explicitly calculate the change in retained earnings based on our projected net income and dividends.

We can now construct a partial pro forma balance sheet for Rosengarten. We do this by using the percentages we have just calculated wherever possible to calculate the projected amounts. For example, net fixed assets are 180 percent of sales; so, with a new sales level of $1,250, the net fixed asset amount will be 1.80 × $1,250 = $2,250, representing an increase of $2,250 − 1,800 = $450 in plant and equipment. It is important to note that for items that don't vary directly with sales, we initially assume no change and write in the

TABLE 4.4

ROSENGARTEN CORPORATION Partial Pro Forma Balance Sheet					
Assets			**Liabilities and Owners' Equity**		
	Projected	Change from Previous Year		Projected	Change from Previous Year
Current assets			Current liabilities		
Cash	$ 200	$ 40	Accounts payable	$ 375	$ 75
Accounts receivable	550	110	Notes payable	100	0
Inventory	750	150	Total	$ 475	$ 75
Total	$1,500	$300	Long-term debt	$ 800	$ 0
Fixed assets					
Net plant and equipment	$2,250	$450	Owners' equity		
			Common stock and paid-in surplus	$ 800	$ 0
			Retained earnings	1,110	110
			Total	$1,910	$110
			Total liabilities and owners' equity	$3,185	$185
Total assets	$3,750	$750	External financing needed	$ 565	$565

original amounts. The result is shown in Table 4.4. Notice that the change in retained earnings is equal to the $110 addition to retained earnings we calculated earlier.

Inspecting our pro forma balance sheet, we notice that assets are projected to increase by $750. However, without additional financing, liabilities and equity will increase by only $185, leaving a shortfall of $750 − 185 = $565. We label this amount *external financing needed* (EFN).

A PARTICULAR SCENARIO

Our financial planning model now reminds us of one of those good news–bad news jokes. The good news is we're projecting a 25 percent increase in sales. The bad news is that this isn't going to happen unless Rosengarten can somehow raise $565 in new financing.

This is a good example of how the planning process can point out problems and potential conflicts. If, for example, Rosengarten has a goal of not borrowing any additional funds and not selling any new equity, then a 25 percent increase in sales is probably not feasible.

If we take the need for $565 in new financing as given, we know that Rosengarten has three possible sources: short-term borrowing, long-term borrowing, and new equity. The choice of some combination among these three is up to management; we will illustrate only one of the many possibilities.

Suppose Rosengarten decides to borrow the needed funds. In this case, the firm might choose to borrow some over the short term and some over the long term. For example, current assets increased by $300, whereas current liabilities rose by only $75. Rosengarten could borrow $300 − 75 = $225 in short-term notes payable and leave total net working capital unchanged. With $565 needed, the remaining $565 − 225 = $340 would have to come from long-term debt. Table 4.5 shows the completed pro forma balance sheet for Rosengarten.

TABLE 4.5

ROSENGARTEN CORPORATION Pro Forma Balance Sheet					
Assets			**Liabilities and Owners' Equity**		
	Projected	Change from Previous Year		Projected	Change from Previous Year
Current assets			Current liabilities		
Cash	$ 200	$ 40	Accounts payable	$ 375	$ 75
Accounts receivable	550	110	Notes payable	325	225
Inventory	750	150	Total	$ 700	$300
Total	$1,500	$300	Long-term debt	$1,140	$340
Fixed assets					
Net plant and equipment	$2,250	$450	Owners' equity		
			Common stock and paid-in surplus	$ 800	$ 0
			Retained earnings	1,110	110
			Total	$1,910	$110
Total assets	$3,750	$750	Total liabilities and owners' equity	$3,750	$750

We have used a combination of short- and long-term debt as the plug here, but we emphasize that this is just one possible strategy; it is not necessarily the best one by any means. There are many other scenarios we could (and should) investigate. The various ratios we discussed in Chapter 3 come in handy here. For example, with the scenario we have just examined, we would surely want to examine the current ratio and the total debt ratio to see if we were comfortable with the new projected debt levels.

Now that we have finished our balance sheet, we have all of the projected sources and uses of cash. We could finish off our pro formas by drawing up the projected statement of cash flows along the lines discussed in Chapter 3. We will leave this as an exercise and instead investigate an important alternative scenario.

AN ALTERNATIVE SCENARIO

The assumption that assets are a fixed percentage of sales is convenient, but it may not be suitable in many cases. In particular, note that we effectively assumed that Rosengarten was using its fixed assets at 100 percent of capacity because any increase in sales led to an increase in fixed assets. For most businesses, there would be some slack or excess capacity, and production could be increased by perhaps running an extra shift.

For example, in July 2016, Fiat Chrysler announced that it would spend $1.05 billion in assembly plants in Ohio and Illinois to expand production of its Jeep product line. Later that year, Ford announced plans to close two Mexican plants. Ford also announced that it would idle four of its plants for a week, or longer. Evidently Ford had excess capacity, whereas Fiat Chrysler did not.

In another example, in November 2016, automotive replacement parts manufacturer Standard Motor Products announced that it was closing a plant in Texas. The company stated that it would increase production at other plants to compensate for the closings. Apparently, Standard Motor had significant excess capacity at its production facilities. Overall, according to the Federal Reserve, capacity utilization for U.S. manufacturing companies in September 2017 was 76.2 percent, up slightly from the 76.1 percent in the previous month.

If we assume that Rosengarten is operating at only 70 percent of capacity, then the need for external funds will be quite different. When we say "70 percent of capacity," we mean that the current sales level is 70 percent of the full-capacity sales level:

Current sales = $1,000 = .70 × Full-capacity sales
Full-capacity sales = $1,000/.70 = $1,429

This tells us that sales could increase by almost 43 percent—from $1,000 to $1,429—before any new fixed assets would be needed.

In our previous scenario, we assumed it would be necessary to add $450 in net fixed assets. In the current scenario, no spending on net fixed assets is needed because sales are projected to rise only to $1,250, which is substantially less than the $1,429 full-capacity level.

As a result, our original estimate of $565 in external funds needed is too high. We estimated that $450 in new net fixed assets would be needed. Instead, no spending on new net fixed assets is necessary. Thus, if we are currently operating at 70 percent capacity, we need only $565 − 450 = $115 in external funds. The excess capacity thus makes a considerable difference in our projections.

EFN and Capacity Usage

EXAMPLE 4.1

Suppose Rosengarten is operating at 90 percent capacity. What would sales be at full capacity? What is the capital intensity ratio at full capacity? What is EFN in this case?

Full-capacity sales would be $1,000/.90 = $1,111. From Table 4.3, we know that fixed assets are $1,800. At full capacity, the ratio of fixed assets to sales is this:

Fixed assets/Full-capacity sales = $1,800/$1,111 = 1.62

So, Rosengarten needs $1.62 in fixed assets for every $1 in sales once it reaches full capacity. At the projected sales level of $1,250, then, it needs $1,250 × 1.62 = $2,025 in fixed assets. Compared to the $2,250 we originally projected, this is $225 less, so EFN is $565 − 225 = $340.

Current assets would still be $1,500, so total assets would be $1,500 + 2,025 = $3,525. The capital intensity ratio would thus be $3,525/$1,250 = 2.82, which is less than our original value of 3 because of the excess capacity.

These alternative scenarios illustrate that it is inappropriate to blindly manipulate financial statement information in the planning process. The results depend critically on the assumptions made about the relationships between sales and asset needs. We return to this point a little later.

One thing should be clear by now. Projected growth rates play an important role in the planning process. They are also important to outside analysts and potential investors. Our nearby *Work the Web* box shows you how to obtain growth rate estimates for real companies.

Concept Questions

4.3a What is the basic idea behind the percentage of sales approach?
4.3b Unless it is modified, what does the percentage of sales approach assume about fixed asset capacity usage?

WORK THE WEB

Calculating company growth rates can involve detailed research, and a major part of a stock analyst's job is to estimate them. One place to find earnings and sales growth rates on the web is Yahoo! Finance at finance.yahoo.com. We pulled up a quote for 3M Company and followed the "Analysts" link. Here is an abbreviated look at the results:

Revenue Estimate	Current Qtr. (Mar 2017)	Next Qtr. (Jun 2017)	Current Year	Next Year
No. of Analysts	12	12	16	15
Avg. Estimate	7.47B	7.71B	30.44B	31.44B
Low Estimate	7.33B	7.58B	30.14B	31.1B
High Estimate	7.57B	7.85B	30.91B	31.89B
Year Ago Sales	7.41B	7.66B	30.11B	30.44B
Sales Growth (year/est)	0.90%	0.70%	1.10%	3.30%

As shown, analysts expect, on average, revenue (sales) of $30.44 billion in 2017, growing to $31.44 billion in 2018, an increase of 3.3 percent. We also have the following table showing estimates for estimated growth in 3M's EPS:

Earnings Estimate	Current Qtr. (Mar 2017)	Next Qtr. (Jun 2017)	Current Year	Next Year
No. of Analysts	16	15	18	17
Avg. Estimate	2.06	2.23	8.62	9.38
Low Estimate	2.02	2.14	8.4	9
High Estimate	2.14	2.29	8.8	10.2
Year Ago EPS	2.05	2.08	8.16	8.62

As you can see, the average EPS estimate for 3M in 2017 is $8.62, while the average EPS estimate for 2018 is $9.38, an increase of 8.8 percent. What does this mean for 3M stock? We'll get to that in a later chapter.

Questions
1. *One of the things shown here is the projected sales growth for 3M during 2017 at the time this was captured from finance.yahoo.com. How does the current sales projection or the actual sales number differ from this projection? Can you think of any reasons for the difference?*
2. *On the same web page, you can find the earnings history for 3M. How close have analysts been to estimating 3M's earnings? In other words, what has the "surprise" been in 3M's earnings?*

External Financing and Growth

4.4

Excel Master It!
xlsx Excel Master
coverage online

External financing needed and growth are obviously related. All other things staying the same, the higher the rate of growth in sales or assets, the greater will be the need for external financing. In the previous section, we took a growth rate as given, and then we determined the amount of external financing needed to support that growth. In this section, we turn things around a bit. We will take the firm's financial policy as given and then examine the relationship between that financial policy and the firm's ability to finance new investments and thereby grow.

Once again, we emphasize that we are focusing on growth but not because growth is an appropriate goal; instead, for our purposes, growth is a convenient means of examining the interactions between investment and financing decisions. In effect, we assume that the use of growth as a basis for planning is a reflection of the very high level of aggregation used in the planning process.

EFN AND GROWTH

The first thing we need to do is establish the relationship between EFN and growth. To do this, we introduce the simplified income statement and balance sheet for the Hoffman Company in Table 4.6. Notice that we have simplified the balance sheet by combining short-term and long-term debt into a single total debt figure. Effectively, we are assuming that none of the current liabilities varies spontaneously with sales. This assumption isn't as restrictive as it sounds. If any current liabilities (such as accounts payable) vary with sales, we can assume that any such accounts have been netted out in current assets. Also, we continue to combine depreciation, interest, and costs on the income statement.

Suppose the Hoffman Company is forecasting next year's sales level at $600, a $100 increase. Notice that the percentage increase in sales is $100/$500 = .20, or 20%. Using the percentage of sales approach and the figures in Table 4.6, we can prepare a pro forma income statement and balance sheet as in Table 4.7. As Table 4.7 illustrates, at a 20 percent growth

TABLE 4.6

HOFFMAN COMPANY Income Statement and Balance Sheet				
Income Statement				
Sales		$500.0		
Costs		416.5		
Taxable income		$ 83.5		
Taxes (21%)		17.5		
Net income		$ 66.0		
Dividends	$22			
Addition to retained earnings	44			

Balance Sheet				
Assets			**Liabilities and Owners' Equity**	
	$	Percentage of Sales		$	Percentage of Sales
Current assets	$200	40%	Total debt	$250	n/a
Net fixed assets	300	60	Owners' equity	250	n/a
Total assets	$500	100%	Total liabilities and owners' equity	$500	n/a

TABLE 4.7

HOFFMAN COMPANY					
Pro Forma Income Statement and Balance Sheet					
Income Statement					
Sales (projected)		$600.0			
Costs (83.3% of sales)		499.8			
Taxable income		$100.2			
Taxes (21%)		21.0			
Net income		$ 79.2			
Dividends	$26.4				
Addition to retained earnings	52.8				

Balance Sheet					
Assets			**Liabilities and Owners' Equity**		
	$	**Percentage of Sales**		**$**	**Percentage of Sales**
Current assets	$240.0	40%	Total debt	$250.0	n/a
Net fixed assets	360.0	60	Owners' equity	302.8	n/a
Total assets	$600.0	100%	Total liabilities and owners' equity	$552.8	n/a
			External financing needed	$ 47.2	n/a

rate, Hoffman needs $100 in new assets (assuming full capacity). The projected addition to retained earnings is $52.8, so the external financing needed (EFN) is $100 − 52.8 = $47.2.

Notice that the debt-equity ratio for Hoffman was originally (from Table 4.6) equal to $250/$250 = 1.0. We will assume that the Hoffman Company does not wish to sell new equity. In this case, the $47.2 in EFN will have to be borrowed. What will the new debt-equity ratio be? From Table 4.7, we know that total owners' equity is projected at $302.8. The new total debt will be the original $250 plus $47.2 in new borrowing, or $297.2 total. The debt-equity ratio thus falls from 1.0 to $297.2/$302.8 = .98.

Table 4.8 shows EFN for several different growth rates. The projected addition to re-tained earnings and the projected debt-equity ratio for each scenario are also given (you should probably calculate a few of these for practice). In determining the debt-equity ratios, we assumed that any needed funds were borrowed, and we also assumed any surplus funds were used to pay off debt. Thus, for the zero growth case, debt falls by $44, from $250 to $206. In Table 4.8, notice that the increase in assets required is equal to the original assets

TABLE 4.8

Growth and Projected EFN for the Hoffman Company

Projected Sales Growth	Increase in Assets Required	Addition to Retained Earnings	External Financing Needed, EFN	Projected Debt-Equity Ratio
0%	$ 0	$44.0	−$44.0	.70
5	25	46.2	−21.2	.77
10	50	48.4	1.6	.84
15	75	50.6	24.4	.91
20	100	52.8	47.2	.98
25	125	55.0	70.0	1.05

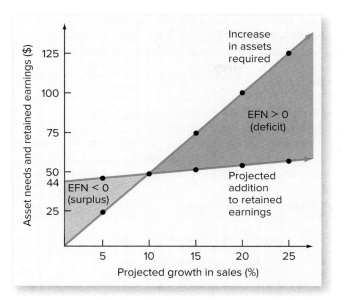

FIGURE 4.1

Growth and Related Financing Needed for the Hoffman Company

of $500 multiplied by the growth rate. Similarly, the addition to retained earnings is equal to the original $44 plus $44 times the growth rate.

Table 4.8 shows that for relatively low growth rates, Hoffman will run a surplus, and its debt-equity ratio will decline. Once the growth rate increases to about 10 percent, however, the surplus becomes a deficit. Furthermore, as the growth rate exceeds approximately 20 percent, the debt-equity ratio surpasses its original value of 1.0.

Figure 4.1 illustrates the connection between growth in sales and external financing needed in more detail by plotting asset needs and additions to retained earnings from Table 4.8 against the growth rates. As shown, the need for new assets grows at a much faster rate than the addition to retained earnings, so the internal financing provided by the addition to retained earnings rapidly disappears.

As this discussion shows, whether a firm runs a cash surplus or deficit depends on growth. Microsoft is a good example. Its revenue growth in the 1990s was amazing, averaging well over 30 percent per year for the decade. Growth slowed down noticeably over the 2000–2010 period; nonetheless, Microsoft's combination of growth and substantial profit margins led to enormous cash surpluses. In part because Microsoft pays a relatively small dividend, the cash really piled up; in 2017, Microsoft's cash horde exceeded $137 billion.

FINANCIAL POLICY AND GROWTH

Based on our preceding discussion, we see that there is a direct link between growth and external financing. In this section, we discuss two growth rates that are particularly useful in long-range planning.

The Internal Growth Rate   The first growth rate of interest is the maximum growth rate that can be achieved with no external financing of any kind. We will call this the **internal growth rate** because this is the rate the firm can maintain with internal financing only. In Figure 4.1, this internal growth rate is represented by the point where the two lines cross. At this point, the required increase in assets is exactly equal to the addition

internal growth rate
The maximum growth rate a firm can achieve without external financing of any kind.

to retained earnings, and EFN is therefore zero. We have seen that this happens when the growth rate is slightly less than 10 percent. With a little algebra (see Problem 31 at the end of the chapter), we can define this growth rate more precisely:

$$\textbf{Internal growth rate} = \frac{\textbf{ROA} \times \textbf{\textit{b}}}{\textbf{1} - \textbf{ROA} \times \textbf{\textit{b}}}$$ **4.2**

Here, ROA is the return on assets we discussed in Chapter 3, and b is the plowback, or retention, ratio defined earlier in this chapter.

For the Hoffman Company, net income was $66 and total assets were $500. ROA is thus $66/$500 = .132, or 13.2%. Of the $66 net income, $44 was retained, so the plowback ratio, b, is $44/$66 = 2/3. With these numbers, we can calculate the internal growth rate:

$$
\begin{aligned}
\text{Internal growth rate} &= \frac{\text{ROA} \times b}{1 - \text{ROA} \times b} \\
&= \frac{.132 \times (2/3)}{1 - .132 \times (2/3)} \\
&= .0964, \text{ or } 9.64\%
\end{aligned}
$$

Thus, the Hoffman Company can expand at a maximum rate of 9.64 percent per year without external financing.

The Sustainable Growth Rate   We have seen that if the Hoffman Company wishes to grow more rapidly than at a rate of 9.64 percent per year, external financing must be arranged. The second growth rate of interest is the maximum growth rate a firm can achieve with no external *equity* financing while it maintains a constant debt-equity ratio. This rate is commonly called the **sustainable growth rate** because it is the maximum rate of growth a firm can maintain without increasing its financial leverage.

sustainable growth rate
The maximum growth rate a firm can achieve without external equity financing while maintaining a constant debt-equity ratio.

There are various reasons why a firm might wish to avoid equity sales. For example, as we discuss in Chapter 15, new equity sales can be expensive. Alternatively, the current owners may not wish to bring in new owners or contribute additional equity. Why a firm might view a particular debt-equity ratio as optimal is discussed in Chapters 14 and 16; for now, we will take it as given.

Based on Table 4.8, the sustainable growth rate for Hoffman is approximately 20 percent because the debt-equity ratio is near 1.0 at that growth rate. The precise value can be calculated (see Problem 31 at the end of the chapter):

$$\textbf{Sustainable growth rate} = \frac{\textbf{ROE} \times \textbf{\textit{b}}}{\textbf{1} - \textbf{ROE} \times \textbf{\textit{b}}}$$ **4.3**

This is identical to the internal growth rate except that ROE, return on equity, is used instead of ROA.

For the Hoffman Company, net income was $66 and total equity was $250; ROE is thus $66/$250 = .264, or 26.4%. The plowback ratio, b, is still 2/3, so we can calculate the sustainable growth rate as follows:

$$
\begin{aligned}
\text{Sustainable growth rate} &= \frac{\text{ROE} \times b}{1 - \text{ROE} \times b} \\
&= \frac{.264 \times (2/3)}{1 - .264 \times (2/3)} \\
&= .2135, \text{ or } 21.35\%
\end{aligned}
$$

Thus, the Hoffman Company can expand at a maximum rate of 21.35 percent per year without external equity financing.

| Sustainable Growth | **EXAMPLE 4.2** |

Suppose Hoffman grows at exactly the sustainable growth rate of 21.35 percent. What will the pro forma statements look like?

At a 21.35 percent growth rate, sales will rise from $500 to $606.7. The pro forma income statement will look like this:

HOFFMAN COMPANY Pro Forma Income Statement		
Sales (projected)		$606.7
Costs (83.3% of sales)		505.4
Taxable income		$101.3
Taxes (21%)		21.3
Net income		$ 80.0
Dividends	$26.7	
Addition to retained earnings	53.4	

We construct the balance sheet as we did before. Notice, in this case, that owners' equity will rise from $250 to $303.4 because the addition to retained earnings is $53.4.

HOFFMAN COMPANY Pro Forma Balance Sheet					
Assets			**Liabilities and Owners' Equity**		
	$	Percentage of Sales		$	Percentage of Sales
Current assets	$242.7	40%	Total debt	$250.0	n/a
Net fixed assets	364.0	60	Owners' equity	303.4	n/a
Total assets	$606.7	100%	Total liabilities and owners' equity	$553.4	n/a
			External financing needed	$ 53.4	n/a

As illustrated, EFN is $53.4. If Hoffman borrows this amount, then total debt will rise to $303.4, and the debt-equity ratio will be exactly 1.0, which verifies our earlier calculation. At any other growth rate, something would have to change.

Determinants of Growth   In the last chapter, we saw that the return on equity, ROE, could be decomposed into its various components using the DuPont identity. Because ROE appears so prominently in the determination of the sustainable growth rate, it is obvious that the factors important in determining ROE are also important determinants of growth.

From Chapter 3, we know that ROE can be written as the product of three factors:

ROE = Profit margin × Total asset turnover × Equity multiplier

If we examine our expression for the sustainable growth rate, we see that anything that increases ROE will increase the sustainable growth rate by making the top bigger and the bottom smaller. Increasing the plowback ratio will have the same effect.

Putting it all together, what we have is that a firm's ability to sustain growth depends explicitly on the following four factors:

1. *Profit margin*: An increase in profit margin will increase the firm's ability to generate funds internally and thereby increase its sustainable growth.

2. *Dividend policy*: A decrease in the percentage of net income paid out as dividends will increase the retention ratio. This increases internally generated equity and thus increases sustainable growth.
3. *Financial policy*: An increase in the debt-equity ratio increases the firm's financial leverage. Because this makes additional debt financing available, it increases the sustainable growth rate.
4. *Total asset turnover*: An increase in the firm's total asset turnover increases the sales generated for each dollar in assets. This decreases the firm's need for new assets as sales grow and thereby increases the sustainable growth rate. Notice that increasing total asset turnover is the same thing as decreasing capital intensity.

The sustainable growth rate is a very useful planning number. What it illustrates is the explicit relationship between the firm's four major areas of concern: Its operating efficiency as measured by profit margin, its asset use efficiency as measured by total asset turnover, its dividend policy as measured by the retention ratio, and its financial policy as measured by the debt-equity ratio.

Given values for all four of these, there is only one growth rate that can be achieved. This is an important point, so it bears restating:

> If a firm does not wish to sell new equity and its profit margin, dividend policy, financial policy, and total asset turnover (or capital intensity) are all fixed, then there is only one possible growth rate.

As we described early in this chapter, one of the primary benefits of financial planning is that it ensures internal consistency among the firm's various goals. The concept of the sustainable growth rate captures this element nicely. Also, we now see how a financial planning model can be used to test the feasibility of a planned growth rate. If sales are to grow at a rate higher than the sustainable growth rate, the firm must increase profit margins, increase total asset turnover, increase financial leverage, increase earnings retention, or sell new shares.

The two growth rates, internal and sustainable, are summarized in Table 4.9.

TABLE 4.9

Summary of Internal and Sustainable Growth Rates

I. Internal Growth Rate
$\text{Internal growth rate} = \dfrac{\text{ROA} \times b}{1 - \text{ROA} \times b}$
where
ROA = Return on assets = Net income/Total assets
b = Plowback (retention) ratio
= Addition to retained earnings/Net income
The internal growth rate is the maximum growth rate that can be achieved with no external financing of any kind.
II. Sustainable Growth Rate
$\text{Sustainable growth rate} = \dfrac{\text{ROE} \times b}{1 - \text{ROE} \times b}$
where
ROE = Return on equity = Net income/Total equity
b = Plowback (retention) ratio
= Addition to retained earnings/Net income
The sustainable growth rate is the maximum growth rate that can be achieved with no external equity financing while maintaining a constant debt-equity ratio.

Most financial officers know intuitively that it takes money to make money. Rapid sales growth requires increased assets in the form of accounts receivable, inventory, and fixed plant, which, in turn, require money to pay for assets. They also know that if their company does not have the money when needed, it can literally "grow broke." The sustainable growth equation states these intuitive truths explicitly.

Sustainable growth is often used by bankers and other external analysts to assess a company's creditworthiness. They are aided in this exercise by several sophisticated computer software packages that provide detailed analyses of the company's past financial performance, including its annual sustainable growth rate.

Bankers use this information in several ways. Quick comparison of a company's actual growth rate to its sustainable rate tells the banker what issues will be at the top of management's financial agenda. If actual growth consistently exceeds sustainable growth, management's problem will be where to get the cash to finance growth. The banker thus can anticipate interest in loan products. Conversely, if sustainable growth consistently exceeds actual, the banker had best be prepared to talk about investment products, because management's problem will be what to do with all the cash that keeps piling up in the till.

Bankers also find the sustainable growth equation useful for explaining to financially inexperienced small business owners and overly optimistic entrepreneurs that, for the long-run viability of their business, it is necessary to keep growth and profitability in proper balance.

Finally, comparison of actual to sustainable growth rates helps a banker understand why a loan applicant needs money and for how long the need might continue. In one instance, a loan applicant requested $100,000 to pay off several insistent suppliers and promised to repay in a few months when he collected some accounts receivable that were coming due. A sustainable growth analysis revealed that the firm had been growing at four to six times its sustainable growth rate and that this pattern was likely to continue in the foreseeable future. This alerted the banker to the fact that impatient suppliers were only a symptom of the much more fundamental disease of overly rapid growth, and that a $100,000 loan would likely prove to be only the down payment on a much larger, multiyear commitment.

Robert C. Higgins is the Marguerite Reimers Professor of Finance, Emeritus, at the Foster School of Business at the University of Washington. He pioneered the use of sustainable growth as a tool for financial analysis.

A NOTE ABOUT SUSTAINABLE GROWTH RATE CALCULATIONS

Very commonly, the sustainable growth rate is calculated using just the numerator in our expression, $ROE \times b$. This causes some confusion, which we can clear up here. The issue has to do with how ROE is computed. Recall that ROE is calculated as net income divided by total equity. If total equity is taken from an ending balance sheet (as we have done consistently, and is commonly done in practice), then our formula is the right one. However, if total equity is from the beginning of the period, then the simpler formula is the correct one.

In principle, you'll get exactly the same sustainable growth rate regardless of which way you calculate it (as long as you match up the ROE calculation with the right formula). In reality, you may see some differences because of accounting-related complications. By the way, if you use the average of beginning and ending equity (as some advocate), yet another formula is needed. Also, all of our comments here apply to the internal growth rate as well.

A simple example is useful to illustrate these points. Suppose a firm has a net income of $20 and a retention ratio of .60. Beginning assets are $100. The debt-equity ratio is .25, so beginning equity is $80.

If we use beginning numbers, we get the following:

ROE = $20/$80 = .25, or 25%

Sustainable growth = .60 × .25 = .15, or 15%

For the same firm, ending equity is $80 + .60 × $20 = $92. So, we can calculate this:

ROE = $20/$92 = .2174, or 21.74%

Sustainable growth = .60 × .2174/(1 − .60 × .2174) = .15, or 15%

These growth rates are exactly the same (after accounting for a small rounding error in the second calculation). See if you don't agree that the internal growth rate is 12 percent.

EXAMPLE 4.3	Profit Margins and Sustainable Growth

The Sandar Co. has a debt-equity ratio of .5, a profit margin of 3 percent, a dividend payout ratio of 40 percent, and a capital intensity ratio of 1. What is its sustainable growth rate? If Sandar desired a 10 percent sustainable growth rate and planned to achieve this goal by improving profit margins, what would you think?

ROE is $.03 \times 1 \times 1.5 = .045$, or 4.5%. The retention ratio is $1 - .40 = .60$. Sustainable growth is thus $.045(.60)/[1 - .045(.60)] = .0277$, or 2.77%.

For the company to achieve a 10 percent growth rate, the profit margin will have to rise. To see this, assume that sustainable growth is equal to 10 percent and then solve for profit margin, PM:

$$.10 = PM(1.5)(.6)/[1 - PM(1.5)(.6)]$$
$$PM = .1/.99 = .101, \text{ or } 10.1\%$$

For the plan to succeed, the necessary increase in profit margin is substantial, from 3 percent to about 10 percent. This may not be feasible.

Concept Questions

4.4a   How is a firm's sustainable growth related to its accounting return on equity (ROE)?

4.4b   What are the determinants of growth?

4.5 Some Caveats Regarding Financial Planning Models

Financial planning models do not always ask the right questions. A primary reason is that they tend to rely on accounting relationships and not financial relationships. In particular, the three basic elements of firm value tend to get left out—namely, cash flow size, risk, and timing.

Because of this, financial planning models sometimes do not produce meaningful clues about what strategies will lead to increases in value. Instead, they divert the user's attention to questions concerning the association of, say, the debt-equity ratio and firm growth.

The financial model we used for the Hoffman Company was simple—in fact, too simple. Our model, like many in use today, is really an accounting statement generator at heart. Such models are useful for pointing out inconsistencies and reminding us of financial needs, but they offer little guidance concerning what to do about these problems.

In closing our discussion, we should add that financial planning is an iterative process. Plans are created, examined, and modified over and over. The final plan will be a result negotiated between all the different parties to the process. In fact, long-term financial planning in most corporations relies on what might be called the Procrustes approach.[1] Upper-level managers have a goal in mind, and it is up to the planning staff to rework and ultimately deliver a feasible plan that meets that goal.

---

[1]In Greek mythology, Procrustes is a giant who seizes travelers and ties them to an iron bed. He stretches them or cuts off their legs as needed to make them fit the bed.

The final plan will therefore implicitly contain different goals in different areas and also satisfy many constraints. For this reason, such a plan need not be a dispassionate assessment of what we think the future will bring; it may instead be a means of reconciling the planned activities of different groups and a way of setting common goals for the future.

Concept Questions

4.5a   What are some important elements that are often missing in financial planning models?

4.5b   Why do we say planning is an iterative process?

Summary and Conclusions   4.6

Financial planning forces the firm to think about the future. We have examined a number of features of the planning process. We described what financial planning can accomplish and the components of a financial model. We went on to develop the relationship between growth and financing needs, and we discussed how a financial planning model is useful in exploring that relationship.

Corporate financial planning should not become a purely mechanical activity. If it does, it will probably focus on the wrong things. In particular, plans all too often are formulated in terms of a growth target with no explicit linkage to value creation, and they frequently are overly concerned with accounting statements. Nevertheless, the alternative to financial planning is stumbling into the future. Perhaps the immortal Yogi Berra (the baseball catcher, not the cartoon character) put it best when he said, "Ya gotta watch out if you don't know where you're goin'. You just might not get there."[2]

CONNECT TO FINANCE

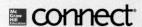 If you are using *Connect* Finance in your course, get online to take a Practice Test, check out study tools, and find out where you need additional practice.

Can you answer the following *Connect* Quiz questions?

Section 4.1   Murphy's, Inc., is in the process of preparing a financial plan for the firm for the next five years. This five-year period is referred to as the

_____.

Section 4.2   What is generally the first step in the financial planning process?

Section 4.3   A firm has current sales of $272,600 with total assets of $311,000. What is the full-capacity capital intensity ratio if the firm is currently operating at 68 percent capacity?

Section 4.4   What growth rate assumes that the debt-equity ratio is held constant?

Section 4.5   What is generally considered when compiling a financial plan?

---

[2] We're not *exactly* sure what this means either, but we like the sound of it.

CHAPTER REVIEW AND SELF-TEST PROBLEMS

4.1 Calculating EFN Based on the following information for the Skandia Mining Company, what is EFN if sales are predicted to grow by 10 percent? Use the percentage of sales approach and assume the company is operating at full capacity. The payout ratio is constant.

SKANDIA MINING COMPANY
Financial Statements

Income Statement		Balance Sheet			
		Assets		**Liabilities and Owners' Equity**	
Sales	$4,250.0	Current assets	$ 900.0	Current liabilities	$ 500.0
Costs	3,936.7	Net fixed assets	2,200.0	Long-term debt	1,800.0
Taxable income	$ 313.3			Owners' equity	800.0
Taxes (21%)	65.8			Total liabilities and owners'	
Net income	$ 247.5	Total assets	$3,100.0	equity	$3,100.0
Dividends	$ 82.6				
Addition to retained earnings	164.9				

4.2 EFN and Capacity Use Based on the information in Problem 4.1, what is EFN, assuming 60 percent capacity usage for net fixed assets? Assuming 95 percent capacity?

4.3 Sustainable Growth Based on the information in Problem 4.1, what growth rate can Skandia maintain if no external financing is used? What is the sustainable growth rate?

ANSWERS TO CHAPTER REVIEW AND SELF-TEST PROBLEMS

4.1 We can calculate EFN by preparing the pro forma statements using the percentage of sales approach. Note that sales are forecast to be $4,250 × 1.10 = $4,675.

SKANDIA MINING COMPANY
Pro Forma Financial Statements

Income Statement

Sales	$4,675.0	Forecast
Costs	4,330.4	92.63% of sales
Taxable income	$ 344.6	
Taxes (21%)	72.4	
Net income	$ 272.3	
Dividends	$ 90.9	33.37% of net income
Addition to retained earnings	181.4	

Balance Sheet

Assets			Liabilities and Owners' Equity		
Current assets	$ 990.0	21.18%	Current liabilities	$ 550.0	11.76%
Net fixed assets	2,420.0	51.76%	Long-term debt	1,800.0	n/a
			Owners' equity	981.4	n/a
Total assets	$3,410.0	72.94%	Total liabilities and owners' equity	$3,331.4	n/a
			EFN	$ 78.6	n/a

4.2   Full-capacity sales are equal to current sales divided by the capacity utilization. At 60 percent of capacity:

$4,250 = .60 \times$ Full-capacity sales

$7,083 =$ Full-capacity sales

With a sales level of $4,675, no net new fixed assets will be needed, so our earlier estimate is too high. We estimated an increase in fixed assets of $2,420 − 2,200 = $220. The new EFN will thus be $78.6 − 220 = −$141.4, a surplus. No external financing is needed in this case.

At 95 percent capacity, full-capacity sales are $4,474. The ratio of fixed assets to full-capacity sales is thus $2,200/$4,474 = .4918, or 49.18%. At a sales level of $4,675, we will thus need $4,675 × .4918 = $2,299.0 in net fixed assets, an increase of $99.0. This is $220 − 99 = $121 less than we originally predicted, so the EFN is now $78.6 − 121 = −$42.4, a surplus. No additional financing is needed.

4.3   Skandia retains $b = 1 - .3337 = .6663$, or 66.63% of net income. Return on assets is $247.5/$3,100 = .0798$, or 7.98%. The internal growth rate is thus:

$$\frac{\text{ROA} \times b}{1 - \text{ROA} \times b} = \frac{.0798 \times .6663}{1 - .0798 \times .6663}$$

$$= .0562, \text{ or } 5.62\%$$

Return on equity for Skandia is $247.5/$800 = .3094$, or 30.94%, so we can calculate the sustainable growth rate as follows:

$$\frac{\text{ROE} \times b}{1 - \text{ROE} \times b} = \frac{.3094 \times .6663}{1 - .3094 \times .6663}$$

$$= .2597, \text{ or } 25.97\%$$

CONCEPTS REVIEW AND CRITICAL THINKING QUESTIONS

1. **Sales Forecast [LO1]** Why do you think most long-term financial planning begins with sales forecasts? Put differently, why are future sales the key input?

2. **Sustainable Growth [LO3]** In the chapter, we used Rosengarten Corporation to demonstrate how to calculate EFN. The ROE for Rosengarten is about 7.3 percent, and the plowback ratio is about 67 percent. If you calculate the sustainable growth rate for Rosengarten, you will find it is only 5.14 percent. In our calculation for EFN, we used a growth rate of 25 percent. Is this possible? (*Hint*: Yes. How?)

3. **External Financing Needed [LO2]** Testaburger, Inc., uses no external financing and maintains a positive retention ratio. When sales grow by 15 percent, the firm has a negative projected EFN. What does this tell you about the firm's internal growth rate? How about the sustainable growth rate? At this same level of sales growth, what will happen to the projected EFN if the retention ratio is increased? What if the retention ratio is decreased? What happens to the projected EFN if the firm pays out all of its earnings in the form of dividends?

4. **EFN and Growth Rates [LO2, 3]** Broslofski Co. maintains a positive retention ratio and keeps its debt-equity ratio constant every year. When sales grow by 20 percent, the firm has a negative projected EFN. What does this tell you about the firm's sustainable growth rate? Do you know, with certainty, if the internal growth rate is greater than or less than 20 percent? Why? What happens to the projected EFN if the retention ratio is increased? What if the retention ratio is decreased? What if the retention ratio is zero?

Use the following information to answer Questions 5–10: A small business called The Grandmother Calendar Company began selling personalized photo calendar kits. The kits were a hit, and sales soon sharply exceeded forecasts. The rush of orders created a huge backlog, so the company leased more space and expanded capacity; but it still could not keep up with demand. Equipment failed from overuse and quality suffered. Working capital was drained to expand production, and, at the same time, payments from customers were often delayed until the product was shipped. Unable to deliver on orders, the company became so strapped for cash that employee paychecks began to bounce. Finally, out of cash, the company ceased operations entirely three years later.

5. **Product Sales [LO4]** Do you think the company would have suffered the same fate if its product had been less popular? Why or why not?

6. **Cash Flow [LO4]** The Grandmother Calendar Company clearly had a cash flow problem. In the context of the cash flow analysis we developed in Chapter 2, what was the impact of customers not paying until orders were shipped?

7. **Product Pricing [LO4]** The firm actually priced its product to be about 20 percent less than that of competitors, even though the Grandmother calendar was more detailed. In retrospect, was this a wise choice?

8. **Corporate Borrowing [LO4]** If the firm was so successful at selling, why wouldn't a bank or some other lender step in and provide it with the cash it needed to continue?

9. **Cash Flow [LO4]** Which was the biggest culprit here: Too many orders, too little cash, or too little production capacity?

10. **Cash Flow [LO4]** What are some of the actions that a small company like The Grandmother Calendar Company can take if it finds itself in a situation in which growth in sales outstrips production capacity and available financial resources? What other options (besides expansion of capacity) are available to a company when orders exceed capacity?

QUESTIONS AND PROBLEMS

BASIC

(Questions 1–15)

1. **Forma Statements [LO1]** Consider the following simplified financial statements for the Wims Corporation (assuming no income taxes):

Income Statement		Balance Sheet			
Sales	$38,000	Assets	$27,300	Debt	$ 6,700
Costs	32,600			Equity	20,600
Net income	$ 5,400	Total	$27,300	Total	$27,300

The company has predicted a sales increase of 15 percent. It has predicted that every item on the balance sheet will increase by 15 percent as well. Create the pro forma statements and reconcile them. What is the plug variable here?

2. **Pro Forma Statements and EFN [LO1, 2]** In Question 1, assume the company pays out half of net income in the form of a cash dividend. Costs and assets vary with sales, but debt and equity do not. Prepare the pro forma statements and determine the external financing needed.

3. **Calculating EFN** [LO2] The most recent financial statements for Kerch, Inc., are shown here (assuming no income taxes):

Income Statement		Balance Sheet			
Sales	$7,200	Assets	$21,700	Debt	$ 9,100
Costs	4,730			Equity	12,600
Net income	$2,470	Total	$21,700	Total	$21,700

Assets and costs are proportional to sales. Debt and equity are not. No dividends are paid. Next year's sales are projected to be $8,424. What is the external financing needed?

4. **EFN** [LO2] The most recent financial statements for Cardinal, Inc., are shown here:

Income Statement		Balance Sheet			
Sales	$25,400	Assets	$61,000	Debt	$26,900
Costs	17,300			Equity	34,100
Taxable income	$ 8,100	Total	$61,000	Total	$61,000
Taxes (21%)	1,701				
Net income	$ 6,399				

Assets and costs are proportional to sales. Debt and equity are not. A dividend of $2,100 was paid, and the company wishes to maintain a constant payout ratio. Next year's sales are projected to be $29,210. What is the external financing needed?

5. **EFN** [LO2] The most recent financial statements for Assouad, Inc., are shown here: ✗

Income Statement		Balance Sheet			
Sales	$7,900	Current assets	$ 3,900	Current liabilities	$ 2,100
Costs	5,500	Fixed assets	8,600	Long-term debt	3,700
Taxable income	$2,400			Equity	6,700
Taxes (25%)	600	Total	$12,500	Total	$12,500
Net income	$1,800				

Assets, costs, and current liabilities are proportional to sales. Long-term debt and equity are not. The company maintains a constant 40 percent dividend payout ratio. As with every other firm in its industry, next year's sales are projected to increase by exactly 15 percent. What is the external financing needed?

6. **Calculating Internal Growth** [LO3] The most recent financial statements for ✗ Bello Co. are shown here:

Income Statement		Balance Sheet			
Sales	$18,900	Current assets	$11,700	Debt	$15,700
Costs	12,800	Fixed assets	26,500	Equity	22,500
Taxable income	$ 6,100	Total	$38,200	Total	$38,200
Taxes (21%)	1,281				
Net income	$ 4,819				

Assets and costs are proportional to sales. Debt and equity are not. The company maintains a constant 30 percent dividend payout ratio. What is the internal growth rate?

7. **Calculating Sustainable Growth** [LO3] For the company in Problem 6, what is the sustainable growth rate?

8. **Sales and Growth [LO2]** The most recent financial statements for Alexander Co. are shown here:

Income Statement		Balance Sheet			
Sales	$42,800	Current assets	$17,500	Long-term debt	$37,000
Costs	35,500	Fixed assets	68,300	Equity	48,800
Taxable income	$ 7,300	Total	$85,800	Total	$85,800
Taxes (23%)	1,679				
Net income	$ 5,621				

Assets and costs are proportional to sales. The company maintains a constant 40 percent dividend payout ratio and a constant debt-equity ratio. What is the maximum increase in sales that can be sustained assuming no new equity is issued?

9. **Calculating Retained Earnings from Pro Forma Income [LO1]** Consider the following income statement for the Heir Jordan Corporation:

HEIR JORDAN CORPORATION Income Statement	
Sales	$49,000
Costs	40,300
Taxable income	$ 8,700
Taxes (22%)	1,914
Net income	$ 6,786
Dividends	$2,400
Addition to retained earnings	4,386

A 20 percent growth rate in sales is projected. Prepare a pro forma income statement assuming costs vary with sales and the dividend payout ratio is constant. What is the projected addition to retained earnings?

10. **Applying Percentage of Sales [LO1]** The balance sheet for the Heir Jordan Corporation follows. Based on this information and the income statement in the previous problem, supply the missing information using the percentage of sales approach. Assume that accounts payable vary with sales, whereas notes payable do not. Put "n/a" where needed.

HEIR JORDAN CORPORATION Balance Sheet					
Assets			**Liabilities and Owners' Equity**		
	$	Percentage of Sales		$	Percentage of Sales
Current assets			Current liabilities		
Cash	$ 2,950	—	Accounts payable	$ 2,400	—
Accounts receivable	4,100	—	Notes payable	5,400	—
Inventory	6,400	—	Total	$ 7,800	—
Total	$13,450	—	Long-term debt	$28,000	—
Fixed assets					
Net plant and equipment	$41,300	—	Owners' equity		
			Common stock and paid-in surplus	$15,000	—
			Retained earnings	3,950	—
			Total	$18,950	—
			Total liabilities and		
Total assets	$54,750	—	owners' equity	$54,750	—

11. **EFN and Sales** [LO2] From the previous two questions, prepare a pro forma balance sheet showing EFN, assuming an increase in sales of 15 percent, no new external debt or equity financing, and a constant payout ratio.

12. **Internal Growth** [LO3] If A7X Co. has an ROA of 7.6 percent and a payout ratio of 25 percent, what is its internal growth rate?

13. **Sustainable Growth** [LO3] If Synyster Corp. has an ROE of 14.7 percent and a payout ratio of 30 percent, what is its sustainable growth rate?

14. **Sustainable Growth** [LO3] Based on the following information, calculate the sustainable growth rate for Kaleb's Heavy Equipment:

Profit margin	= 7.3%
Capital intensity ratio	= .80
Debt–equity ratio	= .95
Net income	= $73,000
Dividends	= $24,000

15. **Sustainable Growth** [LO3] Assuming the following ratios are constant, what is the sustainable growth rate?

Total asset turnover	= 2.90
Profit margin	= 5.2%
Equity multiplier	= 1.10
Payout ratio	= 35%

16. **Full-Capacity Sales** [LO1] Hodgkiss Mfg., Inc., is currently operating at only 91 percent of fixed asset capacity. Current sales are $715,000. How fast can sales grow before any new fixed assets are needed?

17. **Fixed Assets and Capacity Usage** [LO1] For the company in Problem 16, suppose fixed assets are $520,000 and sales are projected to grow to $790,000. How much in new fixed assets are required to support this growth in sales? Assume the company wants to operate at full capacity.

18. **Growth and Profit Margin** [LO3] Ramble On Co. wishes to maintain a growth rate of 12 percent per year, a debt-equity ratio of .90, and a dividend payout ratio of 25 percent. The ratio of total assets to sales is constant at .85. What profit margin must the firm achieve?

19. **Growth and Assets** [LO3] A firm wishes to maintain an internal growth rate of 7.1 percent and a dividend payout ratio of 25 percent. The current profit margin is 6.5 percent, and the firm uses no external financing sources. What must total asset turnover be?

20. **Sustainable Growth** [LO3] Based on the following information, calculate the sustainable growth rate for Hendrix Guitars, Inc.:

Profit margin	= 6.3%
Total asset turnover	= 1.75
Total debt ratio	= .35
Payout ratio	= 30%

21. **Sustainable Growth and Outside Financing** [LO3] You've collected the following information about Molino, Inc.:

Sales	= $215,000
Net income	= $17,300
Dividends	= $9,400
Total debt	= $77,000
Total equity	= $59,000

INTERMEDIATE
(Questions 16–26)

What is the sustainable growth rate for the company? If it does grow at this rate, how much new borrowing will take place in the coming year, assuming a constant debt-equity ratio? What growth rate could be supported with no outside financing at all?

22. **Sustainable Growth Rate [LO3]** Gilmore, Inc., had equity of $145,000 at the beginning of the year. At the end of the year, the company had total assets of $210,000. During the year, the company sold no new equity. Net income for the year was $27,000 and dividends were $5,800. What is the sustainable growth rate for the company? What is the sustainable growth rate if you use the formula ROE × b and beginning of period equity? What is the sustainable growth rate if you use end of period equity in this formula? Is this number too high or too low? Why?

23. **Internal Growth Rates [LO3]** Calculate the internal growth rate for the company in Problem 22. Now calculate the internal growth rate using ROA × b for both beginning of period and end of period total assets. What do you observe?

24. **Calculating EFN [LO2]** The most recent financial statements for Crosby, Inc., follow. Sales for 2018 are projected to grow by 20 percent. Interest expense will remain constant; the tax rate and the dividend payout rate will also remain constant. Costs, other expenses, current assets, fixed assets, and accounts payable increase spontaneously with sales. If the firm is operating at full capacity and no new debt or equity is issued, what external financing is needed to support the 20 percent growth rate in sales?

CROSBY, INC.	
2017 Income Statement	
Sales	$980,760
Costs	792,960
Other expenses	20,060
Earnings before interest and taxes	$167,740
Interest paid	14,740
Taxable income	$153,000
Taxes (21%)	32,130
Net income	$120,870
Dividends	$39,250
Addition to retained earnings	81,620

CROSBY, INC.			
Balance Sheet as of December 31, 2017			
Assets		**Liabilities and Owners' Equity**	
Current assets		Current liabilities	
Cash	$ 27,920	Accounts payable	$ 71,720
Accounts receivable	42,630	Notes payable	17,620
Inventory	95,910	Total	$ 89,340
Total	$166,460	Long-term debt	$170,000
Fixed assets		Owners' equity	
Net plant and equipment	$455,980	Common stock and paid-in surplus	$140,000
		Retained earnings	223,100
		Total	$363,100
Total assets	$622,440	Total liabilities and owners' equity	$622,440

25. **Capacity Usage and Growth [LO2]** In the previous problem, suppose the firm was operating at only 80 percent capacity in 2017. What is EFN now?

26. **Calculating EFN [LO2]** In Problem 24, suppose the firm wishes to keep its debt-equity ratio constant. What is EFN now?

27. **EFN and Internal Growth [LO2, 3]** Redo Problem 24 using sales growth rates of 15 and 25 percent in addition to 20 percent. Illustrate graphically the relationship between EFN and the growth rate, and use this graph to determine the relationship between them. At what growth rate is the EFN equal to zero? Why is this internal growth rate different from that found by using the equation in the text?

28. **EFN and Sustainable Growth [LO2, 3]** Redo Problem 26 using sales growth rates of 30 and 35 percent in addition to 20 percent. Assume the firm wishes to maintain its debt-equity ratio. Illustrate graphically the relationship between EFN and the growth rate, and use this graph to determine the relationship between them. At what growth rate is the EFN equal to zero? Why is this sustainable growth rate different from that found by using the equation in the text?

29. **Constraints on Growth [LO3]** Sig, Inc., wishes to maintain a growth rate of 12 percent per year and a debt-equity ratio of .43. The profit margin is 5.9 percent, and the ratio of total assets to sales is constant at 1.80. Is this growth rate possible? To answer, determine what the dividend payout ratio must be. How do you interpret the result?

30. **EFN [LO2]** Define the following:

    S = Previous year's sales

    A = Total assets

    E = Total equity

    g = Projected growth in sales

    PM = Profit margin

    b = Retention (plowback) ratio

    Assuming all debt is constant, show that EFN can be written as follows:

    EFN = −PM(S)b + (A − PM(S)b) × g

    Hint: Asset needs will equal A × g. The addition to retained earnings will equal PM(S)b × (1 + g).

31. **Growth Rates [LO3]** Based on the result in Problem 30, show that the internal and sustainable growth rates are as given in the chapter. *Hint*: For the internal growth rate, set EFN equal to zero and solve for g.

32. **Sustainable Growth Rate [LO3]** In the chapter, we discussed the two versions of the sustainable growth rate formula. Derive the formula ROE × b from the formula given in the chapter, where ROE is based on beginning of period equity. Also, derive the formula ROA × b from the internal growth rate formula.

CHALLENGE
(Questions 27–32)

EXCEL MASTER IT! PROBLEM

Financial planning can be more complex than the percentage of sales approach indicates. Often, the assumptions behind the percentage of sales approach may be too simple. A more sophisticated model allows important items to vary without being a strict percentage of sales.

Consider a new model in which depreciation is calculated as a percentage of beginning fixed assets and interest expense depends directly on the amount of debt. Debt is still the plug variable. Note that since depreciation and interest now do not necessarily vary directly with sales, the profit margin is no longer constant. Also, for the same reason, taxes and dividends will no longer be a fixed percentage of sales. The parameter estimates used in the new model are:

Cost percentage	= Costs / Sales
Depreciation rate	= Depreciation / Beginning fixed assets
Interest rate	= Interest paid / Total debt
Tax rate	= Taxes / Net income
Payout ratio	= Dividends / Net income
Capital intensity ratio	= Fixed assets / Sales
Fixed assets ratio	= Fixed assets / Total assets

The model parameters can be determined by whatever methods the company deems appropriate. For example, they might be based on average values for the last several years, industry standards, subjective estimates, or even company targets. Alternatively, sophisticated statistical techniques can be used to estimate them.

The Moore Company is preparing its pro forma financial statements for the next year using this model. The abbreviated financial statements are presented below.

Sales growth	20%
Tax rate	21%
Income Statement	
Sales	$780,000
Costs	415,000
Depreciation	135,000
Interest	68,000
Taxable income	$162,000
Taxes	34,020
Net income	$127,980
Dividends	$ 30,000
Additions to retained earnings	$ 97,980

Balance Sheet			
Assets		**Liabilities and Equity**	
Current assets	$ 240,000	Total debt	$ 880,000
Net fixed assets	1,350,000	Owners' equity	710,000
Total assets	$1,590,000	Total debt and equity	$1,590,000

a. Calculate each of the parameters necessary to construct the pro forma balance sheet.

b. Construct the pro forma balance sheet. What is the total debt necessary to balance the pro forma balance sheet?

c. In this financial planning model, show that it is possible to solve algebraically for the amount of new borrowing.

MINICASE

Planning for Growth at S&S Air

After Chris completed the ratio analysis for S&S Air (see Chapter 3), Mark and Todd approached him about planning for next year's sales. The company had historically used little planning for investment needs. As a result, the company experienced some challenging times because of cash flow problems. The lack of planning resulted in missed sales, as well as periods when Mark and Todd were unable to draw salaries. To this end, they would like Chris to prepare a financial plan for the next year so the company can begin to address any outside investment requirements. The income statement and balance sheet are shown here:

S&S AIR, INC. 2018 Income Statement	
Sales	$46,298,115
Cost of goods sold	34,536,913
Other expenses	5,870,865
Depreciation	2,074,853
EBIT	$ 3,815,484
Interest	725,098
Taxable income	$ 3,090,386
Taxes (21%)	772,597
Net income	$ 2,317,789
Dividends	$ 705,000
Add to retained earnings	1,612,789

S&S AIR, INC.
2018 Balance Sheet

Assets		Liabilities and Equity	
Current assets		Current liabilities	
Cash	$ 524,963	Accounts payable	$ 1,068,356
Accounts receivable	843,094	Notes payable	2,439,553
Inventory	1,235,161	Total current liabilities	$ 3,507,909
Total current assets	$ 2,603,218	Long-term debt	$ 6,300,000
Fixed assets			
Net plant and equipment	$20,381,945	Shareholder equity	
		Common stock	$ 460,000
		Retained earnings	12,717,254
		Total equity	$13,177,254
Total assets	$22,985,163	Total liabilities and equity	$22,985,163

QUESTIONS

1. Calculate the internal growth rate and sustainable growth rate for S&S Air. What do these numbers mean?

2. S&S Air is planning for a growth rate of 12 percent next year. Calculate the EFN for the company assuming the company is operating at full capacity. Can the company's sales increase at this growth rate?

3. Most assets can be increased as a percentage of sales. For instance, cash can be increased by any amount. However, fixed assets must be increased in specific amounts because it is impossible, as a practical matter, to buy part of a new plant or machine. In this case, a company has a "staircase" or "lumpy" fixed cost structure. Assume S&S Air is currently producing at 100 percent capacity. As a result, to increase production, the company must set up an entirely new line at a cost of $5,000,000. Calculate the new EFN with this assumption. What does this imply about capacity utilization for the company next year?

Chapter

5 | Introduction to Valuation: The Time Value of Money

AS YOU ARE PROBABLY AWARE, the United States government has a significant amount of debt. That debt, which is widely owned by investors, comes in different varieties, including Series EE U.S. Treasury savings bonds. With a Series EE bond, you pay a particular amount today of, say, $25, and the bond accrues interest over the time you hold it. In early 2017, the U.S. Treasury promised to pay .10 percent per year on EE savings bonds. In an interesting (and important) wrinkle, if you hold the bond for 20 years, the Treasury promises to "step up" the value to double your cost. That is, if the $25 bond you purchased and all the accumulated interest earned are worth less than $50, the Treasury will automatically increase the value of the bond to $50.

Is giving up $25 in exchange for $50 in 20 years a good deal? On the plus side, you get back $2 for every $1 you put up. That probably sounds good, but, on the downside, you have to wait 20 years to get it. What you need to know is how to analyze this trade-off. This chapter gives you the tools you need.

Learning Objectives

After studying this chapter, you should be able to:

LO1 Determine the future value of an investment made today.

LO2 Determine the present value of cash to be received at a future date.

LO3 Find the return on an investment.

LO4 Calculate how long it takes for an investment to reach a desired value.

For updates on the latest happenings in finance, visit fundamentalsofcorporatefinance.blogspot.com.

One of the basic problems faced by the financial manager is how to determine the value today of cash flows expected in the future. For example, the jackpot in a Powerball™ lottery drawing was $110 million. Does this mean the winning ticket was worth $110 million? The answer is no because the jackpot was actually going to pay out over a 20-year period at a rate of $5.5 million per year. How much was the ticket worth then? The answer depends on the time value of money, the subject of this chapter.

In the most general sense, the phrase *time value of money* refers to the fact that a dollar in hand today is worth more than a dollar promised at some time in the future. On a practical level, one reason for this is that you could earn interest while you waited; so, a dollar today would grow to more than a dollar later. The trade-off between money now and money later thus depends on, among other things, the rate you can earn by investing. Our goal in this chapter is to explicitly evaluate this trade-off between dollars today and dollars at some future time.

A thorough understanding of the material in this chapter is critical to understanding material in subsequent chapters, so you should study it with particular care. We will present a number of examples in this chapter. In many problems, your answer may differ from ours slightly. This can happen because of rounding and is not a cause for concern.

Future Value and Compounding

5.1

The first thing we will study is future value. **Future value (FV)** refers to the amount of money an investment will grow to over some period of time at some given interest rate. Put another way, future value is the cash value of an investment at some time in the future. We start out by considering the simplest case: A single-period investment.

future value (FV)
The amount an investment is worth after one or more periods.

INVESTING FOR A SINGLE PERIOD

Suppose you invest $100 in a savings account that pays 10 percent interest per year. How much will you have in one year? You will have $110. This $110 is equal to your original *principal* of $100 plus $10 in interest that you earn. We say that $110 is the future value of $100 invested for one year at 10 percent, and we mean that $100 today is worth $110 in one year, given that 10 percent is the interest rate.

In general, if you invest for one period at an interest rate of r, your investment will grow to $(1 + r)$ per dollar invested. In our example, r is 10 percent, so your investment grows to $1 + .10 = 1.1$ dollars per dollar invested. You invested $100 in this case, so you ended up with $100 \times 1.10 = $110.

INVESTING FOR MORE THAN ONE PERIOD

Going back to our $100 investment, what will you have after two years, assuming the interest rate doesn't change? If you leave the entire $110 in the bank, you will earn $110 \times .10 = $11 in interest during the second year, so you will have a total of $110 + 11 = $121. This $121 is the future value of $100 in two years at 10 percent. Another way of looking at it is that one year from now you are effectively investing $110 at 10 percent for a year. This is a single-period problem, so you'll end up with $1.10 for every dollar invested, or $110 \times 1.1 = $121 total.

This $121 has four parts. The first part is the $100 original principal. The second part is the $10 in interest you earned in the first year, and the third part is another $10 you earned in the second year, for a total of $120. The last $1 you end up with (the fourth part) is interest you earned in the second year on the interest paid in the first year: $10 \times .10 = $1.

This process of leaving your money and any accumulated interest in an investment for more than one period, thereby *reinvesting* the interest, is called **compounding**. Compounding the interest means earning **interest on interest**, so we call the result **compound interest**. With **simple interest**, the interest is not reinvested, so interest is earned each period only on the original principal.

compounding
The process of accumulating interest on an investment over time to earn more interest.

interest on interest
Interest earned on the reinvestment of previous interest payments.

compound interest
Interest earned on both the initial principal and the interest reinvested from prior periods.

simple interest
Interest earned only on the original principal amount invested.

Interest on Interest	**EXAMPLE 5.1**

Suppose you locate a two-year investment that pays 14 percent per year. If you invest $325, how much will you have at the end of the two years? How much of this is simple interest? How much is compound interest?

> At the end of the first year, you will have $325 × (1 + .14) = $370.50. If you reinvest this entire amount and thereby compound the interest, you will have $370.50 × 1.14 = $422.37 at the end of the second year. The total interest you earn is thus $422.37 − 325 = $97.37. Your $325 original principal earns $325 × .14 = $45.50 in interest each year, for a two-year total of $91 in simple interest. The remaining $97.37 − 91 = $6.37 results from compounding. You can check this by noting that the interest earned in the first year is $45.50. The interest on interest earned in the second year thus amounts to $45.50 × .14 = $6.37, as we calculated.

We now take a closer look at how we calculated the $121 future value. We multiplied $110 by 1.1 to get $121. The $110, however, was $100 also multiplied by 1.1. In other words:

$$\$121 = \$110 \times 1.1$$
$$= (\$100 \times 1.1) \times 1.1$$
$$= \$100 \times (1.1 \times 1.1)$$
$$= \$100 \times 1.1^2$$
$$= \$100 \times 1.21$$

At the risk of belaboring the obvious, let's ask: How much would our $100 grow to after three years? Once again, in two years, we'll be investing $121 for one period at 10 percent. We'll end up with $1.10 for every dollar we invest, or $121 × 1.1 = $133.10 total. This $133.10 is thus:

$$\$133.10 = \$121 \times 1.1$$
$$= (\$110 \times 1.1) \times 1.1$$
$$= (\$100 \times 1.1) \times 1.1 \times 1.1$$
$$= \$100 \times (1.1 \times 1.1 \times 1.1)$$
$$= \$100 \times 1.1^3$$
$$= \$100 \times 1.331$$

You're probably noticing a pattern to these calculations, so we can now go ahead and state the general result. As our examples suggest, the future value of $1 invested for t periods at a rate of r per period is this:

Future value = $1 × (1 + r)^t   5.1

The expression $(1 + r)^t$ is sometimes called the *future value interest factor* (or just *future value factor*) for $1 invested at r percent for t periods and can be abbreviated as FVIF(r, t).

In our example, what would your $100 be worth after five years? We can first compute the relevant future value factor as follows:

$$(1 + r)^t = (1 + .10)^5 = 1.1^5 = 1.6105$$

Your $100 will thus grow to:

$$\$100 \times 1.6105 = \$161.05$$

The growth of your $100 each year is illustrated in Table 5.1. As shown, the interest earned in each year is equal to the beginning amount multiplied by the interest rate of 10 percent.

In Table 5.1, notice the total interest you earn is $61.05. Over the five-year span of this investment, the simple interest is $100 × .10 = $10 per year, so you accumulate $50 this way. The other $11.05 is from compounding.

Year	Beginning Amount	Simple Interest	Compound Interest	Total Interest Earned	Ending Amount
1	$100.00	$10	$ .00	$10.00	$110.00
2	110.00	10	1.00	11.00	121.00
3	121.00	10	2.10	12.10	133.10
4	133.10	10	3.31	13.31	146.41
5	146.41	10	4.64	14.64	161.05
Total		$50	$11.05	$61.05	

TABLE 5.1

Future Value of $100 at 10 percent

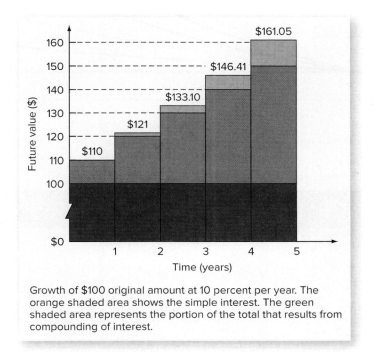

FIGURE 5.1

Future Value, Simple Interest, and Compound Interest

Growth of $100 original amount at 10 percent per year. The orange shaded area shows the simple interest. The green shaded area represents the portion of the total that results from compounding of interest.

Figure 5.1 illustrates the growth of the compound interest in Table 5.1. Notice how the simple interest is constant each year, but the amount of compound interest you earn gets bigger every year. The amount of the compound interest keeps increasing because more and more interest builds up and there is thus more to compound.

Future values depend critically on the assumed interest rate, particularly for long-lived investments. Figure 5.2 illustrates this relationship by plotting the growth of $1 for different rates and lengths of time. Notice the future value of $1 after 10 years is about $6.20 at a 20 percent rate, but it is only about $2.60 at 10 percent. In this case, doubling the interest rate more than doubles the future value.

To solve future value problems, we need to come up with the relevant future value factors. There are several different ways of doing this. In our example, we could have multiplied 1.1 by itself five times. This would work just fine, but it would get to be very tedious for, say, a 30-year investment.

A brief introduction to key financial concepts is available at **www.teachmefinance.com**.

FIGURE 5.2

Future Value of $1 for Different Periods and Rates

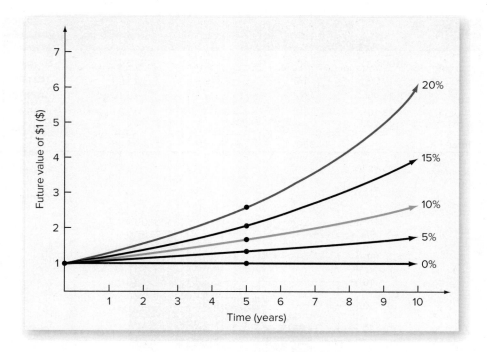

TABLE 5.2

Future Value Interest Factors

Number of Periods	Interest Rate			
	5%	**10%**	**15%**	**20%**
1	1.0500	1.1000	1.1500	1.2000
2	1.1025	1.2100	1.3225	1.4400
3	1.1576	1.3310	1.5209	1.7280
4	1.2155	1.4641	1.7490	2.0736
5	1.2763	1.6105	2.0114	2.4883

Fortunately, there are several easier ways to get future value factors. Most calculators have a key labeled "y^x". You can usually just enter 1.1, press this key, enter 5, and press the "=" key to get the answer. This is an easy way to calculate future value factors because it's quick and accurate.

Alternatively, you can use a table that contains future value factors for some common interest rates and time periods. Table 5.2 contains some of these factors. Table A.1 in the appendix at the end of the book contains a much larger set. To use the table, find the column that corresponds to 10 percent. Then look down the rows until you come to five periods. You should find the factor that we calculated, 1.6105.

Future value interest factor tables such as Table 5.2 are not as common as they once were because they predate inexpensive calculators and are available only for a relatively small number of rates. Interest rates are often quoted to three or four decimal places, so the tables needed to deal with these accurately would be quite large. As a result, the real world has moved away from using them. We will emphasize the use of a calculator in this chapter.

These tables still serve a useful purpose, however. To make sure you are doing the calculations correctly, pick a factor from the table and then calculate it yourself to see that you get the same answer. There are plenty of numbers to choose from.

Compound Interest   EXAMPLE 5.2

You've located an investment that pays 12 percent per year. That rate sounds good to you, so you invest $400. How much will you have in three years? How much will you have in seven years? At the end of seven years, how much interest will you have earned? How much of that interest results from compounding?

Based on our discussion, we can calculate the future value factor for 12 percent and three years as follows:

$$(1 + r)^t = 1.12^3 = 1.4049$$

Your $400 thus grows to:

$$\$400 \times 1.4049 = \$561.97$$

After seven years, you will have:

$$\$400 \times 1.12^7 = \$400 \times 2.2107 = \$884.27$$

Thus, you will more than double your money over seven years.

Because you invested $400, the interest in the $884.27 future value is $884.27 − 400 = $484.27. At 12 percent, your $400 investment earns $400 × .12 = $48 in simple interest every year. Over seven years, the simple interest thus totals 7 × $48 = $336. The other $484.27 − 336 = $148.27 is from compounding.

The effect of compounding is not great over short time periods, but it really starts to add up as the horizon grows. To take an extreme case, suppose one of your more frugal ancestors had invested $5 for you at a 6 percent interest rate 200 years ago. How much would you have today? The future value factor is a substantial $1.06^{200} = 115{,}125.90$ (you won't find this one in a table), so you would have $5 × 115,125.90 = $575,629.52 today. Notice that the simple interest is just $5 × .06 = $.30 per year. After 200 years, this amounts to $60. The rest is from reinvesting. Such is the power of compound interest!

How Much for That Island?   EXAMPLE 5.3

To further illustrate the effect of compounding for long horizons, consider the case of Peter Minuit and the American Indians. In 1626, Minuit bought all of Manhattan Island for about $24 in goods and trinkets. This sounds cheap, but the Indians may have gotten the better end of the deal. To see why, suppose the Indians had sold the goods and invested the $24 at 10 percent. How much would it be worth today?

About 391 years have passed since the transaction. At 10 percent, $24 will grow by quite a bit over that time. How much? The future value factor is roughly:

$$(1 + r)^t = 1.1^{391} \approx 15{,}295{,}000{,}000{,}000{,}000$$

That is, 15.295 followed by 12 zeroes. The future value is thus on the order of $24 × 15.295 = $367 *quadrillion* (give or take a few hundreds of trillions).

Well, $367 quadrillion is a lot of money. How much? If you had it, you could buy the United States. All of it. Cash. With money left over to buy Canada, Mexico, and the rest of the world, for that matter.

This example is something of an exaggeration, of course. In 1626, it would not have been easy to locate an investment that would pay 10 percent every year without fail for the next 391 years.

CALCULATOR HINTS

Using a Financial Calculator

Although there are the various ways of calculating future values we have described so far, many of you will decide that a financial calculator is the way to go. If you are planning on using one, you should read this extended hint; otherwise, skip it.

A financial calculator is an ordinary calculator with a few extra features. In particular, it knows some of the most commonly used financial formulas, so it can directly compute things like future values.

Financial calculators have the advantage that they handle a lot of the computation, but that is really all. In other words, you still have to understand the problem; the calculator just does some of the arithmetic. In fact, there is an old joke (somewhat modified) that goes like this: Anyone can make a mistake on a time value of money problem, but to really screw one up takes a financial calculator! We therefore have two goals for this section. First, we'll discuss how to compute future values. After that, we'll show you how to avoid the most common mistakes people make when they start using financial calculators.

How to Calculate Future Values with a Financial Calculator

Examining a typical financial calculator, you will find five keys of particular interest. They usually look like this:

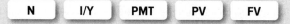

For now, we need to focus on four of these. The keys labeled **PV** and **FV** are just what you would guess: present value and future value. The key labeled **N** refers to the number of periods, which is what we have been calling t. Finally, **I/Y** stands for the interest rate, which we have called r.[1]

If we have the financial calculator set up right (see our next section), then calculating a future value is very simple. Take a look back at our question involving the future value of $100 at 10 percent for five years. We have seen that the answer is $161.05. The exact keystrokes will differ depending on what type of calculator you use, but here is basically all you do:

1. Enter −100. Press the **PV** key. (The negative sign is explained in the next section.)
2. Enter 10. Press the **I/Y** key. (Notice that we entered 10, not .10; see the next section.)
3. Enter 5. Press the **N** key.

Now we have entered all of the relevant information. To solve for the future value, we need to ask the calculator what the FV is. Depending on your calculator, either you press the button labeled "CPT" (for compute) and then press **FV**, or you just press **FV**. Either way, you should get 161.05. If you don't (and you probably won't if this is the first time you have used a financial calculator!), we will offer some help in our next section.

Before we explain the kinds of problems you are likely to run into, we want to establish a standard format for showing you how to use a financial calculator. Using the example we just looked at, in the future, we will illustrate such problems like this:

Enter 5   10   − 100

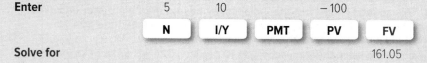

Solve for   161.05

Here is an important tip: Appendix D contains more detailed instructions for the most common types of financial calculators. See if yours is included; if it is, follow the instructions there if you need help. Of course, if all else fails, you can read the manual that came with the calculator.

How to Get the Wrong Answer Using a Financial Calculator

There are a couple of common (and frustrating) problems that cause a lot of trouble with financial calculators. In this section, we provide some important *dos* and *don'ts*. If you just can't seem to get a problem to work out, you should refer back to this section.

---

[1]The reason financial calculators use N and I/Y is that the most common use for these calculators is determining loan payments. In this context, N is the number of payments and I/Y is the interest rate on the loan. But as we will see, there are many other uses of financial calculators that don't involve loan payments and interest rates.

There are two categories we examine: Three things you need to do only once and three things you need to do every time you work a problem. The things you need to do just once deal with the following calculator settings:

1. *Make sure your calculator is set to display a large number of decimal places.* Most financial calculators display only two decimal places; this causes problems because we frequently work with numbers—like interest rates—that are very small.

2. *Make sure your calculator is set to assume only one payment per period or per year.* Most financial calculators assume monthly payments (12 per year) unless you specify otherwise.

3. *Make sure your calculator is in "end" mode.* This is usually the default, but you can accidentally change to "begin" mode.

If you don't know how to set these three things, see Appendix D or your calculator's operating manual. There are also three things you need to do *every time you work a problem*:

1. *Before you start, completely clear out the calculator.* This is very important. Failure to do this is the number one reason for wrong answers; you must get in the habit of clearing the calculator every time you start a problem. How you do this depends on the calculator (see Appendix D), but you must do more than just clear the display. For example, on a Texas Instruments BA II Plus you must press **2nd** then **CLR TVM** for *clear time value of money*. There is a similar command on your calculator. Learn it!

   Note that turning the calculator off and back on won't do it. Most financial calculators remember everything you enter, even after you turn them off. In other words, they remember all your mistakes unless you explicitly clear them out. Also, if you are in the middle of a problem and make a mistake, *clear it out and start over*. Better to be safe than sorry.

2. *Put a negative sign on cash outflows.* Most financial calculators require you to put a negative sign on cash outflows and a positive sign on cash inflows. As a practical matter, this usually just means that you should enter the present value amount with a negative sign (because normally the present value represents the amount you give up today in exchange for cash inflows later). By the same token, when you solve for a present value, you shouldn't be surprised to see a negative sign.

3. *Enter the rate correctly.* Financial calculators assume that rates are quoted in percent, so if the rate is .08 (or 8 percent), you should enter 8, not .08.

If you follow these guidelines (especially the one about clearing out the calculator), you should have no problem using a financial calculator to work almost all of the problems in this and the next few chapters. We'll provide some additional examples and guidance where appropriate.

A NOTE ABOUT COMPOUND GROWTH

If you are considering depositing money in an interest-bearing account, then the interest rate on that account is just the rate at which your money grows, assuming you don't remove any of it. If that rate is 10 percent, then each year you have 10 percent more money than you had the year before. In this case, the interest rate is just an example of a compound growth rate.

The way we calculated future values is actually quite general and lets you answer some other types of questions related to growth. For example, say your company currently has 10,000 employees. You've estimated that the number of employees grows by 3 percent per year. How many employees will there be in five years? Here, we start with 10,000 people instead of dollars, and we don't think of the growth rate as an interest rate, but the calculation is exactly the same:

$$10{,}000 \times 1.03^5 = 10{,}000 \times 1.1593 = 11{,}593 \text{ employees}$$

There will be about 1,593 net new hires over the coming five years.

To give another example, according to the company, Walmart's 2016 sales were about $481 billion. Suppose sales are projected to increase at a rate of 15 percent per year. What will Walmart's sales be in the year 2021 if this is correct? Verify for yourself that the answer is about $968 billion—just over twice as large.

EXAMPLE 5.4   Dividend Growth

The TICO Corporation currently pays a cash dividend of $5 per share. You believe the dividend will be increased by 4 percent each year indefinitely. How big will the dividend be in eight years?

Here we have a cash dividend growing because it is being increased by management; but once again the calculation is the same:

Future value = $5 × 1.04⁸ = $5 × 1.3686 = $6.84

The dividend will grow by $1.84 over that period. Dividend growth is a subject we will return to in a later chapter.

Concept Questions

5.1a What do we mean by the future value of an investment?

5.1b What does it mean to compound interest? How does compound interest differ from simple interest?

5.1c In general, what is the future value of $1 invested at r per period for t periods?

5.2 Present Value and Discounting

Excel Master It!

xlsx Excel Master coverage online

When we discuss future value, we are thinking of questions like: What will my $2,000 investment grow to if it earns a 6.5 percent return every year for the next six years? The answer to this question is what we call the future value of $2,000 invested at 6.5 percent for six years (verify that the answer is about $2,918).

Another type of question that comes up even more often in financial management is obviously related to future value. Suppose you need to have $10,000 in 10 years, and you can earn 6.5 percent on your money. How much do you have to invest today to reach your goal? You can verify that the answer is $5,327.26. How do we know this? Read on.

THE SINGLE-PERIOD CASE

present value (PV)
The current value of future cash flows discounted at the appropriate discount rate.

We've seen that the future value of $1 invested for one year at 10 percent is $1.10. We now ask a slightly different question: How much do we have to invest today at 10 percent to get $1 in one year? In other words, we know the future value here is $1, but what is the **present value (PV)**? The answer isn't too hard to figure out. Whatever we invest today will be 1.1 times bigger at the end of the year. Because we need $1 at the end of the year:

Present value × 1.1 = $1

Or solving for the present value:

Present value = $1/1.1 = $.909

discount
Calculate the present value of some future amount.

In this case, the present value is the answer to the following question: What amount, invested today, will grow to $1 in one year if the interest rate is 10 percent? Present value is thus the reverse of future value. Instead of compounding the money forward into the future, we **discount** it back to the present.

Single-Period PV

EXAMPLE 5.5

Suppose you need $400 to buy textbooks next year. You can earn 7 percent on your money. How much do you have to put up today?

We need to know the PV of $400 in one year at 7 percent. Proceeding as in the previous example:

Present value × 1.07 = $400

We can now solve for the present value:

Present value = $400 × (1/1.07) = $373.83

Thus, $373.83 is the present value. Again, this means that investing this amount for one year at 7 percent will give you a future value of $400.

From our examples, the present value of $1 to be received in one period is generally given as follows:

$$PV = \$1 \times [1/(1 + r)] = \$1/(1 + r)$$

We next examine how to get the present value of an amount to be paid in two or more periods into the future.

PRESENT VALUES FOR MULTIPLE PERIODS

Suppose you need to have $1,000 in two years. If you can earn 7 percent, how much do you have to invest to make sure you have the $1,000 when you need it? In other words, what is the present value of $1,000 in two years if the relevant rate is 7 percent?

Based on your knowledge of future values, you know the amount invested must grow to $1,000 over the two years. In other words, it must be the case that:

$$\begin{aligned}\$1,000 &= PV \times 1.07 \times 1.07 \\ &= PV \times 1.07^2 \\ &= PV \times 1.1449\end{aligned}$$

Given this, we can solve for the present value:

Present value = $1,000/1.1449 = $873.44

Therefore, $873.44 is the amount you must invest to achieve your goal.

Saving Up

EXAMPLE 5.6

You would like to buy a new automobile. You have $50,000 or so, but the car costs $68,500. If you can earn 9 percent, how much do you have to invest today to buy the car in two years? Do you have enough? Assume the price will stay the same.

What we need to know is the present value of $68,500 to be paid in two years, assuming a 9 percent rate. Based on our discussion, this is:

$$PV = \$68,500/1.09^2 = \$68,500/1.1881 = \$57,655.08$$

You're still about $7,655 short, even if you're willing to wait two years.

TABLE 5.3

Present Value Interest Factors

Number of Periods	Interest Rate			
	5%	10%	15%	20%
1	.9524	.9091	.8696	.8333
2	.9070	.8264	.7561	.6944
3	.8638	.7513	.6575	.5787
4	.8227	.6830	.5718	.4823
5	.7835	.6209	.4972	.4019

As you have probably recognized by now, calculating present values is quite similar to calculating future values, and the general result looks much the same. The present value of $1 to be received t periods into the future at a discount rate of r is:

$$\text{PV} = \$1 \times [1/(1 + r)^t] = \$1/(1 + r)^t$$

5.2

The quantity in brackets, $1/(1 + r)^t$, goes by several different names. Because it's used to discount a future cash flow, it is often called a *discount factor*. With this name, it is not surprising that the rate used in the calculation is often called the **discount rate**. We will tend to call it this in talking about present values. The quantity in brackets is also called the *present value interest factor* (or just *present value factor*) for $1 at r percent for t periods and is sometimes abbreviated as PVIF(r, t). Finally, calculating the present value of a future cash flow to determine its worth today is commonly called **discounted cash flow (DCF) valuation**.

discount rate
The rate used to calculate the present value of future cash flows.

discounted cash flow (DCF) valuation
Calculating the present value of a future cash flow to determine its value today.

To illustrate, suppose you need $1,000 in three years. You can earn 15 percent on your money. How much do you have to invest today? To find out, we have to determine the present value of $1,000 in three years at 15 percent. We do this by discounting $1,000 back three periods at 15 percent. With these numbers, the discount factor is:

$$1/(1 + .15)^3 = 1/1.5209 = .6575$$

The amount you must invest is thus:

$$\$1,000 \times .6575 = \$657.50$$

We say that $657.50 is the present or discounted value of $1,000 to be received in three years at 15 percent.

There are tables for present value factors just as there are tables for future value factors, and you use them in the same way (if you use them at all). Table 5.3 contains a small set. A much larger set can be found in Table A.2 in the book's appendix.

In Table 5.3, the discount factor we just calculated (.6575) can be found by looking down the column labeled "15%" until you come to the third row.

CALCULATOR HINTS

You solve present value problems on a financial calculator just as you do future value problems. For the example we just examined (the present value of $1,000 to be received in three years at 15 percent), you would do the following:

Enter	3	15			1,000
	N	**I/Y**	**PMT**	**PV**	**FV**
Solve for				−657.52	

Notice that the answer has a negative sign; as we discussed earlier, that's because it represents an outflow today in exchange for the $1,000 inflow later.

Deceptive Advertising?

EXAMPLE 5.7

Businesses sometimes advertise that you should "Come try our product. If you do, we'll give you $100 just for coming by!" If you read the fine print, what you find out is that they will give you a savings certificate that will pay you $100 in 25 years or so. If the going interest rate on such certificates is 10 percent per year, how much are they really giving you today?

What you're actually getting is the present value of $100 to be paid in 25 years. If the discount rate is 10 percent per year, then the discount factor is:

$$1/1.1^{25} = 1/10.8347 = .0923$$

This tells you that a dollar in 25 years is worth a little more than nine cents today, assuming a 10 percent discount rate. Given this, the promotion is actually paying you about .0923 × $100 = $9.23. Maybe this is enough to draw customers, but it's not $100.

As the length of time until payment grows, present values decline. As Example 5.7 illustrates, present values tend to become small as the time horizon grows. If you look out far enough, they will always approach zero. Also, for a given length of time, the higher the discount rate is, the lower the present value will be. Put another way, present values and discount rates are inversely related. Increasing the discount rate decreases the PV and vice versa.

The relationship between time, discount rates, and present values is illustrated in Figure 5.3. Notice that by the time we get to 10 years, the present values are all substantially smaller than the future amounts.

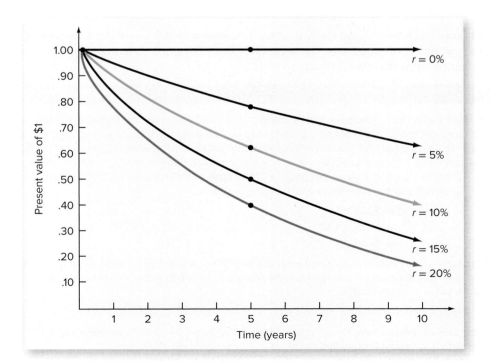

FIGURE 5.3

Present Value of $1 for Different Periods and Rates

5.3

Concept Questions

5.2a   What do we mean by the *present value* of an investment?

5.2b   The process of discounting a future amount back to the present is the opposite of doing what?

5.2c   What do we mean by *discounted cash flow*, or *DCF, valuation*?

5.2d   In general, what is the present value of $1 to be received in *t* periods, assuming a discount rate of *r* per period?

5.3 More about Present and Future Values

Excel Master It!

xlsx Excel Master coverage online

If you look back at the expressions we came up with for present and future values, you will see a simple relationship between the two. We explore this relationship and some related issues in this section.

PRESENT VERSUS FUTURE VALUE

What we called the present value factor is the reciprocal of (that is, 1 divided by) the future value factor:

$$\text{Future value factor} = (1 + r)^t$$

$$\text{Present value factor} = 1/(1 + r)^t$$

In fact, the easy way to calculate a present value factor on many calculators is to first calculate the future value factor and then press the "$1/x$" key to flip it over.

If we let FV_t stand for the future value after t periods, then the relationship between future value and present value can be written as one of the following:

$$\mathbf{PV \times (1 + r)^t = FV_t}$$
$$\mathbf{PV = FV_t / (1 + r)^t = FV_t \times [1/(1 + r)^t]}$$

This last result we will call the *basic present value equation*. We will use it throughout the text. A number of variations come up, but this simple equation underlies many of the most important ideas in corporate finance.

EXAMPLE 5.8   Evaluating Investments

To give you an idea of how we will be using present and future values, consider the following simple investment. Your company proposes to buy an asset for $335. This investment is very safe. You would sell off the asset in three years for $400. You know you could invest the $335 elsewhere at 10 percent with very little risk. What do you think of the proposed investment?

This is not a good investment. Why not? Because you can invest the $335 elsewhere at 10 percent. If you do, after three years it will grow to:

$$\$335 \times (1 + r)^t = \$335 \times 1.1^3$$
$$= \$335 \times 1.331$$
$$= \$445.89$$

Because the proposed investment pays out only $400, it is not as good as other alternatives we have. Another way of seeing the same thing is to notice that the present value of $400 in three years at 10 percent is:

$$\$400 \times [1/(1 + r)^t] = \$400/1.1^3 = \$400/1.331 = \$300.53$$

This tells us that we have to invest only about $300 to get $400 in three years, not $335. We will return to this type of analysis later on.

DETERMINING THE DISCOUNT RATE

We frequently need to determine what discount rate is implicit in an investment. We can do this by looking at the basic present value equation:

$$PV = FV_t/(1 + r)^t$$

There are only four parts to this equation: The present value (PV), the future value (FV$_t$), the discount rate (r), and the life of the investment (t). Given any three of these, we can always find the fourth.

For a downloadable, Windows-based financial calculator, go to **www.calculator.org**.

Finding *r* for a Single-Period Investment   EXAMPLE 5.9

You are considering a one-year investment. If you put up $1,250, you will get back $1,350. What rate is this investment paying?

First, in this single-period case, the answer is fairly obvious. You are getting a total of $100 in addition to your $1,250. The implicit rate on this investment is thus $100/$1,250 = 8 percent.

More formally, from the basic present value equation, the present value (the amount you must put up today) is $1,250. The future value (what the present value grows to) is $1,350. The time involved is one period, so we have:

$1,250 = $1,350/(1 + r)^1
$1 + r$ = $1,350/$1,250 = 1.08
r = .08, or 8%

In this simple case, of course, there was no need to go through this calculation. But as we describe next, it gets a little harder with more than one period.

To illustrate what happens with multiple periods, let's say we are offered an investment that costs us $100 and will double our money in eight years. To compare this to other investments, we would like to know what discount rate is implicit in these numbers. This discount rate is called the *rate of return*, or sometimes just the *return*, on the investment. In this case, we have a present value of $100, a future value of $200 (double our money), and an eight-year life. To calculate the return, we can write the basic present value equation as:

$$PV = FV_t /(1 + r)^t$$
$$\$100 = \$200/(1 + r)^8$$

It could also be written as:

$$(1 + r)^8 = \$200/\$100 = 2$$

We now need to solve for r. There are three ways to do this:

1. Use a financial calculator.
2. Solve the equation for $1 + r$ by taking the eighth root of both sides. Because this is the same thing as raising both sides to the power of ⅛ or .125, this is actually easy to do with the "y^x" key on a calculator. Just enter 2, then press "y^x," enter .125, and press the "=" key. The eighth root should be about 1.09, which implies that r is 9 percent.
3. Use a future value table. The future value factor after eight years is equal to 2. If you look across the row corresponding to eight periods in Table A.1, you will see that a future value factor of 2 corresponds to the 9 percent column, again implying that the return here is 9 percent.

Actually, in this particular example, there is a useful "back of the envelope" means of solving for r—the Rule of 72. For reasonable rates of return, the time it takes to double your money is given approximately by $72/r\%$. In our example, this means that $72/r\% = 8$ years, implying that r is 9 percent, as we calculated. This rule is fairly accurate for discount rates in the 5 percent to 20 percent range.

EXAMPLE 5.10   **Sneakers as Investments**

In December 2016, a pair of game-worn shoes with graffiti-style writing that said "Oakland Strong" used by Stephen Curry were auctioned off to benefit the Oakland Fire Relief Fund. The shoes sold for $30,101. The record for game-worn shoes by an active NBA player is $37,740 for a pair of Kobe Bryant shoes used in the 2008 Olympics. "Experts" often argue that collectibles such as this will double in value over a 10-year period.

So were the sneakers a good investment? By the Rule of 72, you already know the experts were predicting that the sneakers would double in value in 10 years; so the return predicted would be about $72/10 = 7.2$ percent per year, which is only so-so.

Why does the Rule of 72 work? See **www.moneychimp.com**.

At one time at least, a rule of thumb in the rarefied world of fine art collecting was "your money back in 5 years, double your money in 10 years." Given this, let's see how an investment stacked up. In 2013, the Pablo Picasso painting *Le Rêve* was sold for $155 million. The painting had reached a level of notoriety in part because its owner, casino magnate Steve Wynn, had put his elbow through the middle of the painting. Wynn had purchased the painting 12 years earlier in 2001 for an estimated $60 million. So was Wynn's gamble a winner?

The rule of thumb has us doubling our money in 10 years; so, from the Rule of 72, we have that 7.2 percent per year was the norm. The painting was resold in about 12 years. The present value is $60 million, and the future value is $155 million. We need to solve for the unknown rate, r, as follows:

$$\$60,000,000 = \$155,000,000/(1 + r)^{12}$$
$$(1 + r)^{12} = 2.5833$$

Solving for r, we find that Wynn earned about 8.23 percent per year—a little better than the 7.2 percent rule of thumb.

What about other collectibles? To a philatelist (a stamp collector to you and us), one of the most prized stamps is the 1918 24-cent inverted Jenny C3a. The stamp is a collectible because it has a picture of an upside-down biplane. One of these stamps sold at auction for $1,175,000 in 2016. At what rate did its value grow? Verify for yourself that the answer is about 17.02 percent, assuming a 98-year period.

Collectible autos can also have good returns. For example, a 1939 Alfa Romeo 8C 2900B Lungo Spider was reported to have sold for £1,150 when it was brand new. When it was auctioned in 2016, it became the most expensive prewar car to date when it sold for £19.8 million. Assuming that 77 years had passed, see if you don't agree that the increase in the value of the car was 13.50 percent per year.

Not all collectibles do as well. In 2016, a 1792 Silver Center Cent, believed to be the first coin produced outside the U.S. Mint, was auctioned for $352,500. While this seems like a huge return to the untrained eye, check that, over the 224-year period, the gain was only about 8.07 percent.

One of the rarest coins is the 1894-S dime, struck at the San Francisco mint. Only 24 were ever produced, with nine believed to be still in existence. In 2016, one of these dimes sold at auction for $2 million. See if you agree that this collectible gained about 14.77 percent per year.

A slightly more extreme example involves money bequeathed by Benjamin Franklin, who died on April 17, 1790. In his will, he gave 1,000 pounds sterling to Massachusetts and the city of Boston. He gave a like amount to Pennsylvania and the city of Philadelphia. The money had been paid to Franklin when he held political office, but he believed that politicians should not be paid for their service (it appears that this view is not widely shared by modern politicians).

Franklin originally specified that the money should be paid out 100 years after his death and used to train young people. Later, however, after some legal wrangling, it was agreed that the money would be paid out in 1990, 200 years after Franklin's death. By that time, the Pennsylvania bequest had grown to about $2 million; the Massachusetts bequest had grown to $4.5 million. The money was used to fund the Franklin Institutes in Boston and Philadelphia. Assuming that 1,000 pounds sterling was equivalent to $1,000, what rate of return did the two states earn? (The dollar did not become the official U.S. currency until 1792.)

For Pennsylvania, the future value is $2 million and the present value is $1,000. There are 200 years involved, so we need to solve for r in the following:

$$\$1,000 = \$2 \text{ million}/(1 + r)^{200}$$
$$(1 + r)^{200} = 2,000$$

Solving for r, we see that the Pennsylvania money grew at about 3.87 percent per year. The Massachusetts money did better; verify that the rate of return in this case was 4.3 percent. Small differences in returns can add up!

CALCULATOR HINTS

We can illustrate how to calculate unknown rates using a financial calculator with these numbers. For Pennsylvania, you would do the following:

Enter	200			−1,000	2,000,000
	N	**I/Y**	**PMT**	**PV**	**FV**
Solve for		3.87			

As in our previous examples, notice the minus sign on the present value, representing Franklin's outlay made many years ago. What do you change to work the problem for Massachusetts?

Saving for College

EXAMPLE 5.11

You estimate that you will need about $80,000 to send your child to college in eight years. You have about $35,000 now. If you can earn 20 percent per year, will you make it? At what rate will you just reach your goal?

If you can earn 20 percent, the future value of your $35,000 in eight years will be:

$$FV = \$35,000 \times 1.20^8 = \$35,000 \times 4.2998 = \$150,493.59$$

So, you will make it easily. The minimum rate is the unknown *r* in the following:

$$FV = \$35,000 \times (1 + r)^8 = \$80,000$$

$$(1 + r)^8 = \$80,000/\$35,000 = 2.2857$$

Therefore, the future value factor is 2.2857. Looking at the row in Table A.1 that corresponds to eight periods, we see that our future value factor is roughly halfway between the ones shown for 10 percent (2.1436) and 12 percent (2.4760), so you will just reach your goal if you earn approximately 11 percent. To get the exact answer, we could use a financial calculator or we could solve for *r*:

$$(1 + r)^8 = \$80,000/\$35,000 = 2.2857$$

$$1 + r = 2.2857^{1/8} = 2.2857^{.125} = 1.1089$$

$$r = .1089, \text{ or } 10.89\%$$

EXAMPLE 5.12   **Only 18,262.5 Days to Retirement**

You would like to retire in 50 years as a millionaire. If you have $10,000 today, what rate of return do you need to earn to achieve your goal?

The future value is $1,000,000. The present value is $10,000, and there are 50 years until payment. We need to calculate the unknown discount rate in the following:

$$\$10,000 = \$1,000,000/(1 + r)^{50}$$

$$(1 + r)^{50} = 100$$

The future value factor is thus 100. You can verify that the implicit rate is about 9.65 percent.

Not taking the time value of money into account when computing growth rates or rates of return often leads to some misleading numbers in the real world. For example, the most loved (and hated) team in baseball, the New York Yankees, had the highest payroll during the 1988 season, about $19 million. In 2016, the Los Angeles Dodgers had the highest payroll, a staggering $223 million—an increase of 1,074 percent! If history is any guide, we can get a rough idea of the future growth in baseball payrolls. See if you don't agree that this represents an annual increase of 9.19 percent, a substantial growth rate, but much less than the gaudy 1,074 percent.

How about classic maps? A few years ago, the first map of America, printed in Rome in 1507, was valued at about $135,000, 69 percent more than the $80,000 it was worth 10 years earlier. Your return on investment if you were the proud owner of the map over those 10 years? Verify that it's about 5.4 percent per year—far worse than the 69 percent reported increase in price.

Whether with maps or baseball payrolls, it's easy to be misled when returns are quoted without considering the time value of money. However, it's not just the uninitiated who are guilty of this slight form of deception. The title of a feature article in a leading business magazine predicted the Dow Jones Industrial Average would soar to a 70 percent gain over the coming five years. Do you think it meant a 70 percent return per year on your money? Think again!

FINDING THE NUMBER OF PERIODS

Suppose we are interested in purchasing an asset that costs $50,000. We currently have $25,000. If we can earn 12 percent on this $25,000, how long until we have the $50,000?

Finding the answer involves solving for the last variable in the basic present value equation, the number of periods. You already know how to get an approximate answer to this particular problem. Notice that we need to double our money. From the Rule of 72, this will take about $72/12 = 6$ years at 12 percent.

To come up with the exact answer, we can again manipulate the basic present value equation. The present value is $25,000, and the future value is $50,000. With a 12 percent discount rate, the basic equation takes one of the following forms:

$$\$25{,}000 = \$50{,}000/1.12^t$$

$$\$50{,}000/\$25{,}000 = 1.12^t = 2$$

We thus have a future value factor of 2 for a 12 percent rate. We now need to solve for t. If you look down the column in Table A.1 that corresponds to 12 percent, you will see that a future value factor of 1.9738 occurs at six periods. It will thus take about six years, as we calculated. To get the exact answer, we have to explicitly solve for t (or use a financial calculator). If you do this, you will see that the answer is 6.1163 years, so our approximation was quite close in this case.

CALCULATOR HINTS

If you use a financial calculator, here are the relevant entries:

Enter		12		-25,000	50,000
	N	**I/Y**	**PMT**	**PV**	**FV**
Solve for	6.1163				

Waiting for Godot   **EXAMPLE 5.13**

You've been saving up to buy the Godot Company. The total cost will be $10 million. You currently have about $2.3 million. If you can earn 5 percent on your money, how long will you have to wait? At 16 percent, how long must you wait?

At 5 percent, you'll have to wait a long time. From the basic present value equation:

$$\$2.3 \text{ million} = \$10 \text{ million}/1.05^t$$

$$1.05^t = 4.35$$

$$t = 30 \text{ years}$$

At 16 percent, things are a little better. Verify for yourself that it will take about 10 years.

Consider the U.S. EE Savings Bonds that we discussed at the beginning of the chapter. You purchase them for half of their $50 face value. In other words, you pay $25 today and get $50 at some point in the future when the bond "matures." You receive no interest in between, and the interest rate is adjusted every six months, so the length of time until your $25 grows to $50 depends on future interest rates. However, at worst, the bonds are guaranteed to be worth $50 at the end of 20 years, so this is the longest you would ever have to wait. If you do have to wait the full 20 years, what rate do you earn?

Learn more about using Excel for time value and other calculations at **www.studyfinance.com.**

TABLE 5.4

Summary of Time Value Calculations

I. Symbols:
PV = Present value, what future cash flows are worth today FV_t = Future value, what cash flows are worth in the future r = Interest rate, rate of return, or discount rate per period—typically, but not always, one year t = Number of periods—typically, but not always, the number of years C = Cash amount
II. Future Value of C Invested at r Percent for t Periods:
$FV_t = C \times (1 + r)^t$ The term $(1 + r)^t$ is called the *future value factor*.
III. Present Value of C to Be Received in t Periods at r Percent per Period:
$PV = C/(1 + r)^t$ The term $1/(1 + r)^t$ is called the *present value factor*.
IV. The Basic Present Value Equation Giving the Relationship between Present and Future Value:
$PV = FV_t/(1 + r)^t$

Because this investment is doubling in value in 20 years, the Rule of 72 tells you the answer right away: $72/20 = .036$, or 3.6%. Remember, this is the *minimum* guaranteed return, so you might do better. This example finishes our introduction to basic time value concepts. Table 5.4 summarizes present and future value calculations for future reference. As our nearby *Work the Web* box shows, online calculators are widely available to handle these calculations; however, it is still important to know what is really going on.

SPREADSHEET STRATEGIES

Using a Spreadsheet for Time Value of Money Calculations

More and more, businesspeople from many different areas (not just finance and accounting) rely on spreadsheets to do all the different types of calculations that come up in the real world. As a result, in this section, we will show you how to use a spreadsheet to handle the various time value of money problems we presented in this chapter. We will use Microsoft Excel™, but the commands are similar for other types of software. We assume you are already familiar with basic spreadsheet operations.

As we have seen, you can solve for any one of the following four potential unknowns: Future value, present value, the discount rate, or the number of periods. With a spreadsheet, there is a separate formula for each. In Excel, these are shown in a nearby box.

In these formulas, *pv* and *fv* are present and future value, respectively; *nper* is the number of periods; and *rate* is the discount, or interest, rate. We will talk about *pmt* in the next chapter.

Two things are a little tricky here. First, unlike a financial calculator, the spreadsheet requires that the rate be entered as a decimal. Second, as with most financial

To Find	Enter This Formula
Future value	= FV (rate,nper,pmt,pv)
Present value	= PV (rate,nper,pmt,fv)
Discount rate	= RATE (nper,pmt,pv,fv)
Number of periods	= NPER (rate,pmt,pv,fv)

calculators, you have to put a negative sign on either the present value or the future value to solve for the rate or the number of periods. For the same reason, if you solve for a present value, the answer will have a negative sign unless you input a negative future value. The same is true when you compute a future value.

To illustrate how you might use these formulas, we will go back to an example in the chapter. If you invest $25,000 at 12 percent per year, how long until you have $50,000? You might set up a spreadsheet like this:

	A	B	C	D	E	F	G	H
1								
2	Using a spreadsheet for time value of money calculations							
3								
4	If we invest $25,000 at 12 percent, how long until we have $50,000? We need to solve							
5	for the unknown number of periods, so we use the formula NPER(rate,pmt,pv,fv).							
6								
7	Present value (pv):	$25,000						
8	Future value (fv):	$50,000						
9	Rate (rate):	.12						
10								
11	Periods:	**6.1162554**						
12								
13	The formula entered in cell B11 is =NPER(B9,0,-B7,B8); notice that pmt is zero and that pv							
14	has a negative sign on it. Also notice that rate is entered as a decimal, not a percentage.							

SOURCE: Microsoft Excel

Concept Questions

5.3a   What is the basic present value equation?

5.3b   What is the Rule of 72?

WORK THE WEB

How important is the time value of money? A recent search on one web search engine returned over 689 million hits! Although you must understand the calculations behind the time value of money, the advent of financial calculators and spreadsheets has eliminated the need for tedious calculations. In fact, many websites offer time value of money calculators. The following is one example from www .investopedia.com.

You have $20,000 today and will invest it at 9.75 percent for 40 years. How much will it be worth at that time? With the Investopedia calculator, you enter the values and hit "Calculate". The results look like this:

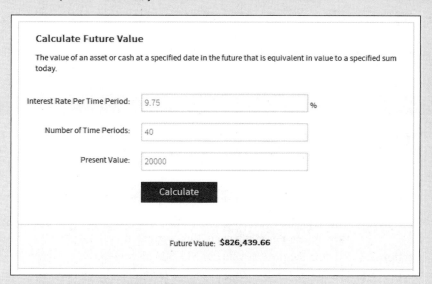

Calculate Future Value

The value of an asset or cash at a specified date in the future that is equivalent in value to a specified sum today.

Interest Rate Per Time Period: 9.75   %

Number of Time Periods: 40

Present Value: 20000

[Calculate]

Future Value: **$826,439.66**

Who said time value of money calculations are hard?

Questions
1. Use the present value calculator on this website to answer the following: Suppose you want to have $140,000 in 25 years. If you can earn a 10 percent return, how much do you have to invest today?
2. Use the future value calculator on this website to answer the following question: Suppose you have $8,000 today that you plan to save for your retirement in 40 years. If you earn a return of 10.8 percent per year, how much will this account be worth when you are ready to retire?

5.4 Summary and Conclusions

This chapter has introduced you to the basic principles of present value and discounted cash flow valuation. In it, we explained a number of things about the time value of money, including these:

1. For a given rate of return, we can determine the value at some point in the future of an investment made today by calculating the future value of that investment.

2. We can determine the current worth of a future cash flow or series of cash flows for a given rate of return by calculating the present value of the cash flow(s) involved.

3. The relationship between present value (PV) and future value (FV) for a given rate r and time t is given by the basic present value equation:

$$PV = FV_t/(1 + r)^t$$

As we have shown, it is possible to find any one of the four components (PV, FV$_t$, r, or t) given the other three.

The principles developed in this chapter will figure prominently in the chapters to come. The reason for this is that most investments, whether they involve real assets or financial assets, can be analyzed using the discounted cash flow (DCF) approach. As a result, the DCF approach is broadly applicable and widely used in practice. Before going on you might want to do some of the problems that follow.

CONNECT TO FINANCE

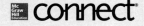 *Connect Finance* offers you plenty of opportunities to practice mastering time value of money concepts. Log on to connect.mheducation.com to learn more. If you like what you see, ask your professor about using *Connect Finance!*

Can you answer the following *Connect* Quiz questions?

Section 5.1 You deposited $2,000 in a bank account that pays 5 percent simple interest. How much will you have in this account after three years?

Section 5.2 What is the present value of $11,500 discounted at 9 percent for 11 years?

Section 5.3 Charlie invested $6,200 in a stock last year. Currently, this investment is worth $6,788.38. What is the rate of return on this investment?

CHAPTER REVIEW AND SELF-TEST PROBLEMS

5.1 **Calculating Future Values** Assume you deposit $10,000 today in an account that pays 6 percent interest. How much will you have in five years?

5.2 **Calculating Present Values** Suppose you have just celebrated your 19th birthday. A rich uncle has set up a trust fund for you that will pay you $150,000 when you turn 30. If the relevant discount rate is 9 percent, how much is this fund worth today?

5.3 **Calculating Rates of Return** You've been offered an investment that will double your money in 10 years. What rate of return are you being offered? Check your answer using the Rule of 72.

5.4 **Calculating the Number of Periods** You've been offered an investment that will pay you 9 percent per year. If you invest $15,000, how long until you have $30,000? How long until you have $45,000?

ANSWERS TO CHAPTER REVIEW AND SELF-TEST PROBLEMS

5.1 We need to calculate the future value of $10,000 at 6 percent for five years. The future value factor is:

$$1.06^5 = 1.3382$$

The future value is thus $10,000 \times 1.3382 = \$13,382.26$.

5.2 We need the present value of $150,000 to be paid in 11 years at 9 percent. The discount factor is:

$$1/1.09^{11} = 1/2.5804 = .3875$$

The present value is thus about $58,130.

5.3 Suppose you invest $1,000. You will have $2,000 in 10 years with this investment. So, $1,000 is the amount you have today, or the present value, and $2,000 is the amount you will have in 10 years, or the future value. From the basic present value equation, we have:

$$\$2,000 = \$1,000 \times (1 + r)^{10}$$
$$2 = (1 + r)^{10}$$

From here, we need to solve for r, the unknown rate. As shown in the chapter, there are several different ways to do this. We will take the 10th root of 2 (by raising 2 to the power of 1/10):

$$2^{1/10} = 1 + r$$
$$1.0718 = 1 + r$$
$$r = .0718, \text{ or } 7.18\%$$

Using the Rule of 72, we have $72/t = r\%$, or $72/10 = .072$, or 7.2%; so, our answer looks good (remember that the Rule of 72 is only an approximation).

5.4 The basic equation is this:

$$\$30,000 = \$15,000 \times (1 + .09)^t$$
$$2 = (1 + .09)^t$$

If we solve for t, we find that $t = 8.04$ years. Using the Rule of 72, we get $72/9 = 8$ years, so once again our answer looks good. To get $45,000, verify for yourself that you will have to wait 12.75 years.

CONCEPTS REVIEW AND CRITICAL THINKING QUESTIONS

1. **Present Value [LO2]** The basic present value equation has four parts. What are they?

2. **Compounding [LO1, 2]** What is compounding? What is discounting?

3. **Compounding and Periods [LO1, 2]** As you increase the length of time involved, what happens to future values? What happens to present values?

4. **Compounding and Interest Rates [LO1, 2]** What happens to a future value if you increase the rate r? What happens to a present value?

5. **Ethical Considerations [LO2]** Take a look back at Example 5.7. Is it deceptive advertising? Is it unethical to advertise a future value like this without a disclaimer?

Use the following information for Questions 6–10:

On March 28, 2008, Toyota Motor Credit Corporation (TMCC), a subsidiary of Toyota Motor, offered some securities for sale to the public. Under the terms of the deal, TMCC promised to repay the owner of one of these securities $100,000 on March 28, 2038, but investors would receive nothing until then. Investors paid TMCC $24,099 for each of these securities; so they gave up $24,099 on March 28, 2008, for the promise of a $100,000 payment 30 years later.

6. **Time Value of Money [LO2]** Why would TMCC be willing to accept such a small amount today ($24,099) in exchange for a promise to repay about four times that amount ($100,000) in the future?

7. **Call Provisions [LO2]** TMCC has the right to buy back the securities on the anniversary date at a price established when the securities were issued (this feature is a term of this particular deal). What impact does this feature have on the desirability of this security as an investment?

8. **Time Value of Money [LO2]** Would you be willing to pay $24,099 today in exchange for $100,000 in 30 years? What would be the key considerations in answering yes or no? Would your answer depend on who is making the promise to repay?

9. **Investment Comparison [LO2]** Suppose that when TMCC offered the security for $24,099, the U.S. Treasury had offered an essentially identical security. Do you think it would have had a higher or lower price? Why?

10. **Length of Investment [LO2]** The TMCC security is bought and sold on the New York Stock Exchange. If you looked at the price today, do you think the price would exceed the $24,099 original price? Why? If you looked in the year 2019, do you think the price would be higher or lower than today's price? Why?

QUESTIONS AND PROBLEMS

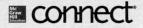

BASIC

(Questions 1–14)

1. **Simple Interest versus Compound Interest [LO1]** First City Bank pays 9 percent simple interest on its savings account balances, whereas Second City Bank pays 9 percent interest compounded annually. If you made a deposit of $7,500 in each bank, how much more money would you earn from your Second City Bank account at the end of eight years?

2. **Calculating Future Values [LO1]** For each of the following, compute the future value:

Present Value	Years	Interest Rate	Future Value
$ 2,328	11	13%	
7,513	7	9	
74,381	14	12	
192,050	16	6	

3. **Calculating Present Values [LO2]** For each of the following, compute the present value:

Present Value	Years	Interest Rate	Future Value
	13	9%	$ 16,832
	4	7	48,318
	29	13	886,073
	40	21	550,164

4. **Calculating Interest Rates [LO3]** Solve for the unknown interest rate in each of the following:

Present Value	Years	Interest Rate	Future Value
$ 181	5		$ 317
335	17		1,080
48,000	13		185,382
40,353	30		531,618

5. **Calculating the Number of Periods [LO4]** Solve for the unknown number of years in each of the following:

Present Value	Years	Interest Rate	Future Value
$ 560		7%	$ 1,389
810		8	1,821
18,400		9	289,715
21,500		11	430,258

6. **Calculating Interest Rates [LO3]** Assume the total cost of a college education will be $345,000 when your child enters college in 18 years. You presently have $73,000 to invest. What annual rate of interest must you earn on your investment to cover the cost of your child's college education?

7. **Calculating the Number of Periods [LO4]** At 6.1 percent interest, how long does it take to double your money? To quadruple it?

8. **Calculating Interest Rates [LO3]** According to the Census Bureau, in October 2016, the average house price in the United States was $354,900. In October 2000, the average price was $215,100. What was the annual increase in the price of the average house sold?

9. **Calculating the Number of Periods [LO4]** You're trying to save to buy a new $245,000 Ferrari. You have $50,000 today that can be invested at your bank. The bank pays 4.3 percent annual interest on its accounts. How long will it be before you have enough to buy the car?

10. **Calculating Present Values [LO2]** Imprudential, Inc., has an unfunded pension liability of $415 million that must be paid in 20 years. To assess the value of the firm's stock, financial analysts want to discount this liability back to the present. If the relevant discount rate is 5.2 percent, what is the present value of this liability?

11. **Calculating Present Values [LO2]** You have just received notification that you have won the $2 million first prize in the Centennial Lottery. However, the prize will be awarded on your 100th birthday (assuming you're around to collect), 80 years from now. What is the present value of your windfall if the appropriate discount rate is 8.4 percent?

12. **Calculating Future Values [LO1]** Your coin collection contains fifty 1952 silver dollars. If your grandparents purchased them for their face value when they were new, how much will your collection be worth when you retire in 2067, assuming they appreciate at an annual rate of 4.3 percent?

13. **Calculating Interest Rates and Future Values [LO1, 3]** In 1895, the first U.S. Open Golf Championship was held. The winner's prize money was $150. In 2016, the winner's check was $1,800,000. What was the percentage increase per year in the winner's check over this period? If the winner's prize increases at the same rate, what will it be in 2040?

14. **Calculating Rates of Return [LO3]** Although appealing to more refined tastes, art as a collectible has not always performed so profitably. During 2003, Sotheby's sold the Edgar Degas bronze sculpture *Petite Danseuse de Quatorze Ans* at auction for a price of $10,311,500. Unfortunately for the previous owner, he had purchased it in 1999 at a price of $12,377,500. What was his annual rate of return on this sculpture?

INTERMEDIATE
(Questions 15–20)

15. **Calculating Rates of Return [LO3]** The "Brasher doubloon," which was featured in the plot of the Raymond Chandler novel, *The High Window*, was sold at auction in 2014 for $4,582,500. The coin had a face value of $15 when it was first issued in 1787 and had been previously sold for $430,000 in 1979. At what annual rate did the coin appreciate from its minting to the 1979 sale? What annual rate did the 1979 buyer earn on his purchase? At what annual rate did the coin appreciate from its minting to the 2014 sale?

16. **Calculating Rates of Return [LO3]** Refer back to the Series EE savings bonds we discussed at the very beginning of the chapter.

    a. Assuming you purchased a $50 face value bond, what is the exact rate of return you would earn if you held the bond for 20 years until it doubled in value?

    b. If you purchased a $50 face value bond in early 2017 at the then current interest rate of .10 percent per year, how much would the bond be worth in 2027?

    c. In 2027, instead of cashing the bond in for its then current value, you decide to hold the bond until it doubles in face value in 2037. What rate of return will you earn over the last 10 years?

17. **Calculating Present Values [LO2]** Suppose you are still committed to owning a $245,000 Ferrari (see Problem 9). If you believe your mutual fund can achieve an annual rate of return of 11.2 percent and you want to buy the car in 9 years (on the day you turn 30), how much must you invest today?

18. **Calculating Future Values [LO1]** You have just made your first $5,500 contribution to your retirement account. Assuming you earn a return of 10 percent per year and make no additional contributions, what will your account be worth when you retire in 45 years? What if you wait 10 years before contributing? (Does this suggest an investment strategy?)

19. **Calculating Future Values [LO1]** You are scheduled to receive $20,000 in two years. When you receive it, you will invest it for six more years at 6.8 percent per year. How much will you have in eight years?

20. **Calculating the Number of Periods [LO4]** You expect to receive $10,000 at graduation in two years. You plan on investing it at 9 percent until you have $60,000. How long will you wait from now?

Discounted Cash Flow Valuation

THE SIGNING OF BIG-NAME ATHLETES is frequently accompanied by great fanfare, but the numbers are often misleading. For example, in late 2016, catcher Jason Castro reached a deal with the Minnesota Twins, signing a contract with a reported value of $24.5 million. Not bad, especially for someone who makes a living using the "tools of ignorance" (jock jargon for a catcher's equipment). Another example is the contract signed by DeMar DeRozan with the Toronto Raptors, which had a stated value of $139 million.

It looks like Jason and DeMar did pretty well, but now consider Andrew Luck, who signed to play in front of the Indianapolis Colts' fans. Andrew's contract also had a stated value of about $139 million, but this amount was actually payable over several years. The contract consisted of a $6.4 million signing bonus, along with $12 million in salary in the first year plus $120.725 million in future salary to be paid in the years 2017 through 2021. The payments to Jason and DeMar were similarly spread over time.

Because all three contracts call for payments to be made at future dates, we must consider the time value of money, which means none of these players received the quoted amounts. How much did they really get? This chapter gives you the "tools of knowledge" to answer this question.

Learning Objectives

After studying this chapter, you should be able to:

LO1 Determine the future and present value of investments with multiple cash flows.

LO2 Explain how loan payments are calculated and how to find the interest rate on a loan.

LO3 Describe how loans are amortized or paid off.

LO4 Show how interest rates are quoted (and misquoted).

©by_adri/iStockPhotoGettyImages

For updates on the latest happenings in finance, visit fundamentalsofcorporatefinance.blogspot.com.

In our previous chapter, we covered the basics of discounted cash flow valuation. However, so far, we have dealt with only single cash flows. In reality, most investments have multiple cash flows. For example, if Target is thinking of opening a new department store, there will be a large cash outlay in the beginning and then cash inflows for many years. In this chapter, we begin to explore how to value such investments.

When you finish this chapter, you should have some very practical skills. For example, you will know how to calculate your own car payments or student loan payments. You will also be able to determine how long it will take to pay off a credit card if you make the minimum payment each month (a practice we do not recommend). We will show you how to compare interest rates to determine which are the highest and which are the lowest, and we will also show you how interest rates can be quoted in different—and at times deceptive—ways.

FIGURE 6.1

Drawing and Using a Time Line

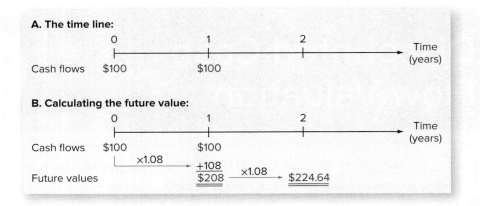

A. The time line:

B. Calculating the future value:

6.1 Future and Present Values of Multiple Cash Flows

Excel Master It!

xlsx Excel Master coverage online

Thus far, we have restricted our attention to either the future value of a lump sum present amount or the present value of some single future cash flow. In this section, we begin to study ways to value multiple cash flows. We start with future value.

FUTURE VALUE WITH MULTIPLE CASH FLOWS

Suppose you deposit $100 today in an account paying 8 percent interest. In one year, you will deposit another $100. How much will you have in two years? This particular problem is relatively easy. At the end of the first year, you will have $108 plus the second $100 you deposit, for a total of $208. You leave this $208 on deposit at 8 percent for another year. At the end of this second year, it is worth:

$208 × 1.08 = $224.64

Figure 6.1 is a *time line* that illustrates the process of calculating the future value of these two $100 deposits. Figures such as this are useful for solving complicated problems. Almost anytime you are having trouble with a present or future value problem, drawing a time line will help you see what is happening.

In the first part of Figure 6.1, we show the cash flows on the time line. The most important thing is that we write them down where they actually occur. Here, the first cash flow occurs today, which we label as Time 0. We therefore put $100 at Time 0 on the time line. The second $100 cash flow occurs one year from today, so we write it down at the point labeled as Time 1. In the second part of Figure 6.1, we calculate the future values one period at a time to come up with the final $224.64.

EXAMPLE 6.1 | **Saving Up Revisited**

You think you will be able to deposit $4,000 at the end of each of the next three years in a bank account paying 8 percent interest. You currently have $7,000 in the account. How much will you have in three years? In four years?

At the end of the first year, you will have:

$7,000 × 1.08 + 4,000 = $11,560

At the end of the second year, you will have:

$11,560 × 1.08 + 4,000 = $16,484.80

Repeating this for the third year gives:

$16,484.80 × 1.08 + 4,000 = $21,803.58

Therefore, you will have $21,803.58 in three years. If you leave this on deposit for one more year (and don't add to it), at the end of the fourth year, you'll have:

$21,803.58 × 1.08 = $23,547.87

When we calculated the future value of the two $100 deposits, we calculated the balance as of the beginning of each year and then rolled that amount forward to the next year. We could have done it another, quicker way. The first $100 is on deposit for two years at 8 percent, so its future value is:

$100 × 1.08² = $100 × 1.1664 = $116.64

The second $100 is on deposit for one year at 8 percent, and its future value is thus:

$100 × 1.08 = $108

The total future value, as we previously calculated, is equal to the sum of these two future values:

$116.64 + 108 = $224.64

Based on this example, there are two ways to calculate future values for multiple cash flows: (1) Compound the accumulated balance forward one year at a time or (2) calculate the future value of each cash flow first and then add them up. Both give the same answer, so you can do it either way.

To illustrate the two different ways of calculating future values, consider the future value of $2,000 invested at the end of each of the next five years. The current balance is zero, and the rate is 10 percent. We first draw a time line, as shown in Figure 6.2.

On the time line, notice that nothing happens until the end of the first year, when we make the first $2,000 investment. This first $2,000 earns interest for the next four (not five) years. Also notice that the last $2,000 is invested at the end of the fifth year, so it earns no interest at all.

Figure 6.3 illustrates the calculations involved if we compound the investment one period at a time. As illustrated, the future value is $12,210.20.

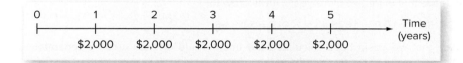

FIGURE 6.2

Time Line for $2,000 per Year for Five Years

FIGURE 6.3   **Future Value Calculated by Compounding Forward One Period at a Time**

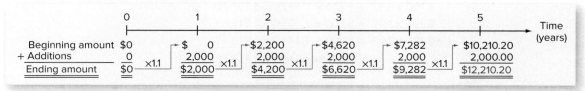

FIGURE 6.4   **Future Value Calculated by Compounding Each Cash Flow Separately**

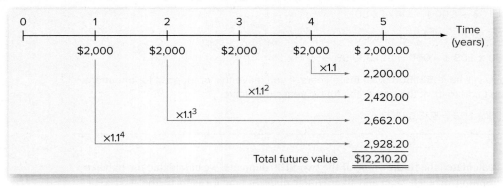

Figure 6.4 goes through the same calculations, but the second technique is used. Naturally, the answer is the same.

EXAMPLE 6.2   **Saving Up Once Again**

If you deposit $100 in one year, $200 in two years, and $300 in three years, how much will you have in three years? How much of this is interest? How much will you have in five years if you don't add additional amounts? Assume a 7 percent interest rate throughout.

We will calculate the future value of each amount in three years. Notice that the $100 earns interest for two years, and the $200 earns interest for one year. The final $300 earns no interest. The future values are thus:

$$\begin{aligned} \$100 \times 1.07^2 &= \$114.49 \\ \$200 \times 1.07 &= 214.00 \\ +\$300 &= \underline{300.00} \\ \text{Total future value} &= \underline{\underline{\$628.49}} \end{aligned}$$

The total future value is thus $628.49. The total interest is:

$628.49 − (100 + 200 + 300) = $28.49

How much will you have in five years? We know that you will have $628.49 in three years. If you leave that in for two more years, it will grow to:

$628.49 × 1.07² = $628.49 × 1.1449 = $719.56

Notice that we could have calculated the future value of each amount separately. Once again, be careful about the lengths of time. As we previously calculated, the first $100 earns interest for only four years, the second ($200) deposit earns three years' interest, and the last ($300) deposit earns two years' interest:

$$\begin{aligned} \$100 \times 1.07^4 &= \$100 \times 1.3108 = \$131.08 \\ \$200 \times 1.07^3 &= \$200 \times 1.2250 = 245.01 \\ +\$300 \times 1.07^2 &= \$300 \times 1.1449 = \underline{343.47} \\ \text{Total future value} &= \underline{\underline{\$719.56}} \end{aligned}$$

PRESENT VALUE WITH MULTIPLE CASH FLOWS

We often need to determine the present value of a series of future cash flows. As with future values, there are two ways we can do it. We can either discount back one period at a time, or we can calculate the present values individually and add them up.

Suppose you need $1,000 in one year and $2,000 more in two years. If you can earn 9 percent on your money, how much do you have to put up today to exactly cover these amounts in the future? In other words, what is the present value of the two cash flows at 9 percent?

The present value of $2,000 in two years at 9 percent is:

$$\$2,000/1.09^2 = \$1,683.36$$

The present value of $1,000 in one year at 9 percent is:

$$\$1,000/1.09 = \$917.43$$

Therefore, the total present value is:

$$\$1,683.36 + 917.43 = \$2,600.79$$

To see why $2,600.79 is the right answer, we can check to see that after the $2,000 is paid out in two years, there is no money left. If we invest $2,600.79 for one year at 9 percent, we will have:

$$\$2,600.79 \times 1.09 = \$2,834.86$$

We take out $1,000, leaving $1,834.86. This amount earns 9 percent for another year, leaving us with:

$$\$1,834.86 \times 1.09 = \$2,000$$

This is just as we planned. As this example illustrates, the present value of a series of future cash flows is the amount you would need today to exactly duplicate those future cash flows (for a given discount rate).

An alternative way of calculating present values for multiple future cash flows is to discount back to the present, one period at a time. To illustrate, suppose we had an investment that was going to pay $1,000 at the end of every year for the next five years. To find the present value, we could discount each $1,000 back to the present separately and then add them up. Figure 6.5 illustrates this approach for a 6 percent discount rate; as shown, the answer is $4,212.37 (ignoring a small rounding error).

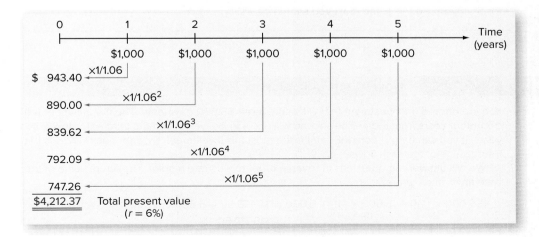

FIGURE 6.5

Present Value Calculated by Discounting Each Cash Flow Separately

FIGURE 6.6   Present Value Calculated by Discounting Back One Period at a Time

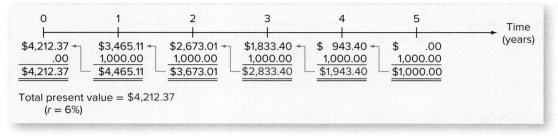

Total present value = $4,212.37
  (*r* = 6%)

Alternatively, we could discount the last cash flow back one period and add it to the next-to-the-last cash flow:

$$(\$1,000/1.06) + 1,000 = \$943.40 + 1,000 = \$1,943.40$$

We could then discount this amount back one period and add it to the Year 3 cash flow:

$$(\$1,943.40/1.06) + 1,000 = \$1,833.40 + 1,000 = \$2,833.40$$

This process could be repeated as necessary. Figure 6.6 illustrates this approach and the remaining calculations.

EXAMPLE 6.3   **How Much Is It Worth?**

You are offered an investment that will pay you $200 in one year, $400 the next year, $600 the next year, and $800 at the end of the fourth year. You can earn 12 percent on very similar investments. What is the most you should pay for this one?

We need to calculate the present value of these cash flows at 12 percent. Taking them one at a time gives:

$$\$200 \times 1/1.12^1 = \$200/1.1200 = \$\ \ 178.57$$
$$\$400 \times 1/1.12^2 = \$400/1.2544 = \ \ \ 318.88$$
$$\$600 \times 1/1.12^3 = \$600/1.4049 = \ \ \ 427.07$$
$$+\$800 \times 1/1.12^4 = \$800/1.5735 = \ \ \underline{508.41}$$
$$\text{Total present value} = \underline{\$1,432.93}$$

If you can earn 12 percent on your money, then you can duplicate this investment's cash flows for $1,432.93, so this is the most you should be willing to pay.

EXAMPLE 6.4   **How Much Is It Worth? Part 2**

You are offered an investment that will make three $5,000 payments. The first payment will occur four years from today. The second will occur in five years, and the third will follow in six years. If you can earn 11 percent, what is the most this investment is worth today? What is the future value of the cash flows?

We will answer the questions in reverse order to illustrate a point. The future value of the cash flows in six years is:

$$(\$5,000 \times 1.11^2) + (5,000 \times 1.11) + 5,000 = \$6,160.50 + 5,550 + 5,000$$
$$= \$16,710.50$$

The present value must be:

$16,710.50/1.11^6 = $8,934.12

Let's check this. Taking them one at a time, the PVs of the cash flows are:

$5,000 × 1/1.11^6 = $5,000/1.8704 = $2,673.20
$5,000 × 1/1.11^5 = $5,000/1.6851 =   2,967.26
+$5,000 × 1/1.11^4 = $5,000/1.5181 =   3,293.65
                Total present value = $8,934.12

This is as we previously calculated. The point we want to make is that we can calculate present and future values in any order and convert between them using whatever way seems most convenient. The answers will always be the same as long as we stick with the same discount rate and are careful to keep track of the right number of periods.

CALCULATOR HINTS

How to Calculate Present Values with Multiple Future Cash Flows Using a Financial Calculator

To calculate the present value of multiple cash flows with a financial calculator, we will discount the individual cash flows one at a time using the same technique we used in our previous chapter, so this is not really new. However, we can show you a shortcut. We will use the numbers in Example 6.3 to illustrate.

To begin, of course, we first remember to clear out the calculator! Next, from Example 6.3, the first cash flow is $200 to be received in one year and the discount rate is 12 percent, so we do the following:

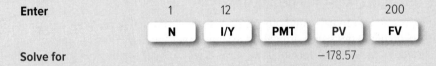

Enter   1   12   200

Solve for   −178.57

Now, you can write down this answer to save it, but that's inefficient. All calculators have a memory where you can store numbers. Why not just save it there? Doing so cuts down on mistakes because you don't have to write down and/or rekey numbers, and it's much faster.

Next, we value the second cash flow. We need to change N to 2 and FV to 400. As long as we haven't changed anything else, we don't have to reenter I/Y or clear out the calculator, so we have:

Enter   2   400

Solve for   −318.88

You save this number by adding it to the one you saved in your first calculation, and so on for the remaining two calculations.

As we will see in a later chapter, some financial calculators will let you enter all of the future cash flows at once, but we'll discuss that subject when we get to it.

SPREADSHEET STRATEGIES

How to Calculate Present Values with Multiple Future Cash Flows Using a Spreadsheet

Just as we did in our previous chapter, we can set up a basic spreadsheet to calculate the present values of the individual cash flows as follows. Notice that we have calculated the present values one at a time and added them up:

	A	B	C	D	E
1					
2			Using a spreadsheet to value multiple future cash flows		
3					
4	What is the present value of $200 in one year, $400 the next year, $600 the next year, and				
5	$800 the last year if the discount rate is 12 percent?				
6					
7	Rate:	.12			
8					
9	Year	Cash flows	Present values	Formula used	
10	1	$200	$178.57	=PV($B$7,A10,0,−B10)	
11	2	$400	$318.88	=PV($B$7,A11,0,−B11)	
12	3	$600	$427.07	=PV($B$7,A12,0,−B12)	
13	4	$800	$508.41	=PV($B$7,A13,0,−B13)	
14					
15		Total PV:	$1,432.93	=SUM(C10:C13)	
16					
17	Notice the negative signs inserted in the PV formulas. These just make the present values have				
18	positive signs. Also, the discount rate in cell B7 is entered as $B$7 (an "absolute" reference)				
19	because it is used over and over. We could have just entered ".12" instead, but our approach is				
20	more flexible.				
21					
22					

SOURCE: Microsoft Excel

A NOTE ABOUT CASH FLOW TIMING

In working present and future value problems, cash flow timing is critically important. In almost all such calculations, it is implicitly assumed that the cash flows occur at the *end* of each period. In fact, all the formulas we have discussed, all the numbers in a standard present value or future value table, and (very important) all the preset (or default) settings on a financial calculator assume that cash flows occur at the end of each period. Unless you are explicitly told otherwise, you should always assume that this is what is meant.

As a quick illustration of this point, suppose you are told that a three-year investment has a first-year cash flow of $100, a second-year cash flow of $200, and a third-year cash flow of $300. You are asked to draw a time line. Without further information, you should always assume that the time line looks like this:

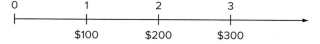

On our time line, notice how the first cash flow occurs at the end of the first period, the second at the end of the second period, and the third at the end of the third period.

We will close this section by answering the question we posed at the beginning of the chapter concerning quarterback Andrew Luck's contract. Recall that the contract called for a $6.4 million signing bonus and $12 million in salary in 2016. The remaining $120.725 million was to be paid as $19.4 million in 2017, $24.4 million in 2018, $27.525 million in 2019, $28.4 million in 2020, and $21 million in 2021. If 12 percent is the appropriate discount rate, how much money was really thrown at the Colts' quarterback?

To answer, we can calculate the present value by discounting each year's salary back to the present as follows (notice we assume that all the payments are made at year-end):

Year 0 (2016): $18,400,000   = $18,400,000.00
Year 1 (2017): $19,400,000 × 1 / 1.12^1 = $17,321,428.57
Year 2 (2018): $24,400,000 × 1 / 1.12^2 = $19,451,530.61
...
...
Year 5 (2021): $ 21,000,000 × 1 / 1.12^5 = $11,915,963.97

If you fill in the missing rows and then add (do it for practice), you will see that Andrew's contract had a present value of $104.7 million, or about 75 percent of the stated $139.125 million value.

Valuing Level Cash Flows: Annuities and Perpetuities

6.2

Excel Master It!
Excel Master coverage online

We will frequently encounter situations in which we have multiple cash flows that are all the same amount. For example, a common type of loan repayment plan calls for the borrower to repay the loan by making a series of equal payments over some length of time. Almost all consumer loans (such as car loans) and home mortgages feature equal payments, usually made each month.

More generally, a series of constant or level cash flows that occur at the end of each period for some fixed number of periods is called an ordinary **annuity**; more correctly, the cash flows are said to be in *ordinary annuity form*. Annuities appear frequently in financial arrangements, and there are some useful shortcuts for determining their values. We consider these next.

annuity
A level stream of cash flows for a fixed period of time.

PRESENT VALUE FOR ANNUITY CASH FLOWS

Suppose we were examining an asset that promised to pay $500 at the end of each of the next three years. The cash flows from this asset are in the form of a three-year, $500 annuity. If we wanted to earn 10 percent on our money, how much would we offer for this annuity?

From the previous section, we know that we can discount each of these $500 payments back to the present at 10 percent to determine the total present value:

$$\text{Present value} = (\$500/1.1^1) + (500/1.1^2) + (500/1.1^3)$$
$$= (\$500/1.1) + (500/1.21) + (500/1.331)$$
$$= \$454.55 + 413.22 + 375.66$$
$$= \$1,243.43$$

This approach works just fine. However, we will often encounter situations in which the number of cash flows is quite large. For example, a typical home mortgage calls for monthly payments over 30 years, for a total of 360 payments. If we were trying to determine the present value of those payments, it would be useful to have a shortcut.

Because the cash flows of an annuity are all the same, we can come up with a handy variation on the basic present value equation. The present value of an annuity of C dollars per period for t periods when the rate of return or interest rate is r is given by:

$$\text{Annuity present value} = C \times \left(\frac{1 - \text{Present value factor}}{r}\right)$$

$$= C \times \left\{\frac{1 - [1/(1 + r)^t]}{r}\right\}$$

6.1

The term in parentheses on the first line is sometimes called the *present value interest factor for annuities* and abbreviated PVIFA(r, t).

The expression for the annuity present value may look a little complicated, but it isn't difficult to use. Notice that the term in square brackets on the second line, $1/(1 + r)^t$, is the same present value factor we've been calculating. In our example from the beginning of this section, the interest rate is 10 percent and there are three years involved. The usual present value factor is:

Present value factor $= 1/1.1^3 = 1/1.331 = .751315$

To calculate the annuity present value factor, we just plug this in:

Annuity present value factor $= (1 - \text{Present value factor})/r$

$= (1 - .751315)/.10$

$= .248685/.10 = 2.48685$

As we calculated before, the present value of our $500 annuity is therefore:

Annuity present value $= \$500 \times 2.48685 = \$1,243.43$

EXAMPLE 6.5   **How Much Can You Afford?**

After carefully going over your budget, you have determined you can afford to pay $632 per month toward a new sports car. You call your local bank and find out that the going rate is 1 percent per month for 48 months. How much can you borrow?

To determine how much you can borrow, we need to calculate the present value of $632 per month for 48 months at 1 percent per month. The loan payments are in ordinary annuity form, so the annuity present value factor is:

Annuity PV factor $= (1 - \text{Present value factor})/r$

$= [1 - (1/1.01^{48})]/.01$

$= (1 - .6203)/.01 = 37.9740$

With this factor, we can calculate the present value of the 48 payments of $632 each as:

Present value $= \$632 \times 37.9740 = \$24,000$

Therefore, $24,000 is what you can afford to borrow and repay.

Annuity Tables   Just as there are tables for ordinary present value factors, there are tables for annuity factors as well. Table 6.1 contains a few such factors; Table A.3 in the appendix to the book contains a larger set. To find the annuity present value factor we calculated just before Example 6.5, look for the row corresponding to three periods and then find the column for 10 percent. The number you see at that intersection should be 2.4869 (rounded to four decimal places), as we calculated. Once again, try calculating a few of

	Interest Rate				TABLE 6.1
Number of Periods	5%	10%	15%	20%	**Annuity Present Value Interest Factors**
1	.9524	.9091	.8696	.8333	
2	1.8594	1.7355	1.6257	1.5278	
3	2.7232	2.4869	2.2832	2.1065	
4	3.5460	3.1699	2.8550	2.5887	
5	4.3295	3.7908	3.3522	2.9906	

these factors yourself and compare your answers to the ones in the table to make sure you know how to do it. If you are using a financial calculator, just enter $1 as the payment and calculate the present value; the result should be the annuity present value factor.

CALCULATOR HINTS

Annuity Present Values

To find annuity present values with a financial calculator, we need to use the **PMT** key (you were probably wondering what it was for). Compared to finding the present value of a single amount, there are two important differences. First, we enter the annuity cash flow using the **PMT** key. Second, we don't enter anything for the future value, **FV**. So, for example, the problem we have been examining is a three-year, $500 annuity. If the discount rate is 10 percent, we need to do the following (after clearing out the calculator!):

Enter	3	10	500		
	N	**I/Y**	**PMT**	**PV**	**FV**
Solve for				−1,243.43	

As usual, we get a negative sign on the PV.

SPREADSHEET STRATEGIES

Annuity Present Values

Using a spreadsheet to find annuity present values goes like this:

	A	B	C	D	E	F	G
1							
2			Using a spreadsheet to find annuity present values				
3							
4	What is the present value of $500 per year for three years if the discount rate is 10 percent?						
5	We need to solve for the unknown present value, so we use the formula PV(rate,nper,pmt,fv).						
6							
7	Payment amount per period:	$500					
8	Number of payments:	3					
9	Discount rate:	.1					
10							
11	Annuity present value:	$1,243.43					
12							
13	The formula entered in cell B11 is =PV(B9,B8,-B7,0); notice that fv is zero and that						
14	pmt has a negative sign on it. Also notice that rate is entered as a decimal, not a percentage.						
15							
16							
17							

SOURCE: Microsoft Excel

TABLE 6.1

Annuity Present Value Interest Factors

	Interest Rate			
Number of Periods	5%	10%	15%	20%
1	.9524	.9091	.8696	.8333
2	1.8594	1.7355	1.6257	1.5278
3	2.7232	2.4869	2.2832	2.1065
4	3.5460	3.1699	2.8550	2.5887
5	4.3295	3.7908	3.3522	2.9906

these factors yourself and compare your answers to the ones in the table to make sure you know how to do it. If you are using a financial calculator, just enter $1 as the payment and calculate the present value; the result should be the annuity present value factor.

CALCULATOR HINTS

Annuity Present Values

To find annuity present values with a financial calculator, we need to use the **PMT** key (you were probably wondering what it was for). Compared to finding the present value of a single amount, there are two important differences. First, we enter the annuity cash flow using the **PMT** key. Second, we don't enter anything for the future value, **FV**. So, for example, the problem we have been examining is a three-year, $500 annuity. If the discount rate is 10 percent, we need to do the following (after clearing out the calculator!):

Enter	3	10	500		
	N	I/Y	PMT	PV	FV
Solve for				−1,243.43	

As usual, we get a negative sign on the PV.

SPREADSHEET STRATEGIES

Annuity Present Values

Using a spreadsheet to find annuity present values goes like this:

	A	B	C	D	E	F	G
1							
2	Using a spreadsheet to find annuity present values						
3							
4	What is the present value of $500 per year for three years if the discount rate is 10 percent?						
5	We need to solve for the unknown present value, so we use the formula PV(rate,nper,pmt,fv).						
6							
7	Payment amount per period:	$500					
8	Number of payments:	3					
9	Discount rate:	.1					
10							
11	Annuity present value:	$1,243.43					
12							
13	The formula entered in cell B11 is =PV(B9,B8,-B7,0); notice that fv is zero and that						
14	pmt has a negative sign on it. Also notice that rate is entered as a decimal, not a percentage.						
15							
16							
17							

SOURCE: Microsoft Excel

Finding the Payment   Suppose you wish to start up a new business that specializes in the latest of health food trends, frozen yak milk. To produce and market your product, the Yakkee Doodle Dandy, you need to borrow $100,000. Because it strikes you as unlikely that this particular fad will be long-lived, you propose to pay off the loan quickly by making five equal annual payments. If the interest rate is 18 percent, what will the payment be?

In this case, we know the present value is $100,000. The interest rate is 18 percent, and there are five years. The payments are all equal, so we need to find the relevant annuity factor and solve for the unknown cash flow:

$$\text{Annuity present value} = \$100,000 = C \times [(1 - \text{Present value factor})/r]$$
$$= C \times \{[1 - (1/1.18^5)]/.18\}$$
$$= C \times [(1 - .4371)/.18]$$
$$= C \times 3.1272$$
$$C = \$100,000/3.1272 = \$31,977.78$$

Therefore, you'll make five payments of just under $32,000 each.

CALCULATOR HINTS

Annuity Payments

Finding annuity payments is easy with a financial calculator. In our yak milk example, the PV is $100,000, the interest rate is 18 percent, and there are five years. We find the payment as follows:

Enter	5	18		100,000	
	N	**I/Y**	**PMT**	**PV**	**FV**
Solve for			−31,977.78		

Here, we get a negative sign on the payment because the payment is an outflow for us.

SPREADSHEET STRATEGIES

Annuity Payments

Using a spreadsheet to work the same problem goes like this:

	A	B	C	D	E	F	G
1							
2		Using a spreadsheet to find annuity payments					
3							
4	What is the annuity payment if the present value is $100,000, the interest rate is 18 percent, and						
5	there are five periods? We need to solve for the unknown payment in an annuity, so we use the						
6	formula PMT(rate,nper,pv,fv).						
7							
8	Annuity present value:	$100,000					
9	Number of payments:	5					
10	Discount rate:	.18					
11							
12	Annuity payment:	-$31,977.78					
13							
14	The formula entered in cell B12 is =PMT(B10,B9,B8,0); notice that fv is zero and that the payment						
15	has a negative sign because it is an outflow for us.						
16							

Source: Microsoft Excel

Finding the Number of Payments

EXAMPLE 6.6

You ran a little short on your spring break vacation, so you put $1,000 on your credit card. You can afford only the minimum payment of $20 per month. The interest rate on the credit card is 1.5 percent per month. How long will you need to pay off the $1,000?

What we have here is an annuity of $20 per month at 1.5 percent per month for some unknown length of time. The present value is $1,000 (the amount you owe today). We need to do a little algebra (or use a financial calculator):

$$\$1,000 = \$20 \times [(1 - \text{Present value factor})/.015]$$
$$(\$1,000/20) \times .015 = 1 - \text{Present value factor}$$
$$\text{Present value factor} = .25 = 1/(1 + r)^t$$
$$1.015^t = 1/.25 = 4$$

At this point, the problem boils down to asking: How long does it take for your money to quadruple at 1.5 percent per month? Based on our previous chapter, the answer is about 93 months:

$$1.015^{93} = 3.99 \approx 4$$

It will take you about 93/12 = 7.75 years to pay off the $1,000 at this rate. If you use a financial calculator for problems like this, you should be aware that some automatically round up to the next whole period.

CALCULATOR HINTS

Finding the Number of Payments

To solve Example 6.6 on a financial calculator, do the following:

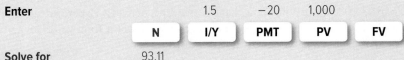

Enter		1.5	−20	1,000	
	N	**I/Y**	**PMT**	**PV**	**FV**
Solve for	93.11				

Notice that we put a negative sign on the payment you must make, and we have solved for the number of months. You still have to divide by 12 to get our answer. Also, some financial calculators won't report a fractional value for N; they automatically (without telling you) round up to the next whole period (not to the nearest value). With a spreadsheet, use the function =NPER(rate,pmt,pv,fv); be sure to put in a zero for fv and to enter −20 as the payment.

Finding the Rate   The last question we might want to ask concerns the interest rate implicit in an annuity. For example, an insurance company offers to pay you $1,000 per year for 10 years if you will pay $6,710 up front. What rate is implicit in this 10-year annuity?

In this case, we know the present value ($6,710), we know the cash flows ($1,000 per year), and we know the life of the investment (10 years). What we don't know is the discount rate:

$$\$6,710 = \$1,000 \times [(1 - \text{Present value factor})/r]$$
$$\$6,710/\$1,000 = 6.71 = \{1 - [1/(1 + r)^{10}]\}/r$$

So, the annuity factor for 10 periods is equal to 6.71, and we need to solve this equation for the unknown value of r. Unfortunately, this is mathematically impossible to do directly. The only way to do it is to use a table or trial and error to find a value for r.

If you look across the row corresponding to 10 periods in Table A.3, you will see a factor of 6.7101 for 8 percent, so we see right away that the insurance company is offering just about 8 percent. Alternatively, we could start trying different values until we got very close to the answer. Using this trial-and-error approach can be a little tedious, but fortunately machines are good at that sort of thing.[1]

To illustrate how to find the answer by trial and error, suppose a relative of yours wants to borrow $3,000. She offers to repay you $1,000 every year for four years. What interest rate are you being offered?

The cash flows here have the form of a four-year, $1,000 annuity. The present value is $3,000. We need to find the discount rate, r. Our goal in doing so is primarily to give you a feel for the relationship between annuity values and discount rates.

We need to start somewhere, and 10 percent is probably as good a place as any to begin. At 10 percent, the annuity factor is:

Annuity present value factor $= [1 - (1/1.10^4)]/.10 = 3.1699$

The present value of the cash flows at 10 percent is thus:

Present value $= \$1,000 \times 3.1699 = \$3,169.90$

You can see that we're already in the right ballpark.

Is 10 percent too high or too low? Recall that present values and discount rates move in opposite directions: Increasing the discount rate lowers the PV and vice versa. Our present value here is too high, so the discount rate is too low. If we try 12 percent, we're almost there:

Present value $= \$1,000 \times \{[1 - (1/1.12^4)]/.12\} = \$3,037.35$

We are still a little low on the discount rate (because the PV is a little high), so we'll try 13 percent:

Present value $= \$1,000 \times \{[1 - (1/1.13^4)]/.13\} = \$2,974.47$

This is less than $3,000, so we now know that the answer is between 12 percent and 13 percent, and it looks to be about 12.5 percent. For practice, work at it for a while longer and see if you find that the answer is about 12.59 percent.

CALCULATOR HINTS

Finding the Rate

Alternatively, you could use a financial calculator to do the following:

Enter	4		1,000	−3,000	
	N	I/Y	PMT	PV	FV
Solve for		12.59			

Notice that we put a negative sign on the present value (why?). With a spreadsheet, use the function =RATE(nper,pmt,pv,fv); be sure to put in a zero for fv and to enter 1,000 as the payment and −3,000 as the pv.

To illustrate a situation in which finding the unknown rate can be useful, let us consider that the Tri-State Megabucks lottery in Maine, Vermont, and New Hampshire offers you a choice of how to take your winnings (most lotteries do this). In a recent drawing, participants were offered the option of receiving a lump sum payment of $250,000 or an annuity

---

[1] Financial calculators rely on trial and error to find the answer. That's why they sometimes appear to be "thinking" before coming up with the answer. Actually, it is possible to directly solve for r if there are fewer than five periods, but it's usually not worth the trouble.

of $500,000 to be received in equal installments over a 25-year period. (At the time, the lump sum payment was always half the annuity option.) Which option was better?

To answer, suppose you were to compare $250,000 today to an annuity of $500,000/25 = $20,000 per year for 25 years. At what rate do these have the same value? This is the same type of problem we've been looking at; we need to find the unknown rate, r, for a present value of $250,000, a $20,000 payment, and a 25-year period. If you grind through the calculations (or get a little machine assistance), you should find that the unknown rate is about 6.24 percent. You should take the annuity option if that rate is attractive relative to other investments available to you. Notice that we have ignored taxes in this example, and taxes can significantly affect our conclusion. Be sure to consult your tax adviser anytime you win the lottery.

In another example, in early 2014, Warren Buffett and Dan Gilbert, founder of Quicken Loans, teamed up to offer $1 billion to anyone who could correctly predict a perfect NCAA March Madness bracket. The odds of winning: 1 in 9.2 quintillion! Of course, you wouldn't receive the $1 billion today, but rather $25 million per year for 40 years, or a lump sum of $500 million. See if you don't agree that the rate of return on this arrangement is 3.93 percent. Unfortunately, this was a one-time event, as legal and financial disagreements squashed the challenge.

FUTURE VALUE FOR ANNUITIES

On occasion, it's also handy to know a shortcut for calculating the future value of an annuity. As you might guess, there are future value factors for annuities as well as present value factors. In general, here is the future value factor for an annuity:

Annuity FV factor = (Future value factor − 1)/r
$$= [(1 + r)^t − 1]/r$$

To see how we use annuity future value factors, suppose you plan to contribute $2,000 every year to a retirement account paying 8 percent. If you retire in 30 years, how much will you have?

The number of years here, t, is 30, and the interest rate, r, is 8 percent; so we can calculate the annuity future value factor as:

Annuity FV factor = (Future value factor − 1)/r
$$= (1.08^{30} − 1)/.08$$
$$= (10.0627 − 1)/.08$$
$$= 113.2832$$

The future value of this 30-year, $2,000 annuity is thus:

Annuity future value = $2,000 × 113.28
$$= \$226,566.42$$

CALCULATOR HINTS

Future Values of Annuities

Of course, you could solve this problem using a financial calculator by doing the following:

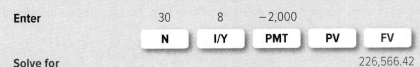

Enter	30	8	−2,000		
	N	I/Y	PMT	PV	FV
Solve for					226,566.42

Notice that we put a negative sign on the payment (why?). With a spreadsheet, use the function =FV(rate,nper, pmt,pv); be sure to put in a zero for pv and to enter −2,000 as the payment.

Sometimes we need to find the unknown rate, r, in the context of an annuity future value. For example, if you had invested $100 per month in stocks over the 25-year period ended December 1978, your investment would have grown to $76,374. This period had the *worst* stretch of stock returns of any 25-year period between 1925 and 2016. How bad was it?

Here we have the cash flows ($100 per month), the *future* value ($76,374), and the time period (25 years, or 300 months). We need to find the implicit rate, r:

$76,374 = $100 \times$ [(Future value factor $-$ 1)/r]

$763.74 = [(1 + r)^{300} - 1]/r$

Because this is the worst period, let's try 1 percent:

Annuity future value factor $= (1.01^{300} - 1)/.01 = 1,878.85$

We see that 1 percent is too high. From here, it's trial and error. See if you agree that r is about .55 percent per month. As you will see later in the chapter, this works out to be about 6.8 percent per year.

A NOTE ABOUT ANNUITIES DUE

annuity due
An annuity for which the cash flows occur at the beginning of the period.

So far we have only discussed ordinary annuities. These are the most important, but there is a fairly common variation. Remember that with an ordinary annuity, the cash flows occur at the end of each period. When you take out a loan with monthly payments, for example, the first loan payment normally occurs one month after you get the loan. However, when you lease an apartment, the first lease payment is usually due immediately. The second payment is due at the beginning of the second month, and so on. A lease is an example of an **annuity due**. An annuity due is an annuity for which the cash flows occur at the beginning of each period. Almost any type of arrangement in which we have to prepay the same amount each period is an annuity due.

There are several different ways to calculate the value of an annuity due. With a financial calculator, you switch it into "due" or "beginning" mode. (Remember to switch it back when you are done!) Another way to calculate the present value of an annuity due can be illustrated with a time line. Suppose an annuity due has five payments of $400 each, and the relevant discount rate is 10 percent. The time line looks like this:

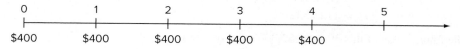

Notice how the cash flows here are the same as those for a *four*-year ordinary annuity, except that there is an extra $400 at Time 0. For practice, check to see that the value of a four-year ordinary annuity at 10 percent is $1,267.95. If we add on the extra $400, we get $1,667.95, which is the present value of this annuity due.

There is an even easier way to calculate the present or future value of an annuity due. If we assume cash flows occur at the end of each period when they really occur at the beginning, then we discount each one by one period too many. We could fix this by multiplying our answer by $(1 + r)$, where r is the discount rate. In fact, the relationship between the value of an annuity due and an ordinary annuity is:

Time value applications abound on the web. See, for example, **www .collegeboard.org** and **personal.fidelity.com**.

Annuity due value = Ordinary annuity value × (1 + r)   6.3

This works for both present and future values, so calculating the value of an annuity due involves two steps: (1) Calculate the present or future value as though it were an ordinary annuity and (2) multiply your answer by $(1 + r)$.

TABLE 6.2
Summary of Annuity and Perpetuity Calculations

I.	**Symbols:**
	PV = Present value, what future cash flows are worth today
	FV_t = Future value, what cash flows are worth in the future
	r = Interest rate, rate of return, or discount rate per period—typically, but not always, one year
	t = Number of periods—typically, but not always, the number of years
	C = Cash amount
II.	**Future Value of *C* per Period for *t* Periods at *r* Percent per Period:**
	$FV_t = C \times \{[(1 + r)^t - 1]/r\}$
	A series of identical cash flows is called an *annuity*, and the term $[(1 + r)^t - 1]/r$ is called the *annuity future value factor*.
III.	**Present Value of *C* per Period for *t* Periods at *r* Percent per Period:**
	$PV = C \times \{1 - [1/(1 + r)^t]\}/r$
	The term $\{1 - [1/(1 + r)^t]\}/r$ is called the *annuity present value factor*.
IV.	**Present Value of a Perpetuity of *C* per Period:**
	$PV = C/r$
	A *perpetuity* has the same cash flow every year forever.

PERPETUITIES

We've seen that a series of level cash flows can be valued by treating those cash flows as an annuity. An important special case of an annuity arises when the level stream of cash flows continues forever. Such an asset is called a **perpetuity** because the cash flows are perpetual. Perpetuities are also called **consols**, particularly in Canada and the United Kingdom. See Example 6.7 for an important example of a perpetuity.

perpetuity
An annuity in which the cash flows continue forever.

Because a perpetuity has an infinite number of cash flows, we obviously can't compute its value by discounting each one. Fortunately, valuing a perpetuity turns out to be the easiest possible case. The present value of a perpetuity is:

consol
A type of perpetuity.

PV for a perpetuity = *C*/*r*

For example, an investment offers a perpetual cash flow of $500 every year. The return you require on such an investment is 8 percent. What is the value of this investment? The value of this perpetuity is:

Perpetuity PV = *C*/*r* = $500/.08 = $6,250

For future reference, Table 6.2 contains a summary of the annuity and perpetuity basic calculations we have described in this section. By now, you probably think that you'll just use online calculators to handle annuity problems. Before you do, see our nearby *Work the Web* box!

Preferred Stock	**EXAMPLE 6.7**

Preferred stock (or preference stock) is an important example of a perpetuity. When a corporation sells preferred stock, the buyer is promised a fixed cash dividend every period (usually every quarter) forever. This dividend must be paid before any dividend can be paid to regular stockholders—hence the term *preferred*.

Suppose the Fellini Co. wants to sell preferred stock at $100 per share. A similar issue of preferred stock already outstanding has a price of $40 per share and offers a dividend of $1 every quarter. What dividend will Fellini have to offer if the preferred stock is going to sell?

The issue that is already out has a present value of $40 and a cash flow of $1 every quarter forever. Because this is a perpetuity:

Present value = $40 = $1 × (1/r)

r = .025, or 2.5%

To be competitive, the new Fellini issue will also have to offer 2.5 percent *per quarter*; so if the present value is to be $100, the dividend must be such that:

Present value = $100 = C × (1/.025)

C = $2.50 (per quarter)

WORK THE WEB

As we discussed in our previous chapter, many websites have financial calculators. One of these sites is Calculatoredge, which is located at www.calculatoredge.com. Suppose you retire with $1,750,000 and want to withdraw an equal amount each year for the next 30 years. If you can earn a 7 percent return, how much can you withdraw each year? Here is what Calculatoredge says:

Enter your values:

Currency:	US Dollars ▾	
Starting Principal:	1750000	**US Dollars**
Annual Interest Rate:	7	%
Repayment Period:	30	**Years**

[Calculate]   [Clear]

Results:

Annuity Payment: 131800.19   **US Dollars / Year**

According to the Calculatoredge calculator, the answer is $131,800.19. How important is it to understand what you are doing? Calculate this one for yourself, and you should get $141,026.21. Who is right? You are, of course! What's going on is that Calculatoredge assumes (but does not tell you) that the annuity is in the form of an annuity due, not an ordinary annuity. Recall that with an annuity due, the payments occur at the beginning of the period rather than the end of the period. The moral of the story is clear: *Caveat calculator.*

Questions

1. *Go to the calculator at www.calculatoredge.com and find out how much the website says you could withdraw each year if you have $2,500,000, earn an 8 percent interest rate, and make annual withdrawals for 35 years. How much more are the withdrawals if they are in the form of an ordinary annuity?*

2. *Suppose you have $500,000 and want to make withdrawals each month for the next 10 years. The first withdrawal is today and the appropriate interest rate is 9 percent compounded monthly. Using the calculator at this website, how much are your withdrawals?*

GROWING ANNUITIES AND PERPETUITIES

Annuities commonly have payments that grow over time. Suppose, for example, that we are looking at a lottery payout over a 20-year period. The first payment, made one year from now, will be $200,000. Every year thereafter, the payment will grow by 5 percent, so the payment in the second year will be $200,000 × 1.05 = $210,000. The payment in the third year will be $210,000 × 1.05 = $220,500, and so on. What's the present value if the appropriate discount rate is 11 percent?

If we use the symbol g to represent the growth rate, we can calculate the value of a growing annuity using a modified version of our regular annuity formula:

$$\text{Growing annuity present value} = C \times \left[\frac{1 - \left(\frac{1+g}{1+r} \right)^t}{r - g} \right]$$ **6.5**

Plugging in the numbers from our lottery example (and letting $g = .05$), we get:

$$PV = \$200,000 \times \left[\frac{1 - \left(\frac{1 + .05}{1 + .11} \right)^{20}}{.11 - .05} \right] = \$200,000 \times 11.18169 = \$2,236,337.06$$

There is also a formula for the present value of a growing perpetuity:

$$\text{Growing perpetuity present value} = C \times \left[\frac{1}{r - g} \right] = \frac{C}{r - g}$$ **6.6**

Returning to our lottery example, now suppose the payments continue forever. In this case, the present value is:

$$PV = \$200,000 \times \frac{1}{.11 - .05} = \$200,000 \times 16.6667 = \$3,333,333.33$$

The notion of a growing perpetuity may seem a little odd because the payments get bigger every period forever; but, as we will see in a later chapter, growing perpetuities play a key role in our analysis of stock prices.

Before we go on, there is one important item to note in regard to our formulas for growing annuities and perpetuities. In both cases, the cash flow in the formula, C, is the cash flow that is going to occur exactly one period from today.

Concept Questions

6.2a   In general, what is the present value of an annuity of C dollars per period at a discount rate of r per period? The future value?

6.2b   In general, what is the present value of a perpetuity?

Comparing Rates: The Effect of Compounding   6.3

The next issue we need to discuss has to do with the way interest rates are quoted. This subject causes a fair amount of confusion because rates are quoted in many different ways. Sometimes the way a rate is quoted is the result of tradition, and sometimes it's the result of legislation. Unfortunately, at times, rates are quoted in deliberately deceptive ways to mislead borrowers and investors. We will discuss these topics in this section.

Excel Master It!
Excel Master coverage online

EFFECTIVE ANNUAL RATES AND COMPOUNDING

If a rate is quoted as 10 percent compounded semiannually, this means the investment actually pays 5 percent every six months. A natural question then arises: Is 5 percent every six months the same thing as 10 percent per year? It's easy to see that it is not. If you invest $1 at 10 percent per year, you will have $1.10 at the end of the year. If you invest at 5 percent every six months, then you'll have the future value of $1 at 5 percent for two periods:

$$\$1 \times 1.05^2 = \$1.1025$$

This is $.0025 more. The reason is simple: Your account was credited with $1 × .05 = 5 cents in interest after six months. In the following six months, you earned 5 percent on that nickel, for an extra 5 × .05 = .25 cents.

As our example illustrates, 10 percent compounded semiannually is actually equivalent to 10.25 percent per year. Put another way, we would be indifferent between 10 percent compounded semiannually and 10.25 percent compounded annually. Anytime we have compounding during the year, we need to be concerned about what the rate really is.

In our example, the 10 percent is called a **stated**, or **quoted, interest rate**. Other names are used as well. The 10.25 percent, which is actually the rate you will earn, is called the **effective annual rate (EAR)**. To compare different investments or interest rates, we will always need to convert to effective rates. Some general procedures for doing this are discussed next.

stated interest rate
The interest rate expressed in terms of the interest payment made each period. Also known as the *quoted interest rate*.

effective annual rate (EAR)
The interest rate expressed as if it were compounded once per year.

CALCULATING AND COMPARING EFFECTIVE ANNUAL RATES

To see why it is important to work only with effective rates, suppose you've shopped around and come up with the following three rates:

Bank A: 15 percent compounded daily
Bank B: 15.5 percent compounded quarterly
Bank C: 16 percent compounded annually

Which of these is the best if you are thinking of opening a savings account? Which of these is best if they represent loan rates?

To begin, Bank C is offering 16 percent per year. Because there is no compounding during the year, this is the effective rate. Bank B is actually paying .155/4 = .03875 or 3.875 percent per quarter. At this rate, an investment of $1 for four quarters would grow to:

$$\$1 \times 1.03875^4 = \$1.1642$$

The EAR, therefore, is 16.42 percent. For a saver, this is much better than the 16 percent rate Bank C is offering; for a borrower, it's worse.

Bank A is compounding every day. This may seem a little extreme, but it is common to calculate interest daily. In this case, the daily interest rate is actually:

$$.15/365 = .000411$$

This is .0411 percent per day. At this rate, an investment of $1 for 365 periods would grow to:

$$\$1 \times 1.000411^{365} = \$1.1618$$

The EAR is 16.18 percent. This is not as good as Bank B's 16.42 percent for a saver, and not as good as Bank C's 16 percent for a borrower.

This example illustrates two things. First, the highest quoted rate is not necessarily the best. Second, compounding during the year can lead to a significant difference between the quoted rate and the effective rate. Remember that the effective rate is what you actually get or what you pay.

If you look at our examples, you see that we computed the EARs in three steps. We first divided the quoted rate by the number of times that the interest is compounded. We then added 1 to the result and raised it to the power of the number of times the interest is compounded. Finally, we subtracted the 1. If we let m be the number of times the interest is compounded during the year, these steps can be summarized as:

EAR = [1 + (Quoted rate/m)]^m − 1   **6.7**

For example, suppose you are offered 12 percent compounded monthly. In this case, the interest is compounded 12 times a year; so m is 12. You can calculate the effective rate as:

$$EAR = [1 + (\text{Quoted rate}/m)]^m - 1$$
$$= [1 + (.12/12)]^{12} - 1$$
$$= 1.01^{12} - 1$$
$$= 1.126825 - 1$$
$$= .126825, \text{ or } 12.6825\%$$

What's the EAR?   **EXAMPLE 6.8**

A bank is offering 12 percent compounded quarterly. If you put $100 in an account, how much will you have at the end of one year? What's the EAR? How much will you have at the end of two years?

   The bank is effectively offering 12%/4 = 3% every quarter. If you invest $100 for four periods at 3 percent per period, the future value is:

Future value = $100 × 1.03^4
            = $100 × 1.1255
            = $112.55

The EAR is 12.55 percent: $100 × (1 + .1255) = $112.55.

   We can determine what you would have at the end of two years in two different ways. One way is to recognize that two years is the same as eight quarters. At 3 percent per quarter, after eight quarters, you would have:

$100 × 1.03^8 = $100 × 1.2668 = $126.68

Alternatively, we could determine the value after two years by using an EAR of 12.55 percent; so after two years you would have:

$100 × 1.1255^2 = $100 × 1.2668 = $126.68

Thus, the two calculations produce the same answer. This illustrates an important point. Anytime we do a present or future value calculation, the rate we use must be an actual or effective rate. In this case, the actual rate is 3 percent per quarter. The effective annual rate is 12.55 percent. It doesn't matter which one we use once we know the EAR.

Quoting a Rate   **EXAMPLE 6.9**

Now that you know how to convert a quoted rate to an EAR, consider going the other way. As a lender, you know you want to actually earn 18 percent on a particular loan. You want to quote a rate that features monthly compounding. What rate do you quote?

In this case, we know the EAR is 18 percent, and we know this is the result of monthly compounding. Let q stand for the quoted rate. We have:

$$\text{EAR} = [1 + (\text{Quoted rate}/m)]^m - 1$$
$$.18 = [1 + (q/12)]^{12} - 1$$
$$1.18 = [1 + (q/12)]^{12}$$

We need to solve this equation for the quoted rate. This calculation is the same as the ones we did to find an unknown interest rate in Chapter 5:

$$1.18^{(1/12)} = 1 + (q/12)$$
$$1.18^{.08333} = 1 + (q/12)$$
$$1.0139 = 1 + (q/12)$$
$$q = .0139 \times 12$$
$$= .1667, \text{ or } 16.67\%$$

Therefore, the rate you would quote is 16.67 percent, compounded monthly.

EARs AND APRs

Sometimes it's not altogether clear whether a rate is an effective annual rate. A case in point concerns what is called the **annual percentage rate (APR)** on a loan. Truth-in-lending laws in the United States require that lenders disclose an APR on virtually all consumer loans. This rate must be displayed on a loan document in a prominent and unambiguous way.[2]

Given that an APR must be calculated and displayed, an obvious question arises: Is an APR an effective annual rate? Put another way, if a bank quotes a car loan at 12 percent APR, is the consumer actually paying 12 percent interest? Surprisingly, the answer is no. There is some confusion over this point, which we discuss next.

The confusion over APRs arises because lenders are required by law to compute the APR in a particular way. By law, the APR is equal to the interest rate per period multiplied by the number of periods in a year. For example, if a bank is charging 1.2 percent per month on car loans, then the APR that must be reported is $1.2\% \times 12 = 14.4\%$. So, an APR is in fact a quoted, or stated, rate in the sense we've been discussing. For example, an APR of 12 percent on a loan calling for monthly payments is really 1 percent per month. The EAR on such a loan is thus:

$$\text{EAR} = [1 + (\text{APR}/12)]^{12} - 1$$
$$= 1.01^{12} - 1 = .126825, \text{ or } 12.6825\%$$

---

[2] By law, lenders are required to report the APR on all consumer loans. In this text, we compute the APR as the interest rate per period multiplied by the number of periods in a year. According to federal law, the APR is a measure of the cost of consumer credit expressed as a yearly rate, and it includes interest and certain noninterest charges and fees. In practice, the APR can be much higher than the interest rate on the loan if the lender charges substantial fees that must be included in the federally mandated APR calculation.

EXAMPLE 6.10 **What Rate Are You Paying?**

Depending on the issuer, a typical credit card agreement quotes an interest rate of 18 percent APR. Monthly payments are required. What is the actual interest rate you pay on such a credit card?

Based on our discussion, an APR of 18 percent with monthly payments is really .18/12 = .015 or 1.5 percent per month. The EAR is thus:

$$EAR = [1 + (.18/12)]^{12} - 1$$
$$= 1.015^{12} - 1$$
$$= 1.1956 - 1$$
$$= .1956, \text{ or } 19.56\%$$

This is the rate you actually pay.

It is somewhat ironic that truth-in-lending laws sometimes require lenders to be *un*truthful about the actual rate on a loan. There are also truth-in-savings laws that require banks and other borrowers to quote an "annual percentage yield," or APY, on things like savings accounts. To make things a little confusing, an APY is an EAR. As a result, by law, the rates quoted to borrowers (APRs) and those quoted to savers (APYs) are not computed the same way.

There can be a huge difference between the APR and EAR when interest rates are large. For example, consider "payday loans." Payday loans are short-term loans made to consumers, often for less than two weeks, and are offered by companies such as AmeriCash Advance and National Payday. The loans work like this: You write a check today that is postdated (the date on the check is in the future) and give it to the company. They give you some cash. When the check date arrives, you either go to the store and pay the cash amount of the check, or the company cashes it (or else automatically renews the loan).

For example, in one particular state, Check Into Cash allows you to write a check for $115 dated 14 days in the future, for which you get $100 today. So what are the APR and EAR on this arrangement? First, we need to find the interest rate, which we can find by the FV equation as follows:

$$FV = PV \times (1 + r)^1$$
$$\$115 = \$100 \times (1 + r)^1$$
$$1.15 = (1 + r)$$
$$r = .15, \text{ or } 15\%$$

That doesn't seem too bad until you remember this is the interest rate for *14 days*! The APR of the loan is:

$$APR = .15 \times 365/14$$
$$APR = 3.9107, \text{ or } 391.07\%$$

And the EAR for this loan is:

$$EAR = (1 + \text{Quoted rate}/m)^m - 1$$
$$EAR = (1 + .15)^{365/14} - 1$$
$$EAR = 37.2366, \text{ or } 3,723.66\%$$

Now that's an interest rate! Just to see what a difference a small difference in fees can make, Advance America Cash Advance will let you write a check for $117.50 in exchange for the same $100 amount. Check for yourself that the APR of this arrangement is 456.25 percent and the EAR is 6,598.65 percent—not a loan we would like to take out!

TABLE 6.3

Compounding Frequency and Effective Annual Rates

Compounding Period	Number of Times Compounded	Effective Annual Rate
Year	1	10.00000%
Quarter	4	10.38129
Month	12	10.47131
Week	52	10.50648
Day	365	10.51558
Hour	8,760	10.51703
Minute	525,600	10.51709

TAKING IT TO THE LIMIT:
A NOTE ABOUT CONTINUOUS COMPOUNDING

If you made a deposit in a savings account, how often could your money be compounded during the year? If you think about it, there isn't really any upper limit. We've seen that daily compounding, for example, isn't a problem. There is no reason to stop here, however. We could compound every hour or minute or second. How high would the EAR get in this case? Table 6.3 illustrates the EARs that result as 10 percent is compounded at shorter and shorter intervals. Notice that the EARs do keep getting larger, but the differences get very small.

As the numbers in Table 6.3 seem to suggest, there is an upper limit to the EAR. If we let q stand for the quoted rate, then, as the number of times the interest is compounded gets extremely large, the EAR approaches:

EAR = $e^q - 1$

6.8

where e is the number 2.71828 (look for a key labeled "e^x" on your calculator). For example, with our 10 percent rate, the highest possible EAR is:

$$EAR = e^q - 1$$
$$= 2.71828^{.10} - 1$$
$$= 1.1051709 - 1$$
$$= .1051709, \text{ or } 10.51709\%$$

In this case, we say that the money is continuously, or instantaneously, compounded. Interest is being credited the instant it is earned, so the amount of interest grows continuously.

EXAMPLE 6.11   **What's the Law?**

At one time, commercial banks and savings and loan associations (S&Ls) were restricted in the interest rates they could offer on savings accounts. Under what was known as Regulation Q, S&Ls were allowed to pay at most 5.5 percent, and banks were not allowed to pay more than 5.25 percent (the idea was to give the S&Ls a competitive advantage; it didn't work). The law did not say how often these rates could be compounded, however. Under Regulation Q, then, what were the maximum allowed interest rates?

The maximum allowed rates occurred with continuous, or instantaneous, compounding. For the commercial banks, 5.25 percent compounded continuously would be:

$$EAR = e^{.0525} - 1$$
$$= 2.71828^{.0525} - 1$$
$$= 1.0539026 - 1$$
$$= .0539026, \text{ or } 5.39026\%$$

This is what banks could actually pay. Check for yourself to see that S&Ls could effectively pay 5.65406 percent.

Loan Types and Loan Amortization

6.4

Whenever a lender extends a loan, some provision will be made for repayment of the principal (the original loan amount). A loan might be repaid in equal installments, for example, or it might be repaid in a single lump sum. Because the way that the principal and interest are paid is up to the parties involved, there are actually an unlimited number of possibilities.

In this section, we describe a few forms of repayment that come up quite often, and more complicated forms can usually be built up from these. The three basic types of loans are pure discount loans, interest-only loans, and amortized loans. Working with these loans is a very straightforward application of the present value principles that we have already developed.

Excel Master It!
Excel Master coverage online

PURE DISCOUNT LOANS

The *pure discount loan* is the simplest form of loan. With such a loan, the borrower receives money today and repays a single lump sum at some time in the future. A one-year, 10 percent pure discount loan, for example, would require the borrower to repay $1.10 in one year for every dollar borrowed today.

Because a pure discount loan is so simple, we already know how to value one. Suppose a borrower was able to repay $25,000 in five years. If we, acting as the lender, wanted a 12 percent interest rate on the loan, how much would we be willing to lend? Put another way, what value would we assign today to that $25,000 to be repaid in five years? Based on our work in Chapter 5, we know the answer is the present value of $25,000 at 12 percent for five years:

$$\text{Present value} = \$25,000/1.12^5$$
$$= \$25,000/1.7623$$
$$= \$14,186$$

Pure discount loans are common when the loan term is short—say a year or less. In recent years, they have become increasingly common for much longer periods.

Treasury Bills

EXAMPLE 6.12

When the U.S. government borrows money on a short-term basis (a year or less), it does so by selling what are called *Treasury bills*, or *T-bills* for short. A T-bill is a promise by the government to repay a fixed amount at some time in the future—for example, in 3 months or 12 months.

Treasury bills are pure discount loans. If a T-bill promises to repay $10,000 in 12 months, and the market interest rate is 7 percent, how much will the bill sell for in the market?

Because the going rate is 7 percent, the T-bill will sell for the present value of $10,000 to be repaid in one year at 7 percent:

Present value = $10,000/1.07 = $9,345.79

INTEREST-ONLY LOANS

A second type of loan repayment plan calls for the borrower to pay interest each period and to repay the entire principal (the original loan amount) at some point in the future. Loans with such a repayment plan are called *interest-only loans*. Notice that if there is just one period, a pure discount loan and an interest-only loan are the same thing.

For example, with a three-year, 10 percent, interest-only loan of $1,000, the borrower would pay $1,000 × .10 = $100 in interest at the end of the first and second years. At the end of the third year, the borrower would return the $1,000 along with another $100 in interest for that year. Similarly, a 50-year interest-only loan would call for the borrower to pay interest every year for the next 50 years and then repay the principal. In the extreme, the borrower pays the interest every period forever and never repays any principal. As we discussed earlier in the chapter, the result is a perpetuity.

Most corporate bonds have the general form of an interest-only loan. Because we will be considering bonds in some detail in the next chapter, we will defer further discussion of them for now.

AMORTIZED LOANS

With a pure discount or interest-only loan, the principal is repaid all at once. An alternative is an *amortized loan*, with which the lender may require the borrower to repay parts of the loan amount over time. The process of providing for a loan to be paid off by making regular principal reductions is called *amortizing* the loan.

A simple way of amortizing a loan is to have the borrower pay the interest each period plus some fixed amount. This approach is common with medium-term business loans. For example, suppose a business takes out a $5,000, five-year loan at 9 percent. The loan agreement calls for the borrower to pay the interest on the loan balance each year and to reduce the loan balance each year by $1,000. Because the loan amount declines by $1,000 each year, it is fully paid in five years.

In the case we are considering, notice that the total payment will decline each year. The reason is that the loan balance goes down, resulting in a lower interest charge each year, whereas the $1,000 principal reduction is constant. For example, the interest in the first year will be $5,000 × .09 = $450. The total payment will be $1,000 + 450 = $1,450. In the second year, the loan balance is $4,000, so the interest is $4,000 × .09 = $360, and the total payment is $1,360. We can calculate the total payment in each of the remaining years by preparing a simple *amortization schedule* as follows:

Year	Beginning Balance	Total Payment	Interest Paid	Principal Paid	Ending Balance
1	$5,000	$1,450	$ 450	$1,000	$4,000
2	4,000	1,360	360	1,000	3,000
3	3,000	1,270	270	1,000	2,000
4	2,000	1,180	180	1,000	1,000
5	1,000	1,090	90	1,000	0
Totals		$6,350	$1,350	$5,000	

Notice that in each year, the interest paid is given by the beginning balance multiplied by the interest rate. Also notice that the beginning balance is given by the ending balance from the previous year.

Probably the most common way of amortizing a loan is to have the borrower make a single, fixed payment every period. Almost all consumer loans (such as car loans) and mortgages work this way. For example, suppose our five-year, 9 percent, $5,000 loan was amortized this way. How would the amortization schedule look?

We first need to determine the payment. From our discussion earlier in the chapter, we know that this loan's cash flows are in the form of an ordinary annuity. In this case, we can solve for the payment as follows:

$$\$5,000 = C \times \{[1 - (1/1.09^5)]/.09\}$$
$$= C \times [(1 - .6499)/.09]$$

This gives us:

$$C = \$5,000/3.8897$$
$$= \$1,285.46$$

The borrower will therefore make five equal payments of $1,285.46. Will this pay off the loan? We will check by filling in an amortization schedule.

In our previous example, we knew the principal reduction each year. We then calculated the interest owed to get the total payment. In this example, we know the total payment. We will calculate the interest and then subtract it from the total payment to calculate the principal portion in each payment.

In the first year, the interest is $450, as we calculated before. Because the total payment is $1,285.46, the principal paid in the first year must be:

Principal paid = $1,285.46 − 450 = $835.46

The ending loan balance is:

Ending balance = $5,000 − 835.46 = $4,164.54

The interest in the second year is $4,164.54 × .09 = $374.81, and the loan balance declines by $1,285.46 − 374.81 = $910.65. We can summarize all of the relevant calculations in the following schedule:

Year	Beginning Balance	Total Payment	Interest Paid	Principal Paid	Ending Balance
1	$5,000.00	$1,285.46	$ 450.00	$ 835.46	$4,164.54
2	4,164.54	1,285.46	374.81	910.65	3,253.88
3	3,253.88	1,285.46	292.85	992.61	2,261.27
4	2,261.27	1,285.46	203.51	1,081.95	1,179.32
5	1,179.32	1,285.46	106.14	1,179.32	0.00
Totals		$6,427.31	$1,427.31	$5,000.00	

Because the loan balance declines to zero, the five equal payments do pay off the loan. Notice that the interest paid declines each period. This isn't surprising because the loan balance is going down. Given that the total payment is fixed, the principal paid must be rising each period.

If you compare the two loan amortizations in this section, you will see that the total interest is greater for the equal total payment case: $1,427.31 versus $1,350. The reason for this is that the loan is repaid more slowly early on, so the interest is somewhat higher. This doesn't mean that one loan is better than the other; it means that one is effectively paid off faster than the other. For example, the principal reduction in the first year is $835.46 in the equal total payment case as compared to $1,000 in the first case. Many websites offer loan amortization schedules. See our nearby *Work the Web* box for an example.

WORK THE WEB

Preparing an amortization table is one of the more tedious time value of money applications. Using a spreadsheet makes it relatively easy, but there are also websites available that will prepare an amortization schedule very quickly. One such site is www.bankrate.com. This site has a mortgage calculator for home loans, but the same calculations apply to most other types of loans such as car loans and student loans. Suppose you graduate with a student loan of $25,000 and will repay the loan over the next 10 years at 5.3 percent. What are your monthly payments? Using the calculator we get:

Home price ⑦

| $ 25,000 |

Down payment ⑦

| $ 0 | 0.00 % |

Mortgage term ⑦

| 10.000 years | 120 months |

Annual interest rate ⑦

| 5.30 % | TODAY'S RATES |

CALCULATE

Your estimated monthly payment ⑦

$268.84

Try this example yourself and click the "Show Amortization Schedule" button. You will find that your first payment will consist of $158.43 in principal and $110.42 in interest. Over the life of the loan you will pay a total of $7,261 in interest.

Questions

1. *Suppose you take out a 30-year mortgage for $250,000 at an interest rate of 6.8 percent. Use this website to construct an amortization table for the loan. What are the interest payment and principal amounts in the 110th payment? How much in total interest will you pay over the life of the loan?*

2. *You take out a 30-year mortgage for $275,000 at an interest rate of 7.3 percent. How much will you pay in interest over the life of this loan? Now assume you pay an extra $100 per month on this loan. How much is your total interest now? How much sooner will the mortgage be paid off?*

We will close this chapter with an example that may be of particular relevance. Federal Stafford loans are an important source of financing for many college students, helping to cover the cost of tuition, books, new cars, condominiums, and many other things. Sometimes students do not seem to fully realize that Stafford loans have a serious drawback: They must be repaid in monthly installments, usually beginning six months after the student leaves school.

Some Stafford loans are subsidized, meaning that the interest does not begin to accrue until repayment begins (this is a good thing). If you are a dependent undergraduate student under this particular option, the total debt you can run up is, at most, $23,000. The interest rate in 2017–2018 is 4.45 percent, or $4.45/12 = .3708$ percent per month. Under the "standard repayment plan," the loans are amortized over 10 years (subject to a minimum payment of $50).

Suppose you max out borrowing under this program. Beginning six months after you graduate (or otherwise depart the ivory tower), what will your monthly payment be? How much will you owe after making payments for four years?

Given our earlier discussions, see if you don't agree that your monthly payment (assuming a $23,000 total loan) is $237.81 per month. Also, as explained in Example 6.13, after making payments for four years, you still owe the present value of the remaining payments. There are 120 payments in all. After you make 48 of them (the first four years), you have 72 to go. By now, it should be easy for you to verify that the present value of $237.81 per month for 72 months at .3708 percent per month is about $15,003.07, so you still have a long way to go.

Partial Amortization, or "Bite the Bullet"   EXAMPLE 6.13

A common arrangement in real estate lending might call for a 5-year loan with, say, a 15-year amortization. What this means is that the borrower makes a payment every month of a fixed amount based on a 15-year amortization. However, after 60 months, the borrower makes a single, much larger payment called a "balloon" or "bullet" to pay off the loan. Because the monthly payments don't fully pay off the loan, the loan is said to be partially amortized.

Suppose we have a $100,000 commercial mortgage with a 12 percent APR and a 20-year (240-month) amortization. Further suppose the mortgage has a five-year balloon. What will the monthly payment be? How big will the balloon payment be?

The monthly payment can be calculated based on an ordinary annuity with a present value of $100,000. There are 240 payments, and the interest rate is 1 percent per month. The payment is:

$$\$100,000 = C \times [(1 - 1/1.01^{240})/.01]$$
$$= C \times 90.8194$$
$$C = \$1,101.09$$

Now, there is an easy way and a hard way to determine the balloon payment. The hard way is to actually amortize the loan for 60 months to see what the balance is at that time. The easy way is to recognize that after 60 months, we have a $240 - 60 = 180$-month loan. The payment is still $1,101.09 per month, and the interest rate is still 1 percent per month. The loan balance is thus the present value of the remaining payments:

$$\text{Loan balance} = \$1,101.09 \times [(1 - 1/1.01^{180})/.01]$$
$$= \$1,101.09 \times 83.3217$$
$$= \$91,744.33$$

The balloon payment is a substantial $91,744.33. Why is it so large? To get an idea, consider the first payment on the mortgage. The interest in the first month is $100,000 \times .01 = \$1,000$. Your payment is $1,101.09, so the loan balance declines by only $101.09. Because the loan balance declines so slowly, the cumulative "pay down" over five years is not great.

SPREADSHEET STRATEGIES

Loan Amortization Using a Spreadsheet

Loan amortization is a common spreadsheet application. To illustrate, we will set up the problem that we examined earlier in this section: a five-year, $5,000, 9 percent loan with constant payments. Our spreadsheet looks like this:

	A	B	C	D	E	F	G	H
1								
2				**Using a spreadsheet to amortize a loan**				
3								
4			Loan amount:	$5,000				
5			Interest rate:	.09				
6			Loan term:	5				
7			Loan payment:	**$1,285.46**				
8				*Note:* Payment is calculated using PMT(rate,nper,-pv,fv).				
9			*Amortization table:*					
10								
11		Year	Beginning	Total	Interest	Principal	Ending	
12			Balance	Payment	Paid	Paid	Balance	
13		1	$5,000.00	$1,285.46	$450.00	$835.46	$4,164.54	
14		2	4,164.54	1,285.46	374.81	910.65	3,253.88	
15		3	3,253.88	1,285.46	292.85	992.61	2,261.27	
16		4	2,261.27	1,285.46	203.51	1,081.95	1,179.32	
17		5	1,179.32	1,285.46	106.14	1,179.32	.00	
18		Totals		6,427.31	1,427.31	5,000.00		
19								
20			*Formulas in the amortization table:*					
21								
22		Year	Beginning	Total	Interest	Principal	Ending	
23			Balance	Payment	Paid	Paid	Balance	
24		1	=+D4	=$D$7	=+$D$5*C13	=+D13-E13	=+C13-F13	
25		2	=+G13	=$D$7	=+$D$5*C14	=+D14-E14	=+C14-F14	
26		3	=+G14	=$D$7	=+$D$5*C15	=+D15-E15	=+C15-F15	
27		4	=+G15	=$D$7	=+$D$5*C16	=+D16-E16	=+C16-F16	
28		5	=+G16	=$D$7	=+$D$5*C17	=+D17-E17	=+C17-F17	
29								
30			*Note:* Totals in the amortization table are calculated using the SUM formula.					
31								

SOURCE: Microsoft Excel

Of course, it is possible to rack up much larger debts. According to the Association of American Medical Colleges, medical students who borrowed to attend medical school and graduated in 2015 had an average student loan balance of $180,723. Ouch! In fact, it was reported that former Federal Reserve Chairman Ben Bernanke's son was on track to graduate with over $400,000 in student loans, although that included his undergraduate degree as well. How long will it take the average student to pay off her medical school loans?

Let's say she makes a monthly payment of $1,200, and the loan has an interest rate of 7 percent per year, or .5833 percent per month. See if you agree that it will take about 362 months, or about 30 years, to pay off the loan. Maybe MD really stands for "mucho debt"!

Concept Questions

6.4a   What is a pure discount loan? An interest-only loan?

6.4b   What does it mean to amortize a loan?

6.4c   What is a balloon payment? How do you determine its value?

Summary and Conclusions   6.5

This chapter rounded out your understanding of fundamental concepts related to the time value of money and discounted cash flow valuation. Several important topics were covered:

1. There are two ways of calculating present and future values when there are multiple cash flows. Both approaches are straightforward extensions of our earlier analysis of single cash flows.

2. A series of constant cash flows that arrive or are paid at the end of each period is called an ordinary annuity, and we described some useful shortcuts for determining the present and future values of annuities.

3. Interest rates can be quoted in a variety of ways. For financial decisions, any rates being compared must first be converted to effective rates. The relationship between a quoted rate, such as an annual percentage rate (APR), and an effective annual rate (EAR) is given by:

$$\text{EAR} = [1 + (\text{Quoted rate}/m)]^m - 1$$

where m is the number of times during the year the money is compounded or, equivalently, the number of payments during the year.

4. Many loans are annuities. The process of providing for a loan to be paid off gradually is called amortizing the loan, and we discussed how amortization schedules are prepared and interpreted.

The principles developed in this chapter will figure prominently in the chapters to come. The reason for this is that most investments, whether they involve real assets or financial assets, can be analyzed using the discounted cash flow (DCF) approach. As a result, the DCF approach is broadly applicable and widely used in practice. For example, the next two chapters show how to value bonds and stocks using an extension of the techniques presented in this chapter. Before going on, therefore, you might want to do some of the problems that follow.

CONNECT TO FINANCE

 Do you use *Connect Finance* to practice what you learn? If you don't, you should—we can help you master the topics presented in this chapter. Log on to connect.mheducation.com to learn more!

Can you answer the following *Connect* Quiz questions?

Section 6.1   Two years ago, you opened an investment account and deposited $5,000. One year ago, you added another $2,000 to the account. Today, you are making a final deposit of $7,500. How much will you have in this account three years from today if you earn a 14 percent rate of return?

Section 6.2   A stream of equal payments that occur at the beginning of each month for one year is called a(n) _____.

Section 6.3   Your credit card charges interest of 1.2 percent per month. What is the annual percentage rate?

Section 6.4   What type of loan is repaid in a single lump sum?

CHAPTER REVIEW AND SELF-TEST PROBLEMS

6.1 **Present Values with Multiple Cash Flows** A first-round draft choice quarterback has been signed to a three-year, $25 million contract. The details provide for an immediate cash bonus of $2 million. The player is to receive $5 million in salary at the end of the first year, $8 million the next, and $10 million at the end of the last year. Assuming a 15 percent discount rate, is this package worth $25 million? If not, how much is it worth?

6.2 **Future Value with Multiple Cash Flows** You plan to make a series of deposits in an individual retirement account. You will deposit $1,000 today, $2,000 in two years, and $2,000 in five years. If you withdraw $1,500 in three years and $1,000 in seven years, assuming no withdrawal penalties, how much will you have after eight years if the interest rate is 7 percent? What is the present value of these cash flows?

6.3 **Annuity Present Value** You are looking into an investment that will pay you $12,000 per year for the next 10 years. If you require a 15 percent return, what is the most you would pay for this investment?

6.4 **APR versus EAR** The going rate on student loans is quoted as 8 percent APR. The terms of the loans call for monthly payments. What is the effective annual rate (EAR) on such a student loan?

6.5 **It's the Principal That Matters** Suppose you borrow $10,000. You are going to repay the loan by making equal annual payments for five years. The interest rate on the loan is 14 percent per year. Prepare an amortization schedule for the loan. How much interest will you pay over the life of the loan?

6.6 **Just a Little Bit Each Month** You've recently finished your MBA at the Darnit School. Naturally, you must purchase a new BMW immediately. The car costs about $36,000. The bank quotes an interest rate of 15 percent APR for a 72-month loan with a 10 percent down payment. You plan on trading the car in for a new one in two years. What will your monthly payment be? What is the effective interest rate on the loan? What will the loan balance be when you trade the car in?

ANSWERS TO CHAPTER REVIEW AND SELF-TEST PROBLEMS

6.1 Obviously, the package is not worth $25 million because the payments are spread out over three years. The bonus is paid today, so it's worth $2 million. The present values for the three subsequent salary payments are:

$$(\$5/1.15) + (8/1.15^2) + (10/1.15^3) = (\$5/1.15) + (8/1.3225) + (10/1.5209)$$
$$= \$16.9721 \text{ million}$$

The package is worth a total of $18.9721 million.

6.2 We will calculate the future values for each of the cash flows separately and then add them up. Notice that we treat the withdrawals as negative cash flows:

$$\$1,000 \times 1.07^8 = \ \$1,000 \times 1.7182 = \$\ 1,718.19$$
$$2,000 \times 1.07^6 = \ 2,000 \times 1.5007 = \ 3,001.46$$
$$-1,500 \times 1.07^5 = -1,500 \times 1.4026 = -2,103.83$$
$$2,000 \times 1.07^3 = \ 2,000 \times 1.2250 = \ 2,450.09$$
$$-1,000 \times 1.07^1 = -1,000 \times 1.0700 = \underline{-1,070.00}$$

Total future value = $\underline{\underline{\$\ 3,995.91}}$

To calculate the present value, we could discount each cash flow back to the present or we could discount back a single year at a time. However, because we already know that the future value in eight years is $3,995.91, the easy way to get the PV is just to discount this amount back eight years:

$$\text{Present value} = \$3,995.91/1.07^8$$
$$= \$3,995.91/1.7182$$
$$= \$2,325.65$$

For practice, you can verify that this is what you get if you discount each cash flow back separately.

6.3 The most you would be willing to pay is the present value of $12,000 per year for 10 years at a 15 percent discount rate. The cash flows here are in ordinary annuity form, so the relevant present value factor is:

$$\text{Annuity present value factor} = (1 - \text{Present value factor})/r$$
$$= [1 - (1/1.15^{10})]/.15$$
$$= (1 - .2472)/.15$$
$$= 5.0188$$

The present value of the 10 cash flows is thus:

$$\text{Present value} = \$12,000 \times 5.0188$$
$$= \$60,225$$

This is the most you would pay.

6.4 A rate of 8 percent APR with monthly payments is actually $8\%/12 = .67\%$ per month. The EAR is thus:

$$\text{EAR} = [1 + (.08/12)]^{12} - 1 = .0830, \text{ or } 8.30\%$$

6.5 We first need to calculate the annual payment. With a present value of $10,000, an interest rate of 14 percent, and a term of five years, the payment can be determined from:

$$\$10,000 = \text{Payment} \times \{[1 - (1/1.14^5)]/.14\}$$
$$= \text{Payment} \times 3.4331$$

Therefore, the payment is $10,000/3.4331 = $2,912.84 (actually, it's $2,912.8355; this will create some small rounding errors in the following schedule). We can now prepare the amortization schedule as follows:

Year	Beginning Balance	Total Payment	Interest Paid	Principal Paid	Ending Balance
1	$10,000.00	$ 2,912.84	$1,400.00	$ 1,512.84	$8,487.16
2	8,487.16	2,912.84	1,188.20	1,724.63	6,762.53
3	6,762.53	2,912.84	946.75	1,966.08	4,796.45
4	4,796.45	2,912.84	671.50	2,241.33	2,555.12
5	2,555.12	2,912.84	357.72	2,555.12	0.00
Totals		$14,564.17	$4,564.17	$10,000.00	

6.6   The cash flows on the car loan are in annuity form, so we need to find only the payment. The interest rate is 15%/12 = 1.25% per month, and there are 72 months. The first thing we need is the annuity factor for 72 periods at 1.25 percent per period:

$$\text{Annuity present value factor} = (1 - \text{Present value factor})/r$$
$$= [1 - (1/1.0125^{72})]/.0125$$
$$= [1 - (1/2.4459)]/.0125$$
$$= (1 - .4088)/.0125$$
$$= 47.2925$$

The present value is the amount we finance. With a 10 percent down payment, we will be borrowing 90 percent of $36,000, or $32,400. To find the payment, we need to solve for C:

$$\$32,400 = C \times \text{Annuity present value factor}$$
$$= C \times 47.2925$$

Rearranging things a bit, we have:

$$C = \$32,400 \times (1/47.2925)$$
$$= \$32,400 \times .02115$$
$$= \$685.10$$

Your payment is just over $685 per month.

The actual interest rate on this loan is 1.25 percent per month. Based on our work in the chapter, we can calculate the effective annual rate as:

$$\text{EAR} = (1.0125)^{12} - 1 = .1608, \text{ or } 16.08\%$$

The effective rate is about one point higher than the quoted rate.

To determine the loan balance in two years, we could amortize the loan to see what the balance is at that time. This would be fairly tedious to do by hand. Using the information already determined in this problem, we can instead calculate the present value of the remaining payments. After two years, we have made 24 payments, so there are 72 − 24 = 48 payments left. What is the present value of 48 monthly payments of $685.10 at 1.25 percent per month? The relevant annuity factor is:

$$\text{Annuity present value factor} = (1 - \text{Present value factor})/r$$
$$= [1 - (1/1.0125^{48})]/.0125$$
$$= [1 - (1/1.8154)]/.0125$$
$$= (1 - .5509)/.0125$$
$$= 35.9315$$

The present value is thus:

$$\text{Present value} = \$685.10 \times 35.9315 = \$24,616.60$$

You will owe about $24,617 on the loan in two years.

CONCEPTS REVIEW AND CRITICAL THINKING QUESTIONS

1. **Annuity Factors [LO1]** There are four pieces to an annuity present value. What are they?

2. **Annuity Period [LO1]** As you increase the length of time involved, what happens to the present value of an annuity? What happens to the future value?

3. **Interest Rates** [LO1] What happens to the future value of an annuity if you increase the rate r? What happens to the present value?

4. **Present Value** [LO1] What do you think about the Tri-State Megabucks lottery discussed in the chapter advertising a $500,000 prize when the lump sum option is $250,000? Is it deceptive advertising?

5. **Present Value** [LO1] If you were an athlete negotiating a contract, would you want a big signing bonus payable immediately and smaller payments in the future, or vice versa? How about looking at it from the team's perspective?

6. **Present Value** [LO1] Suppose two athletes each sign 10-year contracts for $80 million. In one case, we're told that the $80 million will be paid in 10 equal installments. In the other case, we're told that the $80 million will be paid in 10 installments, but the installments will increase by 5 percent per year. Who got the better deal?

7. **APR and EAR** [LO4] Should lending laws be changed to require lenders to report EARs instead of APRs? Why or why not?

8. **Time Value** [LO1] On subsidized Stafford loans, a common source of financial aid for college students, interest does not begin to accrue until repayment begins. Who receives a bigger subsidy, a freshman or a senior? Explain. In words, how would you go about valuing the subsidy on a subsidized Stafford loan?

9. **Time Value** [LO1] Eligibility for a subsidized Stafford loan is based on current financial need. However, both subsidized and unsubsidized Stafford loans are repaid out of future income. Given this, do you see a possible objection to having two types?

10. **Time Value** [LO1] A viatical settlement is a lump sum of money given to a terminally ill individual in exchange for his life insurance policy. When the insured person dies, the purchaser receives the payout from the life insurance policy. What factors determine the value of the viatical settlement? Do you think such settlements are ethical? Why or why not?

11. **Perpetuity Values** [LO1] What happens to the future value of a perpetuity if interest rates increase? What if interest rates decrease?

12. **Loans and Interest Rates** [LO4] In the chapter, we gave several examples of so-called payday loans. As you saw, the interest rates on these loans can be extremely high and are even called predatory by some. Do you think such high interest loans are ethical? Why or why not?

QUESTIONS AND PROBLEMS

1. **Present Value and Multiple Cash Flows** [LO1] McCann Co. has identified an investment project with the following cash flows. If the discount rate is 10 percent, what is the present value of these cash flows? What is the present value at 18 percent? At 24 percent?

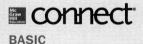

BASIC
(Questions 1–28)

Year	Cash Flow
1	$ 530
2	690
3	875
4	1,090

2. **Present Value and Multiple Cash Flows** [LO1] Investment X offers to pay you $4,200 per year for eight years, whereas Investment Y offers to pay you $6,100 per year for five years. Which of these cash flow streams has the higher present value if the discount rate is 5 percent? If the discount rate is 15 percent?

✗   3. **Future Value and Multiple Cash Flows** [LO1] Fuente, Inc., has identified an investment project with the following cash flows. If the discount rate is 8 percent, what is the future value of these cash flows in Year 4? What is the future value at a discount rate of 11 percent? At 24 percent?

Year	Cash Flow
1	$1,075
2	1,210
3	1,340
4	1,420

4. **Calculating Annuity Present Value** [LO1] An investment offers $4,350 per year for 15 years, with the first payment occurring one year from now. If the required return is 6 percent, what is the value of the investment? What would the value be if the payments occurred for 40 years? For 75 years? Forever?

5. **Calculating Annuity Cash Flows** [LO1] If you put up $41,000 today in exchange for a 5.1 percent, 15-year annuity, what will the annual cash flow be?

✗   6. **Calculating Annuity Values** [LO1] Your company will generate $47,000 in annual revenue each year for the next seven years from a new information database. If the appropriate interest rate is 7.1 percent, what is the present value of the savings?

7. **Calculating Annuity Values** [LO1] If you deposit $4,500 at the end of each of the next 20 years into an account paying 9.7 percent interest, how much money will you have in the account in 20 years? How much will you have if you make deposits for 40 years?

8. **Calculating Annuity Values** [LO1] You want to have $60,000 in your savings account 12 years from now, and you're prepared to make equal annual deposits into the account at the end of each year. If the account pays 6.4 percent interest, what amount must you deposit each year?

9. **Calculating Annuity Values** [LO2] Prescott Bank offers you a five-year loan for $75,000 at an annual interest rate of 6.8 percent. What will your annual loan payment be?

✗   10. **Calculating Perpetuity Values** [LO1] The Maybe Pay Life Insurance Co. is trying to sell you an investment policy that will pay you and your heirs $35,000 per year forever. If the required return on this investment is 4.7 percent, how much will you pay for the policy?

11. **Calculating Perpetuity Values** [LO1] In the previous problem, suppose a sales associate told you the policy costs $800,000. At what interest rate would this be a fair deal?

12. **Calculating EAR** [LO4] Find the EAR in each of the following cases:

Stated Rate (APR)	Number of Times Compounded	Effective Rate (EAR)
9%	Quarterly	
16	Monthly	
12	Daily	
11	Infinite	

13. **Calculating APR** [LO4] Find the APR, or stated rate, in each of the following cases:

Stated Rate (APR)	Number of Times Compounded	Effective Rate (EAR)
	Semiannually	11.1%
	Monthly	19.6
	Weekly	10.5
	Infinite	8.4

14. **Calculating EAR** [LO4] First National Bank charges 13.1 percent compounded monthly on its business loans. First United Bank charges 13.4 percent compounded semiannually. As a potential borrower, which bank would you go to for a new loan?

15. **Calculating APR** [LO4] Elliott Credit Corp. wants to earn an effective annual return on its consumer loans of 17.1 percent per year. The bank uses daily compounding on its loans. What interest rate is the bank required by law to report to potential borrowers? Explain why this rate is misleading to an uninformed borrower.

16. **Calculating Future Values** [LO1] What is the future value of $3,100 in 17 years assuming an interest rate of 8.4 percent compounded semiannually?

17. **Calculating Future Values** [LO1] Spartan Credit Bank is offering 8.1 percent compounded daily on its savings accounts. If you deposit $6,500 today, how much will you have in the account in 5 years? In 10 years? In 20 years?

18. **Calculating Present Values** [LO1] An investment will pay you $80,000 in 10 years. If the appropriate discount rate is 9 percent compounded daily, what is the present value?

19. **EAR versus APR** [LO4] Big Dom's Pawn Shop charges an interest rate of 27 percent per month on loans to its customers. Like all lenders, Big Dom must report an APR to consumers. What rate should the shop report? What is the effective annual rate?

20. **Calculating Loan Payments** [LO2, 4] You want to buy a new sports coupe for $84,500, and the finance office at the dealership has quoted you an APR of 5.2 percent for a 60-month loan to buy the car. What will your monthly payments be? What is the effective annual rate on this loan?

21. **Calculating Number of Periods** [LO3] One of your customers is delinquent on his accounts payable balance. You've mutually agreed to a repayment schedule of $450 per month. You will charge 1.3 percent per month interest on the overdue balance. If the current balance is $18,000, how long will it take for the account to be paid off?

22. **Calculating EAR** [LO4] Friendly's Quick Loans, Inc., offers you "three for four or I knock on your door." This means you get $3 today and repay $4 when you get your paycheck in one week (or else). What's the effective annual return Friendly's earns on this lending business? If you were brave enough to ask, what APR would Friendly's say you were paying?

23. **Valuing Perpetuities** [LO1] Live Forever Life Insurance Co. is selling a perpetuity contract that pays $1,250 monthly. The contract currently sells for $245,000. What is the monthly return on this investment vehicle? What is the APR? The effective annual return?

24. **Calculating Annuity Future Values** [LO1] You are planning to make monthly deposits of $475 into a retirement account that pays 10 percent interest compounded monthly. If your first deposit will be made one month from now, how large will your retirement account be in 30 years?

25. **Calculating Annuity Future Values** [LO1] In the previous problem, suppose you make $5,700 annual deposits into the same retirement account. How large will your account balance be in 30 years?

26. **Calculating Annuity Present Values** [LO1] Beginning three months from now, you want to be able to withdraw $2,500 each quarter from your bank account to cover college expenses over the next four years. If the account pays .57 percent interest per quarter, how much do you need to have in your bank account today to meet your expense needs over the next four years?

27. **Discounted Cash Flow Analysis** [LO1] If the appropriate discount rate for the following cash flows is 9 percent compounded quarterly, what is the present value of the cash flows?

Year	Cash Flow
1	$ 815
2	990
3	0
4	1,520

28. **Discounted Cash Flow Analysis** [LO1] If the appropriate discount rate for the following cash flows is 7.17 percent per year, what is the present value of the cash flows?

Year	Cash Flow
1	$2,480
2	0
3	3,920
4	2,170

INTERMEDIATE
(Questions 29–56)

29. **Simple Interest versus Compound Interest** [LO4] First Simple Bank pays 6.4 percent simple interest on its investment accounts. If First Complex Bank pays interest on its accounts compounded annually, what rate should the bank set if it wants to match First Simple Bank over an investment horizon of 10 years?

30. **Calculating EAR** [LO4] You are looking at an investment that has an effective annual rate of 11.6 percent. What is the effective semiannual return? The effective quarterly return? The effective monthly return?

31. **Calculating Interest Expense** [LO2] You receive a credit card application from Shady Banks Savings and Loan offering an introductory rate of 1.25 percent per year, compounded monthly for the first six months, increasing thereafter to 17.8 percent compounded monthly. Assuming you transfer the $8,000 balance from your existing credit card and make no subsequent payments, how much interest will you owe at the end of the first year?

32. **Calculating Annuities** [LO1] You are planning to save for retirement over the next 30 years. To do this, you will invest $750 per month in a stock account and $250 per month in a bond account. The return of the stock account is expected to be 10 percent, and the bond account will pay 6 percent. When you retire, you will combine your money into an account with a return of 5 percent. How much can you withdraw each month from your account assuming a 25-year withdrawal period?

33. **Calculating Future Values** [LO1] You have an investment that will pay you .67 percent per month. How much will you have per dollar invested in one year? In two years?

34. **Calculating Annuity Payments** [LO1] You want to be a millionaire when you retire in 40 years. How much do you have to save each month if you can earn an annual return of 9.7 percent? How much do you have to save each month if you wait 10 years before you begin your deposits? 20 years?

35. **Calculating Rates of Return** [LO2] Suppose an investment offers to triple your money in 12 months (don't believe it). What rate of return per quarter are you being offered?

36. **Comparing Cash Flow Streams** [LO1] You've just joined the investment bank- ✂
ing firm of Dewey, Cheatum, and Howe. They've offered you two different salary
arrangements. You can have $85,000 per year for the next two years, or you can have
$74,000 per year for the next two years, along with a $20,000 signing bonus today.
The bonus is paid immediately, and the salary is paid in equal amounts at the end
of each month. If the interest rate is 7 percent compounded monthly, which do you
prefer?

37. **Growing Annuity** [LO1] You have just won the lottery and will receive $1,500,000
in one year. You will receive payments for 30 years, and the payments will increase
by 2.7 percent per year. If the appropriate discount rate is 6.8 percent, what is the
present value of your winnings?

38. **Growing Annuity** [LO1] Your job pays you only once a year for all the work
you did over the previous 12 months. Today, December 31, you just received your
salary of $55,000 and you plan to spend all of it. However, you want to start saving
for retirement beginning next year. You have decided that one year from today you
will begin depositing 9 percent of your annual salary in an account that will earn
10 percent per year. Your salary will increase at 3 percent per year throughout your
career. How much money will you have on the date of your retirement 40 years
from today?

39. **Present Value and Interest Rates** [LO1] What is the relationship between the
value of an annuity and the level of interest rates? Suppose you just bought an annuity with 11 annual payments of $8,500 per year at the current interest rate of 10 per-
cent per year. What happens to the value of your investment if interest rates suddenly
drop to 5 percent? What if interest rates suddenly rise to 15 percent?

40. **Calculating the Number of Payments** [LO2] You're prepared to make monthly
payments of $175, beginning at the end of this month, into an account that pays
7 percent interest compounded monthly. How many payments will you have made
when your account balance reaches $15,000?

41. **Calculating Annuity Present Values** [LO2] You want to borrow $115,000 from
your local bank to buy a new sailboat. You can afford to make monthly payments of
$2,250, but no more. Assuming monthly compounding, what is the highest rate you
can afford on a 60-month APR loan?

42. **Calculating Loan Payments** [LO2] You need a 30-year, fixed-rate mortgage to
buy a new home for $235,000. Your mortgage bank will lend you the money at an
APR of 5.35 percent for this 360-month loan. However, you can afford monthly payments of only $925, so you offer to pay off any remaining loan balance at the end of
the loan in the form of a single balloon payment. How large will this balloon payment
have to be for you to keep your monthly payments at $925?

43. **Present and Future Values** [LO1] The present value of the following cash flow
stream is $7,500 when discounted at 9 percent annually. What is the value of the
missing cash flow?

Year	Cash Flow
1	$1,700
2	?
3	2,450
4	2,980

44. Calculating Present Values [LO1] You just won the TVM Lottery. You will receive $1 million today plus another 10 annual payments that increase by $375,000 per year. Thus, in one year, you receive $1.375 million. In two years, you get $1.75 million, and so on. If the appropriate interest rate is 6.5 percent, what is the value of your winnings today?

✗ 45. EAR versus APR [LO4] You have just purchased a new warehouse. To finance the purchase, you've arranged for a 30-year mortgage loan for 80 percent of the $3,400,000 purchase price. The monthly payment on this loan will be $16,500. What is the APR on this loan? The EAR?

✗ 46. Present Value and Break-Even Interest [LO1] Consider a firm with a contract to sell an asset for $145,000 four years from now. The asset costs $91,700 to produce today. Given a relevant discount rate of 11 percent per year, will the firm make a profit on this asset? At what rate does the firm just break even?

47. Present Value and Multiple Cash Flows [LO1] What is the value today of $4,400 per year, at a discount rate of 8.3 percent, if the first payment is received 6 years from today and the last payment is received 20 years from today?

48. Variable Interest Rates [LO1] A 15-year annuity pays $1,475 per month, and payments are made at the end of each month. If the interest rate is 9 percent compounded monthly for the first seven years, and 6 percent compounded monthly thereafter, what is the present value of the annuity?

49. Comparing Cash Flow Streams [LO1] You have your choice of two investment accounts. Investment A is a 13-year annuity that features end-of-month $1,250 payments and has an interest rate of 7.5 percent compounded monthly. Investment B is a 7 percent continuously compounded lump sum investment, also good for 13 years. How much money would you need to invest in Investment B today for it to be worth as much as Investment A 13 years from now?

✗ 50. Calculating Present Value of a Perpetuity [LO1] Given an interest rate of 5.3 percent per year, what is the value at date $t = 7$ of a perpetual stream of $6,400 payments that begins at date $t = 15$?

51. Calculating EAR [LO4] A local finance company quotes an interest rate of 17.1 percent on one-year loans. So, if you borrow $20,000, the interest for the year will be $3,420. Because you must repay a total of $23,420 in one year, the finance company requires you to pay $23,420/12, or $1,951.67, per month over the next 12 months. Is the interest rate on this loan 17.1 percent? What rate would legally have to be quoted? What is the effective annual rate?

52. Calculating Present Values [LO1] A five-year annuity of 10 $5,900 semiannual payments will begin 9 years from now, with the first payment coming 9.5 years from now. If the discount rate is 8 percent compounded monthly, what is the value of this annuity five years from now? What is the value three years from now? What is the current value of the annuity?

53. Calculating Annuities Due [LO1] Suppose you are going to receive $13,500 per year for five years. The appropriate interest rate is 6.8 percent.

    a. What is the present value of the payments if they are in the form of an ordinary annuity? What is the present value if the payments are an annuity due?

    b. Suppose you plan to invest the payments for five years. What is the future value if the payments are an ordinary annuity? What if the payments are an annuity due?

    c. Which has the highest present value, the ordinary annuity or the annuity due? Which has the highest future value? Will this always be true?

54. **Calculating Annuities Due [LO1]** You want to buy a new sports car from Muscle Motors for $57,500. The contract is in the form of a 60-month annuity due at an APR of 5.9 percent. What will your monthly payment be?

55. **Amortization with Equal Payments [LO3]** Prepare an amortization schedule for a five-year loan of $71,500. The interest rate is 7 percent per year, and the loan calls for equal annual payments. How much interest is paid in the third year? How much total interest is paid over the life of the loan?

56. **Amortization with Equal Principal Payments [LO3]** Rework Problem 55 assuming that the loan agreement calls for a principal reduction of $14,300 every year instead of equal annual payments.

57. **Calculating Annuity Values [LO1]** Bilbo Baggins wants to save money to meet three objectives. First, he would like to be able to retire 30 years from now with retirement income of $17,500 per month for 25 years, with the first payment received 30 years and 1 month from now. Second, he would like to purchase a cabin in Rivendell in 10 years at an estimated cost of $345,000. Third, after he passes on at the end of the 25 years of withdrawals, he would like to leave an inheritance of $2,000,000 to his nephew Frodo. He can afford to save $2,350 per month for the next 10 years. If he can earn an EAR of 10 percent before he retires and an EAR of 7 percent after he retires, how much will he have to save each month in Years 11 through 30?

CHALLENGE
(Questions 57–80)

58. **Calculating Annuity Values [LO1]** After deciding to buy a new car, you can either lease the car or purchase it on a three-year loan. The car you wish to buy costs $43,000. The dealer has a special leasing arrangement where you pay $4,300 today and $505 per month for the next three years. If you purchase the car, you will pay it off in monthly payments over the next three years at an APR of 6 percent. You believe you will be able to sell the car for $28,000 in three years. Should you buy or lease the car? What break-even resale price in three years would make you indifferent between buying and leasing?

59. **Calculating Annuity Values [LO1]** An All-Pro defensive lineman is in contract negotiations. The team has offered the following salary structure:

Time	Salary
0	$8,400,000
1	$4,700,000
2	$5,100,000
3	$5,700,000
4	$6,400,000
5	$7,100,000
6	$7,800,000

All salaries are to be paid in lump sums. The player has asked you as his agent to renegotiate the terms. He wants a $10 million signing bonus payable today and a contract value increase of $2 million. He also wants an equal salary paid every three months, with the first paycheck three months from now. If the interest rate is 4.8 percent compounded daily, what is the amount of his quarterly check? Assume 365 days in a year.

60. **Discount Interest Loans [LO4]** This question illustrates what is known as *discount interest*. Imagine you are discussing a loan with a somewhat unscrupulous lender. You want to borrow $25,000 for one year. The interest rate is 14.9 percent. You and

the lender agree that the interest on the loan will be .149 × $25,000 = $3,725. So the lender deducts this interest amount from the loan up front and gives you $21,275. In this case, we say that the discount is $3,725. What's wrong here?

61. **Calculating Annuity Values** [LO1] You are serving on a jury. A plaintiff is suing the city for injuries sustained after a freak street sweeper accident. In the trial, doctors testified that it will be five years before the plaintiff is able to return to work. The jury has already decided in favor of the plaintiff. You are the foreperson of the jury and propose that the jury give the plaintiff an award to cover the following: (a) The present value of two years' back pay. The plaintiff's annual salary for the last two years would have been $43,000 and $46,000, respectively. (b) The present value of five years' future salary. You assume the salary will be $51,000 per year. (c) $150,000 for pain and suffering. (d) $20,000 for court costs. Assume that the salary payments are equal amounts paid at the end of each month. If the interest rate you choose is an EAR of 6.5 percent, what is the size of the settlement? If you were the plaintiff, would you like to see a higher or lower interest rate?

62. **Calculating EAR with Points** [LO4] You are looking at a one-year loan of $10,000. The interest rate is quoted as 9.8 percent plus 2 points. A *point* on a loan is 1 percent (one percentage point) of the loan amount. Quotes similar to this one are common with home mortgages. The interest rate quotation in this example requires the borrower to pay 2 points to the lender up front and repay the loan later with 9.8 percent interest. What rate would you actually be paying here?

63. **Calculating EAR with Points** [LO4] The interest rate on a one-year loan is quoted as 12 percent plus 3 points (see the previous problem). What is the EAR? Is your answer affected by the loan amount?

64. **Calculating Interest Rates** [LO2] You are buying a house and will borrow $225,000 on a 30-year fixed rate mortgage with monthly payments to finance the purchase. Your loan officer has offered you a mortgage with an APR of 4.3 percent. Alternatively, she tells you that you can "buy down" the interest rate to 4.05 percent if you pay points up front on the loan. A point on a loan is 1 percent (one percentage point) of the loan value. How many points, at most, would you be willing to pay to buy down the interest rate?

65. **Calculating Interest Rates** [LO2] In the previous problem, suppose that you believe that you will only live in the house for eight years before selling the house and buying another house. This means that in eight years, you will pay off the remaining balance of the original mortgage. What is the maximum number of points that you would be willing to pay now?

66. **EAR versus APR** [LO4] Two banks in the area offer 30-year, $275,000 mortgages at 5.1 percent and charge a $4,300 loan application fee. However, the application fee charged by Insecurity Bank and Trust is refundable if the loan application is denied, whereas that charged by I.M. Greedy and Sons Mortgage Bank is not. The current disclosure law requires that any fees that will be refunded if the applicant is rejected be included in calculating the APR, but this is not required with nonrefundable fees (presumably because refundable fees are part of the loan rather than a fee). What are the EARs on these two loans? What are the APRs?

67. **Calculating EAR with Add-On Interest** [LO4] This problem illustrates a deceptive way of quoting interest rates called *add-on interest*. Imagine that you see an advertisement for Crazy Judy's Stereo City that reads something like this: "$1,000 Instant Credit! 17.3% Simple Interest! Three Years to Pay! Low, Low Monthly Payments!" You're not exactly sure what all this means and somebody has spilled ink over the APR on the loan contract, so you ask the manager for clarification.

Judy explains that if you borrow $1,000 for three years at 17.3 percent interest, in three years you will owe:

$$\$1,000 \times 1.173^3 = \$1,000 \times 1.61396 = \$1,613.96$$

Now, Judy recognizes that coming up with $1,613.96 all at once might be a strain, so she lets you make "low, low monthly payments" of $1,613.96/36 = $44.83 per month, even though this is extra bookkeeping work for her.

    Is the interest rate on this loan 17.3 percent? Why or why not? What is the APR on this loan? What is the EAR? Why do you think this is called add-on interest?

68. **Growing Annuities [LO1]** You have successfully started and operated a company for the past 10 years. You have decided that it is time to sell your company and spend time on the beaches of Hawaii. A potential buyer is interested in your company, but he does not have the necessary capital to pay you a lump sum. Instead, he has offered $500,000 today and annuity payments for the balance. The first payment will be for $150,000 in three months. The payments will increase at 2 percent per quarter and a total of 25 quarterly payments will be made. If you require an EAR of 11 percent, how much are you being offered for your company?

69. **Calculating the Number of Periods [LO2]** Your Christmas ski vacation was great, but it unfortunately ran a bit over budget. All is not lost: You just received an offer in the mail to transfer your $15,000 balance from your current credit card, which charges an annual rate of 17.5 percent, to a new credit card charging a rate of 8.9 percent. How much faster could you pay the loan off by making your planned monthly payments of $250 with the new card? What if there was a fee of 2 percent charged on any balances transferred?

70. **Future Value and Multiple Cash Flows [LO1]** An insurance company is offering a new policy to its customers. Typically, the policy is bought by a parent or grandparent for a child at the child's birth. The purchaser (say, the parent) makes the following six payments to the insurance company:

First birthday:	$700
Second birthday:	$700
Third birthday:	$800
Fourth birthday:	$800
Fifth birthday:	$900
Sixth birthday:	$900

After the child's sixth birthday, no more payments are made. When the child reaches age 65, he or she receives $300,000. If the relevant interest rate is 10 percent for the first six years and 7 percent for all subsequent years, is the policy worth buying?

71. **Calculating a Balloon Payment [LO2]** You have just arranged for a $2,350,000 mortgage to finance the purchase of a large tract of land. The mortgage has an APR of 5.2 percent, and it calls for monthly payments over the next 30 years. However, the loan has an eight-year balloon payment, meaning that the loan must be paid off then. How big will the balloon payment be?

72. **Calculating Interest Rates [LO4]** A financial planning service offers a college savings program. The plan calls for you to make six annual payments of $15,000 each, with the first payment occurring today, your child's 12th birthday. Beginning

on your child's 18th birthday, the plan will provide $32,000 per year for four years. What return is this investment offering?

73. **Break-Even Investment Returns** [LO4] Your financial planner offers you two different investment plans. Plan X is an annual perpetuity of $35,000 per year. Plan Y is an annuity for 15 years and an annual payment of $47,000. Both plans will make their first payment one year from today. At what discount rate would you be indifferent between these two plans?

74. **Perpetual Cash Flows** [LO1] What is the value of an investment that pays $25,000 every *other* year forever, if the first payment occurs one year from today and the discount rate is 7 percent compounded daily? What is the value today if the first payment occurs four years from today?

75. **Ordinary Annuities and Annuities Due** [LO1] As discussed in the text, an annuity due is identical to an ordinary annuity except that the periodic payments occur at the beginning of each period instead of at the end of the period. Show that the relationship between the value of an ordinary annuity and the value of an otherwise equivalent annuity due is:

Annuity due value = Ordinary annuity value $\times (1 + r)$

Show this for both present and future values.

76. **Calculating Growing Annuities** [LO1] You have 45 years left until retirement and want to retire with $4 million. Your salary is paid annually, and you will receive $50,000 at the end of the current year. Your salary will increase at 3 percent per year, and you can earn an annual return of 9 percent on the money you invest. If you save a constant percentage of your salary, what percentage of your salary must you save each year?

77. **Calculating EAR** [LO4] A check-cashing store is in the business of making personal loans to walk-up customers. The store makes only one-week loans at 6.8 percent interest per week.

   a. What APR must the store report to its customers? What EAR are customers actually paying?

   b. Now suppose the store makes one-week loans at 6.8 percent discount interest per week (see Problem 60). What's the APR now? The EAR?

   c. The check-cashing store also makes one-month add-on interest loans at 6.8 percent discount interest per week. Thus if you borrow $100 for one month (four weeks), the interest will be ($100 $\times$ 1.068^4) − 100 = $30.10. Because this is discount interest, your net loan proceeds today will be $69.90. You must then repay the store $100 at the end of the month. To help you out, though, the store lets you pay off this $100 in installments of $25 per week. What is the APR of this loan? What is the EAR?

78. **Present Value of a Growing Perpetuity** [LO1] What is the equation for the present value of a growing perpetuity with a payment of C one period from today if the payments grow by C each period?

79. **Rule of 72** [LO4] Earlier, we discussed the Rule of 72, a useful approximation for many interest rates and periods for the time it takes a lump sum to double in value. For a 10 percent interest rate, show that the "Rule of 73" is slightly better. For what rate is the Rule of 72 exact? (*Hint*: Use the Solver function in Excel.)

80. **Rule of 69.3** [LO4] A corollary to the Rule of 72 is the Rule of 69.3. The Rule of 69.3 is exactly correct except for rounding when interest rates are compounded continuously. Prove the Rule of 69.3 for continuously compounded interest.

EXCEL MASTER-IT! PROBLEM

This is a classic retirement problem. A friend is celebrating her birthday and wants to start saving for her anticipated retirement. She has the following years to retirement and retirement spending goals:

Years until retirement:	30
Amount to withdraw each year:	$90,000
Years to withdraw in retirement:	20
Interest rate:	8%

Because your friend is planning ahead, the first withdrawal will not take place until one year after she retires. She wants to make equal annual deposits into her account for her retirement fund.

a. If she starts making these deposits in one year and makes her last deposit on the day she retires, what amount must she deposit annually to be able to make the desired withdrawals at retirement?

b. Suppose your friend has just inherited a large sum of money. Rather than making equal annual payments, she has decided to make one lump sum deposit today to cover her retirement needs. What amount does she have to deposit today?

c. Suppose your friend's employer will contribute to the account each year as part of the company's profit sharing plan. In addition, your friend expects a distribution from a family trust 20 years from now. What amount must she deposit annually now to be able to make the desired withdrawals at retirement?

Employer's annual contribution:	$ 1,500
Years until trust fund distribution:	20
Amount of trust fund distribution:	$25,000

MINICASE

The MBA Decision

Ben Bates graduated from college six years ago with a finance undergraduate degree. Although he is satisfied with his current job, his goal is to become an investment banker. He feels that an MBA degree would allow him to achieve this goal. After examining schools, he has narrowed his choice to either Wilton University or Mount Perry College. Although internships are encouraged by both schools, to get class credit for the internship, no salary can be paid. Other than internships, neither school will allow its students to work while enrolled in its MBA program.

Ben currently works at the money management firm of Dewey and Louis. His annual salary at the firm is $53,000 per year, and his salary is expected to increase at 3 percent per year until retirement. He is currently 28 years old and expects to work for 38 more years. His current job includes a fully paid health insurance plan, and his current average tax rate is 26 percent. Ben has a savings account with enough money to cover the entire cost of his MBA program.

The Ritter College of Business at Wilton University is one of the top MBA programs in the country. The MBA degree requires two years of full-time enrollment at the university. The annual tuition is $58,000, payable at the beginning of each school year. Books and other supplies are estimated to cost $2,000 per year. Ben expects that after graduation from Wilton, he will receive a job offer for about $87,000 per year, with a $10,000 signing bonus. The salary at this job will increase at 4 percent per year. Because of the higher salary, his average income tax rate will increase to 31 percent.

The Bradley School of Business at Mount Perry College began its MBA program 16 years ago. The Bradley School is smaller and less well known than the Ritter College. Bradley offers an accelerated one-year program, with a tuition cost of $75,000 to be paid upon matriculation. Books and other supplies for the program are expected to cost $4,200. Ben thinks that he will receive an offer of $78,000 per year upon graduation, with an $8,000 signing bonus. The salary at this job will increase at 3.5 percent per year. His average tax rate at this level of income will be 29 percent.

Both schools offer a health insurance plan that will cost $3,000 per year, payable at the beginning of the year. Ben has also found that both schools offer graduate housing. His room and board expenses will decrease by $4,000 per year at either school he attends. The appropriate discount rate is 5.5 percent.

QUESTIONS

1. How does Ben's age affect his decision to get an MBA?

2. What other, perhaps nonquantifiable, factors affect Ben's decision to get an MBA?

3. Assuming all salaries are paid at the end of each year, what is the best option for Ben from a strictly financial standpoint?

4. Ben believes that the appropriate analysis is to calculate the future value of each option. How would you evaluate this statement?

5. What initial salary would Ben need to receive to make him indifferent between attending Wilton University and staying in his current position?

6. Suppose, instead of being able to pay cash for his MBA, Ben must borrow the money. The current borrowing rate is 5.4 percent. How would this affect his decision?

Interest Rates and Bond Valuation

7
Chapter

GENERALLY, WHEN AN INVESTMENT is made, you expect that you will get back more money in the future than you invested today. In December 2017, this wasn't the case for many bond investors. The yield on a 5-year German government bond was about negative .20 percent, and the yields on 2-year and 5-year Japanese government bonds were negative .14 percent and negative .09 percent, respectively. In fact, in 2016, the amount of debt worldwide that had a negative yield reached a record $13.4 trillion! And negative yields were not restricted to government bonds, as the yield on the chocolate maker Nestlé's bond was negative as well.

As you will see in this chapter, a bond's yield is an important determinant of a bond's price. In addition to showing you how to value a bond, we will talk about various bond features and the factors that affect bond yields.

Learning Objectives

After studying this chapter, you should be able to:

LO1 Define important bond features and types of bonds.

LO2 Explain bond values and yields and why they fluctuate.

LO3 Describe bond ratings and what they mean.

LO4 Outline the impact of inflation on interest rates.

LO5 Illustrate the term structure of interest rates and the determinants of bond yields.

©by_adri/iStockPhotoGettyImages

For updates on the latest happenings in finance, visit fundamentalsofcorporatefinance.blogspot.com.

Our goal in this chapter is to introduce you to bonds. We begin by showing how the techniques we developed in Chapters 5 and 6 can be applied to bond valuation. From there, we go on to discuss bond features and how bonds are bought and sold. One important thing we learn is that bond values depend, in large part, on interest rates. We therefore close the chapter with an examination of interest rates and their behavior.

196 **PART 3** Valuation of Future Cash Flows

7.1 Bonds and Bond Valuation

Excel Master It!

xlsx Excel Master coverage online

When a corporation or government wishes to borrow money from the public on a long-term basis, it usually does so by issuing or selling debt securities that are generically called *bonds*. In this section, we describe the various features of corporate bonds and some of the terminology associated with bonds. We then discuss the cash flows associated with a bond and how bonds can be valued using our discounted cash flow procedure.

BOND FEATURES AND PRICES

As we mentioned in our previous chapter, a bond is normally an interest-only loan, meaning that the borrower will pay the interest every period, but none of the principal will be repaid until the end of the loan. For example, suppose the Beck Corporation wants to borrow $1,000 for 30 years. The interest rate on similar debt issued by similar corporations is 12 percent. Beck will thus pay .12 × $1,000 = $120 in interest every year for 30 years. At the end of 30 years, Beck will repay the $1,000. As this example suggests, a bond is a fairly simple financing arrangement. There is, however, a rich jargon associated with bonds, so we will use this example to define some of the more important terms.

In our example, the $120 regular interest payments that Beck promises to make are called the bond's **coupons**. Because the coupon is constant and paid every year, the type of bond we are describing is sometimes called a *level coupon bond*. The amount that will be repaid at the end of the loan is called the bond's **face value**, or **par value**. As in our example, this par value is usually $1,000 for corporate bonds, and a bond that sells for its par value is called a *par value bond*. Government bonds frequently have much larger face, or par, values. Finally, the annual coupon divided by the face value is called the **coupon rate** on the bond; in this case, because $120/1,000 = 12%, the bond has a 12 percent coupon rate.

The number of years until the face value is paid is called the bond's time to **maturity**. A corporate bond will frequently have a maturity of 30 years when it is originally issued, but this varies. Once the bond has been issued, the number of years to maturity declines as time goes by.

BOND VALUES AND YIELDS

As time passes, interest rates change in the marketplace. The cash flows from a bond, however, stay the same. As a result, the value of the bond will fluctuate. When interest rates rise, the present value of the bond's remaining cash flows declines, and the bond is worth less. When interest rates fall, the bond is worth more.

To determine the value of a bond at a particular point in time, we need to know the number of periods remaining until maturity, the face value, the coupon, and the market interest rate for bonds with similar features. This interest rate required in the market on a bond is called the bond's **yield to maturity (YTM)**. This rate is sometimes called the bond's *yield* for short. Given all this information, we can calculate the present value of the cash flows as an estimate of the bond's current market value.

For example, suppose the Xanth (pronounced "zanth") Co. were to issue a bond with 10 years to maturity. The Xanth bond has an annual coupon of $80. Similar bonds have a yield to maturity of 8 percent. Based on our preceding discussion, the Xanth bond will pay $80 per year for the next 10 years in coupon interest. In 10 years, Xanth will pay $1,000 to the owner of the bond. The cash flows from the bond are shown in Figure 7.1. What would this bond sell for?

As illustrated in Figure 7.1, the Xanth bond's cash flows have an annuity component (the coupons) and a lump sum (the face value paid at maturity). We thus estimate the market

coupon
The stated interest payment made on a bond.

face value
The principal amount of a bond that is repaid at the end of the term. Also called *par value*.

coupon rate
The annual coupon divided by the face value of a bond.

maturity
The specified date on which the principal amount of a bond is paid.

yield to maturity (YTM)
The rate required in the market on a bond.

FIGURE 7.1   **Cash Flows for Xanth Co. Bond**

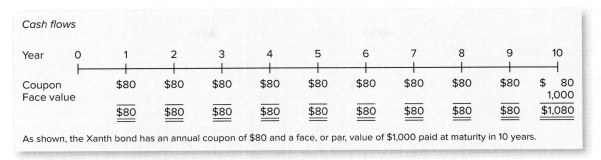

As shown, the Xanth bond has an annual coupon of $80 and a face, or par, value of $1,000 paid at maturity in 10 years.

value of the bond by calculating the present value of these two components separately and adding the results together. First, at the going rate of 8 percent, the present value of the $1,000 paid in 10 years is:

Present value = $1,000/1.08^{10} = $1,000/2.1589 = $463.19

Second, the bond offers $80 per year for 10 years; the present value of this annuity stream is:

$$Annuity\ present\ value = \$80 \times (1-1/1.08^{10})/.08$$
$$= \$80 \times (1-1/2.1589)/.08$$
$$= \$80 \times 6.7101$$
$$= \$536.81$$

We can now add the values for the two parts together to get the bond's value:

Total bond value = $463.19 + 536.81 = $1,000

This bond sells for exactly its face value. This is not a coincidence. The going interest rate in the market is 8 percent. Considered as an interest-only loan, what interest rate does this bond have? With an $80 coupon, this bond pays exactly 8 percent interest only when it sells for $1,000.

To illustrate what happens as interest rates change, suppose a year has gone by. The Xanth bond now has nine years to maturity. If the interest rate in the market has risen to 10 percent, what will the bond be worth? To find out, we repeat the present value calculations with 9 years instead of 10, and a 10 percent yield instead of an 8 percent yield. First, the present value of the $1,000 paid in nine years at 10 percent is:

Present value = $1,000/1.10^9 = $1,000/2.3579 = $424.10

Second, the bond now offers $80 per year for nine years; the present value of this annuity stream at 10 percent is:

$$Annuity\ present\ value = \$80 \times (1-1/1.10^9)/.10$$
$$= \$80 \times (1-1/2.3579)/.10$$
$$= \$80 \times 5.7590$$
$$= \$460.72$$

We can now add the values for the two parts together to get the bond's value:

Total bond value = $424.10 + 460.72 = $884.82

A good bond site to visit is **finance.yahoo.com/bonds**, which has loads of useful information.

Therefore, the bond should sell for about $885. In the vernacular, we say that this bond, with its 8 percent coupon, is priced to yield 10 percent at $885.

The Xanth Co. bond now sells for less than its $1,000 face value. Why? The market interest rate is 10 percent. Considered as an interest-only loan of $1,000, this bond pays only 8 percent, its coupon rate. Because this bond pays less than the going rate, investors are willing to lend only something less than the $1,000 promised repayment. Because the bond sells for less than face value, it is said to be a *discount bond*.

The only way to get the interest rate up to 10 percent is to lower the price to less than $1,000 so that the purchaser, in effect, has a built-in gain. For the Xanth bond, the price of $885 is $115 less than the face value, so an investor who purchases and keeps the bond will get $80 per year and will have a $115 gain at maturity as well. This gain compensates the lender for the below-market coupon rate.

Another way to see why the bond is discounted by $115 is to note that the $80 coupon is $20 below the coupon on a newly issued par value bond, based on current market conditions. The bond would be worth $1,000 only if it had a coupon of $100 per year. In a sense, an investor who buys and keeps the bond gives up $20 per year for nine years. At 10 percent, this annuity stream is worth:

$$\text{Annuity present value} = \$20 \times (1 - 1/1.10^9)/.10$$
$$= \$20 \times 5.7590$$
$$= \$115.18$$

This is the amount of the discount.

What would the Xanth bond sell for if interest rates had dropped by 2 percent instead of rising by 2 percent? As you might guess, the bond would sell for more than $1,000. Such a bond is said to sell at a *premium* and is called a *premium bond*.

Online bond calculators are available at **personal .fidelity.com**; interest rate information is available at **money.cnn.com/data/bonds** and **www.bankrate.com**.

This case is the opposite of that of a discount bond. The Xanth bond now has a coupon rate of 8 percent when the market rate is only 6 percent. Investors are willing to pay a premium to get this extra coupon amount. In this case, the relevant discount rate is 6 percent, and there are nine years remaining. The present value of the $1,000 face amount is:

$$\text{Present value} = \$1,000/1.06^9 = \$1,000/1.6895 = \$591.90$$

The present value of the coupon stream is:

$$\text{Annuity present value} = \$80 \times (1 - 1/1.06^9)/.06$$
$$= \$80 \times (1 - 1/1.6895)/.06$$
$$= \$80 \times 6.8017$$
$$= \$544.14$$

We can now add the values for the two parts together to get the bond's value:

$$\text{Total bond value} = \$591.90 + 544.14 = \$1,136.03$$

Total bond value is therefore about $136 in excess of par value. Once again, we can verify this amount by noting that the coupon is now $20 too high, based on current market conditions. The present value of $20 per year for nine years at 6 percent is:

$$\text{Annuity present value} = \$20 \times (1 - 1/1.06^9)/.06$$
$$= \$20 \times 6.8017$$
$$= \$136.03$$

This is just as we calculated.

Based on our examples, we can now write the general expression for the value of a bond. If a bond has (1) a face value of F paid at maturity, (2) a coupon of C paid per period, (3) t periods to maturity, and (4) a yield of r per period, its value is:

Bond value = $C \times [1 - 1/(1 + r)^t]/r$ + $F/(1 + r)^t$

Bond value =   Present value   +   Present value
**   of the coupons   of the face amount**

7.1

Semiannual Coupons   **EXAMPLE 7.1**

In practice, bonds issued in the United States usually make coupon payments twice a year. So, if an ordinary bond has a coupon rate of 14 percent, then the owner will get a total of $140 per year, but this $140 will come in two payments of $70 each. Suppose we are examining such a bond. The yield to maturity is quoted at 16 percent.

Bond yields are quoted like APRs; the quoted rate is equal to the actual rate per period multiplied by the number of periods. In this case, with a 16 percent quoted yield and semiannual payments, the true yield is 8 percent per six months. The bond matures in seven years. What is the bond's price? What is the effective annual yield on this bond?

Based on our discussion, we know the bond will sell at a discount because it has a coupon rate of 7 percent every six months when the market requires 8 percent every six months. So, if our answer exceeds $1,000, we know we have made a mistake.

To get the exact price, we first calculate the present value of the bond's face value of $1,000 paid in seven years. This seven-year period has 14 periods of six months each. At 8 percent per period, the value is:

Present value = $1,000/1.08^{14}$ = $1,000/2.9372 = $340.46

The coupons can be viewed as a 14-period annuity of $70 per period. At an 8 percent discount rate, the present value of such an annuity is:

Annuity present value = $70 \times (1 - 1/1.08^{14})/.08$
                      = $70 \times (1 - .3405)/.08$
                      = 70×8.2442
                      = $577.10

The total present value gives us what the bond should sell for:

Total present value = $340.46 + 577.10 = $917.56

To calculate the effective yield on this bond, note that 8 percent every six months is equivalent to:

Effective annual rate = $(1 + .08)^2 - 1 = 16.64\%$

The effective yield is 16.64 percent.

As we have illustrated in this section, bond prices and interest rates always move in opposite directions. When interest rates rise, a bond's value, like any other present value, will decline. Similarly, when interest rates fall, bond values rise. Even if we are considering a bond that is riskless in the sense that the borrower is certain to make all the payments, there is still risk in owning a bond. We discuss this next.

Visit **investorguide.com** to learn more about bonds.

INTEREST RATE RISK

The risk that arises for bond owners from fluctuating interest rates is called *interest rate risk*. How much interest rate risk a bond has depends on how sensitive its price is to interest rate changes. This sensitivity directly depends on two things: The time to maturity and the coupon rate. As we will see momentarily, you should keep the following in mind when looking at a bond:

1. All other things being equal, the longer the time to maturity, the greater the interest rate risk.
2. All other things being equal, the lower the coupon rate, the greater the interest rate risk.

We illustrate the first of these two points in Figure 7.2. As shown, we compute and plot prices under different interest rate scenarios for 10 percent coupon bonds with maturities of 1 year and 30 years. Notice how the slope of the line connecting the prices is much steeper for the 30-year maturity than it is for the 1-year maturity. This steepness tells us that a relatively small change in interest rates will lead to a substantial change in the bond's value. In comparison, the 1-year bond's price is relatively insensitive to interest rate changes.

Intuitively, we can see that longer-term bonds have greater interest rate sensitivity because a large portion of a bond's value comes from the $1,000 face amount. The present value of this amount isn't greatly affected by a small change in interest rates if the

FIGURE 7.2

Interest Rate Risk and Time to Maturity

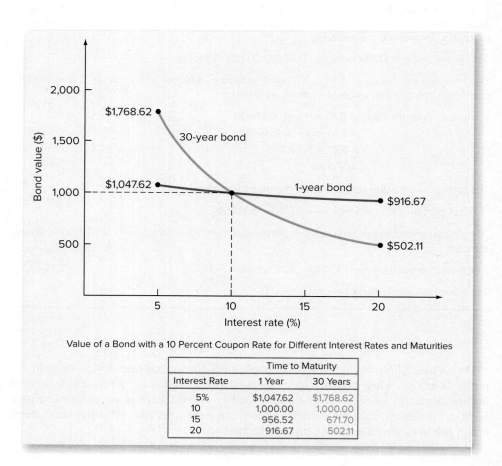

Value of a Bond with a 10 Percent Coupon Rate for Different Interest Rates and Maturities

Interest Rate	Time to Maturity	
	1 Year	30 Years
5%	$1,047.62	$1,768.62
10	1,000.00	1,000.00
15	956.52	671.70
20	916.67	502.11

amount is to be received in one year. Even a small change in the interest rate, however, once it is compounded for 30 years, can have a significant effect on the present value. As a result, the present value of the face amount will be much more volatile with a longer-term bond.

The other thing to know about interest rate risk is that, like most things in finance and economics, it increases at a decreasing rate. In other words, if we compared a 10-year bond to a 1-year bond, we would see that the 10-year bond has much greater interest rate risk. If you were to compare a 20-year bond to a 30-year bond, you would find that the 30-year bond has somewhat greater interest rate risk because it has a longer maturity, but the difference in the risk would be fairly small.

The reason that bonds with lower coupons have greater interest rate risk is essentially the same. As we discussed earlier, the value of a bond depends on the present value of its coupons and the present value of the face amount. If two bonds with different coupon rates have the same maturity, then the value of the one with the lower coupon is proportionately more dependent on the face amount to be received at maturity. As a result, all other things being equal, its value will fluctuate more as interest rates change. Put another way, the bond with the higher coupon has a larger cash flow early in its life, so its value is less sensitive to changes in the discount rate.

Bonds are rarely issued with maturities longer than 30 years. However, low interest rates in recent years have led to the issuance of much longer-term issues. In the 1990s, Walt Disney issued "Sleeping Beauty" bonds with a 100-year maturity. Similarly, BellSouth (now known as AT&T), Coca-Cola, and Dutch banking giant ABN AMRO all issued bonds with 100-year maturities. These companies evidently wanted to lock in the historical low interest rates for a *long* time. The current record holder for corporations looks to be Republic National Bank, which sold bonds with 1,000 years to maturity. Although somewhat rare, 100-year bond issues still occur, and recently they have even been issued by governments. For example, Belgium issued 100-year bonds in 2015, and Ireland issued 100-year bonds in 2016. The Irish bonds had a yield to maturity of only 2.35 percent when they were originally issued, something to keep in mind when we discuss the term structure of interest rates later in this chapter.

We can illustrate the effect of interest rate risk using the 100-year BellSouth (AT&T) issue. The following table provides some basic information about this issue, along with its prices on December 31, 1995, March 6, 2009, and December 29, 2017:

Maturity	Coupon Rate	Price on 12/31/95	Price on 3/6/09	Percentage Change in Price 1995–2009	Price on 12/29/17	Percentage Change in Price 2009–2017
2095	7.00%	$1,000.00	$803.43	−19.66%	$1,166.10	45.14%

Several things emerge from this table. First, interest rates apparently increased between December 31, 1995, and March 6, 2009 (why?). After that, they fell (why?). The bond's price first lost 19.66 percent and then gained 45.14 percent.

FINDING THE YIELD TO MATURITY: MORE TRIAL AND ERROR

Frequently, we will know a bond's price, coupon rate, and maturity date, but not its yield to maturity. For example, suppose we are interested in a six-year, 8 percent coupon bond with annual payments. A broker quotes a price of $955.14. What is the yield on this bond?

We've seen that the price of a bond can be written as the sum of its annuity and lump sum components. Knowing that there is an $80 coupon for six years and a $1,000 face value, we can say that the price is:

$$\$955.14 = \$80 \times [1 - 1/(1 + r)^6]/r + 1,000/(1 + r)^6$$

where r is the unknown discount rate, or yield to maturity. We have one equation here and one unknown, but we cannot solve it for r explicitly. The only way to find the answer is to use trial and error.

This problem is essentially identical to the one we examined in the last chapter when we tried to find the unknown interest rate on an annuity. Finding the rate (or yield) on a bond is even more complicated because of the $1,000 face amount.

We can speed up the trial-and-error process by using what we know about bond prices and yields. In this case, the bond has an $80 coupon and is selling at a discount. We know that the yield is greater than 8 percent. If we compute the price at 10 percent:

$$\begin{aligned} \text{Bond value} &= \$80 \times (1 - 1/1.10^6)/.10 + 1,000/1.10^6 \\ &= \$80 \times 4.3553 + 1,000/1.7716 \\ &= \$912.89 \end{aligned}$$

Current market rates are available at **www.bankrate.com**.

current yield
A bond's annual coupon divided by its price.

At 10 percent, the value we calculate is lower than the actual price, so 10 percent is too high. The true yield must be somewhere between 8 and 10 percent. At this point, it's "plug and chug" to find the answer. You would probably want to try 9 percent next. If you did, you would see that this is in fact the bond's yield to maturity.

A bond's yield to maturity should not be confused with its **current yield**, which is a bond's annual coupon divided by its price. In the example we just worked, the bond's annual coupon was $80, and its price was $955.14. Given these numbers, we see that the current yield is $80/955.14 = 8.38 percent, which is less than the yield to maturity of 9 percent. The reason the current yield is too low is that it considers only the coupon portion of your return; it doesn't consider the built-in gain from the price discount. For a premium bond, the reverse is true, meaning that current yield would be higher because it ignores the built-in loss.

Our discussion of bond valuation is summarized in Table 7.1.

TABLE 7.1

Summary of Bond Valuation

I. Finding the Value of a Bond

Bond value = $C \times [1 - 1/(1 + r)^t]/r + F/(1 + r)^t$
where:
   C = Coupon paid each period
   r = Rate per period
   t = Number of periods
   F = Bond's face value

II. Finding the Yield on a Bond
Given a bond value, coupon, time to maturity, and face value, it is possible to find the implicit discount rate, or yield to maturity, by trial and error only. To do this, try different discount rates until the calculated bond value equals the given value (or let a financial calculator do it for you). Remember that increasing the rate *decreases* the bond value.

Current Events

EXAMPLE 7.2

A bond has a quoted price of $1,080.42. It has a face value of $1,000, a semiannual coupon of $30, and a maturity of five years. What is its current yield? What is its yield to maturity? Which is bigger? Why?

Notice that this bond makes semiannual payments of $30, so the annual payment is $60. The current yield is thus $60/1,080.42 = 5.55 percent. To calculate the yield to maturity, refer back to Example 7.1. In this case, the bond pays $30 every six months and has 10 six-month periods until maturity. So, we need to find r as follows:

$$\$1,080.42 = \$30 \times [1 - 1/(1 + r)^{10}]/r + 1,000/(1 + r)^{10}$$

After some trial and error, we find that r is equal to about 2.1 percent. But, the tricky part is that this 2.1 percent is the yield *per six months*. We have to double it to get the yield to maturity, so the yield to maturity is 4.2 percent, which is less than the current yield. The reason is that the current yield ignores the built-in loss of the premium between now and maturity.

Bond Yields

EXAMPLE 7.3

You're looking at two bonds identical in every way except for their coupons and, of course, their prices. Both have 12 years to maturity. The first bond has a 10 percent annual coupon rate and sells for $935.08. The second has a 12 percent annual coupon rate. What do you think it would sell for?

Because the two bonds are similar, they will be priced to yield about the same rate. We first need to calculate the yield on the 10 percent coupon bond. Proceeding as before, we know that the yield must be greater than 10 percent because the bond is selling at a discount. The bond has a fairly long maturity of 12 years. We've seen that long-term bond prices are relatively sensitive to interest rate changes, so the yield is probably close to 10 percent. A little trial and error reveals that the yield is actually 11 percent:

$$\begin{aligned}
\text{Bond value} &= \$100 \times (1 - 1/1.11^{12})/.11 + 1,000/1.11^{12} \\
&= \$100 \times 6.4924 + 1,000/3.4985 \\
&= \$649.24 + 285.84 \\
&= \$935.08
\end{aligned}$$

With an 11 percent yield, the second bond will sell at a premium because of its $120 coupon. Its value is:

$$\begin{aligned}
\text{Bond value} &= \$120 \times (1 - 1/1.11^{12})/.11 + 1,000/1.11^{12} \\
&= \$120 \times 6.4924 + 1,000/3.4985 \\
&= \$779.08 + 285.84 \\
&= \$1,064.92
\end{aligned}$$

CALCULATOR HINTS

How to Calculate Bond Prices and Yields Using a Financial Calculator

Many financial calculators have fairly sophisticated built-in bond valuation routines. However, these vary quite a lot in implementation, and not all financial calculators have them. As a result, we will illustrate a simple way to handle bond problems that will work on about any financial calculator.

To begin, of course, we first remember to clear out the calculator! Returning to Example 7.3, we have two bonds to consider, both with 12 years to maturity. The first one sells for $935.08 and has a 10 percent annual coupon rate. To find its yield, we can do the following:

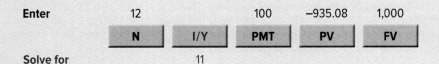

Enter	12		100	−935.08	1,000
	N	**I/Y**	**PMT**	**PV**	**FV**
Solve for		11			

Notice that here we have entered both a future value of $1,000, representing the bond's face value, and a payment of 10 percent of $1,000, or $100, per year, representing the bond's annual coupon. Also, notice that we have a negative sign on the bond's price, which we have entered as the present value.

For the second bond, we now know that the relevant yield is 11 percent. It has a 12 percent annual coupon and 12 years to maturity, so what's the price? To answer, we enter the relevant values and solve for the present value of the bond's cash flows:

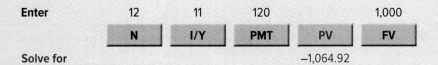

Enter	12	11	120		1,000
	N	**I/Y**	**PMT**	**PV**	**FV**
Solve for				−1,064.92	

There is an important detail that comes up here. Suppose we have a bond with a price of $902.29, 10 years to maturity, and a coupon rate of 6 percent. As we mentioned earlier, most bonds actually make semiannual payments. Assuming that this is the case for the bond here, what's the bond's yield? To answer, we need to enter the relevant numbers like this:

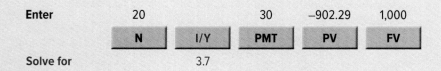

Enter	20		30	−902.29	1,000
	N	**I/Y**	**PMT**	**PV**	**FV**
Solve for		3.7			

Notice that we entered $30 as the payment because the bond actually makes payments of $30 every six months. Similarly, we entered 20 for N because there are actually 20 six-month periods. When we solve for the yield, we get 3.7 percent. The tricky thing to remember is that this is the yield *per six months*, so we have to double it to get the right answer: 2 × 3.7 = 7.4 percent, which would be the bond's reported yield.

SPREADSHEET STRATEGIES

How to Calculate Bond Prices and Yields Using a Spreadsheet

Most spreadsheets have fairly elaborate routines available for calculating bond values and yields; many of these routines involve details we have not discussed. Setting up a spreadsheet to calculate prices or yields is straightforward, as our next two spreadsheets show:

	A	B	C	D	E	F	G	H
1								
2	**Using a spreadsheet to calculate bond values**							
3								
4	Suppose we have a bond with 22 years to maturity, a coupon rate of 8 percent, and a yield to							
5	maturity of 9 percent. If the bond makes semiannual payments, what is its price today?							
6								
7	Settlement date:	1/1/00						
8	Maturity date:	1/1/22						
9	Annual coupon rate:	.08						
10	Yield to maturity:	.09						
11	Face value (% of par):	100						
12	Coupons per year:	2						
13	Bond price (% of par):	**90.49**						
14								
15	The formula entered in cell B13 is =PRICE(B7,B8,B9,B10,B11,B12); notice that face value and bond							
16	price are given as a percentage of face value.							

	A	B	C	D	E	F	G	H
1								
2	**Using a spreadsheet to calculate bond yields**							
3								
4	Suppose we have a bond with 22 years to maturity, a coupon rate of 8 percent, and a price of							
5	$960.17. If the bond makes semiannual payments, what is its yield to maturity?							
6								
7	Settlement date:	1/1/00						
8	Maturity date:	1/1/22						
9	Annual coupon rate:	.08						
10	Bond price (% of par):	96.017						
11	Face value (% of par):	100						
12	Coupons per year:	2						
13	Yield to maturity:	**.084**						
14								
15	The formula entered in cell B13 is =YIELD(B7,B8,B9,B10,B11,B12); notice that face value and bond							
16	price are entered as a percentage of face value.							
17								

In our spreadsheets, notice that we had to enter two dates: A settlement date and a maturity date. The settlement date is the date you actually pay for the bond, and the maturity date is the day the bond actually matures. In most of our problems, we don't explicitly have these dates, so we have to make them up. For example, because our bond has 22 years to maturity, we picked 1/1/2000 (January 1, 2000) as the settlement date and 1/1/2022 (January 1, 2022) as the maturity date. Any two dates would do as long as they are exactly 22 years apart, but these are particularly easy to work with. Finally, notice that we had to enter the coupon rate and yield to maturity in annual terms and then explicitly provide the number of coupon payments per year.

Concept Questions

7.1a   What are the cash flows associated with a bond?

7.1b   What is the general expression for the value of a bond?

7.1c   Is it true that the only risk associated with owning a bond is that the issuer will not make all the payments? Explain.

7.2 More about Bond Features

In this section, we continue our discussion of corporate debt by describing in some detail the basic terms and features that make up a typical long-term corporate bond. We discuss additional issues associated with long-term debt in subsequent sections.

Securities issued by corporations may be classified roughly as *equity securities* and *debt securities*. At the crudest level, a debt represents something that must be repaid; it is the result of borrowing money. When corporations borrow, they generally promise to make regularly scheduled interest payments and to repay the original amount borrowed (that is, the principal). The person or firm making the loan is called the *creditor* or *lender*. The corporation borrowing the money is called the *debtor* or *borrower*.

From a financial point of view, the main differences between debt and equity are the following:

1. Debt is not an ownership interest in the firm. Creditors generally do not have voting power.
2. The corporation's payment of interest on debt is considered a cost of doing business and is tax deductible (up to certain limits). Dividends paid to stockholders are *not* tax deductible.
3. Unpaid debt is a liability of the firm. If it is not paid, the creditors can legally claim the assets of the firm. This action can result in liquidation or reorganization, two of the possible consequences of bankruptcy. Thus, one of the costs of issuing debt is the possibility of financial failure. This possibility does not arise when equity is issued.

IS IT DEBT OR EQUITY?

Sometimes it is unclear if a particular security is debt or equity. For example, suppose a corporation issues a perpetual bond with interest payable solely from corporate income if and only if earned. Whether this is really a debt is hard to say and is primarily a legal and semantic issue. Courts and taxing authorities would have the final say.

Corporations are adept at creating exotic, hybrid securities that have many features of equity but are treated as debt. Obviously, the distinction between debt and equity is important for tax purposes. So, one reason that corporations try to create a debt security that is really equity is to obtain the tax benefits of debt and the bankruptcy benefits of equity.

As a general rule, equity represents an ownership interest, and it is a residual claim. This means that equity holders are paid after debt holders. As a result of this, the risks and benefits associated with owning debt and equity are different. To give just one example, note that the maximum reward for owning a debt security is ultimately fixed by the amount of the loan, whereas there is no upper limit to the potential reward from owning an equity interest.

LONG-TERM DEBT: THE BASICS

Ultimately, all long-term debt securities are promises made by the issuing firm to pay principal when due and to make timely interest payments on the unpaid balance. Beyond this, a number of features distinguish these securities from one another. We discuss some of these features next.

The maturity of a long-term debt instrument is the length of time the debt remains outstanding with some unpaid balance. Debt securities can be *short-term* (with maturities of one year or less) or *long-term* (with maturities of more than one year).[1] Short-term debt is sometimes referred to as *unfunded debt*.[2]

Debt securities are typically called *notes, debentures,* or *bonds.* Strictly speaking, a bond is a secured debt. However, in common usage, the word *bond* refers to all kinds of secured and unsecured debt. We will continue to use the term generically to refer to long-term debt. Also, usually the only difference between a note and a bond is the original maturity. Issues with an original maturity of 10 years or less are often called notes. Longer-term issues are called bonds.

The two major forms of long-term debt are public-issue and privately placed. We concentrate on public-issue bonds. Most of what we say about them holds true for private-issue, long-term debt as well. The main difference between public-issue and privately placed debt is that the latter is directly placed with a lender and not offered to the public. Because this is a private transaction, the specific terms are up to the parties involved.

There are many other dimensions to long-term debt, including such things as security, call features, sinking funds, ratings, and protective covenants. The following table illustrates these features for a bond issued by technology giant Microsoft. If some of these terms are unfamiliar, have no fear. We will discuss them all presently.

Information about individual bonds can be found at **finra-markets.morningstar .com**.

Features of a Microsoft Bond		
Term		**Explanation**
Amount of issue	$4.5 billion	The company issued $4.5 billion worth of bonds.
Date of issue	8/8/2016	The bonds were sold on 8/8/2016.
Maturity	8/8/2046	The bonds mature on 8/8/2046.
Face value	$2,000	The denomination of the bonds is $2,000.
Annual coupon	3.700	Each bondholder will receive $74 per bond per year (3.700% of face value).
Offer price	99.515	The offer price will be 99.515% of the $2,000 face value, or $1,990, per bond.
Coupon payment dates	2/8, 8/8	Coupons of $74/2 = $37 will be paid on these dates.
Security	None	The bonds are not secured by specific assets.
Sinking fund	None	The bonds have no sinking fund.
Call provision	At any time	The bonds do not have a deferred call.
Call price	Treasury rate plus .25%	The bonds have a "make-whole" call price.
Rating	Moody's Aaa S&P AAA	The bonds have the highest possible credit rating.

Many of these features will be detailed in the bond indenture, so we discuss this first.

---

[1]There is no universally agreed-upon distinction between short-term and long-term debt. In addition, people often refer to *intermediate-term debt,* which has a maturity of more than 1 year and less than 3 to 5, or even 10, years.

[2]The word *funding* is part of the jargon of finance. It generally refers to the long term. A firm planning to "fund" its debt requirements may be replacing short-term debt with long-term debt.

THE INDENTURE

indenture
The written agreement between the corporation and the lender detailing the terms of the debt issue.

The **indenture** is the written agreement between the corporation (the borrower) and its creditors. It is sometimes referred to as the *deed of trust*.[3] Usually, a trustee (a bank, perhaps) is appointed by the corporation to represent the bondholders. The trust company must (1) make sure the terms of the indenture are obeyed, (2) manage the sinking fund (described in the following pages), and (3) represent the bondholders in default—that is, if the company defaults on its payments to them.

The bond indenture is a legal document. It can run several hundred pages and generally makes for tedious reading. It is an important document because it generally includes the following provisions:

1. The basic terms of the bonds.
2. The total amount of bonds issued.
3. A description of property used as security.
4. The repayment arrangements.
5. The call provisions.
6. Details of the protective covenants.

We discuss these features next.

Terms of a Bond   Corporate bonds usually have a face value (that is, a denomination) of $1,000, although par values of $2,000 like the Microsoft bond have become relatively common. Other par values also exist. For example, municipal bonds often have par values of $5,000, and Treasury bonds with par values of $10,000 or $100,000 are often sold. This *principal value* is stated on the bond certificate. So, if a corporation wanted to borrow $1 million, 1,000 bonds would have to be sold. The par value (that is, the initial accounting value) of a bond is almost always the same as the face value, and the terms are used interchangeably in practice.

registered form
The form of bond issue in which the registrar of the company records ownership of each bond; payment is made directly to the owner of record.

Corporate bonds are usually in **registered form**. For example, the indenture might read as follows:

> **Interest is payable semiannually on July 1 and January 1 of each year to the person in whose name the bond is registered at the close of business on June 15 or December 15, respectively.**

This means that the company has a registrar who will record the ownership of each bond and record any changes in ownership. The company will pay the interest and principal by check mailed directly to the address of the owner of record. A corporate bond may be registered and have attached "coupons." To obtain an interest payment, the owner must separate a coupon from the bond certificate and send it to the company registrar (the paying agent).

bearer form
The form of bond issue in which the bond is issued without record of the owner's name; payment is made to whomever holds the bond.

Alternatively, the bond could be in **bearer form**. This means that the certificate is the basic evidence of ownership, and the corporation will "pay the bearer." Ownership is not otherwise recorded, and, as with a registered bond with attached coupons, the holder of the bond certificate detaches the coupons and sends them to the company to receive payment.

There are two drawbacks to bearer bonds. First, they are difficult to recover if they are lost or stolen. Second, because the company does not know who owns its bonds, it cannot notify bondholders of important events. Bearer bonds were once the dominant type, but they are now much less common (in the United States) than registered bonds.

---

[3]The words *loan agreement* or *loan contract* are usually used for privately placed debt and term loans.

Security   Debt securities are classified according to the collateral and mortgages used to protect the bondholder.

Collateral is a general term that frequently means securities (for example, bonds and stocks) that are pledged as security for payment of debt. For example, collateral trust bonds often involve a pledge of common stock held by the corporation. However, the term *collateral* is commonly used to refer to any asset pledged on a debt.

Mortgage securities are secured by a mortgage on the real property of the borrower. The property involved is usually real estate—for example, land or buildings. The legal document that describes the mortgage is called a *mortgage trust indenture* or *trust deed*.

Sometimes mortgages are on specific property, such as a railroad car. More often, blanket mortgages are used. A *blanket mortgage* pledges all the real property owned by the company.[4]

Bonds frequently represent unsecured obligations of the company. A **debenture** is an unsecured bond, for which no specific pledge of property is made. The term **note** is generally used for such instruments if the maturity of the unsecured bond is less than 10 years when the bond is originally issued. Debenture holders have a claim only on property not otherwise pledged—in other words, the property that remains after mortgages and collateral trusts are taken into account. The Microsoft bonds in the table are an example of such an issue.

The terminology that we use here and elsewhere in this chapter is standard in the United States. Outside the United States, these same terms can have different meanings. For example, bonds issued by the British government ("gilts") are called treasury "stock." Also, in the United Kingdom, a debenture is a *secured* obligation.

At the current time, public bonds issued in the United States by industrial and financial companies are typically debentures. Most utility and railroad bonds are secured by a pledge of assets.

> **debenture**
> An unsecured debt, usually with a maturity of 10 years or more.
>
> **note**
> An unsecured debt, usually with a maturity under 10 years.

Seniority   In general terms, *seniority* indicates preference in position over other lenders, and debts are sometimes labeled as *senior* or *junior* to indicate seniority. Some debt is *subordinated*, as in, for example, a subordinated debenture.

In the event of default, holders of subordinated debt must give preference to other specified creditors. Usually, this means that the subordinated lenders will be paid off only after the specified creditors have been compensated. However, debt cannot be subordinated to equity.

The Securities Industry and Financial Markets Association (SIFMA) website is **www.sifma.org**.

Repayment   Bonds can be repaid at maturity, at which time the bondholder will receive the stated, or face, value of the bond; or they may be repaid in part or in entirety before maturity. Early repayment in some form is more typical and is often handled through a sinking fund.

A **sinking fund** is an account managed by the bond trustee for the purpose of repaying the bonds. The company makes annual payments to the trustee, who then uses the funds to retire a portion of the debt. The trustee does this by either buying up some of the bonds in the market or calling in a fraction of the outstanding bonds. This second option is discussed in the next section.

There are many different kinds of sinking fund arrangements, and the details are spelled out in the indenture. For example:

> **sinking fund**
> An account managed by the bond trustee for early bond redemption.

1. Some sinking funds start about 10 years after the initial issuance.
2. Some sinking funds establish equal payments over the life of the bond.

---

[4]Real property includes land and things "affixed thereto." It does not include cash or inventories.

3. Some high-quality bond issues establish payments to the sinking fund that are not sufficient to redeem the entire issue. As a consequence, there is the possibility of a large "balloon payment" at maturity.

call provision
An agreement giving the corporation the option to repurchase a bond at a specified price prior to maturity.

call premium
The amount by which the call price exceeds the par value of a bond.

deferred call provision
A call provision prohibiting the company from redeeming a bond prior to a certain date.

call-protected bond
A bond that, during a certain period, cannot be redeemed by the issuer.

The Call Provision

A **call provision** allows the company to repurchase or "call" part or all of the bond issue at stated prices over a specific period. Corporate bonds are usually callable.

Generally, the call price is above the bond's stated value (that is, the par value). The difference between the call price and the stated value is the **call premium**. The amount of the call premium may become smaller over time. One arrangement is to initially set the call premium equal to the annual coupon payment and then make it decline to zero as the call date moves closer to the time of maturity.

Call provisions are often not operative during the first part of a bond's life. This makes the call provision less of a worry for bondholders in the bond's early years. For example, a company might be prohibited from calling its bonds for the first 10 years. This is a **deferred call provision**. During this period of prohibition, the bond is said to be **call-protected**.

In recent years, a new type of call provision, a "make-whole" call, has become widespread in the corporate bond market. With such a feature, bondholders receive approximately what the bonds are worth if they are called. Because bondholders don't suffer a loss in the event of a call, they are "made whole."

To determine the make-whole call price, we calculate the present value of the remaining interest and principal payments at a rate specified in the indenture. For example, looking at our Microsoft issue, we see that the discount rate is "Treasury rate plus .25%." What this means is that we determine the discount rate by first finding a U.S. Treasury issue with the same maturity. We calculate the yield to maturity on the Treasury issue and then add on .25 percent to get the discount rate we use.

Notice that with a make-whole call provision, the call price is higher when interest rates are lower and vice versa (why?). Also notice that, as is common with a make-whole call, the Microsoft issue does not have a deferred call feature. Why might investors not be too concerned about the absence of this feature?

protective covenant
A part of the indenture limiting certain actions that might be taken during the term of the loan, usually to protect the lender's interest.

Protective Covenants

A **protective covenant** is that part of the indenture or loan agreement that limits certain actions a company might otherwise wish to take during the term of the loan. Protective covenants can be classified into two types: negative covenants and positive (or affirmative) covenants.

A *negative covenant* is a "thou shalt not" type of covenant. It limits or prohibits actions the company might take. Here are some typical examples:

1. The firm must limit the amount of dividends it pays according to some formula.
2. The firm cannot pledge any assets to other lenders.
3. The firm cannot merge with another firm.
4. The firm cannot sell or lease any major assets without approval by the lender.
5. The firm cannot issue additional long-term debt.

A *positive covenant* is a "thou shalt" type of covenant. It specifies an action the company agrees to take or a condition the company must abide by. Here are some examples:

1. The company must maintain its working capital at or above some specified minimum level.
2. The company must periodically furnish audited financial statements to the lender.
3. The firm must maintain any collateral or security in good condition.

Want detailed information about the amount and terms of the debt issued by a particular firm? Check out its latest financial statements by searching SEC filings at **www.sec.gov**

This is only a partial list of covenants; a particular indenture may feature many different ones.

Concept Questions

7.2a   What are the distinguishing features of debt compared to equity?

7.2b   What is the indenture? What are protective covenants? Give some examples.

7.2c   What is a sinking fund?

Bond Ratings   7.3

Firms frequently pay to have their debt rated. The two leading bond-rating firms are Moody's and Standard & Poor's (S&P). The debt ratings are an assessment of the creditworthiness of the corporate issuer. The definitions of creditworthiness used by Moody's and S&P are based on how likely the firm is to default and the protection creditors have in the event of a default.

It is important to recognize that bond ratings are concerned *only* with the possibility of default. Earlier, we discussed interest rate risk, which we defined as the risk of a change in the value of a bond resulting from a change in interest rates. Bond ratings do not address this issue. As a result, the price of a highly rated bond can still be quite volatile.

Bond ratings are constructed from information supplied by the corporation. The rating classes and some information concerning them are shown in the following table:

	Investment-Quality Bond Ratings				Low-Quality, Speculative, and/or "Junk" Bond Ratings					
	High Grade		Medium Grade		Low Grade			Very Low Grade		
Standard & Poor's	AAA	AA	A	BBB	BB	B	CCC	CC	C	D
Moody's	Aaa	Aa	A	Baa	Ba	B	Caa	Ca	C	

Moody's	S&P	
Aaa	AAA	Debt rated Aaa and AAA has the highest rating. Capacity to pay interest and principal is extremely strong.
Aa	AA	Debt rated Aa and AA has a very strong capacity to pay interest and repay principal. Together with the highest rating, this group comprises the high-grade bond class.
A	A	Debt rated A has a strong capacity to pay interest and repay principal, although it is somewhat more susceptible to the adverse effects of changes in circumstances and economic conditions than debt in high-rated categories.
Baa	BBB	Debt rated Baa and BBB is regarded as having an adequate capacity to pay interest and repay principal. Whereas it normally exhibits adequate protection parameters, adverse economic conditions or changing circumstances are more likely to lead to a weakened capacity to pay interest and repay principal for debt in this category than in higher-rated categories. These bonds are medium-grade obligations.
Ba; B Caa Ca C	BB; B CCC CC C	Debt rated in these categories is regarded, on balance, as predominantly speculative with respect to capacity to pay interest and repay principal in accordance with the terms of the obligation. BB and Ba indicate the lowest degree of speculation, and Ca, CC, and C the highest degree of speculation. Although such debt is likely to have some quality and protective characteristics, these are outweighed by large uncertainties or major risk exposures to adverse conditions. Issues rated C by Moody's are typically in default.
	D	Debt rated D is in default, and payment of interest and/or repayment of principal is in arrears.

NOTE: At times, both Moody's and S&P use adjustments (called notches) to these ratings. S&P uses plus and minus signs: A+ is the strongest A rating and A− the weakest. Moody's uses a 1, 2, or 3 designation, with 1 being the highest.

Want to know what criteria are commonly used to rate corporate and municipal bonds? Go to **www.standardandpoors .com, www.moodys.com**, or **www.fitchinv.com.**

The highest rating a firm's debt can have is AAA or Aaa, and such debt is judged to be the best quality and to have the lowest degree of risk. For example, the 100-year BellSouth issue we discussed earlier was originally rated AAA. This rating is not awarded very often: As of January 2018, only two nonfinancial U.S. companies, Johnson & Johnson and Microsoft, had AAA ratings. AA or Aa ratings indicate very good quality debt and are much more common.

A large part of corporate borrowing takes the form of low-grade, or "junk," bonds. If these low-grade corporate bonds are rated at all, they are rated below investment grade by the major rating agencies. Investment-grade bonds are bonds rated at least BBB by S&P or Baa by Moody's.

Rating agencies don't always agree. To illustrate, some bonds are known as "crossover" or "5B" bonds. The reason is that they are rated triple-B (or Baa) by one rating agency and double-B (or Ba) by another, a "split rating." For example, in February 2016, India-based textile and chemical company Standard Industries sold an issue of 10-year notes rated BBB– by S&P and Ba2 by Moody's.

A bond's credit rating can change as the issuer's financial strength improves or deteriorates. For example, in May 2016, Fitch Ratings cut the bond rating on retailer The Gap from BBB– to BB+, lowering the company's bond rating from investment grade to junk bond status. Bonds that drop into junk territory like this are called *fallen angels*. Fitch was concerned about the decline in same-store sales and gross margin at the company.

Credit ratings are important because defaults really do occur, and when they do, investors can lose heavily. For example, in 2000, AmeriServe Food Distribution, Inc., which supplied restaurants such as Burger King with everything from burgers to giveaway toys, defaulted on $200 million in junk bonds. After the default, the bonds traded at just 18 cents on the dollar, leaving investors with a loss of more than $160 million.

Even worse in AmeriServe's case, the bonds had been issued only four months earlier, thereby making AmeriServe an NCAA champion. Although that might be a good thing for a college basketball team such as the University of Kentucky Wildcats, in the bond market it means "No Coupon At All," and it's not a good thing for investors.

If you're nervous about the level of debt piled up by the U.S. government, don't go to **www.fiscal.treasury.gov** or to **www.usdebtclock .org/world-debt-clock.html**! Learn all about government bonds at **www.newyorkfed .org**.

Concept Questions

7.3a   What does a bond rating say about the risk of fluctuations in a bond's value resulting from interest rate changes?

7.3b   What is a junk bond?

7.4 Some Different Types of Bonds

Thus far we have considered only "plain vanilla" corporate bonds. In this section, we briefly look at bonds issued by governments and also at bonds with unusual features.

GOVERNMENT BONDS

The biggest borrower in the world—by a wide margin—is everybody's favorite family member, Uncle Sam. In early 2018, the total debt of the U.S. government was $20 *trillion*, or about $63,000 per citizen (and growing!). When the government wishes to borrow money for more than one year, it sells what are known as Treasury notes and bonds to the public (in fact, it does so every month). Currently, outstanding Treasury notes and bonds have original maturities ranging from 2 to 30 years.

Most U.S. Treasury issues are just ordinary coupon bonds. There are two important things to keep in mind. First, U.S. Treasury issues, unlike essentially all other bonds, have no default risk because (we hope) the Treasury can always come up with the money to make the payments. Second, Treasury issues are exempt from state income taxes (though not federal income taxes). In other words, the coupons you receive on a Treasury note or bond are taxed only at the federal level.

State and local governments also borrow money by selling notes and bonds. Such issues are called *municipal* notes and bonds, or just "munis." Unlike Treasury issues, munis have varying degrees of default risk, and, in fact, they are rated much like corporate issues. Also, they are almost always callable. The most intriguing thing about munis is that their coupons are exempt from federal income taxes (though not necessarily state income taxes). This makes them very attractive to high-income, high-tax bracket investors.

For information on municipal bonds, including prices, check out **emma.msrb.org**.

Because of the enormous tax break they receive, the yields on municipal bonds are much lower than the yields on taxable bonds. For example, in December 2017, long-term Aa-rated corporate bonds were yielding about 3.42 percent. At the same time, long-term Aa munis were yielding about 2.20 percent. Suppose an investor was in a 30 percent tax bracket. All else being the same, would this investor prefer a Aa corporate bond or a Aa municipal bond?

To answer, we need to compare the *aftertax* yields on the two bonds. Ignoring state and local taxes, the muni pays 2.20 percent on both a pretax and an aftertax basis. The corporate issue pays 3.42 percent before taxes, but it pays only $.0342 \times (1 - .30) = .0239$, or 2.39 percent, once we account for the 30 percent tax bite. Given this, the corporate bond has a better yield, but the difference is much smaller after we account for the tax bite.

Another good bond market site is **money.cnn.com/data /bonds**.

Taxable versus Municipal Bonds	**EXAMPLE 7.4**

Suppose taxable bonds are currently yielding 8 percent, while at the same time, munis of comparable risk and maturity are yielding 6 percent. Which is more attractive to an investor in a 40 percent bracket? What is the break-even tax rate? How do you interpret this rate?

For an investor in a 40 percent tax bracket, a taxable bond yields $8 \times (1 - .40) = 4.8$ percent after taxes, so the muni is much more attractive. The break-even tax rate is the tax rate at which an investor would be indifferent between a taxable and a nontaxable issue. If we let t^* stand for the break-even tax rate, then we can solve for it as follows:

$$.08 \times (1 - t^*) = .06$$
$$1 - t^* = .06/.08 = .75$$
$$t^* = .25$$

An investor in a 25 percent tax bracket would make 6 percent after taxes from either bond.

ZERO COUPON BONDS

A bond that pays no coupons at all must be offered at a price that is much lower than its stated value. Such bonds are called **zero coupon bonds**, or just *zeroes*.[5]

zero coupon bond
A bond that makes no coupon payments and is thus initially priced at a deep discount.

---

[5]A bond issued with a very low coupon rate (as opposed to a zero coupon rate) is an *original-issue discount* (*OID*) *bond.*

TABLE 7.2

Interest Expense for EIN's Zeroes

Year	Beginning Value	Ending Value	Implicit Interest Expense	Straight-Line Interest Expense
1	$508.35	$ 582.01	$ 73.66	$ 98.33
2	582.01	666.34	84.33	98.33
3	666.34	762.90	96.56	98.33
4	762.90	873.44	110.54	98.33
5	873.44	1,000.00	126.56	98.33
Total			$491.65	$491.65

Suppose the Eight-Inch Nails (EIN) Company issues a $1,000 face value, five-year zero coupon bond. The initial price is set at $508.35. Even though no interest payments are made on the bond, zero coupon bond calculations use semiannual periods to be consistent with coupon bond calculations. Using semiannual periods, it is straightforward to verify that, at this price, the bond yields about 14 percent to maturity. The total interest paid over the life of the bond is $1,000 − 508.35 = $491.65.

For tax purposes, the issuer of a zero coupon bond deducts interest every year even though no interest is actually paid. Similarly, the owner must pay taxes on interest accrued every year, even though no interest is actually received.

The way in which the yearly interest on a zero coupon bond is calculated is governed by tax law. Before 1982, corporations could calculate the interest deduction on a straight-line basis. For EIN, the annual interest deduction would have been $491.65/5 = $98.33 per year.

Under current tax law, the implicit interest is determined by amortizing the loan. We do this by first calculating the bond's value at the beginning of each year. For example, after one year, the bond will have four years until maturity, so it will be worth $1,000/1.07^8 = $582.01; the value in two years will be $1,000/1.07^6 = $666.34; and so on. The implicit interest each year is the change in the bond's value for the year. The values and interest expenses for the EIN bond are listed in Table 7.2.

Notice that under the old rules, zero coupon bonds were more attractive because the deductions for interest expense were larger in the early years (compare the implicit interest expense with the straight-line expense).

Under current tax law, EIN could deduct $73.66 in interest paid the first year and the owner of the bond would pay taxes on $73.66 in taxable income (even though no interest was actually received). This second tax feature makes taxable zero coupon bonds less attractive to individuals. They are still a very attractive investment for tax-exempt investors with long-term dollar-denominated liabilities, such as pension funds, because the future dollar value is known with relative certainty.

Some bonds are zero coupon bonds for only part of their lives. For example, General Motors has a debenture outstanding that matures on March 15, 2036. For the first 20 years of its life, no coupon payments will be made; but, after 20 years, it will begin paying coupons semiannually at a rate of 7.75 percent per year.

FLOATING-RATE BONDS

The conventional bonds we have talked about in this chapter have fixed-dollar obligations because the coupon rates are set as fixed percentages of the par values. Similarly, the principal amounts are set equal to the par values. Under these circumstances, the coupon payments and principal are completely fixed.

With *floating-rate bonds (floaters)*, the coupon payments are adjustable. The adjustments are tied to an interest rate index such as the Treasury bill interest rate or the 30-year Treasury bond rate.

The value of a floating-rate bond depends on exactly how the coupon payment adjustments are defined. In most cases, the coupon adjusts with a lag to some base rate. For example, suppose a coupon rate adjustment is made on June 1. The adjustment might be based on the simple average of Treasury bond yields during the previous three months. In addition, the majority of floaters have the following features:

1. The holder has the right to redeem the note at par on the coupon payment date after some specified amount of time. This is called a *put* provision, and it is discussed in the following section.
2. The coupon rate has a floor and a ceiling, meaning that the coupon is subject to a minimum and a maximum. In this case, the coupon rate is said to be "capped," and the upper and lower rates are sometimes called the *collar*.

A particularly interesting type of floating-rate bond is an *inflation-linked* bond. Such bonds have coupons that are adjusted according to the rate of inflation (the principal amount may be adjusted as well). The U.S. Treasury began issuing such bonds in January of 1997. The issues are sometimes called "TIPS," or Treasury Inflation-Protected Securities. Other countries, including Canada, Israel, and Britain, have issued similar securities.

Official information about U.S. inflation-indexed bonds is at **www.treasurydirect.gov**.

OTHER TYPES OF BONDS

Many bonds have unusual or exotic features. So-called catastrophe, or cat, bonds provide an interesting example. In May 2016, United Services Automobile Association (USAA), the company that specializes in insurance for military veterans, issued $250 million in cat bonds. These cat bonds covered U.S. storms, wildfires, meteor strikes, and solar flares. In the event of one of these triggering events, investors would lose some or all of their money.

The largest single cat bond issue to date is a series of six bonds sold by Merna Reinsurance in 2007 (reinsurance companies sell insurance to insurance companies). The six bond issues were to cover various catastrophes the company faced due to its reinsurance of State Farm. The six bonds totaled about $1.2 billion in par value. During 2016, about $7.1 billion in cat bonds were issued, and there was about $26.8 billion par value in cat bonds outstanding at the end of the year.

At this point, cat bonds probably seem pretty risky. It might be surprising to learn that since cat bonds were first issued in 1997, only four have not been paid in full. Because of Hurricane Katrina, cat bondholders lost $190 million. Cat bondholders also lost $300 million due to the 2011 tsunami in Japan. During 2011, two other cat bond issues, each worth $100 million, were triggered due to an unusually active tornado season.

Another possible bond feature is a *warrant*. A warrant gives the buyer of a bond the right to purchase shares of stock in the company at a fixed price. Such a right is very valuable if the stock price climbs substantially (a later chapter discusses this subject in greater depth). Because of the value of this feature, bonds with warrants are often issued at a very low coupon rate.

As these examples illustrate, bond features are really limited only by the imaginations of the parties involved. Unfortunately, there are far too many variations for us to cover in detail here. We close this discussion by mentioning a few of the more common types.

Income bonds are similar to conventional bonds, except that coupon payments depend on company income. Specifically, coupons are paid to bondholders only if the firm's income is sufficient. This would appear to be an attractive feature, but income bonds are not very common.

A *convertible bond* can be swapped for a fixed number of shares of stock anytime before maturity at the holder's option. Convertibles are relatively common, but the number has been decreasing in recent years.

A *put bond* allows the *holder* to force the issuer to buy back the bond at a stated price. For example, International Paper Co. has bonds outstanding that allow the holder to force International Paper to buy the bonds back at 100 percent of face value if certain "risk" events happen. One such event is a change in credit rating from investment grade to lower than investment grade by Moody's or S&P. The put feature is therefore just the reverse of the call provision.

The *reverse convertible* is a relatively new type of structured note. One type generally offers a high coupon rate, but the redemption at maturity can be paid in cash at par value or paid in shares of stock. For example, one recent General Motors (GM) reverse convertible had a coupon rate of 16 percent, which is a very high coupon rate in today's interest rate environment. However, at maturity, if GM's stock declined sufficiently, bondholders would receive a fixed number of GM shares that were worth less than par value. So, while the income portion of the bond return would be high, the potential loss in par value could easily erode the extra return.

Perhaps the most unusual bond (and certainly the most ghoulish) is the "death bond." Companies such as Stone Street Financial purchase life insurance policies from individuals who are expected to die within the next 10 years. They then sell bonds that are paid off from the life insurance proceeds received when the policyholders pass away. The return on the bonds to investors depends on how long the policyholders live. A major risk is that if medical treatment advances quickly, it will raise the life expectancy of the policyholders, thereby decreasing the return to the bondholder.

Structured notes are bonds that are based on stocks, bonds, commodities, or currencies. One particular type of structured note has a return based on a stock market index. At expiration, if the stock index has declined, the bond returns the principal. However, if the stock index has increased, the bond will return a portion of the stock index return, say 80 percent. Another type of structured note will return twice the stock index return, but with the potential for loss of principal.

A given bond may have many unusual features. Two of the most recent exotic bonds are *CoCo bonds*, which have a coupon payment, and *NoNo bonds*, which are zero coupon bonds. CoCo and NoNo bonds are contingent convertible, putable, callable, subordinated bonds. The contingent convertible clause is similar to the normal conversion feature, except the contingent feature must be met. For example, a contingent feature may require that the company stock trade at 110 percent of the conversion price for 20 out of the most recent 30 days. Valuing a bond of this sort can be quite complex, and the yield to maturity calculation is often meaningless.

SUKUK

You can find out more about sukuk at **www.sukuk.com**.

Worldwide demand for assets that comply with sharia, or Islamic law and cultural tradition, has grown dramatically. Assets, including deposits at Islamic financial institutions, totaled about $2.1 trillion in 2016, up from $1.3 trillion in 2011. One of the major differences between Western financial practices and sharia is that Islamic law does not permit charging or paying *riba*, or interest. Given our current discussion about bonds, this means that anyone following sharia cannot buy or issue conventional bonds.

To accommodate the restriction on interest payments, Islamic bonds, or *sukuk*, have been created. There are many possible structures to sukuk, such as partial ownership in a debt (sukuk al-murabaha) or an asset (sukuk al-ijara). In the case of a sukuk al-ijara, there is a binding promise to repurchase a certain asset by the issuer at maturity. Before the sukuk matures, rent is paid on the asset. While we have noted that traditional bonds can be relatively illiquid, most sukuk are bought and held to maturity. As a result, secondary markets in sukuk are extremely illiquid.

One of the most important developments in corporate finance over the last 40 years has been the reemergence of publicly owned and traded low-rated corporate debt. Originally offered to the public in the early 1900s to help finance some of our emerging growth industries, these high-yield, high-risk bonds (sometimes called "junk bonds") virtually disappeared after the rash of bond defaults during the Depression. Starting in the late 1970s, however, the junk bond market catapulted from being an insignificant element in the corporate fixed-income market to being one of the fastest-growing and most controversial types of financing mechanisms. Technically, high-yield bonds are bonds issued by companies whose rating given by one or more of the major rating agencies, i.e., Fitch, Moody's or Standard & Poor's, is below investment grade, e.g., below BBB– by S&P.

The term *junk* emanates from the dominant type of low-rated bond issues outstanding prior to 1977 when the "market" consisted almost exclusively of original-issue investment-grade bonds that fell from their lofty status to a higher-default risk, speculative-grade level. These so-called fallen angels amounted to about $8.5 billion in 1977. In 2016, fallen angels comprised about 12 percent of the $1.6 trillion publicly owned junk bond market. The balance are "original-issue," high-yield bonds.

The high-yield bond market in Europe, although in existence for decades, only began to grow significantly starting in 2009 from about €100 billion to about €500 billion at the end of 2016, and is now a fairly well diversified market, about 1/3 the size of the U.S. market.

Beginning in 1977, some speculative-grade issuers began to go directly to the public to raise debt capital for growth purposes. Early issuers of junk bonds were energy-related firms, cable TV companies, airlines, and assorted other industrial companies. The emerging growth company rationale coupled with relatively high returns to early investors helped legitimize this asset class and attract interest from the more established investment banks and asset managers in the mid-1980s. The pioneers in the high-yield market were Drexel Burnham Lambert, a boutique bank, and its junk bond "king," Michael Milken. I, personally, became interested in this new financing innovation in the early 1980s, when a major bank asked me to assess the market's potential.

By far the most important and controversial aspect of the early junk bond financings was its role in the corporate restructuring movement from 1985 to 1989. High-leverage transactions and acquisitions, such as leveraged buyouts (LBOs), which occur when a firm is taken private and the old shareholders are paid a premium to sell their shares, became numerous and threatening to many firms. Funds for this buyout were raised from traditional bank loans and high-yield bonds, plus equity. These leveraged recapitalizations helped to transform the face of corporate America, leading to a heated debate as to the economic and social consequences of firms' being bought by private-equity firms with debt-equity ratios of at least 6:1 in the restructured firm. Similar, but less emotional, comments accompanied a second LBO movement in 2004–2007, and even less so in the most recent heavy activity by private-equity firms in what is now (in 2017) an established and impressive market. The latter trend is not without some concerns, as the prices paid to buyout firms soared to above 10 times EBITA in 2015 and 2016, a very high multiple.

LBOs involved increasingly large companies, and the multi-billion dollar takeover became fairly common in the 1980s. The first mega-buyout was the huge $25+ billion RJR Nabisco LBO in 1989. LBOs were typically financed with about 60 percent senior bank and insurance company debt, about 25–30 percent subordinated public debt (usually junk bonds), and 10–15 percent equity. The junk bond segment is sometimes referred to as "mezzanine" financing because it lies between the "balcony" senior debt and the "basement" equity. In the most recent LBO binge, however, more than 30 percent of the financing has been equity but the transactions are, on average, much larger than in the late 1980s.

These restructurings resulted in huge fees to advisers and underwriters and large premiums (at least 30 to 40 percent in most cases) to the old shareholders who were bought out. They continued as long as the market was willing to buy these new debt offerings at what appeared to be a favorable risk–return trade-off. The bottom fell out of the market in the last six months of 1989 due to a number of factors, including a marked increase in defaults, government regulation against S&Ls holding junk bonds, and at least one highly publicized bankruptcy of a highly leveraged financial restructuring—Federated Department Stores. In addition, the leading underwriter, Drexel Burnham, went bankrupt and Milken was prosecuted and sent to jail. As a result, in the early 1990s, the financial market was questioning the very survival of the junk bond market. The answer as to its survival was a resounding "yes," as the amount of new issues soared to record annual levels of $40 billion in 1992, almost $80 billion in 1993, and in 1997 reached an impressive $119 billion. Coupled with plummeting default rates (under 2 percent each year in the 1993–97 period) and attractive returns in these years, the risk–return characteristics were extremely favorable. Despite legal and financial problems, Drexel's and Milken's positive legacy for pioneering the high-yield market is clear and important.

The junk bond market in the late 1990s was a quieter one compared to that of the 1980s, but, in terms of growth and returns, it was healthier than ever before. While the low default rates in 1992–1998 helped to fuel new investment funds and new issues, the market experienced its ups and downs in subsequent years. Indeed, default rates started to rise in 1999 and accelerated in 2000–2002. The latter year saw default rates reach record levels of over 12 percent as the economy slipped into a recession and investors suffered from the excesses of lending in the late 1990s.

Since the mid-1990s, a "sister" high-yield debt market developed in the private leveraged loan (LL) market. This low-quality (non-investment grade), higher-interest rate market grew enormously in the United States and Europe in the 2005–2007 period and was at least 30 percent larger than the high-yield bond market in 2008. Since the great financial crisis of 2008, the private LL market has once again become extremely popular and is a major source of funds in the private debt market. One of the main reasons for the recent growth and popularity of leveraged loans was that the issuing bank could, in most environments, easily sell these loans into structured finance vehicles called collateralized loan obligations (CLOs).

Private, leveraged loan debt facilities have registered lower default rates than high-yield bonds and higher recovery rates due to their senior status. They have continued to be a major source of corporate debt at levels exceeding $400 billion a year in the last five years, and with attractive risk–return trade-offs for major banks and the new and growing "shadow-banking" markets made up of non-bank lenders. I estimate that the shadow-banking market has perhaps more than $200 billion under management in 2017.

The market for leveraged financing rebounded quickly in 2003 and continued to prosper until the credit crisis of 2008–2009. With the "flight-to-quality" caused by the sub-prime mortgage market meltdown in the second half of 2007 and 2008, returns to investors in high-yield bonds and leveraged loans fell considerably, new issues dried up, and default rates increased from the unusually low-risk years that coincided with the leveraged excesses. Despite these highly volatile events and problems with liquidity, we were convinced that high-yield bonds, and their private debt companion, leveraged loans, would continue in the future to be a major source of corporate debt financing and a legitimate asset class for investors.

Indeed, the high yield bond market, as well as all risky bonds and common stocks, staged a remarkable recovery after the first quarter of 2009, and for the entire year 2009 the returns to high yield bond and leveraged loan investors were the highest in the almost 40 years of the modern era of leveraged finance markets. This amazing turnaround, despite near-record defaults in 2009, was remarkable in the speed and extent of the recovery, with returns of about 60 percent for high-yield bond investors. Impressive positive returns and record new issuance of highly leveraged financed projects and refinancing has continued almost unabated through 2016. And, the market was incredibly accepting of higher yielding bonds and loans, especially in the low interest rate environment of 2012–2016. But, we are now (2017) concerned about another bubble building as the current benign credit cycle, with low default rates and highly risky new issuance, continues for more than seven years since the last market downturn. Perhaps the next few years will be quite volatile with rising default rates and lower recoveries and returns. But, as always, the leveraged finance market will continue to exist and probably expand in the U.S., in Europe, and in other parts of the world.

Edward I. Altman is Max L. Heine Professor of Finance Emeritus and Director of Credit and Debt Markets Research at the NYU Salomon Center at the Stern School of Business. He is widely recognized as one of the world's leading experts on bankruptcy and credit analysis as well as the high-yield and distressed debt markets.

Concept Questions

7.4a   Why might an income bond be attractive to a corporation with volatile cash flows? Can you think of a reason why income bonds are not more popular?

7.4b   What do you think would be the effect of a put feature on a bond's coupon? How about a convertibility feature? Why?

7.5 Bond Markets

Bonds are bought and sold in enormous quantities every day. You may be surprised to learn that the trading volume in bonds on a typical day is many, many times larger than the trading volume in stocks (by *trading volume* we mean the amount of money that changes hands). Here is a finance trivia question: What is the largest securities market in the world?

WORK THE WEB

Bond quotes have become more available with the rise of the Internet. One site where you can find current bond prices is finra-markets.morningstar.com. We went to the website and searched for bonds issued by Coca-Cola. Here is a look at part of what we found for one of the bonds:

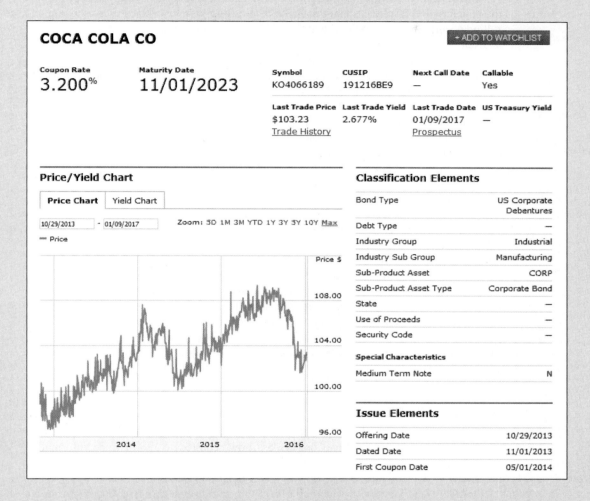

The bond has a coupon rate of 3.20 percent and matures on November 1, 2023. The last sale on this bond was at a price of 103.23 percent of par, which gives a yield to maturity of about 2.677 percent. Not only does the site provide the most recent price and yield information, but it also provides other important information about the bond, such as the credit rating, coupon date, call date, and call price. We'll leave it up to you to have a look at the page and the rest of the information available there.

Questions
1. *Go to this website and find the bond shown above. What is the credit rating on this bond? What was the size of the bond issue? What were the yield to maturity and price when the bond was issued?*
2. *If you search for Chevron bonds (CVX), you will find bonds for several companies listed. Why do you think Chevron has bonds issued with different corporate names?*

Most people would guess the New York Stock Exchange. In fact, the largest securities market in the world in terms of trading volume is the U.S. Treasury market.

HOW BONDS ARE BOUGHT AND SOLD

As we mentioned all the way back in Chapter 1, most trading in bonds takes place over the counter, or OTC. Recall that this means there is no particular place where buying and selling occur. Instead, dealers around the country (and around the world) stand ready to buy and sell. The various dealers are connected electronically.

One reason the bond markets are so big is that the number of bond issues far exceeds the number of stock issues. There are two reasons for this. First, a corporation would typically have only one common stock issue outstanding (there are exceptions to this that we discuss in our next chapter). A large corporation could easily have a dozen or more note and bond issues outstanding. Beyond this, federal, state, and local borrowing is enormous. For example, even a small city would usually have a wide variety of notes and bonds outstanding, representing money borrowed to pay for things like roads, sewers, and schools. When you think about how many small cities there are in the United States, you begin to get the picture!

Because the bond market is almost entirely OTC, it has historically had little or no transparency. A financial market is *transparent* if it is possible to easily observe its prices and trading volume. On the New York Stock Exchange, for example, it is possible to see the price and quantity for every single transaction. In contrast, in the bond market, it is often not possible to observe either. Transactions are privately negotiated between parties, and there is little or no centralized reporting of transactions.

Although the total volume of trading in bonds far exceeds that in stocks, only a small fraction of the total bond issues that exist actually trade on a given day. This fact, combined with the lack of transparency in the bond market, means that getting up-to-date prices on individual bonds can be difficult or impossible, particularly for smaller corporate or municipal issues. Instead, a variety of sources of estimated prices exist and are commonly used.

BOND PRICE REPORTING

To learn more about TRACE, visit **www.finra.org**.

In 2002, transparency in the corporate bond market began to improve dramatically. Under new regulations, corporate bond dealers are now required to report trade information through what is known as the Trade Reporting and Compliance Engine (TRACE). Our nearby *Work the Web* box shows you how to get bond quotes.

TRACE bond quotes are available at finra-markets.morningstar.com. As shown in Figure 7.3, the Financial Industry Regulatory Authority (FINRA) provides a daily snapshot from TRACE by reporting the most active issues. The information shown is largely self-explanatory. Notice that the price of the Microsoft bond dropped about 1.92 percentage points on this day. What do you think happened to the yield to maturity for this bond? Figure 7.3 focuses on the most active bonds with investment grade ratings, but the most active high-yield and convertible bonds are also available on the website.

The Federal Reserve Bank of St. Louis maintains dozens of online files containing macroeconomic data as well as rates on U.S. Treasury issues. Go to **fred.stlouisfed.org**

If you go to the website and click on a particular bond, you will get a lot of information about the bond, including the credit rating, the call schedule, original issue information, and trade information.

As we mentioned before, the U.S. Treasury market is the largest securities market in the world. As with bond markets in general, it is an OTC market, so there is limited transparency. Unlike the situation with bond markets in general, trading in Treasury issues,

FIGURE 7.3   **Sample TRACE Bond Quotations**

Most Active Investment Grade Bonds

Issuer Name	Symbol	Coupon	Maturity	Moody's/S&P/Fitch	High	Low	Last	Change	Yield%
COMCAST CORP NEW	CMCS4442549	3.300%	02/01/2027	//A-	101.35700	99.42200	99.63300	-0.484000	
TEVA PHARMACEUTICAL FIN NETH III B V	TEVA4384553	3.150%	10/01/2026	Baa2//BBB	94.39000	92.20800	92.22400	-1.096000	4.127938
MPLX LP	MPLX4403827	4.500%	07/15/2023	Baa3/BBB-/BBB-	102.83800	102.67100	102.68200	-0.442000	4.012035
COMCAST CORP NEW	CMCS4442550	3.000%	02/01/2024	//A-	100.04300	99.50700	99.55100	-0.492000	
BARCLAYS PLC	BCS4442016	4.950%	01/10/2047	Baa2//	102.77500	101.17600	101.17600	-1.438000	
ANHEUSER-BUSCH INBEV FIN INC	BUD4327588	4.900%	02/01/2046	A3/A-/BBB	108.92900	107.37500	107.83800	-1.034000	4.414289
MICROSOFT CORP	MSFT4389880	3.700%	08/08/2046	Aaa/AAA/AA+	95.82700	94.54000	94.68900	-1.918286	4.008024
ROYAL BK CDA	RY4297754	2.100%	10/14/2020	Aaa//AAA	99.83700	99.55300	99.73300	-0.035000	2.173974
ANHEUSER-BUSCH INBEV FIN INC	BUD4327481	3.650%	02/01/2026	A3/A-/BBB	103.01100	101.01600	101.07700	-0.598000	3.506954
ACTAVIS FDG SCS	ACT4218879	3.800%	03/15/2025	Baa3//BBB-	100.49600	99.55800	100.14200	-0.566000	3.778990

particularly recently issued ones, is very heavy. Each day, representative prices for outstanding Treasury issues are reported.

Figure 7.4 shows a portion of the daily Treasury note and bond listings from the website wsj.com. Examine the entry that begins "2/15/2036." Reading from left to right, the "2/15/2036" tells us that the bond's maturity is February 15, 2036. The next column is the coupon rate, which is 4.500 percent for this bond. Treasury bonds all make semiannual payments and have a minimum face value of $1,000, so this bond will pay $22.50 every six months until it matures.

The next two pieces of information are the **bid** and **asked prices**. In general, in any OTC or dealer market, the bid price represents what a dealer is willing to pay for a security, and the asked price (or "ask" price) is what a dealer is willing to take for it. The difference between the two prices is called the **bid-ask spread** (or just "spread"), and it represents the dealer's profit.

Treasury prices are quoted as a percentage of face value. The bid price, or what a dealer is willing to pay, on the 2/15/2036 bond is 128.0781. With a $1,000 face value, this quote represents $1,280.781. The asked price, or the price at which the dealer is willing to sell the bond, is 128.1406, or $1,281.406.

The next number quoted is the change in the asked price from the previous day, measured as a percentage of face value, so this issue's asked price increased by .7031 percent, or $7.031, in value from the previous day. Finally, the last number reported is the yield to maturity, based on the asked price. Notice that this is a premium bond because it sells for more than its face value. Not surprisingly, its yield to maturity (2.618 percent) is less than its coupon rate (4.50 percent).

The very last ordinary bond listed, the 11/15/2046, is often called the "bellwether" bond. This bond's yield is the one that is usually reported in the evening news. So, for example, when you hear that long-term interest rates rose, what is really being said is that the yield on this bond went up (and its price went down).

If you examine the yields on the various issues in Figure 7.4, you will clearly see that they vary by maturity. Why this occurs and what it might mean is one of the things we discuss in our next section. Government (referred to as "sovereign") bond yields also vary by country of origin. Nearby, we show the 10-year bond yields of several countries. The yields vary according to default risks and foreign exchange risks (to be discussed later in the text).

bid price
The price a dealer is willing to pay for a security.

asked price
The price a dealer is willing to take for a security.

bid–ask spread
The difference between the bid price and the asked price.

Current and historical Treasury yield information is available at **www.treasury.gov**.

FIGURE 7.4

Sample *Wall Street Journal* U.S. Treasury Note and Bond Prices

SOURCE: Table recreated with data from wsj.com, January 9, 2017.

Treasury Notes and Bonds					
Maturity	Coupon	Bid	Asked	Chg	Asked Yield
11/15/2018	1.250	100.1484	100.1641	0.0391	1.160
4/15/2019	0.875	99.0703	99.0859	0.0625	1.286
4/30/2020	1.125	98.5938	98.6094	0.1016	1.558
8/15/2021	8.125	127.4844	127.5000	0.2344	1.857
7/31/2022	2.000	99.9609	99.9766	0.2266	2.004
2/28/2023	1.500	96.5703	96.5859	0.2500	2.096
5/15/2024	2.500	101.9375	101.9531	0.3125	2.210
8/15/2025	6.875	135.8438	135.8594	0.3438	2.262
8/15/2026	1.500	92.4766	92.4922	0.2969	2.380
8/15/2027	6.375	136.8281	136.8438	0.4688	2.414
8/15/2028	5.500	130.2891	130.3516	0.4531	2.473
11/15/2028	5.250	128.1563	128.2188	0.4453	2.485
2/15/2029	5.250	128.7578	128.8203	0.4609	2.478
8/15/2029	6.125	139.1875	139.2500	0.5391	2.478
5/15/2030	6.250	142.5781	142.6406	0.5938	2.478
2/15/2031	5.375	134.3438	134.4063	0.5625	2.470
2/15/2036	4.500	128.0781	128.1406	0.7031	2.618
2/15/2037	4.750	131.7891	131.8516	0.7500	2.688
5/15/2037	5.000	135.9531	136.0156	0.7656	2.690
5/15/2038	4.500	128.0625	128.1250	0.6875	2.749
2/15/2039	3.500	110.9844	111.0469	0.6406	2.824
8/15/2039	4.500	127.4922	127.5547	0.7344	2.839
2/15/2040	4.625	129.7188	129.7813	0.6953	2.855
11/15/2040	4.250	123.3438	123.4063	0.7422	2.885
2/15/2041	4.750	132.4688	132.5000	0.7578	2.872
2/15/2042	3.125	103.3516	103.3828	0.6484	2.934
2/15/2043	3.125	103.1406	103.1719	0.6250	2.950
5/15/2043	2.875	98.3594	98.3906	0.5625	2.963
2/15/2044	3.625	112.7266	112.7578	0.6484	2.939
2/15/2045	2.500	90.7578	90.7891	0.6016	2.987
11/15/2046	2.875	98.1172	98.1484	0.6719	2.969

SELECTED INTERNATIONAL GOVERNMENT 10-YEAR BOND YIELDS	Yield (%)
United States	2.41
United Kingdom	1.19
Japan	.04
Canada	2.04
Australia	2.63
Greece	4.03
Spain	1.55
Italy	2.00
India	7.32

SOURCE: Data pulled from www.bloomberg.com, December 30, 2017.

A NOTE ABOUT BOND PRICE QUOTES

If you buy a bond between coupon payment dates, the price you pay is usually more than the price you are quoted. The reason is that standard convention in the bond market is to quote prices net of "accrued interest," meaning that accrued interest is deducted to arrive at the quoted price. This quoted price is called the **clean price**. The price you actually pay, however, includes the accrued interest. This price is the **dirty price**, also known as the "full" or "invoice" price.

An example is the easiest way to understand these issues. Suppose you buy a bond with a 12 percent annual coupon, payable semiannually. You actually pay $1,080 for this bond, so $1,080 is the dirty, or invoice, price. Further, on the day you buy it, the next coupon is due in four months, so you are between coupon dates. Notice that the next coupon will be $60.

The accrued interest on a bond is calculated by taking the fraction of the coupon period that has passed, in this case two months out of six, and multiplying this fraction by the next coupon, $60. So, the accrued interest in this example is $2/6 \times \$60 = \$20$. The bond's quoted price (that is, its clean price) would be $1,080 - 20 = \$1,060$.[6]

clean price
The price of a bond net of accrued interest; this is the price that is typically quoted.

dirty price
The price of a bond including accrued interest, also known as the *full* or *invoice price*. This is the price the buyer actually pays.

Concept Questions

7.5a   Why do we say bond markets may have little or no transparency?
7.5b   In general, what are bid and ask prices?
7.5c   What is the difference between a bond's clean price and its dirty price?

Inflation and Interest Rates   7.6

So far, we haven't considered the role of inflation in our various discussions of interest rates, yields, and returns. Because this is an important consideration, we consider the impact of inflation next.

REAL VERSUS NOMINAL RATES

In examining interest rates, or any other financial market rates such as discount rates, bond yields, rates of return, and required returns, it is often necessary to distinguish between **real rates** and **nominal rates**. Nominal rates are called "nominal" because they have not been adjusted for inflation. Real rates are rates that have been adjusted for inflation.

To see the effect of inflation, suppose prices are currently rising by 5 percent per year. In other words, the rate of inflation is 5 percent. An investment is available that will be worth $115.50 in one year. It costs $100 today. Notice that with a present value of $100 and a future value in one year of $115.50, this investment has a 15.5 percent rate of return. In calculating this 15.5 percent return, we did not consider the effect of inflation, so this is the nominal return.

What is the impact of inflation here? To answer, suppose pizzas cost $5 apiece at the beginning of the year. With $100, we can buy 20 pizzas. Because the inflation rate is

real rates
Interest rates or rates of return that have been adjusted for inflation.

nominal rates
Interest rates or rates of return that have not been adjusted for inflation.

---

[6]The way accrued interest is calculated actually depends on the type of bond being quoted—for example, Treasury or corporate. The difference has to do with exactly how the fractional coupon period is calculated. In our example here, we implicitly treated the months as having exactly the same length (30 days each, 360 days in a year), which is consistent with the way corporate bonds are quoted. In contrast, for Treasury bonds, actual day counts are used.

5 percent, pizzas will cost 5 percent more, or $5.25, at the end of the year. If we take the investment, how many pizzas can we buy at the end of the year? Measured in pizzas, what is the rate of return on this investment?

Our $115.50 from the investment will buy us $115.50/$5.25 = 22 pizzas. This is up from 20 pizzas, so our pizza rate of return is 10 percent. What this illustrates is that even though the nominal return on our investment is 15.5 percent, our buying power goes up by only 10 percent because of inflation. Put another way, we are really only 10 percent richer. In this case, we say that the real return is 10 percent.

Alternatively, we can say that with 5 percent inflation, each of the $115.50 nominal dollars we get is worth 5 percent less in real terms, so the real dollar value of our investment in a year is:

$$\$115.50/1.05 = \$110$$

What we have done is to *deflate* the $115.50 by 5 percent. Because we give up $100 in current buying power to get the equivalent of $110, our real return is again 10 percent. Because we have removed the effect of future inflation here, this $110 is said to be measured in current dollars.

The difference between nominal and real rates is important and bears repeating:

> **The nominal rate on an investment is the percentage change in the number of dollars you have.**
>
> **The real rate on an investment is the percentage change in how much you can buy with your dollars—in other words, the percentage change in your buying power.**

THE FISHER EFFECT

Fisher effect
The relationship between nominal returns, real returns, and inflation.

Our discussion of real and nominal returns illustrates a relationship often called the **Fisher effect** (after the great economist Irving Fisher). Because investors are ultimately concerned with what they can buy with their money, they require compensation for inflation. Let R stand for the nominal rate and r stand for the real rate. The Fisher effect tells us that the relationship between nominal rates, real rates, and inflation can be written as:

$$1 + R = (1 + r) \times (1 + h) \tag{7.2}$$

where h is the inflation rate.

In the preceding example, the nominal rate was 15.50 percent and the inflation rate was 5 percent. What was the real rate? We can determine it by plugging in these numbers:

$$1 + .1550 = (1 + r) \times (1 + .05)$$
$$1 + r = 1.1550/1.05 = 1.10$$
$$r = .10, \text{ or } 10\%$$

This real rate is the same as we found before. If we take another look at the Fisher effect, we can rearrange things a little as follows:

$$1 + R = (1 + r) \times (1 + h)$$
$$R = r + h + r \times h \tag{7.3}$$

What this tells us is that the nominal rate has three components. First, there is the real rate on the investment, r. Next, there is the compensation for the decrease in the value of the money originally invested because of inflation, h. The third component represents compensation for the fact that the dollars earned on the investment are also worth less because of inflation.

This third component is usually small, so it is often dropped. The nominal rate is then approximately equal to the real rate plus the inflation rate:

$$R \approx r + h \qquad \text{[7.4]}$$

The Fisher Effect

EXAMPLE 7.5

If investors require a 10 percent real rate of return, and the inflation rate is 8 percent, what must be the approximate nominal rate? The exact nominal rate?

The nominal rate is approximately equal to the sum of the real rate and the inflation rate: 10% + 8% = 18%. From the Fisher effect, we have:

$$1 + R = (1 + r) \times (1 + h)$$
$$= 1.10 \times 1.08$$
$$= 1.1880$$

Therefore, the nominal rate will actually be closer to 19 percent.

You would expect that investors would always require a positive real return since a primary purpose of investing is to be able to spend more in the future than you could today. This means that the only time investors would accept a negative yield on a bond would be if there was deflation, or negative inflation. Going back to our discussion at the beginning of the chapter about negative yields, while inflation rates were low at the time, they were not negative, so investors were willing to accept a negative real return. Why? After all, holding cash has a zero real return, which is better. One answer is that holding a huge amount of cash is both expensive and difficult to do, so investors were willing to accept a real return slightly below zero, at what amounts to a storage cost.

It is important to note that financial rates, such as interest rates, discount rates, and rates of return, are almost always quoted in nominal terms. To remind you of this, we will henceforth use the symbol R instead of r in most of our discussions about such rates.

INFLATION AND PRESENT VALUES

One question that often comes up is the effect of inflation on present value calculations. The basic principle is simple: Either discount nominal cash flows at a nominal rate or discount real cash flows at a real rate. As long as you are consistent, you will get the same answer.

To illustrate, suppose you want to withdraw money each year for the next three years, and you want each withdrawal to have $25,000 worth of purchasing power as measured in current dollars. If the inflation rate is 4 percent per year, then the withdrawals will have to increase by 4 percent each year to compensate. The withdrawals each year will thus be:

$$C_1 = \$25,000(1.04) = \$26,000$$
$$C_2 = \$25,000(1.04)^2 = \$27,040$$
$$C_3 = \$25,000(1.04)^3 = \$28,121.60$$

What is the present value of these cash flows if the appropriate nominal discount rate is 10 percent? This is a standard calculation, and the answer is:

$$PV = \$26,000/1.10 + \$27,040/1.10^2 + \$28,121.60/1.10^3 = \$67,111.65$$

Notice that we discounted the nominal cash flows at a nominal rate.

To calculate the present value using real cash flows, we need the real discount rate. Using the Fisher equation, the real discount rate is:

$$1 + R = (1 + r)(1 + h)$$
$$1 + .10 = (1 + r)(1 + .04)$$
$$r = .0577, \text{ or } 5.77\%$$

By design, the real cash flows are an annuity of $25,000 per year. So, the present value in real terms is:

$$PV = \$25,000[1 - (1/1.0577^3)]/.0577 = \$67,111.65$$

Thus, we get exactly the same answer (after allowing for a small rounding error in the real rate). Of course, you could also use the growing annuity equation we discussed in the previous chapter. The withdrawals are increasing at 4 percent per year; so using the growing annuity formula, the present value is:

$$PV = \$26,000 \left[\frac{1 - \left(\frac{1 + .04}{1 + .10} \right)^3}{.10 - .04} \right] = \$26,000(2.58122) = \$67,111.65$$

This is exactly the same present value we calculated before.

Concept Questions

7.6a　What is the difference between a nominal and a real return? Which is more important to a typical investor?

7.6b　What is the Fisher effect?

7.7 Determinants of Bond Yields

We are now in a position to discuss the determinants of a bond's yield. As we will see, the yield on any particular bond reflects a variety of factors, some common to all bonds and some specific to the issue under consideration.

THE TERM STRUCTURE OF INTEREST RATES

At any point in time, short-term and long-term interest rates will generally be different. Sometimes short-term rates are higher, sometimes lower. Figure 7.5 gives us a long-range perspective on this by showing over two centuries of short- and long-term interest rates. As shown, through time, the difference between short- and long-term rates has ranged from essentially zero to up to several percentage points, both positive and negative.

The relationship between short- and long-term interest rates is known as the **term structure of interest rates**. To be a little more precise, the term structure of interest rates tells us what *nominal* interest rates are on *default-free*, *pure discount* bonds of all maturities. These rates are, in essence, "pure" interest rates because they involve no risk of default and a single, lump sum future payment. In other words, the term structure tells us the pure time value of money for different lengths of time.

When long-term rates are higher than short-term rates, we say that the term structure is upward sloping; when short-term rates are higher, we say it is downward sloping. The term structure can also be "humped." When this occurs, it is usually because rates increase at first, but then begin to decline as we look at longer- and longer-term rates. The most

Excel Master It!

Excel Master coverage online

term structure of interest rates
The relationship between nominal interest rates on default-free, pure discount securities and time to maturity; that is, the pure time value of money.

FIGURE 7.5   **U.S. Interest Rates: 1800–2016**

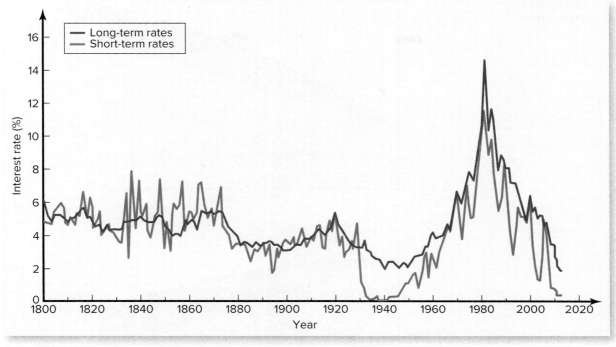

SOURCE: Siegel, Jeremy J., *Stocks for the Long Run*, 4th edition. New York: McGraw-Hill, 2008, updated by the authors.

common shape of the term structure, particularly in modern times, is upward sloping; but the degree of steepness has varied quite a bit.

What determines the shape of the term structure? There are three basic components. The first two are the ones we discussed in our previous section: the real rate of interest and the rate of inflation. The real rate of interest is the compensation investors demand for forgoing the use of their money. You can think of it as the pure time value of money after adjusting for the effects of inflation.

The real rate of interest is the basic component underlying every interest rate, regardless of the time to maturity. When the real rate is high, all interest rates will tend to be higher, and vice versa. Thus, the real rate doesn't really determine the shape of the term structure; instead, it mostly influences the overall level of interest rates.

In contrast, the prospect of future inflation strongly influences the shape of the term structure. Investors thinking about lending money for various lengths of time recognize that future inflation erodes the value of the dollars that will be returned. As a result, investors demand compensation for this loss in the form of higher nominal rates. This extra compensation is called the **inflation premium**.

If investors believe the rate of inflation will be higher in the future, then long-term nominal interest rates will tend to be higher than short-term rates. Thus, an upward-sloping term structure may reflect anticipated increases in inflation. Similarly, a downward-sloping term structure probably reflects the belief that inflation will be falling in the future.

The third, and last, component of the term structure has to do with interest rate risk. As we discussed earlier in the chapter, longer-term bonds have much greater risk of loss resulting from changes in interest rates than do shorter-term bonds. Investors recognize this risk, and they demand extra compensation in the form of higher rates for bearing it. This extra compensation is called the **interest rate risk premium**. The longer the term to maturity, the greater the interest rate risk, so the interest rate risk premium increases with

inflation premium
The portion of a nominal interest rate that represents compensation for expected future inflation.

interest rate risk premium
The compensation investors demand for bearing interest rate risk.

FIGURE 7.6

**The Term Structure
of Interest Rates**

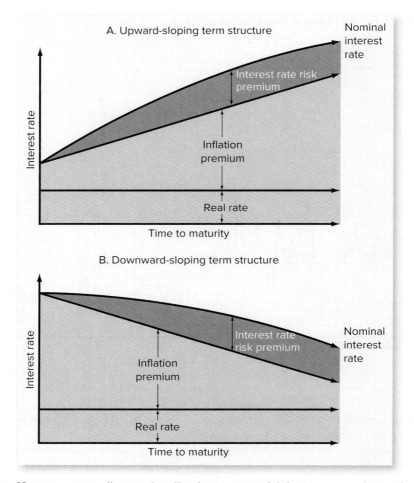

maturity. However, as we discussed earlier, interest rate risk increases at a decreasing rate, so the interest rate risk premium does as well.[7]

Putting the pieces together, we see that the term structure reflects the combined effect of the real rate of interest, the inflation premium, and the interest rate risk premium. Figure 7.6 shows how these can interact to produce an upward-sloping term structure (in Part A of Figure 7.6) or a downward-sloping term structure (in Part B).

In Part A of Figure 7.6, notice how the rate of inflation is expected to rise gradually. At the same time, the interest rate risk premium increases at a decreasing rate, so the combined effect is to produce a pronounced upward-sloping term structure. In Part B of Figure 7.6, the rate of inflation is expected to fall in the future, and the expected decline is enough to offset the interest rate risk premium and produce a downward-sloping term structure. Notice that if the rate of inflation was expected to decline by only a small amount, we could still get an upward-sloping term structure because of the interest rate risk premium.

We assumed in drawing Figure 7.6 that the real rate would remain the same. Actually, expected future real rates could be larger or smaller than the current real rate. Also, for simplicity, we used straight lines to show expected future inflation rates as rising or declining, but they do not necessarily have to look like this. They could, for example, rise and then fall, leading to a humped yield curve.

---

[7]In days of old, the interest rate risk premium was called a "liquidity" premium. Today, the term *liquidity premium* has an altogether different meaning, which we explore in our next section. Also, the interest rate risk premium is sometimes called a *maturity risk premium*. Our terminology is consistent with the modern view of the term structure.

FIGURE 7.7 **The Treasury Yield Curve: December 29, 2017**

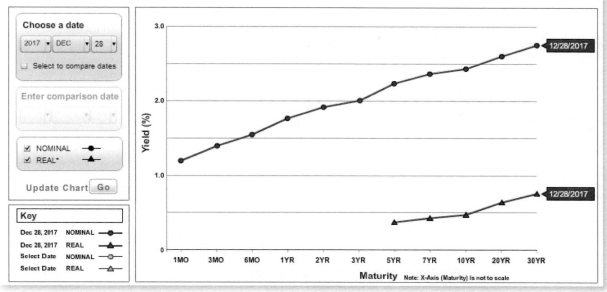

SOURCE: www.treasury.gov, December 29, 2017.

BOND YIELDS AND THE YIELD CURVE: PUTTING IT ALL TOGETHER

Going back to Figure 7.4, recall that we saw that the yields on Treasury notes and bonds of different maturities are not the same. Each day, in addition to the Treasury prices and yields shown in Figure 7.4, the U.S. Treasury provides a plot of Treasury yields relative to maturity. This plot is called the **Treasury yield curve** (or just the yield curve). Figure 7.7 shows the yield curve as of December 29, 2017. Note, the yield curve available on the U.S. Treasury website will display both the nominal and real yield curves.

As you probably now suspect, the shape of the yield curve reflects the term structure of interest rates. In fact, the Treasury yield curve and the term structure of interest rates are almost the same thing. The only difference is that the term structure is based on pure discount bonds, whereas the yield curve is based on coupon bond yields. As a result, Treasury yields depend on the three components that underlie the term structure—the real rate, expected future inflation, and the interest rate risk premium.

Treasury notes and bonds have three important features that we need to remind you of: They are default-free, they are taxable, and they are highly liquid. This is not true of bonds in general, so we need to examine what additional factors come into play when we look at bonds issued by corporations or municipalities.

The first thing to consider is credit risk—that is, the possibility of default. Investors recognize that issuers other than the Treasury may or may not make all the promised payments on a bond, so they demand a higher yield as compensation for this risk. This extra compensation is called the **default risk premium**. Earlier in the chapter, we saw how bonds were rated based on their credit risk. What you will find if you start looking at bonds of different ratings is that lower-rated bonds have higher yields.

An important thing to recognize about a bond's yield is that it is calculated assuming that all the promised payments will be made. As a result, it is really a promised yield, and it may or may not be what you will earn. In particular, if the issuer defaults, your actual yield will be lower—probably much lower. This fact is particularly important when it comes to junk bonds. Thanks

Treasury yield curve
A plot of the yields on Treasury notes and bonds relative to maturity.

Online yield curve information is available at **www.bloomberg.com /markets**.

default risk premium
The portion of a nominal interest rate or bond yield that represents compensation for the possibility of default.

To see how the yield curve has changed over time, check out the "living yield curve" at **stockcharts.com /freecharts/yieldcurve.php**.

to a clever bit of marketing, such bonds are now commonly called high-yield bonds, which has a much nicer ring to it; but now you recognize that these are really high *promised* yield bonds.

Next, recall that we discussed earlier how municipal bonds are free from most taxes and, as a result, have much lower yields than taxable bonds. Investors demand the extra yield on a taxable bond as compensation for the unfavorable tax treatment. This extra compensation is the **taxability premium**.

Finally, bonds have varying degrees of liquidity. As we discussed earlier, there are an enormous number of bond issues, most of which do not trade regularly. As a result, if you wanted to sell quickly, you would probably not get as good a price as you could otherwise. Investors prefer liquid assets to illiquid ones, so they demand a **liquidity premium** on top of all the other premiums we have discussed. As a result, all else being the same, less liquid bonds will have higher yields than more liquid bonds.

taxability premium
The portion of a nominal interest rate or bond yield that represents compensation for unfavorable tax status.

liquidity premium
The portion of a nominal interest rate or bond yield that represents compensation for lack of liquidity.

CONCLUSION

If we combine all of the things we have discussed regarding bond yields, we find that bond yields represent the combined effect of no fewer than six things. The first is the real rate of interest. On top of the real rate are five premiums representing compensation for (1) expected future inflation, (2) interest rate risk, (3) default risk, (4) taxability, and (5) lack of liquidity. As a result, determining the appropriate yield on a bond requires careful analysis of each of these effects.

> ### Concept Questions
>
> **7.7a**   What is the term structure of interest rates? What determines its shape?
> **7.7b**   What is the Treasury yield curve?
> **7.7c**   What six components make up a bond's yield?

7.8 Summary and Conclusions

This chapter has explored bonds, bond yields, and interest rates:

1. Determining bond prices and yields is an application of basic discounted cash flow principles.
2. Bond values move in the direction opposite that of interest rates, leading to potential gains or losses for bond investors.
3. Bonds have a variety of features spelled out in a document called the indenture.
4. Bonds are rated based on their default risk. Some bonds, such as Treasury bonds, have no risk of default, whereas so-called junk bonds have substantial default risk.
5. A wide variety of bonds exist, many of which contain exotic or unusual features.
6. Almost all bond trading is OTC, with little or no market transparency in many cases. As a result, bond price and volume information can be difficult to find for some types of bonds.
7. Bond yields and interest rates reflect the effect of six different things: the real interest rate and five premiums that investors demand as compensation for inflation, interest rate risk, default risk, taxability, and lack of liquidity.

In closing, we note that bonds are a vital source of financing to governments and corporations of all types. Bond prices and yields are a rich subject, and our one chapter, necessarily, touches on only the most important concepts and ideas. There is a great deal more we could say, but, instead, we will move on to stocks in our next chapter.

CONNECT TO FINANCE

 Do you use *Connect Finance* to practice what you learned? If you don't, you should—we can help you master the topics presented in this chapter. Log on to connect.mheducation.com to learn more!

Can you answer the following *Connect* Quiz questions?

Section 7.1   An 8 percent, semiannual coupon bond has a face value of $1,000 and a current market value of $1,030. What is the current yield?

Section 7.3   The 10-year bonds issued by KP Enterprises were rated as BBB and Baa last year. This year, the bonds are rated as CC and Ca. What term best applies to these bonds today?

Section 7.4   What type of bonds is most apt to have a "collar"?

Section 7.6   Kate wants to earn a 4 percent real rate of return. To do this, what nominal rate must she earn if the inflation rate is 3.6 percent?

Section 7.7   The term structure of interest rates is based on what type of bonds?

CHAPTER REVIEW AND SELF-TEST PROBLEMS

7.1   **Bond Values** A Microgates Industries bond has a 10 percent coupon rate and a $1,000 face value. Interest is paid semiannually, and the bond has 20 years to maturity. If investors require a 12 percent yield, what is the bond's value? What is the effective annual yield on the bond?

7.2   **Bond Yields** A Macrohard Corp. bond carries an 8 percent coupon, paid semiannually. The par value is $1,000, and the bond matures in six years. If the bond currently sells for $911.37, what is its yield to maturity? What is the effective annual yield?

ANSWERS TO CHAPTER REVIEW AND SELF-TEST PROBLEMS

7.1   Because the bond has a 10 percent coupon yield and investors require a 12 percent return, we know that the bond must sell at a discount. Notice that, because the bond pays interest semiannually, the coupons amount to $100/2 = $50 every six months. The required yield is 12%/2 = 6% every six months. Finally, the bond matures in 20 years, so there are a total of 40 six-month periods.

The bond's value is thus equal to the present value of $50 every six months for the next 40 six-month periods plus the present value of the $1,000 face amount:

$$\text{Bond value} = \$50 \times [(1 - 1/1.06^{40})/.06] + 1{,}000/1.06^{40}$$
$$= \$50 \times 15.0463 + 1{,}000/10.2857$$
$$= \$849.54$$

Notice that we discounted the $1,000 back 40 periods at 6 percent per period, rather than 20 years at 12 percent. The reason is that the effective annual yield on the bond is $1.06^2 - 1 = .1236$, or 12.36%, not 12 percent. We thus could have used 12.36 percent per year for 20 years when we calculated the present value of the $1,000 face amount, and the answer would have been the same.

7.2 The present value of the bond's cash flows is its current price, $911.37. The coupon is $40 every six months for 12 periods. The face value is $1,000. So the bond's yield is the unknown discount rate in the following:

$$\$911.37 = \$40 \times [1 - 1/(1 + r)^{12}]/r + 1,000/(1 + r)^{12}$$

The bond sells at a discount. Because the coupon rate is 8 percent, the yield must be something in excess of that.

  If we were to solve this by trial and error, we might try 12 percent (or 6 percent per six months):

$$\text{Bond value} = \$40 \times (1 - 1/1.06^{12})/.06 + 1,000/1.06^{12}$$
$$= \$832.32$$

This is less than the actual value, so our discount rate is too high. We now know that the yield is somewhere between 8 and 12 percent. With further trial and error (or a little machine assistance), the yield works out to be 10 percent, or 5 percent every six months.

  By convention, the bond's yield to maturity would be quoted as $2 \times 5\% = 10\%$. The effective yield is thus $1.05^2 - 1 = .1025$, or 10.25%.

CONCEPTS REVIEW AND CRITICAL THINKING QUESTIONS

1. **Treasury Bonds** [LO1] Is it true that a U.S. Treasury security is risk-free?

2. **Interest Rate Risk** [LO2] Which has greater interest rate risk, a 30-year Treasury bond or a 30-year BB corporate bond?

3. **Treasury Pricing** [LO1] With regard to bid and ask prices on a Treasury bond, is it possible for the bid price to be higher? Why or why not?

4. **Yield to Maturity** [LO2] Treasury bid and ask quotes are sometimes given in terms of yields, so there would be a bid yield and an ask yield. Which do you think would be larger? Explain.

5. **Call Provisions** [LO1] A company is contemplating a long-term bond issue. It is debating whether to include a call provision. What are the benefits to the company from including a call provision? What are the costs? How do these answers change for a put provision?

6. **Coupon Rate** [LO1] How does a bond issuer decide on the appropriate coupon rate to set on its bonds? Explain the difference between the coupon rate and the required return on a bond.

7. **Real and Nominal Returns** [LO4] Are there any circumstances under which an investor might be more concerned about the nominal return on an investment than the real return?

8. **Bond Ratings** [LO3] Companies pay rating agencies such as Moody's and S&P to rate their bonds, and the costs can be substantial. However, companies are not required to have their bonds rated; doing so is strictly voluntary. Why do you think they do it?

9. **Bond Ratings** [LO3] Often, junk bonds are not rated. Why?

10. **Term Structure** [LO5] What is the difference between the term structure of interest rates and the yield curve?

11. **Crossover Bonds** [LO3] Looking back at the crossover bonds we discussed in the chapter, why do you think split ratings such as these occur?

12. **Municipal Bonds** [LO1] Why is it that municipal bonds are not taxed at the federal level, but are taxable across state lines? Why are U.S. Treasury bonds not taxable at the state level? (You may need to dust off the history books for this one.)

13. **Bond Market** [LO1] What does the lack of transparency in the bond market imply for bond investors?

14. **Rating Agencies** [LO3] A controversy erupted regarding bond-rating agencies when some agencies began to provide unsolicited bond ratings. Why do you think this is controversial?

15. **Bonds as Equity** [LO1] The 100-year bonds we discussed in the chapter have something in common with junk bonds. Critics charge that, in both cases, the issuers are really selling equity in disguise. What are the issues here? Why would a company want to sell "equity in disguise"?

QUESTIONS AND PROBLEMS

1. **Interpreting Bond Yields** [LO1] Is the yield to maturity on a bond the same thing as the required return? Is YTM the same thing as the coupon rate? Suppose today a 10 percent coupon bond sells at par. Two years from now, the required return on the same bond is 8 percent. What is the coupon rate on the bond then? The YTM?

BASIC
(Questions 1–17)

2. **Interpreting Bond Yields** [LO2] Suppose you buy a 7 percent coupon, 20-year bond today when it's first issued. If interest rates suddenly rise to 15 percent, what happens to the value of your bond? Why?

3. **Valuing Bonds** [LO2] Even though most corporate bonds in the United States make coupon payments semiannually, bonds issued elsewhere often have annual coupon payments. Suppose a German company issues a bond with a par value of €1,000, 23 years to maturity, and a coupon rate of 3.8 percent paid annually. If the yield to maturity is 4.7 percent, what is the current price of the bond?

4. **Bond Yields** [LO2] A Japanese company has a bond outstanding that sells for 105.43 percent of its ¥100,000 par value. The bond has a coupon rate of 3.4 percent paid annually and matures in 16 years. What is the yield to maturity of this bond?

5. **Coupon Rates** [LO2] Gabriele Enterprises has bonds on the market making annual payments, with eight years to maturity, a par value of $1,000, and selling for $948. At this price, the bonds yield 5.1 percent. What must the coupon rate be on the bonds?

6. **Bond Prices** [LO2] Weismann Co. issued 15-year bonds a year ago at a coupon rate of 4.9 percent. The bonds make semiannual payments and have a par value of $1,000. If the YTM on these bonds is 4.5 percent, what is the current bond price?

7. **Bond Yields** [LO2] West Corp. issued 25-year bonds two years ago at a coupon rate of 5.3 percent. The bonds make semiannual payments. If these bonds currently sell for 105 percent of par value, what is the YTM?

8. **Coupon Rates** [LO2] McConnell Corporation has bonds on the market with 14.5 years to maturity, a YTM of 5.3 percent, a par value of $1,000, and a current price of $1,045. The bonds make semiannual payments. What must the coupon rate be on these bonds?

9. **Zero Coupon Bonds** [LO2] You find a zero coupon bond with a par value of $10,000 and 17 years to maturity. If the yield to maturity on this bond is 4.2 percent, what is the price of the bond? Assume semiannual compounding periods.

10. **Valuing Bonds** [LO2] Yan Yan Corp. has a $2,000 par value bond outstanding with a coupon rate of 4.4 percent paid semiannually and 13 years to maturity. The yield to maturity of the bond is 4.8 percent. What is the price of the bond?

11. **Valuing Bonds** [LO2] Union Local School District has a bond outstanding with a coupon rate of 2.8 percent paid semiannually and 16 years to maturity. The yield to maturity on this bond is 3.4 percent, and the bond has a par value of $5,000. What is the price of the bond?

12. **Calculating Real Rates of Return** [LO4] If Treasury bills are currently paying 4.7 percent and the inflation rate is 2.2 percent, what is the approximate real rate of interest? The exact real rate?

13. **Inflation and Nominal Returns** [LO4] Suppose the real rate is 2.1 percent and the inflation rate is 3.4 percent. What rate would you expect to see on a Treasury bill?

14. **Nominal and Real Returns** [LO4] An investment offers a total return of 12.3 percent over the coming year. Janice Yellen thinks the total real return on this investment will be only 8 percent. What does Janice believe the inflation rate will be over the next year?

15. **Nominal versus Real Returns** [LO4] Say you own an asset that had a total return last year of 11.65 percent. If the inflation rate last year was 2.75 percent, what was your real return?

16. **Using Treasury Quotes** [LO2] Locate the Treasury issue in Figure 7.4 maturing in May 2038. What is its coupon rate? What is its bid price? What was the *previous* day's asked price? Assume a par value of $10,000.

17. **Using Treasury Quotes** [LO2] Locate the Treasury bond in Figure 7.4 maturing in February 2040. Is this a premium or a discount bond? What is its current yield? What is its yield to maturity? What is the bid-ask spread in dollars? Assume a par value of $10,000.

INTERMEDIATE
(Questions 18–31)

18. **Bond Price Movements** [LO2] Bond X is a premium bond making semiannual payments. The bond pays a coupon rate of 7.4 percent, has a YTM of 6.8 percent, and has 13 years to maturity. Bond Y is a discount bond making semiannual payments. This bond pays a coupon rate of 6.8 percent, has a YTM of 7.4 percent, and also has 13 years to maturity. What is the price of each bond today? If interest rates remain unchanged, what do you expect the price of these bonds to be one year from now? In three years? In eight years? In 12 years? In 13 years? What's going on here? Illustrate your answers by graphing bond prices versus time to maturity.

19. **Interest Rate Risk** [LO2] Both Bond Sam and Bond Dave have 7.3 percent coupons, make semiannual payments, and are priced at par value. Bond Sam has three years to maturity, whereas Bond Dave has 20 years to maturity. If interest rates suddenly rise by 2 percent, what is the percentage change in the price of Bond Sam? Of Bond Dave? If rates were to suddenly fall by 2 percent instead, what would the percentage change in the price of Bond Sam be then? Of Bond Dave? Illustrate your answers by graphing bond prices versus YTM. What does this problem tell you about the interest rate risk of longer-term bonds?

20. **Interest Rate Risk** [LO2] Bond J has a coupon rate of 3 percent. Bond K has a coupon rate of 9 percent. Both bonds have 14 years to maturity, make semiannual payments, and have a YTM of 6 percent. If interest rates suddenly rise by 2 percent, what is the percentage price change of these bonds? What if rates suddenly fall by 2 percent instead? What does this problem tell you about the interest rate risk of lower-coupon bonds?

21. **Bond Yields** [LO2] Workman Software has 6.4 percent coupon bonds on the market with 18 years to maturity. The bonds make semiannual payments and currently sell for 94.31 percent of par. What is the current yield on the bonds? The YTM? The effective annual yield?

22. **Bond Yields** [LO2] Chamberlain Co. wants to issue new 20-year bonds for some much-needed expansion projects. The company currently has 6 percent coupon bonds on the market that sell for $1,083, make semiannual payments, and mature in 20 years. What coupon rate should the company set on its new bonds if it wants them to sell at par?

23. **Accrued Interest** [LO2] You purchase a bond with an invoice price of $948. The bond has a coupon rate of 5.9 percent, and there are four months to the next semiannual coupon date. What is the clean price of the bond?

24. **Accrued Interest** [LO2] You purchase a bond with a coupon rate of 5.3 percent and a clean price of $951. If the next semiannual coupon payment is due in two months, what is the invoice price?

25. **Finding the Bond Maturity** [LO2] Excey Corp. has 8 percent coupon bonds making annual payments with a YTM of 7.2 percent. The current yield on these bonds is 7.55 percent. How many years do these bonds have left until they mature?

26. **Using Bond Quotes** [LO2] Suppose the following bond quotes for IOU Corporation appear in the financial page of today's newspaper. Assume the bond has a face value of $2,000 and the current date is April 19, 2018. What is the yield to maturity of the bond? What is the current yield?

Company (Ticker)	Coupon	Maturity	Last Price	Last Yield	EST Vol (000s)
IOU (IOU)	5.7	Apr 19, 2034	108.96	??	1,827

27. **Bond Prices versus Yields** [LO2]

    a. What is the relationship between the price of a bond and its YTM?

    b. Explain why some bonds sell at a premium over par value while other bonds sell at a discount. What do you know about the relationship between the coupon rate and the YTM for premium bonds? What about for discount bonds? For bonds selling at par value?

    c. What is the relationship between the current yield and YTM for premium bonds? For discount bonds? For bonds selling at par value?

28. **Interest on Zeroes** [LO2] Imagination Dragons Corporation needs to raise funds to finance a plant expansion, and it has decided to issue 25-year zero coupon bonds with a par value of $1,000 each to raise the money. The required return on the bonds will be 4.9 percent. Assume semiannual compounding periods.

    a. What will these bonds sell for at issuance?

    b. Using the IRS amortization rule, what interest deduction can the company take on these bonds in the first year? In the last year?

    c. Repeat part (b) using the straight-line method for the interest deduction.

    d. Based on your answers in (b) and (c), which interest deduction method would the company prefer? Why?

29. **Zero Coupon Bonds** [LO2] Suppose your company needs to raise $53 million and you want to issue 20-year bonds for this purpose. Assume the required return on your bond issue will be 5.3 percent, and you're evaluating two issue alternatives: a semiannual coupon bond with a coupon rate of 5.3 percent, and a zero coupon bond. Your company's tax rate is 21 percent. Both bonds will have a par value of $1,000.

    a. How many of the coupon bonds would you need to issue to raise the $53 million? How many of the zeroes would you need to issue?

b. In 20 years, what will your company's repayment be if you issue the coupon bonds? What if you issue the zeroes?

c. Based on your answers in (a) and (b), why would you ever want to issue the zeroes? To answer, calculate the firm's aftertax cash flows for the first year under the two different scenarios. Assume the IRS amortization rules apply for the zero coupon bonds.

30. Finding the Maturity [LO2] You've just found a 10 percent coupon bond on the market that sells for par value. What is the maturity on this bond?

31. Real Cash Flows [LO4] You want to have $2.5 million in real dollars in an account when you retire in 40 years. The nominal return on your investment is 10.3 percent and the inflation rate is 3.7 percent. What real amount must you deposit each year to achieve your goal?

CHALLENGE
(Questions 32–38)

32. Components of Bond Returns [LO2] Bond P is a premium bond with a coupon rate of 9 percent. Bond D has a coupon rate of 5 percent and is currently selling at a discount. Both bonds make annual payments, have a YTM of 7 percent, and have 10 years to maturity. What is the current yield for Bond P? For Bond D? If interest rates remain unchanged, what is the expected capital gains yield over the next year for Bond P? For Bond D? Explain your answers and the interrelationships among the various types of yields.

33. Holding Period Yield [LO2] The YTM on a bond is the interest rate you earn on your investment if interest rates don't change. If you actually sell the bond before it matures, your realized return is known as the *holding period yield* (HPY).

a. Suppose that today you buy a bond with an annual coupon rate of 7 percent for $1,060. The bond has 21 years to maturity. What rate of return do you expect to earn on your investment? Assume a par value of $1,000.

b. Two years from now, the YTM on your bond has declined by 1 percent, and you decide to sell. What price will your bond sell for? What is the HPY on your investment? Compare this yield to the YTM when you first bought the bond. Why are they different?

34. Valuing Bonds [LO2] Jallouk Corporation has two different bonds currently outstanding. Bond M has a face value of $20,000 and matures in 20 years. The bond makes no payments for the first six years, then pays $900 every six months over the subsequent eight years, and finally pays $1,300 every six months over the last six years. Bond N also has a face value of $20,000 and a maturity of 20 years; it makes no coupon payments over the life of the bond. If the required return on both these bonds is 5.4 percent compounded semiannually, what is the current price of Bond M? Of Bond N?

35. Valuing the Call Feature [LO2] At one point, certain U.S. Treasury bonds were callable. Consider the prices in the following three Treasury issues as of May 15, 2017:

5/15/2023	6.500	106.31250	106.37500	–.31250	5.28
5/15/2023	8.250	103.43750	103.50000	–.09375	5.24
5/15/2023	12.000	134.78125	134.96875	–.46875	5.32

The bond in the middle is callable in February 2018. What is the implied value of the call feature? Assume a par value of $1,000. (*Hint*: Is there a way to combine the two noncallable issues to create an issue that has the same coupon as the callable bond?)

36. Treasury Bonds [LO2] The following Treasury bond quote appeared in *The Wall Street Journal* on May 11, 2004:

5/15/2009	9.125	100.09375	100.12500	0	−2.15

Why would anyone buy this Treasury bond with a negative yield to maturity? How is this possible?

37. Real Cash Flows [LO4] When Marilyn Monroe died, ex-husband Joe DiMaggio vowed to place fresh flowers on her grave every Sunday as long as he lived. The week after she died in 1962, a bunch of fresh flowers that the former baseball player thought appropriate for the star cost about $7. Based on actuarial tables, "Joltin' Joe" could expect to live for 30 years after the actress died. Assume that the EAR is 6.4 percent. Also, assume that the price of the flowers will increase at 3.7 percent per year, when expressed as an EAR. Assuming that each year has exactly 52 weeks, what is the present value of this commitment? Joe began purchasing flowers the week after Marilyn died.

38. Real Cash Flows [LO4] You are planning to save for retirement over the next 30 years. To save for retirement, you will invest $800 per month in a stock account in real dollars and $400 per month in a bond account in real dollars. The effective annual return of the stock account is expected to be 11 percent, and the bond account will earn 7 percent. When you retire, you will combine your money into an account with an effective return of 9 percent. The returns are stated in nominal terms. The inflation rate over this period is expected to be 4 percent. How much can you withdraw each month from your account in real terms assuming a 25-year withdrawal period? What is the nominal dollar amount of your last withdrawal?

EXCEL MASTER IT! PROBLEM

Companies often buy bonds to meet a future liability or cash outlay. Such an investment is called a dedicated portfolio because the proceeds of the portfolio are dedicated to the future liability. In such a case, the portfolio is subject to reinvestment risk. Reinvestment risk occurs because the company will be reinvesting the coupon payments it receives. If the YTM on similar bonds falls, these coupon payments will be reinvested at a lower interest rate, which will result in a portfolio value that is lower than desired at maturity. Of course, if interest rates increase, the portfolio value at maturity will be higher than needed.

Suppose Ice Cubes, Inc., has the following liability due in five years. The company is going to buy five-year bonds today to meet the future obligation. The liability and current YTM are below.

Amount of liability:	$100,000,000
Current YTM:	8%

a. At the current YTM, what is the face value of the bonds the company has to purchase today to meet its future obligation? Assume that the bonds in the relevant range will have the same coupon rate as the current YTM and these bonds make semiannual coupon payments.

b. Assume that the interest rates remain constant for the next five years. Thus, when the company reinvests the coupon payments, it will reinvest at the current YTM. What is the value of the portfolio in five years?

c. Assume that immediately after the company purchases the bonds, interest rates either rise or fall by 1 percent. What is the value of the portfolio in five years under these circumstances?

One way to eliminate reinvestment risk is called *immunization*. Rather than buying bonds with the same maturity as the liability, the company instead buys bonds with the same duration as the liability. If you think about the dedicated portfolio, if the interest rate falls, the future value of the reinvested coupon payments decreases. However, as interest rates fall, the price of the bond increases. These effects offset each other in an immunized portfolio.

Another advantage of using duration to immunize a portfolio is that the duration of a portfolio is the weighted average of the duration of the assets in the portfolio. In other words, to find the duration of a portfolio, you take the weight of each asset multiplied by its duration and then sum the results.

d. What is the duration of the liability for Ice Cubes, Inc.?

e. Suppose the two bonds shown below are the only bonds available to immunize the liability. What face amount of each bond will the company need to purchase to immunize the portfolio?

	Bond A	Bond B
Settlement:	1/1/2000	1/1/2000
Maturity:	1/1/2003	1/1/2008
Coupon rate:	7.00%	8.00%
YTM:	7.50%	9.00%
Coupons per year:	2	2

MINICASE

Financing S&S Air's Expansion Plans with a Bond Issue

Mark Sexton and Todd Story, the owners of S&S Air, have decided to expand their operations. They instructed their newly hired financial analyst, Chris Guthrie, to enlist an underwriter to help sell $35 million in new 10-year bonds to finance construction. Chris has entered into discussions with Renata Harper, an underwriter from the firm of Raines and Warren, about which bond features S&S Air should consider and what coupon rate the issue will likely have.

Although Chris is aware of the bond features, he is uncertain about the costs and benefits of some features, so he isn't sure how each feature would affect the coupon rate of the bond issue. You are Renata's assistant, and she has asked you to prepare a memo to Chris describing the effect of each of the following bond features on the coupon rate of the bond. She would also like you to list any advantages or disadvantages of each feature.

QUESTIONS

1. The security of the bond—that is, whether the bond has collateral.
2. The seniority of the bond.
3. The presence of a sinking fund.
4. A call provision with specified call dates and call prices.
5. A deferred call accompanying the call provision.
6. A make-whole call provision.
7. Any positive covenants. Also, discuss several possible positive covenants S&S Air might consider.
8. Any negative covenants. Also, discuss several possible negative covenants S&S Air might consider.
9. A conversion feature (note that S&S Air is not a publicly traded company).
10. A floating-rate coupon.

Stock Valuation

WHEN THE STOCK MARKET CLOSED on December 29, 2017, the common stock of video game retailer GameStop was going for $17.95 per share. On that same day, stock in industrial giant General Electric closed at $17.45, while stock in data center and technology company Switch, Inc., closed at $18.19. Because the stock prices of these three companies were so similar, you might expect that they would be offering similar dividends to their stockholders, but you would be wrong. In fact, GameStop's annual dividend was $1.52 per share, General Electric's was $.48 per share, and Switch was paying no dividend at all!

As we will see in this chapter, the dividends currently being paid are one of the primary factors we look at when attempting to value common stocks. However, it is obvious from looking at Micron Technology that current dividends are not the end of the story. This chapter explores dividends, stock values, and the connection between the two.

Learning Objectives

After studying this chapter, you should be able to:

LO1 Explain how stock prices depend on future dividends and dividend growth.

LO2 Show how to value stocks using multiples.

LO3 Lay out the different ways corporate directors are elected to office.

LO4 Define how the stock markets work.

For updates on the latest happenings in finance, visit fundamentalsofcorporatefinance.blogspot.com.

©by_adri/iStockPhotoGetty/Images

In our previous chapter, we introduced you to bonds and bond valuation. In this chapter, we turn to the other major source of financing for corporations: Common and preferred stock. We first describe the cash flows associated with a share of stock and then go on to develop a famous result, the dividend growth model. From there, we move on to examine various important features of common and preferred stock, focusing on shareholder rights. We close the chapter with a discussion of how shares of stock are traded and how stock prices and other important information are reported in the financial press.

8.1 Common Stock Valuation

A share of common stock is more difficult to value in practice than a bond for at least three reasons. First, with common stock, not even the promised cash flows are known in advance. Second, the life of the investment is essentially forever because common stock has no maturity. Third, there is no way to easily observe the rate of return that the market requires. Nonetheless, as we will see, there are cases in which we can come up with the present value of the future cash flows for a share of stock and thus determine its value.

CASH FLOWS

Imagine that you are considering buying a share of stock today. You plan to sell the stock in one year. You somehow know that the stock will be worth $70 at that time. You predict that the stock will also pay a $10 per share dividend at the end of the year. If you require a 25 percent return on your investment, what is the most you would pay for the stock? In other words, what is the present value of the $10 dividend along with the $70 ending value at 25 percent?

If you buy the stock today and sell it at the end of the year, you will have a total of $80 in cash. At 25 percent:

Present value = ($10 + 70)/1.25 = $64

Therefore, $64 is the value you would assign to the stock today.

More generally, let P_0 be the current price of the stock, and assign P_1 to be the price in one period. If D_1 is the cash dividend paid at the end of the period, then:

$$P_0 = (D_1 + P_1)/(1 + R)$$

8.1

where R is the required return in the market on this investment.

Notice that we really haven't said much so far. If we wanted to determine the value of a share of stock today (P_0), we would first have to come up with the value in one year (P_1). This is even harder to do, so we've only made the problem more complicated.

What is the price in one period, P_1? We don't know in general. Instead, suppose we somehow knew the price in two periods, P_2. Given a predicted dividend in two periods, D_2, the stock price in one period would be:

$$P_1 = (D_2 + P_2)/(1 + R)$$

If we were to substitute this expression for P_1 into our expression for P_0, we would have:

$$P_0 = \frac{D_1 + P_1}{1 + R} = \frac{D_1 + \dfrac{D_2 + P_2}{1 + R}}{1 + R}$$

$$= \frac{D_1}{(1 + R)^1} + \frac{D_2}{(1 + R)^2} + \frac{P_2}{(1 + R)^2}$$

Now we need to get a price in two periods. We don't know this either, so we can procrastinate again and write:

$$P_2 = (D_3 + P_3)/(1 + R)$$

If we substitute this back in for P_2, we have:

$$P_0 = \frac{D_1}{(1+R)^1} + \frac{D_2}{(1+R)^2} + \frac{P_2}{(1+R)^2}$$

$$= \frac{D_1}{(1+R)^1} + \frac{D_2}{(1+R)^2} + \frac{\dfrac{D_3 + P_3}{1+R}}{(1+R)^2}$$

$$= \frac{D_1}{(1+R)^1} + \frac{D_2}{(1+R)^2} + \frac{D_3}{(1+R)^3} + \frac{P_3}{(1+R)^3}$$

You should start to notice that we can push the problem of coming up with the stock price off into the future forever. Note that no matter what the stock price is, the present value is essentially zero if we push the sale of the stock far enough away.[1] What we are eventually left with is the result that the current price of the stock can be written as the present value of the dividends beginning in one period and extending out forever:

$$P_0 = \frac{D_1}{(1+R)^1} + \frac{D_2}{(1+R)^2} + \frac{D_3}{(1+R)^3} + \frac{D_4}{(1+R)^4} + \frac{D_5}{(1+R)^5} + \cdots$$

We have illustrated here that the price of the stock today is equal to the present value of all of the future dividends. How many future dividends are there? In principle, there can be an infinite number. This means that we still can't compute a value for the stock because we would have to forecast an infinite number of dividends and then discount them all. In the next section, we consider some special cases in which we can get around this problem.

---

[1] The only assumption we make about the stock price is that it is a finite number no matter how far away we push it. It can be extremely large, just not infinitely so. Because no one has ever observed an infinite stock price, this assumption is plausible.

Growth Stocks   EXAMPLE 8.1

You might be wondering about shares of stock in companies such as Alphabet that currently pay no dividends. Small, growing companies frequently plow back everything and pay no dividends. Are such shares worth nothing? It depends. When we say that the value of the stock is equal to the present value of the future dividends, we don't rule out the possibility that some number of those dividends are zero. They just can't *all* be zero.

Imagine a company that has a provision in its corporate charter that prohibits the paying of dividends now or ever. The corporation never borrows any money, never pays out any money to stockholders in any form whatsoever, and never sells any assets. Such a corporation couldn't really exist because the IRS wouldn't like it, and the stockholders could always vote to amend the charter if they wanted to. If it did exist, however, what would the stock be worth?

The stock would be worth absolutely nothing. Such a company would be a financial "black hole." Money goes in, but nothing valuable ever comes out. Because nobody would ever get any return on this investment, the investment would have no value. This example is a little absurd, but it illustrates that when we speak of companies that don't pay dividends, what we really mean is that they are not *currently* paying dividends.

SOME SPECIAL CASES

In a few useful special circumstances, we can come up with a value for the stock. What we have to do is make some simplifying assumptions about the pattern of future dividends. The three cases we consider are the following: (1) The dividend has a zero growth rate, (2) the dividend grows at a constant rate, and (3) the dividend grows at a constant rate after some length of time. We consider each of these separately.

Zero Growth   The case of zero growth is one we've already seen. A share of common stock in a company with a constant dividend is much like a share of preferred stock. From Chapter 6 (see Example 6.7), we know that the dividend on a share of preferred stock has zero growth and is constant through time. For a zero-growth share of common stock, this implies that:

$$D_1 = D_2 = D_3 = D = \text{constant}$$

So, the value of the stock is:

$$P_0 = \frac{D}{(1+R)^1} + \frac{D}{(1+R)^2} + \frac{D}{(1+R)^3} + \frac{D}{(1+R)^4} + \frac{D}{(1+R)^5} + \cdots$$

Because the dividend is always the same, the stock can be viewed as an ordinary perpetuity with a cash flow equal to D every period. The per-share value is given by:

$$\boldsymbol{P_0 = D/R} \qquad \textbf{8.2}$$

where R is the required return.

For example, suppose the Paradise Prototyping Company has a policy of paying a $10 per share dividend every year. If this policy is to be continued indefinitely, what is the value of a share of stock if the required return is 20 percent? The stock in this case amounts to an ordinary perpetuity, so the stock is worth $10/.20 = $50 per share.

Constant Growth   Suppose we know that the dividend for some company always grows at a steady rate. Call this growth rate g. If we let D_0 be the dividend just paid, then the next dividend, D_1, is:

$$D_1 = D_0 \times (1 + g)$$

The dividend in two periods is:

$$D_2 = D_1 \times (1 + g)$$
$$= [D_0 \times (1 + g)] \times (1 + g)$$
$$= D_0 \times (1 + g)^2$$

We could repeat this process to come up with the dividend at any point in the future. In general, from our discussion of compound growth in Chapter 6, we know that the dividend t periods into the future, D_t, is given by:

$$D_t = D_0 \times (1 + g)^t$$

As we have previously seen, an asset with cash flows that grow at a constant rate forever is called a *growing perpetuity*.

The assumption of steady dividend growth might strike you as peculiar. Why would the dividend grow at a constant rate? The reason is that, for many companies, steady growth in dividends is an explicit goal. For example, in 2016, Procter & Gamble, the Cincinnati-based maker of personal care and household products, increased its dividend by 1 percent to $2.68 per share; this increase was notable because it was the 60th in a row. The subject of dividend growth falls under the general heading of dividend policy, so we will defer further discussion of it to a later chapter.

| **Dividend Growth** | **EXAMPLE 8.2** |

The Hedless Corporation has just paid a dividend of $3 per share. The dividend of this company grows at a steady rate of 8 percent per year. Based on this information, what will the dividend be in five years?

Here we have a $3 current amount that grows at 8 percent per year for five years. The future amount is thus:

$3 \times 1.08^5 = \$3 \times 1.4693 = \$4.41$

The dividend will increase by $1.41 over the coming five years.

If the dividend grows at a steady rate, then we have replaced the problem of forecasting an infinite number of future dividends with the problem of coming up with a single growth rate, a considerable simplification. In this case, if we take D_0 to be the dividend just paid and g to be the constant growth rate, the value of a share of stock can be written as:

$$P_0 = \frac{D_1}{(1+R)^1} + \frac{D_2}{(1+R)^2} + \frac{D_3}{(1+R)^3} + \cdots$$
$$= \frac{D_0(1+g)^1}{(1+R)^1} + \frac{D_0(1+g)^2}{(1+R)^2} + \frac{D_0(1+g)^3}{(1+R)^3} + \cdots$$

As long as the growth rate, g, is less than the discount rate, r, the present value of this series of cash flows can be written as:

$$P_0 = \frac{D_0 \times (1+g)}{R-g} = \frac{D_1}{R-g}$$

[8.3]

This elegant result goes by a lot of different names. We will call it the **dividend growth model**. By any name, it is easy to use. To illustrate, suppose D_0 is $2.30, R is 13 percent, and g is 5 percent. The price per share in this case is:

$$P_0 = D_0 \times (1+g)/(R-g)$$
$$= \$2.30 \times 1.05/(.13 - .05)$$
$$= \$2.415/.08$$
$$= \$30.19$$

dividend growth model
A model that determines the current price of a stock as its dividend next period divided by the discount rate less the dividend growth rate.

We can actually use the dividend growth model to get the stock price at any point in time, not just today. In general, the price of the stock as of Time t is:

$$P_t = \frac{D_t \times (1+g)}{R-g} = \frac{D_{t+1}}{R-g}$$

[8.4]

In our example, suppose we are interested in the price of the stock in five years, P_5. We first need the dividend at Time 5, D_5. Because the dividend just paid is $2.30 and the growth rate is 5 percent per year, D_5 is:

$$D_5 = \$2.30 \times 1.05^5 = \$2.30 \times 1.2763 = \$2.935$$

From the dividend growth model, we get the price of the stock in five years:

$$P_5 = \frac{D_5 \times (1+g)}{R-g} = \frac{\$2.935 \times 1.05}{.13 - .05} = \frac{\$3.0822}{.08} = \$38.53$$

EXAMPLE 8.3   **Gordon Growth Company**

The next dividend for the Gordon Growth Company will be $4 per share. Investors require a
16 percent return on companies such as Gordon. Gordon's dividend increases by 6 percent
every year. Based on the dividend growth model, what is the value of Gordon's stock today?
What is the value in four years?

The only tricky thing here is that the next dividend, D_1, is given as $4, so we won't multiply
this by $(1 + g)$. With this in mind, the price per share is given by:

$$P_0 = D_1/(R - g)$$
$$= \$4/(.16 - .06)$$
$$= \$4/.10$$
$$= \$40$$

Because we already have the dividend in one year, we know that the dividend in four
years is equal to $D_1 \times (1 + g)^3 = \$4 \times 1.06^3 = \$4.764$. So, the price in four years is:

$$P_4 = D_4 \times (1 + g)/(R - g)$$
$$= \$4.764 \times 1.06/(.16 - .06)$$
$$= \$5.05/.10$$
$$= \$50.50$$

Notice in this example that P_4 is equal to $P_0 \times (1 + g)^4$.

$$P_4 = \$50.50 = \$40 \times 1.06^4 = P_0 \times (1 + g)^4$$

To see why this is so, notice first that:

$$P_4 = D_5/(R - g)$$

However, D_5 is just equal to $D_1 \times (1 + g)^4$, so we can write P_4 as:

$$P_4 = D_1 \times (1 + g)^4/(R - g)$$
$$= [D_1/(R - g)] \times (1 + g)^4$$
$$= P_0 \times (1 + g)^4$$

This last example illustrates that the dividend growth model makes the implicit assumption that the stock price will grow at the same constant rate as the dividend. This really isn't
too surprising. What it tells us is that if the cash flows on an investment grow at a constant
rate through time, so does the value of that investment.

You might wonder what would happen with the dividend growth model if the growth
rate, g, were greater than the discount rate, R. It looks like we would get a negative stock
price because $R - g$ would be less than zero. This is not what would happen.

Instead, if the constant growth rate exceeds the discount rate, then the stock price is
infinitely large. Why? If the growth rate is bigger than the discount rate, the present value
of the dividends keeps getting bigger. Essentially the same is true if the growth rate and
the discount rate are equal. In both cases, the simplification that allows us to replace the
infinite stream of dividends with the dividend growth model is "illegal," so the answers we
get from the dividend growth model are nonsense unless the growth rate is less than the
discount rate.

Finally, the expression we came up with for the constant growth case will work for any
growing perpetuity, not just dividends on common stock. As we saw in Chapter 6, if C_1 is the
next cash flow on a growing perpetuity, then the present value of the cash flows is given by:

$$\text{Present value} = C_1/(R - g) = C_0(1 + g)/(R - g)$$

Notice that this expression looks like the result for an ordinary perpetuity except that we have $R - g$ on the bottom instead of just R.

Nonconstant Growth   The next case we consider is nonconstant growth. The main reason to consider this case is to allow for "supernormal" growth rates over some finite length of time. As we discussed earlier, the growth rate cannot exceed the required return indefinitely, but it certainly could do so for some number of years. To avoid the problem of having to forecast and discount an infinite number of dividends, we will require that the dividends start growing at a constant rate sometime in the future.

For a simple example of nonconstant growth, consider the case of a company that is currently not paying dividends. You predict that, in five years, the company will pay a dividend for the first time. The dividend will be $.50 per share. You expect that this dividend will then grow at a rate of 10 percent per year indefinitely. The required return on companies such as this one is 20 percent. What is the price of the stock today?

To see what the stock is worth today, we first find out what it will be worth once dividends are paid. We can then calculate the present value of that future price to get today's price. The first dividend will be paid in five years, and the dividend will grow steadily from then on. Using the dividend growth model, we can say that the price in four years will be:

$$
\begin{aligned}
P_4 &= D_4 \times (1 + g)/(R - g) \\
&= D_5/(R - g) \\
&= \$.50/(.20 - .10) \\
&= \$5
\end{aligned}
$$

If the stock will be worth $5 in four years, then we can get the current value by discounting this price back four years at 20 percent:

$$P_0 = \$5/1.20^4 = \$5/2.0736 = \$2.41$$

The stock is worth $2.41 today.

The problem of nonconstant growth is only slightly more complicated if the dividends are not zero for the first several years. For example, suppose you have come up with the following dividend forecasts for the next three years:

Year	Expected Dividend
1	$1.00
2	$2.00
3	$2.50

After the third year, the dividend will grow at a constant rate of 5 percent per year. The required return is 10 percent. What is the value of the stock today?

In dealing with nonconstant growth, a time line can be helpful. Figure 8.1 illustrates a time line for this problem. The important thing to notice is when constant growth starts. As we've shown, for this problem, constant growth starts at Time 3. This means we can use our constant growth model to determine the stock price at Time 3, P_3. By far the most common mistake in this situation is to incorrectly identify the start of the constant growth phase and, as a result, calculate the future stock price at the wrong time.

As always, the value of the stock is the present value of all the future dividends. To calculate this present value, we first have to compute the present value of the stock price three years down the road, just as we did before. We then have to add in the present

FIGURE 8.1

Nonconstant Growth

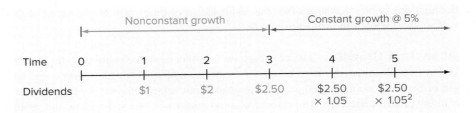

value of the dividends that will be paid between now and then. So, the price in three years is:

$$P_3 = D_3 \times (1 + g)/(R - g)$$
$$= \$2.50 \times 1.05/(.10 - .05)$$
$$= \$52.50$$

We can now calculate the total value of the stock as the present value of the first three dividends plus the present value of the price at Time 3, P_3:

$$P_0 = \frac{D_1}{(1 + R)^1} + \frac{D_2}{(1 + R)^2} + \frac{D_3}{(1 + R)^3} + \frac{P_3}{(1 + R)^3}$$
$$= \frac{\$1}{1.10} + \frac{2}{1.10^2} + \frac{2.50}{1.10^3} + \frac{52.50}{1.10^3}$$
$$= \$.91 + 1.65 + 1.88 + 39.44$$
$$= \$43.88$$

The value of the stock today is thus $43.88.

EXAMPLE 8.4   **Supernormal Growth**

Chain Reaction, Inc., has been growing at a phenomenal rate of 30 percent per year because of its rapid expansion and explosive sales. You believe this growth rate will last for three more years and will then drop to 10 percent per year. If the growth rate then remains at 10 percent indefinitely, what is the total value of the stock? Total dividends just paid were $5 million, and the required return is 20 percent.

Chain Reaction's situation is an example of supernormal growth. It is unlikely that a 30 percent growth rate can be sustained for any extended time. To value the equity in this company, we first need to calculate the total dividends over the supernormal growth period:

Year	Total Dividends (in millions)
1	$5.00 × 1.3 = $ 6.500
2	6.50 × 1.3 = 8.450
3	8.45 × 1.3 = 10.985

The price at Time 3 can be calculated as:

$$P_3 = D_3 \times (1 + g)/(R - g)$$

where g is the long-run growth rate. So, we have:

$$P_3 = \$10.985 \times 1.10/(.20 - .10) = \$120.835$$

To determine the value today, we need the present value of this amount plus the present value of the total dividends:

$$P_0 = \frac{D_1}{(1+R)^1} + \frac{D_2}{(1+R)^2} + \frac{D_3}{(1+R)^3} + \frac{P_3}{(1+R)^3}$$

$$= \frac{\$6.50}{1.20} + \frac{8.45}{1.20^2} + \frac{10.985}{1.20^3} + \frac{120.835}{1.20^3}$$

$$= \$5.42 + 5.87 + 6.36 + 69.93$$

$$= \$87.57$$

The total value of the stock today is thus $87.57 million. If there were, for example, 20 million shares, then the stock would be worth $87.57/20 = $4.38 per share.

Two-Stage Growth   The last case we consider is a special case of nonconstant growth: Two-stage growth. Here, the idea is that the dividend will grow at a rate of g_1 for t years and then grow at a rate of g_2 thereafter, forever. In this case, the value of the stock can be written as:

$$P_0 = \frac{D_1}{R - g_1} \times \left[1 - \left(\frac{1 + g_1}{1 + R} \right)^t \right] + \frac{P_t}{(1 + R)^t}$$ **8.5**

Notice that the first term in our expression is the present value of a growing annuity, which we discussed in Chapter 6. In this first stage, g_1 can be greater than R. The second part is the present value of the stock price once the second stage begins at Time t.
We can calculate P_t as follows:

$$P_t = \frac{D_{t+1}}{R - g_2} = \frac{D_0 \times (1 + g_1)^t \times (1 + g_2)}{R - g_2}$$ **8.6**

In this calculation, we need the dividend at Time $t + 1$, D_{t+1}, to get the stock price at Time t, P_t. Notice that to get the dividend at Time $t + 1$, we grew the current dividend, D_0, at rate g_1 for t periods and then grew it one period at rate g_2. Also, in this second stage, g_2 must be less than R.

Two-Stage Growth

EXAMPLE 8.5

The Highfield Company's dividend is expected to grow at 20 percent for the next five years. After that, the growth is expected to be 4 percent forever. If the required return is 10 percent, what's the value of the stock? The dividend just paid was $2.
There is a fair amount of computation here, but it is mostly just "plug and chug" with a calculator. We can start by calculating the stock price five years from now, P_5:

$$P_5 = \frac{D_6}{R - g_2} = \frac{D_0 \times (1 + g_1)^5 \times (1 + g_2)}{R - g_2}$$

$$= \frac{\$2 \times (1 + .20)^5 \times (1 + .04)}{.10 - .04} = \frac{\$5.18}{.06}$$

$$= \$86.26$$

We then plug this result into our two-stage growth formula to get the price today:

$$P_0 = \frac{D_1}{R - g_1} \times \left[1 - \left(\frac{1 + g_1}{1 + R} \right)^t \right] + \frac{P_t}{(1 + R)^t}$$

$$= \frac{\$2 \times (1 + .20)}{.10 - .20} \times \left[1 - \left(\frac{1 + .20}{1 + .10} \right)^5 \right] + \frac{\$86.26}{(1 + .10)^5}$$

$$= \$66.64$$

> Notice that we were given $D_0 = \$2$ here, so we had to grow it by 20 percent for one period to get D_1. Notice also that g_1 is bigger than R in this problem, but that fact does not cause a problem.

COMPONENTS OF THE REQUIRED RETURN

Thus far, we have taken the required return, or discount rate, R, as given. We will have quite a bit to say about this subject in Chapters 12 and 13. For now, we want to examine the implications of the dividend growth model for this required return. Earlier, we calculated P_0 as:

$$P_0 = D_1/(R - g)$$

If we rearrange this to solve for R, we get:

8.7

$$R - g = D_1/P_0$$
$$R = D_1/P_0 + g$$

dividend yield
A stock's expected cash dividend divided by its current price.

capital gains yield
The dividend growth rate, or the rate at which the value of an investment grows.

This tells us that the total return, R, has two components. The first of these, D_1/P_0, is called the **dividend yield**. Because this is calculated as the expected cash dividend divided by the current price, it is conceptually similar to the current yield on a bond.

The second part of the total return is the growth rate, g. We know that the dividend growth rate is also the rate at which the stock price grows (see Example 8.3). This growth rate can be interpreted as the **capital gains yield**—that is, the rate at which the value of the investment grows.[2]

To illustrate the components of the required return, suppose we observe a stock selling for $20 per share. The next dividend will be $1 per share. You think that the dividend will grow by 10 percent per year more or less indefinitely. What return does this stock offer if this is correct?

The dividend growth model calculates total return as:

$$R = \text{Dividend yield} + \text{Capital gains yield}$$
$$R = \qquad D_1/P_0 \qquad + \qquad \qquad g$$

In this case, total return works out to be:

$$R = \$1/20 + 10\%$$
$$= 5\% + 10\%$$
$$= 15\%$$

This stock has an expected return of 15 percent.

We can verify this answer by calculating the price in one year, P_1, using 15 percent as the required return. Based on the dividend growth model, this price is:

$$P_1 = D_1 \times (1 + g)/(R - g)$$
$$= \$1 \times 1.10/(.15 - .10)$$
$$= \$1.10/.05$$
$$= \$22$$

---

[2]Here and elsewhere, we use the term *capital gains* a little loosely. For the record, a capital gain (or loss) is, strictly speaking, something defined by the IRS. For our purposes, it would be more accurate (but less common) to use the term *price appreciation* instead of *capital gain*.

Notice that this $22 is $20 × 1.1, so the stock price has grown by 10 percent, as it should. If you pay $20 for the stock today, you will get a $1 dividend at the end of the year, and you will have a $22 − 20 = $2 gain. Your dividend yield is thus $1/20 = 5%. Your capital gains yield is $2/20 = 10%, so your total return is 5% + 10% = 15%.

To get a feel for actual numbers in this context, consider that, according to the December 2016 Value Line *Investment Survey,* Procter & Gamble's dividends were expected to grow by 5 percent over the next 5 or so years, compared to a historical growth rate of 7.5 percent over the preceding 5 years and 9.5 percent over the preceding 10 years. In 2017, the projected dividend for the coming year was given as $2.85. The stock price at that time was about $85 per share. What is the return investors require on P&G? Here, the dividend yield is 3.35 percent and the capital gains yield is 5 percent, giving a total required return of 8.35 percent on P&G stock.

STOCK VALUATION USING MULTIPLES

An obvious problem with our dividend-based approach to stock valuation is that many companies don't pay dividends. What do we do in such cases? A common approach is to make use of the PE ratio, which we defined in Chapter 3 as the ratio of a stock's price per share to its earnings per share (EPS) over the previous year. The idea here is to have some sort of benchmark or reference PE ratio, which we then multiply by earnings to come up with a price:

Price at Time $t = P_t$ = Benchmark PE ratio × EPS$_t$ 8.8

The benchmark PE ratio could come from one of several possible sources. It could be based on similar companies (perhaps an industry average or median), or it could be based on a company's own historical values. For example, suppose we are trying to value Inactivision, Inc., a video game developer known for its hit *Slack Ops* series. Inactivision does not pay dividends, but after studying the industry, you feel that a PE ratio of 20 is appropriate for a company like this one. Total earnings over the four most recent quarters combined are $2 per share, so you think the stock should sell for 20 × $2 = $40. You might view this stock as an attractive purchase if it is going for less than $40, but not attractive if it sells for more than $40.

Security analysts spend a lot of time forecasting future earnings, particularly for the coming year. A PE ratio that is based on estimated future earnings is called a *forward* PE ratio. For example, suppose you felt that Inactivision's earnings for the coming year were going to be $2.50, reflecting the growing popularity of the company's *World of Slackcraft* massively multiplayer online role-playing game (MMORPG). In this case, if the current stock price is $40, the forward PE ratio is $40/$2.50 = 16.

Finally, notice that your benchmark PE of 20 applies to earnings over the previous year. If earnings over the coming year turn out to be $2.50, then the stock price one year from today should be 20 × $2.50 = $50. Forecast prices such as this one are often called *target* prices.

Often we will be interested in valuing newer companies that both don't pay dividends and are not yet profitable, meaning that earnings are negative. What do we do then? One answer is to use the price-sales ratio, which we also introduced in Chapter 3. As the name suggests, this ratio is the price per share on the stock divided by sales per share. You use this ratio just like you use the PE ratio, except you use sales per share instead of earnings per share. As with PE ratios, price-sales ratios vary depending on company age and industry. Typical values are in the .8–2.0 range, but they can be much higher for younger, faster-growing companies.

For future reference, our discussion of stock valuation techniques is summarized in Table 8.1.

TABLE 8.1

Summary of Stock Valuation

I. The General Case

In general, the price today of a share of stock, P_0, is the present value of all of its future dividends, $D_1, D_2, D_3, \ldots$:

$$P_0 = \frac{D_1}{(1+R)^1} + \frac{D_2}{(1+R)^2} + \frac{D_3}{(1+R)^3} + \cdots$$

where R is the required return.

II. Constant Growth Case

If the dividend grows at a steady rate, g, then the price can be written as:

$$P_0 = \frac{D_1}{R-g}$$

This result is called the *dividend growth model*.

III. Nonconstant Growth

If the dividend grows steadily after t periods, then the price can be written as:

$$P_0 = \frac{D_1}{(1+R)^1} + \frac{D_2}{(1+R)^2} + \cdots + \frac{D_t}{(1+R)^t} + \frac{P_t}{(1+R)^t}$$

where

$$P_t = \frac{D_t \times (1+g)}{(R-g)}$$

IV. Two-Stage Growth

If the dividend grows at rate g_1 for t periods and then grows at rate g_2 thereafter, then the price can be written as:

$$P_0 = \frac{D_1}{R-g_1} \times \left[1 - \left(\frac{1+g_1}{1+R} \right)^t \right] + \frac{P_t}{(1+R)^t}$$

where

$$P_t = \frac{D_{t+1}}{R-g_2} = \frac{D_0 \times (1+g_1)^t \times (1+g_2)}{R-g_2}$$

V. Valuation Using Multiples

For stocks that don't pay dividends (or have erratic dividend growth rates), we can value them using the PE ratio and/or the price-sales ratio:

P_t = Benchmark PE ratio × EPS_t

P_t = Benchmark price-sales ratio × Sales per share$_t$

VI. The Required Return

The required return, R, can be written as the sum of two things:

$R = D_1/P_0 + g$

where D_1/P_0 is the *dividend yield* and g is the *capital gains yield* (which is the same thing as the growth rate in dividends for the steady growth case).

Concept Questions

8.1a   What are the relevant cash flows for valuing a share of common stock?

8.1b   Does the value of a share of stock depend on how long you expect to keep it?

8.1c   What is the value of a share of stock when the dividend grows at a constant rate?

Some Features of Common and Preferred Stocks

8.2

In discussing common stock features, we focus on shareholder rights and dividend payments. For preferred stock, we explain what *preferred* means, and we also debate whether preferred stock is really debt or equity.

COMMON STOCK FEATURES

The term **common stock** means different things to different people, but it is usually applied to stock that has no special preference either in receiving dividends or in bankruptcy.

common stock
Equity without priority for dividends or in bankruptcy.

Shareholder Rights   The conceptual structure of the corporation assumes that shareholders elect directors who, in turn, hire managers to carry out their directives. Shareholders, therefore, control the corporation through the right to elect the directors. Generally, only shareholders have this right.

Directors are elected each year at an annual meeting. Although there are exceptions (discussed next), the general idea is "one share, one vote" (*not* one share*holder*, one vote). Corporate democracy is thus very different from our political democracy. With corporate democracy, the "golden rule" prevails absolutely.[3]

Directors are elected at an annual shareholders' meeting by a vote of the holders of a majority of shares who are present and entitled to vote. However, the exact mechanism for electing directors differs across companies. The most important difference is whether shares must be voted cumulatively or voted straight.

To illustrate the two different voting procedures, imagine that a corporation has two shareholders: Smith with 20 shares and Jones with 80 shares. Both want to be a director. Jones does not want Smith to be a director, however. We assume there are a total of four directors to be elected.

The effect of **cumulative voting** is to permit minority participation.[4] If cumulative voting is permitted, the total number of votes that each shareholder may cast is determined first. This is usually calculated as the number of shares (owned or controlled) multiplied by the number of directors to be elected.

cumulative voting
A procedure in which a shareholder may cast all votes for one member of the board of directors.

With cumulative voting, the directors are elected all at once. In our example, this means that the top four vote getters will be the new directors. A shareholder can distribute votes however he or she wishes.

Will Smith get a seat on the board? If we ignore the possibility of a five-way tie, then the answer is yes. Smith will cast $20 \times 4 = 80$ votes, and Jones will cast $80 \times 4 = 320$ votes. If Smith gives all his votes to himself, he is assured of a directorship. The reason is that Jones can't divide 320 votes among four candidates in such a way as to give all of them more than 80 votes, so Smith will finish fourth at worst.

In general, if there are N directors up for election, then $1/(N + 1)$ percent of the stock plus one share will guarantee you a seat. In our current example, this is $1/(4 + 1) = .20$, or 20%. So the more seats that are up for election at one time, the easier (and cheaper) it is to win one.

With **straight voting**, the directors are elected one at a time. Each time, Smith can cast 20 votes and Jones can cast 80. As a consequence, Jones will elect all of the candidates. The

straight voting
A procedure in which a shareholder may cast all votes for each member of the board of directors.

---

[3]The golden rule: Whosoever has the gold makes the rules.

[4]By *minority participation*, we mean participation by shareholders with relatively small amounts of stock.

only way to guarantee a seat is to own 50 percent plus one share. This also guarantees that you will win every seat, so it's really all or nothing.

EXAMPLE 8.6   **Buying the Election**

Stock in JRJ Corporation sells for $20 per share and features cumulative voting. There are 10,000 shares outstanding. If three directors are up for election, how much does it cost to ensure yourself a seat on the board?

The question here is how many shares of stock it will take to get a seat. The answer is 2,501, so the cost is 2,501 × $20 = $50,020. Why 2,501? Because there is no way the remaining 7,499 votes can be divided among three people to give all of them more than 2,501 votes. For example, suppose two people receive 2,502 votes and the first two seats. A third person can receive at most 10,000 − 2,502 − 2,502 − 2,501 = 2,495, so the third seat is yours.

Many companies have staggered elections for directors. With staggered elections, only a fraction of the directorships (often one-third) are up for election at a particular time. If only two directors are up for election at any one time, it will take $1/(2 + 1) = .3333$, or 33.33% of the stock plus one share to guarantee a seat. Staggered boards are often called *classified* boards because directors are placed into different classes with terms that expire at different times. In recent years, corporations have come under pressure to declassify their boards, meaning that all directors would stand for election every year, and many have done so.

Overall, staggering has two basic effects:

1. Staggering makes it more difficult for a minority to elect a director because there are fewer directors to be elected at one time.

2. Staggering makes takeover attempts less likely to be successful because it makes it more difficult to vote in a majority of new directors.

We should note that staggering may serve a beneficial purpose. It provides "institutional memory"—that is, continuity on the board of directors. This may be important for corporations with significant long-range plans and projects.

proxy
A grant of authority by a shareholder allowing another individual to vote his or her shares.

Proxy Voting   A **proxy** is the grant of authority by a shareholder to someone else to vote his or her shares. For convenience, much of the voting in large public corporations is actually done by proxy.

As we have seen, with straight voting, each share of stock has one vote. The owner of 10,000 shares has 10,000 votes. Large companies have hundreds of thousands or even millions of shareholders. Shareholders can come to the annual meeting and vote in person, or they can transfer their right to vote to another party.

Obviously, management always tries to get as many proxies as possible transferred to it. If shareholders are not satisfied with management, an "outside" group of shareholders can try to obtain votes via proxy. They can vote by proxy in an attempt to replace management by electing enough directors. The resulting battle is called a *proxy fight*.

Classes of Stock   Some firms have more than one class of common stock. Often the classes are created with unequal voting rights. The Ford Motor Company, for example, has Class B common stock, which is not publicly traded (it is held by Ford family interests and trusts). This class has 40 percent of the voting power, even though it represents less than 10 percent of the total number of shares outstanding.

There are many other cases of corporations with different classes of stock. For example, at one time, General Motors had its "GM Classic" shares (the original) and two additional classes, Class E ("GME") and Class H ("GMH"). These classes were created to help pay for two large acquisitions, Electronic Data Systems and Hughes Aircraft. Another good example is Alphabet, the web search company, which became publicly owned in 2004. Alphabet originally had two classes of common stock, A and B. The Class A shares are held by the public, and each share has one vote. The Class B shares are held by company insiders, and each Class B share has 10 votes. Then, in 2014, the company had a stock split of its Class B shares, creating Class C shares, which have no vote at all. As a result, Alphabet's founders and managers control the company. Facebook joined Alphabet when it created its own nonvoting Class C shares in 2016.

Historically, the New York Stock Exchange did not allow companies to create classes of publicly traded common stock with unequal voting rights. Exceptions (like Ford) appear to have been made. In addition, many non-NYSE companies have dual classes of common stock.

A primary reason for creating dual or multiple classes of stock has to do with control of the firm. If such stock exists, management of a firm can raise equity capital by issuing nonvoting or limited-voting stock while maintaining control.

The subject of unequal voting rights is controversial in the United States, and the idea of one share, one vote has a strong following and a long history. Interestingly, shares with unequal voting rights are quite common in the United Kingdom and elsewhere around the world.

Other Rights   The value of a share of common stock in a corporation is directly related to the general rights of shareholders. In addition to the right to vote for directors, shareholders usually have the following rights:

1. The right to share proportionally in dividends paid.
2. The right to share proportionally in assets remaining after liabilities have been paid in a liquidation.
3. The right to vote on stockholder matters of great importance, such as a merger. Voting is usually done at the annual meeting or a special meeting.

In addition, stockholders sometimes have the right to share proportionally in any new stock sold. This is called the *preemptive right*.

Essentially, a preemptive right means that a company that wishes to sell stock must first offer it to the existing stockholders before offering it to the general public. The purpose is to give stockholders the opportunity to protect their proportionate ownership in the corporation.

Dividends   A distinctive feature of corporations is that they have shares of stock on which they are authorized by law to pay dividends to their shareholders. **Dividends** paid to shareholders represent a return on the capital directly or indirectly contributed to the corporation by the shareholders. The payment of dividends is at the discretion of the board of directors.

dividends
Payments by a corporation to shareholders, made in either cash or stock.

Some important characteristics of dividends include the following:

1. Unless a dividend is declared by the board of directors of a corporation, it is not a liability of the corporation. A corporation cannot default on an undeclared dividend. As a consequence, corporations cannot become bankrupt because of nonpayment of dividends. The amount of the dividend and even whether it is paid are decisions based on the business judgment of the board of directors.

2. The payment of dividends by the corporation is not a business expense. Dividends are not deductible for corporate tax purposes. In short, dividends are paid out of the corporation's aftertax profits.

3. Dividends received by individual shareholders are taxable. In 2018, the tax rate was 15 to 20 percent. However, corporations that own stock in other corporations are permitted to exclude 50 percent of the dividend amounts they receive and are taxed on only the remaining 50 percent (the 50 percent exclusion was reduced from 70 percent by the Tax Cuts and Jobs Act of 2017).[5]

PREFERRED STOCK FEATURES

preferred stock
Stock with dividend priority over common stock, normally with a fixed dividend rate, sometimes without voting rights.

Preferred stock differs from common stock because it has preference over common stock in the payment of dividends and in the distribution of corporation assets in the event of liquidation. *Preference* means only that the holders of the preferred shares must receive a dividend (in the case of an ongoing firm) before holders of common shares are entitled to anything.

Preferred stock is a form of equity from a legal and tax standpoint. It is important to note that holders of preferred stock sometimes have no voting privileges.

Stated Value   Preferred shares have a stated liquidating value, usually $100 per share. The cash dividend is described in terms of dollars per share. For example, General Motors "$5 preferred" easily translates into a dividend yield of 5 percent of stated value.

Cumulative and Noncumulative Dividends   A preferred dividend is *not* like interest on a bond. The board of directors may decide not to pay the dividends on preferred shares, and their decision may have nothing to do with the current net income of the corporation.

Dividends payable on preferred stock are either *cumulative* or *noncumulative*; most are cumulative. If preferred dividends are cumulative and are not paid in a particular year, they will be carried forward as an *arrearage*. Usually, both the accumulated (past) preferred dividends and the current preferred dividends must be paid before the common shareholders can receive anything.

Unpaid preferred dividends are *not* debts of the firm. Directors elected by the common shareholders can defer preferred dividends indefinitely. In such cases, common shareholders must also forgo dividends. In addition, holders of preferred shares are often granted voting and other rights if preferred dividends have not been paid for some time. For example, at one point, USAir (now part of American Airlines) had failed to pay dividends on one of its preferred stock issues for six quarters. As a consequence, the holders of the shares were allowed to nominate two people to represent their interests on the airline's board. Because preferred stockholders receive no interest on the accumulated dividends, some have argued that firms have an incentive to delay paying preferred dividends; but, as we have seen, this may mean sharing control with preferred stockholders.

Is Preferred Stock Really Debt?   A good case can be made that preferred stock is really debt in disguise, a kind of equity bond. Preferred shareholders receive a stated dividend only; and if the corporation is liquidated, preferred shareholders get a stated value. Often, preferred stocks carry credit ratings much like those of bonds. Furthermore,

---

[5]For the record, the 70 percent exclusion applies when the recipient owns less than 20 percent of the outstanding stock in a corporation. If a corporation owns more than 20 percent but less than 80 percent, the exclusion is 80 percent. If more than 80 percent is owned, the corporation can file a single "consolidated" return and the exclusion is effectively 100 percent.

preferred stock is sometimes convertible into common stock, and preferred stocks are often callable.

In addition, many issues of preferred stock have obligatory sinking funds. The existence of such a sinking fund effectively creates a final maturity because it means that the entire issue will ultimately be retired. For these reasons, preferred stock seems to be a lot like debt. For tax purposes, preferred dividends are treated like common stock dividends.

In the 1990s, firms began to sell securities that looked a lot like preferred stocks but were treated as debt for tax purposes. The new securities were given interesting acronyms like TOPrS (trust-originated preferred securities, or toppers), MIPS (monthly income preferred securities), and QUIPS (quarterly income preferred securities), among others. Because of various specific features, these instruments can be counted as debt for tax purposes, making the interest payments tax deductible (up to certain limits). Payments made to investors in these instruments are treated as interest for personal income taxes. Until 2003, interest payments and dividends were taxed at the same marginal tax rate. When the tax rate on dividend payments was reduced, these instruments were not included, so individuals must still pay their higher income tax rate on dividend payments received from these instruments.

Concept Questions

8.2a   What is a proxy?

8.2b   What rights do stockholders have?

8.2c   Why is preferred stock called *preferred*?

The Stock Markets

8.3

Back in Chapter 1, we briefly mentioned that shares of stock are bought and sold on various stock exchanges, the two most important of which are the New York Stock Exchange and NASDAQ. From our earlier discussion, recall that the stock market consists of a **primary market** and a **secondary market**. In the primary, or new issue, market, shares of stock are first brought to the market and sold to investors. In the secondary market, existing shares are traded among investors.

In the primary market, companies sell securities to raise money. We will discuss this process in detail in a later chapter. We focus mainly on secondary market activity in this section. We conclude with a discussion of how stock prices are quoted in the financial press.

DEALERS AND BROKERS

Because most securities transactions involve dealers and brokers, it is important to understand exactly what is meant by the terms *dealer* and *broker*. A **dealer** maintains an inventory and stands ready to buy and sell at any time. In contrast, a **broker** brings buyers and sellers together but does not maintain an inventory. When we speak of used car dealers and real estate brokers, we recognize that the used car dealer maintains an inventory, whereas the real estate broker does not.

In the securities markets, a dealer stands ready to buy securities from investors wishing to sell them and sell securities to investors wishing to buy them. Recall from our previous chapter that the price the dealer is willing to pay is called the *bid price*. The price at which the dealer will sell is called the *ask price* (sometimes called the asked, offered, or offering price). The difference between the bid and ask prices is called the *spread,* and it is the basic source of dealer profits.

primary market
The market in which new securities are originally sold to investors.

secondary market
The market in which previously issued securities are traded among investors.

dealer
An agent who buys and sells securities from inventory.

broker
An agent who arranges security transactions among investors.

How big is the bid-ask spread on your favorite stock? Check out the latest quotes at **www.bloomberg.com**.

Dealers exist in all areas of the economy, not just the stock markets. For example, your local college bookstore is probably both a primary and a secondary market textbook dealer. If you buy a new book, this is a primary market transaction. If you buy a used book, this is a secondary market transaction, and you pay the store's ask price. If you sell the book back, you receive the store's bid price (often half of the ask price). The bookstore's spread is the difference between the two prices.

In contrast, a securities broker arranges transactions between investors, matching investors wishing to buy securities with investors wishing to sell securities. The distinctive characteristic of security brokers is that they do not buy or sell securities for their own accounts. Facilitating trades by others is their business.

ORGANIZATION OF THE NYSE

The New York Stock Exchange, or NYSE, popularly known as the Big Board, celebrated its bicentennial a few years ago. It has occupied its current location on Wall Street since the turn of the twentieth century. Measured in terms of the total value of shares listed, it is the largest stock market in the world.

members

As of 2006, a member is the owner of a trading license on the NYSE.

Members   The NYSE has 1,366 exchange **members**. Prior to 2006, the exchange members were said to own "seats" on the exchange, and collectively the members of the exchange were also the owners. For this and other reasons, seats were valuable and were bought and sold fairly regularly. Seat prices reached a record $4 million in 2005.

In 2006, all of this changed when the NYSE became a publicly owned corporation. Naturally, its stock was listed on the NYSE. Now, instead of purchasing seats, exchange members must purchase trading licenses, the number of which is still limited to 1,366. In 2017, a license would set you back a cool $40,000—per year. Having a license entitles you to buy and sell securities on the floor of the exchange. Different members play different roles in this regard.

On April 4, 2007, the NYSE grew even larger when it merged with Euronext to form NYSE Euronext. Euronext was a stock exchange in Amsterdam, with subsidiaries in Belgium, France, Portugal, and the United Kingdom. With the merger, NYSE Euronext became the world's "first global exchange." Further expansion occurred in 2008 when NYSE Euronext merged with the American Stock Exchange. Then, in November 2013, the acquisition of the NYSE by the Intercontinental Exchange (ICE) was completed. ICE, which was founded in May 2000, was originally a commodities exchange, but its rapid growth gave it the necessary $8.2 billion for the acquisition of the NYSE.

designated market makers (DMMs)

NYSE members who act as dealers in particular stocks. Formerly known as "specialists."

floor brokers

NYSE members who execute customer buy and sell orders.

supplemental liquidity providers (SLPs)

Investment firms that are active participants in stocks assigned to them. Their job is to make a one-sided market (i.e., offering to either buy or sell). They trade purely for their own accounts.

As we briefly describe how the NYSE operates, keep in mind that other markets owned by NYSE Euronext and ICE may function differently. What makes the NYSE somewhat unique is that it is a *hybrid market*. In a hybrid market, trading takes place both electronically and face-to-face.

With electronic trading, orders to buy and orders to sell are submitted to the exchange. Orders are compared by a computer and whenever there is a match, the orders are executed with no human intervention. Most trades on the NYSE occur this way. For orders that are not handled electronically, the NYSE relies on its license holders. There are three different types of license holders, **designated market makers (DMMs)**, **floor brokers**, and **supplemental liquidity providers (SLPs)**, and we now discuss the role played by each.

The DMMs, formerly known as "specialists," act as dealers in particular stocks. Typically, each stock on the NYSE is assigned to a single DMM. As a dealer, a DMM maintains a two-sided market, meaning that the DMM continually posts and updates bid and ask prices. By doing so, the DMM ensures that there is always a buyer or seller available, thereby promoting market liquidity.

The job of a floor broker is to execute trades for customers, with an emphasis on getting the best price possible. Floor brokers are generally employees of large brokerage firms such as Merrill Lynch, the wealth management division of Bank of America. The interaction between floor brokers and DMMs is the key to nonelectronic trading on the NYSE. We discuss this interaction in detail in just a moment.

The SLPs are essentially investment firms that agree to be active participants in stocks assigned to them. Their job is to regularly make a one-sided market (i.e., offering to either buy or sell). They trade purely for their own accounts (using their own money), so they do not represent customers. They are given a small rebate on their buys and sells, thereby encouraging them to be more aggressive. The NYSE's goal is to generate as much liquidity as possible, which makes it easier for ordinary investors to quickly buy and sell at prevailing prices. Unlike DMMs and floor brokers, SLPs do not operate on the floor of the stock exchange.

In recent years, floor brokers have become less important on the exchange floor because of the efficient Pillar system, which allows orders to be transmitted electronically directly to the DMM. Additionally, the NYSE has an electronic platform called Arca, which accounts for a substantial percentage of all trading on the NYSE, particularly for smaller orders. The average time for a trade on the NYSE Arca is less than 1 second.

Finally, a small number of NYSE members are floor traders who independently trade for their own accounts. Floor traders try to anticipate temporary price fluctuations and profit from them by buying low and selling high. In recent decades, the number of floor traders has declined substantially, suggesting that it has become increasingly difficult to profit from short-term trading on the exchange floor.

Operations   Now that we have a basic idea of how the NYSE is organized and who the major players are, we turn to the question of how trading actually takes place. Fundamentally, the business of the NYSE is to attract and process **order flow**. The term *order flow* refers to the flow of customer orders to buy and sell stocks. The customers of the NYSE are the millions of individual investors and tens of thousands of institutional investors who place their orders to buy and sell shares in NYSE-listed companies. The NYSE has been quite successful in attracting order flow. Currently, it is not unusual for well over a billion shares to change hands in a single day.

> **order flow**
> The flow of customer orders to buy and sell securities.

Floor Activity   It is quite likely that you have seen footage of the NYSE trading floor on television. If so, you would have seen a big room, about the size of a basketball gym. This big room is called, technically, "the Big Room." There are a few other, smaller rooms that you normally don't see, one of which is called "the Garage," because that is what it was before it was taken over for trading.

On the floor of the exchange are a number of stations, each with a roughly figure-eight shape. These stations have multiple counters with numerous terminal screens above and on the sides. People operate behind and in front of the counters in relatively stationary positions.

Other people move around on the exchange floor, frequently returning to the many telephones positioned along the exchange walls. In all, you may be reminded of worker ants moving around an ant colony. It is natural to wonder, "What are all those people doing down there (and why are so many wearing funny-looking coats)?"

Take a virtual field trip to the New York Stock Exchange at **www.nyse.com**.

As an overview of exchange floor activity, here is a quick look at what goes on. Each of the counters is a **DMM's post**. DMMs normally operate in front of their posts to monitor and manage trading in the stocks assigned to them. Clerical employees working for the DMMs operate behind the counter. Moving from the many workstations lining the walls of the exchange out to the exchange floor and back again are swarms of floor brokers, receiving customer orders, walking out to DMMs' posts where the orders can be executed, and returning to confirm order executions and receive new customer orders.

> **DMM's post**
> A fixed place on the exchange floor where the DMM operates.

To better understand activity on the NYSE trading floor, imagine yourself as a floor broker. Your phone clerk has just handed you an order to sell 20,000 shares of Walmart for a customer of the brokerage company that employs you. The customer wants to sell the stock at the best possible price as soon as possible. You immediately walk (running violates exchange rules) to the DMM's post where Walmart stock is traded.

As you approach the DMM's post where Walmart is traded, you check the terminal screen for information on the current market price. The screen reveals that the last executed trade was at $60.10 and that the DMM is bidding $60 per share. You could immediately sell to the DMM at $60, but that would be too easy.

Instead, as the customer's representative, you are obligated to get the best possible price. It is your job to "work" the order, and your job depends on providing satisfactory order execution service. So, you look around for another broker who represents a customer who wants to buy Walmart stock. Luckily, you quickly find another broker at the DMM's post with an order to buy 20,000 shares. Noticing that the DMM is asking $60.10 per share, you both agree to execute your orders with each other at a price of $60.05. This price is exactly halfway between the DMM's bid and ask prices, and it saves each of your customers $.05 × 20,000 = $1,000 as compared to dealing at the posted prices.

For a very actively traded stock, there may be many buyers and sellers around the DMM's post, and most of the trading will be done directly between brokers. This is called trading in the "crowd." In such cases, the DMM's responsibility is to maintain order and to make sure that all buyers and sellers receive a fair price. In other words, the DMM essentially functions as a referee.

More often, there will be no crowd at the DMM's post. Going back to our Walmart example, suppose you are unable to quickly find another broker with an order to buy 20,000 shares. Because you have an order to sell immediately, you may have no choice but to sell to the DMM at the bid price of $60. In this case, the need to execute an order quickly takes priority, and the DMM provides the liquidity necessary to allow immediate order execution.

Finally, note that colored coats are worn by many of the people on the floor of the exchange. The color of the coat indicates the person's job or position. Clerks, runners, visitors, exchange officials, and so on wear particular colors to identify themselves. Also, things can get a little hectic on a busy day, with the result that good clothing doesn't last long; the cheap coats offer some protection.

NASDAQ OPERATIONS

In terms of total dollar volume of trading, the second largest stock market in the United States is NASDAQ (say "Naz-dak"). The somewhat odd name originally was an acronym for the National Association of Securities Dealers Automated Quotations system, but NASDAQ is now a name in its own right.

Introduced in 1971, the NASDAQ market is a computer network of securities dealers and others that disseminates timely security price quotes to computer screens worldwide. NASDAQ dealers act as market makers for securities listed on the NASDAQ. As market makers, NASDAQ dealers post bid and ask prices at which they accept sell and buy orders, respectively. With each price quote, they also post the number of shares that they obligate themselves to trade at their quoted prices.

Like NYSE DMMs, NASDAQ market makers trade on an inventory basis—that is, using their inventory as a buffer to absorb buy and sell order imbalances. Unlike the NYSE specialist system, NASDAQ features multiple market makers for actively traded stocks. There are two key differences between the NYSE and NASDAQ:

1. NASDAQ is a computer network and has no physical location where trading takes place.
2. NASDAQ has a multiple market maker system rather than a DMM system.

over-the-counter (OTC) market
Securities market in which trading is almost exclusively done through dealers who buy and sell for their own inventories.

Traditionally, a securities market largely characterized by dealers who buy and sell securities for their own inventories is called an **over-the-counter (OTC) market**. Consequently, NASDAQ is often referred to as an OTC market. In their efforts to promote a distinct image, NASDAQ officials prefer that the term OTC not be used when referring to the NASDAQ market. Nevertheless, old habits die hard, and many people still refer to NASDAQ as an OTC market.

The NASDAQ network operates with three levels of information access. Level 1 is designed to provide a timely, accurate source of price quotations. These prices are freely available over the Internet.

Level 2 allows users to view price quotes from all NASDAQ market makers. In particular, this level allows access to **inside quotes**. Inside quotes are the highest bid quotes and the lowest asked quotes for a NASDAQ-listed security. Level 2 is now available on the web, sometimes for a small fee. Level 3 is for the use of market makers only. This access level allows NASDAQ dealers to enter or change their price quote information. See our nearby *Work the Web* box for an example of inside quotes.

inside quotes
The highest bid quotes and the lowest ask quotes for a security.

NASDAQ is actually made up of three separate markets: The NASDAQ Global Select Market, the NASDAQ Global Market, and the NASDAQ Capital Market. As the market for NASDAQ's larger and more actively traded securities, the Global Select Market lists about 1,600 companies (as of early 2017), including some of the best-known companies in the world, such as Microsoft and Intel. Global Market companies are somewhat smaller in size, and NASDAQ lists about 810 of these. Finally, the smallest companies listed on NASDAQ are in the NASDAQ Capital Market; about 820 are currently listed. Of course, as Capital Market companies become more established, they may move up to the Global Market or Global Select Market.

NASDAQ (**www.nasdaq.com**) has a great website; check it out!

WORK THE WEB

You can actually watch trading taking place on the web by visiting www.batstrading.com. The BATS Exchange is somewhat unique in that the "order book," meaning the list of all buy and sell orders, is public in real time. As shown below, we have captured a sample of the order book for Intel (INTC). On the top in blue are sell orders (asks); buy orders (bids) are in green on the bottom. All orders are "limit" orders, which means the customer has specified the most he or she will pay (for buy orders) or the least he or she will accept (for sell orders). The inside quotes (the highest bid, or buy, and the lowest ask, or sell) in the market are in the middle of the quotes.

INTC		Orders Accepted		Total Volume
INTEL CORP COM		238,440		905,015
TOP OF BOOK			LAST 10 TRADES	
Shares	Price	Time	Price	Shares
1,900	36.8000	13:51:33	36.7500	100
2,302	36.7900	13:51:33	36.7500	200
2,201	36.7800	13:51:33	36.7500	100
2,723	36.7700	13:50:56	36.7500	100
982	36.7600	13:50:56	36.7500	100
801	36.7500	13:50:56	36.7500	100
2,274	36.7400	13:50:56	36.7500	100
2,262	36.7300	13:50:56	36.7500	100
2,561	36.7200	13:50:56	36.7500	100
2,602	36.7100	13:50:47	36.7550	66

(ASKS for the top rows; BIDS for the lower rows)

If you visit the site, you can see trading take place as orders are entered and executed. Notice that on this particular day, about 905,000 shares of Intel had traded on BATS. At that time, the inside quotes for Intel were 801 shares bid at $36.75 and 982 shares offered at $36.76. This is not the entire order book for Intel, as there are more buy orders below $36.75 and more sell orders above $36.76.

electronic communications networks (ECNs)
A website that allows investors to trade directly with each other.

ECNs In a very important development in the late 1990s, the NASDAQ system was opened to so-called **electronic communications networks (ECNs)**. ECNs are basically websites that allow investors to trade directly with one another. Investor buy and sell orders placed on ECNs are transmitted to the NASDAQ and displayed along with market maker bid and ask prices. As a result, the ECNs open up the NASDAQ by essentially allowing individual investors, not just market makers, to enter orders. As a result, the ECNs act to increase liquidity and competition.

Of course, the NYSE and the NASDAQ are not the only places stocks are traded. See our nearby *Work the Web* box for a discussion of somewhat wilder markets.

You can get real-time stock quotes on the web. See **finance.yahoo.com** for details.

STOCK MARKET REPORTING

In recent years, the reporting of stock prices and related information has increasingly moved from traditional print media, such as *The Wall Street Journal*, to various websites. Yahoo! Finance (finance.yahoo.com) is a good example. We went there and requested a stock quote on wholesale club Costco, which is listed on the NASDAQ. Here is a portion of what we found:

Costco Wholesale Corporation (COST)
NasdaqGS - NasdaqGS Real Time Price. Currency in USD

☆ Add to watchlist

160.63 -1.03 (-0.64%)
As of 1:49PM EST. Market open.

Summary Conversations Statistics Profile Financials Options Holders Historical Data Analysts

Previous Close	161.66	Market Cap	70.56B	
Open	161.47	Beta	0.90	
Bid	160.33 x 100	PE Ratio (TTM)	29.31	
Ask	160.41 x 200	EPS (TTM)	5.48	
Day's Range	160.35 - 162.35	Earnings Date	Mar 2, 2017	
52 Week Range	138.57 - 169.59	Dividend & Yield	1.80 (1.12%)	
Volume	686,350	Ex-Dividend Date	N/A	
Avg. Volume	2,289,400	1y Target Est	173.12	

1D 5D 1M 6M 1Y 2Y 5Y 10Y MAX   ↗ Interactive chart

WORK THE WEB

Where do companies trade when they can't (or don't want to) meet the listing requirements of the larger stock markets? Mostly, they trade on the OTCQX®, OTCQB®, and OTC Pink® marketplaces operated by OTC Markets Group. The OTCQX® marketplace includes qualitative and quantitative standards and the OTCQB® marketplace imposes some requirements as well, though these requirements are less restrictive than those enforced by the larger stock markets. OTC Pink® is called the "Open Marketplace" because there are no filing or financial requirements.

A small portion of companies also continue to trade on the Over-the-Counter Bulletin Board, or OTCBB, operated by the Financial Industry Regulatory Authority, known as FINRA. The OTCBB began as an electronic bulletin board that was created to facilitate OTC trading in non-listed stocks. It has effectively been replaced by OTC Markets Group's OTCQB® marketplace as the primary marketplace for these types of companies. Like the OTCQX® and OTCQB®, the OTCBB imposes some requirements, though they are not as restrictive as the larger markets. For example, OTCBB only requires that listed firms file financial statements with the SEC (or other relevant agency).

Trading at any of the OTC Markets Group marketplaces, as well as the OTCBB, is conducted under a dealer-driven framework. So, aside from the minimal requirements for inclusion on these marketplaces, all that is necessary for a particular security to begin trading is a registered broker-dealer willing (and approved) to quote and make a market in the security. Investors can trade OTCQX®, OTCQB®, and OTC Pink® securities in a manner similar to the trading in an exchange-listed stock. Given the ease of trading, these marketplaces (OTCQX®, in particular) are attractive to foreign firms that file with regulators in their home countries, but do not have interest in filing with U.S. regulators. These markets are also an option for companies that have been delisted from the larger markets either by choice or for failure to maintain their listing requirements.

Stocks traded on these markets often have very low prices and are frequently referred to as *penny stocks*, *microcaps*, or even *nanocaps*. Relatively few brokers do any research on these companies, so information is often spread through word of mouth or the Internet (not the most reliable of sources). To get a feel for what trading looks like, we captured a typical screen from the OTCBB website (http://finra-markets.morningstar.com/MarketData/EquityOptions/default.jsp):

OOTC Equity

| Most Actives | % Gainers | % Losers | Exchange by | OOTC ▼ |

Symbol		Last	Chg	Chg %	Vol (mil) ▼
MLCG	▲	0.0003	0.0000	0.0000	307.3956
TPAC	▲	0.0006	0.0001	20.0000	220.4887
GAWK	▲	0.0002	0.0000	0.0000	157.7228
ICNM	▲	0.0002	0.0001	100.0000	136.8407
GDGI	▲	0.0002	0.0001	100.0000	128.5851
SNMN	▲	0.0017	0.0010	142.8571	121.8124
SDVI	▼	0.0012	-0.0003	-20.0000	105.6642
KGET	▼	0.0001	-0.0001	-25.0000	103.3502
FWDG	▲	0.0001	0.0000	0.0000	99.8849
ASTI	▲	0.0019	0.0002	11.7647	94.4509

First, take a look at the returns. SNM Global Holdings (SNMN) had an intraday return on this day of 142.86 percent. That's not something you see very often. Of course, the big return was generated by a whopping price increase of $.0010 per share. A stock listed on the OTCBB is often the most actively traded stock on any particular day. For example, by the end of this particular day, Bank of America was the most active stock on the NYSE, trading about 81.3 million shares. In contrast, Alumifuel Power Corp. traded about 480 million shares. But, at an average price of, say, $.0001 per share, the total dollar volume in Alumifuel was all of $48,000. In contrast, trades in Bank of America amounted to about $1.88 billion.

All in all, the OTC markets can be pretty wild places to trade. Low stock prices allow for huge percentage returns on small stock price movements. Be advised that attempts at manipulation and fraud are possible. Also, stocks on these markets are often thinly traded, meaning there is little volume. It is not unusual for a stock listed on any of these markets to have no trades on a given day. Even two or three days in a row without a trade in a particular stock is not uncommon.

You can get real-time stock quotes on the web. See **finance.yahoo.com** for details.

Most of this information is self-explanatory. The price $160.63 is the real-time price of the last trade. Availability of real-time prices for free is a relatively new development. The reported change is from the previous day's closing price. The opening price is the first trade of the day. We see the bid and ask prices of $160.33 and $160.41, respectively, along with the market "depth," which is the number of shares sought at the bid price and offered at the ask price. The "1y Target Est" is the average estimated stock price one year ahead based on estimates from security analysts who follow the stock.

We also have the range of prices for this day, followed by the range over the previous 52 weeks. Volume is the number of shares traded today, followed by average daily volume over the last three months. In the second column, Market Cap is number of shares outstanding (from the most recent quarterly financial statements) multiplied by the current price per share. The PE ratio was discussed in Chapter 3. The earnings per share (EPS) used in the calculation is "TTM," meaning "trailing twelve months." Finally, we have the dividend on the stock, which is actually the most recent quarterly dividend multiplied by 4, and the dividend yield. Notice that the yield is the reported dividend divided by the stock price: $1.80/$160.63 = .0112, or 1.12%.

Concept Questions

8.3a   What is the difference between a securities broker and a securities dealer?

8.3b   Which is bigger, the bid price or the ask price? Why?

8.3c   How does NASDAQ differ from the NYSE?

8.4 Summary and Conclusions

This chapter has covered the basics of stocks and stock valuation:

1. The cash flows from owning a share of stock come in the form of future dividends. We saw that in certain special cases it is possible to calculate the present value of all the future dividends and come up with a value for the stock.

2. As the owner of shares of common stock in a corporation, you have various rights, including the right to vote to elect corporate directors. Voting in corporate elections can be either cumulative or straight. Most voting is actually done by proxy, and a proxy battle breaks out when competing sides try to gain enough votes to elect their candidates for the board.

3. In addition to common stock, some corporations have issued preferred stock. The name stems from the fact that preferred stockholders must be paid first, before common stockholders can receive anything. Preferred stock has a fixed dividend.

4. The two biggest stock markets in the United States are the NYSE and the NASDAQ. We discussed the organization and operation of these two markets, and we saw how stock price information is reported.

This chapter completes Part 3 of our book. By now, you should have a good grasp of what we mean by *present value*. You should also be familiar with how to calculate present values, loan payments, and so on. In Part 4, we cover capital budgeting decisions. As you will see, the techniques you learned in Chapters 5–8 form the basis for our approach to evaluating business investment decisions.

CONNECT TO FINANCE

For more practice, you should be using *Connect Finance*. Log on to connect.mheducation.com to get started!

Can you answer the following *Connect* Quiz questions?

Section 8.1   A stock is selling for $11.90 a share given a market return of 14 percent and a capital gains yield of 5 percent. What was the amount of the last annual dividend that was paid?

Section 8.2   An 8 percent preferred stock sells for $54 a share. What is the rate of return?

Section 8.3   What kind of market is the NYSE?

CHAPTER REVIEW AND SELF-TEST PROBLEMS

8.1   **Dividend Growth and Stock Valuation** The Brigapenski Co. has just paid a cash dividend of $2 per share. Investors require a 16 percent return from investments such as this. If the dividend is expected to grow at a steady 8 percent per year, what is the current value of the stock? What will the stock be worth in five years?

8.2   **More Dividend Growth and Stock Valuation** In Self-Test Problem 8.1, what would the stock sell for today if the dividend was expected to grow at 20 percent per year for the next three years and then settle down to 8 percent per year indefinitely?

ANSWERS TO CHAPTER REVIEW AND SELF-TEST PROBLEMS

8.1   The last dividend, D_0, was $2. The dividend is expected to grow steadily at 8 percent. The required return is 16 percent. Based on the dividend growth model, we can say that the current price is:

$$P_0 = D_1/(R - g) = D_0 \times (1 + g)/(R - g)$$
$$= \$2 \times 1.08/(.16 - .08)$$
$$= \$2.16/.08$$
$$= \$27$$

We could calculate the price in five years by calculating the dividend in five years and then using the growth model again. Alternatively, we could recognize that the stock price will increase by 8 percent per year and calculate the future price directly. We'll do both. First, the dividend in five years will be:

$$D_5 = D_0 \times (1 + g)^5$$
$$= \$2 \times 1.08^5$$
$$= \$2.9387$$

The price in five years would therefore be:

$$P_5 = D_5 \times (1 + g)/(R - g)$$
$$= \$2.9387 \times 1.08/.08$$
$$= \$3.1738/.08$$
$$= \$39.67$$

Once we understand the dividend model, however, it's easier to notice that:

$$P_5 = P_0 \times (1 + g)^5$$
$$= \$27 \times 1.08^5$$
$$= \$27 \times 1.4693$$
$$= \$39.67$$

Notice that both approaches yield the same price in five years.

8.2   In this scenario, we have supernormal growth for the next three years. We'll need to calculate the dividends during the rapid growth period and the stock price in three years. The dividends are:

$$D_1 = \$2.00 \times 1.20 = \$2.400$$
$$D_2 = \$2.40 \times 1.20 = \$2.880$$
$$D_3 = \$2.88 \times 1.20 = \$3.456$$

After three years, the growth rate falls to 8 percent indefinitely. The price at that time, P_3, is thus:

$$P_3 = D_3 \times (1 + g)/(R - g)$$
$$= \$3.456 \times 1.08/(.16 - .08)$$
$$= \$3.7325/.08$$
$$= \$46.656$$

To complete the calculation of the stock's present value, we have to determine the present value of the three dividends and the future price:

$$P_0 = \frac{D_1}{(1 + R)^1} + \frac{D_2}{(1 + R)^2} + \frac{D_3}{(1 + R)^3} + \frac{P_3}{(1 + R)^3}$$
$$= \frac{\$2.40}{1.16} + \frac{2.88}{1.16^2} + \frac{3.456}{1.16^3} + \frac{46.656}{1.16^3}$$
$$= \$2.07 + 2.14 + 2.21 + 29.89$$
$$= \$36.31$$

CONCEPTS REVIEW AND CRITICAL THINKING QUESTIONS

1. **Stock Valuation [LO1]** Why does the value of a share of stock depend on dividends?

2. **Stock Valuation [LO1]** A substantial percentage of the companies listed on the NYSE and NASDAQ don't pay dividends, but investors are nonetheless willing to buy shares in them. How is this possible given your answer to the previous question?

3. **Dividend Policy [LO1]** Referring to the previous questions, under what circumstances might a company choose not to pay dividends?

4. **Dividend Growth Model [LO1]** Under what two assumptions can we use the dividend growth model presented in the chapter to determine the value of a share of stock? Comment on the reasonableness of these assumptions.

5. **Common versus Preferred Stock** [LO1] Suppose a company has a preferred stock issue and a common stock issue. Both have just paid a $2 dividend. Which do you think will have a higher price, a share of the preferred or a share of the common?

6. **Dividend Growth Model** [LO1] Based on the dividend growth model, what are the two components of the total return on a share of stock? Which do you think is typically larger?

7. **Growth Rate** [LO1] In the context of the dividend growth model, is it true that the growth rate in dividends and the growth rate in the price of the stock are identical?

8. **Voting Rights** [LO3] When it comes to voting in elections, what are the differences between U.S. political democracy and U.S. corporate democracy?

9. **Corporate Ethics** [LO3] Is it unfair or unethical for corporations to create classes of stock with unequal voting rights?

10. **Voting Rights** [LO3] Some companies, such as Alphabet, have created classes of stock with no voting rights at all. Why would investors buy such stock?

11. **Stock Valuation** [LO1] Evaluate the following statement: Managers should not focus on the current stock value because doing so will lead to an overemphasis on short-term profits at the expense of long-term profits.

12. **Two-Stage Dividend Growth Model** [LO1] One of the assumptions of the two-stage growth model is that the dividends drop immediately from the high growth rate to the perpetual growth rate. What do you think about this assumption? What happens if this assumption is violated?

13. **Voting Rights** [LO3] In the chapter, we mentioned that many companies have been under pressure to declassify their boards of directors. Why would investors want a board to be declassified? What are the advantages of a classified board?

14. **Price Ratio Valuation** [LO2] What are the difficulties in using the PE ratio to value stock?

QUESTIONS AND PROBLEMS

1. **Stock Values** [LO1] The Jackson-Timberlake Wardrobe Co. just paid a dividend of $2.15 per share on its stock. The dividends are expected to grow at a constant rate of 4 percent per year indefinitely. If investors require a return of 10.5 percent on the company's stock, what is the current price? What will the price be in three years? In 15 years?

2. **Stock Values** [LO1] The next dividend payment by Savitz, Inc., will be $2.34 per share. The dividends are anticipated to maintain a growth rate of 4.5 percent forever. If the stock currently sells for $37 per share, what is the required return?

3. **Stock Values** [LO1] For the company in the previous problem, what is the dividend yield? What is the expected capital gains yield?

4. **Stock Values** [LO1] Hudson Corporation will pay a dividend of $3.28 per share next year. The company pledges to increase its dividend by 3.75 percent per year indefinitely. If you require a return of 10 percent on your investment, how much will you pay for the company's stock today?

5. **Stock Valuation** [LO1] Grateful Eight Co. is expected to maintain a constant 3.7 percent growth rate in its dividends indefinitely. If the company has a dividend yield of 5.6 percent, what is the required return on the company's stock?

6. **Stock Valuation** [LO1] Suppose you know that a company's stock currently sells for $74 per share and the required return on the stock is 10.6 percent. You also know that the total return on the stock is evenly divided between a capital gains yield and a dividend yield. If it's the company's policy to always maintain a constant growth rate in its dividends, what is the current dividend per share?

BASIC
(Questions 1–13)

7. **Stock Valuation [LO1]** Burnett Corp. pays a constant $8.25 dividend on its stock. The company will maintain this dividend for the next 13 years and will then cease paying dividends forever. If the required return on this stock is 11.2 percent, what is the current share price?

8. **Valuing Preferred Stock [LO1]** Bedekar, Inc., has an issue of preferred stock outstanding that pays a $3.40 dividend every year in perpetuity. If this issue currently sells for $91 per share, what is the required return?

9. **Stock Valuation and Required Return [LO1]** Red, Inc., Yellow Corp., and Blue Company each will pay a dividend of $3.65 next year. The growth rate in dividends for all three companies is 4 percent. The required return for each company's stock is 8 percent, 11 percent, and 14 percent, respectively. What is the stock price for each company? What do you conclude about the relationship between the required return and the stock price?

10. **Voting Rights [LO3]** After successfully completing your corporate finance class, you feel the next challenge ahead is to serve on the board of directors of Schenkel Enterprises. Unfortunately, you will be the only person voting for you. If the company has 650,000 shares outstanding, and the stock currently sells for $43, how much will it cost you to buy a seat if the company uses straight voting?

11. **Voting Rights [LO3]** In the previous problem, assume that the company uses cumulative voting, and there are four seats in the current election. How much will it cost you to buy a seat now?

12. **Stock Valuation and PE [LO2]** The Perfect Rose Co. has earnings of $3.18 per share. The benchmark PE for the company is 18. What stock price would you consider appropriate? What if the benchmark PE were 21?

13. **Stock Valuation and PS [LO2]** TwitterMe, Inc., is a new company and currently has negative earnings. The company's sales are $2.1 million and there are 130,000 shares outstanding. If the benchmark price-sales ratio is 4.3, what is your estimate of an appropriate stock price? What if the price-sales ratio were 3.6?

INTERMEDIATE
(Questions 14–31)

14. **Stock Valuation [LO1]** Moody Farms just paid a dividend of $2.65 on its stock. The growth rate in dividends is expected to be a constant 3.8 percent per year indefinitely. Investors require a return of 15 percent for the first three years, a return of 13 percent for the next three years, and a return of 11 percent thereafter. What is the current share price?

15. **Nonconstant Growth [LO1]** Metallica Bearings, Inc., is a young start-up company. No dividends will be paid on the stock over the next nine years because the firm needs to plow back its earnings to fuel growth. The company will pay a dividend of $17 per share 10 years from today and will increase the dividend by 3.9 percent per year thereafter. If the required return on this stock is 12.5 percent, what is the current share price?

16. **Nonconstant Dividends [LO1]** Maurer, Inc., has an odd dividend policy. The company has just paid a dividend of $2.75 per share and has announced that it will increase the dividend by $4.50 per share for each of the next five years and then never pay another dividend. If you require a return of 11 percent on the company's stock, how much will you pay for a share today?

17. **Nonconstant Dividends [LO1]** Lohn Corporation is expected to pay the following dividends over the next four years: $13, $9, $6, and $2.75. Afterward, the company pledges to maintain a constant 5 percent growth rate in dividends forever. If the required return on the stock is 10.75 percent, what is the current share price?

18. **Supernormal Growth** [LO1] Synovec Co. is growing quickly. Dividends are expected to grow at a rate of 30 percent for the next three years, with the growth rate falling off to a constant 4 percent thereafter. If the required return is 11 percent, and the company just paid a dividend of $2.45, what is the current share price?

19. **Supernormal Growth** [LO1] Mobray Corp. is experiencing rapid growth. Dividends are expected to grow at 25 percent per year during the next three years, 15 percent over the following year, and then 6 percent per year indefinitely. The required return on this stock is 10 percent, and the stock currently sells for $79 per share. What is the projected dividend for the coming year?

20. **Negative Growth** [LO1] Antiques R Us is a mature manufacturing firm. The company just paid a dividend of $9.80, but management expects to reduce the payout by 4 percent per year indefinitely. If you require a return of 9.5 percent on this stock, what will you pay for a share today?

21. **Finding the Dividend** [LO1] Mannix Corporation stock currently sells for $57 per share. The market requires a return of 11 percent on the firm's stock. If the company maintains a constant 3.75 percent growth rate in dividends, what was the most recent dividend per share paid on the stock?

22. **Valuing Preferred Stock** [LO1] E-Eyes.com just issued some new preferred stock. The issue will pay an annual dividend of $20 in perpetuity, beginning 20 years from now. If the market requires a return of 5.65 percent on this investment, how much does a share of preferred stock cost today?

23. **Using Stock Quotes** [LO4] You have found the following stock quote for RJW Enterprises, Inc., in the financial pages of today's newspaper. What was the closing price for this stock that appeared in *yesterday's* paper? If the company currently has 25 million shares of stock outstanding, what was net income for the most recent four quarters?

52-WEEK							
HI	LO	STOCK (DIV)	YLD %	PE	VOL 100s	CLOSE	NET CHG
84.13	53.17	RJW 1.75	2.35	19	17652	??	−.23

24. **Two-Stage Dividend Growth Model** [LO1] A7X Corp. just paid a dividend of $1.55 per share. The dividends are expected to grow at 21 percent for the next eight years and then level off to a growth rate of 3.5 percent indefinitely. If the required return is 12 percent, what is the price of the stock today?

25. **Two-Stage Dividend Growth Model** [LO1] Navel County Choppers, Inc., is experiencing rapid growth. The company expects dividends to grow at 18 percent per year for the next 11 years before leveling off at 4 percent into perpetuity. The required return on the company's stock is 10 percent. If the dividend per share just paid was $1.94, what is the stock price?

26. **Stock Valuation and PE** [LO2] Domergue Corp. currently has an EPS of $3.76, and the benchmark PE for the company is 21. Earnings are expected to grow at 5.1 percent per year.

   a. What is your estimate of the current stock price?

   b. What is the target stock price in one year?

   c. Assuming the company pays no dividends, what is the implied return on the company's stock over the next year? What does this tell you about the implicit stock return using PE valuation?

27. Stock Valuation and PE [LO2] You have found the following historical information for the Daniela Company over the past four years:

	Year 1	Year 2	Year 3	Year 4
Stock price	$49.18	$53.18	$58.14	$56.32
EPS	2.35	2.47	2.78	3.04

Earnings are expected to grow at 11 percent for the next year. Using the company's historical average PE as a benchmark, what is the target stock price one year from today?

28. Stock Valuation and PE [LO2] In the previous problem, we assumed that the stock had a single stock price for the year. However, if you look at stock prices over any year, you will find a high and low stock price for the year. Instead of a single benchmark PE ratio, we now have a high and low PE ratio for each year. We can use these ratios to calculate a high and a low stock price for the next year. Suppose we have the following information on a particular company over the past four years:

	Year 1	Year 2	Year 3	Year 4
High price	$27.43	$26.32	$30.42	$37.01
Low price	19.86	20.18	25.65	26.41
EPS	1.35	1.58	1.51	1.85

Earnings are projected to grow at 9 percent over the next year. What are your high and low target stock prices over the next year?

29. Stock Valuation and PE [LO2] RAK, Inc., currently has an EPS of $2.45 and an earnings growth rate of 8 percent. If the benchmark PE ratio is 23, what is the target share price five years from now?

30. PE and Terminal Stock Price [LO2] In practice, a common way to value a share of stock when a company pays dividends is to value the dividends over the next five years or so, then find the "terminal" stock price using a benchmark PE ratio. Suppose a company just paid a dividend of $1.36. The dividends are expected to grow at 13 percent over the next five years. In five years, the estimated payout ratio is 40 percent and the benchmark PE ratio is 19. What is the target stock price in five years? What is the stock price today assuming a required return of 11 percent on this stock?

31. Stock Valuation and PE [LO2] Perine, Inc., has balance sheet equity of $6.8 million. At the same time, the income statement shows net income of $815,000. The company paid dividends of $285,000 and has 245,000 shares of stock outstanding. If the benchmark PE ratio is 16, what is the target stock price in one year?

CHALLENGE
(Questions 32–38)

32. Capital Gains versus Income [LO1] Consider four different stocks, all of which have a required return of 13 percent and a most recent dividend of $3.75 per share. Stocks W, X, and Y are expected to maintain constant growth rates in dividends for the foreseeable future of 10 percent, 0 percent, and −5 percent per year, respectively. Stock Z is a growth stock that will increase its dividend by 20 percent for the next two years and then maintain a constant 5 percent growth rate thereafter. What is the dividend yield for each of these four stocks? What is the expected capital gains yield? Discuss the relationship among the various returns that you find for each of these stocks.

33. Stock Valuation [LO1] Most corporations pay quarterly dividends on their common stock rather than annual dividends. Barring any unusual circumstances during the year, the board raises, lowers, or maintains the current dividend once a year and then pays this dividend out in equal quarterly installments to its shareholders.

a. Suppose a company currently pays an annual dividend of $3.40 on its common stock in a single annual installment, and management plans on raising this dividend by 3.8 percent per year indefinitely. If the required return on this stock is 10.5 percent, what is the current share price?

b. Now suppose the company in (a) actually pays its annual dividend in equal quarterly installments; thus, the company has just paid a dividend of $.85 per share, as it has for the previous three quarters. What is your value for the current share price now? (*Hint*: Find the equivalent annual end-of-year dividend for each year.) Comment on whether you think this model of stock valuation is appropriate.

34. **Nonconstant Growth [LO1]** Storico Co. just paid a dividend of $3.15 per share. The company will increase its dividend by 20 percent next year and then reduce its dividend growth rate by 5 percentage points per year until it reaches the industry average of 5 percent dividend growth, after which the company will keep a constant growth rate forever. If the required return on the company's stock is 12 percent, what will a share of stock sell for today?

35. **Nonconstant Growth [LO1]** This one's a little harder. Suppose the current share price for the firm in the previous problem is $54.50 and all the dividend information remains the same. What required return must investors be demanding on the company's stock? (*Hint*: Set up the valuation formula with all the relevant cash flows, and use trial and error to find the unknown rate of return.)

36. **Constant Dividend Growth Model [LO1]** Assume a stock has dividends that grow at a constant rate forever. If you value the stock using the constant dividend growth model, how many years worth of dividends constitute one-half of the stock's current price?

37. **Two-Stage Dividend Growth [LO1]** Regarding the two-stage dividend growth model in the chapter, show that the price of a share of stock today can be written as follows:

$$P_0 = \frac{D_0 \times (1 + g_1)}{R - g_1} \times \left[1 - \left(\frac{1 + g_1}{1 + R}\right)^t\right] + \left(\frac{1 + g_1}{1 + R}\right)^t \times \frac{D_0 \times (1 + g_2)}{R - g_2}$$

Can you provide an intuitive interpretation of this expression?

38. **Two-Stage Dividend Growth [LO1]** The chapter shows that in the two-stage dividend growth model, the growth rate in the first stage, g_1, can be greater than or less than the discount rate, R. Can they be exactly equal? (*Hint*: Yes, but what does the expression for the value of the stock look like?)

EXCEL MASTER IT! PROBLEM

In practice, the use of the dividend discount model is refined from the method we presented in the textbook. Many analysts will estimate the dividend for the next 5 years and then estimate a perpetual growth rate at some point in the future, typically 10 years. Rather than have the dividend growth fall dramatically from the fast growth period to the perpetual growth period, linear interpolation is applied. That is, the dividend growth is projected to fall by an equal amount each year. For example, if the fast growth period is 15 percent for the next 5 years and the dividends are expected to fall to a 5 percent perpetual growth rate 5 years later, the dividend growth rate would decline by 2 percent each year.

Suppose you find the following information about a particular stock:

Current dividend: $3.95
5-year dividend growth rate: 9.5%
Perpetual growth rate: 4%
Required return: 11%

a. Assume that the perpetual growth rate begins 10 years from now and use linear interpolation between the high growth rate and perpetual growth rate. Construct a table that shows the dividend growth rate and dividend each year. What is the stock price at Year 10? What is the stock price today?

b. How sensitive is the current stock price to changes in the perpetual growth rate? Graph the current stock price against the perpetual growth rate in 10 years to find out.

Instead of applying the constant dividend growth model to find the stock price in the future, analysts will often combine the dividend discount method with price ratio valuation, often with the PE ratio. Remember that the PE ratio is the price per share divided by the earnings per share. So, if we know the PE ratio, the dividend, and the payout ratio, we can solve for the stock price. To illustrate, suppose we also have the following information about the company:

Payout ratio: 25%
PE ratio at constant growth rate: 15

c. Use the PE ratio to calculate the stock price when the company reaches a perpetual growth rate in dividends. Now find the value of the stock today using the present value of the dividends during the nonconstant growth period and the price you calculated using the PE ratio.

d. How sensitive is the current stock price to changes in the PE ratio when the stock reaches the perpetual growth rate? Graph the current stock price against the PE ratio in 10 years to find out.

MINICASE

Stock Valuation at Ragan, Inc.

Ragan, Inc., was founded nine years ago by brother and sister Carrington and Genevieve Ragan. The company manufactures and installs commercial heating, ventilation, and cooling (HVAC) units. Ragan, Inc., has experienced rapid growth because of a proprietary technology that increases the energy efficiency of its units. The company is equally owned by Carrington and Genevieve. The original partnership agreement between the siblings gave each 50,000 shares of stock. In the event either wished to sell stock, the shares first had to be offered to the other at a discounted price.

Although neither sibling wants to sell, they have decided they should value their holdings in the company. To get started,

they have gathered the information about their main competitors in the table below.

Expert HVAC Corporation's negative earnings per share were the result of an accounting write-off last year. Without the write-off, earnings per share for the company would have been $1.10. The ROE for Expert HVAC is based on net income excluding the write-off.

Last year, Ragan, Inc., had an EPS of $3.15 and paid a dividend to Carrington and Genevieve of $45,000 each. The company also had a return on equity of 17 percent. The siblings believe that 14 percent is an appropriate required return for the company.

Ragan, Inc., Competitors					
	EPS	DPS	Stock Price	ROE	R
Arctic Cooling, Inc.	$1.30	$.16	$25.34	8.50%	10.00%
National Heating & Cooling	1.95	.23	29.85	10.50	13.00
Expert HVAC Corp.	−.37	.14	22.13	9.78	12.00
Industry Average	$ .96	$.18	$25.77	9.59%	11.67%

QUESTIONS

1. Assuming the company continues its current growth rate, what is the value per share of the company's stock?

2. To verify their calculations, Carrington and Genevieve have hired Josh Schlessman as a consultant. Josh was previously an equity analyst and covered the HVAC industry. Josh has examined the company's financial statements, as well as examining its competitors' financials. Although Ragan, Inc., currently has a technological advantage, his research indicates that other companies are investigating methods to improve efficiency. Given this, Josh believes that the company's technological advantage will last only for the next five years. After that period, the company's growth will likely slow to the industry growth average. Additionally, Josh believes that the required return used by the company is too high. He believes the industry average required return is more appropriate. Under this growth rate assumption, what is your estimate of the stock price?

3. What is the industry average price-earnings ratio? What is the price-earnings ratio for Ragan, Inc.? Is this the relationship you would expect between the two ratios? Why?

4. Carrington and Genevieve are unsure how to interpret the price-earnings ratio. After some head scratching, they've come up with the following expression for the price-earnings ratio:

$$\frac{P_0}{E_1} = \frac{1 - b}{R - (\text{ROE} \times b)}$$

Beginning with the constant dividend growth model, verify this result. What does this expression imply about the relationship between the dividend payout ratio, the required return on the stock, and the company's ROE?

5. Assume the company's growth rate slows to the industry average in five years. What future return on equity does this imply, assuming a constant payout ratio?

6. After discussing the stock value with Josh, Carrington and Genevieve agree that they would like to increase the value of the company stock. Like many small business owners, they want to retain control of the company, so they do not want to sell stock to outside investors. They also feel that the company's debt is at a manageable level and do not want to borrow more money. How can they increase the price of the stock? Are there any conditions under which this strategy would *not* increase the stock price?

Chapter 9 | Net Present Value and Other Investment Criteria

ALTHOUGH KNOWN AS Apple's largest supplier, Foxconn does have other buyers. In December 2016, Foxconn announced a joint venture with Sharp to build an $8.8 billion plant in China. The new plant would be a Gen-10.5 facility used to manufacture large-screen LCDs. And while the price tag of the new LCD plant may seem large, it wasn't even the biggest project announced by Foxconn that year. Earlier, Foxconn announced that it was looking to invest $10 billion to build a new plant to manufacture iPhones in India.

Foxconn's new plants are examples of capital budgeting decisions. Decisions such as these, with price tags well over $1 billion, are obviously major undertakings, and the risks and rewards must be carefully weighed. In this chapter, we discuss the basic tools used in making such decisions.

In Chapter 1, we saw that increasing the value of the stock in a company is the goal of financial management. Thus, what we need to know is how to tell whether a particular investment will achieve that or not. This chapter considers a variety of techniques that are used in practice for this purpose. More important, it shows how many of these techniques can be misleading, and it explains why the net present value approach is the right one.

Learning Objectives

After studying this chapter, you should be able to:

LO1 Show the reasons why the net present value criterion is the best way to evaluate proposed investments.

LO2 Discuss the payback rule and some of its shortcomings.

LO3 Discuss the discounted payback rule and some of its shortcomings.

LO4 Explain accounting rates of return and some of the problems with them.

LO5 Present the internal rate of return criterion and its strengths and weaknesses.

LO6 Calculate the modified internal rate of return.

LO7 Illustrate the profitability index and its relation to net present value.

For updates on the latest happenings in finance, visit fundamentalsofcorporatefinance.blogspot.com.

In Chapter 1, we identified the three key areas of concern to the financial manager. The first of these involved the question: What fixed assets should we buy? We called this the *capital budgeting decision*. In this chapter, we begin to deal with the issues that arise in answering this question.

The process of allocating or budgeting capital is usually more involved than deciding whether to buy a particular fixed asset. We frequently face broader issues, like whether we should launch a new product or enter a new market. Decisions such as these determine the nature of a firm's operations and products for years to come, primarily because fixed asset investments are generally long-lived and not easily reversed once they are made.

The most fundamental decision a business must make concerns its product line. What services will we offer or what will we sell? In what markets will we compete? What new products will we introduce? The answer to any of these questions will require that the firm commit its scarce and valuable capital to certain types of assets. As a result, all of these strategic issues fall under the general heading of capital budgeting. The process of capital budgeting could be given a more descriptive (not to mention impressive) name: *Strategic asset allocation.*

For the reasons we have discussed, the capital budgeting question is probably the most important issue in corporate finance. How a firm chooses to finance its operations (the capital structure question) and how a firm manages its short-term operating activities (the working capital question) are certainly issues of concern, but the fixed assets define the business of the firm. Airlines, for example, are airlines because they operate airplanes, regardless of how they finance them.

Any firm possesses a huge number of possible investments. Each possible investment is an option available to the firm. Some options are valuable and some are not. The essence of successful financial management, of course, is learning to identify which ones are which. With this in mind, our goal in this chapter is to introduce you to the techniques used to analyze potential business ventures to decide which are worth undertaking.

We present and compare a number of different procedures used in practice. Our primary goal is to acquaint you with the advantages and disadvantages of the various approaches. As we will see, the most important concept in this area is the idea of net present value. We consider this next.

Net Present Value

9.1

In Chapter 1, we argued that the goal of financial management is to create value for the stockholders. The financial manager must examine a potential investment in light of its likely effect on the price of the firm's shares. In this section, we describe a widely used procedure for doing this: The net present value approach.

Excel Master It!
Excel Master coverage online

THE BASIC IDEA

An investment is worth undertaking if it creates value for its owners. In the most general sense, we create value by identifying an investment worth more in the marketplace than it costs us to acquire. How can something be worth more than it costs? It's a case of the whole being worth more than the cost of the parts.

For example, suppose you buy a run-down house for $25,000 and spend another $25,000 on painters, plumbers, and so on to get it fixed up. Your total investment is $50,000. When the work is completed, you place the house back on the market and find that it's worth $60,000. The market value ($60,000) exceeds the cost ($50,000) by $10,000. What you have done here is to act as a manager to bring together some fixed assets (a house), some labor (plumbers, carpenters, and others), and some materials (carpeting, paint, and so on). The net result is that you have created $10,000 in value. Put another way, this $10,000 is the *value added* by management.

net present value (NPV)

The difference between an investment's market value and its cost.

With our house example, it turned out *after the fact* that $10,000 in value had been created. Things worked out nicely. The real challenge, of course, would have been to somehow identify *ahead of time* whether investing the necessary $50,000 was a good idea in the first place. This is what capital budgeting is all about—namely, trying to determine whether a proposed investment or project will be worth more, once it is in place, than it costs.

For reasons that will be obvious in a moment, the difference between an investment's market value and its cost is called the **net present value** of the investment, abbreviated **NPV**. In other words, net present value is a measure of how much value is created or added today by undertaking an investment. Given our goal of creating value for the stockholders, the capital budgeting process can be viewed as a search for investments with positive net present values.

With our run-down house, you can probably imagine how we would go about making the capital budgeting decision. We would first look at what comparable, fixed-up properties were selling for in the market. We would then get estimates of the cost of buying a particular property and bringing it to market. At this point, we would have an estimated total cost and an estimated market value. If the difference was positive, then this investment would be worth undertaking because it would have a positive estimated net present value. There is risk, of course, because there is no guarantee that our estimates will turn out to be correct.

As our example illustrates, investment decisions are greatly simplified when there is a market for assets similar to the investment we are considering. Capital budgeting becomes much more difficult when we cannot observe the market price for at least roughly comparable investments. The reason is that we then face the problem of estimating the value of an investment using only indirect market information. Unfortunately, this is precisely the situation the financial manager usually encounters. We examine this issue next.

ESTIMATING NET PRESENT VALUE

Imagine we are thinking of starting a business to produce and sell a new product—say, organic fertilizer. We can estimate the start-up costs with reasonable accuracy because we know what we will need to buy to begin production. Would this be a good investment? Based on our discussion, you know that the answer depends on whether the value of the new business exceeds the cost of starting it. In other words, does this investment have a positive NPV?

This problem is much more difficult than our "fixer upper" house example because entire fertilizer companies are not routinely bought and sold in the marketplace, so it is essentially impossible to observe the market value of a similar investment. As a result, we must somehow estimate this value by other means.

Based on our work in Chapters 5 and 6, you may be able to guess how we will go about estimating the value of our fertilizer business. We will first try to estimate the future cash flows we expect the new business to produce. We will then apply our basic discounted cash flow procedure to estimate the present value of those cash flows. Once we have this estimate, we will then estimate NPV as the difference between the present value of the future cash flows and the cost of the investment. As we mentioned in Chapter 5, this procedure is often called **discounted cash flow (DCF) valuation**.

discounted cash flow (DCF) valuation

The process of valuing an investment by discounting its future cash flows.

To see how we might go about estimating NPV, suppose we believe the cash revenues from our fertilizer business will be $20,000 per year, assuming everything goes as expected. Cash costs (including taxes) will be $14,000 per year. We will wind down the business in eight years. The plant, property, and equipment will be worth $2,000 as salvage at that time. The project costs $30,000 to launch. We use a 15 percent discount rate on new projects such as this one. Is this a good investment? If there are 1,000 shares of stock outstanding, what will be the effect on the price per share of taking this investment?

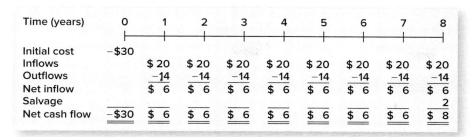

Time (years)	0	1	2	3	4	5	6	7	8
Initial cost	−$30								
Inflows		$ 20	$ 20	$ 20	$ 20	$ 20	$ 20	$ 20	$ 20
Outflows		−14	−14	−14	−14	−14	−14	−14	−14
Net inflow		$ 6	$ 6	$ 6	$ 6	$ 6	$ 6	$ 6	$ 6
Salvage									2
Net cash flow	−$30	$ 6	$ 6	$ 6	$ 6	$ 6	$ 6	$ 6	$ 8

FIGURE 9.1

Project Cash Flows ($000)

From a purely mechanical perspective, we need to calculate the present value of the future cash flows at 15 percent. The net cash inflow will be $20,000 cash income less $14,000 in costs per year for eight years. These cash flows are illustrated in Figure 9.1. As Figure 9.1 suggests, we effectively have an eight-year annuity of $20,000 − 14,000 = $6,000 per year, along with a single lump sum inflow of $2,000 in eight years. Calculating the present value of the future cash flows comes down to the same type of problem we considered in Chapter 6. The total present value is:

$$\text{Present value} = \$6{,}000 \times [1 - (1/1.15^8)]/.15 + (2{,}000/1.15^8)$$
$$= (\$6{,}000 \times 4.4873) + (2{,}000/3.0590)$$
$$= \$26{,}924 + 654$$
$$= \$27{,}578$$

When we compare this to the $30,000 estimated cost, we see that the NPV is:

$$\text{NPV} = -\$30{,}000 + 27{,}578 = -\$2{,}422$$

Therefore, this is *not* a good investment. Based on our estimates, taking it would *decrease* the total value of the stock by $2,422. With 1,000 shares outstanding, our best estimate of the impact of taking this project is a loss of value of $2,422/1,000 = $2.42 per share.

Our fertilizer example illustrates how NPV estimates can be used to determine whether an investment is desirable. From our example, notice that if the NPV is negative, the effect on share value will be unfavorable. If the NPV were positive, the effect would be favorable. As a consequence, all we need to know about a particular proposal for the purpose of making an accept–reject decision is whether the NPV is positive or negative.

Given that the goal of financial management is to increase share value, our discussion in this section leads us to the *net present value rule*:

> **An investment should be accepted if the net present value is positive and rejected if it is negative.**

In the unlikely event that the net present value turned out to be exactly zero, we would be indifferent between taking the investment and not taking it.

Two comments about our example are in order. First and foremost, it is not the rather mechanical process of discounting the cash flows that is important. Once we have the cash flows and the appropriate discount rate, the required calculations are fairly straightforward. The task of coming up with the cash flows and the discount rate is much more challenging. We will have much more to say about this in the next several chapters. For the remainder of this chapter, we take it as a given that we have estimates of the cash revenues and costs and, where needed, an appropriate discount rate.

The second thing to keep in mind about our example is that the −$2,422 NPV is an estimate. Like any estimate, it can be high or low. The only way to find out the true NPV would be to place the investment up for sale and see what we could get for it. We generally won't be doing this, so it is important that our estimates be reliable. Once again, we will say more about this later. For the rest of this chapter, we will assume the estimates are accurate.

EXAMPLE 9.1   **Using the NPV Rule**

Suppose we are asked to decide whether a new consumer product should be launched. Based on projected sales and costs, we expect that the cash flows over the five-year life of the project will be $2,000 in the first two years, $4,000 in the next two, and $5,000 in the last year. It will cost about $10,000 to begin production. We use a 10 percent discount rate to evaluate new products. What should we do here?

Given the cash flows and discount rate, we can calculate the total value of the product by discounting the cash flows back to the present:

$$\text{Present value} = (\$2,000/1.1) + (2,000/1.1^2) + (4,000/1.1^3)$$
$$+ (4,000/1.1^4) + (5,000/1.1^5)$$
$$= \$1,818 + 1,653 + 3,005 + 2,732 + 3,105$$
$$= \$12,313$$

The present value of the expected cash flows is $12,313, but the cost of getting those cash flows is only $10,000, so the NPV is $12,313 − 10,000 = $2,313. This is positive; so, based on the net present value rule, we should take on the project.

As we have seen in this section, estimating NPV is one way of assessing the profitability of a proposed investment. It is certainly not the only way profitability is assessed, and we now turn to some alternatives. As we will see, when compared to NPV, each of the alternative ways of assessing profitability that we will examine is flawed in some key way; so NPV is the preferred approach in principle, if not always in practice.

SPREADSHEET STRATEGIES

Calculating NPVs with a Spreadsheet

Spreadsheets are commonly used to calculate NPVs. Examining the use of spreadsheets in this context also allows us to issue an important warning. Let's rework Example 9.1:

You can get a freeware NPV calculator at **www.wheatworks.com**

	A	B	C	D	E	F	G	H
1								
2			Using a spreadsheet to calculate net present values					
3								
4	From Example 9.1, the project's cost is $10,000. The cash flows are $2,000 per year for the first							
5	two years, $4,000 per year for the next two, and $5,000 in the last year. The discount rate is							
6	10 percent; what's the NPV?							
7								
8		Year	Cash Flow					
9		0	−$10,000		Discount rate =	10%		
10		1	2,000					
11		2	2,000		NPV =	$2,102.72	(*wrong* answer)	
12		3	4,000		NPV =	$2,312.99	(*right* answer)	
13		4	4,000					
14		5	5,000					
15								
16	The formula entered in cell F11 is =NPV(F9, C9:C14). This gives the wrong answer because the							
17	NPV function actually calculates present values, not *net* present values.							
18								
19	The formula entered in cell F12 is =NPV(F9, C10:C14) + C9. This gives the right answer because the							
20	NPV function is used to calculate the present value of the cash flows and then the initial cost is							
21	subtracted to calculate the answer. Notice that we added cell C9 because it is already negative.							

Source: Microsoft Excel

In our spreadsheet example, notice that we have provided two answers. By comparing the answers to that found in Example 9.1, we see that the first answer is wrong even though we used the spreadsheet's NPV formula. What happened is that the "NPV" function in our spreadsheet is actually a PV function; unfortunately, one of the original spreadsheet programs many years ago got the definition wrong, and subsequent spreadsheets have copied it! Our second answer shows how to use the formula properly.

The example here illustrates the danger of blindly using calculators or computers without understanding what is going on; we shudder to think of how many capital budgeting decisions in the real world are based on incorrect use of this particular function. We will see another example of something that can go wrong with a spreadsheet later in the chapter.

Concept Questions

9.1a   What is the net present value rule?

9.1b   If we say an investment has an NPV of $1,000, what exactly do we mean?

The Payback Rule

9.2

Excel Master It!

xlsx Excel Master coverage online

It is common in practice to talk of the payback on a proposed investment. Loosely, the *payback* is the length of time it takes to recover our initial investment or "get our bait back." Because this idea is widely understood and used, we will examine it in some detail.

DEFINING THE RULE

We can illustrate how to calculate a payback with an example. Figure 9.2 shows the cash flows from a proposed investment. How many years do we have to wait until the accumulated cash flows from this investment equal or exceed the cost of the investment? As Figure 9.2 indicates, the initial investment is $50,000. After the first year, the firm has recovered $30,000, leaving $20,000. The cash flow in the second year is exactly $20,000, so this investment "pays for itself" in exactly two years. Put another way, the **payback period** is two years. If we require a payback of, say, three years or less, then this investment is acceptable. This illustrates the *payback period rule*:

payback period
The amount of time required for an investment to generate cash flows sufficient to recover its initial cost.

> Based on the payback rule, an investment is acceptable if its calculated payback period is less than some prespecified number of years.

In our example, the payback works out to be exactly two years. This won't usually happen, of course. When the numbers don't work out exactly, it is customary to work with fractional years. For example, suppose the initial investment is $60,000, and the cash flows are $20,000 in the first year and $90,000 in the second. The cash flows over the first two years

FIGURE 9.2

Net Project Cash Flows

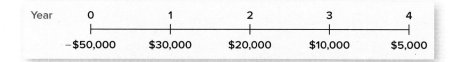

Year	0	1	2	3	4
	−$50,000	$30,000	$20,000	$10,000	$5,000

are $110,000, so the project obviously pays back sometime in the second year. After the first year, the project has paid back $20,000, leaving $40,000 to be recovered. To figure out the fractional year, note that this $40,000 is $40,000/$90,000 = 4/9 of the second year's cash flow. Assuming that the $90,000 cash flow is received uniformly throughout the year, the payback would be $1\frac{4}{9}$ years.

EXAMPLE 9.2	Calculating Payback

Here are the projected cash flows from a proposed investment:

Year	Cash Flow
1	$100
2	200
3	500

This project costs $500. What is the payback period for this investment?

The initial cost is $500. After the first two years, the cash flows total $300. After the third year, the total cash flow is $800, so the project pays back sometime between the end of Year 2 and the end of Year 3. Because the accumulated cash flows for the first two years are $300, we need to recover $200 in the third year. The third-year cash flow is $500, so we will have to wait $200/$500 = .4 years to do this. The payback period is thus 2.4 years, or about two years and five months.

Now that we know how to calculate the payback period on an investment, using the payback period rule for making decisions is straightforward. A particular cutoff time is selected—say, two years—and all investment projects that have payback periods of two years or less are accepted, whereas any that pay off in more than two years are rejected.

Table 9.1 illustrates cash flows for five different projects. The figures shown as the Year 0 cash flows are the costs of the investments. We examine these to indicate some peculiarities that can, in principle, arise with payback periods.

The payback for the first project, A, is easily calculated. The sum of the cash flows for the first two years is $70, leaving us with $100 − 70 = $30 to go. Because the cash flow in the third year is $50, the payback occurs sometime in that year. When we compare the $30 we need to the $50 that will be coming in, we get $30/$50 = .6; so, payback will occur 60 percent of the way into the year. The payback period is thus 2.6 years.

Project B's payback is also easy to calculate: It *never* pays back because the cash flows never total up to the original investment. Project C has a payback of exactly four years because it supplies the $130 that B is missing in Year 4. Project D is a little strange. Because of the negative cash flow in Year 3, you can easily verify that it has two different payback periods, two years and four years. Which of these is correct? Both of them; the way the

TABLE 9.1

Expected Cash Flows for Projects A through E

Year	A	B	C	D	E
0	−$100	−$200	−$200	−$200	−$ 50
1	30	40	40	100	100
2	40	20	20	100	−50,000,000
3	50	10	10	−200	
4	60		130	200	

payback period is calculated doesn't guarantee a single answer. Finally, Project E is obviously unrealistic, but it does pay back in six months, thereby illustrating the point that a rapid payback does not guarantee a good investment.

ANALYZING THE RULE

When compared to the NPV rule, the payback period rule has some rather severe shortcomings. First, we calculate the payback period by adding up the future cash flows. There is no discounting involved, so the time value of money is completely ignored. The payback rule also fails to consider any risk differences. The payback would be calculated the same way for both very risky and very safe projects.

Perhaps the biggest problem with the payback period rule is coming up with the right cutoff period: We don't really have an objective basis for choosing a particular number. Put another way, there is no economic rationale for looking at payback in the first place, so we have no guide for how to pick the cutoff. As a result, we end up using a number that is arbitrarily chosen.

Suppose we have somehow decided on an appropriate payback period of two years or less. As we have seen, the payback period rule ignores the time value of money for the first two years. More seriously, cash flows after the second year are ignored entirely. To see this, consider the two investments, Long and Short, in Table 9.2. Both projects cost $250. Based on our discussion, the payback on Long is 2 + ($50/$100) = 2.5 years, and the payback on Short is 1 + ($150/$200) = 1.75 years. With a cutoff of two years, Short is acceptable and Long is not.

Is the payback period rule guiding us to the right decisions? Maybe not. Suppose we require a 15 percent return on this type of investment. We can calculate the NPV for these two investments as:

$$\text{NPV(Short)} = -\$250 + (100/1.15) + (200/1.15^2) = -\$11.81$$
$$\text{NPV(Long)} = -\$250 + (100 \times \{[1 - (1/1.15^4)]/.15\}) = \$35.50$$

Now we have a problem. The NPV of the shorter-term investment is actually negative, meaning that taking it diminishes the value of the shareholders' equity. The opposite is true for the longer-term investment—it increases share value.

Our example illustrates two primary shortcomings of the payback period rule. First, by ignoring time value, we may be led to take investments (like Short) that actually are worth less than they cost. Second, by ignoring cash flows beyond the cutoff, we may be led to reject profitable longer-term investments (like Long). More generally, using a payback period rule will tend to bias us toward shorter-term investments.

REDEEMING QUALITIES OF THE RULE

Despite its shortcomings, the payback period rule is often used by large and sophisticated companies when they are making relatively minor decisions. There are several reasons for this. The primary reason is that many decisions do not warrant detailed analysis because

Year	Long	Short
0	−$250	−$250
1	100	100
2	100	200
3	100	0
4	100	0

TABLE 9.2

Investment Projected Cash Flows

the cost of the analysis would exceed the possible loss from a mistake. As a practical matter, it can be said that an investment that pays back rapidly and has benefits extending beyond the cutoff period probably has a positive NPV.

Small investment decisions are made by the hundreds every day in large organizations. Moreover, they are made at all levels. As a result, it would not be uncommon for a corporation to require, for example, a two-year payback on all investments of less than $10,000. Investments larger than this would be subjected to greater scrutiny. The requirement of a two-year payback is not perfect for reasons we have seen, but it does exercise some control over expenditures and limits possible losses.

In addition to its simplicity, the payback rule has two other positive features. First, because it is biased toward short-term projects, it is biased toward liquidity. In other words, a payback rule tends to favor investments that free up cash for other uses quickly. This could be important for a small business; it would be less so for a large corporation. Second, the cash flows that are expected to occur later in a project's life are probably more uncertain. Arguably, a payback period rule adjusts for the extra riskiness of later cash flows, but it does so in a rather draconian fashion—by ignoring them altogether.

We should note here that some of the apparent simplicity of the payback rule is an illusion. The reason is that we still must come up with the cash flows first, and, as we discussed earlier, this is not at all easy to do. It would probably be more accurate to say that the *concept* of a payback period is both intuitive and easy to understand.

SUMMARY OF THE RULE

To summarize, the payback period is a kind of "break-even" measure. Because time value is ignored, you can think of the payback period as the length of time it takes to break even in an accounting sense, but not in an economic sense. The biggest drawback to the payback period rule is that it doesn't ask the right question. The relevant issue is the impact an investment will have on the value of the stock, not how long it takes to recover the initial investment.

Nevertheless, because it is so simple, companies often use it as a screen for dealing with the myriad minor investment decisions they have to make. There is certainly nothing wrong with this practice. As with any simple rule of thumb, there will be some errors in using it; but it wouldn't have survived all this time if it weren't useful. Now that you understand the rule, you can be on the alert for circumstances under which it might lead to problems. To help you remember, the following table lists the pros and cons of the payback period rule:

Advantages and Disadvantages of the Payback Period Rule	
Advantages	Disadvantages
1. Easy to understand.	1. Ignores the time value of money.
2. Adjusts for uncertainty of later cash flows.	2. Requires an arbitrary cutoff point.
3. Biased toward liquidity.	3. Ignores cash flows beyond the cutoff date.
	4. Biased against long-term projects, such as research and development, and new projects.

Concept Questions

9.2a   In words, what is the payback period? The payback period rule?

9.2b   Why do we say that the payback period is, in a sense, an accounting break-even measure?

The Discounted Payback

We saw that one shortcoming of the payback period rule was that it ignored time value. A variation of the payback period, the discounted payback period, fixes this particular problem. The **discounted payback period** is the length of time until the sum of the discounted cash flows is equal to the initial investment. The *discounted payback rule* is therefore:

> Based on the discounted payback rule, an investment is acceptable if its discounted payback is less than some prespecified number of years.

To see how we might calculate the discounted payback period, suppose we require a 12.5 percent return on new investments. We have an investment that costs $300 and has cash flows of $100 per year for five years. To get the discounted payback, we have to discount each cash flow at 12.5 percent and then start adding them. We do this in Table 9.3. In Table 9.3, we have both the discounted and the undiscounted cash flows. Looking at the accumulated cash flows, we see that the regular payback is almost exactly three years (look for the highlighted figure in Year 3). The discounted cash flows total $301 only after four years, so the discounted payback is four years, as shown.[1]

How do we interpret the discounted payback? Recall that the ordinary payback is the time it takes to break even in an accounting sense. Because it includes the time value of money, the discounted payback is the time it takes to break even in an economic or financial sense. Loosely speaking, in our example, we get our money back, along with the interest we could have earned elsewhere, in four years.

Figure 9.3 illustrates this idea by comparing the *future* value of the $300 investment at 12.5 percent to the *future* value of the $100 annual cash flows at 12.5 percent. Notice that the two lines cross at exactly four years. This tells us that the value of the project's cash flows catches up and then passes the original investment in four years.

Table 9.3 and Figure 9.3 illustrate another interesting feature of the discounted payback period. If a project ever pays back on a discounted basis, then it must have a positive NPV.[2] This is true because, by definition, the NPV is zero when the sum of the discounted cash flows equals the initial investment. For example, the present value of all the cash flows in

Excel Master It!

xlsx   Excel Master coverage online

discounted payback period
The length of time required for an investment's discounted cash flows to equal its initial cost.

	Cash Flow		Accumulated Cash Flow	
Year	**Undiscounted**	**Discounted**	**Undiscounted**	**Discounted**
1	$100	$89	$100	$ 89
2	100	79	200	168
3	100	70	300	238
4	100	62	400	301
5	100	55	500	356

TABLE 9.3

Ordinary and Discounted Payback

---

[1] In this case, the discounted payback is an even number of years. This won't ordinarily happen, of course. Calculating a fractional year for the discounted payback period is more involved than it is for the ordinary payback, and it is not commonly done.

[2] This argument assumes the cash flows, other than the first, are all positive. If they are not, then these statements are not necessarily correct. Also, there may be more than one discounted payback.

FIGURE 9.3

Future Value of Project Cash Flows

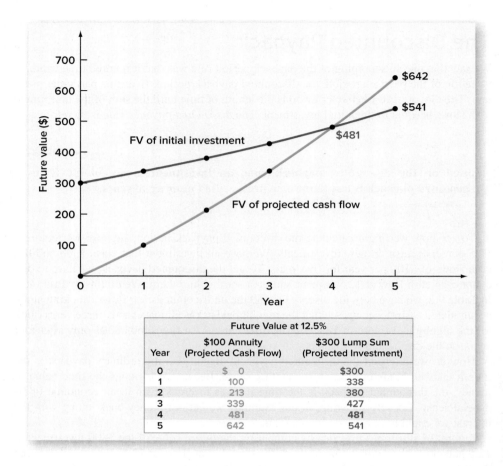

Future Value at 12.5%		
Year	$100 Annuity (Projected Cash Flow)	$300 Lump Sum (Projected Investment)
0	$ 0	$300
1	100	338
2	213	380
3	339	427
4	481	481
5	642	541

Table 9.3 is $356. The cost of the project was $300, so the NPV is obviously $56. This $56 is the value of the cash flow that occurs *after* the discounted payback (see the last line in Table 9.3). In general, if we use a discounted payback rule, we won't accidentally take any projects with a negative estimated NPV.

Based on our example, the discounted payback would seem to have much to recommend it. You may be surprised to find out that it is rarely used in practice. Why? Probably because it really isn't any simpler to use than NPV. To calculate a discounted payback, you have to discount cash flows, add them up, and compare them to the cost, just as you do with NPV. So, unlike an ordinary payback, the discounted payback is not especially simple to calculate.

A discounted payback period rule has a couple of other significant drawbacks. The biggest one is that the cutoff still has to be arbitrarily set, and cash flows beyond that point are ignored.[3] As a result, a project with a positive NPV may be found unacceptable because the cutoff is too short. Also, just because one project has a shorter discounted payback than another does not mean it has a larger NPV.

All things considered, the discounted payback is a compromise between a regular payback and NPV that lacks the simplicity of the first and the conceptual rigor of the second. Nonetheless, if we need to assess the time it will take to recover the investment required by a project, then the discounted payback is better than the ordinary payback because it

---

[3]If the cutoff were forever, then the discounted payback rule would be the same as the NPV rule. It would also be the same as the profitability index rule considered in a later section.

considers time value. In other words, the discounted payback recognizes that we could have invested the money elsewhere and earned a return on it. The ordinary payback does not take this into account. The advantages and disadvantages of the discounted payback rule are summarized in the following table:

Advantages and Disadvantages of the Discounted Payback Period Rule	
Advantages	**Disadvantages**
1. Includes time value of money.	1. May reject positive NPV investments.
2. Easy to understand.	2. Requires an arbitrary cutoff point.
3. Does not accept negative estimated NPV investments.	3. Ignores cash flows beyond the cutoff date.
4. Biased toward liquidity.	4. Biased against long-term projects, such as research and development, and new projects.

Calculating Discounted Payback   EXAMPLE 9.3

Consider an investment that costs $400 and pays $100 per year forever. We use a 20 percent discount rate on this type of investment. What is the ordinary payback? What is the discounted payback? What is the NPV?

The NPV and ordinary payback are easy to calculate in this case because the investment is a perpetuity. The present value of the cash flows is $100/.2 = $500, so the NPV is $500 − 400 = $100. The ordinary payback is obviously four years.

To get the discounted payback, we need to find the number of years such that a $100 annuity has a present value of $400 at 20 percent. In other words, the present value annuity factor is $400/$100 = 4, and the interest rate is 20 percent per period; so what's the number of periods? If we solve for the number of periods, we find that the answer is a little less than nine years, so this is the discounted payback.

Concept Questions

9.3a   In words, what is the discounted payback period? Why do we say it is, in a sense, a financial or economic break-even measure?

9.3b   What advantage(s) does the discounted payback have over the ordinary payback?

The Average Accounting Return

9.4

Another attractive, but flawed, approach to making capital budgeting decisions involves the **average accounting return (AAR)**. There are many different definitions of the AAR. However, in one form or another, the AAR is always defined as:

$$\frac{\text{Some measure of average accounting profit}}{\text{Some measure of average accounting value}}$$

The specific definition we will use is:

$$\frac{\text{Average net income}}{\text{Average book value}}$$

To see how we might calculate this number, suppose we are deciding whether to open a store in a new shopping mall. The required investment in improvements is $500,000.

Excel Master It!
xlsx Excel Master
coverage online

average accounting return (AAR)
An investment's average net income divided by its average book value.

TABLE 9.4

Projected Yearly Revenue and Costs for Average Accounting Return

	Year 1	Year 2	Year 3	Year 4	Year 5
Revenue	$433,333	$450,000	$266,667	$200,000	$133,333
Expenses	200,000	150,000	100,000	100,000	100,000
Earnings before depreciation	$233,333	$300,000	$166,667	$100,000	$ 33,333
Depreciation	100,000	100,000	100,000	100,000	100,000
Earnings before taxes	$133,333	$200,000	$ 66,667	$ 0	− $ 66,667
Taxes (25%)	33,333	50,000	16,667	0	− 16,667
Net income	$100,000	$150,000	$ 50,000	$ 0	−$ 50,000

$$\text{Average net income} = \frac{\$100,000 + 150,000 + 50,000 + 0 - 50,000}{5} = \$50,000$$

$$\text{Average book value} = \frac{\$500,000 + 0}{2} = \$250,000$$

The store would have a five-year life because everything reverts to the mall owners after that time. The required investment would be 100 percent depreciated (straight-line) over five years, so the depreciation would be $500,000/5 = $100,000 per year. The tax rate is 25 percent. Table 9.4 contains the projected revenues and expenses. Net income in each year, based on these figures, is also shown.

To calculate the average book value for this investment, we note that we started out with a book value of $500,000 (the initial cost) and ended up at $0. The average book value during the life of the investment is ($500,000 + 0)/2 = $250,000. As long as we use straight-line depreciation, the average investment will always be one-half of the initial investment.[4]

Looking at Table 9.4, we see that net income is $100,000 in the first year, $150,000 in the second year, $50,000 in the third year, $0 in Year 4, and −$50,000 in Year 5. The average net income, then, is:

[$100,000 + 150,000 + 50,000 + 0 + (−50,000)]/5 = $50,000

The average accounting return is:

$$\text{AAR} = \frac{\text{Average net income}}{\text{Average book value}} = \frac{\$50,000}{\$250,000} = .20, \text{ or } 20\%$$

If the firm has a target AAR of less than 20 percent, then this investment is acceptable; otherwise, it is not. The *average accounting return rule* is:

Based on the average accounting return rule, a project is acceptable if its average accounting return exceeds a target average accounting return.

As we will now see, the use of this rule has a number of problems.

You should recognize the chief drawback to the AAR immediately. Above all else, the AAR is not a rate of return in any meaningful economic sense. Instead, it is the ratio of

---

[4]We could, of course, calculate the average of the six book values directly. In thousands, we would have ($500 + 400 + 300 + 200 + 100 + 0)/6 = $250.

two accounting numbers, and it is not comparable to the returns offered, for example, in financial markets.[5]

One of the reasons the AAR is not a true rate of return is that it ignores time value. When we average figures that occur at different times, we are treating the near future and the more distant future in the same way. There was no discounting involved when we computed the average net income, for example.

The second problem with the AAR is similar to the problem we had with the payback period rule concerning the lack of an objective cutoff period. Because a calculated AAR is really not comparable to a market return, the target AAR must somehow be specified. There is no generally agreed-upon way to do this. One way of doing it is to calculate the AAR for the firm as a whole and use this as a benchmark, but there are lots of other ways as well.

The third, and perhaps worst, flaw in the AAR is that it doesn't even look at the right things. Instead of cash flow and market value, it uses net income and book value. These are both poor substitutes. As a result, an AAR doesn't tell us what we really want to know—which is, What effect will taking this investment have on share price?

Does the AAR have any redeeming features? About the only one is that it almost always can be computed. The reason is that accounting information will almost always be available, both for the project under consideration and for the firm as a whole. We hasten to add that once the accounting information is available, we can always convert it to cash flows, so even this is not a particularly important fact. The AAR is summarized in the following table:

Advantages and Disadvantages of the Average Accounting Return	
Advantages	**Disadvantages**
1. Easy to calculate. 2. Needed information will usually be available.	1. Not a true rate of return; time value of money is ignored. 2. Uses an arbitrary benchmark cutoff rate. 3. Based on accounting (book) values, not cash flows and market values.

Concept Questions

9.4a   What is an average accounting rate of return (AAR)?
9.4b   What are the weaknesses of the AAR rule?

The Internal Rate of Return

9.5

We now come to the most important alternative to NPV, the **internal rate of return**, universally known as the **IRR**. As we will see, the IRR is closely related to NPV. With the IRR, we try to find a single rate of return that summarizes the merits of a project. Furthermore, we want this rate to be an "internal" rate in the sense that it depends only on the cash flows of a particular investment, not on rates offered elsewhere.

To illustrate the idea behind the IRR, consider a project that costs $100 today and pays $110 in one year. Suppose you were asked, "What is the return on this investment?" What would you say? It seems both natural and obvious to say that the return is 10 percent

Excel Master It!

xlsx   Excel Master
coverage online

internal rate of return (IRR)
The discount rate that makes the NPV of an investment zero.

---

[5]The AAR is closely related to the return on assets (ROA) discussed in Chapter 3. In practice, the AAR is sometimes computed by first calculating the ROA for each year and then averaging the results. This produces a number that is similar, but not identical, to the one we computed.

because, for every dollar we put in, we get $1.10 back. In fact, as we will see in a moment, 10 percent is the internal rate of return, or IRR, on this investment.

Is this project with its 10 percent IRR a good investment? Once again, it would seem apparent that this is a good investment only if our required return is less than 10 percent. This intuition is also correct and illustrates the *IRR rule*:

> **Based on the IRR rule, an investment is acceptable if the IRR exceeds the required return. It should be rejected otherwise.**

Imagine that we want to calculate the NPV for our simple investment. At a discount rate of R, the NPV is:

$$NPV = -\$100 + [110/(1 + R)]$$

Now, suppose we don't know the discount rate. This presents a problem, but we can still ask how high the discount rate would have to be before this project would be deemed unacceptable. We know that we are indifferent between taking and not taking this investment when its NPV is just equal to zero. In other words, this investment is *economically* a break-even proposition when the NPV is zero because value is neither created nor destroyed. To find the break-even discount rate, we set NPV equal to zero and solve for R:

$$NPV = 0 = -\$100 + [110/(1 + R)]$$
$$\$100 = \$110/(1 + R)$$
$$1 + R = \$110/\$100 = 1.1$$
$$R = .10, \text{ or } 10\%$$

This 10 percent is what we already have called the return on this investment. What we have now illustrated is that the internal rate of return on an investment (or just "return" for short) is the discount rate that makes the NPV equal to zero. This is an important observation, so it bears repeating:

> **The IRR on an investment is the required return that results in a zero NPV when it is used as the discount rate.**

The fact that the IRR is the discount rate that makes the NPV equal to zero is important because it tells us how to calculate the returns on more complicated investments. As we have seen, finding the IRR turns out to be relatively easy for a single-period investment. Suppose you were now looking at an investment with the cash flows shown in Figure 9.4. As illustrated, this investment costs $100 and has a cash flow of $60 per year for two years, so it's only slightly more complicated than our single-period example. If you were asked for the return on this investment, what would you say? There doesn't seem to be any obvious answer (at least not to us). Based on what we now know, we can set the NPV equal to zero and solve for the discount rate:

$$NPV = 0 = -\$100 + [60/(1 + IRR)] + [60/(1 + IRR)^2]$$

FIGURE 9.4

Project Cash Flows

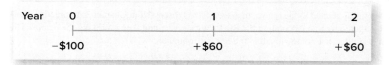

Year	0	1	2
	−$100	+$60	+$60

Discount Rate	NPV
0%	$20.00
5	11.56
10	4.13
15	− 2.46
20	− 8.33

TABLE 9.5

NPV at Different Discount Rates

Unfortunately, the only way to find the IRR in general is by trial and error, either by hand or by calculator. This is precisely the same problem that came up in Chapter 5, when we found the unknown rate for an annuity, and in Chapter 7, when we found the yield to maturity on a bond. In fact, we now see that in both of those cases, we were finding an IRR.

In this particular case, the cash flows form a two-period, $60 annuity. To find the unknown rate, we can try some different rates until we get the answer. If we were to start with a 0 percent rate, the NPV would obviously be $120 − 100 = $20. At a 10 percent discount rate, we would have:

$$NPV = -\$100 + (60/1.1) + (60/1.1^2) = \$4.13$$

Now, we're getting close. We can summarize these and some other possibilities as shown in Table 9.5. From our calculations, the NPV appears to be zero with a discount rate between 10 percent and 15 percent, so the IRR is somewhere in that range. With a little more effort, we can find that the IRR is about 13.1 percent.[6] So, if our required return were less than 13.1 percent, we would take this investment. If our required return exceeded 13.1 percent, we would reject it.

By now, you have probably noticed that the IRR rule and the NPV rule appear to be quite similar. In fact, the IRR is sometimes called the *discounted cash flow*, or *DCF*, *return*. The easiest way to illustrate the relationship between NPV and IRR is to plot the numbers we calculated for Table 9.5. We put the different NPVs on the vertical axis, or *y*-axis, and the discount rates on the horizontal axis, or *x*-axis. If we had a very large number of points, the resulting picture would be a smooth curve called a **net present value profile**. Figure 9.5 illustrates the NPV profile for this project. Beginning with a 0 percent discount

net present value profile
A graphical representation of the relationship between an investment's NPVs and various discount rates.

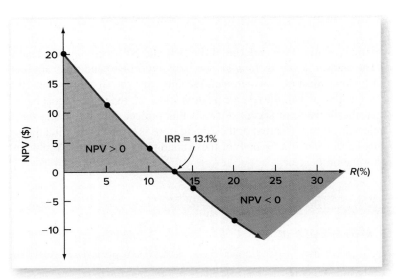

FIGURE 9.5

An NPV Profile

[6]With a lot more effort (or a personal computer), we can find that the IRR is approximately (to 9 decimal places) 13.066238629 percent—not that anybody would ever want this many decimal places!

rate, we have $20 plotted directly on the *y*-axis. As the discount rate increases, the NPV declines smoothly. Where will the curve cut through the *x*-axis? This will occur where the NPV is just equal to zero, so it will happen right at the IRR of 13.1 percent.

In our example, the NPV rule and the IRR rule lead to identical accept–reject decisions. We will accept an investment using the IRR rule if the required return is less than 13.1 percent. As Figure 9.5 illustrates, the NPV is positive at any discount rate less than 13.1 percent, so we would accept the investment using the NPV rule as well. The two rules give equivalent results in this case.

EXAMPLE 9.4   **Calculating the IRR**

A project has a total up-front cost of $435.44. The cash flows are $100 in the first year, $200 in the second year, and $300 in the third year. What's the IRR? If we require an 18 percent return, should we take this investment?

We'll describe the NPV profile and find the IRR by calculating some NPVs at different discount rates. You should check our answers for practice. Beginning with 0 percent, we have:

Discount Rate	NPV
0%	$164.56
5	100.36
10	46.15
15	.00
20	− 39.61

The NPV is zero at 15 percent, so 15 percent is the IRR. If we require an 18 percent return, then we should not take the investment. The reason is that the NPV is negative at 18 percent (verify that it is −$24.47). The IRR rule tells us the same thing in this case. We shouldn't take this investment because its 15 percent return is below our required 18 percent return.

At this point, you may be wondering if the IRR and NPV rules always lead to identical decisions. The answer is yes, as long as two very important conditions are met. First, the project's cash flows must be *conventional*, meaning that the first cash flow (the initial investment) is negative and all the rest are positive. Second, the project must be *independent*, meaning that the decision to accept or reject this project does not affect the decision to accept or reject any other. The first of these conditions is typically met, but the second often is not. In any case, when one or both of these conditions are not met, problems can arise. We discuss some of these next.

SPREADSHEET STRATEGIES

Calculating IRRs with a Spreadsheet

Because IRRs are so tedious to calculate by hand, financial calculators and especially spreadsheets are generally used. The procedures used by various financial calculators are too different for us to illustrate here, so we will focus on using a spreadsheet (financial calculators are covered in Appendix D). As the following example illustrates, using a spreadsheet is easy.

	A	B	C	D	E	F	G	H
1								
2			Using a spreadsheet to calculate internal rates of return					
3								
4	Suppose we have a four-year project that costs $500. The cash flows over the four-year life will be							
5	$100, $200, $300, and $400. What is the IRR?							
6								
7		Year	Cash Flow					
8		0	−$500					
9		1	100		IRR =	27.3%		
10		2	200					
11		3	300					
12		4	400					
13								
14								
15	The formula entered in cell F9 is =IRR(C8:C12). Notice that the Year 0 cash flow has a negative							
16	sign representing the initial cost of the project.							
17								

SOURCE: Microsoft Excel

PROBLEMS WITH THE IRR

The problems with the IRR come about when the cash flows are not conventional or when we are trying to compare two or more investments to see which is best. In the first case, surprisingly, the simple question "What's the return?" can become difficult to answer. In the second case, the IRR can be a misleading guide.

Nonconventional Cash Flows   Suppose we have a strip-mining project that requires a $60 investment. Our cash flow in the first year will be $155. In the second year, the mine will be depleted, but we will have to spend $100 to restore the terrain. As Figure 9.6 illustrates, both the first and third cash flows are negative.

To find the IRR on this project, we can calculate the NPV at various rates:

Discount Rate	NPV
0%	−$5.00
10	− 1.74
20	− .28
30	.06
40	− .31

The NPV appears to be behaving in a peculiar fashion here. First, as the discount rate increases from 0 percent to 30 percent, the NPV starts out negative and becomes positive. This seems backward because the NPV is rising as the discount rate rises. It then starts getting smaller and becomes negative again. What's the IRR? To find out, we draw the NPV profile as shown in Figure 9.7.

In Figure 9.7, notice that the NPV is zero when the discount rate is 25 percent, so this is the IRR. Or is it? The NPV is also zero at $33\frac{1}{3}$ percent. Which of these is correct? The answer is both or neither; more precisely, there is no unambiguously correct answer.

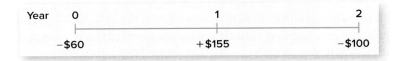

Year   0   1   2

−$60   +$155   −$100

FIGURE 9.6

Project Cash Flows

FIGURE 9.7

NPV Profile

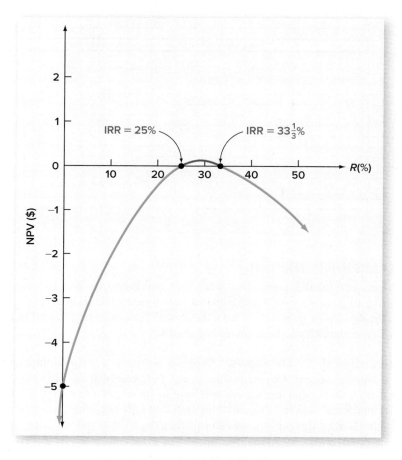

This is the **multiple rates of return** problem. Many financial computer packages (including a best seller for personal computers) aren't aware of this problem and just report the first IRR that is found. Others report only the smallest positive IRR, even though this answer is no better than any other.

In our current example, the IRR rule breaks down completely. Suppose our required return is 10 percent. Should we take this investment? Both IRRs are greater than 10 percent, so, by the IRR rule, maybe we should. As Figure 9.7 shows, the NPV is negative at any discount rate less than 25 percent, so this is not a good investment. When should we take it? Looking at Figure 9.7 one last time, we see that the NPV is positive only if our required return is between 25 percent and $33\frac{1}{3}$ percent.

Nonconventional cash flows can occur in a variety of ways. For example, Northeast Utilities, owner of the Connecticut-located Millstone nuclear power plant, had to shut down the plant's three reactors in November 1995. The reactors were expected to be back online in January 1997. By some estimates, the cost of the shutdown would run about $334 million. In fact, all nuclear plants eventually have to be shut down forever, and the costs associated with decommissioning a plant are enormous, creating large negative cash flows at the end of the project's life. The four companies in Germany that operate nuclear power plants have set aside $45 billion to decommission nuclear plants in that country.

The moral of the story is that when the cash flows aren't conventional, strange things can start to happen to the IRR. This is not anything to get upset about because the NPV rule, as always, works just fine. This illustrates the fact that, oddly enough, the obvious question—What's the rate of return?—may not always have a good answer.

What's the IRR?   EXAMPLE 9.5

You are looking at an investment that requires you to invest $51 today. You'll get $100 in one year, but you must pay out $50 in two years. What is the IRR on this investment?

You're on the alert now for the nonconventional cash flow problem, so you probably wouldn't be surprised to see more than one IRR. If you start looking for an IRR by trial and error, it will take you a long time. The reason is that there is no IRR. The NPV is negative at every discount rate, so we shouldn't take this investment under any circumstances. What's the return on this investment? Your guess is as good as ours.

"I Think; Therefore, I Know How Many IRRs There Can Be."   EXAMPLE 9.6

We've seen that it's possible to get more than one IRR. If you wanted to make sure that you had found all of the possible IRRs, how could you do it? The answer comes from the great mathematician, philosopher, and financial analyst Descartes (of "I think; therefore, I am" fame). Descartes' Rule of Sign says that the maximum number of IRRs that there can be is equal to the number of times that the cash flows change sign from positive to negative and/or negative to positive.[7]

In our example with the 25 percent and $33\frac{1}{3}$ percent IRRs, could there be yet another IRR? The cash flows flip from negative to positive, then back to negative, for a total of two sign changes. Therefore, according to Descartes' rule, the maximum number of IRRs is two, and we don't need to look for any more. Note that the actual number of IRRs can be less than the maximum (see Example 9.5).

Mutually Exclusive Investments   Even if there is a single IRR, another problem can arise concerning **mutually exclusive investment decisions**. If two investments, X and Y, are mutually exclusive, then taking one of them means that we cannot take the other. Two projects that are not mutually exclusive are said to be independent. For example, if we own one corner lot, then we can build a gas station or an apartment building, but not both. These are mutually exclusive alternatives.

mutually exclusive investment decisions
A situation in which taking one investment prevents the taking of another.

Thus far, we have asked whether a given investment is worth undertaking. A related question comes up often: Given two or more mutually exclusive investments, which one is the best? The answer is simple enough: The best one is the one with the largest NPV. Can we also say that the best one has the highest return? As we show, the answer is no.

To illustrate the problem with the IRR rule and mutually exclusive investments, consider the following cash flows from two mutually exclusive investments:

Year	Investment A	Investment B
0	−$100	−$100
1	50	20
2	40	40
3	40	50
4	30	60

[7]To be more precise, the number of IRRs that are bigger than −100 percent is equal to the number of sign changes, or it differs from the number of sign changes by an even number. Thus, for example, if there are five sign changes, there are five IRRs, three IRRs, or one IRR. If there are two sign changes, there are either two IRRs or no IRRs.

The IRR for A is 24 percent, and the IRR for B is 21 percent. Because these investments are mutually exclusive, we can take only one of them. Simple intuition suggests that Investment A is better because of its higher return. Unfortunately, simple intuition is not always correct.

To see why Investment A is not necessarily the better of the two investments, we've calculated the NPV of these investments for different required returns:

Discount Rate	NPV(A)	NPV(B)
0%	$60.00	$70.00
5	43.13	47.88
10	29.06	29.79
15	17.18	14.82
20	7.06	2.31
25	− 1.63	− 8.22

The IRR for A (24 percent) is larger than the IRR for B (21 percent). However, if you compare the NPVs, you'll see that which investment has the higher NPV depends on our required return. B has greater total cash flow, but it pays back more slowly than A. As a result, it has a higher NPV at lower discount rates.

In our example, the NPV and IRR rankings conflict for some discount rates. If our required return is 10 percent, for instance, then B has the higher NPV and is the better of the two even though A has the higher return. If our required return is 15 percent, then there is no ranking conflict: A is better.

The conflict between the IRR and NPV for mutually exclusive investments can be illustrated by plotting the investments' NPV profiles as we have done in Figure 9.8. In Figure 9.8, notice that the NPV profiles cross at about 11.1 percent. Notice also that at any discount rate less than 11.1 percent, the NPV for B is higher. In this range, taking B benefits us more than taking A, even though A's IRR is higher. At any rate greater than 11.1 percent, Investment A has the greater NPV.

FIGURE 9.8

NPV Profiles for Mutually Exclusive Investments

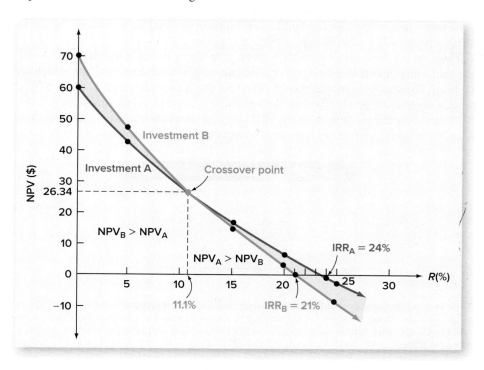

This example illustrates that when we have mutually exclusive projects, we shouldn't rank them based on their returns. More generally, anytime we are comparing investments to determine which is best, looking at IRRs can be misleading. Instead, we need to look at the relative NPVs to avoid the possibility of choosing incorrectly. Remember, we're ultimately interested in creating value for the shareholders, so the option with the higher NPV is preferred, regardless of the relative returns.

If this seems counterintuitive, think of it this way. Suppose you have two investments. One has a 10 percent return and makes you $100 richer immediately. The other has a 20 percent return and makes you $50 richer immediately. Which one do you like better? We would rather have $100 than $50, regardless of the returns, so we like the first one better.

Calculating the Crossover Rate   **EXAMPLE 9.7**

In Figure 9.8, the NPV profiles cross at about 11 percent. How can we determine just what this crossover point is? The *crossover rate*, by definition, is the discount rate that makes the NPVs of two projects equal. To illustrate, suppose we have the following two mutually exclusive investments:

Year	Investment A	Investment B
0	−$400	−$500
1	250	320
2	280	340

What's the crossover rate?

To find the crossover, first consider moving out of Investment A and into Investment B. If you make the move, you'll have to invest an extra $100 (= $500 − 400). For this $100 investment, you'll get an extra $70 (= $320 − 250) in the first year and an extra $60 (= $340 − 280) in the second year. Is this a good move? In other words, is it worth investing the extra $100?

Based on our discussion, the NPV of the switch, NPV(B − A), is:

$$\text{NPV}(B - A) = -\$100 + [70/(1 + R)] + [60/(1 + R)^2]$$

We can calculate the return on this investment by setting the NPV equal to zero and solving for the IRR:

$$\text{NPV}(B - A) = 0 = -\$100 + [70/(1 + IRR)] + [60/(1 + IRR)^2]$$

If you go through this calculation, you will find the IRR is exactly 20 percent. What this tells us is that at a 20 percent discount rate, we are indifferent between the two investments because the NPV of the difference in their cash flows is zero. As a consequence, the two investments have the same value, so this 20 percent is the crossover rate. Check to see that the NPV at 20 percent is $2.78 for both investments.

In general, you can find the crossover rate by taking the difference in the cash flows and calculating the IRR using the difference. It doesn't make any difference which one you subtract from which. To see this, find the IRR for (A − B); you'll see it's the same number. Also, for practice, you might want to find the exact crossover in Figure 9.8. (*Hint:* It's 11.0704 percent.)

Investing or Financing?   Consider the following two independent investments:

Year	Investment A	Investment B
0	−$100	$100
1	130	− 130

FIGURE 9.9   **NPV Profile for Investing and Financing Investments**

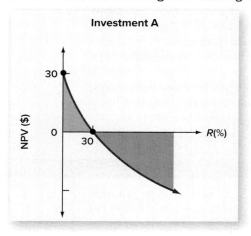
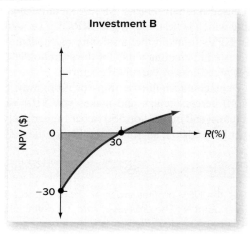

The company initially pays out cash with Investment A and initially receives cash for Investment B. While most projects are more like Investment A, projects like Investment B also occur. For example, consider a corporation conducting a seminar where the participants pay in advance. Because large expenses are frequently incurred at the seminar date, cash inflows precede cash outflows.

For these two projects, suppose the required return for each investment project is 12 percent. According to the IRR decision rule, which, if either, project should we accept? If you calculate the IRRs, you will find that they are 30 percent for both projects.

According to the IRR decision rule, we should accept both projects. However, if we calculate the NPV of B at 12 percent, we get:

$$\$100 - \frac{\$130}{1.12} = -\$16.07$$

In this case, the NPV and IRR decision rules disagree. To see what's going on, Figure 9.9 shows the NPV profile for each project. As you can see, the NPV profile for B is upward sloping. The project should be accepted if the required return is *greater* than 30 percent.

When a project has cash flows like Investment B's, the IRR is really a rate that you are paying, not receiving. For this reason, we say that the project has *financing type* cash flows, whereas Investment A has *investing type* cash flows. You should take a project with financing-type cash flows only if it is an inexpensive source of financing, meaning that its IRR is *lower* than your required return.

REDEEMING QUALITIES OF THE IRR

Despite its flaws, the IRR is very popular in practice—more so than even the NPV. It probably survives because it fills a need that the NPV does not. In analyzing investments, people in general, and financial analysts in particular, seem to prefer talking about rates of return rather than dollar values.

In a similar vein, the IRR also appears to provide a simple way of communicating information about a proposal. One manager might say to another, "Remodeling the clerical wing has a 20 percent return." This may somehow seem simpler than saying, "At a 10 percent discount rate, the net present value is $4,000."

Finally, under certain circumstances, the IRR may have a practical advantage over the NPV. We can't estimate the NPV unless we know the appropriate discount rate, but we can still estimate the IRR. Suppose we didn't know the required return on an investment, but we found, for example, that it had a 40 percent return. We would probably be inclined to take it because it would be unlikely that the required return would be that high. The advantages and disadvantages of the IRR are summarized as follows:

Advantages and Disadvantages of the Internal Rate of Return	
Advantages	**Disadvantages**
1. Closely related to NPV, often leading to identical decisions.	1. May result in multiple answers or not deal with nonconventional cash flows.
2. Easy to understand and communicate.	2. May lead to incorrect decisions in comparisons of mutually exclusive investments.

THE MODIFIED INTERNAL RATE OF RETURN (MIRR)

To address some of the problems that can crop up with the standard IRR, it is often proposed that a modified version be used. As we will see, there are several different ways of calculating a modified IRR, or MIRR, but the basic idea is to modify the cash flows first and then calculate an IRR using the modified cash flows.

To illustrate, let's go back to the cash flows in Figure 9.6: −$60, +$155, and −$100. As we saw, there are two IRRs, 25 percent and $33\frac{1}{3}$ percent. We next illustrate three different MIRRs, all of which have the property that only one answer will result, thereby eliminating the multiple IRR problem.

Method #1: The Discounting Approach   With the discounting approach, the idea is to discount all negative cash flows back to the present at the required return and add them to the initial cost. Then, calculate the IRR. Because only the first modified cash flow is negative, there will be only one IRR. The discount rate used might be the required return, or it might be some other externally supplied rate. We will use the project's required return.

If the required return on the project is 20 percent, then the modified cash flows look like this:

Time 0: $-\$60 + \dfrac{-\$100}{1.20^2} = -\$129.44$

Time 1:   +$155

Time 2:   +$0

If you calculate the MIRR now, you should get 19.74 percent.

Method #2: The Reinvestment Approach   With the reinvestment approach, we compound *all* cash flows (positive and negative) except the first out to the end of the project's life and then calculate the IRR. In a sense, we are "reinvesting" the cash flows and not taking them out of the project until the very end. The rate we use could be the required return on the project, or it could be a separately specified "reinvestment rate." We will use the project's required return. When we do, here are the modified cash flows:

Time 0:   −$60

Time 1:   +0

Time 2: $-\$100 + (\$155 \times 1.2) = \$86$

The MIRR on this set of cash flows is 19.72 percent, or a little lower than we got using the discounting approach.

Method #3: The Combination Approach   As the name suggests, the combination approach blends our first two methods. Negative cash flows are discounted back to the present, and positive cash flows are compounded to the end of the project. In practice, different discount or compounding rates might be used, but we will again stick with the project's required return.

With the combination approach, the modified cash flows are as follows:

Time 0: $-\$60 + \dfrac{-\$100}{1.20^2} = -\$129.44$

Time 1: $+0$

Time 2: $\$155 \times 1.2 = \$186$

See if you don't agree that the MIRR is 19.87 percent, the highest of the three.

MIRR or IRR: Which Is Better?   MIRRs are controversial. At one extreme are those who claim that MIRRs are superior to IRRs, period. For example, by design, they clearly don't suffer from the multiple rate of return problem.

At the other end, detractors say that MIRR should stand for "meaningless internal rate of return." As our example makes clear, one problem with MIRRs is that there are different ways of calculating them, and there is no clear reason to say one of our three methods is better than any other. The differences are small with our simple cash flows, but they could be much larger for a more complex project. Further, it's not clear how to interpret an MIRR. It may look like a rate of return, but it's a rate of return on a modified set of cash flows, not the project's actual cash flows.

We're not going to take sides. However, notice that calculating an MIRR requires discounting, compounding, or both, which leads to two obvious observations. First, if we have the relevant discount rate, why not calculate the NPV and be done with it? Second, because an MIRR depends on an externally supplied discount (or compounding) rate, the answer you get is not truly an "internal" rate of return, which, by definition, depends on only the project's cash flows.

We *will* take a stand on one issue that frequently comes up in this context. The value of a project does not depend on what the firm does with the cash flows generated by that project. A firm might use a project's cash flows to fund other projects, to pay dividends, or to buy an executive jet. It doesn't matter: How the cash flows are spent in the future does not affect their value today. As a result, there is generally no need to consider reinvestment of interim cash flows.

Concept Questions

9.5a   Under what circumstances will the IRR and NPV rules lead to the same accept-reject decisions? When might they conflict?

9.5b   Is it generally true that an advantage of the IRR rule over the NPV rule is that we don't need to know the required return to use the IRR rule?

9.6 The Profitability Index

Another tool used to evaluate projects is called the **profitability index (PI)** or benefit-cost ratio. This index is defined as the present value of the future cash flows divided by the initial investment. So, if a project costs $200 and the present value of its future cash flows is $220, the profitability index value would be $220/$200 = 1.1. Notice that the NPV for this investment is $20, so it is a desirable investment.

More generally, if a project has a positive NPV, then the present value of the future cash flows must be bigger than the initial investment. The profitability index will be bigger than 1 for a positive NPV investment and less than 1 for a negative NPV investment.

How do we interpret the profitability index? In our example, the PI was 1.1. This tells us that, per dollar invested, $1.10 in value or $.10 in NPV results. The profitability index measures "bang for the buck"—that is, the value created per dollar invested. For this reason, it is often proposed as a measure of performance for government or other not-for-profit investments. Also, when capital is scarce, it may make sense to allocate it to projects with the highest PIs. We will return to this issue in a later chapter.

The PI is obviously similar to the NPV. However, consider an investment that costs $5 and has a $10 present value and an investment that costs $100 with a $150 present value. The first of these investments has an NPV of $5 and a PI of 2. The second has an NPV of $50 and a PI of 1.5. If these are mutually exclusive investments, then the second one is preferred even though it has a lower PI. This ranking problem is similar to the IRR ranking problem we saw in the previous section. In all, there seems to be little reason to rely on the PI instead of the NPV. Our discussion of the PI is summarized as follows:

profitability index (PI)
The present value of an investment's future cash flows divided by its initial cost. Also called the benefit-cost ratio.

Advantages and Disadvantages of the Profitability Index	
Advantages	**Disadvantages**
1. Closely related to NPV, generally leading to identical decisions.	1. May lead to incorrect decisions in comparisons of mutually exclusive investments.
2. Easy to understand and communicate.	
3. May be useful when available investment funds are limited.	

Concept Questions

9.6a What does the profitability index measure?

9.6b How would you state the profitability index rule?

The Practice of Capital Budgeting   9.7

Given that NPV seems to be telling us directly what we want to know, you might be wondering why there are so many other procedures and why alternative procedures are commonly used. Recall that we are trying to make an investment decision and that we are frequently operating under considerable uncertainty about the future. We can only *estimate* the NPV of an investment in this case. The resulting estimate can be very "soft," meaning that the true NPV might be quite different.

Because the true NPV is unknown, the astute financial manager seeks clues to help in assessing whether the estimated NPV is reliable. For this reason, firms would typically use multiple criteria for evaluating a proposal. For example, suppose we have an investment with a positive estimated NPV. Based on our experience with other projects, this one appears to have a short payback and a very high AAR. In this case, the different indicators seem to agree that it's "all systems go." Put another way, the payback and the AAR are consistent with the conclusion that the NPV is positive.

On the other hand, suppose we had a positive estimated NPV, a long payback, and a low AAR. This could still be a good investment, but it looks like we need to be much more careful in making the decision because we are getting conflicting signals. If the estimated

NPV is based on projections in which we have little confidence, then further analysis is probably in order. We will consider how to evaluate NPV estimates in more detail in the next two chapters.

Large firms often have huge capital budgets. For example, for 2017, ExxonMobil announced that it expected to have about $22 billion in capital outlays during the year, down from its record $42.5 billion in 2013. About the same time, competitor Chevron announced that it would decrease its capital budgeting for 2017 to $19.8 billion, down from $26.6 billion in 2016. Other companies with large capital spending budgets included Walmart, which projected capital spending of about $11 billion for 2017, and Apple, which projected capital spending of about $16 billion for 2017.

According to information released by the Census Bureau in 2017, capital investment for the economy as a whole was $1.401 trillion in 2013, $1.507 trillion in 2014, and $1.545 trillion in 2015. The total for the three years therefore exceeded $4.4 trillion! Given the sums at stake, it is not too surprising that careful analysis of capital expenditures is something at which successful businesses seek to become adept.

There have been a number of surveys conducted asking firms what types of investment criteria they actually use. Table 9.6 summarizes the results of several of these. Panel A of the table is a historical comparison looking at the primary capital budgeting techniques used by large firms through time. In 1959, only 19 percent of the firms surveyed used either IRR or NPV, and 68 percent used either payback periods or accounting returns. It is clear that by the 1980s, IRR and NPV had become the dominant criteria.

Panel B of Table 9.6 summarizes the results of a 1999 survey of chief financial officers (CFOs) at both large and small firms in the United States. A total of 392 CFOs responded. What is shown is the percentage of CFOs who always or almost always used

TABLE 9.6   Capital Budgeting Techniques in Practice

A. Historical Comparison of the Primary Use of Various Capital Budgeting Techniques							
	1959	1964	1970	1975	1977	1979	1981
Payback period	34%	24%	12%	15%	9%	10%	5%
Average accounting return (AAR)	34	30	26	10	25	14	11
Internal rate of return (IRR)	19	38	57	37	54	60	65
Net present value (NPV)	—	—	—	26	10	14	17
IRR or NPV	19	38	57	63	64	74	82

B. Percentage of CFOs Who Always or Almost Always Used a Given Technique in 1999				
Capital Budgeting Technique	Percentage Always or Almost Always Using	Average Score [Scale is 4 (always) to 0 (never)]		
		Overall	Large Firms	Small Firms
Internal rate of return	76%	3.09	3.41	2.87
Net present value	75	3.08	3.42	2.83
Payback period	57	2.53	2.25	2.72
Discounted payback period	29	1.56	1.55	1.58
Accounting rate of return	20	1.34	1.25	1.41
Profitability index	12	.83	.75	.88

SOURCES: Graham, J. R., and Harvey, C. R., "The Theory and Practice of Corporate Finance: Evidence from the Field," Journal of Financial Economics, May–June 2001, 187–243; Moore, J. S, and Reichert, A. K., "An Analysis of the Financial Management Techniques Currently Employed by Large U.S. Corporations," Journal of Business Finance and Accounting, Winter 1983, 623–45; and Stanley, M. T., and Block, S. R., "A Survey of Multinational Capital Budgeting," The Financial Review, March 1984, 36–51.

the various capital budgeting techniques we describe in this chapter. Not surprisingly, IRR and NPV were the two most widely used techniques, particularly at larger firms. However, over half of the respondents always, or almost always, used the payback criterion as well. In fact, among smaller firms, payback was used just about as much as NPV and IRR. Less commonly used were discounted payback, accounting rates of return, and the profitability index. For future reference, the various criteria we have discussed are summarized in Table 9.7.

TABLE 9.7

Summary of Investment Criteria

I.   Discounted Cash Flow Criteria
A. *Net present value (NPV)*: The NPV of an investment is the difference between its market value and its cost. The NPV rule is to take a project if its NPV is positive. NPV is frequently estimated by calculating the present value of the future cash flows (to estimate market value) and then subtracting the cost. NPV has no serious flaws; it is the preferred decision criterion.
B. *Internal rate of return (IRR)*: The IRR is the discount rate that makes the estimated NPV of an investment equal to zero; it is sometimes called the *discounted cash flow (DCF) return*. The IRR rule is to take a project when its IRR exceeds the required return. IRR is closely related to NPV, and it leads to exactly the same decisions as NPV for conventional, independent projects. When project cash flows are not conventional, there may be no IRR or there may be more than one. More seriously, the IRR cannot be used to rank mutually exclusive projects; the project with the highest IRR is not necessarily the preferred investment.
C. *Modified internal rate of return (MIRR)*: The MIRR is a modification to the IRR. A project's cash flows are modified by (1) discounting the negative cash flows back to the present; (2) compounding cash flows to the end of the project's life; or (3) combining (1) and (2). An IRR is then computed on the modified cash flows. MIRRs are guaranteed to avoid the multiple rate of return problem, but it is unclear how to interpret them; and they are not truly "internal" because they depend on externally supplied discounting or compounding rates.
D. *Profitability index (PI)*: The PI, also called the *benefit-cost ratio*, is the ratio of present value to cost. The PI rule is to take an investment if the index exceeds 1. The PI measures the present value of an investment per dollar invested. It is quite similar to NPV; but, like IRR, it cannot be used to rank mutually exclusive projects. However, it is sometimes used to rank projects when a firm has more positive NPV investments than it can currently finance.
II.
A. *Payback period*: The payback period is the length of time until the sum of an investment's cash flows equals its cost. The payback period rule is to take a project if its payback is less than some cutoff. The payback period is a flawed criterion, primarily because it ignores risk, the time value of money, and cash flows beyond the cutoff point.
B. *Discounted payback period*: The discounted payback period is the length of time until the sum of an investment's discounted cash flows equals its cost. The discounted payback period rule is to take an investment if the discounted payback is less than some cutoff. The discounted payback rule is flawed, primarily because it ignores cash flows after the cutoff.
III.
A. *Average accounting return (AAR)*: The AAR is a measure of accounting profit relative to book value. It is not related to the IRR, but it is similar to the accounting return on assets (ROA) measure in Chapter 3. The AAR rule is to take an investment if its AAR exceeds a benchmark AAR. The AAR is seriously flawed for a variety of reasons, and it has little to recommend it.

Concept Questions

9.7a   What are the most commonly used capital budgeting procedures?

9.7b   If NPV is conceptually the best procedure for capital budgeting, why do you think multiple measures are used in practice?

9.8 Summary and Conclusions

This chapter has covered the different criteria used to evaluate proposed investments. The seven criteria, in the order we discussed them, are these:

1. Net present value (NPV).
2. Payback period.
3. Discounted payback period.
4. Average accounting return (AAR).
5. Internal rate of return (IRR).
6. Modified internal rate of return (MIRR).
7. Profitability index (PI).

We illustrated how to calculate each of these and discussed the interpretation of the results. We also described the advantages and disadvantages of each of them. Ultimately a good capital budgeting criterion must tell us two things. First, is a particular project a good investment? Second, if we have more than one good project, but we can take only one of them, which one should we take? The main point of this chapter is that only the NPV criterion can always provide the correct answer to both questions.

For this reason, NPV is one of the two or three most important concepts in finance, and we will refer to it many times in the chapters ahead. When we do, keep two things in mind: (1) NPV is always the difference between the market value of an asset or project and its cost and (2) the financial manager acts in the shareholders' best interests by identifying and taking positive NPV projects.

Finally, we noted that NPVs can't normally be observed in the market; instead, they must be estimated. Because there is always the possibility of a poor estimate, financial managers use multiple criteria for examining projects. The other criteria provide additional information about whether a project truly has a positive NPV.

CONNECT TO FINANCE

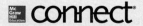 If you are using *Connect Finance* in your course, get online to take a Practice Test, check out study tools, and find out where you need additional practice.

Can you answer the following *Connect* Quiz questions?

Section 9.1   The net present value rule states that you should accept a project if its net present value _____.

Section 9.2   A drawback of the payback method of project analysis is _____.

Section 9.3   The discounted payback period for a project will be _____ the payback period for the project given a positive, nonzero discount rate.

Section 9.4   What is an advantage of the average accounting return method of project analysis?

Section 9.6   What is a benefit-cost ratio?

Section 9.7   What method of analysis tends to be least utilized by CFOs, according to the survey conducted in 1999 as presented in your textbook?

CHAPTER REVIEW AND SELF-TEST PROBLEMS

9.1   Investment Criteria This problem will give you some practice calculating NPVs and paybacks. A proposed overseas expansion has the following cash flows:

Year	Cash Flow
0	−$200
1	50
2	60
3	70
4	200

Calculate the payback, the discounted payback, and the NPV at a required return of 10 percent.

9.2   Mutually Exclusive Investments Consider the following two mutually exclusive investments. Calculate the IRR for each and the crossover rate. Under what circumstances will the IRR and NPV criteria rank the two projects differently?

Year	Investment A	Investment B
0	−$75	−$75
1	20	60
2	40	50
3	70	15

9.3   Average Accounting Return You are looking at a three-year project with a projected net income of $2,000 in Year 1, $4,000 in Year 2, and $6,000 in Year 3. The cost is $12,000, which will be depreciated straight-line to zero over the three-year life of the project. What is the average accounting return (AAR)?

ANSWERS TO CHAPTER REVIEW AND SELF-TEST PROBLEMS

9.1   In the following table, we have listed the cash flow, cumulative cash flow, discounted cash flow (at 10 percent), and cumulative discounted cash flow for the proposed project.

	Cash Flow		Accumulated Cash Flow	
Year	Undiscounted	Discounted	Undiscounted	Discounted
1	$ 50	$ 45.45	$ 50	$ 45.45
2	60	49.59	110	95.04
3	70	52.59	180	147.63
4	200	136.60	380	284.24

Recall that the initial investment was $200. When we compare this to accumulated undiscounted cash flows, we see that payback occurs between Years 3 and 4. The cash flows for the first three years are $180 total, so, going into the fourth year, we are short by $20. The total cash flow in Year 4 is $200, so the payback is 3 + ($20/200) = 3.10 years.

Looking at the accumulated discounted cash flows, we see that the discounted payback occurs between Years 3 and 4. The sum of the discounted cash flows is $284.24, so the NPV is $84.24. Notice that this is the present value of the cash flows that occur after the discounted payback.

9.2 To calculate the IRR, we might try some guesses, as in the following table:

Discount Rate	NPV(A)	NPV(B)
0%	$55.00	$50.00
10	28.83	32.14
20	9.95	18.40
30	− 4.09	7.57
40	− 14.80	− 1.17

Several things are immediately apparent from our guesses. First, the IRR for A must be between 20 percent and 30 percent (why?). With some more effort, we find that it's 26.79 percent. For B, the IRR must be a little less than 40 percent (again, why?); it works out to be 38.54 percent. Also, notice that at rates between 0 percent and 10 percent, the NPVs are very close, indicating that the crossover is in that vicinity.

To find the crossover exactly, we can compute the IRR on the difference in the cash flows. If we take the cash flows from A minus the cash flows from B, the resulting cash flows are:

Year	A − B
0	$ 0
1	− 40
2	− 10
3	55

These cash flows look a little odd; but the sign changes only once, so we can find an IRR. With some trial and error, you'll see that the NPV is zero at a discount rate of 5.42 percent, so this is the crossover rate.

The IRR for B is higher. However, as we've seen, A has the larger NPV for any discount rate less than 5.42 percent, so the NPV and IRR rankings will conflict in that range. Remember, if there's a conflict, we will go with the higher NPV. Our decision rule is thus simple: Take A if the required return is less than 5.42 percent, take B if the required return is between 5.42 percent and 38.54 percent (the IRR on B), and take neither if the required return is more than 38.54 percent.

9.3   Here we need to calculate the ratio of average net income to average book value to get the AAR. Average net income is:

Average net income = ($2,000 + 4,000 + 6,000)/3 = $4,000

Average book value is:

Average book value = $12,000/2 = $6,000

So the average accounting return is:

AAR = $4,000/6,000 = .6667, or 66.67%

This is an impressive return. Remember, however, that it isn't really a rate of return like an interest rate or an IRR, so the size doesn't tell us a lot. In particular, our money is probably not going to grow at a rate of 66.67 percent per year, sorry to say.

CONCEPTS REVIEW AND CRITICAL THINKING QUESTIONS

1. **Payback Period and Net Present Value [LO1, 2]** If a project with conventional cash flows has a payback period less than the project's life, can you definitively state the algebraic sign of the NPV? Why or why not? If you know that the discounted payback period is less than the project's life, what can you say about the NPV? Explain.

2. **Net Present Value [LO1]** Suppose a project has conventional cash flows and a positive NPV. What do you know about its payback? Its discounted payback? Its profitability index? Its IRR? Explain.

3. **Payback Period [LO2]** Concerning payback:
   a. Describe how the payback period is calculated, and describe the information this measure provides about a sequence of cash flows. What is the payback criterion decision rule?
   b. What are the problems associated with using the payback period to evaluate cash flows?
   c. What are the advantages of using the payback period to evaluate cash flows? Are there any circumstances under which using payback might be appropriate? Explain.

4. **Discounted Payback [LO3]** Concerning discounted payback:
   a. Describe how the discounted payback period is calculated, and describe the information this measure provides about a sequence of cash flows. What is the discounted payback criterion decision rule?
   b. What are the problems associated with using the discounted payback period to evaluate cash flows?
   c. What conceptual advantage does the discounted payback method have over the regular payback method? Can the discounted payback ever be longer than the regular payback? Explain.

5. **Average Accounting Return [LO4]** Concerning AAR:
   a. Describe how the average accounting return is usually calculated, and describe the information this measure provides about a sequence of cash flows. What is the AAR criterion decision rule?
   b. What are the problems associated with using the AAR to evaluate a project's cash flows? What underlying feature of AAR is most troubling to you from a financial perspective? Does the AAR have any redeeming qualities?

6. **Net Present Value** [LO1] Concerning NPV:

   a. Describe how NPV is calculated, and describe the information this measure provides about a sequence of cash flows. What is the NPV criterion decision rule?

   b. Why is NPV considered a superior method of evaluating the cash flows from a project? Suppose the NPV for a project's cash flows is computed to be $2,500. What does this number represent with respect to the firm's shareholders?

7. **Internal Rate of Return** [LO5] Concerning IRR:

   a. Describe how the IRR is calculated, and describe the information this measure provides about a sequence of cash flows. What is the IRR criterion decision rule?

   b. What is the relationship between IRR and NPV? Are there any situations in which you might prefer one method over the other? Explain.

   c. Despite its shortcomings in some situations, why do most financial managers use IRR along with NPV when evaluating projects? Can you think of a situation in which IRR might be a more appropriate measure to use than NPV? Explain.

8. **Profitability Index** [LO7] Concerning the profitability index:

   a. Describe how the profitability index is calculated, and describe the information this measure provides about a sequence of cash flows. What is the profitability index decision rule?

   b. What is the relationship between the profitability index and NPV? Are there any situations in which you might prefer one method over the other? Explain.

9. **Payback and Internal Rate of Return** [LO2, 5] A project has perpetual cash flows of *C* per period, a cost of *I*, and a required return of *R*. What is the relationship between the project's payback and its IRR? What implications does your answer have for long-lived projects with relatively constant cash flows?

10. **International Investment Projects** [LO1] In 2016, automobile manufacturer BMW completed its $1 billion investment to increase production at its South Carolina plant by 50 percent. BMW apparently felt that it would be better able to compete and create value with U.S-based facilities. Other companies such as Fuji Film and Swiss chemical company Lonza have reached similar conclusions and taken similar actions. What are some of the reasons that foreign manufacturers of products as diverse as automobiles, film, and chemicals might arrive at this same conclusion?

11. **Capital Budgeting Problems** [LO1] What difficulties might come up in actual applications of the various criteria we discussed in this chapter? Which one would be the easiest to implement in actual applications? The most difficult?

12. **Capital Budgeting in Not-for-Profit Entities** [LO1] Are the capital budgeting criteria we discussed applicable to not-for-profit corporations? How should such entities make capital budgeting decisions? What about the U.S. government? Should it evaluate spending proposals using these techniques?

13. **Modified Internal Rate of Return** [LO6] One of the less flattering interpretations of the acronym MIRR is "meaningless internal rate of return." Why do you think this term is applied to MIRR?

14. **Net Present Value** [LO1] It is sometimes stated that "the net present value approach assumes reinvestment of the intermediate cash flows at the required return." Is this claim correct? To answer, suppose you calculate the NPV of a project in the usual way. Next, suppose you do the following:

   a. Calculate the future value (as of the end of the project) of all the cash flows other than the initial outlay assuming they are reinvested at the required return, producing a single future value figure for the project.

b. Calculate the NPV of the project using the single future value calculated in the previous step and the initial outlay. It is easy to verify that you will get the same NPV as in your original calculation only if you use the required return as the reinvestment rate in the previous step.

15. **Internal Rate of Return [LO5]** It is sometimes stated that "the internal rate of return approach assumes reinvestment of the intermediate cash flows at the internal rate of return." Is this claim correct? To answer, suppose you calculate the IRR of a project in the usual way. Next, suppose you do the following:

a. Calculate the future value (as of the end of the project) of all the cash flows other than the initial outlay assuming they are reinvested at the IRR, producing a single future value figure for the project.

b. Calculate the IRR of the project using the single future value calculated in the previous step and the initial outlay. It is easy to verify that you will get the same IRR as in your original calculation only if you use the IRR as the reinvestment rate in the previous step.

QUESTIONS AND PROBLEMS

1. **Calculating Payback [LO2]** What is the payback period for the following set of cash flows?

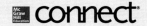

BASIC

(Questions 1–19)

Year	Cash Flow
0	−$8,300
1	2,100
2	3,000
3	2,300
4	1,700

2. **Calculating Payback [LO2]** An investment project provides cash inflows of $745 per year for eight years. What is the project payback period if the initial cost is $1,700? What if the initial cost is $3,300? What if it is $6,100?

3. **Calculating Payback [LO2]** Bronco, Inc., imposes a payback cutoff of three years for its international investment projects. If the company has the following two projects available, should it accept either of them?

Year	Cash Flow (A)	Cash Flow (B)
0	−$35,000	−$ 45,000
1	12,000	11,000
2	17,000	13,000
3	14,000	16,000
4	9,000	255,000

4. **Calculating Discounted Payback [LO3]** An investment project has annual cash inflows of $2,800, $3,700, $5,100, and $4,300, for the next four years, respectively. The discount rate is 11 percent. What is the discounted payback period for these cash flows if the initial cost is $5,200? What if the initial cost is $6,400? What if it is $10,400?

5. **Calculating Discounted Payback [LO3]** An investment project costs $17,000 and has annual cash flows of $4,700 for six years. What is the discounted payback period if the discount rate is zero percent? What if the discount rate is 5 percent? If it is 19 percent?

6. Calculating AAR [LO4] You're trying to determine whether to expand your business by building a new manufacturing plant. The plant has an installation cost of $13.5 million, which will be depreciated straight-line to zero over its four-year life. If the plant has projected net income of $1,570,000, $1,684,200, $1,716,300, and $1,097,400 over these four years, respectively, what is the project's average accounting return (AAR)?

7. Calculating IRR [LO5] A firm evaluates all of its projects by applying the IRR rule. If the required return is 14 percent, should the firm accept the following project?

Year	Cash Flow
0	−$34,000
1	15,000
2	17,000
3	13,000

8. Calculating NPV [LO1] For the cash flows in the previous problem, suppose the firm uses the NPV decision rule. At a required return of 11 percent, should the firm accept this project? What if the required return is 24 percent?

9. Calculating NPV and IRR [LO1, 5] A project that provides annual cash flows of $11,700 for nine years costs $63,000 today. Is this a good project if the required return is 8 percent? What if it's 20 percent? At what discount rate would you be indifferent between accepting the project and rejecting it?

10. Calculating IRR [LO5] What is the IRR of the following set of cash flows?

Year	Cash Flow
0	−$15,400
1	7,300
2	9,100
3	5,900

11. Calculating NPV [LO1] For the cash flows in the previous problem, what is the NPV at a discount rate of zero percent? What if the discount rate is 10 percent? If it is 20 percent? If it is 30 percent?

12. NPV versus IRR [LO1, 5] Bruin, Inc., has identified the following two mutually exclusive projects:

Year	Cash Flow (A)	Cash Flow (B)
0	−$37,500	−$37,500
1	17,300	5,700
2	16,200	12,900
3	13,800	16,300
4	7,600	27,500

a. What is the IRR for each of these projects? Using the IRR decision rule, which project should the company accept? Is this decision necessarily correct?

b. If the required return is 11 percent, what is the NPV for each of these projects? Which project will the company choose if it applies the NPV decision rule?

c. Over what range of discount rates would the company choose Project A? Project B? At what discount rate would the company be indifferent between these two projects? Explain.

13. **NPV versus IRR [LO1, 5]** Consider the following two mutually exclusive projects:

Year	Cash Flow (X)	Cash Flow (Y)
0	−$23,000	−$23,000
1	10,490	12,000
2	10,900	9,360
3	10,500	10,400

Sketch the NPV profiles for X and Y over a range of discount rates from zero to 25 percent. What is the crossover rate for these two projects?

14. **Problems with IRR [LO5]** Light Sweet Petroleum, Inc., is trying to evaluate a generation project with the following cash flows:

Year	Cash Flow
0	−$48,000,000
1	71,000,000
2	− 13,000,000

a. If the company requires a return of 12 percent on its investments, should it accept this project? Why?

b. Compute the IRR for this project. How many IRRs are there? Using the IRR decision rule, should the company accept the project? What's going on here?

15. **Calculating Profitability Index [LO7]** What is the profitability index for the following set of cash flows if the relevant discount rate is 10 percent? What if the discount rate is 15 percent? If it is 22 percent?

Year	Cash Flow
0	−$16,700
1	9,700
2	7,800
3	4,300

16. **Problems with Profitability Index [LO1, 7]** The Sloan Corporation is trying to choose between the following two mutually exclusive design projects:

Year	Cash Flow (I)	Cash Flow (II)
0	−$63,000	−$15,500
1	28,900	7,900
2	28,900	7,900
3	28,900	7,900

a. If the required return is 10 percent and the company applies the profitability index decision rule, which project should the firm accept?

b. If the company applies the NPV decision rule, which project should it take?

c. Explain why your answers in (a) and (b) are different.

17. **Comparing Investment Criteria** [LO1, 2, 3, 5, 7] Consider the following two mutually exclusive projects:

Year	Cash Flow (A)	Cash Flow (B)
0	−$364,000	−$52,000
1	46,000	25,000
2	68,000	22,000
3	68,000	21,500
4	458,000	17,500

Whichever project you choose, if any, you require a return of 11 percent on your investment.

a. If you apply the payback criterion, which investment will you choose? Why?

b. If you apply the discounted payback criterion, which investment will you choose? Why?

c. If you apply the NPV criterion, which investment will you choose? Why?

d. If you apply the IRR criterion, which investment will you choose? Why?

e. If you apply the profitability index criterion, which investment will you choose? Why?

f. Based on your answers in (a) through (e), which project will you finally choose? Why?

18. **NPV and Discount Rates** [LO1] An investment has an installed cost of $527,630. The cash flows over the four-year life of the investment are projected to be $212,200, $243,800, $203,500, and $167,410, respectively. If the discount rate is zero, what is the NPV? If the discount rate is infinite, what is the NPV? At what discount rate is the NPV just equal to zero? Sketch the NPV profile for this investment based on these three points.

19. **MIRR** [LO6] Solo Corp. is evaluating a project with the following cash flows:

Year	Cash Flow
0	−$47,000
1	16,900
2	20,300
3	25,800
4	19,600
5	− 9,500

The company uses an interest rate of 10 percent on all of its projects. Calculate the MIRR of the project using all three methods.

20. **MIRR** [LO6] Suppose the company in the previous problem uses a discount rate of 11 percent and a reinvestment rate of 8 percent on all of its projects. Calculate the MIRR of the project using all three methods using these interest rates.

21. **NPV and the Profitability Index** [LO1, 7] If we define the NPV index as the ratio of NPV to cost, what is the relationship between this index and the profitability index?

22. **Cash Flow Intuition** [LO1, 2] A project has an initial cost of I, a required return of R, and pays C annually for N years.

a. Find C in terms of I and N such that the project has a payback period just equal to its life.

b. Find C in terms of I, N, and R such that this is a profitable project according to the NPV decision rule.

c. Find C in terms of I, N, and R such that the project has a benefit-cost ratio of 2.

23. **Payback and NPV [LO1, 2]** An investment under consideration has a payback of seven years and a cost of $685,000. If the required return is 11 percent, what is the worst-case NPV? The best-case NPV? Explain. Assume the cash flows are conventional.

CHALLENGE
(Questions 23–28)

24. **Multiple IRRs [LO5]** This problem is useful for testing the ability of financial calculators and spreadsheets. Consider the following cash flows. How many different IRRs are there? (*Hint*: Search between 20 percent and 70 percent.) When should we take this project?

Year	Cash Flow
0	−$ 3,024
1	17,172
2	− 36,420
3	34,200
4	− 12,000

25. **NPV Valuation [LO1]** The Yurdone Corporation wants to set up a private ceme-tery business. According to the CFO, Barry M. Deep, business is "looking up." As a result, the cemetery project will provide a net cash inflow of $145,000 for the firm during the first year, and the cash flows are projected to grow at a rate of 4 percent per year forever. The project requires an initial investment of $1,900,000.

a. If the company requires an 11 percent return on such undertakings, should the cemetery business be started?

b. The company is somewhat unsure about the assumption of a growth rate of 4 per-cent in its cash flows. At what constant growth rate would the company just break even if it still required a return of 11 percent on investment?

26. **Problems with IRR [LO5]** A project has the following cash flows:

Year	Cash Flow
0	$59,000
1	− 34,000
2	− 39,000

What is the IRR for this project? If the required return is 12 percent, should the firm accept the project? What is the NPV of this project? What is the NPV of the project if the required return is 0 percent? 24 percent? What is going on here? Sketch the NPV profile to help you with your answer.

27. **Problems with IRR [LO5]** McKeekin Corp. has a project with the following cash flows:

Year	Cash Flow
0	$25,000
1	− 11,000
2	7,000

What is the IRR of the project? What is happening here?

28. **NPV and IRR** [LO1, 5] Anderson International Limited is evaluating a project in Erewhon. The project will create the following cash flows:

Year	Cash Flow
0	−$1,275,000
1	435,000
2	505,000
3	415,000
4	345,000

All cash flows will occur in Erewhon and are expressed in dollars. In an attempt to improve its economy, the Erewhonian government has declared that all cash flows created by a foreign company are "blocked" and must be reinvested with the government for one year. The reinvestment rate for these funds is 4 percent. If Anderson uses a required return of 11 percent on this project, what are the NPV and IRR of the project? Is the IRR you calculated the MIRR of the project? Why or why not?

EXCEL MASTER IT! PROBLEM

As you have already seen, Excel does not have a function to calculate the payback period, so you will create your own. Below, the cash flows for a project are shown. You need to calculate the payback period using two different methods.

a. Calculate the payback period in a table. The first three columns of the table will be the year, the cash flow for that year, and the cumulative cash flow. The fourth column will show the whole year for the payback. In other words, if the payback period is three-plus years, this column will have a 3, otherwise it will be a 0. The next column will calculate the fractional part of the payback period, or else it will display 0. The last column will add the previous two columns and display the final payback period calculation. You should also have a cell that displays the final payback period by itself and a cell that returns the correct accept or reject decision based on the payback criteria.

b. Write a nested IF statement that calculates the payback period using only the project cash flow column. The IF statement should return a value of "Never" if the project has no payback period. In contrast to the example we showed previously, the nested IF function should test for the payback period starting with shorter payback periods and working toward longer payback periods. Another cell should display the correct accept or reject decision based on the payback criteria.

t	Cash Flow
0	−$250,000
1	41,000
2	48,000
3	63,000
4	79,000
5	88,000
6	64,000
7	41,000
Required payback:	5

MINICASE

Bullock Gold Mining

Seth Bullock, the owner of Bullock Gold Mining, is evaluating a new gold mine in South Dakota. Dan Dority, the company's geologist, has just finished his analysis of the mine site. He has estimated that the mine would be productive for eight years, after which the gold would be completely mined. Dan has taken an estimate of the gold deposits to Alma Garrett, the company's financial officer. Alma has been asked by Seth to perform an analysis of the new mine and present her recommendation on whether the company should open the new mine.

Alma has used the estimates provided by Dan to determine the revenues that could be expected from the mine. She has also projected the expense of opening the mine and the annual operating expenses. If the company opens the mine, it will cost $635 million today, and it will have a cash outflow of $45 million nine years from today in costs associated with closing the mine and reclaiming the area surrounding it. The expected cash flows each year from the mine are shown in the table. Bullock Mining has a required return of 12 percent on all of its gold mines.

Year	Cash Flow
0	−$635,000,000
1	89,000,000
2	105,000,000
3	130,000,000
4	173,000,000
5	205,000,000
6	155,000,000
7	145,000,000
8	122,000,000
9	− 45,000,000

QUESTIONS

1. Construct a spreadsheet to calculate the payback period, internal rate of return, modified internal rate of return, and net present value of the proposed mine.

2. Based on your analysis, should the company open the mine?

3. Bonus question: Most spreadsheets do not have a built-in formula to calculate the payback period. Write a VBA script that calculates the payback period for a project.

10 | Making Capital Investment Decisions

IS THERE GREEN IN GREEN? General Electric (GE) thinks so. Through its "Ecomagination" program, the company planned to double research and development spending on green products. By 2015, GE had invested over $13 billion in its Ecomagination program, and currently about one-half of the company's R&D budget is spent on green projects. As an example, GE's Evolution® Series Locomotive required over $600 million in development, but it allows railroads to move one ton of freight more than 480 miles with a single gallon of fuel. GE's green initiative seems to be paying off. Revenue from green products has totaled more than $230 billion since its launch in 2005, with $36 billion in 2015 alone. Even further, revenues from Ecomagination products were growing at twice the rate of the rest of the company's revenues. The company's internal commitment to green was increased when it announced its goal to decrease greenhouse gas emissions and water consumption by an additional 20 percent by 2020.

As you no doubt recognize from your study of the previous chapter, GE's decision to develop and market green technology represents a capital budgeting decision. In this chapter, we further investigate such decisions, how they are made, and how to look at them objectively.

This chapter follows up on our previous one by delving more deeply into capital budgeting. We have two main tasks. First, recall that in the last chapter, we saw that cash flow estimates are the critical input in a net present value analysis, but we didn't say much about where these cash flows come from; so we will now examine this question in some detail. Our second goal is to learn how to critically examine NPV estimates, and, in particular, how to evaluate the sensitivity of NPV estimates to assumptions made about the uncertain future.

Learning Objectives

After studying this chapter, you should be able to:

LO1 Determine the relevant cash flows for a proposed project.

LO2 Evaluate whether a project is acceptable.

LO3 Explain how to set a bid price for a project.

LO4 Evaluate the equivalent annual cost of a project.

For updates on the latest happenings in finance, visit fundamentalsofcorporatefinance.blogspot.com.

So far, we've covered various parts of the capital budgeting decision. Our task in this chapter is to start bringing these pieces together. In particular, we will show you how to "spread the numbers" for a proposed investment or project and, based on those numbers, make an initial assessment about whether the project should be undertaken.

In the discussion that follows, we focus on the process of setting up a discounted cash flow analysis. From the last chapter, we know that the projected future cash flows are the key element in such an evaluation. Accordingly, we emphasize working with financial and accounting information to come up with these figures.

In evaluating a proposed investment, we pay special attention to deciding what information is relevant to the decision at hand and what information is not. As we will see, it is easy to overlook important pieces of the capital budgeting puzzle.

We will wait until the next chapter to describe in detail how to go about evaluating the results of our discounted cash flow analysis. Also, where needed, we will assume that we know the relevant required return, or discount rate. We continue to defer in-depth discussion of this subject to Part 5.

Project Cash Flows: A First Look   10.1

The effect of taking a project is to change the firm's overall cash flows today and in the future. To evaluate a proposed investment, we must consider these changes in the firm's cash flows and then decide whether they add value to the firm. The first (and most important) step, therefore, is to decide which cash flows are relevant.

RELEVANT CASH FLOWS

What is a relevant cash flow for a project? The general principle is simple enough: A relevant cash flow for a project is a change in the firm's overall future cash flow that comes about as a direct consequence of the decision to take that project. Because the relevant cash flows are defined in terms of changes in, or increments to, the firm's existing cash flow, they are called the **incremental cash flows** associated with the project.

The concept of incremental cash flow is central to our analysis, so we will state a general definition and refer back to it as needed:

incremental cash flows
The difference between a firm's future cash flows with a project and those without the project.

> The incremental cash flows for project evaluation consist of *any and all* changes in the firm's future cash flows that are a direct consequence of taking the project.

This definition of incremental cash flows has an obvious and important corollary: Any cash flow that exists regardless of *whether or not* a project is undertaken is *not* relevant.

THE STAND-ALONE PRINCIPLE

In practice, it would be cumbersome to actually calculate the future total cash flows to the firm with and without a project, especially for a large firm. Fortunately, it is not really necessary to do so. Once we identify the effect of undertaking the proposed project on the firm's cash flows, we need focus only on the project's resulting incremental cash flows. This is called the **stand-alone principle**.

What the stand-alone principle says is that once we have determined the incremental cash flows from undertaking a project, we can view that project as a kind of "minifirm" with its own future revenues and costs, its own assets, and, of course, its own cash flows. We will then be primarily interested in comparing the cash flows from this minifirm to the cost of acquiring it. An important consequence of this approach is that we will be evaluating the proposed project purely on its own merits, in isolation from any other activities or projects.

stand-alone principle
The assumption that evaluation of a project may be based on the project's incremental cash flows.

10.2 Incremental Cash Flows

We are concerned here with only cash flows that are incremental and that result from a project. Looking back at our general definition, we might think it would be easy enough to decide whether a cash flow is incremental. Even so, in a few situations it is easy to make mistakes. In this section, we describe some common pitfalls and how to avoid them.

SUNK COSTS

sunk cost
A cost that has already been incurred and cannot be removed and therefore should not be considered in an investment decision.

A **sunk cost**, by definition, is a cost we have already paid or have already incurred the liability to pay. Such a cost cannot be changed by the decision today to accept or reject a project. Put another way, the firm will have to pay this cost no matter what. Based on our general definition of incremental cash flow, such a cost is clearly irrelevant to the decision at hand. So, we will always be careful to exclude sunk costs from our analysis.

That a sunk cost is irrelevant seems obvious given our discussion. Nonetheless, it's easy to fall prey to the fallacy that a sunk cost should be associated with a project. Suppose General Milk Company hires a financial consultant to help evaluate whether a line of chocolate milk should be launched. When the consultant turns in the report, General Milk objects to the analysis because the consultant did not include the hefty consulting fee as a cost of the chocolate milk project.

Who is correct? By now, we know that the consulting fee is a sunk cost: It must be paid whether or not the chocolate milk line is actually launched (this is an attractive feature of the consulting business).

OPPORTUNITY COSTS

opportunity cost
The most valuable alternative that is given up if a particular investment is undertaken.

When we think of costs, we normally think of out-of-pocket costs—namely those that require us to actually spend some amount of cash. An **opportunity cost** is slightly different; it requires us to give up a benefit. A common situation arises in which a firm already owns some of the assets a proposed project will be using. For example, we might be thinking of converting an old rustic cotton mill we bought years ago for $100,000 into upmarket condominiums.

If we undertake this project, there will be no direct cash outflow associated with buying the old mill because we already own it. For purposes of evaluating the condo project, should we then treat the mill as "free"? The answer is no. The mill is a valuable resource used by the project. If we didn't use it here, we could do something else with it. Like what? The obvious answer is that, at a minimum, we could sell it. Using the mill for the condo complex has an opportunity cost: We give up the valuable opportunity to do something else with the mill.[1]

There is another issue here. Once we agree that the use of the mill has an opportunity cost, how much should we charge the condo project for this use? Given that we paid $100,000, it might seem that we should charge this amount to the condo project. Is this correct? The answer is no, and the reason is based on our discussion concerning sunk costs.

The fact that we paid $100,000 some years ago is irrelevant. That cost is sunk. At a minimum, the opportunity cost that we charge the project is what the mill would sell for today

---

[1]Economists sometimes use the acronym TANSTAAFL, which is short for "There ain't no such thing as a free lunch," to describe the fact that only very rarely is something truly free.

(net of any selling costs) because this is the amount we give up by using the mill instead of selling it.[2]

SIDE EFFECTS

Remember that the incremental cash flows for a project include all the resulting changes in the *firm's* future cash flows. It would not be unusual for a project to have side, or spillover, effects, both good and bad. For example, in 2017, the time between the theatrical release of a feature film and the release of the DVD had shrunk to 17 weeks compared to 29 weeks in 1998, although several studios have shorter times. This shortened release time was blamed for at least part of the decline in movie theater box office receipts. Of course, retailers cheered the move because it was credited with increasing DVD sales. A negative impact on the cash flows of an existing product from the introduction of a new product is called **erosion**.[3] In this case, the cash flows from the new line should be adjusted downward to reflect lost profits on other lines.

erosion
The cash flows of a new project that come at the expense of a firm's existing projects.

In accounting for erosion, it is important to recognize that any sales lost as a result of launching a new product might be lost anyway because of future competition. Erosion is relevant only when the sales would not otherwise be lost.

Side effects show up in a lot of different ways. For example, one of The Walt Disney Company's concerns when it built Euro Disney (now known as Disneyland Paris) was that the new park would drain visitors from the Florida park, a popular vacation destination for Europeans.

There are beneficial spillover effects, of course. For example, you might think that Hewlett-Packard would have been concerned when the price of a printer that sold for $500 to $600 in 1994 declined to below $100 by 2017, but such was not the case. HP realized that the big money is in the consumables that printer owners buy to keep their printers going, such as ink-jet cartridges, laser toner cartridges, and special paper. The profit margins for these products are substantial.

NET WORKING CAPITAL

Normally a project will require that the firm invest in net working capital in addition to long-term assets. For example, a project will generally need some amount of cash on hand to pay any expenses that arise. In addition, a project will need an initial investment in inventories and accounts receivable (to cover credit sales). Some of the financing for this will be in the form of amounts owed to suppliers (accounts payable), but the firm will have to supply the balance. This balance represents the investment in net working capital.

It's easy to overlook an important feature of net working capital in capital budgeting. As a project winds down, inventories are sold, receivables are collected, bills are paid, and cash balances can be drawn down. These activities free up the net working capital originally invested. So the firm's investment in project net working capital closely resembles a loan. The firm supplies working capital at the beginning and recovers it toward the end.

FINANCING COSTS

In analyzing a proposed investment, we will *not* include interest paid or any other financing costs such as dividends or principal repaid because we are interested in the cash flow generated by the assets of the project. As we mentioned in Chapter 2, interest paid, for example, is a component of cash flow to creditors, not cash flow from assets.

---

[2]If the asset in question is unique, then the opportunity cost might be higher because there might be other valuable projects we could undertake that would use it. However, if the asset in question is of a type that is routinely bought and sold (a used car, perhaps), then the opportunity cost is always the going price in the market because that is the cost of buying another similar asset.

[3]More colorfully, erosion is sometimes called *piracy* or *cannibalism*.

More generally, our goal in project evaluation is to compare the cash flow from a project to the cost of acquiring that project in order to estimate NPV. The particular mixture of debt and equity a firm actually chooses to use in financing a project is a managerial variable and primarily determines how project cash flow is divided between owners and creditors. This is not to say that financing arrangements are unimportant. They are just something to be analyzed separately. We will cover this in later chapters.

OTHER ISSUES

There are some other things to watch out for. First, we are interested only in measuring cash flow. Moreover, we are interested in measuring it when it actually occurs, not when it accrues in an accounting sense. Second, we are always interested in *aftertax* cash flow because taxes are definitely a cash outflow. In fact, whenever we write *incremental cash flows*, we mean aftertax incremental cash flows. Remember, aftertax cash flow and accounting profit, or net income, are entirely different things.

Concept Questions

10.2a What is a sunk cost? An opportunity cost?

10.2b Explain what erosion is and why it is relevant.

10.2c Explain why interest paid is an irrelevant cash flow for project evaluation.

10.3 Pro Forma Financial Statements and Project Cash Flows

Excel Master It!

xlsx Excel Master coverage online

The first thing we need when we begin evaluating a proposed investment is a set of pro forma, or projected, financial statements. Given these, we can develop the projected cash flows from the project. Once we have the cash flows, we can estimate the value of the project using the techniques we described in the previous chapter.

GETTING STARTED: PRO FORMA FINANCIAL STATEMENTS

pro forma financial statements
Financial statements projecting future years' operations.

Pro forma financial statements are a convenient and easily understood means of summarizing much of the relevant information for a project. To prepare these statements, we will need estimates of quantities such as unit sales, the selling price per unit, the variable cost per unit, and total fixed costs. We will also need to know the total investment required, including any investment in net working capital.

To illustrate, suppose we think we can sell 50,000 cans of shark attractant per year at a price of $4 per can. It costs us about $2.50 per can to make the attractant, and a new product such as this one typically has only a three-year life (perhaps because the customer base dwindles rapidly). We require a 20 percent return on new products.

Fixed costs for the project, including such things as rent on the production facility, will run $17,430 per year.[4] Further, we will need to invest a total of $90,000 in manufacturing equipment. For simplicity, we will assume that this $90,000 will be 100 percent depreciated over the three-year life of the project.[5] Furthermore, the cost of removing the equipment will roughly equal its actual value in three years, so it will be essentially worthless on

---

[4]By *fixed cost*, we literally mean a cash outflow that will occur regardless of the level of sales. This should not be confused with some sort of accounting period charge.

[5]We will also assume that a full year's depreciation can be taken in the first year.

Sales (50,000 units at $4/unit)	$200,000
Variable costs ($2.50/unit)	125,000
Fixed costs	17,430
Depreciation ($90,000/3)	30,000
EBIT	$ 27,570
Taxes (21%)	5,790
Net income	$ 21,780

TABLE 10.1

Projected Income Statement, Shark Attractant Project

	Year			
	0	1	2	3
Net working capital	$ 20,000	$20,000	$20,000	$20,000
Net fixed assets	90,000	60,000	30,000	0
Total investment	$110,000	$80,000	$50,000	$20,000

TABLE 10.2

Projected Capital Requirements, Shark Attractant Project

a market value basis as well. Finally, the project will require an initial $20,000 investment in net working capital, and the tax rate is 21 percent.

In Table 10.1, we organize these initial projections by first preparing the pro forma income statement. Once again, notice that we have *not* deducted any interest expense. This will always be so. As we described earlier, interest paid is a financing expense, not a component of operating cash flow.

We can also prepare a series of abbreviated balance sheets that show the capital requirements for the project as we've done in Table 10.2. Here we have net working capital of $20,000 in each year. Fixed assets are $90,000 at the start of the project's life (Year 0), and they decline by the $30,000 in depreciation each year, ending up at zero. Notice that the total investment given here for future years is the total book, or accounting, value—not market value.

At this point, we need to start converting this accounting information into cash flows. We consider how to do this next.

PROJECT CASH FLOWS

To develop the cash flows from a project, we need to recall (from Chapter 2) that cash flow from assets has three components: Operating cash flow, capital spending, and changes in net working capital. To evaluate a project, or minifirm, we need to estimate each of these.

Once we have estimates of the components of cash flow, we will calculate cash flow for our minifirm just as we did in Chapter 2 for an entire firm:

Project cash flow = Project operating cash flow
　　　　　　　　　 − Project change in net working capital
　　　　　　　　　 − Project capital spending

We consider these components next.

Project Operating Cash Flow   To determine the operating cash flow associated with a project, we first need to recall the definition of operating cash flow:

Operating cash flow = Earnings before interest and taxes
　　　　　　　　　　 + Depreciation
　　　　　　　　　　 − Taxes

TABLE 10.3

Projected Income Statement, Abbreviated, Shark Attractant Project

Sales	$200,000
Variable costs	125,000
Fixed costs	17,430
Depreciation	30,000
EBIT	$ 27,570
Taxes (21%)	5,790
Net income	$ 21,780

TABLE 10.4

Projected Operating Cash Flow, Shark Attractant Project

EBIT	$27,570
Depreciation	+ 30,000
Taxes	− 5,790
Operating cash flow	$51,780

TABLE 10.5

Projected Total Cash Flows, Shark Attractant Project

	Year			
	0	1	2	3
Operating cash flow		$51,780	$51,780	$51,780
Changes in NWC	−$ 20,000			+ 20,000
Capital spending	− 90,000			
Total project cash flow	−$110,000	$51,780	$51,780	$71,780

To illustrate the calculation of operating cash flow, we will use the projected information from the shark attractant project. For ease of reference, Table 10.3 repeats the income statement in more abbreviated form.

Given the income statement in Table 10.3, calculating the operating cash flow is straightforward. As we see in Table 10.4, projected operating cash flow for the shark attractant project is $51,780.

Project Net Working Capital and Capital Spending   We next need to take care of the fixed asset and net working capital requirements. Based on our balance sheets, we know that the firm must spend $90,000 up front for fixed assets and invest an additional $20,000 in net working capital. The immediate outflow is a total of $110,000. At the end of the project's life, the fixed assets will be worthless, but the firm will recover the $20,000 that was tied up in working capital.[6] This will lead to a $20,000 *inflow* in the last year.

On a purely mechanical level, notice that whenever we have an investment in net working capital, that same investment has to be recovered; in other words, the same number needs to appear at some time in the future with the opposite sign.

PROJECTED TOTAL CASH FLOW AND VALUE

Given the information we've accumulated, we can finish the preliminary cash flow analysis as illustrated in Table 10.5.

---

[6]In reality, the firm would probably recover something less than 100 percent of this amount because of bad debts, inventory loss, and so on. If we wanted to, we could just assume that, for example, only 90 percent was recovered and proceed from there.

Now that we have cash flow projections, we are ready to apply the various criteria we discussed in the last chapter. First, the NPV at the 20 percent required return is:

$$NPV = -\$110,000 + 51,780/1.2 + 51,780/1.2^2 + 71,780/1.2^3$$
$$= \$10,648$$

Based on these projections, the project creates over $10,000 in value and should be accepted. Also, the return on this investment obviously exceeds 20 percent (because the NPV is positive at 20 percent). After some trial and error, we find that the IRR works out to be about 25.8 percent.

In addition, if required, we could calculate the payback and the average accounting return, or AAR. Inspection of the cash flows shows that the payback on this project is a little over two years (verify that it's about 2.1 years).[7]

From the last chapter, we know that the AAR is average net income divided by average book value. The net income each year is $21,780. The average (in thousands) of the four book values (from Table 10.2) for total investment is ($110 + 80 + 50 + 20)/4 = $65. So the AAR is $21,780/$65,000 = .3351, or 33.51 percent.[8] We've already seen that the return on this investment (the IRR) is about 26 percent. The fact that the AAR is larger illustrates again why the AAR cannot be meaningfully interpreted as the return on a project.

Concept Questions

10.3a   What is the definition of project operating cash flow? How does this differ from net income?

10.3b   For the shark attractant project, why did we add back the firm's net working capital investment in the final year?

More about Project Cash Flow

10.4

In this section, we take a closer look at some aspects of project cash flow. In particular, we discuss project net working capital in more detail. We then examine current tax laws regarding depreciation. Finally, we work through a more involved example of the capital investment decision.

Excel Master It!

Excel Master coverage online

A CLOSER LOOK AT NET WORKING CAPITAL

In calculating operating cash flow, we did not explicitly consider the fact that some of our sales might be on credit. Also, we may not have actually paid some of the costs shown. In either case, the cash flow in question would not yet have occurred. We show here that these possibilities are not a problem as long as we don't forget to include changes in net working capital in our analysis. This discussion emphasizes the importance and the effect of doing so.

---

[7]We're guilty of a minor inconsistency here. When we calculated the NPV and the IRR, we assumed that all the cash flows occurred at end of year. When we calculated the payback, we assumed that the cash flows occurred uniformly throughout the year.

[8]Notice that the average total book value is not the initial total of $110,000 divided by 2. The reason is that the $20,000 in working capital doesn't "depreciate."

Suppose that during a particular year of a project we have the following simplified income statement:

Sales	$500
Costs	310
Net income	$190

Depreciation and taxes are zero. No fixed assets are purchased during the year. Also, to illustrate a point, we assume that the only components of net working capital are accounts receivable and payable. The beginning and ending amounts for these accounts are as follows:

	Beginning of Year	End of Year	Change
Accounts receivable	$880	$910	+$30
Accounts payable	550	605	+ 55
Net working capital	$330	$305	−$25

Based on this information, what is total cash flow for the year? We can first just mechanically apply what we have been discussing to come up with the answer. Operating cash flow in this particular case is the same as EBIT because there are no taxes or depreciation; thus, it equals $190. Also, notice that net working capital actually *declined* by $25. This just means that $25 was freed up during the year. There was no capital spending, so the total cash flow for the year is:

$$\text{Total cash flow} = \text{Operating cash flow} - \text{Change in NWC} - \text{Capital spending}$$
$$= \$190 - (-25) - 0$$
$$= \$215$$

Now, we know that this $215 total cash flow has to be "dollars in" less "dollars out" for the year. We could therefore ask a different question: What were cash revenues for the year? Also, what were cash costs?

To determine cash revenues, we need to look more closely at net working capital. During the year, we had sales of $500. However, accounts receivable rose by $30 over the same time period. What does this mean? The $30 increase tells us that sales exceeded collections by $30. In other words, we haven't yet received the cash from $30 of the $500 in sales. As a result, our cash inflow is $500 − 30 = $470. In general, cash income is sales minus the increase in accounts receivable.

Cash outflows can be similarly determined. We show costs of $310 on the income statement, but accounts payable increased by $55 during the year. This means that we have not yet paid $55 of the $310, so cash costs for the period are just $310 − 55 = $255. In other words, in this case, cash costs equal costs less the increase in accounts payable.[9]

Putting this information together, we calculate that cash inflows less cash outflows are $470 − 255 = $215, just as we had before. Notice that:

$$\text{Cash flow} = \text{Cash inflow} - \text{Cash outflow}$$
$$= (\$500 - 30) - (310 - 55)$$
$$= (\$500 - 310) - (30 - 55)$$
$$= \text{Operating cash flow} - \text{Change in NWC}$$
$$= \$190 - (-25)$$
$$= \$215$$

---

[9]If there were other accounts, we might have to make some further adjustments. For example, a net increase in inventory would be a cash outflow.

Samuel Weaver on Capital Budgeting at The Hershey Company

The capital program at The Hershey Company and most Fortune 500 or Fortune 1,000 companies involves a three-phase approach: Planning or budgeting, evaluation, and postcompletion reviews.

The first phase involves identification of likely projects at strategic planning time. These are selected to support the strategic objectives of the corporation. This identification is generally broad in scope with minimal financial evaluation attached. Projects are classified as new product, cost savings, capacity expansion, etc. As the planning process focuses more closely on the short-term plans (or budgets), major capital expenditures are discussed more rigorously. Project costs are more closely honed, and specific projects may be reconsidered.

Each project is then individually reviewed and authorized. Planning, developing, and refining cash flows underlie capital analysis at Hershey. Once the cash flows have been determined, the application of capital evaluation techniques such as those using net present value, internal rate of return, and payback period is routine. Presentation of the results is enhanced using sensitivity analysis, which plays a major role for management in assessing the critical assumptions and resulting impact.

The final phase relates to postcompletion reviews in which the original forecasts of the project's performance are compared to actual results and/or revised expectations.

Capital expenditure analysis is only as good as the assumptions that underlie the project. The old cliché of GIGO (garbage in, garbage out) applies in this case. Incremental cash flows primarily result from incremental sales or margin improvements (cost savings). For the most part, a range of incremental cash flows can be identified from marketing research or engineering studies. However, for a number of projects, correctly discerning the implications and the relevant cash flows is analytically challenging. For example, when a new product is introduced and is expected to generate millions of dollars' worth of sales, the appropriate analysis focuses on the incremental sales after accounting for cannibalization of existing products.

One of the problems that we face at Hershey deals with the application of net present value, NPV, versus internal rate of return, IRR. NPV offers us the correct investment indication when dealing with mutually exclusive alternatives. However, decision makers at all levels sometimes find it difficult to comprehend the result. Specifically, an NPV of, say, $535,000 needs to be interpreted. It is not enough to know that the NPV is positive or even that it is more positive than an alternative. Decision makers seek to determine a level of "comfort" regarding how profitable the investment is by relating it to other standards.

Although the IRR may provide a misleading indication of which project to select, the result is provided in a way that can be interpreted by all parties. The resulting IRR can be mentally compared to expected inflation, current borrowing rates, the cost of capital, an equity portfolio's return, and so on. An IRR of, say, 18 percent is readily interpretable by management. Perhaps this ease of understanding is why surveys indicate that many Fortune 500 or Fortune 1,000 companies use the IRR method (in conjunction with NPV) as a primary evaluation technique.

In addition to the NPV versus IRR problem, there are a limited number of projects for which traditional capital expenditure analysis is difficult to apply because the cash flows can't be determined. When new computer equipment is purchased, an office building is renovated, or a parking lot is repaved, it is essentially impossible to identify the cash flows, so the use of traditional evaluation techniques is limited. These types of "capital expenditure" decisions are made using other techniques that hinge on management's judgment.

Samuel Weaver, Ph.D., is the former director, financial planning and analysis, for Hershey. He is a certified management accountant and certified financial manager. His position combined the theoretical with the pragmatic and involved the analysis of many different facets of finance in addition to capital expenditure analysis.

More generally, this example illustrates that including net working capital changes in our calculations has the effect of adjusting for the discrepancy between accounting sales and costs and actual cash receipts and payments.

Cash Collections and Costs	**EXAMPLE 10.1**

For the year just completed, the Combat Wombat Telestat Co. (CWT) reports sales of $998 and costs of $734. You have collected the following beginning and ending balance sheet information:

	Beginning	Ending
Accounts receivable	$100	$110
Inventory	100	80
Accounts payable	100	70
Net working capital	$100	$120

Based on these figures, what are cash inflows? Cash outflows? What happened to each account? What is net cash flow?

Sales were $998, but receivables rose by $10. So cash collections were $10 less than sales, or $988. Costs were $734, but inventories fell by $20. This means that we didn't replace $20 worth of inventory, so costs are actually overstated by this amount. Also, payables fell by $30. This means that, on a net basis, we actually paid our suppliers $30 more than we received from them, resulting in a $30 understatement of costs. Adjusting for these events, we calculate that cash costs are $734 − 20 + 30 = $744. Net cash flow is $988 − 744 = $244.

Finally, notice that net working capital increased by $20 overall. We can check our answer by noting that the original accounting sales less costs (= $998 − 734) are $264. In addition, CWT spent $20 on net working capital, so the net result is a cash flow of $264 − 20 = $244, as we calculated.

DEPRECIATION

As we note elsewhere, accounting depreciation is a noncash deduction. As a result, depreciation has cash flow consequences only because it influences the tax bill. The way that depreciation is computed for tax purposes is the relevant method for capital investment decisions. Not surprisingly, the procedures are governed by tax law. We now discuss some specifics of the depreciation system enacted by the Tax Reform Act of 1986. This system is a modification of the **accelerated cost recovery system (ACRS)** instituted in 1981.

accelerated cost recovery system (ACRS)
A depreciation method under U.S. tax law allowing for the accelerated write-off of property under various classifications.

Modified ACRS Depreciation (MACRS)   Calculating depreciation is normally mechanical. Although there are a number of *ifs*, *ands*, and *buts* involved, the basic idea under MACRS is that every asset is assigned to a particular class. An asset's class establishes its life for tax purposes. Once an asset's tax life is determined, the depreciation for each year is computed by multiplying the cost of the asset by a fixed percentage.[10] The expected salvage value (what we think the asset will be worth when we dispose of it) and the expected economic life (how long we expect the asset to be in service) are not explicitly considered in the calculation of depreciation.

Some typical depreciation classes are given in Table 10.6, and associated percentages (as specified by the IRS) are shown in Table 10.7.[11]

A nonresidential real property, such as an office building, is depreciated over 31.5 years using straight-line depreciation. A residential real property, such as an apartment building, is depreciated straight-line over 27.5 years. Remember that land cannot be depreciated.[12]

---

[10]Under certain circumstances, the cost of the asset may be adjusted before computing depreciation. The result is called the *depreciable basis*, and depreciation is calculated using this number instead of the actual cost.

[11]For the curious, these depreciation percentages are derived from a double-declining balance scheme with a switch to straight-line when the latter becomes advantageous. Further, there is a half-year convention, meaning that all assets are assumed to be placed in service midway through the tax year. This convention is maintained unless more than 40 percent of an asset's cost is incurred in the final quarter. In this case, a midquarter convention is used. The odd-looking rounding is courtesy of the IRS.

[12]There are, however, depletion allowances for firms in extraction-type lines of business (such as mining). These are somewhat similar to depreciation allowances.

Class	Examples
Three-year	Equipment used in research
Five-year	Autos, computers
Seven-year	Most industrial equipment

TABLE 10.6

Modified ACRS Property Classes

	Property Class		
Year	Three-Year	Five-Year	Seven-Year
1	33.33%	20.00%	14.29%
2	44.45	32.00	24.49
3	14.81	19.20	17.49
4	7.41	11.52	12.49
5		11.52	8.93
6		5.76	8.92
7			8.93
8			4.46

TABLE 10.7

Modified ACRS Depreciation Allowances

To illustrate how depreciation is calculated, we consider an automobile costing $12,000. Autos are normally classified as five-year property. Looking at Table 10.7, we see that the relevant figure for the first year of a five-year asset is 20 percent.[13] The depreciation in the first year is thus $12,000 × .20 = $2,400. The relevant percentage in the second year is 32 percent, so the depreciation in the second year is $12,000 × .32 = $3,840, and so on. We can summarize these calculations as follows:

Year	MACRS Percentage	Depreciation		
1	20.00%	.2000 × $12,000 =	$ 2,400.00
2	32.00	.3200 × 12,000 =	3,840.00
3	19.20	.1920 × 12,000 =	2,304.00
4	11.52	.1152 × 12,000 =	1,382.40
5	11.52	.1152 × 12,000 =	1,382.40
6	5.76	.0576 × 12,000 =	691.20
	100.00%		$12,000.00

Notice that the MACRS percentages sum up to 100 percent. As a result, we write off 100 percent of the cost of the asset, or $12,000 in this case.

Bonus Depreciation   For a number of years prior to 2018, various tax rules and regulations were enacted that allowed "bonus" depreciation. Based on the Protecting Americans from Tax Hikes (PATH) Act of 2015, the size of the bonus in 2017 was 50%. What this means is that a firm can take a depreciation deduction of 50% of the cost on an eligible asset in the first year and then depreciate the remaining 50% using the MACRS schedules as we have just described. Significantly, in late 2017, Congress passed the Tax Cuts and Jobs Act, which increased the bonus depreciation to 100% for 2018, lasting until the end of 2022. After that it, drops by 20% per year until it reaches zero after 2026. The implication is that most firms will not use the MACRS schedules until 2023 unless they wish to (taking the bonus depreciation is optional). Of course, future legislation may change things.

Book Value versus Market Value   In calculating depreciation under current tax law, the economic life and future market value of the asset are not an issue. As a result, the

---

[13]It may appear odd that five-year property is depreciated over six years. The tax accounting reason is that it is assumed we have the asset for only six months in the first year and, consequently, six months in the last year. As a result, there are five 12-month periods, but we have some depreciation in each of six different tax years.

TABLE 10.8

MACRS Book Values

Year	Beginning Book Value	Depreciation	Ending Book Value
1	$12,000.00	$2,400.00	$9,600.00
2	9,600.00	3,840.00	5,760.00
3	5,760.00	2,304.00	3,456.00
4	3,456.00	1,382.40	2,073.60
5	2,073.60	1,382.40	691.20
6	691.20	691.20	.00

book value of an asset can differ substantially from its actual market value. For example, with our $12,000 car, book value after the first year is $12,000 less the first year's depreciation of $2,400, or $9,600. The remaining book values are summarized in Table 10.8. After six years, the book value of the car is zero.

Suppose we wanted to sell the car after five years. Based on historical averages, it would be worth, say, 25 percent of the purchase price, or .25 × $12,000 = $3,000. If we actually sold it for this, then we would have to pay taxes at the ordinary income tax rate on the difference between the sale price of $3,000 and the book value of $691.20. For a corporation in the 21 percent bracket, the tax liability would be .21 × $2,308.80 = $484.85.[14]

The reason taxes must be paid in this case is that the difference between market value and book value is "excess" depreciation, and it must be "recaptured" when the asset is sold. What this means is that, as it turns out, we overdepreciated the asset by $3,000 − 691.20 = $2,308.80. Because we deducted $2,308.80 too much in depreciation, we paid $484.85 too little in taxes, and we have to make up the difference.

Notice that this is *not* a tax on a capital gain. As a general (albeit rough) rule, a capital gain occurs only if the market price exceeds the original cost. However, what is and what is not a capital gain is ultimately up to taxing authorities, and the specific rules can be complex. We will ignore capital gains taxes for the most part.

Finally, if the book value exceeds the market value, then the difference is treated as a loss for tax purposes. For example, if we sell the car after two years for $4,000, then the book value exceeds the market value by $1,760. In this case, a tax savings of .21 × $1,760 = $369.60 occurs.

---

[14]The rules are different and more complicated with real property. Essentially, in this case, only the difference between the actual book value and the book value that would have existed if straight-line depreciation had been used is recaptured. Anything above the straight-line book value is considered a capital gain.

EXAMPLE 10.2

MACRS Depreciation

The Staple Supply Co. has just purchased a new computerized information system with an installed cost of $160,000. The computer is treated as five-year property. What are the yearly depreciation allowances? Based on historical experience, we think that the system will be worth only $10,000 when Staple gets rid of it in four years. What are the tax consequences of the sale? What is the total aftertax cash flow from the sale?

The yearly depreciation allowances are calculated by multiplying $160,000 by the five-year percentages found in Table 10.7:

Year	MACRS Percentage	Depreciation	Ending Book Value
1	20.00%	.2000 × $160,000 = $ 32,000	$128,000
2	32.00	.3200 × 160,000 = 51,200	76,800
3	19.20	.1920 × 160,000 = 30,720	46,080
4	11.52	.1152 × 160,000 = 18,432	27,648
5	11.52	.1152 × 160,000 = 18,432	9,216
6	5.76	.0576 × 160,000 = 9,216	0
	100.00%	$160,000	

Notice that we have also computed the book value of the system as of the end of each year. The book value at the end of Year 4 is $27,648. If Staple sells the system for $10,000 at that time, it will have a loss of $17,648 (the difference) for tax purposes. This loss, of course, is like depreciation because it isn't a cash expense.

What really happens? Two things. First, Staple gets $10,000 from the buyer. Second, it saves .21 × $17,648 = $3,706 in taxes. So, the total aftertax cash flow from the sale is a $13,706 cash inflow.

AN EXAMPLE: THE MAJESTIC MULCH AND COMPOST COMPANY (MMCC)

At this point, we want to go through a somewhat more involved capital budgeting analysis. Keep in mind as you read that the basic approach here is exactly the same as that in the shark attractant example used earlier. We have just added some real-world detail (and a lot more numbers).

MMCC is investigating the feasibility of a new line of power mulching tools aimed at the growing number of home composters. Based on exploratory conversations with buyers for large garden shops, MMCC projects unit sales as follows:

Year	Unit Sales
1	3,000
2	5,000
3	6,000
4	6,500
5	6,000
6	5,000
7	4,000
8	3,000

The new power mulcher will sell for $120 per unit to start. When the competition catches up after three years, however, MMCC anticipates that the price will drop to $110.

The power mulcher project will require $20,000 in net working capital at the start. Subsequently, total net working capital at the end of each year will be about 15 percent of sales for that year. The variable cost per unit is $60, and total fixed costs are $25,000 per year.

It will cost about $800,000 to buy the equipment necessary to begin production. This investment is primarily in industrial equipment, which qualifies as seven-year MACRS property. We assume there is no bonus depreciation, so we apply MACRS to the entire cost. The equipment will actually be worth about 20 percent of its cost in eight years, or .20 × $800,000 = $160,000. The relevant tax rate is 21 percent, and the required return is 15 percent. Based on this information, should MMCC proceed?

Operating Cash Flows   There is a lot of information here that we need to organize. The first thing we can do is calculate projected sales. Sales in the first year are projected at 3,000 units at $120 apiece, or $360,000 total. The remaining figures are shown in Table 10.9.

Next, we compute the depreciation on the $800,000 investment in Table 10.10 (remember, there is no bonus depreciation in this case). With this information, we can prepare the pro forma income statements, as shown in Table 10.11. From here, computing the operating cash flows is straightforward. The results are shown in the first part of Table 10.13.

TABLE 10.9

Projected Revenues, Power Mulcher Project

Year	Unit Price	Unit Sales	Revenues
1	$120	3,000	$360,000
2	120	5,000	600,000
3	120	6,000	720,000
4	110	6,500	715,000
5	110	6,000	660,000
6	110	5,000	550,000
7	110	4,000	440,000
8	110	3,000	330,000

TABLE 10.10

Annual Depreciation, Power Mulcher Project

Year	MACRS Percentage	Depreciation	Ending Book Value
1	14.29%	.1429 × $800,000 = $114,320	$685,680
2	24.49	.2449 × 800,000 = 195,920	489,760
3	17.49	.1749 × 800,000 = 139,920	349,840
4	12.49	.1249 × 800,000 = 99,920	249,920
5	8.93	.0893 × 800,000 = 71,440	178,480
6	8.92	.0892 × 800,000 = 71,360	107,120
7	8.93	.0893 × 800,000 = 71,440	35,680
8	4.46	.0446 × 800,000 = 35,680	0
	100.00%	$800,000	

TABLE 10.11   Projected Income Statements, Power Mulcher Project

	Year							
	1	2	3	4	5	6	7	8
Unit price	$ 120	$ 120	$ 120	$ 110	$ 110	$ 110	$ 110	$ 110
Unit sales	3,000	5,000	6,000	6,500	6,000	5,000	4,000	3,000
Revenues	$360,000	$600,000	$720,000	$715,000	$660,000	$550,000	$440,000	$330,000
Variable costs	180,000	300,000	360,000	390,000	360,000	300,000	240,000	180,000
Fixed costs	25,000	25,000	25,000	25,000	25,000	25,000	25,000	25,000
Depreciation	114,320	195,920	139,920	99,920	71,440	71,360	71,440	35,680
EBIT	$ 40,680	$ 79,080	$195,080	$200,080	$203,560	$153,640	$103,560	$ 89,320
Taxes (21%)	8,543	16,607	40,967	42,017	42,748	32,264	21,748	18,757
Net income	$ 32,137	$ 62,473	$154,113	$158,063	$160,812	$121,376	$ 81,812	$ 70,563

Change in NWC   Now that we have the operating cash flows, we need to determine the changes in NWC. By assumption, net working capital requirements change as sales change. In each year, MMCC will generally either add to or recover some of its project net working capital. Recalling that NWC starts out at $20,000 and then rises to 15 percent of sales, we can calculate the amount of NWC for each year as shown in Table 10.12.

As illustrated, during the first year, net working capital grows from $20,000 to .15 × $360,000 = $54,000. The increase in net working capital for the year is thus $54,000 − 20,000 = $34,000. The remaining figures are calculated in the same way.

TABLE 10.12

Changes in Net Working Capital, Power Mulcher Project

Year	Revenues	Net Working Capital	Cash Flow
0		$ 20,000	−$20,000
1	$360,000	54,000	− 34,000
2	600,000	90,000	− 36,000
3	720,000	108,000	− 18,000
4	715,000	107,250	750
5	660,000	99,000	8,250
6	550,000	82,500	16,500
7	440,000	66,000	16,500
8	330,000	49,500	16,500

TABLE 10.13   Projected Cash Flows, Power Mulcher Project

	0	1	2	3	4	5	6	7	8
I. Operating Cash Flow									
EBIT		$ 40,680	$ 79,080	$195,080	$200,080	$203,560	$153,640	$103,560	$ 89,320
Depreciation		114,320	195,920	139,920	99,920	71,440	71,360	71,440	35,680
Taxes		− 8,543	− 16,607	− 40,967	− 42,017	− 42,748	− 32,264	− 21,748	− 18,757
Operating cash flow		$146,457	$258,393	$294,033	$257,983	$232,252	$192,736	$153,252	$106,243
II. Net Working Capital									
Initial NWC	−$ 20,000								
Change in NWC		−$ 34,000	−$ 36,000	−$ 18,000	$ 750	$ 8,250	$ 16,500	$ 16,500	$ 16,500
NWC recovery									49,500
Total change in NWC	−$ 20,000	−$ 34,000	−$ 36,000	−$ 18,000	$ 750	$ 8,250	$ 16,500	$ 16,500	$ 66,000
III. Capital Spending									
Initial outlay	−$800,000								
Aftertax salvage									$126,400
Capital spending	−$800,000								$126,400

Remember that an increase in net working capital is a cash outflow, so we use a negative sign in this table to indicate an additional investment that the firm makes in net working capital. A positive sign represents net working capital returning to the firm. For example, $16,500 in NWC flows back to the firm in Year 6. Over the project's life, net working capital builds to a peak of $108,000 and declines from there as sales begin to drop off.

We show the result for changes in net working capital in the second part of Table 10.13. Notice that at the end of the project's life, there is $49,500 in net working capital still to be recovered. Therefore, in the last year, the project returns $16,500 of NWC during the year and then returns the remaining $49,500 at the end of the year, for a total of $66,000.

TABLE 10.14   **Projected Total Cash Flows, Power Mulcher Project**

	Year								
	0	1	2	3	4	5	6	7	8
Operating cash flow		$146,457	$258,393	$ 294,033	$257,983	$232,252	$192,736	$153,252	$ 106,243
Change in NWC	–$ 20,000	– 34,000	– 36,000	– 18,000	750	8,250	16,500	16,500	66,000
Capital spending	– 800,000								126,400
Total project cash flow	–$820,000	$112,457	$222,393	$276,033	$258,733	$240,502	$209,236	$169,752	$298,643
Cumulative cash flow	–$820,000	–$707,543	–$485,150	–$209,116	–$ 49,617	$290,119	$499,355	$669,107	$967,750
Discounted cash flow @ 15%	– 820,000	97,789	168,161	181,496	147,932	119,572	90,458	63,816	97,627

Net present value (15%) = $146,852
Internal rate of return   = 19.86%
Payback   = 3.81 years

Capital Spending   Finally, we have to account for the long-term capital invested in the project. In this case, MMCC invests $800,000 at Year 0. By assumption, this equipment will be worth $160,000 at the end of the project. It will have a book value of zero at that time. As we discussed earlier, this $160,000 excess of market value over book value is taxable, so the aftertax proceeds will be $160,000 × (1 − .21) = $126,400. These figures are shown in the third part of Table 10.13.

Total Cash Flow and Value   We now have all the cash flow pieces, and we put them together in Table 10.14. If you notice, the project cash flows each year are the same as the cash flow from assets that we calculated in Chapter 3. In addition to the total project cash flows, we have calculated the cumulative cash flows and the discounted cash flows. At this point, it's essentially plug-and-chug to calculate the net present value, internal rate of return, and payback.

If we sum the discounted flows and the initial investment, the net present value (at 15 percent) works out to be $146,852. This is positive, so, based on these preliminary projections, the power mulcher project is acceptable. The internal, or DCF, rate of return is greater than 15 percent because the NPV is positive. It works out to be 19.86 percent, again indicating that the project is acceptable.

Looking at the cumulative cash flows, we can see that the project is paid back between three and four years because the table shows that the cumulative cash flow becomes positive at that time. As indicated, the fractional year works out to be $209,116/$258,733 = .81, so the payback is 3.81 years. We can't say whether or not this is good because we don't have a benchmark for MMCC. This is the usual problem with payback periods.

Conclusion   This completes our preliminary DCF analysis. Where do we go from here? If we have a great deal of confidence in our projections, there is no further analysis to be done. MMCC should begin production and marketing immediately. It is unlikely that this will be the case. It is important to remember that the result of our analysis is an estimate of NPV, and we will usually have less than complete confidence in our projections. This means we have more work to do. In particular, we will almost surely want to spend some time evaluating the quality of our estimates. We will take up this subject in the next chapter. For now, we look at some alternative definitions of operating cash flow, and we illustrate some different cases that arise in capital budgeting.

Alternative Definitions of Operating Cash Flow

10.5

The analysis we went through in the previous section is quite general and can be adapted to almost any capital investment problem. In the next section, we illustrate some particularly useful variations. Before we do so, we need to discuss the fact that there are different definitions of project operating cash flow that are commonly used, both in practice and in finance texts.

As we will see, the different approaches to operating cash flow that exist all measure the same thing. If they are used correctly, they all produce the same answer, and one is not necessarily any better or more useful than another. Unfortunately, the fact that alternative definitions are used does sometimes lead to confusion. For this reason, we examine several of these variations next to see how they are related.

In the discussion that follows, keep in mind that when we speak of cash flow, we literally mean dollars in less dollars out. This is all we are concerned with. Different definitions of operating cash flow amount to different ways of manipulating basic information about sales, costs, depreciation, and taxes to get at cash flow.

For a particular project and year under consideration, suppose we have the following estimates:

Sales = $1,500
Costs = $700
Depreciation = $600

With these estimates, notice that EBIT is:

$$EBIT = Sales - Costs - Depreciation$$
$$= \$1,500 - 700 - 600$$
$$= \$200$$

Once again, we assume that no interest is paid, so the tax bill is:

$$Taxes = EBIT \times T_C$$
$$= \$200 \times .21 = \$42$$

where T_C, the corporate tax rate, is 21 percent.

When we put all of this together, we see that project operating cash flow, OCF, is:

$$OCF = EBIT + Depreciation - Taxes$$
$$= \$200 + 600 - 42 = \$758$$

There are some other ways to determine OCF that could be (and are) used. We consider these next.

THE BOTTOM-UP APPROACH

Because we are ignoring any financing expenses, such as interest, in our calculations of project OCF, we can write project net income as:

$$\text{Project net income} = \text{EBIT} - \text{Taxes}$$
$$= \$200 - 42$$
$$= \$158$$

If we add the depreciation to both sides, we arrive at a slightly different and very common expression for OCF:

OCF = Net income + Depreciation   **10.1**
$$= \$158 + 600$$
$$= \$758$$

This is the *bottom-up* approach. Here, we start with the accountant's bottom line (net income) and add back any noncash deductions such as depreciation. It is crucial to remember that this definition of operating cash flow as net income plus depreciation is correct only if there is no interest expense subtracted in the calculation of net income.

Applying this approach to the shark attractant project (see Section 10.3), net income was $21,780 and depreciation was $30,000, so the bottom-up calculation is:

$$\text{OCF} = \$21{,}780 + 30{,}000 = \$51{,}780$$

This is exactly the same OCF we had previously.

THE TOP-DOWN APPROACH

Perhaps the most obvious way to calculate OCF is:

OCF = Sales − Costs − Taxes   **10.2**
$$= \$1{,}500 - 700 - 42 = \$758$$

This is the *top-down* approach, the second variation on the basic OCF definition. Here, we start at the top of the income statement with sales and work our way down to net cash flow by subtracting costs, taxes, and other expenses. Along the way, we leave out any strictly noncash items such as depreciation.

For the shark attractant project, the operating cash flow can be readily calculated using the top-down approach. With sales of $200,000, total costs (fixed plus variable) of $142,430, and a tax bill of $5,790, the OCF is:

$$\text{OCF} = \$200{,}000 - 142{,}430 - 5{,}790 = \$51{,}780$$

This is as we had before.

THE TAX SHIELD APPROACH

The third variation on our basic definition of OCF is the *tax shield* approach. This approach will be useful for some problems we consider in the next section. The tax shield definition of OCF is:

OCF = (Sales − Costs) × (1 − T_c) + Depreciation × T_c   **10.3**

where T_c is again the corporate tax rate. Assuming that $T_c = 21\%$, the OCF works out to be:

$$\text{OCF} = (\$1{,}500 - 700) \times .79 + 600 \times .21$$
$$= \$632 + 126$$
$$= \$758$$

This is as we had before.

This approach views OCF as having two components. The first part is what the project's cash flow would be if there were no depreciation expense. In this case, this would-have-been cash flow is $632.

The second part of OCF in this approach is the depreciation deduction multiplied by the tax rate. This is called the **depreciation tax shield**. We know that depreciation is a noncash expense. The only cash flow effect of deducting depreciation is to reduce our taxes, a benefit to us. At the current 21 percent corporate tax rate, every dollar in depreciation expense saves us 21 cents in taxes. So, in our example, the $600 depreciation deduction saves us $600 × .21 = $126 in taxes.

For the shark attractant project we considered earlier in the chapter, the depreciation tax shield would be $30,000 × .21 = $6,300. The aftertax value for sales less costs would be ($200,000 − 142,430) × (1 − .21) = $45,480. Adding these together yields the value of OCF:

OCF = $45,480 + 6,300 = $51,780

This calculation verifies that the tax shield approach is completely equivalent to the approach we used before.

> **depreciation tax shield**
> The tax saving that results from the depreciation deduction, calculated as depreciation multiplied by the corporate tax rate.

CONCLUSION

Now that we've seen that all of these approaches are the same, you're probably wondering why everybody doesn't just agree on one of them. One reason, as we will see in the next section, is that different approaches are useful in different circumstances. The best approach to use is whichever one happens to be the most convenient for the problem at hand.

Concept Questions

10.5a   What are the top-down and bottom-up definitions of operating cash flow?

10.5b   What is meant by the term *depreciation tax shield*?

Some Special Cases of Discounted Cash Flow Analysis

10.6

To finish our chapter, we look at three common cases involving discounted cash flow analysis. The first case involves investments that are primarily aimed at improving efficiency and thereby cutting costs. The second case we consider comes up when a firm is involved in submitting competitive bids. The third and final case arises in choosing between equipment options with different economic lives.

We could consider many other special cases, but these three are particularly important because problems similar to these are so common. Also, they illustrate some diverse applications of cash flow analysis and DCF valuation.

Excel Master It!
xlsx   Excel Master coverage online

EVALUATING COST-CUTTING PROPOSALS

One decision we frequently face is whether to upgrade existing facilities to make them more cost-effective. The issue is whether the cost savings are large enough to justify the necessary capital expenditure.

For example, suppose we are considering automating some part of an existing production process. The necessary equipment costs $80,000 to buy and install. The automation will save $22,000 per year (before taxes) by reducing labor and material costs. For simplicity, assume that the equipment has a five-year life and is depreciated to zero on a straight-line basis over that period. It will actually be worth $20,000 in five years. Should we automate? The tax rate is 21 percent, and the discount rate is 10 percent.

As always, the first step in making such a decision is to identify the relevant incremental cash flows. First, determining the relevant capital spending is easy enough. The initial cost is $80,000. The aftertax salvage value is $20,000 × (1 − .21) = $15,800 because the book value will be zero in five years. Second, there are no working capital consequences here, so we don't need to worry about changes in net working capital.

Operating cash flows are the third component to consider. Buying the new equipment affects our operating cash flows in two ways. First, we save $22,000 before taxes every year. In other words, the firm's operating income increases by $22,000, so this is the relevant incremental project operating income.

Second (and it's easy to overlook this), we have an additional depreciation deduction. In this case, the depreciation is $80,000/5 = $16,000 per year.

Because the project has an operating income of $22,000 (the annual pretax cost saving) and a depreciation deduction of $16,000, taking the project will increase the firm's EBIT by $22,000 − 16,000 = $6,000, so this is the project's EBIT.

Finally, because EBIT is rising for the firm, taxes will increase. This increase in taxes will be $6,000 × .21 = $1,260. With this information, we can compute operating cash flow in the usual way:

EBIT	$ 6,000
+ Depreciation	16,000
− Taxes	1,260
Operating cash flow	$20,740

So, our aftertax operating cash flow is $20,740.

It might be somewhat more enlightening to calculate operating cash flow using a different approach. What is actually going on here is very simple. First, the cost savings increase our pretax income by $22,000. We have to pay taxes on this amount, so our tax bill increases by .21 × $22,000 = $4,620. In other words, the $22,000 pretax saving amounts to $22,000 × (1 − .21) = $17,380 after taxes.

Second, the extra $16,000 in depreciation isn't really a cash outflow, but it does reduce our taxes by $16,000 × .21 = $3,360. The sum of these two components is $17,380 + 3,360 = $20,740, as we had before. Notice that the $3,360 is the depreciation tax shield we discussed earlier, and we have effectively used the tax shield approach here.

We can now finish our analysis. Based on our discussion, here are the relevant cash flows:

			Year			
	0	1	2	3	4	5
Operating cash flow		$20,740	$20,740	$20,740	$20,740	$20,740
Capital spending	−$80,000					15,800
Total cash flow	−$80,000	$20,740	$20,740	$20,740	$20,740	$36,540

At 10 percent, it's straightforward to verify that the NPV here is $8,431, so we should go ahead and automate.

| To Buy or Not to Buy | EXAMPLE 10.3 |

We are considering the purchase of a $200,000 computer-based inventory management system. It will be depreciated straight-line to zero over its four-year life. It will be worth $30,000 at the end of that time. The system will save us $60,000 before taxes in inventory-related costs. The relevant tax rate is 21 percent. Because the new setup is more efficient than our existing one, we will be able to carry less total inventory and thus free up $45,000 in net working capital. What is the NPV at 16 percent? What is the DCF return (the IRR) on this investment?

We can first calculate the operating cash flow. The aftertax cost savings are $60,000 × (1 − .21) = $47,400. The depreciation is $200,000/4 = $50,000 per year, so the depreciation tax shield is $50,000 × .21 = $10,500. Operating cash flow is $47,400 + 10,500 = $57,900 per year.

The capital spending involves $200,000 up front to buy the system. The aftertax salvage is $30,000 × (1 − .21) = $23,700. Finally, and this is the somewhat tricky part, the initial investment in net working capital is a $45,000 *inflow* because the system frees up working capital. Furthermore, we will have to put this back in at the end of the project's life. What this really means is simple: While the system is in operation, we have $45,000 to use elsewhere.

To finish our analysis, we can compute the total cash flows:

| | Year | | | | |
	0	1	2	3	4
Operating cash flow		$57,900	$57,900	$57,900	$57,900
Change in NWC	$ 45,000				− 45,000
Capital spending	− 200,000				23,700
Total cash flow	−$155,000	$57,900	$57,900	$57,900	$36,600

At 16 percent, the NPV is −$4,749, so the investment is not attractive. After some trial and error, we find that the NPV is zero when the discount rate is 14.36 percent, so the IRR on this investment is about 14.4 percent.

SETTING THE BID PRICE

Early on, we used discounted cash flow analysis to evaluate a proposed new product. A somewhat different (and common) scenario arises when we must submit a competitive bid to win a job. Under such circumstances, the winner is whoever submits the lowest bid.

There is an old joke concerning this process: The low bidder is whoever makes the biggest mistake. This is called the winner's curse. In other words, if you win, there is a good chance you underbid. In this section, we look at how to go about setting the bid price to avoid the winner's curse. The procedure we describe is useful anytime we have to set a price on a product or service.

To illustrate how to go about setting a bid price, imagine we are in the business of buying stripped-down truck platforms and then modifying them to customer specifications for resale. A local distributor has requested bids for five specially modified trucks each year for the next four years, for a total of 20 trucks in all.

We need to decide what price per truck to bid. The goal of our analysis is to determine the lowest price we can profitably charge. This maximizes our chances of being awarded the contract while guarding against the winner's curse.

Suppose we can buy the truck platforms for $10,000 each. The facilities we need can be leased for $24,000 per year. The labor and material cost to do the modification works out to be about $4,000 per truck. Total cost per year will thus be $24,000 + 5 × (10,000 + 4,000) = $94,000.

We will need to invest $60,000 in new equipment. This equipment will be depreciated straight-line to a zero salvage value over the four years. It will be worth about $5,000 at the end of that time. We will also need to invest $40,000 in raw materials inventory and other working capital items. The relevant tax rate is 21 percent. What price per truck should we bid if we require a 20 percent return on our investment?

We start by looking at the capital spending and net working capital investment. We have to spend $60,000 today for new equipment. The aftertax salvage value is $5,000 × (1 − .21) = $3,950. Furthermore, we have to invest $40,000 today in working capital. We will get this back in four years.

We can't determine the operating cash flow just yet because we don't know the sales price. If we draw a time line, here is what we have so far:

	Year				
	0	1	2	3	4
Operating cash flow		+OCF	+OCF	+OCF	+OCF
Change in NWC	−$ 40,000				$40,000
Capital spending	− 60,000				3,950
Total cash flow	−$100,000	+OCF	+OCF	+OCF	+OCF + $43,950

With this in mind, note that the key observation is the following: The lowest possible price we can profitably charge will result in a zero NPV at 20 percent. At that price, we earn exactly 20 percent on our investment.

Given this observation, we first need to determine what the operating cash flow must be for the NPV to equal zero. To do this, we calculate the present value of the $43,050 non-operating cash flow from the last year and subtract it from the $100,000 initial investment:

$$\$100,000 − 43,950/1.20^4 = \$100,000 − 21,195 = \$78,805$$

Once we have done this, our time line is as follows:

	Year				
	0	1	2	3	4
Total cash flow	−$78,805	+OCF	+OCF	+OCF	+OCF

As the time line suggests, the operating cash flow is now an unknown ordinary annuity amount. The four-year annuity factor for 20 percent is 2.58873, so we have:

$$NPV = 0 = −\$78,805 + OCF × 2.58873$$

This implies that:

$$OCF = \$78,805/2.58873 = \$30,442$$

So the operating cash flow needs to be $30,442 each year.

We're not quite finished. The final problem is to find out what sales price results in an operating cash flow of $30,442. The easiest way to do this is to recall that operating cash flow can be written as net income plus depreciation (the bottom-up definition). The depreciation here is $60,000/4 = $15,000. Given this, we can determine what net income must be:

$$\text{Operating cash flow} = \text{Net income} + \text{Depreciation}$$
$$\$30,442 = \text{Net income} + \$15,000$$
$$\text{Net income} = \$15,442$$

From here, we work our way backward up the income statement. If net income is $15,442, then our income statement is as follows:

Sales	?
Costs	$94,000
Depreciation	15,000
Taxes (21%)	?
Net income	$15,442

We can solve for sales by noting that:

$$\text{Net income} = (\text{Sales} - \text{Costs} - \text{Depreciation}) \times (1 - T_C)$$
$$\$15,442 = (\text{Sales} - \$94,000 - \$15,000) \times (1 - .21)$$
$$\text{Sales} = \$15,442/.79 + 94,000 + 15,000$$
$$= \$128,546$$

Sales per year must be $128,546. Because the contract calls for five trucks per year, the sales price has to be $128,546/5 = $25,709. If we round this up a bit, it looks as though we need to bid about $26,000 per truck. At this price, were we to get the contract, our return would be just over 20 percent.

EVALUATING EQUIPMENT OPTIONS WITH DIFFERENT LIVES

The final problem we consider involves choosing among different possible systems, equipment setups, or procedures. Our goal is to choose the most cost-effective alternative. The approach we consider here is necessary only when two special circumstances exist. First, the possibilities under evaluation have different economic lives. Second, and just as important, we will need whatever we buy more or less indefinitely. As a result, when it wears out, we will buy another one.

We can illustrate this problem with a simple example. Imagine we are in the business of manufacturing stamped metal subassemblies. Whenever a stamping mechanism wears out, we have to replace it with a new one to stay in business. We are considering which of two stamping mechanisms to buy.

Machine A costs $100 to buy and $10 per year to operate. It wears out and must be replaced every two years. Machine B costs $140 to buy and $8 per year to operate. It lasts for three years and must then be replaced. Ignoring taxes, which one should we choose if we use a 10 percent discount rate?

In comparing the two machines, we notice that the first is cheaper to buy, but it costs more to operate and it wears out more quickly. How can we evaluate these trade-offs? We can start by computing the present value of the costs for each:

Machine A: $PV = -\$100 + -10/1.1 + -10/1.1^2 = -\$117.36$
Machine B: $PV = -\$140 + -8/1.1 + -8/1.1^2 + -8/1.1^3 = -\$159.89$

Notice that *all* the numbers here are costs, so they all have negative signs. If we stopped here, it might appear that A is more attractive because the PV of the costs is less. However, all we have really discovered so far is that A effectively provides two years' worth of stamping service for $117.36, whereas B effectively provides three years' worth for $159.89. These costs are not directly comparable because of the difference in service periods.

We need to somehow work out a cost per year for these two alternatives. To do this, we ask: What amount, paid each year over the life of the machine, has the same PV of costs? This amount is called the **equivalent annual cost (EAC)**.

Calculating the EAC involves finding an unknown payment amount. For example, for Machine A, we need to find a two-year ordinary annuity with a PV of −$117.36 at 10 percent. Going back to Chapter 6, we know that the two-year annuity factor is:

equivalent annual cost (EAC)

The present value of a project's costs calculated on an annual basis.

$$\text{Annuity factor} = (1 - 1/1.10^2)/.10 = 1.7355$$

For Machine A, then, we have:

$$\text{PV of costs} = -\$117.36 = \text{EAC} \times 1.7355$$
$$\text{EAC} = -\$117.36/1.7355$$
$$= -\$67.62$$

For Machine B, the life is three years, so we first need the three-year annuity factor:

$$\text{Annuity factor} = (1 - 1/1.10^3)/.10 = 2.4869$$

We calculate the EAC for B just as we did for A:

$$\text{PV of costs} = -\$159.89 = \text{EAC} \times 2.4869$$
$$\text{EAC} = -\$159.89/2.4869$$
$$= -\$64.30$$

Based on this analysis, we should purchase B because it effectively costs $64.30 per year versus $67.62 for A. In other words, all things considered, B is cheaper. In this case, the longer life and lower operating cost are more than enough to offset the higher initial purchase price.

EXAMPLE 10.4   **Equivalent Annual Costs**

This extended example illustrates what happens to the EAC when we consider taxes. You are evaluating two different pollution control options. A filtration system will cost $1.1 million to install and $60,000 annually, before taxes, to operate. It will have to be completely replaced every five years. A precipitation system will cost $1.9 million to install but only $10,000 per year to operate. The precipitation equipment has an effective operating life of eight years. Straight-line depreciation is used throughout, and neither system has any salvage value. Which option should we select if we use a 12 percent discount rate? The tax rate is 21 percent.

We need to consider the EACs for the two systems because they have different service lives and will be replaced as they wear out. The relevant information can be summarized as follows:

	Filtration System	Precipitation System
Aftertax operating cost	−$ 47,400	−$ 7,900
Depreciation tax shield	46,200	49,875
Operating cash flow	−$ 1,200	$ 41,975
Economic life	5 years	8 years
Annuity factor (12%)	3.6048	4.9676
Present value of operating cash flow	−$ 4,326	$ 208,517
Capital spending	− 1,100,000	− 1,900,000
Total PV of costs	−$1,104,326	−$1,691,483

Notice that the operating cash flow is actually positive in the second case because of the large depreciation tax shield. This can occur whenever the operating cost is small relative to the purchase price.

To decide which system to purchase, we compute the EACs for both using the appropriate annuity factors:

Filtration system: −$1,104,326 = EAC × 3.6048
EAC = −$306,351
Precipitation system: −$1,691,483 = EAC × 4.9676
EAC = −$340,500

The filtration system is the cheaper of the two, so we select it. In this case, the longer life and smaller operating cost of the precipitation system are insufficient to offset its higher initial cost.

Concept Questions

10.6a In setting a bid price, we used a zero NPV as our benchmark. Explain why this is appropriate.

10.6b Under what circumstances do we have to worry about unequal economic lives? How do you interpret the EAC?

Summary and Conclusions   10.7

This chapter has described how to put together a discounted cash flow analysis. In it, we covered:

1. The identification of relevant project cash flows: We discussed project cash flows and described how to handle some issues that often come up, including sunk costs, opportunity costs, financing costs, net working capital, and erosion.

2. Preparing and using pro forma, or projected, financial statements: We showed how information from such financial statements is useful in coming up with projected cash flows, and we also looked at some alternative definitions of operating cash flow.

3. The role of net working capital and depreciation in determining project cash flows: We saw that including the change in net working capital was important in cash flow analysis because it adjusted for the discrepancy between accounting revenues and costs and cash revenues and costs. We also went over the calculation of depreciation expense under current tax law.

4. Some special cases encountered in using discounted cash flow analysis: Here we looked at three special issues. First, we evaluated cost-cutting investments. Next, we examined how to go about setting a bid price. Finally, we looked at unequal lives problem.

The discounted cash flow analysis we've covered here is a standard tool in the business world. It is a very powerful tool, so care should be taken in its use. The most important thing is to identify the cash flows in a way that makes economic sense. This chapter gives you a good start in learning how to do this.

CONNECT TO FINANCE

 *Connect Finance* offers you plenty of opportunities to practice mastering these concepts. Log on to connect.mheducation.com to learn more. If you like what you see, ask your professor about using *Connect Finance*!

Can you answer the following *Connect* Quiz questions?

Section 10.1   The analysis of a project based on the project's relevant cash flows is referred to as the _____.

Section 10.2   What should NOT be included as an incremental cash flow for a proposed project?

Section 10.3   A project has projected sales of $62,000, costs of $48,000, depreciation expense of $6,200, and a tax rate of 21 percent. What is the operating cash flow for this project?

Section 10.4   An asset costs $24,000 and is classified as three-year MACRS property. What is the depreciation expense in Year 2?

Section 10.5   A firm has sales for the year of $92,000, costs of $46,000, and taxes of $21,000. What is the operating cash flow for the year?

Section 10.6   What rate of return will a firm earn if it accepts a project with a sales price per unit set equal to the bid price?

CHAPTER REVIEW AND SELF-TEST PROBLEMS

10.1   **Capital Budgeting for Project X** Based on the following information for Project X, should we undertake the venture? To answer, first prepare a pro forma income statement for each year. Next calculate operating cash flow. Finish the problem by determining total cash flow and then calculating NPV assuming a 28 percent required return. Use a 21 percent tax rate throughout. For help, look back at our shark attractant and power mulcher examples.

     Project X involves a new type of graphite composite in-line skate wheel. We think we can sell 6,000 units per year at a price of $1,000 each. Variable costs will run about $400 per unit, and the product should have a four-year life.

     Fixed costs for the project will run $450,000 per year. Further, we will need to invest a total of $1,250,000 in manufacturing equipment. This equipment is seven-year MACRS property for tax purposes. In four years, the equipment will be worth about half of what we paid for it. We will have to invest $1,150,000 in net working capital at the start. After that, net working capital requirements will be 25 percent of sales.

10.2   **Calculating Operating Cash Flow** Mont Blanc Livestock Pens, Inc., has projected a sales volume of $1,650 for the second year of a proposed expansion project. Costs normally run 60 percent of sales, or about $990 in this case. The depreciation expense will be $100, and the tax rate is 21 percent. What is the operating cash flow? Calculate your answer using all of the approaches (including the top-down, bottom-up, and tax shield approaches) described in the chapter.

10.3   **Spending Money to Save Money?** For help on this one, refer back to the computerized inventory management system in Example 10.3. Here, we're contemplating a new automatic surveillance system to replace our current contract security system. It will cost $450,000 to get the new system. The cost will be depreciated straight-line to zero over the system's four-year expected life. The system is expected to be worth $250,000 at the end of four years after removal costs.

We think the new system will save us $125,000 per year, before taxes, in contract security costs. The tax rate is 21 percent. What are the NPV and IRR for buying the new system? The required return is 17 percent.

ANSWERS TO CHAPTER REVIEW AND SELF-TEST PROBLEMS

10.1 To develop the pro forma income statements, we need to calculate the depreciation for each of the four years. The relevant MACRS percentages, depreciation allowances, and book values for the first four years are shown here:

Year	MACRS Percentage	Depreciation	Ending Book Value
1	14.29%	.1429 × $1,250,000 = $178,625	$1,071,375
2	24.49	.2449 × 1,250,000 = 306,125	765,250
3	17.49	.1749 × 1,250,000 = 218,625	546,625
4	12.49	.1249 × 1,250,000 = 156,125	390,500

The projected income statements, therefore, are as follows:

	Year			
	1	**2**	**3**	**4**
Sales	$6,000,000	$6,000,000	$6,000,000	$6,000,000
Variable costs	2,400,000	2,400,000	2,400,000	2,400,000
Fixed costs	450,000	450,000	450,000	450,000
Depreciation	178,625	306,125	218,625	156,125
EBIT	$2,971,375	$2,843,875	$2,931,375	$2,993,875
Taxes (21%)	623,989	597,214	615,589	628,714
Net income	$2,347,386	$2,246,661	$2,315,786	$2,365,161

Based on this information, here are the operating cash flows:

	Year			
	1	**2**	**3**	**4**
EBIT	$2,971,375	$2,843,875	$2,931,375	$2,993,875
Depreciation	178,625	306,125	218,625	156,125
Taxes	623,989	597,214	615,589	628,714
Operating cash flow	$2,526,011	$2,552,786	$2,534,411	$2,521,286

We now have to worry about the nonoperating cash flows. Net working capital starts out at $1,150,000 and then rises to 25 percent of sales, or $1,500,000. This is a $350,000 change in net working capital.

Finally, we have to invest $1,250,000 to get started. In four years, the book value of this investment will be $390,500, compared to an estimated market value of $625,000 (half of the cost). The aftertax salvage is thus $625,000 − .21 × ($625,000 − 390,500) = $575,755.

When we combine all this information, the projected cash flows for Project X are as follows:

		Year			
	0	1	2	3	4
Operating cash flow		$2,526,011	$2,552,786	$2,534,411	$2,521,286
Change in NWC	−$1,150,000	− 350,000			1,500,000
Capital spending	− 1,250,000				575,755
Total cash flow	−$2,400,000	$2,176,011	$2,552,786	$2,534,411	$4,597,041

With these cash flows, the NPV at 28 percent is:

$$NPV = -\$2,400,000 + 2,176,011/1.28 + 2,552,786/1.28^2$$
$$+2,534,411/1.28^3 + 4,597,041/1.28^4$$
$$= \$3,779,139$$

So, this project appears to be quite profitable.

10.2 First, we can calculate the project's EBIT, its tax bill, and its net income:

$$EBIT = Sales - Costs - Depreciation$$
$$= \$1,650 - 990 - 100 = \$560$$
$$Taxes = \$560 \times .21 = \$118$$
$$Net\ income = \$560 - 118 = \$442$$

With these numbers, operating cash flow is:

$$OCF = EBIT + Depreciation - Taxes$$
$$= \$560 + 100 - 118$$
$$= \$542$$

Using the other OCF definitions, we have:

$$Bottom\text{-}up\ OCF = Net\ income + Depreciation$$
$$= \$442 + 100$$
$$= \$542$$

$$Top\text{-}down\ OCF = Sales - Costs - Taxes$$
$$= \$1,650 - 990 - 118$$
$$= \$542$$

$$Tax\ shield\ OCF = (Sales - Costs) \times (1 - .21) + Depreciation \times .21$$
$$= (\$1,650 - 990) \times .79 + 100 \times .21$$
$$= \$542$$

As expected, all of these definitions produce exactly the same answer.

10.3 The $125,000 pretax saving amounts to $(1 - .21) \times \$125,000 = \$98,750$ after taxes. The annual depreciation of $\$450,000/4 = \$112,500$ generates a tax shield of $.21 \times \$112,500 = \$23,625$ each year. Putting these together, we calculate that the operating cash flow is $\$98,750 + 23,625 = \$122,375$. Because the book value is zero in four years, the aftertax salvage value is $(1 - .21) \times \$250,000 = \$197,500$. There are no working capital consequences, so here are the cash flows:

	Year			
	0	**1**	**2**	**3**	**4**
Operating cash flow		$122,375	$122,375	$122,375	$122,375
Capital spending	−$450,000				165,000
Total cash flow	−$450,000	$122,375	$122,375	$122,375	$287,375

You can verify that the NPV at 17 percent is −$26,244, and the return on the new surveillance system is only about 14.40 percent. The project does not appear to be profitable.

CONCEPTS REVIEW AND CRITICAL THINKING QUESTIONS

1. **Opportunity Cost [LO1]** In the context of capital budgeting, what is an opportunity cost?

2. **Depreciation [LO1]** Given the choice, would a firm prefer to use MACRS depreciation or straight-line depreciation? Why?

3. **Net Working Capital [LO1]** In our capital budgeting examples, we assumed that a firm would recover all of the working capital it invested in a project. Is this a reasonable assumption? When might it not be valid?

4. **Stand-Alone Principle [LO1]** Suppose a financial manager is quoted as saying, "Our firm uses the stand-alone principle. Because we treat projects like minifirms in our evaluation process, we include financing costs because they are relevant at the firm level." Critically evaluate this statement.

5. **Equivalent Annual Cost [LO4]** When is EAC analysis appropriate for comparing two or more projects? Why is this method used? Are there any implicit assumptions required by this method that you find troubling? Explain.

6. **Cash Flow and Depreciation [LO1]** "When evaluating projects, we're concerned with only the relevant incremental aftertax cash flows. Therefore, because depreciation is a noncash expense, we should ignore its effects when evaluating projects." Critically evaluate this statement.

7. **Capital Budgeting Considerations [LO1]** A major college textbook publisher has an existing finance textbook. The publisher is debating whether to produce an "essentialized" version, meaning a shorter (and lower-priced) book. What are some of the considerations that should come into play?

To answer the next three questions, refer to the following example. In 2003, Porsche unveiled its new sports utility vehicle (SUV), the Cayenne. With a price tag of over $40,000, the Cayenne went from zero to 62 mph in 9.7 seconds. Porsche's decision to enter the SUV market was a response to the runaway success of other high-priced SUVs such as the Mercedes-Benz M-class. Vehicles in this class had generated years of high profits. The Cayenne certainly spiced up the market, and Porsche subsequently introduced the Cayenne Turbo S, which goes from zero to 60 mph in 3.8 seconds and has a top speed of 176 mph. The price tag for the Cayenne Turbo S in 2018? About $130,000!

Some analysts questioned Porsche's entry into the luxury SUV market. The analysts were concerned not only that Porsche was a late entry into the market, but also that the introduction of the Cayenne would damage Porsche's reputation as a maker of high-performance automobiles.

8. **Erosion** [LO1] In evaluating the Cayenne, would you use the term *erosion* to describe the possible damage to Porsche's reputation?

9. **Capital Budgeting** [LO1] Porsche was one of the last manufacturers to enter the sports utility vehicle market. Why would one company decide to proceed with a product when other companies, at least initially, decide not to enter the market?

10. **Capital Budgeting** [LO1] In evaluating the Cayenne, what do you think Porsche needs to assume regarding the substantial profit margins that exist in this market? Is it likely they will be maintained as the market becomes more competitive, or will Porsche be able to maintain the profit margin because of its image and the performance of the Cayenne?

QUESTIONS AND PROBLEMS

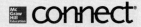

BASIC

(Questions 1–20)

1. **Relevant Cash Flows** [LO1] Parker & Stone, Inc., is looking at setting up a new manufacturing plant in South Park to produce garden tools. The company bought some land six years ago for $3.6 million in anticipation of using it as a warehouse and distribution site, but the company has since decided to rent these facilities from a competitor instead. If the land were sold today, the company would net $4.1 million. The company wants to build its new manufacturing plant on this land; the plant will cost $18.1 million to build, and the site requires $950,000 worth of grading before it is suitable for construction. What is the proper cash flow amount to use as the initial investment in fixed assets when evaluating this project? Why?

2. **Relevant Cash Flows** [LO1] Winnebagel Corp. currently sells 20,000 motor homes per year at $97,000 each and 14,000 luxury motor coaches per year at $145,000 each. The company wants to introduce a new portable camper to fill out its product line; it hopes to sell 30,000 of these campers per year at $21,000 each. An independent consultant has determined that if the company introduces the new campers, it should boost the sales of its existing motor homes by 2,700 units per year and reduce the sales of its motor coaches by 1,300 units per year. What is the amount to use as the annual sales figure when evaluating this project? Why?

3. **Calculating Projected Net Income** [LO1] A proposed new investment has projected sales of $585,000. Variable costs are 44 percent of sales, and fixed costs are $187,000; depreciation is $51,000. Prepare a pro forma income statement assuming a tax rate of 21 percent. What is the projected net income?

4. **Calculating OCF** [LO1] Consider the following income statement:

Sales	$747,300
Costs	582,600
Depreciation	89,300
EBIT	?
Taxes (22%)	?
Net income	?

Fill in the missing numbers and then calculate the OCF. What is the depreciation tax shield?

5. **OCF from Several Approaches** [LO1] A proposed new project has projected sales of $175,000, costs of $93,000, and depreciation of $24,800. The tax rate is 23 percent. Calculate operating cash flow using the four different approaches described in the chapter and verify that the answer is the same in each case.

6. **Calculating Depreciation [LO1]** A piece of newly purchased industrial equipment ✗
costs $1,375,000 and is classified as seven-year property under MACRS. Calculate the
annual depreciation allowances and end-of-the-year book values for this equipment.

7. **Calculating Salvage Value [LO1]** Consider an asset that costs $680,000 and is de- ✗
preciated straight-line to zero over its eight-year tax life. The asset is to be used in a
five-year project; at the end of the project, the asset can be sold for $143,000. If the
relevant tax rate is 21 percent, what is the aftertax cash flow from the sale of this asset?

8. **Calculating Salvage Value [LO1]** An asset used in a four-year project falls in
the five-year MACRS class for tax purposes. The asset has an acquisition cost of
$5,100,000 and will be sold for $1,600,000 at the end of the project. If the tax rate is
21 percent, what is the aftertax salvage value of the asset?

9. **Calculating Project OCF [LO1]** Quad Enterprises is considering a new three-year
expansion project that requires an initial fixed asset investment of $2.32 million. The
fixed asset will be depreciated straight-line to zero over its three-year tax life, after
which time it will be worthless. The project is estimated to generate $1.735 million
in annual sales, with costs of $650,000. If the tax rate is 21 percent, what is the OCF
for this project?

10. **Calculating Project NPV [LO1]** In the previous problem, suppose the required
return on the project is 12 percent. What is the project's NPV?

11. **Calculating Project Cash Flow from Assets [LO1]** In the previous problem, suppose the project requires an initial investment in net working capital of $250,000, and
the fixed asset will have a market value of $180,000 at the end of the project. What is
the project's Year 0 net cash flow? Year 1? Year 2? Year 3? What is the new NPV?

12. **NPV and MACRS [LO1]** In the previous problem, suppose the fixed asset actually
falls into the three-year MACRS class. All the other facts are the same. What is the
project's Year 1 net cash flow now? Year 2? Year 3? What is the new NPV?

13. **NPV and Bonus Depreciation [LO1]** In the previous problem, suppose the fixed
asset actually qualifies for 100 percent bonus depreciation in the first year. All the
other facts are the same. What is the project's Year 1 net cash flow now? Year 2?
Year 3? What is the new NPV?

14. **Project Evaluation [LO1]** Dog Up! Franks is looking at a new sausage system
with an installed cost of $460,000. This cost will be depreciated straight-line to
zero over the project's five-year life, at the end of which the sausage system can be
scrapped for $55,000. The sausage system will save the firm $155,000 per year in
pretax operating costs, and the system requires an initial investment in net working
capital of $29,000. If the tax rate is 21 percent and the discount rate is 10 percent,
what is the NPV of this project?

15. **NPV and Bonus Depreciation [LO1]** In the previous problem, suppose the fixed
asset actually qualifies for 100 percent bonus depreciation in the first year. What is
the new NPV?

16. **Project Evaluation [LO1]** Your firm is contemplating the purchase of a new
$485,000 computer-based order entry system. The system will be depreciated
straight-line to zero over its five-year life. It will be worth $35,000 at the end of that
time. You will save $140,000 before taxes per year in order processing costs, and you
will be able to reduce working capital by $60,000 (this is a one-time reduction). If the
tax rate is 24 percent, what is the IRR for this project?

17. **Project Evaluation [LO2]** In the previous problem, suppose your required return
on the project is 11 percent and your pretax cost savings are $150,000 per year. Will
you accept the project? What if the pretax cost savings are $100,000 per year? At

what level of pretax cost savings would you be indifferent between accepting the project and not accepting it?

18. **Calculating EAC [LO4]** A five-year project has an initial fixed asset investment of $315,000, an initial NWC investment of $25,000, and an annual OCF of −$35,000. The fixed asset is fully depreciated over the life of the project and has no salvage value. If the required return is 11 percent, what is this project's equivalent annual cost, or EAC?

19. **Calculating EAC [LO4]** You are evaluating two different silicon wafer milling machines. The Techron I costs $245,000, has a three-year life, and has pretax operating costs of $63,000 per year. The Techron II costs $420,000, has a five-year life, and has pretax operating costs of $35,000 per year. For both milling machines, use straight-line depreciation to zero over the project's life and assume a salvage value of $40,000. If your tax rate is 22 percent and your discount rate is 10 percent, compute the EAC for both machines. Which do you prefer? Why?

20. **Calculating a Bid Price [LO3]** Martin Enterprises needs someone to supply it with 125,000 cartons of machine screws per year to support its manufacturing needs over the next five years, and you've decided to bid on the contract. It will cost you $910,000 to install the equipment necessary to start production; you'll depreciate this cost straight-line to zero over the project's life. You estimate that, in five years, this equipment can be salvaged for $85,000. Your fixed production costs will be $485,000 per year, and your variable production costs should be $17.35 per carton. You also need an initial investment in net working capital of $90,000. If your tax rate is 21 percent and you require a return of 12 percent on your investment, what bid price should you submit?

INTERMEDIATE
(Questions 21–33)

21. **Cost-Cutting Proposals [LO2]** Masters Machine Shop is considering a four-year project to improve its production efficiency. Buying a new machine press for $385,000 is estimated to result in $145,000 in annual pretax cost savings. The press falls in the MACRS five-year class, and it will have a salvage value at the end of the project of $45,000. The press also requires an initial investment in spare parts inventory of $20,000, along with an additional $3,100 in inventory for each succeeding year of the project. If the shop's tax rate is 22 percent and its discount rate is 9 percent, should the company buy and install the machine press?

22. **NPV and Bonus Depreciation [LO1]** Eggz, Inc., is considering the purchase of new equipment that will allow the company to collect loose hen feathers for sale. The equipment will cost $425,000 and will be eligible for 100 percent bonus depreciation. The equipment can be sold for $25,000 at the end of the project in 5 years. Sales would be $275,000 per year, with annual fixed costs of $47,000 and variable costs equal to 35 percent of sales. The project would require an investment of $25,000 in NWC that would be returned at the end of the project. The tax rate is 22 percent and the required return is 9 percent. What is the project's NPV?

23. **Comparing Mutually Exclusive Projects [LO1]** Letang Industrial Systems Company (LISC) is trying to decide between two different conveyor belt systems. System A costs $265,000, has a four-year life, and requires $73,000 in pretax annual operating costs. System B costs $345,000, has a six-year life, and requires $67,000 in pretax annual operating costs. Both systems are to be depreciated straight-line to zero over their lives and will have zero salvage value. Whichever project is chosen, it will *not* be replaced when it wears out. If the tax rate is 21 percent and the discount rate is 8 percent, which project should the firm choose?

24. **Comparing Mutually Exclusive Projects [LO4]** Suppose in the previous problem that the company always needs a conveyor belt system; when one wears out, it must be replaced. Which project should the firm choose now?

25. **Calculating a Bid Price** [LO3] Consider a project to supply 100 million postage stamps per year to the U.S. Postal Service for the next five years. You have an idle parcel of land available that cost $750,000 five years ago; if the land were sold today, it would net you $1,125,000 aftertax. The land can be sold for $1,295,000 after taxes in five years. You will need to install $5.1 million in new manufacturing plant and equipment to actually produce the stamps; this plant and equipment will be depreciated straight-line to zero over the project's five-year life. The equipment can be sold for $450,000 at the end of the project. You will also need $425,000 in initial net working capital for the project, and an additional investment of $50,000 in every year thereafter. Your production costs are .38 cents per stamp, and you have fixed costs of $1.1 million per year. If your tax rate is 23 percent and your required return on this project is 10 percent, what bid price should you submit on the contract?

26. **Interpreting a Bid Price** [LO3] In the previous problem, suppose you were going to use a three-year MACRS depreciation schedule for your manufacturing equipment and you could keep working capital investments down to only $25,000 per year. How would this new information affect your calculated bid price? What if you used 100 bonus depreciation?

27. **Comparing Mutually Exclusive Projects** [LO4] Vandelay Industries is considering the purchase of a new machine for the production of latex. Machine A costs $2,900,000 and will last for six years. Variable costs are 35 percent of sales, and fixed costs are $210,000 per year. Machine B costs $5,800,000 and will last for nine years. Variable costs for this machine are 30 percent of sales and fixed costs are $245,000 per year. The sales for each machine will be $13 million per year. The required return is 10 percent, and the tax rate is 24 percent. Both machines will be depreciated on a straight-line basis. If the company plans to replace the machine when it wears out on a perpetual basis, which machine should it choose?

28. **Equivalent Annual Cost** [LO4] Light-emitting diode (LED) light bulbs have become required in recent years, but do they make financial sense? Suppose a typical 60-watt incandescent light bulb costs $.45 and lasts for 1,000 hours. A 7-watt LED, which provides the same light, costs $2.25 and lasts for 40,000 hours. A kilowatt-hour of electricity costs $.121, which is about the national average. A kilowatt-hour is 1,000 watts for 1 hour. If you require a 10 percent return and use a light fixture 500 hours per year, what is the equivalent annual cost of each lightbulb?

29. **Break-Even Cost** [LO2] The previous problem suggests that using LEDs instead of incandescent bulbs is a no-brainer. However, electricity costs actually vary quite a bit depending on location and user type (you can get information on your rates from your local power company). An industrial user in West Virginia might pay $.04 per kilowatt-hour whereas a residential user in Hawaii might pay $.25. What's the break-even cost per kilowatt-hour in Problem 25?

30. **Break-Even Replacement** [LO2] The previous two problems suggest that using LEDs is a good idea from a purely financial perspective unless you live in an area where power is relatively inexpensive, but there is another wrinkle. Suppose you have a residence with a lot of incandescent bulbs that are used on average 500 hours a year. The average bulb will be about halfway through its life, so it will have 500 hours remaining (and you can't tell which bulbs are older or newer). At what cost per kilowatt-hour does it make sense to replace your incandescent bulbs today?

31. **Issues in Capital Budgeting** [LO1] Before LEDs became a popular replacement for incandescent light bulbs, compact fluorescent lamps (CFLs) were hailed as the new generation of lighting. However, CFLs had even more wrinkles. In no particular order:

    1. Incandescent bulbs generate a lot more heat than CFLs.

2. CFL prices will probably decline relative to incandescent bulbs.

3. CFLs unavoidably contain small amounts of mercury, a significant environmental hazard, and special precautions must be taken in disposing of burned-out units (and also in cleaning up a broken lamp). Currently, there is no agreed-upon way to recycle a CFL. Incandescent bulbs pose no disposal/breakage hazards.

4. Depending on a light's location (or the number of lights), there can be a nontrivial cost to change bulbs (i.e., labor cost in a business).

5. Coal-fired power generation accounts for a substantial portion of the mercury emissions in the U.S., though the emissions will drop sharply in the relatively near future.

6. Power generation accounts for a substantial portion of CO_2 emissions in the U.S.

7. CFLs are more energy and material intensive to manufacture. On-site mercury contamination and worker safety are issues.

8. If you install a CFL in a permanent lighting fixture in a building, you will probably move long before the CFL burns out.

9. Even as CFLs began to replace incandescent light bulbs, LEDs were in the latter stages of development. At the time, LEDs were much more expensive than CFLs, but costs were coming down. LEDs last much longer than CFLs and use even less power. Plus, LEDs don't contain mercury.

Qualitatively, how would these issues affect your position in the CFL versus incandescent light bulb debate? Some countries banned incandescent bulbs. Does your analysis suggest such a move was wise? Are there other regulations short of an outright ban that make sense to you?

32. **Replacement Decisions** [LO2] Your small remodeling business has two work vehicles. One is a small passenger car used for job site visits and for other general business purposes. The other is a heavy truck used to haul equipment. The car gets 25 miles per gallon (mpg). The truck gets 10 mpg. You want to improve gas mileage to save money, and you have enough money to upgrade one vehicle. The upgrade cost will be the same for both vehicles. An upgraded car will get 40 mpg; an upgraded truck will get 12.5 mpg. The cost of gasoline is $2.65 per gallon. Assuming an upgrade is a good idea in the first place, which one should you upgrade? Both vehicles are driven 12,000 miles per year.

33. **Replacement Decisions** [LO2] In the previous problem, suppose you drive the truck x miles per year. How many miles would you have to drive the car before upgrading the car would be the better choice? *Hint*: Look at the relative gas savings.

CHALLENGE
(Questions 34–40)

34. **Calculating Project NPV** [LO1] You have been hired as a consultant for Pristine Urban-Tech Zither, Inc. (PUTZ), manufacturers of fine zithers. The market for zithers is growing quickly. The company bought some land three years ago for $1.9 million in anticipation of using it as a toxic waste dump site but has recently hired another company to handle all toxic materials. Based on a recent appraisal, the company believes it could sell the land for $2.1 million on an aftertax basis. In four years, the land could be sold for $2.3 million after taxes. The company also hired a marketing firm to analyze the zither market, at a cost of $175,000. An excerpt of the marketing report is as follows:

> The zither industry will have a rapid expansion in the next four years. With the brand name recognition that PUTZ brings to bear, we feel that the company will be able to sell 5,100, 5,800, 6,400, and 4,700 units each year for the next four years, respectively.

Again, capitalizing on the name recognition of PUTZ, we feel that a premium price of $425 can be charged for each zither. Because zithers appear to be a fad, we feel at the end of the four-year period, sales should be discontinued.

PUTZ believes that fixed costs for the project will be $345,000 per year, and variable costs are 15 percent of sales. The equipment necessary for production will cost $2.65 million and will be depreciated according to a three-year MACRS schedule. At the end of the project, the equipment can be scrapped for $395,000. Net working capital of $125,000 will be required immediately. PUTZ has a tax rate of 22 percent, and the required return on the project is 13 percent. What is the NPV of the project?

35. **NPV and Bonus Depreciation** [LO1] In the previous problem, suppose the fixed asset actually qualifies for 100 percent bonus depreciation in the first year. What is the new NPV?

36. **Project Evaluation** [LO1] Aria Acoustics, Inc. (AAI), projects unit sales for a new seven-octave voice emulation implant as follows:

Year	Unit Sales
1	73,000
2	86,000
3	105,000
4	97,000
5	67,000

Production of the implants will require $1,500,000 in net working capital to start and additional net working capital investments each year equal to 15 percent of the projected sales increase for the following year. Total fixed costs are $3,200,000 per year, variable production costs are $255 per unit, and the units are priced at $375 each. The equipment needed to begin production has an installed cost of $16,500,000. Because the implants are intended for professional singers, this equipment is considered industrial machinery and thus qualifies as seven-year MACRS property. In five years, this equipment can be sold for about 20 percent of its acquisition cost. The tax rate is 21 percent and the required return is 18 percent. Based on these preliminary project estimates, what is the NPV of the project? What is the IRR?

37. **Calculating Required Savings** [LO2] A proposed cost-saving device has an installed cost of $735,000. The device will be used in a five-year project but is classified as three-year MACRS property for tax purposes. The required initial net working capital investment is $55,000, the tax rate is 22 percent, and the project discount rate is 9 percent. The device has an estimated Year 5 salvage value of $85,000. What level of pretax cost savings do we require for this project to be profitable?

38. **Financial Break-Even Analysis** [LO2] To solve the bid price problem presented in the text, we set the project NPV equal to zero and found the required price using the definition of OCF. Thus the bid price represents a financial break-even level for the project. This type of analysis can be extended to many other types of problems.

a. In Problem 20, assume that the price per carton is $26 and find the project NPV. What does your answer tell you about your bid price? What do you know about the number of cartons you can sell and still break even? How about your level of costs?

b. Solve Problem 20 again with the price still at $26, but find the quantity of cartons per year that you can supply and still break even. *Hint*: It's less than 125,000.

c. Repeat (b) with a price of $26 and a quantity of 125,000 cartons per year, and find the highest level of fixed costs you could afford and still break even. *Hint*: It's more than $485,000.

39. Calculating a Bid Price [LO3] Your company has been approached to bid on a contract to sell 4,800 voice recognition (VR) computer keyboards per year for four years. Due to technological improvements, beyond that time they will be outdated and no sales will be possible. The equipment necessary for the production will cost $3.1 million and will be depreciated on a straight-line basis to a zero salvage value. Production will require an investment in net working capital of $395,000 to be returned at the end of the project, and the equipment can be sold for $305,000 at the end of production. Fixed costs are $570,000 per year, and variable costs are $75 per unit. In addition to the contract, you feel your company can sell 11,400, 13,500, 17,900, and 10,400 additional units to companies in other countries over the next four years, respectively, at a price of $170. This price is fixed. The tax rate is 23 percent, and the required return is 10 percent. Additionally, the president of the company will undertake the project only if it has an NPV of $100,000. What bid price should you set for the contract?

40. Replacement Decisions [LO2] Suppose we are thinking about replacing an old computer with a new one. The old one cost us $1,560,000; the new one will cost $1,872,000. The new machine will be depreciated straight-line to zero over its five-year life. It will probably be worth about $360,000 after five years.

The old computer is being depreciated at a rate of $312,000 per year. It will be completely written off in three years. If we don't replace it now, we will have to replace it in two years. We can sell it now for $504,000; in two years, it will probably be worth $144,000. The new machine will save us $348,000 per year in operating costs. The tax rate is 22 percent, and the discount rate is 12 percent.

a. Suppose we recognize that if we don't replace the computer now, we will be replacing it in two years. Should we replace it now or should we wait? *Hint*: What we effectively have here is a decision either to "invest" in the old computer (by not selling it) or to invest in the new one. Notice that the two investments have unequal lives.

b. Suppose we consider only whether we should replace the old computer now without worrying about what's going to happen in two years. What are the relevant cash flows? Should we replace it or not? *Hint*: Consider the net change in the firm's aftertax cash flows if we do the replacement.

EXCEL MASTER IT! PROBLEM

For this Master It! assignment, refer to the Conch Republic Electronics minicase below. For your convenience, we have entered the relevant values in the case such as the price and variable cost. For this project, answer the following questions:

a. What is the profitability index of the project?

b. What is the IRR of the project?

c. What is the NPV of the project?

d. At what price would Conch Republic Electronics be indifferent to accepting the project?

e. At what level of variable costs per unit would Conch Republic Electronics be indifferent to accepting the project?

MINICASE

Conch Republic Electronics, Part 1

Conch Republic Electronics is a midsized electronics manufacturer located in Key West, Florida. The company president is Shelley Couts, who inherited the company. When it was founded over 70 years ago, the company originally repaired radios and other household appliances. Over the years, the company expanded into manufacturing and is now a reputable manufacturer of various electronic items. Jay McCanless, a recent MBA graduate, has been hired by the company's finance department.

One of the major revenue-producing items manufactured by Conch Republic is a smartphone. Conch Republic currently has one smartphone model on the market, and sales have been excellent. The smartphone is a unique item in that it comes in a variety of tropical colors and is preprogrammed to play Jimmy Buffett music. However, as with any electronic item, technology changes rapidly, and the current smartphone has limited features in comparison with newer models. Conch Republic spent $750,000 to develop a prototype for a new smartphone that has all the features of the existing smartphone but adds new features such as WiFi tethering. The company has spent a further $200,000 for a marketing study to determine the expected sales figures for the new smartphone.

Conch Republic can manufacture the new smartphones for $220 each in variable costs. Fixed costs for the operation are estimated to run $6.4 million per year. The estimated sales volume is 155,000, 165,000, 125,000, 95,000, and 75,000 per year for the next five years, respectively. The unit price of the new smartphone will be $535. The necessary equipment can be purchased for $43.5 million and will be depreciated on a seven-year MACRS schedule. It is believed the value of the equipment in five years will be $6.5 million.

As previously stated, Conch Republic currently manufactures a smartphone. Production of the existing model is expected to be terminated in two years. If Conch Republic does not introduce the new smartphone, sales will be 95,000 units and 65,000 units for the next two years, respectively. The price of the existing smartphone is $385 per unit, with variable costs of $145 each and fixed costs of $4.3 million per year. If Conch Republic does introduce the new smartphone, sales of the existing smartphone will fall by 30,000 units per year, and the price of the existing units will have to be lowered to $215 each. Net working capital for the smartphones will be 20 percent of sales and will occur with the timing of the cash flows for the year; for example, there is no initial outlay for NWC, but changes in NWC will first occur in Year 1 with the first year's sales. Conch Republic has a 21 percent corporate tax rate and a required return of 12 percent.

Shelley has asked Jay to prepare a report that answers the following questions.

QUESTIONS

1. What is the payback period of the project?
2. What is the profitability index of the project?
3. What is the IRR of the project?
4. What is the NPV of the project?

11 Project Analysis and Evaluation

IN THE SUMMER OF 2016, the movie *Ben-Hur*, starring Jack Huston and Morgan Freeman, thundered into theaters with the slogan, "First to finish. Last to die." But what died was the film's box office. One critic called it "a dull, clunking return to one of cinema's great warhorses." Others were even more harsh, saying the movie was "a digitalized eyesore hobbled in every department by staggering incompetence."

Looking at the numbers, *Ben-Hur*'s losses were epic. After production, distribution, and marketing costs, movie maker MGM and its partners were estimated to have lost as much as $120 million on the film. In fact, about 4 out of 10 movies lose money at the box office, though DVD sales often help the final tally. Of course, there are movies that do quite well. Also in 2016, the Twentieth Century Fox production *Deadpool* raked in about $782 million worldwide at a production cost of $58 million.

Obviously, MGM didn't *plan* to lose $120 million on *Ben-Hur*, but it happened. As this particular box office bomb shows, projects don't always go as companies think they will. This chapter explores how this can happen and what companies can do to analyze and possibly avoid these situations.

Learning Objectives

After studying this chapter, you should be able to:

LO1 Perform and interpret a sensitivity analysis for a proposed investment.

LO2 Perform and interpret a scenario analysis for a proposed investment.

LO3 Determine and interpret cash, accounting, and financial break-even points.

LO4 Explain how the degree of operating leverage can affect the cash flows of a project.

LO5 Discuss how capital rationing affects the ability of a company to accept projects.

For updates on the latest happenings in finance, visit fundamentalsofcorporatefinance.blogspot.com.

In the previous chapter, we discussed how to identify and organize the relevant cash flows for capital investment decisions. Our primary interest there was in coming up with a preliminary estimate of the net present value for a proposed project. In this chapter, we focus on assessing the reliability of such an estimate and on some additional considerations in project analysis.

We begin by discussing the need for an evaluation of cash flow and NPV estimates. We go on to develop some useful tools for such an evaluation. We also examine additional complications and concerns that can arise in project evaluation.

Evaluating NPV Estimates   11.1

As we discussed in Chapter 9, an investment has a positive net present value if its market value exceeds its cost. Such an investment is desirable because it creates value for its owner. The primary problem in identifying such opportunities is that most of the time we can't actually observe the relevant market value. Instead, we estimate it. Having done so, it is only natural to wonder whether our estimates are at least close to the true values. We consider this question next.

THE BASIC PROBLEM

Suppose we are working on a preliminary discounted cash flow analysis along the lines we described in the previous chapter. We carefully identify the relevant cash flows, avoiding such things as sunk costs, and we remember to consider working capital requirements. We add back any depreciation; we account for possible erosion; and we pay attention to opportunity costs. Finally, we double-check our calculations; when all is said and done, the bottom line is that the estimated NPV is positive.

Now what? Do we stop here and move on to the next proposal? Probably not. The fact that the estimated NPV is positive is definitely a good sign; but, more than anything, this tells us that we need to take a closer look.

If you think about it, there are two circumstances under which a DCF analysis could lead us to conclude that a project has a positive NPV. The first possibility is that the project really does have a positive NPV. That's the good news. The bad news is the second possibility: A project may appear to have a positive NPV because our estimate is inaccurate.

Notice that we could also err in the opposite way. If we conclude that a project has a negative NPV when the true NPV is positive, we lose a valuable opportunity.

PROJECTED VERSUS ACTUAL CASH FLOWS

There is a somewhat subtle point we need to make here. When we say something like, "The projected cash flow in Year 4 is $700," what exactly do we mean? Does this mean that we think the cash flow will actually be $700? Not really. It could happen, of course, but we would be surprised to see it turn out exactly that way. The reason is that the $700 projection is based on only what we know today. Almost anything could happen between now and then to change that cash flow.

Loosely speaking, we really mean that if we took all the possible cash flows that could occur in four years and averaged them, the result would be $700. So, we don't really expect a projected cash flow to be exactly right in any one case. What we do expect is that if we evaluate a large number of projects, our projections will be right on average.

FORECASTING RISK

The key inputs into a discounted cash flow (DCF) analysis are projected future cash flows. If the projections are seriously in error, then we have a classic GIGO (garbage in, garbage out) system. In such a case, no matter how carefully we arrange the numbers and manipulate them, the resulting answer can still be grossly misleading. This is the danger in using a relatively sophisticated technique like DCF. It is sometimes easy to get caught up in number crunching and forget the underlying nuts-and-bolts economic reality.

forecasting risk
The possibility that errors in projected cash flows will lead to incorrect decisions. Also known as *estimation risk*.

The possibility that we will make a bad decision because of errors in the projected cash flows is called **forecasting risk** (or *estimation risk*). Because of forecasting risk, there is the danger that we will think a project has a positive NPV when it really does not. How is this possible? It happens if we are overly optimistic about the future, and, as a result, our projected cash flows don't realistically reflect the possible future cash flows.

Forecasting risk can take many forms. For example, Microsoft spent several billion dollars developing and bringing the Xbox One game console to market. Technologically more sophisticated than its competition, the Xbox One was the best way to play against competitors over the Internet and included other features, such as the Kinect motion detector. However, Microsoft sold only four million Xboxes in the first four months of sales, which was at the low end of Microsoft's expected range and noticeably fewer than the 6.6 million Sony PS4s sold. Since the Xbox was arguably the best available game console at the time, why didn't it sell better? A major reason given by analysts was that the Xbox cost $100 more than the PS4.

So far, we have not explicitly considered what to do about the possibility of errors in our forecasts; so one of our goals in this chapter is to develop some tools that are useful in identifying areas where potential errors exist and where they might be especially damaging. In one form or another, we will be trying to assess the economic "reasonableness" of our estimates. We will also be wondering how much damage will be done by errors in those estimates.

SOURCES OF VALUE

The first line of defense against forecasting risk is to ask, "What is it about this investment that leads to a positive NPV?" We should be able to point to something specific as the source of value. For example, if the proposal under consideration involves a new product, then we might ask questions such as the following: Are we certain that our new product is significantly better than that of the competition? Can we truly manufacture at lower cost, or distribute more effectively, or identify undeveloped market niches, or gain control of a market?

These are just a few of the potential sources of value. There are many others. For example, in 2004, Google announced a new, free email service: Gmail. Why? Free email service is widely available from big hitters like Microsoft and Yahoo! and, obviously, it's free! The answer is that Google's email service is integrated with its acclaimed search engine, thereby giving it an edge. Also, offering email lets Google expand its lucrative keyword-based advertising delivery. So, Google's source of value is leveraging its proprietary web search and ad delivery technologies.

A key factor to keep in mind is the degree of competition in the market. A basic principle of economics is that positive NPV investments will be rare in a highly competitive environment. Therefore, proposals that appear to show significant value in the face of stiff competition are particularly troublesome, and the likely reaction of the competition to any innovations must be closely examined.

To give an example, in 2008, demand for flat-screen LCD televisions was high, prices were high, and profit margins were fat for retailers. But, also in 2008, manufacturers of the screens, such as Samsung and Sony, were projected to pour several billion dollars into new production facilities. Anyone thinking of entering this highly profitable market would have done well to reflect on what the supply (and profit margin) situation would look like in just a few years. And, in fact, the high prices did not last. By 2017, television sets that had been selling for well over $1,000 only a few years before were selling for around $300–$400. And, it is likely that the new 4K television sets will experience a similar price drop in the next few years.

It is also necessary to think about *potential* competition. For example, suppose home improvement retailer Lowe's identifies an area that is underserved and is thinking about opening a store. If the store is successful, what will happen? The answer is that Home Depot (or another competitor) will likely also build a store, thereby driving down volume and profits. So, we always need to keep in mind that success attracts imitators and competitors.

The point to remember is that positive NPV investments are probably not all that common, and the number of positive NPV projects is almost certainly limited for any given firm. If we can't articulate some sound economic basis for thinking ahead of time that we have found something special, then the conclusion that our project has a positive NPV should be viewed with some suspicion.

Concept Questions

11.1a   What is forecasting risk? Why is it a concern for the financial manager?

11.1b   What are some potential sources of value in a new project?

Scenario and Other What-If Analyses

11.2

Our basic approach to evaluating cash flow and NPV estimates involves asking what-if questions. Accordingly, we discuss some organized ways of going about a what-if analysis. Our goal in performing such an analysis is to assess the degree of forecasting risk and to identify the most critical components of the success or failure of an investment.

Excel Master It!

Excel Master coverage online

GETTING STARTED

We are investigating a new project. Naturally, the first thing we do is estimate NPV based on our projected cash flows. We will call this initial set of projections the *base case*. Now, we recognize the possibility of error in these cash flow projections. After completing the base case, we wish to investigate how different assumptions about the future will impact our estimates.

One way to organize this investigation is to put upper and lower bounds on the various components of the project. For example, suppose we forecast sales at 100 units per year. We know this estimate may be high or low, but we are relatively certain it is not off by more than 10 units in either direction. In this situation, we would pick a lower bound of 90 and an upper bound of 110. We go on to assign such bounds to any other cash flow components we are unsure about.

When we pick these upper and lower bounds, we are not ruling out the possibility that the actual values could be outside this range. What we are saying, again loosely speaking, is that it is unlikely that the true average (as opposed to our estimated average) of the possible values is outside this range.

An example is useful to illustrate the idea here. The project under consideration costs $200,000, has a five-year life, and has no salvage value. Depreciation is straight-line to zero. The required return is 12 percent, and the tax rate is 21 percent. In addition, we have compiled the following information:

	Base Case	Lower Bound	Upper Bound
Unit sales	6,000	5,500	6,500
Price per unit	$ 80	$ 75	$ 85
Variable costs per unit	$ 60	$ 58	$ 62
Fixed costs per year	$50,000	$45,000	$55,000

With this information, we can calculate the base-case NPV by first calculating net income:

Sales	$480,000
Variable costs	360,000
Fixed costs	50,000
Depreciation	40,000
EBIT	$ 30,000
Taxes (21%)	6,300
Net income	$ 23,700

Operating cash flow is $30,000 + 40,000 − 6,300 = $63,700 per year. At 12 percent, the five-year annuity factor is 3.6048, so the base-case NPV is:

$$\text{Base-case NPV} = -\$200,000 + 63,700 \times 3.6048$$
$$= \$29,624$$

The project looks good so far.

SCENARIO ANALYSIS

scenario analysis
The determination of what happens to NPV estimates when we ask what-if questions.

The basic form of what-if analysis is called **scenario analysis**. What we do is investigate the changes in our NPV estimates that result from asking questions like: What if unit sales realistically should be projected at 5,500 units instead of 6,000?

Once we start looking at alternative scenarios, we might find that most of the plausible ones result in positive NPVs. In this case, we have some confidence in proceeding with the project. If a substantial percentage of the scenarios look bad, the degree of forecasting risk is high and further investigation is in order.

We can consider a number of possible scenarios. A good place to start is with the worst-case scenario. This will tell us the minimum NPV of the project. If this turns out to be positive, we will be in good shape. While we are at it, we will go ahead and determine the other extreme, the best case. This puts an upper bound on our NPV.

To get the worst case, we assign the least favorable value to each item. This means *low* values for items like units sold and price per unit and *high* values for costs. We do the reverse for the best case. For our project, these values would be the following:

	Worst Case	Best Case
Unit sales	5,500	6,500
Price per unit	$ 75	$ 85
Variable costs per unit	$ 62	$ 58
Fixed costs per year	$55,000	$45,000

With this information, we can calculate the net income and cash flows under each scenario (check these for yourself):

Scenario	Net Income	Cash Flow	Net Present Value	IRR
Base case	$23,700	$63,700	$ 29,624	17.8%
Worst case*	−18,565	21,435	−122,732	−17.7
Best case	71,495	111,495	201,915	47.9

*We assume a tax credit is created in our worst-case scenario.

What we learn is that under the worst scenario, the cash flow is still positive at $21,435. That's good news. The bad news is that the return is −17.7 percent in this case, and the NPV is −$122,732. Because the project costs $200,000, we stand to lose more than half of the original investment under the worst possible scenario. The best case offers an attractive 47.9 percent return.

The terms *best case* and *worst case* are commonly used, and we will stick with them; but they are somewhat misleading. The absolutely best thing that could happen would be some-thing absurdly unlikely, such as launching a new diet soda and subsequently learning that our (patented) formulation also just happens to cure the common cold. Similarly, the true worst case would involve some incredibly remote possibility of total disaster. We're not claiming that these things don't happen; once in a while they do. Some products, such as personal computers, succeed beyond the wildest expectations; and some turn out to be absolute catastrophes. For example, in April 2010, BP's Gulf of Mexico oil rig *Deepwater Horizon* caught fire and sank following an explosion, leading to a massive oil spill. The leak was finally stopped in July after releasing over 200 million gallons of crude oil into the Gulf. When everything was included, BP's costs associated with the disaster were about $62 billion, not including opportunity costs such as lost government contracts. Nonetheless, our point is that in assessing the reasonable-ness of an NPV estimate, we need to stick to cases that are reasonably likely to occur.

Instead of *best* and *worst*, then, it is probably more accurate to use the words *optimistic* and *pessimistic*. In broad terms, if we were thinking about a reasonable range for, say, unit sales, then what we call the best case would correspond to something near the upper end of that range. The worst case would correspond to the lower end.

Not all companies complete (or at least publish) all three estimates. For example, Almaden Minerals, Ltd., made a press release with information concerning its Elk Gold Project in British Columbia. Here is a table of the possible outcomes given by the company:

Project Summary	Base Case	$1,200 Case	Unit
Assumed gold price	1,000	1,200	$US/tr.oz
Tonnes per day treated	500	1,000	tpd
Life	7	9	years
Total tonnes treated	1.1	2.6	MT
Grade	4.14	3.89	g/t
Waste: Ore ratio	16.4	30.1	
Plant recovery	92	92	%
Ounces Au produced	139,198	297,239	tr.oz
Initial capital expense	9.91	17.50	$CADM
Working and preproduction capital	2.27	9.60	$CADM
Waste mining	2.42	1.90	$CAD/tonne waste
Ore mining	8.38	5.87	$CAD/tonne ore
Processing	20.68	14.74	$CAD/tonne ore
Administration and overheads	2.07	1.27	$CAD/tonne ore
Total operating cost	70.30	78.91	$CAD/tonne ore
Pretax NPV @ 8%	28.7	67.9	$CADM
Pretax IRR	51%	39%	
Max exposure	13.66	33.53	$CADM
Payback, years from start production	1.85	3.30	years
Ratio, gross earnings: max exposure	5.02	6.00	
Ratio, NPV: max exposure	2.10	2.03	

As you can see, the NPV is projected at C$28.7 million in the base case and C$67.9 million in the best ($1,200 price) case. Unfortunately, Almaden did not release a worst-case analysis, but we hope the company also examined this possibility.

As we have mentioned, there are an unlimited number of different scenarios that we could examine. At a minimum, we might want to investigate two intermediate cases by going halfway between the base amounts and the extreme amounts. This would give us five scenarios in all, including the base case.

Beyond this point, it is hard to know when to stop. As we generate more and more possibilities, we run the risk of experiencing "paralysis of analysis." The difficulty is that no matter how many scenarios we run, all we can learn are possibilities—some good and some bad. Beyond that, we don't get any guidance as to what to do. Scenario analysis is useful in telling us what can happen and in helping us gauge the potential for disaster, but it does not tell us whether to take a project.

Unfortunately, in practice, even the worst-case scenarios may not be low enough. Two recent examples show what we mean. The Eurotunnel, or Chunnel, may be one of the new wonders of the world. The tunnel under the English Channel connects England to France and covers 24 miles. It took 8,000 workers eight years to remove 9.8 million cubic yards of rock. When the tunnel was finally built, it cost $17.9 billion, or slightly more than twice the original estimate of $8.8 billion. And things got worse. Forecasts called for 16.8 million passengers in the first year, but only 4 million actually used it. Revenue estimates for 2003 were $2.88 billion, but actual revenue was only about one-third of that. The major problems faced by the Eurotunnel were increased competition from ferry services, which dropped their prices, and the rise of low-cost airlines. In 2006, things got so bad that the company operating the Eurotunnel was forced into negotiations with creditors to chop its $11.1 billion debt in half to avoid bankruptcy. The debt reduction appeared to help. In 2007, the Eurotunnel reported its first profit of €1 million ($1.6 million). By 2013, the Chunnel had a profit of €101 million ($138 million). Sales for the year were €1.09 billion ($1.49 billion), the first year its sales exceeded €1 billion, and for the first time it transported more than 10 million passengers in a year. And, by 2016, the Chunnel's profit reached €535 million ($700 million).

Another example is the Samsung Note 7 cell phone, which caught fire with consumers when it was introduced in August 2016. Unfortunately, the phones subsequently began to actually catch fire, causing the Federal Aviation Administration to ban them from flights, even in a checked bag. In early September, Samsung recalled 2.5 million Note 7s. The company halted all further production and sales in early October, which caused Samsung's market capitalization to drop about $17 billion. The company was expected to eventually write off about $5 billion, a "Note-able" loss.

SENSITIVITY ANALYSIS

sensitivity analysis
Investigation of what happens to NPV when only one variable is changed.

Sensitivity analysis is a variation on scenario analysis that is useful in pinpointing the areas where forecasting risk is especially severe. The basic idea with a sensitivity analysis is to freeze all of the variables except one and then see how sensitive our estimate of NPV is to changes in that one variable. If our NPV estimate turns out to be very sensitive to relatively small changes in the projected value of some component of project cash flow, then the forecasting risk associated with that variable is high.

To illustrate how sensitivity analysis works, we go back to our base case for every item except unit sales. We can then calculate cash flow and NPV using the largest and smallest unit sales figures.

Scenario	Unit Sales	Cash Flow	Net Present Value	IRR
Base case	6,000	$63,700	$29,624	17.8%
Worst case	5,500	55,800	1,147	12.2
Best case	6,500	71,600	58,102	23.2

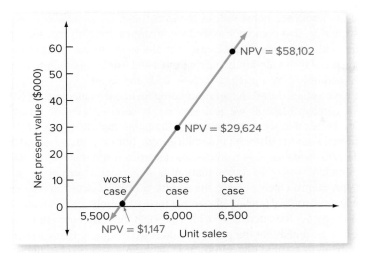

FIGURE 11.1

Sensitivity Analysis for Unit Sales

For comparison, we now freeze everything except fixed costs and repeat the analysis:

Scenario	Fixed Costs	Cash Flow	Net Present Value	IRR
Base case	$50,000	$63,700	$29,624	17.8%
Worst case	55,000	59,750	15,385	15.1
Best case	45,000	67,650	43,863	20.5

What we see here is that given our ranges, the estimated NPV of this project is more sensitive to changes in projected unit sales than it is to changes in projected fixed costs. In fact, under the worst case for fixed costs, the NPV is still positive.

The results of our sensitivity analysis for unit sales can be illustrated graphically as in Figure 11.1. Here we place NPV on the vertical axis and unit sales on the horizontal axis. When we plot the combinations of unit sales versus NPV, we see that all possible combinations fall on a straight line. The steeper the resulting line is, the greater the sensitivity of the estimated NPV to changes in the projected value of the variable being investigated.

Sensitivity analysis can produce results that vary dramatically depending on the assumptions. For example, Bard Ventures Ltd. announced its projections for a molybdenum mine in British Columbia. At a cost of capital of 10 percent and an average molybdenum price of $19 per ton, the NPV of the new mine would be $112 million with an IRR of 12.4 percent. At a high price of $30 per ton, the NPV would be $1.152 billion, and the IRR would be 32.0 percent.

As we have illustrated, sensitivity analysis is useful in pinpointing which variables deserve the most attention. If we find that our estimated NPV is especially sensitive to changes in a variable that is difficult to forecast (such as unit sales), then the degree of forecasting risk is high. We might decide that further market research would be a good idea in this case.

Because sensitivity analysis is a form of scenario analysis, it suffers from the same drawbacks. Sensitivity analysis is useful for pointing out where forecasting errors will do the most damage, but it does not tell us what to do about possible errors.

SIMULATION ANALYSIS

Scenario analysis and sensitivity analysis are widely used. With scenario analysis, we let all the different variables change, but let them take on only a few values. With sensitivity analysis, we let only one variable change, but we let it take on many values. If we combine the two approaches, the result is a crude form of **simulation analysis**.

simulation analysis
A combination of scenario and sensitivity analysis.

If we want to let all the items vary at the same time, we have to consider a very large number of scenarios, and computer assistance is almost certainly needed. In the simplest case, we start with unit sales and assume that any value in our 5,500 to 6,500 range is equally likely. We start by randomly picking one value (or by instructing a computer to do so). We then randomly pick a price, a variable cost, and so on.

Once we have values for all the relevant components, we calculate an NPV. We repeat this sequence as many times as we desire, probably several thousand times. The result is many NPV estimates that we summarize by calculating the average value and some measure of how spread out the different possibilities are. For example, it would be of some interest to know what percentage of the possible scenarios result in negative estimated NPVs.

Because simulation analysis (or simulation) is an extended form of scenario analysis, it has the same problems. Once we have the results, no simple decision rule tells us what to do. Also, we have described a relatively simple form of simulation. To really do it right, we would have to consider the interrelationships between the different cash flow components. Furthermore, we assumed that the possible values were equally likely to occur. It is probably more realistic to assume that values near the base case are more likely than extreme values, but coming up with the probabilities is difficult, to say the least.

For these reasons, the use of simulation is somewhat limited in practice. However, recent advances in computer software and hardware (and user sophistication) lead us to believe it may become more common in the future, particularly for large-scale projects.

Concept Questions

11.2a   What are scenario, sensitivity, and simulation analysis?

11.2b   What are the drawbacks to the various types of what-if analysis?

11.3 Break-Even Analysis

It will frequently turn out that the crucial variable for a project is sales volume. If we are thinking of creating a new product or entering a new market, for example, the hardest thing to forecast accurately is how much we can sell. For this reason, sales volume is usually analyzed more closely than other variables.

Break-even analysis is a popular and commonly used tool for analyzing the relationship between sales volume and profitability. There are a variety of different break-even measures, and we have already seen several types. For example, we discussed (in Chapter 9) how the payback period can be interpreted as the length of time until a project breaks even, ignoring time value.

All break-even measures have a similar goal. Loosely speaking, we will always be asking, "How bad do sales have to get before we actually begin to lose money?" Implicitly, we will also be asking, "Is it likely that things will get that bad?" To get started on this subject, we first discuss fixed and variable costs.

FIXED AND VARIABLE COSTS

In discussing break-even, the difference between fixed and variable costs becomes very important. As a result, we need to be a little more explicit about the difference than we have been so far.

variable costs
Costs that change when the quantity of output changes.

Variable Costs   By definition, **variable costs** change as the quantity of output changes, and they are zero when production is zero. For example, direct labor costs and raw

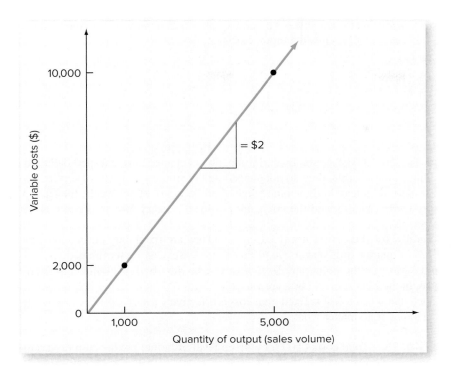

FIGURE 11.2

**Output Level and
Variable Costs**

material costs are usually considered variable. This makes sense because if we shut down operations tomorrow, there will be no future costs for labor or raw materials.

We will assume that variable costs are a constant amount per unit of output. This means that total variable cost is equal to the cost per unit multiplied by the number of units. In other words, the relationship between total variable cost (VC), cost per unit of output (v), and total quantity of output (Q) can be written as:

Total variable cost = Total quantity of output × Cost per unit of output

$$VC = Q \times v$$

For example, suppose variable costs (v) are $2 per unit. If total output (Q) is 1,000 units, what will total variable costs (VC) be?

$$
\begin{aligned}
VC &= Q \times v \\
&= 1{,}000 \times \$2 \\
&= \$2{,}000
\end{aligned}
$$

Similarly, if Q is 5,000 units, then VC will be 5,000 × $2 = $10,000. Figure 11.2 illustrates the relationship between output level and variable costs in this case. In Figure 11.2, notice that increasing output by one unit results in variable costs rising by $2, so "the rise over the run" (the slope of the line) is given by $2/1 = $2.

Variable Costs

EXAMPLE 11.1

The Blume Corporation is a manufacturer of pencils. It has received an order for 5,000 pencils, and the company has to decide whether to accept the order. From recent experience, the company knows that each pencil requires 5 cents in raw materials and 50 cents in direct labor costs. These variable costs are expected to continue to apply in the future. What will Blume's total variable costs be if it accepts the order?

In this case, the cost per unit is 50 cents in labor plus 5 cents in material for a total of 55 cents per unit. At 5,000 units of output, we have:

$$VC = Q \times v$$
$$= 5{,}000 \times \$.55$$
$$= \$2{,}750$$

Therefore, total variable costs will be $2,750.

fixed costs
Costs that do not change when the quantity of output changes during a particular time period.

Fixed Costs   **Fixed costs**, by definition, do not change during a specified time period. So, unlike variable costs, they do not depend on the amount of goods or services produced during a period (at least within some range of production). For example, the lease payment on a production facility and the company president's salary are fixed costs, at least over some period.

Naturally, fixed costs are not fixed forever. They are fixed only during some particular time, say, a quarter or a year. Beyond that time, leases can be terminated and executives "retired." More to the point, any fixed cost can be modified or eliminated given enough time; so, in the long run, all costs are variable.

Notice that when a cost is fixed, that cost is effectively a sunk cost because we are going to have to pay it no matter what.

Total Costs   Total costs (TC) for a given level of output are the sum of variable costs (VC) and fixed costs (FC):

$$TC = VC + FC$$
$$= v \times Q + FC$$

So, for example, if we have variable costs of $3 per unit and fixed costs of $8,000 per year, our total cost is:

$$TC = \$3 \times Q + \$8{,}000$$

If we produce 6,000 units, our total production cost will be $3 × 6,000 + $8,000 = $26,000. At other production levels, we have the following:

Quantity Produced	Total Variable Costs	Fixed Costs	Total Costs
0	$ 0	$8,000	$ 8,000
1,000	3,000	8,000	11,000
5,000	15,000	8,000	23,000
10,000	30,000	8,000	38,000

marginal cost
The change in costs that occurs when there is a small change in output. Also called *incremental cost*.

By plotting these points in Figure 11.3, we see that the relationship between quantity produced and total costs is given by a straight line. In Figure 11.3, notice that total costs equal fixed costs when sales are zero. Beyond that point, every one-unit increase in production leads to a $3 increase in total costs, so the slope of the line is 3. In other words, the **marginal**, or **incremental, cost** of producing one more unit is $3.

EXAMPLE 11.2   **Average Cost versus Marginal Cost**

Suppose the Blume Corporation has a variable cost per pencil of 55 cents. The lease payment on the production facility runs $5,000 per month. If Blume produces 100,000 pencils per year, what are the total costs of production? What is the average cost per pencil?

The fixed costs are $5,000 per month, or $60,000 per year. The variable cost is $.55 per pencil. So the total cost for the year, assuming that Blume produces 100,000 pencils, is:

Total cost = $v \times Q$ + FC
            = $.55 × 100,000 + $60,000
            = $115,000

The average cost per pencil is $115,000/100,000 = $1.15.

Now suppose that Blume has received a special, one-shot order for 5,000 pencils. Blume has sufficient capacity to manufacture the 5,000 pencils on top of the 100,000 already produced, so no additional fixed costs will be incurred. Also, there will be no effect on existing orders. If Blume can get 75 cents per pencil for this order, should the order be accepted?

What this boils down to is a simple proposition. It costs 55 cents to make another pencil. Anything Blume can get for this pencil in excess of the 55-cent incremental cost contributes in a positive way toward covering fixed costs. The 75-cent **marginal**, or **incremental**, **revenue** exceeds the 55-cent marginal cost, so Blume should take the order.

The fixed cost of $60,000 is irrelevant to this decision because it is effectively sunk, at least for the current period. In the same way, the fact that the average cost is $1.15 is irrelevant because this average reflects the fixed cost. As long as producing the extra 5,000 pencils truly does not cost anything beyond the 55 cents per pencil, then Blume should accept any price above 55 cents.

marginal revenue
The change in revenue that occurs when there is a small change in output. Also called *incremental revenue.*

ACCOUNTING BREAK-EVEN

The most widely used measure of break-even is **accounting break-even**. The accounting break-even point is the sales level that results in a zero project net income.

To determine a project's accounting break-even, we start off with some common sense. Suppose we retail one-petabyte computer disks for $5 apiece. We can buy disks from a wholesale supplier for $3 apiece. We have accounting expenses of $600 in fixed costs and $300 in depreciation. How many disks do we have to sell to break even—that is, for net income to be zero?

accounting break-even
The sales level that results in zero project net income.

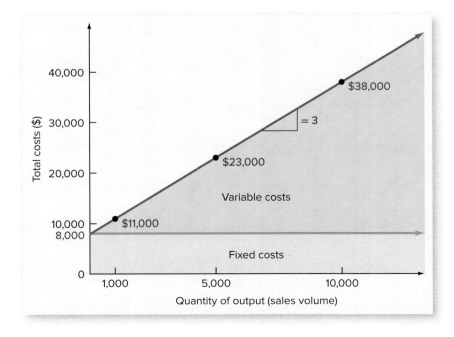

FIGURE 11.3
Output Level and Total Costs

For every disk we sell, we pick up $5 − 3 = $2 toward covering our other expenses (this $2 difference between the selling price and the variable cost is often called the *contribution margin per unit*). We have to cover a total of $600 + 300 = $900 in accounting expenses, so we obviously need to sell $900/$2 = 450 disks. We can check this by noting that at a sales level of 450 units, our revenues are $5 × 450 = $2,250 and our variable costs are $3 × 450 = $1,350. Here is the income statement:

Sales	$2,250
Variable costs	1,350
Fixed costs	600
Depreciation	300
EBIT	$ 0
Taxes (21%)	0
Net income	$ 0

Remember, because we are discussing a proposed new project, we do not consider any interest expense in calculating net income or cash flow from the project. Also, notice that we include depreciation in calculating expenses here, even though depreciation is not a cash outflow. That is why we call it an accounting break-even. Finally, notice that when net income is zero, so are pretax income and, of course, taxes. In accounting terms, our revenues are equal to our costs, so there is no profit to tax.

Figure 11.4 presents another way to see what is happening. This figure looks a lot like Figure 11.3 except that we add a line for revenues. As indicated, total revenues are zero when output is zero. Beyond that, each unit sold brings in another $5, so the slope of the revenue line is 5.

From our preceding discussion, we know that we break even when revenues are equal to total costs. The line for revenues and the line for total costs cross right where output is at

FIGURE 11.4

Accounting Break-Even

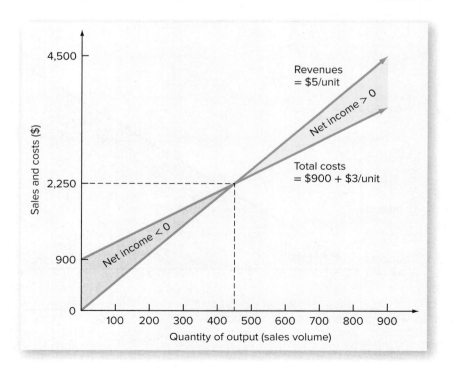

450 units. As illustrated, at any level of output below 450, our accounting profit is negative, and at any level above 450, we have a positive net income.

ACCOUNTING BREAK-EVEN: A CLOSER LOOK

In our numerical example, notice that the break-even level is equal to the sum of fixed costs and depreciation, divided by price per unit less variable costs per unit. This is always true. To see why, we recall all of the following variables:

P = Selling price per unit
v = Variable cost per unit
Q = Total units sold
S = Total sales = $P \times Q$
VC = Total variable costs = $v \times Q$
FC = Fixed costs
D = Depreciation
T_C = Tax rate

Project net income is given by:

Net income = (Sales − Variable costs − Fixed costs − Depreciation) × $(1 − T_C)$
$$= (S − \text{VC} − \text{FC} − D) \times (1 − T_C)$$

From here, it is not difficult to calculate the break-even point. If we set this net income equal to zero, we get:

Net income $\overset{\text{SET}}{=} 0 = (S − \text{VC} − \text{FC} − D) \times \left(1 − T_C\right)$

Divide both sides by $(1 − T_C)$ to get:

$$S − \text{VC} − \text{FC} − D = 0$$

As we have seen, this says that when net income is zero, so is pretax income. If we recall that $S = P \times Q$ and VC = $v \times Q$, then we can rearrange the equation to solve for the break-even level:

$$S − \text{VC} = \text{FC} + D$$
$$P \times Q − v \times Q = \text{FC} + D$$
$$(P − v) \times Q = \text{FC} + D$$
$$\mathbf{Q = (FC + D)/(P − v)}$$

11.1

This is the same result we described earlier.

USES FOR THE ACCOUNTING BREAK-EVEN

Why would anyone be interested in knowing the accounting break-even point? To illustrate how it can be useful, suppose we are a small specialty ice cream manufacturer with a strictly local distribution. We are thinking about expanding into new markets. Based on the estimated cash flows, we find that the expansion has a positive NPV.

Going back to our discussion of forecasting risk, we know that it is likely that what will make or break our expansion is sales volume. The reason is that, in this case at least, we probably have a fairly good idea of what we can charge for the ice cream. Further, we know relevant production and distribution costs reasonably well because we are already in the business. What we do not know with any real precision is how much ice cream we can sell.

Given the costs and selling price, we can immediately calculate the break-even point. Once we have done so, we might find that we need to get 30 percent of the market just to break even. If we think that this is unlikely to occur, because, for example, we have only 10 percent of our current market, then we know our forecast is questionable and there is a real possibility that the true NPV is negative. On the other hand, we might find that we already have firm commitments from buyers for about the break-even amount, so we are almost certain we can sell more. In this case, the forecasting risk is much lower, and we have greater confidence in our estimates.

There are several other reasons why knowing the accounting break-even can be useful. First, as we will discuss in more detail later, accounting break-even and payback period are similar measures. Like payback period, accounting break-even is relatively easy to calculate and explain.

Second, managers are often concerned with the contribution a project will make to the firm's total accounting earnings. A project that does not break even in an accounting sense actually reduces total earnings.

Third, a project that just breaks even on an accounting basis loses money in a financial or opportunity cost sense. This is true because we could have earned more by investing elsewhere. Such a project does not lose money in an out-of-pocket sense. As described in the following sections, we get back exactly what we put in. For noneconomic reasons, opportunity losses may be easier to live with than out-of-pocket losses.

Concept Questions

11.3a How are fixed costs similar to sunk costs?
11.3b What is net income at the accounting break-even point? What about taxes?
11.3c Why might a financial manager be interested in the accounting break-even point?

11.4 Operating Cash Flow, Sales Volume, and Break-Even

Excel Master It!
Excel Master coverage online

Accounting break-even is one tool that is useful for project analysis. Ultimately, we are more interested in cash flow than accounting income. So, for example, if sales volume is the critical variable, then we need to know more about the relationship between sales volume and cash flow than just the accounting break-even.

Our goal in this section is to illustrate the relationship between operating cash flow and sales volume. We also discuss some other break-even measures. To simplify matters somewhat, we will ignore the effect of taxes. We start off by looking at the relationship between accounting break-even and cash flow.

ACCOUNTING BREAK-EVEN AND CASH FLOW

Now that we know how to find the accounting break-even, it is natural to wonder what happens with cash flow. To illustrate, suppose the Wettway Sailboat Corporation is considering whether to launch its new Margo-class sailboat. The selling price will be $40,000 per boat. The variable costs will be about half that, or $20,000 per boat, and fixed costs will be $500,000 per year.

The Base Case   The total investment needed to undertake the project is $3,500,000. This amount will be depreciated straight-line to zero over the five-year life of the equipment.

The salvage value is zero, and there are no working capital consequences. Wettway has a 20 percent required return on new projects.

Based on market surveys and historical experience, Wettway projects total sales for the five years at 425 boats, or about 85 boats per year. Ignoring taxes, should this project be launched?

To begin, ignoring taxes, the operating cash flow at 85 boats per year is:

$$
\begin{aligned}
\text{Operating cash flow} &= \text{EBIT} + \text{Depreciation} - \text{Taxes} \\
&= (S - \text{VC} - \text{FC} - D) + D - 0 \\
&= 85 \times (\$40,000 - 20,000) - \$500,000 \\
&= \$1,200,000 \text{ per year}
\end{aligned}
$$

At 20 percent, the five-year annuity factor is 2.9906, so the NPV is:

$$
\begin{aligned}
\text{NPV} &= -\$3,500,000 + \$1,200,000 \times 2.9906 \\
&= -\$3,500,000 + 3,588,735 \\
&= \$88,735
\end{aligned}
$$

In the absence of additional information, the project should be launched.

Calculating the Break-Even Level   To begin looking a little closer at this project, you might ask a series of questions. For example, how many new boats does Wettway need to sell for the project to break even on an accounting basis? If Wettway does break even, what will be the annual cash flow from the project? What will be the return on the investment in this case?

Before fixed costs and depreciation are considered, Wettway generates $40,000 − 20,000 = $20,000 per boat (this is revenue less variable cost). Depreciation is $3,500,000/5 = $700,000 per year. Fixed costs and depreciation together total $1.2 million, so Wettway needs to sell $(FC + D)/(P − v) = $1.2 million/$20,000 = 60 boats per year to break even on an accounting basis. This is 25 boats less than projected sales; so, assuming that Wettway is confident its projection is accurate to within, say, 15 boats, it appears unlikely that the new investment will fail to at least break even on an accounting basis.

To calculate Wettway's cash flow in this case, we note that if 60 boats are sold, net income will be exactly zero. Recalling from the previous chapter that operating cash flow for a project can be written as net income plus depreciation (the bottom-up definition), we can see that the operating cash flow is equal to the depreciation, or $700,000 in this case. The internal rate of return is exactly zero (why?).

Payback and Break-Even   As our example illustrates, whenever a project breaks even on an accounting basis, the cash flow for that period will equal the depreciation. This result makes perfect accounting sense. For example, suppose we invest $100,000 in a five-year project. The depreciation is straight-line to a zero salvage, or $20,000 per year. If the project exactly breaks even every period, then the cash flow will be $20,000 per period.

The sum of the cash flows for the life of this project is 5 × $20,000 = $100,000, the original investment. What this shows is that a project's payback period is exactly equal to its life if the project breaks even every period. Similarly, a project that does better than break even has a payback that is shorter than the life of the project and has a positive rate of return.

The bad news is that a project that just breaks even on an accounting basis has a negative NPV and a zero return. For our sailboat project, the fact that Wettway will almost surely break even on an accounting basis is partially comforting because it means that the firm's "downside" risk (its potential loss) is limited, but we still don't know if the project is truly profitable. More work is needed.

SALES VOLUME AND OPERATING CASH FLOW

At this point, we can generalize our example and introduce some other break-even measures. From our discussion in the previous section, we know that, ignoring taxes, a project's
operating cash flow, OCF, can be written as EBIT plus depreciation:

$$\textbf{OCF} = [(P - v) \times Q - \text{FC} - D] + D$$
$$= (\textbf{\textit{P}} - \textbf{\textit{v}}) \times \textbf{\textit{Q}} - \textbf{FC}$$

For the Wettway sailboat project, the general relationship (in thousands of dollars) between operating cash flow and sales volume is:

$$\text{OCF} = (P - v) \times Q - \text{FC}$$
$$= (\$40 - 20) \times Q - 500$$
$$= -\$500 + \$20 \times Q$$

What this tells us is that the relationship between operating cash flow and sales volume is
given by a straight line with a slope of $20 and a *y*-intercept of −$500. If we calculate some
different values, we get:

Quantity Sold	Operating Cash Flow
0	−$ 500
15	− 200
30	100
50	500
75	1,000

These points are plotted in Figure 11.5, where we have indicated three different break-even
points. We discuss these next.

CASH FLOW, ACCOUNTING, AND FINANCIAL BREAK-EVEN POINTS

We know from the preceding discussion that the relationship between operating cash flow
and sales volume (ignoring taxes) is:

$$\text{OCF} = (P - v) \times Q - \text{FC}$$

If we rearrange this and solve for *Q*, we get:

$$\textbf{\textit{Q}} = (\textbf{FC} + \textbf{OCF})/(\textbf{\textit{P}} - \textbf{\textit{v}})$$

FIGURE 11.5

**Operating Cash Flow
and Sales Volume**

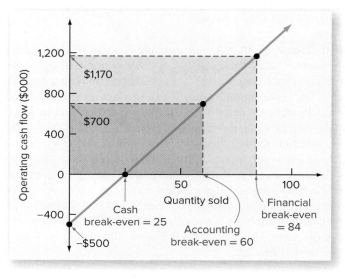

This tells us what sales volume (Q) is necessary to achieve any given OCF, so this result is more general than the accounting break-even. We use it to find the various break-even points in Figure 11.5.

Accounting Break-Even Revisited   Looking at Figure 11.5, suppose operating cash flow is equal to depreciation (D). Recall that this situation corresponds to our break-even point on an accounting basis. To find the sales volume, we substitute the $700 depreciation amount for OCF in our general expression:

$Q = (FC + OCF)/(P - v)$
$\quad = (\$500 + 700)/\$20$
$\quad = 60$

This is the same quantity we had before.

Cash Break-Even   We have seen that a project that breaks even on an accounting basis has a net income of zero, but it still has a positive cash flow. At some sales level below the accounting break-even, the operating cash flow actually goes negative. This is a particularly unpleasant occurrence. If it happens, we actually have to supply additional cash to the project to keep it afloat.

To calculate the **cash break-even** (the point where operating cash flow is equal to zero), we put in a zero for OCF:

cash break-even
The sales level that results in a zero operating cash flow.

$Q = (FC + 0)/(P - v)$
$\quad = \$500/\$20$
$\quad = 25$

Wettway must therefore sell 25 boats to cover the $500 in fixed costs. As we show in Figure 11.5, this point occurs right where the operating cash flow line crosses the horizontal axis.

Notice that a project that just breaks even on a cash flow basis can cover its own fixed operating costs, but that is all. It never pays back anything, so the original investment is a complete loss (the IRR is −100 percent).

Financial Break-Even   The last case we consider is that of **financial break-even**, the sales level that results in a zero NPV. To the financial manager, this is the most interesting case. What we do is first determine what operating cash flow has to be for the NPV to be zero. We then use this amount to determine the sales volume.

financial break-even
The sales level that results in a zero NPV.

To illustrate, recall that Wettway requires a 20 percent return on its $3,500 (in thousands) investment. How many sailboats does Wettway have to sell to break even once we account for the 20 percent per year opportunity cost?

The sailboat project has a five-year life. The project has a zero NPV when the present value of the operating cash flows equals the $3,500 investment. Because the cash flow is the same each year, we can solve for the unknown amount by viewing it as an ordinary annuity. The five-year annuity factor at 20 percent is 2.9906, and the OCF can be determined as follows:

$\$3,500 = OCF \times 2.9906$
$\quad OCF = \$3,500/2.9906$
$\qquad\quad = \$1,170$

Wettway needs an operating cash flow of $1,170 each year to break even. We can now plug this OCF into the equation for sales volume:

$Q = (\$500 + 1,170)/\$20$
$\quad = 83.5$

So, Wettway needs to sell about 84 boats per year. This is not good news.

As indicated in Figure 11.5, the financial break-even is substantially higher than the accounting break-even. This will often be the case. Moreover, what we have discovered is that the sailboat project has a substantial degree of forecasting risk. We project sales of 85 boats per year, but it takes 84 just to earn the required return.

Conclusion   Overall, it seems unlikely that the Wettway sailboat project would fail to break even on an accounting basis. However, there appears to be a very good chance that the true NPV is negative. This illustrates the danger in looking at just the accounting break-even.

What should Wettway do? Is the new project all wet? The decision at this point is essentially a managerial issue—a judgment call. The crucial questions are these:

1. How much confidence do we have in our projections?
2. How important is the project to the future of the company?
3. How badly will the company be hurt if sales turn out to be low? What options are available to the company in this case?

We will consider questions such as these in a later section. For future reference, our discussion of the different break-even measures is summarized in Table 11.1.

TABLE 11.1

Summary of Break-Even Measures

I.	The General Break-Even Expression
	Ignoring taxes, the relation between operating cash flow (OCF) and quantity of output or sales volume (Q) is:
	$$Q = \frac{FC + OCF}{P - v}$$
	where
	FC = Total fixed costs
	P = Price per unit
	v = Variable cost per unit
	As shown next, this relation can be used to determine the accounting, cash, and financial break-even points.

II.	The Accounting Break-Even Point
	Accounting break-even occurs when net income is zero. Operating cash flow is equal to depreciation when net income is zero, so the accounting break-even point is:
	$$Q = \frac{FC + D}{P - v}$$
	A project that always just breaks even on an accounting basis has a payback exactly equal to its life, a negative NPV, and an IRR of zero.

III.	The Cash Break-Even Point
	Cash break-even occurs when operating cash flow is zero. The cash break-even point is:
	$$Q = \frac{FC}{P - v}$$
	A project that always just breaks even on a cash basis never pays back, has an NPV that is negative and equal to the initial outlay, and has an IRR of −100 percent.

IV.	The Financial Break-Even Point
	Financial break-even occurs when the NPV of the project is zero. The financial break-even point is:
	$$Q = \frac{FC + OCF^*}{P - v}$$
	where OCF^* is the level of OCF that results in a zero NPV. A project that breaks even on a financial basis has a discounted payback equal to its life, a zero NPV, and an IRR just equal to the required return.

Operating Leverage

11.5

Excel Master It!

xlsx   Excel Master coverage online

We have discussed how to calculate and interpret various measures of break-even for a proposed project. What we have not explicitly discussed is what determines these points and how they might be changed. We now turn to this subject.[1]

THE BASIC IDEA

Operating leverage is the degree to which a project or firm is committed to fixed production costs. A firm with low operating leverage will have low fixed costs compared to a firm with high operating leverage. Generally speaking, projects with a relatively heavy investment in plant and equipment will have a relatively high degree of operating leverage. Such projects are said to be *capital intensive*.

Anytime we are thinking about a new venture, there will normally be alternative ways of producing and delivering the product. For example, Wettway Sailboat Corporation can purchase the necessary equipment and build all of the components for its sailboats in-house. Alternatively, some of the work could be farmed out to other firms. The first option involves a greater investment in plant and equipment, greater fixed costs and depreciation, and, as a result, a higher degree of operating leverage.

operating leverage
The degree to which a firm or project relies on fixed costs.

IMPLICATIONS OF OPERATING LEVERAGE

Regardless of how it is measured, operating leverage has important implications for project evaluation. Fixed costs act like a lever in the sense that a small percentage change in operating revenue can be magnified into a large percentage change in operating cash flow and NPV. This explains why we call it operating "leverage."

The higher the degree of operating leverage, the greater is the potential danger from forecasting risk. The reason is that relatively small errors in forecasting sales volume can get magnified, or "levered up," into large errors in cash flow projections.

From a managerial perspective, one way of coping with highly uncertain projects is to keep the degree of operating leverage as low as possible. This will generally have the effect of keeping the break-even point (however measured) at its minimum level. We will illustrate this point in a bit, but first we need to discuss how to measure operating leverage.

MEASURING OPERATING LEVERAGE

One way of measuring operating leverage is to ask: If quantity sold rises by 5 percent, what will be the percentage change in operating cash flow? In other words, the **degree of operating leverage (DOL)** is defined such that:

Percentage change in OCF = DOL × Percentage change in Q

degree of operating leverage (DOL)
The percentage change in operating cash flow relative to the percentage change in quantity sold.

---

[1]The assumption of no taxes still holds. To see the effect of taxes on break-even and DOL, see Problems 25 and 26.

Based on the relationship between OCF and Q, DOL can be written as:[2]

DOL = 1 + FC/OCF

11.4

The ratio FC/OCF measures fixed costs as a percentage of total operating cash flow. Notice that zero fixed costs would result in a DOL of 1, implying that percentage changes in quantity sold would show up one for one in operating cash flow. In other words, no magnification, or leverage, effect would exist.

To illustrate this measure of operating leverage, we go back to the Wettway sailboat project. Fixed costs were $500 and $(P - v)$ was $20, so OCF was:

$$OCF = -\$500 + \$20 \times Q$$

Suppose Q is currently 50 boats. At this level of output, OCF is $-\$500 + 1{,}000 = \$500$.

If Q rises by 1 unit to 51, then the percentage change in Q is $(51 - 50)/50 = .02$, or 2%. OCF rises to $520, a change of $P - v = \$20$. The percentage change in OCF is $(\$520 - 500)/\$500 = .04$, or 4%. So a 2 percent increase in the number of boats sold leads to a 4 percent increase in operating cash flow. The degree of operating leverage must be exactly 2.00. We can check this by noting that:

$$\begin{aligned} DOL &= 1 + FC/OCF \\ &= 1 + \$500/\$500 \\ &= 2 \end{aligned}$$

This verifies our previous calculations.

Our formulation of DOL depends on the current output level, Q. However, it can handle changes from the current level of any size, not just one unit. For example, suppose Q rises from 50 to 75, a 50 percent increase. With DOL equal to 2, operating cash flow should increase by 100 percent, or exactly double. Does it? The answer is yes, because, at a Q of 75, OCF is:

$$OCF = -\$500 + \$20 \times 75 = \$1{,}000$$

Notice that operating leverage declines as output (Q) rises. For example, at an output level of 75, we have:

$$\begin{aligned} DOL &= 1 + \$500/\$1{,}000 \\ &= 1.50 \end{aligned}$$

The reason DOL declines is that fixed costs, considered as a percentage of operating cash flow, get smaller and smaller, so the leverage effect diminishes.

---

[2]To see this, note that if Q goes up by one unit, OCF will go up by $(P - v)$. In this case, the percentage change in Q is $1/Q$, and the percentage change in OCF is $(P - v)/OCF$. Given this, we have:

Percentage change in OCF = DOL × Percentage change in Q

$$(P - v)/OCF = DOL \times 1/Q$$
$$DOL = (P - v) \times Q/OCF$$

Also, based on our definitions of OCF:

$$OCF + FC = (P - v) \times Q$$

Thus, DOL can be written as:

$$\begin{aligned} DOL &= (OCF + FC)/OCF \\ &= 1 + FC/OCF \end{aligned}$$

Operating Leverage	**EXAMPLE 11.3**

The Sasha Corp. currently sells gourmet dog food for $1.20 per can. The variable cost is 80 cents per can, and the packaging and marketing operations have fixed costs of $360,000 per year. Depreciation is $60,000 per year. What is the accounting break-even? Ignoring taxes, what will be the increase in operating cash flow if the quantity sold rises to 10 percent above the break-even point?

The accounting break-even is $420,000/$.40 = 1,050,000 cans. As we know, the operating cash flow is equal to the $60,000 depreciation at this level of production, so the degree of operating leverage is:

$$DOL = 1 + FC/OCF$$
$$= 1 + \$360,000/\$60,000$$
$$= 7$$

Given this, a 10 percent increase in the number of cans of dog food sold will increase operating cash flow by a substantial 70 percent.

To check this answer, we note that if sales rise by 10 percent, then the quantity sold will rise to 1,050,000 × 1.1 = 1,155,000. Ignoring taxes, the operating cash flow will be 1,155,000 × $.40 − $360,000 = $102,000. Compared to the $60,000 cash flow we had, this is exactly 70 percent more: $102,000/$60,000 = 1.70.

OPERATING LEVERAGE AND BREAK-EVEN

We illustrate why operating leverage is an important consideration by examining the Wettway sailboat project under an alternative scenario. At a Q of 85 boats, the degree of operating leverage for the sailboat project under the original scenario is:

$$DOL = 1 + FC/OCF$$
$$= 1 + \$500/\$1,200$$
$$= 1.42$$

Also, recall that the NPV at a sales level of 85 boats was $88,735, and the accounting break-even was 60 boats.

An option available to Wettway is to subcontract production of the boat hull assemblies. If the company does this, the necessary investment falls to $3,200,000 and the fixed operating costs fall to $180,000. Variable costs will rise to $25,000 per boat because subcontracting is more expensive than producing in-house. Ignoring taxes, evaluate this option.

For practice, see if you don't agree with the following:

NPV at 20% (85 units) = $74,720
Accounting break-even = 55 boats
Degree of operating leverage = 1.16

What has happened? This option results in a slightly lower estimated net present value, and the accounting break-even point falls to 55 boats from 60 boats.

Given that this alternative has the lower NPV, is there any reason to consider it further? Maybe there is. The degree of operating leverage is substantially lower in the second case. If Wettway is worried about the possibility of an overly optimistic projection, then it might prefer to subcontract.

There is another reason why Wettway might consider the second arrangement. If sales turn out to be better than expected, the company still has the option of starting to produce in-house at a later date. As a practical matter, it is much easier to increase operating leverage (by purchasing equipment) than to decrease it (by selling off equipment). As we discuss in a later chapter, one of the drawbacks to discounted cash flow analysis is that it is difficult to explicitly include options of this sort in the analysis, even though they may be quite important.

Concept Questions

11.5a   What is operating leverage?

11.5b   How is operating leverage measured?

11.5c   What are the implications of operating leverage for the financial manager?

11.6 Capital Rationing

capital rationing
The situation that exists if a firm has positive NPV projects but cannot find the necessary financing.

Capital rationing is said to exist when we have profitable (positive NPV) investments available but we can't get the funds needed to undertake them. For example, as division managers for a large corporation, we might identify $5 million in excellent projects but find that, for whatever reason, we can spend only $2 million. Now what? Unfortunately, for reasons we will discuss, there may be no truly satisfactory answer.

SOFT RATIONING

soft rationing
The situation that occurs when units in a business are allocated a certain amount of financing for capital budgeting.

The situation we have just described is called **soft rationing**. This occurs when, for example, different units in a business are allocated some fixed amount of money each year for capital spending. Such an allocation is primarily a means of controlling and keeping track of overall spending. The important thing to note about soft rationing is that the corporation as a whole isn't short of capital; more can be raised on ordinary terms if management so desires.

If we face soft rationing, the first thing to do is to try to get a larger allocation. Failing that, one common suggestion is to generate as large a net present value as possible within the existing budget. This amounts to choosing projects with the largest benefit-cost ratio (profitability index).

Strictly speaking, this is the correct thing to do only if the soft rationing is a one-time event—that is, it won't exist next year. If the soft rationing is a chronic problem, then something is amiss. The reason goes all the way back to Chapter 1. Ongoing soft rationing means we are constantly bypassing positive NPV investments. This contradicts the goal of our firm. If we are not trying to maximize value, then the question of which projects to take becomes ambiguous because we no longer have an objective goal in the first place.

HARD RATIONING

hard rationing
The situation that occurs when a business cannot raise financing for a project under any circumstances.

With **hard rationing**, a business cannot raise capital for a project under any circumstances. For large, healthy corporations, this situation probably does not occur very often. This is fortunate because, with hard rationing, our DCF analysis breaks down, and the best course of action is ambiguous.

The reason DCF analysis breaks down has to do with the required return. Suppose we say our required return is 20 percent. Implicitly, we are saying we will take a project with a return that exceeds this. However, if we face hard rationing, then we are not going to take a new project no matter what the return on that project is, so the whole concept of a required return is ambiguous. About the only interpretation we can give this situation is that the required return is so large that no project has a positive NPV in the first place.

Hard rationing can occur when a company experiences financial distress, meaning that bankruptcy is a possibility. Also, a firm may not be able to raise capital without violating a preexisting contractual agreement. We discuss these situations in greater detail in a later chapter.

Concept Questions

11.6a   What is capital rationing? What types are there?

11.6b   What problems does capital rationing create for discounted cash flow analysis?

Summary and Conclusions   11.7

In this chapter, we looked at some ways of evaluating the results of a discounted cash flow analysis; we also touched on some of the problems that can come up in practice:

1. Net present value estimates depend on projected future cash flows. If there are errors in those projections, then our estimated NPVs can be misleading. We called this possibility *forecasting risk*.

2. Scenario and sensitivity analysis are useful tools for identifying which variables are critical to the success of a project and where forecasting problems can do the most damage.

3. Break-even analysis in its various forms is a particularly common type of scenario analysis that is useful for identifying critical levels of sales.

4. Operating leverage is a key determinant of break-even levels. It reflects the degree to which a project or a firm is committed to fixed costs. The degree of operating leverage tells us the sensitivity of operating cash flow to changes in sales volume.

5. Projects usually have future managerial options associated with them. These options may be important, but standard discounted cash flow analysis tends to ignore them.

6. Capital rationing occurs when apparently profitable projects cannot be funded. Standard discounted cash flow analysis is troublesome in this case because NPV is not necessarily the appropriate criterion.

The most important thing to carry away from reading this chapter is that estimated NPVs or returns should not be taken at face value. They depend critically on projected cash flows. If there is room for significant disagreement about those projected cash flows, the results from the analysis have to be taken with a grain of salt.

Despite the problems we have discussed, discounted cash flow analysis is still *the* way of attacking problems because it forces us to ask the right questions. What we have learned in this chapter is that knowing the questions to ask does not guarantee we will get all the answers.

CONNECT TO FINANCE

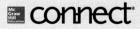 Do you use *Connect Finance* to practice what you learned? If you don't, you should—we can help you master the topics presented in this chapter. Log on to connect.mheducation.com to learn more!

Can you answer the following *Connect* Quiz questions?

Section 11.1 The potential for believing that a project has a positive net present value when it does not is referred to as _____.

Section 11.2 Marcos Entertainment expects to sell 84,000 theater tickets at $12 each during the coming year. What is the worst-case sales revenue if all estimates are accurate to within a ±3 percent range?

Section 11.3 Delta Tool has projected sales of 8,500 units at a sales price per unit of $9,400. Fixed costs are estimated at $5.2 million, and estimated variable costs per unit are $8,300. What is the amount of the total costs if the firm temporarily stops production?

Section 11.4 What is true for a project if that project is operating at its financial break-even point?

Section 11.5 A capital-intensive project is one that has a _____.

Section 11.6 Pavloki, Inc., has three proposed projects with positive net present values. These projects and their net present values are: Project A−NPV $46,300; Project B−NPV $31,900; Project C−NPV $6,400. If the firm is faced with hard rationing, which of the projects will it accept?

CHAPTER REVIEW AND SELF-TEST PROBLEMS

Use the following base-case information to work the self-test problems:

A project under consideration costs $750,000, has a five-year life, and has no salvage value. Depreciation is straight-line to zero. The required return is 17 percent, and the tax rate is 21 percent. Sales are projected at 500 units per year. Price per unit is $2,500, variable cost per unit is $1,500, and fixed costs are $200,000 per year.

11.1 Scenario Analysis Suppose you think that the unit sales, price, variable cost, and fixed cost projections given here are accurate to within 5 percent. What are the upper and lower bounds for these projections? What is the base-case NPV? What are the best- and worst-case scenario NPVs?

11.2 Break-Even Analysis Given the base-case projections in the previous problem, what are the cash, accounting, and financial break-even sales levels for this project? Ignore taxes in answering.

ANSWERS TO CHAPTER REVIEW AND SELF-TEST PROBLEMS

11.1 We can summarize the relevant information as follows:

	Base Case	Lower Bound	Upper Bound
Unit sales	500	475	525
Price per unit	$ 2,500	$ 2,375	$ 2,625
Variable cost per unit	$ 1,500	$ 1,425	$ 1,575
Fixed cost per year	$200,000	$190,000	$210,000

Depreciation is $150,000 per year; knowing this, we can calculate the cash flows under each scenario. Remember that we assign high costs and low prices and volume for the worst case and just the opposite for the best case:

Scenario	Unit Sales	Unit Price	Unit Variable Cost	Fixed Costs	Cash Flow
Base case	500	$2,500	$1,500	$200,000	$268,500
Best case	525	2,625	1,425	190,000	379,100
Worst case	475	2,375	1,575	210,000	165,800

At 17 percent, the five-year annuity factor is 3.19935, so the NPVs are:

$$\text{Base-case NPV} = -\$750,000 + 3.19935 \times \$268,500$$
$$= \$109,024$$
$$\text{Best-case NPV} = -\$750,000 + 3.19935 \times \$379,100$$
$$= \$462,872$$
$$\text{Worst-case NPV} = -\$750,000 + 3.19935 \times \$165,800$$
$$= -\$219,548$$

11.2 In this case, we have $200,000 in cash fixed costs to cover. Each unit contributes $2,500 − 1,500 = $1,000 toward covering fixed costs. The cash break-even is thus $200,000/$1,000 = 200 units. We have another $150,000 in depreciation, so the accounting break-even is ($200,000 + 150,000)/$1,000 = 350 units.

To get the financial break-even, we need to find the OCF such that the project has a zero NPV. As we have seen, the five-year annuity factor is 3.19935 and the project costs $750,000, so the OCF must be such that:

$$\$750,000 = \text{OCF} \times 3.19935$$

So, for the project to break even on a financial basis, the project's cash flow must be $750,000/3.19935, or $234,423 per year. If we add this to the $200,000 in cash fixed costs, we get a total of $434,423 that we have to cover. At $1,000 per unit, we need to sell $434,423/$1,000 = 435 units.

CONCEPTS REVIEW AND CRITICAL THINKING QUESTIONS

1. **Forecasting Risk [LO1]** What is forecasting risk? In general, would the degree of forecasting risk be greater for a new product or a cost-cutting proposal? Why?

2. **Sensitivity Analysis and Scenario Analysis [LO1, 2]** What is the essential difference between sensitivity analysis and scenario analysis?

3. **Marginal Cash Flows [LO3]** A co-worker claims that looking at all this marginal this and incremental that is just a bunch of nonsense, saying, "Listen, if our average revenue doesn't exceed our average cost, then we will have a negative cash flow, and we will go broke!" How do you respond?

4. **Operating Leverage [LO4]** At one time at least, many Japanese companies had a "no-layoff" policy (for that matter, so did IBM). What are the implications of such a policy for the degree of operating leverage a company faces?

5. **Operating Leverage [LO4]** Airlines offer an example of an industry in which the degree of operating leverage is fairly high. Why?

6. **Break-Even [LO3]** As a shareholder of a firm that is contemplating a new project, would you be more concerned with the accounting break-even point, the cash break-even point, or the financial break-even point? Why?

7. **Break-Even [LO3]** Assume a firm is considering a new project that requires an initial investment and has equal sales and costs over its life. Will the project reach the accounting, cash, or financial break-even point first? Which will it reach next? Last? Will this ordering always apply?

8. **Capital Rationing [LO5]** How do soft rationing and hard rationing differ? What are the implications if a firm is experiencing soft rationing? Hard rationing?

9. **Capital Rationing [LO5]** Going all the way back to Chapter 1, recall that we saw that partnerships and proprietorships can face difficulties when it comes to raising capital. In the context of this chapter, the implication is that small businesses will generally face what problem?

10. **Scenario Analysis [LO2]** You are at work when a co-worker excitedly comes to your desk and shows you the scenario analysis that he has just completed for a potential new project. All three scenarios show a positive NPV. He states, "We have to take this project!" What is your initial reaction regarding this new project. Do you believe the results of the scenario analysis?

QUESTIONS AND PROBLEMS

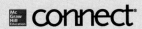

BASIC

(Questions 1–15)

1. **Calculating Costs and Break-Even [LO3]** Night Shades, Inc. (NSI), manufactures biotech sunglasses. The variable materials cost is $11.13 per unit, and the variable labor cost is $7.29 per unit.

   a. What is the variable cost per unit?

   b. Suppose the company incurs fixed costs of $875,000 during a year in which total production is 190,000 units. What are the total costs for the year?

   c. If the selling price is $44.99 per unit, does the company break even on a cash basis? If depreciation is $435,000 per year, what is the accounting break-even point?

2. **Computing Average Cost [LO3]** K-Too Everwear Corporation can manufacture mountain climbing shoes for $33.18 per pair in variable raw material costs and $24.36 per pair in variable labor expense. The shoes sell for $170 per pair. Last year, production was 145,000 pairs. Fixed costs were $1,750,000. What were total production costs? What is the marginal cost per pair? What is the average cost? If the company is considering a one-time order for an extra 5,000 pairs, what is the minimum acceptable total revenue from the order? Explain.

3. **Scenario Analysis [LO2]** Sloan Transmissions, Inc., has the following estimates for its new gear assembly project: Price = $1,440 per unit; variable costs = $460 per unit; fixed costs = $3.9 million; quantity = 85,000 units. Suppose the company believes all of its estimates are accurate only to within ±15 percent. What values should the company use for the four variables given here when it performs its best-case scenario analysis? What about the worst-case scenario?

4. **Sensitivity Analysis [LO1]** For the company in the previous problem, suppose management is most concerned about the impact of its price estimate on the project's profitability. How could you address this concern? Describe how you would calculate your answer. What values would you use for the other forecast variables?

5. **Sensitivity Analysis and Break-Even [LO1, 3]** We are evaluating a project that costs $786,000, has an eight-year life, and has no salvage value. Assume that depreciation is straight-line to zero over the life of the project. Sales are projected at 65,000 units per year. Price per unit is $48, variable cost per unit is $25, and fixed costs are $725,000 per year. The tax rate is 22 percent, and we require a return of 10 percent on this project.

   a. Calculate the accounting break-even point. What is the degree of operating leverage at the accounting break-even point?

b. Calculate the base-case cash flow and NPV. What is the sensitivity of NPV to changes in the quantity sold? Explain what your answer tells you about a 500-unit decrease in the quantity sold.

c. What is the sensitivity of OCF to changes in the variable cost figure? Explain what your answer tells you about a $1 decrease in estimated variable costs.

6. **Scenario Analysis [LO2]** In the previous problem, suppose the projections given for price, quantity, variable costs, and fixed costs are all accurate to within ±10 percent. Calculate the best-case and worst-case NPV figures.

7. **Calculating Break-Even [LO3]** In each of the following cases, calculate the accounting break-even and the cash break-even points. Ignore any tax effects in calculating the cash break-even.

Unit Price	Unit Variable Cost	Fixed Costs	Depreciation
$2,980	$2,135	$8,100,000	$3,100,000
46	41	185,000	183,000
9	3	2,770	1,050

8. **Calculating Break-Even [LO3]** In each of the following cases, find the unknown variable:

Accounting Break-Even	Unit Price	Unit Variable Cost	Fixed Costs	Depreciation
125,736	$39	$30	$ 820,000	?
165,000	?	27	2,320,000	$975,000
21,430	92	?	237,000	128,700

9. **Calculating Break-Even [LO3]** A project has the following estimated data: Price = $62 per unit; variable costs = $28 per unit; fixed costs = $27,300; required return = 12 percent; initial investment = $34,800; life = four years. Ignoring the effect of taxes, what is the accounting break-even quantity? The cash break-even quantity? The financial break-even quantity? What is the degree of operating leverage at the financial break-even level of output?

10. **Using Break-Even Analysis [LO3]** Consider a project with the following data: Accounting break-even quantity = 13,700 units; cash break-even quantity = 9,600 units; life = five years; fixed costs = $185,000; variable costs = $23 per unit; required return = 12 percent. Ignoring the effect of taxes, find the financial break-even quantity.

11. **Calculating Operating Leverage [LO4]** At an output level of 45,000 units, you calculate that the degree of operating leverage is 2.79. If output rises to 48,000 units, what will the percentage change in operating cash flow be? Will the new level of operating leverage be higher or lower? Explain.

12. **Leverage [LO4]** In the previous problem, suppose fixed costs are $175,000. What is the operating cash flow at 43,000 units? The degree of operating leverage?

13. **Operating Cash Flow and Leverage [LO4]** A proposed project has fixed costs of $89,000 per year. The operating cash flow at 10,400 units is $127,400. Ignoring the effect of taxes, what is the degree of operating leverage? If units sold rise from 10,400 to 11,100, what will be the increase in operating cash flow? What is the new degree of operating leverage?

14. **Cash Flow and Leverage** **[LO4]** At an output level of 17,500 units, you have calculated that the degree of operating leverage is 3.26. The operating cash flow is $78,000 in this case. Ignoring the effect of taxes, what are fixed costs? What will the operating cash flow be if output rises to 18,500 units? If output falls to 16,500 units?

15. **Leverage** **[LO4]** In the previous problem, what will be the new degree of operating leverage in each case?

INTERMEDIATE
(Questions 16–24)

16. **Break-Even Intuition** **[LO3]** Consider a project with a required return of R percent that costs $\$I$ and will last for N years. The project uses straight-line depreciation to zero over the N-year life; there is no salvage value or net working capital requirements.

    a. At the accounting break-even level of output, what is the IRR of this project? The payback period? The NPV?

    b. At the cash break-even level of output, what is the IRR of this project? The payback period? The NPV?

    c. At the financial break-even level of output, what is the IRR of this project? The payback period? The NPV?

17. **Sensitivity Analysis** **[LO1]** Consider a four-year project with the following information: Initial fixed asset investment = $575,000; straight-line depreciation to zero over the four-year life; zero salvage value; price = $29; variable costs = $19; fixed costs = $235,000; quantity sold = 76,000 units; tax rate = 21 percent. How sensitive is OCF to changes in quantity sold?

18. **Operating Leverage** **[LO4]** In the previous problem, what is the degree of operating leverage at the given level of output? What is the degree of operating leverage at the accounting break-even level of output?

19. **Project Analysis** **[LO1, 2, 3, 4]** You are considering a new product launch. The project will cost $1,950,000, have a four-year life, and have no salvage value; depreciation is straight-line to zero. Sales are projected at 210 units per year; price per unit will be $17,500, variable cost per unit will be $10,600, and fixed costs will be $560,000 per year. The required return on the project is 12 percent, and the relevant tax rate is 21 percent.

    a. Based on your experience, you think the unit sales, variable cost, and fixed cost projections given here are probably accurate to within ±10 percent. What are the upper and lower bounds for these projections? What is the base-case NPV? What are the best-case and worst-case scenarios?

    b. Evaluate the sensitivity of your base-case NPV to changes in fixed costs.

    c. What is the cash break-even level of output for this project (ignoring taxes)?

    d. What is the accounting break-even level of output for this project? What is the degree of operating leverage at the accounting break-even point? How do you interpret this number?

20. **Project Analysis** **[LO1, 2]** McGilla Golf has decided to sell a new line of golf clubs. The clubs will sell for $845 per set and have a variable cost of $405 per set. The company has spent $150,000 for a marketing study that determined the company will sell 60,000 sets per year for seven years. The marketing study also determined that the company will lose sales of 10,000 sets of its high-priced clubs. The high-priced clubs sell at $1,175 and have variable costs of $620. The company will also increase sales of its cheap clubs by 12,000 sets. The cheap clubs sell for $435 and have variable costs of $200 per set. The fixed costs each year will be $9.75 million. The company has also spent $1 million on research and development for the new clubs. The plant and equipment required will cost $37.1 million and will be depreciated on a straight-line basis. The new clubs will also require an increase in net working

capital of $1.7 million that will be returned at the end of the project. The tax rate is 25 percent, and the cost of capital is 10 percent. Calculate the payback period, the NPV, and the IRR.

21. **Scenario Analysis [LO2]** In the previous problem, you feel that the values are accurate to within only ±10 percent. What are the best-case and worst-case NPVs? *Hint*: The price and variable costs for the two existing sets of clubs are known with certainty; only the sales gained or lost are uncertain.

22. **Sensitivity Analysis [LO1]** In Problem 20, McGilla Golf would like to know the sensitivity of NPV to changes in the price of the new clubs and the quantity of new clubs sold. What is the sensitivity of the NPV to each of these variables?

23. **Break-Even Analysis [LO3]** Hybrid cars are touted as a "green" alternative; however, the financial aspects of hybrid ownership are not as clear. Consider the 2016 Toyota Camry Hybrid LE, which had a list price of $5,500 (including tax consequences) more than the comparable Volkswagen Touareg VR6. Additionally, the annual ownership costs (other than fuel) for the hybrid were expected to be $350 more than the traditional sedan. The EPA mileage estimate was 39 mpg for the hybrid and 30 mpg for the traditional sedan.

    a. Assume that gasoline costs $2.85 per gallon and you plan to keep either car for six years. How many miles per year would you need to drive to make the decision to buy the hybrid worthwhile, ignoring the time value of money?

    b. If you drive 15,000 miles per year and keep either car for six years, what price per gallon would make the decision to buy the hybrid worthwhile, ignoring the time value of money?

    c. Rework parts (a) and (b) assuming the appropriate interest rate is 10 percent and all cash flows occur at the end of the year.

    d. What assumption did the analysis in the previous parts make about the resale value of each car?

24. **Break-Even Analysis [LO3]** In an effort to capture the large jet market, Airbus invested $13 billion developing its A380, which is capable of carrying 800 passengers. The plane had a list price of $280 million. In discussing the plane, Airbus stated that the company would break even when 249 A380s were sold.

    a. Assuming the break-even sales figure given is the accounting break-even, what is the cash flow per plane?

    b. Airbus promised its shareholders a 20 percent rate of return on the investment. If sales of the plane continue in perpetuity, how many planes must the company sell per year to deliver on this promise?

    c. Suppose instead that the sales of the A380 last for only 10 years. How many planes must Airbus sell per year to deliver the same rate of return?

25. **Break-Even and Taxes [LO3]** This problem concerns the effect of taxes on the various break-even measures.

    CHALLENGE
    (Questions 25–30)

    a. Show that, when we consider taxes, the general relationship between operating cash flow, OCF, and sales volume, Q, can be written as:

$$Q = \frac{FC + \dfrac{OCF - T_c \times D}{1 - T_c}}{P - v}$$

    b. Use the expression in part (a) to find the cash, accounting, and financial break-even points for the Wettway sailboat example in the chapter. Assume a 21 percent tax rate.

c. In part (b), the accounting break-even should be the same as before. Why? Verify this algebraically.

26. **Operating Leverage and Taxes [LO4]** Show that if we consider the effect of taxes, the degree of operating leverage can be written as:

$$DOL = 1 + [FC \times (1 - T_C) - T_C \times D]/OCF$$

Notice that this reduces to our previous result if $T_C = 0$. Can you interpret this in words?

27. **Scenario Analysis [LO2]** Consider a project to supply Detroit with 30,000 tons of machine screws annually for automobile production. You will need an initial $4.3 million investment in threading equipment to get the project started; the project will last for five years. The accounting department estimates that annual fixed costs will be $1.025 million and that variable costs should be $190 per ton; accounting will depreciate the initial fixed asset investment straight-line to zero over the five-year project life. It also estimates a salvage value of $400,000 after dismantling costs. The marketing department estimates that the automakers will let the contract at a selling price of $290 per ton. The engineering department estimates you will need an initial net working capital investment of $410,000. You require a return of 13 percent and face a tax rate of 22 percent on this project.

    a. What is the estimated OCF for this project? The NPV? Should you pursue this project?

    b. Suppose you believe that the accounting department's initial cost and salvage value projections are accurate only to within ±15 percent; the marketing department's price estimate is accurate only to within ±10 percent; and the engineering department's net working capital estimate is accurate only to within ±5 percent. What is your worst-case scenario for this project? Your best-case scenario? Do you still want to pursue the project?

28. **Sensitivity Analysis [LO1]** In Problem 27, suppose you're confident about your own projections, but you're a little unsure about Detroit's actual machine screw requirement. What is the sensitivity of the project OCF to changes in the quantity supplied? What about the sensitivity of NPV to changes in quantity supplied? Given the sensitivity number you calculated, is there some minimum level of output below which you wouldn't want to operate? Why?

29. **Break-Even Analysis [LO3]** Use the results of Problem 25 to find the accounting, cash, and financial break-even quantities for the company in Problem 27.

30. **Operating Leverage [LO4]** Use the results of Problem 26 to find the degree of operating leverage for the company in Problem 27 at the base-case output level of 30,000 tons. How does this number compare to the sensitivity figure you found in Problem 28? Verify that either approach will give you the same OCF figure at any new quantity level.

EXCEL MASTER IT! PROBLEM

Harper Industries is examining a new project to manufacture cell phones. The company has examined several alternatives for the manufacturing process. With Process I, the company would manufacture the cell phone entirely in-house. This would require the highest initial cost and fixed costs. Process II would involve subcontracting the manufacture of the electronics. While this choice would reduce the initial cost and fixed costs, it would result in higher variable costs. Finally, Process III would subcontract all production, with Harper Industries only completing the final assembly and testing. Below you are given the information for each of the options available to the company.

	Process I	Process II	Process III
Initial cost:	$75,000,000	$55,000,000	$36,000,000
Life (years):	7		
Units:	450,000		
Price per unit:	$ 345		
VC per unit:	$ 85	$ 137	$ 182
Fixed costs:	$81,000,000	$63,000,000	$48,000,000
Required return:	13%		
Tax rate:	21%		

a. Calculate the NPV for each of the three manufacturing processes available to the company.

b. What are the accounting break-even, cash break-even, and financial break-even points for each manufacturing process?

c. What is the DOL for each manufacturing process? Graph the DOL for each manufacturing process on the same graph for different unit sales.

MINICASE

Conch Republic Electronics, Part 2

Shelley Couts, the owner of Conch Republic Electronics, has received the capital budgeting analysis from Jay McCanless for the new smartphone the company is considering. Shelley is pleased with the results, but she still has concerns about the new smartphone. Conch Republic has used a small market research firm for the past 20 years, but recently the founder of that firm has retired. Because of this, Shelley is not convinced the sales projections presented by the market research firm are entirely accurate. Additionally, because of rapid changes in technology, she is concerned that a competitor may enter the market. This would likely force Conch Republic to lower the sales price of its new smartphone. For these reasons, she has asked Jay to analyze how changes in the price of the new smartphone and changes in the quantity sold will affect the NPV of the project.

Shelley has asked Jay to prepare a memo answering the following questions.

QUESTIONS

1. How sensitive is the NPV to changes in the price of the new smartphone?

2. How sensitive is the NPV to changes in the quantity sold of the new smartphone?

12 | Some Lessons from Capital Market History

WITH THE S&P 500 UP about 12 percent and the NASDAQ index up about 9 percent in 2016, stock market performance overall was mixed for the year. The S&P 500 return was about average, while the NASDAQ return was below average. However, investors in AK Steel had to be thrilled with the 359 percent gain in that stock, and investors in United States Steel had to feel pleased with its 332 percent gain. Of course, not all stocks increased during the year. Stock in pharmaceutical company Endo International fell 73 percent during the year, and stock in First Solar fell 51 percent.

These examples show that there were tremendous potential profits to be made during 2016, but there was also the risk of losing money—lots of it. So what should you, as a stock market investor, expect when you invest your own money? In this chapter, we study almost nine decades of market history to find out.

Learning Objectives

After studying this chapter, you should be able to:

LO1   Calculate the return on an investment.

LO2   Discuss the historical returns on various important types of investments.

LO3   Discuss the historical risks on various important types of investments.

LO4   Explain the implications of market efficiency.

For updates on the latest happenings in finance, visit fundamentalsofcorporatefinance.blogspot.com.

Thus far, we haven't had much to say about what determines the required return on an investment. In one sense, the answer is simple: The required return depends on the risk of the investment. The greater the risk, the greater is the required return.

Having said this, we are left with a somewhat more difficult problem. How can we measure the amount of risk present in an investment? Put another way, what does it mean to say that one investment is riskier than another? Obviously, we need to define what we mean by *risk* if we are going to answer these questions. This is our task in this chapter and the next.

From the last several chapters, we know that one of the responsibilities of the financial manager is to assess the value of proposed real asset investments. In doing this, it is important that we first look at what financial investments have to offer. At a minimum, the return we require from a proposed nonfinancial investment must be greater than what we can get by buying financial assets of similar risk.

Our goal in this chapter is to provide a perspective on what capital market history can tell us about risk and return. The most important thing to get out of this chapter is a feel for the numbers. What is a high return? What is a low return? More generally, what returns should we expect from financial assets, and what are the risks of such investments? This perspective is essential for understanding how to analyze and value risky investment projects.

We start our discussion of risk and return by describing the historical experience of investors in U.S. financial markets. In 1931, for example, the stock market lost 44 percent of its value. Just two years later, the stock market gained 54 percent. In more recent memory, the market lost about 25 percent of its value on October 19, 1987, alone. What lessons, if any, can financial managers learn from such shifts in the stock market? We will explore almost a century of market history to find out.

Not everyone agrees on the value of studying history. On the one hand, there is philosopher George Santayana's famous comment: "Those who do not remember the past are condemned to repeat it."* On the other hand, there is industrialist Henry Ford's equally famous comment: "History is more or less bunk."† Nonetheless, perhaps everyone would agree with Mark Twain's observation: "October. This is one of the peculiarly dangerous months to speculate in stocks. The others are July, January, September, April, November, May, March, June, December, August, and February."‡

Two central lessons emerge from our study of market history. First, there is a reward for bearing risk. Second, the greater is the potential reward, the greater is the risk. To illustrate these facts about market returns, we devote much of this chapter to reporting the statistics and numbers that make up the modern capital market history of the United States. In the next chapter, these facts provide the foundation for our study of how financial markets put a price on risk.

Returns

12.1

Excel Master It!

xlsx   Excel Master coverage online

We wish to discuss historical returns on different types of financial assets. The first thing we need to do, then, is to briefly discuss how to calculate the return from investing.

DOLLAR RETURNS

If you buy an asset of any sort, your gain (or loss) from that investment is called the *return on your investment*. This return will usually have two components. First, you may receive some cash directly while you own the investment. This is called the *income component* of your return. Second, the value of the asset you purchase will often change. In this case, you have a capital gain or capital loss on your investment.[1]

How did the market do today? Find out at **finance.yahoo.com**.

To illustrate, suppose the Video Concept Company has several thousand shares of stock outstanding. You purchased some of these shares of stock in the company at the beginning of the year. It is now year-end, and you want to determine how well you have done on your investment.

First, over the year, a company may pay cash dividends to its shareholders. As a stockholder in Video Concept Company, you are a part owner of the company. If the company is profitable, it may choose to distribute some of its profits to shareholders (we discuss the details of dividend policy in a later chapter). So, as the owner of some stock, you will receive some cash. This cash is the income component from owning the stock.

In addition to the dividend, the other part of your return is the capital gain or capital loss on the stock. This part arises from changes in the value of your investment. For example, consider the cash flows illustrated in Figure 12.1. At the beginning of the year, the stock was selling for $37 per share. If you had bought 100 shares, you would have had a total outlay of $3,700. Suppose that, over the year, the stock paid a dividend of $1.85 per share. By the end of the year, then, you would have received income of:

Dividend = $1.85 × 100 = $185

---

*Source: George Santayana, Philosopher (1863–1952)

†Source: Henry Ford, Industrialist (1863–1947)

‡Source: Mark Twain (1835–1910)

[1]As we mentioned in an earlier chapter, strictly speaking, what is and what is not a capital gain (or loss) is determined by the IRS. We use the terms loosely.

FIGURE 12.1

Dollar Returns

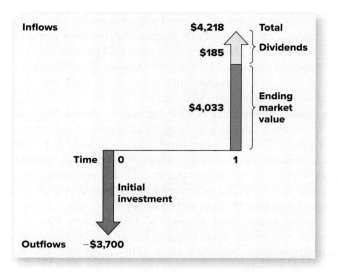

Also, the value of the stock has risen to $40.33 per share by the end of the year. Your 100 shares are now worth $4,033, so you have a capital gain of:

Capital gain = ($40.33 − 37) × 100 = $333

On the other hand, if the price had dropped to, say, $34.78, you would have a capital loss of:

Capital loss = ($34.78 − 37) × 100 = −$222

Notice that a capital loss is the same thing as a negative capital gain.

The total dollar return on your investment is the sum of the dividend and the capital gain:

Total dollar return = Dividend income + Capital gain (or loss)   **12.1**

In our first example, the total dollar return is given by:

Total dollar return = $185 + 333 = $518

Notice that if you sold the stock at the end of the year, the total amount of cash you would have would equal your initial investment plus the total return. In the preceding example, then:

Total cash if stock is sold = Initial investment + Total return   **12.2**
$$= \$3,700 + 518$$
$$= \$4,218$$

As a check, notice that this is the same as the proceeds from the sale of the stock plus the dividends:

Proceeds from stock sale + Dividends = $40.33 × 100 + 185
$$= \$4,033 + 185$$
$$= \$4,218$$

Suppose you hold on to your Video Concept stock and don't sell it at the end of the year. Should you still consider the capital gain as part of your return? Isn't this only a "paper" gain and not really a cash flow if you don't sell the stock?

The answer to the first question is a strong yes, and the answer to the second is an equally strong no. The capital gain is every bit as much a part of your return as the dividend, and you should certainly count it as part of your return. That you actually decided to keep the stock and not sell (you don't "realize" the gain) is irrelevant because you could have converted it to cash if you had wanted to. Whether you choose to do so or not is up to you.

After all, if you insisted on converting your gain to cash, you could always sell the stock at year-end and immediately reinvest by buying the stock back. There is no net difference between doing this and just not selling (assuming, of course, that there are no tax consequences from selling the stock). Again, the point is that your decision to actually cash out and buy sodas (or whatever) or to reinvest by not selling doesn't affect the return you earn.

PERCENTAGE RETURNS

It is usually more convenient to summarize information about returns in percentage terms, rather than dollar terms, because that way your return doesn't depend on how much you actually invest. The question we want to answer is this: How much do we get for each dollar we invest?

To answer this question, let P_t be the price of the stock at the beginning of the year and let D_{t+1} be the dividend paid on the stock during the year. Consider the cash flows in Figure 12.2. These are the same as those in Figure 12.1, except that we have now expressed everything on a per-share basis.

In our example, the price at the beginning of the year was $37 per share and the dividend paid during the year on each share was $1.85. As we discussed in Chapter 8, expressing the dividend as a percentage of the beginning stock price results in the dividend yield:

Dividend yield $= D_{t+1}/P_t$

$\qquad = \$1.85/\$37 = .05$, or 5%

This says that for each dollar we invest, we get five cents in dividends.

The second component of our percentage return is the capital gains yield. Recall (from Chapter 8) that this is calculated as the change in the price during the year (the capital gain) divided by the beginning price:

Capital gains yield $= (P_{t+1} - P_t)/P_t$

$\qquad = (\$40.33 - 37)/\$37$

$\qquad = \$3.33/\$37$

$\qquad = .09$, or 9%

So, per dollar invested, we get nine cents in capital gains.

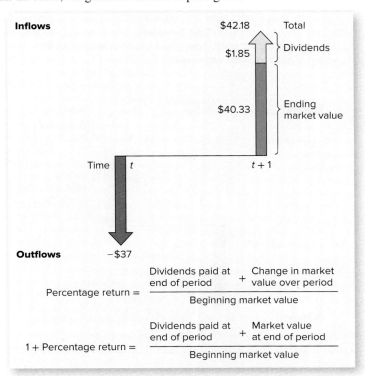

FIGURE 12.2

Percentage Returns

Putting it together, per dollar invested, we get 5 cents in dividends and 9 cents in capital gains; so we get a total of 14 cents. Our percentage return is 14 cents on the dollar, or 14 percent.

To check this, notice that we invested $3,700 and ended up with $4,218. By what percentage did our $3,700 increase? As we saw, we picked up $4,218 − 3,700 = $518. This is a $518/$3,700 = 14% increase.

EXAMPLE 12.1   Calculating Returns

Suppose you buy some stock at the beginning of the year for $25 per share. At the end of the year, the price is $35 per share. During the year, you receive a $2 dividend per share. This is the situation illustrated in Figure 12.3. What is the dividend yield? The capital gains yield? The percentage return? If your total investment was $1,000, how much do you have at the end of the year?

Your $2 dividend per share works out to a dividend yield of:

Dividend yield = D_{t+1}/P_t
$$= \$2/\$25 = .08, \text{ or } 8\%$$

The per-share capital gain is $10, so the capital gains yield is:

Capital gains yield = $(P_{t+1} - P_t)/P_t$
$$= (\$35 - 25)/\$25$$
$$= \$10/\$25$$
$$= .40, \text{ or } 40\%$$

The total percentage return is 48 percent.

If you had invested $1,000, you would have $1,480 at the end of the year, representing a 48 percent increase. To check this, note that your $1,000 would have bought you $1,000/$25 = 40 shares. Your 40 shares would then have paid you a total of 40 × $2 = $80 in cash dividends. Your $10 per-share gain would give you a total capital gain of $10 × 40 = $400. Add these together, and you get the $480 increase.

FIGURE 12.3 Cash Flow—An Investment Example

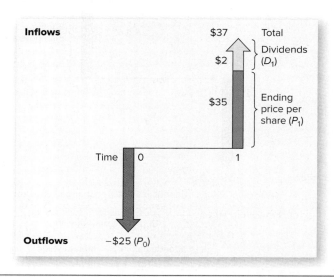

To give another example, stock in entertainment company Time Warner began 2016 at $70.65 per share. Time Warner paid dividends of $1.61 during 2016, and the stock price at the end of the year was $93.85. What was the return on Time Warner for the year? For practice, see if you agree that the answer is 35.12 percent. Of course, negative returns occur as well. For example, again in 2016, the stock price of shoe giant Nike was $62.50 per share at the beginning of the year and dividends of $.66 were paid. The stock ended the year at $50.83 per share. Verify that the loss was 17.62 percent for the year.

Concept Questions

12.1a   What are the two parts of total return?

12.1b   Why are unrealized capital gains or losses included in the calculation of returns?

12.1c   What is the difference between a dollar return and a percentage return? Why are percentage returns more convenient?

The Historical Record

12.2

Roger Ibbotson and Rex Sinquefield conducted a famous set of studies dealing with rates of return in U.S. financial markets.[2] They presented year-to-year historical rates of return on five important types of financial investments. The returns can be interpreted as what you would have earned if you had held portfolios of the following:

1. *Large-company stocks:* This common stock portfolio is based on the Standard & Poor's (S&P) 500 index, which contains 500 of the largest companies (in terms of total market value of outstanding stock) in the United States.

2. *Small-company stocks:* This is a portfolio composed of the stock corresponding to the smallest 20 percent of the companies listed on the New York Stock Exchange, again as measured by market value of outstanding stock.

3. *Long-term corporate bonds:* This is based on high-quality bonds with 20 years to maturity.

4. *Long-term U.S. government bonds:* This is based on U.S. government bonds with 20 years to maturity.

5. *U.S. Treasury bills:* This is based on Treasury bills (T-bills for short) with a one-month maturity.

These returns are not adjusted for inflation or taxes; they are nominal, pretax returns.

In addition to the year-to-year returns on these financial instruments, the year-to-year percentage change in the consumer price index (CPI) is also computed. This is a commonly used measure of inflation, so we can calculate real returns using this as the inflation rate.

For more about market history, visit **www.globalfinancialdata.com**.

A FIRST LOOK

Before looking closely at the different portfolio returns, we take a look at the big picture. Figure 12.4 shows what happened to $1 invested in these different portfolios at the end of 1925. The growth in value for each of the different portfolios over the 91-year period ending in 2016 is given separately (the long-term corporate bonds are omitted). Notice that to get everything on a single graph, some modification in scaling is used. As is commonly

---

[2]R. G. Ibbotson and R. A. Sinquefield, *Stocks, Bonds, Bills, and Inflation* [SBBI] (Charlottesville, VA: Financial Analysis Research Foundation, 1982).

FIGURE 12.4   A $1 Investment in Different Types of Portfolios: 1926–2016 (Year-End 1925 = $1)

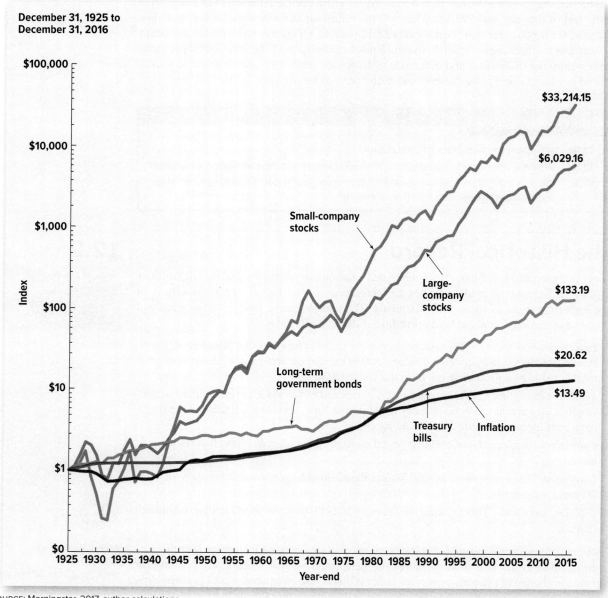

SOURCE: Morningstar, 2017, author calculations.

Go to
bigcharts.marketwatch.com
to see both intraday and long-term charts.

done with financial series, the vertical axis is scaled so that equal distances measure equal percentage (as opposed to dollar) changes in values.[3]

Looking at Figure 12.4, we see that the "small-cap" (short for small-capitalization) investment did the best overall. Every dollar invested grew to a remarkable $33,214.15 over the 91 years. The large-company common stock portfolio did less well; a dollar invested in it grew to $6,029.16.

---

[3]In other words, the scale is logarithmic.

At the other end, the T-bill portfolio grew to only $20.62. This is even less impressive when we consider the inflation over the period in question. As illustrated, the increase in the price level was such that $13.49 was needed at the end of the period just to replace the original $1.

Given the historical record, why would anybody buy anything other than small-cap stocks? If you look closely at Figure 12.4, you will probably see the answer. The T-bill and long-term government bond portfolios grew more slowly than did the stock portfolios, but they also grew much more steadily. The small stocks ended up on top; but as you can see, they grew quite erratically at times. For example, the small stocks were the worst performers for about the first 10 years and had a smaller return than long-term government bonds for over 15 years.

A CLOSER LOOK

To illustrate the variability of the different investments, Figures 12.5 through 12.8 plot the year-to-year percentage returns in the form of vertical bars drawn from the horizontal

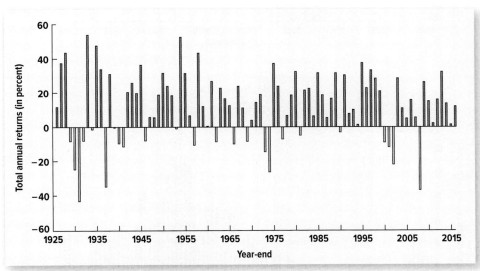

FIGURE 12.5

Year-by-Year Total Returns on Large-Company Common Stocks

SOURCE: Morningstar, 2017

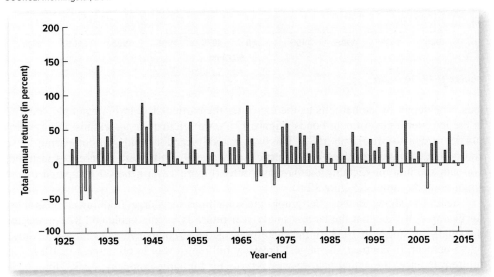

FIGURE 12.6

Year-by-Year Total Returns on Small-Company Stocks

SOURCE: Morningstar, 2017

FIGURE 12.7

**Year-by-Year Total
Returns on Bonds
and Bills**

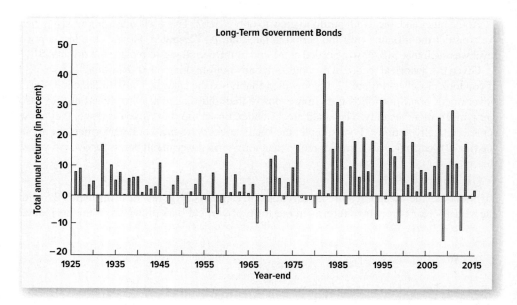

SOURCE: Morningstar, 2017

axis. The height of the bar tells us the return for the particular year. For example, looking at the long-term government bonds (Figure 12.7), we see that the largest historical return (44.28 percent) occurred in 1982. This was a good year for bonds. In comparing these charts, notice the differences in the vertical axis scales. With these differences in mind, you can see how predictably the Treasury bills (Figure 12.7) behaved compared to the small-company stocks (Figure 12.6).

The returns shown in these bar graphs are sometimes very large. Looking at the graphs, for example, we see that the largest single-year return is a remarkable 142.87 percent for the small-cap stocks in 1933. In the same year, the large-company stocks returned "only" 52.95 percent. In contrast, the largest Treasury bill return was 14.60 percent in 1981. For future reference, the actual year-to-year returns for the large-company stocks, long-term government bonds, Treasury bills, and the CPI are shown in Table 12.1.

The financial markets are the most carefully documented human phenomena in history. Every day, almost 2,000 NYSE stocks are traded, and at least 8,000 more stocks are listed on other U.S. exchanges and trading venues. Bonds, commodities, futures, and options also provide a wealth of data. These data are available across a wide spectrum of electronic media, including newswires, websites, and market data platforms like Bloomberg. A record actually exists of almost every transaction, providing not only a real-time database but also a historical record extending back, in many cases, more than a century.

The global market adds another dimension to this wealth of data. Over 2,500 stocks trade on Japanese stock markets while the London Exchange reports on over 2,000 domestic and foreign issues a day. Altogether, more than 20 billion shares trade globally on a typical day.

The data generated by these transactions are quantifiable, quickly analyzed and disseminated, and are easily accessible. Because of this, finance has increasingly come to resemble one of the exact sciences. The use of financial market data ranges from the simple, such as using the S&P 500 index to compare the performance of a portfolio, to the incredibly complex. For example, only a few decades ago, the bond market was the most staid province on Wall Street. Today, it attracts swarms of traders seeking to exploit arbitrage opportunities—small temporary mispricings—using real-time data and computers to analyze them.

Financial market data are the foundation for the extensive empirical understanding we now have of the financial markets. The following is a list of some of the principal findings of such research:

- Trading is more automated and its cost is lower than ever.
- Risky securities, such as stocks, have higher average returns than riskless securities, such as Treasury bills.
- Stocks of small companies have higher average returns than those of larger companies.
- More liquid stocks have higher valuations, but lower returns than less liquid stocks.
- The cost of capital for a company, project, or division can be estimated using data from the markets.

Because phenomena in the financial markets are so well measured, finance is the most readily quantifiable branch of economics. Researchers are able to do more extensive empirical research than in any other economic field, and the research can be quickly translated into action in the marketplace.

Roger Ibbotson is Professor in the Practice of Management at the Yale School of Management. He is also chairman of Zebra Capital, an equity investment manager. He is the founder of Ibbotson Associates, now part of Morningstar, Inc., a major supplier of financial data and analysis. An outstanding scholar, he is best known for his original estimates of the historical rates of return realized by investors in different markets.

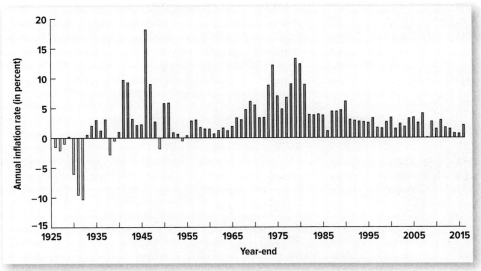

FIGURE 12.8

Year-by-Year Inflation

SOURCE: Morningstar, 2017

TABLE 12.1   Year-to-Year Total Returns: 1926–2016

Year	Large-Company Stocks	Long-Term Government Bonds	U.S. Treasury Bills	Consumer Price Index	Year	Large-Company Stocks	Long-Term Government Bonds	U.S. Treasury Bills	Consumer Price Index
1926	13.75%	5.69%	3.30%	−1.12%	1972	18.99%	2.39%	4.23%	3.41%
1927	35.70	6.58	3.15	−2.26	1973	−14.69	3.30	7.29	8.71
1928	45.08	1.15	4.05	−1.16	1974	−26.47	4.00	7.99	12.34
1929	−8.80	4.39	4.47	.58	1975	37.23	5.52	5.87	6.94
1930	−25.13	4.47	2.27	−6.40	1976	23.93	15.56	5.07	4.86
1931	−43.60	−2.15	1.15	−9.32	1977	−7.16	.38	5.45	6.70
1932	−8.75	8.51	.88	−10.27	1978	6.57	−1.26	7.64	9.02
1933	52.95	1.92	.52	.76	1979	18.61	−2.76	10.56	13.29
1934	−2.31	7.59	.27	1.52	1980	32.50	−2.48	12.10	12.52
1935	46.79	4.20	.17	2.99	1981	−4.92	4.04	14.60	8.92
1936	32.49	5.13	.17	1.45	1982	21.55	44.28	10.94	3.83
1937	−35.45	1.44	.27	2.86	1983	22.56	1.29	8.99	3.79
1938	31.63	4.21	.06	−2.78	1984	6.27	15.29	9.90	3.95
1939	−1.43	3.84	.04	.00	1985	31.73	32.27	7.71	3.80
1940	−10.36	5.70	.04	.71	1986	18.67	22.39	6.09	1.10
1941	−12.02	.47	.14	9.93	1987	5.25	−3.03	5.88	4.43
1942	20.75	1.80	.34	9.03	1988	16.61	6.84	6.94	4.42
1943	25.38	2.01	.38	2.96	1989	31.69	18.54	8.44	4.65
1944	19.49	2.27	.38	2.30	1990	−3.10	7.74	7.69	6.11
1945	36.21	5.29	.38	2.25	1991	30.46	19.36	5.43	3.06
1946	−8.42	.54	.38	18.13	1992	7.62	7.34	3.48	2.90
1947	5.05	−1.02	.62	8.84	1993	10.08	13.06	3.03	2.75
1948	4.99	2.66	1.06	2.99	1994	1.32	−7.32	4.39	2.67
1949	17.81	4.58	1.12	−2.07	1995	37.58	25.94	5.61	2.54
1950	30.05	−.98	1.22	5.93	1996	22.96	.13	5.14	3.32
1951	23.79	−.20	1.56	6.00	1997	33.36	12.02	5.19	1.70
1952	18.39	2.43	1.75	.75	1998	28.58	14.45	4.86	1.61
1953	−1.07	2.28	1.87	.75	1999	21.04	−7.51	4.80	2.68
1954	52.23	3.08	.93	−.74	2000	−9.10	17.22	5.98	3.39
1955	31.62	−.73	1.80	.37	2001	−11.89	5.51	3.33	1.55
1956	6.91	−1.72	2.66	2.99	2002	−22.10	15.15	1.61	2.38
1957	−10.50	6.82	3.28	2.90	2003	28.89	2.01	.94	1.88
1958	43.57	−1.72	1.71	1.76	2004	10.88	8.12	1.14	3.26
1959	12.01	−2.02	3.48	1.73	2005	4.91	6.89	2.79	3.42
1960	.47	11.21	2.81	1.36	2006	15.79	.28	4.97	2.54
1961	26.84	2.20	2.40	.67	2007	5.49	10.85	4.52	4.08
1962	−8.75	5.72	2.82	1.33	2008	−37.00	41.78	1.24	.09
1963	22.70	1.79	3.23	1.64	2009	26.46	−25.61	.15	2.72
1964	16.43	3.71	3.62	.97	2010	15.06	7.73	.14	1.50
1965	12.38	.93	4.06	1.92	2011	2.11	35.75	.06	2.96
1966	−10.06	5.12	4.94	3.46	2012	16.00	1.80	.08	1.74
1967	23.98	−2.86	4.39	3.04	2013	32.39	−14.69	.05	1.50
1968	11.03	2.25	5.49	4.72	2014	13.69	24.74	.03	.75
1969	−8.43	−5.63	6.90	6.20	2015	1.41	−.64	.04	.74
1970	3.94	18.92	6.50	5.57	2016	11.98	1.76	.21	2.11
1971	14.30	11.24	4.36	3.27					

SOURCE: Authors' calculation based on data obtained from *Global Financial Data* and other sources.

12.2a   With 20/20 hindsight, what do you say was the best investment for the period from 1926 through 1935?

12.2b   Why doesn't everyone just buy small stocks as investments?

12.2c   What was the smallest return observed over the 91 years for each of these investments? Approximately when did it occur?

12.2d   About how many times did large-company stocks return more than 30 percent? How many times did they return less than −20 percent?

12.2e   What was the longest "winning streak" (years without a negative return) for large-company stocks? For long-term government bonds?

12.2f   How often did the T-bill portfolio have a negative return?

Average Returns: The First Lesson

12.3

Excel Master It!

xlsx   Excel Master coverage online

As you've probably begun to notice, the history of capital market returns is too complicated to be of much use in its undigested form. We need to begin summarizing all these numbers. Accordingly, we discuss how to go about condensing the detailed data. We start out by calculating average returns.

CALCULATING AVERAGE RETURNS

The obvious way to calculate the average returns on the different investments in Table 12.1 is to add up the yearly returns and divide by 91. The result is the historical average of the individual values.

For example, if you add up the returns for the large-company stocks in Figure 12.5 for the 91 years, you will get about 10.88. The average annual return is 10.88/91 = .120, or 12.0%. You interpret this 12.0 percent just like any other average. If you were to pick a year at random from the 91-year history and you had to guess what the return in that year was, the best guess would be 12.0 percent.

AVERAGE RETURNS: THE HISTORICAL RECORD

Table 12.2 shows the average returns for the investments we have discussed. As shown, in a typical year, the small-company stocks increased in value by 16.6 percent. Notice also how much larger the returns are for stocks, compared to the returns on bonds.

These averages are, of course, nominal because we haven't worried about inflation. Notice that the average inflation rate was 3.0 percent per year over this 91-year span. The nominal return on U.S. Treasury bills was 3.4 percent per year. The average real return on

Investment	Average Return
Large-company stocks	12.0%
Small-company stocks	16.6
Long-term corporate bonds	6.3
Long-term government bonds	6.0
U.S. Treasury bills	3.4
Inflation	3.0

SOURCE: Morningstar, 2017, author calculations.

TABLE 12.2

Average Annual Returns: 1926–2016

Treasury bills was approximately .4 percent per year; so the real return on T-bills has been quite low historically.

At the other extreme, small stocks had an average real return of about $16.6\% - 3.0 = 13.6\%$, which is relatively large. If you remember the Rule of 72 (Chapter 5), then you know that a quick back-of-the-envelope calculation tells us that 13.6 percent real growth doubles your buying power about every five years. Notice also that the real value of the large-company stock portfolio increased by about 9 percent in a typical year.

RISK PREMIUMS

Now that we have computed some average returns, it seems logical to see how they compare with each other. One such comparison involves government-issued securities. These are free of much of the variability we see in, for example, the stock market.

The government borrows money by issuing bonds in different forms. The ones we will focus on are the Treasury bills. These have the shortest time to maturity of the different government bonds. Because the government can always raise taxes to pay its bills, the debt represented by T-bills is virtually free of any default risk over its short life. We will call the rate of return on such debt the *risk-free return*, and we will use it as a kind of benchmark.

A particularly interesting comparison involves the virtually risk-free return on T-bills and the very risky return on common stocks. The difference between these two returns can be interpreted as a measure of the *excess return* on the average risky asset (assuming that the stock of a large U.S. corporation has about average risk compared to all risky assets).

We call this the "excess" return because it is the additional return we earn by moving from a relatively risk-free investment to a risky one. Because it can be interpreted as a reward for bearing risk, we will call it a **risk premium**.

risk premium
The excess return required from an investment in a risky asset over that required from a risk-free investment.

Using Table 12.2, we can calculate the risk premiums for the different investments; these are shown in Table 12.3. We report only the nominal risk premiums because there is only a slight difference between the historical nominal and real risk premiums.

The risk premium on T-bills is shown as zero in the table because we have assumed that they are riskless.

THE FIRST LESSON

Looking at Table 12.3, we see that the average risk premium earned by a typical large-company stock is $12.0\% - 3.4 = 8.6\%$. This is a significant reward. The fact that it exists historically is an important observation, and it is the basis for our first lesson: Risky assets, on average, earn a risk premium. Put another way, there is a reward for bearing risk.

Why is this so? Why, for example, is the risk premium for small stocks so much larger than the risk premium for large stocks? More generally, what determines the relative sizes of the risk premiums for the different assets? The answers to these questions are at the heart of modern finance, and the next chapter is devoted to them. For now, we can find part of the answer by looking at the historical variability of the returns on these different investments. So, to get started, we now turn our attention to measuring variability in returns.

TABLE 12.3

Average Annual Returns and Risk Premiums: 1926–2016

Investment	Average Return	Risk Premium
Large-company stocks	12.0%	8.6%
Small-company stocks	16.6	13.2
Long-term corporate bonds	6.3	2.9
Long-term government bonds	6.0	2.6
U.S. Treasury bills	3.4	0.0

SOURCE: Morningstar, 2017, author calculations.

The Variability of Returns: The Second Lesson   **12.4**

Excel Master It!
Excel Master coverage online

We have already seen that the year-to-year returns on common stocks tend to be more volatile than the returns on, say, long-term government bonds. We now discuss measuring this variability of stock returns so we can begin examining the subject of risk.

FREQUENCY DISTRIBUTIONS AND VARIABILITY

To get started, we can draw a *frequency distribution* for the common stock returns like the one in Figure 12.9. What we have done here is to count the number of times the annual return on the common stock portfolio falls within each 10 percent range. For example, in Figure 12.9, the height of 17 times in the range of 10 to 20 percent means that 17 of the 91 annual returns were in that range.

What we need to do now is to actually measure the spread in returns. We know, for example, that the return on small stocks in a typical year was 16.6 percent. We now want

FIGURE 12.9   **Frequency Distribution of Returns on Large-Company Stocks: 1926–2016**

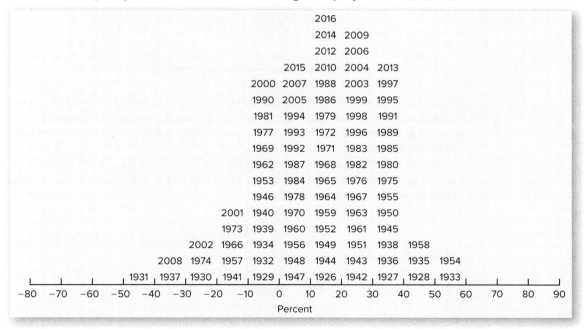

SOURCE: Morningstar, 2017, author calculations.

variance
The average squared difference between the actual return and the average return.

standard deviation
The positive square root of the variance.

For an easy-to-read review of basic stats, check out **www.robertniles.com/stats/**.

to know how much the actual return deviates from this average in a typical year. In other words, we need a measure of the volatility of the return. The **variance** and its square root, the **standard deviation**, are the most commonly used measures of volatility. We describe how to calculate them next.

THE HISTORICAL VARIANCE AND STANDARD DEVIATION

The variance essentially measures the average squared difference between the actual returns and the average return. The bigger this number is, the more the actual returns tend to differ from the average return. Also, the larger the variance or standard deviation is, the more spread out the returns will be.

The way we will calculate the variance and standard deviation will depend on the specific situation. In this chapter, we are looking at historical returns; so the procedure we describe here is the correct one for calculating the *historical* variance and standard deviation. If we were examining projected future returns, then the procedure would be different. We describe this procedure in the next chapter.

To illustrate how we calculate the historical variance, suppose a particular investment had returns of 10 percent, 12 percent, 3 percent, and −9 percent over the last four years. The average return is $(.10 + .12 + .03 − .09)/4 = .04$, or 4%. Notice that the return is never actually equal to 4 percent. Instead, the first return deviates from the average by $.10 − .04 = .06$, the second return deviates from the average by $.12 − .04 = .08$, and so on. To compute the variance, we square each of these deviations, add them, and divide the result by the number of returns less 1, or 3 in this case. Most of this information is summarized in the following table:

	(1) Actual Return	(2) Average Return	(3) Deviation (1) − (2)	(4) Squared Deviation
	.10	.04	.06	.0036
	.12	.04	.08	.0064
	.03	.04	−.01	.0001
	−.09	.04	−.13	.0169
Totals	.16		.00	.0270

In the first column, we write the four actual returns. In the third column, we calculate the difference between the actual returns and the average by subtracting 4 percent. Finally, in the fourth column, we square the numbers in the third column to get the squared deviations from the average.

The variance can now be calculated by dividing .0270, the sum of the squared deviations, by the number of returns less 1. Let Var(R), or σ^2 (read this as "sigma squared"), stand for the variance of the return:

$$\text{Var}(R) = \sigma^2 = .027/(4 − 1) = .009$$

The standard deviation is the square root of the variance. So, if SD(R), or σ, stands for the standard deviation of return:

$$\text{SD}(R) = \sigma = \sqrt{.009} = .09487$$

The square root of the variance is used because the variance is measured in "squared" percentages and is hard to interpret. The standard deviation is an ordinary percentage, so the answer could be written as 9.487 percent.

In the preceding table, notice that the sum of the deviations is equal to zero. This will always be the case, and it provides a good way to check your work. In general, if we have T historical returns, where T is some number, we can write the historical variance as:

$$\text{Var}(R) = \frac{1}{T-1}[(R_1 - \bar{R})^2 + \cdots + (R_T - \bar{R})^2]$$

12.3

This formula tells us to do what we just did: Take each of the T individual returns $(R_1, R_2, \ldots)$ and subtract the average return, $\bar{R}$; square the results, and add them; and finally, divide this total by the number of returns less 1, $(T - 1)$. The standard deviation is always the square root of Var(R). Standard deviations are a widely used measure of volatility. Our nearby *Work the Web* box gives a real-world example.

Calculating the Variance and Standard Deviation

EXAMPLE 12.2

Suppose the Supertech Company and the Hyperdrive Company have experienced the following returns in the last four years:

Year	Supertech Return	Hyperdrive Return
2014	−.20	.05
2015	.50	.09
2016	.30	−.12
2017	.10	.20

What are the average returns? The variances? The standard deviations? Which investment was more volatile?

To calculate the average returns, we add the returns and divide by 4. The results are:

Supertech average return = $\bar{R}$ = .70/4 = .175
Hyperdrive average return = $\bar{R}$ = .22/4 = .055

To calculate the variance for Supertech, we can summarize the relevant calculations as follows:

Year	(1) Actual Return	(2) Average Return	(3) Deviation (1) − (2)	(4) Squared Deviation
2014	−.20	.175	−.375	.140625
2015	.50	.175	.325	.105625
2016	.30	.175	.125	.015625
2017	.10	.175	−.075	.005625
Totals	.70		.000	.267500

Because there are four years of returns, we calculate the variance by dividing .2675 by (4 − 1) = 3:

	Supertech	Hyperdrive
Variance (σ^2)	.2675/3 = .0892	.0529/3 = .0176
Standard deviation (σ)	$\sqrt{.0892}$ = .2986	$\sqrt{.0176}$ = .1328

For practice, verify that you get the same answer as we do for Hyperdrive. Notice that the standard deviation for Supertech, 29.86 percent, is a little more than twice Hyperdrive's 13.28 percent; Supertech is the more volatile investment.

THE HISTORICAL RECORD

Figure 12.10 summarizes much of our discussion of capital market history so far. It displays average returns, standard deviations, and frequency distributions of annual returns on a common scale. In Figure 12.10, for example, notice that the standard deviation for the small-stock portfolio (31.9 percent per year) is more than 10 times larger than the T-bill portfolio's standard deviation (3.1 percent per year). We will return to these figures momentarily.

WORK THE WEB

Standard deviations are widely reported for mutual funds. For example, the Fidelity Magellan Fund was one of the better-known mutual funds in the United States at the time this was written. How volatile is it? To find out, we went to www.morningstar.com, entered the ticker symbol FMAGX, and clicked the "Ratings & Risk" link. Here is what we found:

MPT Statistics FMAGX

3-Year	5-Year	10-Year	15-Year

3-Year Trailing	Index	R-Squared	Beta	Alpha	Treynor Ratio	Currency
vs. Best-Fit Index						
FMAGX	Russell 3000 Growth TR USD	95.66	0.99	-0.42	—	USD
vs. Standard Index						
FMAGX	S&P 500 TR USD	92.53	1.04	-1.36	7.26	USD
Category: LG	S&P 500 TR USD	83.21	1.02	-3.04	5.47	USD

12/31/2016

Volatility Measures FMAGX

3-Year	5-Year	10-Year	15-Year

3-Year Trailing	Standard Deviation	Return	Sharpe Ratio	Sortino Ratio	Bear Market Percentile Rank
FMAGX	11.63	7.70	0.68	1.21	—
S&P 500 TR USD	10.74	8.87	0.83	1.51	—
Category: LG	12.12	5.70	0.51	0.89	—

12/31/2016

The standard deviation for the Fidelity Magellan Fund is 11.63 percent. When you consider that the average stock has a standard deviation of about 50 percent, this seems like a low number. The reason for the low standard deviation has to do with the power of diversification, a topic we discuss in the next chapter. The return column is the average return, so over the last three years, investors in the Magellan Fund gained 7.70 percent per year. Also, under the Volatility Measures section, you will see the Sharpe ratio. The Sharpe ratio is calculated as the risk premium of the asset divided by the standard deviation. As such, it is a measure of return relative to the level of risk taken (as measured by standard deviation). The "beta" for the Fidelity Magellan Fund is .99. We will have more to say about this number—lots more—in the next chapter.

Questions

1. Go to the Morningstar website at www.morningstar.com. What does the Sortino ratio measure? What does the Bear Market Percentile Rank measure?
2. Get a quote for the Fidelity Magellan Fund at Morningstar. What are the five sectors that have the highest percentage investment for this fund? What are the five stocks with the highest percentage investment?

FIGURE 12.10 **Historical Returns, Standard Deviations, and Frequency Distributions: 1926–2016**

Series	Average Return	Standard Deviation	Frequency Distribution
Large-company stocks	12.0%	19.9%	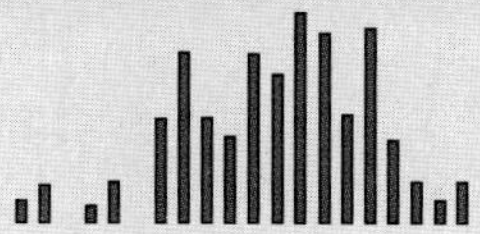
Small-company stocks	16.6	31.9	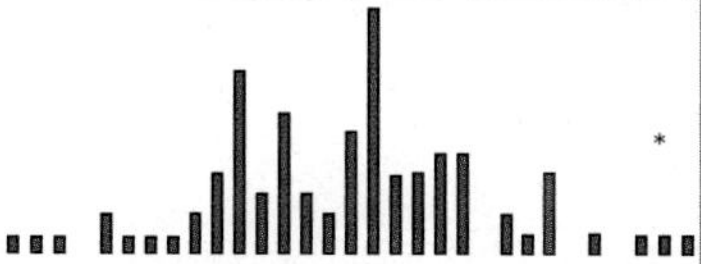 *
Long-term corporate bonds	6.3	8.4	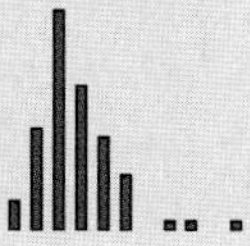
Long-term government bonds	6.0	9.9	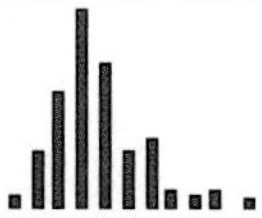
Intermediate-term government bonds	5.3	5.6	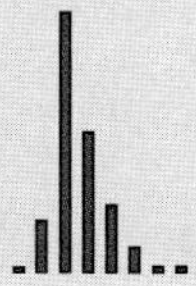
U.S. Treasury bills	3.4	3.1	
Inflation	3.0	4.1	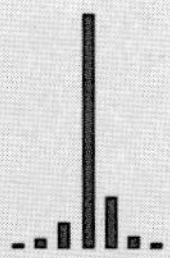

*The 1933 small-company stocks total return was 142.9 percent.
SOURCE: Morningstar, 2017, author calculations.

NORMAL DISTRIBUTION

For many different random events in nature, a particular frequency distribution, the **normal distribution** (or *bell curve*), is useful for describing the probability of ending up in a given range. For example, the idea behind "grading on a curve" comes from the fact that exam score distributions often resemble a bell curve.

normal distribution
A symmetric, bell-shaped frequency distribution that is completely defined by its mean and standard deviation.

Figure 12.11 illustrates a normal distribution and its distinctive bell shape. As you can see, this distribution has a much cleaner appearance than the actual return distributions illustrated in Figure 12.10. Even so, like the normal distribution, the actual distributions do appear to be at least roughly mound-shaped and symmetric. When this is true, the normal distribution is often a very good approximation.

Also, keep in mind that the distributions in Figure 12.10 are based on only 91 yearly observations, whereas Figure 12.11 is, in principle, based on an infinite number. So,

FIGURE 12.11

The Normal Distribution

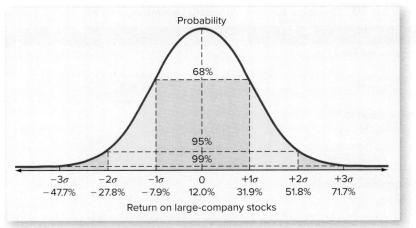

NOTE: Illustrated returns are based on the historical return and standard deviation for a portfolio of large-company common stocks.

if we had been able to observe returns for, say, 1,000 years, we might have filled in a lot of the irregularities and ended up with a much smoother picture in Figure 12.10. For our purposes, it is enough to observe that the returns are at least roughly normally distributed.

The usefulness of the normal distribution stems from the fact that it is completely described by the average and the standard deviation. If you have these two numbers, then there is nothing else to know. For example, with a normal distribution, the probability that we will end up within one standard deviation of the average is about 2/3. The probability that we will end up within two standard deviations is about 95 percent. Finally, the probability of being more than three standard deviations away from the average is less than 1 percent. These ranges and the probabilities are illustrated in Figure 12.11.

To see why this is useful, recall from Figure 12.10 that the standard deviation of returns on the large-company stocks is 19.9 percent. The average return is 12.0 percent. So, assuming that the frequency distribution is at least approximately normal, the probability that the return in a given year is in the range of −7.9 to 31.9 percent (12.0 percent plus or minus one standard deviation, 19.9 percent) is about 2/3. This range is illustrated in Figure 12.11. In other words, there is about one chance in three that the return will be *outside* this range. This literally tells you that, if you buy stocks in large companies, you should expect to be outside this range in one year out of every three. This reinforces our earlier observations about stock market volatility. However, there is only a 5 percent chance (approximately) that we would end up outside the range of −27.8 to 51.8 percent (12.0% plus or minus 2 × 19.9%). These points are also illustrated in Figure 12.11.

THE SECOND LESSON

Our observations concerning the year-to-year variability in returns are the basis for our second lesson from capital market history. On average, bearing risk is handsomely rewarded; but in a given year, there is a significant chance of a dramatic change in value. Our second lesson is this: The greater the potential reward, the greater is the risk.

2008: A YEAR TO REMEMBER

To reinforce our point concerning stock market volatility, consider that just a few short years ago, 2008 entered the record books as one of the worst years for stock market investors in

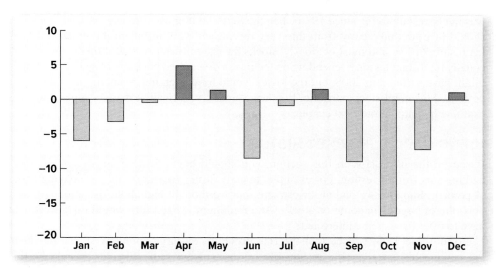

FIGURE 12.12

**S&P 500 Monthly
Returns: 2008**

U.S. history. How bad was it? As shown in several exhibits in the chapter (e.g., Table 12.1), the widely followed S&P 500 index plunged 37 percent. Of the 500 stocks in the index, 485 were down for the year.

Over the period 1926–2016, only the year 1931 had a lower return than 2008 (−44 percent versus −37 percent). Making matters worse, the downdraft continued with a further decline of 8.43 percent in January 2009. In all, from November 2007 (when the decline began) through March 2009 (when it ended), the S&P 500 lost 50 percent of its value.

Figure 12.12 shows the month-by-month performance of the S&P 500 during 2008. As indicated, returns were negative in 8 of the 12 months. Most of the damage occurred in the fall, with investors losing almost 17 percent in October alone. Small stocks fared no better. They also fell 37 percent for the year (with a 21 percent drop in October), their worst performance since losing 58 percent in 1937.

As Figure 12.12 suggests, stock prices were highly volatile during the year. Oddly, the S&P had 126 up days and 126 down days (remember the markets are closed weekends and holidays). Of course, the down days were much worse on average. To see how extraordinary volatility was in 2008, consider that there were 18 days during which the value of the S&P changed by more than 5 percent. There were only 17 such moves between 1956 and 2007!

The drop in stock prices was a global phenomenon, and many of the world's major markets were off by much more than the S&P. China, India, and Russia, for example, all experienced declines of more than 50 percent. Tiny Iceland saw share prices drop by more than 90 percent for the year. Trading on the Icelandic exchange was temporarily suspended on October 9. In what has to be a modern record for a single day, stocks fell by 76 percent when trading resumed on October 14.

Were there any bright spots in 2008 for U.S. investors? The answer is yes because, as stocks tanked, bonds soared, particularly U.S. Treasury bonds. In fact, long-term Treasuries gained 40 percent, while shorter-term Treasury bonds were up 13 percent. Long-term corporate bonds did less well, but still managed to finish in positive territory, up 9 percent. These returns were especially impressive considering that the rate of inflation, as measured by the CPI, was essentially zero.

Of course, stock prices can be volatile in both directions. From March 2009 through February 2011, a period of about 700 days, the S&P 500 doubled in value. This climb was the fastest doubling since 1936 when the S&P did it in just 500 days. So, what lessons should investors take away from this very recent, and very turbulent, bit of capital market history? First, and most obviously, stocks have significant risk! But there is a second, equally important lesson. Depending on the mix, a diversified portfolio of stocks and bonds might have suffered in 2008, but the losses would have been much smaller than those experienced by an all-stock portfolio. In other words, diversification matters, a point we will examine in detail in our next chapter.

USING CAPITAL MARKET HISTORY

Based on the discussion in this section, you should begin to have an idea of the risks and rewards from investing. For example, in early 2017, Treasury bills were paying about .4 percent. Suppose we had an investment that we thought had about the same risk as a portfolio of large-firm common stocks. At a minimum, what return would this investment have to offer for us to be interested?

From Table 12.3, we see that the risk premium on large-company stocks has been 8.6 percent historically, so a reasonable estimate of our required return would be this premium plus the T-bill rate, $.4\% + 8.6 = 9\%$. This may strike you as being high; but if we were thinking of starting a new business, then the risks of doing so might resemble those of investing in small-company stocks. In this case, the historical risk premium is 13.2 percent, so, at a minimum, we might require as much as 13.6 percent from such an investment.

We will discuss the relationship between risk and required return in more detail in the next chapter. For now, you should notice that a projected internal rate of return, or IRR, on a risky investment in the 10 to 20 percent range isn't particularly outstanding. It depends on the level of risk. This, too, is an important lesson from capital market history.

EXAMPLE 12.3   Investing in Growth Stocks

The term *growth stock* is frequently used as a euphemism for small-company stock. Are such investments suitable for "widows and orphans"? Before answering, you should consider the historical volatility. For example, from the historical record, what is the approximate probability that you will actually lose more than 15 percent of your money in a single year if you buy a portfolio of stocks of such companies?

Looking back at Figure 12.10, we see that the average return on small-company stocks is 16.6 percent and the standard deviation is 31.9 percent. Assuming the returns are approximately normal, there is about a 1/3 probability that you will experience a return outside the range of −15.3 to 48.5 percent (16.6% ± 31.9%).

Because the normal distribution is symmetric, the odds of being above or below this range are equal. There is a 1/6 chance (half of 1/3) that you will lose more than −15.3 percent. You should expect this to happen once in every six years, on average. Such investments can be *very* volatile, and they are not well suited for those who cannot afford the risk.

MORE ON THE STOCK MARKET RISK PREMIUM

As we have discussed, the historical stock market risk premium has been substantial. In fact, based on standard economic models, it has been argued that the historical risk premium is *too* big and is an overestimate of what is likely to happen in the future.

Of course, any time we use the past to predict the future, there is the danger that the past period we observe isn't representative of what the future will hold. For example, in

FIGURE 12.13   **Stock Market Risk Premiums for 17 Countries: 1900–2005**

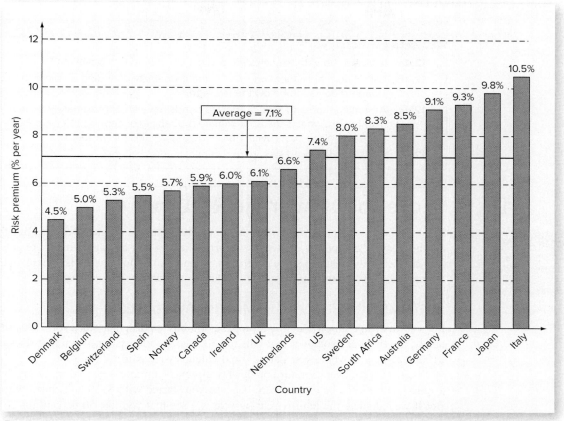

SOURCE: Based on Dimson, Elroy et al., "The Worldwide Equity Premium: A Smaller Puzzle," in *Handbook of the Equity Risk Premium*, Rajnish Mehra, ed., Amsterdam: Elsevier, 2007.

this chapter, we studied the period 1926–2016. Perhaps investors got lucky over this period and earned particularly high returns. Data from earlier years is available, though it is not of the same quality. With that caveat in mind, researchers have traced returns back to 1802, and the risk premiums seen in the pre-1926 era are perhaps a little smaller, but not dramatically so.

Another possibility is that the U.S. stock market experience was unusually good. Investors in at least some other major countries did not do as well because their financial markets were nearly or completely wiped out because of revolution, war, and/or hyperinflation. A recent study addresses this issue by examining data from 1900–2005 for 17 countries.

Figure 12.13 shows the historical average stock market risk premium for all 17 countries over the 106-year period. Looking at the numbers, the U.S. risk premium is the 8th highest at 7.4 percent (which differs from our earlier estimate because of the differing time periods examined). The overall average risk premium is 7.1 percent. These numbers make it clear that U.S. investors did well, but not exceptionally so relative to investors in many other countries.

So, is the U.S. stock market risk premium estimated from 1926–2016 too high? The evidence seems to suggest that the answer is "maybe a little." One thing we haven't stressed so far is that even with 106 years of data, the average risk premium is still not measured with great precision. From a statistical standpoint, the standard error associated with the U.S.

estimated risk premium of 7.4 percent is about 2 percent.[4] Even a one standard error range covers 5.4 to 9.4 percent.

Concept Questions

12.4a In words, how do we calculate a variance? A standard deviation?

12.4b With a normal distribution, what is the probability of ending up more than one standard deviation below the average?

12.4c Assuming that long-term corporate bonds have an approximately normal distribution, what is the approximate probability of earning 14.7 percent or more in a given year? With T-bills, roughly what is this probability?

12.4d What is the second lesson from capital market history?

12.5 More about Average Returns

Excel Master It!

xlsx Excel Master coverage online

Thus far in this chapter, we have looked closely at simple average returns. But there is another way of computing an average return. The fact that average returns are calculated two different ways leads to some confusion, so our goal in this section is to explain the two approaches and also the circumstances under which each is appropriate.

ARITHMETIC VERSUS GEOMETRIC AVERAGES

Let's start with a simple example. Suppose you buy a particular stock for $100. Unfortunately, the first year you own it, it falls to $50. The second year you own it, it rises back to $100, leaving you where you started (no dividends were paid).

What was your average return on this investment? Common sense seems to say that your average return must be exactly zero because you started with $100 and ended with $100. But if we calculate the returns year-by-year, we see that you lost 50 percent the first year (you lost half of your money). The second year, you made 100 percent (you doubled your money). Your average return over the two years was $(-50\% + 100)/2 = 25\%$!

geometric average return

The average compound return earned per year over a multiyear period.

Which is correct, 0 percent or 25 percent? Both are correct: They just answer different questions. The 0 percent is called the **geometric average return**. The 25 percent is called the **arithmetic average return**. The geometric average return answers the question, "What was your average compound return per year over a particular period?" The arithmetic average return answers the question, "What was your return in an average year over a particular period?"

arithmetic average return

The return earned in an average year over a multiyear period.

Notice that, in previous sections, the average returns we calculated were all arithmetic averages and we already know how to calculate them. What we need to do now is (1) learn how to calculate geometric averages and (2) learn the circumstances under which one average is more meaningful than the other.

CALCULATING GEOMETRIC AVERAGE RETURNS

First, to illustrate how we calculate a geometric average return, suppose a particular investment had annual returns of 10 percent, 12 percent, 3 percent, and −9 percent over the last four years. The geometric average return over this four-year period is calculated as $(1.10 \times 1.12 \times 1.03 \times .91)^{1/4} - 1 = .0366$, or 3.66%. In contrast, the average arithmetic return we have been calculating is $(.10 + .12 + .03 - .09)/4 = .04$, or 4.0%.

---

[4]Recall from basic "sadistics" that the standard error of a sample mean is the sample standard deviation divided by the square root of the sample size. In our case, the standard deviation over the 1900–2005 period was 19.6 percent, so the standard error is $.196/\sqrt{106} = .019$.

In general, if we have T years of returns, the geometric average return over these T years is calculated using this formula:

$$\text{Geometric average return} = [(1 + R_1) \times (1 + R_2) \times \ldots \times (1 + R_T)]^{1/T} - 1 \qquad \textbf{12.4}$$

This formula tells us that four steps are required:

1. Take each of the T annual returns $R_1, R_2, \ldots, R_T$ and add 1 to each (after converting them to decimals!).
2. Multiply the numbers from Step 1 together.
3. Take the result from Step 2 and raise it to the power of $1/T$.
4. Finally, subtract 1 from the result of Step 3. The result is the geometric average return.

Calculating the Geometric Average Return   EXAMPLE 12.4

Calculate the geometric average return for S&P 500 large-cap stocks for the first five years in Table 12.1, 1926–1930.

First, convert percentages to decimal returns, add 1, and then calculate their product:

S&P 500 Returns	Product
13.75	1.1375
35.70	×1.3570
45.08	×1.4508
−8.80	× .9120
−25.13	× .7487
	1.5291

Notice that the number 1.5291 is what our investment is worth after five years if we started with a $1 investment. The geometric average return is then calculated as follows:

Geometric average return = $1.5291^{1/5} - 1 = .0887$, or 8.87%

The geometric average return is about 8.87 percent in this example. Here is a tip: If you are using a financial calculator, you can enter $1 as the present value, $1.5291 as the future value, and 5 as the number of periods. Then, solve for the unknown rate. You should get the same answer we did.

One thing you may have noticed in our examples thus far is that the geometric average returns seem to be smaller. This will always be true (as long as the returns are not all identical, in which case the two "averages" would be the same). To illustrate, Table 12.4 shows the arithmetic averages and standard deviations from Figure 12.10, along with the geometric average returns.

As shown in Table 12.4, the geometric averages are all smaller (before rounding), but the magnitude of the difference varies quite a bit. The reason is that the difference is greater for more volatile investments. In fact, there is a useful approximation. Assuming all the numbers are expressed in decimals (as opposed to percentages), the geometric average return is approximately equal to the arithmetic average return minus half the variance. For example, looking at the large-company stocks, the arithmetic average is .120 and the standard deviation is .199, implying that the variance is .040. The approximate geometric average is thus .120 − .040/2 = .100, which is the same as the actual value in this case.

EXAMPLE 12.5   More Geometric Averages

Take a look back at Figure 12.4. There, we showed the value of a $1 investment after 91 years. Use the value for the large-company stock investment to check the geometric average in Table 12.4.

In Figure 12.4, the large-company investment grew to $6,029.16 over 91 years. The geometric average return is thus

Geometric average return = $6,029.16^{1/91} - 1 = .1000$, or 10.0%

This 10.0% is the value shown in Table 12.4. For practice, check some of the other numbers in Table 12.4 the same way.

TABLE 12.4

Geometric versus Arithmetic Average Returns: 1926–2016

Series	Average Return		Standard Deviation
	Geometric	Arithmetic	
Large-company stocks	10.0%	12.0%	19.9%
Small-company stocks	12.0	16.6	31.9
Long-term corporate bonds	6.0	6.3	8.4
Long-term government bonds	5.5	6.0	9.9
Intermediate-term government bonds	5.3	5.3	5.6
U.S. Treasury bills	3.4	3.4	3.1
Inflation	2.9	3.0	4.1

SOURCE: Morningstar, 2017, author calculations.

ARITHMETIC AVERAGE RETURN OR GEOMETRIC AVERAGE RETURN?

When we look at historical returns, the difference between the geometric and arithmetic average returns isn't too hard to understand. To put it slightly differently, the geometric average tells you what you actually earned per year on average, compounded annually. The arithmetic average tells you what you earned in a typical year. You should use whichever one answers the question you want answered.

A somewhat trickier question concerns which average return to use when forecasting future wealth levels, and there's a lot of confusion on this point among analysts and financial planners. First, let's get one thing straight: If you *know* the true arithmetic average return, then this is what you should use in your forecast. For example, if you know the arithmetic return is 10 percent, then your best guess of the value of a $1,000 investment in 10 years is the future value of $1,000 at 10 percent for 10 years, or $2,593.74.

The problem we face is that we usually have only *estimates* of the arithmetic and geometric returns, and estimates have errors. In this case, the arithmetic average return is probably too high for longer periods and the geometric average is probably too low for shorter periods. You should regard long-run projected wealth levels calculated using arithmetic averages as optimistic. Short-run projected wealth levels calculated using geometric averages are probably pessimistic.

The good news is that there is a simple way of combining the two averages, which we will call *Blume's formula*.[5] Suppose we have calculated geometric and arithmetic return averages from N years of data, and we wish to use these averages to form a T-year average return forecast, $R(T)$, where T is less than N. Here's how we do it:

$$R(T) = \frac{T-1}{N-1} \times \textbf{\textit{Geometric average}} + \frac{N-T}{N-1} \times \textbf{\textit{Arithmetic average}}$$

12.5

For example, suppose that, from 25 years of annual returns data, we calculate an arithmetic average return of 12 percent and a geometric average return of 9 percent. From these averages, we wish to make 1-year, 5-year, and 10-year average return forecasts. These three average return forecasts are calculated as follows:

$$R(1) = \frac{1-1}{24} \times 9\% + \frac{25-1}{24} \times 12\% = 12\%$$

$$R(5) = \frac{5-1}{24} \times 9\% + \frac{25-5}{24} \times 12\% = 11.5\%$$

$$R(10) = \frac{10-1}{24} \times 9\% + \frac{25-10}{24} \times 12\% = 10.875\%$$

We see that 1-year, 5-year, and 10-year forecasts are 12 percent, 11.5 percent, and 10.875 percent, respectively.

As a practical matter, Blume's formula says that if you are using averages calculated over a long period (such as the 91 years we use) to forecast up to a decade or so into the future, then you should use the arithmetic average. If you are forecasting a few decades into the future (as you might do for retirement planning), then you should split the difference between the arithmetic and geometric average returns. Finally, if for some reason you are doing very long forecasts covering many decades, use the geometric average.

This concludes our discussion of geometric versus arithmetic averages. One last note: In the future, when we say "average return," we mean arithmetic unless we explicitly say otherwise.

---

[5]This elegant result is due to Marshall Blume ("Unbiased Estimates of Long-Run Expected Rates of Return," *Journal of the American Statistical Association,* September 1974, pp. 634–38).

12.5a If you want to forecast what the stock market is going to do over the next year, should you use an arithmetic or geometric average?

12.5b If you want to forecast what the stock market is going to do over the next century, should you use an arithmetic or geometric average?

12.6 Capital Market Efficiency

Capital market history suggests that the market values of stocks and bonds can fluctuate widely from year to year. Why does this occur? At least part of the answer is that prices change because new information arrives, and investors reassess asset values based on that information.

efficient capital market
A market in which security prices reflect available information.

The behavior of market prices has been extensively studied. A question that has received particular attention is whether prices adjust quickly and correctly when new information arrives. A market is said to be "efficient" if this is the case. To be more precise, in an **efficient capital market**, current market prices fully reflect available information. By this we mean that, based on available information, there is no reason to believe that the current price is too low or too high.

The concept of market efficiency is a rich one, and much has been written about it. A full discussion of the subject goes beyond the scope of our study of corporate finance. Because the concept figures so prominently in studies of market history, we briefly describe the key points here.

PRICE BEHAVIOR IN AN EFFICIENT MARKET

To illustrate how prices behave in an efficient market, suppose the F-Stop Camera Corporation (FCC) has, through years of secret research and development, developed a camera with an autofocusing system whose speed will double that of the autofocusing systems now available. FCC's capital budgeting analysis suggests that launching the new camera will be a highly profitable move; in other words, the NPV appears to be positive and substantial. The key assumption thus far is that FCC has not released any information about the new system; the fact of its existence is "inside" information only.

Now consider a share of stock in FCC. In an efficient market, its price reflects what is known about FCC's current operations and profitability, and it reflects the market opinion about FCC's potential for future growth and profits. The value of the new autofocusing system is not reflected because the market is unaware of the system's existence.

If the market agrees with FCC's assessment of the value of the new project, FCC's stock price will rise when the decision to launch is made public. For example, assume the announcement is made in a press release on Wednesday morning. In an efficient market, the price of shares in FCC will adjust quickly to this new information. Investors should not be able to buy the stock on Wednesday afternoon and make a profit on Thursday. This would imply that it took the stock market a full day to realize the implication of the FCC press release. If the market is efficient, the price of shares of FCC stock on Wednesday afternoon will already reflect the information contained in the Wednesday morning press release.

Figure 12.14 presents three possible stock price adjustments for FCC. In Figure 12.14, Day 0 represents the announcement day. As illustrated, before the announcement, FCC's stock sells for $140 per share. The NPV per share of the new system is, say, $40, so the new price will be $180 once the value of the new project is fully reflected.

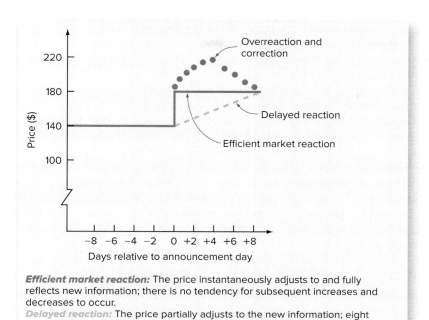

FIGURE 12.14

Reaction of Stock Price to New Information in Efficient and Inefficient Markets

Efficient market reaction: The price instantaneously adjusts to and fully reflects new information; there is no tendency for subsequent increases and decreases to occur.
Delayed reaction: The price partially adjusts to the new information; eight days elapse before the price completely reflects the new information.
Overreaction: The price overadjusts to the new information; it overshoots the new price and subsequently corrects.

The solid line in Figure 12.14 represents the path taken by the stock price in an efficient market. In this case, the price adjusts immediately to the new information and no further changes in the price of the stock take place. The broken line in Figure 12.14 depicts a delayed reaction. Here it takes the market eight days or so to fully absorb the information. Finally, the dotted line illustrates an overreaction and subsequent adjustment to the correct price.

The broken line and the dotted line in Figure 12.14 illustrate paths that the stock price might take in an inefficient market. If, for example, stock prices don't adjust immediately to new information (the broken line), then buying stock immediately following the release of new information and then selling it several days later would be a positive NPV activity because the price is too low for several days after the announcement.

THE EFFICIENT MARKETS HYPOTHESIS

The **efficient markets hypothesis (EMH)** asserts that well-organized capital markets, such as the NYSE, are efficient markets, at least as a practical matter. In other words, an advocate of the EMH might argue that although inefficiencies may exist, they are relatively small and uncommon.

If a market is efficient, then there is a very important implication for market participants: All investments in that market are zero NPV investments. The reason is not complicated. If prices are neither too low nor too high, then the difference between the market value of an investment and its cost is zero; hence, the NPV is zero. As a result, in an efficient market, investors get exactly what they pay for when they buy securities, and firms receive exactly what their stocks and bonds are worth when they sell them.

What makes a market efficient is competition among investors. Many individuals spend their entire lives trying to find mispriced stocks. For any given stock, they study what has

efficient markets hypothesis (EMH)
The hypothesis that actual capital markets, such as the NYSE, are efficient.

Look under the "Contents" link at **www.investorhome.com** for more info on the EMH.

happened in the past to the stock price and the stock's dividends. They learn, to the extent possible, what a company's earnings have been, how much the company owes to creditors, what taxes it pays, what businesses it is in, what new investments are planned, how sensitive it is to changes in the economy, and so on.

Not only is there a great deal to know about any particular company, but there is also a powerful incentive for knowing it—namely, the profit motive. If you know more about some company than other investors in the marketplace, you can profit from that knowledge by investing in the company's stock if you have good news and by selling it if you have bad news.

The logical consequence of all this information gathering and analysis is that mispriced stocks will become fewer and fewer. In other words, because of competition among investors, the market will become increasingly efficient. A kind of equilibrium comes into being with which there is just enough mispricing around for those who are best at identifying it to make a living at it. For most other investors, the activity of information gathering and analysis will not pay.[6]

SOME COMMON MISCONCEPTIONS ABOUT THE EMH

No other idea in finance has attracted as much attention as that of efficient markets, and not all of the attention has been flattering. Rather than rehash the arguments here, we will be content to observe that some markets are more efficient than others. For example, financial markets on the whole are probably much more efficient than real asset markets.

Having said this, we can also say that much of the criticism of the EMH is misguided because it is based on a misunderstanding of what the hypothesis says and what it doesn't say. For example, when the notion of market efficiency was first publicized and debated in the popular financial press, it was often characterized by words to the effect that "throwing darts at the financial page will produce a portfolio that can be expected to do as well as any managed by professional security analysts."[7]

Confusion over statements of this sort has often led to a failure to understand the implications of market efficiency. For example, sometimes it is wrongly argued that market efficiency means that it doesn't matter how you invest your money because the efficiency of the market will protect you from making a mistake. However, a random dart thrower might wind up with all of the darts sticking into one or two high-risk stocks that deal in genetic engineering. Would you really want all of your money in two such stocks?

A contest run by *The Wall Street Journal* provides a good example of the controversy surrounding market efficiency. Each month, the *Journal* asked four professional money managers to pick one stock each. At the same time, it threw four darts at the stock page to select a comparison group. In the 147 five-and one-half month contests from July 1990 to September 2002, the pros won 90 times.

The fact that the pros are ahead of the darts by 90 to 57 suggests that markets are not efficient. Or does it? One problem is that the darts naturally tend to select stocks of average risk. The pros are playing to win and naturally select riskier stocks, or so it is argued. If this is true, then, on average, we *expect* the pros to win. Furthermore, the pros' picks are

---

[6]The idea behind the EMH can be illustrated by the following short story: A student was walking down the hall with her finance professor when they both saw a $20 bill on the ground. As the student bent down to pick it up, the professor shook his head slowly and, with a look of disappointment on his face, said patiently to the student, "Don't bother. If it were really there, someone else would have picked it up already." The moral of the story reflects the logic of the efficient markets hypothesis: If you think you have found a pattern in stock prices or a simple device for picking winners, you probably have not.

[7]Malkiel, B. G., *A Random Walk Down Wall Street,* revised and updated ed. New York: Norton, 2016.

The concept of an efficient market is a special application of the "no free lunch" principle. In an efficient financial market, costless trading policies will not generate "excess" returns. After adjusting for the riskiness of the policy, the trader's return will be no larger than the return of a randomly selected portfolio, at least on average.

This is often thought to imply something about the amount of "information" reflected in asset prices. However, it really doesn't mean that prices reflect all information nor even that they reflect publicly available information. Instead it means that the connection between unreflected information and prices is too subtle and tenuous to be easily or costlessly detected.

Relevant information is difficult and expensive to uncover and evaluate. Thus, if costless trading policies are ineffective, there must exist some traders who make a living by "beating the market." They cover their costs (including the opportunity cost of their time) by trading. The existence of such traders is actually a necessary precondition for markets to become efficient. Without such professional traders, prices would fail to reflect everything that is cheap and easy to evaluate.

Efficient market prices should approximate a random walk, meaning that they will appear to fluctuate more or less randomly. Prices can fluctuate nonrandomly to the extent that their departure from randomness is expensive to discern. Also, observed price series can depart from apparent randomness due to changes in preferences and expectations, but this is really a technicality and does not imply a free lunch relative to current investor sentiments.

Richard Roll is Linde Institute Professor of Finance at the California Institute of Technology. He is a preeminent financial researcher, and he has written extensively in almost every area of modern finance. He is particularly well known for his insightful analyses and great creativity in understanding empirical phenomena.

announced to the public at the start. This publicity may boost the prices of the shares involved somewhat, leading to a partially self-fulfilling prophecy. Unfortunately, the *Journal* discontinued the contest in 2002, so this test of market efficiency is no longer ongoing.

More than anything else, what efficiency implies is that the price a firm will obtain when it sells a share of its stock is a "fair" price in the sense that it reflects the value of that stock given the information available about the firm. Shareholders do not have to worry that they are paying too much for a stock with a low dividend or some other sort of characteristic because the market has already incorporated that characteristic into the price. We sometimes say that the information has been "priced out."

The concept of efficient markets can be explained further by replying to a frequent objection. It is sometimes argued that the market cannot be efficient because stock prices fluctuate from day to day. If the prices are right, the argument goes, then why do they change so much and so often? From our discussion of the market, we can see that these price movements are in no way inconsistent with efficiency. Investors are bombarded with information every day. The fact that prices fluctuate is, at least in part, a reflection of that information flow. In fact, the absence of price movements in a world that changes as rapidly as ours would suggest inefficiency.

THE FORMS OF MARKET EFFICIENCY

It is common to distinguish between three forms of market efficiency. Depending on the degree of efficiency, we say that markets are either *weak form efficient, semistrong form efficient*, or *strong form efficient*. The difference between these forms relates to what information is reflected in prices.

We start with the extreme case. If the market is strong form efficient, then *all* information of *every* kind is reflected in stock prices. In such a market, there is no such thing as inside information. Therefore, in our FCC example, we apparently were assuming that the market was not strong form efficient.

Casual observation, particularly in recent years, suggests that inside information does exist, and it can be valuable to possess. Whether it is lawful or ethical to use that information is another issue. In any event, we conclude that private information about a particular stock may exist and may not be currently reflected in the price of the stock. For example, prior knowledge of a takeover attempt could be very valuable.

The second form of efficiency, semistrong form efficiency, is the most controversial. If a market is semistrong form efficient, then all *public* information is reflected in the stock price. The reason this form is controversial is that it implies that a security analyst who tries to identify mispriced stocks using, for example, financial statement information, is wasting time because that information is already reflected in the current price.

The third form of efficiency, weak form efficiency, suggests that, at a minimum, the current price of a stock reflects the stock's own past prices. In other words, studying past prices in an attempt to identify mispriced securities is futile if the market is weak form efficient. Although this form of efficiency might seem rather mild, it implies that searching for patterns in historical prices that will be useful in identifying mispriced stocks will not work (although this practice is quite common).

What does capital market history say about market efficiency? Here again, there is great controversy. At the risk of going out on a limb, we can say that the evidence seems to tell us three things. First, prices appear to respond rapidly to new information, and the response is at least not grossly different from what we would expect in an efficient market. Second, the future of market prices, particularly in the short run, is difficult to predict based on publicly available information. Third, if mispriced stocks exist, then there is no obvious means of identifying them. Put another way, simpleminded schemes based on public information will probably not be successful.

Concept Questions

12.6a   What is an efficient market?
12.6b   What are the forms of market efficiency?

12.7 Summary and Conclusions

This chapter has explored the subject of capital market history. Such history is useful because it tells us what to expect in the way of returns from risky assets. We summarized our study of market history with two key lessons:

1. Risky assets, on average, earn a risk premium. There is a reward for bearing risk.
2. The greater the potential reward from a risky investment, the greater is the risk.

These lessons have significant implications for the financial manager. We will consider these implications in the chapters ahead.

We also discussed the concept of market efficiency. In an efficient market, prices adjust quickly and correctly to new information. Consequently, asset prices in efficient markets are rarely too high or too low. How efficient capital markets (such as the NYSE) are is a matter of debate; but, at a minimum, they are probably much more efficient than most real asset markets.

CONNECT TO FINANCE

connect If you are using *Connect Finance* in your course, get online to take a Practice Test, check out study tools, and find out where you need additional practice. Log on to connect.mheducation.com to learn more!

Can you answer the following *Connect* Quiz questions?

Section 12.1 Chase Bank pays an annual dividend of $1.05 per share on its common stock. One year ago, this stock sold for $48 per share. Today, the stock is priced to sell at $31 per share. What is the capital gains yield?

Section 12.3 The risk premium is computed as the excess return that a security earns over and above the rate for what?

Section 12.4 How are risk and reward related?

Section 12.5 A stock produced annual rates of return of 11 percent, −17 percent, 2 percent, and 14 percent over the past four years, respectively. What is the geometric average return for this period?

Section 12.6 Corporate insiders cannot benefit financially from the inside information they possess in what type of market?

CHAPTER REVIEW AND SELF-TEST PROBLEMS

12.1 **Recent Return History** Use Table 12.1 to calculate the average return over the years 1996 through 2000 for large-company stocks, long-term government bonds, and Treasury bills.

12.2 **More Recent Return History** Calculate the standard deviation for each security type using information from Problem 12.1. Which of the investments was the most volatile over this period?

ANSWERS TO CHAPTER REVIEW AND SELF-TEST PROBLEMS

12.1 We calculate the averages as follows:

| | Actual Returns | | |
Year	Large-Company Stocks	Long-Term Government Bonds	Treasury Bills
1996	.2296	.0013	.0514
1997	.3336	.1202	.0519
1998	.2858	.1445	.0486
1999	.2104	−.0751	.0480
2000	−.0910	.1722	.0598
Average	.1937	.0726	.0519

12.2 We first need to calculate the deviations from the average returns. Using the averages from Problem 12.1, we get the following values:

	Deviations from Average Returns		
Year	Large-Company Stocks	Long-Term Government Bonds	Treasury Bills
1996	.0359	−.0713	−.0005
1997	.1399	.0476	.0000
1998	.0921	.0719	−.0033
1999	.0167	−.1477	−.0039
2000	−.2847	.0996	.0079
Total	.0000	.0000	.0000

We square these deviations and calculate the variances and standard deviations:

	Squared Deviations from Average Returns		
Year	Large-Company Stocks	Long-Term Government Bonds	Treasury Bills
1996	.0012902	.0050865	.0000003
1997	.0195776	.0022639	.0000000
1998	.0084861	.0051667	.0000112
1999	.0002796	.0218212	.0000155
2000	.0810427	.0099162	.0000618
Variance	.0276691	.0110636	.0000222
Std dev	.1663402	.1051838	.0047104

To calculate the variances, we added the squared deviations and divided by 4, the number of returns less 1. Notice that the stocks had much more volatility than the bonds, with a much larger average return. For large-company stocks, this was a particularly good period: The average return was 19.37 percent.

CONCEPTS REVIEW AND CRITICAL THINKING QUESTIONS

1. **Investment Selection** [LO4] Given that AK Steel was up by about 359 percent for 2016, why didn't all investors hold this stock?

2. **Investment Selection** [LO4] Given that Endo International was down by 73 percent for 2016, why did some investors hold the stock? Why didn't they sell out before the price declined so sharply?

3. **Risk and Return** [LO2, 3] We have seen that over long periods, stock investments have tended to substantially outperform bond investments. However, it is common to observe investors with long horizons holding portfolios composed entirely of bonds. Are such investors irrational?

4. **Market Efficiency Implications** [LO4] Explain why a characteristic of an efficient market is that investments in that market have zero NPVs.

5. **Efficient Markets Hypothesis [LO4]** A stock market analyst is able to identify mispriced stocks by comparing the average price for the last 10 days to the average price for the last 60 days. If this is true, what do you know about the market?

6. **Semistrong Efficiency [LO4]** If a market is semistrong form efficient, is it also weak form efficient? Explain.

7. **Efficient Markets Hypothesis [LO4]** What are the implications of the efficient markets hypothesis for investors who buy and sell stocks in an attempt to "beat the market"?

8. **Stocks versus Gambling [LO4]** Critically evaluate the following statement: Playing the stock market is like gambling. Such speculative investing has no social value other than the pleasure people get from this form of gambling.

9. **Efficient Markets Hypothesis [LO4]** Several celebrated investors and stock pickers frequently mentioned in the financial press have recorded huge returns on their investments over the past two decades. Is the success of these particular investors an invalidation of the EMH? Explain.

10. **Efficient Markets Hypothesis [LO4]** For each of the following scenarios, discuss whether profit opportunities exist from trading in the stock of the firm under the conditions that (1) the market is not weak form efficient, (2) the market is weak form but not semistrong form efficient, (3) the market is semistrong form but not strong form efficient, and (4) the market is strong form efficient.

    a. The stock price has risen steadily each day for the past 30 days.

    b. The financial statements for a company were released three days ago, and you believe you've uncovered some anomalies in the company's inventory and cost control reporting techniques that are causing the firm's true liquidity strength to be understated.

    c. You observe that the senior managers of a company have been buying a lot of the company's stock on the open market over the past week.

QUESTIONS AND PROBLEMS

1. **Calculating Returns [LO1]** Suppose a stock had an initial price of $65 per share, paid a dividend of $1.45 per share during the year, and had an ending share price of $71. Compute the percentage total return.

2. **Calculating Yields [LO1]** In Problem 1, what was the dividend yield? The capital gains yield?

3. **Return Calculations [LO1]** Rework Problems 1 and 2 assuming the ending share price is $58.

4. **Calculating Returns [LO1]** Suppose you bought a bond with an annual coupon of 7 percent one year ago for $1,010. The bond sells for $985 today.

    a. Assuming a $1,000 face value, what was your total dollar return on this investment over the past year?

    b. What was your total nominal rate of return on this investment over the past year?

    c. If the inflation rate last year was 3 percent, what was your total real rate of return on this investment?

5. **Nominal versus Real Returns [LO2]** What was the average annual return on large-company stocks from 1926 through 2016:

    a. In nominal terms?

    b. In real terms?

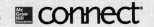

BASIC
(Questions 1–12)

6. **Bond Returns [LO2]** What is the historical real return on long-term government bonds? On long-term corporate bonds?

7. **Calculating Returns and Variability [LO1]** Using the following returns, calculate the arithmetic average returns, the variances, and the standard deviations for X and Y.

	Returns	
Year	X	Y
1	12%	25%
2	28	34
3	9	13
4	−7	−27
5	10	14

8. **Risk Premiums [LO2, 3]** Refer to Table 12.1 in the text and look at the period from 1970 through 1975.

    a. Calculate the arithmetic average returns for large-company stocks and T-bills over this period.

    b. Calculate the standard deviation of the returns for large-company stocks and T-bills over this period.

    c. Calculate the observed risk premium in each year for the large-company stocks versus the T-bills. What was the average risk premium over this period? What was the standard deviation of the risk premium over this period?

    d. Is it possible for the risk premium to be negative before an investment is undertaken? Can the risk premium be negative after the fact? Explain.

9. **Calculating Returns and Variability [LO1]** You've observed the following returns on Crash-n-Burn Computer's stock over the past five years: 8 percent, −15 percent, 19 percent, 31 percent, and 21 percent.

    a. What was the arithmetic average return on the company's stock over this five-year period?

    b. What was the variance of the company's returns over this period? The standard deviation?

10. **Calculating Real Returns and Risk Premiums [LO1]** For Problem 9, suppose the average inflation rate over this period was 3.1 percent and the average T-bill rate over the period was 3.9 percent.

    a. What was the average real return on the company's stock?

    b. What was the average nominal risk premium on the company's stock?

11. **Calculating Real Rates [LO1]** Given the information in Problem 10, what was the average real risk-free rate over this time period? What was the average real risk premium?

12. **Effects of Inflation [LO2]** Look at Table 12.1 and Figure 12.7 in the text. When were T-bill rates at their highest over the period from 1926 through 2016? Why do you think they were so high during this period? What relationship underlies your answer?

13. **Calculating Investment Returns [LO1]** You bought one of Great White Shark Repellant Co.'s 5.8 percent coupon bonds one year ago for $1,030. These bonds make annual payments and mature 14 years from now. Suppose you decide to sell your bonds today, when the required return on the bonds is 5.1 percent. If the inflation rate was 3.9 percent over the past year, what was your total real return on investment?

14. **Calculating Returns and Variability** [LO1] You find a certain stock that had returns of 9 percent, −16 percent, 18 percent, and 14 percent for four of the last five years. If the average return of the stock over this period was 10.3 percent, what was the stock's return for the missing year? What is the standard deviation of the stock's return?

15. **Arithmetic and Geometric Returns** [LO1] A stock has had returns of 8 percent, 26 percent, 14 percent, −17 percent, 31 percent, and −1 percent over the last six years. What are the arithmetic and geometric average returns for the stock?

16. **Arithmetic and Geometric Returns** [LO1] A stock has had the following year-end prices and dividends:

Year	Price	Dividend
1	$63.40	—
2	70.20	$.85
3	79.18	.95
4	75.32	1.03
5	84.18	1.11
6	98.62	1.20

What are the arithmetic and geometric average returns for the stock?

17. **Using Return Distributions** [LO3] Suppose the returns on long-term corporate bonds are normally distributed. Based on the historical record, what is the approximate probability that your return on these bonds will be less than −2.1 percent in a given year? What range of returns would you expect to see 95 percent of the time? What range would you expect to see 99 percent of the time?

18. **Using Return Distributions** [LO3] Assuming that the returns from holding small-company stocks are normally distributed, what is the approximate probability that your money will double in value in a single year? What about triple in value?

19. **Distributions** [LO3] In Problem 18, what is the probability that the return is less than −100 percent (think)? What are the implications for the distribution of returns?

20. **Blume's Formula** [LO1] Over a 40-year period, an asset had an arithmetic return of 11.2 percent and a geometric return of 9.4 percent. Using Blume's formula, what is your best estimate of the future annual returns over 5 years? 10 years? 20 years?

21. **Blume's Formula** [LO1, 2] Assume that the historical return on large-company stocks is a predictor of the future returns. What return would you estimate for large-company stocks over the next year? The next 10 years? 20 years? 40 years?

22. **Calculating Returns** [LO2, 3] Refer to Table 12.1 in the text and look at the period from 1973 through 1980:

    a. Calculate the average return for Treasury bills and the average annual inflation rate (consumer price index) for this period.

    b. Calculate the standard deviation of Treasury bill returns and inflation over this period.

    c. Calculate the real return for each year. What is the average real return for Treasury bills?

    d. Many people consider Treasury bills risk-free. What do these calculations tell you about the potential risks of Treasury bills?

CHALLENGE
(Questions 23–24)

23. **Using Probability Distributions** [LO3] Suppose the returns on large-company stocks are normally distributed. Based on the historical record, use the NORMDIST function in Excel® to determine the probability that in any given year you will lose money by investing in common stock.

24. **Using Probability Distributions** [LO3] Suppose the returns on long-term corporate bonds and T-bills are normally distributed. Based on the historical record, use the NORMDIST function in Excel® to answer the following questions:

   a. What is the probability that in any given year, the return on long-term corporate bonds will be greater than 10 percent? Less than 0 percent?

   b. What is the probability that in any given year, the return on T-bills will be greater than 10 percent? Less than 0 percent?

   c. In 1979, the return on long-term government bonds was −2.76 percent. How likely is it that such a low return will recur at some point in the future? T-bills had a return of 10.56 percent in this same year. How likely is it that such a high return on T-bills will recur at some point in the future?

EXCEL MASTER IT! PROBLEM

As we have seen, over the 1926–2016 period, small company stocks had the highest return and the highest risk, while U.S. Treasury bills had the lowest return and the lowest risk. While we certainly hope you have a 91-year holding period, likely your investment will be for fewer years. One way risk and return is examined over a shorter investment period is by using rolling returns and standard deviations. Suppose you have a series of annual returns and you want to calculate a three-year rolling average return. You would calculate the first rolling average at Year 3 using the returns for the first three years. The next rolling average would be calculated using the returns from Years 2, 3, and 4.

   a. Using the annual returns for large company stocks and Treasury bills, and inflation, calculate both the 5- and 10-year rolling average return and standard deviation.

   b. Over how many 5-year periods did Treasury bills outperform large company stocks? How many 10-year periods?

   c. Over how many 5-year periods did Treasury bills have a larger standard deviation than large company stocks? Over how many 10-year periods?

   d. Graph the rolling 5-year and 10-year average returns for large company stocks and Treasury bills.

   e. What conclusions do you draw from the above results?

MINICASE

A Job at S&S Air

You recently graduated from college, and your job search led you to S&S Air. Because you felt the company's business was taking off, you accepted a job offer. The first day on the job, while you are finishing your employment paperwork, Chris Guthrie, who works in Finance, stops by to inform you about the company's 401(k) plan.

A 401(k) plan is a retirement plan offered by many companies. Such plans are tax-deferred savings vehicles, meaning that any deposits you make into the plan are deducted from your current pretax income, so no current taxes are paid on the money. For example, assume your salary will be $50,000 per year. If you contribute $3,000 to the 401(k) plan, you will pay taxes on only $47,000 in income. There are also no taxes paid on any capital gains or income while you are invested in the plan, but you do pay taxes when you withdraw money at retirement. As is fairly common, the company also has a 5 percent match. This means that the company will match your contribution up to 5 percent of your salary, but you must contribute to get the match.

The 401(k) plan has several options for investments, most of which are mutual funds. A mutual fund is a portfolio of assets. When you purchase shares in a mutual fund, you are actually purchasing partial ownership of the fund's assets. The return of the fund is the weighted average of the return of the assets owned by the fund, minus any expenses. The largest expense is typically the management fee, paid to the fund manager. The management fee is compensation for the manager, who makes all of the investment decisions for the fund.

S&S Air uses Bledsoe Financial Services as its 401(k) plan administrator. Here are the investment options offered for employees:

Company Stock One option in the 401(k) plan is stock in S&S Air. The company is currently privately held. However, when you interviewed with the owners, Mark Sexton and Todd Story, they informed you the company stock was expected to go public in the next three to four years. Until then, a company stock price is simply set each year by the board of directors.

Bledsoe S&P 500 Index Fund This mutual fund tracks the S&P 500. Stocks in the fund are weighted exactly the same as the S&P 500. This means the fund return is approximately the return on the S&P 500, minus expenses. Because an index fund purchases assets based on the composition of the index it is following, the fund manager is not required to research stocks and make investment decisions. The result is that the fund expenses are usually low. The Bledsoe S&P 500 Index Fund charges expenses of .15 percent of assets per year.

Bledsoe Small-Cap Fund This fund primarily invests in small-capitalization stocks. As such, the returns of the fund are more volatile. The fund can also invest 10 percent of its assets in companies based outside the United States. This fund charges 1.70 percent in expenses.

Bledsoe Large-Company Stock Fund This fund invests primarily in large-capitalization stocks of companies based in the United States. The fund is managed by Evan Bledsoe and has outperformed the market in six of the last eight years. The fund charges 1.50 percent in expenses.

Bledsoe Bond Fund This fund invests in long-term corporate bonds issued by U.S.-domiciled companies. The fund is restricted to investments in bonds with an investment-grade credit rating. This fund charges 1.40 percent in expenses.

Bledsoe Money Market Fund This fund invests in short-term, high credit-quality debt instruments, which include Treasury bills. As such, the return on the money market fund is only slightly higher than the return on Treasury bills. Because of the credit quality and short-term nature of the investments, there is only a very slight risk of a negative return. The fund charges .60 percent in expenses.

QUESTIONS

1. What advantages do the mutual funds offer compared to the company stock?

2. Assume that you invest 5 percent of your salary and receive the full 5 percent match from S&S Air. What EAR do you earn from the match? What conclusions do you draw about matching plans?

3. Assume you decide you should invest at least part of your money in large-capitalization stocks of companies based in the United States. What are the advantages and disadvantages of choosing the Bledsoe Large-Company Stock Fund compared to the Bledsoe S&P 500 Index Fund?

4. The returns on the Bledsoe Small-Cap Fund are the most volatile of all the mutual funds offered in the 401(k) plan. Why would you ever want to invest in this fund? When you examine the expenses of the mutual funds, you will notice that this fund also has the highest expenses. Does this affect your decision to invest in this fund?

5. A measure of risk-adjusted performance that is often used is the Sharpe ratio. The Sharpe ratio is calculated as the risk premium of an asset divided by its standard deviation. The standard deviation and return of the funds over the past 10 years are listed in the following table. Calculate the Sharpe ratio for each of these funds. Assume that the expected return and standard deviation of the company stock will be 17 percent and 70 percent, respectively. Calculate the Sharpe ratio for the company stock. How appropriate is the Sharpe ratio for these assets? When would you use the Sharpe ratio?

	10-Year Annual Return	Standard Deviation
Bledsoe S&P 500 Index Fund	6.88%	10.75%
Bledsoe Small-Cap Fund	9.29	12.81
Bledsoe Large-Company Stock Fund	3.56	10.99
Bledsoe Bond Fund	5.27	7.12

6. What portfolio allocation would you choose? Why? Explain your thinking carefully.

13 | Return, Risk, and the Security Market Line

IN JANUARY 2017, Constellation Brands, Volkswagen, and Chipotle all made major announcements. Constellation Brands, best-known as the importer of Modelo and Corona beers, announced that its sales were up 10 percent from the previous year and that profits had exceeded analysts' estimates. German auto maker Volkswagen announced that it had agreed in principle to pay a $4.3 billion fine to settle a U.S. Justice Department probe into the company's diesel engine emissions scandal. For Chipotle, the company announced that its fourth quarter profit would be 50 to 58 cents per share, well below analysts' estimates of 96 cents. You might expect that these three cases represent good news for Constellation Brands and bad news for Volkswagen and Chipotle, and usually you would be right. But here, Constellation Brands's stock price dropped about 7 percent, Volkswagen's stock jumped by about 3.4 percent, and Chipotle's stock price rose about 5 percent.

So we see that stock price reactions do not always match what we might expect based on news. So when is good news really good news? The answer is fundamental to understanding risk and return, and—the good news is—this chapter explores it in some detail.

Learning Objectives

After studying this chapter, you should be able to:

LO1 Show how to calculate expected returns, variance, and standard deviation.

LO2 Discuss the impact of diversification.

LO3 Summarize the systematic risk principle.

LO4 Describe the security market line and the risk–return trade-off.

For updates on the latest happenings in finance, visit fundamentalsofcorporatefinance.blogspot.com.

In our last chapter, we learned some important lessons from capital market history. Most important, we learned that there is a reward, on average, for bearing risk. We called this reward a *risk premium*. The second lesson is that this risk premium is larger for riskier investments. This chapter explores the economic and managerial implications of this basic idea.

Thus far, we have concentrated mainly on the return behavior of a few large portfolios. We need to expand our consideration to include individual assets. Specifically, we have two tasks to accomplish. First, we have to define risk and discuss how to measure it. We then must quantify the relationship between an asset's risk and its required return.

When we examine the risks associated with individual assets, we find there are two types of risk: Systematic and unsystematic. This distinction is crucial because, as we will see, systematic risk affects almost all assets in the economy, at least to some degree, whereas unsystematic risk affects at most a small number of assets. We then develop the principle of diversification, which shows that highly diversified portfolios will tend to have almost no unsystematic risk.

The principle of diversification has an important implication: To a diversified investor, only systematic risk matters. It follows that in deciding whether to buy a particular individual asset, a diversified investor will be concerned only with that asset's systematic risk. This is a key observation, and it allows us to say a great deal about the risks and returns on individual assets. In particular, it is the basis for a famous relationship between risk and return called the *security market line*, or the SML. To develop the SML, we introduce the equally famous "beta" coefficient, one of the centerpieces of modern finance. Beta and the SML are key concepts because they supply us with at least part of the answer to the question of how to determine the required return on an investment.

Expected Returns and Variances

13.1

In our previous chapter, we discussed how to calculate average returns and variances using historical data. We now begin to discuss how to analyze returns and variances when the information we have concerns future possible returns and their probabilities.

EXPECTED RETURN

We start with a straightforward case. Consider a single period of time—say a year. We have two stocks, L and U, which have the following characteristics: Stock L is expected to have a return of 25 percent in the coming year. Stock U is expected to have a return of 20 percent for the same period.

In a situation like this, if all investors agreed on the expected returns, why would anyone want to hold Stock U? After all, why invest in one stock when the expectation is that another will do better? Clearly, the answer must depend on the risk of the two investments. The return on Stock L, although it is *expected* to be 25 percent, could actually turn out to be higher or lower.

For example, suppose the economy booms. In this case, we think Stock L will have a 70 percent return. If the economy enters a recession, we think the return will be −20 percent. In this case, we say that there are two *states of the economy*, which means that these are the only two possible situations. This setup is oversimplified, of course, but it allows us to illustrate some key ideas without a lot of computation.

Suppose we think a boom and a recession are equally likely to happen, for a 50–50 chance of each. Table 13.1 illustrates the basic information we have described and some additional information about Stock U. Notice that Stock U earns 30 percent if there is a recession and 10 percent if there is a boom.

Obviously, if you buy one of these stocks, say Stock U, what you earn in any particular year depends on what the economy does during that year. However, suppose the probabilities stay the same through time. If you hold Stock U for a number of years, you'll earn 30 percent about half the time and 10 percent the other half. In this case, we say that your **expected return** on Stock U, $E(R_U)$, is 20 percent:

$$E(R_U) = .50 \times 30\% + .50 \times 10\% = 20\%$$

In other words, you should expect to earn 20 percent from this stock, on average.

expected return
The return on a risky asset expected in the future.

TABLE 13.1

States of the Economy and Stock Returns

State of Economy	Probability of State of Economy	Rate of Return If State Occurs	
		Stock L	Stock U
Recession	.50	−20%	30%
Boom	.50	70	10
	1.00		

TABLE 13.2

Calculation of Expected Return

		Stock L			Stock U	
(1) State of Economy	(2) Probability of State of Economy	(3) Rate of Return If State Occurs	(4) Product (2) × (3)	(5) Rate of Return If State Occurs	(6) Product (2) × (5)
Recession	.50	−.20	−.10	.30	.15
Boom	.50	.70	.35	.10	.05
	1.00		$E(R_L) = .25$, or 25%		$E(R_U) = .20$, or 20%

For Stock L, the probabilities are the same, but the possible returns are different. Here, we lose 20 percent half the time, and we gain 70 percent the other half. The expected return on L, $E(R_L)$, is 25 percent:

$$E(R_L) = .50 \times -20\% + .50 \times 70\% = 25\%$$

Table 13.2 illustrates these calculations.

In our previous chapter, we defined the risk premium as the difference between the return on a risky investment and that on a risk-free investment, and we calculated the historical risk premiums on some different investments. Using our projected returns, we can calculate the *projected*, or *expected*, *risk premium* as the difference between the expected return on a risky investment and the certain return on a risk-free investment.

For example, suppose risk-free investments are currently offering 8 percent. We will say that the risk-free rate, which we label as R_f, is 8 percent. Given this, what is the projected risk premium on Stock U? On Stock L? Because the expected return on Stock U, $E(R_U)$, is 20 percent, the projected risk premium is:

Risk premium = Expected return − Risk-free rate   13.1

$$= E(R_U) - R_f$$
$$= 20\% - 8$$
$$= 12\%$$

Similarly, the risk premium on Stock L is $25\% - 8 = 17\%$.

In general, the expected return on a security or other asset is equal to the sum of the possible returns multiplied by their probabilities. So, if we had 100 possible returns, we would multiply each one by its probability and sum the results. The result would be the expected return. The risk premium would then be the difference between this expected return and the risk-free rate.

EXAMPLE 13.1   **Unequal Probabilities**

Look again at Tables 13.1 and 13.2. Suppose you think a boom will occur only 20 percent of the time instead of 50 percent. What are the expected returns on Stocks U and L in this case? If the risk-free rate is 10 percent, what are the risk premiums?

The first thing to notice is that a recession must occur 80 percent of the time (1 − .20 = .80) because there are only two possibilities. With this in mind, we see that Stock U has a 30 percent return in 80 percent of the years and a 10 percent return in 20 percent of the years. To calculate the expected return, we again just multiply the possibilities by the probabilities and add up the results:

$$E(R_U) = .80 \times 30\% + .20 \times 10\% = 26\%$$

Table 13.3 summarizes the calculations for both stocks. Notice that the expected return on L is −2 percent.

(1) State of Economy	(2) Probability of State of Economy	Stock L		Stock U	
		(3) Rate of Return If State Occurs	(4) Product (2) × (3)	(5) Rate of Return If State Occurs	(6) Product (2) × (5)
Recession	.80	−.20	−.16	.30	.24
Boom	.20	.70	.14	.10	.02
			$E(R_L) = -.02$, or −2%		$E(R_U) = .26 =$, or 26%

TABLE 13.3

Calculation of Expected Return

The risk premium for Stock U is 26% − 10 = 16% in this case. The risk premium for Stock L is: −2% − 10 = −12%. This is a little odd; but, for reasons we discuss later, it is not impossible.

CALCULATING THE VARIANCE

To calculate the variances of the returns on our two stocks, we first determine the squared deviations from the expected return. We then multiply each possible squared deviation by its probability. We add these, and the result is the variance. The standard deviation, as always, is the square root of the variance.

To illustrate, let us return to the Stock U we originally discussed, which has an expected return of $E(R_U) = 20\%$. In a given year, it will actually return either 30 percent or 10 percent. The possible deviations are 30% − 20% = 10% and 10% − 20% = −10%. In this case, the variance is:

$$\text{Variance} = \sigma^2 = .50 \times .10^2 + .50 \times (-.10)^2 = .01$$

The standard deviation is the square root of this:

$$\text{Standard deviation} = \sigma = \sqrt{.01} = .10, \text{ or } 10\%$$

Table 13.4 summarizes these calculations for both stocks. Notice that Stock L has a much larger variance.

When we put the expected return and variability information for our two stocks together, we have the following:

	Stock L	Stock U
Expected return, E(R)	25%	20%
Variance, σ^2	.2025	.0100
Standard deviation, σ	45%	10%

Stock L has a higher expected return, but U has less risk. You could get a 70 percent return on your investment in L, but you could also lose 20 percent. Notice that an investment in U will always pay at least 10 percent.

Which of these two stocks should you buy? We can't really say; it depends on your personal preferences. We can be reasonably sure that some investors would prefer L to U and some would prefer U to L.

You've probably noticed that the way we have calculated expected returns and variances here is somewhat different from the way we did it in the last chapter. The reason is that, in Chapter 12, we were examining actual historical returns, so we estimated the average return and the variance based on some actual events. Here, we have projected *future* returns and their associated probabilities, so this is the information with which we must work.

TABLE 13.4

Calculation of Variance

(1) State of Economy	(2) Probability of State of Economy	(3) Return Deviation from Expected Return	(4) Squared Return Deviation from Expected Return	(5) Product (2) × (4)
Stock L				
Recession	.50	$-.20 - .25 = -.45$	$-.45^2 = .2025$	.10125
Boom	.50	$.70 - .25 = .45$	$.45^2 = .2025$	.10125
				$\sigma_L^2 = .20250$
Stock U				
Recession	.50	$.30 - .20 = .10$	$.10^2 = .01$	.005
Boom	.50	$.10 - .20 = -.10$	$-.10^2 = .01$	.005
				$\sigma_U^2 = .010$

EXAMPLE 13.2   **More Unequal Probabilities**

Going back to Example 13.1, what are the variances on the two stocks once we have unequal probabilities? The standard deviations?

We can summarize the needed calculations as follows:

(1) State of Economy	(2) Probability of State of Economy	(3) Return Deviation from Expected Return	(4) Squared Return Deviation from Expected Return	(5) Product (2) × (4)
Stock L				
Recession	.80	$-.20 - (-.02) = -.18$	.0324	.02592
Boom	.20	$.70 - (-.02) = .72$	.5184	.10368
				$\sigma_L^2 = .12960$
Stock U				
Recession	.80	$.30 - .26 = .04$	.0016	.00128
Boom	.20	$.10 - .26 = -.16$	.0256	.00512
				$\sigma_U^2 = .00640$

Based on these calculations, the standard deviation for L is $\sigma_L = \sqrt{.1296} = .36$, or 36%. The standard deviation for U is much smaller: $\sigma_U = \sqrt{.0064} = .08$, or 8%.

Concept Questions

13.1a   How do we calculate the expected return on a security?

13.1b   In words, how do we calculate the variance of the expected return?

13.2 Portfolios

Excel Master It!

xlsx Excel Master coverage online

Thus far in this chapter, we have concentrated on individual assets considered separately. However, most investors actually hold a **portfolio** of assets. All we mean by this is that investors tend to own more than just a single stock, bond, or other asset. Given this, portfolio return and portfolio risk are of obvious relevance. Accordingly, we now discuss portfolio expected returns and variances.

(1) State of Economy	(2) Probability of State of Economy	(3) Portfolio Return If State Occurs	(4) Product (2) × (3)
Recession	.50	.50 × −20% + .50 × 30% = 5%	.025
Boom	.50	.50 × 70% + .50 × 10% = 40%	.200
			$E(R_p)$ = .225, or 22.5%

TABLE 13.5

Expected Return on an Equally Weighted Portfolio of Stock L and Stock U

PORTFOLIO WEIGHTS

There are many equivalent ways of describing a portfolio. The most convenient approach is to list the percentage of the total portfolio's value that is invested in each portfolio asset. We call these percentages the **portfolio weights**.

For example, if we have $50 in one asset and $150 in another, our total portfolio is worth $200. The percentage of our portfolio in the first asset is $50/$200 = .25. The percentage of our portfolio in the second asset is $150/$200, or .75. Our portfolio weights are .25 and .75. Notice that the weights have to sum to 1.00 because all of our money is invested somewhere.[1]

portfolio
A group of assets such as stocks and bonds held by an investor.

portfolio weight
The percentage of a portfolio's total value that is invested in a particular asset.

PORTFOLIO EXPECTED RETURNS

Let's go back to Stocks L and U. You put half your money in each. The portfolio weights are obviously .50 and .50. What is the pattern of returns on this portfolio? The expected return?

To answer these questions, suppose the economy actually enters a recession. In this case, half your money (the half in L) loses 20 percent. The other half (the half in U) gains 30 percent. Your portfolio return, R_p, in a recession is:

$$R_p = .50 \times -20\% + .50 \times 30\% = 5\%$$

Table 13.5 summarizes the remaining calculations. Notice that when a boom occurs, your portfolio will return 40 percent:

$$R_p = .50 \times 70\% + .50 \times 10\% = 40\%$$

As indicated in Table 13.5, the expected return on your portfolio, $E(R_p)$, is 22.5 percent.

We can save ourselves some work by calculating the expected return more directly. Given these portfolio weights, we could have reasoned that we expect half of our money to earn 25 percent (the half in L) and half of our money to earn 20 percent (the half in U). Our portfolio expected return is thus:

$$E(R_p) = .50 \times E(R_L) + .50 \times E(R_U)$$
$$= .50 \times 25\% + .50 \times 20\%$$
$$= 22.5\%$$

This is the same portfolio expected return we calculated previously.

This method of calculating the expected return on a portfolio works no matter how many assets there are in the portfolio. Suppose we had n assets in our portfolio, where n is any number. If we let x_i stand for the percentage of our money in Asset i, then the expected return would be:

$$E(R_P) = x_1 \times E(R_1) + x_2 \times E(R_2) + \cdots + x_n \times E(R_n)$$

Want more information about investing? Visit **www.thestreet.com**.

---

[1] Some of it could be in cash, of course, but we would then just consider the cash to be one of the portfolio assets.

This says that the expected return on a portfolio is a straightforward combination of the expected returns on the assets in that portfolio. This seems somewhat obvious; but, as we will examine next, the obvious approach is not always the right one.

EXAMPLE 13.3   **Portfolio Expected Return**

Suppose we have the following projections for three stocks:

State of Economy	Probability of State of Economy	Returns If State Occurs		
		Stock A	Stock B	Stock C
Boom	.40	10%	15%	20%
Bust	.60	8	4	0

We want to calculate portfolio expected returns in two cases. First, what would be the expected return on a portfolio with equal amounts invested in each of the three stocks? Second, what would be the expected return if half of the portfolio were in A, with the remainder equally divided between B and C?

Based on what we've learned from our earlier discussions, we can determine that the expected returns on the individual stocks are (check these for practice):

$E(R_A) = 8.8\%$
$E(R_B) = 8.4\%$
$E(R_C) = 8.0\%$

If a portfolio has equal investments in each asset, the portfolio weights are all the same. Such a portfolio is said to be *equally weighted*. Because there are three stocks in this case, the weights are all equal to 1/3. The portfolio expected return is thus:

$E(R_P) = (1/3) \times 8.8\% + (1/3) \times 8.4\% + (1/3) \times 8\% = 8.4\%$

In the second case, verify that the portfolio expected return is 8.5 percent.

PORTFOLIO VARIANCE

From our earlier discussion, the expected return on a portfolio that contains equal investments in Stocks U and L is 22.5 percent. What is the standard deviation of return on this portfolio? Simple intuition might suggest that because half of the money has a standard deviation of 45 percent and the other half has a standard deviation of 10 percent, the portfolio's standard deviation might be calculated as:

$\sigma_P = .50 \times 45\% + .50 \times 10\% = 27.5\%$

Unfortunately, this approach is completely incorrect!

Let's see what the standard deviation really is. Table 13.6 summarizes the relevant calculations. As we see, the portfolio's variance is about .031, and its standard deviation is less than we thought—it's only 17.5 percent. What is illustrated here is that the variance on a portfolio is not generally a simple combination of the variances of the assets in the portfolio.

We can illustrate this point a little more dramatically by considering a slightly different set of portfolio weights. Suppose we put 2/11 (about 18 percent) in L and the other 9/11 (about 82 percent) in U. If a recession occurs, this portfolio will have a return of:

$R_P = (2/11) \times -20\% + (9/11) \times 30\% = 20.91\%$

(1)\nState of\nEconomy	(2)\nProbability\nof State of\nEconomy	(3)\nPortfolio\nReturn If\nState Occurs	(4)\nSquared\nDeviation from\nExpected Return	(5)\nProduct\n(2) × (4)
Recession	.50	5%	$(.05 - .225)^2 = .030625$	.0153125
Boom	.50	40	$(.40 - .225)^2 = .030625$	.0153125
			$\sigma_P^2 = .030625$	
			$\sigma_P = \sqrt{.030625} = .175$, or 17.5%	

TABLE 13.6

Variance on an Equally Weighted Portfolio of Stock L and Stock U

If a boom occurs, this portfolio will have a return of:

$$R_p = (2/11) \times 70\% + (9/11) \times 10\% = 20.91\%$$

Notice that the return is the same no matter what happens. No further calculations are needed: This portfolio has a zero variance. Apparently, combining assets into portfolios can substantially alter the risks faced by the investor. This is a crucial observation, and we will begin to explore its implications in the next section.

Portfolio Variance and Standard Deviation   EXAMPLE 13.4

In Example 13.3, what are the standard deviations on the two portfolios? To answer, we first have to calculate the portfolio returns in the two states. We will work with the second portfolio, which has 50 percent in Stock A and 25 percent in each of Stocks B and C. The relevant calculations can be summarized as follows:

State of\nEconomy	Probability of\nState of Economy	Rate of Return If State Occurs			
		Stock A	Stock B	Stock C	Portfolio
Boom	.40	10%	15%	20%	13.75%
Bust	.60	8	4	0	5.00

The portfolio return when the economy booms is calculated as:

$$E(R_p) = .50 \times 10\% + .25 \times 15\% + .25 \times 20\% = 13.75\%$$

The return when the economy goes bust is calculated the same way. The expected return on the portfolio is 8.5 percent. The variance is thus:

$$\sigma_P^2 = .40 \times (.1375 - .085)^2 + .60 \times (.05 - .085)^2$$

$$= .0018375$$

The standard deviation is about 4.3 percent. For our equally weighted portfolio, check to see that the standard deviation is about 5.4 percent.

Concept Questions

13.2a What is a portfolio weight?

13.2b How do we calculate the expected return on a portfolio?

13.2c Is there a simple relationship between the standard deviation on a portfolio and the standard deviations of the assets in the portfolio?

13.3 Announcements, Surprises, and Expected Returns

Now that we know how to construct portfolios and evaluate their returns, we begin to describe more carefully the risks and returns associated with individual securities. Thus far, we have measured volatility by looking at the difference between the actual return on an asset or portfolio, R, and the expected return, $E(R)$. We now look at why those deviations exist.

EXPECTED AND UNEXPECTED RETURNS

To begin, for concreteness, we consider the return on the stock of a company called Flyers. What will determine this stock's return in, say, the coming year?

The return on any stock traded in a financial market is composed of two parts. First, the normal, or expected, return from the stock is the part of the return that shareholders in the market predict or expect. This return depends on the information shareholders have that bears on the stock, and it is based on the market's understanding today of the important factors that will influence the stock in the coming year.

The second part of the return on the stock is the uncertain, or risky, part. This is the portion that comes from unexpected information revealed within the year. A list of all possible sources of such information would be endless, but here are a few examples:

- News about Flyers research.
- Government figures released on gross domestic product (GDP).
- The results from the latest arms control talks.
- The news that Flyers sales figures are higher than expected.
- A sudden, unexpected drop in interest rates.

Based on this discussion, one way to express the return on Flyers stock in the coming year would be:

Total return = Expected return + Unexpected return

$$R = E(R) + U$$

(13.3)

where R stands for the actual total return in the year, $E(R)$ stands for the expected part of the return, and U stands for the unexpected part of the return. What this says is that the actual return, R, differs from the expected return, $E(R)$, because of surprises that occur during the year. In any given year, the unexpected return will be positive or negative; but, through time, the average value of U will be zero. This means that on average, the actual return equals the expected return.

ANNOUNCEMENTS AND NEWS

We need to be careful when we talk about the effect of news items on the return. For example, suppose Flyers's business is such that the company prospers when GDP grows at a relatively high rate and suffers when GDP is relatively stagnant. In this case, in deciding what return to expect this year from owning stock in Flyers, shareholders either implicitly or explicitly must think about what GDP is likely to be for the year.

When the government actually announces GDP figures for the year, what will happen to the value of Flyers's stock? Obviously, the answer depends on what figure is released. More to the point, however, the impact depends on how much of that figure is *new* information.

At the beginning of the year, market participants will have some idea or forecast of what the yearly GDP will be. To the extent that shareholders have predicted GDP, that prediction will already be factored into the expected part of the return on the stock, $E(R)$. On the other hand, if the announced GDP is a surprise, the effect will be part of U, the unanticipated portion of the return. As an example, suppose shareholders in the market had forecast that the GDP increase this year would be .5 percent. If the actual announcement this year is exactly .5 percent, the same as the forecast, then the shareholders don't really learn anything, and the announcement isn't news. There will be no impact on the stock price as a result. This is like receiving confirmation of something you suspected all along; it doesn't reveal anything new.

A common way of saying that an announcement isn't news is to say that the market has already "discounted" the announcement. The use of the word *discount* here is different from the use of the term in computing present values, but the spirit is the same. When we discount a dollar in the future, we say it is worth less to us because of the time value of money. When we discount an announcement or a news item, we say that it has less of an impact on the price because the market already knew much of it.

Going back to Flyers, suppose the government announces that the actual GDP increase during the year has been 1.5 percent. Now shareholders have learned something—namely, that the increase is one percentage point higher than they had forecast. This difference between the actual result and the forecast, one percentage point in this example, is sometimes called the *innovation* or the *surprise*.

This distinction explains why what seems to be good news can actually be bad news (and vice versa). Going back to the companies we discussed in our chapter opener, even though Constellation Brands beat sales and profit estimates, investors were concerned about slowing beer sales and the potential for tariffs on the company's imports. For Chipotle, earnings were below estimates and same-store sales had declined, but the decline was lower than previous quarters, indicating a possible reversal in falling sales caused by a previous foodborne contamination problem. An additional cause of the decreased earnings—an increase in the price of avocados—was not expected to continue.

In the case of Volkswagen, even though its $4.3 billion settlement seems negative, it actually was a positive for investors. The Justice Department probe had centered on "dieselgate," a reference to excess emissions from diesel engines in Volkswagen vehicles. Volkswagen had programmed certain models to activate controls that worked only during emissions tests, allowing the cars to meet the emissions standards for NO_X. During normal operations, the cars emitted as much as 40 times more NO_X than under testing conditions. Even though the settlement was large, investors had been worried that the probe would drag on much longer and that the fine would be much higher.

To summarize, an announcement can be broken into two parts: the anticipated, or expected, part and the surprise, or innovation:

Announcement = Expected part + Surprise   13.4

The expected part of any announcement is the part of the information that the market uses to form the expectation, $E(R)$, of the return on the stock. The surprise is the news that influences the unanticipated return on the stock, U.

Our discussion of market efficiency in the previous chapter bears on this discussion. We are assuming that relevant information known today is already reflected in the expected return. This is identical to saying that the current price reflects relevant publicly available information. We are implicitly assuming that markets are at least reasonably efficient in the semistrong form.

Henceforth, when we speak of news, we will mean the surprise part of an announcement and not the portion that the market has expected and therefore already discounted.

13.4 Risk: Systematic and Unsystematic

The unanticipated part of the return, that portion resulting from surprises, is the true risk of any investment. After all, if we always receive exactly what we expect, then the investment is perfectly predictable and, by definition, risk-free. In other words, the risk of owning an asset comes from surprises—unanticipated events.

There are important differences, though, among various sources of risk. Returning to our example in the previous section, look back at the list of news stories that could impact the return on Flyers's stock. Some of these stories are directed specifically at Flyers, and some are more general. Which of the news items are of specific importance to Flyers?

Announcements about interest rates or GDP are clearly important for nearly all companies, whereas news about Flyers's president, its research, or its sales is of specific interest to Flyers. We will distinguish between these two types of events because, as we will see, they have different implications.

SYSTEMATIC AND UNSYSTEMATIC RISK

systematic risk
A risk that influences a large number of assets. Also called *market risk*.

unsystematic risk
A risk that affects at most a small number of assets. Also called *unique* or *asset-specific risk*.

The first type of surprise—the one that affects many assets—we will label **systematic risk**. A systematic risk is one that influences a large number of assets, each to a greater or lesser extent. Because systematic risks have marketwide effects, they are sometimes called *market risks*.

The second type of surprise we will call **unsystematic risk**. An unsystematic risk is one that affects a single asset or a small group of assets. Because these risks are unique to individual companies or assets, they are sometimes called *unique* or *asset-specific risks*. We will use these terms interchangeably.

As we have seen, uncertainties about general economic conditions (such as GDP, interest rates, or inflation) are examples of systematic risks. These conditions affect nearly all companies to some degree. An unanticipated increase, or surprise, in inflation, for example, affects wages and the costs of the supplies that companies buy; it affects the value of the assets that companies own; and it affects the prices at which companies sell their products. Forces such as these, to which all companies are susceptible, are the essence of systematic risk.

In contrast, the announcement of an oil strike by a company will primarily affect that company and, perhaps, a few others (such as primary competitors and suppliers). It is unlikely to have much of an effect on the world oil market, or on the affairs of companies not in the oil business, so this is an unsystematic event.

SYSTEMATIC AND UNSYSTEMATIC COMPONENTS OF RETURN

The distinction between a systematic risk and an unsystematic risk is never really as exact as we make it out to be. Even the most narrow and peculiar bit of news about a company ripples through the economy. This is true because every enterprise, no matter how tiny, is a part of the economy. It's like the tale of a kingdom that was lost because one horse lost a shoe. This is mostly hairsplitting. Some risks are clearly much more general than others. We'll see some evidence on this point in just a moment.

The distinction between the types of risk allows us to break down the surprise portion, U, of the return on the Flyers stock into two parts. Earlier, we had the actual return broken down into its expected and surprise components:

$$R = E(R) + U$$

We now recognize that the total surprise component for Flyers, U, has a systematic and an unsystematic component, so:

R = E(R) + Systematic portion + Unsystematic portion

Because it is traditional, we will use the Greek letter epsilon, ϵ, to stand for the unsystematic portion. Because systematic risks are often called market risks, we will use the letter m to stand for the systematic part of the surprise. With these symbols, we can rewrite the formula for the total return:

$$R = E(R) + U$$
$$= E(R) + m + \epsilon$$

The important thing about the way we have broken down the total surprise, U, is that the unsystematic portion, ϵ, is more or less unique to Flyers. For this reason, it is unrelated to the unsystematic portion of the return on most other assets. To see why this is important, we need to return to the subject of portfolio risk.

Concept Questions

13.4a   What are the two basic types of risk?

13.4b   What is the distinction between the two types of risk?

Diversification and Portfolio Risk

13.5

We've seen earlier that portfolio risks can, in principle, be quite different from the risks of the assets that make up the portfolio. We now look more closely at the riskiness of an individual asset versus the risk of a portfolio of many different assets. We will once again examine some market history to get an idea of what happens with actual investments in U.S. capital markets.

Excel Master It!
Excel Master coverage online

THE EFFECT OF DIVERSIFICATION: ANOTHER LESSON FROM MARKET HISTORY

In our previous chapter, we saw that the standard deviation of the annual return on a portfolio of 500 large common stocks has historically been about 20 percent per year. Does this mean that the standard deviation of the annual return on a typical stock in that group of 500 is about 20 percent? As you might suspect by now, the answer is no. This is an extremely important observation.

For more about risk and diversification, visit **www .investopedia.com/university.**

To illustrate the relationship between portfolio size and portfolio risk, Table 13.7 illustrates typical average annual standard deviations for equally weighted portfolios that contain different numbers of randomly selected NYSE securities.

In Column 2 of Table 13.7, we see that the standard deviation for a "portfolio" of one security is about 49 percent. What this means is that if you randomly selected a single NYSE stock and put all your money into it, your standard deviation of return would typically be a substantial 49 percent per year. If you were to randomly select two stocks and invest

TABLE 13.7

Standard Deviations of Annual Portfolio Returns

(1) Number of Stocks in Portfolio	(2) Average Standard Deviation of Annual Portfolio Returns	(3) Ratio of Portfolio Standard Deviation to Standard Deviation of a Single Stock
1	49.24%	1.00
2	37.36	.76
4	29.69	.60
6	26.64	.54
8	24.98	.51
10	23.93	.49
20	21.68	.44
30	20.87	.42
40	20.46	.42
50	20.20	.41
100	19.69	.40
200	19.42	.39
300	19.34	.39
400	19.29	.39
500	19.27	.39
1,000	19.21	.39

SOURCE: These figures are from Table 1 in Statman, M., "How Many Stocks Make a Diversified Portfolio?" *Journal of Financial and Quantitative Analysis* 22, September 1987, 353–63. They were derived from Elton, E. J. and Gruber, M. J., "Risk Reduction and Portfolio Size: An Analytical Solution," *Journal of Business* 50, October 1977, 415–37.

half your money in each, your standard deviation would be about 37 percent on average, and so on.

The important thing to notice in Table 13.7 is that the standard deviation declines as the number of securities is increased. By the time we have 100 randomly chosen stocks, the portfolio's standard deviation has declined by about 60 percent, from 49 percent to about 20 percent. With 500 securities, the standard deviation is 19.27 percent, similar to the 20 percent we saw in our previous chapter for the large common stock portfolio. The small difference exists because the portfolio securities and time periods examined are not identical.

THE PRINCIPLE OF DIVERSIFICATION

Figure 13.1 illustrates the point we've been discussing. What we have plotted is the standard deviation of return versus the number of stocks in the portfolio. Notice in Figure 13.1 that the benefit in terms of risk reduction from adding securities drops off as we add more and more. By the time we have 10 securities, most of the effect is already realized; and by the time we get to 30 or so, there is little remaining benefit.

Figure 13.1 illustrates two key points. First, some of the riskiness associated with individual assets can be eliminated by forming portfolios. The process of spreading an investment across assets (and thereby forming a portfolio) is called *diversification*. The **principle of diversification** tells us that spreading an investment across many assets will eliminate some of the risk. The blue shaded area in Figure 13.1, labeled "diversifiable risk," is the part that can be eliminated by diversification.

The second point is equally important. There is a minimum level of risk that cannot be eliminated by diversifying. This minimum level is labeled "nondiversifiable risk" in

principle of diversification

Spreading an investment across a number of assets will eliminate some, but not all, of the risk.

FIGURE 13.1

Portfolio Diversification

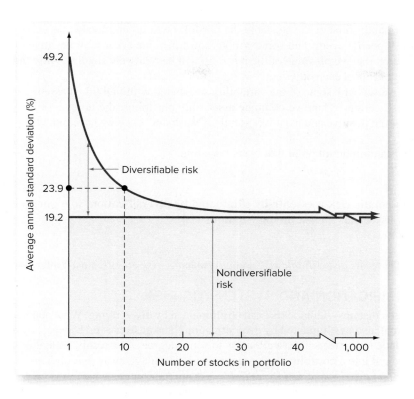

Figure 13.1. Taken together, these two points are another important lesson from capital market history: Diversification reduces risk, but only up to a point. Put another way, some risk is diversifiable and some is not.

To give a recent example of the impact of diversification, the S&P 500, which is a widely followed stock market index of 500 large, well-known U.S. stocks, was up about 12 percent in 2016. As we saw in our previous chapter, this gain represents an average year for a portfolio of large-cap stocks. The biggest individual winners for the year were Nvidia (up a whopping 224 percent), ONEOK (up 147 percent), and Freeport-McMoRan (up 95 percent). But not all 500 stocks were up: The losers included TripAdvisor (down 46 percent), Perrigo (down 42 percent), and Vertex Pharmaceuticals (down 41 percent). Again, the lesson is clear: Diversification reduces exposure to extreme outcomes, both good and bad.

DIVERSIFICATION AND UNSYSTEMATIC RISK

From our discussion of portfolio risk, we know that some of the risk associated with individual assets can be diversified away and some cannot. We are left with an obvious question: Why is this so? It turns out that the answer hinges on the distinction we made earlier between systematic and unsystematic risk.

By definition, an unsystematic risk is one that is particular to a single asset or, at most, a small group. For example, if the asset under consideration is stock in a single company, the discovery of positive NPV projects such as successful new products and innovative cost savings will tend to increase the value of the stock. Unanticipated lawsuits, industrial accidents, strikes, and similar events will tend to decrease future cash flows and thereby reduce share values.

Here is the important observation: If we held only a single stock, the value of our investment would fluctuate because of company-specific events. If we hold a large portfolio, on the other hand, some of the stocks in the portfolio will go up in value because of positive company-specific events and some will go down in value because of negative events. The net effect on the overall value of the portfolio will be relatively small because these effects will tend to cancel each other out.

Now we see why some of the variability associated with individual assets is eliminated by diversification. When we combine assets into portfolios, the unique, or unsystematic, events—both positive and negative—tend to "wash out" once we have more than just a few assets.

This is an important point that bears repeating:

> **Unsystematic risk is essentially eliminated by diversification, so a portfolio with many assets has almost no unsystematic risk.**

In fact, the terms *diversifiable risk* and *unsystematic risk* are often used interchangeably.

DIVERSIFICATION AND SYSTEMATIC RISK

We've seen that unsystematic risk can be eliminated by diversifying. What about systematic risk? Can it also be eliminated by diversification? The answer is no because, by definition, a systematic risk affects almost all assets to some degree. As a result, no matter how many assets we put into a portfolio, the systematic risk doesn't go away. For obvious reasons, the terms *systematic risk* and *nondiversifiable risk* are used interchangeably.

Because we have introduced so many different terms, it is useful to summarize our discussion before moving on. What we have seen is that the total risk of an investment, as measured by the standard deviation of its return, can be written as:

Total risk = Systematic risk + Unsystematic risk   **13.6**

Systematic risk is also called *nondiversifiable risk* or *market risk*. Unsystematic risk is also called *diversifiable risk*, *unique risk*, or *asset-specific risk*. For a well-diversified portfolio, the unsystematic risk is negligible. For such a portfolio, essentially all of the risk is systematic.

Concept Questions

13.5a What happens to the standard deviation of return for a portfolio if we increase the number of securities in the portfolio?

13.5b What is the principle of diversification?

13.5c Why is some risk diversifiable? Why is some risk not diversifiable?

13.5d Why can't systematic risk be diversified away?

13.6 Systematic Risk and Beta

Excel Master It!
Excel Master coverage online

The question that we now begin to address is this: What determines the size of the risk premium on a risky asset? Put another way, why do some assets have a larger risk premium than other assets? The answer to these questions, as we discuss next, is also based on the distinction between systematic and unsystematic risk.

THE SYSTEMATIC RISK PRINCIPLE

Thus far, we've seen that the total risk associated with an asset can be decomposed into two components: Systematic and unsystematic risk. We have also seen that unsystematic risk can be essentially eliminated by diversification. The systematic risk present in an asset, on the other hand, cannot be eliminated by diversification.

Based on our study of capital market history, we know that there is a reward, on average, for bearing risk. We now need to be more precise about what we mean by risk. The **systematic risk principle** states that the reward for bearing risk depends only on the systematic risk of an investment. The underlying rationale for this principle is straightforward: Because unsystematic risk can be eliminated at virtually no cost (by diversifying), there is no reward for bearing it. Put another way, the market does not reward risks that are borne unnecessarily.

systematic risk principle
The expected return on a risky asset depends only on that asset's systematic risk.

The systematic risk principle has a remarkable and very important implication:

> **The expected return on an asset depends only on that asset's systematic risk.**

There is an obvious corollary to this principle: No matter how much total risk an asset has, only the systematic portion is relevant in determining the expected return (and the risk premium) on that asset.

For more about beta, see **www.investools.com** and **money.msn.com.**

MEASURING SYSTEMATIC RISK

Because systematic risk is the crucial determinant of an asset's expected return, we need some way of measuring the level of systematic risk for different investments. The specific measure we will use is called the **beta coefficient**, for which we will use the Greek symbol β. A beta coefficient, or beta for short, tells us how much systematic risk a particular asset has relative to an average asset. By definition, an average asset has a beta of 1.0 relative to itself. An asset with a beta of .50, therefore, has half as much systematic risk as an average asset; an asset with a beta of 2.0 has twice as much.

beta coefficient
The amount of systematic risk present in a particular risky asset relative to that in an average asset.

Table 13.8 contains the estimated beta coefficients for the stocks of some well-known companies. The range of betas in Table 13.8 is typical for stocks of large U.S. corporations. Betas outside this range occur, but they are less common.

The important thing to remember is that the expected return, and thus the risk premium, of an asset depends only on its systematic risk. Because assets with larger betas have greater systematic risks, they will have greater expected returns. From Table 13.8, an investor who buys stock in Coca-Cola, with a beta of .74, should expect to earn less, on average, than an investor who buys stock in Apple, with a beta of about 1.44.

	Beta Coefficient (β)
Johnson & Johnson	.67
Coca-Cola	.74
Twitter	.85
Pfizer	.99
Tesla	1.19
Ford	1.29
Apple	1.44
CBS Corporation	1.71

SOURCE: Yahoo! Finance, 2017.

TABLE 13.8

Beta Coefficients for Selected Companies

One cautionary note is in order: Not all betas are created equal. Different providers use somewhat different methods for estimating betas, and significant differences sometimes occur. As a result, it is a good idea to look at several sources. See our nearby *Work the Web* box for more about beta.

WORK THE WEB

You can find beta estimates at many sites on the web. One of the best is finance.yahoo.com. Here is a snapshot of the "Statistics" screen for Sears Holdings (SHLD), parent of Sears and K-Mart stores:

Stock Price History

Beta	1.44
52-Week Change [3]	-52.89%
S&P500 52-Week Change [3]	20.11%
52 Week High [3]	19.12
52 Week Low [3]	8.00

Management Effectiveness

Return on Assets (ttm)	-8.07%
Return on Equity (ttm)	N/A

Balance Sheet

Total Cash (mrq)	258M
Total Cash Per Share (mrq)	2.41
Total Debt (mrq)	4.46B
Total Debt/Equity (mrq)	N/A
Current Ratio (mrq)	1.04
Book Value Per Share (mrq)	-22.12

The reported beta for Sears is 1.44, which means that Sears has about one and one-half times the systematic risk of a typical stock. You would expect that the company is very risky and, looking at the other numbers, we agree. Sears's ROA is negative 8.07 percent, which indicates the company lost money over the past year, but the ROE is not reported. Why? If you look at the book value per share, it is negative. In this case, the larger the loss, the larger the ROE! That's not good. Given this, Sears appears to be a good candidate for a high beta.

Questions

1. As we mentioned, the book value per share of stock for Sears is negative. What is the current book value per share reported on this website?
2. What growth rate are analysts projecting for Sears? How does this growth rate compare to the industry?

| **Total Risk versus Beta** | EXAMPLE 13.5 |

Consider the following information about two securities. Which has greater total risk? Which has greater systematic risk? Greater unsystematic risk? Which asset will have a higher risk premium?

	Standard Deviation	Beta
Security A	40%	.50
Security B	20	1.50

From our discussion in this section, Security A has greater total risk, but it has substantially less systematic risk. Because total risk is the sum of systematic and unsystematic risk, Security A must have greater unsystematic risk. Finally, from the systematic risk principle, Security B will have a higher risk premium and a greater expected return, despite the fact that it has less total risk.

PORTFOLIO BETAS

Earlier, we saw that the riskiness of a portfolio has no simple relationship to the risks of the assets in the portfolio. A portfolio beta, however, can be calculated, just like a portfolio expected return. For example, looking again at Table 13.8, suppose you put half of your money in Apple and half in Coca-Cola. What would the beta of this combination be? Because Apple has a beta of 1.44 and Coca-Cola has a beta of .74, the portfolio's beta, β_P, would be:

$$\beta_P = .50 \times \beta_{Apple} + .50 \times \beta_{Coca\text{-}Cola}$$
$$= .50 \times 1.44 + .50 \times .74$$
$$= 1.09$$

In general, if we had many assets in a portfolio, we would multiply each asset's beta by its portfolio weight and then add the results to get the portfolio's beta.

| **Portfolio Betas** | EXAMPLE 13.6 |

Suppose we had the following investments:

Security	Amount Invested	Expected Return	Beta
Stock A	$1,000	8%	.80
Stock B	2,000	12	.95
Stock C	3,000	15	1.10
Stock D	4,000	18	1.40

What is the expected return on this portfolio? What is the beta of this portfolio? Does this portfolio have more or less systematic risk than an average asset?

To answer, we first have to calculate the portfolio weights. Notice that the total amount invested is $10,000. Of this, $1,000/10,000 = 10\%$ is invested in Stock A. Similarly, 20 percent is invested in Stock B, 30 percent is invested in Stock C, and 40 percent is invested in Stock D. The expected return, $E(R_p)$, is:

$$E(R_P) = .10 \times E(R_A) + .20 \times E(R_B) + .30 \times E(R_C) + .40 \times E(R_D)$$
$$= .10 \times 8\% + .20 \times 12\% + .30 \times 15\% + .40 \times 18\%$$
$$= 14.9\%$$

Similarly, the portfolio beta, β_p, is:

$$\beta_P = .10 \times \beta_A + .20 \times \beta_B + .30 \times \beta_C + .40 \times \beta_D$$
$$= .10 \times .80 + .20 \times .95 + .30 \times 1.10 + .40 \times 1.40$$
$$= 1.16$$

This portfolio has an expected return of 14.9 percent and a beta of 1.16. Because the beta is larger than 1, this portfolio has greater systematic risk than an average asset.

Betas are easy to find on the web. Try **finance.yahoo.com** and **money.cnn.com**.

Concept Questions

13.6a   What is the systematic risk principle?

13.6b   What does a beta coefficient measure?

13.6c   True or false: The expected return on a risky asset depends on that asset's total risk. Explain.

13.6d   How do you calculate a portfolio beta?

13.7   The Security Market Line

We're now in a position to see how risk is rewarded in the marketplace. To begin, suppose that Asset A has an expected return of $E(R_A) = 20\%$ and a beta of $\beta_A = 1.6$. Furthermore, suppose that the risk-free rate is $R_f = 8\%$. Notice that a risk-free asset, by definition, has no systematic risk (or unsystematic risk), so a risk-free asset has a beta of zero.

BETA AND THE RISK PREMIUM

Consider a portfolio made up of Asset A and a risk-free asset. We can calculate some different possible portfolio expected returns and betas by varying the percentages invested in these two assets. For example, if 25 percent of the portfolio is invested in Asset A, then the expected return is:

$$E(R_P) = .25 \times E(R_A) + (1 - .25) \times R_f$$
$$= .25 \times 20\% + .75 \times 8\%$$
$$= 11\%$$

Similarly, the beta on the portfolio, β_p, would be:

$$\beta_P = .25 \times \beta_A + (1 - .25) \times 0$$
$$= .25 \times 1.6$$
$$= .40$$

Notice that because the weights have to add up to 1, the percentage invested in the risk-free asset is equal to 1 minus the percentage invested in Asset A.

One thing that you might wonder about is whether it is possible for the percentage invested in Asset A to exceed 100 percent. The answer is yes. This can happen if the investor borrows at the risk-free rate. For example, suppose an investor has $100 and borrows an additional $50 at 8 percent, the risk-free rate. The total investment in Asset A would be $150, or 150 percent of the investor's wealth. The expected return in this case would be:

$$E(R_p) = 1.50 \times E(R_A) + (1 - 1.50) \times R_f$$
$$= 1.50 \times 20\% - .50 \times 8\%$$
$$= 26\%$$

The beta on the portfolio would be:

$$\beta_P = 1.50 \times \beta_A + (1 - 1.50) \times 0$$
$$= 1.50 \times 1.6$$
$$= 2.4$$

We can calculate some other possibilities, as follows:

Percentage of Portfolio in Asset A	Portfolio Expected Return	Portfolio Beta
0%	8%	.0
25	11	.4
50	14	.8
75	17	1.2
100	20	1.6
125	23	2.0
150	26	2.4

In Figure 13.2A, these portfolio expected returns are plotted against the portfolio betas. Notice that all the combinations fall on a straight line.

The Reward-to-Risk Ratio What is the slope of the straight line in Figure 13.2A? As always, the slope of a straight line is equal to "the rise over the run." In this case, as we move out of the risk-free asset into Asset A, the beta increases from zero to 1.6

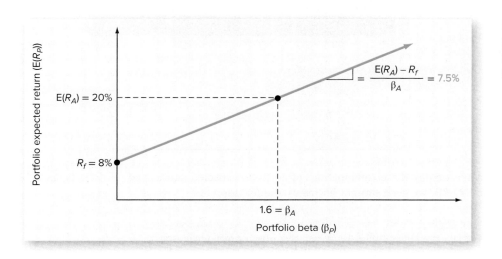

FIGURE 13.2A

Portfolio Expected Returns and Betas for Asset A

(a "run" of 1.6). At the same time, the expected return goes from 8 percent to 20 percent, a "rise" of 12 percent. The slope of the line is thus 12%/1.6 = 7.5%.

Notice that the slope of our line is the risk premium on Asset A, $E(R_A) - R_f$, divided by Asset A's beta, β_A:

$$\text{Slope} = \frac{E(R_A) - R_f}{\beta_A}$$
$$= \frac{.20 - .08}{1.6} = .075, \text{ or } 7.5\%$$

What this tells us is that Asset A offers a *reward-to-risk* ratio of 7.5 percent.[2] In other words, Asset A has a risk premium of 7.5 percent per "unit" of systematic risk.

The Basic Argument   Now suppose we consider a second asset, Asset B. This asset has a beta of 1.2 and an expected return of 16 percent. Which investment is better, Asset A or Asset B? You might think that, once again, we really cannot say—some investors might prefer A; some investors might prefer B. Actually, we can say: A is better because, as we will demonstrate, B offers inadequate compensation for its level of systematic risk, at least, relative to A.

To begin, we calculate different combinations of expected returns and betas for portfolios of Asset B and a risk-free asset, just as we did for Asset A. For example, if we put 25 percent in Asset B and the remaining 75 percent in the risk-free asset, the portfolio's expected return will be:

$$E(R_P) = .25 \times E(R_B) + (1 - .25) \times R_f$$
$$= .25 \times 16\% + .75 \times 8\%$$
$$= 10\%$$

Similarly, the beta on the portfolio, β_P, will be:

$$\beta_P = .25 \times \beta_B + (1 - .25) \times 0$$
$$= .25 \times 1.2$$
$$= .30$$

Some other possibilities are as follows:

Percentage of Portfolio in Asset B	Portfolio Expected Return	Portfolio Beta
0%	8%	.0
25	10	.3
50	12	.6
75	14	.9
100	16	1.2
125	18	1.5
150	20	1.8

When we plot these combinations of portfolio expected returns and portfolio betas in Figure 13.2B, we get a straight line as we did for Asset A.

---

[2]This ratio is sometimes called the *Treynor index*, after one of its originators.

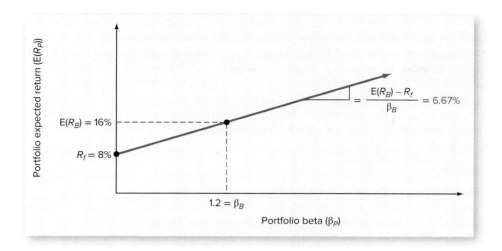

FIGURE 13.2B

Portfolio Expected Returns and Betas for Asset B

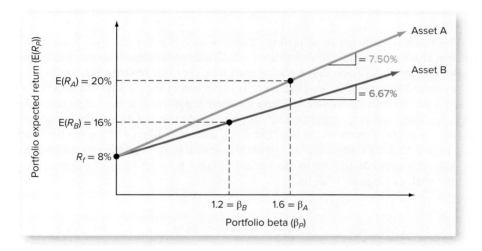

FIGURE 13.2C

Portfolio Expected Returns and Betas for Both Assets

The key thing to notice is that when we compare the results for Assets A and B, as in Figure 13.2C, the line describing the combinations of expected returns and betas for Asset A is higher than the one for Asset B. This tells us that for any given level of systematic risk (as measured by β), some combination of Asset A and the risk-free asset always offers a larger return. This is why we were able to state that Asset A is a better investment than Asset B.

Another way of seeing that A offers a superior return for its level of risk is to note that the slope of our line for Asset B is:

$$\text{Slope} = \frac{\text{E}(R_B) - R_f}{\beta_B}$$

$$= \frac{.16 - .08}{1.2} = .0667, \text{ or } 6.67\%$$

Asset B has a reward-to-risk ratio of 6.67 percent, which is less than the 7.5 percent offered by Asset A.

The Fundamental Result   The situation we have described for Assets A and B could not persist in a well-organized, active market, because investors would be attracted to Asset A and away from Asset B. As a result, Asset A's price would rise and Asset B's price would fall. Because prices and returns move in opposite directions, A's expected return would decline and B's would rise.

This buying and selling would continue until the two assets plotted on exactly the same line, which means they would offer the same reward for bearing risk. In other words, in an active, competitive market, we must have the situation that:

$$\frac{E(R_A) - R_f}{\beta_A} = \frac{E(R_B) - R_f}{\beta_B}$$

This is the fundamental relationship between risk and return.

Our basic argument can be extended to more than just two assets. In fact, no matter how many assets we have, we will always reach the same conclusion:

> **The reward-to-risk ratio must be the same for all the assets in the market.**

This result is really not so surprising. What it says is that, for example, if one asset has twice as much systematic risk as another asset, its risk premium will be twice as large.

Because all of the assets in the market must have the same reward-to-risk ratio, they all must plot on the same line. This argument is illustrated in Figure 13.3. As shown, Assets A and B plot directly on the line and have the same reward-to-risk ratio. If an asset plotted above the line, such as C in Figure 13.3, its price would rise and its expected return would fall until it plotted exactly on the line. Similarly, if an asset plotted below the line, such as D in Figure 13.3, its expected return would rise until it too plotted directly on the line. As an aside, it is common to refer to the vertical distance between an asset's expected return and the SML as the asset's "alpha."

FIGURE 13.3

Expected Returns and Systematic Risk

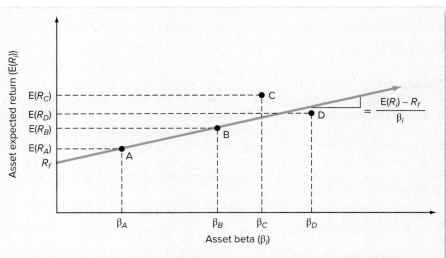

The fundamental relationship between beta and expected return is that all assets must have the same reward-to-risk ratio, $[E(R_i) - R_f]/\beta_i$. This means that they would all plot on the same straight line. Assets A and B are examples of this behavior. Asset C's expected return is too high; Asset D's is too low.

The arguments we have presented apply to active, competitive, well-functioning markets. The financial markets, such as the NYSE, best meet these criteria. Other markets, such as real asset markets, may or may not meet these criteria. For this reason, these concepts are most useful in examining financial markets. We will focus on such markets here. As we discuss in a later section, the information about risk and return gleaned from financial markets is crucial in evaluating the investments that a corporation makes in real assets.

Buy Low, Sell High   EXAMPLE 13.7

An asset is said to be *overvalued* if its price is too high given its expected return and risk. Suppose you observe the following situation:

Security	Beta	Expected Return
SWMS Co.	1.3	14%
Insec Co.	.8	10

The risk-free rate is currently 6 percent. Is one of the two securities overvalued relative to the other?

To answer, we compute the reward-to-risk ratio for both. For SWMS, this ratio is (14% − 6)/1.3 = 6.15%. For Insec, this ratio is 5 percent. What we conclude is that Insec offers an insufficient expected return for its level of risk, at least relative to SWMS. Because its expected return is too low, its price is too high. In other words, Insec is overvalued relative to SWMS, and we would expect to see its price fall relative to SWMS's. Notice that we could also say SWMS is undervalued relative to Insec.

THE SECURITY MARKET LINE

The line that results when we plot expected returns and beta coefficients is obviously of some importance, so it's time we gave it a name. This line, which we use to describe the relationship between systematic risk and expected return in financial markets, is usually called the **security market line (SML)**. After NPV, the SML is arguably the most important concept in modern finance.

security market line (SML)
A positively sloped straight line displaying the relationship between expected return and beta.

Market Portfolios   It will be very useful to know the equation of the SML. There are many different ways we could write it, but one way is particularly common. Suppose we consider a portfolio made up of all of the assets in the market. Such a portfolio is called a market portfolio, and we will express the expected return on this market portfolio as $E(R_M)$.

Because all the assets in the market must plot on the SML, so must a market portfolio made up of those assets. To determine where it plots on the SML, we need to know the beta of the market portfolio, β_M. Because this portfolio is representative of all of the assets in the market, it must have average systematic risk. In other words, it has a beta of 1. We could express the slope of the SML as:

$$\text{SML slope} = \frac{E(R_M) - R_f}{\beta_M} = \frac{E(R_M) - R_f}{1} = E(R_M) - R_f$$

The term $E(R_M) - R_f$ is often called the **market risk premium** because it is the risk premium on a market portfolio.

market risk premium
The slope of the SML, which is the difference between the expected return on a market portfolio and the risk-free rate.

The Capital Asset Pricing Model   To finish up, if we let $E(R_i)$ and β_i stand for the expected return and beta, respectively, on any asset in the market, then we know that asset must plot on the SML. As a result, we know that its reward-to-risk ratio is the same as the overall market's:

$$\frac{E(R_i) - R_f}{\beta_i} = E(R_M) - R_f$$

If we rearrange this, then we can write the equation for the SML as:

$$E(R_i) = R_f + [E(R_M) - R_f] \times \beta_i$$

13.7

capital asset pricing model (CAPM)
The equation of the SML showing the relationship between expected return and beta.

This result is the famous **capital asset pricing model (CAPM)**.

The CAPM shows that the expected return for a particular asset depends on three things:

1. *The pure time value of money*: As measured by the risk-free rate, R_f, this is the reward for merely waiting for your money, without taking any risk.
2. *The reward for bearing systematic risk*: As measured by the market risk premium, $E(R_M) - R_f$, this component is the reward the market offers for bearing an average amount of systematic risk in addition to waiting.
3. *The amount of systematic risk*: As measured by β_i, this is the amount of systematic risk present in a particular asset or portfolio, relative to that in an average asset.

By the way, the CAPM works for portfolios of assets just as it does for individual assets. In an earlier section, we saw how to calculate a portfolio's β. To find the expected return on a portfolio, we use this β in the CAPM equation.

Figure 13.4 summarizes our discussion of the SML and the CAPM. As before, we plot expected return against beta. Now we recognize that, based on the CAPM, the slope of the SML is equal to the market risk premium, $E(R_M) - R_f$.

This concludes our presentation of concepts related to the risk–return trade-off. For future reference, Table 13.9 summarizes the various concepts in the order in which we discussed them.

FIGURE 13.4

The Security Market Line (SML)

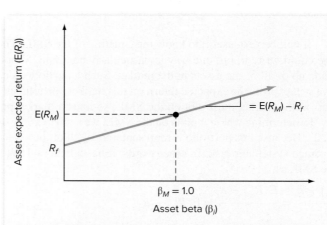

The slope of the security market line is equal to the market risk premium—that is, the reward for bearing an average amount of systematic risk. The equation describing the SML can be written:

$$E(R_i) = R_f + [E(R_M) - R_f] \times \beta_i$$

which is the capital asset pricing model (CAPM).

Risk and Return   EXAMPLE 13.8

Suppose the risk-free rate is 4 percent, the market risk premium is 8.6 percent, and a particular stock has a beta of 1.3. Based on the CAPM, what is the expected return on this stock? What would the expected return be if the beta were to double?

   With a beta of 1.3, the risk premium for the stock is 1.3 × 8.6%, or 11.18 percent. The risk-free rate is 4 percent, so the expected return is 15.18 percent. If the beta were to double to 2.6, the risk premium would double to 22.36 percent, so the expected return would be 26.36 percent.

TABLE 13.9

Summary of Risk and Return

I.	Total Risk
	The *total risk* of an investment is measured by the variance or, more commonly, the standard deviation of its return.

II.	Total Return
	The *total return* on an investment has two components: The expected return and the unexpected return. The unexpected return comes about because of unanticipated events. The risk from investing stems from the possibility of an unanticipated event.

III.	Systematic and Unsystematic Risks
	Systematic risks (also called *market risks*) are unanticipated events that affect almost all assets to some degree because the effects are economy-wide. *Unsystematic risks* are unanticipated events that affect single assets or small groups of assets. Unsystematic risks are also called *unique* or *asset-specific risks*.

IV.	The Effect of Diversification
	Some, but not all, of the risk associated with a risky investment can be eliminated by diversification. The reason is that unsystematic risks, which are unique to individual assets, tend to wash out in a large portfolio, but systematic risks, which affect all of the assets in a portfolio to some extent, do not.

V.	The Systematic Risk Principle and Beta
	Because unsystematic risk can be freely eliminated by diversification, the *systematic risk principle* states that the reward for bearing risk depends only on the level of systematic risk. The level of systematic risk in a particular asset, relative to the average, is given by the beta of that asset.

VI.	The Reward-to-Risk Ratio and the Security Market Line
	The *reward-to-risk ratio* for Asset i is the ratio of its risk premium, $E(R_i) - R_f$, to its beta, β_i: $$\frac{E(R_i) - R_f}{\beta_i}$$ In a well-functioning market, this ratio is the same for every asset. As a result, when asset expected returns are plotted against asset betas, all assets plot on the same straight line, called the *security market line* (SML).

VII.	The Capital Asset Pricing Model
	From the SML, the expected return on Asset i can be written: $$E(R_i) = R_f + [E(R_M) - R_f] \times \beta_i$$ This is the *capital asset pricing model* (CAPM). The expected return on a risky asset has three components. The first is the pure time value of money (R_f), the second is the market risk premium $[E(R_M) - R_f]$, and the third is the beta for that asset (β_i).

13.8 The SML and the Cost of Capital: A Preview

Our goal in studying risk and return is twofold. First, risk is an extremely important consideration in almost all business decisions, so we want to discuss what risk is and how it is rewarded in the market. Our second purpose is to learn what determines the appropriate discount rate for future cash flows. We briefly discuss this second subject now; we will discuss it in more detail in a subsequent chapter.

THE BASIC IDEA

The security market line tells us the reward for bearing risk in financial markets. At an absolute minimum, any new investment our firm undertakes must offer an expected return that is no worse than what the financial markets offer for the same risk. The reason for this is that our shareholders can always invest for themselves in the financial markets.

The only way we benefit our shareholders is by finding investments with expected returns that are superior to what the financial markets offer for the same risk. Such an investment will have a positive NPV. So, if we ask, "What is the appropriate discount rate?" the answer is that we should use the expected return offered in financial markets on investments with the same systematic risk.

In other words, to determine whether an investment has a positive NPV, we essentially compare the expected return on that new investment to what the financial market offers on an investment with the same beta. This is why the SML is so important: It tells us the "going rate" for bearing risk in the economy.

THE COST OF CAPITAL

cost of capital
The minimum required return on a new investment.

The appropriate discount rate on a new project is the minimum expected rate of return an investment must offer to be attractive. This minimum required return is often called the **cost of capital** associated with the investment. It is called this because the required return is what the firm must earn on its capital investment in a project just to break even. It can be interpreted as the opportunity cost associated with the firm's capital investment.

Notice that when we say an investment is attractive if its expected return exceeds what is offered in financial markets for investments of the same risk, we are effectively using the internal rate of return (IRR) criterion that we developed and discussed in Chapter 9. The only difference is that now we have a much better idea of what determines the required return on an investment. This understanding will be critical when we discuss cost of capital and capital structure in Part 6 of our book.

Concept Questions

13.8a   If an investment has a positive NPV, would it plot above or below the SML? Why?

13.8b   What is meant by the term *cost of capital*?

Summary and Conclusions   13.9

This chapter has covered the essentials of risk. Along the way, we have introduced a number of definitions and concepts. The most important of these is the security market line, or SML. The SML is important because it tells us the reward offered in financial markets for bearing risk. Once we know this, we have a benchmark against which we can compare the returns expected from real asset investments to determine if they are desirable.

Because we have covered quite a bit of ground, it's useful to summarize the basic economic logic underlying the SML as follows:

1. Based on capital market history, there is a reward for bearing risk. This reward is the risk premium on an asset.

2. The total risk associated with an asset has two parts: Systematic risk and unsystematic risk. Unsystematic risk can be freely eliminated by diversification (this is the principle of diversification), so only systematic risk is rewarded. As a result, the risk premium on an asset is determined by its systematic risk. This is the systematic risk principle.

3. An asset's systematic risk, relative to the average, can be measured by its beta coefficient, β_i. The risk premium on an asset is then given by its beta coefficient multiplied by the market risk premium, $[E(R_M) - R_f] \times \beta_i$.

4. The expected return on an asset, $E(R_i)$, is equal to the risk-free rate, R_f, plus the risk premium:

$$E(R_i) = R_f + [E(R_M) - R_f] \times \beta_i$$

This is the equation of the SML, and it is often called the capital asset pricing model (CAPM).

This chapter completes our discussion of risk and return. Now that we have a better understanding of what determines a firm's cost of capital for an investment, the next several chapters will examine more closely how firms raise the long-term capital needed for investment.

CONNECT TO FINANCE

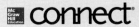 *Connect Finance* offers you plenty of opportunities to practice mastering these concepts. Log on to connect.mheducation.com to learn more. If you like what you see, ask your professor about using *Connect Finance*!

Can you answer the following *Connect* Quiz questions?

Section 13.1 A stock is expected to earn 15 percent in a boom economy and 7 percent in a normal economy. There is a 35 percent chance the economy will boom and a 65 percent chance the economy will be normal. What is the standard deviation of these returns?

Section 13.5 Which type of risk can be eliminated through diversification?

Section 13.6 Beta is a measure of what?

Section 13.7 The slope of the security market line is equal to what?

Section 13.8 Where would a negative net present value project appear on a security market line graph?

CHAPTER REVIEW AND SELF-TEST PROBLEMS

13.1 Expected Return and Standard Deviation This problem will give you some practice calculating measures of prospective portfolio performance. There are two assets and three states of the economy:

State of Economy	Probability of State of Economy	Rate of Return If State Occurs	
		Stock A	Stock B
Recession	.20	−.15	.20
Normal	.50	.20	.30
Boom	.30	.60	.40

What are the expected returns and standard deviations for these two stocks?

13.2 Portfolio Risk and Return Using the information in the previous problem, suppose you have $20,000 total. If you put $15,000 in Stock A and the remainder in Stock B, what will be the expected return and standard deviation of your portfolio?

13.3 Risk and Return Suppose you observe the following situation:

Security	Beta	Expected Return
Cooley, Inc.	1.8	22.00%
Moyer Co.	1.6	20.44

If the risk-free rate is 7 percent, are these securities correctly priced? What would the risk-free rate have to be if they are correctly priced?

13.4 CAPM Suppose the risk-free rate is 8 percent. The expected return on the market is 16 percent. If a particular stock has a beta of .7, what is its expected return based on the CAPM? If another stock has an expected return of 24 percent, what must its beta be?

ANSWERS TO CHAPTER REVIEW AND SELF-TEST PROBLEMS

13.1 The expected returns are just the possible returns multiplied by the associated probabilities:

$$E(R_A) = (.20 \times -.15) + (.50 \times .20) + (.30 \times .60) = .25, \text{ or } 25\%$$
$$E(R_B) = (.20 \times .20) + (.50 \times .30) + (.30 \times .40) = .31, \text{ or } 31\%$$

The variances are given by the sums of the squared deviations from the expected returns multiplied by their probabilities:

$$\sigma_A^2 = .20 \times (-.15 - .25)^2 + .50 \times (.20 - .25)^2 + .30 \times (.60 - .25)^2$$
$$= (.20 \times -.40^2) + (.50 \times -.05^2) + (.30 \times .35^2)$$
$$= (.20 \times .16) + (.50 \times .0025) + (.30 \times .1225)$$
$$= .0700$$

$$\sigma_B^2 = .20 \times (.20 - .31)^2 + .50 \times (.30 - .31)^2 + .30 \times (.40 - .31)^2$$
$$= (.20 \times -.11^2) + (.50 \times -.01^2) + (.30 \times .09^2)$$
$$= (.20 \times .0121) + (.50 \times .0001) + (.30 \times .0081)$$
$$= .0049$$

The standard deviations are thus:

$$\sigma_A = \sqrt{.0700} = .2646, \text{ or } 26.46\%$$
$$\sigma_B = \sqrt{.0049} = .07, \text{ or } 7\%$$

13.2 The portfolio weights are $15,000/$20,000 = .75$ and $5,000/$20,000 = .25$. The expected return is thus:

$$E(R_P) = .75 \times E(R_A) + .25 \times E(R_B)$$
$$= (.75 \times .25) + (.25 \times .31)$$
$$= .265, \text{ or } 26.5\%$$

Alternatively, we could calculate the portfolio's return in each of the states:

State of Economy	Probability of State of Economy	Portfolio Return If State Occurs
Recession	.20	$(.75 \times -.15) + (.25 \times .20) = -.0625$
Normal	.50	$(.75 \times .20) + (.25 \times .30) = .2250$
Boom	.30	$(.75 \times .60) + (.25 \times .40) = .5500$

The portfolio's expected return is:

$$E(R_P) = (.20 \times -.0625) + (.50 \times .2250) + (.30 \times .5500) = .265, \text{ or } 26.5\%$$

This is the same as we had before.
The portfolio's variance is:

$$\sigma_P^2 = .20 \times (-.0625 - .265)^2 + .50 \times (.225 - .265)^2$$
$$+ .30 \times (.55 - .265)^2$$
$$= .0466$$

So the standard deviation is $\sqrt{.0466} = .2159$, or 21.59%.

13.3 If we compute the reward-to-risk ratios, we get $(.22 - .07)/1.8 = .0833$, or 8.33% for Cooley versus 8.4% for Moyer. Relative to that of Cooley, Moyer's expected return is too high, so its price is too low. If they are correctly priced, then they must offer the same reward-to-risk ratio. The risk-free rate would have to be such that:

$$(.22 - R_f)/1.8 = (.2044 - R_f)/1.6$$

With a little algebra, we find that the risk-free rate must be 8 percent:

$$.2\% - R_f = (.2044 - R_f)(1.8/1.6)$$
$$.22 - .2044 \times 1.125 = R_f - R_f \times 1.125$$
$$R_f = .08, \text{ or } 8\%$$

13.4 Because the expected return on the market is 16 percent, the market risk premium is $.16 - .08 = .08$, or 8%. The first stock has a beta of .7, so its expected return is $.08 + .7 \times .08 = .136$, or 13.6%.

For the second stock, notice that the risk premium is $.24\% - .08 = .16$, or 16%. Because this is twice as large as the market risk premium, the beta must be exactly equal to 2. We can verify this using the CAPM:

$$E(R_i) = R_f + [E(R_M) - R_f] \times \beta_i$$
$$.24 = .08 + (.16 - .08) \times \beta_i$$
$$\beta_i = .16/.08$$
$$= 2.0$$

CONCEPTS REVIEW AND CRITICAL THINKING QUESTIONS

1. **Diversifiable and Nondiversifiable Risks [LO3]** In broad terms, why are some risks diversifiable? Why are some risks nondiversifiable? Does it follow that an investor can control the level of unsystematic risk in a portfolio, but not the level of systematic risk?

2. **Information and Market Returns [LO3]** Suppose the government announces that, based on a just-completed survey, the growth rate in the economy is likely to be 2 percent in the coming year, as compared to 5 percent for the past year. Will security prices increase, decrease, or stay the same following this announcement? Does it make any difference whether the 2 percent figure was anticipated by the market? Explain.

3. **Systematic versus Unsystematic Risk [LO3]** Classify the following events as mostly systematic or mostly unsystematic. Is the distinction clear in every case?
   a. Short-term interest rates increase unexpectedly.
   b. The interest rate a company pays on its short-term debt borrowing is increased by its bank.
   c. Oil prices unexpectedly decline.
   d. An oil tanker ruptures, creating a large oil spill.
   e. A manufacturer loses a multimillion-dollar product liability suit.
   f. A Supreme Court decision substantially broadens producer liability for injuries suffered by product users.

4. **Systematic versus Unsystematic Risk [LO3]** Indicate whether the following events might cause stocks in general to change price, and whether they might cause Big Widget Corp.'s stock to change price:
   a. The government announces that inflation unexpectedly jumped by 2 percent last month.
   b. Big Widget's quarterly earnings report, just issued, generally fell in line with analysts' expectations.
   c. The government reports that economic growth last year was at 3 percent, which generally agreed with most economists' forecasts.
   d. The directors of Big Widget die in a plane crash.
   e. Congress approves changes to the tax code that will increase the top marginal corporate tax rate. The legislation had been debated for the previous six months.

5. **Expected Portfolio Returns** [LO1] If a portfolio has a positive investment in every asset, can the expected return on the portfolio be greater than that on every asset in the portfolio? Can it be less than that on every asset in the portfolio? If you answer yes to one or both of these questions, give an example to support your answer.

6. **Diversification** [LO2] True or false: The most important characteristic in determining the expected return of a well-diversified portfolio is the variance of the individual assets in the portfolio. Explain.

7. **Portfolio Risk** [LO2] If a portfolio has a positive investment in every asset, can the standard deviation on the portfolio be less than that on every asset in the portfolio? What about the portfolio beta?

8. **Beta and CAPM** [LO4] Is it possible that a risky asset could have a beta of zero? Explain. Based on the CAPM, what is the expected return on such an asset? Is it possible that a risky asset could have a negative beta? What does the CAPM predict about the expected return on such an asset? Can you give an explanation for your answer?

9. **Alpha** [LO4] In our discussion of the SML, we defined alpha. What does alpha measure? What alpha would you like to see on your investments?

10. **Alpha** [LO4] Common advice on Wall Street is "Keep your alpha high and your beta low." Why?

11. **Corporate Downsizing** [LO1] In recent years, it has been common for companies to experience significant stock price changes in reaction to announcements of massive layoffs. Critics charge that such events encourage companies to fire long-time employees and that Wall Street is cheering them on. Do you agree or disagree?

12. **Earnings and Stock Returns** [LO1] As indicated by a number of examples in this chapter, earnings announcements by companies are closely followed by, and frequently result in, share price revisions. Two issues should come to mind. First, earnings announcements concern past periods. If the market values stocks based on expectations of the future, why are numbers summarizing past performance relevant? Second, these announcements concern accounting earnings. Going back to Chapter 2, such earnings may have little to do with cash flow—so, again, why are they relevant?

QUESTIONS AND PROBLEMS

1. **Determining Portfolio Weights** [LO1] What are the portfolio weights for a portfolio that has 115 shares of Stock A that sell for $43 per share and 180 shares of Stock B that sell for $19 per share?

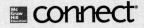

BASIC
(Questions 1–19)

2. **Portfolio Expected Return** [LO1] You own a portfolio that has $3,480 invested in Stock A and $7,430 invested in Stock B. If the expected returns on these stocks are 8 percent and 11 percent, respectively, what is the expected return on the portfolio?

3. **Portfolio Expected Return** [LO1] You own a portfolio that is invested 35 percent in Stock X, 20 percent in Stock Y, and 45 percent in Stock Z. The expected returns on these three stocks are 9 percent, 15 percent, and 12 percent, respectively. What is the expected return on the portfolio?

4. **Portfolio Expected Return** [LO1] You have $10,000 to invest in a stock portfolio. Your choices are Stock X with an expected return of 12.1 percent and Stock Y with

an expected return of 9.8 percent. If your goal is to create a portfolio with an expected return of 10.85 percent, how much money will you invest in Stock X? In Stock Y?

5. **Calculating Expected Return** [LO1] Based on the following information, calculate the expected return:

State of Economy	Probability of State of Economy	Portfolio Return If State Occurs
Recession	.20	−.08
Boom	.80	.15

6. **Calculating Expected Return** [LO1] Based on the following information, calculate the expected return:

State of Economy	Probability of State of Economy	Portfolio Return If State Occurs
Recession	.10	−.15
Normal	.60	.09
Boom	.30	.23

7. **Calculating Returns and Standard Deviations** [LO1] Based on the following information, calculate the expected return and standard deviation for Stock A and Stock B:

State of Economy	Probability of State of Economy	Rate of Return If State Occurs	
		Stock A	Stock B
Recession	.10	.04	−.17
Normal	.60	.09	.12
Boom	.30	.17	.27

8. **Calculating Expected Returns** [LO1] A portfolio is invested 25 percent in Stock G, 55 percent in Stock J, and 20 percent in Stock K. The expected returns on these stocks are 11 percent, 9 percent, and 15 percent, respectively. What is the portfolio's expected return? How do you interpret your answer?

9. **Returns and Variances** [LO1] Consider the following information:

State of Economy	Probability of State of Economy	Rate of Return If State Occurs		
		Stock A	Stock B	Stock C
Boom	.75	.08	.17	.24
Bust	.25	.11	−.05	−.08

a. What is the expected return on an equally weighted portfolio of these three stocks?

b. What is the variance of a portfolio invested 20 percent each in A and B and 60 percent in C?

10. **Returns and Standard Deviations** [LO1] Consider the following information:

State of Economy	Probability of State of Economy	Rate of Return If State Occurs		
		Stock A	Stock B	Stock C
Boom	.10	.35	.40	.27
Good	.60	.16	.17	.08
Poor	.25	−.01	−.03	−.04
Bust	.05	−.12	−.18	−.09

   a. Your portfolio is invested 30 percent each in A and C, and 40 percent in B. What is the expected return of the portfolio?

   b. What is the variance of this portfolio? The standard deviation?

11. **Calculating Portfolio Betas** [LO4] You own a stock portfolio invested 20 percent in Stock Q, 30 percent in Stock R, 35 percent in Stock S, and 15 percent in Stock T. The betas for these four stocks are .79, 1.23, 1.13, and 1.36, respectively. What is the portfolio beta?

12. **Calculating Portfolio Betas** [LO4] You own a portfolio equally invested in a risk-free asset and two stocks. If one of the stocks has a beta of 1.17 and the total portfolio is equally as risky as the market, what must the beta be for the other stock in your portfolio?

13. **Using CAPM** [LO4] A stock has a beta of 1.15, the expected return on the market is 10.3 percent, and the risk-free rate is 3.1 percent. What must the expected return on this stock be?

14. **Using CAPM** [LO4] A stock has an expected return of 10.2 percent, the risk-free rate is 3.9 percent, and the market risk premium is 7.2 percent. What must the beta of this stock be?

15. **Using CAPM** [LO4] A stock has an expected return of 10.45 percent, its beta is .93, and the risk-free rate is 3.6 percent. What must the expected return on the market be?

16. **Using CAPM** [LO4] A stock has an expected return of 11.85 percent, its beta is 1.24, and the expected return on the market is 10.2 percent. What must the risk-free rate be?

17. **Using the SML** [LO4] Asset W has an expected return of 11.8 percent and a beta of 1.10. If the risk-free rate is 3.3 percent, complete the following table for portfolios of Asset W and a risk-free asset. Illustrate the relationship between portfolio expected return and portfolio beta by plotting the expected returns against the betas. What is the slope of the line that results?

Percentage of Portfolio in Asset W	Portfolio Expected Return	Portfolio Beta
0%		
25		
50		
75		
100		
125		
150		

18. **Reward-to-Risk Ratios** [LO4] Stock Y has a beta of 1.2 and an expected return of 11.1 percent. Stock Z has a beta of .80 and an expected return of 7.85 percent. If the risk-free rate is 2.4 percent and the market risk premium is 7.2 percent, are these stocks correctly priced?

19. **Reward-to-Risk Ratios** [LO4] In the previous problem, what would the risk-free rate have to be for the two stocks to be correctly priced?

20. **Using CAPM** [LO4] A stock has a beta of 1.12 and an expected return of 10.8 percent. A risk-free asset currently earns 2.7 percent.

   INTERMEDIATE
   (Questions 20–24)

   a. What is the expected return on a portfolio that is equally invested in the two assets?

   b. If a portfolio of the two assets has a beta of .92, what are the portfolio weights?

   c. If a portfolio of the two assets has an expected return of 9 percent, what is its beta?

   d. If a portfolio of the two assets has a beta of 2.24, what are the portfolio weights? How do you interpret the weights for the two assets in this case? Explain.

21. Portfolio Returns [LO2] Using information from the previous chapter on capital market history, determine the return on a portfolio that is equally invested in large-company stocks and long-term government bonds. What is the return on a portfolio that is equally invested in small-company stocks and Treasury bills?

22. CAPM [LO4] Using the CAPM, show that the ratio of the risk premiums on two assets is equal to the ratio of their betas.

23. Portfolio Returns and Deviations [LO2] Consider the following information about three stocks:

State of Economy	Probability of State of Economy	Rate of Return If State Occurs		
		Stock A	Stock B	Stock C
Boom	.25	.21	.33	.55
Normal	.60	.17	.11	.09
Bust	.15	.00	−.21	−.45

   a. If your portfolio is invested 40 percent each in A and B and 20 percent in C, what is the portfolio expected return? The variance? The standard deviation?

   b. If the expected T-bill rate is 3.80 percent, what is the expected risk premium on the portfolio?

   c. If the expected inflation rate is 3.30 percent, what are the approximate and exact expected real returns on the portfolio? What are the approximate and exact expected real risk premiums on the portfolio?

24. Analyzing a Portfolio [LO2, 4] You want to create a portfolio equally as risky as the market, and you have $1,000,000 to invest. Given this information, fill in the rest of the following table:

Asset	Investment	Beta
Stock A	$165,000	.80
Stock B	$350,000	1.09
Stock C		1.27
Risk-free asset		

CHALLENGE
(Questions 25–28)

25. Analyzing a Portfolio [LO2, 4] You have $100,000 to invest in a portfolio containing Stock X and Stock Y. Your goal is to create a portfolio that has an expected return of 12.7 percent. If Stock X has an expected return of 11.4 percent and a beta of 1.25, and Stock Y has an expected return of 8.68 percent and a beta of .85, how much money will you invest in Stock Y? How do you interpret your answer? What is the beta of your portfolio?

26. Systematic versus Unsystematic Risk [LO3] Consider the following information about Stocks I and II:

State of Economy	Probability of State of Economy	Rate of Return If State Occurs	
		Stock I	Stock II
Recession	.15	.03	−.23
Normal	.70	.20	.09
Irrational exuberance	.15	.08	.43

The market risk premium is 7 percent, and the risk-free rate is 3.5 percent. Which stock has the most systematic risk? Which one has the most unsystematic risk? Which stock is "riskier"? Explain.

27. **SML [LO4]** Suppose you observe the following situation:

Security	Beta	Expected Return
Pete Corp.	1.25	.1323
Repete Co.	.87	.0967

Assume these securities are correctly priced. Based on the CAPM, what is the expected return on the market? What is the risk-free rate?

28. **SML [LO4]** Suppose you observe the following situation:

	Probability of	Return If State Occurs	
State of Economy	State of Economy	Stock A	Stock B
Bust	.15	−.08	−.10
Normal	.60	.11	.09
Boom	.25	.30	.27

a. Calculate the expected return on each stock.

b. Assuming the capital asset pricing model holds and Stock A's beta is greater than Stock B's beta by .35, what is the expected market risk premium?

EXCEL MASTER IT! PROBLEM

The CAPM is one of the most thoroughly researched models in financial economics. When beta is estimated in practice, a variation of CAPM called the market model is often used. To derive the market model, we start with the CAPM:

$$E(R_i) = R_f + \beta[E(R_M) - R_f]$$

Since CAPM is an equation, we can subtract the risk-free rate from both sides, which gives us:

$$E(R_i) - R_f = \beta[E(R_M) - R_f]$$

This equation is deterministic, by which we mean it is exact. In a regression, we realize that there is some indeterminate error. We need to formally recognize this in the equation by adding epsilon, ε, which represents this error:

$$E(R_i) - R_f = \beta[E(R_M) - R_f] + \varepsilon$$

Finally, think of the above equation in a regression. Since there is no intercept in the equation, the intercept is zero. However, when we estimate the regression equation, we can add an intercept term, which we will call alpha:

$$E(R_i) - R_f = \alpha_i + \beta[E(R_M) - R_f] + \varepsilon$$

This equation is often called the "market" model, though it is not the only equation with that name, which is a source of confusion. The intercept term is known as Jensen's alpha, and it represents the "excess" return. If CAPM holds exactly, this intercept should be zero.

If you think of alpha in terms of the SML, then if the alpha is positive, the stock plots above the SML, and if alpha is negative, the stock plots below the SML.

a. You want to estimate the market model for an individual stock and a mutual fund. First, go to finance.yahoo.com and download the adjusted prices for the last 61 months for an individual stock, a mutual fund, and the S&P 500. Next, go to the St. Louis Federal Reserve website at www.stlouisfed.org. You should find the FRED® database there. Look for the 1-Month Treasury Constant Maturity Rate and download this data. This series will be the proxy for the risk-free rate. When using this rate, you should be aware that this interest rate is the annualized interest rate. Since we are using monthly stock returns, you will need to adjust the 1-month T-bill rate. For the stock and mutual fund you select, estimate the beta and alpha using the market model. When you estimate the regression model, find the box that says "Residuals" and check this box when you do each regression. Because you are saving the residuals, you may want to save the regression output in a new worksheet.

1. Are the alpha and beta for each regression statistically different from zero?
2. How do you interpret the alpha and beta for the stock and the mutual fund?
3. Which of the two regression estimates has the highest R-squared? Is this what you would have expected? Why?

b. In part (a), you asked Excel to return the residuals of the regression, which is the epsilon in the regression equation. If you remember back to basic statistics, the residuals are the distance from each observation to the regression line. In this context, the residuals are the part of the monthly return that is not explained by the market model estimate. The residuals can be used to calculate the appraisal ratio, which is the alpha divided by the standard deviation of the residuals.

1. What do you think the appraisal ratio is intended to measure?
2. Calculate the appraisal ratios for the stock and the mutual fund. Which has a better appraisal ratio?
3. Often, the appraisal ratio is used to evaluate the performance of mutual fund managers. Why do you think the appraisal ratio is used more often for mutual funds, which are portfolios, than for individual stocks?

MINICASE

The Beta for Colgate-Palmolive

Joey Moss, a recent finance graduate, has just begun his job with the investment firm of Covili and Wyatt. Paul Covili, one of the firm's founders, has been talking to Joey about the firm's investment portfolio.

As with any investment, Paul is concerned about the risk of the investment as well as the potential return. More specifically, because the company holds a diversified portfolio, Paul is concerned about the systematic risk of current and potential investments. One such position the company currently holds is stock in Colgate-Palmolive (CL). Colgate-Palmolive is the well-known manufacturer of consumer products under brand names such as Colgate, Palmolive, Softsoap, Irish Spring, Ajax, and others.

Covili and Wyatt currently uses a commercial data vendor for information about its positions. Because of this, Paul is unsure exactly how the numbers provided are calculated. The data provider considers its methods proprietary, and it will not disclose how stock betas and other information are calculated. Paul is uncomfortable with not knowing exactly how these numbers are being computed and also believes that it could be less expensive to calculate the necessary statistics in-house. To explore this question, Paul has asked Joey to do the following assignments.

QUESTIONS

1. Go to finance.yahoo.com and download the ending monthly stock prices for Colgate-Palmolive for the last 60 months. Use the adjusted closing price, which adjusts for dividend payments and stock splits. Next, download the ending value of the S&P 500 index over the same

period. For the historical risk-free rate, go to the St. Louis Federal Reserve website (www.stlouisfed.org) and find the three-month Treasury bill secondary market rate. Download this file. What are the monthly returns, average monthly returns, and standard deviations for Colgate-Palmolive stock, the three-month Treasury bill, and the S&P 500 for this period?

2. Beta is often estimated by linear regression. A model commonly used is called the *market model*, which is:

$$R_t - R_{ft} = \alpha_i + \beta_i [R_{Mt} - R_{ft}] + \varepsilon_t$$

In this regression, R_t is the return on the stock and R_{ft} is the risk-free rate for the same period. R_{Mt} is the return on a stock market index such as the S&P 500 index; α_i is the regression intercept; β_i is the slope (and the stock's estimated beta); and ε_t represents the residuals for the regression. What do you think is the motivation for this particular regression? The intercept, α, is often called *Jensen's alpha*. What does it measure? If an asset has a positive Jensen's alpha, where would it plot with respect to the SML? What is the financial interpretation of the residuals in the regression?

3. Use the market model to estimate the beta for Colgate-Palmolive using the last 36 months of returns (the regression procedure in Excel is one easy way to do this). Plot the monthly returns on Colgate-Palmolive against the index and also show the fitted line.

4. When the beta of a stock is calculated using monthly returns, there is a debate over the number of months that should be used in the calculation. Rework the previous questions using the last 60 months of returns. How does this answer compare to what you calculated previously? What are some arguments for and against using shorter versus longer periods? Also, you've used monthly data, which is a common choice. You could have used daily, weekly, quarterly, or even annual data. What do you think are the issues here?

5. Compare your beta for Colgate-Palmolive to the beta you find on finance.yahoo.com. How similar are they? Why might they be different?

Chapter

14 | Cost of Capital

WITH OVER 112,000 EMPLOYEES ON FIVE CONTINENTS, Germany-based BASF is a major international company. The company operates in a variety of industries, including agriculture, oil and gas, chemicals, and plastics. In an attempt to increase value, BASF launched Vision 2020, a comprehensive plan that included all functions within the company and challenged and encouraged all employees to act in an entrepreneurial manner. The major financial component of the strategy was that the company expected to earn its weighted average cost of capital, or WACC, plus a premium. So, what exactly is the WACC?

The WACC is the minimum return a company needs to earn to satisfy all of its investors, including stockholders, bondholders, and preferred stockholders. In 2017, for example, BASF pegged its cost of capital at 10 percent, the same WACC that it used during 2016, but down slightly from the 11 percent used in 2015. In this chapter, we learn how to compute a firm's cost of capital and find out what it means to the firm and its investors. We will also learn when to use the firm's cost of capital, and, perhaps more important, when not to use it.

Learning Objectives

After studying this chapter, you should be able to:

LO1 Determine a firm's cost of equity capital.

LO2 Determine a firm's cost of debt.

LO3 Determine a firm's overall cost of capital and how to use it to value a company.

LO4 Explain how to correctly include flotation costs in capital budgeting projects.

LO5 Describe some of the pitfalls associated with a firm's overall cost of capital and what to do about them.

For updates on the latest happenings in finance, visit fundamentalsofcorporatefinance.blogspot.com.

©by_adri/iStockPhoto/GettyImages

Suppose you have just become the president of a large company, and the first decision you face is whether to go ahead with a plan to renovate the company's warehouse distribution system. The plan will cost the company $50 million, and it is expected to save $12 million per year after taxes over the next six years.

This is a familiar problem in capital budgeting. To address it, you would determine the relevant cash flows, discount them, and, if the net present value is positive, take on the project; if the NPV is negative, you would scrap it. So far, so good; but what should you use as the discount rate?

From our discussion of risk and return, you know that the correct discount rate depends on the riskiness of the project to renovate the warehouse distribution system. In particular, the new project will have a positive NPV only if its return exceeds what the financial markets offer on investments of similar risk. We called this minimum required return the *cost of capital* associated with the project.[1]

To make the right decision as president, you must examine what the capital markets have to offer and use this information to arrive at an estimate of the project's cost of capital. Our primary purpose in this chapter is to describe how to go about doing this. There are a variety of approaches to this task, and a number of conceptual and practical issues arise.

One of the most important concepts we develop is that of the *weighted average cost of capital* (WACC). This is the cost of capital for the firm as a whole, and it can be interpreted as the required return on the overall firm. In discussing the WACC, we will recognize the fact that a firm will normally raise capital in a variety of forms and that these different forms of capital may have different costs associated with them.

We also recognize in this chapter that taxes are an important consideration in determining the required return on an investment: We are always interested in valuing the aftertax cash flows from a project. We will therefore discuss how to incorporate taxes explicitly into our estimates of the cost of capital.

The Cost of Capital: Some Preliminaries   14.1

In Chapter 13, we developed the security market line, or SML, and used it to explore the relationship between the expected return on a security and its systematic risk. In our examination of the risky returns from buying securities, we took the viewpoint of, for example, a shareholder in the firm. This helped us to better understand the alternatives available to an investor in the capital markets.

In this chapter, we turn things around a bit and look more closely at the other side of the problem, which is how these returns and securities look from the viewpoint of the companies that issue them. The important fact to note is that the return an investor in a security receives is the cost of that security to the company that issued it.

REQUIRED RETURN VERSUS COST OF CAPITAL

When we say that the required return on an investment is, say, 10 percent, we usually mean that the investment will have a positive NPV only if its return exceeds 10 percent. Another way of interpreting the required return is to observe that the firm must earn 10 percent on the investment to compensate its investors for the use of the capital needed to finance the project. This is why we could also say that 10 percent is the cost of capital associated with the investment.

To illustrate the point further, imagine that we are evaluating a risk-free project. In this case, how to determine the required return is obvious: We look at the capital markets and observe the current rate offered by risk-free investments, and we use this rate to discount the project's cash flows. Thus, the cost of capital for a risk-free investment is the risk-free rate.

If a project is risky, then, assuming that all the other information is unchanged, the required return is obviously higher. In other words, the cost of capital for this project, if it is risky, is greater than the risk-free rate, and the appropriate discount rate would exceed the risk-free rate.

We will henceforth use the terms *required return*, *appropriate discount rate*, and *cost of capital* more or less interchangeably because, as the discussion in this section suggests,

---

[1] The term *cost of money* is also used.

they all mean essentially the same thing. The key fact to grasp is that the cost of capital associated with an investment depends on the risk of that investment. This is one of the most important lessons in corporate finance, so it bears repeating:

> **The cost of capital depends primarily on the use of the funds, not the source.**

It is a common error to forget this crucial point and fall into the trap of thinking that the cost of capital for an investment depends primarily on how and where the capital is raised.

FINANCIAL POLICY AND COST OF CAPITAL

We know that the particular mixture of debt and equity a firm chooses to employ—its capital structure—is a managerial variable. In this chapter, we will take the firm's financial policy as given. In particular, we will assume that the firm has a fixed debt-equity ratio that it maintains. This ratio reflects the firm's *target* capital structure. How a firm might choose that ratio is the subject of a later chapter.

From the preceding discussion, we know that a firm's overall cost of capital will reflect the required return on the firm's assets as a whole. Given that a firm uses both debt and equity capital, this overall cost of capital will be a mixture of the returns needed to compensate its creditors and those needed to compensate its stockholders. In other words, a firm's cost of capital will reflect both its cost of debt capital and its cost of equity capital. We discuss these costs separately in the sections that follow.

Concept Questions

14.1a   What is the primary determinant of the cost of capital for an investment?

14.1b   What is the relationship between the required return on an investment and the cost of capital associated with that investment?

14.2   The Cost of Equity

Excel Master It!

Excel Master coverage online

cost of equity
The return that equity investors require on their investment in the firm.

To open our discussion of cost of capital, we begin with the most difficult question: What is the firm's overall **cost of equity**? The reason this is a difficult question is that there is no way of directly observing the return that the firm's equity investors require on their investment. Instead, we must somehow estimate it. This section discusses two approaches to determining the cost of equity: The dividend growth model approach and the security market line (SML) approach.

THE DIVIDEND GROWTH MODEL APPROACH

The easiest way to estimate the cost of equity capital is to use the dividend growth model we developed in Chapter 8. Recall that, under the assumption that the firm's dividend will grow at a constant rate, g, the price per share of the stock, P_0, can be written as:

$$P_0 = \frac{D_0 \times (1 + g)}{R_E - g} = \frac{D_1}{R_E - g}$$

where D_0 is the dividend just paid and D_1 is the next period's projected dividend. Notice that we have used the symbol R_E (the E stands for equity) for the required return on the stock.

As we discussed in Chapter 8, we can rearrange this to solve for R_E as follows:

$$R_E = D_1/P_0 + g$$

Because R_E is the return that the shareholders require on the stock, it can be interpreted as the firm's cost of equity capital.

Implementing the Approach   To estimate R_E using the dividend growth model approach, we obviously need three pieces of information: P_0, D_0, and g.[2] Of these, for a publicly traded, dividend-paying company, the first two can be observed directly, so they are easily obtained. Only the third component, the expected growth rate for dividends, must be estimated.

To illustrate how we estimate R_E, suppose Greater States Public Service, a large public utility, paid a dividend of $4 per share last year. The stock currently sells for $60 per share. You estimate that the dividend will grow steadily at a rate of 6 percent per year into the indefinite future. What is the cost of equity capital for Greater States?

Using the dividend growth model, we can calculate that the expected dividend for the coming year, D_1, is:

$$
\begin{aligned}
D_1 &= D_0 \times (1 + g) \\
&= \$4 \times 1.06 \\
&= \$4.24
\end{aligned}
$$

Given this, the cost of equity, R_E, is:

$$
\begin{aligned}
R_E &= D_1/P_0 + g \\
&= \$4.24/\$60 + .06 \\
&= .1307, \text{ or } 13.07\%
\end{aligned}
$$

The cost of equity is 13.07 percent.

Estimating g   To use the dividend growth model, we must come up with an estimate for g, the growth rate. There are essentially two ways of doing this: (1) Use historical growth rates or (2) use analysts' forecasts of future growth rates. Analysts' forecasts are available from a variety of sources. Naturally, different sources will have different estimates, so one approach might be to obtain multiple estimates and then average them.

Alternatively, we might observe dividends for the previous, say, five years, calculate the year-to-year growth rates, and average them. For example, suppose we observe the following for some company:

Year	Dividend
2013	$1.10
2014	1.20
2015	1.35
2016	1.40
2017	1.55

Growth estimates can be found at **www.zacks.com.**

We can calculate the percentage change in the dividend for each year as follows:

Year	Dividend	Dollar Change	Percentage Change
2013	$1.10	—	—
2014	1.20	$.10	9.09%
2015	1.35	.15	12.50
2016	1.40	.05	3.70
2017	1.55	.15	10.71

---

[2]Notice that if we have D_0 and g, we can simply calculate D_1 by multiplying D_0 by $(1 + g)$.

Notice that we calculated the change in the dividend on a year-to-year basis and then expressed the change as a percentage. In 2014 for example, the dividend rose from $1.10 to $1.20, an increase of $.10. This represents a $.10/$1.10 = .0909, or 9.09% increase.

If we average the four growth rates, the result is (.0909 + .1250 + .0370 + .1071)/4 = .09, or 9%, so we could use this as an estimate for the expected growth rate, g. Notice that this 9 percent growth rate we have calculated is a simple, or arithmetic, average. Going back to Chapter 12, we also could calculate a geometric growth rate. Here, the dividend grows from $1.10 to $1.55 over a four-year period. What's the compound, or geometric, growth rate? See if you don't agree that it's 8.95 percent; you can view this as a simple time value of money problem where $1.10 is the present value and $1.55 is the future value.

As usual, the geometric average (8.95 percent) is lower than the arithmetic average (9 percent), but the difference here is not likely to be of any practical significance. In general, if the dividend has grown at a relatively steady rate, as we assume when we use this approach, then it can't make much difference which way we calculate the average dividend growth rate.

Advantages and Disadvantages of the Approach   The primary advantage of the dividend growth model approach is its simplicity. It is both easy to understand and easy to use. There are a number of associated practical problems and disadvantages.

First and foremost, the dividend growth model is obviously applicable only to companies that pay dividends. This means that the approach is useless in many cases. Furthermore, even for companies that pay dividends, the key underlying assumption is that the dividend grows at a constant rate. As our previous example illustrates, this will never be *exactly* the case. More generally, the model is really applicable only to cases in which reasonably steady growth is likely to occur.

A second problem is that the estimated cost of equity is very sensitive to the estimated growth rate. For a given stock price, an upward revision of g by just one percentage point, for example, increases the estimated cost of equity by at least a full percentage point. Because D_1 will probably be revised upward as well, the increase will actually be somewhat larger than that.

Finally, this approach really does not explicitly consider risk. Unlike the SML approach (which we consider next), there is no direct adjustment for the riskiness of the investment. For example, there is no allowance for the degree of certainty or uncertainty surrounding the estimated growth rate for dividends. As a result, it is difficult to say whether or not the estimated return is commensurate with the level of risk.[3]

THE SML APPROACH

In Chapter 13, we discussed the security market line, or SML. Our primary conclusion was that the required or expected return on a risky investment depends on three things:

1. The risk-free rate, R_f.
2. The market risk premium, $E(R_M) - R_f$.
3. The systematic risk of the asset relative to average, which we called its beta coefficient, β.

Using the SML, we can write the expected return on the company's equity, $E(R_E)$, as:

$$E(R_E) = R_f + \beta_E \times [E(R_M) - R_f]$$

where β_E is the estimated beta. To make the SML approach consistent with the dividend growth model, we will drop the Es denoting expectations and henceforth write the required return from the SML, R_E, as:

$$R_E = R_f + \beta_E \times (R_M - R_f)$$

14.2

---
[3]There is an implicit adjustment for risk because the current stock price is used. All other things being equal, the higher the risk, the lower is the stock price. Further, the lower the stock price, the greater is the cost of equity, again assuming all the other information is the same.

Implementing the Approach

To use the SML approach, we need a risk-free rate, R_f, an estimate of the market risk premium, $R_M - R_f$, and an estimate of the relevant beta, β_E. In Chapter 12, we saw that one estimate of the market risk premium (based on large common stocks) is about 7 percent. U.S. Treasury bills are paying about .40 percent as this chapter is being written, so we will use this as our risk-free rate. Beta coefficients for publicly traded companies are widely available.[4]

Betas and T-bill rates both can be found at **www.bloomberg.com**.

To illustrate, in Chapter 13, we saw that Tesla had an estimated beta of 1.19 (Table 13.8). We could estimate Tesla's cost of equity as:

$$R_{Tesla} = R_f + \beta_{Tesla} \times (R_M - R_f)$$
$$= .0040 + 1.19 \times .07$$
$$= .0873, \text{ or } 8.73\%$$

Using the SML approach, we calculate that Tesla's cost of equity is about 8.73 percent.

Advantages and Disadvantages of the Approach

The SML approach has two primary advantages. First, it explicitly adjusts for risk. Second, it is applicable to companies other than just those with steady dividend growth. It may be useful in a wider variety of circumstances.

There are drawbacks, of course. The SML approach requires that two things be estimated: The market risk premium and the beta coefficient. To the extent that our estimates are poor, the resulting cost of equity will be inaccurate. For example, our estimate of the market risk premium, 7 percent, is based on about 100 years of returns on particular stock portfolios and markets. Using different time periods or different stocks and markets could result in very different estimates.

Finally, as with the dividend growth model, we essentially rely on the past to predict the future when we use the SML approach. Economic conditions can change quickly; so as always, the past may not be a good guide to the future. In the best of all worlds, both approaches (the dividend growth model and the SML) are applicable and the two result in similar answers. If this happens, we might have some confidence in our estimates. We might also wish to compare the results to those for other similar companies as a reality check.

---

[4]We can also estimate beta coefficients directly by using historical data. For a discussion of how to do this, see Chapters 10, 11, and 13 in S. A. Ross, R. W. Westerfield, J. J. Jaffe, and B. D. Jordan, *Corporate Finance*, 11th ed. (New York: McGraw-Hill, 2016).

The Cost of Equity	**EXAMPLE 14.1**

Suppose stock in Alpha Air Freight has a beta of 1.2. The market risk premium is 7 percent, and the risk-free rate is 6 percent. Alpha's last dividend was $2 per share, and the dividend is expected to grow at 8 percent indefinitely. The stock currently sells for $30. What is Alpha's cost of equity capital?

We can start off by using the SML. Doing this, we find that the expected return on the common stock of Alpha Air Freight is:

$$R_E = R_f + \beta_E \times (R_M - R_f)$$
$$= .06 + 1.2 \times .07$$
$$= .144, \text{ or } 14.4\%$$

This suggests that 14.4 percent is Alpha's cost of equity. We next use the dividend growth model. The projected dividend is $D_0 \times (1 + g) = \$2 \times 1.08 = \$2.16$, so the expected return using this approach is:

$$R_E = D_1/P_0 + g$$
$$= \$2.16/\$30 + .08$$
$$= .152, \text{ or } 15.2\%$$

Our two estimates are reasonably close, so we might just average them to find that Alpha's cost of equity is approximately 14.8 percent.

Concept Questions

14.2a What do we mean when we say that a corporation's cost of equity capital is 16 percent?

14.2b What are two approaches to estimating the cost of equity capital?

14.3 The Costs of Debt and Preferred Stock

In addition to ordinary equity, firms use debt and, to a lesser extent, preferred stock to finance their investments. As we discuss next, determining the costs of capital associated with these sources of financing is much easier than determining the cost of equity.

THE COST OF DEBT

cost of debt
The return that lenders require on the firm's debt.

The **cost of debt** is the return the firm's creditors demand on new borrowing. In principle, we could determine the beta for the firm's debt and then use the SML to estimate the required return on debt just as we estimated the required return on equity. This isn't really necessary, however.

Unlike a firm's cost of equity, its cost of debt can normally be observed either directly or indirectly: The cost of debt is the interest rate the firm must pay on new borrowing, and we can observe interest rates in the financial markets. For example, if the firm already has bonds outstanding, then the yield to maturity on those bonds is the market-required rate on the firm's debt.

Alternatively, if we know that the firm's bonds are rated, say, AA, then we can find the interest rate on newly issued AA-rated bonds. Either way, there is no need to estimate a beta for the debt because we can directly observe the rate we want to know.

There is one thing to be careful about, though. The coupon rate on the firm's outstanding debt is irrelevant here. That rate tells us roughly what the firm's cost of debt was back when the bonds were issued, not what the cost of debt is today.[5] This is why we have to look at the yield on the debt in today's marketplace. For consistency with our other notation, we will use the symbol R_D for the cost of debt.

EXAMPLE 14.2 **The Cost of Debt**

Suppose the General Tool Company issued a 30-year, 7 percent bond 8 years ago. The bond is currently selling for 96 percent of its face value, or $960. What is General Tool's cost of debt?

Going back to Chapter 7, we need to calculate the yield to maturity on this bond. Because the bond is selling at a discount, the yield is apparently greater than 7 percent, but not much greater because the discount is fairly small. You can check to see that the yield to maturity is about 7.37 percent, assuming annual coupons. General Tool's cost of debt, R_D, is 7.37 percent.

THE COST OF PREFERRED STOCK

Determining the *cost of preferred stock* is quite straightforward. As we discussed in Chapters 6 and 8, preferred stock has a fixed dividend paid every period forever, so a share of preferred stock is essentially a perpetuity. The cost of preferred stock, R_P, is thus:

$$R_P = D/P_0$$

[14.3]

[5]The firm's cost of debt based on its historical borrowing is sometimes called the *embedded debt cost*.

where D is the fixed dividend and P_0 is the current price per share of the preferred stock. Notice that the cost of preferred stock is equal to the dividend yield on the preferred stock. Alternatively, because preferred stocks are rated in much the same way as bonds, the cost of preferred stock can be estimated by observing the required returns on other, similarly rated shares of preferred stock.

Alabama Power Co.'s Cost of Preferred Stock   **EXAMPLE 14.3**

On January 2, 2018, Alabama Power Co. had two issues of ordinary preferred stock with a $100 par value that traded on the NYSE. One issue paid $4.64 annually per share and sold for $99.70 per share. The other paid $4.92 per share annually and sold for $98.97 per share. What is Alabama Power's cost of preferred stock?

Using the first issue, we calculate that the cost of preferred stock is:

$R_P = D/P_0$
     $= \$4.64/\$99.70$
     $= .0465$, or 4.65%

Using the second issue, we calculate that the cost is:

$R_P = D/P_0$
     $= \$4.92/98.97$
     $= .0497$, or 4.97%

So, Alabama Power's cost of preferred stock appears to be about 4.81 percent.

Concept Questions

14.3a   Why is the coupon rate a bad estimate of a firm's cost of debt?
14.3b   How can the cost of debt be calculated?
14.3c   How can the cost of preferred stock be calculated?

The Weighted Average Cost of Capital   14.4

Now that we have the costs associated with the main sources of capital the firm employs, we need to worry about the specific mix. As we mentioned earlier, we will take this mix, which is the firm's capital structure, as given for now. Also, we will focus mostly on debt and ordinary equity in this discussion.

In Chapter 3, we mentioned that financial analysts frequently focus on a firm's total capitalization, which is the sum of its long-term debt and equity. This is particularly true in determining cost of capital; short-term liabilities are often ignored in the process. We will not explicitly distinguish between total value and total capitalization in the following discussion; the general approach is applicable with either.

THE CAPITAL STRUCTURE WEIGHTS

We will use the symbol E (for equity) to stand for the *market* value of the firm's equity. We calculate this by taking the number of shares outstanding and multiplying it by the price per share. Similarly, we will use the symbol D (for debt) to stand for the *market* value of the firm's debt. For long-term debt, we calculate this by multiplying the market price of a single bond by the number of bonds outstanding.

Excel Master It!
Excel Master coverage online

If there are multiple bond issues (as there normally would be), we repeat this calculation of D for each and then add up the results. If there is debt that is not publicly traded (because it is held by a life insurance company, for example), we must observe the yield on similar publicly traded debt and then estimate the market value of the privately held debt using this yield as the discount rate. For short-term debt, the book (accounting) values and market values should be somewhat similar, so we might use the book values as estimates of the market values.

Finally, we will use the symbol V (for value) to stand for the combined market value of the debt and equity:

$$V = E + D$$

14.4

If we divide both sides by V, we can calculate the percentages of the total capital represented by the debt and equity:

$$100\% = E/V + D/V$$

14.5

These percentages can be interpreted just like portfolio weights, and they are often called the *capital structure weights*.

For example, if the total market value of a company's stock were calculated as $200 million and the total market value of the company's debt were calculated as $50 million, then the combined value would be $250 million. Of this total, $E/V = \$200$ million/$\$250$ million $= .80$, so 80 percent of the firm's financing would be equity and the remaining 20 percent would be debt.

We emphasize here that the correct way to proceed is to use the *market* values of the debt and equity. Under certain circumstances, such as when calculating figures for a privately owned company, it may not be possible to get reliable estimates of these quantities. In this case, we might go ahead and use the accounting values for debt and equity. Although this would probably be better than nothing, we would have to take the answer with a grain of salt.

TAXES AND THE WEIGHTED AVERAGE COST OF CAPITAL

There is one final issue we need to discuss. Recall that we are always concerned with aftertax cash flows. If we are determining the discount rate appropriate to those cash flows, then the discount rate also needs to be expressed on an aftertax basis.

As we discussed previously in various places in this book (and as we will discuss later), the interest paid by a corporation is deductible for tax purposes. Payments to stockholders, such as dividends, are not. What this means, effectively, is that the government pays some of the interest. In determining an aftertax discount rate, we need to distinguish between the pretax and the aftertax cost of debt.

To illustrate, suppose a firm borrows $1 million at 9 percent interest. The corporate tax rate is 21 percent. What is the aftertax interest rate on this loan? The total interest bill will be $90,000 per year. This amount is tax deductible, however, so the $90,000 interest reduces the firm's tax bill by $.21 \times \$90,000 = \$18,900$. The aftertax interest bill is $\$90,000 - 18,900 = \$71,100$. The aftertax interest rate is $\$71,100/\$1$ million $= .0711$, or 7.11%.

To get a feel for actual, industry-level WACCs, visit Professor Aswath Damodaran at **pages .stern.nyu.edu/~adamodar/** and look for "cost of capital by sector."

Notice that, in general, the aftertax interest rate is equal to the pretax rate multiplied by 1 minus the tax rate. If we use the symbol T_C to stand for the corporate tax rate, then the aftertax rate can be written as $R_D \times (1 - T_C)$. Using the numbers from the preceding paragraph, we find that the aftertax interest rate is $9\% \times (1 - .21) = 7.11\%$.

The Tax Cuts and Jobs Act of 2017 placed limitations on the amount of interest that can be deducted in certain situations. Throughout this chapter, we will assume all interest can be deducted. We will discuss this issue in greater detail in a subsequent chapter.

Bringing together the various topics we have discussed in this chapter, we now have the capital structure weights along with the cost of equity and the aftertax cost of debt. To calculate the firm's overall cost of capital, we multiply the capital structure weights by the associated costs and add them up. The total is the **weighted average cost of capital (WACC)**:

$$\textbf{WACC} = (\textbf{\textit{E/V}}) \times \textbf{\textit{R}}_E + (\textbf{\textit{D/V}}) \times \textbf{\textit{R}}_D \times (\textbf{1} - \textbf{\textit{T}}_c)$$

weighted average cost of capital (WACC)
The weighted average of the cost of equity and the aftertax cost of debt.

This WACC has a straightforward interpretation. It is the overall return the firm must earn on its existing assets to maintain the value of its stock. It is also the required return on any investments by the firm that have essentially the same risks as existing operations. So, if we were evaluating the cash flows from a proposed expansion of our existing operations, this is the discount rate we would use.

If a firm uses preferred stock in its capital structure, then our expression for the WACC needs a simple extension. If we define *P/V* as the percentage of the firm's financing that comes from preferred stock, then the WACC is:

$$\textbf{WACC} = (\textbf{\textit{E/V}}) \times \textbf{\textit{R}}_E + (\textbf{\textit{P/V}}) \times \textbf{\textit{R}}_P + (\textbf{\textit{D/V}}) \times \textbf{\textit{R}}_D \times (\textbf{1} - \textbf{\textit{T}}_c)$$

where R_p is the cost of preferred stock.

Calculating the WACC | EXAMPLE 14.4

The B.B. Lean Co. has 1.4 million shares of stock outstanding. The stock currently sells for $20 per share. The firm's debt is publicly traded and was recently quoted at 93 percent of face value. It has a total face value of $5 million, and it is currently priced to yield 11 percent. The risk-free rate is 8 percent, and the market risk premium is 7 percent. You've estimated that Lean has a beta of .74. If the corporate tax rate is 21 percent, what is the WACC of Lean Co.?

We can first determine the cost of equity and the cost of debt. Using the SML, we find that the cost of equity is 8% + .74 × 7% = 13.18%. The total value of the equity is 1.4 million × $20 = $28 million. The pretax cost of debt is the current yield to maturity on the outstanding debt, 11 percent. The debt sells for 93 percent of its face value, so its current market value is .93 × $5 million = $4.65 million. The total market value of the equity and debt together is $28 million + 4.65 million = $32.65 million.

From here, we can calculate the WACC easily enough. The percentage of equity used by Lean to finance its operations is $28 million/$32.65 million = .8576, or 85.76%. Because the weights have to add up to 1, the percentage of debt is 1 − .8576 = .1424, or 14.24%. The WACC is:

$$
\begin{aligned}
\text{WACC} &= (E/V) \times R_E + (D/V) \times R_D \times (1 - T_c) \\
&= .8576 \times .1318 + .1424 \times .11 \times (1 - .21) \\
&= .1254, \text{ or } 12.54\%
\end{aligned}
$$

B.B. Lean has an overall weighted average cost of capital of 12.54 percent.

CALCULATING THE WACC FOR EASTMAN CHEMICAL

In this section, we illustrate how to calculate the WACC for Eastman Chemical Co., a leading international chemical company and maker of plastics such as those used in soft drink containers. It was created in 1993, when its former parent company, Eastman Kodak, split off the division as a separate company. Our goal is to take you through, on a step-by-step basis, the process of finding and using the information needed from online sources. As you will see, there is a fair amount of detail involved, but the necessary information is, for the most part, readily available.

Eastman's Cost of Equity   Our first stop is the main screen for Eastman available at finance.yahoo.com (ticker: EMN). As of early 2017, here's what it looked like:

Eastman Chemical Company (EMN)
NYSE - NYSE Real Time Price. Currency in USD

☆ Add to watchlist

77.72 -1.35 (-1.71%)
As of 2:01PM EST. Market open.

| Summary | Conversations | Statistics | Profile | Financials | Options | Holders | Historical Data | Analysts |

Previous Close	79.07	Market Cap	11.41B	
Open	78.71	Beta	1.35	
Bid	0.00 x	PE Ratio (TTM)	13.09	
Ask	0.00 x	EPS (TTM)	5.94	
Day's Range	76.99 - 79.23	Earnings Date	Jan 26, 2017	
52 Week Range	56.03 - 79.23	Dividend & Yield	2.04 (2.64%)	
Volume	730,190	Ex-Dividend Date	N/A	
Avg. Volume	1,463,619	1y Target Est	82.24	

1D 5D 1M 6M 1Y 2Y 5Y 10Y MAX   ↗ Interactive chart

Next, we went to the "Statistics" screen. According to this screen, Eastman has 146.75 million shares of stock outstanding. The book value per share is $29.62, but the stock sells for $77.72. Total equity is therefore about $4.347 billion on a book value basis, but it is closer to $11.405 billion on a market value basis.

Balance Sheet

Total Cash (mrq)	207M
Total Cash Per Share (mrq)	1.41
Total Debt (mrq)	6.68B
Total Debt/Equity (mrq)	148.01
Current Ratio (mrq)	1.32
Book Value Per Share (mrq)	29.62

Stock Price History

Beta	1.35
52-Week Change [3]	25.49%
S&P500 52-Week Change [3]	17.36%
52 Week High [3]	79.23
52 Week Low [3]	56.03
50-Day Moving Average [3]	76.18
200-Day Moving Average [3]	69.95

Share Statistics

Avg Vol (3 month) [3]	1.46M
Avg Vol (10 day) [3]	1.33M
Shares Outstanding [5]	146.75M
Float	146M
% Held by Insiders [1]	0.68%
% Held by Institutions [1]	85.50%
Shares Short [3]	2.94M
Short Ratio [3]	1.98
Short % of Float [3]	2.00%
Shares Short (prior month) [3]	2.95M

To estimate Eastman's cost of equity, we will assume a market risk premium of 7 percent, similar to what we calculated in Chapter 12. Eastman's beta on Yahoo! is 1.35, which is higher than the beta of the average stock. To check this number, we went to the well-known Value Line *Investment Survey*, which uses an approach that moderates very large and very small betas. Here, the beta is reported as 1.30, so we will stick with the Yahoo! estimate. According to the Bonds section of finance.yahoo.com, T-bills were paying about .45 percent. Using the CAPM to estimate the cost of equity, we find:

$$R_E = .0045 + 1.35(.07) = .0990, \text{ or } 9.90\%$$

Eastman has paid dividends for only a few years, so calculating the growth rate for the dividend discount model is problematic. However, under the Analysts link at finance .yahoo.com, we found the following:

Growth Estimates	EMN
Current Qtr.	-6.30%
Next Qtr.	4.10%
Current Year	-7.40%
Next Year	8.20%
Next 5 Years (per annum)	5.06%
Past 5 Years (per annum)	11.06%

Analysts estimate the growth in earnings per share for the company will be 5.06 percent for the next five years. For now, we will use this growth rate in the dividend discount model to estimate the cost of equity; the link between earnings growth and dividends is discussed in a later chapter. The estimated cost of equity using the dividend discount model is:

$$R_E = \frac{\$2.04(1 + .0506)}{77.72} + .0506 = .0782, \text{ or } 7.82\%$$

Notice that our two estimates for the cost of equity are not identical. This is essentially always the case. Remember that each method of estimating the cost of equity relies on different assumptions, so different estimates of the cost of equity should not surprise us. If the estimates are different, there are two simple solutions. First, we could ignore one of the estimates. In this case, we would look at each estimate to see if one of them seemed too high or too low to be reasonable. Second, we could average the two estimates. For Eastman, our estimates of 9.90 percent and 7.82 percent are relatively close, so we would average them to get 8.86 percent as the cost of equity.

Eastman's Cost of Debt   Eastman has 13 relatively long-term bond issues that account for essentially all of its long-term debt. To calculate the cost of debt, we will have to combine these 13 issues. What we will do is compute a weighted average. We went to www.finra.org/marketdata to find quotes on the bonds. We should note here that finding the yield to maturity for all of a company's outstanding bond issues on a single day is unusual. If you remember our previous discussion of bonds, the bond market is not as liquid as the stock market; on many days, individual bond issues may not trade. To find the book value of the bonds, we went to www.sec.gov and found the 10-Q report dated September 30, 2016, and filed with the SEC on November 4, 2016. The basic information is as follows:

Coupon Rate	Maturity	Book Value (face value, in millions)	Price (% of par)	Yield to Maturity
2.40%	2017	$ 499	100.675	.920%
6.30	2018	166	109.498	1.077
5.50	2019	249	108.301	2.462
2.70	2020	795	101.276	2.245
4.50	2021	249	105.684	2.897
3.60	2022	890	102.866	3.014
1.50	2023	607	90.484	3.168
7.25	2024	244	124.376	3.322
7.625	2024	54	128.187	3.311
3.80	2025	792	101.611	3.565
7.60	2027	222	134.007	3.548
4.80	2042	492	102.564	4.626
4.65	2044	870	97.750	4.797
		$6,129		

To calculate the weighted average cost of debt, we take the percentage of the total debt represented by each issue and multiply by the yield on the issue. We then add to get the overall weighted average debt cost. We use both book values and market values here for comparison. The results of the calculations are as follows:

Coupon Rate	Book Value (face value, in millions)	Percentage of Total	Market Value (in millions)	Percentage of Total	Yield to Maturity	Book Values	Market Values
2.40%	$ 499	.08	$ 502.37	.08	.92%	.07%	.07%
6.30	166	.03	181.77	.03	1.08	.03	.03
5.50	249	.04	269.67	.04	2.46	.10	.11
2.70	795	.13	805.14	.13	2.25	.29	.29
4.50	249	.04	263.15	.04	2.90	.12	.12
3.60	890	.15	915.51	.14	3.01	.44	.44
1.50	607	.10	549.24	.09	3.17	.31	.28
7.25	244	.04	303.48	.05	3.32	.13	.16
7.625	54	.01	69.22	.01	3.31	.03	.04
3.80	792	.13	804.76	.13	3.57	.46	.45
7.60	222	.04	297.50	.05	3.55	.13	.17
4.80	492	.08	504.61	.08	4.63	.37	.37
4.65	875	.14	850.43	.13	4.80	.68	.65
	$6,129	1.00	$6,316.84	1.00		3.17%	3.16%

As these calculations show, Eastman's cost of debt is 3.17 percent on a book value basis and 3.16 percent on a market value basis. For Eastman, whether market values or book values are used makes no difference. The reason is that the market values and book values are similar. This will often be the case and explains why companies frequently use book values for debt in WACC calculations. Also, Eastman has no preferred stock, so we don't need to consider its cost.

Eastman's WACC   We now have the various pieces necessary to calculate Eastman's WACC. First, we need to calculate the capital structure weights. On a book value basis, Eastman's equity and debt are worth $4.347 billion and $6.129 billion, respectively. The total value is $10.476 billion, so the equity and debt weights are $4.347 billion/$10.476 billion = .41 and $6.129 billion/$10.476 billion = .59, respectively. Assuming a tax rate of 21 percent, Eastman's WACC is:

$$\text{WACC} = .41 \times .0886 + .59 \times .0317 \times (1 - .21) = .0514, \text{ or } 5.14\%$$

Using book value capital structure weights (and more decimal points than shown here), we get about 5.14 percent for Eastman's WACC.

If we use market value weights, the WACC will be higher. To see why, notice that on a market value basis, Eastman's equity and debt are worth $11.405 billion and $6.317 billion, respectively. The capital structure weights are therefore $11.405 billion/$17.722 billion = .64 and $6.317 billion/$17.722 billion = .36, so the equity percentage is much higher. With these weights (and more decimal points than shown here), Eastman's WACC is:

$$\text{WACC} = .64 \times .0886 + .36 \times .0316 \times (1 - .21) = .0659, \text{ or } 6.59\%$$

Using market value weights, we get about 6.59 percent for Eastman's WACC, which is noticeably larger than the 5.14 percent WACC we got using book value weights.

As this example illustrates, using book values can lead to trouble, particularly if equity book values are used. Going back to Chapter 3, recall that we discussed the market-to-book

WORK THE WEB

So how does our estimate of the WACC for Eastman Chemical compare to others? One place to find estimates for WACC is www.valuepro.net. We went there and found the following information for Eastman:

Online Valuation for EMN - 1 / 12 / 2017

Intrinsic Stock Value	130.74	Recalculate Value Another Stock

Excess Return Period (yrs)	10	Depreciation Rate (% of Rev)	4.44
Revenues ($mil)	8588	Investment Rate (% of Rev)	5.8
Growth Rate (%)	11.5	Working Capital (% of Rev)	9.21
Net Oper. Profit Margin (%)	14.68	Short-Term Assets ($mil)	2737
Tax Rate (%)	32.583	Short-Term Liab. ($mil)	1335
Stock Price ($)	71.99	Equity Risk Premium (%)	3
Shares Outstanding (mil)	154.8	Company Beta	1.365
10-Yr Treasury Yield (%)	5	Value Debt Out. ($mil)	4779
Bond Spread Treasury (%)	1.5	Value Pref. Stock Out. ($mil)	0
Preferred Stock Yield (%)	7.5	Company WACC (%)	7.68

As you can see, ValuePro estimates the WACC (cost of capital) for Eastman as 7.68 percent, which is a little over one percent higher than our estimate of 6.59 percent. However, different inputs were used in the computations. For example, ValuePro uses an equity risk premium of only 3 percent. ValuePro also used the historic tax rate, which we chose not to change. Calculating WACC requires the estimation of various inputs, and you must use your best judgment in these estimates.

Questions

1. *Go to www.valuepro.net and look up the current WACC for Eastman Chemical on this website. How has the WACC changed? What are the possible reasons for the change?*
2. *Celgene (CELG) is a biopharmaceutical company. Would you expect the WACC for this company to be higher or lower than the WACC for Eastman Chemical? Why? Go to www.valuepro.net and find the estimated WACC for CELG. Was your assumption correct?*

ratio (the ratio of market value per share to book value per share). This ratio is usually substantially bigger than 1. For Eastman, for example, verify that it's about 2.62; so book values significantly overstate the percentage of Eastman's financing that comes from debt. In addition, if we were computing a WACC for a company that did not have publicly traded stock, we would try to come up with a suitable market-to-book ratio by looking at similar, publicly traded companies, and we would then use this ratio to adjust the book value of the company under consideration. As we have seen, failure to do so can lead to significant underestimation of the WACC.

Our nearby *Work the Web* box explains more about the WACC and related topics.

SOLVING THE WAREHOUSE PROBLEM AND SIMILAR CAPITAL BUDGETING PROBLEMS

Now we can use the WACC to solve the warehouse problem we posed at the beginning of the chapter. However, before we rush to discount the cash flows at the WACC to estimate NPV, we need to make sure we are doing the right thing.

Going back to first principles, we need to find an alternative in the financial markets that is comparable to the warehouse renovation. To be comparable, an alternative must be of the same level of risk as the warehouse project. Projects that have the same risk are said to be in the same risk class.

The WACC for a firm reflects the risk and the target capital structure of the firm's existing assets as a whole. As a result, strictly speaking, the firm's WACC is the appropriate discount rate only if the proposed investment is a replica of the firm's existing operating activities.

In broader terms, whether or not we can use the firm's WACC to value the warehouse project depends on whether the warehouse project is in the same risk class as the firm. We will assume that this project is an integral part of the overall business of the firm. In such cases, it is natural to think that the cost savings will be as risky as the general cash flows of the firm, and the project will be in the same risk class as the overall firm. More generally, projects like the warehouse renovation that are intimately related to the firm's existing operations are often viewed as being in the same risk class as the overall firm.

We can now see what the president should do. Suppose the firm has a target debt-equity ratio of 1/3. From Chapter 3, we know that a debt-equity ratio of $D/E = 1/3$ implies that E/V is .75 and D/V is .25. The cost of debt is 10 percent, and the cost of equity is 20 percent. Assuming a 21 percent tax rate, the WACC will be:

$$
\begin{aligned}
\text{WACC} &= (E/V) \times R_E + (D/V) \times R_D \times (1 - T_C) \\
&= .75 \times 20\% + .25 \times 10\% \times (1 - .21) \\
&= .1698, \text{ or } 16.98\%
\end{aligned}
$$

Recall that the warehouse project had a cost of $50 million and expected aftertax cash flows (the cost savings) of $12 million per year for six years. The NPV (in millions) is:

$$
\text{NPV} = -\$50 + \frac{12}{(1 + \text{WACC})^1} + \cdots + \frac{12}{(1 + \text{WACC})^6}
$$

Because the cash flows are in the form of an ordinary annuity, we can calculate this NPV using 16.65 percent (the WACC) as the discount rate as follows:

$$
\begin{aligned}
\text{NPV} &= -\$50 + 12 \times \frac{1 - [1/(1 + .1698)^6]}{.1698} \\
&= -\$50 + 12 \times 3.5915 \\
&= -\$6.90
\end{aligned}
$$

Should the firm take on the warehouse renovation? The project has a negative NPV using the firm's WACC. This means that the financial markets offer superior projects in the same risk class (namely, the firm itself). The answer is clear: The project should be rejected. For future reference, our discussion of the WACC is summarized in Table 14.1.

TABLE 14.1

Summary of Capital Cost Calculations

I.　The Cost of Equity, R_E

A.　Dividend growth model approach (from Chapter 8):

$$R_E = D_1/P_0 + g$$

where D_1 is the expected dividend in one period, g is the dividend growth rate, and P_0 is the current stock price.

B.　SML approach (from Chapter 13):

$$R_E = R_f + \beta_E \times (R_M - R_f)$$

where R_f is the risk-free rate, R_M is the expected return on the overall market, and β_E is the systematic risk of the equity.

II.　The Cost of Debt, R_D

A.　For a firm with publicly held debt, the cost of debt can be measured as the yield to maturity on the outstanding debt. The coupon rate is irrelevant. Yield to maturity is covered in Chapter 7.

B.　If the firm has no publicly traded debt, then the cost of debt can be measured as the yield to maturity on similarly rated bonds (bond ratings are discussed in Chapter 7).

III.　The Weighted Average Cost of Capital, WACC

A.　The firm's WACC is the overall required return on the firm as a whole. It is the appropriate discount rate to use for cash flows similar in risk to those of the overall firm.

B.　The WACC is calculated as:

$$\text{WACC} = (E/V) \times R_E + (D/V) \times R_D \times (1 - T_C)$$

where T_C is the corporate tax rate, E is the *market* value of the firm's equity, D is the *market* value of the firm's debt, and $V = E + D$. Note that E/V is the percentage of the firm's financing (in market value terms) that is equity, and D/V is the percentage that is debt.

EXAMPLE 14.5	**Using the WACC**

A firm is considering a project that will result in initial aftertax cash savings of $5 million at the end of the first year. These savings will grow at the rate of 5 percent per year. The firm has a debt-equity ratio of .5, a cost of equity of 29.2 percent, and a cost of debt of 10 percent. The cost-saving proposal is closely related to the firm's core business, so it is viewed as having the same risk as the overall firm. Should the firm take on the project?

Assuming a 21 percent tax rate, the firm should take on this project if it costs less than $30 million. To see this, first note that the PV is:

$$PV = \frac{\$5 \text{ million}}{\text{WACC} - .05}$$

This is an example of a growing perpetuity as discussed in Chapter 6. The WACC is:

$$\begin{aligned} \text{WACC} &= (E/V) \times R_E + (D/V) \times R_D \times (1 - T_C) \\ &= 2/3 \times 29.2\% + 1/3 \times 10\% \times (1 - .21) \\ &= 22.10\% \end{aligned}$$

The PV is thus:

$$PV = \frac{\$5 \text{ million}}{.2210 - .05} = \$29.2 \text{ million}$$

The NPV will be positive only if the cost is less than $29.2 million.

A firm's weighted average cost of capital has important applications other than the discount rate in capital project evaluations. For instance, it is a key ingredient to measure a firm's true economic profit, or what I like to call EVA, standing for economic value added. Accounting rules dictate that the interest expense a company incurs on its debt financing be deducted from its reported profit, but those same rules ironically forbid deducting a charge for the shareholders' funds a firm uses. In economic terms, equity capital is in fact a very costly financing source, because shareholders bear the risk of being paid last, after all other stakeholders and investors are paid first. But according to accountants, shareholders' equity is free.

This egregious oversight has dire practical consequences. For one thing, it means that the profit figure accountants certify to be correct is inherently at odds with the net present value decision rule. For instance, it is a simple matter for management to inflate its reported earnings and earnings per share in ways that actually harm the shareholders by investing capital in projects that earn less than the overall cost of capital but more than the aftertax cost of borrowing money, which amounts to a trivial hurdle in most cases, a couple percentage points at most. In effect, EPS requires management to vault a mere three-foot hurdle when to satisfy shareholders managers must jump a ten-foot hurdle that includes the cost of equity. A prime example of the way accounting profit leads smart managers to do dumb things was Enron, where former top executives Ken Lay and Jeff Skilling boldly declared in the firm's 2000 annual report that they were "laser-focused on earnings per share," and so they were. Bonuses were funded out of book profit, and project developers were paid for signing up new deals and not generating a decent return on investment. Consequently, Enron's EPS was on the rise while its true economic profit—its EVA—measured after deducting the full cost of capital, was plummeting in the years leading up to the firm's demise—the result of massive misallocations of capital to ill-advised energy and new economy projects. The point is, EVA measures economic profit, the profit that actually discounts to net present value, and the maximization of which is every company's most important financial goal; yet, for all its popularity, EPS is just an accounting contrivance that is wholly unrelated to the maximization of shareholder wealth or sending the right decision signals to management.

Starting in the early 1990s, firms around the world—ranging from Coca-Cola, to Briggs & Stratton, Herman Miller, and Eli Lilly in America, Siemens in Germany, Tata Consulting and the Godrej Group out of India, Brahma Beer in Brazil, and many, many more—began to turn to EVA as a new and better way to measure performance and set goals, make decisions and determine bonuses, and to communicate with investors and to teach business and finance basics to managers and employees. Properly tailored and implemented, EVA is a natural way to bring the cost of capital to life and to turn everyone in a company into a capital conscientious, owner-entrepreneur.

Bennett Stewart is a cofounder of Stern Stewart & Co. and also the CEO of EVA Dimensions, a firm providing EVA data, valuation modeling, and hedge fund management. Stewart pioneered the practical development of EVA as chronicled in his original book, The Quest for Value, *and latest book,* Best-Practice EVA.

PERFORMANCE EVALUATION: ANOTHER USE OF THE WACC

Performance evaluation is another use of the WACC. Probably the best-known approach in this area is the economic value added (EVA) method developed by Stern Stewart & Co. Companies such as AT&T, Coca-Cola, Quaker Oats, and Briggs & Stratton are among the firms that have been using EVA as a means of evaluating corporate performance. Similar approaches include market value added (MVA) and shareholder value added (SVA).

Visit **www.sternstewart.com** for more about EVA.

Although the details differ, the basic idea behind EVA and similar strategies is straightforward. Suppose we have $100 million in capital (debt and equity) tied up in our firm, and our overall WACC is 12 percent. If we multiply these together, we get $12 million. Referring back to Chapter 2, if our cash flow from assets is less than this, we are, on an overall basis, destroying value; if cash flow from assets exceeds $12 million, we are creating value.

In practice, evaluation strategies such as these suffer to a certain extent from problems with implementation. For example, it appears that many companies make extensive use of book values for debt and equity in computing cost of capital. Even so, by focusing on value creation, WACC-based evaluation procedures force employees and management to pay attention to the real bottom line: Increasing share prices.

14.5 Divisional and Project Costs of Capital

As we have seen, using the WACC as the discount rate for future cash flows is appropriate only when the proposed investment is similar to the firm's existing activities. This is not as restrictive as it sounds. If we are in the pizza business, for example, and we are thinking of opening a new location, then the WACC is the discount rate to use. The same is true of a retailer thinking of a new store, a manufacturer considering expanding production, or a consumer products company considering expanding its markets.

Despite the usefulness of the WACC as a benchmark, there will clearly be situations in which the cash flows under consideration have risks distinctly different from those of the overall firm. We consider how to cope with this problem next.

THE SML AND THE WACC

When we are evaluating investments with risks that are substantially different from those of the overall firm, use of the WACC will potentially lead to poor decisions. Figure 14.1 illustrates why.

In Figure 14.1, we have plotted an SML corresponding to a risk-free rate of 7 percent and a market risk premium of 8 percent. To keep things simple, we consider an all-equity company with a beta of 1. As we have indicated, the WACC and the cost of equity are exactly equal to 15 percent for this company because there is no debt.

FIGURE 14.1

The Security Market Line (SML) and the Weighted Average Cost of Capital (WACC)

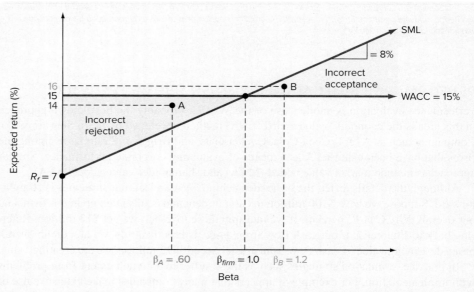

If a firm uses its WACC to make accept–reject decisions for all types of projects, it will have a tendency toward incorrectly accepting risky projects and incorrectly rejecting less risky projects.

Suppose our firm uses its WACC to evaluate all investments. This means that any investment with a return of greater than 15 percent will be accepted and any investment with a return of less than 15 percent will be rejected. We know from our study of risk and return that a desirable investment is one that plots above the SML. As Figure 14.1 illustrates, using the WACC for all types of projects can result in the firm incorrectly accepting relatively risky projects and incorrectly rejecting relatively safe ones.

For example, consider Point A. This project has a beta of $\beta_A = .60$, as compared to the firm's beta of 1.0. It has an expected return of 14 percent. Is this a desirable investment? The answer is yes because its required return is only:

$$\text{Required return} = R_f + \beta_A \times (R_M - R_f)$$
$$= .07 + .60 \times .08$$
$$= .118, \text{ or } 11.8\%$$

If we use the WACC as a cutoff, then this project will be rejected because its return is less than 15 percent. This example illustrates that a firm that uses its WACC as a cutoff will tend to reject profitable projects with risks less than those of the overall firm.

At the other extreme, consider Point B. This project has a beta of $\beta_B = 1.2$. It offers a 16 percent return, which exceeds the firm's cost of capital. This is not a good investment, because, given its level of systematic risk, its return is inadequate. Nonetheless, if we use the WACC to evaluate it, it will appear to be attractive. So the second error that will arise if we use the WACC as a cutoff is that we will tend to make unprofitable investments with risks greater than those of the overall firm. As a consequence, through time, a firm that uses its WACC to evaluate all projects will have a tendency to both accept unprofitable investments and become increasingly risky.

DIVISIONAL COST OF CAPITAL

The same type of problem with the WACC can arise in a corporation with more than one line of business. Imagine a corporation that has two divisions: A regulated electric company and an electronics manufacturing operation. The first of these (the electricity operation) has relatively low risk; the second has relatively high risk.

In this case, the firm's overall cost of capital is really a mixture of two different costs of capital, one for each division. If the two divisions were competing for resources, and the firm used a single WACC as a cutoff, which division would tend to be awarded greater funds for investment?

The answer is that the riskier division would tend to have greater returns (ignoring the greater risk), so it would tend to be the "winner." The less glamorous operation might have great profit potential that would end up being ignored. Large corporations in the United States are aware of this problem, and many work to develop separate divisional costs of capital.

THE PURE PLAY APPROACH

We've seen that using the firm's WACC inappropriately can lead to problems. How can we come up with the appropriate discount rates in such circumstances? Because we cannot observe the returns on these investments, there generally is no direct way of coming up with a beta. Instead, what we must do is examine other investments outside the firm that are in the same risk class as the one we are considering, and use the market-required return on these investments as the discount rate. In other words, we will try to determine what the cost of capital is for such investments by trying to locate some similar investments in the marketplace.

Going back to our electricity division, suppose we wanted to come up with a discount rate to use for that division. What we could do is identify several other electric companies that have publicly traded securities. We might find that a typical electric company has a beta of .80, AA-rated debt, and a capital structure that is about 50 percent debt and 50 percent equity. Using this information, we could develop a WACC for a typical electric company and use this as our discount rate.

Alternatively, if we were considering entering a new line of business, we would try to develop the appropriate cost of capital by looking at the market-required returns on companies already in that business. In the language of Wall Street, a company that focuses on a single line of business is called a *pure play*. If you wanted to bet on the price of crude oil by purchasing common stocks, you would try to identify companies that deal exclusively with this product because they would be the most affected by changes in the price of crude oil. Such companies would be called "pure plays on the price of crude oil."

What we try to do here is to find companies that focus as exclusively as possible on the type of project in which we are interested. Our approach, therefore, is called the **pure play approach** to estimating the required return on an investment. To illustrate, suppose McDonald's decides to enter the cell phone and tablet business with a line of electronics called McPhones. The risks involved are quite different from those in the fast-food business. As a result, McDonald's would need to look at companies already in the consumer electronics business to compute a cost of capital for the new division. An obvious pure play candidate would be Apple, which is predominantly in this line of business. Samsung, on the other hand, would not be as good a choice because it sells more product lines, such as televisions and appliances, which likely have a different level of risk.

In Chapter 3, we discussed the subject of identifying similar companies for comparison purposes. The same problems we described there come up here. The most obvious one is that we may not be able to find any suitable companies. In this case, how to objectively determine a discount rate becomes a difficult question. Even so, the important thing is to be aware of the issue so that we at least reduce the possibility of the kinds of mistakes that can arise when the WACC is used as a cutoff on all investments.

pure play approach
The use of a WACC that is unique to a particular project, based on companies in similar lines of business.

THE SUBJECTIVE APPROACH

Because of the difficulties that exist in objectively establishing discount rates for individual projects, firms often adopt an approach that involves making subjective adjustments to the overall WACC. To illustrate, suppose a firm has an overall WACC of 14 percent. It places all proposed projects into four categories as follows:

Category	Examples	Adjustment Factor	Discount Rate
High risk	New products	+6%	20%
Moderate risk	Cost savings, expansion of existing lines	+0	14
Low risk	Replacement of existing equipment	−4	10
Mandatory	Pollution control equipment	n/a	n/a

n/a = Not applicable.

The effect of this crude partitioning is to assume that all projects either fall into one of three risk classes or else are mandatory. In the last case, the cost of capital is irrelevant because the project must be taken. With the subjective approach, the firm's WACC may change through time as economic conditions change. As this happens, the discount rates for the different types of projects will also change.

Within each risk class, some projects will presumably have more risk than others, and the danger of making incorrect decisions still exists. Figure 14.2 illustrates this point.

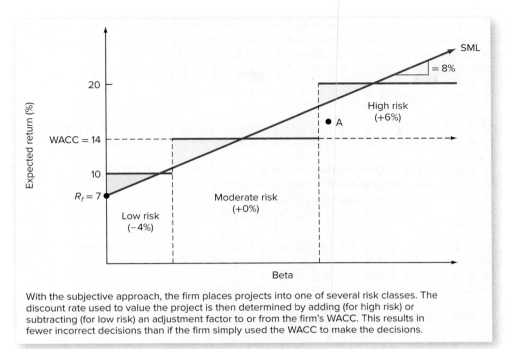

FIGURE 14.2

The Security Market Line (SML) and the Subjective Approach

With the subjective approach, the firm places projects into one of several risk classes. The discount rate used to value the project is then determined by adding (for high risk) or subtracting (for low risk) an adjustment factor to or from the firm's WACC. This results in fewer incorrect decisions than if the firm simply used the WACC to make the decisions.

Comparing Figures 14.1 and 14.2, we see that similar problems exist; but the magnitude of the potential error is less with the subjective approach. The project labeled A would be accepted if the WACC were used, but it is rejected once it is classified as a high-risk investment. What this illustrates is that some risk adjustment, even if it is subjective, is probably better than no risk adjustment.

It would be better, in principle, to objectively determine the required return for each project separately. As a practical matter, it may not be possible to go much beyond subjective adjustments because either the necessary information is unavailable or the cost and effort required are not worthwhile.

Concept Questions

14.5a   What are the likely consequences if a firm uses its WACC to evaluate all proposed investments?

14.5b   What is the pure play approach to determining the appropriate discount rate? When might it be used?

Company Valuation with the WACC   **14.6**

When valuing a company, our approach is the same as the one we used for individual capital projects like the warehouse renovation, but there is one issue we have to deal with. When we look at an entire company, we will often see an interest deduction because the company has borrowed money. But as we have consistently emphasized, interest paid is a financing cost, not an operating cost. However, because interest paid is a tax deductible expense, a company's tax bill is lower than it would have been had the company not used debt financing. We will have much more to say about this in a later chapter.

For now, to calculate cash flow from assets, we need to first calculate what the firm's tax bill would have been if it had not used debt financing. To do that, we take earnings before interest and taxes (EBIT) and multiply it by the firm's tax rate (T_C) to get the firm's "would-have-been" tax bill, which we will call the "adjusted" taxes and label Taxes*:

Taxes* = EBIT × T_c (14.8)

Next, we will calculate cash flow from assets the usual way, except we will use the adjusted taxes. We will call this the "adjusted" cash flow from assets, CFA*, which we calculate as:

CFA* = EBIT + Depreciation − Taxes*   (14.9)
**   − Change in NWC − Capital spending**
**   = EBIT + Depreciation − EBIT × T_c**
**   − Change in NWC − Capital spending**

Our adjusted cash flow, CFA*, is often called "free cash flow," but as we mentioned much earlier in our book, that phrase means different things to different people, so we will stick with CFA* to avoid confusion.

Notice that we could simplify our CFA* calculation a bit by writing it as:

CFA* = EBIT × (1 − T_c) + Depreciation
**   − Change in NWC − Capital spending**

The term EBIT × $(1 - T_C)$ is what net income would have been if the firm had used no debt, and the sum of the first two terms is our bottom-up definition of operating cash flow from Chapter 10.

At this point, if the firm is growing steadily, we can value it using our growing perpetuity formula (as we did earlier in this chapter). For example, suppose you project CFA* for the coming year as $CFA_1^* = \$120$ million. You think this amount will grow indefinitely at $g = 5$ percent per year. You've estimated the firm's WACC to be 9 percent, so the value of the firm today (V_0) is:

$$\text{Firm value today} = V_0 = \frac{CFA_1^*}{WACC - g} = \frac{\$120}{.09 - .05} = \$3 \text{ billion}$$

In sum, valuing a firm is no different from valuing a project, except for the fact that we have to adjust the taxes to remove the effect of any debt financing.

We can also consider the impact of nonconstant growth (as we did in an earlier chapter on stock valuation using the dividend growth model). In this case, we assume that constant growth begins at Time t in the future. In that case, we can write the value of the firm today as:

$$V_0 = \frac{CFA_1^*}{1 + WACC} + \frac{CFA_2^*}{(1 + WACC)^2} + \frac{CFA_3^*}{(1 + WACC)^3} + \cdots$$
$$+ \frac{CFA_t^* + V_t}{(1 + WACC)^t}$$

Here, V_t is the value of the firm at Time t, which we again calculate using the growing perpetuity formula:

$$V_t = \frac{CFA_{t+1}^*}{WACC - g}$$ (14.12)

As always, notice that the tricky part is that to get the value at Time t, we have to use the cash flow that occurs at the end of that period at Time $t + 1$. Also, the value of the firm in the future, V_t, is often referred to as the "terminal value."

Valuing a Company

EXAMPLE 14.6

A guest on the popular show *Great White Tank* is attempting to raise money for her new company, Feline Fancy, which makes cat toys. The potential investor wants to value the company, which is privately held. Because of this, she uses the pure play approach to determine that the appropriate WACC for the company is 8 percent. The relevant tax rate is 21 percent.

Feline Fancy currently has $40 million in debt and 3.5 million shares outstanding. Sales this year are expected to be $30 million, and that amount is expected to grow at 15 percent per year for the following four years. After that, sales are expected to grow at 2 percent indefinitely. EBIT this year will be $10 million. EBIT, depreciation, capital spending, and the change in net working capital will grow at the same rate as sales. What value would you assign to Feline Fancy as a whole? What price per share would you assign?

To value the company, we begin by estimating adjusted cash flow from assets (CFA*) for the next five years. The Year 1 values are the projections in millions for next year:

	Year 1	Year 2	Year 3	Year 4	Year 5
EBIT	$10.00	$11.50	$13.23	$15.21	$17.49
Depreciation	1.50	1.73	1.98	2.28	2.62
Taxes*	2.10	2.42	2.78	3.19	3.67
Change in NWC	.80	.92	1.06	1.22	1.40
Capital spending	2.40	2.76	3.17	3.65	4.20
CFA*	$ 6.20	$ 7.13	$ 8.20	$ 9.43	$10.84

Since the adjusted cash flow from assets will grow at 2 percent after Year 5, the terminal value of the company in Year 5 will be:

$$V_5 = \frac{\$10.84(1 + .02)}{.08 - .02} = \$184.35 \text{ million}$$

We can now find the value of the company today by discounting the first five CFA* values and the terminal value back to the present using the WACC. Doing so, we find:

$$V_0 = \frac{\$6.20}{1 + .08} + \frac{\$7.13}{(1 + .08)^2} + \frac{\$8.20}{(1 + .08)^3} + \frac{\$9.43}{(1 + .08)^4} + \frac{\$10.84 + 184.35}{(1 + .08)^5}$$
$$= \$158.14 \text{ million}$$

To find the value of equity, we subtract the $40 million in debt, resulting in a total equity value of $118.14 million. To find the share price, we divide this by the number of shares (3.5 million), which gives us a share price of:

Price per share = $118.14/3.5 = $33.75

Another common way to calculate the terminal value is to use a target ratio, similar to the way we used the PE and price-sales ratios in Chapter 8. For example, suppose the potential investor believes the appropriate price-sales ratio when the company's growth rate slows is three times. Sales in Year 5 are projected at $30 million × 1.15⁴ = $52.47 million (notice that we compounded the $30 million forward four years because $30 million is sales by the end of Year 1, not sales from last year). So, the new estimated terminal value is:

$$V_5 = 3 \times \$52.47 \text{ million} = \$157.41 \text{ million}$$

With this new terminal value, the value of the company today will be:

$$V_0 = \frac{\$6.20}{1 + .08} + \frac{\$7.13}{(1 + .08)^2} + \frac{\$8.20}{(1 + .08)^3} + \frac{\$9.43}{(1 + .08)^4} + \frac{\$10.84 + 157.41}{(1 + .08)^5}$$
$$= \$139.80 \text{ million}$$

See for yourself if you don't agree that using this terminal value will result in an estimated per share value of $28.52.

14.7 Flotation Costs and the Average Cost of Capital

So far, we have not included issue, or flotation, costs in our discussion of the weighted average cost of capital. If a company accepts a new project, it may be required to issue, or float, new bonds and stocks. This means that the firm will incur some costs, which we call *flotation costs*. The nature and magnitude of flotation costs are discussed in some detail in Chapter 15.

Sometimes it is suggested that the firm's WACC should be adjusted upward to reflect flotation costs. This is really not the best approach because, once again, the required return on an investment depends on the risk of the investment, not the source of the funds. This is not to say that flotation costs should be ignored. Because these costs arise as a consequence of the decision to undertake a project, they are relevant cash flows. We briefly discuss how to include them in project analysis.

THE BASIC APPROACH

We start with a simple case. The Spatt Company, an all-equity firm, has a cost of equity of 20 percent. Because this firm is 100 percent equity, its WACC and its cost of equity are the same. Spatt is contemplating a large-scale, $100 million expansion of its existing operations. The expansion would be funded by selling new stock.

Based on conversations with its investment banker, Spatt believes its flotation costs will run 10 percent of the amount issued. This means that Spatt's proceeds from the equity sale will be only 90 percent of the amount sold. When flotation costs are considered, what is the cost of the expansion?

As we discuss in more detail in Chapter 15, Spatt needs to sell enough equity to raise $100 million *after* covering the flotation costs. In other words:

$100 million = (1 − .10) × Amount raised
Amount raised = $100 million/.90 = $111.11 million

Spatt's flotation costs are $11.11 million, and the true cost of the expansion is $111.11 million once we include flotation costs.

Things are only slightly more complicated if the firm uses both debt and equity. Suppose Spatt's target capital structure is 60 percent equity, 40 percent debt. The flotation costs associated with equity are still 10 percent, but the flotation costs for debt are less—say 5 percent.

Earlier, when we had different capital costs for debt and equity, we calculated a weighted average cost of capital using the target capital structure weights. Here we will do much the same thing. We can calculate a weighted average flotation cost, f_A, by multiplying the equity flotation cost, f_E, by the percentage of equity (E/V) and the debt flotation cost, f_D, by the percentage of debt (D/V) and then adding the two together:

$$f_A = (E/V) \times f_E + (D/V) \times f_D$$
$$= .60 \times .10 + .40 \times .05$$
$$= .08, \text{ or } 8\%$$

14.13

The weighted average flotation cost is 8 percent. What this tells us is that for every dollar in outside financing needed for new projects, the firm must actually raise $1/(1 − .08) = $1.087. In our example, the project cost is $100 million when we ignore flotation costs. If we include them, then the true cost is $100 million/(1 − f_A) = $100 million/.92 = $108.7 million.

In taking issue costs into account, the firm must be careful not to use the wrong weights. The firm should use the target weights, even if it can finance the entire cost of the project with either debt or equity. The fact that a firm can finance a specific project with debt or equity is not directly relevant. If a firm has a target debt-equity ratio of 1, for example, but chooses to finance a particular project with all debt, it will have to raise additional equity later on to maintain its target debt-equity ratio. To take this into account, the firm should always use the target weights in calculating the flotation cost.

Calculating the Weighted Average Flotation Cost   EXAMPLE 14.7

The Weinstein Corporation has a target capital structure that is 80 percent equity, 20 percent debt. The flotation costs for equity issues are 20 percent of the amount raised; the flotation costs for debt issues are 6 percent. If Weinstein needs $65 million for a new manufacturing facility, what is the true cost once flotation costs are considered?

We first calculate the weighted average flotation cost, f_A:

$$f_A = (E/V) \times f_E + (D/V) \times f_D$$
$$= .80 \times .20 + .20 \times .06$$
$$= .172, \text{ or } 17.2\%$$

The weighted average flotation cost is 17.2 percent. The project cost is $65 million when we ignore flotation costs. If we include them, then the true cost is $65 million/(1 − f_A) = $65 million/.828 = $78.5 million, again illustrating that flotation costs can be a considerable expense.

FLOTATION COSTS AND NPV

To illustrate how flotation costs can be included in an NPV analysis, suppose the Tripleday Printing Company is currently at its target debt-equity ratio of 100 percent. It is considering building a new $500,000 printing plant in Kansas. This new plant is expected to generate aftertax cash flows of $73,150 per year forever. The tax rate is 21 percent. There are two financing options:

1. A $500,000 new issue of common stock: The issuance costs of the new common stock would be about 10 percent of the amount raised. The required return on the company's new equity is 20 percent.

2. A $500,000 issue of 30-year bonds: The issuance costs of the new debt would be 2 percent of the proceeds. The company can raise new debt at 10 percent.

What is the NPV of the new printing plant?

To begin, because printing is the company's main line of business, we will use the company's weighted average cost of capital to value the new printing plant:

$$\text{WACC} = (E/V) \times R_E + (D/V) \times R_D \times (1 − T_C)$$
$$= .50 \times .20 + .50 \times .10 \times (1 − .21)$$
$$= .1395, \text{ or } 13.95\%$$

Because the cash flows are $73,150 per year forever, the PV of the cash flows at 13.95 percent per year is:

$$\text{PV} = \frac{\$73,150}{.1395} = \$524,373$$

If we ignore flotation costs, the NPV is:

$$\text{NPV} = \$524{,}373 - 500{,}000 = \$24{,}373$$

With no flotation costs, the project generates an NPV that is greater than zero, so it should be accepted.

What about financing arrangements and issue costs? Because new financing must be raised, the flotation costs are relevant. From the information given, we know that the flotation costs are 2 percent for debt and 10 percent for equity. Because Tripleday uses equal amounts of debt and equity, the weighted average flotation cost, f_A, is:

$$f_A = (E/V) \times f_E + (D/V) \times f_D = .50 \times .10 + .50 \times .02$$
$$= .06, \text{ or } 6\%$$

Remember, the fact that Tripleday can finance the project with all debt or all equity is irrelevant. Because Tripleday needs $500,000 to fund the new plant, the true cost, once we include flotation costs, is $500,000/(1 − f_A) = $500,000/.94 = $531,915. Because the PV of the cash flows is $524,373, the plant has an NPV of $524,373 − 531,915 = −$7,542, so it is no longer a good investment.

INTERNAL EQUITY AND FLOTATION COSTS

Our discussion of flotation costs to this point implicitly assumes that firms always have to raise the capital needed for new investments. In reality, most firms rarely sell equity at all. Instead, their internally generated cash flow is sufficient to cover the equity portion of their capital spending. Only the debt portion must be raised externally.

The use of internal equity doesn't change our approach. We now assign a value of zero to the flotation cost of equity because there is no such cost. In our Tripleday example, the weighted average flotation cost would therefore be:

$$f_A = (E/V) \times f_E + (D/V) \times f_D$$
$$= .50 \times 0 + .50 \times .02$$
$$= .01, \text{ or } 1\%$$

Notice that whether equity is generated internally or externally makes a big difference because external equity has a relatively high flotation cost.

Concept Questions

14.7a   What are flotation costs?

14.7b   How are flotation costs included in an NPV analysis?

Summary and Conclusions   14.8

This chapter has discussed cost of capital. The most important concept is the weighted average cost of capital, or WACC, which we interpreted as the required rate of return on the overall firm. It is also the discount rate appropriate for cash flows that are similar in risk to those of the overall firm. We described how the WACC can be calculated, and we illustrated how it can be used in certain types of analyses.

We also pointed out situations in which it is inappropriate to use the WACC as the discount rate. To handle such cases, we described some alternative approaches to developing discount rates, such as the pure play approach. We also discussed how the flotation costs associated with raising new capital can be included in an NPV analysis.

CONNECT TO FINANCE

 Do you use *Connect Finance* to practice what you learned? If you don't, you should—we can help you master the topics presented in this material. Log on to connect.mheducation.com to learn more!

Can you answer the following *Connect* Quiz questions?

Section 14.2 A firm has paid dividends of $1.02, $1.10, $1.25, and $1.35 over the past four years, respectively. What is the average dividend growth rate?

Section 14.3 A semiannual, 7 percent bond matures in 14 years and has a face value of $1,000. The market quote on this bond is 101.4. What is the aftertax cost of debt if the tax rate is 21 percent?

Section 14.4 Why is the tax rate applied to the cost of debt but not to the cost of equity or preferred stock when computing a firm's weighted average cost of capital?

Section 14.5 What approach to a project's cost of capital entails the use of another firm's cost of capital rather than the use of your own firm's cost of capital?

Section 14.6 What is the flotation cost of equity for a firm that generates sufficient internal cash flows to cover the equity portion of any capital expenditure?

CHAPTER REVIEW AND SELF-TEST PROBLEMS

14.1 Calculating the Cost of Equity Suppose stock in Watta Corporation has a beta of .80. The market risk premium is 6 percent, and the risk-free rate is 6 percent. Watta's last dividend was $1.20 per share, and the dividend is expected to grow at 8 percent indefinitely. The stock currently sells for $45 per share. What is Watta's cost of equity capital?

14.2 Calculating the WACC In addition to the information given in the previous problem, suppose Watta has a target debt-equity ratio of 50 percent. Its cost of debt is 9 percent before taxes. If the tax rate is 21 percent, what is the WACC?

14.3 Flotation Costs Suppose in the previous problem Watta is seeking $30 million for a new project. The necessary funds will have to be raised externally. Watta's flotation costs for selling debt and equity are 2 percent and 16 percent, respectively. If flotation costs are considered, what is the true cost of the new project?

ANSWERS TO CHAPTER REVIEW AND SELF-TEST PROBLEMS

14.1 We start off with the SML approach. Based on the information given, the expected return on Watta's common stock is:

$$R_E = R_f + \beta_E \times (R_M - R_f)$$
$$= .06 + .80 \times .06$$
$$= .1080, \text{ or } 10.80\%$$

We now use the dividend growth model. The projected dividend is $D_0 \times (1 + g) = \$1.20 \times 1.08 = \$1.296$, so the expected return using this approach is:

$$R_E = D_1/P_0 + g$$
$$= \$1.296/\$45 + .08$$
$$= .1088, \text{ or } 10.88\%$$

Because these two estimates, 10.80 percent and 10.88 percent, are fairly close, we will average them. Watta's cost of equity is approximately 10.84 percent.

14.2 Because the target debt-equity ratio is .50, Watta uses $.50 in debt for every $1 in equity. In other words, Watta's target capital structure is 1/3 debt and 2/3 equity. The WACC is thus:

$$WACC = (E/V) \times R_E + (D/V) \times R_D \times (1 - T_C)$$
$$= 2/3 \times .1084 + 1/3 \times .09 \times (1 - .21)$$
$$= .0960, \text{ or } 9.60\%$$

14.3 Because Watta uses both debt and equity to finance its operations, we first need the weighted average flotation cost. As in the previous problem, the percentage of equity financing is 2/3, so the weighted average cost is:

$$f_A = (E/V) \times f_E + (D/V) \times f_D$$
$$= 2/3 \times .16 + 1/3 \times .02$$
$$= .1133, \text{ or } 11.33\%$$

If Watta needs $30 million after flotation costs, then the true cost of the project is $30 million/$(1 - f_A)$ = $30 million/.8867 = $33.83 million.

CONCEPTS REVIEW AND CRITICAL THINKING QUESTIONS

1. **WACC [LO3]** On the most basic level, if a firm's WACC is 12 percent, what does this mean?
2. **Book Values versus Market Values [LO3]** In calculating the WACC, if you had to use book values for either debt or equity, which would you choose? Why?
3. **Project Risk [LO5]** If you can borrow all the money you need for a project at 6 percent, doesn't it follow that 6 percent is your cost of capital for the project?
4. **WACC and Taxes [LO3]** Why do we use an aftertax figure for cost of debt but not for cost of equity?
5. **DCF Cost of Equity Estimation [LO1]** What are the advantages of using the DCF model for determining the cost of equity capital? What are the disadvantages? What specific piece of information do you need to find the cost of equity using this model? What are some of the ways in which you could get this estimate?
6. **SML Cost of Equity Estimation [LO1]** What are the advantages of using the SML approach to finding the cost of equity capital? What are the disadvantages? What specific pieces of information are needed to use this method? Are all of these variables observable, or do they need to be estimated? What are some of the ways in which you could get these estimates?
7. **Cost of Debt Estimation [LO2]** How do you determine the appropriate cost of debt for a company? Does it make a difference if the company's debt is privately placed as opposed to being publicly traded? How would you estimate the cost of debt for a firm whose only debt issues are privately held by institutional investors?
8. **Cost of Capital [LO5]** Suppose Tom O'Bedlam, president of Bedlam Products, Inc., has hired you to determine the firm's cost of debt and cost of equity capital.
   a. The stock currently sells for $50 per share, and the dividend per share will probably be about $5. Tom argues, "It will cost us $5 per share to use the stockholders' money this year, so the cost of equity is equal to 10 percent (= $5/50)." What's wrong with this conclusion?
   b. Based on the most recent financial statements, Bedlam Products's total liabilities are $8 million. Total interest expense for the coming year will be about

$1 million. Tom therefore reasons, "We owe $8 million, and we will pay $1 million interest. Therefore, our cost of debt is obviously $1 million/8 million = .125, or 12.5%." What's wrong with this conclusion?

c. Based on his own analysis, Tom is recommending that the company increase its use of equity financing because "Debt costs 12.5 percent, but equity costs only 10 percent; thus equity is cheaper." Ignoring all the other issues, what do you think about the conclusion that the cost of equity is less than the cost of debt?

9. **Company Risk versus Project Risk [LO5]** Both Dow Chemical Company, a large natural gas user, and Superior Oil, a major natural gas producer, are thinking of investing in natural gas wells near Houston. Both companies are all equity financed. Dow and Superior are looking at identical projects. They've analyzed their respective investments, which would involve a negative cash flow now and positive expected cash flows in the future. These cash flows would be the same for both firms. No debt would be used to finance the projects. Both companies estimate that their projects would have a net present value of $1 million at an 18 percent discount rate and a −$1.1 million NPV at a 22 percent discount rate. Dow has a beta of 1.25, whereas Superior has a beta of .75. The expected risk premium on the market is 8 percent, and risk-free bonds are yielding 12 percent. Should either company proceed? Should both? Explain.

10. **Divisional Cost of Capital [LO5]** Under what circumstances would it be appropriate for a firm to use different costs of capital for its different operating divisions? If the overall firm WACC were used as the hurdle rate for all divisions, would the riskier divisions or the more conservative divisions tend to get most of the investment projects? Why? If you were to try to estimate the appropriate cost of capital for different divisions, what problems might you encounter? What are two techniques you could use to develop a rough estimate for each division's cost of capital?

QUESTIONS AND PROBLEMS

BASIC
(Questions 1–19)

1. **Calculating Cost of Equity [LO1]** The Drogon Co. just issued a dividend of $2.80 per share on its common stock. The company is expected to maintain a constant 4.5 percent growth rate in its dividends indefinitely. If the stock sells for $58 a share, what is the company's cost of equity?

2. **Calculating Cost of Equity [LO1]** The Rhaegel Corporation's common stock has a beta of 1.07. If the risk-free rate is 3.5 percent and the expected return on the market is 10 percent, what is the company's cost of equity capital?

3. **Calculating Cost of Equity [LO1]** Stock in Daenerys Industries has a beta of 1.05. The market risk premium is 7 percent, and T-bills are currently yielding 3.4 percent. The company's most recent dividend was $2.35 per share, and dividends are expected to grow at an annual rate of 4.1 percent indefinitely. If the stock sells for $43 per share, what is your best estimate of the company's cost of equity?

4. **Estimating the DCF Growth Rate [LO1]** Suppose Stark, Ltd., just issued a dividend of $2.51 per share on its common stock. The company paid dividends of $2.01, $2.17, $2.25, and $2.36 per share in the last four years. If the stock currently sells for $43, what is your best estimate of the company's cost of equity capital using the arithmetic average growth rate in dividends? What if you use the geometric average growth rate?

5. **Calculating Cost of Preferred Stock [LO1]** Holdup Bank has an issue of preferred stock with a stated dividend of $4.25 that just sold for $93 per share. What is the bank's cost of preferred stock?

6. **Calculating Cost of Debt** [LO2] Viserion, Inc., is trying to determine its cost of debt. The firm has a debt issue outstanding with 23 years to maturity that is quoted at 103 percent of face value. The issue makes semiannual payments and has an embedded cost of 6 percent annually. What is the company's pretax cost of debt? If the tax rate is 21 percent, what is the aftertax cost of debt?

7. **Calculating Cost of Debt** [LO2] Jiminy's Cricket Farm issued a 30-year, 6 percent semiannual bond three years ago. The bond currently sells for 93 percent of its face value. The company's tax rate is 22 percent.

    a. What is the pretax cost of debt?

    b. What is the aftertax cost of debt?

    c. Which is more relevant, the pretax or the aftertax cost of debt? Why?

8. **Calculating Cost of Debt** [LO2] For the firm in Problem 7, suppose the book value of the debt issue is $95 million. In addition, the company has a second debt issue on the market, a zero coupon bond with eight years left to maturity; the book value of this issue is $40 million, and the bonds sell for 67 percent of par. What is the company's total book value of debt? The total market value? What is your best estimate of the aftertax cost of debt now?

9. **Calculating WACC** [LO3] Targaryen Corporation has a target capital structure of 70 percent common stock, 5 percent preferred stock, and 25 percent debt. Its cost of equity is 10 percent, the cost of preferred stock is 5 percent, and the pretax cost of debt is 6 percent. The relevant tax rate is 23 percent.

    a. What is the company's WACC?

    b. The company president has approached you about the company's capital structure. He wants to know why the company doesn't use more preferred stock financing because it costs less than debt. What would you tell the president?

10. **Taxes and WACC** [LO3] Lannister Manufacturing has a target debt-equity ratio of .55. Its cost of equity is 11 percent, and its cost of debt is 6 percent. If the tax rate is 21 percent, what is the company's WACC?

11. **Finding the Target Capital Structure** [LO3] Fama's Llamas has a weighted average cost of capital of 7.9 percent. The company's cost of equity is 11 percent, and its pretax cost of debt is 5.8 percent. The tax rate is 25 percent. What is the company's target debt-equity ratio?

12. **Book Value versus Market Value** [LO3] Dinklage Corp. has 7 million shares of common stock outstanding. The current share price is $68, and the book value per share is $8. The company also has two bond issues outstanding. The first bond issue has a face value of $70 million, a coupon rate of 6 percent, and sells for 97 percent of par. The second issue has a face value of $40 million, a coupon rate of 6.5 percent, and sells for 108 percent of par. The first issue matures in 21 years, the second in 6 years. Both bonds make semiannual coupon payments.

    a. What are the company's capital structure weights on a book value basis?

    b. What are the company's capital structure weights on a market value basis?

    c. Which are more relevant, the book or market value weights? Why?

13. **Calculating the WACC** [LO3] In Problem 12, suppose the most recent dividend was $3.25 and the dividend growth rate is 5 percent. Assume that the overall cost of debt is the weighted average of that implied by the two outstanding debt issues. Both bonds make semiannual payments. The tax rate is 21 percent. What is the company's WACC?

14. **WACC [LO3]** Starset, Inc., has a target debt-equity ratio of .85. Its WACC is 9.1 percent, and the tax rate is 23 percent.

    a. If the company's cost of equity is 14 percent, what is its pretax cost of debt?

    b. If instead you know that the aftertax cost of debt is 6.5 percent, what is the cost of equity?

15. **Finding the WACC [LO3]** Given the following information for Watson Power Co., find the WACC. Assume the company's tax rate is 21 percent.

Debt:	15,000 bonds with a 5.8 percent coupon outstanding, $1,000 par value, 25 years to maturity, selling for 108 percent of par; the bonds make semiannual payments.
Common stock:	575,000 shares outstanding, selling for $64 per share; the beta is 1.09.
Preferred stock:	35,000 shares of 2.8 percent preferred stock outstanding, currently selling for $65 per share.
Market:	7 percent market risk premium and 3.2 percent risk-free rate.

16. **Finding the WACC [LO3]** Titan Mining Corporation has 7.5 million shares of common stock outstanding, 250,000 shares of 4.2 percent preferred stock outstanding, and 140,000 bonds with a semiannual coupon of 5.1 percent outstanding, par value $1,000 each. The common stock currently sells for $51 per share and has a beta of 1.15, the preferred stock currently sells for $103 per share, and the bonds have 15 years to maturity and sell for 107 percent of par. The market risk premium is 7.5 percent, T-bills are yielding 2.4 percent, and the company's tax rate is 22 percent.

    a. What is the firm's market value capital structure?

    b. If the company is evaluating a new investment project that has the same risk as the firm's typical project, what rate should the firm use to discount the project's cash flows?

17. **SML and WACC [LO1]** An all-equity firm is considering the following projects:

Project	Beta	IRR
W	.85	8.9%
X	.92	10.8
Y	1.09	12.8
Z	1.35	13.3

The T-bill rate is 4 percent, and the expected return on the market is 11 percent.

    a. Which projects have a higher expected return than the firm's 11 percent cost of capital?

    b. Which projects should be accepted?

    c. Which projects would be incorrectly accepted or rejected if the firm's overall cost of capital were used as a hurdle rate?

18. **Calculating Flotation Costs [LO4]** Suppose your company needs $24 million to build a new assembly line. Your target debt-equity ratio is .75. The flotation cost for new equity is 7 percent, but the flotation cost for debt is only 3 percent. Your boss has decided to fund the project by borrowing money because the flotation costs are lower and the needed funds are relatively small.

    a. What do you think about the rationale behind borrowing the entire amount?

    b. What is your company's weighted average flotation cost, assuming all equity is raised externally?

   c. What is the true cost of building the new assembly line after taking flotation costs into account? Does it matter in this case that the entire amount is being raised from debt?

19. **Calculating Flotation Costs** [LO4] Cully Company needs to raise $80 million to start a new project and will raise the money by selling new bonds. The company will generate no internal equity for the foreseeable future. The company has a target capital structure of 70 percent common stock, 5 percent preferred stock, and 25 percent debt. Flotation costs for issuing new common stock are 7 percent, for new preferred stock, 4 percent, and for new debt, 2 percent. What is the true initial cost figure the company should use when evaluating its project?

20. **WACC and NPV** [LO3, 5] Sommer, Inc., is considering a project that will result in initial aftertax cash savings of $2.3 million at the end of the first year, and these savings will grow at a rate of 2 percent per year indefinitely. The firm has a target debt-equity ratio of .60, a cost of equity of 10 percent, and an aftertax cost of debt of 4.6 percent. The cost-saving proposal is somewhat riskier than the usual project the firm undertakes; management uses the subjective approach and applies an adjustment factor of +3 percent to the cost of capital for such risky projects. Under what circumstances should the company take on the project?

INTERMEDIATE
(Questions 20–25)

21. **Flotation Costs** [LO4] Being Human, Inc., recently issued new securities to finance a new TV show. The project cost $35 million, and the company paid $2.2 million in flotation costs. In addition, the equity issued had a flotation cost of 7 percent of the amount raised, whereas the debt issued had a flotation cost of 3 percent of the amount raised. If the company issued new securities in the same proportion as its target capital structure, what is the company's target debt-equity ratio?

22. **Calculating the Cost of Debt** [LO2] Ying Import has several bond issues outstanding, each making semiannual interest payments. The bonds are listed in the following table. If the corporate tax rate is 22 percent, what is the aftertax cost of the company's debt?

Bond	Coupon Rate	Price Quote	Maturity	Face Value
1	5.00%	103.18	5 years	$45,000,000
2	7.10	112.80	8 years	40,000,000
3	6.30	107.45	$15\frac{1}{2}$ years	50,000,000
4	5.90	102.75	25 years	65,000,000

23. **Calculating the Cost of Equity** [LO1] Minder Industries stock has a beta of 1.08. The company just paid a dividend of $.65, and the dividends are expected to grow at 4 percent. The expected return on the market is 10.5 percent, and Treasury bills are yielding 3.4 percent. The most recent stock price for the company is $72.

   a. Calculate the cost of equity using the DCF method.

   b. Calculate the cost of equity using the SML method.

   c. Why do you think your estimates in (a) and (b) are so different?

24. **Adjusted Cash Flow from Assets** [LO3] Pearl Corp. is expected to have an EBIT of $1.8 million next year. Depreciation, the increase in net working capital, and capital spending are expected to be $155,000, $75,000, and $115,000, respectively. All are expected to grow at 18 percent per year for four years. The company currently has $9.5 million in debt and 750,000 shares outstanding. After Year 5, the adjusted cash flow from assets is expected to grow at 3 percent indefinitely. The company's

WACC is 8.5 percent and the tax rate is 21 percent. What is the price per share of the company's stock?

25. **Adjusted Cash Flow from Assets [LO3]** In the previous problem, instead of a perpetual growth rate in adjusted cash flow from assets, you decide to calculate the terminal value of the company with the price-sales ratio. You believe that Year 5 sales will be $16.9 million and the appropriate price-sales ratio is 2.9. What is your new estimate of the current share price?

CHALLENGE
(Questions 26–31)

26. **Adjusted Cash Flow from Assets [LO3]** You have looked at the current financial statements for Reigle Homes, Co. The company has an EBIT of $3.15 million this year. Depreciation, the increase in net working capital, and capital spending were $265,000, $105,000, and $495,000, respectively. You expect that over the next five years, EBIT will grow at 15 percent per year, depreciation and capital spending will grow at 20 percent per year, and NWC will grow at 10 percent per year. The company has $19.5 million in debt and 400,000 shares outstanding. After Year 5, the adjusted cash flow from assets is expected to grow at 3.5 percent indefinitely. The company's WACC is 9.25 percent, and the tax rate is 22 percent. What is the price per share of the company's stock?

27. **Adjusted Cash Flow from Assets [LO3]** In the previous problem, suppose you believe that sales in five years will be $29.2 million and the price-sales ratio will be 2.45. What is the share price now?

28. **Flotation Costs and NPV [LO3, 4]** Photochronograph Corporation (PC) manufactures time series photographic equipment. It is currently at its target debt-equity ratio of .60. It's considering building a new $65 million manufacturing facility. This new plant is expected to generate aftertax cash flows of $9.4 million in perpetuity. The company raises all equity from outside financing. There are three financing options:

1. *A new issue of common stock*: The flotation costs of the new common stock would be 8 percent of the amount raised. The required return on the company's new equity is 14 percent.

2. *A new issue of 20-year bonds*: The flotation costs of the new bonds would be 4 percent of the proceeds. If the company issues these new bonds at an annual coupon rate of 8 percent, they will sell at par.

3. *Increased use of accounts payable financing*: Because this financing is part of the company's ongoing daily business, it has no flotation costs, and the company assigns it a cost that is the same as the overall firm WACC. Management has a target ratio of accounts payable to long-term debt of .15. (Assume there is no difference between the pretax and aftertax accounts payable cost.)

What is the NPV of the new plant? Assume that PC has a 21 percent tax rate.

29. **Flotation Costs [LO3]** Lucas Corp. has a debt-equity ratio of .65. The company is considering a new plant that will cost $51 million to build. When the company issues new equity, it incurs a flotation cost of 7 percent. The flotation cost on new debt is 2.7 percent. What is the initial cost of the plant if the company raises all equity externally? What if it typically uses 60 percent retained earnings? What if all equity investment is financed through retained earnings?

30. **Project Evaluation [LO3, 4]** This is a comprehensive project evaluation problem bringing together much of what you have learned in this and previous chapters. Suppose you have been hired as a financial consultant to Defense Electronics, Inc. (DEI), a large, publicly traded firm that is the market share leader in radar detection systems (RDSs). The company is looking at setting up a manufacturing plant overseas to produce a new line of RDSs. This will be a five-year project.

The company bought some land three years ago for $2.7 million in anticipation of using it as a toxic dump site for waste chemicals, but it built a piping system to safely discard the chemicals instead. The land was appraised last week for $3.8 million on an aftertax basis. In five years, the aftertax value of the land will be $4.1 million, but the company expects to keep the land for a future project. The company wants to build its new manufacturing plant on this land; the plant and equipment will cost $34 million to build. The following market data on DEI's securities are current:

Debt:	195,000 bonds with a coupon rate of 6.2 percent outstanding, 25 years to maturity, selling for 106 percent of par; the bonds have a $1,000 par value each and make semiannual payments.
Common stock:	8,100,000 shares outstanding, selling for $63 per share; the beta is 1.1.
Preferred stock:	450,000 shares of 4.25 percent preferred stock outstanding, selling for $83 per share.
Market:	7 percent expected market risk premium; 3.1 percent risk- free rate.

DEI uses G.M. Wharton as its lead underwriter. Wharton charges DEI spreads of 7 percent on new common stock issues, 5 percent on new preferred stock issues, and 3 percent on new debt issues. Wharton has included all direct and indirect issuance costs (along with its profit) in setting these spreads. Wharton has recommended to DEI that it raise the funds needed to build the plant by issuing new shares of common stock. DEI's tax rate is 25 percent. The project requires $1,500,000 in initial net working capital investment to get operational. Assume DEI raises all equity for new projects externally.

a. Calculate the project's initial Time 0 cash flow, taking into account all side effects.

b. The new RDS project is somewhat riskier than a typical project for DEI, primarily because the plant is being located overseas. Management has told you to use an adjustment factor of +2 percent to account for this increased riskiness. Calculate the appropriate discount rate to use when evaluating DEI's project.

c. The manufacturing plant has an eight-year tax life, and DEI uses straight-line depreciation to a zero salvage value. At the end of the project (that is, the end of Year 5), the plant and equipment can be scrapped for $4.9 million. What is the aftertax salvage value of this plant and equipment?

d. The company will incur $6.9 million in annual fixed costs. The plan is to manufacture 12,100 RDSs per year and sell them at $11,450 per machine; the variable production costs are $9,500 per RDS. What is the annual operating cash flow (OCF) from this project?

e. DEI's comptroller is primarily interested in the impact of DEI's investments on the bottom line of reported accounting statements. What will you tell her is the accounting break-even quantity of RDSs sold for this project?

f. Finally, DEI's president wants you to throw all your calculations, assumptions, and everything else into the report for the chief financial officer; all he wants to know is what the RDS project's internal rate of return (IRR) and net present value (NPV) are. What will you report?

31. **Adjusted Cash Flow from Assets [LO3]** Suppose you are looking at a company with no change in capital spending, no change in net working capital, and no depreciation. Since the company is not increasing its assets, EBIT is constant. What is the value of the company?

EXCEL MASTER IT! PROBLEM

You want to calculate the WACC for auto parts retailer AutoZone (AZO). Complete the following steps to construct a spreadsheet that can be updated.

   a. Using an input for the ticker symbol, create hyperlinks to the web pages that you will need to find all of the information necessary to calculate the cost of equity. Use a market risk premium of 7 percent when using CAPM.

   b. Create hyperlinks to go to the FINRA bond quote website and the SEC EDGAR database and find the information for the company's bonds. Create a table that calculates the cost of debt for the company. Assume the tax rate is 21 percent.

   c. Finally, calculate the market value weights for debt and equity. What is the WACC for AutoZone?

MINICASE

Cost of Capital for Swan Motors

You have recently been hired by Swan Motors, Inc. (SMI), in its relatively new treasury management department. SMI was founded eight years ago by Joe Swan. Joe found a method to manufacture a cheaper battery that will hold a larger charge, giving a car powered by the battery a range of 700 miles before requiring a charge. The cars manufactured by SMI are mid-sized and carry a price that allows the company to compete with other mainstream auto manufacturers. The company is privately owned by Joe and his family, and it had sales of $97 million last year.

SMI primarily sells to customers who buy the cars online, although it does have a limited number of company-owned dealerships. The customer selects any customization and makes a deposit of 20 percent of the purchase price. After the order is taken, the car is made to order, typically within 45 days. SMI's growth to date has come from its profits. When the company had sufficient capital, it would expand production. Relatively little formal analysis has been used in its capital budgeting process. Joe has just read about capital budgeting techniques and has come to you for help. For starters, the company has never attempted to determine its cost of capital, and Joe would like you to perform the analysis. Because the company is privately owned, it is difficult to determine the cost of equity for the company. Joe wants you to use the pure play approach to estimate the cost of capital for SMI, and he has chosen Tesla Motors as a representative company. The following questions will lead you through the steps to calculate this estimate.

QUESTIONS

1. Most publicly traded corporations are required to submit quarterly (10-Q) and annual (10-K) reports to the SEC detailing the financial operations of the company over the past quarter or year, respectively. These corporate filings are available on the SEC website at www.sec.gov. Go to the SEC website, follow the "Search for Company Filings" link, and search for SEC filings made by Tesla Motors (TSLA). Find the most recent 10-Q or 10-K, and download the form. Look on the balance sheet to find the book value of debt and the book value of equity.

2. To estimate the cost of equity for TSLA, go to finance.yahoo.com and enter the ticker symbol TSLA. Follow the links to answer the following questions: What is the most recent stock price listed for TSLA? What is the market value of equity, or market capitalization? How many shares of stock does TSLA have outstanding? What is the most recent annual dividend? Can you use the dividend discount model in this case? What is the beta for TSLA? Now go back to finance.yahoo.com and follow the "Bonds" link. What is the yield on three-month Treasury bills? Using the historical market risk premium, what is the cost of equity for TSLA using CAPM?

3. You now need to calculate the cost of debt for TSLA. Go to finra-markets.morningstar.com, enter TSLA as the company, and find the yield to maturity for each of TSLA's bonds. What is the weighted average cost of debt for TSLA using the book value weights and using the market value weights? Does it make a difference in this case if you use book value weights or market value weights?

4. You now have all the necessary information to calculate the weighted average cost of capital for TSLA. Calculate this using book value weights and market value weights, assuming TSLA has a 21 percent tax rate. Which number is more relevant?

5. You used TSLA as a pure play company to estimate the cost of capital for SMI. Are there any potential problems with this approach in this situation?

Raising Capital

ON MARCH 2, 2017, in one of the most anticipated IPOs of the year, video messaging company Snap, operator of Snapchat, went public. Assisted by investment banks Morgan Stanley, Goldman Sachs, J.P. Morgan, and a host of others, the company offered 145 million shares of stock at a price of $17 per share. The first trade on the New York Stock Exchange was at $24 per share, a 41 percent jump from the initial stock price. The stock quickly rose to $26.05, before closing at $24.48. What made Snap's stock offering particularly unique was that the company sold Class A shares, which had no voting rights, in the IPO. The company also had Class B shares, with one vote per share, and Class C stock, with 10 votes per share. The Class C stock was held entirely by the company's founders. In this chapter, we will examine the process by which companies such as Snap sell stock to the public, the costs of doing so, and the role of investment banks in the process.

Learning Objectives

After studying this chapter, you should be able to:

LO1 Describe the venture capital market and its role in the financing of new, high-risk ventures.

LO2 Explain how securities are sold to the public and the role of investment banks in the process.

LO3 Define initial public offerings and some of the costs of going public.

LO4 Demonstrate how rights are issued to existing shareholders and how to value those rights.

For updates on the latest happenings in finance, visit fundamentalsofcorporatefinance.blogspot.com.

All firms must, at varying times, obtain capital. To do so, a firm must either borrow the money (debt financing), sell a portion of the firm (equity financing), or both. How a firm raises capital depends a great deal on the size of the firm, its life-cycle stage, and its growth prospects.

In this chapter, we examine some of the ways in which firms actually raise capital. We begin by looking at companies in the early stages of their lives and the importance of venture capital for such firms. We then look at the process of going public and the role of investment banks. Along the way, we discuss many of the issues associated with selling securities to the public and their implications for all types of firms. We close the chapter with a discussion of sources of debt capital.[1]

---

[1]We are indebted to Jay R. Ritter of the University of Florida and M. Shane Hadden of *The Currency Report* (www.globalcurrencyreport.com) for helpful comments and suggestions for this chapter.

15.1 The Financing Life Cycle of a Firm: Early-Stage Financing and Venture Capital

One day, you and a friend have a great idea for a new computer software product that helps users communicate using the next-generation meganet. Filled with entrepreneurial zeal, you christen the product Megacomm and set about bringing it to market.

Working nights and weekends, you are able to create a prototype of your product. It doesn't actually work, but at least you can show it around to illustrate your idea. To actually develop the product, you need to hire programmers, buy computers, rent office space, and so on. Unfortunately, because you are both college students, your combined assets are not sufficient to fund a pizza party, much less a start-up company. You need what is often referred to as OPM—other people's money.

Your first thought might be to approach a bank for a loan. You would probably discover that banks are generally not interested in making loans to start-up companies with no assets (other than an idea) run by fledgling entrepreneurs with no track record. Instead your search for capital would likely lead you to the **venture capital (VC)** market.

venture capital (VC)
Financing for new, often high-risk, ventures.

VENTURE CAPITAL

The term *venture capital* does not have a precise meaning, but it generally refers to financing for new, often high-risk, ventures. For example, before it went public, Google was VC financed. Individual venture capitalists invest their own money; so-called "angels" are usually individual VC investors, but they tend to specialize in smaller deals. Venture capital firms specialize in pooling funds from various sources and investing them. The underlying sources of funds for such firms include individuals, pension funds, insurance companies, large corporations, and even university endowment funds. The broad term *private equity* is often used to label the rapidly growing area of equity financing for nonpublic companies.[2]

Venture capitalists and venture capital firms recognize that many or even most new ventures will not fly, but the occasional one will. The potential profits are enormous in such cases. To limit their risk, venture capitalists generally provide financing in stages. At each stage, enough money is invested to reach the next milestone or planning stage. For example, the *first-stage financing* might be enough to get a prototype built and a manufacturing plan completed. Based on the results, the *second-stage financing* might be a major investment needed to actually begin manufacturing, marketing, and distribution. There might be many such stages, each of which represents a key step in the process of growing the company.

Venture capital firms often specialize in different stages. Some specialize in very early "seed money," or ground floor, financing. In contrast, financing in the later stages might come from venture capitalists specializing in so-called mezzanine-level financing, where *mezzanine level* refers to the level just above the ground floor.

The fact that financing is available in stages and is contingent on specified goals being met is a powerful motivating force for the firm's founders. Often, the founders receive relatively little in the way of salary and have substantial portions of their personal assets tied up in the business. At each stage of financing, the value of the founders' stake grows and the probability of success rises.

In addition to providing financing, venture capitalists often actively participate in running the firm, providing the benefit of experience with previous start-ups as well as general business expertise. This is especially true when the firm's founders have little or no hands-on experience in running a company.

For more on the VC industry, check out **nvca.org**.

---

[2]So-called "vulture capitalists" specialize in high-risk investments in established, but financially distressed, firms. Vulgar capitalists invest in firms that have bad taste (OK, we made up this last bit).

SOME VENTURE CAPITAL REALITIES

Although there is a large venture capital market, the truth is that access to venture capital is really very limited. Venture capital companies receive huge numbers of unsolicited proposals, the vast majority of which end up in the circular file unread. Venture capitalists rely heavily on informal networks of lawyers, accountants, bankers, and other venture capitalists to help identify potential investments. As a result, personal contacts are important in gaining access to the venture capital market; it is very much an "introduction" market.

Another simple fact about venture capital is that it is incredibly expensive. In a typical deal, the venture capitalist will demand (and get) 40 percent or more of the equity in the company. Venture capitalists frequently hold voting preferred stock, giving them various priorities in the event that the company is sold or liquidated. The venture capitalist will typically demand (and get) several seats on the company's board of directors and may even appoint one or more members of senior management.

CHOOSING A VENTURE CAPITALIST

Some start-up companies, particularly those headed by experienced, previously successful entrepreneurs, will be in such demand that they will have the luxury of looking beyond the money in choosing a venture capitalist. There are some key considerations in such a case, some of which can be summarized as follows:

The Internet is a tremendous source of venture capital information, both for suppliers and demanders of capital. For example, the site at **www.dealflow.com** prompts you to search the firm's database as either an entrepreneur (capital seeker) or a venture capitalist (capital supplier).

1. *Financial strength is important:* The venture capitalist needs to have the resources and financial reserves for additional financing stages should they become necessary. This doesn't mean that bigger is necessarily better because of our next consideration.

2. *Style is important:* Some venture capitalists will wish to be very much involved in day-to-day operations and decision making, whereas others will be content with monthly reports. Which type is better depends on the firm and also on the venture capitalists' business skills. In addition, a large venture capital firm may be less flexible and more bureaucratic than a smaller "boutique" firm.

3. *References are important:* Has the venture capitalist been successful with similar firms? Of equal importance, how has the venture capitalist dealt with situations that didn't work out?

4. *Contacts are important:* A venture capitalist may be able to help the business in ways other than helping with financing and management by providing introductions to potentially important customers, suppliers, and other industry contacts. Venture capitalist firms frequently specialize in a few particular industries, and such specialization could prove quite valuable.

5. *Exit strategy is important:* Venture capitalists are generally not long-term investors. How and under what circumstances the venture capitalist will "cash out" of the business should be carefully evaluated.

CONCLUSION

If a start-up succeeds, the big payoff frequently comes when the company is sold to another company or goes public. Either way, investment bankers are often involved in the process. We discuss the process of selling securities to the public in the next several sections, paying particular attention to the process of going public.

Concept Questions

15.1a   What is venture capital?
15.1b   Why is venture capital often provided in stages?

15.2 Selling Securities to the Public: The Basic Procedure

Many rules and regulations surround the process of selling securities. The Securities Act of 1933 is the origin of federal regulations for all new interstate securities issues. The Securities Exchange Act of 1934 is the basis for regulating securities already outstanding. The Securities and Exchange Commission, or SEC, administers both acts.

A series of steps is involved in issuing securities to the public. In general terms, the basic procedure is as follows:

1. Management's first step in issuing any securities to the public is to obtain approval from the board of directors. In some cases, the number of authorized shares of common stock must be increased. This requires a vote of the shareholders.

2. The firm must prepare a **registration statement** and file it with the SEC. The registration statement is required for all public, interstate issues of securities, with two exceptions:

   a. Loans that mature within nine months.

   b. Issues that involve less than $5 million.

registration statement
A statement filed with the SEC that discloses all material information concerning the corporation making a public offering.

The second exception is known as the *small-issues exemption*. In such a case, simplified procedures are used. Under the basic small-issues exemption, issues of less than $5 million are governed by **Regulation A**, for which only a brief offering statement is needed. Normally, a registration statement contains many pages (50 or more) of financial information, including a financial history, details of the existing business, proposed financing, and plans for the future.

Regulation A
An SEC regulation that exempts public issues of less than $5 million from most registration requirements.

3. The SEC examines the registration statement during a waiting period. During this time, the firm may distribute copies of a preliminary **prospectus**. The prospectus contains much of the information in the registration statement, and it is given to potential investors by the firm. The preliminary prospectus is sometimes called a **red herring**, in part because bold red letters are printed on the cover.

prospectus
A legal document describing details of the issuing corporation and the proposed offering to potential investors.

red herring
A preliminary prospectus distributed to prospective investors in a new issue of securities.

A registration statement becomes effective on the 20th day after its filing unless the SEC sends a *letter of comment* suggesting changes. In that case, after the changes are made, the 20-day waiting period starts again. It is important to note that the SEC does not consider the economic merits of the proposed sale; it merely makes sure that various rules and regulations are followed. Also, the SEC generally does not check the accuracy or truthfulness of information in the prospectus.

The registration statement does not initially contain the price of the new issue. Usually, a price amendment is filed at or near the end of the waiting period, and the registration becomes effective.

4. The company cannot sell these securities during the waiting period. However, oral offers can be made.

5. On the effective date of the registration statement, a price is determined and a full-fledged selling effort gets under way. A final prospectus must accompany the delivery of securities or confirmation of sale, whichever comes first.

tombstone
An advertisement announcing a public offering.

Tombstone advertisements (or *tombstones*) are used by underwriters during and after the waiting period. An example is reproduced in Figure 15.1. The tombstone contains the name of the issuer (the World Wrestling Federation, now known as World Wrestling Entertainment). It provides some information about the issue, and it lists the investment banks (the underwriters) involved with selling the issue. The role of the investment banks in selling securities is discussed more fully in the following sections.

The investment banks on the tombstone are divided into groups called *brackets* based on their participation in the issue, and the names of the banks are listed alphabetically within each bracket. The brackets are often viewed as a kind of pecking order. In general,

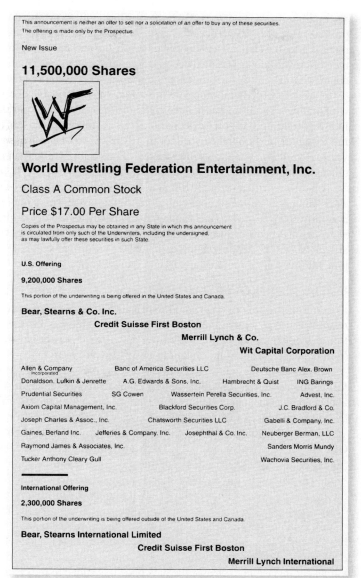

This announcement is neither an offer to sell nor a solicitation of an offer to buy any of these securities. The offering is made only by the Prospectus.

New Issue

11,500,000 Shares

World Wrestling Federation Entertainment, Inc.

Class A Common Stock

Price $17.00 Per Share

Copies of the Prospectus may be obtained in any State in which this announcement is circulated from only such of the Underwriters, including the undersigned, as may lawfully offer these securities in such State.

U.S. Offering

9,200,000 Shares

This portion of the underwriting is being offered in the United States and Canada.

Bear, Stearns & Co. Inc.

Credit Suisse First Boston

Merrill Lynch & Co.

Wit Capital Corporation

Allen & Company Incorporated	Banc of America Securities LLC	Deutsche Banc Alex. Brown
Donaldson, Lufkin & Jenrette	A.G. Edwards & Sons, Inc. Hambrecht & Quist ING Barings	
Prudential Securities	SG Cowen Wasserstein Perella Securities, Inc.	Advest, Inc.
Axiom Capital Management, Inc.	Blackford Securities Corp.	J.C. Bradford & Co.
Joseph Charles & Assoc., Inc.	Chatsworth Securities LLC	Gabelli & Company, Inc.
Gaines, Berland Inc. Jefferies & Company, Inc. Josephthal & Co. Inc.		Neuberger Berman, LLC
Raymond James & Associates, Inc.		Sanders Morris Mundy
Tucker Anthony Cleary Gull		Wachovia Securities, Inc.

International Offering

2,300,000 Shares

This portion of the underwriting is being offered outside of the United States and Canada.

Bear, Stearns International Limited

Credit Suisse First Boston

Merrill Lynch International

FIGURE 15.1

An Example of a Tombstone Advertisement

the higher the bracket, the greater is the underwriter's prestige. In recent years, the use of printed tombstones has declined, in part as a cost-saving measure.

CROWDFUNDING

On April 5, 2012, the Jumpstart Our Business Startups ("JOBS") Act was signed into law. A provision of this act allows companies to raise money through *crowdfunding*, which is the practice of raising small amounts of capital from a large number of people, typically via the Internet. Crowdfunding was first used to underwrite the U.S. tour of British rock band Marillion. The JOBS Act allows companies to sell equity by crowdfunding. Originally, the JOBS Act allowed a company to issue up to $1 million in securities in a 12-month period, although this limit was later raised to a maximum of $50 million.

We should make an important distinction about two types of crowdfunding—project crowdfunding and equity crowdfunding. As an example of project crowdfunding, consider the card game Exploding Kittens, which exploded on the crowdfunding website Kickstarter and raised

Learn more about crowdfunding at the Crowdfunding Professional Association website, **www.cfpa.org**.

Check out two of the more well-known project and charitable crowdfunding websites at **www.kickstarter.com** and **www.gofundme.com**.

Crowd Expert has a lot more info on equity crowdfunding at **www.crowdexpert.com**.

See upcoming ICOs at **tokenmarket.net/ico-calendar**.

The SEC has some warnings on ICOs at **www.sec.gov/news /public-statement/statement -clayton-2017-12-11**.

To see the market value of tokens at **coinmarketcap.com/**

$8.8 million from about 220,000 backers. During the crowdfunding campaign, the company presold card decks. Every backer was shipped a deck of cards for the game, beginning about six months after the campaign ended. In this case, the backers were purchasers, not investors. This type of crowdfunding has also become a popular way to raise money for charitable causes. In contrast, with equity crowdfunding, the backers receive equity in the company.

In May 2016, Regulation CF (also known as Title III of the JOBS Act) kicked in, which allows small investors access to new crowdfunding "portals." Previously, investors in crowdfunding had to be "accredited." For an individual, this requirement translates to more than $1 million in net worth or more than $200,000 in income for two of the past three years. Regulation CF allows investors with less than $100,000 in income or assets to invest at least $2,000 per year, up to a maximum of $5,000.

To sell securities through Regulation CF, a company must file a form with the SEC. This filing makes the company eligible to list its securities on a crowdfunding portal that is approved by FINRA (the Financial Industry Regulatory Authority), the same agency we mentioned earlier in the textbook for bond price reporting. Crowdfunding portals are already specializing. For example, there are portals that specialize in only accredited investors, all investors, or real estate, to name just a few.

INITIAL COIN OFFERINGS (ICOs)

In addition to sales of traditional debt and equity, a company can raise funds by selling *tokens*. These tokens often grant the holder the right to use the company's service in the future. For example, a company building a railroad may issue a token that can be used as a train ticket after the railroad is built.

Token sales occur on digital currency platforms and can be easily transferred on the platform or converted to U.S. dollars on specialized token exchanges. This liquidity has made tokens a popular means of funding since their introduction in 2015. Tokens are now purchased by both customers and investors who may never use the token for the service being offered.

The initial sale of a token on a digital currency platform is often called an Initial Coin Offering or ICO (to sound like IPO). Many start-up companies are now choosing to raise funding through an ICO rather than the traditional venture capital channels. The most common platform for issuing new tokens is Ethereum, but there are many competitors. In 2017, there were 234 ICOs with a total value of about $3.7 billion.

Token sales are most popular among companies that are building services based on blockchain technology. This technology is at the heart of bitcoin and other cryptocurrencies. A blockchain is a timestamped ledger of transactions that is kept among a network of users without centralized control. It is similar to a traditional database, except that cryptography is used to make it infeasible to change the data once it is added to the chain. Many industries, including finance, are now updating their recordkeeping infrastructure with blockchain technology.

Token sales can also serve as an effective marketing tool. This is especially true if the business benefits from network effects as the potential for price appreciation in the tokens attracts new customers. The increase in customers increases the value of the service, which in turn increases the value of the tokens. For example, Civic is building a blockchain-based identity platform, and its currency is used to purchase identity verification services from trusted parties. The company raised $33 million in June 2017 through an ICO of the CVC token. The total value of the tokens at the end of 2017 was $224 million.

Concept Questions

15.2a　What are the basic procedures involved in selling a new issue?
15.2b　What is a registration statement?

Alternative Issue Methods

When a company decides to issue a new security, it can sell it as a public issue or a private issue. In the case of a public issue, the firm is required to register the issue with the SEC. If the issue is to be sold to fewer than 35 investors, the sale can be carried out privately. In this case, a registration statement is not required.[3]

For equity sales, there are two kinds of public issues: a **general cash offer** and a **rights offer** (or *rights offering*). With a cash offer, securities are offered to the general public. With a rights offer, securities are initially offered only to existing owners. Rights offers are fairly common in other countries, but they are relatively rare in the United States, particularly in recent years. We therefore focus primarily on cash offers in this chapter.

The first public equity issue that is made by a company is referred to as an **initial public offering (IPO)**, or an *unseasoned new issue*. This issue occurs when a company decides to go public. Obviously, all initial public offerings are cash offers. If the firm's existing shareholders wanted to buy the shares, the firm wouldn't have to sell them publicly in the first place.

A **seasoned equity offering (SEO)** is a new issue for a company with securities that have been previously issued.[4] A seasoned equity offering of common stock can be made by using a cash offer or a rights offer.

These methods of issuing new securities are shown in Table 15.1. They are discussed in more detail in Sections 15.4 through 15.8.

Method	Type	Definition
Public Traditional negotiated cash offer	Firm commitment cash offer	The company negotiates an agreement with an investment banker to underwrite and distribute the new shares. A specified number of shares are bought by underwriters and sold at a higher price.
	Best efforts cash offer	The company has investment bankers sell as many of the new shares as possible at the agreed-upon price. There is no guarantee concerning how much cash will be raised.
	Dutch auction cash offer	The company has investment bankers auction shares to determine the highest offer price obtainable for a given number of shares to be sold.
Privileged subscription	Direct rights offer	The company offers the new stock directly to its existing shareholders.
	Standby rights offer	Like the direct rights offer, this contains a privileged subscription arrangement with existing shareholders. The net proceeds are guaranteed by the underwriters.
Nontraditional cash offer	Shelf cash offer	Qualifying companies can authorize all shares they expect to sell over a two-year period and sell them when needed.
	Competitive firm cash offer	The company can elect to award the underwriting contract through a public auction instead of negotiation.
Private	Direct placement	Securities are sold directly to the purchaser, who, at least until recently, generally could not resell securities for at least two years.

15.3

general cash offer
An issue of securities offered for sale to the general public on a cash basis.

rights offer
A public issue of securities in which securities are first offered to existing shareholders. Also called a *rights offering*.

initial public offering (IPO)
A company's first equity issue made available to the public. Also called an *unseasoned new issue*.

seasoned equity offering (SEO)
A new equity issue of securities by a company that has previously issued securities to the public.

TABLE 15.1

The Methods of Issuing New Securities

IPO information is widely available. Try IPO Scoop at **www.iposcoop.com**.

---

[3]A variety of different arrangements can be made for private equity issues. Selling unregistered securities avoids the costs of complying with the Securities Exchange Act of 1934. Regulation significantly restricts the resale of unregistered equity securities. For example, the purchaser may be required to hold the securities for at least one year (or more). Many of the restrictions were significantly eased in 1990 for very large institutional investors. The private placement of bonds is discussed in a later section.

[4]The terms *follow-on offering* and *secondary offering* are also commonly used.

15.4 Underwriters

underwriters
Investment firms that act as intermediaries between a company selling securities and the investing public.

If the public issue of securities is a cash offer, **underwriters** are usually involved. Underwriting is an important line of business for large investment firms such as Morgan Stanley. Underwriters perform services such as the following for corporate issuers:

1. Formulating the method used to issue the securities.
2. Pricing the new securities.
3. Selling the new securities.

Typically, the underwriter buys the securities for less than the offering price and accepts the risk of not being able to sell them. Because underwriting involves risk, underwriters usually combine to form an underwriting group called a **syndicate** to share the risk and to help sell the issue.

syndicate
A group of underwriters formed to share the risk and to help sell an issue.

In a syndicate, one or more managers arrange, or co-manage, the offering. The lead manager typically has the responsibility of dealing with the issuer and pricing the securities. The other underwriters in the syndicate serve primarily to distribute the issue and produce research reports later on. In recent years, it has become fairly common for a syndicate to consist of only a small number of co-managers.

gross spread
Compensation to the underwriter, determined by the difference between the underwriter's buying price and the offering price.

The difference between the underwriter's buying price and the offering price is called the **gross spread**, or underwriting discount. It is the basic compensation received by the underwriter. Sometimes, on smaller deals, the underwriter will get noncash compensation in the form of warrants and stock in addition to the spread.[5]

CHOOSING AN UNDERWRITER

A firm can offer its securities to the highest bidding underwriter on a *competitive offer* basis, or it can negotiate directly with an underwriter. Except for a few large firms, companies usually offer new issues of debt and equity on a *negotiated offer* basis. The exception is public utility holding companies, which are essentially required to use competitive underwriting.

There is evidence that competitive underwriting is cheaper to use than negotiated underwriting. The underlying reasons for the dominance of negotiated underwriting in the United States are the subject of ongoing debate.

TYPES OF UNDERWRITING

Three basic types of underwriting are involved in a cash offer: firm commitment, best efforts, and Dutch auction.

firm commitment underwriting
The type of underwriting in which the underwriter buys the entire issue, assuming full financial responsibility for any unsold shares.

Firm Commitment Underwriting   In **firm commitment underwriting**, the issuer sells the entire issue to the underwriters, who then attempt to resell it. This is the most prevalent type of underwriting in the United States. This is really just a purchase-resale arrangement, and the underwriter's fee is the spread. For a new issue of seasoned equity, the underwriters can look at the market price to determine what the issue should sell for, and more than 95 percent of all such new issues are firm commitments.

If the underwriter cannot sell all of the issue at the agreed-upon offering price, it may have to lower the price on the unsold shares. Nonetheless, with firm commitment

---

[5] Warrants are options to buy newly issued stock at a fixed price for some fixed period.

underwriting, the issuer receives the agreed-upon amount, and all the risk associated with selling the issue is transferred to the underwriter.

Because the offering price usually isn't set until the underwriters have investigated how receptive the market is to the issue, this risk is usually minimal. Also, because the offering price usually is not set until just before selling commences, the issuer doesn't know precisely what its net proceeds will be until that time.

To determine the offering price, the underwriter will meet with potential buyers, typically large institutional buyers such as mutual funds. Often, the underwriter and company management will do presentations in multiple cities, pitching the stock in what is known as a *road show*. Potential buyers provide information on the price they would be willing to pay and the number of shares they would purchase at a particular price. This process of soliciting information about buyers and the prices and quantities they would demand is known as *bookbuilding*. As we will see, despite the bookbuilding process, underwriters frequently get the price wrong, or so it seems.

Learn more about investment banks at Merrill Lynch (**www.ml.com**).

Best Efforts Underwriting

In **best efforts underwriting**, the underwriter is legally bound to use "best efforts" to sell the securities at the agreed-upon offering price. Beyond this, the underwriter does not guarantee any particular amount of money to the issuer. This form of underwriting has become uncommon in recent years.

Dutch Auction Underwriting

With **Dutch auction underwriting**, the underwriter does not set a fixed price for the shares to be sold. Instead, the underwriter conducts an auction in which investors bid for shares. The offer price is determined based on the submitted bids. A Dutch auction is also known by the more descriptive name *uniform price auction*. This approach to selling securities to the public is relatively new in the IPO market and has not been widely used there, but it is very common in the bond markets. For example, it is the sole procedure used by the U.S. Treasury to sell enormous quantities of notes, bonds, and bills to the public.

The best way to understand a Dutch or uniform price auction is to consider a simple example. Suppose the Rial Company wants to sell 400 shares to the public. The company receives five bids as follows:

Bidder	Quantity	Price
A	100 shares	$16
B	100 shares	14
C	200 shares	12
D	100 shares	12
E	200 shares	10

best efforts underwriting
The type of underwriting in which the underwriter sells as much of the issue as possible, but can return any unsold shares to the issuer without financial responsibility.

Dutch auction underwriting
The type of underwriting in which the offer price is set based on competitive bidding by investors. Also known as a *uniform price auction*.

Bidder A is willing to buy 100 shares at $16 each, Bidder B is willing to buy 100 shares at $14, and so on. The Rial Company examines the bids to determine the highest price that will result in all 400 shares being sold. So, for example, at $14, A and B would buy only 200 shares, so that price is too high. Working our way down, all 400 shares won't be sold until we hit a price of $12, so $12 will be the offer price in the IPO. Bidders A through D will receive shares; Bidder E will not.

There are two additional important points to observe in our example. First, all the winning bidders will pay $12—even Bidders A and B, who actually bid a higher price. The fact that all successful bidders pay the same price is the reason for the name "uniform price auction." The idea in such an auction is to encourage bidders to bid aggressively by providing some protection against bidding a price that is too high.

Second, notice that at the $12 offer price, there are actually bids for 500 shares, which exceeds the 400 shares Rial wants to sell. There has to be some sort of allocation. How this is done varies a bit; but in the IPO market, the approach has been to compute the ratio of shares offered to shares bid at the offer price or better, which, in our example, is

Learn all about Dutch auction IPOs at **www.wrhambrecht.com**.

400/500 = .8, and allocate bidders that percentage of their bids. In other words, Bidders A through D would each receive 80 percent of the shares they bid at a price of $12 per share.

THE AFTERMARKET

The period after a new issue is initially sold to the public is referred to as the *aftermarket*. During this time, the members of the underwriting syndicate generally do not sell securities for less than the offering price.

The principal underwriter is permitted to buy shares if the market price falls below the offering price. The purpose of this would be to support the market and stabilize the price against temporary downward pressure. If the issue remains unsold after a time (for example, 30 days), members can leave the group and sell their shares at whatever price the market will allow.[6]

THE GREEN SHOE PROVISION

Green Shoe provision
A contract provision giving the underwriter the option to purchase additional shares from the issuer at the offering price. Also called the *overallotment option*.

Many underwriting contracts contain a **Green Shoe provision** (sometimes called the *overallotment option*), which gives the members of the underwriting group the option to purchase additional shares from the issuer at the offering price.[7] Essentially all IPOs and SEOs include this provision, but ordinary debt offerings generally do not. The stated reason for the Green Shoe option is to cover excess demand and oversubscriptions. Green Shoe options usually last for 30 days and involve 15 percent of the newly issued shares.

In practice, usually underwriters initially go ahead and sell 115 percent of the shares offered. If the demand for the issue is strong after the offering, the underwriters exercise the Green Shoe option to get the extra 15 percent from the company. If demand for the issue is weak, the underwriters buy the needed shares in the open market, thereby helping to support the price of the issue in the aftermarket.

LOCKUP AGREEMENTS

lockup agreement
The part of the underwriting contract that specifies how long insiders must wait after an IPO before they can sell stock.

Although they are not required by law, almost all underwriting contracts contain so-called **lockup agreements**. Such agreements specify how long insiders must wait after an IPO before they can sell some or all of their stock. Lockup periods have become fairly standardized in recent years at 180 days. Following an IPO, insiders can't cash out until six months have gone by, which ensures that they maintain a significant economic interest in the company going public.

Lockup periods are also important because it is not unusual for the number of locked-up shares to exceed the number of shares held by the public, sometimes by a substantial multiple. On the day the lockup period expires, there is the possibility that a large number of shares will hit the market on the same day and thereby depress values. The evidence suggests that, on average, venture capital-backed companies are particularly likely to experience a loss in value on the lockup expiration day.

THE QUIET PERIOD

Once a firm begins to seriously contemplate an IPO, the SEC requires that a firm and its managing underwriters observe a "quiet period." This means that all communications with the public must be limited to ordinary announcements and other purely factual matters. The quiet period ends 40 calendar days after an IPO (for most IPOs). The SEC's logic is that all relevant information should be contained in the prospectus. An important result of this requirement is that the underwriters' analysts are prohibited from making recommendations

---

[6] Occasionally, the price of a security falls dramatically when the underwriter ceases to stabilize the price. In such cases, Wall Street humorists (the ones who didn't buy any of the stock) have referred to the period following the aftermarket as the *aftermath*.

[7] The term *Green Shoe provision* sounds quite exotic, but the origin is relatively mundane. The term comes from the name of the Green Shoe Manufacturing Company, which, in 1963, was the first issuer that granted such an option.

to investors. As soon as the quiet period ends, the managing underwriters typically publish research reports, usually accompanied by a favorable "buy" recommendation.

In 2004, two firms experienced notable quiet period-related problems. Just before the Google (now Alphabet) IPO, an interview with Google cofounders Sergey Brin and Larry Page appeared in *Playboy*. The interview almost caused a postponement of the IPO, but Google was able to amend its prospectus in time. In May 2004, Salesforce.com's IPO was delayed because an interview with CEO Marc Benioff appeared in *The New York Times*. Salesforce.com finally went public two months later.

DIRECT LISTING

While firms usually use underwriters to help their stock become publicly traded, it is not required. If it wishes to do so, and it meets the requirements of the stock exchange, a company can do a **direct listing**. In this case, the firm arranges for its stock to be listed on the exchange without marketing and other help from an underwriter. Direct listings are not common for large firms, but music-streaming giant Spotify, with a valuation well into the billions of dollars, was proposing to do one on the NYSE in 2018. Among other things, a direct listing is much less expensive because there are no underwriting fees and other associated costs. Such fees are discussed in detail in a subsequent section, and they can be substantial.

direct listing
In a direct listing, a firm arranges for its stock to be listed on an exchange without marketing and other help from an underwriter.

Concept Questions

15.4a What do underwriters do?
15.4b What is the Green Shoe provision?

IPOs and Underpricing

15.5

Determining the correct offering price is the most difficult thing an underwriter must do for an initial public offering. The issuing firm faces a potential cost if the offering price is set too high or too low. If the issue is priced too high, it may be unsuccessful and have to be withdrawn. If the issue is priced below the true market value, the issuer's existing shareholders will experience an opportunity loss when the issuer sells shares for less than they are worth.

Underpricing is fairly common. It obviously helps new shareholders earn a higher return on the shares they buy. The existing shareholders of the issuing firm are not helped by underpricing. To them, it is an indirect cost of issuing new securities. For example, consider the 2017 Snap IPO. Snap sold 145 million shares in the IPO at a price of $17. The stock opened at $24 and rose to a first-day high of $26.05, before closing at $24.48. Based on these numbers, Snap was underpriced by about $7.48 per share, which means the company missed out on an additional $1.085 billion or so "left on the table." In 1999, eToys's 8.2-million-share IPO was underpriced by $57 per share, or almost a half a billion dollars in all. eToys could have used the money: It was bankrupt within two years.

Find out which firms are going public this week at **www.marketwatch.com**.

IPO UNDERPRICING: THE 1999–2000 EXPERIENCE

Table 15.2, along with Figures 15.2 and 15.3, shows that 1999 and 2000 were extraordinary years in the IPO market. Almost 900 companies went public, and the average first-day return across the two years was about 64 percent. During this time, 194 IPOs doubled, or more than doubled, in value on the first day. In contrast, only 39 did so in the preceding 24 years combined. One company, VA Linux, shot up 698 percent!

The dollar amount raised in 1999, $64.91 billion, was a record, followed closely by the $64.88 billion raised in 2000. The underpricing was so severe in 1999 that companies left

TABLE 15.2

Number of Offerings,
Average First-Day
Return, and Gross
Proceeds of Initial
Public Offerings:
1960–2016

Year	Number of Offerings*	Average First-Day Return, %†	Gross Proceeds, $ Millions‡
1960	269	17.8	553
1961	435	34.1	1,243
1962	298	−1.6	431
1963	83	3.9	246
1964	97	5.3	380
1965	146	12.7	409
1966	85	7.1	275
1967	100	37.7	641
1968	368	55.9	1,205
1969	780	12.5	2,605
1970	358	−.7	780
1971	391	21.2	1,655
1972	562	7.5	2,724
1973	105	−17.8	330
1974	9	−7.0	51
1975	12	−.2	261
1976	26	1.9	214
1977	15	3.6	128
1978	19	12.6	207
1979	39	8.5	313
1980	75	13.9	934
1981	196	6.2	2,367
1982	80	10.5	1,014
1983	524	8.9	11,370
1984	218	2.8	2,622
1985	218	6.5	4,964
1986	477	6.1	15,938
1987	336	5.7	12,481
1988	129	5.4	3,922
1989	122	7.8	5,308
1990	116	10.4	4,334
1991	293	11.8	16,431
1992	416	10.2	22,750
1993	527	12.7	31,756
1994	411	9.8	17,493
1995	464	21.1	29,511
1996	690	17.3	42,481
1997	486	13.9	32,559
1998	316	20.3	34,465
1999	486	69.7	64,913
2000	382	56.2	64,876
2001	79	14.2	34,241
2002	70	8.6	22,136
2003	68	11.9	10,075

TABLE 15.2
(*continued*)

Year	Number of Offerings*	Average First-Day Return, %[†]	Gross Proceeds, $ Millions[‡]
2004	183	12.3	31,927
2005	168	10.1	28,593
2006	162	11.9	30,648
2007	160	14.0	35,704
2008	21	5.7	22,762
2009	43	10.6	13,307
2010	100	9.2	30,708
2011	82	13.2	27,750
2012	105	17.1	32,074
2013	162	20.9	39,093
2014	224	14.9	46,940
2015	122	18.1	22,020
2016	77	14.4	12,736
1960–69	2,661	21.2	7,988
1970–79	1,536	7.1	6,663
1980–89	2,375	6.9	60,380
1990–99	4,205	21.0	296,693
2000–16	2,208	21.1	505,590
1960–2016	**12,985**	**16.8**	**877,314**

SOURCE: Data from 1960–1974 are taken from Ibbotson, Roger, Sindelar, Jody, and Ritter, Jay R., "The Market's Problems with the Pricing of Initial Public Offerings," *Journal of Applied Corporate Finance* 7, no. 1, Spring 1994, 66–74 (Table 1). Data from 1975–2016 are compiled by Jay R. Ritter using Thomson Financial, Dealogic, and other sources. The 1975–1993 numbers are different from those reported in the 1994 JACF article because the published article included IPOs that did not qualify for listing on Nasdaq, the Amex, or NYSE (mainly penny stocks).

*Beginning in 1975, the number of offerings excludes IPOs with an offer price of less than $5.00, ADRs, small best efforts offers, units, Regulation A offers (small issues, raising less than $1.5 million during the 1980s and $5 million until 2012), real estate investment trusts (REITs), natural resource limited partnerships, and closed-end funds. Banks and S&L IPOs are included. From 2012 and later, Regulation A offerings (issues raising up to $50 million are eligible) are included.

[†]First-day returns are computed as the percentage return from the offering price to the first closing market price.

[‡]Gross proceeds exclude overallotment options but include the international tranche, if any. No adjustments for inflation have been made.

FIGURE 15.2   Average Initial Returns by Month for SEC-Registered Initial Public Offerings: 1960–2016

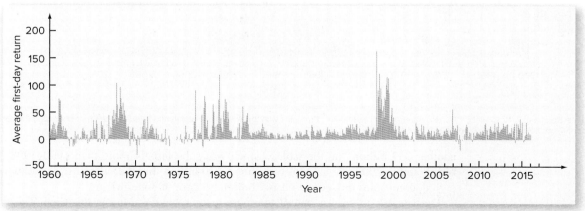

SOURCE: Ibbotson, R. G., Sindelar, J. L., and Ritter, J. R., "The Market's Problems with the Pricing of Initial Public Offerings," *Journal of Applied Corporate Finance* 7, no. 1, Spring 1994, as updated by the authors.

WORK THE WEB

So, do the high returns IPOs sometimes earn have you excited? Do you wonder how recent IPOs have performed? You can find out at www.ipomonitor.com. We went to the website and looked in the Best-Worst Performers area. Here is part of what we found:

5 Best Performers			
Date	**Company**	**Symbol**	**% Chg.**
2017-01-27	JELD-WEN Holding, Inc.	JELD	+17.6%
2017-01-20	Keane Group, Inc.	FRAC	+16.7%
2017-01-27	REV Group, Inc.	REVG	+14.8%
2017-01-26	AnaptysBio, Inc.	ANAB	+10.8%
2017-01-27	Jounce Therapeutics, Inc.	JNCE	+6.8%

As you can see, in January 2017, JELD-WEN Holding and Keane Group had the largest first-day returns.

Questions

1. Go to www.ipomonitor.com and find the companies that have had the biggest first-day gains in the most recent quarter. How do those gains compare with the biggest gains shown above? Which companies had the biggest first-day price drop?
2. Go to www.ipomonitor.com and find out which companies have filed for an IPO but have yet to start trading.

FIGURE 15.3   **Number of Offerings by Month for SEC-Registered Initial Public Offerings: 1960–2016**

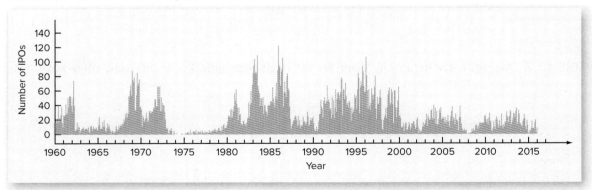

SOURCE: Ibbotson, R. G., Sindelar, J. L., and Ritter, J. R., "The Market's Problems with the Pricing of Initial Public Offerings," *Journal of Applied Corporate Finance* 7, no. 1, Spring 1994, as updated by the authors.

another $37 billion "on the table," which was substantially more than 1990–1998 combined; and in 2000, the amount was almost $30 billion. In other words, over the two-year period, companies missed out on $67 billion because of underpricing.

October 19, 1999, was one of the more memorable days during this time. The World Wrestling Federation (WWF) (now known as World Wrestling Entertainment, or WWE) and Martha Stewart Omnimedia both went public. When the closing bell rang, it was a

The United States is not the only country in which initial public offerings (IPOs) of common stock are underpriced. The phenomenon exists in every country with a stock market, although the extent of underpricing varies from country to country.

In general, countries with developed capital markets have more moderate underpricing than in emerging markets. During the Internet bubble of 1999–2000, however, underpricing in the developed capital markets increased dramatically. In the United States, for example, the average first-day return during 1999–2000 was 65 percent. Since the bursting of the Internet bubble in mid-2000, the level of underpricing in the United States, Germany, and other developed capital markets has returned to more traditional levels.

The underpricing of Chinese IPOs used to be extreme, but in recent years it has moderated. In the 1990s, Chinese government regulations required that the offer price could not be more than 15 times earnings, even when comparable stocks had a price-earnings ratio of 45. In 2011–2012, the average first-day return was 21 percent. But in 2013, there were no IPOs in China at all, due to a moratorium that the government imposed because it thought that an increase in the supply of shares would depress stock prices.

The following table gives a summary of the average first-day returns on IPOs in a number of countries around the world, with the figures collected from a number of studies by various authors.

Country	Sample Size	Time Period	Avg. Initial Return, %	Country	Sample Size	Time Period	Avg. Initial Return, %
Argentina	26	1991–2013	4.2	Malaysia	474	1980–2013	56.2
Australia	1,562	1976–2011	21.8	Mauritius	40	1989–2005	15.2
Austria	103	1971–2013	6.4	Mexico	123	1987–2002	11.6
Belgium	114	1984–2006	13.5	Morocco	33	2004–2011	33.3
Brazil	275	1979–2011	33.1	Netherlands	181	1982–2006	10.2
Bulgaria	9	2004–2007	36.5	New Zealand	242	1979–2013	18.6
Canada	720	1971–2013	6.5	Nigeria	122	1989–2013	13.1
Chile	81	1982–2013	7.4	Norway	209	1984–2013	8.1
China	2,637	1990–2014	113.5	Pakistan	80	2000–2013	22.1
Cyprus	73	1997–2012	20.3	Philippines	155	1987–2013	18.1
Denmark	164	1984–2011	7.4	Poland	309	1991–2014	12.7
Egypt	62	1990–2010	10.4	Portugal	32	1992–2006	11.9
Finland	168	1971–2013	16.9	Russia	64	1999–2013	3.3
France	697	1983–2010	10.5	Saudi Arabia	80	2003–2011	239.8
Germany	779	1978–2014	23.0	Singapore	609	1973–2013	25.8
Greece	373	1976–2013	50.8	South Africa	316	1980–2013	17.4
Hong Kong	1,486	1980–2013	15.8	Spain	143	1986–2013	10.3
India	2,983	1990–2014	88.0	Sri Lanka	105	1987–2008	33.5
Indonesia	464	1990–2014	24.9	Sweden	405	1980–2015	25.9
Iran	279	1991–2004	22.4	Switzerland	164	1983–2013	27.3
Ireland	38	1991–2013	21.6	Taiwan	1,620	1980–2013	38.1
Israel	348	1990–2006	13.8	Thailand	500	1987–2012	35.1
Italy	312	1985–2013	15.2	Tunisia	38	2001–2014	21.7
Japan	3,313	1970–2014	42.8	Turkey	404	1990–2014	9.6
Jordan	53	1999–2008	149.0	United Kingdom	4,932	1959–2012	16.0
Korea	1,758	1980–2014	58.8	United States	12,819	1960–2015	16.9

Jay R. Ritter is Cordell Professor of Finance at the University of Florida. An outstanding scholar, he is well known for his insightful analyses of new issues and going public.

SOURCE: *Jay R. Ritter's website.*

clear smack-down as Martha Stewart gained 98 percent on the first day compared to 48 percent for the WWF. If you're interested in finding out how IPOs have done recently, check out our nearby *Work the Web* box.

EVIDENCE ON UNDERPRICING

Figure 15.2 provides a more general illustration of the underpricing phenomenon. What is shown is the month-by-month history of underpricing for SEC-registered IPOs.[8] The period covered is 1960 through 2016. Figure 15.3 presents the number of offerings in each month for the same period.

Figure 15.2 shows that underpricing can be quite dramatic, exceeding 100 percent in some months. In such months, the average IPO more than doubled in value, sometimes in a matter of hours. Also, the degree of underpricing varies through time, and periods of severe underpricing ("hot issue" markets) are followed by periods of little underpricing ("cold issue" markets). For example, in the 1960s, the average IPO was underpriced by 21.2 percent. In the 1970s, the average underpricing was much smaller (7.1 percent), and the amount of underpricing was actually very small or even negative for much of that time. Underpricing in the 1980s ran about 6.9 percent. For 1990–1999, IPOs were underpriced by 21 percent on average, and they were underpriced by 21.1 percent in 2000–2016.

From Figure 15.3, it is apparent that the number of IPOs is also highly variable through time. Further, there are pronounced cycles in both the degree of underpricing and the number of IPOs. Comparing Figures 15.2 and 15.3, we see that increases in the number of new offerings tend to follow periods of significant underpricing by roughly six months. This probably occurs because companies decide to go public when they perceive that the market is highly receptive to new issues.

Table 15.2 contains a year-by-year summary of underpricing for the years 1960–2016. As indicated, a grand total of 12,985 companies were included in this analysis. The degree of underpricing averaged 16.8 percent overall for the 57 years examined. Securities were overpriced on average in only 5 of the 57 years. At the other extreme, in 1999, the 486 issues were underpriced, on average, by a remarkable 69.7 percent.

THE PARTIAL ADJUSTMENT PHENOMENON

When a company files its registration statement with the SEC, it will at some point in the process indicate a range of stock prices between which it expects to offer shares. This range is called the "file price range" or words to that effect. A file price range of $10 to $12 is common, but many others exist. For example, when Fitbit first filed its IPO on June 2, 2015, the company indicated a maximum anticipated price of $16.

Just before a company's shares are sold to investors, the final IPO offer price is determined. As shown in Section A of Table 15.3, that price can be above, within, or below the price range originally indicated by the company. Over the period 1980–2016, 48 percent of IPOs were within the file range, with 29 percent below and 23 percent above.

Section B of Table 15.3 illustrates an interesting and very clear pattern. IPO underpricing is much more severe when an offer is priced above the file range. Again over the 1980–2016 period, IPOs that priced above the file range were underpriced by 50 percent, on average, compared to only 3 percent for firms priced below it. The 1999–2000 period again stands out. Issues that "went off" above the file range were underpriced by an average of 121 percent!

This pattern is known as the "partial adjustment" phenomenon. The name refers to the fact that when firms raise their IPO offer prices, they only do so partially, meaning that they don't move the price high enough. In Fitbit's case, for example, the final offer price

[8]The discussion in this section draws on R. G. Ibbotson, J. L. Sindelar, and J. R. Ritter, "The Market's Problems with the Pricing of Initial Public Offerings," *Journal of Applied Corporate Finance* 7, no. 1 (Spring 1994).

TABLE 15.3

IPO Underpricing and File Price Range

A: Percentage of IPOs Relative to File Price Range	Below	Within	Above
1980–1989	30%	57%	13%
1990–1998	27	49	24
1999–2000	18	38	44
2001–2016	36	43	22
1980–2016	29	48	23

B: Average First-Day Returns Relative to File Price Range	Below	Within	Above
1980–1989	0%	6%	20%
1990–1998	4	11	31
1999–2000	8	26	121
2001–2016	3	11	37
1980–2016	3	11	50

was $20, an amount 25 percent higher than the original maximum price: The stock jumped 48 percent on the first day of trading. The Snap IPO we discussed to open the chapter is another good example. The company indicated a preliminary price range of $14–$16, but the final offer price was $17, and the stock soared on the first day of trading.

Why does the partial adjustment phenomenon exist? The answer is unknown. The question is related to the broader question of why IPO underpricing exists, which we consider next.

WHY DOES UNDERPRICING EXIST?

Based on the evidence we've examined, an obvious question is, Why does underpricing continue to exist? As we discuss, there are various explanations; but to date, there is a lack of complete agreement among researchers as to which of these is correct.

We present some pieces of the underpricing puzzle by stressing two important caveats to our preceding discussion. First, the average figures we have examined tend to obscure the fact that much of the apparent underpricing is attributable to the smaller, more highly speculative issues. This point is illustrated in Table 15.4, which shows the extent of underpricing for IPOs over the period from 1980 through 2016. Here, the firms are grouped based on their total sales in the 12 months prior to the IPO.

TABLE 15.4   Average First-Day Returns, Categorized by Sales, for IPOs: 1980–2016*

Annual Sales of Issuing Firms	1980–1989 Return	N	1990–1998 Return	N	1999–2000 Return	N	2001–2016 Return	N
0 ≤ sales < $10m	10.3%	420	17.2%	741	68.9%	331	9.7%	338
$10m ≤ sales < $20m	8.7	243	18.7	393	81.4	138	13.8	72
$20m ≤ sales < $50m	7.8	500	18.8	791	75.0	155	14.4	213
$50m ≤ sales < $100m	6.3	356	12.9	589	61.8	87	20.8	273
$100m ≤ sales < $200m	5.1	234	11.8	454	35.8	56	17.5	231
$200m ≤ sales	3.4	290	8.7	645	25.0	91	11.9	607
All	7.3	2,043	14.8	3,613	64.5	858	14.0	1,734

*Sales, measured in millions, are for the last 12 months prior to going public. All sales have been converted into dollars of 2003 purchasing power, using the Consumer Price Index. There are 8,248 IPOs, after excluding IPOs with an offer price of less than $5.00 per share, units, REITs, ADRs, closed-end funds, banks and S&Ls, firms not listed on CRSP within six months of the offering, and energy-related limited partnerships. Sales are from Thomson Financial's SDC, Dealogic, EDGAR, and the Graeme Howard-Todd Huxster collection of pre-EDGAR prospectuses. The average first-day return is 17.9 percent.
SOURCE: Professor Jay R. Ritter, University of Florida.

As illustrated in Table 15.4, the underpricing tends to be higher for firms with few to no sales in the previous year. These firms tend to be young firms, and such young firms can be very risky investments. Arguably, they must be significantly underpriced, on average, just to attract investors, and this is one explanation for the underpricing phenomenon.

The second caveat is that relatively few IPO buyers will actually get the initial high average returns observed in IPOs, and many will actually lose money. Although it is true that, on average, IPOs have positive initial returns, a significant fraction of them have price drops. Furthermore, when the price is too low, the issue is often "oversubscribed." This means investors will not be able to buy all of the shares they want, and the underwriters will allocate the shares among investors.

The average investor will find it difficult to get shares in a "successful" offering (one in which the price increases) because there will not be enough shares to go around. On the other hand, an investor blindly submitting orders for IPOs tends to get more shares in issues that go down in price.

To illustrate, consider this tale of two investors. Smith knows very accurately what the Bonanza Corporation is worth when its shares are offered. She is confident that the shares are underpriced. Jones knows only that prices usually rise one month after an IPO. Armed with this information, Jones decides to buy 1,000 shares of every IPO. Does he actually earn an abnormally high return on the initial offering?

The answer is no, and at least one reason is Smith. Knowing about the Bonanza Corporation, Smith invests all her money in its IPO. When the issue is oversubscribed, the underwriters have to somehow allocate the shares between Smith and Jones. The net result is that when an issue is underpriced, Jones doesn't get to buy as much of it as he wanted.

Smith also knows that the Blue Sky Corporation IPO is overpriced. In this case, she avoids its IPO altogether, and Jones ends up with a full 1,000 shares. To summarize this tale, Jones gets fewer shares when more knowledgeable investors swarm to buy an underpriced issue and he gets all he wants when the smart money avoids the issue.

This is an example of a "winner's curse," and it is thought to be another reason why IPOs have such a large average return. When the average investor "wins" and gets the entire allocation, it may be because those who knew better avoided the issue. The only way underwriters can counteract the winner's curse and attract the average investor is to underprice new issues (on average) so that the average investor still makes a profit.

Another reason for underpricing is that the underpricing is a kind of insurance for the investment banks. Conceivably, an investment bank could be sued successfully by angry customers if it consistently overpriced securities. Underpricing guarantees that, at least on average, customers will come out ahead.

A final reason for underpricing is that before the offer price is established, investment banks talk to big institutional investors to gauge the level of interest in the stock and to gather opinions about a suitable price. Underpricing is a way that the bank can reward these investors for truthfully revealing what they think the stock is worth and the number of shares they would like to buy.

Concept Questions

15.5a Why is underpricing a cost to the issuing firm?

15.5b Suppose a stockbroker calls you up out of the blue and offers to sell you "all the shares you want" of a new issue. Do you think the issue will be more or less underpriced than average?

New Equity Sales and the Value of the Firm   15.6

We now turn to a consideration of seasoned offerings, which, as we discussed earlier, are offerings by firms that already have outstanding securities. It seems reasonable to believe that new long-term financing is arranged by firms after positive net present value projects are put together. As a consequence, when the announcement of external financing is made, the firm's market value should go up. Interestingly, this is not what happens. Stock prices tend to decline following the announcement of a new equity issue, although they tend to not change much following a debt announcement. A number of researchers have studied this issue. Plausible reasons for this strange result include the following:

1. *Managerial information*: If management has superior information about the market value of the firm, it may know when the firm is overvalued. If it does, then it will attempt to issue new shares of stock when the market value exceeds the correct value. This will benefit existing shareholders. However, the potential new shareholders are not stupid, and they will anticipate this superior information and discount it in lower market prices at the new-issue date.

2. *Debt usage*: A company's decision to issue new equity may reveal that the company has too much debt or too little liquidity. One version of this argument says that the equity issue is a bad signal to the market. After all, if the new projects are favorable ones, why should the firm let new shareholders in on them? It could just issue debt and let the existing shareholders have all the gain.

3. *Issue costs*: As we discuss next, there are substantial costs associated with selling securities.

The drop in value of the existing stock following the announcement of a new issue is an example of an indirect cost of selling securities. This drop might typically be on the order of 3 percent for an industrial corporation (and somewhat smaller for a public utility); so, for a large company, it can represent a substantial amount of money. In our discussion of the costs of new issues (see Section 15.7), we label this drop the *abnormal return*.

To give a couple of recent examples, in December 2017, biopharmeceutical company Cascadian Therapeutics announced a secondary offering. Its stock fell about 3.4 percent on the day of the announcement. Also in December 2017, power systems company Digital Power announced a secondary offering. Its stock dropped 11.1 percent on the day of the announcement.

Concept Questions

15.6a What are some possible reasons why the price of a stock drops on the announcement of a new equity issue?

15.6b Explain why we might expect a firm with a positive NPV investment to finance it with debt instead of equity.

The Costs of Issuing Securities   15.7

Issuing securities to the public isn't free, and the costs of different methods are important determinants of which is used. These costs associated with *floating* a new issue are generically called *flotation costs*. In this section, we take a closer look at the flotation costs associated with equity sales to the public.

THE COSTS OF SELLING STOCK TO THE PUBLIC

The costs of selling stock are classified in the following list and fall into six categories: (1) the gross spread, (2) other direct expenses, (3) indirect expenses, (4) abnormal returns (discussed previously), (5) underpricing, and (6) the Green Shoe provision.

THE COSTS OF ISSUING SECURITIES

1. *Gross spread*	The gross spread consists of direct fees paid by the issuer to the underwriting syndicate—the difference between the price the issuer receives and the offer price.
2. *Other direct expenses*	These are direct costs, incurred by the issuer, that are not part of the compensation to underwriters. These costs include filing fees, legal fees, and taxes—all reported on the prospectus.
3. *Indirect expenses*	These costs are not reported on the prospectus and include the costs of management time spent working on the new issue.
4. *Abnormal returns*	In a seasoned issue of stock, the price of the existing stock drops on average by 3 percent on the announcement of the issue. This drop is called the *abnormal return*.
5. *Underpricing*	For initial public offerings, losses arise from selling the stock below the true value.
6. *Green Shoe option*	The Green Shoe option gives the underwriters the right to buy additional shares at the offer price to cover overallotments.

Table 15.5 reports direct costs as a percentage of the gross amount raised for IPOs, SEOs, straight (ordinary) bonds, and convertible bonds sold by U.S. companies over the 19-year period from 1990 through 2008. These are direct costs only. Not included are indirect expenses, the cost of the Green Shoe provision, underpricing (for IPOs), and abnormal returns (for SEOs).

As Table 15.5 shows, the direct costs alone can be very large, particularly for smaller issues (less than $10 million). On a smaller IPO, for example, the total direct costs amount to 25.22 percent of the amount raised. This means that if a company sells $10 million in stock, it will net only about $7.5 million; the other $2.5 million goes to cover the underwriter spread and other direct expenses. Typical underwriter spreads on an IPO range from about 5 percent up to 10 percent or so, but for well over half of the IPOs in Table 15.5, the spread is exactly 7 percent; so this is, by far, the most common spread.

Overall, four clear patterns emerge from Table 15.5. First, with the possible exception of straight debt offerings (about which we will have more to say later), there are substantial economies of scale. The underwriter spreads are smaller on larger issues, and the other direct costs fall sharply as a percentage of the amount raised—a reflection of the mostly fixed nature of such costs. Second, the costs associated with selling debt are substantially less than the costs of selling equity. Third, IPOs have higher expenses than SEOs, but the difference is not as great as might originally be guessed. Finally, straight bonds are cheaper to float than convertible bonds.

As we have discussed, the underpricing of IPOs is an additional cost to the issuer. To give a better idea of the total cost of going public, Table 15.6 combines the information in Table 15.5 for IPOs with data on the underpricing experienced by these firms. Overall, across all size groups, the total direct costs amount to about 10 percent of the amount raised, and the underpricing amounts to about 19 percent.

Finally, with regard to debt offerings, there is a general pattern in issue costs that is somewhat obscured in Table 15.5. Recall from Chapter 7 that bonds carry different credit

TABLE 15.5 Direct Costs as a Percentage of Gross Proceeds for Equity (IPOs and SEOs) and Straight and Convertible Bonds Offered by Domestic Operating Companies: 1990–2008

Proceeds ($ millions)	IPOs				SEOs			
	Number of Issues	Gross Spread	Other Direct Expense	Total Direct Cost	Number of Issues	Gross Spread	Other Direct Expense	Total Direct Cost
2.00–9.99	1,007	9.40%	15.82%	25.22%	515	8.11%	26.99%	35.11%
10.00–19.99	810	7.39	7.30	14.69	726	6.11	7.76	13.86
20.00–39.99	1,422	6.96	7.06	14.03	1,393	5.44	4.10	9.54
40.00–59.99	880	6.89	2.87	9.77	1,129	5.03	8.93	13.96
60.00–79.99	522	6.79	2.16	8.94	841	4.88	1.98	6.85
80.00–99.99	327	6.71	1.84	8.55	536	4.67	2.05	6.72
100.00–199.99	702	6.39	1.57	7.96	1,372	4.34	.89	5.23
200.00–499.99	440	5.81	1.03	6.84	811	3.72	1.22	4.94
500.00 and up	155	5.01	.49	5.50	264	3.10	.27	3.37
Total/Avg	**6,265**	**7.19**	**3.18**	**10.37**	**7,587**	**5.02**	**2.68**	**7.69**

Proceeds ($ millions)	Straight Bonds				Convertible Bonds			
	Number of Issues	Gross Spread	Other Direct Expense	Total Direct Cost	Number of Issues	Gross Spread	Other Direct Expense	Total Direct Cost
2.00–9.99	3,962	1.64%	2.40%	4.03%	14	6.39%	3.43%	9.82%
10.00–19.99	3,400	1.50	1.71	3.20	23	5.52	3.09	8.61
20.00–39.99	2,690	1.25	.92	2.17	30	4.63	1.67	6.30
40.00–59.99	3,345	.81	.79	1.59	35	3.49	1.04	4.54
60.00–79.99	891	1.65	.80	2.44	60	2.79	.62	3.41
80.00–99.99	465	1.41	.57	1.98	16	2.30	.62	2.92
100.00–199.99	4,949	1.61	.52	2.14	82	2.66	.42	3.08
200.00–499.99	3,305	1.38	.33	1.71	46	2.65	.33	2.99
500.00 and up	1,261	.61	.15	.76	7	2.16	.13	2.29
Total/Avg	**24,268**	**1.38**	**.61**	**2.00**	**313**	**3.07**	**.85**	**3.92**

SOURCE: Lee, I. et al., "The Costs of Raising Capital," *Journal of Financial Research* 19, Spring 1996, updated by the authors.

TABLE 15.6

Direct and Indirect Costs, in Percentages, of Equity IPOs: 1990–2008

Proceeds ($ millions)	Number of Issues	Gross Spread	Other Direct Expense	Total Direct Cost	Underpricing
2.00–9.99	1,007	9.40%	15.82%	25.22%	20.42%
10.00–19.99	810	7.39	7.30	14.69	10.33
20.00–39.99	1,422	6.96	7.06	14.03	17.03
40.00–59.99	880	6.89	2.87	9.77	28.26
60.00–79.99	522	6.79	2.16	8.94	28.36
80.00–99.99	327	6.71	1.84	8.55	32.92
100.00–199.99	702	6.39	1.57	7.96	21.55
200.00–499.99	440	5.81	1.03	6.84	6.19
500.00 and up	155	5.01	.49	5.50	6.64
Total/Avg	**6,265**	**7.19**	**3.18**	**10.37**	**19.34**

SOURCE: Lee, I. et al., "The Costs of Raising Capital," *Journal of Financial Research* 19, Spring 1996, updated by the authors.

ratings. Higher-rated bonds are said to be investment grade, whereas lower-rated bonds are noninvestment grade. Table 15.7 contains a breakdown of direct costs for bond issues after the investment and noninvestment grades have been separated.

Table 15.7 clarifies two things regarding debt issues. First, there are substantial economies of scale here as well. Second, investment-grade issues have much lower direct costs, particularly for straight bonds.

THE COSTS OF GOING PUBLIC: A CASE STUDY

On July 21, 2016, Impinj, the Seattle-based radio-frequency identification company, went public via an IPO. Impinj issued 4.8 million shares of stock at a price of $14 each. The lead underwriter on the IPO was RBC Capital Markets, assisted by a syndicate of other investment banks. Even though the IPO raised a gross sum of $67.2 million, Impinj only got to keep $62.496 million after expenses. The biggest expense was the 7 percent underwriter spread, which is the usual spread for an offering of that size. Impinj sold each of the 4.8 million shares to the underwriters for $13.02, and the underwriters in turn sold the shares to the public for $14 each.

But wait—there's more. Impinj spent $7,458 in SEC registration fees and $11,609 in FINRA filing fees. The company also spent $125,000 in exchange listing fees, $1.6 million in legal fees, $417,000 on accounting to obtain the necessary audits, $5,000 for a transfer agent to physically transfer the shares and maintain a list of shareholders, $255,000 for printing and engraving expenses, and finally, $261,000 in miscellaneous expenses.

As Impinj's outlays show, an IPO can be a costly undertaking! In the end, Impinj's expenses totaled $7.39 million, of which $4.7 million went to the underwriters and $2.69 million went to other parties. All told, the total direct cost to Impinj was 11.8 percent of the issue proceeds raised by the company.

Concept Questions

15.7a What are the different costs associated with security offerings?

15.7b What lessons do we learn from studying issue costs?

TABLE 15.7 Average Gross Spreads and Total Direct Costs for Domestic Debt Issues: 1990–2008

Convertible Bonds

Proceeds ($ millions)	Investment Grade				Junk or Not Rated			
	Number of Issues	Gross Spread	Other Direct Expense	Total Direct Cost	Number of Issues	Gross Spread	Other Direct Expense	Total Direct Cost
2.00–9.99	–	–	–	–	14	6.39%	3.43%	9.82%
10.00–19.99	1	14.12%	1.87%	15.98%	23	5.52	3.09	8.61
20.00–39.99	–	–	–	–	30	4.63	1.67	6.30
40.00–59.99	3	1.92	.51	2.43	35	3.49	1.04	4.54
60.00–79.99	6	1.65	.44	2.09	60	2.79	.62	3.41
80.00–99.99	4	.89	.27	1.16	16	2.30	.62	2.92
100.00–199.99	27	2.22	.33	2.55	82	2.66	.42	3.08
200.00–499.99	27	2.03	.19	2.22	46	2.65	.33	2.99
500.00 and up	11	1.94	.13	2.06	7	2.16	.13	2.29
Total/Avg	**79**	**2.15**	**.29**	**2.44**	**313**	**3.31**	**.98**	**4.29**

Straight Bonds

Proceeds ($ millions)	Investment Grade				Junk or Not Rated			
	Number of Issues	Gross Spread	Other Direct Expense	Total Direct Cost	Number of Issues	Gross Spread	Other Direct Expense	Total Direct Cost
2.00–9.99	2,709	.62%	1.28%	1.90%	1,253	2.77%	2.50%	5.27%
10.00–19.99	2,564	.59	1.17	1.76	836	3.15	1.97	5.12
20.00–39.99	2,400	.63	.74	1.37	290	3.07	1.13	4.20
40.00–59.99	3,146	.40	.52	.92	199	2.93	1.20	4.14
60.00–79.99	792	.58	.38	.96	99	3.12	1.16	4.28
80.00–99.99	385	.66	.29	.96	80	2.73	.93	3.66
100.00–199.99	4,427	.54	.25	.79	522	2.73	.68	3.41
200.00–499.99	3,031	.52	.25	.76	274	2.59	.39	2.98
500.00 and up	1,207	.31	.08	.39	54	2.38	.25	2.63
Total/Avg	**20,661**	**.52**	**.35**	**.87**	**3,607**	**2.76**	**.81**	**3.57**

Source: Lee, I. et al., "The Costs of Raising Capital," *Journal of Financial Research* 19, Spring 1996, updated by the authors.

15.8 Rights

When new shares of common stock are sold to the general public, the proportional owner-ship of existing shareholders is likely to be reduced. If a preemptive right is contained in the firm's articles of incorporation, the firm must first offer any new issue of common stock to existing shareholders. If the articles of incorporation do not include a preemptive right, the firm has a choice of offering the issue of common stock directly to existing shareholders or to the public.

An issue of common stock offered to existing stockholders is called a *rights offering* (or *offer*, for short) or a *privileged subscription*. In a rights offering, each shareholder is issued rights to buy a specified number of new shares from the firm at a specified price within a specified time, after which the rights are said to *expire*. The terms of the rights offering are evidenced by certificates known as *share warrants* or *rights*. Such rights are often traded on securities exchanges or over the counter.

Rights offerings have some interesting advantages relative to cash offers. For example, they appear to be cheaper for the issuing firm than cash offers. In fact, a firm can do a rights offering without using an underwriter; whereas, as a practical matter, an underwriter is almost a necessity in a cash offer. Despite this, rights offerings are fairly rare in the United States; in many other countries, they are more common than cash offers. Why this is true is a bit of a mystery and the source of much debate; but to our knowledge, no definitive answer exists.

THE MECHANICS OF A RIGHTS OFFERING

To illustrate the various considerations a financial manager faces in a rights offering, we will examine the situation faced by the National Power Company, whose abbreviated initial financial statements are given in Table 15.8.

As indicated in Table 15.8, National Power earns $2 million after taxes and has 1 million shares outstanding. Earnings per share are $2, and the stock sells for $20, or 10 times earnings (that is, the price-earnings ratio is 10). To fund a planned expansion, the company intends to raise $5 million worth of new equity funds through a rights offering.

TABLE 15.8

National Power Company Financial Statements Before Rights Offering

NATIONAL POWER COMPANY			
Balance Sheet			
Assets		Shareholders' Equity	
Assets	$15,000,000	Common stock	$ 5,000,000
		Retained earnings	10,000,000
Total	$15,000,000	Total	$15,000,000
Income Statement			
Earnings before taxes	$ 2,531,646		
Taxes (21%)	531,646		
Net income	$ 2,000,000		
Shares outstanding	1,000,000		
Earnings per share	$ 2		
Market price per share	$ 20		
Total market value	$20,000,000		

To execute a rights offering, the financial management of National Power will have to answer the following questions:

1. What should the price per share be for the new stock?
2. How many shares will have to be sold?
3. How many shares will each shareholder be allowed to buy?

Also, management will probably want to ask this:

4. What is likely to be the effect of the rights offering on the per-share value of the existing stock?

It turns out that the answers to these questions are highly interrelated. We will get to them in just a moment.

The early stages of a rights offering are the same as those for a general cash offer. The difference between a rights offering and a general cash offer lies in how the shares are sold. In a rights offer, National Power's existing shareholders are informed that they own one right for each share of stock they own. National Power will then specify how many rights a shareholder needs to buy one additional share at a specified price.

To take advantage of the rights offering, shareholders have to exercise the rights by filling out a subscription form and sending it, along with payment, to the firm's subscription agent (the subscription agent is usually a bank). Shareholders of National Power will actually have several choices: (1) Exercise their rights and subscribe for some or all of the entitled shares, (2) order some or all of the rights sold, or (3) do nothing and let the rights expire. As we will discuss, this third course of action is inadvisable.

NUMBER OF RIGHTS NEEDED TO PURCHASE A SHARE

National Power wants to raise $5 million in new equity. Suppose the subscription price is set at $10 per share. How National Power arrives at that price we will discuss later; but notice that the subscription price is substantially less than the current $20 per share market price.

At $10 per share, National Power will have to issue 500,000 new shares. This can be determined by dividing the total amount of funds to be raised by the subscription price:

$$\text{Number of new shares} = \frac{\text{Funds to be raised}}{\text{Subscription price}} \qquad \textbf{15.1}$$

$$= \frac{\$5,000,000}{\$10} = 500,000 \text{ shares}$$

Because stockholders always get one right for each share of stock they own, 1 million rights will be issued by National Power. To determine how many rights will be needed to buy one new share of stock, we can divide the number of existing outstanding shares of stock by the number of new shares:

$$\frac{\text{Number of rights needed}}{\text{to buy a share of stock}} = \frac{\text{Old shares}}{\text{New shares}} \qquad \textbf{15.2}$$

$$= \frac{1,000,000}{500,000} = 2 \text{ rights}$$

A shareholder will need to give up two rights plus $10 to receive a share of new stock. If all the stockholders do this, National Power will raise the required $5 million.

It should be clear that the subscription price, the number of new shares, and the number of rights needed to buy a new share of stock are interrelated. For example, National Power can lower the subscription price. If it does, then more new shares will have to be issued to raise $5 million in new equity. Several alternatives are worked out here:

Subscription Price	Number of New Shares	Number of Rights Needed to Buy a Share of Stock
$20	250,000	4
10	500,000	2
5	1,000,000	1

THE VALUE OF A RIGHT

Rights clearly have value. In the case of National Power, the right to buy a share of stock worth $20 for $10 is definitely worth something. In fact, if you think about it, a right is essentially a call option, which we will discuss in more detail in later chapters. The most important difference between a right and an ordinary call option is that rights are issued by the firm, so they more closely resemble warrants. In general, the valuation of options, rights, and warrants can be fairly complex, so we defer a full discussion of this subject to a later chapter. However, we can discuss the value of a right just prior to expiration to illustrate some important points.

Suppose a shareholder of National Power owns two shares of stock just before the rights offering is about to expire. This situation is depicted in Table 15.9. Initially, the price of National Power is $20 per share, so the shareholder's total holding is worth $2 \times \$20 = \$40$. The National Power rights offer gives shareholders with two rights the opportunity to purchase one additional share for $10. The additional share does not carry a right.

The stockholder who has two shares will receive two rights. The holding of the shareholder who exercises these rights and buys the new share will increase to three shares. The total investment will be $\$40 + 10 = \$50$ (the $40 initial value plus the $10 paid to the company).

The stockholder now holds three shares, all of which are identical because the new share does not have a right and the rights attached to the old shares have been exercised. Because the total cost of buying these three shares is $\$40 + 10 = \$50$, the price per share must end up at $50/3 = \$16.67$ (rounded to two decimal places).

TABLE 15.9

The Value of Rights: The Individual Shareholder

Initial Position	
Number of shares	2
Share price	$20
Value of holding	$40
Terms of Offer	
Subscription price	$10
Number of rights issued	2
Number of rights for a new share	2
After Offer	
Number of shares	3
Value of holding	$50
Share price	$16.67
Value of one right: Old price − New price	$20 − 16.67 = $3.33

Initial Position	
Number of shares	1 million
Share price	$20
Value of firm	$20 million
Terms of Offer	
Subscription price	$10
Number of rights issued	1 million
Number of rights for a new share	2
After Offer	
Number of shares	1.5 million
Share price	$16.67
Value of firm	$25 million
Value of one right	$20 − 16.67 = $3.33

TABLE 15.10

National Power Company Rights Offering

Table 15.10 summarizes what happens to National Power's stock price. If all shareholders exercise their rights, the number of shares will increase to 1 million + .5 million = 1.5 million. The value of the firm will increase to $20 million + 5 million = $25 million. The value of each share will drop to $25 million/1.5 million = $16.67 after the rights offering.

The difference between the old share price of $20 and the new share price of $16.67 reflects the fact that the old shares carried rights to subscribe to the new issue. The difference must be equal to the value of one right—that is, $20 − 16.67 = $3.33.

An investor holding no shares of outstanding National Power stock who wants to subscribe to the new issue can do so by buying some rights. Suppose an outside investor buys two rights. This will cost $3.33 × 2 = $6.67 (to account for previous rounding). If the investor exercises the rights at a subscription price of $10, the total cost will be $10 + 6.67 = $16.67. In return for this expenditure, the investor will receive a share of the new stock, which, as we have seen, is worth $16.67.

Exercising Your Rights: Part 1	**EXAMPLE 15.1**

In the National Power example, suppose the subscription price is set at $8. How many shares will have to be sold? How many rights will you need to buy a new share? What is the value of a right? What will the price per share be after the rights offer?

To raise $5 million, $5 million/$8 = 625,000 shares will need to be sold. There are 1 million shares outstanding, so it will take 1 million/625,000 = 8/5 = 1.6 rights to buy a new share of stock (you can buy five new shares for every eight you own). After the rights offer, there will be 1.625 million shares, worth $25 million altogether, so the per-share value will be $25/1.625 = $15.38. The value of a right in this case is the $20 original price less the $15.38 ending price, or $4.62.

EX RIGHTS

National Power's rights have a substantial value. In addition, the rights offering will have a large impact on the market price of National Power's stock. That price will drop by $3.33 on the **ex-rights date**.

ex-rights date
The beginning of the period when stock is sold without a recently declared right, normally two trading days before the holder-of-record date.

FIGURE 15.4

Ex-Rights Stock Prices

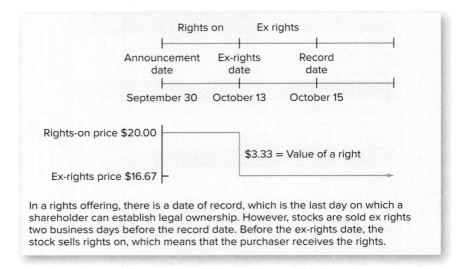

In a rights offering, there is a date of record, which is the last day on which a shareholder can establish legal ownership. However, stocks are sold ex rights two business days before the record date. Before the ex-rights date, the stock sells rights on, which means that the purchaser receives the rights.

holder-of-record date

The date on which existing shareholders on company records are designated as the recipients of stock rights. Also, the date of record.

The standard procedure for issuing rights involves the firm's setting a **holder-of-record date**. Following stock exchange rules, the stock typically goes ex rights two trading days before the holder-of-record date. If the stock is sold before the ex-rights date—"rights on," "with rights," or "cum rights"—the new owner will receive the rights. After the ex-rights date, an investor who purchases the shares will not receive the rights. This is depicted for National Power in Figure 15.4.

As illustrated, on September 30, National Power announces the terms of the rights offering, stating that the rights will be mailed on, say, November 1 to stockholders of record as of October 15. Because October 13 is the ex-rights date, only shareholders who own the stock on or before October 12 will receive the rights.

EXAMPLE 15.2   **Exercising Your Rights: Part II**

The Lagrange Point Co. has proposed a rights offering. The stock currently sells for $40 per share. Under the terms of the offer, stockholders will be allowed to buy one new share for every five that they own at a price of $25 per share. What is the value of a right? What is the ex-rights price?

You can buy five rights-on shares for 5 × $40 = $200 and then exercise the rights for another $25. Your total investment is $225, and you end up with six ex-rights shares. The ex-rights price per share is $225/6 = $37.50. The rights are worth $40 − 37.50 = $2.50 apiece.

EXAMPLE 15.3   **Right On**

In Example 15.2, suppose the rights sell for only $2 instead of the $2.50 we calculated. What can you do?

You can get rich quickly because you have found a money machine. Here's the recipe: Buy five rights for $10. Exercise them and pay $25 to get a new share. Your total investment to get one ex-rights share is 5 × $2 + 25 = $35. Sell the share for $37.50 and pocket the $2.50 difference. Repeat as desired.

THE UNDERWRITING ARRANGEMENTS

Rights offerings are typically arranged using **standby underwriting**. In standby underwriting, the issuer makes a rights offering, and the underwriter makes a firm commitment to "take up" (that is, purchase) the unsubscribed portion of the issue. The underwriter usually gets a **standby fee** and additional amounts based on the securities taken up.

Standby underwriting protects the firm against undersubscription, which can occur if investors throw away rights or if bad news causes the market price of the stock to fall below the subscription price.

In practice, only a small percentage (fewer than 10 percent) of shareholders fail to exercise valuable rights. This failure can probably be attributed to ignorance or vacations. Furthermore, shareholders are usually given an **oversubscription privilege**, which enables them to purchase unsubscribed shares at the subscription price. The oversubscription privilege makes it unlikely that the corporate issuer would have to turn to its underwriter for help.

standby underwriting
The type of underwriting in which the underwriter agrees to purchase the unsubscribed portion of the issue.

standby fee
An amount paid to an underwriter participating in a standby underwriting agreement.

oversubscription privilege
A privilege that allows shareholders to purchase unsubscribed shares in a rights offering at the subscription price.

EFFECTS ON SHAREHOLDERS

Shareholders can exercise their rights or sell them. In either case, the stockholder will neither win nor lose because of the rights offering. The hypothetical holder of two shares of National Power has a portfolio worth $40. If the shareholder exercises the rights, she or he ends up with three shares worth a total of $50. In other words, with an expenditure of $10, the investor's holding increases in value by $10, which means the shareholder is neither better nor worse off.

On the other hand, if the shareholder sells the two rights for $3.33 each, he or she would obtain $3.33 × 2 = $6.67 and end up with two shares worth $16.67 and the cash from selling the right:

Shares held = 2 × $16.67 = $33.33
Rights sold = 2 × $3.33 =   6.67
    Total = $40.00

The new $33.33 market value plus $6.67 in cash is exactly the same as the original holding of $40. Thus, stockholders cannot lose or gain by exercising or selling rights.

It is obvious that after the rights offering, the new market price of the firm's stock will be lower than the price before the rights offering. As we have seen, stockholders have suffered no loss because of the rights offering. The stock price decline is very much like that in a stock split, a device described in Chapter 17. The lower the subscription price, the greater is the price decline resulting from a rights offering. Because shareholders receive rights equal in value to the price drop, the rights offering does *not* hurt stockholders.

There is one last issue. How do we set the subscription price in a rights offering? If you think about it, you will see that the subscription price really does not matter. It has to be below the market price of the stock for the rights to have value; but beyond this, the price is arbitrary. In principle, it can be as low as we care to make it, as long as it is not zero. In other words, it is impossible to underprice a rights offer.

Concept Questions

15.8a How does a rights offering work?

15.8b What questions must financial managers answer in a rights offering?

15.8c How is the value of a right determined?

15.8d When does a rights offering affect the value of a company's shares?

15.8e Does a rights offering cause share prices to decrease? How are existing shareholders affected by a rights offering?

15.9 Dilution

dilution
Loss in existing shareholders' value in terms of ownership, market value, book value, or EPS.

A subject that comes up quite a bit in discussions involving the selling of securities is **dilution**. Dilution refers to a loss in existing shareholders' value. There are several kinds:

1. Dilution of percentage ownership.
2. Dilution of market value.
3. Dilution of book value and earnings per share.

The differences between these three types can be a little confusing, and there are some common misconceptions about dilution, so we discuss it in this section.

DILUTION OF PROPORTIONATE OWNERSHIP

The first type of dilution can arise whenever a firm sells shares to the general public. For example, Joe Smith owns 5,000 shares of Merit Shoe Company. Merit Shoe currently has 50,000 shares of stock outstanding; each share gets one vote. Joe controls 10 percent (= 5,000/50,000) of the votes and gets 10 percent of the dividends.

If Merit Shoe issues 50,000 new shares of common stock to the public via a general cash offer, Joe's ownership in Merit Shoe may be diluted. If Joe does not participate in the new issue, his ownership will drop to 5 percent (= 5,000/100,000). Notice that the value of Joe's shares is unaffected; he just owns a smaller percentage of the firm.

As this example illustrates, a rights offering ensures Joe Smith an opportunity to maintain his proportionate 10 percent share; therefore, dilution of the ownership of existing shareholders can be avoided by using a rights offering.

DILUTION OF VALUE: BOOK VERSUS MARKET VALUES

We now examine dilution of value by looking at some accounting numbers. We do this to illustrate a fallacy concerning dilution; we do not mean to suggest that accounting value dilution is more important than market value dilution. As we illustrate, quite the reverse is true.

Suppose Upper States Manufacturing (USM) wants to build a new electricity-generating plant to meet future anticipated demands. As shown in Table 15.11, USM currently has

TABLE 15.11

New Issues and Dilution: The Case of Upper States Manufacturing

	Initial	After Taking on New Project	
		With Dilution	**With No Dilution**
Number of shares	1,000,000	1,400,000	1,400,000
Book value	$10,000,000	$12,000,000	$12,000,000
Book value per share (B)	$10	$8.57	$8.57
Market value	$5,000,000	$6,000,000	$8,000,000
Market price (P)	$5	$4.29	$5.71
Net income	$1,000,000	$1,200,000	$1,600,000
Return on equity (ROE)	.10	.10	.13
Earnings per share (EPS)	$1	$.86	$1.14
EPS/P	.20	.20	.20
P/EPS	5	5	5
P/B	.5	.5	.67
Project cost $2,000,000		NPV = −$1,000,000	NPV = $1,000,000

1 million shares outstanding and no debt. Each share is selling for $5, and the company has a $5 million market value. USM's book value is $10 million total, or $10 per share.

USM has experienced a variety of difficulties in the past, including cost overruns, regulatory delays in building a nuclear-powered electricity-generating plant, and below-normal profits. These difficulties are reflected in the fact that USM's market-to-book ratio is $5/$10 = .50 (successful firms rarely have market prices below book values).

Net income for USM is currently $1 million. With 1 million shares, earnings per share are $1, and the return on equity is $1/$10 = .10, or 10%.[9] USM sells for five times earnings (the price-earnings ratio is 5). USM has 200 shareholders, each of whom holds 5,000 shares. The new plant will cost $2 million, so USM will have to issue 400,000 new shares ($5 × 400,000 = $2 million). There will be 1.4 million shares outstanding after the issue.

The ROE on the new plant is expected to be the same as for the company as a whole. In other words, net income is expected to go up by .10 × $2 million = $200,000. Total net income will be $1.2 million. The following will result if the plant is built:

1. With 1.4 million shares outstanding, EPS will be $1.2/1.4 = $.857, down from $1.
2. The proportionate ownership of each old shareholder will drop to 5,000/1.4 million = .0036, or .36 percent from .50 percent.
3. If the stock continues to sell for five times earnings, then the value will drop to 5 × $.857 = $4.29, representing a loss of $.71 per share.
4. The total book value will be the old $10 million plus the new $2 million, for a total of $12 million. Book value per share will fall to $12 million/1.4 million = $8.57.

If we take this example at face value, then dilution of proportionate ownership, accounting dilution, and market value dilution all occur. USM's stockholders appear to suffer significant losses.

A Misconception   Our example appears to show that selling stock when the market-to-book ratio is less than 1 is detrimental to stockholders. Some managers claim that the resulting dilution occurs because EPS will go down whenever shares are issued when the market value is less than the book value.

When the market-to-book ratio is less than 1, increasing the number of shares does cause EPS to go down. Such a decline in EPS is accounting dilution, and accounting dilution will always occur under these circumstances.

Is it also true that market value dilution will necessarily occur? The answer is no. There is nothing incorrect about our example, but why the market price has decreased is not obvious. We discuss this next.

The Correct Arguments   In this example, the market price falls from $5 per share to $4.29. This is true dilution, but why does it occur? The answer has to do with the new project. USM is going to spend $2 million on the new plant. As shown in Table 15.11, the total market value of the company is going to rise from $5 million to $6 million, an increase of only $1 million. This means that the NPV of the new project is −$1 million. With 1.4 million shares, the loss per share is $1/1.4 = $.71, as we calculated before.

So, true dilution takes place for the shareholders of USM because the NPV of the project is negative, not because the market-to-book ratio is less than 1. This negative NPV causes the market price to drop, and the accounting dilution has nothing to do with it.

---

[9] Return on equity, or ROE, is equal to earnings per share divided by book value per share, or, equivalently, net income divided by common equity. We discuss this and other financial ratios in some detail in Chapter 3.

Suppose the new project has a positive NPV of $1 million. The total market value rises by $2 million + 1 million = $3 million. As shown in Table 15.11 (third column), the price per share rises to $5.71. Notice that accounting dilution still takes place because the book value per share still falls, but there is no economic consequence of that fact. The market value of the stock rises.

The $.71 increase in share value comes about because of the $1 million NPV, which amounts to an increase in value of about $.71 per share. Also, as shown, if the ratio of price to EPS remains at 5, then EPS must rise to $5.71/5 = $1.14. Total earnings (net income) rises to $1.14 per share × 1.4 million shares = $1.6 million. Finally, ROE will rise to $1.6 million/$12 million = 13.33%.

Concept Questions

15.9a   What are the different kinds of dilution?
15.9b   Is dilution important?

15.10 Issuing Long-Term Debt

The general procedures followed in a public issue of bonds are the same as those for stocks. The issue must be registered with the SEC, there must be a prospectus, and so on. The registration statement for a public issue of bonds is different from the one for common stock. For bonds, the registration statement must indicate an indenture.

Another important difference is that more than 50 percent of all debt is issued privately. There are two basic forms of direct private long-term financing: Term loans and private placement.

term loans
Direct business loans of typically one to five years.

private placements
Loans (usually long-term) provided directly by a limited number of investors.

Term loans are direct business loans. These loans have maturities of between one and five years. Most term loans are repayable during the life of the loan. The lenders include commercial banks, insurance companies, and other lenders that specialize in corporate finance. **Private placements** are similar to term loans except that the maturity is longer.

The important differences between direct private long-term financing and public issues of debt are these:

1. A direct long-term loan avoids the cost of Securities and Exchange Commission registration.
2. Direct placement is likely to have more restrictive covenants.
3. It is easier to renegotiate a term loan or a private placement in the event of a default. It is harder to renegotiate a public issue because hundreds of holders are usually involved.
4. Life insurance companies and pension funds dominate the private placement segment of the bond market. Commercial banks are significant participants in the term loan market.
5. The costs of distributing bonds are lower in the private market.

The interest rates on term loans and private placements are usually higher than those on an equivalent public issue. This difference reflects the trade-off between a higher interest rate and more flexible arrangements in the event of financial distress, as well as the lower costs associated with private placements.

An additional, and very important, consideration is that the flotation costs associated with selling debt are much less than the comparable costs associated with selling equity.

Concept Questions

15.10a What is the difference between private and public bond issues?

15.10b A private placement is likely to have a higher interest rate than a public issue. Why?

Shelf Registration

15.11

To simplify the procedures for issuing securities, in March 1982, the SEC adopted Rule 415 on a temporary basis, and it was made permanent in November 1983. Rule 415 allows shelf registration. Both debt and equity securities can be shelf registered.

Shelf registration permits a corporation to register an offering that it reasonably expects to sell within the next two years and then sell the issue whenever it wants during that two-year period. For example, in March 2017, cargo ship operator DryShips announced a shelf registration of $2 billion in securities, including debt, preferred stock, common stock, and warrants. Not all companies can use Rule 415. The primary qualifications are these:

shelf registration
Registration permitted by SEC Rule 415, which allows a company to register all issues it expects to sell within two years at one time, with subsequent sales at any time within those two years.

1. The company must be rated investment grade.
2. The firm cannot have defaulted on its debt in the past three years.
3. The aggregate market value of the firm's outstanding stock must be more than $150 million.
4. The firm must not have violated the Securities Act of 1934 in the past three years.

Shelf registration allows firms to use a *dribble* method of new equity issuance. In dribbling, a company registers the issue and hires an underwriter as its selling agent. The company sells shares in "dribs and drabs" from time to time directly via a stock exchange (for example, the NYSE). Companies that have used dribble programs include Wells Fargo & Co., Pacific Gas and Electric Co., and Southern Company.

The rule has been controversial. The following arguments have been constructed against shelf registration:

1. The costs of new issues might go up because underwriters are unable to provide as much current information to potential investors as they would otherwise; therefore, investors may pay less. The expense of selling the issue piece by piece might therefore be higher than that of selling it all at once.
2. Some investment bankers have argued that shelf registration will cause a "market overhang" that will depress market prices. In other words, the possibility that the company may increase the supply of stock at any time will have a negative impact on the current stock price.

Concept Questions

15.11a What is shelf registration?
15.11b What are the arguments against shelf registration?

15.12 Summary and Conclusions

This chapter has looked at how corporate securities are issued. The following are the main points:

1. The costs of issuing securities can be quite large. They are much lower (as a percentage) for larger issues.

2. The direct and indirect costs of going public can be substantial. However, once a firm is public, it can raise additional capital with much greater ease.

3. Rights offerings are cheaper than general cash offers. Even so, most new equity issues in the United States are underwritten general cash offers.

CONNECT TO FINANCE

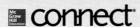 For more practice, you should be using *Connect Finance*. Log on to connect .mheducation.com to get started!

Can you answer the following *Connect* Quiz questions?

Section 15.1 What stage of venture capital funding is most apt to provide the funding needed to actually commence the manufacturing operations of a firm?

Section 15.2 Smythe Enterprises is issuing securities under Regulation A. Given this, you know that the securities are valued at _____ or less, or are debt securities that mature in less than _____.

Section 15.4 The gross spread is defined as the difference between the _____ and the _____.

Section 15.7 What is referred to as the *abnormal return*?

CHAPTER REVIEW AND SELF-TEST PROBLEMS

15.1 **Flotation Costs** The L5 Corporation is considering an equity issue to finance a new space station. A total of $15 million in new equity is needed. If the direct costs are estimated at 7 percent of the amount raised, how large does the issue need to be? What is the dollar amount of the flotation cost?

15.2 **Rights Offerings** The Hadron Corporation currently has 3 million shares outstanding. The stock sells for $40 per share. To raise $20 million for a new particle accelerator, the firm is considering a rights offering at $25 per share. What is the value of a right in this case? The ex-rights price?

ANSWERS TO CHAPTER REVIEW AND SELF-TEST PROBLEMS

15.1 The firm needs to net $15 million after paying the 7 percent flotation costs. So the amount raised is given by:

$$\text{Amount raised} \times (1 - .07) = \$15 \text{ million}$$
$$\text{Amount raised} = \$15 \text{ million}/.93 = \$16.129 \text{ million}$$

The total flotation cost is thus $1.129 million.

15.2   To raise $20 million at $25 per share, $20 million/$25 = 800,000 shares will have to be sold. Before the offering, the firm is worth 3 million × $40 = $120 million. The issue will raise $20 million, and there will be 3.8 million shares outstanding. The price of an ex-rights share will therefore be $140 million/3.8 million = $36.84. The value of a right is thus $40 − 36.84 = $3.16.

CONCEPTS REVIEW AND CRITICAL THINKING QUESTIONS

1. **Debt versus Equity Offering Size** [LO2] In the aggregate, debt offerings are much more common than equity offerings and typically much larger as well. Why?

2. **Debt versus Equity Flotation Costs** [LO2] Why are the costs of selling equity so much larger than the costs of selling debt?

3. **Bond Ratings and Flotation Costs** [LO2] Why do noninvestment-grade bonds have much higher direct costs than investment-grade issues?

4. **Underpricing in Debt Offerings** [LO2] Why is underpricing not a great concern with bond offerings?

   Use the following information to answer the next three questions. Zipcar, the car-sharing company, went public in April 2011. Assisted by the investment bank Goldman, Sachs & Co., Zipcar sold 9.68 million shares at $18 each, thereby raising a total of $174.24 million. By the end of the first day of trading, the stock had zipped to $28 per share, down from a high of $31.50. Based on the end-of-day numbers, Zipcar shares were apparently underpriced by about $10 each, meaning that the company missed out on an additional $96.8 million.

5. **IPO Pricing** [LO3] The Zipcar IPO was underpriced by about 56 percent. Should Zipcar be upset at Goldman over the underpricing?

6. **IPO Pricing** [LO3] In the previous question, how would it affect your thinking to know that the company was incorporated about 10 years earlier, had only $186 million in revenues in 2010, and had never earned a profit? Additionally, the viability of the company's business model was still unproven.

7. **IPO Pricing** [LO3] In the previous two questions, how would it affect your thinking to know that in addition to the 9.68 million shares offered in the IPO, Zipcar had an additional 30 million shares outstanding? Of those 30 million shares, 14.1 million shares were owned by four venture capital firms, and 15.5 million shares were owned by the 12 directors and executive officers.

8. **Cash Offer versus Rights Offer** [LO4] Ren-Stimpy International is planning to raise fresh equity capital by selling a large new issue of common stock. Ren-Stimpy is currently a publicly traded corporation, and it is trying to choose between an underwritten cash offer and a rights offering (not underwritten) to current shareholders. Ren-Stimpy management is interested in minimizing the selling costs and has asked you for advice on the choice of issue methods. What is your recommendation and why?

9. **IPO Underpricing** [LO3] In 1980, a certain assistant professor of finance bought 12 initial public offerings of common stock. He held each of these for approximately one month and then sold them. The investment rule he followed was to submit a purchase order for every firm commitment initial public offering of oil and gas exploration companies. There were 22 of these offerings, and he submitted a purchase order for approximately $1,000 in stock for each of the companies. With 10 of these, no shares were allocated to this assistant professor. With 5 of the 12 offerings that were purchased, fewer than the requested number of shares were allocated.

The year 1980 was very good for oil and gas exploration company owners: On average, for the 22 companies that went public, the stocks were selling for 80 percent above the offering price a month after the initial offering date. The assistant professor looked at his performance record and found that the $8,400 invested in the 12 companies had grown to $10,000, representing a return of only about 20 percent (commissions were negligible). Did he have bad luck, or should he have expected to do worse than the average initial public offering investor? Explain.

10. **IPO Pricing [LO3]** The following material represents the cover page and summary of the prospectus for the initial public offering of the Pest Investigation Control Corporation (PICC), which is going public tomorrow with a firm commitment initial public offering managed by the investment banking firm of Erlanger and Ritter. Answer the following questions:

   a. Assume you know nothing about PICC other than the information contained in the prospectus. Based on your knowledge of finance, what is your prediction for

---

PROSPECTUS   PICC

200,000 SHARES
PEST INVESTIGATION CONTROL CORPORATION

Of the shares being offered hereby, all 200,000 are being sold by the Pest Investigation Control Corporation, Inc. ("the Company"). Before the offering there has been no public market for the shares of PICC, and no guarantee can be given that any such market will develop.

These securities have not been approved or disapproved by the SEC nor has the commission passed upon the accuracy or adequacy of this prospectus. Any representation to the contrary is a criminal offense.

	Price to Public	Underwriting Discount	Proceeds to Company*
Per share	$11.00	$1.10	$9.90
Total	$2,200,000	$220,000	$1,980,000

*Before deducting expenses estimated at $27,000 and payable by the Company.

This is an initial public offering. The common shares are being offered, subject to prior sale, when, as, and if delivered to and accepted by the Underwriters and subject to approval of certain legal matters by their Counsel and by Counsel for the Company. The Underwriters reserve the right to withdraw, cancel, or modify such offer and to reject offers in whole or in part.

Erlanger and Ritter, Investment Bankers
July 12, 2018
Prospectus Summary

The Company	The Pest Investigation Control Corporation (PICC) breeds and markets toads and tree frogs as ecologically safe insect-control mechanisms.
The Offering	200,000 shares of common stock, no par value.
Listing	The Company will seek listing on NASDAQ and will trade over the counter.
Shares Outstanding	As of June 30, 2018, 400,000 shares of common stock were outstanding. After the offering, 600,000 shares of common stock will be outstanding.
Use of Proceeds	To finance expansion of inventory and receivables and general working capital, and to pay for country club memberships for certain finance professors.

Selected Financial Information
(amounts in thousands except per-share data)

	Fiscal Year Ended June 30				As of June 30, 2018	
	2016	2017	2018		Actual	As Adjusted for This Offering
Revenues	$60.00	$120.00	$240.00	Working capital	$ 8	$1,961
Net earnings	3.80	15.90	36.10	Total assets	511	2,464
Earnings per share	.01	.04	.09	Stockholders' equity	423	2,376

the price of PICC tomorrow? Provide a short explanation of why you think this will occur.

b. Assume you have several thousand dollars to invest. When you get home from class tonight, you find that your stockbroker, whom you have not talked to for weeks, has called. She has left a message that PICC is going public tomorrow and that she can get you several hundred shares at the offering price if you call her back first thing in the morning. Discuss the merits of this opportunity.

QUESTIONS AND PROBLEMS

1. **Rights Offerings** [LO4] Leah, Inc., is proposing a rights offering. Presently there are 375,000 shares outstanding at $67 each. There will be 50,000 new shares offered at $58 each.

   BASIC
   (Questions 1–8)

   a. What is the new market value of the company?
   b. How many rights are associated with one of the new shares?
   c. What is the ex-rights price?
   d. What is the value of a right?
   e. Why might a company have a rights offering rather than a general cash offer?

2. **Rights Offerings** [LO4] The Clifford Corporation has announced a rights offer to raise $35 million for a new journal, the *Journal of Financial Excess*. This journal will review potential articles after the author pays a nonrefundable reviewing fee of $5,000 per page. The stock currently sells for $53 per share, and there are 3.9 million shares outstanding.

   a. What is the maximum possible subscription price? What is the minimum?
   b. If the subscription price is set at $47 per share, how many shares must be sold? How many rights will it take to buy one share?
   c. What is the ex-rights price? What is the value of a right?
   d. Show how a shareholder with 1,000 shares before the offering and no desire (or money) to buy additional shares is not harmed by the rights offer.

3. **Rights** [LO4] Red Shoe Co. has concluded that additional equity financing will be needed to expand operations and that the needed funds will be best obtained through a rights offering. It has correctly determined that as a result of the rights offering, the share price will fall from $49 to $47.60 ($49 is the rights-on price; $47.60 is the ex-rights price, also known as the *when-issued* price). The company is seeking $16.5 million in additional funds with a per-share subscription price equal to $34. How many shares are there currently, before the offering? (Assume that the increment to the market value of the equity equals the gross proceeds from the offering.)

4. **IPO Underpricing** [LO3] The Woods Co. and the Spieth Co. have both announced IPOs at $40 per share. One of these is undervalued by $9, and the other is overvalued by $4, but you have no way of knowing which is which. You plan to buy 1,000 shares of each issue. If an issue is underpriced, it will be rationed, and only half your order will be filled. If you *could* get 1,000 shares in Woods and 1,000 shares in Spieth, what would your profit be? What profit do you actually expect? What principle have you illustrated?

5. **Calculating Flotation Costs** [LO3] The Whistling Straits Corporation needs to raise $60 million to finance its expansion into new markets. The company will sell new shares of equity via a general cash offering to raise the needed funds. If the offer price is $21 per share and the company's underwriters charge a spread of 7 percent, how many shares need to be sold?

6. **Calculating Flotation Costs [LO3]** In Problem 5, if the SEC filing fee and associated administrative expenses of the offering are $1.2 million, how many shares need to be sold?

7. **Calculating Flotation Costs [LO3]** The Raven Co. has just gone public. Under a firm commitment agreement, Raven received $21.39 for each of the 20 million shares sold. The initial offering price was $23 per share, and the stock rose to $28.41 per share in the first few minutes of trading. Raven paid $950,000 in direct legal and other costs and $320,000 in indirect costs. What was the flotation cost as a percentage of funds raised?

8. **Price Dilution [LO3]** Nemesis, Inc., has 165,000 shares of stock outstanding. Each share is worth $77, so the company's market value of equity is $12,705,000. Suppose the firm issues 30,000 new shares at the following prices: $77, $73, and $65. What effect will each of these alternative offering prices have on the existing price per share?

INTERMEDIATE
(Questions 9–15)

9. **Dilution [LO3]** Wayne, Inc., wishes to expand its facilities. The company currently has 6 million shares outstanding and no debt. The stock sells for $64 per share, but the book value per share is $19. Net income is currently $11.5 million. The new facility will cost $30 million, and it will increase net income by $675,000.

    a. Assuming a constant price-earnings ratio, what will the effect be of issuing new equity to finance the investment? To answer, calculate the new book value per share, the new total earnings, the new EPS, the new stock price, and the new market-to-book ratio. What is going on here?

    b. What would the new net income for the company have to be for the stock price to remain unchanged?

10. **Dilution [LO3]** The Metallica Heavy Metal Mining (MHMM) Corporation wants to diversify its operations. Some recent financial information for the company is shown here:

Stock price	$ 75
Number of shares	64,000
Total assets	$9,400,000
Total liabilities	$4,100,000
Net income	$ 980,000

MHMM is considering an investment that has the same PE ratio as the firm. The cost of the investment is $1.5 million, and it will be financed with a new equity issue. The return on the investment will equal MHMM's current ROE. What will happen to the book value per share, the market value per share, and the EPS? What is the NPV of this investment? Does dilution take place?

11. **Dilution [LO3]** In Problem 10, what would the ROE on the investment have to be if we wanted the price after the offering to be $75 per share? (Assume the PE ratio remains constant.) What is the NPV of this investment? Does any dilution take place?

12. **Rights [LO4]** Bell Hill Mfg. is considering a rights offer. The company has determined that the ex-rights price would be $63. The current price is $68 per share, and there are 26 million shares outstanding. The rights offer would raise a total of $70 million. What is the subscription price?

13. **Value of a Right [LO4]** Show that the value of a right just prior to expiration can be written as:

$$\text{Value of a right} = P_{RO} - P_X = (P_{RO} - P_S)/(N + 1)$$

where P_{RO}, P_S, and P_X stand for the rights-on price, the subscription price, and the ex-rights price, respectively, and N is the number of rights needed to buy one new share at the subscription price.

14. **Selling Rights** [LO4] Prahm Corp. wants to raise $4.7 million via a rights offering. The company currently has 530,000 shares of common stock outstanding that sell for $55 per share. Its underwriter has set a subscription price of $30 per share and will charge the company a spread of 6 percent. If you currently own 5,000 shares of stock in the company and decide not to participate in the rights offering, how much money can you get by selling your rights?

15. **Valuing a Right** [LO4] Knight Inventory Systems, Inc., has announced a rights offer. The company has announced that it will take four rights to buy a new share in the offering at a subscription price of $35. At the close of business the day before the ex-rights day, the company's stock sells for $60 per share. The next morning, you notice that the stock sells for $53 per share and the rights sell for $3 each. Are the stock and the rights correctly priced on the ex-rights day? Describe a transaction in which you could use these prices to create an immediate profit.

MINICASE

S&S Air Goes Public

Mark Sexton and Todd Story have been discussing the future of S&S Air. The company has been experiencing fast growth, and the two see only clear skies in the company's future. However, the fast growth can no longer be funded by internal sources, so Mark and Todd have decided the time is right to take the company public. To this end, they have entered into discussions with the investment bank of Crowe & Mallard. The company has a working relationship with Renata Harper, the underwriter who assisted with the company's previous bond offering. Crowe & Mallard have assisted numerous small companies in the IPO process, so Mark and Todd feel confident with this choice.

Renata begins by telling Mark and Todd about the process. Although Crowe & Mallard charged an underwriter fee of 4 percent on the bond offering, the underwriter fee is 7 percent on all initial stock offerings of the size of S&S Air's offering. Renata tells Mark and Todd that the company can expect to pay about $2.1 million in legal fees and expenses, $12,000 in SEC registration fees, and $15,000 in other filing fees. Additionally, to be listed on the NASDAQ, the company must pay $100,000. There are also transfer agent fees of $6,500 and engraving expenses of $520,000. The company should also expect to pay $110,000 for other expenses associated with the IPO.

Finally, Renata tells Mark and Todd that to file with the SEC, the company must provide three years' audited financial statements. She is unsure about the costs of the audit. Mark tells Renata that the company provides audited financial statements as part of the bond covenant, and the company pays $300,000 per year for the outside auditor.

QUESTIONS

1. At the end of the discussion, Mark asks Renata about the Dutch auction IPO process. What are the differences in the expenses to S&S Air if it uses a Dutch auction IPO versus a traditional IPO? Should the company go public through a Dutch auction or use a traditional underwritten offering?

2. During the discussion of the potential IPO and S&S Air's future, Mark states that he feels the company should raise $85 million. However, Renata points out that if the company needs more cash in the near future, a secondary offering close to the IPO would be problematic. Instead she suggests that the company should raise $95 million in the IPO. How can we calculate the optimal size of the IPO? What are the advantages and disadvantages of increasing the size of the IPO to $95 million?

3. After deliberation, Mark and Todd have decided that the company should use a firm commitment offering with Crowe & Mallard as the lead underwriter. The IPO will be for $85 million. Ignoring underpricing, how much will the IPO cost the company as a percentage of the funds received?

4. Many employees of S&S Air have shares of stock in the company because of an existing employee stock purchase plan. To sell the stock, the employees can tender their shares to be sold in the IPO at the offering price, or the employees can retain their stock and sell it in the secondary market after S&S Air goes public. Todd asks you to advise the employees about which option is best. What would you suggest to the employees?

NO MATTER HOW YOU you look at it, 2017 was a tough year for brick-and-mortar retailers. In January, women's retailer The Limited announced it was filing for bankruptcy after more than 50 years in business. Then in March, electronics retailer RadioShack filed for bankruptcy. What made RadioShack's bankruptcy unique is that the company had emerged from a previous bankruptcy in 2015. After that bankruptcy, the company was left with 1,200 stores, which were co-branded as Sprint stores, but it quickly failed again. And in September, Toys "R" Us filed for Chapter 11 bankruptcy. The toy retailer had $4.9 billion in debt on its balance sheet at the time of the bankruptcy filing. Overall, more than 19 publicly traded retailers filed for bankruptcy during 2017.

A firm's choice of how much debt it should have relative to equity is known as a *capital structure decision*. Such a choice has many implications for a firm and is far from being a settled issue in either theory or practice. In this chapter, we discuss the basic ideas underlying capital structures and how firms choose them.

A firm's capital structure is really just a reflection of its borrowing policy. Should we borrow a lot of money, or just a little? At first glance, it probably seems that debt is something to be avoided. After all, the more debt a firm has, the greater is the risk of bankruptcy. What we learn is that debt is really a double-edged sword, and, properly used, debt can be enormously beneficial to a firm.

A good understanding of the effects of debt financing is important because the role of debt is so misunderstood, and many firms (and individuals) are far too conservative in their use of debt. Having said this, we can also say that firms sometimes err in the opposite direction, becoming much too heavily indebted, with bankruptcy as the unfortunate consequence. Striking the right balance is what the capital structure issue is all about.

Learning Objectives

After studying this chapter, you should be able to:

LO1 Explain the effect of financial leverage.

LO2 Show the impact of taxes and bankruptcy on capital structure choice.

LO3 Describe the essentials of the bankruptcy process.

©by_adril/iStockPhoto/GettyImages

For updates on the latest happenings in finance, visit fundamentalsofcorporatefinance.blogspot.com.

Thus far, we have taken the firm's capital structure as given. Debt-equity ratios don't just drop on firms from the sky, of course, so now it's time to wonder where they come from. Going back to Chapter 1, recall that we refer to decisions about a firm's debt-equity ratio as *capital structure decisions.*[1]

For the most part, a firm can choose any capital structure it wants. If management so desired, a firm could issue some bonds and use the proceeds to buy back some stock, thereby increasing the debt-equity ratio. Alternatively, it could issue stock and use the money to pay off some debt, thereby reducing the debt-equity ratio. Activities such as these, which alter the firm's existing capital structure, are called capital *restructurings*. In general, such restructurings take place whenever the firm substitutes one capital structure for another while leaving the firm's assets unchanged.

Because the assets of a firm are not directly affected by a capital restructuring, we can examine the firm's capital structure decision separately from its other activities. This means that a firm can consider capital restructuring decisions in isolation from its investment decisions. In this chapter, then, we will ignore investment decisions and focus on the long-term financing, or capital structure, question.

What we will see in this chapter is that capital structure decisions can have important implications for the value of the firm and its cost of capital. We will also find that important elements of the capital structure decision are easy to identify, but precise measures of these elements are generally not obtainable. As a result, we are able to give only an incomplete answer to the question of what the best capital structure might be for a particular firm at a particular time.

The Capital Structure Question   16.1

How should a firm go about choosing its debt-equity ratio? Here, as always, we assume that the guiding principle is to choose the course of action that maximizes the value of a share of stock. As we discuss next, when it comes to capital structure decisions, this is essentially the same thing as maximizing the value of the whole firm, and, for convenience, we will tend to frame our discussion in terms of firm value.

FIRM VALUE AND STOCK VALUE: AN EXAMPLE

The following example illustrates that the capital structure that maximizes the value of the firm is the one financial managers should choose for the shareholders, so there is no conflict in our goals. To begin, suppose the market value of the J.J. Sprint Company is $1,000. The company currently has no debt, and J.J. Sprint's 100 shares sell for $10 each. Further suppose that J.J. Sprint restructures itself by borrowing $500 and then paying out the proceeds to shareholders as an extra dividend of $500/100 = $5 per share.

This restructuring will change the capital structure of the firm with no direct effect on the firm's assets. The immediate effect will be to increase debt and decrease equity. What will be the final impact of the restructuring? Table 16.1 illustrates three possible outcomes in addition to the original no-debt case. Notice that in Scenario II, the value of the firm is unchanged at $1,000. In Scenario I, firm value rises to $1,250; it falls by $250, to $750, in Scenario III. We haven't yet said what might lead to these changes. For now, we just take them as possible outcomes to illustrate a point.

Because our goal is to benefit the shareholders, we next examine, in Table 16.2, the net payoffs to the shareholders in these scenarios. We see that, if the value of the firm stays the

---

[1] It is conventional to refer to decisions regarding debt and equity as *capital structure decisions*. The term *financial structure decisions* would be more accurate, and we use the terms interchangeably.

TABLE 16.1

Possible Firm Values: No Debt versus Debt plus Dividend

	No Debt	Debt plus Dividend		
		I	II	III
Debt	$ 0	$ 500	$ 500	$500
Equity	1,000	750	500	250
Firm value	$1,000	$1,250	$1,000	$750

TABLE 16.2

Possible Payoffs to Shareholders: Debt plus Dividend

	Debt plus Dividend		
	I	II	III
Equity value reduction	−$250	−$500	−$750
Dividends	500	500	500
Net effect	+$250	$ 0	−$250

same, shareholders will experience a capital loss exactly offsetting the extra dividend. This is Scenario II. In Scenario I, the value of the firm increases to $1,250 and the shareholders come out ahead by $250. In other words, the restructuring has an NPV of $250 in this scenario. The NPV in Scenario III is −$250.

The key observation to make here is that the change in the value of the firm is the same as the net effect on the stockholders. Financial managers can try to find the capital structure that maximizes the value of the firm. Put another way, the NPV rule applies to capital structure decisions, and the change in the value of the overall firm is the NPV of a restructuring. J.J. Sprint should borrow $500 if it expects Scenario I. The crucial question in determining a firm's capital structure is, of course, which scenario is likely to occur.

CAPITAL STRUCTURE AND THE COST OF CAPITAL

In Chapter 14, we discussed the concept of the firm's weighted average cost of capital, or WACC. You may recall that the WACC tells us that the firm's overall cost of capital is a weighted average of the costs of the various components of the firm's capital structure. When we described the WACC, we took the firm's capital structure as given. One important issue that we will want to explore in this chapter is what happens to the cost of capital when we vary the amount of debt financing, or the debt-equity ratio.

A primary reason for studying the WACC is that the value of the firm is maximized when the WACC is minimized. To see this, recall that the WACC is the appropriate discount rate for the firm's overall cash flows. Because values and discount rates move in opposite directions, minimizing the WACC will maximize the value of the firm's cash flows.

We will want to choose the firm's capital structure so that the WACC is minimized. For this reason, we will say that one capital structure is better than another if it results in a lower weighted average cost of capital. Further, we say that a particular debt-equity ratio represents the *optimal capital structure* if it results in the lowest possible WACC. This optimal capital structure is sometimes called the firm's *target* capital structure as well.

Concept Questions

16.1a Why should financial managers choose the capital structure that maximizes the value of the firm?

16.1b What is the relationship between the WACC and the value of the firm?

16.1c What is an optimal capital structure?

The Effect of Financial Leverage

The previous section described why the capital structure that produces the highest firm value (or the lowest cost of capital) is the one most beneficial to stockholders. In this section, we examine the impact of financial leverage on the payoffs to stockholders. As you may recall, *financial leverage* refers to the extent to which a firm relies on debt. The more debt financing a firm uses in its capital structure, the more financial leverage it employs.

As we describe, financial leverage can dramatically alter the payoffs to shareholders in the firm. Remarkably, financial leverage may not affect the overall cost of capital. If this is true, then a firm's capital structure is irrelevant because changes in capital structure won't affect the value of the firm. We will return to this issue a little later.

THE BASICS OF FINANCIAL LEVERAGE

We start by illustrating how financial leverage works. For now, we ignore the impact of taxes. Also, for ease of presentation, we describe the impact of leverage in terms of its effects on earnings per share, EPS, and return on equity, ROE. These are accounting numbers and, as such, are not our primary concern. Using cash flows instead of these accounting numbers would lead to precisely the same conclusions, but a little more work would be needed. We discuss the impact on market values in a subsequent section.

Financial Leverage, EPS, and ROE: An Example   The Trans Am Corporation currently has no debt in its capital structure. The CFO, Ms. Morris, is considering a restructuring that would involve issuing debt and using the proceeds to buy back some of the outstanding equity. Table 16.3 presents both the current and proposed capital structures. As shown, the firm's assets have a market value of $8 million, and there are 400,000 shares outstanding. Because Trans Am is an all-equity firm, the price per share is $20.

The proposed debt issue would raise $4 million; the interest rate would be 10 percent. Because the stock sells for $20 per share, the $4 million in new debt would be used to purchase $4 million/$20 = 200,000 shares, leaving 200,000. After the restructuring, Trans Am would have a capital structure that was 50 percent debt, so the debt-equity ratio would be 1. Notice that, for now, we assume that the stock price will remain at $20.

To investigate the impact of the proposed restructuring, Ms. Morris has prepared Table 16.4, which compares the firm's current capital structure to the proposed capital structure under three scenarios. The scenarios reflect different assumptions about the firm's EBIT. Under the expected scenario, the EBIT is $1 million. In the recession scenario, EBIT falls to $500,000. In the expansion scenario, it rises to $1.5 million.

To illustrate some of the calculations behind the figures in Table 16.4, consider the expansion case. EBIT is $1.5 million. With no debt (the current capital structure) and no taxes, net income is also $1.5 million. In this case, there are 400,000 shares worth $8 million total.

	Current	Proposed
Assets	$8,000,000	$8,000,000
Debt	$ 0	$4,000,000
Equity	$8,000,000	$4,000,000
Debt-equity ratio	0	1
Share price	$ 20	$ 20
Shares outstanding	400,000	200,000
Interest rate	10%	10%

TABLE 16.3

Current and Proposed Capital Structures for the Trans Am Corporation

TABLE 16.4

Capital Structure Scenarios for the Trans Am Corporation

Current Capital Structure: No Debt			
	Recession	Expected	Expansion
EBIT	$500,000	$1,000,000	$1,500,000
Interest	0	0	0
Net income	$500,000	$1,000,000	$1,500,000
ROE	6.25%	12.50%	18.75%
EPS	$ 1.25	$ 2.50	$ 3.75
Proposed Capital Structure: Debt = $4 million			
EBIT	$500,000	$1,000,000	$1,500,000
Interest	400,000	400,000	400,000
Net income	$100,000	$ 600,000	$1,100,000
ROE	2.50%	15.00%	27.50%
EPS	$ .50	$ 3.00	$ 5.50

EPS is $1.5 million/400,000 = $3.75. Also, because accounting return on equity, ROE, is net income divided by total equity, ROE is $1.5 million/$8 million = .1875, or 18.75%.[2]

With $4 million in debt (the proposed capital structure), things are somewhat different. Because the interest rate is 10 percent, the interest bill is $400,000. With EBIT of $1.5 million, interest of $400,000, and no taxes, net income is $1.1 million. Now there are only 200,000 shares worth $4 million total. EPS is therefore $1.1 million/200,000 = $5.50, versus the $3.75 that we calculated in the previous, no-debt, scenario. Furthermore, ROE is $1.1 million/$4 million = .275, or 27.5%. This is well above the 18.75 percent we calculated for the current capital structure.

EPS versus EBIT   The impact of leverage is evident when the effect of the restructuring on EPS and ROE is examined. In particular, the variability in both EPS and ROE is much larger under the proposed capital structure. This illustrates how financial leverage acts to magnify gains and losses to shareholders.

In Figure 16.1, we take a closer look at the effect of the proposed restructuring. This figure plots earnings per share, EPS, against earnings before interest and taxes, EBIT, for the current and proposed capital structures. The first line, labeled "No debt," represents the case of no leverage. This line begins at the origin, indicating that EPS would be $0 if EBIT were $0. From there, every $400,000 increase in EBIT increases EPS by $1 (because there are 400,000 shares outstanding).

The second line represents the proposed capital structure. Here, EPS is negative if EBIT is $0. This follows because $400,000 of interest must be paid regardless of the firm's profits. Because there are 200,000 shares in this case, the EPS is −$2 as shown. Similarly, if EBIT were $400,000, EPS would be exactly $0.

The important thing to notice in Figure 16.1 is that the slope of the line in this second case is steeper. In fact, for every $400,000 increase in EBIT, EPS rises by $2, so the line is twice as steep. This tells us that EPS is twice as sensitive to changes in EBIT because of the financial leverage employed.

Another observation to make in Figure 16.1 is that the lines intersect. At that point, EPS is exactly the same for both capital structures. To find this point, note that EPS is equal to EBIT/400,000 in the no-debt case. In the with-debt case, EPS is (EBIT − $400,000)/200,000. If we set these equal to each other, EBIT is:

EBIT/400,000 = (EBIT − $400,000)/200,000
EBIT = 2 × (EBIT − $400,000)
= $800,000

[2]ROE is discussed in some detail in Chapter 3.

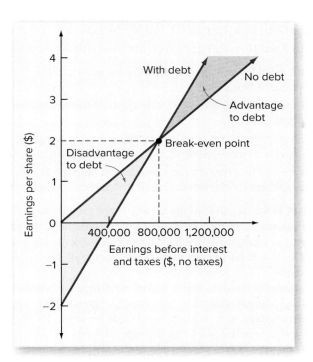

FIGURE 16.1

Financial Leverage: EPS and EBIT for the Trans Am Corporation

When EBIT is $800,000, EPS is $2 under either capital structure. This is labeled as the break-even point in Figure 16.1; we could also call it the indifference point. If EBIT is above this level, leverage is beneficial; if it is below this point, it is not.

There is another, more intuitive, way of seeing why the break-even point is $800,000. Notice that, if the firm has no debt and its EBIT is $800,000, its net income is also $800,000. In this case, the ROE is 10 percent. This is precisely the same as the interest rate on the debt, so the firm earns a return that is just sufficient to pay the interest.

Break-Even EBIT   **EXAMPLE 16.1**

The MPD Corporation has decided in favor of a capital restructuring. Currently, MPD uses no debt financing. Following the restructuring, debt will be $1 million. The interest rate on the debt will be 9 percent. MPD currently has 200,000 shares outstanding, and the price per share is $20. If the restructuring is expected to increase EPS, what is the minimum level for EBIT that MPD's management must be expecting? Ignore taxes in answering.

To answer, we calculate the break-even EBIT. At any EBIT above this, the increased financial leverage will increase EPS, so this will tell us the minimum level for EBIT. Under the old capital structure, EPS is EBIT/200,000. Under the new capital structure, the interest expense will be $1 million × .09 = $90,000. Furthermore, with the $1 million proceeds, MPD will repurchase $1 million/$20 = 50,000 shares of stock, leaving 150,000 shares outstanding. EPS will be (EBIT − $90,000)/150,000.

Now that we know how to calculate EPS under both scenarios, we set them equal to each other and solve for the break-even EBIT:

$$\text{EBIT}/200{,}000 = (\text{EBIT} - \$90{,}000)/150{,}000$$
$$\text{EBIT} = 4/3 \times (\text{EBIT} - \$90{,}000)$$
$$= \$360{,}000$$

Verify that, in either case, EPS is $1.80 when EBIT is $360,000. Management at MPD is apparently of the opinion that EPS will exceed $1.80.

CORPORATE BORROWING AND HOMEMADE LEVERAGE

Based on Tables 16.3 and 16.4 and Figure 16.1, Ms. Morris draws the following conclusions:

1. The effect of financial leverage depends on the company's EBIT. When EBIT is relatively high, leverage is beneficial.
2. Under the expected scenario, leverage increases the returns to shareholders, as measured by both ROE and EPS.
3. Shareholders are exposed to more risk under the proposed capital structure because the EPS and ROE are much more sensitive to changes in EBIT in this case.
4. Because of the impact that financial leverage has on both the expected return to stockholders and the riskiness of the stock, capital structure is an important consideration.

The first three of these conclusions are clearly correct. Does the last conclusion necessarily follow? Surprisingly, the answer is no. As we discuss next, the reason is that shareholders can adjust the amount of financial leverage by borrowing and lending on their own. This use of personal borrowing to alter the degree of financial leverage is called **homemade leverage**.

homemade leverage
The use of personal borrowing to change the overall amount of financial leverage to which the individual is exposed.

We will now illustrate that it actually makes no difference whether or not Trans Am adopts the proposed capital structure, because any stockholder who prefers the proposed capital structure can create it using homemade leverage. To begin, the first part of Table 16.5 shows what will happen to an investor who buys $2,000 worth of Trans Am stock if the proposed capital structure is adopted. This investor purchases 100 shares of stock. From Table 16.4, we know that EPS will be $.50, $3, or $5.50, so the total earnings for 100 shares will be either $50, $300, or $550 under the proposed capital structure.

Now, suppose that Trans Am does not adopt the proposed capital structure. In this case, EPS will be $1.25, $2.50, or $3.75. The second part of Table 16.5 demonstrates how a stockholder who prefers the payoffs under the proposed structure can create them using personal borrowing. To do this, the stockholder borrows $2,000 at 10 percent on his or her own. Our investor uses this amount, along with the original $2,000, to buy 200 shares of stock. As shown, the net payoffs are exactly the same as those for the proposed capital structure.

How did we know to borrow $2,000 to create the right payoffs? We are trying to replicate Trans Am's proposed capital structure at the personal level. The proposed capital structure results in a debt-equity ratio of 1. To replicate this structure at the personal level, the stockholder must borrow enough to create this same debt-equity ratio. Because the stockholder has $2,000 in equity invested, the borrowing of another $2,000 will create a personal debt-equity ratio of 1.

TABLE 16.5

Proposed Capital Structure versus Original Capital Structure with Homemade Leverage

	Proposed Capital Structure		
	Recession	Expected	Expansion
EPS	$ .50	$ 3.00	$ 5.50
Earnings for 100 shares	50.00	300.00	550.00
Net cost = 100 shares × $20 = $2,000			
	Original Capital Structure and Homemade Leverage		
EPS	$ 1.25	$ 2.50	$ 3.75
Earnings for 200 shares	250.00	500.00	750.00
Less: Interest on $2,000 at 10%	200.00	200.00	200.00
Net earnings	$ 50.00	$300.00	$550.00
Net cost = 200 shares × $20 − Amount borrowed = $4,000 − 2,000 = $2,000			

This example demonstrates that investors can always increase financial leverage themselves to create a different pattern of payoffs. It makes no difference whether Trans Am chooses the proposed capital structure.

Unlevering the Stock   **EXAMPLE 16.2**

In our Trans Am example, suppose management adopts the proposed capital structure. Further suppose that an investor who owns 100 shares prefers the original capital structure. Show how this investor could "unlever" the stock to re-create the original payoffs.

To create leverage, investors borrow on their own. To undo leverage, investors must lend money. In the case of Trans Am, the corporation borrowed an amount equal to half its value. The investor can unlever the stock by lending money in the same proportion. In this case, the investor sells 50 shares for $1,000 total and then lends the $1,000 at 10 percent. The payoffs are calculated in the following table:

	Recession	Expected	Expansion
EPS (proposed structure)	$ .50	$ 3.00	$ 5.50
Earnings for 50 shares	25.00	150.00	275.00
Plus: Interest on $1,000	100.00	100.00	100.00
Total payoff	$125.00	$250.00	$375.00

These are precisely the payoffs the investor would have experienced under the original capital structure.

Concept Questions

16.2a What is the impact of financial leverage on stockholders?
16.2b What is homemade leverage?
16.2c Why is Trans Am's capital structure irrelevant?

Capital Structure and the Cost of Equity Capital

16.3

We have seen that there is nothing special about corporate borrowing because investors can borrow or lend on their own. As a result, whichever capital structure Trans Am chooses, the stock price will be the same. Trans Am's capital structure is irrelevant, at least in the simple world we have examined.

Our Trans Am example is based on a famous argument advanced by two Nobel laureates, Franco Modigliani and Merton Miller, whom we will henceforth call M&M. What we illustrated for the Trans Am Corporation is a special case of **M&M Proposition I**. M&M Proposition I states that it is completely irrelevant how a firm chooses to arrange its finances.

M&M Proposition I
The proposition that the value of the firm is independent of the firm's capital structure.

M&M PROPOSITION I: THE PIE MODEL

One way to illustrate M&M Proposition I is to imagine two firms that are identical on the left side of the balance sheet. Their assets and operations are exactly the same. The right sides are different because the two firms finance their operations differently. In this case, we can view the capital structure question in terms of a "pie" model. Why we choose this

FIGURE 16.2

Two Pie Models of Capital Structure

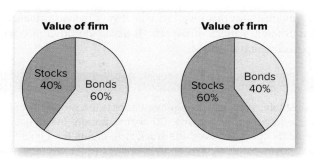

name is apparent from Figure 16.2. Figure 16.2 gives two possible ways of cutting up the pie between the equity slice, E, and the debt slice, D: 40%–60% and 60%–40%. However, the size of the pie in Figure 16.2 is the same for both firms because the value of the assets is the same. This is precisely what M&M Proposition I states: The size of the pie doesn't depend on how it is sliced.

THE COST OF EQUITY AND FINANCIAL LEVERAGE: M&M PROPOSITION II

Although changing the capital structure of the firm does not change the firm's *total* value, it does cause important changes in the firm's debt and equity. We now examine what happens to a firm financed with debt and equity when the debt-equity ratio is changed. To simplify our analysis, we will continue to ignore taxes.

Based on our discussion in Chapter 14, if we ignore taxes, the weighted average cost of capital, WACC, is:

$$\text{WACC} = (E/V) \times R_E + (D/V) \times R_D$$

where $V = E + D$. We also saw that one way of interpreting the WACC is as the required return on the firm's overall assets. To remind us of this, we will use the symbol R_A to stand for the WACC and write:

$$R_A = (E/V) \times R_E + (D/V) \times R_D$$

If we rearrange this to solve for the cost of equity capital, we see that:

$$R_E = R_A + (R_A - R_D) \times (D/E)$$ **16.1**

M&M Proposition II
The proposition that a firm's cost of equity capital is a positive linear function of the firm's capital structure.

This is the famous **M&M Proposition II**, which tells us that the cost of equity depends on three things: The required rate of return on the firm's assets, R_A; the firm's cost of debt, R_D; and the firm's debt-equity ratio, D/E.

Figure 16.3 summarizes our discussion thus far by plotting the cost of equity capital, R_E, against the debt-equity ratio. As shown, M&M Proposition II indicates that the cost of equity, R_E, is given by a straight line with a slope of $(R_A - R_D)$. The y-intercept corresponds to a firm with a debt-equity ratio of zero, so $R_A = R_E$ in that case. Figure 16.3 shows that as the firm raises its debt-equity ratio, the increase in leverage raises the risk of the equity and therefore the required return or cost of equity (R_E).

Notice in Figure 16.3 that the WACC doesn't depend on the debt-equity ratio; it's the same no matter what the debt-equity ratio is. This is another way of stating M&M Proposition I: The firm's overall cost of capital is unaffected by its capital structure. As illustrated, the fact that the cost of debt is lower than the cost of equity is exactly offset by the increase in the cost of equity from borrowing. In other words, the change in the capital structure weights (E/V and D/V) is exactly offset by the change in the cost of equity (R_E), so the WACC stays the same.

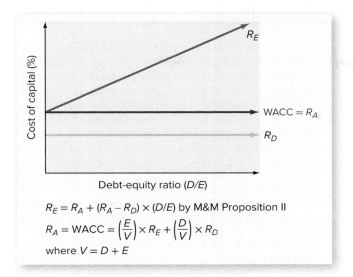

FIGURE 16.3

The Cost of Equity and the WACC: M&M Propositions I and II with No Taxes

$R_E = R_A + (R_A - R_D) \times (D/E)$ by M&M Proposition II

$R_A = \text{WACC} = \left(\dfrac{E}{V}\right) \times R_E + \left(\dfrac{D}{V}\right) \times R_D$

where $V = D + E$

The Cost of Equity Capital

EXAMPLE 16.3

The Ricardo Corporation has a weighted average cost of capital (ignoring taxes) of 12 percent. It can borrow at 8 percent. Assuming that Ricardo has a target capital structure of 80 percent equity and 20 percent debt, what is its cost of equity? What is the cost of equity if the target capital structure is 50 percent equity? Calculate the WACC using your answers to verify that it is the same.

According to M&M Proposition II, the cost of equity, R_E, is:

$$R_E = R_A + (R_A - R_D) \times (D/E)$$

In the first case, the debt-equity ratio is .2/.8 = .25, so the cost of the equity is:

$$R_E = .12 + (.12 - .08) \times .25$$
$$= .13, \text{ or } 13\%$$

In the second case, verify that the debt-equity ratio is 1.0, so the cost of equity is 16 percent.

We can now calculate the WACC assuming that the percentage of equity financing is 80 percent, the cost of equity is 13 percent, and the tax rate is zero:

$$\text{WACC} = (E/V) \times R_E + (D/V) \times R_D$$
$$= .80 \times .13 + .20 \times .08$$
$$= .12, \text{ or } 12\%$$

In the second case, the percentage of equity financing is 50 percent and the cost of equity is 16 percent. The WACC is:

$$\text{WACC} = (E/V) \times R_E + (D/V) \times R_D$$
$$= .50 \times .16 + .50 \times .08$$
$$= .12, \text{ or } 12\%$$

As we have calculated, the WACC is 12 percent in both cases.

BUSINESS AND FINANCIAL RISK

business risk
The equity risk that comes from the nature of the firm's operating activities.

M&M Proposition II shows that the firm's cost of equity can be broken down into two components. The first component, R_A, is the required return on the firm's assets overall, and it depends on the nature of the firm's operating activities. The risk inherent in a firm's operations is called the **business risk** of the firm's equity. Referring back to Chapter 13, note that this business risk depends on the systematic risk of the firm's assets. The greater a firm's business risk, the greater R_A will be, and, all other things being the same, the greater will be the firm's cost of equity.

financial risk
The equity risk that comes from the financial policy (the capital structure) of the firm.

The second component in the cost of equity, $(R_A - R_D) \times (D/E)$, is determined by the firm's financial structure. For an all-equity firm, this component is zero. As the firm begins to rely on debt financing, the required return on equity rises. This occurs because the debt financing increases the risks borne by the stockholders. This extra risk that arises from the use of debt financing is called the **financial risk** of the firm's equity.

The total systematic risk of the firm's equity has two parts: Business risk and financial risk. The first part (the business risk) depends on the firm's assets and operations and is unaffected by capital structure. Given the firm's business risk (and its cost of debt), the second part (the financial risk) is completely determined by financial policy. As we have illustrated, the firm's cost of equity rises when the firm increases its use of financial leverage because the financial risk of the equity increases while the business risk remains the same.

Concept Questions

16.3a   What does M&M Proposition I state?

16.3b   What are the three determinants of a firm's cost of equity?

16.3c   The total systematic risk of a firm's equity has two parts. What are they?

M&M Propositions I and II with Corporate Taxes

16.4

Debt has two distinguishing features that we have not taken into proper account. First, as we have mentioned in a number of places, interest paid on debt is tax deductible. This is good for the firm, and it may be an added benefit of debt financing. Second, failure to meet debt obligations can result in bankruptcy. This is not good for the firm, and it may be an added cost of debt financing. Because we haven't explicitly considered either of these two features of debt, we realize that we may get a different answer about capital structure once we do. Accordingly, we consider taxes in this section and bankruptcy in the next one.

Our discussion here will assume that all interest paid is tax deductible. In reality, however, the Tax Cuts and Jobs Act of 2017 placed limits on the amount of interest that can be deducted. Specifically, for 2018 through 2021, the net interest deduction is limited to at most 30 percent of EBITDA. After 2021, it drops to 30 percent of EBIT. The term "net interest" means interest paid less interest earned (if any). Also, the limits aren't exactly based on EBITDA and EBIT because of some adjustments, but the differences will be minor in most cases. Importantly, any interest that can't be deducted in a particular year can be carried forward and deducted later. Thus, the tax deductibility isn't lost; it is deferred.

We can start by considering what happens to M&M Propositions I and II when we consider the effect of corporate taxes. To do this, we will examine two firms: Firm U (unlevered) and Firm L (levered). These two firms are identical on the left side of the balance sheet, so their assets and operations are the same.

We assume that EBIT is expected to be $1,000 every year forever for both firms. The difference between the firms is that Firm L has issued $1,000 worth of perpetual bonds on which it pays 8 percent interest each year. The interest bill is $.08 \times \$1,000 = \$80$ every year forever. Also, we assume that the corporate tax rate is 21 percent.

For our two firms, U and L, we can now calculate the following:

	Firm U	Firm L
EBIT	$1,000	$1,000.00
Interest	0	80.00
Taxable income	$1,000	$ 920.00
Taxes (21%)	210	193.20
Net income	$ 790	$ 726.80

THE INTEREST TAX SHIELD

To simplify things, we will assume that depreciation is zero. We will also assume that capital spending is zero and that there are no changes in NWC. In this case, cash flow from assets is equal to EBIT − Taxes. For Firms U and L, we have:

Cash Flow from Assets	Firm U	Firm L
EBIT	$1,000	$1,000.00
−Taxes	210	193.20
Total	$ 790	$ 806.80

We immediately see that capital structure is now having some effect because the cash flows from U and L are not the same even though the two firms have identical assets.

To see what's going on, we can compute the cash flow to stockholders and bondholders:

Cash Flow	Firm U	Firm L
To stockholders	$790	$726.80
To bondholders	0	80.00
Total	$790	$806.80

What we are seeing is that the total cash flow to L is $16.80 more. This occurs because L's tax bill (which is a cash outflow) is $16.80 less. The fact that interest is deductible for tax purposes has generated a tax savings equal to the interest payment ($80) multiplied by the corporate tax rate (21 percent): $80 × .21 = $16.80. We call this tax savings the **interest tax shield**.

interest tax shield
The tax savings attained by a firm from interest expense.

TAXES AND M&M PROPOSITION I

Because the debt is perpetual, the same $16.80 shield will be generated every year forever. The aftertax cash flow to L will be the same $790 that U earns plus the $16.80 tax shield. Because L's cash flow is always $16.80 greater, Firm L is worth more than Firm U, the difference being the value of this $16.80 perpetuity.

Because the tax shield is generated by paying interest, it has the same risk as the debt, and 8 percent (the cost of debt) is the appropriate discount rate. The value of the tax shield is:

$$PV = \frac{\$16.80}{.08} = \frac{.21 \times \$1,000 \times .08}{.08} = .21 \times \$1,000 = \$210$$

As our example illustrates, the present value of the interest tax shield can be written as:

Present value of the interest tax shield = $(T_c \times D \times R_D)/R_D$

$$= T_c \times D$$

We have now come up with another famous result, M&M Proposition I with corporate taxes. We have seen that the value of Firm L, V_L, exceeds the value of Firm U, V_U, by the present value of the interest tax shield, $T_c \times D$. M&M Proposition I with taxes states that:

$V_L = V_U + T_c \times D$

The effect of borrowing in this case is illustrated in Figure 16.4. We have plotted the value of the levered firm, V_L, against the amount of debt, D. M&M Proposition I with corporate taxes implies that the relationship is given by a straight line with a slope of T_c and a y-intercept of V_U.

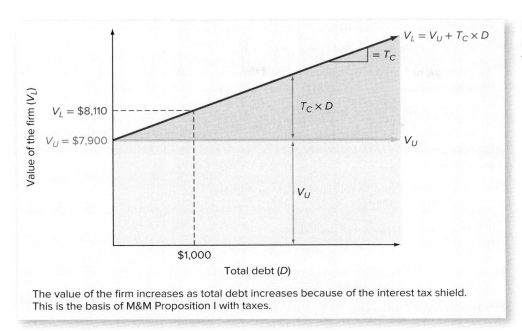

FIGURE 16.4

M&M Proposition I with Taxes

The value of the firm increases as total debt increases because of the interest tax shield. This is the basis of M&M Proposition I with taxes.

In Figure 16.4, we have also drawn a horizontal line representing V_U. As indicated, the distance between the two lines is $T_C \times D$, the present value of the tax shield.

Suppose that the cost of capital for Firm U is 10 percent. We will call this the **unlevered cost of capital**, and we will use the symbol R_U to represent it. We can think of R_U as the cost of capital a firm would have if it had no debt. Firm U's cash flow is $790 every year forever, and, because U has no debt, the appropriate discount rate is $R_U = 10\%$. The value of the unlevered firm, V_U, is:

unlevered cost of capital
The cost of capital for a firm that has no debt.

$$V_U = \frac{\text{EBIT} \times (1 - T_C)}{R_U}$$

$$= \frac{\$790}{.10}$$

$$= \$7,900$$

The value of the levered firm, V_L, is:

$$V_L = V_U + T_C \times D$$

$$= \$7,900 + .21 \times 1,000$$

$$= \$8,110$$

As Figure 16.4 indicates, the value of the firm goes up by $.21 for every $1 in debt. In other words, the NPV *per dollar* of debt is $.21. It is difficult to imagine why any corporation would not borrow to the absolute maximum under these circumstances.

The result of our analysis in this section is the realization that, once we include taxes, capital structure definitely matters. However, we immediately reach the illogical conclusion that the optimal capital structure is 100 percent debt.

TAXES, THE WACC, AND PROPOSITION II

We can also conclude that the best capital structure is 100 percent debt by examining the weighted average cost of capital. From Chapter 14, we know that once we consider the effect of taxes, the WACC is:

$$\text{WACC} = (E/V) \times R_E + (D/V) \times R_D \times (1 - T_C)$$

To calculate this WACC, we need to know the cost of equity. M&M Proposition II with corporate taxes states that the cost of equity is:

$$R_E = R_U + (R_U - R_D) \times (D/E) \times (1 - T_C)$$ **16.4**

To illustrate, recall that we saw a moment ago that Firm L is worth $8,110 total. Because the debt is worth $1,000, the equity must be worth $8,110 − 1,000 = $7,110. For Firm L, the cost of equity is:

$$R_E = .10 + (.10 - .08) \times (\$1,000/\$7,110) \times (1 - .21)$$
$$= .1022, \text{ or } 10.22\%$$

The weighted average cost of capital is:

$$\text{WACC} = (\$7,110/\$8,110) \times .1022 + (\$1,000/\$8,110) \times .08 \times (1 - .21)$$
$$= .0974, \text{ or } 9.74\%$$

Without debt, the WACC is over 10 percent; with debt, it is 9.74 percent. Therefore, the firm is better off with debt.

CONCLUSION

Figure 16.5 summarizes our discussion concerning the relationship between the cost of equity, the aftertax cost of debt, and the weighted average cost of capital. For reference,

FIGURE 16.5

The Cost of Equity and the WACC: M&M Proposition II with Taxes

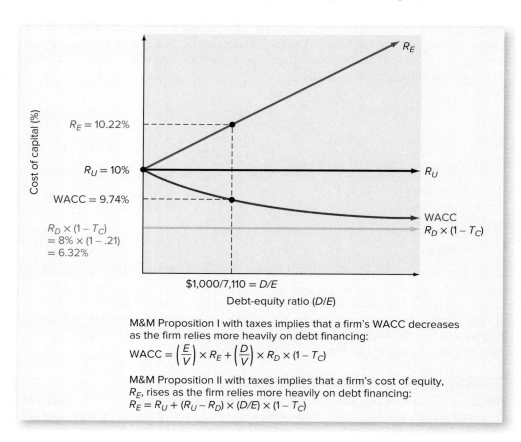

M&M Proposition I with taxes implies that a firm's WACC decreases as the firm relies more heavily on debt financing:
$$\text{WACC} = \left(\frac{E}{V}\right) \times R_E + \left(\frac{D}{V}\right) \times R_D \times (1 - T_C)$$

M&M Proposition II with taxes implies that a firm's cost of equity, R_E, rises as the firm relies more heavily on debt financing:
$$R_E = R_U + (R_U - R_D) \times (D/E) \times (1 - T_C)$$

TABLE 16.6

Modigliani and Miller Summary

I.	**The No-Tax Case**

A. Proposition I: The value of the firm levered (V_L) is equal to the value of the firm unlevered (V_U):

$$V_L = V_U$$

Implications of Proposition I:

1. A firm's capital structure is irrelevant.

2. A firm's weighted average cost of capital (WACC) is the same no matter what mixture of debt and equity is used to finance the firm.

B. Proposition II: The cost of equity, R_E, is:

$$R_E = R_A + (R_A - R_D) \times (D/E)$$

where R_A is the WACC, R_D is the cost of debt, and D/E is the debt-equity ratio.

Implications of Proposition II:

1. The cost of equity rises as the firm increases its use of debt financing.

2. The risk of the equity depends on two things: The riskiness of the firm's operations (*business risk*) and the degree of financial leverage (*financial risk*). Business risk determines R_A; financial risk is determined by D/E.

II.	**The Tax Case**

A. Proposition I with taxes: The value of the firm levered (V_L) is equal to the value of the firm unlevered (V_U) plus the present value of the interest tax shield:

$$V_L = V_U + T_C \times D$$

where T_C is the corporate tax rate and D is the amount of debt.

Implications of Proposition I:

1. Debt financing is highly advantageous, and, in the extreme, a firm's optimal capital structure is 100 percent debt.

2. A firm's weighted average cost of capital (WACC) decreases as the firm relies more heavily on debt financing.

B. Proposition II with taxes: The cost of equity, R_E, is:

$$R_E = R_U + (R_U - R_D) \times (D/E) \times (1 - T_C)$$

where R_U is the *unlevered cost of capital*—that is, the cost of capital for the firm if it has no debt. Unlike the case with Proposition I, the general implications of Proposition II are the same whether or not there are taxes.

we have included R_U, the unlevered cost of capital. In Figure 16.5, we have the debt-equity ratio on the horizontal axis. Notice how the WACC declines as the debt-equity ratio grows. This illustrates again that the more debt the firm uses, the lower is its WACC. Table 16.6 summarizes the key results of our analysis of the M&M propositions for future reference.

The Cost of Equity and the Value of the Firm	**EXAMPLE 16.4**

This is a comprehensive example that illustrates most of the points we have discussed thus far. You are given the following information for the Format Co.:

EBIT = $126.58
T_C = .21
D = $500
R_U = .20

The cost of debt capital is 10 percent. What is the value of Format's equity? What is the cost of equity capital for Format? What is the WACC?

This one's easier than it looks. Remember that all the cash flows are perpetuities. The value of the firm if it has no debt, V_U, is:

$$V_U = \frac{EBIT - Taxes}{R_U} = \frac{EBIT \times (1 - T_C)}{R_U}$$

$$= \frac{\$100}{.20}$$

$$= \$500$$

From M&M Proposition I with taxes, we know that the value of the firm with debt is:

$$V_L = V_U + T_C \times D$$
$$= \$500 + .21 \times \$500$$
$$= \$605$$

Because the firm is worth \$605 total and the debt is worth \$500, the equity is worth \$105:

$$E = V_L - D$$
$$= \$605 - 500$$
$$= \$105$$

Based on M&M Proposition II with taxes, the cost of equity is:

$$R_E = R_U + (R_U - R_D) \times (D/E) \times (1 - T_C)$$
$$= .20 + (.20 - .10) \times (\$500/\$105) \times (1 - .21)$$
$$= .5762, \text{ or } 57.62\%$$

Finally, the WACC is:

$$WACC = (\$105/\$605) \times .5762 + (\$500/\$605) \times .10 \times (1 - .21)$$
$$= .1653, \text{ or } 16.53\%$$

Notice that this is lower than the cost of capital for the firm with no debt ($R_U = 20\%$), so debt financing is advantageous.

Concept Questions

16.4a What is the relationship between the value of an unlevered firm and the value of a levered firm once we consider the effect of corporate taxes?

16.4b If we consider only the effect of taxes, what is the optimal capital structure?

16.5 Bankruptcy Costs

One limiting factor affecting the amount of debt a firm might use comes in the form of *bankruptcy costs*. As the debt-equity ratio rises, so too does the probability that the firm will be unable to pay its bondholders what was promised to them. When this happens, ownership of the firm's assets is ultimately transferred from the stockholders to the bondholders.

In principle, a firm becomes bankrupt when the value of its assets equals the value of its debt. When this occurs, the value of equity is zero, and the stockholders turn over control of the firm to the bondholders. When this takes place, the bondholders hold assets whose value is exactly equal to what is owed on the debt. In a perfect world, there are no costs associated with this transfer of ownership, and the bondholders don't lose anything.

This idealized view of bankruptcy is not, of course, what happens in the real world. Ironically, it is expensive to go bankrupt. As we discuss, the costs associated with bankruptcy may eventually offset the tax-related gains from leverage.

DIRECT BANKRUPTCY COSTS

When the value of a firm's assets equals the value of its debt, then the firm is economically bankrupt in the sense that the equity has no value. However, the formal turning over of the assets to the bondholders is a *legal* process, not an economic one. There are legal and administrative costs to bankruptcy, and it has been remarked that bankruptcies are to lawyers what blood is to sharks.

For example, in September 2008, famed investment bank Lehman Brothers filed for bankruptcy in the largest U.S. bankruptcy to date. The company emerged from bankruptcy in March 2012 as a liquidating trust, with the goal of selling off assets and paying creditors. The direct bankruptcy costs were eye-watering: Lehman spent more than $2.2 billion (that's "billion" with a "b") on lawyers, accountants, consultants, and examiners for its U.S. and European operations. The individual costs submitted by one law firm were equally amazing: The firm requested $200,000 for business meals, $439,000 for computerized and other research, $115,000 for local transportation, and $287,000 for copying charges at 10 cents per page. The other costs of bankruptcy may have been even larger. Some experts estimated that because Lehman rushed into bankruptcy it lost out on $75 billion that it could have earned if the sale of many of its assets had been better planned.

Because of the expenses associated with bankruptcy, bondholders won't get all that they are owed. Some fraction of the firm's assets will "disappear" in the legal process of going bankrupt. These are the legal and administrative expenses associated with the bankruptcy proceeding. We call these costs **direct bankruptcy costs**.

These direct bankruptcy costs are a disincentive to debt financing. If a firm goes bankrupt, then, suddenly, a piece of the firm disappears. This amounts to a bankruptcy "tax." So a firm faces a trade-off: Borrowing saves a firm money on its corporate taxes, but the more a firm borrows, the more likely it is that the firm will become bankrupt and have to pay the bankruptcy tax.

direct bankruptcy costs
The costs that are directly associated with bankruptcy, such as legal and administrative expenses.

INDIRECT BANKRUPTCY COSTS

Because it is expensive to go bankrupt, a firm will spend resources to avoid doing so. When a firm is having significant problems in meeting its debt obligations, we say that it is experiencing financial distress. Some financially distressed firms ultimately file for bankruptcy, but most do not because they are able to recover or otherwise survive.

The costs of avoiding a bankruptcy filing incurred by a financially distressed firm are called **indirect bankruptcy costs**. We use the term **financial distress costs** to refer generically to the direct and indirect costs associated with going bankrupt or avoiding a bankruptcy filing.

The problems that come up in financial distress are particularly severe, and the financial distress costs are larger, when the stockholders and the bondholders are different groups. Until the firm is legally bankrupt, the stockholders control it. They, of course, will take actions in their own economic interests. Because the stockholders can be wiped out in a legal bankruptcy, they have a very strong incentive to avoid a bankruptcy filing.

The bondholders, on the other hand, are primarily concerned with protecting the value of the firm's assets and will try to take control away from stockholders. They have a strong incentive to seek bankruptcy to protect their interests and keep stockholders from further dissipating the assets of the firm. The net effect of all this fighting is that a long, drawn-out, and potentially quite expensive legal battle gets started.

indirect bankruptcy costs
The costs of avoiding a bankruptcy filing incurred by a financially distressed firm.

financial distress costs
The direct and indirect costs associated with going bankrupt or experiencing financial distress.

Meanwhile, as the wheels of justice turn in their ponderous ways, the assets of the firm lose value because management is busy trying to avoid bankruptcy instead of running the business. Normal operations are disrupted, and sales are lost. Valuable employees leave, potentially fruitful programs are dropped to preserve cash, and otherwise profitable investments are not taken.

For example, in 2008, both General Motors and Chrysler were experiencing significant financial difficulty, and many people felt that one or both companies would eventually file for bankruptcy (both later did). As a result of the bad news surrounding them, there was a loss of confidence in the companies' automobiles. A study showed that 75 percent of Americans would not purchase an automobile from a bankrupt company because the company might not honor the warranty, and it might be difficult to obtain replacement parts. This concern resulted in lost potential sales for both companies, which only added to their financial distress.

These are all indirect bankruptcy costs, or costs of financial distress. Whether or not the firm ultimately goes bankrupt, the net effect is a loss of value because the firm chose to use debt in its capital structure. It is this possibility of loss that limits the amount of debt that a firm will choose to use.

Concept Questions

16.5a   What are direct bankruptcy costs?
16.5b   What are indirect bankruptcy costs?

16.6 Optimal Capital Structure

Our previous two sections have established the basis for determining an optimal capital structure. A firm will borrow because the interest tax shield is valuable. At relatively low debt levels, the probability of bankruptcy and financial distress is low, and the benefit from debt outweighs the cost. At very high debt levels, the possibility of financial distress is a chronic, ongoing problem for the firm, so the benefits from debt financing may be more than offset by the financial distress costs. Based on our discussion, it would appear that an optimal capital structure exists somewhere in between these extremes.

THE STATIC THEORY OF CAPITAL STRUCTURE

static theory of capital structure
The theory that a firm borrows up to the point where the tax benefit from an extra dollar in debt is exactly equal to the cost that comes from the increased probability of financial distress.

The theory of capital structure that we have outlined is called the **static theory of capital structure**. It says that firms borrow up to the point where the tax benefit from an extra dollar in debt is exactly equal to the cost that comes from the increased probability of financial distress. We call this the static theory because it assumes that the firm is fixed in terms of its assets and operations and it considers only possible changes in the debt-equity ratio.

The static theory is illustrated in Figure 16.6, which plots the value of the firm, V_L, against the amount of debt, D. In Figure 16.6, we have drawn lines corresponding to three different stories. The first represents M&M Proposition I with no taxes. This is the horizontal line extending from V_U, and it indicates that the value of the firm is unaffected by its capital structure. The second case, M&M Proposition I with corporate taxes, is represented by the upward-sloping straight line. These two cases are exactly the same as the ones we previously illustrated in Figure 16.4.

FIGURE 16.6   **The Static Theory of Capital Structure: The Optimal Capital Structure and the Value of the Firm**

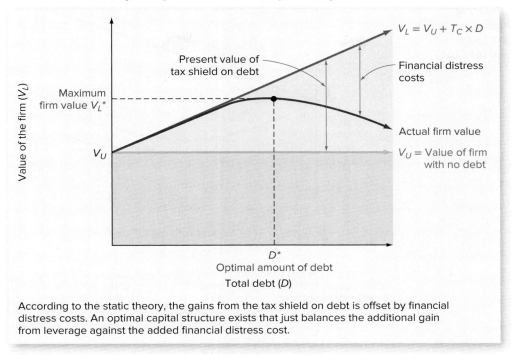

According to the static theory, the gains from the tax shield on debt is offset by financial distress costs. An optimal capital structure exists that just balances the additional gain from leverage against the added financial distress cost.

The third case in Figure 16.6 illustrates our current discussion: The value of the firm rises to a maximum and then declines beyond that point. This is the picture that we get from our static theory. The maximum value of the firm, V_L^*, is reached at D^*, so this point represents the optimal amount of borrowing. Put another way, the firm's optimal capital structure is composed of D^*/V_L^* in debt and $(1 - D^*/V_L^*)$ in equity.

The final thing to notice in Figure 16.6 is that the difference between the value of the firm in our static theory and the M&M value of the firm with taxes is the loss in value from the possibility of financial distress. Also, the difference between the static theory value of the firm and the M&M value with no taxes is the gain from leverage, net of distress costs.

OPTIMAL CAPITAL STRUCTURE AND THE COST OF CAPITAL

As we discussed earlier, the capital structure that maximizes the value of the firm is also the one that minimizes the cost of capital. Figure 16.7 illustrates the static theory of capital structure in terms of the weighted average cost of capital and the costs of debt and equity. Notice in Figure 16.7 that we have plotted the various capital costs against the debt-equity ratio, D/E.

Figure 16.7 is much the same as Figure 16.5 except that we have added a new line for the WACC. This line, which corresponds to the static theory, declines at first. This occurs because the aftertax cost of debt is cheaper than equity, so, at least initially, the overall cost of capital declines.

At some point, the cost of debt begins to rise, and the fact that debt is cheaper than equity is more than offset by the financial distress costs. From this point, further increases in debt actually increase the WACC. As illustrated, the minimum WACC* occurs at the point D^*/E^*, just as we described before.

FIGURE 16.7

The Static Theory of Capital Structure: The Optimal Capital Structure and the Cost of Capital

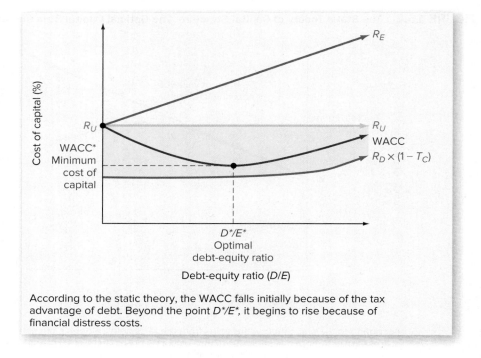

According to the static theory, the WACC falls initially because of the tax advantage of debt. Beyond the point D^*/E^*, it begins to rise because of financial distress costs.

OPTIMAL CAPITAL STRUCTURE: A RECAP

With the help of Figure 16.8, we can recap (no pun intended) our discussion of capital structure and cost of capital. As we have noted, there are essentially three cases. We will use the simplest of the three cases as a starting point and then build up to the static theory of capital structure. Along the way, we will pay particular attention to the connection between capital structure, firm value, and cost of capital.

Figure 16.8 presents the original Modigliani and Miller no-tax, no-bankruptcy argument as Case I. This is the most basic case. In the top part of the figure, we have plotted the value of the firm, V_L, against total debt, D. When there are no taxes, bankruptcy costs, or other real-world imperfections, we know that the total value of the firm is not affected by its debt policy, so V_L is constant. The bottom part of Figure 16.8 tells the same story in terms of the cost of capital. Here, the weighted average cost of capital, WACC, is plotted against the debt-equity ratio, D/E. As with total firm value, the overall cost of capital is not affected by debt policy in this basic case, so the WACC is constant.

Next, we consider what happens to the original M&M argument once taxes are introduced. As Case II illustrates, we now see that the firm's value critically depends on its debt policy. The more the firm borrows, the more it is worth. From our earlier discussion, we know this happens because interest payments are tax deductible, and the gain in firm value is equal to the present value of the interest tax shield.

In the bottom part of Figure 16.8, notice how the WACC declines as the firm uses more and more debt financing. As the firm increases its financial leverage, the cost of equity does increase; but this increase is more than offset by the tax break associated with debt financing. As a result, the firm's overall cost of capital declines.

To finish our story, we include the impact of bankruptcy, or financial distress costs, to get Case III. As shown in the top part of Figure 16.8, the value of the firm will not be as large as we previously indicated. The reason is that the firm's value is reduced by the present value of the potential future bankruptcy costs. These costs grow as the

FIGURE 16.8

The Capital Structure Question

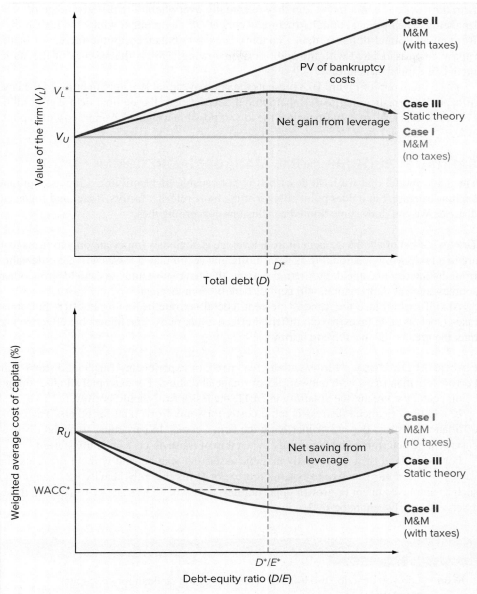

Case I
With no taxes or bankruptcy costs, the value of the firm and its weighted average cost of capital are not affected by capital structures.

Case II
With corporate taxes and no bankruptcy costs, the value of the firm increases and the weighted average cost of capital decreases as the amount of debt goes up.

Case III
With corporate taxes and bankruptcy costs, the value of the firm, V_L, reaches a maximum at D^*, the point representing the optimal amount of borrowing. At the same time, the weighted average cost of capital, WACC, is minimized at D^*/E^*.

firm borrows more and more, and they eventually overwhelm the tax advantage of debt financing. The optimal capital structure occurs at D^*, the point at which the tax savings from an additional dollar in debt financing is exactly balanced by the increased bankruptcy costs associated with the additional borrowing. This is the essence of the static theory of capital structure.

The bottom part of Figure 16.8 presents the optimal capital structure in terms of the cost of capital. Corresponding to D^*, the optimal debt level, is the optimal debt-equity ratio, D^*/E^*. At this level of debt financing, the lowest possible weighted average cost of capital, WACC*, occurs.

CAPITAL STRUCTURE: SOME MANAGERIAL RECOMMENDATIONS

The static model that we have described is not capable of identifying a precise optimal capital structure, but it does point out two of the more relevant factors: Taxes and financial distress. We can draw some limited conclusions concerning these.

Taxes   First of all, the tax benefit from leverage is obviously important only to firms that are in a tax-paying position. Firms with substantial accumulated losses will get little value from the interest tax shield. Furthermore, firms that have substantial tax shields from other sources, such as depreciation, will get less benefit from leverage.

Also, firms all face the same 21 percent federal tax rate beginning in 2018, but other taxes (such as state taxes) create different effective tax rates. The higher the effective tax rate, the greater the incentive to borrow.

Financial Distress   Firms with a greater risk of experiencing financial distress will borrow less than firms with a lower risk of financial distress. For example, all other things being equal, the greater the volatility in EBIT, the less a firm should borrow.

In addition, financial distress is more costly for some firms than for others. The costs of financial distress depend primarily on the firm's assets. In particular, financial distress costs will be determined by how easily ownership of those assets can be transferred.

For example, a firm with mostly tangible assets that can be sold without great loss in value will have an incentive to borrow more. For firms that rely heavily on intangibles, such as employee talent or growth opportunities, debt will be less attractive because these assets effectively cannot be sold.

Concept Questions

16.6a   Can you describe the trade-off that defines the static theory of capital structure?
16.6b   What are the important factors in making capital structure decisions?

16.7 The Pie Again

Although it is comforting to know that the firm might have an optimal capital structure when we take into account real-world matters such as taxes and financial distress costs, it is disquieting to see the elegant original M&M intuition (that is, the no-tax version) fall apart in the face of these matters.

Critics of the M&M theory often say that it fails to hold as soon as we add in real-world issues and that the M&M theory is really just that: A theory that doesn't have much to say about the real world that we live in. In fact, they would argue that it is the M&M theory that is irrelevant, not capital structure. As we discuss next, taking that view blinds critics to the real value of the M&M theory.

THE EXTENDED PIE MODEL

To illustrate the value of the original M&M intuition, we briefly consider an expanded version of the pie model that we introduced earlier. In the extended pie model, taxes represent just another claim on the cash flows of the firm. Because taxes are reduced as leverage is increased, the value of the government's claim (G) on the firm's cash flows decreases with leverage.

Bankruptcy costs are also a claim on the cash flows of the firm. They come into play as the firm comes close to bankruptcy and has to alter its behavior to attempt to stave off the event itself, and they become large when bankruptcy actually takes place. The value of this claim (B) on the cash flows rises with increases in the debt-equity ratio.

The extended pie model holds that all of these claims can be paid from only one source: The cash flows (CF) of the firm. Algebraically, we must have:

CF = Payments to stockholders

    + Payments to creditors

    + Payments to the government

    + Payments to bankruptcy courts and lawyers

    + Payments to any and all other claimants to the cash flows of the firm

The extended pie model is illustrated in Figure 16.9. Notice that we have added a few slices for the additional groups. Notice also the change in the relative sizes of the slices as the firm's use of debt financing is increased.

With the list we have developed, we have not even begun to exhaust the potential claims to the firm's cash flows. To give an unusual example, we might say that everyone reading this book has an economic claim on the cash flows of General Motors. After all, if you are injured in an accident, you might sue GM, and, win or lose, GM will expend some of its cash flow in dealing with the matter. For GM, or any other company, there should be a slice of the pie representing potential lawsuits. This is the essence of the M&M intuition

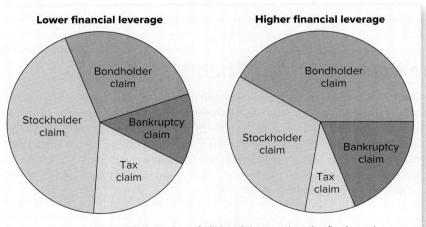

FIGURE 16.9

The Extended Pie Model

In the extended pie model, the value of all the claims against the firm's cash flows is unaffected by capital structure, but the *relative* values of claims change as the amount of debt financing is increased.

and theory: The value of the firm depends on the total cash flow of the firm. The firm's capital structure just cuts that cash flow up into slices without altering the total. What we recognize now is that the stockholders and the bondholders may not be the only ones who can claim a slice.

MARKETED CLAIMS VERSUS NONMARKETED CLAIMS

With our extended pie model, there is an important distinction between claims such as those of stockholders and bondholders, on the one hand, and those of the government and potential litigants in lawsuits on the other. The first set of claims are *marketed claims*, and the second set are *nonmarketed claims*. A key difference is that the marketed claims can be bought and sold in financial markets and the nonmarketed claims cannot be sold in financial markets.

When we speak of the value of the firm, we are generally referring to just the value of the marketed claims, V_M, and not the value of the nonmarketed claims, V_N. If we write V_T for the total value of *all* the claims against a corporation's cash flows, then:

$$V_T = E + D + G + B + \cdots$$
$$= V_M + V_N$$

The essence of our extended pie model is that this total value, V_T, of all the claims to the firm's cash flows is unaltered by capital structure. However, the value of the marketed claims, V_M, may be affected by changes in the capital structure.

Based on the extended pie model, any increase in V_M must imply an identical decrease in V_N. The optimal capital structure is the one that maximizes the value of the marketed claims or, equivalently, minimizes the value of nonmarketed claims such as taxes and bankruptcy costs.

> **Concept Questions**
>
> **16.7a**   What are some of the claims to a firm's cash flows?
> **16.7b**   What is the difference between a marketed claim and a nonmarketed claim?
> **16.7c**   What does the extended pie model say about the value of all the claims to a firm's cash flows?

16.8   The Pecking-Order Theory

The static theory we have developed in this chapter has dominated thinking about capital structure for a long time, but it has some shortcomings. Perhaps the most obvious is that many large, financially sophisticated, and highly profitable firms use little debt. This is the opposite of what we would expect. Under the static theory, these are the firms that should use the *most* debt because there is little risk of bankruptcy and the value of the tax shield is substantial. Why do they use so little debt? The pecking-order theory, which we consider next, may be part of the answer.

INTERNAL FINANCING AND THE PECKING ORDER

The pecking-order theory is an alternative to the static theory. A key element in the pecking-order theory is that firms prefer to use internal financing whenever possible.

A simple reason is that selling securities to raise cash can be expensive, so it makes sense to avoid doing so if possible. If a firm is very profitable, it might never need external financing; so it would end up with little or no debt. For example, in late 2017, Alphabet's balance sheet showed assets of $189.5 billion, of which almost $100.3 billion were classified as either cash or marketable securities. In fact, Alphabet held so much of its assets in the form of securities that, at one point, it was in danger of being regulated as a mutual fund!

There is a more subtle reason that companies may prefer internal financing. Suppose you are the manager of a firm, and you need to raise external capital to fund a new venture. As an insider, you are privy to a lot of information that isn't known to the public. Based on your knowledge, the firm's future prospects are considerably brighter than outside investors realize. As a result, you think your stock is currently undervalued. Should you issue debt or equity to finance the new venture?

If you think about it, you definitely don't want to issue equity in this case. The reason is that your stock is undervalued, and you don't want to sell it too cheaply. So, you issue debt instead.

Would you ever want to issue equity? Suppose you thought your firm's stock was overvalued. It makes sense to raise money at inflated prices, but a problem crops up. If you try to sell equity, investors will realize that the shares are probably overvalued, and your stock price will take a hit. In other words, if you try to raise money by selling equity, you run the risk of signaling to investors that the price is too high. In fact, in the real world, companies rarely sell new equity, and the market reacts negatively to such sales when they occur.

So, we have a pecking order. Companies will use internal financing first. Then, they will issue debt if necessary. Equity will be sold pretty much as a last resort.

IMPLICATIONS OF THE PECKING ORDER

The pecking-order theory has several significant implications, a couple of which are at odds with our static theory:

1. *No target capital structure*: Under the pecking-order theory, there is no target or optimal debt-equity ratio. Instead, a firm's capital structure is determined by its need for external financing, which dictates the amount of debt the firm will have.

2. *Profitable firms use less debt*: Because profitable firms have greater internal cash flow, they will need less external financing and will therefore have less debt. As we mentioned earlier, this is a pattern that we seem to observe, at least for some companies.

3. *Companies will want financial slack*: To avoid selling new equity, companies will want to stockpile internally generated cash. Such a cash reserve is known as *financial slack*. It gives management the ability to finance projects as they appear and to move quickly if necessary.

Which theory, static or pecking-order, is correct? Financial researchers have not reached a definitive conclusion on this issue, but we can make a few observations. The static theory speaks more to long-run financial goals or strategies. The issues of tax shields and financial distress costs are plainly important in that context. The pecking-order theory is more concerned with the shorter-run, tactical issue of raising external funds to finance investments. So both theories are useful ways of understanding corporate use of debt. For example, it is probably the case that firms have long-run, target capital structures, but it is also probably true that they will deviate from those long-run targets as needed to avoid issuing new equity.

Concept Questions

16.8a Under the pecking-order theory, what is the order in which firms will obtain financing?

16.8b Why might firms prefer not to issue new equity?

16.8c What are some differences in implications of the static and pecking-order theories?

16.9 Observed Capital Structures

No two firms have identical capital structures. Nonetheless, we see some regular elements when we start looking at actual capital structures. We discuss a few of these next.

The most striking thing we observe about capital structures, particularly in the United States, is that most corporations seem to have relatively low debt-equity ratios. In fact, most corporations use much less debt financing than equity financing. To illustrate, Table 16.7 presents median debt ratios and debt-equity ratios for various U.S. industries classified by SIC code (we discussed such codes in Chapter 3).

In Table 16.7, what is most striking is the wide variation across industries, ranging from essentially no debt for drug and computer companies to relatively heavy debt usage in the airline and cable television industries. Notice that these last two industries are the only ones for which more debt is used than equity, and most of the other industries rely far more heavily on equity than debt. This is true even though many of the companies in these industries pay substantial taxes. Table 16.7 makes it clear that corporations have not, in general, issued debt up to the point that tax shelters have been completely used up, and we conclude that there must be limits to the amount of debt corporations can use. Take a look at our nearby *Work the Web* box for more about actual capital structures.

TABLE 16.7

Capital Structures for U.S. Industries

SOURCE: *Ibbotson Cost of Capital Yearbook.* Chicago: Morningstar, 2010.

Industry	Ratio of Debt to Total Capital*	Ratio of Debt to Equity	Number of Companies	SIC Code	Representative Companies
Electric utilities	48.54%	94.31%	33	491	American Electric Power, Southern Co.
Computer equipment	9.09	10.02	48	357	Apple, Cisco
Paper	27.75	38.40	24	26	Avery Dennison, Weyerhaeuser
Petroleum refining	32.27	47.65	18	29	Chevron, Sunoco
Airlines	63.92	177.19	10	4512	Delta, Southwest
Pay television	63.56	193.88	5	484	Dish Network, TiVo
Motor vehicles	17.77	21.60	25	371	Ford, Winnebago
Fabric apparel	15.86	18.84	14	23	Guess, Nine West
Department stores	27.40	37.73	8	531	J.C. Penney, Macy's
Eating places	23.40	30.54	42	5812	McDonald's, Papa John's
Drugs	7.80	8.46	194	283	Merck, Pfizer
Steel works	19.96	24.95	9	331	Nucor, U.S. Steel

*Debt is the book value of preferred stock and long-term debt, including amounts due in one year. Equity is the market value of outstanding shares. Total capital is the sum of debt and equity. Median values are shown.

WORK THE WEB

When it comes to capital structure, all companies (and industries) are not created equal. To illustrate, we looked up some capital structure information on American Airlines (AAL) and Pfizer (PFE) using the Financials area of www.reuters.com. American Airlines's capital structure looks like this (note that leverage ratios are expressed as percentages on this site):

FINANCIAL STRENGTH			
	Company	industry	sector
Quick Ratio (MRQ)	0.68	0.90	2.07
Current Ratio (MRQ)	0.76	0.97	2.49
LT Debt to Equity (MRQ)	490.66	92.30	65.25
Total Debt to Equity (MRQ)	531.61	143.06	90.49
Interest Coverage (TTM)	8.55	13.73	14.40

For every dollar of equity, American Airlines has long-term debt of $4.9066 and total debt of $5.3161. Compare this result to Pfizer:

FINANCIAL STRENGTH			
	Company	industry	sector
Quick Ratio (MRQ)	0.89	2.29	2.41
Current Ratio (MRQ)	1.11	3.21	3.31
LT Debt to Equity (MRQ)	48.08	21.38	21.99
Total Debt to Equity (MRQ)	69.61	30.44	30.99
Interest Coverage (TTM)	23.64	38.25	38.48

For every dollar of equity, Pfizer has only $.4808 of long-term debt and total debt of $.6961. When we examine the industry and sector averages, the differences are again apparent. Although the choice of capital structure is a management decision, it is clearly influenced by industry characteristics.

Questions
1. *The ratios shown for these companies were based on January 2017 figures. Go to www.reuters.com and find the current long-term debt-to-equity and total debt-to-equity ratios for both American Airlines and Pfizer. How have these ratios changed over this time?*
2. *Go to www.reuters.com and find the long-term debt-to-equity and total debt-to-equity ratios for Bank of America (BAC), Cisco (CSCO), and Chevron (CVX). Why do you think these three companies use such differing amounts of debt?*

Because different industries have different operating characteristics in terms of, for example, EBIT volatility and asset types, there does appear to be some connection between these characteristics and capital structure. Our story involving tax savings, financial distress costs, and potential pecking orders undoubtedly supplies part of the reason; but, to date, there is no fully satisfactory theory that explains these regularities in capital structures.

Concept Questions

16.9a Do U.S. corporations rely heavily on debt financing?
16.9b What regularities do we observe in capital structures?

16.10 A Quick Look at the Bankruptcy Process

As we have discussed, one consequence of using debt is the possibility of financial distress, which can be defined in several ways:

1. *Business failure*: This term is usually used to refer to a situation in which a business has terminated with a loss to creditors; but even an all-equity firm can fail.
2. *Legal bankruptcy*: Firms or creditors bring petitions to a federal court for bankruptcy. **Bankruptcy** is a legal proceeding for liquidating or reorganizing a business.
3. *Technical insolvency*: Technical insolvency occurs when a firm is unable to meet its financial obligations.
4. *Accounting insolvency*: Firms with negative net worth are insolvent on the books. This happens when the total book liabilities exceed the book value of the total assets.

bankruptcy
A legal proceeding for liquidating or reorganizing a business.

We now very briefly discuss some of the terms and more relevant issues associated with bankruptcy and financial distress.

LIQUIDATION AND REORGANIZATION

Firms that cannot or choose not to make contractually required payments to creditors have two basic options: Liquidation or reorganization. **Liquidation** means termination of the firm as a going concern, and it involves selling off the assets of the firm. The proceeds, net of selling costs, are distributed to creditors in order of established priority. **Reorganization** is the option of keeping the firm a going concern; it often involves issuing new securities to replace old securities. Liquidation or reorganization is the result of a bankruptcy proceeding. Which occurs depends on whether the firm is worth more "dead or alive."

liquidation
Termination of the firm as a going concern.

reorganization
Financial restructuring of a failing firm to attempt to continue operations as a going concern.

Bankruptcy Liquidation   Chapter 7 of the Federal Bankruptcy Reform Act of 1978 deals with "straight" liquidation. The following sequence of events is typical:

1. A petition is filed in a federal court. Corporations may file a voluntary petition, or involuntary petitions may be filed against the corporation by several of its creditors.
2. A trustee-in-bankruptcy is elected by the creditors to take over the assets of the debtor corporation. The trustee will attempt to liquidate the assets.
3. When the assets are liquidated, after payment of the bankruptcy administration costs, the proceeds are distributed among the creditors.
4. If any proceeds remain, after expenses and payments to creditors, they are distributed to the shareholders.

The SEC has a good overview of the bankruptcy process in its "Online Publications" section at **www.sec.gov**.

The distribution of the proceeds of the liquidation occurs according to the following priority list:

1. Administrative expenses associated with the bankruptcy.
2. Other expenses arising after the filing of an involuntary bankruptcy petition but before the appointment of a trustee.
3. Wages, salaries, and commissions.
4. Contributions to employee benefit plans.
5. Consumer claims.
6. Government tax claims.
7. Payment to unsecured creditors.
8. Payment to preferred stockholders.
9. Payment to common stockholders.

This priority list for liquidation is a reflection of the **absolute priority rule (APR)**. The higher a claim is on this list, the more likely it is to be paid. In many of these categories, there are various limitations and qualifications that we omit for the sake of brevity.

absolute priority rule (APR)
The rule establishing priority of claims in liquidation.

Two qualifications to this list are in order. The first concerns secured creditors. Such creditors are entitled to the proceeds from the sale of the security and are outside this ordering. If the secured property is liquidated and provides cash insufficient to cover the amount owed, the secured creditors join with unsecured creditors in dividing the remaining liquidated value. In contrast, if the secured property is liquidated for proceeds greater than the secured claim, the net proceeds are used to pay unsecured creditors and others. The second qualification to the APR is that, in reality, what happens, and who gets what, in the event of bankruptcy are subject to much negotiation; as a result, the APR is frequently not followed.

Bankruptcy Reorganization   Corporate reorganization takes place under Chapter 11 of the Federal Bankruptcy Reform Act of 1978. The general objective of a proceeding under Chapter 11 is to plan to restructure the corporation with some provision for repayment of creditors. A typical sequence of events follows:

Get the latest on bankruptcy at **www.bankruptcydata.com**.

1. A voluntary petition can be filed by the corporation, or an involuntary petition can be filed by creditors.
2. A federal judge either approves or denies the petition. If the petition is approved, a time for filing proofs of claims is set.
3. In most cases, the corporation (the "debtor in possession") continues to run the business.
4. The corporation (and, in certain cases, the creditors) submits a reorganization plan.
5. Creditors and shareholders are divided into classes. A class of creditors accepts the plan if a majority of the class agrees to the plan.
6. After its acceptance by creditors, the plan is confirmed by the court.
7. Payments in cash, property, and securities are made to creditors and shareholders. The plan may provide for the issuance of new securities.
8. For some fixed length of time, the firm operates according to the provisions of the reorganization plan.

The corporation may wish to allow the old stockholders to retain some participation in the firm. Needless to say, this may involve some protest by the holders of unsecured debt.

So-called prepackaged bankruptcies are a relatively common phenomenon. What happens is that the corporation secures the necessary approval of a bankruptcy plan from a majority of its creditors first, and then it files for bankruptcy. As a result, the company enters bankruptcy and reemerges almost immediately.

For example, one of the largest Chapter 11 prepackaged bankruptcies to date began when business lender CIT Group filed for bankruptcy on November 1, 2009. Under the terms of the agreement, stockholders were wiped out entirely and bondholders' claims were reduced by $10.5 billion. At the same time, the maturity on the company's debt was extended by three years. An additional debt reduction occurred when $2.3 billion in "bailout" funds received by the company under the U.S. government's Troubled Asset Relief Program (TARP) were wiped out. Thanks to the prepack, the company moved quickly through the bankruptcy process, emerging from bankruptcy proceedings on December 10, 2009.

In another recent example, on October 24, 2016, Houston-based Key Energy Services filed for a prepack bankruptcy. Under the terms of the plan, the company's debt would be reduced from $1.2 billion to $250 million, existing creditors would be granted shares of the company's new stock, and rights would be issued on the company's new stock to repay principal and interest on an outstanding loan. Surprisingly, existing shareholders received a reduced number of shares of new stock, with rights and warrants to buy more. Key Energy Services exited its prepack bankruptcy on December 15, 2016, only 52 days after entering bankruptcy.

In some cases, the bankruptcy procedure is needed to invoke the "cram-down" power of the bankruptcy court. Under certain circumstances, a class of creditors can be forced to accept a bankruptcy plan even if they vote not to approve it—hence the remarkably apt description "cram down."

In 2005, Congress passed the most significant overhaul of U.S. bankruptcy laws in the last 25 years, the Bankruptcy Abuse Prevention and Consumer Protection Act of 2005 (BAPCPA). Most of the changes were aimed at individual debtors, but corporations were also affected. Before BAPCPA, a bankrupt company had the exclusive right to submit reorganization plans to the bankruptcy court. It has been argued that this exclusivity is one reason some companies have remained in bankruptcy for so long. Under the new law, after 18 months, creditors can submit their own plan for the court's consideration. This change is likely to speed up bankruptcies and also lead to more prepacks.

One controversial change made by BAPCPA has to do with so-called key employee retention plans, or KERPs. Strange as it may sound, bankrupt companies routinely give bonus payments to executives, even though the executives may be the same ones who led the company into bankruptcy in the first place. Such bonuses are intended to keep valuable employees from moving to more successful firms, but critics have argued they are often abused. The new law permits KERPs only if the employee in question actually has a job offer from another company.

Recently, Section 363 of the bankruptcy code has been in the news. In a traditional Chapter 11 filing, the bankruptcy plan is described to creditors and shareholders in a prospectus-like disclosure. The plan must then be approved by a vote involving the interested parties. A Section 363 bankruptcy is more like an auction. An initial bidder, known as a *stalking horse*, bids on all or part of the bankrupt company's assets. Other bidders are then invited into the process to determine the highest bid for the company's assets. The main advantage of a Section 363 bankruptcy is speed. Since a traditional bankruptcy requires the approval of interested parties, it is not uncommon for the process to take several years, while a Section 363 bankruptcy is generally much quicker. For example, in the middle of 2009, both General Motors and Chrysler sped through the bankruptcy process in less than 45 days with the help of Section 363 sales.

FINANCIAL MANAGEMENT AND THE BANKRUPTCY PROCESS

It may seem a little odd, but the right to go bankrupt is very valuable. There are several reasons why this is true. First, from an operational standpoint, when a firm files for bankruptcy, there is an immediate "stay" on creditors, usually meaning that payments to creditors will cease, and creditors will have to await the outcome of the bankruptcy process to find out if and how much they will be paid. This stay gives the firm time to evaluate its options, and it prevents what is usually termed a "race to the courthouse steps" by creditors and others.

Beyond this, some bankruptcy filings are actually strategic actions intended to improve a firm's competitive position, and firms have filed for bankruptcy even though they were not insolvent at the time. Probably the most famous example is Continental Airlines. In 1983, following deregulation of the airline industry, Continental found itself competing with newly established airlines that had much lower labor costs. Continental filed for reorganization under Chapter 11 even though it was not insolvent.

Continental argued that, based on pro forma data, it would become insolvent in the future, and a reorganization was therefore necessary. By filing for bankruptcy, Continental was able to terminate its existing labor agreements, lay off large numbers of workers, and slash wages for the remaining employees. In other words, at least in the eyes of critics, Continental essentially used the bankruptcy process as a vehicle for reducing labor costs. Congress subsequently modified bankruptcy laws to make it more difficult, though not impossible, for companies to abrogate a labor contract through the bankruptcy process. For example, Delta Air Lines filed for bankruptcy in 2005, in part to renegotiate the contracts with its union employees.

Other famous examples of strategic bankruptcies exist. For example, Manville (then known as Johns-Manville) and Dow Corning filed for bankruptcies because of expected future losses resulting from litigation associated with asbestos and silicone breast implants, respectively. Similarly, in the then-largest-ever bankruptcy, Texaco filed in 1987 after Pennzoil was awarded a $10.3 billion judgment against the company. Texaco later settled for $3.5 billion and emerged from bankruptcy. As of early 2018, the largest bankruptcies in the United States in terms of assets were the 2008 bankruptcy of Lehman Brothers (with $691 billion in assets) and the collapse of Washington Mutual (with $328 billion in assets), also in 2008. However, the 2003 bankruptcy filing of Italian dairy company Parmalat may have topped them both in terms of relative importance. This company, by itself, represented 1.5 percent of the Italian gross national product!

AGREEMENTS TO AVOID BANKRUPTCY

When a firm defaults on an obligation, it can avoid a bankruptcy filing. Because the legal process of bankruptcy can be lengthy and expensive, it is often in everyone's best interest to devise a "workout" that avoids a bankruptcy filing. Much of the time, creditors can work with the management of a company that has defaulted on a loan contract. Voluntary arrangements to restructure or "reschedule" the company's debt can be, and often are, made. This may involve *extension*, which postpones the date of payment, or *composition*, which involves a reduced payment.

Concept Questions

16.10a   What is the APR?
16.10b   What is the difference between liquidation and reorganization?

16.11 Summary and Conclusions

The ideal mixture of debt and equity for a firm—its optimal capital structure—is the one that maximizes the value of the firm and minimizes the overall cost of capital. If we ignore taxes, financial distress costs, and any other imperfections, we find that there is no ideal mixture. Under these circumstances, the firm's capital structure is irrelevant.

If we consider the effect of corporate taxes, we find that capital structure matters a great deal. This conclusion is based on the fact that interest is tax deductible and generates a valuable tax shield. Unfortunately, we also find that the optimal capital structure is 100 percent debt, which is not something we observe in healthy firms.

When we introduce costs associated with bankruptcy, or, more generally, financial distress, we see that these costs reduce the attractiveness of debt financing. We conclude that an optimal capital structure exists when the net tax savings from an additional dollar in interest just equals the increase in expected financial distress costs. This is the essence of the static theory of capital structure.

In this chapter we also considered the pecking-order theory of capital structure as an alternative to the static theory. This theory suggests that firms will use internal financing as much as possible, followed by debt financing if needed. Equity will not be issued if possible. As a result, a firm's capital structure just reflects its historical needs for external financing, so there is no optimal capital structure.

When we examine actual capital structures, we find two regularities. First, firms in the United States typically do not use great amounts of debt, but they pay substantial taxes. This suggests that there is a limit to the use of debt financing to generate tax shields. Second, firms in similar industries tend to have similar capital structures, suggesting that the nature of their assets and operations is an important determinant of capital structure.

CONNECT TO FINANCE

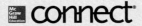 *Connect Finance* offers you plenty of opportunities to practice mastering these concepts. Log on to connect.mheducation.com to learn more. If you like what you see, ask your professor about using *Connect Finance*!

Can you answer the following *Connect* Quiz questions?

Section 16.1   Maximizing what will maximize shareholder value?
Section 16.3   What is most closely related to a firm's use of debt in its capital structure?
Section 16.5   Give an example of a direct cost of bankruptcy.
Section 16.7   What claims increase when the debt-equity ratio is increased?

CHAPTER REVIEW AND SELF-TEST PROBLEMS

16.1   EBIT and EPS   Suppose the BDJ Corporation has decided in favor of a capital restructuring that involves increasing its existing $80 million in debt to $125 million. The interest rate on the debt is 9 percent and is not expected to change. The firm currently has 10 million shares outstanding, and the price per share is $45. If the restructuring is expected to increase the ROE, what is the minimum level for EBIT that BDJ's management must be expecting? Ignore taxes in your answer.

16.2 M&M Proposition II (no taxes) The Habitat Corporation has a WACC of 16 percent. Its cost of debt is 13 percent. If Habitat's debt-equity ratio is 2, what is its cost of equity capital? Ignore taxes in your answer.

16.3 M&M Proposition I (with corporate taxes) Gypco expects an EBIT of $10,000 every year forever. Gypco can borrow at 7 percent. Suppose Gypco currently has no debt, and its cost of equity is 17 percent. If the corporate tax rate is 21 percent, what is the value of the firm? What will the value be if Gypco borrows $15,000 and uses the proceeds to repurchase stock?

ANSWERS TO CHAPTER REVIEW AND SELF-TEST PROBLEMS

16.1 To answer, we can calculate the break-even EBIT. At any EBIT above this, the increased financial leverage will increase EPS. Under the old capital structure, the interest bill is $80 million × .09 = $7,200,000. There are 10 million shares of stock; so, ignoring taxes, EPS is (EBIT − $7.2 million)/10 million.

Under the new capital structure, the interest expense will be $125 million × .09 = $11.25 million. Furthermore, the debt rises by $45 million. This amount is sufficient to repurchase $45 million/$45 = 1 million shares of stock, leaving 9 million outstanding. EPS is thus (EBIT − $11.25 million)/9 million.

Now that we know how to calculate EPS under both scenarios, we set the two calculations equal to each other and solve for the break-even EBIT:

$$(EBIT − \$7.2 \text{ million})/10 \text{ million} = (EBIT − \$11.25 \text{ million})/9 \text{ million}$$
$$EBIT − \$7.2 \text{ million} = 1.11 × (EBIT − \$11.25 \text{ million})$$
$$EBIT = \$47,700,000$$

Verify that, in either case, EPS is $4.05 when EBIT is $47.7 million.

16.2 According to M&M Proposition II (no taxes), the cost of equity is:

$$R_E = R_A + (R_A − R_D) × (D/E)$$
$$= .16 + (.16 − .13) × 2$$
$$= .22, \text{ or } 22\%$$

16.3 With no debt, Gypco's WACC is 17 percent. This is also the unlevered cost of capital. The aftertax cash flow is $10,000 × (1 − .21) = $7,900, so the value is just $V_U = \$7,900/.17 = \$46,471$.

After the debt issue, Gypco will be worth the original $46,471 plus the present value of the tax shield. According to M&M Proposition I with taxes, the present value of the tax shield is $T_C × D$, or .21 × $15,000 = $3,150; so the firm is worth $46,471 + 3,150 = $49,621.

CONCEPTS REVIEW AND CRITICAL THINKING QUESTIONS

1. **Business Risk versus Financial Risk [LO1]** Explain what is meant by *business risk* and *financial risk*. Suppose Firm A has greater business risk than Firm B. Is it true that Firm A also has a higher cost of equity capital? Explain.

2. **M&M Propositions [LO1]** How would you answer in the following debate?
   Q: Isn't it true that the riskiness of a firm's equity will rise if the firm increases its use of debt financing?
   A: Yes, that's the essence of M&M Proposition II.

Q: And isn't it true that, as a firm increases its use of borrowing, the likelihood of default increases, thereby increasing the risk of the firm's debt?

A: Yes.

Q: In other words, increased borrowing increases the risk of the equity *and* the debt?

A: That's right.

Q: Well, given that the firm uses only debt and equity financing, and given that the risks of both are increased by increased borrowing, does it not follow that increasing debt increases the overall risk of the firm and therefore decreases the value of the firm?

A: ?

3. **Optimal Capital Structure [LO1]** Is there an easily identifiable debt-equity ratio that will maximize the value of a firm? Why or why not?

4. **Observed Capital Structures [LO1]** Refer to the observed capital structures given in Table 16.7 of the text. What do you notice about the types of industries with respect to their average debt-equity ratios? Are certain types of industries more likely to be highly leveraged than others? What are some possible reasons for this observed segmentation? Do the operating results and tax history of the firms play a role? How about their future earnings prospects? Explain.

5. **Financial Leverage [LO1]** Why is the use of debt financing referred to as financial "leverage"?

6. **Interest Deductibility and Financial Ratios [LO1]** Take a look back at the times interest earned (TIE) ratio we discussed in Chapter 3. For interest paid to be fully deductible by a company after the Tax Cuts and Jobs Act of 2017, what must be true about this ratio? Assume the company has no interest income.

7. **Bankruptcy and Corporate Ethics [LO3]** As mentioned in the text, some firms have filed for bankruptcy because of actual or likely litigation-related losses. Is this a proper use of the bankruptcy process?

8. **Bankruptcy and Corporate Ethics [LO3]** Firms sometimes use the threat of a bankruptcy filing to force creditors to renegotiate terms. Critics argue that in such cases, the firm is using bankruptcy laws "as a sword rather than a shield." Is this an ethical tactic?

9. **Bankruptcy and Corporate Ethics [LO3]** As mentioned in the text, Continental Airlines filed for bankruptcy, at least in part, as a means of reducing labor costs. Whether this move was ethical, or proper, was hotly debated. Give both sides of the argument.

10. **Capital Structure Goal [LO1]** What is the basic goal of financial management with regard to capital structure?

QUESTIONS AND PROBLEMS

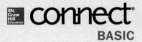

BASIC

(Questions 1–15)

1. **EBIT and Leverage [LO1]** Ghost, Inc., has no debt outstanding and a total market value of $185,000. Earnings before interest and taxes, EBIT, are projected to be $29,000 if economic conditions are normal. If there is strong expansion in the economy, then EBIT will be 30 percent higher. If there is a recession, then EBIT will be 40 percent lower. The company is considering a $65,000 debt issue with an interest rate of 7 percent. The proceeds will be used to repurchase shares of stock. There are currently 7,400 shares outstanding. Ignore taxes for this problem.

   a. Calculate earnings per share (EPS) under each of the three economic scenarios before any debt is issued. Also calculate the percentage changes in EPS when the economy expands or enters a recession.

b. Repeat part (a) assuming that the company goes through with recapitalization. What do you observe?

2. **EBIT, Taxes, and Leverage** [LO2] Repeat parts (a) and (b) in Problem 1 assuming the company has a tax rate of 21 percent, a market-to-book ratio of 1.0, and the stock price remains constant.

3. **ROE and Leverage** [LO1, 2] Suppose the company in Problem 1 has a market-to-book ratio of 1.0 and the stock price remains constant.

   a. Calculate return on equity (ROE) under each of the three economic scenarios before any debt is issued. Also calculate the percentage changes in ROE for economic expansion and recession, assuming no taxes.

   b. Repeat part (a) assuming the firm goes through with the proposed recapitalization.

   c. Repeat parts (a) and (b) of this problem assuming the firm has a tax rate of 21 percent.

4. **Break-Even EBIT** [LO1] Round Hammer is comparing two different capital structures: An all-equity plan (Plan I) and a levered plan (Plan II). Under Plan I, the company would have 180,000 shares of stock outstanding. Under Plan II, there would be 130,000 shares of stock outstanding and $1.925 million in debt outstanding. The interest rate on the debt is 8 percent, and there are no taxes.

   a. If EBIT is $400,000, which plan will result in the higher EPS?

   b. If EBIT is $600,000, which plan will result in the higher EPS?

   c. What is the break-even EBIT?

5. **M&M and Stock Value** [LO1] In Problem 4, use M&M Proposition I to find the price per share of equity under each of the two proposed plans. What is the value of the firm?

6. **Break-Even EBIT and Leverage** [LO1, 2] Bellwood Corp. is comparing two different capital structures. Plan I would result in 12,700 shares of stock and $109,250 in debt. Plan II would result in 9,800 shares of stock and $247,000 in debt. The interest rate on the debt is 10 percent.

   a. Ignoring taxes, compare both of these plans to an all-equity plan assuming that EBIT will be $79,000. The all-equity plan would result in 15,000 shares of stock outstanding. Which of the three plans has the highest EPS? The lowest?

   b. In part (a), what are the break-even levels of EBIT for each plan as compared to that for an all-equity plan? Is one higher than the other? Why?

   c. Ignoring taxes, when will EPS be identical for Plans I and II?

   d. Repeat parts (a), (b), and (c) assuming that the corporate tax rate is 21 percent. Are the break-even levels of EBIT different from before? Why or why not?

7. **Leverage and Stock Value** [LO1] Ignoring taxes in Problem 6, what is the price per share of equity under Plan I? Plan II? What principle is illustrated by your answers?

8. **Homemade Leverage** [LO1] FCOJ, Inc., a prominent consumer products firm, is debating whether to convert its all-equity capital structure to one that is 30 percent debt. Currently, there are 5,800 shares outstanding, and the price per share is $57. EBIT is expected to remain at $32,000 per year forever. The interest rate on new debt is 8 percent, and there are no taxes.

   a. Allison, a shareholder of the firm, owns 100 shares of stock. What is her cash flow under the current capital structure, assuming the firm has a dividend payout rate of 100 percent?

   b. What will Allison's cash flow be under the proposed capital structure of the firm? Assume she keeps all 100 of her shares.

c. Suppose the company does convert, but Allison prefers the current all-equity capital structure. Show how she could unlever her shares of stock to re-create the original capital structure.

d. Using your answer to part (c), explain why the company's choice of capital structure is irrelevant.

9. **Homemade Leverage and WACC [LO1]** ABC Co. and XYZ Co. are identical firms in all respects except for their capital structure. ABC is all-equity financed with $720,000 in stock. XYZ uses both stock and perpetual debt; its stock is worth $360,000 and the interest rate on its debt is 7 percent. Both firms expect EBIT to be $73,000. Ignore taxes.

a. Rico owns $43,500 worth of XYZ's stock. What rate of return is he expecting?

b. Show how Rico could generate exactly the same cash flows and rate of return by investing in ABC and using homemade leverage.

c. What is the cost of equity for ABC? What is it for XYZ?

d. What is the WACC for ABC? For XYZ? What principle have you illustrated?

10. **M&M [LO1]** Thrice Corp. uses no debt. The weighted average cost of capital is 8.4 percent. If the current market value of the equity is $16.3 million and there are no taxes, what is EBIT?

11. **M&M and Taxes [LO2]** In Problem 10, suppose the corporate tax rate is 22 percent. What is EBIT in this case? What is the WACC? Explain.

12. **Calculating WACC [LO1]** Blitz Industries has a debt-equity ratio of 1.25. Its WACC is 8.3 percent, and its cost of debt is 5.1 percent. The corporate tax rate is 21 percent.

a. What is the company's cost of equity capital?

b. What is the company's unlevered cost of equity capital?

c. What would the cost of equity be if the debt-equity ratio were 2? What if it were 1? What if it were zero?

13. **Calculating WACC [LO1]** Citee Corp. has no debt but can borrow at 6.1 percent. The firm's WACC is currently 9.4 percent, and the tax rate is 21 percent.

a. What is the company's cost of equity?

b. If the firm converts to 25 percent debt, what will its cost of equity be?

c. If the firm converts to 50 percent debt, what will its cost of equity be?

d. What is the company's WACC in part (b)? In part (c)?

14. **M&M and Taxes [LO2]** Meyer & Co. expects its EBIT to be $97,000 every year forever. The firm can borrow at 8 percent. The company currently has no debt, and its cost of equity is 13 percent. If the tax rate is 24 percent, what is the value of the firm? What will the value be if the company borrows $195,000 and uses the proceeds to repurchase shares?

15. **M&M and Taxes [LO2]** In Problem 14, what is the cost of equity after recapitalization? What is the WACC? What are the implications for the firm's capital structure decision?

INTERMEDIATE
(Questions 16–18)

16. **M&M [LO2]** Tool Manufacturing has an expected EBIT of $51,000 in perpetuity and a tax rate of 21 percent. The firm has $126,000 in outstanding debt at an interest rate of 5.35 percent, and its unlevered cost of capital is 9.6 percent. What is the value of the firm according to M&M Proposition I with taxes? Should the company change its debt-equity ratio if the goal is to maximize the value of the firm? Explain.

17. **Firm Value** [LO2] Change Corporation expects an EBIT of $31,200 every year forever. The company currently has no debt, and its cost of equity is 11 percent.

    a. What is the current value of the company?

    b. Suppose the company can borrow at 6 percent. If the corporate tax rate is 22 percent, what will the value of the firm be if the company takes on debt equal to 50 percent of its unlevered value? What if it takes on debt equal to 100 percent of its unlevered value?

    c. What will the value of the firm be if the company takes on debt equal to 50 percent of its levered value? What if the company takes on debt equal to 100 percent of its levered value?

18. **Homemade Leverage** [LO1] The Day Company and the Knight Company are identical in every respect except that Day is not levered. Financial information for the two firms appears in the following table. All earnings streams are perpetuities, and neither firm pays taxes. Both firms distribute all earnings available to common stockholders immediately.

	Day	Knight
Projected operating income	$ 375,000	$ 375,000
Year-end interest on debt	—	$ 54,000
Market value of stock	$2,300,000	$1,650,000
Market value of debt	—	$ 900,000

    a. An investor who can borrow at 6 percent per year wishes to purchase 5 percent of Knight's equity. Can he increase his dollar return by purchasing 5 percent of Day's equity if he borrows so that the initial net costs of the strategies are the same?

    b. Given the two investment strategies in (a), which will investors choose? When will this process cease?

19. **Weighted Average Cost of Capital** [LO1] In a world of corporate taxes only, show that the WACC can be written as $\text{WACC} = R_U \times [1 - T_C(D/V)]$.

    CHALLENGE
    (Questions 19–22)

20. **Cost of Equity and Leverage** [LO1] Assuming a world of corporate taxes only, show that the cost of equity, R_E, is as given in the chapter by M&M Proposition II with corporate taxes.

21. **Business and Financial Risk** [LO1] Assume a firm's debt is risk-free, so that the cost of debt equals the risk-free rate, R_f. Define β_A as the firm's *asset* beta—that is, the systematic risk of the firm's assets. Define β_E to be the beta of the firm's equity. Use the capital asset pricing model (CAPM) along with M&M Proposition II to show that $\beta_E = \beta_A \times (1 + D/E)$, where D/E is the debt-equity ratio. Assume the tax rate is zero.

22. **Stockholder Risk** [LO1] Suppose a firm's business operations are such that they mirror movements in the economy as a whole very closely; that is, the firm's asset beta is 1.0. Use the result of Problem 21 to find the equity beta for this firm for debt-equity ratios of 0, 1, 5, and 20. What does this tell you about the relationship between capital structure and shareholder risk? How is the shareholders' required return on equity affected? Explain.

EXCEL MASTER IT! PROBLEM

The TL Corporation currently has no debt outstanding. Josh Culberson, the CFO, is considering restructuring the company by issuing debt and using the proceeds to repurchase outstanding equity. The company's assets are worth $40 million, the stock price is $25 per share, and there are 1,600,000 shares outstanding. In the expected state of the economy, EBIT is predicted to be $3 million. If there is a recession, EBIT would fall to $1.8 million, and in an expansion, EBIT would increase to $4.3 million. If the company issues debt, it will issue a combination of short-term debt and long-term debt. The ratio of short-term debt to long-term debt will be .20. The short-term debt will have an interest rate of 3 percent and the long-term debt will have an interest rate of 8 percent.

a. On the next worksheet, fill in the values in each table. For the debt-equity ratio, create a spinner that changes the debt-equity ratio. The resulting debt-equity ratio should range from 0 to 10 at increments of .1.

b. Graph the EBIT and EPS for the TL Corporation on the same graph using a scatter plot.

c. What is the break-even EBIT between the current capital structure and the new capital structure?

d. To illustrate the new capital structure, you would like to create a pie chart. Another pie chart that is available is the pie in pie chart. Using the pie in pie chart, graph the equity and total debt in the main pie chart and the short-term debt and long-term debt in the secondary pie chart. Note, if you right-click on a data series in the chart and select Format Data Series, the Series Options will permit you to display the series by a customized choice. In the customization, you can select which data series you want displayed in the primary pie chart and the secondary pie chart.

MINICASE

Stephenson Real Estate Recapitalization

Stephenson Real Estate Company was founded 25 years ago by the current CEO, Robert Stephenson. The company purchases real estate, including land and buildings, and rents the property to tenants. The company has shown a profit every year for the past 18 years, and the shareholders are satisfied with the company's management. Prior to founding Stephenson Real Estate, Robert was the founder and CEO of a failed alpaca farming operation. The resulting bankruptcy made him extremely averse to debt financing. As a result, the company is entirely equity financed, with 8 million shares of common stock outstanding. The stock currently trades at $37.80 per share.

Stephenson is evaluating a plan to purchase a huge tract of land in the southeastern United States for $85 million. The land will subsequently be leased to tenant farmers. This purchase is expected to increase Stephenson's annual pretax earnings by $14.125 million in perpetuity. Jennifer Weyand, the company's new CFO, has been put in charge of the project. Jennifer has determined that the company's current cost of capital is 10.2 percent. She feels that the company would be more valuable

if it included debt in its capital structure, so she is evaluating whether the company should issue debt to entirely finance the project. Based on some conversations with investment banks, she thinks that the company can issue bonds at par value with a 6 percent coupon rate. From her analysis, she also believes that a capital structure in the range of 70 percent equity/30 percent debt would be optimal. If the company goes beyond 30 percent debt, its bonds would carry a lower rating and a much higher coupon because the possibility of financial distress and the associated costs would rise sharply. Stephenson has a 23 percent corporate tax rate (state and federal).

QUESTIONS

1. If Stephenson wishes to maximize its total market value, would you recommend that it issue debt or equity to finance the land purchase? Explain.

2. Construct Stephenson's market value balance sheet before it announces the purchase.

3. Suppose Stephenson decides to issue equity to finance the purchase.
   a. What is the net present value of the project?
   b. Construct Stephenson's market value balance sheet after it announces that the firm will finance the purchase using equity. What would be the new price per share of the firm's stock? How many shares will Stephenson need to issue to finance the purchase?
   c. Construct Stephenson's market value balance sheet after the equity issue but before the purchase has been made. How many shares of common stock does Stephenson have outstanding? What is the price per share of the firm's stock?

d. Construct Stephenson's market value balance sheet after the purchase has been made.

4. Suppose Stephenson decides to issue debt to finance the purchase.
   a. What will the market value of the Stephenson Real Estate Company be if the purchase is financed with debt?
   b. Construct Stephenson's market value balance sheet after both the debt issue and the land purchase. What is the price per share of the firm's stock?

5. Which method of financing maximizes the per-share stock price of Stephenson's equity?

17 | Dividends and Payout Policy

ON JANUARY 26, 2017, cable TV giant Comcast announced a broad plan to reward stockholders for the recent success of the firm's business. Under the plan, Comcast would (1) boost its annual dividend by 15 percent, from $1.10 per share to $1.26 per share; (2) undertake a two-for-one stock split, meaning each share of common stock would be replaced with two new shares; and (3) repurchase about $5 billion of Comcast's common stock during the next year. Investors cheered, bidding up the stock price by about 3 percent on the day of the announcement, on a day when the stock market as a whole fell. Why were investors so pleased? To find out, this chapter explores these actions and their implications for shareholders.

Learning Objectives

After studying this chapter, you should be able to:

LO1 Define dividend types and how dividends are paid.

LO2 Explain the issues surrounding dividend policy decisions.

LO3 Describe the difference between cash and stock dividends.

LO4 Explain why share repurchases are an alternative to dividends.

For updates on the latest happenings in finance, visit fundamentalsofcorporatefinance.blogspot.com.

Dividend policy is an important subject in corporate finance, and dividends are a major cash outlay for many corporations. For example, S&P 500 companies paid about $397 billion in dividends in 2016, an increase from the $383 billion paid in 2015, and a record for dividends paid. In fact, dividends globally were $1.024 trillion. ExxonMobil and Apple were the biggest payers. How big? ExxonMobil paid out about $12.5 billion in dividends during 2016 and Apple paid out about $12 billion. In contrast, about 16 percent of the companies in the S&P 500 paid no dividend at all.

At first glance, it may seem obvious that a firm would always want to give as much as possible back to its shareholders by paying dividends. It might seem equally obvious that a firm could always invest the money for its shareholders instead of paying it out. The heart of the dividend policy question is this: Should the firm pay out money to its shareholders, or should the firm take that money and invest it for its shareholders?

In this chapter, we will cover a variety of topics related to dividends and corporate payout policies. We first discuss the various types of cash dividends and how they are paid. We ask whether dividend policy matters, and we consider arguments in favor of both high and low dividend payouts. Next, we examine stock repurchases, which have become an important alternative to cash dividends. We then bring together several decades of research on dividends and corporate payouts to describe the key trade-offs involved in establishing a payout policy. We conclude the chapter by discussing stock splits and stock dividends.

Cash Dividends and Dividend Payment

17.1

The term **dividend** usually refers to cash paid out of earnings. If a payment is made from sources other than current or accumulated retained earnings, the term **distribution**, rather than *dividend*, is used. It is acceptable to refer to a distribution from earnings as a dividend and a distribution from capital as a liquidating dividend. More generally, any direct payment by the corporation to the shareholders may be considered a dividend or a part of dividend policy.

Dividends come in several different forms. The basic types of cash dividends are these:

1. Regular cash dividends.
2. Extra dividends.
3. Special dividends.
4. Liquidating dividends.

Later in the chapter, we discuss dividends paid in stock instead of cash. We also consider another alternative to cash dividends: Stock repurchase.

dividend
A payment made out of a firm's earnings to its owners, in the form of either cash or stock.

distribution
A payment made by a firm to its owners from sources other than current or accumulated retained earnings.

CASH DIVIDENDS

The most common type of dividend is a cash dividend. Commonly, public companies pay **regular cash dividends** four times per year. As the name suggests, these are cash payments made directly to shareholders, and they are made in the regular course of business. In other words, management sees nothing unusual about the dividend and no reason why it won't be continued.

Sometimes firms will pay a regular cash dividend and an *extra cash dividend*. By calling part of the payment "extra," management is indicating that the "extra" part may or may not be repeated in the future. A *special dividend* is similar, but the name usually indicates that this dividend is viewed as a truly unusual or one-time event and won't be repeated. For example, in December 2004, Microsoft paid a special dividend of $3 per share. The total payout of $32 billion was the largest one-time corporate dividend in history. Founder Bill Gates received about $3 *billion*, which he pledged to donate to charity. To give you another idea of the size of the special dividend, consider that in December, when the dividend was sent to investors, personal income in the United States rose 3.7 percent. Without the dividend, personal income rose only .3 percent, so the dividend payment accounted for about 3 percent of all personal income in the United States for the month! Finally, the payment of a *liquidating dividend* usually means that some or all of the business has been liquidated—that is, sold off.

regular cash dividend
A cash payment made by a firm to its owners in the normal course of business, usually paid four times per year.

For a list of companies that are paying dividends today, go to **www.thestreet.com /dividends/**.

However it is labeled, a cash dividend payment reduces corporate cash and retained earnings, except in the case of a liquidating dividend (which may reduce paid-in capital).

STANDARD METHOD OF CASH DIVIDEND PAYMENT

The decision to pay a dividend rests in the hands of the board of directors of the corporation. When a dividend has been declared, it becomes a debt of the firm and cannot easily be rescinded. Sometime after it has been declared, a dividend is distributed to all shareholders as of some specific date.

FIGURE 17.1

Example of Procedure for Dividend Payment

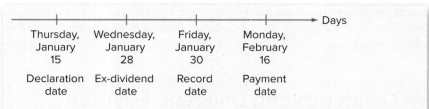

1. *Declaration date*: The board of directors declares a payment of dividends.
2. *Ex-dividend date*: A share of stock goes ex-dividend on the date the seller is entitled to keep the dividend; under NYSE rules, shares are traded ex dividend on and after the second business day before the record date.
3. *Record date*: The declared dividends are distributable to people who are shareholders of record as of this specific date.
4. *Payment date*: The dividend checks are mailed to shareholders of record.

Commonly, the amount of the cash dividend is expressed in terms of dollars per share (*dividends per share*). As we have seen in other chapters, it is also expressed as a percentage of the market price (the *dividend yield*) or as a percentage of net income or earnings per share (the *dividend payout*).

DIVIDEND PAYMENT: A CHRONOLOGY

The mechanics of a cash dividend payment can be illustrated by the example in Figure 17.1 and the following description:

declaration date
The date on which the board of directors passes a resolution to pay a dividend.

1. **Declaration date**: On January 15, the board of directors passes a resolution to pay a dividend of $1 per share on February 16 to all holders of record as of January 30.

ex-dividend date
The date two business days before the date of record, establishing those individuals entitled to a dividend.

2. **Ex-dividend date**: To make sure that dividend checks go to the right people, brokerage firms and stock exchanges establish an ex-dividend date. This date is two business days before the date of record (discussed next). If you buy the stock before this date, you are entitled to the dividend. If you buy on this date or after, the previous owner will get the dividend.

   In Figure 17.1, Wednesday, January 28, is the ex-dividend date. Before this date, the stock is said to trade "with dividend" or "cum dividend." Afterward, the stock trades "ex dividend."

   The ex-dividend date convention removes any ambiguity about who is entitled to the dividend. Because the dividend is valuable, the stock price will be affected when the stock goes "ex." We examine this effect in a moment.

date of record
The date by which a holder must be on record to be designated to receive a dividend.

3. **Date of record**: Based on its records, the corporation prepares a list on January 30 of all individuals believed to be stockholders. These are the *holders of record*, and January 30 is the date of record (or record date). The word *believed* is important here. If you buy the stock just before this date, the corporation's records may not reflect that fact because of mailing or other delays. Without some modification, some of the dividend checks will get mailed to the wrong people. This is the reason for the ex-dividend date convention.

date of payment
The date on which the dividend checks are mailed.

4. **Date of payment**: The dividend checks are mailed on February 16.

MORE ABOUT THE EX-DIVIDEND DATE

The ex-dividend date is important and is a common source of confusion. We examine what happens to the stock when it goes ex, meaning that the ex-dividend date arrives.

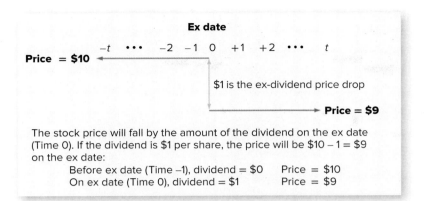

FIGURE 17.2

Price Behavior around the Ex-Dividend Date for a $1 Cash Dividend

To illustrate, suppose we have a stock that sells for $10 per share. The board of directors declares a dividend of $1 per share, and the record date is set to be Tuesday, June 12. Based on our previous discussion, we know that the ex date will be two business (not calendar) days earlier, on Friday, June 8.

If you buy the stock on Thursday, June 7, just as the market closes, you'll get the $1 dividend because the stock is trading cum dividend. If you wait and buy it just as the market opens on Friday, you won't get the $1 dividend. What happens to the value of the stock overnight?

If you think about it, you will see that the stock is worth about $1 less on Friday morning, so its price will drop by this amount between close of business on Thursday and the Friday opening. In general, we expect that the value of a share of stock will go down by about the dividend amount when the stock goes ex dividend. The key word here is *about*. Because dividends are taxed, the actual price drop might be closer to some measure of the aftertax value of the dividend. Determining this value is complicated because of the different tax rates and tax rules that apply for different buyers.

The series of events described here is illustrated in Figure 17.2.

"Ex" Marks the Day	EXAMPLE 17.1

The board of directors of Divided Airlines has declared a dividend of $2.50 per share payable on Tuesday, May 30, to shareholders of record as of Tuesday, May 9. Cal Icon buys 100 shares of Divided on Tuesday, May 2, for $150 per share. What is the ex date? Describe the events that will occur with regard to the cash dividend and the stock price.

The ex date is two business days before the date of record, Tuesday, May 9; so the stock will go ex on Friday, May 5. Cal buys the stock on Tuesday, May 2, so Cal purchases the stock cum dividend. In other words, Cal will get $2.50 × 100 = $250 in dividends. The check will be mailed on Tuesday, May 30. Just before the stock does go ex on Friday, its value will drop overnight by about $2.50 per share.

As an example of the price drop on the ex-dividend date, we examine the large dividend paid by Warrior Met Coal, operator of coal mines in Alabama, in November 2017. The dividend was $11.21 per share at a time when the stock price was around $30, so the dividend was about 40 percent of the total stock price, a truly special dividend. The stock went ex dividend on November 24, 2017. The stock price chart here shows the change in Warrior stock four days prior to the ex-dividend date and on the ex-dividend date.

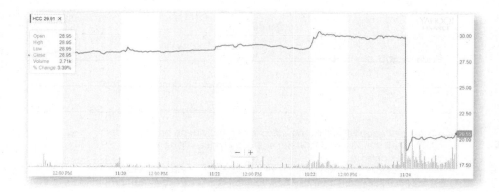

The stock closed at $29.90 on November 22 (November 23 was a holiday) and opened at $18.65 on November 24—a drop of $11.25. With a 20 percent tax rate on dividends, we would have expected a drop of about $9, so the actual price dropped more than we would have expected. We discuss dividends and taxes in more detail in a subsequent section.

Concept Questions

17.1a   What are the different types of cash dividends?
17.1b   What are the mechanics of the cash dividend payment?
17.1c   How should the price of a stock change when it goes ex dividend?

17.2 Does Dividend Policy Matter?

To decide whether or not dividend policy matters, we first have to define what we mean by dividend *policy*. All other things being the same, of course dividends matter. Dividends are paid in cash, and cash is something that everybody likes. The question we will be discussing here is whether the firm should pay out cash now or invest the cash and pay it out later. Dividend policy is the time pattern of dividend payout. In particular, should the firm pay out a large percentage of its earnings now or a small (or even zero) percentage? This is the dividend policy question.

AN ILLUSTRATION OF THE IRRELEVANCE OF DIVIDEND POLICY

A powerful argument can be made that dividend policy does not matter. We illustrate this by considering the simple case of Wharton Corporation. Wharton is an all-equity firm that has existed for 10 years. The current financial managers plan to dissolve the firm in two years. The total cash flows the firm will generate, including the proceeds from liquidation, will be $10,000 in each of the next two years.

Current Policy: Dividends Set Equal to Cash Flow   At the present time, dividends at each date are set equal to the cash flow of $10,000. There are 100 shares outstanding, so the dividend per share is $100. In Chapter 6, we showed that the value of the stock is equal to the present value of the future dividends. Assuming a 10 percent required return, the value of a share of stock today, P_0, is:

$$P_0 = \frac{D_1}{(1+R)^1} + \frac{D_2}{(1+R)^2}$$

$$= \frac{\$100}{1.10} + \frac{\$100}{1.10^2} = \$173.55$$

The firm as a whole is worth $100 \times \$173.55 = \$17,355$.

Several members of the board of Wharton have expressed dissatisfaction with the current dividend policy and have asked you to analyze an alternative policy.

Alternative Policy: Initial Dividend Greater than Cash Flow Another possible policy is for the firm to pay a dividend of $110 per share on the first date (Date 1), which is, of course, a total dividend of $11,000. Because the cash flow is only $10,000, an extra $1,000 must somehow be raised. One way to do this is to issue $1,000 worth of bonds or stock at Date 1. Assume that stock is issued. The new stockholders will desire enough cash flow at Date 2 so that they earn the required 10 percent return on their Date 1 investment.[1]

What is the value of the firm with this new dividend policy? The new stockholders invest $1,000. They require a 10 percent return, so they will demand $1,000 \times 1.10 = \$1,100$ of the Date 2 cash flow, leaving only $8,900 to the old stockholders. The dividends to the old stockholders will be as follows:

	Date 1	Date 2
Aggregate dividends to old stockholders	$11,000	$8,900
Dividends per share	110	89

The present value of the dividends per share is:

$$P_0 = \frac{\$110}{1.10} + \frac{89}{1.10^2} = \$173.55$$

This is the same value we had before.

The value of the stock is unaffected by this switch in dividend policy even though we have to sell some new stock to finance the new dividend. In fact, no matter what pattern of dividend payout the firm chooses, the value of the stock will always be the same in this example. In other words, for the Wharton Corporation, dividend policy makes no difference. The reason is simple: Any increase in a dividend at some point in time is exactly offset by a decrease at some other time; so the net effect, once we account for time value, is zero.

HOMEMADE DIVIDENDS

There is an alternative and perhaps more intuitively appealing explanation of why dividend policy doesn't matter in our example. Suppose individual Investor X prefers dividends per share of $100 at both Dates 1 and 2. Would she be disappointed if informed that the firm's management was adopting the alternative dividend policy (dividends of $110 and $89 on the two dates, respectively)? Not necessarily: She could easily reinvest the $10 of unneeded

---

[1]The same results would occur after an issue of bonds, though the arguments would be less easily presented.

funds received on Date 1 by buying more Wharton stock. At 10 percent, this investment would grow to $11 by Date 2. Investor X would receive her desired net cash flow of $110 − 10 = $100 at Date 1 and $89 + 11 = $100 at Date 2.

Conversely, imagine that Investor Z, preferring $110 of cash flow at Date 1 and $89 of cash flow at Date 2, finds that management will pay dividends of $100 at both Dates 1 and 2. This investor can sell $10 worth of stock to boost his total cash at Date 1 to $110. Because this investment returns 10 percent, Investor Z gives up $11 at Date 2 (= $10 × 1.1), leaving him with $100 − 11 = $89.

Our two investors are able to transform the corporation's dividend policy into a different policy by buying or selling on their own. The result is that investors are able to create a **homemade dividend policy**. This means that dissatisfied stockholders can alter the firm's dividend policy to suit themselves. As a result, there is no particular advantage to any one dividend policy the firm might choose.

Many corporations actually assist their stockholders in creating homemade dividend policies by offering *automatic dividend reinvestment plans* (ADRs or DRIPs). McDonald's, Walmart, and Procter & Gamble, for example, have set up such plans. As the name suggests, with such a plan, stockholders have the option of automatically reinvesting some or all of their cash dividend in shares of stock. In some cases, they actually receive a discount on the stock, which makes such plans very attractive.

homemade dividend policy

The tailored dividend policy created by individual investors who undo corporate dividend policy by reinvesting dividends or selling shares of stock.

For more information on DRIPs, check out the Motley Fool at **www.fool.com**.

A TEST

Our discussion to this point can be summarized by considering the following true-false test questions:

1. True or false: Dividends are irrelevant.
2. True or false: Dividend policy is irrelevant.

The first statement is surely false, and the reason follows from common sense. Clearly, investors prefer higher dividends to lower dividends at any single date if the dividend level is held constant at every other date. To be more precise regarding the first question, if the dividend per share at a given date is raised while the dividend per share at every other date is held constant, the stock price will rise. The reason is that the present value of the future dividends must go up if this occurs. This action can be accomplished by management decisions that improve productivity, increase tax savings, strengthen product marketing, or otherwise improve cash flow.

The second statement is true, at least in the simple case we have been examining. Dividend policy by itself cannot raise the dividend at one date while keeping it the same at all other dates. Rather, dividend policy merely establishes the trade-off between dividends at one date and dividends at another date. Once we allow for time value, the present value of the dividend stream is unchanged. In this simple world, dividend policy does not matter because managers choosing either to raise or to lower the current dividend do not affect the current value of their firm. However, we have ignored several real-world factors that might lead us to change our minds; we pursue some of these in subsequent sections.

Concept Questions

17.2a   How can an investor create a homemade dividend?
17.2b   Are dividends irrelevant?

Real-World Factors Favoring a Low Dividend Payout

17.3

The example we used to illustrate the irrelevance of dividend policy ignored taxes and flotation costs. In this section, we will see that these factors might lead us to prefer a low dividend payout.

TAXES

U.S. tax laws are complex, and they affect dividend policy in a number of ways. The key tax feature has to do with the taxation of dividend income and capital gains. For individual shareholders, *effective* tax rates on dividend income are higher than the tax rates on capital gains. Historically, dividends received have been taxed as ordinary income. Capital gains have been taxed at somewhat lower rates, and the tax on a capital gain is deferred until the stock is sold. This second aspect of capital gains taxation makes the effective tax rate much lower because the present value of the tax is less.[2]

Recent tax law changes have led to a renewed interest in the effect of taxes on corporate dividend policies. As we previously noted, historically, dividends have been taxed as ordinary income (at ordinary income tax rates). In 2003, under President G. W. Bush, this changed dramatically. Tax rates on dividends and capital gains were lowered from a maximum in the 35–39 percent range to 15 percent, giving corporations a much larger tax incentive to pay dividends. In 2018, the tax rate on dividends was 0 percent, 15 percent, or 20 percent, depending on the individual's marginal tax rate.

FLOTATION COSTS

In our example illustrating that dividend policy doesn't matter, we saw that the firm could sell some new stock if necessary to pay a dividend. As we mentioned in Chapter 15, selling new stock can be very expensive. If we include flotation costs in our argument, then we will find that the value of the stock decreases if we sell new stock.

More generally, imagine two firms identical in every way except that one pays out a greater percentage of its cash flow in the form of dividends. Because the other firm plows back more cash, its equity grows faster. If these two firms are to remain identical, then the one with the higher payout will have to periodically sell some stock to catch up. Because this is expensive, a firm might be inclined to have a low payout.

DIVIDEND RESTRICTIONS

In some cases, a corporation may face restrictions on its ability to pay dividends. For example, as we discussed in Chapter 7, a common feature of a bond indenture is a covenant prohibiting dividend payments above some level. Also, a corporation may be prohibited by state law from paying dividends if the dividend amount exceeds the firm's retained earnings.

---

[2]In fact, capital gains taxes can sometimes be avoided altogether. Although we do not recommend this particular tax avoidance strategy, the capital gains tax may be avoided by dying. Your heirs are not considered to have a capital gain, so the tax liability dies when you do. In this instance, you *can* take it with you.

17.4   Real-World Factors Favoring a High Dividend Payout

In this section, we consider reasons why a firm might pay its shareholders higher dividends even if it means the firm must issue more shares of stock to finance the dividend payments.

In a classic textbook, Benjamin Graham, David Dodd, and Sidney Cottle argue that firms should generally have high dividend payouts because:

1. "The discounted value of near dividends is higher than the present worth of distant dividends."

2. Between "two companies with the same general earning power and same general position in an industry, the one paying the larger dividend will almost always sell at a higher price."[3]

Two additional factors favoring a high dividend payout have also been mentioned frequently by proponents of this view: The desire for current income and the resolution of uncertainty.

DESIRE FOR CURRENT INCOME

It has been argued that many individuals desire current income. The classic example is the group of retired people and others living on a fixed income (the proverbial widows and orphans). It is argued that this group is willing to pay a premium to get a higher dividend yield. If this is true, then it lends support to the second claim made by Graham, Dodd, and Cottle.

It is easy to see that this argument is irrelevant in our simple case. An individual preferring high current cash flow but holding low-dividend securities can easily sell off shares to provide the necessary funds. Similarly, an individual desiring a low current cash flow but holding high-dividend securities can just reinvest the dividend. This is just our homemade dividend argument again. In a world of no transaction costs, a policy of high current dividends would be of no value to the stockholder.

The current income argument may have relevance in the real world. Here the sale of low-dividend stocks would involve brokerage fees and other transaction costs. These direct cash expenses could be avoided by an investment in high-dividend securities. In addition, the expenditure of the stockholder's own time in selling securities and the natural (though not necessarily rational) fear of consuming out of principal might further lead many investors to buy high-dividend securities.

Even so, to put this argument in perspective, remember that financial intermediaries such as mutual funds can (and do) perform these "repackaging" transactions for individuals at very low cost. Such intermediaries could buy low-dividend stocks and, through a controlled policy of realizing gains, they could pay their investors at a higher rate.

---

[3]Graham, B., Dodd, D., and Cottle, S., *Security Analysis*. New York: McGraw-Hill, 1962.

TAX AND OTHER BENEFITS FROM HIGH DIVIDENDS

Earlier, we saw that dividends were taxed unfavorably for individual investors (at least until very recently). This fact is a powerful argument for a low payout. However, there are a number of other investors who do not receive unfavorable tax treatment from holding high-dividend yield, rather than low-dividend yield, securities.

Corporate Investors   A significant tax break on dividends occurs when a corporation owns stock in another corporation. A corporate stockholder receiving either common or preferred dividends is granted a 50 percent (or more) dividend exclusion (reduced from 70 percent or more in the 2017 Tax Cuts and Jobs Act). Because the 50 percent exclusion does not apply to capital gains, this group is taxed unfavorably on capital gains.

As a result of the dividend exclusion, high-dividend, low-capital gains stocks may be more appropriate for corporations to hold. As we discuss elsewhere, this is why corporations hold a substantial percentage of the outstanding preferred stock in the economy. This tax advantage of dividends also leads some corporations to hold high-yielding stocks instead of long-term bonds because there is no similar tax exclusion of interest payments to corporate bondholders.

Tax-Exempt Investors   We have pointed out both the tax advantages and the tax disadvantages of a low dividend payout. Of course, this discussion is irrelevant to those in zero tax brackets. This group includes some of the largest investors in the economy, such as pension funds, endowment funds, and trust funds.

CONCLUSION

Overall, individual investors (for whatever reason) may have a desire for current income and may be willing to pay the dividend tax. In addition, some very large investors such as corporations and tax-free institutions may have a very strong preference for high dividend payouts.

Concept Questions

17.4a   Why might some individual investors favor a high dividend payout?

17.4b   Why might some nonindividual investors prefer a high dividend payout?

A Resolution of Real-World Factors?   17.5

In the previous sections, we presented some factors that favor a low-dividend policy and others that favor a high-dividend policy. In this section, we discuss two important concepts related to dividends and dividend policy: The information content of dividends and the clientele effect. The first topic illustrates both the importance of dividends in general and the importance of distinguishing between dividends and dividend policy. The second topic suggests that, despite the many real-world considerations we have discussed, the dividend payout ratio may not be as important as we originally imagined.

INFORMATION CONTENT OF DIVIDENDS

To begin, we quickly review some of our earlier discussion. Previously, we examined three different positions on dividends:

1. Based on the homemade dividend argument, dividend policy is irrelevant.
2. Because of tax effects for individual investors and new issue costs, a low-dividend policy is best.
3. Because of the desire for current income and related factors, a high-dividend policy is best.

If you wanted to decide which of these positions is the right one, an obvious way to get started would be to look at what happens to stock prices when companies announce dividend changes. You would find with some consistency that stock prices rise when the current dividend is unexpectedly increased, and they generally fall when the dividend is unexpectedly decreased. What does this imply about any of the three positions just stated?

At first glance, the behavior we describe seems consistent with the third position and inconsistent with the other two. In fact, many writers have argued this position. If stock prices rise in response to dividend increases and fall in response to dividend decreases, then isn't the market saying that it approves of higher dividends?

Other authors have pointed out that this observation doesn't really tell us much about dividend policy. Everyone agrees that dividends are important, all other things being equal. Companies cut dividends only with great reluctance. Thus, a dividend cut is often a signal that the firm is in trouble.

More to the point, a dividend cut is usually not a voluntary, planned change in dividend policy. Instead, it usually signals that management does not think that the current dividend policy can be maintained. As a result, expectations of future dividends should generally be revised downward. The present value of expected future dividends falls, and so does the stock price.

In this case, the stock price declines following a dividend cut because future dividends are generally expected to be lower, not because the firm has changed the percentage of its earnings it will pay out in the form of dividends.

For example, on February 4, 2016, oil company ConocoPhillips announced that it was cutting its dividend by two-thirds, from $.74 per year to $.25 per year. The company stated that the drastic fall in oil prices was to blame. Shareholders were in for a big shock. On a typical day, about 7.1 million shares of the company stock traded hands. Following the announcement, about 50 million shares were traded and the stock lost about 9 percent of its value.

Of course, the phenomenon of a stock price decrease in the face of a dividend cut is not restricted to the United States. In February 2016, Australian natural resource company BHP Billiton announced that its annual dividend would be 14 cents, well below the previous year's dividend of 62 cents. In response, the stock dropped by about 5 percent.

In a similar vein, an unexpected increase in the dividend signals good news. Management will raise the dividend only when future earnings, cash flow, and general prospects are expected to rise to such an extent that the dividend will not have to be cut later. A dividend increase is management's signal to the market that the firm is expected to do well. The stock price reacts favorably because expectations of future dividends are revised upward, not because the firm has increased its payout.

information content effect

The market's reaction to a change in corporate dividend payout.

In both of these cases, the stock price reacts to the dividend change. The reaction can be attributed to changes in the expected amount of future dividends, not necessarily a change in dividend payout policy. This reaction is called the **information content effect** of the dividend. The fact that dividend changes convey information about the firm to the market makes it difficult to interpret the effect of the dividend policy of the firm.

THE CLIENTELE EFFECT

In our earlier discussion, we saw that some groups (wealthy individuals, for example) have an incentive to pursue low-payout (or zero-payout) stocks. Other groups (corporations, for example) have an incentive to pursue high-payout stocks. Companies with high payouts will attract one group, and low-payout companies will attract another.

These different groups are called *clienteles*, and what we have described is a **clientele effect**. The clientele effect argument states that different groups of investors desire different levels of dividends. When a firm chooses a particular dividend policy, the only effect is to attract a particular clientele. If a firm changes its dividend policy, then it attracts a different clientele.

What we are left with is a simple supply and demand argument. Suppose 40 percent of all investors prefer high dividends, but only 20 percent of the firms pay high dividends. Here the high-dividend firms will be in short supply; their stock prices will rise. Consequently, low-dividend firms will find it advantageous to switch policies until 40 percent of all firms have high payouts. At this point, the *dividend market* is in equilibrium. Further changes in dividend policy are pointless because all of the clienteles are satisfied. The dividend policy for any individual firm is now irrelevant.

To see if you understand the clientele effect, consider the following statement: In spite of the theoretical argument that dividend policy is irrelevant or that firms should not pay dividends, many investors like high dividends; because of this fact, a firm can boost its share price by having a higher dividend payout ratio. True or false?

The answer is false if clienteles exist. As long as enough high-dividend firms satisfy the dividend-loving investors, a firm won't be able to boost its share price by paying high dividends. An unsatisfied clientele must exist for this to happen, and there is no evidence that this is the case.

> **clientele effect**
> The observable fact that stocks attract particular groups based on dividend yield and the resulting tax effects.

Concept Questions

17.5a How does the market react to unexpected dividend changes? What does this tell us about dividends? About dividend policy?

17.5b What is a dividend clientele? All things considered, would you expect a risky firm with significant but highly uncertain growth prospects to have a low or a high dividend payout?

Stock Repurchases: An Alternative to Cash Dividends

17.6

Thus far in our chapter, we have considered cash dividends. Cash dividends are not the only way corporations distribute cash. Instead, a company can **repurchase** its own stock. Repurchases (or *buybacks*) have become an increasingly popular tool, and the amount spent on repurchases has become huge. For example, in 2016, about $536 billion in share repurchases were announced, a 6 percent decrease over the $572 billion of repurchases in 2015. The record amount of stock buybacks in a single year was the $589 billion announced in 2007.

Another way to see how important repurchases have become is to compare them to cash dividends. Consider Figure 17.3, which shows the aggregate real (inflation-adjusted) dividends and stock repurchases by publicly held U.S. industrial firms for the period 1971–2015, along with the combined total. Aggregate real dividends have grown relatively

> **stock repurchase**
> The purchase, by a corporation, of its own shares of stock; also known as a *buyback*.

FIGURE 17.3

Aggregate Real (2012) Dividends and Stock Repurchases by Publicly Held U.S. Industrial Firms: 1971–2015

SOURCE: Redrawn by authors using Compustat data, following Farre-Mensa, J., Michaely, R., and Schmaltz, M., "Payout Policy," *Annual Review of Financial Economics* 6, 2014, pp. 75–134.

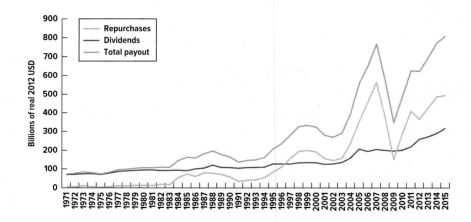

steadily through time, but repurchases have exploded in the last two decades. They reached a peak in 2007 of about 2.5 times the size of aggregate dividends. Repurchases plunged in the 2008–2009 recession as firms conserved cash, but they rebounded in 2010.

Share repurchases are typically accomplished in one of three ways. First, companies may purchase their own stock, just as anyone would buy shares of a particular stock. In these *open market purchases*, the firm does not reveal itself as the buyer. The seller does not know whether the shares were sold back to the firm or sold to another investor.

Second, the firm could institute a *tender offer*. Here, the firm announces to all of its stockholders that it is willing to buy a fixed number of shares at a specific price. For example, suppose Arts and Crafts (A&C), Inc., has 1 million shares of stock outstanding, with a stock price of $50 per share. The firm makes a tender offer to buy back 300,000 shares at $60 per share. A&C chooses a price above $50 to induce shareholders to sell, that is, tender, their shares. In fact, if the tender price is set high enough, shareholders may very well want to sell more than the 300,000 shares. In the extreme case where all outstanding shares are tendered, A&C will buy back 3 out of every 10 shares that a shareholder holds.

Finally, firms may repurchase shares from specific individual stockholders. This procedure has been called a *targeted repurchase*. For example, suppose the International Biotechnology Corporation purchased approximately 10 percent of the outstanding stock of the Prime Robotics Company (P-R Co.) in April at around $38 per share. At that time, International Biotechnology announced to the Securities and Exchange Commission that it might eventually try to take control of P-R Co. In May, P-R Co. repurchased the International Biotechnology holdings at $48 per share, well above the market price at that time. This offer was not extended to other shareholders.

CASH DIVIDENDS VERSUS REPURCHASE

Imagine an all-equity company with excess cash of $300,000. The firm pays no dividends, and its net income for the year just ended is $49,000. The market value balance sheet at the end of the year is represented here:

Market Value Balance Sheet (before paying out excess cash)			
Excess cash	$ 300,000	Debt	$ 0
Other assets	700,000	Equity	1,000,000
Total	$1,000,000	Total	$1,000,000

There are 100,000 shares outstanding. The total market value of the equity is $1 million, so the stock sells for $10 per share. Earnings per share (EPS) are $49,000/100,000 = $.49, and the price-earnings ratio (PE) is $10/$.49 = 20.4.

One option the company is considering is a $300,000/100,000 = $3 per share extra cash dividend. Alternatively, the company is thinking of using the money to repurchase $300,000/$10 = 30,000 shares of stock.

If commissions, taxes, and other imperfections are ignored in our example, the stock-holders shouldn't care which option is chosen. Does this seem surprising? It shouldn't, really. What is happening here is that the firm is paying out $300,000 in cash. The new balance sheet is represented here:

Market Value Balance Sheet (after paying out excess cash)			
Excess cash	$ 0	Debt	$ 0
Other assets	700,000	Equity	700,000
Total	$700,000	Total	$700,000

If the cash is paid out as a dividend, there are still 100,000 shares outstanding, so each is worth $7.

The fact that the per-share value fell from $10 to $7 is not a cause for concern. Consider a stockholder who owns 100 shares. At $10 per share before the dividend, the total value is $1,000.

After the $3 dividend, this same stockholder has 100 shares worth $7 each, for a total of $700, plus 100 × $3 = $300 in cash, for a combined total of $1,000. This illustrates what we saw early on: A cash dividend doesn't affect a stockholder's wealth if there are no imperfections. In this case, the stock price fell by $3 when the stock went ex dividend.

Also, because total earnings and the number of shares outstanding haven't changed, EPS is still 49 cents. The price-earnings ratio falls to $7/$.49 = 14.3. The reason why we are looking at accounting earnings and PE ratios will be apparent in just a moment.

Alternatively, if the company repurchases 30,000 shares, there are 70,000 shares left outstanding. The balance sheet looks the same:

Market Value Balance Sheet (after share repurchase)			
Excess cash	$ 0	Debt	$ 0
Other assets	700,000	Equity	700,000
Total	$700,000	Total	$700,000

The company is worth $700,000 again, so each remaining share is worth $700,000/70,000 = $10. Our stockholder with 100 shares is obviously unaffected. For example, if she was so inclined, she could sell 30 shares and end up with $300 in cash and $700 in stock, just as she has if the firm pays the cash dividend. This is another example of a homemade dividend.

PART 6   Cost of Capital and Long-Term Financial Policy

In this second case, EPS goes up because total earnings remain the same while the number of shares goes down. The new EPS is $49,000/70,000 = $.70. The important thing to notice is that the PE ratio is $10/$.70 = 14.3, as it was following the dividend.

This example illustrates the important point that, if there are no imperfections, a cash dividend and a share repurchase are essentially the same thing. This is another illustration of dividend policy irrelevance when there are no taxes or other imperfections.

REAL-WORLD CONSIDERATIONS IN A REPURCHASE

The example we have just described shows that a repurchase and a cash dividend are the same thing in a world without taxes and transaction costs. In the real world, there are some accounting differences between a share repurchase and a cash dividend, but the most important difference is in the tax treatment.

Under current tax law, a repurchase has a significant tax advantage over a cash dividend. A dividend is taxed, and a shareholder has no choice about whether or not to receive the dividend. In a repurchase, a shareholder pays taxes only if (1) the shareholder actually chooses to sell and (2) the shareholder has a capital gain on the sale.

For example, suppose a dividend of $1 per share is taxed at ordinary rates. Investors in the 28 percent tax bracket who own 100 shares of the security pay $100 × .28 = $28 in taxes. Selling shareholders would pay far lower taxes if $100 worth of stock were repurchased. This is because taxes are paid only on the profit from a sale. The gain on a sale would be only $40 if shares sold at $100 were originally purchased at $60. The capital gains tax would be .28 × $40 = $11.20. Note that the 2003 reductions in dividend and capital gains tax rates do not change the fact that a repurchase has a potentially large tax edge.

To give a few recent examples, in January 2017, Apple announced that it had repurchased $11 billion of its stock in the previous quarter. And General Motors announced that it was increasing its $9 billion repurchase, which it had begun in 2015, by another $5 billion. Also in January 2017, both Pfizer and Swiss drugmaker Novartis announced repurchases of $5 billion.

IBM is well known for its aggressive repurchasing policies. In the first nine months of 2016, it repurchased $2.6 billion of its own stock. Since 2003, the company had spent about $138.8 billion on buybacks through the end of 2016. In fact, from the beginning of 2003 through the end of 2016, the number of shares in the company fell from 1.72 billion shares to 951 million shares.

One thing to note is that not all announced stock repurchase plans are completed. Based on research covering the 2004–2007 period, average completion rates were only 81 percent.[4]

SHARE REPURCHASE AND EPS

You may read in the popular financial press that a share repurchase is beneficial because it causes earnings per share to increase. As we have seen, this will happen. The reason is that a share repurchase reduces the number of outstanding shares, but it has no effect on total earnings. As a result, EPS rises.

---

[4]See A. A. Bonaimé, "Mandatory Disclosure and Firm Behavior: Evidence from Share Repurchases," *The Accounting Review* 90 (2015).

The financial press may place undue emphasis on EPS figures in a repurchase agreement. In our preceding example, we saw that the value of the stock wasn't affected by the EPS change. In fact, the PE ratio was exactly the same when we compared a cash dividend to a repurchase.

Concept Questions

17.6a   Why might a stock repurchase make more sense than an extra cash dividend?

17.6b   What is the effect of a stock repurchase on a firm's EPS? Its PE?

What We Know and Do Not Know about Dividend and Payout Policies

17.7

DIVIDENDS AND DIVIDEND PAYERS

As we have discussed, there are numerous good reasons favoring a dividend policy of low (or no) payout. Nonetheless, in the United States, aggregate dividends paid are quite large. For example, in 1978, U.S. industrial firms listed on the major exchanges paid $31.3 billion in total dividends. By 2000, that number had risen to $101.6 billion (unadjusted for inflation), an increase of over 200 percent (after adjusting for inflation, the increase is smaller, 22.7 percent, but still substantial).

While we know dividends are large in the aggregate, we also know that the number of companies that pay dividends has declined. Over the same 1978–2000 period, the number of industrial companies paying dividends declined from over 2,000 to just under 1,000, and the percentage of these firms paying dividends declined 65 percent, to 19 percent.[5]

The fact that aggregate dividends grew while the number of payers fell so sharply seems a bit paradoxical, but the explanation is straightforward: Dividend payments are heavily concentrated in a relatively small set of large firms. In 2000, for example, about 80 percent of aggregate dividends were paid by just 100 firms. The top 25 payers, which include such well-known giants as ExxonMobil and General Electric, collectively paid about 55 percent of all dividends. The reason that dividends grew while dividend payers shrank is that the decline in dividend payers is almost entirely due to smaller firms, which tend to pay smaller dividends in the first place.

One important reason that the percentage of dividend-paying firms has declined is that the population of firms has changed. There has been a huge increase in the number of newly listed firms over the last 25 or so years. Newly listed firms tend to be younger and less profitable. Such firms need their internally generated cash to fund growth and typically do not pay dividends.

Another factor at work is that firms appear to be more likely to begin making payouts using share repurchases, which are flexible, rather than committing to making cash distributions. Such a policy seems quite sensible given our previous discussions. However, after

---

[5]These figures and those in the following paragraph are from H. DeAngelo, L. DeAngelo, and D. J. Skinner, "Are Dividends Disappearing? Dividend Concentration and the Consolidation of Earnings," *Journal of Financial Economics* 72 (2004).

FIGURE 17.4

Proportion of Dividend Payers, Repurchasers, and Firms with Positive Total Payout among All Publicly Held U.S. Industrial Firms: 1971–2015

SOURCE: Redrawn by authors using Compustat data, following Farre-Mensa, J., Michaely, R., and Schmaltz, M., "Payout Policy," *Annual Review of Financial Economics* 6, 2014, pp. 75–134.

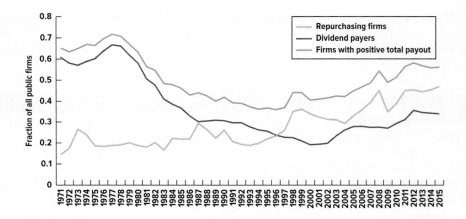

controlling for the changing mix of firms and the increase in share repurchasing activity, there still appears to be a decreased propensity to pay dividends among certain types of older, better established firms, though further research is needed on this question.

The fact that the number of dividend-paying firms has declined so sharply is an interesting phenomenon. Making matters even more interesting is evidence showing that the trend may have begun to reverse itself. Take a look at Figure 17.4, which shows the percentage of industrial firms paying dividends over the period 1971–2015, along with the percentage of (1) firms doing repurchases and (2) firms with a positive payout of one type or the other (or both). As shown, there is a pronounced downward trend, but that trend appears to bottom out in 2000 and then sharply reverse in 2002. So what's going on?

Part of the apparent rebound in Figure 17.4 is probably an illusion. The percentage of firms paying dividends rose because nonpayers dropped out in large numbers.[6] The number of firms listed on the major stock markets dropped sharply, from over 5,000 to under 4,000, during the period 2000–2005. About 2,000 firms delisted over this period, 98 percent of which were not dividend payers. By 2013, the number of listed firms had declined to below 3,000, and the percentage of dividend payers reached 36 percent.

Once we control for the drop-out problem, there is still an increase in the number of dividend payers, but it happens in 2003. As shown in Figure 17.5, the uptick is concentrated in the months following May 2003. What is so special about this month? The answer is that in May 2003, top personal tax rates on dividends were slashed from about 38 to 15 percent. Consistent with our earlier tax arguments, a reduction in personal tax rates led to increases in dividends.

It is important not to read too much into Figure 17.5. It seems clear that the reduction in tax rates did have an effect, but, on balance, what we see is a few hundred firms initiating dividends. There are still thousands of firms that did not initiate dividends, even though the tax rate reduction was very large. The evidence suggests that tax rates matter, but they are not a primary determinant of dividend policy. This interpretation is consistent with the results of a 2005 survey of financial executives, more than two-thirds of whom said that the tax rate cut probably or definitely would not affect their dividend policies.[7]

---

[6]These numbers and this explanation are from R. Chetty and E. Saez, "The Effects of the 2003 Dividend Tax Cut on Corporate Behavior: Interpreting the Evidence," *American Economic Review* Papers and Proceedings 96 (2006).

[7]See A. P. Brav, J. R. Graham, C. R. Harvey, and R. Michaely, "Managerial Response to the May 2003 Dividend Tax Cut," *Financial Management* 37 (2008), pp. 611–624.

FIGURE 17.5   Regular Dividend Initiations, 2001–2006

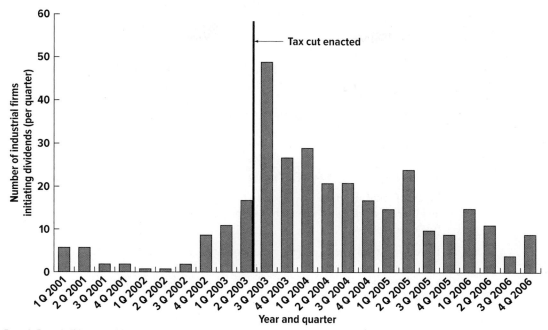

SOURCE: Brav, A. P. et al., "Managerial Response to the May 2003 Dividend Tax Cut," *Financial Management* 37, 2008, pp. 611–624.

A second force that may be at work over time is the maturing of many of the (surviving) newly listed firms we mentioned earlier. As these firms have become better established, their profitability has increased (and, potentially, their investment opportunities have decreased), and they have begun to pay dividends.

A third factor that may be contributing to the increase in the number of dividend payers is a little more subtle. The technology-heavy NASDAQ index plummeted in the spring of 2000 (due to the "dot-com" crash), and it became clear that many newly listed companies were likely to fail. Shortly thereafter, major accounting scandals at companies such as Enron and WorldCom left investors unsure of the trustworthiness of reported earnings. In such an environment, companies may have chosen to initiate dividends in an attempt to signal to investors that they had the cash to make dividend payments now and in the future.

The apparent reversal in the decline of dividend payers is a recent phenomenon, so its significance remains to be seen. It may prove to be just a transient event in the middle of a long decline. We will have to wait and see.

CORPORATIONS SMOOTH DIVIDENDS

As we previously observed, dividend cuts are frequently viewed as very bad news by market participants. As a result, companies only cut dividends when there is no other acceptable alternative. For the same reason, companies are also reluctant to increase dividends unless they are sure the new dividend level can be sustained.

In practice, what we observe is that dividend-paying companies tend to raise dividends only after earnings have risen, and they don't increase or cut dividends in response to temporary earnings fluctuations. In other words, (1) dividend growth lags earnings growth and (2) dividend growth will tend to be much smoother than earnings growth.

To see how important dividend stability and steady growth are to financial managers, consider that, in 2016, 2,634 companies in the United States increased their dividend payments, while only 659 companies decreased their dividend payments. Two companies with long histories of dividend increases are Procter & Gamble and Colgate-Palmolive. At the end of 2016, Procter & Gamble had increased its dividend for 61 consecutive years, and Colgate-Palmolive had increased its dividend for 53 consecutive years. Overall, as of early 2017, 51 companies in the S&P 500 had increased dividends for at least 25 consecutive years.

PUTTING IT ALL TOGETHER

Much of what we have discussed in this chapter (and much of what we know about dividends from decades of research) can be pulled together and summarized in the following five observations:[8]

1. Aggregate dividend and stock repurchases are massive, and they have increased steadily in nominal and real terms over the years.
2. Dividends are heavily concentrated among a relatively small number of large, mature firms.
3. Managers are very reluctant to cut dividends, normally doing so only due to firm-specific problems.
4. Managers smooth dividends, raising them slowly and incrementally as earnings grow.
5. Stock prices react to unanticipated changes in dividends.

The challenge now is to fit these five pieces into a reasonably coherent picture. With regard to payouts in general, meaning the combination of stock repurchases and cash dividends, a simple life cycle theory fits Points 1 and 2. The key ideas are straightforward. First, relatively young and less profitable firms generally should not make cash distributions. They need the cash to fund investments (and flotation costs discourage the raising of outside cash).

As a firm matures, it begins to generate free cash flow (which, you will recall, is internally generated cash flow beyond that needed to fund profitable investment activities). Significant free cash flow can lead to agency problems if it is not distributed. Managers may become tempted to pursue empire building or otherwise spend the excess cash in ways not in the shareholders' best interests. Firms come under pressure to make distributions rather than hoard cash. And, consistent with what we observe, we expect large firms with a history of profitability to make large distributions.

The life cycle theory says that firms trade off the agency costs of excess cash retention against the potential future costs of external equity financing. A firm should begin making distributions when it generates sufficient internal cash flow to fund its investment needs now and into the foreseeable future.

The more complex issue concerns the type of distribution, cash dividends versus repurchases. The tax argument in favor of repurchases is a clear and strong one. Further,

---

[8]This list is distilled in part from a longer list in DeAngelo, H., and DeAngelo, L., "Payout Policy Pedagogy: What Matters and Why," *European Financial Management* 13, 2007.

repurchases are a much more flexible option (and managers greatly value financial flexibility), so the question is: Why would firms ever choose a cash dividend?

If we are to answer this question, we have to ask a different question. What can a cash dividend accomplish that a share repurchase cannot accomplish? One answer is that when a firm makes a commitment to pay a cash dividend now and into the future, it sends a two-part signal to the markets. As we have already discussed, one signal is that the firm anticipates being profitable, with the ability to make the payments on an ongoing basis. Note that a firm cannot benefit by trying to fool the market in this regard because the firm would ultimately be punished when it couldn't make the dividend payment (or couldn't make it without relying on external financing). A cash dividend may let a firm distinguish itself from less profitable rivals.

A second, and more subtle, signal takes us back to the agency problem of free cash flow. By committing to pay cash dividends now and in the future, the firm signals that it won't be hoarding cash (or at least not as much cash), thereby reducing agency costs and enhancing shareholder wealth.

This two-part signaling story is consistent with Points 3–5 above, but an obvious objection remains. Why don't firms just commit to a policy of setting aside whatever money would be used to pay dividends and use it instead to buy back shares? After all, either way, a firm is committing to pay out cash to shareholders.

A fixed repurchase strategy suffers from two drawbacks. The first is verifiability. A firm could announce an open market repurchase and then not do it. By suitably fudging its books, it would be some time before the deception was discovered. It would be necessary for shareholders to develop a monitoring mechanism, meaning some sort of way for stockholders to know for sure that the repurchase was in fact done. Such a mechanism wouldn't be difficult to build (it could be a simple trustee relationship such as we observe in the bond markets), but it currently does not exist. Of course, a tender offer repurchase needs little or no verification, but such offers have expenses associated with them. The beauty of a cash dividend is that it needs no monitoring. A firm is forced to cut and mail checks four times per year, year in and year out.

A second objection to a fixed repurchase strategy is more controversial. Suppose managers, as insiders, are better able than stockholders to judge whether their stock price is too high or too low. (Note that this idea does not conflict with semistrong market efficiency if inside information is the reason.) In this case, a fixed repurchase commitment forces management to buy back stock even in circumstances when the stock is overvalued. In other words, it forces management into making negative NPV investments.

More research on the cash dividend versus share repurchase question is needed, but the historical trend seems to be favoring continued growth in repurchases relative to dividends.

Total corporate payouts seem to be relatively stable over time at roughly 20 percent of aggregate earnings (see Figure 17.3), but repurchases are becoming a larger portion of that total. The split reached about 50-50 in the latter part of the 1990s, but it looks like aggregate repurchases have recently passed aggregate dividends.

One aspect of aggregate cash dividends that has not received much attention is that there may be a strong legacy effect. Before 1982, the regulatory status of stock repurchases was somewhat murky, creating a significant disincentive. In 1982, the SEC, after years of debate, created a clear set of guidelines for firms to follow, thereby making repurchases much more attractive.

The legacy effect arises because many of the giant firms that pay such a large portion of aggregate dividends were paying dividends before (and perhaps long before) 1982. To the extent that these firms are unwilling to cut their dividends, aggregate cash dividends will be large, but only because of a "lock-in" effect for older firms. If locked-in, legacy payers account for much of the aggregate dividend, what we should observe is (1) a sharply reduced tendency for maturing firms to initiate dividends and (2) a growth in repurchases relative to cash dividends over time. We actually do see evidence of both of these trends; legacy effects alone can't account for all cash dividend payers.

The Pros and Cons of Paying Dividends	
Pros	**Cons**
1. Cash dividends can underscore good results and provide support to the stock price.	1. Dividends are taxed to recipients.
2. Dividends may attract institutional investors who prefer some return in the form of dividends. A mix of institutional and individual investors may allow a firm to raise capital at lower cost because of the ability of the firm to reach a wider market.	2. Dividends can reduce internal sources of financing. Dividends may force the firm to forgo positive NPV projects or to rely on costly external equity financing.
3. Stock price usually increases with the announcement of a new or increased dividend.	3. Once established, dividend cuts are hard to make without adversely affecting a firm's stock price.
4. Dividends absorb excess cash flow and may reduce agency costs that arise from conflicts between management and shareholders.	

SOME SURVEY EVIDENCE ON DIVIDENDS

A recent study surveyed a large number of financial executives regarding dividend policy. One of the questions asked was, "Do these statements describe factors that affect your company's dividend decisions?" Table 17.1 shows some of the results.

As shown in Table 17.1, financial managers are very disinclined to cut dividends. Moreover, they are very conscious of their previous dividends and desire to maintain a relatively steady dividend. In contrast, the cost of external capital and the desire to attract "prudent man" investors (those with fiduciary duties) are less important.

TABLE 17.1

Survey Responses on Dividend Decisions*

SOURCE: Adapted from Table 4 of Brav, A. el at., "Payout Policy in the 21st Century," *Journal of Financial Economics,* 2005.

Do These Statements Affect Your Dividend Policy?	Percent Who Agree or Strongly Agree
1. Avoiding dividend cuts	93.8%
2. Maintaining a "smooth" dividend over time	89.6
3. Size of recently paid dividends	88.2
4. Making sure that any changes we make won't have to be reversed later	77.9
5. The rate at which dividends are changing or growing	66.7
6. The cost of cutting dividends exceeds the cost of raising external capital	42.8
7. Using dividends to attract investors subject to "prudent man" investment restrictions	41.7

*Survey respondents were asked the question, "Do these statements describe factors that affect your company's dividend decisions?"

Table 17.2 is drawn from the same survey, but here the responses are to the question, "How important are the following factors to your company's dividend decision?" Not surprisingly given the responses in Table 17.1 and our earlier discussion, the highest priority is maintaining a consistent dividend policy. The next several items are also consistent with our previous analysis. Financial managers are very concerned about earnings stability and future earnings levels in making dividend decisions, and they consider the availability of good investment opportunities. Survey respondents also believed that attracting both institutional and individual (retail) investors was relatively important.

In contrast to our discussion of taxes and flotation costs in the earlier part of this chapter, the financial managers in this survey did not think that personal taxes paid on dividends by shareholders were very important. Even fewer financial managers thought that equity flotation costs were relevant.

TABLE 17.2

Survey Responses on Dividend Decisions*

SOURCE: Adapted from Table 5 of Brav, A. el at., "Payout Policy in the 21st Century," *Journal of Financial Economics*, 2005.

How Important Are the Following?	Percent Who Think This Is Important or Very Important
1. Being consistent with our historic dividend policy	84.1%
2. Future earnings stability	71.9
3. Sustainable earnings changes	67.1
4. Attracting institutional investors	52.5
5. Good quality investments	47.6
6. Attracting retail investors	44.5
7. Personal taxes paid by our shareholders on dividends we pay	21.1
8. Costs associated with issuing new equity	9.3

*Survey respondents were asked the question, "How important are the following factors to your company's dividend decision?"

17.8 Stock Dividends and Stock Splits

stock dividend

A payment made by a firm to its owners in the form of stock, diluting the value of each share outstanding.

Another type of dividend is paid out in shares of stock. This type of dividend is called a **stock dividend**. A stock dividend is not a true dividend because it is not paid in cash. The effect of a stock dividend is to increase the number of shares that each owner holds. Because there are more shares outstanding, each is worth less.

A stock dividend is commonly expressed as a percentage; for example, a 20 percent stock dividend means that a shareholder receives one new share for every five currently owned (a 20 percent increase). Because every shareholder receives 20 percent more stock, the total number of shares outstanding rises by 20 percent. As we will see in a moment, the result is that each share of stock is worth about 20 percent less.

stock split

An increase in a firm's shares outstanding without any change in owners' equity.

A **stock split** is essentially the same thing as a stock dividend, except that a split is expressed as a ratio instead of a percentage. When a split is declared, each share is split up to create additional shares. For example, in a three-for-one stock split, each old share is split into three new shares.

SOME DETAILS ABOUT STOCK SPLITS AND STOCK DIVIDENDS

Stock splits and stock dividends have essentially the same impacts on the corporation and the shareholder: They increase the number of shares outstanding and reduce the value per share. The accounting treatment is not the same and it depends on two things: (1) Whether the distribution is a stock split or a stock dividend and (2) the size of the stock dividend if it is called a dividend. In recent years, stock splits have slowed considerably. During the 1990s, an average of 64 S&P 500 companies split each year. From 2008 through 2012, the number fell to about 12 per year.

By convention, stock dividends of less than 20 to 25 percent are called *small stock dividends*. The accounting procedure for such a dividend is discussed next. A stock dividend greater than this range of 20 to 25 percent is called a *large stock dividend*. Large stock dividends are not uncommon. For example, the Comcast two-for-one stock split we discussed at the beginning of the chapter was to be in the form of a 100 percent stock dividend. In June 2016, Facebook announced its 200 percent stock dividend in the form of a three-for-one stock dividend that created the company's nonvoting Class C shares. Except for some relatively minor accounting differences, a stock dividend has the same effect as a stock split.

Information on upcoming stock splits is available on the splits calendar at **www.investmenthouse.com** and **finance.yahoo.com**.

Example of a Small Stock Dividend   The Peterson Co., a consulting firm specializing in difficult accounting problems, has 10,000 shares of stock outstanding, each selling at $66. The total market value of the equity is $66 \times 10,000 = $660,000. With a 10 percent stock dividend, each stockholder receives one additional share for each 10 owned, and the total number of shares outstanding after the dividend is 11,000.

Before the stock dividend, the equity portion of Peterson's balance sheet might look like this:

Common stock ($1 par, 10,000 shares outstanding)	$ 10,000
Capital in excess of par value	200,000
Retained earnings	290,000
Total owners' equity	$500,000

A seemingly arbitrary accounting procedure is used to adjust the balance sheet after a small stock dividend. Because 1,000 new shares are issued, the common stock account is increased by $1,000 (1,000 shares at $1 par value each), for a total of $11,000. The market price of $66 is $65 greater than the par value, so the "excess" of $65 × 1,000 shares = $65,000 is added to the capital surplus account (capital in excess of par value), producing a total of $265,000.

Total owners' equity is unaffected by the stock dividend because no cash has come in or out, so retained earnings are reduced by the entire $66,000, leaving $224,000. The net effect of these machinations is that Peterson's equity accounts now look like this:

Common stock ($1 par, 11,000 shares outstanding)	$ 11,000
Capital in excess of par value	265,000
Retained earnings	224,000
Total owners' equity	$500,000

Example of a Stock Split A stock split is conceptually similar to a stock dividend, but it is commonly expressed as a ratio. For example, in a three-for-two split, each shareholder receives one additional share of stock for each two held originally, so a three-for-two split amounts to a 50 percent stock dividend. Again, no cash is paid out, and the percentage of the entire firm that each shareholder owns is unaffected.

The accounting treatment of a stock split is a little different from (and simpler than) that of a stock dividend. Suppose Peterson decides to declare a two-for-one stock split. The number of shares outstanding will double to 20,000, and the par value will be halved to $.50 per share. The owners' equity after the split is represented as follows:

Common stock ($.50 par, 20,000 shares outstanding)	$ 10,000
Capital in excess of par value	200,000
Retained earnings	290,000
Total owners' equity	$500,000

For a list of recent stock splits, try **www.stocksplits.net**.

Note that, for all three of the categories, the figures on the right are completely unaffected by the split. The only changes are in the par value per share and the number of shares outstanding. Because the number of shares has doubled, the par value of each is cut in half.

Example of a Large Stock Dividend In our example, if a 100 percent stock dividend were declared, 10,000 new shares would be distributed, so 20,000 shares would be outstanding. At a $1 par value per share, the common stock account would rise by $10,000, for a total of $20,000. The retained earnings account would be reduced by $10,000, leaving $280,000. The result would be the following:

Common stock ($1 par, 20,000 shares outstanding)	$ 20,000
Capital in excess of par value	200,000
Retained earnings	280,000
Total owners' equity	$500,000

VALUE OF STOCK SPLITS AND STOCK DIVIDENDS

The laws of logic tell us that stock splits and stock dividends can (1) leave the value of the firm unaffected, (2) increase its value, or (3) decrease its value. Unfortunately, the issues are complex enough that we cannot easily determine which of the three relationships holds.

The Benchmark Case A strong case can be made that stock dividends and splits do not change either the wealth of any shareholder or the wealth of the firm as a whole. In our preceding example, the equity had a total market value of $660,000. With the small stock dividend, the number of shares increased to 11,000, so it seems that each would be worth $660,000/11,000 = $60.

For example, a shareholder who had 100 shares worth $66 each before the dividend would have 110 shares worth $60 each afterward. The total value of the stock is $6,600 either way; so the stock dividend doesn't really have any economic effect.

After the stock split, there are 20,000 shares outstanding, so each should be worth $660,000/20,000 = $33. In other words, the number of shares doubles and the price halves. From these calculations, it appears that stock dividends and splits are just paper transactions.

Although these results are relatively obvious, reasons are often given to suggest that there may be some benefits to these actions. The typical financial manager is aware of many real-world complexities; for that reason, the stock split or stock dividend decision is not treated lightly in practice.

trading range
The price range between the highest and lowest prices at which a stock is traded.

Popular Trading Range   Proponents of stock dividends and stock splits frequently argue that a security has a proper **trading range**. When the security is priced above this level, many investors do not have the funds to buy the common trading unit of 100 shares, called a *round lot*. Although securities can be purchased in *odd-lot* form (fewer than 100 shares), the commissions are greater. Firms will split the stock to keep the price in this trading range.

For example, Microsoft has split nine times since the company went public in 1986. The stock has split three-for-two on two occasions and two-for-one a total of seven times. So for every share of Microsoft you owned in 1986 when the company first went public, you would own 288 shares as of the most recent stock split. Similarly, since Walmart went public in 1970, it has split its stock two-for-one 11 times, and Apple has split seven-for-one once and two-for-one three times since going public in 1980. For a really long split history, consider Procter & Gamble, which has split five-for-one twice, 1.5-to-1 once, and two-for-one eight times since 1920. Each share of P&G purchased prior to the company's first stock split would now be worth 9,600 shares.

Although this argument is a popular one, its validity is questionable for a number of reasons. Mutual funds, pension funds, and other institutions have steadily increased their trading activity since World War II and now handle a sizable percentage of total trading volume (on the order of 90 percent of NYSE trading volume, for example). Because these institutions buy and sell in huge amounts, the individual share price is of little concern.

Furthermore, we sometimes observe share prices that are quite large that do not appear to cause problems. To take a well-known case, Berkshire Hathaway, a widely respected company headed by legendary investor Warren Buffett, sold for about $300,000 per share in early 2018.

Finally, there is evidence that stock splits may actually decrease the liquidity of the company's shares. Following a two-for-one split, the number of shares traded should more than double if liquidity is increased by the split. This doesn't appear to happen, and the reverse is sometimes observed.

REVERSE SPLITS

reverse split
A stock split in which a firm's number of shares outstanding is reduced.

A less frequently encountered financial maneuver is the **reverse split**. For example, in May 2017, Cobalt Energy announced a 1-for-15 reverse stock split. Also in May 2017, Xerox underwent a 1-for-4 reverse split. In a 1-for-4 reverse split, each investor exchanges 4 old shares for one new share. The par value is increased by a factor of 4 in the process. In what will probably be one of the biggest reverse splits ever (in terms of market cap), banking giant Citigroup announced in March 2011 that it would do a 1-for-10 reverse split, thereby reducing the number of shares outstanding from 29 billion to 2.9 billion. As with stock splits and stock dividends, a case can be made that a reverse split has no real effect.

Given real-world imperfections, three related reasons are cited for reverse splits. First, transaction costs to shareholders may be less after the reverse split. Second, the liquidity and marketability of a company's stock might be improved when its price is raised to the popular trading range. Third, stocks selling at prices below a certain level are not considered respectable, meaning that investors underestimate these firms' earnings, cash flow, growth, and stability. Some financial analysts argue that a reverse split can achieve instant respectability. As was the case with stock splits, none of these reasons is particularly compelling, especially not the third one.

There are two other reasons for reverse splits. First, stock exchanges have minimum price per share requirements. A reverse split may bring the stock price up to such a minimum. For example, NASDAQ begins the delisting process for companies whose stock price drops below $1 per share for 30 days. Following the collapse of the Internet boom in 2001–2002, a large number of Internet-related companies found themselves in danger of being delisted and used reverse splits to boost their stock prices. Second, companies sometimes perform reverse splits and, at the same time, buy out any stockholders who end up with less than a certain number of shares.

For example, in January 2017, Lime Energy completed a reverse/forward split. In this case, the company first did a 1-for-300 reverse stock split and then repurchased all shares held by stockholders with less than one share of stock, eliminating smaller shareholders thus reducing the total number of shareholders. This process allowed the company to delist its stock, or "go dark." What made the proposal especially imaginative was that immediately after the reverse split, the company did a 300-for-1 ordinary split to restore the stock to its original cost!

Concept Questions

17.8a   What is the effect of a stock split on stockholder wealth?

17.8b   How does the accounting treatment of a stock split differ from that used with a small stock dividend?

Summary and Conclusions   17.9

In this chapter, we first discussed the types of dividends and how they are paid. We then defined dividend policy and examined whether or not dividend policy matters. Next, we illustrated how a firm might establish a dividend policy and described an important alternative to cash dividends, a share repurchase.

In covering these subjects, we discussed the following points:

1. Dividend policy is irrelevant when there are no taxes or other imperfections because shareholders can effectively undo the firm's dividend strategy. Shareholders who receive dividends greater than desired can reinvest the excess. Conversely, shareholders who receive dividends smaller than desired can sell off extra shares of stock.

2. Individual shareholder income taxes and new issue flotation costs are real-world considerations that favor a low dividend payout. With taxes and new issue costs, the firm should pay out dividends only after all positive NPV projects have been fully financed.

3. There are groups in the economy that may favor a high payout. These include many large institutions such as pension plans. Recognizing that some groups prefer a high payout and some prefer a low payout, the clientele effect argument supports the idea that dividend policy responds to the needs of stockholders. For example, if 40 percent of the stockholders prefer low dividends and 60 percent of the stockholders prefer high dividends, approximately 40 percent of companies will have a low dividend payout, and 60 percent will have a high payout. This sharply reduces the impact of any individual firm's dividend policy on its market price.

4. A stock repurchase acts much like a cash dividend, but it has a significant tax advantage. Stock repurchases are therefore a very useful part of overall dividend policy.

5. We discussed recent research and thinking on dividend policy. We saw that dividends are heavily concentrated in a relatively small number of larger, older firms and that the use of share repurchases continues to grow. We described a simple life cycle theory of distributions in which firms trade off the agency costs of excess cash retention against the future costs of external equity financing. The implication is that younger firms with significant growth opportunities will not distribute cash, but older, profitable firms with significant free cash flow will distribute cash.

To close our discussion of dividends, we emphasize one last time the difference between dividends and dividend policy. Dividends are important because the value of a share of stock is ultimately determined by the dividends that will be paid. What is less clear is whether the time pattern of dividends (more now versus more later) matters. This is the dividend policy question, and it is not easy to give a definitive answer to it.

CONNECT TO FINANCE

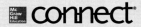 *Connect Finance* offers you plenty of opportunities to practice mastering these concepts. Log on to connect.mheducation.com to learn more. If you like what you see, ask your professor about using *Connect Finance*!

Can you answer the following *Connect* Quiz questions?

Section 17.1 Dividends are paid to the parties listed as shareholders on what date?

Section 17.3 What factors favor a high dividend payout?

Section 17.4 Which parties are most apt to prefer a low dividend payout?

Section 17.8 Tomas currently owns 300 shares of Doo Little Corp. How many shares will he own if the firm does a four-for-five reverse stock split?

CONCEPTS REVIEW AND CRITICAL THINKING QUESTIONS

1. **Dividend Policy Irrelevance [LO2]** How is it possible that dividends are so important, but at the same time, dividend policy is irrelevant?

2. **Stock Repurchases [LO4]** What is the impact of a stock repurchase on a company's debt ratio? Does this suggest another use for excess cash?

3. **Dividend Chronology [LO1]** On Tuesday, December 5, Hometown Power Co.'s board of directors declares a dividend of 75 cents per share payable on Wednesday,

January 17, to shareholders of record as of Wednesday, January 3. When is the ex-dividend date? If a shareholder buys stock before that date, who gets the dividends on those shares, the buyer or the seller?

4. **Alternative Dividends [LO1]** Some corporations, like one British company that offers its large shareholders free crematorium use, pay dividends in kind (that is, offer their services to shareholders at below-market cost). Should mutual funds invest in stocks that pay these dividends in kind? (The fundholders do not receive these services.)

5. **Dividends and Stock Price [LO1]** If increases in dividends tend to be followed by (immediate) increases in share prices, how can it be said that dividend policy is irrelevant?

6. **Dividends and Stock Price [LO1]** Last month, Central Virginia Power Company, which had been having trouble with cost overruns on a nuclear power plant that it had been building, announced that it was "temporarily suspending payments due to the cash flow crunch associated with its investment program." The company's stock price dropped from $28.50 to $25 when this announcement was made. How would you interpret this change in the stock price (that is, what would you say caused it)?

7. **Dividend Reinvestment Plans [LO1]** The DRK Corporation has recently developed a dividend reinvestment plan, or DRIP. The plan allows investors to reinvest cash dividends automatically in DRK in exchange for new shares of stock. Over time, investors in DRK will be able to build their holdings by reinvesting dividends to purchase additional shares of the company.

   A large number of companies offer dividend reinvestment plans. Most companies with DRIPs charge no brokerage or service fees. In fact, the shares of DRK will be purchased at a 10 percent discount from the market price.

   A consultant for DRK estimates that about 75 percent of DRK's shareholders will take part in this plan. This is somewhat higher than the average.

   Evaluate DRK's dividend reinvestment plan. Will it increase shareholder wealth? Discuss the advantages and disadvantages involved here.

8. **Dividend Policy [LO2]** For initial public offerings of common stock, 2017 was a slow year, with about $24.53 billion raised by the process. Relatively few of the 108 firms involved paid cash dividends. Why do you think that most chose not to pay cash dividends?

Use the following information to answer the next two questions:

   Historically, the U.S. tax code treated dividend payments made to shareholders as ordinary income. Thus, dividends were taxed at the investor's marginal tax rate, which was as high as 38.6 percent in 2002. Capital gains were taxed at a capital gains tax rate, which was the same for most investors and fluctuated through the years. In 2002, the capital gains tax rate stood at 20 percent. In an effort to stimulate the economy, President George W. Bush presided over a tax plan overhaul that included changes in dividend and capital gains tax rates. The new tax plan, which was implemented in 2003, called for a 15 percent tax rate on both dividends and capital gains for investors in higher tax brackets. For lower-tax bracket investors, the tax rate on dividends and capital gains was set at 5 percent through 2007, dropping to zero in 2008.

9. **Ex-Dividend Stock Prices [LO1]** How do you think this tax law change affected ex-dividend stock prices?

10. **Stock Repurchases [LO4]** How do you think this tax law change affected the relative attractiveness of stock repurchases compared to dividend payments?

QUESTIONS AND PROBLEMS

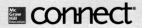

1. **Dividends and Taxes [LO2]** Ginger, Inc., has declared a $5.35 per share dividend. Suppose capital gains are not taxed, but dividends are taxed at 15 percent. New IRS regulations require that taxes be withheld at the time the dividend is paid. The company's stock sells for $74.20 per share, and the stock is about to go ex dividend. What do you think the ex-dividend price will be?

2. **Stock Dividends [LO3]** The owners' equity accounts for Vidi International are shown here:

Common stock ($.50 par value)	$ 25,000
Capital surplus	215,000
Retained earnings	642,700
Total owners' equity	$882,700

   a. If the company's stock currently sells for $32 per share and a 10 percent stock dividend is declared, how many new shares will be distributed? Show how the equity accounts would change.

   b. If the company declared a 25 percent stock dividend, how would the accounts change?

3. **Stock Splits [LO3]** For the company in Problem 2, show how the equity accounts will change if:

   a. The company declares a four-for-one stock split. How many shares are outstanding now? What is the new par value per share?

   b. The company declares a one-for-five reverse stock split. How many shares are outstanding now? What is the new par value per share?

4. **Stock Splits and Stock Dividends [LO3]** Simmons Mineral Operations, Inc. (SMO), currently has 530,000 shares of stock outstanding that sell for $68 per share. Assuming no market imperfections or tax effects exist, what will the share price be after:

   a. SMO has a five-for-three stock split?

   b. SMO has a 15 percent stock dividend?

   c. SMO has a 42.5 percent stock dividend?

   d. SMO has a four-for-seven reverse stock split?

   Determine the new number of shares outstanding in parts (a) through (d).

5. **Regular Dividends [LO1]** The balance sheet for Sinking Ship Corp. is shown here in market value terms. There are 14,000 shares of stock outstanding.

Market Value Balance Sheet			
Cash	$ 53,700	Equity	$438,700
Fixed assets	385,000		
Total	$438,700	Total	$438,700

   The company has declared a dividend of $1.30 per share. The stock goes ex dividend tomorrow. Ignoring any tax effects, what is the stock selling for today? What will it sell for tomorrow? What will the balance sheet look like after the dividends are paid?

6. **Share Repurchase [LO4]** In Problem 5, suppose the company has announced it is going to repurchase $18,200 worth of stock. What effect will this transaction have on the equity of the firm? How many shares will be outstanding? What will the price per

share be after the repurchase? Ignoring tax effects, show how the share repurchase is effectively the same as a cash dividend.

7. **Stock Dividends [LO3]** The market value balance sheet for Bobaflex Manufacturing is shown here. The company has declared a 25 percent stock dividend. The stock goes ex dividend tomorrow (the chronology for a stock dividend is similar to that for a cash dividend). There are 12,000 shares of stock outstanding. What will the ex-dividend price be?

Market Value Balance Sheet			
Cash	$ 79,000	Debt	$116,000
Fixed assets	545,000	Equity	508,000
Total	$624,000	Total	$624,000

8. **Stock Dividends [LO3]** The company with the common equity accounts shown here has declared a 15 percent stock dividend when the market value of its stock is $53 per share. What effects will the distribution of the stock dividend have on the equity accounts?

Common stock ($1 par value)	$ 245,000
Capital surplus	618,000
Retained earnings	2,758,300
Total owners' equity	$3,621,300

9. **Stock Splits [LO3]** In Problem 8, suppose the company instead decides on a four-for-one stock split. The firm's 65-cent per-share cash dividend on the new (postsplit) shares represents an increase of 10 percent over last year's dividend on the presplit stock. What effect does this have on the equity accounts? What was last year's dividend per share?

10. **Homemade Dividends [LO2]** You own 1,000 shares of stock in Avondale Corporation. You will receive a $3.15 per share dividend in one year. In two years, the company will pay a liquidating dividend of $57 per share. The required return on the company's stock is 15 percent. What is the current share price of your stock (ignoring taxes)? If you would rather have equal dividends in each of the next two years, show how you can accomplish this by creating homemade dividends. *Hint:* Dividends will be in the form of an annuity.

11. **Homemade Dividends [LO2]** In Problem 10, suppose you want only $1,500 total in dividends the first year. What will your homemade dividend be in two years?

12. **Stock Repurchase [LO4]** Awake Corporation is evaluating an extra dividend versus a share repurchase. In either case, $17,500 would be spent. Current earnings are $1.89 per share, and the stock currently sells for $64 per share. There are 2,000 shares outstanding. Ignore taxes and other imperfections in answering the first two questions.

   a. Evaluate the two alternatives in terms of the effect on the price per share of the stock and shareholder wealth.

   b. What will be the effect on the company's EPS and PE ratio under the two different scenarios?

   c. In the real world, which of these actions would you recommend? Why?

INTERMEDIATE
(Questions 10–12)

CHALLENGE
(Questions 13–16)

13. **Expected Return, Dividends, and Taxes** [LO2] The Gecko Company and the Gordon Company are two firms that have the same business risk but different dividend policies. Gecko pays no dividend, whereas Gordon has an expected dividend yield of 2.9 percent. Suppose the capital gains tax rate is zero, whereas the income tax rate is 35 percent. Gecko has an expected earnings growth rate of 12 percent annually, and its stock price is expected to grow at this same rate. If the aftertax expected returns on the two stocks are equal (because they are in the same risk class), what is the pretax required return on Gordon's stock?

14. **Dividends and Taxes** [LO2] As discussed in the text, in the absence of market imperfections and tax effects, we would expect the share price to decline by the amount of the dividend payment when the stock goes ex dividend. Once we consider the role of taxes, however, this is not necessarily true. One model has been proposed that incorporates tax effects into determining the ex-dividend price:[9]

$$(P_0 - P_X)/D = (1 - T_P)/(1 - T_G)$$

where P_0 is the price just before the stock goes ex, P_X is the ex-dividend share price, D is the amount of the dividend per share, T_P is the relevant marginal personal tax rate on dividends, and T_G is the effective marginal tax rate on capital gains.

  a. If $T_P = T_G = 0$, how much will the share price fall when the stock goes ex?

  b. If $T_P = 15$ percent and $T_G = 0$, how much will the share price fall?

  c. If $T_P = 15$ percent and $T_G = 30$ percent, how much will the share price fall?

  d. Suppose the only owners of stock are corporations. Recall that corporations get at least a 50 percent exemption from taxation on the dividend income they receive, but they do not get such an exemption on capital gains. If the corporation's income and capital gains tax rates are both 35 percent, what does this model predict the ex-dividend share price will be?

  e. What does this problem tell you about real-world tax considerations and the dividend policy of the firm?

15. **Dividends versus Reinvestment** [LO2] National Business Machine Co. (NBM) has $4 million of extra cash after taxes have been paid. NBM has two choices to make use of this cash. One alternative is to invest the cash in financial assets. The resulting investment income will be paid out as a special dividend at the end of three years. In this case, the firm can invest in Treasury bills yielding 2.5 percent or in 4.3 percent preferred stock. Assume IRS regulations allow the company to exclude from taxable income 70 percent of the dividends received from investing in another company's stock. Another alternative is to pay out the cash now as dividends. This would allow the shareholders to invest on their own in Treasury bills with the same yield, or in preferred stock. The corporate tax rate is 21 percent. Assume the investor has a 31 percent personal income tax rate, which is applied to interest income and preferred stock dividends. Also assume the personal dividend tax rate is 15 percent on common stock dividends. Should the cash be paid today or in three years? Which of the two options generates the highest aftertax income for the shareholders?

16. **Dividends versus Reinvestment** [LO2] After completing its capital spending for the year, Carlson Manufacturing has $1,000 extra cash. Carlson's managers must choose between investing the cash in Treasury bonds that yield 3 percent or paying the cash out to investors who would invest in the bonds themselves.

[9]N. Elton and M. Gruber, "Marginal Stockholder Tax Rates and the Clientele Effect," *Review of Economics and Statistics* 52 (February 1970).

a. If the corporate tax rate is 35 percent, what personal tax rate would make the investors equally willing to receive the dividend or to let Carlson invest the money?

b. Is the answer to (a) reasonable? Why or why not?

c. Suppose the only investment choice is preferred stock that yields 6 percent. The corporate dividend exclusion of 70 percent applies. What personal tax rate will make the stockholders indifferent to the outcome of Carlson's dividend decision?

d. Is this a compelling argument for a low dividend payout ratio? Why or why not?

MINICASE

Electronic Timing, Inc.

Electronic Timing, Inc. (ETI), is a small company founded 15 years ago by electronics engineers Tom Miller and Jessica Kerr. ETI manufactures integrated circuits to capitalize on the complex mixed-signal design technology and has recently entered the market for frequency timing generators, or silicon timing devices, which provide the timing signals or "clocks" necessary to synchronize electronic systems. Its clock products originally were used in PC video graphics applications, but the market has subsequently expanded to include motherboards, PC peripheral devices, and other digital consumer electronics, such as digital television boxes and game consoles. ETI also designs and markets custom application-specific integrated circuits (ASICs) for industrial customers. The ASIC's design combines analog and digital, or mixed-signal, technology. In addition to Tom and Jessica, Nolan Pittman, who provided capital for the company, is the third primary owner. Each owns 25 percent of the 1 million shares outstanding. The company has several other individuals, including current employees, who own the remaining shares.

Recently, the company designed a new computer motherboard. The company's design is both more efficient and less expensive to manufacture, and the ETI design is expected to become standard in many personal computers. After investigating the possibility of manufacturing the new motherboard, ETI determined that the costs involved in building a new plant would be prohibitive. The owners also decided that they were unwilling to bring in another large outside owner. Instead, ETI sold the design to an outside firm. The sale of the motherboard design was completed for an aftertax payment of $30 million.

QUESTIONS

1. Tom believes the company should use the extra cash to pay a special one-time dividend. How will this proposal affect the stock price? How will it affect the value of the company?

2. Jessica believes the company should use the extra cash to pay off debt and upgrade and expand its existing manufacturing capability. How would Jessica's proposals affect the company?

3. Nolan favors a share repurchase. He argues that a repurchase will increase the company's PE ratio, return on assets, and return on equity. Are his arguments correct? How will a share repurchase affect the value of the company?

4. Another option discussed by Tom, Jessica, and Nolan would be to begin a regular dividend payment to shareholders. How would you evaluate this proposal?

5. One way to value a share of stock is the dividend growth, or growing perpetuity, model. Consider the following: The dividend payout ratio is 1 minus b, where b is the "retention" or "plowback" ratio. So, the dividend next year will be the earnings next year, E_1, times 1 minus the retention ratio. The most commonly used equation to calculate the sustainable growth rate is the return on equity times the retention ratio. Substituting these relationships into the dividend growth model, we get the following equation to calculate the price of a share of stock today:

$$P_0 = \frac{E_1(1-b)}{R_s - \text{ROE} \times b}$$

What are the implications of this result in terms of whether the company should pay a dividend or upgrade and expand its manufacturing capability? Explain.

6. Does the question of whether the company should pay a dividend depend on whether the company is organized as a corporation or an LLC?

Chapter

18 | Short-Term Finance and Planning

IN EARLY 2017, car sales were slowing and inventories were climbing. For example, the Buick LaCrosse sat on dealers' lots for an average of 168 days before being sold. At the same time, sales of the Chevrolet Spark were not exactly electrifying, either, as it took 170 days for each of those cars to be sold. In the auto industry, high inventory creates problems, and those problems are often resolved by offering large incentives. For example, Jeep, which had 138 days of inventory of its Renegade, offered $2,500 to entice new buyers. At the other end of the spectrum, it took only 38 days on average to sell a new Honda Pilot.

As this chapter explores, the amount of time goods are carried in inventory until they are sold is an important element of short-term financial management. Industries such as automobile manufacturing pay close attention to it.

Learning Objectives

After studying this chapter, you should be able to:

LO1   Describe the operating and cash cycles and why they are important.

LO2   List the different types of short-term financial policy.

LO3   Summarize the essentials of short-term financial planning.

LO4   Explain the sources and uses of cash on the balance sheet.

©by_adri/iStockPhoto/GettyImages

For updates on the latest happenings in finance, visit fundamentalsofcorporatefinance.blogspot.com.

To this point, we have described many of the decisions of long-term finance, such as those of capital budgeting, dividend policy, and financial structure. In this chapter, we begin to discuss short-term finance. Short-term finance is primarily concerned with the analysis of decisions that affect current assets and current liabilities.

Frequently, the term *net working capital* is associated with short-term financial decision making. As we describe in Chapter 2 and elsewhere, net working capital is the difference between current assets and current liabilities. Often, short-term financial management is called *working capital management*. These terms mean the same thing.

There is no universally accepted definition of *short-term finance*. The most important difference between short-term and long-term finance is in the timing of cash flows. Short-term financial decisions typically involve cash inflows and outflows that occur within a year or less. For example, short-term financial decisions are involved when a firm orders raw materials, pays in cash, and anticipates selling finished goods in one year for cash. In contrast, long-term financial decisions are involved when a firm purchases a special machine that will reduce operating costs over, say, the next five years.

What types of questions fall under the general heading of short-term finance? To name a few:

1. What is a reasonable level of cash to keep on hand (in a bank) to pay bills?
2. How much should the firm borrow in the short term?
3. How much credit should be extended to customers?

This chapter introduces the basic elements of short-term financial decisions. First, we discuss the short-term operating activities of the firm. We then identify some alternative short-term financial policies. Finally, we outline the basic elements in a short-term financial plan and describe short-term financing instruments.

Tracing Cash and Net Working Capital   **18.1**

In this section, we examine the components of cash and net working capital as they change from one year to the next. We have already discussed various aspects of this subject in Chapters 2, 3, and 4. We briefly review some of that discussion as it relates to short-term financing decisions. Our goal is to describe the short-term operating activities of the firm and their impact on cash and working capital.

Interested in a career in short-term finance? Visit the Treasury Management International website at **www .treasury-management.com**.

To begin, recall that *current assets* are cash and other assets that are expected to convert to cash within the year. Current assets are presented on the balance sheet in order of their accounting liquidity—that is, the ease with which they can be converted to cash and the time it takes to convert them. Four of the most important items found in the current assets section of a balance sheet are cash and cash equivalents, marketable securities, accounts receivable, and inventories.

Analogous to their investment in current assets, firms use several kinds of short-term debt, called *current liabilities*. Current liabilities are obligations that are expected to require cash payment within one year (or within the operating period if it is longer than one year). Three major items classified as current liabilities are accounts payable, expenses payable (including accrued wages and taxes), and notes payable.

Because we want to focus on changes in cash, we start off by defining *cash* in terms of the other elements of the balance sheet. This lets us isolate the cash account and explore how cash is impacted by the firm's operating and financing decisions. The basic balance sheet identity can be written as:

Net working capital + Fixed assets = Long-term debt + Equity

Net working capital is cash plus other current assets, less current liabilities—that is:

Net working capital = (Cash + Other current assets) − Current liabilities

If we substitute this for net working capital in the basic balance sheet identity and rearrange things a bit, we see that cash is:

**Cash = Long-term debt + Equity + Current liabilities
    − Current assets other than cash − Fixed assets**

This tells us in general terms that some activities naturally increase cash and some activities decrease it. We can list these various activities, along with an example of each, as follows:

ACTIVITIES THAT INCREASE CASH

Increasing long-term debt (borrowing over the long term)

Increasing equity (selling some stock)

Increasing current liabilities (getting a 90-day loan)

Decreasing current assets other than cash (selling some inventory for cash)

Decreasing fixed assets (selling some property)

ACTIVITIES THAT DECREASE CASH

Decreasing long-term debt (paying off a long-term debt)

Decreasing equity (repurchasing some stock)

Decreasing current liabilities (paying off a 90-day loan)

Increasing current assets other than cash (buying some inventory for cash)

Increasing fixed assets (buying some property)

Notice that our two lists are exact opposites. For example, floating a long-term bond issue increases cash (at least until the money is spent). Paying off a long-term bond issue decreases cash.

As we discussed in Chapter 3, those activities that increase cash are called *sources of cash*. Those activities that decrease cash are called *uses of cash*. Looking back at our list, we see that sources of cash always involve increasing a liability (or equity) account or decreasing an asset account. This makes sense because increasing a liability means that we have raised money by borrowing it or by selling an ownership interest in the firm. A decrease in an asset means that we have sold or otherwise liquidated an asset. In either case, there is a cash inflow.

Uses of cash are just the reverse. A use of cash involves decreasing a liability by paying it off, perhaps, or increasing assets by purchasing something. Both of these activities require that the firm spend some cash.

EXAMPLE 18.1   Sources and Uses

Here is a quick check of your understanding of sources and uses: If accounts payable go up by $100, does this indicate a source or a use? What if accounts receivable go up by $100?

Accounts payable are what we owe our suppliers. This is a short-term debt. If it rises by $100, we have effectively borrowed the money, which is a *source* of cash. Receivables are what our customers owe to us, so an increase of $100 in accounts receivable means that we have lent the money; this is a *use* of cash.

Concept Questions

18.1a   What is the difference between net working capital and cash?
18.1b   Will net working capital always increase when cash increases?
18.1c   List five potential sources of cash.
18.1d   List five potential uses of cash.

18.2 The Operating Cycle and the Cash Cycle

The primary concern in short-term finance is the firm's short-run operating and financing activities. For a typical manufacturing firm, these short-run activities might consist of the following sequence of events and decisions:

Event	Decision
1. Buying raw materials	1. How much inventory to order
2. Paying cash	2. Whether to borrow or draw down cash balances
3. Manufacturing the product	3. What choice of production technology to use
4. Selling the product	4. Whether credit should be extended to a particular customer
5. Collecting cash	5. How to collect

These activities create patterns of cash inflows and cash outflows. These cash flows are both unsynchronized and uncertain. They are unsynchronized because, for example, the payment of cash for raw materials does not happen at the same time as the receipt of cash from selling the product. They are uncertain because future sales and costs cannot be precisely predicted.

DEFINING THE OPERATING AND CASH CYCLES

We can start with a simple case. One day, call it Day 0, we purchase $1,000 worth of inventory on credit. We pay the bill 30 days later; and after 30 more days, someone buys the $1,000 in inventory for $1,400. Our buyer does not actually pay for another 45 days. We can summarize these events chronologically as follows:

Day	Activity	Cash Effect
0	Acquire inventory	None
30	Pay for inventory	−$1,000
60	Sell inventory on credit	None
105	Collect on sale	+$1,400

The Operating Cycle   There are several things to notice in our example. First, the entire cycle, from the time we acquire some inventory to the time we collect the cash, takes 105 days. This is called the **operating cycle**.

As we illustrate, the operating cycle is the length of time it takes to acquire inventory, sell it, and collect for it. This cycle has two distinct components. The first part is the time it takes to acquire and sell the inventory. This period, a 60-day span in our example, is called the **inventory period**. The second part is the time it takes to collect on the sale, 45 days in our example. This is called the **accounts receivable period**.

Based on our definitions, the operating cycle is obviously just the sum of the inventory and accounts receivable periods:

Operating cycle = Inventory period + Accounts receivable period
$$105 \text{ days} = 60 \text{ days} + 45 \text{ days}$$

What the operating cycle describes is how a product moves through the current asset accounts. The product begins life as inventory, is converted to a receivable when it is sold, and is finally converted to cash when we collect from the sale. Notice that, at each step, the asset is moving closer to cash.

The Cash Cycle   The second thing to notice is that the cash flows and other events that occur are not synchronized. For example, we don't actually pay for the inventory until 30 days after we acquire it. The intervening 30-day period is called the **accounts payable period**. Next, we spend cash on Day 30, but we don't collect until Day 105. Somehow, we have to arrange to finance the $1,000 for 105 − 30 = 75 days. This period is called the **cash cycle**.

operating cycle
The period between the acquisition of inventory and the collection of cash from receivables.

inventory period
The time it takes to acquire and sell inventory.

accounts receivable period
The time between sale of inventory and collection of the receivable.

accounts payable period
The time between receipt of inventory and payment for it.

cash cycle
The time between cash disbursement and cash collection.

FIGURE 18.1

Cash Flow Time Line and the Short-Term Operating Activities of a Typical Manufacturing Firm

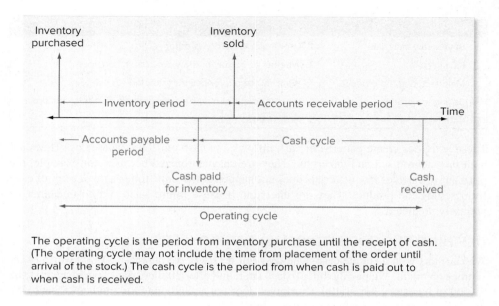

The operating cycle is the period from inventory purchase until the receipt of cash. (The operating cycle may not include the time from placement of the order until arrival of the stock.) The cash cycle is the period from when cash is paid out to when cash is received.

The cash cycle is the number of days that pass before we collect the cash from a sale, measured from when we actually pay for the inventory. Notice that, based on our definitions, the cash cycle is the difference between the operating cycle and the accounts payable period:

Cash cycle = Operating cycle − Accounts payable period   **18.5**
        75 days = 105 days − 30 days

Figure 18.1 depicts the short-term operating activities and cash flows for a typical manufacturing firm by way of a cash flow time line. As shown, the **cash flow time line** presents the operating cycle and the cash cycle in graphical form. In Figure 18.1, the need for short-term financial management is suggested by the gap between the cash inflows and the cash outflows. This is related to the lengths of the operating cycle and the accounts payable period.

The gap between short-term inflows and outflows can be filled either by borrowing or by holding a liquidity reserve in the form of cash or marketable securities. Alternatively, the gap can be shortened by changing the inventory, receivable, and payable periods. These are all managerial options that we discuss in the following sections and in subsequent chapters.

Internet-based bookseller and retailer Amazon.com provides an interesting example of the importance of managing the cash cycle. By early 2017, the market value of Amazon was higher than (in fact more than 500 times as much as) that of Barnes & Noble, king of the brick-and-mortar bookstores.

How could Amazon be worth so much more? There are multiple reasons, but short-term financial management is one factor. During 2016, Amazon turned over its inventory about 8 times per year, twice as fast as Barnes & Noble; so its inventory period was dramatically shorter. Amazon's receivables period is 21 days, but due in part to the company's bargaining power with suppliers, its payables period is almost 135 days. This means Amazon has a *negative* cash cycle! In fact, during 2016, Amazon's cash cycle was negative 69 days. Every sale generates a cash inflow that can be put to work immediately.

cash flow time line
A graphical representation of the operating cycle and the cash cycle.

Title of Manager	Duties Related to Short-Term Financial Management	Assets/Liabilities Influenced
Cash manager	Collection, concentration, disbursement; short-term investments; short-term borrowing; banking relations	Cash, marketable securities, short-term loans
Credit manager	Monitoring and control of accounts receivable; credit policy decisions	Accounts receivable
Marketing manager	Credit policy decisions	Accounts receivable
Purchasing manager	Decisions about purchases, suppliers; may negotiate payment terms	Inventory, accounts payable
Production manager	Setting of production schedules and materials requirements	Inventory, accounts payable
Payables manager	Decisions about payment policies and about whether to take discounts	Accounts payable
Controller	Accounting information about cash flows; reconciliation of accounts payable; application of payments to accounts receivable	Accounts receivable, accounts payable

TABLE 18.1

Managers Who Deal with Short-Term Financial Problems

THE OPERATING CYCLE AND THE FIRM'S ORGANIZATIONAL CHART

Before we examine the operating and cash cycles in greater detail, it is useful for us to take a look at the people involved in managing a firm's current assets and liabilities. As Table 18.1 illustrates, short-term financial management in a large corporation involves a number of different financial and nonfinancial managers. Examining Table 18.1, we see that selling on credit involves at least three different entities: The credit manager, the marketing manager, and the controller. Of these three, only two are responsible to the vice president of finance (the marketing function is usually associated with the vice president of marketing). There is the potential for conflict, particularly if different managers concentrate on only part of the picture. For example, if marketing is trying to land a new account, it may seek more liberal credit terms as an inducement. This may increase the firm's investment in receivables or its exposure to bad-debt risk, and conflict can result.

CALCULATING THE OPERATING AND CASH CYCLES

In our example, the lengths of time that made up the different periods were obvious. If all we have is financial statement information, we will have to do a little more work. We illustrate these calculations next.

To begin, we need to determine various things such as how long it takes, on average, to sell inventory and how long it takes, on average, to collect payment. We start by gathering some balance sheet information such as the following (in thousands):

Item	Beginning	Ending	Average
Inventory	$2,000	$3,000	$2,500
Accounts receivable	1,600	2,000	1,800
Accounts payable	750	1,000	875

Also, from the most recent income statement, we might have the following figures (in thousands):

Net sales	$11,500
Cost of goods sold	8,200

We now need to calculate some financial ratios. We discussed these in some detail in Chapter 3; here, we define them and use them as needed.

The Operating Cycle

First of all, we need the inventory period. We spent $8.2 million on inventory (our cost of goods sold). Our average inventory was $2.5 million. We turned our inventory over $8.2/$2.5 times during the year:[1]

$$\text{Inventory turnover} = \frac{\text{Cost of goods sold}}{\text{Average inventory}}$$

$$= \frac{\$8.2 \text{ million}}{\$2.5 \text{ million}} = 3.28 \text{ times}$$

Loosely speaking, this tells us that we bought and sold off our inventory 3.28 times during the year. This means that, on average, we held our inventory for:

$$\text{Inventory period} = \frac{365 \text{ days}}{\text{Inventory turnover}}$$

$$= \frac{365}{3.28} = 111 \text{ days}$$

So, the inventory period is about 111 days. In other words, on average, inventory sat for about 111 days before it was sold.[2]

Similarly, receivables averaged $1.8 million, and sales were $11.5 million. Assuming that all sales were credit sales, the receivables turnover is:[3]

$$\text{Receivables turnover} = \frac{\text{Credit sales}}{\text{Average accounts receivable}}$$

$$= \frac{\$11.5 \text{ million}}{\$1.8 \text{ million}} = 6.39 \text{ times}$$

If we turn over our receivables 6.39 times, then the receivables period is:

$$\text{Receivables period} = \frac{365 \text{ days}}{\text{Receivables turnover}}$$

$$= \frac{365}{6.39} = 57 \text{ days}$$

The receivables period is also called the *days' sales in receivables* or the *average collection period*. Whatever it is called, it tells us that our customers took an average of 57 days to pay.

The operating cycle is the sum of the inventory and receivables periods:

$$\text{Operating cycle} = \text{Inventory period} + \text{Accounts receivable period}$$

$$= 111 \text{ days} + 57 \text{ days} = 168 \text{ days}$$

This tells us that, on average, 168 days elapse between the time we acquire inventory and, having sold it, the time we collect for the sale.

---

[1]Notice that in calculating inventory turnover here, we use the *average* inventory instead of using the ending inventory as we did in Chapter 3. Both approaches are used in the real world. To gain some practice using average figures, we will stick with this approach in calculating various ratios throughout this chapter.

[2]This measure is conceptually identical to the days' sales in inventory figure we discussed in Chapter 3.

[3]If fewer than 100 percent of our sales were credit sales, then we would just need a little more information—namely, credit sales for the year. See Chapter 3 for more discussion of this measure.

The Cash Cycle   We now need the payables period. From the information given earlier, we know that average payables were $875,000 and cost of goods sold was $8.2 million. Our payables turnover is:

$$\text{Payables turnover} = \frac{\text{Cost of goods sold}}{\text{Average payables}}$$

$$= \frac{\$8.2 \text{ million}}{\$.875 \text{ million}} = 9.37 \text{ times}$$

The payables period is:

$$\text{Payables period} = \frac{365 \text{ days}}{\text{Payables turnover}}$$

$$= \frac{365}{9.37} = 39 \text{ days}$$

We took an average of 39 days to pay our bills.

Finally, the cash cycle is the difference between the operating cycle and the payables period:

$$\text{Cash cycle} = \text{Operating cycle} - \text{Accounts payable period}$$
$$= 168 \text{ days} - 39 \text{ days} = 129 \text{ days}$$

So, on average, there is a 129-day delay between the time we pay for merchandise and the time we collect on the sale.

The Operating and Cash Cycles	**EXAMPLE 18.2**

You have collected the following information for the Slowpay Company:

Item	Beginning	Ending
Inventory	$5,000	$7,000
Accounts receivable	1,600	2,400
Accounts payable	2,700	4,800

Credit sales for the year just ended were $50,000, and cost of goods sold was $30,000. How long does it take Slowpay to collect on its receivables? How long does merchandise stay around before it is sold? How long does Slowpay take to pay its bills?

We can first calculate the three turnover ratios:

Inventory turnover = $30,000/$6,000 = 5 times
Receivables turnover = $50,000/$2,000 = 25 times
Payables turnover = $30,000/$3,750 = 8 times

We use these to get the various periods:

Inventory period = 365/5   = 73 days
Receivables period = 365/25 = 14.6 days
Payables period = 365/8   = 45.6 days

All told, Slowpay collects on a sale in 14.6 days, inventory sits around for 73 days, and bills get paid after about 46 days. The operating cycle here is the sum of the inventory and receivables periods: 73 + 14.6 = 87.6 days. The cash cycle is the difference between the operating cycle and the payables period: 87.6 − 45.6 = 42 days.

INTERPRETING THE CASH CYCLE

Our examples show that the cash cycle depends on the inventory, receivables, and payables periods. The cash cycle increases as the inventory and receivables periods get longer. It decreases if the company can defer payment of payables and thereby lengthen the payables period.

Unlike Amazon.com, most firms have a positive cash cycle, and they require financing for inventories and receivables. The longer the cash cycle, the more financing is required. Also, changes in the firm's cash cycle are often monitored as an early-warning measure. A lengthening cycle can indicate that the firm is having trouble moving inventory or collecting on its receivables. Such problems can be masked, at least partially, by an increased payables cycle; so both cycles should be monitored.

The link between the firm's cash cycle and its profitability can be easily seen by recalling that one of the basic determinants of profitability and growth for a firm is its total asset turnover, which is defined as Sales/Total assets. In Chapter 3, we saw that the higher this ratio is, the greater is the firm's accounting return on assets, ROA, and return on equity, ROE. Thus, all other things being the same, the shorter the cash cycle, the lower is the firm's investment in inventories and receivables. As a result, the firm's total assets are lower, and total asset turnover is higher.

Concept Questions

18.2a Describe the operating cycle and the cash cycle. What are the differences?

18.2b What does it mean to say that a firm has an inventory turnover ratio of 4?

18.2c Explain the connection between a firm's accounting-based profitability and its cash cycle.

18.3 Some Aspects of Short-Term Financial Policy

The short-term financial policy that a firm adopts will be reflected in at least two ways:

1. *The size of the firm's investment in current assets*: This is usually measured relative to the firm's level of total operating revenues. A *flexible*, or accommodative, short-term financial policy would maintain a relatively high ratio of current assets to sales. A *restrictive* short-term financial policy would entail a low ratio of current assets to sales.[4]

2. *The financing of current assets*: This is measured as the proportion of short-term debt (that is, current liabilities) and long-term debt used to finance current assets. A restrictive short-term financial policy means a high proportion of short-term debt relative to long-term financing, and a flexible policy means less short-term debt and more long-term debt.

If we take these two areas together, we see that a firm with a flexible policy would have a relatively large investment in current assets, and it would finance this investment with

---

[4]Some people use the term *conservative* in place of *flexible* and the term *aggressive* in place of *restrictive*.

relatively less short-term debt. The net effect of a flexible policy is a relatively high level of net working capital. Put another way, with a flexible policy, the firm maintains a higher overall level of liquidity.

THE SIZE OF THE FIRM'S INVESTMENT IN CURRENT ASSETS

Short-term financial policies that are flexible with regard to current assets include such actions as:

1. Keeping large balances of cash and marketable securities.
2. Making large investments in inventory.
3. Granting liberal credit terms, which results in a high level of accounts receivable.

Restrictive short-term financial policies would be just the opposite:

1. Keeping low cash balances and making little investment in marketable securities.
2. Making small investments in inventory.
3. Allowing few or no credit sales, thereby minimizing accounts receivable.

Determining the optimal level of investment in short-term assets requires identification of the different costs of alternative short-term financing policies. The objective is to trade off the cost of a restrictive policy against the cost of a flexible one to arrive at the best compromise.

Current asset holdings are highest with a flexible short-term financial policy and lowest with a restrictive policy. So, flexible short-term financial policies are costly in that they require a greater investment in cash and marketable securities, inventory, and accounts receivable. We expect that future cash inflows will be higher with a flexible policy. For example, sales are stimulated by the use of a credit policy that provides liberal financing to customers. A large amount of finished inventory on hand ("on the shelf") enables quick delivery service to customers and may increase sales. Similarly, a large inventory of raw materials may result in fewer production stoppages because of inventory shortages.

A more restrictive short-term financial policy probably reduces future sales to levels below those that would be achieved under flexible policies. It is also possible that higher prices can be charged to customers under flexible working capital policies. Customers may be willing to pay higher prices for the quick delivery service and more liberal credit terms implicit in flexible policies.

Managing current assets can be thought of as involving a trade-off between costs that rise and costs that fall with the level of investment. Costs that rise with increases in the level of investment in current assets are called **carrying costs**. The larger the investment a firm makes in its current assets, the higher its carrying costs will be. Costs that fall with increases in the level of investment in current assets are called **shortage costs**.

In a general sense, carrying costs are the opportunity costs associated with current assets. The rate of return on current assets is very low when compared to that on other assets. For example, the rate of return on U.S. Treasury bills averages about 3 to 4 percent. This is very low compared to the rate of return firms would like to achieve overall. (U.S. Treasury bills are an important component of cash and marketable securities.)

Shortage costs are incurred when the investment in current assets is low. If a firm runs out of cash, it will be forced to sell marketable securities. Of course, if a firm runs out of cash and cannot readily sell marketable securities, it may have to borrow or default on an obligation. This situation is called a *cash-out*. A firm may lose customers if it runs out of inventory (a *stockout*) or if it cannot extend credit to customers.

carrying costs
Costs that rise with increases in the level of investment in current assets.

shortage costs
Costs that fall with increases in the level of investment in current assets.

More generally, there are two kinds of shortage costs:

1. *Trading, or order, costs*: Order costs are the costs of placing an order for more cash (brokerage costs, for example) or more inventory (production setup costs, for example).
2. *Costs related to lack of safety reserves*: These are costs of lost sales, lost customer goodwill, and disruption of production schedules.

The top part of Figure 18.2 illustrates the basic trade-off between carrying costs and shortage costs. On the vertical axis, we have costs measured in dollars; on the horizontal axis, we have the amount of current assets. Carrying costs start out at zero when current assets are zero and then climb steadily as current assets grow. Shortage costs start out very high and then decline as we add current assets. The total cost of holding current assets is the sum of the two. Notice how the combined costs reach a minimum at CA*. This is the optimal level of current assets.

Optimal current asset holdings are highest under a flexible policy. This policy is one in which the carrying costs are perceived to be low relative to shortage costs. This is Case A in Figure 18.2. In comparison, under restrictive current asset policies, carrying costs are perceived to be high relative to shortage costs, resulting in lower current asset holdings. This is Case B in Figure 18.2.

ALTERNATIVE FINANCING POLICIES FOR CURRENT ASSETS

In previous sections, we looked at the basic determinants of the level of investment in current assets, and we focused on the asset side of the balance sheet. Now we turn to the financing side of the question. Here we are concerned with the relative amounts of short-term and long-term debt, assuming that the investment in current assets is constant.

An Ideal Case   We start off with the simplest possible case: An "ideal" economy. In such an economy, short-term assets can always be financed with short-term debt, and long-term assets can be financed with long-term debt and equity. In this economy, net working capital is always zero.

Consider a simplified case for a grain elevator operator. Grain elevator operators buy crops after harvest, store them, and sell them during the year. They have high inventories of grain after the harvest and end up with low inventories just before the next harvest.

Bank loans with maturities of less than one year are used to finance the purchase of grain and the storage costs. These loans are paid off from the proceeds of the sale of grain.

The situation is shown in Figure 18.3. Long-term assets are assumed to grow over time, whereas current assets increase at the end of the harvest and then decline during the year. Short-term assets end up at zero just before the next harvest. Current (short-term) assets are financed by short-term debt, and long-term assets are financed with long-term debt and equity. Net working capital—current assets minus current liabilities—is always zero. Figure 18.3 displays a "sawtooth" pattern that we will see again when we get to our discussion of cash management in the next chapter. For now, we need to discuss some alternative policies for financing current assets under less idealized conditions.

Different Policies for Financing Current Assets   In the real world, it is not likely that current assets will ever drop to zero. For example, a long-term rising level of sales will result in some permanent investment in current assets. Moreover, the firm's investments in long-term assets may show a great deal of variation.

A growing firm can be thought of as having a total asset requirement consisting of the current assets and long-term assets needed to run the business efficiently. The total

Short-term financial policy: the optimal investment in current assets

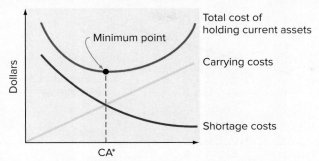

CA* represents the optimal amount of current assets.
Holding this amount minimizes total costs.

Carrying costs increase with the level of investment in current assets. They include the costs of maintaining economic value and opportunity costs. *Shortage costs* decrease with increases in the level of investment in current assets. They include trading costs and the costs related to being short of the current asset (for example, being short of cash). The firm's policy can be characterized as flexible or restrictive.

A. Flexible policy

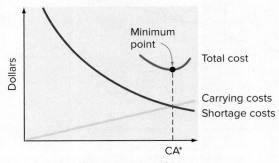

A flexible policy is most appropriate when carrying costs are low relative to shortage costs.

B. Restrictive policy

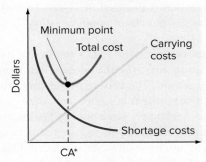

A restrictive policy is most appropriate when carrying costs are high relative to shortage costs.

FIGURE 18.2

Carrying Costs and Shortage Costs

FIGURE 18.3

Financing Policy for an Ideal Economy

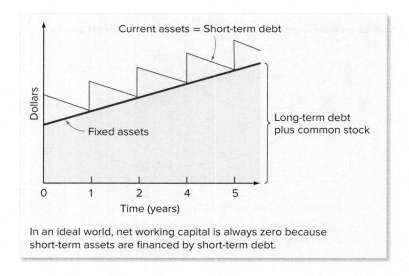

In an ideal world, net working capital is always zero because short-term assets are financed by short-term debt.

FIGURE 18.4

The Total Asset Requirement over Time

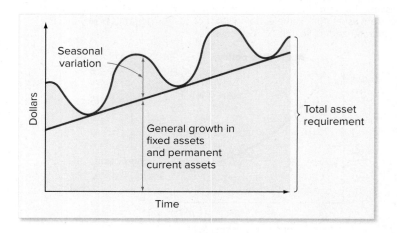

asset requirement may exhibit change over time for many reasons, including (1) a general growth trend, (2) seasonal variation around the trend, and (3) unpredictable day-to-day and month-to-month fluctuations. This fluctuation is depicted in Figure 18.4. (We have not tried to show the unpredictable day-to-day and month-to-month variations in the total asset requirement.)

The peaks and valleys in Figure 18.4 represent the firm's total asset needs through time. For example, for a lawn and garden supply firm, the peaks might represent inventory buildups prior to the spring selling season. The valleys would come about because of lower off-season inventories. Such a firm might consider two strategies to meet its cyclical needs. First, the firm could keep a relatively large pool of marketable securities. As the need for inventory and other current assets begins to rise, the firm could sell off marketable securities and use the cash to purchase whatever is needed. Once the inventory is sold and inventory holdings begin to decline, the firm could reinvest in marketable securities. This approach is the flexible policy illustrated in Figure 18.5 as Policy F. Notice that the firm essentially uses a pool of marketable securities as a buffer against changing current asset needs.

FIGURE 18.5 **Alternative Asset Financing Policies**

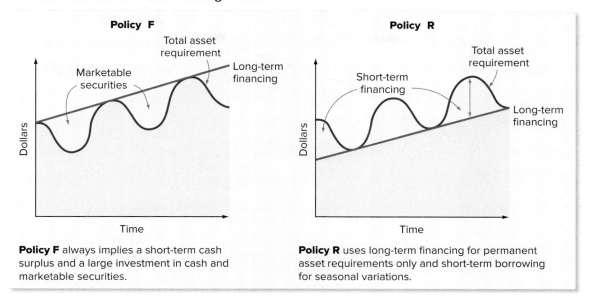

Policy F always implies a short-term cash surplus and a large investment in cash and marketable securities.

Policy R uses long-term financing for permanent asset requirements only and short-term borrowing for seasonal variations.

At the other extreme, the firm could keep relatively little in marketable securities. As the need for inventory and other assets begins to rise, the firm could borrow the needed cash on a short-term basis. The firm could repay the loans as the need for assets cycles back down. This approach is the restrictive policy illustrated in Figure 18.5 as Policy R.

In comparing the two strategies illustrated in Figure 18.5, notice that the chief difference is the way in which the seasonal variation in asset needs is financed. In the flexible case, the firm finances internally, using its own cash and marketable securities. In the restrictive case, the firm finances the variation externally, borrowing the needed funds on a short-term basis. As we discussed previously, all else being the same, a firm with a flexible policy will have a greater investment in net working capital.

WHICH FINANCING POLICY IS BEST?

What is the most appropriate amount of short-term borrowing? There is no definitive answer. Several considerations must be included in a proper analysis:

1. *Cash reserves*: The flexible financing policy implies surplus cash and little short-term borrowing. This policy reduces the probability that a firm will experience financial distress. Firms may not have to worry as much about meeting recurring, short-run obligations. However, investments in cash and marketable securities are zero net present value investments at best.

2. *Maturity hedging*: Most firms attempt to match the maturities of assets and liabilities. They finance inventories with short-term bank loans and fixed assets with long-term financing. Firms tend to avoid financing long-lived assets with short-term borrowing. This type of maturity mismatching would necessitate frequent refinancing and is inherently risky because short-term interest rates are more volatile than longer-term rates.

3. *Relative interest rates*: Short-term interest rates are usually lower than long-term rates. This implies that it is, on average, more costly to rely on long-term borrowing as compared to short-term borrowing.

FIGURE 18.6

A Compromise Financing Policy

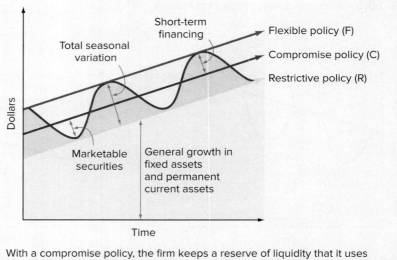

With a compromise policy, the firm keeps a reserve of liquidity that it uses to initially finance seasonal variations in current asset needs. Short-term borrowing is used when the reserve is exhausted.

The two policies depicted in Figure 18.5 are, of course, extreme cases. With F, the firm never does any short-term borrowing; with R, the firm never has a cash reserve (an investment in marketable securities). Figure 18.6 illustrates these two policies along with a compromise, Policy C.

With this compromise approach, the firm borrows in the short term to cover peak financing needs, but it maintains a cash reserve in the form of marketable securities during slow periods. As current assets build up, the firm draws down this reserve before doing any short-term borrowing. This allows for some run-up in current assets before the firm has to resort to short-term borrowing.

CURRENT ASSETS AND LIABILITIES IN PRACTICE

Short-term assets represent a significant portion of a typical firm's overall assets. For U.S. manufacturing, mining, and trade corporations, current assets were about 50 percent of total assets in the 1960s. Today, this figure is closer to 40 percent. Most of the decline is due to more efficient cash and inventory management. Over this same period, current liabilities rose from about 20 percent of total liabilities and equity to almost 30 percent. The result is that liquidity (as measured by the ratio of net working capital to total assets) has declined, signaling a move to more restrictive short-term policies.

Concept Questions

18.3a   What keeps the real world from being an ideal one in which net working capital could always be zero?

18.3b   What considerations determine the optimal size of the firm's investment in current assets?

18.3c   What considerations determine the optimal compromise between flexible and restrictive net working capital policies?

The Cash Budget

The **cash budget** is a primary tool in short-run financial planning. It allows the financial manager to identify short-term financial needs and opportunities. An important function of the cash budget is to help the manager explore the need for short-term borrowing. The idea of the cash budget is simple: It records estimates of cash receipts (cash in) and disbursements (cash out). The result is an estimate of the cash surplus or deficit.

SALES AND CASH COLLECTIONS

We start with an example involving the Fun Toys Corporation. We will prepare a quarterly cash budget. We could just as well use a monthly, weekly, or even daily basis. We choose quarters for convenience and also because a quarter is a common short-term business planning period. (Note that, throughout this example, all figures are in millions of dollars.)

All of Fun Toys' cash inflows come from the sale of toys. Cash budgeting for Fun Toys must start with a sales forecast for the coming year, by quarter:

	Q1	Q2	Q3	Q4
Sales (in millions)	$200	$300	$250	$400

Note that these are predicted sales, so there is forecasting risk here, and actual sales could be more or less. Fun Toys started the year with accounts receivable equal to $120.

Fun Toys has a 45-day receivables, or average collection, period. This means that half of the sales in a given quarter will be collected the following quarter. This happens because sales made during the first 45 days of a quarter will be collected in that quarter, whereas sales made in the second 45 days will be collected in the next quarter. Note that we are assuming that each quarter has 90 days, so the 45-day collection period is the same as a half-quarter collection period.

Based on the sales forecasts, we now need to estimate Fun Toys' projected cash collections. First, any receivables that we have at the beginning of a quarter will be collected within 45 days, so all of them will be collected sometime during the quarter. Second, as we discussed, any sales made in the first half of the quarter will be collected, so total cash collections are:

Cash collections = Beginning accounts receivable + 1/2 × Sales

For example, in the first quarter, cash collections would be the beginning receivables of $120 plus half of sales, 1/2 × $200 = $100, for a total of $220.

Because beginning receivables are all collected along with half of sales, ending receivables for a particular quarter will be the other half of sales. First-quarter sales are projected at $200, so ending receivables will be $100. This will be the beginning receivables in the second quarter. Cash collections in the second quarter will be $100 plus half of the projected $300 in sales, or $250 total.

Continuing this process, we can summarize Fun Toys' projected cash collections as shown in Table 18.2.

	Q1	Q2	Q3	Q4
Beginning receivables	$120	$100	$150	$125
Sales	200	300	250	400
Cash collections	− 220	− 250	− 275	− 325
Ending receivables	$100	$150	$125	$200

Collections = Beginning receivables + 1/2 × Sales
Ending receivables = Beginning receivables + Sales − Collections
= 1/2 × Sales

18.4

Excel Master It!
Excel Master coverage online

cash budget
A forecast of cash receipts and disbursements for the next planning period.

18.6

See the Finance section of **www.toolkit.com** for several useful templates, including a cash flow budget.

TABLE 18.2

Cash Collection for Fun Toys (in millions)

In Table 18.2, collections are shown as the only source of cash. Of course, this need not be the case. Other sources of cash could include asset sales, investment income, and receipts from planned long-term financing.

CASH OUTFLOWS

Next, we consider the cash disbursements, or payments. These come in four basic categories:

1. *Payments of accounts payable*: These are payments for goods or services rendered by suppliers, such as raw materials. Generally, these payments will be made sometime after purchases.
2. *Wages, taxes, and other expenses*: This category includes all other regular costs of doing business that require actual expenditures. Depreciation, for example, is often thought of as a regular cost of business; but it requires no cash outflow and is not included.
3. *Capital expenditures*: These are payments of cash for long-lived assets.
4. *Long-term financing expenses*: This category includes, for example, interest payments on long-term debt outstanding and dividend payments to shareholders.

Fun Toys' purchases from suppliers (in dollars) in a quarter are equal to 60 percent of the next quarter's predicted sales. Fun Toys' payments to suppliers are equal to the previous quarter's purchases, so the accounts payable period is 90 days. For example, in the quarter just ended, Fun Toys ordered $.60 \times \$200 = \$120$ in supplies. This will actually be paid in the first quarter (Q1) of the coming year.

Wages, taxes, and other expenses are routinely 20 percent of sales; interest and dividends are currently $20 per quarter. In addition, Fun Toys plans a major plant expansion (a capital expenditure) costing $100 in the second quarter. If we put all this information together, the cash outflows are as shown in Table 18.3.

THE CASH BALANCE

The predicted *net cash inflow* is the difference between cash collections and cash disbursements. The net cash inflow for Fun Toys is shown in Table 18.4. What we see immediately is that there is a cash surplus in the first and third quarters and a cash deficit in the second and fourth quarters.

TABLE 18.3

Cash Disbursements for Fun Toys (in millions)

	Q1	Q2	Q3	Q4
Payment of accounts (60% of sales)	$ 120	$ 180	$ 150	$ 240
Wages, taxes, other expenses	40	60	50	80
Capital expenditures	0	100	0	0
Long-term financing expenses (interest and dividends)	20	20	20	20
Total cash disbursements	$180	$360	$220	$340

TABLE 18.4

Net Cash Inflow for Fun Toys (in millions)

	Q1	Q2	Q3	Q4
Total cash collections	$220	$250	$275	$325
Total cash disbursements	180	360	220	340
Net cash inflow	$ 40	−$110	$ 55	−$ 15

TABLE 18.5

**Cash Balance for Fun
Toys (in millions)**

	Q1	Q2	Q3	Q4
Beginning cash balance	$20	$ 60	–$50	$ 5
Net cash inflow	40	– 110	55	– 15
Ending cash balance	$60	–$ 50	$ 5	–$10
Minimum cash balance	– 10	– 10	– 10	– 10
Cumulative surplus (deficit)	$50	–$ 60	–$ 5	–$20

We will assume that Fun Toys starts the year with a $20 cash balance. Furthermore, Fun Toys maintains a $10 minimum cash balance to guard against unforeseen contingencies and forecasting errors. So, the company starts the first quarter with $20 in cash. This amount rises by $40 during the quarter, and the ending balance is $60. Of this, $10 is reserved as a minimum, so we subtract it out and find that the first-quarter surplus is $60 – 10 = $50.

Fun Toys starts the second quarter with $60 in cash (the ending balance from the previous quarter). There is a net cash inflow of –$110, so the ending balance is $60 – 110 = –$50. We need another $10 as a buffer, so the total deficit is –$60. These calculations and those for the last two quarters are summarized in Table 18.5.

At the end of the second quarter, Fun Toys has a cash shortfall of $60. This occurs because of the seasonal pattern of sales (higher toward the end of the second quarter), the delay in collections, and the planned capital expenditure.

The cash situation at Fun Toys is projected to improve to a $5 deficit in the third quarter; but, by year's end, Fun Toys still has a $20 deficit. Without some sort of financing, this deficit will carry over into the next year. We explore this subject in the next section.

For now, we can make the following general comments about Fun Toys' cash needs:

1. Fun Toys' large outflow in the second quarter is not necessarily a sign of trouble. It results from delayed collections on sales and a planned capital expenditure (presumably a worthwhile one).
2. The figures in our example are based on a forecast. Sales could be much worse (or better) than the forecast figures.

Concept Questions

18.4a How would you do a sensitivity analysis (discussed in Chapter 11) for Fun Toys' net cash balance?

18.4b What could you learn from such an analysis?

Short-Term Borrowing   18.5

Fun Toys has a short-term financing problem. It cannot meet the forecast cash outflows in the second quarter using internal sources. How it will finance that shortfall depends on its financial policy. With a very flexible policy, Fun Toys might seek up to $60 million in long-term debt financing.

In addition, note that much of the cash deficit comes from the large capital expenditure. Arguably, this is a candidate for long-term financing. Nonetheless, because we have discussed long-term financing elsewhere, we will concentrate here on two short-term borrowing options: (1) unsecured borrowing and (2) secured borrowing.

UNSECURED LOANS

line of credit
A formal (committed) or informal (noncommitted) prearranged, short-term bank loan.

The most common way to finance a temporary cash deficit is to arrange a short-term unsecured bank loan. Firms that use short-term bank loans often arrange for a line of credit. A **line of credit** is an agreement under which a firm is authorized to borrow up to a specified amount. To ensure that the line is used for short-term purposes, the lender will sometimes require the borrower to pay the line down to zero and keep it there for some period during the year, typically 60 days (called a *cleanup period*).

Short-term lines of credit are classified as either *committed* or *noncommitted*. The latter type is an informal arrangement that allows firms to borrow up to a previously specified limit without going through the normal paperwork (much as they would with a credit card). A *revolving credit arrangement* (or *revolver*) is similar to a line of credit, but it is usually open for two or more years, whereas a line of credit would usually be evaluated on an annual basis.

Committed lines of credit are more formal legal arrangements that usually involve a commitment fee paid by the firm to the bank (usually the fee is on the order of .25 percent of the total committed funds per year). The interest rate on the line of credit is usually set equal to the bank's prime lending rate plus an additional percentage, and the rate will usually float. A firm that pays a commitment fee for a committed line of credit is essentially buying insurance to guarantee that the bank can't back out of the agreement (absent some material change in the borrower's status).

compensating balance
Money kept by the firm with a bank in low-interest or non-interest-bearing accounts as part of a loan agreement.

Compensating Balances   As a part of a credit line or other lending arrangement, banks will sometimes require that the firm keep some amount of money on deposit. This is called a compensating balance. A **compensating balance** is some of the firm's money kept by the bank in low-interest or non-interest-bearing accounts. By leaving these funds with the bank and receiving little or no interest, the firm further increases the effective interest rate earned by the bank on the line of credit, thereby "compensating" the bank. A compensating balance might be on the order of 2 to 5 percent of the amount borrowed.

Firms also use compensating balances to pay for noncredit bank services such as cash management services. A traditionally contentious issue is whether the firm should pay for bank credit and noncredit services with fees or with compensating balances. Most major firms have now negotiated for banks to use the corporation's collected funds for compensation and use fees to cover any shortfall. Arrangements such as this one and some similar approaches discussed in the next chapter make the subject of minimum balances less of an issue than it once was.

Cost of a Compensating Balance   A compensating balance requirement has an obvious opportunity cost because the money often must be deposited in an account with a zero or low interest rate. For example, suppose that we have a $100,000 line of credit with a 10 percent compensating balance requirement. This means that 10 percent of the amount actually used must be left on deposit in a non-interest-bearing account.

The quoted interest rate on the credit line is 16 percent. Suppose we need $54,000 to purchase some inventory. How much do we have to borrow? What interest rate are we effectively paying?

If we need $54,000, we have to borrow enough so that $54,000 is left over after we take out the 10 percent compensating balance:

$$\$54,000 = (1 - .10) \times \text{Amount borrowed}$$
$$\text{Amount borrowed} = \$54,000/.90 = \$60,000$$

The interest on the $60,000 for one year at 16 percent is $60,000 × .16 = $9,600. We're actually getting only $54,000 to use, so the effective interest rate is:

$$\text{Effective interest rate} = \text{Interest paid/Amount available}$$
$$= \$9,600/\$54,000$$
$$= .1778, \text{ or } 17.78\%$$

Notice that what effectively happens here is that we pay 16 cents in interest on every 90 cents we borrow because we don't get to use the 10 cents tied up in the compensating balance. The interest rate is .16/.90 = .1778, or 17.78%, as we calculated.

Several points bear mentioning. First, compensating balances are usually computed as a monthly *average* of the daily balances. This means that the effective interest rate may be lower than our example illustrates. Second, it has become common for compensating balances to be based on the *unused* amount of the credit line. The requirement of such a balance amounts to an implicit commitment fee. Third, and most important, the details of any short-term business lending arrangements are highly negotiable. Banks will generally work with firms to design a package of fees and interest.

Letters of Credit   A *letter of credit* is a common arrangement in international finance. With a letter of credit, the bank issuing the letter promises to make a loan if certain conditions are met. Typically, the letter guarantees payment on a shipment of goods provided that the goods arrive as promised. A letter of credit can be revocable (subject to cancellation) or irrevocable (not subject to cancellation if the specified conditions are met).

SECURED LOANS

Banks and other finance companies often require security for a short-term loan just as they do for a long-term loan. Security for short-term loans usually consists of accounts receivable, inventories, or both.

Accounts Receivable Financing   **Accounts receivable financing** involves either *assigning* receivables or *factoring* receivables. Under assignment, the lender has the receivables as security, but the borrower is still responsible if a receivable can't be collected. With *conventional factoring*, the receivable is discounted and sold to the lender (the factor). Once it is sold, collection is the factor's problem, and the factor assumes the full risk of default on bad accounts. With *maturity factoring*, the factor forwards the money on an agreed-upon future date.

> **accounts receivable financing**
> A secured short-term loan that involves either the assignment or the factoring of receivables.

Factors play a particularly important role in the retail industry. Retailers in the clothing business, for example, must buy large amounts of new clothes at the beginning of the season. Because it is typically a long time before they sell anything, they wait to pay their suppliers, sometimes 30 to 60 days. If an apparel maker can't wait that long, it turns to factors, who buy the receivables and take over collection. Historically, the garment industry accounts for about 80 percent of all factoring in the United States.

One of the newest types of factoring is called *credit card receivable funding* or *business cash advances*. The way business cash advances work is that a company goes to a factor and receives cash up front. From that point on, a portion of each credit card sale (perhaps 6 to 8 percent) is routed directly to the factor by the credit card processor until the loan is paid off. This arrangement may be attractive to small businesses in particular, but it can be expensive. The typical premium on the advance is about 35 percent—meaning that with a $100,000 loan, $135,000 must be repaid within a relatively short period.

Purchase order financing (or PO financing) is a popular form of factoring used by small and midsize companies. In a typical scenario, a small business receives a firm order from a customer, but it doesn't have sufficient funds to pay the supplier who manufactures the product. With PO financing, the factor pays the supplier. When the sale is completed and the seller is paid, the factor is repaid. A typical interest rate on purchase order factoring is 3.5 percent for the first 30 days, then 1.25 percent every 10 days after, which results in an annual interest rate above 50 percent.

EXAMPLE 18.3   **Cost of Factoring**

For the year just ended, LuLu's Pies had an average of $50,000 in accounts receivable. Credit sales were $500,000. LuLu's factors its receivables by discounting them 3 percent—in other words, by selling them for 97 cents on the dollar. What is the effective interest rate on this source of short-term financing?

To determine the interest rate, we first have to know the accounts receivable, or average collection, period. During the year, LuLu's turned over its receivables $500,000/$50,000 = 10 times. The average collection period is 365/10 = 36.5 days.

The interest paid here is a form of discount interest (discussed in Chapter 6). In this case, LuLu's is paying 3 cents in interest on every 97 cents of financing. The interest rate per 36.5 days is .03/.97 = .0309, or 3.09%. The APR is 10 × 3.09% = 30.9%, but the effective annual rate is:

$$EAR = 1.0309^{10} - 1 = .356, \text{ or } 35.6\%$$

Factoring is a relatively expensive source of money in this case.

We should note that, if the factor takes on the risk of default by a buyer, then the factor is providing insurance as well as immediate cash. More generally, the factor essentially takes over the firm's credit operations. This can result in a significant savings. The interest rate we calculated is therefore overstated, particularly if default is a significant possibility.

---

inventory loan
A secured short-term loan to purchase inventory.

Inventory Loans   **Inventory loans**, short-term loans to purchase inventory, come in three basic forms: blanket inventory liens, trust receipts, and field warehouse financing:

1. *Blanket inventory lien*: A blanket lien gives the lender a lien against all the borrower's inventories (the blanket "covers" everything).
2. *Trust receipt*: A trust receipt is a device by which the borrower holds specific inventory in "trust" for the lender. Automobile dealer financing, for example, is done by use of trust receipts. This type of secured financing is also called *floor planning*, in reference to inventory on the showroom floor. However, it is somewhat cumbersome to use trust receipts for, say, wheat grain.
3. *Field warehouse financing*: In field warehouse financing, a public warehouse company (an independent company that specializes in inventory management) acts as a control agent to supervise the inventory for the lender.

OTHER SOURCES

A variety of other sources of short-term funds are employed by corporations. Two of the most important are *commercial paper* and *trade credit*.

Commercial paper consists of short-term notes issued by large, highly rated firms. Typically, these notes are of short maturity, ranging up to 270 days (beyond that limit, the firm must file a registration statement with the SEC). Because the firm issues these directly and because it usually backs the issue with a special bank line of credit, the interest rate the firm obtains is often significantly below the rate a bank would charge for a direct loan.

Another option available to a firm is to increase the accounts payable period; in other words, the firm may take longer to pay its bills. This amounts to borrowing from suppliers in the form of trade credit. This is an extremely important form of financing for smaller businesses in particular. As we discuss in Chapter 20, a firm using trade credit may end up paying a much higher price for what it purchases, so this can be a very expensive source of financing.

A Short-Term Financial Plan   18.6

To illustrate a completed short-term financial plan, we will assume that Fun Toys arranges to borrow any needed funds on a short-term basis. The interest rate is a 20 percent APR, and it is calculated on a quarterly basis. From Chapter 6, we know that the rate is 20%/4 = 5% per quarter. We will assume that Fun Toys starts the year with no short-term debt.

From Table 18.5, we know that Fun Toys has a second-quarter deficit of $60 million. The firm will have to borrow this amount. Net cash inflow in the following quarter is $55 million. The firm will now have to pay $60 million × .05 = $3 million in interest out of that, leaving $52 million to reduce the borrowing.

Fun Toys still owes $60 million − 52 million = $8 million at the end of the third quarter. Interest in the last quarter will be $8 million × .05 = $.4 million. In addition, net in-flows in the last quarter are −$15 million; so the company will have to borrow a total of $15.4 million, bringing total borrowing up to $15.4 million + 8 million = $23.4 million. Table 18.6 extends Table 18.5 to include these calculations.

Notice that the ending short-term debt is equal to the cumulative deficit for the entire year, $20 million, plus the interest paid during the year, $3 million + .4 million = $3.4 million, for a total of $23.4 million.

Our plan is very simple. For example, we ignored the fact that the interest paid on the short-term debt is tax deductible. We also ignored the fact that the cash surplus in the first quarter would earn some interest (which would be taxable). We could add on a number of refinements. Even so, our plan highlights the fact that in about 90 days, Fun Toys will need to borrow $60 million or so on a short-term basis. It's time to start lining up the source of the funds.

TABLE 18.6

Short-Term Financial Plan for Fun Toys (in millions)

	Q1	Q2	Q3	Q4
Beginning cash balance	$20	$ 60	$10	$10.0
Net cash inflow	40	− 110	55	− 15.0
New short-term borrowing	0	60	0	15.4
Interest on short-term borrowing	0	0	− 3	− .4
Short-term borrowing repaid	0	0	− 52	0
Ending cash balance	$60	$ 10	$10	$10.0
Minimum cash balance	− 10	− 10	− 10	− 10.0
Cumulative surplus (deficit)	$50	$ 0	$ 0	$ .0
Beginning short-term borrowing	0	0	60	8.0
Change in short-term debt	0	60	− 52	15.4
Ending short-term debt	$ 0	$ 60	$ 8	$23.4

Our plan also illustrates that financing the firm's short-term needs will cost about $3.4 million in interest (before taxes) for the year. This is a starting point for Fun Toys to begin evaluating alternatives to reduce this expense. For example, can the $100 million planned expenditure be postponed or spread out? At 5 percent per quarter, short-term credit is expensive.

Also, if Fun Toys' sales are expected to keep growing, then the deficit of $20 million-plus will probably also keep growing, and the need for additional financing will be permanent. Fun Toys may wish to think about raising money on a long-term basis to cover this need.

Concept Questions

18.6a In Table 18.6, does Fun Toys have a projected deficit or surplus?

18.6b In Table 18.6, what would happen to Fun Toys' deficit or surplus if the minimum cash balance were reduced to $5?

18.7 Summary and Conclusions

1. This chapter has introduced the management of short-term finance. Short-term finance involves short-lived assets and liabilities. We traced and examined the short-term sources and uses of cash as they appear on the firm's financial statements. We saw how current assets and current liabilities arise in the short-term operating activities and the cash cycle of the firm.

2. Managing short-term cash flows involves the minimizing of costs. The two major costs are carrying costs, the return forgone by keeping too much invested in short-term assets such as cash, and shortage costs, the costs of running out of short-term assets. The objective of managing short-term finance and doing short-term financial planning is to find the optimal trade-off between these two costs.

3. In an ideal economy, the firm could perfectly predict its short-term uses and sources of cash, and net working capital could be kept at zero. In the real world, cash and net working capital provide a buffer that lets the firm meet its ongoing obligations. The financial manager seeks the optimal level of each of the current assets.

4. The financial manager can use the cash budget to identify short-term financial needs. The cash budget tells the manager what borrowing is required or what lending will be possible in the short run. The firm has available to it a number of possible ways of acquiring funds to meet short-term shortfalls, including unsecured and secured loans.

CONNECT TO FINANCE

Can you answer the following *Connect* Quiz questions?

Section 18.1   Give an example of an action that will increase cash.

Section 18.2   A firm has an operating cycle of 64 days and a cash cycle of 21 days. How long will the firm's accounts payable period be if the firm decides to increase its accounts payable period by three days?

Section 18.4   Galaxy Sales has a beginning cash balance of $25. During the quarter, the firm had a net cash inflow of $20. What is the cumulative surplus at the end of the quarter if the minimum cash balance is $10?

Section 18.5   What type of lending relies on a control agent to supervise inventory on behalf of a lender?

CHAPTER REVIEW AND SELF-TEST PROBLEMS

18.1   The Operating and Cash Cycles Consider the following financial statement information for the Route 66 Company:

Item	Beginning		Ending
Inventory	$1,273		$1,401
Accounts receivable	3,782		3,368
Accounts payable	1,795		2,025
Net sales		$14,750	
Cost of goods sold		11,375	

Calculate the operating and cash cycles.

18.2   Cash Balance for Greenwell Corporation The Greenwell Corporation has a 60-day average collection period and wishes to maintain a $160 million minimum cash balance. Based on this and the information given in the following cash budget, complete the cash budget. What conclusions do you draw?

GREENWELL CORPORATION Cash Budget (in millions)				
	Q1	Q2	Q3	Q4
Beginning receivables	$240			
Sales	150	$165	$180	$ 135
Cash collections	___	___	___	___
Ending receivables	___	___	___	___
Total cash collections				
Total cash disbursements	170	160	185	190
Net cash inflow	___	___	___	___
Beginning cash balance	$ 45			
Net cash inflow	___	___	___	___
Ending cash balance	___	___	___	___
Minimum cash balance	___	___	___	___
Cumulative surplus (deficit)	___	___	___	___

ANSWERS TO CHAPTER REVIEW AND SELF-TEST PROBLEMS

18.1 We first need the turnover ratios. Note that we use the average values for all balance sheet items and that we base the inventory and payables turnover measures on cost of goods sold:

$$\text{Inventory turnover} = \$11{,}375/[(\$1{,}273 + 1{,}401)/2] = 8.51 \text{ times}$$
$$\text{Receivables turnover} = \$14{,}750/[(\$3{,}782 + 3{,}368)/2] = 4.13 \text{ times}$$
$$\text{Payables turnover} = \$11{,}375/[(\$1{,}795 + 2{,}025)/2] = 5.96 \text{ times}$$

We can now calculate the various periods:

$$\text{Inventory period} = 365 \text{ days}/8.51 \text{ times} = 42.90 \text{ days}$$
$$\text{Receivables period} = 365 \text{ days}/4.13 \text{ times} = 88.47 \text{ days}$$
$$\text{Payables period} = 365 \text{ days}/5.96 \text{ times} = 61.29 \text{ days}$$

So the time it takes to acquire inventory and sell it is about 43 days. Collection takes another 88 days, and the operating cycle is thus 43 + 88 = 131 days. The cash cycle is 131 days less the payables period: 131 − 61 = 70 days.

18.2 Because Greenwell has a 60-day collection period, only sales made in the first 30 days of the quarter will be collected in the same quarter. Total cash collections in the first quarter will thus equal 30/90 = 1/3 of sales plus beginning receivables, or 1/3 × $150 + $240 = $290. Ending receivables for the first quarter (and the second quarter beginning receivables) are the other 2/3 of sales, or 2/3 × $150 = $100. The remaining calculations are straightforward, and the completed budget is as follows:

GREENWELL CORPORATION Cash Budget (in millions)				
	Q1	**Q2**	**Q3**	**Q4**
Beginning receivables	$240	$100	$110	$ 120
Sales	150	165	180	135
Cash collections	290	155	170	165
Ending receivables	$100	$110	$120	$ 90
Total cash collections	$290	$155	$170	$165
Total cash disbursements	170	160	185	190
Net cash inflow	$120	−$ 5	−$15	−$ 25
Beginning cash balance	$ 45	$165	$160	$145
Net cash inflow	120	− 5	− 15	− 25
Ending cash balance	$165	$160	$145	$120
Minimum cash balance	− 160	− 160	− 160	− 160
Cumulative surplus (deficit)	$ 5	$ 0	−$ 15	−$ 40

The primary conclusion from this schedule is that, beginning in the third quarter, Greenwell's cash surplus becomes a cash deficit. By the end of the year, Greenwell will need to arrange for $40 million in cash beyond what will be available.

CONCEPTS REVIEW AND CRITICAL THINKING QUESTIONS

1. **Operating Cycle [LO1]** What are some of the characteristics of a firm with a long operating cycle?

2. **Cash Cycle [LO1]** What are some of the characteristics of a firm with a long cash cycle?

3. **Sources and Uses [LO4]** For the year just ended, you have gathered the following information about the Holly Corporation:

    a. A $200 dividend was paid.

    b. Accounts payable increased by $500.

    c. Fixed asset purchases were $900.

    d. Inventories increased by $625.

    e. Long-term debt decreased by $1,200.

    Label each as a source or use of cash and describe its effect on the firm's cash balance.

4. **Cost of Current Assets [LO2]** Shank Manufacturing, Inc., has recently installed a just-in-time (JIT) inventory system. Describe the effect this is likely to have on the company's carrying costs, shortage costs, and operating cycle.

5. **Operating and Cash Cycles [LO1]** Is it possible for a firm's cash cycle to be longer than its operating cycle? Explain why or why not.

Use the following information to answer Questions 6–10: Last month, BlueSky Airline announced that it would stretch out its bill payments to 45 days from 30 days. The reason given was that the company wanted to "control costs and optimize cash flow." The increased payables period will be in effect for all of the company's 4,000 suppliers.

6. **Operating and Cash Cycles [LO1]** What impact did this change in payables policy have on BlueSky's operating cycle? Its cash cycle?

7. **Operating and Cash Cycles [LO1]** What impact did the announcement have on BlueSky's suppliers?

8. **Corporate Ethics [LO1]** Is it ethical for large firms to unilaterally lengthen their payables periods, particularly when dealing with smaller suppliers?

9. **Payables Period [LO1]** Why don't all firms increase their payables periods to shorten their cash cycles?

10. **Payables Period [LO1]** BlueSky lengthened its payables period to "control costs and optimize cash flow." Exactly what is the cash benefit to BlueSky from this change?

QUESTIONS AND PROBLEMS

1. **Changes in the Cash Account [LO4]** Indicate the impact of the following corporate actions on cash, using the letter *I* for an increase, *D* for a decrease, or *N* when no change occurs:

    a. A dividend is paid with funds received from a sale of debt.

    b. Real estate is purchased and paid for with short-term debt.

    c. Inventory is bought on credit.

    d. A short-term bank loan is repaid.

    e. Next year's taxes are prepaid.

    f. Preferred stock is redeemed.

    g. Sales are made on credit.

    h. Interest on long-term debt is paid.

    i. Payments for previous sales are collected.

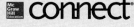

BASIC
(Questions 1–12)

j. The accounts payable balance is reduced.

k. A dividend is paid.

l. Production supplies are purchased and paid for with a short-term note.

m. Utility bills are paid.

n. Cash is paid for raw materials purchased for inventory.

o. Marketable securities are sold.

2. **Cash Equation [LO3]** Cori's Corp. has an equity value of $13,315. Long-term debt is $8,200. Net working capital, other than cash, is $2,750. Fixed assets are $17,380. How much cash does the company have? If current liabilities are $2,025, what are current assets?

3. **Changes in the Operating Cycle [LO1]** Indicate the effect that the following will have on the operating cycle. Use the letter *I* to indicate an increase, the letter *D* for a decrease, and the letter *N* for no change:

a. Average receivables goes up.

b. Credit repayment times for customers are increased.

c. Inventory turnover goes from 3 times to 6 times.

d. Payables turnover goes from 6 times to 11 times.

e. Receivables turnover goes from 7 times to 9 times.

f. Payments to suppliers are accelerated.

4. **Changes in Cycles [LO1]** Indicate the impact of the following on the cash and operating cycles, respectively. Use the letter *I* to indicate an increase, the letter *D* for a decrease, and the letter *N* for no change:

a. The terms of cash discounts offered to customers are made less favorable.

b. The cash discounts offered by suppliers are decreased; thus, payments are made earlier.

c. An increased number of customers begin to pay in cash instead of with credit.

d. Fewer raw materials than usual are purchased.

e. A greater percentage of raw material purchases are paid for with credit.

f. More finished goods are produced for inventory instead of for order.

5. **Calculating Cash Collections [LO3]** The Morning Jolt Coffee Company has projected the following quarterly sales amounts for the coming year:

	Q1	Q2	Q3	Q4
Sales	$850	$880	$960	$1,040

a. Accounts receivable at the beginning of the year are $365. The company has a 45-day collection period. Calculate cash collections in each of the four quarters by completing the following:

	Q1	Q2	Q3	Q4
Beginning receivables				
Sales				
Cash collections				
Ending receivables				

b. Rework (a) assuming a collection period of 60 days.

c. Rework (a) assuming a collection period of 30 days.

6. **Calculating Cycles [LO1]** Consider the following financial statement information
for the Newk Corporation:

Item	Beginning	Ending
Inventory	$11,718	$14,865
Accounts receivable	5,860	6,127
Accounts payable	7,930	8,930
Credit sales	$127,382	
Cost of goods sold	76,157	

Calculate the operating and cash cycles. How do you interpret your answer?

7. **Factoring Receivables [LO3]** Your firm has an average collection period of 31 days. Current practice is to factor all receivables immediately at a discount of 1.25 percent. What is the effective cost of borrowing in this case? Assume that default is extremely unlikely.

8. **Calculating Payments [LO3]** Sexton Corp. has projected the following sales for the coming year:

	Q1	Q2	Q3	Q4
Sales	$810	$880	$840	$930

Sales in the year following this one are projected to be 15 percent greater in each quarter.

a. Calculate payments to suppliers assuming that the company places orders during each quarter equal to 30 percent of projected sales for the next quarter. Assume that the company pays immediately. What is the payables period in this case?

	Q1	Q2	Q3	Q4
Payment of accounts	$	$	$	$

b. Rework (a) assuming a 90-day payables period.
c. Rework (a) assuming a 60-day payables period.

9. **Calculating Payments [LO3]** The Torrey Pine Corporation's purchases from suppliers in a quarter are equal to 75 percent of the next quarter's forecast sales. The payables period is 60 days. Wages, taxes, and other expenses are 20 percent of sales, and interest and dividends are $90 per quarter. No capital expenditures are planned. Projected quarterly sales are shown here:

	Q1	Q2	Q3	Q4
Sales	$1,670	$2,065	$1,810	$1,530

Sales for the first quarter of the following year are projected at $2,025. Calculate the company's cash outlays by completing the following:

	Q1	Q2	Q3	Q4
Payment of accounts				
Wages, taxes, other expenses				
Long-term financing expenses				
(interest and dividends)				
Total				

10. **Calculating Cash Collections [LO3]** The following is the sales budget for Profit, Inc., for the first quarter of 2018:

	January	February	March
Sales budget	$196,000	$215,000	$236,000

Credit sales are collected as follows:

65 percent in the month of the sale

20 percent in the month after the sale

15 percent in the second month after the sale

The accounts receivable balance at the end of the previous quarter was $87,000 ($61,000 of which was uncollected December sales).

a. Compute the sales for November.

b. Compute the sales for December.

c. Compute the cash collections from sales for each month from January through March.

11. **Calculating the Cash Budget [LO3]** Here are some important figures from the budget of Nashville Nougats, Inc., for the second quarter of 2018:

	April	May	June
Credit sales	$336,900	$314,500	$378,400
Credit purchases	134,100	152,400	180,300
Cash disbursements			
Wages, taxes, and expenses	48,910	62,300	67,600
Interest	11,320	11,320	11,320
Equipment purchases	79,900	122,000	0

The company predicts that 5 percent of its credit sales will never be collected, 35 percent of its sales will be collected in the month of the sale, and the remaining 60 percent will be collected in the following month. Credit purchases will be paid in the month following the purchase.

In March 2018, credit sales were $211,500 and credit purchases were $145,200. Using this information, complete the following cash budget:

	April	May	June
Beginning cash balance	$121,000		
Cash receipts			
Cash collections from credit sales			
Total cash available			
Cash disbursements			
Purchases			
Wages, taxes, and expenses			
Interest			
Equipment purchases			
Total cash disbursements			
Ending cash balance			

12. **Sources and Uses [LO4]** Below are the most recent balance sheets for Country Kettles, Inc. Excluding accumulated depreciation, determine whether each item is a source or a use of cash and the amount:

COUNTRY KETTLES, INC. Balance Sheets		
	2016	2017
Assets		
Cash	$ 36,740	$ 35,719
Accounts receivable	84,583	88,746
Inventories	73,568	77,121
Property, plant, and equipment	181,340	190,188
Less: Accumulated depreciation	55,300	60,381
Total assets	$320,931	$331,393
Liabilities and Equity		
Accounts payable	$ 59,863	$ 61,350
Accrued expenses	7,599	6,815
Long-term debt	30,976	33,800
Common stock	19,000	23,000
Accumulated retained earnings	203,493	206,428
Total liabilities and equity	$320,931	$331,393

13. **Costs of Borrowing [LO3]** You've worked out a line of credit arrangement that allows you to borrow up to $40 million at any time. The interest rate is .36 percent per month. In addition, 4 percent of the amount that you borrow must be deposited in a non-interest-bearing account. Assume that your bank uses compound interest on its line of credit loans.

    a. What is the effective annual interest rate on this lending arrangement?

    b. Suppose you need $13 million today and you repay it in six months. How much interest will you pay?

14. **Costs of Borrowing [LO3]** A bank offers your firm a revolving credit arrangement for up to $50 million at an interest rate of 1.65 percent per quarter. The bank also requires you to maintain a compensating balance of 5 percent against the *unused* portion of the credit line, to be deposited in a non-interest-bearing account. Assume you have a short-term investment account at the bank that pays .75 percent per quarter, and assume that the bank uses compound interest on its revolving credit loans.

    a. What is your effective annual interest rate (an opportunity cost) on the revolving credit arrangement if your firm does not use it during the year?

    b. What is your effective annual interest rate on the lending arrangement if you borrow $30 million immediately and repay it in one year?

    c. What is your effective annual interest rate if you borrow $50 million immediately and repay it in one year?

15. **Calculating the Cash Budget [LO3]** Wildcat, Inc., has estimated sales (in millions) for the next four quarters as follows:

INTERMEDIATE
(Questions 13–16)

	Q1	Q2	Q3	Q4
Sales	$170	$185	$200	$225

Sales for the first quarter of the following year are projected at $180 million. Accounts receivable at the beginning of the year were $71 million. Wildcat has a 45-day collection period.

Wildcat's purchases from suppliers in a quarter are equal to 45 percent of the next quarter's forecast sales, and suppliers are normally paid in 36 days. Wages, taxes, and other expenses run about 25 percent of sales. Interest and dividends are $14 million per quarter.

Wildcat plans a major capital outlay in the second quarter of $85 million. Finally, the company started the year with a $54 million cash balance and wishes to maintain a $30 million minimum balance.

a. Complete a cash budget for Wildcat by filling in the following:

WILDCAT, INC. Cash Budget (in millions)	Q1	Q2	Q3	Q4
Beginning cash balance	$54			
Net cash inflow				
Ending cash balance				
Minimum cash balance	30			
Cumulative surplus (deficit)				

b. Assume that Wildcat can borrow any needed funds on a short-term basis at a rate of 3 percent per quarter and can invest any excess funds in short-term marketable securities at a rate of 2 percent per quarter. Prepare a short-term financial plan by filling in the following schedule. What is the net cash cost (total interest paid minus total investment income earned) for the year?

WILDCAT, INC. Short-Term Financial Plan (in millions)	Q1	Q2	Q3	Q4
Target cash balance	$30			
Net cash inflow				
New short-term investments				
Income from short-term investments				
Short-term investments sold				
New short-term borrowing				
Interest on short-term borrowing				
Short-term borrowing repaid				
Ending cash balance				
Minimum cash balance				
Cumulative surplus (deficit)				
Beginning short-term investments				
Ending short-term investments				
Beginning short-term debt				
Ending short-term debt				

16. **Cash Management Policy [LO3]** Rework Problem 15 assuming:

a. Wildcat maintains a minimum cash balance of $40 million.

b. Wildcat maintains a minimum cash balance of $20 million.

Based on your answers in (a) and (b), do you think the firm can boost its profit by changing its cash management policy? Are there other factors that must be considered as well? Explain.

17. **Costs of Borrowing [LO3]** In exchange for a $300 million fixed commitment line of credit, your firm has agreed to do the following:

1. Pay 1.85 percent per quarter on any funds actually borrowed.

2. Maintain a 4.5 percent compensating balance on any funds actually borrowed.

3. Pay an up-front commitment fee of .25 percent of the amount of the line.

Based on this information, answer the following:

a. Ignoring the commitment fee, what is the effective annual interest rate on this line of credit?

b. Suppose your firm immediately uses $115 million of the line and pays it off in one year. What is the effective annual interest rate on this $115 million loan?

18. **Costs of Borrowing [LO3]** Cheap Money Bank offers your firm a *discount* interest loan at 8.25 percent for up to $25 million and, in addition, requires you to maintain a 5 percent compensating balance against the amount borrowed. What is the effective annual interest rate on this lending arrangement?

CHALLENGE
(Questions 17–18)

EXCEL MASTER IT! PROBLEMS

Heidi Pedersen, the treasurer for Wood Products, Inc., has just been asked by Justin Wood, the company's president, to prepare a memo detailing the company's ending cash balance for the next three months. Below, you will see the relevant estimates for this period.

	July	August	September
Credit sales	$1,275,800	$1,483,500	$1,096,300
Credit purchases	765,480	890,160	657,780
Cash disbursements			
Wages, taxes, and expenses	348,600	395,620	337,150
Interest	29,900	29,900	29,900
Equipment	0	158,900	96,300
Credit sales collections			
Collected in month of sale	35%		
Collected month after sale	60%		
Never collected	5%		
June credit sales	$1,135,020		
June credit purchases	$ 681,012		
Beginning cash balance	$ 425,000		

All credit purchases are paid in the month after the purchase.

a. Complete the cash budget for Wood Products for the next three months.

b. Heidi knows that the cash budget will become a standard report completed before each quarter. To help reduce the time preparing the report each quarter, she would like a memo with the appropriate information in Excel linked to the memo. Prepare a memo to Justin that will automatically update when the values are changed in Excel.

MINICASE

Piepkorn Manufacturing Working Capital Management

You have recently been hired by Piepkorn Manufacturing to work in the newly established treasury department. Piepkorn Manufacturing is a small company that produces cardboard boxes in a variety of sizes for different purchasers. Gary Piepkorn, the owner of the company, works primarily in the sales and production areas of the company. Currently, the company puts all receivables in one shoe box and all payables in another. Because of the disorganized system, the finance area needs work, and that's what you've been brought in to do.

The company currently has a cash balance of $305,000, and it plans to purchase new box-folding machinery in the fourth quarter at a cost of $525,000. The machinery will be purchased with cash because of a discount offered. The company's policy is to maintain a minimum cash balance of $125,000. All sales and purchases are made on credit.

Gary Piepkorn has projected the following gross sales for each of the next four quarters:

	Q1	Q2	Q3	Q4
Gross sales	$1,310,000	$1,390,000	$1,440,000	$1,530,000

Also, gross sales for the first quarter of the next year are projected at $1,405,000. Piepkorn currently has an accounts receivable period of 53 days and an accounts receivable balance of $645,000. Twenty percent of the accounts receivable balance is from a company that has just entered bankruptcy, and it is likely this portion of the accounts receivable will never be collected.

Piepkorn typically orders 50 percent of next quarter's projected gross sales in the current quarter, and suppliers are typically paid in 42 days. Wages, taxes, and other costs run about 30 percent of gross sales. The company has a quarterly interest payment of $135,000 on its long-term debt.

The company uses a local bank for its short-term financial needs. It pays 1.5 percent per quarter on all short-term

borrowing and maintains a money market account that pays 1 percent per quarter on all short-term deposits.

Gary has asked you to prepare a cash budget and short-term financial plan for the company under the current policies. He has also asked you to prepare additional plans based on changes in several inputs.

QUESTIONS

1. Use the numbers given to complete the cash budget and short-term financial plan.

2. Rework the cash budget and short-term financial plan assuming Piepkorn changes to a minimum balance of $100,000.

3. You have looked at the credit policy offered by Piepkorn's competitors and have determined that the industry standard credit policy is 1/10, net 40.* The discount will begin to be offered on the first day of the first quarter. You want to examine how this credit policy would affect the cash budget and short-term financial plan. If this credit policy is implemented, you believe that 40 percent of all sales will take advantage of it, and the accounts receivable period will decline to 36 days. Rework the cash budget and short-term financial plan under the new credit policy and a minimum cash balance of $100,000. What interest rate are you effectively offering customers?

4. You have talked to the company's suppliers about the credit terms Piepkorn receives. Currently, the company receives terms of net 45. The suppliers have stated that they would offer new credit terms of 1.5/15, net 40. The discount would begin to be offered on the first day of the first quarter. What interest rate are the suppliers offering the company? Rework the cash budget and short-term financial plan assuming you take the credit terms on all orders and the minimum cash balance is $100,000. Also assume that Piepkorn offers the credit terms detailed in Question 3.

PIEPKORN MANUFACTURING Cash Budget				
	Q1	Q2	Q3	Q4
Target cash balance				
Net cash inflow				
Ending cash balance				
Minimum cash balance	——	——	——	——
Cumulative surplus (deficit)				

*If you are not familiar with credit policy quotations, see Chapter 20.

PIEPKORN MANUFACTURING Short-Term Financial Plan				
	Q1	**Q2**	**Q3**	**Q4**
Target cash balance				
Net cash inflow				
New short-term investments				
Income from short-term investments				
Short-term investments sold				
New short-term borrowing				
Interest on short-term borrowing				
Short-term borrowing repaid	____	____	____	____
Ending cash balance				
Minimum cash balance	____	____	____	____
Cumulative surplus (deficit)				
Beginning short-term investments				
Ending short-term investments				
Beginning short-term debt				
Ending short-term debt				

19 | Cash and Liquidity Management

BY ANY MEASURE, THE CASH BALANCE at U.S. corporations is huge. In the middle of 2017, the cash balance at companies in the S&P 500 excluding financials, transportation, and utilities, reached $1.496 trillion, a record level. Tech giants Cisco and Microsoft, for example, held about $70 billion and $132 billion in cash, respectively. In Cisco's case, the cash amounted to just under one-half of the company's total market cap. It's hard to believe, but these numbers might understate things. Apple, for example, reported about $70 billion in cash and short-term investments, but the company chose to stash most of its cash in longer-term investments. How much? About $180 billion, so Apple's total cash hoard was a mind-boggling $250 billion!

Learning Objectives

After studying this chapter, you should be able to:

LO1 Outline the importance of float and how it affects cash balances.

LO2 Explain how firms manage their cash and some of the collection, concentration, and disbursement techniques used.

LO3 Describe the advantages and disadvantages to holding cash and some of the ways to invest idle cash.

For updates on the latest happenings in finance, visit fundamentalsofcorporatefinance.blogspot.com.

This chapter is about how firms manage cash. The basic objective in cash management is to keep the investment in cash as low as possible while still keeping the firm operating efficiently and effectively. This goal usually reduces to the dictum, "Collect early and pay late." Accordingly, we discuss ways of accelerating collections and managing disbursements.

In addition, firms must invest temporarily idle cash in short-term marketable securities. As we discuss in various places, these securities can be bought and sold in the financial markets. As a group, they have very little default risk, and most are highly marketable. There are different types of these so-called money market securities, and in this chapter we discuss a few of the most important ones.

Reasons for Holding Cash   **19.1**

John Maynard Keynes, in his classic work *The General Theory of Employment, Interest, and Money*, identified three motives for liquidity: The speculative motive, the precautionary motive, and the transaction motive. We discuss these next.

THE SPECULATIVE AND PRECAUTIONARY MOTIVES

The **speculative motive** is the need to hold cash in order to be able to take advantage of, for example, bargain purchases that might arise, attractive interest rates, and (in the case of international firms) favorable exchange rate fluctuations.

For most firms, reserve borrowing ability and marketable securities can be used to satisfy speculative motives. Thus, there might be a speculative motive for maintaining liquidity, but not necessarily for holding cash. Think of it this way: If you have a credit card with a very large credit limit, then you can probably take advantage of any unusual bargains that come along without carrying any cash.

This is also true, to a lesser extent, for precautionary motives. The **precautionary motive** is the need for a safety supply to act as a financial reserve. Once again, there probably is a precautionary motive for maintaining liquidity. However, given that the value of money market instruments is relatively certain and that instruments such as T-bills are extremely liquid, there is no real need to hold substantial amounts of cash for precautionary purposes.

> **speculative motive**
> The need to hold cash to take advantage of additional investment opportunities, such as bargain purchases.

> **precautionary motive**
> The need to hold cash as a safety margin to act as a financial reserve.

THE TRANSACTION MOTIVE

Cash is needed to satisfy the **transaction motive**, the need to have cash on hand to pay bills. Transaction-related needs come from the normal disbursement and collection activities of the firm. The disbursement of cash includes the payment of wages and salaries, trade debts, taxes, and dividends.

Cash is collected from product sales, the selling of assets, and new financing. The cash inflows (collections) and outflows (disbursements) are not perfectly synchronized and some level of cash holdings is necessary to serve as a buffer.

As electronic funds transfers and other high-speed, "paperless" payment mechanisms continue to develop, even the transaction demand for cash may all but disappear. Even if it does, there will still be a demand for liquidity and a need to manage it efficiently.

> **transaction motive**
> The need to hold cash to satisfy normal disbursement and collection activities associated with a firm's ongoing operations.

COMPENSATING BALANCES

Compensating balances are another reason to hold cash. As we discussed in the previous chapter, cash balances are kept at commercial banks to compensate for banking services the firm receives. A minimum compensating balance requirement may impose a lower limit on the level of cash a firm holds.

COSTS OF HOLDING CASH

When a firm holds cash in excess of some necessary minimum, it incurs an opportunity cost. The opportunity cost of excess cash (held in currency or bank deposits) is the interest income that could be earned in the next best use, such as an investment in marketable securities.

Given the opportunity cost of holding cash, why would a firm hold cash in excess of its compensating balance requirements? The answer is that a cash balance must be maintained to provide the liquidity necessary for transaction needs—paying bills. If the firm maintains too small a cash balance, it may run out of cash. If this happens, the firm may have to raise cash on a short-term basis. This could involve, for example, selling marketable securities or borrowing.

Activities such as selling marketable securities and borrowing involve various costs. As we've discussed, holding cash has an opportunity cost. To determine the appropriate cash balance, the firm must weigh the benefits of holding cash against these costs. We discuss this subject in more detail in the sections that follow.

CASH MANAGEMENT VERSUS LIQUIDITY MANAGEMENT

Before we move on, we should note that it is important to distinguish between true cash management and a more general subject, liquidity management. The distinction is a source of confusion because the word *cash* is used in practice in two different ways. First of all, it has its literal meaning: Actual cash on hand. However, financial managers frequently use the word in another way to describe a firm's holdings of cash along with its marketable securities, and marketable securities are sometimes called *cash equivalents* or *near-cash*. In our discussion of Cisco's and Microsoft's cash positions at the beginning of the chapter, for example, what we were actually describing was their total cash and cash equivalents.

The distinction between liquidity management and cash management is straightforward. Liquidity management concerns the optimal quantity of liquid assets a firm should have on hand, and it is one particular aspect of the current asset management policies we discussed in our previous chapter. Cash management is much more closely related to optimizing mechanisms for collecting and disbursing cash, and it is this subject that we primarily focus on in this chapter.

Concept Questions

19.1a   What is the transaction motive, and how does it lead firms to hold cash?
19.1b   What is the cost to the firm of holding excess cash?

19.2 Understanding Float

As you no doubt know, the amount of money you have according to your checkbook can be very different from the amount of money that your bank thinks you have. The reason is that some of the checks you have written haven't yet been presented to the bank for payment. The same thing is true for a business. The cash balance that a firm shows on its books is called the firm's *book*, or *ledger*, *balance*. The balance shown in its bank account as available to spend is called its *available*, or *collected*, *balance*. The difference between the available balance and the ledger balance, called the **float**, represents the net effect of checks in the process of *clearing* (moving through the banking system).

float
The difference between book cash and bank cash, representing the net effect of checks in the process of clearing.

DISBURSEMENT FLOAT

Checks written by a firm generate *disbursement float*, causing a decrease in the firm's book balance but no change in its available balance. For example, suppose General Mechanics, Inc. (GMI), currently has $100,000 on deposit with its bank. On June 8, it buys some raw materials and pays with a check for $100,000. The company's book balance is immediately reduced by $100,000 as a result.

GMI's bank will not find out about this check until it is presented to GMI's bank for payment on, say, June 14. Until the check is presented, the firm's available balance is greater than its book balance by $100,000. In other words, before June 8, GMI has a zero float:

$$\text{Float} = \text{Firm's available balance} - \text{Firm's book balance}$$
$$= \$100,000 - 100,000$$
$$= \$0$$

GMI's position from June 8 to June 14 is:

$$\text{Disbursement float} = \text{Firm's available balance} - \text{Firm's book balance}$$
$$= \$100,000 - 0$$
$$= \$100,000$$

While the check is clearing, GMI has a balance with the bank of $100,000. It can obtain the benefit of this cash during this period. For example, the available balance could be temporarily invested in marketable securities and earn some interest. We will return to this subject a little later.

COLLECTION FLOAT AND NET FLOAT

Checks received by the firm create *collection float*. Collection float increases book balances but does not immediately change available balances. Suppose GMI receives a check from a customer for $100,000 on October 8. Assume, as before, that the company has $100,000 deposited at its bank and a zero float. It deposits the check and increases its book balance by $100,000 to $200,000. However, the additional cash is not available to GMI until its bank has presented the check to the customer's bank and received $100,000. This will occur on, say, October 14. In the meantime, the cash position at GMI will reflect a collection float of $100,000. We can summarize these events. Before October 8, GMI's position is:

$$\text{Float} = \text{Firm's available balance} - \text{Firm's book balance}$$
$$= \$100,000 - 100,000$$
$$= \$0$$

GMI's position from October 8 to October 14 is:

$$\text{Collection float} = \text{Firm's available balance} - \text{Firm's book balance}$$
$$= \$100,000 - 200,000$$
$$= -\$100,000$$

In general, a firm's payment (disbursement) activities generate disbursement float, and its collection activities generate collection float. The net effect—that is, the sum of the total collection and disbursement floats—is the net float. The net float at a point in time is the overall difference between the firm's available balance and its book balance. If the net float is positive, then the firm's disbursement float exceeds its collection float, and its available balance exceeds its book balance. If the available balance is less than the book balance, then the firm has a net collection float.

A firm should be concerned with its net float and available balance more than with its book balance. If a financial manager knows that a check written by the company will not clear for several days, that manager will be able to keep a lower cash balance at the bank than might be possible otherwise. This can generate a great deal of money.

For example, take the case of Walmart. The average daily sales of Walmart are about $1.32 billion. If Walmart's collections could be sped up by a single day, then the company could free up $1.32 billion for investing. At a relatively modest .01 percent daily rate, the interest earned would be on the order of $132,000 *per day*.

EXAMPLE 19.1	**Staying Afloat**

Suppose you have $5,000 on deposit. One day, you write a check for $1,000 to pay for books, and you deposit $2,000. What are your disbursement, collection, and net floats?

After you write the $1,000 check, you show a balance of $4,000 on your books, but the bank shows $5,000 while the check is clearing. The difference is a disbursement float of $1,000.

After you deposit the $2,000 check, you show a balance of $6,000. Your available balance doesn't rise until the check clears. This results in a collection float of −$2,000. Your net float is the sum of the collection and disbursement floats, or −$1,000.

Overall, you show $6,000 on your books. The bank shows a $7,000 balance, but only $5,000 is available because your deposit has not been cleared. The discrepancy between your available balance and your book balance is the net float (−$1,000), and it is bad for you. If you write another check for $5,500, there may not be sufficient available funds to cover it, and it might bounce. This is why financial managers have to be more concerned with available balances than book balances.

FLOAT MANAGEMENT

For a real-world example of float management services, visit **www.carreker.fiserv.com**.

Float management involves controlling the collection and disbursement of cash. The objective in cash collection is to speed up collections and reduce the lag between the time customers pay their bills and the time the cash becomes available. The objective in cash disbursement is to control payments and minimize the firm's costs associated with making payments.

Total collection or disbursement times can be broken down into three parts: Mailing time, processing delay, and availability delay:

1. *Mailing time* is the part of the collection and disbursement process during which checks are trapped in the postal system.
2. *Processing delay* is the time it takes the receiver of a check to process the payment and deposit it in a bank for collection.
3. *Availability delay* refers to the time required to clear a check through the banking system.

Speeding up collections involves reducing one or more of these components. Slowing disbursements involves increasing one of them. We will describe some procedures for managing collection and disbursement times later. First, we need to discuss how float is measured.

Measuring Float   The size of the float depends on both the dollars and the time delay involved. Suppose you mail a check for $500 to another state each month. It takes five days in the mail for the check to reach its destination (the mailing time) and one day for the recipient to get over to the bank (the processing delay). The recipient's bank holds out-of-state checks for three days (availability delay). The total delay is $5 + 1 + 3 = 9$ days.

In this case, what is your average daily disbursement float? There are two equivalent ways of calculating the answer. First, you have a $500 float for nine days, so we say that the total float is $9 \times \$500 = \$4,500$. Assuming 30 days in the month, the average daily float is $\$4,500/30 = \$150$.

Alternatively, your disbursement float is $500 for 9 days out of the month and zero the other 21 days (again assuming 30 days in a month). Your average daily float is:

$$\text{Average daily float} = (9 \times \$500 + 21 \times 0)/30$$
$$= 9/30 \times \$500 + 21/30 \times 0$$
$$= \$4,500/30$$
$$= \$150$$

This means that, on an average day, your book balance is $150 less than your available balance, representing a $150 average disbursement float.

Things are only a little more complicated when there are multiple disbursements or receipts. To illustrate, suppose Concepts, Inc., receives two items each month as follows:

Amount	Processing and availability delay	Total float
Item 1: $5,000,000	× 9	= $45,000,000
Item 2: $3,000,000	× 5	= $15,000,000
Total $8,000,000		$60,000,000

The average daily float is equal to:

Average daily float $= \dfrac{\textbf{Total float}}{\textbf{Total days}}$ **19.1**

$$= \frac{\$60 \text{ million}}{30} = \$2 \text{ million}$$

So, on an average day, there is $2 million that is uncollected and unavailable.

Another way to see this is to calculate the average daily receipts and multiply by the weighted average delay. Average daily receipts are:

$$\text{Average daily receipts} = \frac{\text{Total receipts}}{\text{Total days}} = \frac{\$8 \text{ million}}{30} = \$266,666.67$$

Of the $8 million total receipts, $5 million, or ⅝ of the total, is delayed for nine days. The other ⅜ is delayed for five days. The weighted average delay is thus:

$$\text{Weighted average delay} = (5/8) \times 9 \text{ days} + (3/8) \times 5 \text{ days}$$
$$= 5.625 \text{ days} + 1.875 \text{ days} = 7.50 \text{ days}$$

The average daily float is:

Average daily float = Average daily receipts × Weighted average delay   **19.2**

$$= \$266,666.67 \times 7.50 \text{ days} = \$2 \text{ million}$$

Some Details   In measuring float, there is an important difference to note between collection and disbursement float. We defined *float* as the difference between the firm's available cash balance and its book balance. With a disbursement, the firm's book balance goes down when the check is *mailed*, so the mailing time is an important component in disbursement float. With a collection, the firm's book balance isn't increased until the check is *received*, so mailing time is not a component of collection float.

This doesn't mean that mailing time is not important. The point is that when collection *float* is calculated, mailing time should not be considered. As we will discuss, when total collection *time* is considered, the mailing time is a crucial component.

Also, when we talk about availability delay, how long it actually takes a check to clear isn't really crucial. What matters is how long we must wait before the bank grants availability—that is, use of the funds. Banks actually use availability schedules to determine how long a check is held based on time of deposit and other factors. Beyond this, availability delay can be a matter of negotiation between the bank and a customer. In a similar vein, for outgoing checks, what matters is the date our account is debited, not when the recipient is granted availability.

Cost of the Float   The basic cost of collection float to the firm is the opportunity cost of not being able to use the cash. At a minimum, the firm could earn interest on the cash if it were available for investing.

FIGURE 19.1
Buildup of the Float

	Day 1	Day 2	Day 3	Day 4	Day 5	
Beginning float	$ 0	$1,000	$2,000	$3,000	$3,000	. . .
Checks received	1,000	1,000	1,000	1,000	1,000	. . .
Checks cleared (cash available)	− 0	− 0	− 0	− 1,000	− 1,000	. . .
Ending float	$1,000	$2,000	$3,000	$3,000	$3,000	. . .

FIGURE 19.2
Effect of Eliminating the Float

	Day *t*	Day *t* + 1	Day *t* + 2	
Beginning float	$3,000	$ 0	$ 0	. . .
Checks received	1,000	1,000	1,000	. . .
Checks cleared (cash available)	− 4,000	− 1,000	− 1,000	. . .
Ending float	$ 0	$ 0	$ 0	. . .

Suppose the Lambo Corporation has average daily receipts of $1,000 and a weighted average delay of three days. The average daily float is 3 × $1,000 = $3,000. This means that, on a typical day, there is $3,000 that is not earning interest. Suppose Lambo could eliminate the float entirely. What would be the benefit? If it costs $2,000 to eliminate the float, what is the NPV of doing so?

Figure 19.1 illustrates the situation for Lambo. Suppose Lambo starts with a zero float. On a given day, Day 1, Lambo receives and deposits a check for $1,000. The cash will become available three days later on Day 4. At the end of the day on Day 1, the book balance is $1,000 more than the available balance, so the float is $1,000. On Day 2, the firm receives and deposits another check. It will collect this check (i.e., the cash will become available) three days later on Day 5. At the end of Day 2, there are two uncollected checks, and the books show a $2,000 balance. The bank still shows a zero available balance; so the float is $2,000. The same sequence occurs on Day 3, and the float rises to a total of $3,000.

On Day 4, Lambo again receives and deposits a check for $1,000. It also collects $1,000 from the Day 1 check. The change in book balance and the change in available balance are identical, +$1,000; so the float stays at $3,000. The same thing happens every day after Day 4; the float therefore stays at $3,000 forever.[1]

Figure 19.2 illustrates what happens if the float is eliminated entirely on some Day *t* in the future. After the float is eliminated, daily receipts are still $1,000. The firm collects the same day because the float is eliminated, so daily collections are also still $1,000. As Figure 19.2 illustrates, the only change occurs the first day. On that day, as usual, Lambo collects $1,000 from the sale made three days before. Because the float is gone, it also collects on the sales made two days before, one day before, and that same day, for an additional $3,000. Total collections on Day *t* are $4,000 instead of $1,000.

What we see is that Lambo generates an extra $3,000 on Day *t* by eliminating the float. On every subsequent day, Lambo receives $1,000 in cash just as it did before the float was eliminated. Thus, the only change in the firm's cash flows from eliminating the float is

[1]This permanent float is sometimes called the *steady-state float*.

this extra $3,000 that comes in immediately. No other cash flows are affected, so Lambo is $3,000 richer.

In other words, the PV of eliminating the float is equal to the total float. Lambo could pay this amount out as a dividend, invest it in interest-bearing assets, or do anything else with it. If it costs $2,000 to eliminate the float, then the NPV is $3,000 − 2,000 = $1,000; so Lambo should do it.

Reducing the Float: Part I	EXAMPLE 19.2

Instead of eliminating the float, suppose Lambo can reduce it to one day. What is the maximum Lambo should be willing to pay for this?

If Lambo can reduce the float from three days to one day, then the amount of the float will fall from $3,000 to $1,000. From our discussion immediately preceding, we see right away that the PV of doing this is just equal to the $2,000 float reduction. Lambo should be willing to pay up to $2,000.

Reducing the Float: Part II	EXAMPLE 19.3

Look back at Example 19.2. A large bank is willing to provide the float reduction service for $175 per year, payable at the end of each year. The relevant discount rate is 8 percent. Should Lambo hire the bank? What is the NPV of the investment? How do you interpret this discount rate? What is the most per year that Lambo should be willing to pay?

The PV to Lambo is still $2,000. The $175 would have to be paid out every year forever to maintain the float reduction; so the cost is perpetual, and its PV is $175/.08 = $2,187.50. The NPV is $2,000 − 2,187.50 = −$187.50; therefore, the service is not a good deal.

Ignoring the possibility of bounced checks, the discount rate here corresponds most closely to the cost of short-term borrowing. The reason is that Lambo could borrow $1,000 from the bank every time a check was deposited and pay it back three days later. The cost would be the interest that Lambo would have to pay.

The most Lambo would be willing to pay is whatever charge results in an NPV of zero. This zero NPV occurs when the $2,000 benefit exactly equals the PV of the costs—that is, when $2,000 = C/.08, where C is the annual cost. Solving for C, we find that C = .08 × $2,000 = $160 per year.

Ethical and Legal Questions   The cash manager must work with collected bank cash balances and not the firm's book balance (which reflects checks that have been deposited but not collected). If this is not done, a cash manager could be drawing on uncollected cash as a source of funds for short-term investing. Most banks charge a penalty rate for the use of uncollected funds. However, banks may not have good enough accounting and control procedures to be fully aware of the use of uncollected funds. This raises some ethical and legal questions for the firm.

For example, in May 1985, E.F. Hutton (a large investment bank) pleaded guilty to 2,000 charges of mail and wire fraud in connection with a scheme the firm had operated from 1980 to 1982. E.F. Hutton employees had written checks totaling hundreds of millions of dollars against uncollected cash. The proceeds had then been invested in short-term money market assets. This type of systematic overdrafting of accounts (or check *kiting*, as it is sometimes called) is neither legal nor ethical and is apparently not a widespread practice among corporations. Also, the particular inefficiencies in the banking system that Hutton was exploiting have been largely eliminated.

For its part, E.F. Hutton paid a $2 million fine, reimbursed the government (the U.S. Department of Justice) $750,000, and reserved an additional $8 million for restitution to defrauded banks. We should note that the key issue in the case against Hutton was not its float management per se, but, rather, its practice of writing checks for no economic reason other than to exploit float.

Despite stiff penalties for check kiting, the practice apparently continues. For example, in August 2016, a Michigan woman admitted to a check kiting scheme involving more than $145 million in checks. This fraud cost one financial institution more than $1.8 million.

ELECTRONIC DATA INTERCHANGE AND CHECK 21: THE END OF FLOAT?

Electronic data interchange (EDI) is a general term that refers to the growing practice of direct, electronic information exchange between all types of businesses. One important use of EDI, often called *financial EDI* or *FEDI*, is to electronically transfer financial information and funds between parties, thereby eliminating paper invoices, paper checks, mailing, and handling. It is now possible to arrange to have your checking account directly debited each month to pay many types of bills, and corporations now routinely directly deposit paychecks into employee accounts. More generally, EDI allows a seller to send a bill electronically to a buyer, thereby avoiding the mail. The buyer can then authorize payment, which also occurs electronically. Its bank then transfers the funds to the seller's account at a different bank. The net effect is that the length of time required to initiate and complete a business transaction is shortened considerably, and much of what we normally think of as float is sharply reduced or eliminated. As the use of FEDI increases (which it will), float management will evolve to focus much more on issues surrounding computerized information exchange and funds transfers.

One of the drawbacks of EDI (and FEDI) is that it is expensive and complex to set up. With the growth of the Internet, a new form of EDI has emerged: Internet e-commerce. For example, networking giant Cisco Systems books millions in orders each day on its website from resellers around the world. Firms are also linking to critical suppliers and customers via "extranets," which are business networks that extend a company's internal network. Because of security concerns and lack of standardization, don't look for e-commerce and extranets to eliminate the need for EDI anytime soon. In fact, these are complementary systems that will most likely be used in tandem as the future unfolds.

On October 29, 2004, the Check Clearing Act for the 21st Century, also known as Check 21, took effect. Before Check 21, a bank receiving a check was required to send the physical check to the customer's bank before payment could be made. Now a bank can transmit an electronic image of the check to the customer's bank and receive payment immediately. Previously, an out-of-state check might take three days to clear. But with Check 21, the clearing time is typically one day; and often a check can clear the same day it is written. Check 21 has significantly reduced float.

Concept Questions

19.2a   Which would a firm be most interested in reducing, collection or disbursement float? Why?

19.2b   How is daily average float calculated?

19.2c   What is the benefit from reducing or eliminating float?

Cash Collection and Concentration   19.3

From our previous discussion, we know that collection delays work against the firm. All other things being the same, a firm will adopt procedures to speed up collections and thereby decrease collection times. In addition, even after cash is collected, firms need procedures to funnel, or concentrate, that cash where it can be best used. We discuss some common collection and concentration procedures next.

COMPONENTS OF COLLECTION TIME

Based on our previous discussion, we can depict the basic parts of the cash collection process as follows. The total time in this process is made up of mailing time, check-processing delay, and the bank's availability delay.

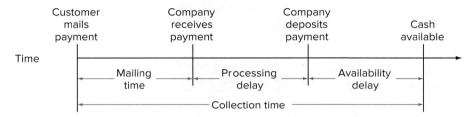

The amount of time that cash spends in each part of the cash collection process depends on where the firm's customers and banks are located and how efficient the firm is in collecting cash.

CASH COLLECTION

How a firm collects from its customers depends in large part on the nature of the business. The simplest case would be a business such as a restaurant chain. Most of its customers will pay with cash, check, or credit card at the point of sale (this is called *over-the-counter collection*), so there is no problem with mailing delay. Normally, the funds will be deposited in a local bank, and the firm will have some means (discussed later) of gaining access to the funds.

When some or all of the payments a company receives are checks that arrive through the mail, all three components of collection time become relevant. The firm may choose to have all the checks mailed to one location; more commonly, the firm might have a number of different mail collection points to reduce mailing times. Also, the firm may run its collection operation itself or might hire an outside firm that specializes in cash collection. We discuss these issues in more detail in the following sections.

Other approaches to cash collection exist. One that is becoming more common is the preauthorized payment arrangement. With this arrangement, the payment amounts and payment dates are fixed in advance. When the agreed-upon date arrives, the amount is automatically transferred from the customer's bank account to the firm's bank account, which sharply reduces or even eliminates collection delays. The same approach is used by firms that have online terminals, meaning that when a sale is rung up, the money is immediately transferred to the firm's accounts.

LOCKBOXES

When a firm receives its payments by mail, it must decide where the checks will be mailed and how the checks will be picked up and deposited. Careful selection of the number and

FIGURE 19.3

Overview of Lockbox Processing

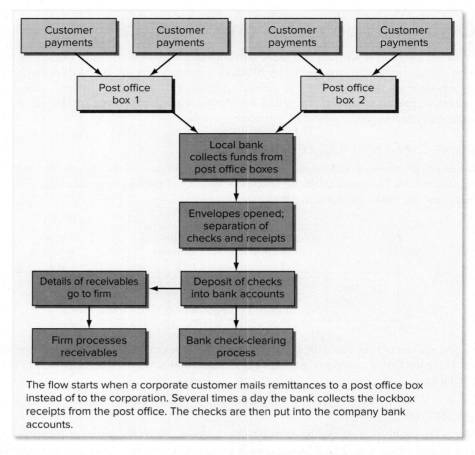

The flow starts when a corporate customer mails remittances to a post office box instead of to the corporation. Several times a day the bank collects the lockbox receipts from the post office. The checks are then put into the company bank accounts.

lockboxes

Special post office boxes set up to intercept and speed up accounts receivable payments.

locations of collection points can greatly reduce collection times. Many firms use special post office boxes called **lockboxes** to intercept payments and speed cash collection.

Figure 19.3 illustrates a lockbox system. The collection process is started by customers mailing their checks to a post office box instead of sending them to the firm. The lockbox is maintained by a local bank. A large corporation may actually maintain more than 20 lockboxes around the country.

In the typical lockbox system, the local bank collects the lockbox checks several times a day. The bank deposits the checks directly into the firm's account. Details of the operation are recorded (in some computer-usable form) and sent to the firm.

A lockbox system reduces mailing time because checks are received at a nearby post office instead of at corporate headquarters. Lockboxes also reduce the processing time because the corporation doesn't have to open the envelopes and deposit checks for collection. In all, a bank lockbox system should enable a firm to get its receipts processed, deposited, and cleared faster than if it were to receive checks at its headquarters and deliver them itself to the bank for deposit and clearing.

Some firms have turned to what are called "electronic lockboxes" as an alternative to traditional lockboxes. In one version of an electronic lockbox, customers use the telephone or the Internet to access their account—say, their credit card account at a bank—review their bill, and authorize payment without paper ever having changed hands on either end of the transaction. Clearly, an electronic lockbox system is far superior to traditional bill payment methods, at least from the biller's perspective. Look for systems like this to continue to grow in popularity.

CASH CONCENTRATION

As we discussed earlier, a firm will typically have a number of cash collection points; as a result, cash collections may end up in many different banks and bank accounts. From here, the firm needs procedures to move the cash into its main accounts. This is called **cash concentration**. By routinely pooling its cash, the firm greatly simplifies its cash management by reducing the number of accounts that must be tracked. Also, by having a larger pool of funds available, a firm may be able to negotiate or otherwise obtain a better rate on any short-term investments.

In setting up a concentration system, firms will typically use one or more *concentration banks*. A concentration bank pools the funds obtained from local banks contained within some geographic region. Concentration systems are often used in conjunction with lockbox systems. Figure 19.4 illustrates how an integrated cash collection and cash concentration system might look. As Figure 19.4 illustrates, a key part of the cash collection and concentration process is the transfer of funds to the concentration bank. There are several options available for accomplishing this transfer. The cheapest is a *depository transfer check* (DTC), which is a preprinted check that usually needs no signature and is valid only for transferring funds between specific accounts within the *same* firm. The money becomes available one to two days later. *Automated clearinghouse* (ACH) transfers are basically electronic versions of paper checks. These may be more expensive, depending on the circumstances, but the funds are available the next day. The most expensive means

cash concentration
The practice of and procedures for moving cash from multiple banks into the firm's main accounts.

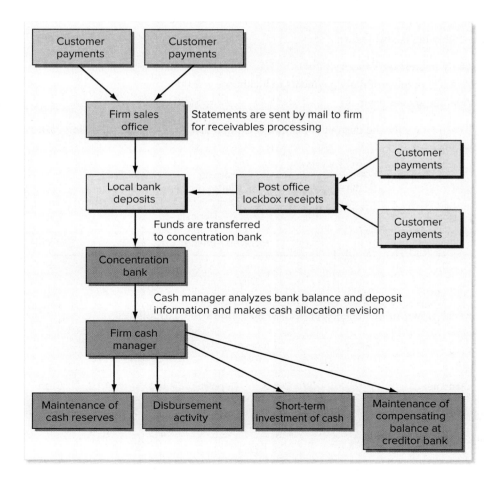

FIGURE 19.4

Lockboxes and Concentration Banks in a Cash Management System

For current info about cash management—especially for international issues—visit Global Treasury News at **www.gtnews.com**.

of transfer are *wire transfers*, which provide same-day availability. Which approach a firm will choose depends on the number and size of payments. A typical ACH transfer might be $200, whereas a typical wire transfer would be several million dollars. Firms with a large number of collection points and relatively small payments will choose the cheaper route, whereas firms that receive smaller numbers of relatively large payments may choose more expensive procedures.

ACCELERATING COLLECTIONS: AN EXAMPLE

The decision of whether or not to use a bank cash management service incorporating lockboxes and concentration banks depends on where a firm's customers are located and the speed of the U.S. postal system. Suppose Atlantic Corporation, located in Philadelphia, is considering a lockbox system. Its collection delay is currently eight days.

Atlantic does business in the southwestern part of the country (New Mexico, Arizona, and California). The proposed lockbox system would be located in Los Angeles and operated by Pacific Bank. Pacific Bank has analyzed Atlantic's cash-gathering system and has concluded that it can decrease collection time by two days. Specifically, the bank has come up with the following information on the proposed lockbox system:

Reduction in mailing time	= 1.0 day
Reduction in clearing time	= .5 day
Reduction in firm processing time	= .5 day
Total	= 2.0 days

The following is also known:

Daily interest on Treasury bills	= .025%
Average number of daily payments to lockboxes	= 2,000
Average size of payment	= $600

The cash flows for the current collection operation are shown in the following cash flow time chart:

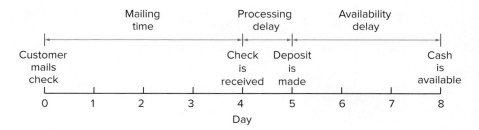

The cash flows for the lockbox collection operation will be as follows:

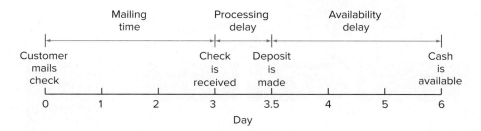

Pacific Bank has agreed to operate this lockbox system for a fee of 25 cents per check processed. Should Atlantic give the go-ahead?

We first need to determine the benefit of the system. The average daily collections from the southwestern region are $1.2 million (= 2,000 × $600). The collection time will be decreased by two days, so the lockbox system will increase the collected bank balance by $1.2 million × 2 = $2.4 million. In other words, the lockbox system releases $2.4 million to the firm by reducing processing, mailing, and clearing time by two days. From our earlier discussion, we know that this $2.4 million is the PV of the proposal.

To calculate the NPV, we need to determine the PV of the costs. There are several different ways to proceed. First, at 2,000 checks per day and $.25 per check, the daily cost is $500. This cost will be incurred every day forever. At an interest rate of .025 percent per day, the PV is therefore $500/.00025 = $2 million. The NPV is $2.4 million − 2 million = $400,000, and the system appears to be desirable.

Alternatively, Atlantic could invest the $2.4 million at .025 percent per day. The interest earned would be $2.4 million × .00025 = $600 per day. The cost of the system is $500 per day; so, running it obviously generates a profit in the amount of $100 per day. The PV of $100 per day forever is $100/.00025 = $400,000, just as we had before.

Finally, each check is for $600 and is available two days sooner if the system is used. The interest on $600 for two days is 2 × $600 × .00025 = $.30. The cost is 25 cents per check, so Atlantic makes a nickel (= $.30 − .25) on every check. With 2,000 checks per day, the profit is $.05 × 2,000 checks = $100 per day, as we calculated.

Accelerating Collections   EXAMPLE 19.4

In our example concerning Atlantic Corporation's proposed lockbox system, suppose Pacific Bank wants a $20,000 fixed fee (paid annually) in addition to the 25 cents per check. Is the system still a good idea?

To answer, we need to calculate the PV of the fixed fee. The daily interest rate is .025 percent. The annual rate is therefore $1.00025^{365} − 1 = .09553$, or 9.553%. The PV of the fixed fee (which is paid each year forever) is $20,000/.09553 = $209,358. Because the NPV without the fee is $400,000, the NPV with the fee is $400,000 − 209,358 = $190,642. It's still a good idea.

Concept Questions

19.3a   What is a lockbox? What purpose does it serve?

19.3b   What is a concentration bank? What purpose does it serve?

Managing Cash Disbursements   19.4

From the firm's point of view, disbursement float is desirable, so the goal in managing disbursement float is to slow down disbursements. To do this, the firm may develop strategies to *increase* mail float, processing float, and availability float on the checks it writes. Beyond this, firms have developed procedures for minimizing cash held for payment purposes. We discuss the most common of these in this section.

INCREASING DISBURSEMENT FLOAT

As we have seen, slowing down payments comes from the time involved in mail delivery, check processing, and collection of funds. Disbursement float can be increased by writing

For a free cash budgeting spreadsheet, go to **finance.toolkit.com.**

a check on a geographically distant bank. For example, a New York supplier might be paid with checks drawn on a Los Angeles bank. This will increase the time required for the checks to clear through the banking system. Mailing checks from remote post offices is another way firms slow down disbursement.

Tactics for maximizing disbursement float are debatable on both ethical and economic grounds. First, as we discuss in some detail in the next chapter, payment terms frequently offer a substantial discount for early payment. The discount is usually much larger than any possible savings from "playing the float game." In such cases, increasing mailing time will be of no benefit if the recipient dates payments based on the date received (as is common) as opposed to the postmark date.

Beyond this, suppliers are not likely to be fooled by attempts to slow down disbursements. The negative consequences of poor relations with suppliers can be costly. In broader terms, intentionally delaying payments by taking advantage of mailing times or unsophisticated suppliers may amount to avoiding paying bills when they are due—an unethical business procedure.

CONTROLLING DISBURSEMENTS

We have seen that maximizing disbursement float is probably poor business practice. However, a firm will still wish to tie up as little cash as possible in disbursements. Firms have therefore developed systems for efficiently managing the disbursement process. The general idea in such systems is to have no more than the minimum amount necessary to pay bills on deposit in the bank. We discuss some approaches to accomplishing this goal next.

zero-balance account
A disbursement account in which the firm maintains a zero balance, transferring funds in from a master account only as needed to cover checks presented for payment.

Zero-Balance Accounts   With a **zero-balance account** system, the firm, in cooperation with its bank, maintains a master account and a set of subaccounts. When a check written on one of the subaccounts must be paid, the necessary funds are transferred in from the master account. Figure 19.5 illustrates how such a system might work. In this case, the firm maintains two disbursement accounts, one for suppliers and one for payroll. As shown, if the firm does not use zero-balance accounts, then each of these accounts must have a safety stock of cash to meet unanticipated demands. If the firm does use zero-balance accounts, then it can keep one safety stock in a master account and transfer the funds to the two subsidiary accounts as needed. The key is that the total amount of cash held as a buffer is smaller under the zero-balance arrangement, which frees up cash to be used elsewhere.

FIGURE 19.5   Zero-Balance Accounts

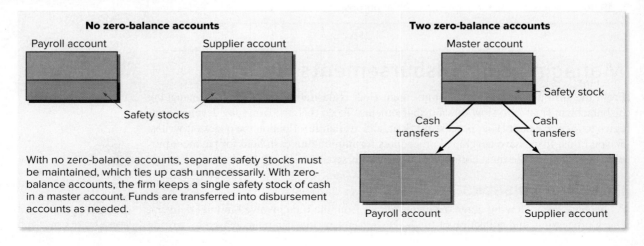

No zero-balance accounts

Payroll account

Supplier account

Safety stocks

Two zero-balance accounts

Master account

Safety stock

Cash transfers

Cash transfers

Payroll account

Supplier account

With no zero-balance accounts, separate safety stocks must be maintained, which ties up cash unnecessarily. With zero-balance accounts, the firm keeps a single safety stock of cash in a master account. Funds are transferred into disbursement accounts as needed.

Controlled Disbursement Accounts   With a **controlled disbursement account** system, almost all payments that must be made in a given day are known in the morning. The bank informs the firm of the total, and the firm transfers (usually by wire) the amount needed.

> **controlled disbursement account**
> A disbursement account to which the firm transfers an amount that is sufficient to cover demands for payment.

Concept Questions

19.4a   Is maximizing disbursement float a sound business practice?

19.4b   What is a zero-balance account? What is the advantage of such an account?

Investing Idle Cash
19.5

If a firm has a temporary cash surplus, it can invest in short-term securities. As we have mentioned at various times, the market for short-term financial assets is called the *money market*. The maturity of short-term financial assets that trade in the money market is one year or less.

Most large firms manage their own short-term financial assets, carrying out transactions through banks and dealers. Some large firms and many small firms use money market mutual funds. These are funds that invest in short-term financial assets for a management fee. The management fee is compensation for the professional expertise and diversification provided by the fund manager.

Among the many money market mutual funds, some specialize in corporate customers. In addition, banks offer arrangements in which the bank takes all excess available funds at the close of each business day and invests them for the firm.

TEMPORARY CASH SURPLUSES

Firms have temporary cash surpluses for various reasons. Two of the most important are the financing of seasonal or cyclical activities of the firm and the financing of planned or possible expenditures.

Seasonal or Cyclical Activities   Some firms have a predictable cash flow pattern. They have surplus cash flows during part of the year and deficit cash flows the rest of the year. For example, Toys "R" Us, a retail toy firm, has a seasonal cash flow pattern influenced by the holiday season.

A firm such as Toys "R" Us may buy marketable securities when surplus cash flows occur and sell marketable securities when deficits occur. Of course, bank loans are another short-term financing device. The use of bank loans and marketable securities to meet temporary financing needs is illustrated in Figure 19.6. In this case, the firm is following a compromise working capital policy in the sense we discussed in the previous chapter.

Planned or Possible Expenditures   Firms frequently accumulate temporary investments in marketable securities to provide the cash for a plant construction program, dividend payment, or other large expenditure. Thus, firms may issue bonds and stocks before the cash is needed, investing the proceeds in short-term marketable securities and then selling the securities to finance the expenditures. Also, firms may face the possibility of having to make a large cash outlay. An obvious example would involve the possibility of losing a large lawsuit. Firms may build up cash surpluses against such a contingency.

FIGURE 19.6

Seasonal Cash Demands

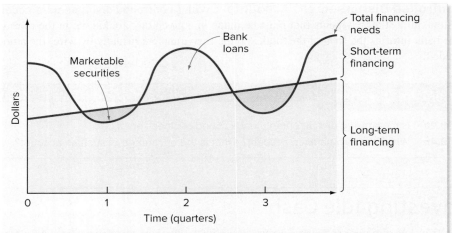

Time 1: A surplus cash flow exists. Seasonal demand for assets is low. The surplus cash flow is invested in short-term marketable securities.

Time 2: A deficit cash flow exists. Seasonal demand for assets is high. The financial deficit is financed by selling marketable securities and by bank borrowing.

CHARACTERISTICS OF SHORT-TERM SECURITIES

Given that a firm has some temporarily idle cash, a variety of short-term securities are available for investing. The most important characteristics of these short-term marketable securities are their maturity, default risk, marketability, and taxability.

Maturity   From Chapter 7, we know that for a given change in the level of interest rates, the prices of longer-maturity securities will change more than those of shorter-maturity securities. As a consequence, firms that invest in long-term securities are accepting greater risk than firms that invest in securities with short-term maturities.

We called this type of risk *interest rate risk*. Firms often limit their investments in marketable securities to those maturing in less than 90 days to avoid the risk of losses in value from changing interest rates. Of course, the expected return on securities with short-term maturities is usually less than the expected return on securities with longer maturities.

Default Risk   *Default risk* refers to the probability that interest and principal will not be paid in the promised amounts on the due dates (or will not be paid at all). In Chapter 7, we observed that various financial reporting agencies, such as Moody's Investors Service and Standard and Poor's, compile and publish ratings of various corporate and other publicly held securities. These ratings are connected to default risk. Of course, some securities have negligible default risk, such as U.S. Treasury bills. Given the purposes of investing idle corporate cash, firms typically avoid investing in marketable securities with significant default risk.

Marketability   *Marketability* refers to how easy it is to convert an asset to cash; so marketability and liquidity mean much the same thing. Some money market instruments are much more marketable than others. At the top of the list are U.S. Treasury bills, which can be bought and sold very cheaply and very quickly.

Taxes   Interest earned on money market securities that are not some kind of government obligation (either federal or state) is taxable at the local, state, and federal levels. U.S. Treasury obligations such as T-bills are exempt from state taxation, but other government-backed debt is not. Municipal securities are exempt from federal taxes, but they may be taxed at the state level.

SOME DIFFERENT TYPES OF MONEY MARKET SECURITIES

Money market securities are generally highly marketable and short-term. They usually have low risk of default. They are issued by the U.S. government (for example, U.S. Treasury bills), domestic and foreign banks (for example, certificates of deposit), and business corporations (for example, commercial paper). There are many types in all, and we illustrate only a few of the most common here.

U.S. Treasury bills are obligations of the U.S. government that mature in 30, 90, or 180 days. Bills are sold by auction every week.

Short-term tax-exempts are short-term securities issued by states, municipalities, local housing agencies, and urban renewal agencies. Because these are all considered municipal securities, they are exempt from federal taxes. RANs, BANs, and TANs are revenue, bond, and tax anticipation notes, respectively. In other words, they represent short-term borrowing by municipalities in anticipation of cash receipts.

Short-term tax-exempts have more default risk than U.S. Treasury issues and are less marketable. Because the interest is exempt from federal income tax, the pretax yield on tax-exempts is lower than that on comparable securities such as Treasury bills. Also, corporations face restrictions on holding tax-exempts as investments.

Commercial paper consists of short-term securities issued by finance companies, banks, and corporations. Typically, commercial paper is unsecured. Maturities range from a few weeks to 270 days.

There is no especially active secondary market in commercial paper. As a consequence, the marketability can be low; however, firms that issue commercial paper will often repurchase it directly before maturity. The default risk of commercial paper depends on the financial strength of the issuer. Moody's and S&P publish quality ratings for commercial paper. These ratings are similar to the bond ratings we discussed in Chapter 7.

Check out short-term rates online at **www.bloomberg.com.**

Certificates of deposit (CDs) are short-term loans to commercial banks. The most common are jumbo CDs—those in excess of $100,000. There are active markets in CDs of 3-month, 6-month, 9-month, and 12-month maturities.

Repurchase agreements (repos) are sales of government securities (for example, U.S. Treasury bills) by a bank or securities dealer with an agreement to repurchase. Typically, an investor buys some Treasury securities from a bond dealer and simultaneously agrees to sell them back at a later date at a specified higher price. Repurchase agreements usually involve a very short term—overnight to a few days.

A corporate stockholder receiving either common or preferred dividends is granted a 50 percent (or more) dividend exclusion (reduced from 70 percent or more in the 2017 Tax Cuts and Jobs Act). As a result, the relatively high dividend yields on preferred stock provide a strong incentive for investment. A problem is that the dividend is fixed with ordinary preferred stock, so the price can fluctuate more than is desirable in a short-term investment. Money market preferred stock (also known as auction rate preferred) features a floating dividend. The dividend is reset fairly often (usually every 49 days); so this type of preferred has much less price volatility than ordinary preferred, and it is a popular short-term investment.

Concept Questions

19.5a   What are some reasons why firms find themselves with idle cash?

19.5b   What are some types of money market securities?

19.5c   Why are money market preferred stocks an attractive short-term investment?

19.6 Summary and Conclusions

In this chapter, we have examined cash and liquidity management. We saw the following:

1. A firm holds cash to conduct transactions and to compensate banks for the various services they render.

2. The difference between a firm's available balance and its book balance is the firm's net float. The float reflects the fact that some checks have not cleared and are uncollected. The financial manager must always work with collected cash balances and not with the company's book balance. To do otherwise is to use the bank's cash without the bank's knowing it, which raises ethical and legal questions.

3. The firm can make use of a variety of procedures to manage the collection and disbursement of cash in such a way as to speed up the collection of cash and slow down the payments. Some methods to speed up collection are the use of lockboxes, concentration banking, and wire transfers.

4. Because of seasonal and cyclical activities, to help finance planned expenditures, or as a contingency reserve, firms temporarily hold a cash surplus. The money market offers a variety of possible vehicles for "parking" this idle cash.

CONNECT TO FINANCE

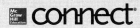 If you are using *Connect Finance* in your course, get online to take a Practice Test, check out study tools, and find out where you need additional practice.

Can you answer the following *Connect* Quiz questions?

Section 19.1 Cash management is defined as _____.

Section 19.2 A firm probably has the most control over what components of collection float?

Section 19.3 What is the primary purpose of a lockbox?

CHAPTER REVIEW AND SELF-TEST PROBLEM

19.1 Float Measurement On a typical day, a firm writes checks totaling $3,000. These checks clear in seven days. Simultaneously, the firm receives $1,700. The cash is available in two days on average. Calculate the disbursement, collection, and net floats. How do you interpret the answer?

ANSWERS TO CHAPTER REVIEW AND SELF-TEST PROBLEM

19.1 The disbursement float is 7 days × $3,000 = $21,000. The collection float is 2 days × (−$1,700) = −$3,400. The net float is $21,000 + (−3,400) = $17,600. In other words, at any given time, the firm typically has uncashed checks outstanding of $21,000. At the same time, it has uncollected receipts of $3,400. Thus the firm's book balance is typically $17,600 less than its available balance, for a positive $17,600 net float.

CONCEPTS REVIEW AND CRITICAL THINKING QUESTIONS

1. **Cash Management** [LO3] Is it possible for a firm to have too much cash? Why would shareholders care if a firm accumulates large amounts of cash?

2. **Cash Management** [LO3] What options are available to a firm if it believes it has too much cash? How about too little?

3. **Agency Issues** [LO3] Are stockholders and creditors likely to agree on how much cash a firm should keep on hand?

4. **Motivations for Holding Cash** [LO3] In the chapter opening, we discussed the enormous cash positions of several companies. Why would firms such as these hold such large quantities of cash?

5. **Cash Management versus Liquidity Management** [LO3] What is the difference between cash management and liquidity management?

6. **Short-Term Investments** [LO3] Why is preferred stock with a dividend tied to short-term interest rates an attractive short-term investment for corporations with excess cash?

7. **Collection and Disbursement Floats** [LO1] Which would a firm prefer: A net collection float or a net disbursement float? Why?

8. **Float** [LO1] Suppose a firm has a book balance of $2 million. On the bank's website, the cash manager finds out that the bank balance is $2.5 million. What is the situation here? If this is an ongoing situation, what ethical dilemma arises?

9. **Short-Term Investments** [LO3] For each of the short-term marketable securities given here, provide an example of the potential disadvantages the investment has for meeting a corporation's cash management goals:
   a. U.S. Treasury bills.
   b. Ordinary preferred stock.
   c. Negotiable certificates of deposit (NCDs).
   d. Commercial paper.
   e. Revenue anticipation notes.
   f. Repurchase agreements.

10. **Agency Issues** [LO3] It is sometimes argued that excess cash held by a firm can aggravate agency problems (discussed in Chapter 1) and, more generally, reduce incentives for shareholder wealth maximization. How would you frame the issue here?

11. **Use of Excess Cash** [LO3] One option a firm usually has with any excess cash is to pay its suppliers more quickly. What are the advantages and disadvantages of this use of excess cash?

12. **Use of Excess Cash** [LO3] One option usually available to a firm with excess cash is to reduce the firm's outstanding debt. What are the advantages and disadvantages of this use of excess cash?

13. **Float** [LO1] An unfortunately common practice goes like this (warning: don't try this at home): Suppose you are out of money in your checking account; however, your local grocery store will, as a convenience to you as a customer, cash a check for you. So, you cash a check for $200. Of course, this check will bounce unless you do something. To prevent this, you go to the grocery the next day and cash another check for $200. You take this $200 and deposit it. You repeat this process every day, and, in doing so, you make sure that no checks bounce. Eventually, manna from heaven arrives (perhaps in the form of money from home), and you are able to cover your outstanding checks.

To make it interesting, suppose you are absolutely certain that no checks will bounce along the way. Assuming this is true, and ignoring any question of legality (what we have described is probably illegal check kiting), is there anything unethical about this? If you say yes, then why? In particular, who is harmed?

QUESTIONS AND PROBLEMS

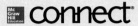

BASIC
(Questions 1–10)

1. **Calculating Float [LO1]** In a typical month, the Monk Corporation receives 80 checks totaling $113,000. These are delayed four days on average. What is the average daily float? Assume 30 days in a month.

2. **Calculating Net Float [LO1]** Each business day, on average, a company writes checks totaling $17,000 to pay its suppliers. The usual clearing time for the checks is four days. Meanwhile, the company is receiving payments from its customers each day, in the form of checks, totaling $22,000. The cash from the payments is available to the firm after two days.
   a. Calculate the company's disbursement float, collection float, and net float.
   b. How would your answer to part (a) change if the collected funds were available in one day instead of two?

3. **Costs of Float [LO1]** Purple Feet Wine, Inc., receives an average of $17,500 in checks per day. The delay in clearing is typically three days. The current interest rate is .017 percent per day.
   a. What is the company's float?
   b. What is the most the company should be willing to pay today to eliminate its float entirely?
   c. What is the highest daily fee the company should be willing to pay to eliminate its float entirely?

4. **Float and Weighted Average Delay [LO1]** Your neighbor goes to the post office once a month and picks up two checks, one for $10,700 and one for $4,600. The larger check takes four days to clear after it is deposited; the smaller one takes three days. Assume 30 days in a month.
   a. What is the total float for the month?
   b. What is the average daily float?
   c. What are the average daily receipts and weighted average delay?

5. **NPV and Collection Time [LO2]** Your firm has an average receipt size of $125. A bank has approached you concerning a lockbox service that will decrease your total collection time by two days. You typically receive 5,100 checks per day. The daily interest rate is .016 percent. If the bank charges a fee of $175 per day, should the lockbox project be accepted? What would the net annual savings be if the service were adopted?

6. **Using Weighted Average Delay [LO1]** A mail-order firm processes 5,300 checks per month. Of these, 60 percent are for $47 and 40 percent are for $79. The $47 checks are delayed two days on average; the $79 checks are delayed three days on average. Assume 30 days in a month.
   a. What is the average daily collection float? How do you interpret your answer?
   b. What is the weighted average delay? Use the result to calculate the average daily float.
   c. How much should the firm be willing to pay to eliminate the float?

d. If the interest rate is 7 percent per year, calculate the daily cost of the float.

e. How much should the firm be willing to pay to reduce the weighted average float to 1.5 days?

7. **Value of Lockboxes [LO2]** Paper Submarine Manufacturing is investigating a lockbox system to reduce its collection time. It has determined the following:

Average number of payments per day	485
Average value of payment	$935
Variable lockbox fee (per transaction)	$.15
Daily interest rate on money market securities	.068%

The total collection time will be reduced by three days if the lockbox system is adopted.

a. What is the PV of adopting the system?

b. What is the NPV of adopting the system?

c. What is the net cash flow per day from adopting the system? Per check?

8. **Lockboxes and Collections [LO2]** It takes Cookie Cutter Modular Homes, Inc., about six days to receive and deposit checks from customers. The company's management is considering a lockbox system to reduce the firm's collection times. It is expected that the lockbox system will reduce receipt and deposit times to three days total. Average daily collections are $175,000, and the required rate of return is 4 percent per year. Assume 365 days per year.

a. What is the reduction in outstanding cash balances as a result of implementing the lockbox system?

b. What is the dollar return that could be earned on these savings?

c. What is the maximum monthly charge the company should pay for this lockbox system if the payment is due at the end of the month? What if the payment is due at the beginning of the month?

9. **Value of Delay [LO2]** Every two weeks, No More Pencils, Inc., disburses checks that average $107,000 and take seven days to clear. How much interest can the company earn annually if it delays transfer of funds from an interest-bearing account that pays .009 percent per day for these seven days? Ignore the effects of compounding interest.

10. **NPV and Reducing Float [LO2]** No More Books Corporation has an agreement with Floyd Bank whereby the bank handles $4.5 million in collections per day and requires a $340,000 compensating balance. No More Books is contemplating canceling the agreement and dividing its eastern region so that two other banks will handle its business. Banks A and B will each handle $2.25 million of collections per day, and each requires a compensating balance of $195,000. No More Books's financial management expects that collections will be accelerated by one day if the eastern region is divided. Should the company proceed with the new system? What will be the annual net savings? Assume that the T-bill rate is 2.5 percent annually.

11. **Lockboxes and Collection Time [LO2]** Bird's Eye Treehouses, Inc., a Kentucky company, has determined that a majority of its customers are located in the Pennsylvania area. It therefore is considering using a lockbox system offered by a bank located in Pittsburgh. The bank has estimated that use of the system will reduce collection time by 1.5 days. Based on the following information, should the lockbox system be adopted?

INTERMEDIATE
(Questions 11–12)

Average number of payments per day	950
Average value of payment	$725
Variable lockbox fee (per transaction)	$.15
Annual interest rate on money market securities	5.5%

How would your answer change if there were a fixed charge of $5,000 per year in addition to the variable charge? Assume 365 days per year.

12. **Calculating Transactions Required** [LO2] Cow Chips, Inc., a large fertilizer distributor based in California, is planning to use a lockbox system to speed up collections from its customers located on the East Coast. A Philadelphia-area bank will provide this service for an annual fee of $6,500 plus 10 cents per transaction. The estimated reduction in collection and processing time is one day. If the average customer payment in this region is $2,900, how many customers each day, on average, are needed to make the system profitable for Cow Chips? Treasury bills are currently yielding 4 percent per year, and there are 365 days per year.

MINICASE

Cash Management at Webb Corporation

Webb Corporation was founded 20 years ago by its president, Bryan Webb. The company originally began as a mail-order company, but it has grown rapidly in recent years, in large part due to its website. Because of the wide geographical dispersion of the company's customers, it currently employs a lockbox system with collection centers in San Francisco, St. Louis, Atlanta, and Boston.

Holly Lennon, the company's treasurer, has been examining the current cash collection policies. On average, each lockbox center handles $207,000 in payments each day. The company's current policy is to invest these payments in short-term marketable securities daily at the collection center banks. Every two weeks, the investment accounts are swept; the proceeds are wire-transferred to Webb's headquarters in Dallas to meet the company's payroll. The investment accounts each earn .013 percent per day, and the wire transfers cost .20 percent of the amount transferred.

Holly has been approached by Third National Bank, located just outside Dallas, about the possibility of setting up a

concentration banking system for Webb Corp. Third National will accept each of the lockbox center's daily payments via automated clearinghouse (ACH) transfers in lieu of wire transfers. The ACH-transferred funds will not be available for use for one day. Once cleared, the funds will be deposited in a short-term account, which will yield .013 percent per day. Each ACH transfer will cost $175. Bryan has asked Holly to determine which cash management system will be the best for the company. As her assistant, Holly has asked you to answer the following questions.

QUESTIONS

1. What is Webb Corporation's total net cash flow available from the current lockbox system to meet payroll?
2. Under the terms outlined by Third National Bank, should the company proceed with the concentration banking system?
3. What cost of ACH transfers would make the company indifferent between the two systems?

19A Determining the Target Cash Balance

target cash balance
A firm's desired cash level as determined by the trade-off between carrying costs and shortage costs.

Based on our general discussion of current assets in the previous chapter, the **target cash balance** involves a trade-off between the opportunity costs of holding too much cash (the carrying costs) and the costs of holding too little cash (the shortage costs, also called **adjustment costs**). The nature of these costs depends on the firm's working capital policy.

If the firm has a flexible working capital policy, it will probably maintain a marketable securities portfolio. In this case, the adjustment, or shortage, costs will be the trading costs associated with buying and selling securities. If the firm has a restrictive working capital policy, it will probably borrow in the short term to meet cash shortages. The costs in this case will be the interest and other expenses associated with arranging a loan.

In our discussion that follows, we will assume the firm has a flexible policy. Its cash management, then, consists of moving money in and out of marketable securities. This is a traditional approach to the subject, and it is a nice way of illustrating the costs and benefits of holding cash.

Keep in mind that the distinction between cash and money market investments is becoming increasingly blurred. For example, how do we classify a money market fund with check-writing privileges? Such near-cash arrangements are becoming more common. It may be that the prime reason they are not universal is regulation limiting their usage. We will return to this subject of such arrangements at various points in the following discussion.

adjustment costs
The costs associated with holding too little cash. Also, *shortage costs*.

THE BASIC IDEA

Figure 19A.1 presents the cash management problem for our flexible firm. If a firm tries to keep its cash holdings too low, it will find itself running out of cash more often than is desirable and selling marketable securities (and perhaps later buying marketable securities to replace those sold) more frequently than would be the case if the cash balance were higher. Trading costs will be high when the cash balance is small. These costs will fall as the cash balance becomes larger.

In contrast, the opportunity costs of holding cash are low if the firm holds little cash. These costs increase as the cash holdings rise because the firm is giving up more interest that could have been earned.

In Figure 19A.1, the sum of the costs is given by the total cost curve. As shown, the minimum total cost occurs where the two individual cost curves cross at Point C^*. At this

FIGURE 19A.1

Cost of Holding Cash

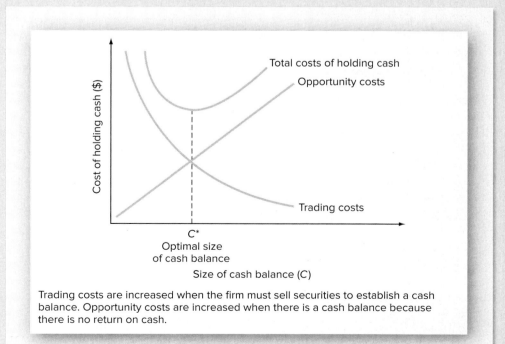

Trading costs are increased when the firm must sell securities to establish a cash balance. Opportunity costs are increased when there is a cash balance because there is no return on cash.

point, the opportunity costs and the trading costs are equal. This point represents the target cash balance, and it is the point the firm should try to find.

Figure 19A.1 is essentially the same as Figure 18.2 in the previous chapter. As we discuss next, we can now say more about the optimal investment in cash and the factors that influence it.

THE BAT MODEL

The Baumol-Allais-Tobin (BAT) model is a classic means of analyzing our cash management problem. We will show how this model can be used to actually establish the target cash balance. It is a straightforward model useful for illustrating the factors in cash management and, more generally, current asset management.

To develop the BAT model, suppose the Golden Socks Corporation starts off at Week 0 with a cash balance of $C = \$1.2$ million. Each week, outflows exceed inflows by $600,000. As a result, the cash balance will drop to zero at the end of Week 2. The average cash balance will be the beginning balance ($1.2 million) plus the ending balance ($0) divided by 2, or ($1.2 million + 0)/2 = $600,000, over the two-week period. At the end of Week 2, Golden Socks replenishes its cash by depositing another $1.2 million.

As we have described, the simple cash management strategy for Golden Socks boils down to depositing $1.2 million every two weeks. This policy is shown in Figure 19A.2. Notice how the cash balance declines by $600,000 per week. Because the company brings the account back up to $1.2 million, the balance hits zero every two weeks. This results in the sawtooth pattern displayed in Figure 19A.2.

Implicitly, we assume that the net cash outflow is the same every day and is known with certainty. These two assumptions make the model easy to handle. We will indicate in the next section what happens when these assumptions do not hold.

If C were set higher, say, at $2.4 million, cash would last four weeks before the firm would have to sell marketable securities; but the firm's average cash balance would increase

FIGURE 19A.2

Cash Balances for the Golden Socks Corporation

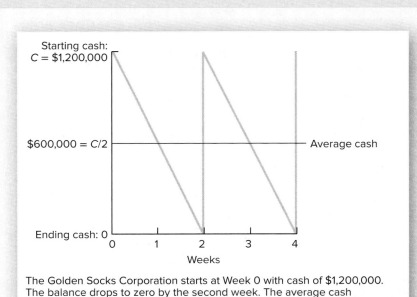

The Golden Socks Corporation starts at Week 0 with cash of $1,200,000. The balance drops to zero by the second week. The average cash balance is C/2 = $1,200,000/2 = $600,000 over the period.

to $1.2 million (from $600,000). If C were set at $600,000, cash would run out in one week, and the firm would have to replenish cash more frequently; but the average cash balance would fall from $600,000 to $300,000.

Because transaction costs (for example, the brokerage costs of selling marketable securities) must be incurred whenever cash is replenished, establishing large initial balances will lower the trading costs connected with cash management. However, the larger the average cash balance, the greater is the opportunity cost (the return that could have been earned on marketable securities).

To determine the optimal strategy, Golden Socks needs to know the following three things:

F = The fixed cost of making a securities trade to replenish cash.

T = The total amount of new cash needed for transaction purposes over the relevant planning period—say, one year.

R = The opportunity cost of holding cash. This is the interest rate on marketable securities.

With this information, Golden Socks can determine the total costs of any particular cash balance policy. It can then determine the optimal cash balance policy.

The Opportunity Costs   To determine the opportunity costs of holding cash, we have to find out how much interest is forgone. Golden Socks has, on average, $C/2$ in cash. This amount could be earning interest at rate R. So the total dollar opportunity costs of cash balances are equal to the average cash balance multiplied by the interest rate:

Opportunity costs = (C/2) × R   19A.1

The opportunity costs of various alternatives are given here, assuming that the interest rate is 10 percent:

Initial Cash Balance	Average Cash Balance	Opportunity Cost (R = .10)
C	$C/2$	$(C/2) \times R$
$4,800,000	$2,400,000	$240,000
2,400,000	1,200,000	120,000
1,200,000	600,000	60,000
600,000	300,000	30,000
300,000	150,000	15,000

In our original case, in which the initial cash balance is $1.2 million, the average balance is $600,000. The interest Golden Socks could have earned on this (at 10 percent) is $60,000, so this is what the firm gives up with this strategy. Notice that the opportunity costs increase as the initial (and average) cash balance rises.

The Trading Costs   To determine the total trading costs for the year, we need to know how many times Golden Socks will have to sell marketable securities during the year. First, the total amount of cash disbursed during the year is $600,000 per week, so $T = $600,000 \times$ 52 weeks = $31.2 million. If the initial cash balance is set at $C = $1.2 million, Golden Socks will sell $1.2 million in marketable securities: $T/C = $31.2 million/$1.2 million = 26 times per year. It costs F dollars each time, so trading costs are given by:

$$\frac{\$31.2 \text{ million}}{\$1.2 \text{ million}} \times F = 26 \times F$$

In general, the total trading costs will be given by:

Trading costs = (T/C) × F

In this example, if F were $1,000 (an unrealistically large amount), the trading costs would be $26,000.

We can calculate the trading costs associated with some different strategies as follows:

Total Amount of Disbursements During Relevant Period	Initial Cash Balance	Trading Costs (F = $1,000)
T	C	(T/C) × F
$31,200,000	$4,800,000	$ 6,500
31,200,000	2,400,000	13,000
31,200,000	1,200,000	26,000
31,200,000	600,000	52,000
31,200,000	300,000	104,000

The Total Cost   Now that we have the opportunity costs and the trading costs, we can calculate the total cost by adding them together:

Total cost = Opportunity costs + Trading costs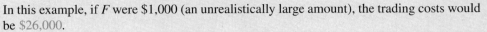
= (C/2) × R + (T/C) × F

Using the numbers generated earlier, we have the following:

Cash Balance	Opportunity Costs	+	Trading Costs	=	Total Cost
$4,800,000	$240,000		$ 6,500		$246,500
2,400,000	120,000		13,000		133,000
1,200,000	60,000		26,000		86,000
600,000	30,000		52,000		82,000
300,000	15,000		104,000		119,000

Notice how the total cost starts out at almost $250,000 ($246,500) and declines to $82,000 before starting to rise again.

The Solution   We can see from the preceding schedule that a $600,000 cash balance results in the lowest total cost of the possibilities presented: $82,000. But what about $700,000 or $500,000 or other possibilities? It appears that the optimal balance is somewhere between $300,000 and $1.2 million. With this in mind, we could easily proceed by trial and error to find the optimal balance. It is not difficult to find it directly so we do this next.

Take a look back at Figure 19A.1. As the figure is drawn, the optimal size of the cash balance, C^*, occurs right where the two lines cross. At this point, the opportunity costs and the trading costs are exactly equal. So at C^*, it must be that:

Opportunity costs = Trading costs
$$(C^*/2) \times R = (T/C^*) \times F$$

With a little algebra, we can write:

$$C^{*2} = (2T \times F)/R$$

To solve for C^*, we take the square root of both sides to get:

$$C^* = \sqrt{(2T \times F)/R}$$

This is the optimal initial cash balance.

For Golden Socks, we have $T = \$31.2$ million, $F = \$1,000$, and $R = 10\%$. We can now find the optimal cash balance:

$$C^* = \sqrt{(2 \times \$31,200,000 \times 1,000)/.10}$$

$$= \sqrt{\$624 \text{ billion}}$$

$$= \$789,937$$

We can verify this answer by calculating the various costs at this balance, as well as a little above and a little below this balance:

Cash Balance	Opportunity Costs	+	Trading Costs	=	Total Cost
$850,000	$42,500		$36,706		$79,206
800,000	40,000		39,000		79,000
789,937	39,497		39,497		78,994
750,000	37,500		41,600		79,100
700,000	35,000		44,571		79,571

The total cost at the optimal cash level is $78,994 and increases as the cash balance moves in either direction.

The BAT Model   EXAMPLE 19A.1

The Vulcan Corporation has cash outflows of $100 per day, seven days a week. The interest rate is 5 percent, and the fixed cost of replenishing cash balances is $10 per transaction. What is the optimal initial cash balance? What is the total cost?

The total cash needed for the year is 365 days × $100 = $36,500. From the BAT model, we have that the optimal initial balance is:

$$C^* = \sqrt{(2T \times F)/R}$$

$$= \sqrt{(2 \times \$36,500 \times 10)/.05}$$

$$= \sqrt{\$14.6 \text{ million}}$$

$$= \$3,821$$

The average cash balance is $3,821/2 = $1,910, so the opportunity cost is $1,910 × .05 = $96. Because Vulcan needs $100 per day, the $3,821 balance will last $3,821/$100 = 38.21 days. The firm needs to resupply the account 365/38.21 = 9.6 times per year, so the trading (order) cost is $96. The total cost is $191.

Conclusion   The BAT model is possibly the simplest model for determining the optimal cash position. Its chief weakness is that it assumes steady, certain cash outflows. Next, we discuss a more involved model designed to deal with this limitation.

THE MILLER-ORR MODEL: A MORE GENERAL APPROACH

We now describe a cash management system designed to deal with cash inflows and out-flows that fluctuate randomly from day to day. With this model, we again concentrate on the cash balance. But in contrast to the situation with the BAT model, we assume that this balance fluctuates up and down randomly and that the average change is zero.

The Basic Idea Figure 19A.3 shows how the system works. It operates in terms of an upper limit (U^*) and a lower limit (L) to the amount of cash, as well as a target cash balance (C^*). The firm allows its cash balance to fluctuate between the lower and upper limits. As long as the cash balance is somewhere between U^* and L, nothing happens.

When the cash balance reaches the upper limit (U^*), as it does at Point X, the firm moves $U^* - C^*$ dollars out of the account and into marketable securities. This action moves the cash balance down to C^*. In the same way, if the cash balance falls to the lower limit (L), as it does at Point Y, the firm will sell $C^* - L$ worth of securities and deposit the cash in the account. This action takes the cash balance up to C^*.

Using the Model To get started, management sets the lower limit (L). This limit essentially defines a safety stock; so where it is set depends on how much risk of a cash shortfall the firm is willing to tolerate. Alternatively, the minimum might equal a required compensating balance.

As with the BAT model, the optimal cash balance depends on trading costs and opportunity costs. Once again, the cost per transaction of buying and selling marketable securities, F, is assumed to be fixed. Also, the opportunity cost of holding cash is R, the interest rate per period on marketable securities.

The only extra piece of information needed is σ^2, the variance of the net cash flow per period. For our purposes, the period can be anything—a day or a week, for example—as long as the interest rate and the variance are based on the same length of time.

FIGURE 19A.3

The Miller-Orr Model

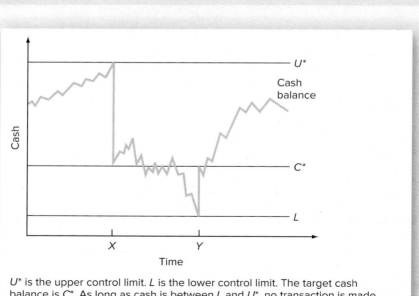

U^* is the upper control limit. L is the lower control limit. The target cash balance is C^*. As long as cash is between L and U^*, no transaction is made.

Given L, which is set by the firm, Miller and Orr show that the cash balance target, C^*, and the upper limit, U^*, that minimize the total costs of holding cash are:[2]

$$C^* = L + (3/4 \times F \times \sigma^2/R)^{(1/3)}$$

$$U^* = 3 \times C^* - 2 \times L$$

Also, the average cash balance in the Miller-Orr model is:

Average cash balance = $(4 \times C^* - L)/3$

The derivation of these expressions is relatively complex, so we will not present it here. Fortunately, as we illustrate next, the results are not difficult to use.

For example, suppose $F = \$10$, the interest rate is 1 percent per month, and the standard deviation of the monthly net cash flows is $200. The variance of the monthly net cash flows is:

$$\sigma^2 = \$200^2 = \$40,000$$

We assume a minimum cash balance of $L = \$100$. We can calculate the cash balance target, C^*, as follows:

$$
\begin{aligned}
C^* &= L + (3/4 \times F \times \sigma^2/R)^{1/3} \\
&= \$100 + (3/4 \times \$10 \times \$40,000/.01)^{1/3} \\
&= \$100 + 30,000,000^{1/3} \\
&= \$100 + 311 = \$411
\end{aligned}
$$

The upper limit, U^*, is:

$$
\begin{aligned}
U^* &= 3 \times C^* - 2 \times L \\
&= 3 \times \$411 - 2 \times \$100 \\
&= \$1,032
\end{aligned}
$$

Finally, the average cash balance will be:

$$
\begin{aligned}
\text{Average cash balance} &= (4 \times C^* - L)/3 \\
&= (4 \times \$411 - \$100)/3 \\
&= \$514
\end{aligned}
$$

IMPLICATIONS OF THE BAT AND MILLER-ORR MODELS

Our two cash management models differ in complexity, but they have some similar implications. In both cases, all other things being equal, we see that:

1. The greater the interest rate, the lower is the target cash balance.
2. The greater the order cost, the higher is the target cash balance.

These implications are both fairly obvious. The advantage of the Miller-Orr model is that it improves our understanding of the problem of cash management by considering the effect of uncertainty as measured by the variation in net cash inflows.

The Miller-Orr model shows that the greater the uncertainty (the higher σ^2 is), the greater the difference between the target balance and the minimum balance will be. Similarly, the greater the uncertainty, the higher the upper limit and the average cash balance will be. These statements all make intuitive sense. For example, the greater the variability, the greater will be the chance that the balance will drop below the minimum. We keep a higher balance to guard against this possibility.

---

[2]M. H. Miller and D. Orr, "A Model of the Demand for Money by Firms," *Quarterly Journal of Economics*, August 1966.

OTHER FACTORS INFLUENCING THE TARGET CASH BALANCE

Before moving on, we briefly discuss two additional considerations that affect the target cash balance.

First, in our discussion of cash management, we assume cash is invested in marketable securities such as Treasury bills. The firm obtains cash by selling these securities. Another alternative is to borrow cash. Borrowing introduces additional considerations to cash management:

1. Borrowing is likely to be more expensive than selling marketable securities because the interest rate is likely to be higher.
2. The need to borrow will depend on management's desire to hold low cash balances. A firm is more likely to have to borrow to cover an unexpected cash outflow with greater cash flow variability and lower investment in marketable securities.

Second, for large firms, the trading costs of buying and selling securities are small when compared to the opportunity costs of holding cash. Suppose a firm has $1 million in cash that won't be needed for 24 hours. Should the firm invest the money or leave it sitting?

Suppose the firm can invest the money at an annualized rate of 7.57 percent per year. The daily rate in this case is about two basis points (.02 percent, or .0002).[3] The daily return earned on $1 million is .0002 × $1 million = $200. In many cases, the order cost will be much less than this; so a large firm will buy and sell securities very often before it will opt to leave substantial amounts of cash idle.

Concept Questions

19A.1a What is a target cash balance?
19A.1b What is the basic trade-off in the BAT model?
19A.1c Describe how the Miller-Orr model works.

APPENDIX REVIEW AND SELF-TEST PROBLEM

19A.1   The BAT Model Given the following information, calculate the target cash balance using the BAT model:

Annual interest rate	12%
Fixed order cost	$100
Total cash needed	$240,000

What are the opportunity cost of holding cash, the trading cost, and the total cost? What would each of these costs be if $15,000 were held instead? If $25,000 were held?

---

[3]A basis point is 1 percent of 1 percent. Also, the annual interest rate is calculated as $(1 + R)^{365} = 1.0757$, implying a daily rate of .02 percent.

ANSWER TO APPENDIX REVIEW AND SELF-TEST PROBLEM

19A.1   From the BAT model, we know that the target cash balance is:

$$C^* = \sqrt{(2T \times F)/R}$$
$$= \sqrt{(2 \times \$240,000 \times \$100)/.12}$$
$$= \sqrt{\$400,000,000}$$
$$= \$20,000$$

The average cash balance will be $C^*/2 = \$20,000/2 = \$10,000$. The opportunity cost of holding $10,000 when the going rate is 12 percent is $10,000 × .12 = $1,200. There will be $240,000/$20,000 = 12 orders during the year, so the order cost, or trading cost, is also 12 × $100 = $1,200. The total cost is thus $2,400.

   If $15,000 is held, the average balance is $7,500. Verify that the opportunity, trading, and total costs in this case are $900, $1,600, and $2,500, respectively. If $25,000 is held, these numbers are $1,500, $960, and $2,460, respectively.

QUESTIONS AND PROBLEMS

1. **Changes in Target Cash Balances [LO2]** Indicate the likely impact of each of the following on a company's target cash balance. Use the letter *I* to denote an increase and *D* to denote a decrease. Briefly explain your reasoning in each case:
   a. Commissions charged by brokers decrease.
   b. Interest rates paid on money market securities rise.
   c. The compensating balance requirement of a bank is raised.
   d. The firm's credit rating improves.
   e. The cost of borrowing increases.
   f. Direct fees for banking services are established.

BASIC
(Questions 1–10)

2. **Using the BAT Model [LO2]** Given the following information, calculate the target cash balance using the BAT model:

Annual interest rate	4.5%
Fixed order cost	$25
Total cash needed	$10,200

   How do you interpret your answer?

3. **Opportunity versus Trading Costs [LO2]** White Whale Corporation has an average daily cash balance of $1,700. Total cash needed for the year is $64,000. The interest rate is 5 percent, and replenishing the cash costs $8 each time. What are the opportunity cost of holding cash, the trading cost, and the total cost? What do you think of White Whale's strategy?

4. **Costs and the BAT Model [LO2]** Debit and Credit Bookkeepers needs a total of $21,000 in cash during the year for transactions and other purposes. Whenever cash runs low, it sells $1,500 in securities and transfers in the cash. The interest rate is 4 percent per year, and selling securities costs $25 per sale.
   a. What is the opportunity cost under the current policy? The trading cost? With no additional calculations, would you say that Debit and Credit keeps too much or too little cash? Explain.
   b. What is the target cash balance derived using the BAT model?

5. **Determining Optimal Cash Balances** [LO2] The All Day Company is currently holding $690,000 in cash. It projects that over the next year its cash outflows will exceed cash inflows by $140,000 per month. How much of the current cash holdings should be retained, and how much should be used to increase the company's holdings of marketable securities? Each time these securities are bought or sold through a broker, the company pays a fee of $250. The annual interest rate on money market securities is 3.2 percent. After the initial investment of excess cash, how many times during the next 12 months will securities be sold?

6. **Interpreting Miller-Orr** [LO2] All Night, Inc., uses a Miller-Orr cash management approach with a lower limit of $43,000, an upper limit of $125,000, and a target balance of $80,000. Explain what each of these points represents; then explain how the system will work.

7. **Using Miller-Orr** [LO2] Slap Shot Corporation has a fixed cost of $40 associated with buying and selling marketable securities. The interest rate is currently .013 percent per day, and the firm has estimated that the standard deviation of its daily net cash flows is $80. Management has set a lower limit of $1,500 on cash holdings. Calculate the target cash balance and upper limit using the Miller-Orr model. Describe how the system will work.

8. **Interpreting Miller-Orr** [LO2] Based on the Miller-Orr model, describe what will happen to the lower limit, the upper limit, and the spread (the distance between the two) if the variation in net cash flow grows. Give an intuitive explanation for why this happens. What happens if the variance drops to zero?

9. **Using Miller-Orr** [LO2] The variance of the daily cash flows for the Pele Bicycle Shop is $890,000. The opportunity cost to the firm of holding cash is 4.1 percent per year. What should the target cash level and the upper limit be if the tolerable lower limit has been established as $160,000? The fixed cost of buying and selling securities is $300 per transaction.

10. **Using BAT** [LO2] Rise Against Corporation has determined that its target cash balance if it uses the BAT model is $5,100. The total cash needed for the year is $31,000, and the order cost is $10. What interest rate must Rise Against be using?

Credit and Inventory Management

IN SEPTEMBER 2016, HANJIN SHIPPING declared bankruptcy. While most people were unaware of the company before the bankruptcy filing, Hanjin controlled just over 3 percent of worldwide shipping traffic. Because banks pulled funding for dock fees, container unloading, and storage, 97 of the company's ships, carrying 500,000 containers worth $14 billion in cargo, were stranded at sea. This delay affected many companies. For example, Samsung had $38 million in inventory on the ocean in Hanjin's ships. Competitor Apple delayed the debut of its new iPhone 7 and iPhone 7 Plus at least three weeks because much of the new iPhone inventory was also sailing the ocean in circles. Meanwhile, Ford, with its cargo sitting portside in Australia for two weeks, was forced to fly in sheet metal, glass, and steering components—a much more expensive process.

As these examples show, inventory disruptions can cause major problems for businesses, but companies also dislike carrying excessive inventory levels for a variety of reasons. In this chapter, we discuss, among other things, how companies arrive at an optimal inventory level.

Learning Objectives

After studying this chapter, you should be able to:

LO1 Explain how firms manage their receivables and the basic components of a firm's credit policies.

LO2 Analyze a firm's decision to grant credit.

LO3 Define the types of inventory and inventory management systems used by firms.

LO4 Determine the costs of carrying inventory and the optimal inventory level.

©by_adri/iStockPhoto/GettyImages

For updates on the latest happenings in finance, visit fundamentalsofcorporatefinance.blogspot.com.

20.1 Credit and Receivables

When a firm sells goods and services, it can demand cash on or before the delivery date or it can extend credit to customers and allow some delay in payment. The next few sections provide an idea of what is involved in the firm's decision to grant credit to its customers. Granting credit is making an investment in a customer—an investment tied to the sale of a product or service.

Why do firms grant credit? Not all do, but the practice is extremely common. The obvious reason is that offering credit is a way of stimulating sales. The costs associated with granting credit are not trivial. First, there is the chance that the customer will not pay. Second, the firm has to bear the costs of carrying the receivables. The credit policy decision thus involves a trade-off between the benefits of increased sales and the costs of granting credit.

From an accounting perspective, when credit is granted, an account receivable is created. Such receivables include credit to other firms, called *trade credit*, and credit granted to consumers, called *consumer credit*. About one-sixth of all the assets of U.S. industrial firms are in the form of accounts receivable, so receivables obviously represent a major investment of financial resources by U.S. businesses.

COMPONENTS OF CREDIT POLICY

If a firm decides to grant credit to its customers, then it must establish procedures for extending credit and collecting payment. In particular, the firm will have to deal with the following components of credit policy:

terms of sale
The conditions under which a firm sells its goods and services for cash or credit.

1. **Terms of sale**: The terms of sale establish how the firm proposes to sell its goods and services. A basic decision is whether the firm will require cash or will extend credit. If the firm does grant credit to a customer, the terms of sale will specify (perhaps implicitly) the credit period, the cash discount and discount period, and the type of credit instrument.

credit analysis
The process of determining the probability that customers will not pay.

2. **Credit analysis**: In granting credit, a firm determines how much effort to expend trying to distinguish between customers who will pay and customers who will not pay. Firms use a number of devices and procedures to determine the probability that customers will not pay; put together, these are called credit analysis.

collection policy
The procedures followed by a firm in collecting accounts receivable.

3. **Collection policy**: After credit has been granted, the firm has the potential problem of collecting the cash, for which it must establish a collection policy.

In the next several sections, we will discuss these components of credit policy that collectively make up the decision to grant credit.

THE CASH FLOWS FROM GRANTING CREDIT

In a previous chapter, we described the accounts receivable period as the time it takes to collect on a sale. There are several events that occur during this period. These events are the cash flows associated with granting credit, and they can be illustrated with a cash flow diagram:

These companies assist businesses with working capital management:
www.treasury.pncbank.com
and **www.treasurystrategies.com**.

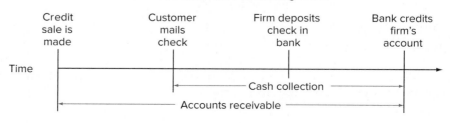

The Cash Flows of Granting Credit

As our time line indicates, the typical sequence of events when a firm grants credit is as follows: (1) The credit sale is made, (2) the customer sends a check to the firm, (3) the firm deposits the check, and (4) the firm's account is credited for the amount of the check.

Based on our discussion in the previous chapter, it is apparent that one of the factors influencing the receivables period is float. One way to reduce the receivables period is to speed up check mailing, processing, and clearing. Because we cover this subject elsewhere, we will ignore float in the subsequent discussion and focus on what is likely to be the major determinant of the receivables period: Credit policy.

THE INVESTMENT IN RECEIVABLES

The investment in accounts receivable for any firm depends on the amount of credit sales and the average collection period. For example, if a firm's average collection period, ACP, is 30 days, then, at any given time, there will be 30 days' worth of sales outstanding. If credit sales run $1,000 per day, the firm's accounts receivable will then be equal to 30 days × $1,000 per day = $30,000, on average.

For more on accounts receivable management, visit **www.insidearm.com**.

As our example illustrates, a firm's receivables generally will be equal to its average daily sales multiplied by its average collection period:

Accounts receivable = Average daily sales × ACP

As this equation shows, a firm's investment in accounts receivable depends on factors that influence credit sales and collections.

We have seen the average collection period in various places, including Chapter 3 and Chapter 18. Recall that we use the terms *days' sales in receivables*, *receivables period*, and *average collection period* interchangeably to refer to the length of time it takes for the firm to collect on a sale.

Concept Questions

20.1a   What are the basic components of credit policy?

20.1b   What are the basic components of the terms of sale if a firm chooses to sell on credit?

Terms of the Sale   20.2

As we described previously, the terms of a sale are made up of three distinct elements:

1. The period for which credit is granted (the credit period).
2. The cash discount and the discount period.
3. The type of credit instrument.

Within a given industry, the terms of sale are usually fairly standard, but these terms vary quite a bit across industries. In many cases, the terms of sale are remarkably archaic and literally date to previous centuries. Organized systems of trade credit that resemble current practice can be easily traced to the great fairs of medieval Europe, and they almost surely existed long before then.

THE BASIC FORM

The easiest way to understand the terms of sale is to consider an example. Terms such as 2/10, net 60 are common. This means that customers have 60 days from the invoice date (discussed a bit later) to pay the full amount; however, if payment is made within 10 days, a 2 percent cash discount can be taken.

Consider a buyer who places an order for $1,000, and assume that the terms of the sale are 2/10, net 60. The buyer has the option of paying $1,000 × (1 − .02) = $980 in 10 days, or paying the full $1,000 in 60 days. If the terms are stated as just net 30, then the customer has 30 days from the invoice date to pay the entire $1,000, and no discount is offered for early payment.

In general, credit terms are interpreted in the following way:

<Take this discount off the invoice price> / <If you pay in this many days>,
<Or pay the full invoice amount in this many days>

Terms of 5/10, net 45 mean: Take a 5 percent discount from the full price if you pay within 10 days, or pay the full amount in 45 days.

THE CREDIT PERIOD

credit period
The length of time for which credit is granted.

The **credit period** is the length of time for which credit is granted. The credit period varies widely from industry to industry, but it is almost always between 30 and 120 days. If a cash discount is offered, then the credit period has two components: The net credit period and the cash discount period.

The net credit period is the length of time the customer has to pay. The cash discount period is the time during which the discount is available. With 2/10, net 30, the net credit period is 30 days and the cash discount period is 10 days.

invoice
A bill for goods or services provided by the seller to the purchaser.

The Invoice Date   The invoice date is the beginning of the credit period. An **invoice** is a written account of merchandise shipped to the buyer. For individual items, by convention, the invoice date is usually the shipping date or the billing date, *not* the date on which the buyer receives the goods or the bill.

Many other arrangements exist. The terms of sale might be ROG, for *receipt of goods*. In this case, the credit period starts when the customer receives the order. This might be used when the customer is in a remote location.

With EOM dating, all sales made during a particular month are assumed to be made at the end of that month. This is useful when a buyer makes purchases throughout the month, but the seller bills only once a month.

Terms of 2/10th, EOM tell the buyer to take a 2 percent discount if payment is made by the 10th of the month; otherwise the full amount is due by the end of the month. Confusingly, the end of the month is sometimes taken to be the 25th day of the month. MOM, for middle of month, is another variation.

Seasonal dating is sometimes used to encourage sales of seasonal products during the off-season. A product sold primarily in the summer (e.g., suntan oil) can be shipped in January with credit terms of 2/10, net 30. However, the invoice might be dated May 1 so that the credit period actually begins at that time. This practice encourages buyers to order early.

Length of the Credit Period   Several factors influence the length of the credit period. Two important ones are the *buyer's* inventory period and operating cycle. All else equal, the shorter these are, the shorter the credit period will be.

As discussed in Chapter 18, the operating cycle has two components: The inventory period and the receivables period. The buyer's inventory period is the time it takes the buyer to acquire inventory (from us), process it, and sell it. The buyer's receivables period is the time it then takes the buyer to collect on the sale. Note that the credit period we offer is effectively the buyer's payables period.

By extending credit, we finance a portion of our buyer's operating cycle and thereby shorten that buyer's cash cycle (see Figure 18.1). If our credit period exceeds the buyer's inventory period, then we are financing not only the buyer's inventory purchases, but part of the buyer's receivables as well.

If our credit period exceeds our buyer's operating cycle, then we are effectively providing financing for aspects of our customer's business beyond the immediate purchase and sale of our merchandise. The reason is that the buyer effectively has a loan from us even after the merchandise is resold, and the buyer can use that credit for other purposes. For this reason, the length of the buyer's operating cycle is often cited as an appropriate upper limit to the credit period.

There are a number of other factors that influence the credit period. Many of these also influence our customer's operating cycles; so, once again, these are related subjects. Among the most important are these:

1. *Perishability and collateral value*: Perishable items have relatively rapid turnover and relatively low collateral value. Credit periods are shorter for such goods. A food wholesaler selling fresh fruit and produce might use net seven days. Alternatively, jewelry might be sold for 5/30, net four months.

2. *Consumer demand*: Products that are well established generally have more rapid turnover. Newer or slow-moving products will often have longer credit periods associated with them to entice buyers. Also, as we have seen, sellers may choose to extend much longer credit periods for off-season sales (when customer demand is low).

3. *Cost, profitability, and standardization*: Relatively inexpensive goods tend to have shorter credit periods. The same is true for relatively standardized goods and raw materials. These all tend to have lower markups and higher turnover rates, both of which lead to shorter credit periods. There are exceptions. Auto dealers, for example, generally pay for cars as they are received.

4. *Credit risk*: The greater the credit risk of the buyer, the shorter the credit period is likely to be (if credit is granted at all).

5. *Size of the account*: If an account is small, the credit period may be shorter because small accounts cost more to manage, and the customers are less important.

6. *Competition*: When the seller is in a highly competitive market, longer credit periods may be offered as a way of attracting customers.

7. *Customer type*: A single seller might offer different credit terms to different buyers. A food wholesaler might supply groceries, bakeries, and restaurants. Each group would probably have different credit terms. More generally, sellers often have both wholesale and retail customers, and they frequently quote different terms to the two types.

CASH DISCOUNTS

As we have seen, **cash discounts** are often part of the terms of sale. The practice of granting discounts for cash purchases in the United States dates to the Civil War and is widespread today. One reason discounts are offered is to speed up the collection of receivables. This will have the effect of reducing the amount of credit being offered, and the firm must trade this off against the cost of the discount.

cash discount
A discount given to induce prompt payment. Also called a *sales discount*.

Notice that when a cash discount is offered, the credit is essentially free during the discount period. The buyer pays for the credit only after the discount expires. With 2/10, net 30, a rational buyer either pays in 10 days to make the greatest possible use of the free credit or pays in 30 days to get the longest possible use of the money in exchange for giving up the discount. By giving up the discount, the buyer effectively gets $30 - 10 = 20$ days' credit.

Another reason for cash discounts is that they are a way of charging higher prices to customers that have had credit extended to them. In this sense, cash discounts are a convenient way of charging for the credit granted to customers.

Visit the National Association of Credit Management at **www.nacm.org**.

Cost of the Credit   In our examples, it might seem that the discounts are rather small. With 2/10, net 30, early payment gets the buyer only a 2 percent discount. Does this provide a significant incentive for early payment? The answer is yes because the implicit interest rate is extremely high.

To see why the discount is important, we will calculate the cost to the buyer of not paying early. To do this, we will find the interest rate that the buyer is effectively paying for the trade credit. Suppose the order is for $1,000. The buyer can pay $980 in 10 days or wait another 20 days and pay $1,000. It's obvious that the buyer is effectively borrowing $980 for 20 days and that the buyer pays $20 in interest on the "loan." What's the interest rate?

This interest is ordinary discount interest, which we discussed in Chapter 5. With $20 in interest on $980 borrowed, the rate is $20/\$980 = .020408$, or 2.0408%. This is relatively low, but remember that this is the rate per 20-day period. There are $365/20 = 18.25$ such periods in a year; so, by not taking the discount, the buyer is paying an effective annual rate (EAR) of:

$$\text{EAR} = 1.020408^{18.25} - 1 = .4459, \text{ or } 44.59\%$$

From the buyer's point of view, this is an expensive source of financing!

Given that the interest rate is so high, it is unlikely that the seller benefits from early payment. Ignoring the possibility of default by the buyer, the decision of a customer to forgo the discount almost surely works to the seller's advantage.

Trade Discounts   In some circumstances, the discount is not really an incentive for early payment but is instead a *trade discount*, a discount routinely given to some type of buyer. With our 2/10th, EOM terms, the buyer takes a 2 percent discount if the invoice is paid by the 10th, but the bill is considered due on the 10th, and overdue after that. In this case, the credit period and the discount period are effectively the same, and there is no reward for paying before the due date.

The Cash Discount and the ACP   To the extent that a cash discount encourages customers to pay early, it will shorten the receivables period and, all other things being equal, reduce the firm's investment in receivables.

Suppose a firm currently has terms of net 30 and an ACP of 30 days. If it offers terms of 2/10, net 30, then perhaps 50 percent of its customers (in terms of volume of purchases) will pay in 10 days. The remaining customers will still take an average of 30 days to pay. What will the new ACP be? If the firm's annual sales are $15 million (before discounts), what will happen to the investment in receivables?

If half of the customers take 10 days to pay and half take 30, then the new average collection period will be:

$$\text{New ACP} = .50 \times 10 \text{ days} + .50 \times 30 \text{ days} = 20 \text{ days}$$

The ACP falls from 30 days to 20 days. Average daily sales are $15 million/365 = $41,096 per day. Receivables will fall by $41,096 \times 10 = \$410,959$.

CREDIT INSTRUMENTS

The **credit instrument** is the basic evidence of indebtedness. Most trade credit is offered on *open account*. This means that the only formal instrument of credit is the invoice, which is sent with the shipment of goods and which the customer signs as evidence that the goods have been received. Afterward, the firm and its customers record the exchange on their books of account.

At times, the firm may require that the customer sign a *promissory note*. This is a basic IOU and might be used when the order is large, when there is no cash discount involved, or when the firm anticipates a problem in collections. Promissory notes are uncommon, but they can eliminate possible controversies later about the existence of debt.

One problem with promissory notes is that they are signed after delivery of the goods. One way to obtain a credit commitment from a customer before the goods are delivered is to arrange a *commercial draft*. Typically, the firm draws up a commercial draft calling for the customer to pay a specific amount by a specified date. The draft is then sent to the customer's bank with the shipping invoices.

If immediate payment is required on the draft, it is called a *sight draft*. If immediate payment is not required, then the draft is a *time draft*. When the draft is presented and the buyer "accepts" it, meaning that the buyer promises to pay it in the future, then it is called a *trade acceptance* and it is sent back to the selling firm. The seller can then keep the acceptance or sell it to someone else. If a bank accepts the draft, meaning that the bank is guaranteeing payment, then the draft becomes a *banker's acceptance*. This arrangement is common in international trade, and banker's acceptances are actively traded in the money market.

A firm can also use a conditional sales contract as a credit instrument. With such an arrangement, the firm retains legal ownership of the goods until the customer has completed payment. Conditional sales contracts usually are paid in installments and have an interest cost built into them.

Concept Questions

20.2a What considerations enter into the determination of the terms of sale?

20.2b Explain what terms of "3/45, net 90" mean. What is the effective interest rate?

Analyzing Credit Policy   20.3

In this section, we take a closer look at the factors that influence the decision to grant credit. Granting credit makes sense only if the NPV from doing so is positive. We need to look at the NPV of the decision to grant credit.

CREDIT POLICY EFFECTS

In evaluating credit policy, there are five basic factors to consider:

1. *Revenue effects*: If the firm grants credit, then there will be a delay in revenue collections as some customers take advantage of the credit offered and pay later. However, the firm may be able to charge a higher price if it grants credit and it may be able to increase the quantity sold. This may increase total revenues.

2. *Cost effects*: Although the firm may experience delayed revenues if it grants credit, it will still incur the costs of sales immediately. Whether the firm sells for cash or credit, it will still have to acquire or produce the merchandise (and pay for it).

3. *The cost of debt*: When the firm grants credit, it must arrange to finance the resulting receivables. As a result, the firm's cost of short-term borrowing is a factor in the decision to grant credit.[1]

4. *The probability of nonpayment*: If the firm grants credit, some percentage of the credit buyers will not pay. This can't happen, of course, if the firm sells for cash.

5. *The cash discount*: When the firm offers a cash discount as part of its credit terms, some customers will choose to pay early to take advantage of the discount.

EVALUATING A PROPOSED CREDIT POLICY

To illustrate how credit policy can be analyzed, we will start with a relatively simple case. Locust Software has been in existence for two years, and it is one of several successful firms that develop computer programs. Currently, Locust sells for cash only.

Locust is evaluating a request from some major customers to change its current policy to net one month (30 days). To analyze this proposal, we define the following:

P = Price per unit

v = Variable cost per unit

Q = Current quantity sold per month

Q' = Quantity sold under new policy

R = Monthly required return

For now, we ignore discounts and the possibility of default. Also, we ignore taxes because they don't affect our conclusions.

NPV of Switching Policies   To illustrate the NPV of switching credit policies, suppose we have the following for Locust:

P = $49

v = $20

Q = 100

Q' = 110

If the required return, R, is 2 percent per month, should Locust make the switch?

Currently, Locust has monthly sales of $P \times Q$ = $4,900. Variable costs each month are $v \times Q$ = $2,000, so the monthly cash flow from this activity is:

Cash flow with old policy = $(P - v)Q$ [20.2]
$$= (\$49 - 20) \times 100$$
$$= \$2,900$$

This is not the total cash flow for Locust, of course, but it is all that we need to look at because fixed costs and other components of cash flow are the same whether or not the switch is made.

If Locust does switch to net 30 days on sales, then the quantity sold will rise to Q' = 110. Monthly revenues will increase to $P \times Q'$, and costs will be $v \times Q'$. The monthly cash flow

---

[1]The cost of short-term debt is not necessarily the required return on receivables, although it is commonly assumed to be. As always, the required return on an investment depends on the risk of the investment, not the source of the financing. The *buyer's* cost of short-term debt is closer in spirit to the correct rate. We will maintain the implicit assumption that the seller and the buyer have the same short-term debt cost. In any case, the time periods in credit decisions are relatively short, so a relatively small error in the discount rate will not have a large effect on our estimated NPV.

under the new policy will be:

Cash flow with new policy = (P − v)Q′   [20.3]

$$= (\$49 - 20) \times 110$$
$$= \$3,190$$

Going back to Chapter 10, we know that the relevant incremental cash flow is the difference between the new and old cash flows:

Incremental cash inflow = $(P - v)(Q' - Q)$
$$= (\$49 - 20) \times (110 - 100)$$
$$= \$290$$

This says that the benefit each month of changing policies is equal to the gross profit per unit sold, $P - v = \$29$, multiplied by the increase in sales, $Q' - Q = 10$. The present value of the future incremental cash flows is:

PV = [(P − v)(Q′ − Q)]/R   [20.4]

For Locust, this present value works out to be:

PV = ($29 × 10)/.02 = $14,500

Notice that we have treated the monthly cash flow as a perpetuity because the same benefit will be realized each month forever.

Now that we know the benefit of switching, what's the cost? There are two components to consider. First, because the quantity sold will rise from Q to Q', Locust will have to produce $Q' - Q$ more units at a cost of $v(Q' - Q) = \$20 \times (110 - 100) = \$200$. Second, the sales that would have been collected this month under the current policy ($P \times Q = \$4,900$) will not be collected. Under the new policy, the sales made this month won't be collected until 30 days later. The cost of the switch is the sum of these two components:

Cost of switching = PQ + v(Q′ − Q)   [20.5]

For Locust, this cost would be $4,900 + 200 = $5,100.

Putting it all together, we see that the NPV of the switch is:

NPV of switching = −[PQ + v(Q′ − Q)] + [(P − v)(Q′ − Q)]/R   [20.6]

For Locust, the cost of switching is $5,100. As we saw earlier, the benefit is $290 per month forever. At 2 percent per month, the NPV is:

NPV = −$5,100 + $290/.02
$$= -\$5,100 + 14,500$$
$$= \$9,400$$

Therefore, the switch is profitable.

We'd Rather Fight Than Switch

EXAMPLE 20.1

Suppose a company is considering a switch from all cash to net 30, but the quantity sold is not expected to change. What is the NPV of the switch? Explain.

In this case, $Q' - Q$ is zero, so the NPV is $-PQ$. What this says is that the effect of the switch is to postpone one month's collections forever, with no benefit from doing so.

A Break-Even Application   Based on our discussion thus far, the key variable for Locust is $Q' - Q$, the increase in unit sales. The projected increase of 10 units is only an estimate, so there is some forecasting risk. Under the circumstances, it's natural to wonder what increase in unit sales is necessary to break even.

Earlier, the NPV of the switch was defined as:

$$\text{NPV} = -[PQ + v(Q' - Q)] + [(P - v)(Q' - Q)]/R$$

We can calculate the break-even point explicitly by setting the NPV equal to zero and solving for $(Q' - Q)$:

$$\textbf{NPV} = 0 = -[PQ + v(Q' - Q)] + [(P - v)(Q' - Q)]/R$$
$$Q' - Q = PQ/[(P - v)/R - v]$$

20.7

For Locust, the break-even sales increase is:

$$Q' - Q = \$4,900/(\$29/.02 - \$20)$$
$$= 3.43 \text{ units}$$

This tells us that the switch is a good idea as long as Locust is confident that it can sell at least 3.43 more units per month.

Concept Questions

20.3a What are the important effects to consider in a decision to offer credit?

20.3b Explain how to estimate the NPV of a credit policy switch.

20.4 Optimal Credit Policy

So far, we've discussed how to compute net present values for a switch in credit policy. We have not discussed the optimal amount of credit or the optimal credit policy. In principle, the optimal amount of credit is determined by the point at which the incremental cash flows from increased sales are exactly equal to the incremental costs of carrying the increased investment in accounts receivable.

THE TOTAL CREDIT COST CURVE

The trade-off between granting credit and not granting credit isn't hard to identify, but it is difficult to quantify precisely. As a result, we can only describe an optimal credit policy.

To begin, the carrying costs associated with granting credit come in three forms:

1. The required return on receivables.
2. The losses from bad debts.
3. The costs of managing credit and credit collections.

We have already discussed the first and second of these. The third cost, the cost of managing credit, consists of the expenses associated with running the credit department. Firms that don't grant credit have no such department and no such expense. These three costs will all increase as credit policy is relaxed.

If a firm has a very restrictive credit policy, then all of the associated costs will be low. In this case, the firm will have a "shortage" of credit, so there will be an opportunity cost.

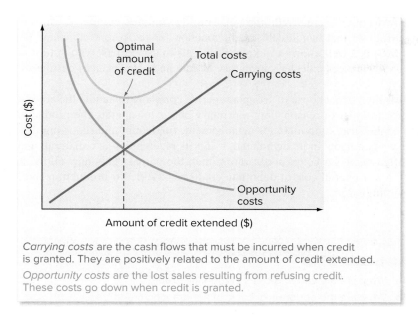

FIGURE 20.1

The Costs of Granting Credit

Carrying costs are the cash flows that must be incurred when credit is granted. They are positively related to the amount of credit extended.

Opportunity costs are the lost sales resulting from refusing credit. These costs go down when credit is granted.

This opportunity cost is the extra potential profit from credit sales that are lost because credit is refused. This forgone benefit comes from two sources: The increase in quantity sold, Q' minus Q, and (potentially) a higher price. The opportunity costs go down as credit policy is relaxed.

The sum of the carrying costs and the opportunity costs of a particular credit policy is called the total **credit cost curve**. We have drawn such a curve in Figure 20.1. As Figure 20.1 illustrates, there is a point where the total credit cost is minimized. This point corresponds to the optimal amount of credit or, equivalently, the optimal investment in receivables.

If the firm extends more credit than this minimum, the additional net cash flow from new customers will not cover the carrying costs of the investment in receivables. If the level of receivables is below this amount, then the firm is forgoing valuable profit opportunities.

In general, the costs and benefits from extending credit will depend on the characteristics of particular firms and industries. All other things being equal, it is likely that firms with (1) excess capacity, (2) low variable operating costs, and (3) repeat customers will extend credit more liberally than other firms. See if you can explain why each of these characteristics contributes to a more liberal credit policy.

credit cost curve
A graphical representation of the sum of the carrying costs and the opportunity costs of a credit policy.

ORGANIZING THE CREDIT FUNCTION

Firms that grant credit have the expense of running a credit department. In practice, firms often choose to contract out all or part of the credit function to a factor, an insurance company, or a captive finance company. Chapter 18 discusses factoring, an arrangement in which the firm sells its receivables. Depending on the specific arrangement, the factor may have full responsibility for credit checking, authorization, and collection. Smaller firms may find such an arrangement cheaper than running a credit department.

Firms that manage internal credit operations are self-insured against default. An alternative is to buy credit insurance through an insurance company. The insurance company offers coverage up to a preset dollar limit for each account. As you would expect, accounts with a higher credit rating merit higher insurance limits. This type of insurance is particularly important for exporters, and government insurance is available for certain types of exports.

captive finance company
A wholly owned subsidiary that handles the credit function for the parent company.

Large firms often extend credit through a **captive finance company**, which is a wholly owned subsidiary that handles the credit function for the parent company. Ford Motor Credit (FMC) is a well-known example. Ford sells to car dealers, who in turn sell to customers. FMC finances a dealer's inventory of cars and also finances customers who buy the cars.

Why would a firm choose to set up a separate company to handle the credit function? There are a number of reasons, but a primary one is to separate the production and financing of the firm's products for management, financing, and reporting. The finance subsidiary can borrow in its own name, using its receivables as collateral, and the subsidiary often carries a better credit rating than the parent. This may allow the firm to achieve a lower overall cost of debt than could be obtained if production and financing were commingled.

Concept Questions

20.4a What are the carrying costs of granting credit?

20.4b What are the opportunity costs of not granting credit?

20.4c What is a captive finance company?

20.5 Credit Analysis

Thus far, we have focused on establishing credit terms. Once a firm decides to grant credit to its customers, it must then establish guidelines for determining who will and who will not be allowed to buy on credit. *Credit analysis* refers to the process of deciding whether or not to extend credit to a particular customer. It usually involves two steps: Gathering relevant information and determining creditworthiness.

Credit analysis is important because potential losses on receivables can be substantial. Companies report the amount of receivables they do not expect to collect on their balance sheets. In late 2017, IBM reported that $689 million of accounts receivable were doubtful, and Microsoft reported $285 million as an allowance for losses.

WHEN SHOULD CREDIT BE GRANTED?

Imagine that a firm is trying to decide whether or not to grant credit to a customer. This decision can get complicated. Note that the answer depends on what will happen if credit is refused. Will the customer pay cash? Or will the customer not make the purchase at all? To avoid being bogged down by this and other difficulties, we will use some special cases to illustrate the key points.

A One-Time Sale We start by considering the simplest case. A new customer wishes to buy one unit on credit at a price of P per unit. If credit is refused, the customer will not make the purchase.

Furthermore, we assume that, if credit is granted, then, in one month, the customer will either pay up or default. The probability of the second of these events is π. In this case, the probability (π) can be interpreted as the percentage of *new* customers who will not pay. Our business does not have repeat customers, so this is strictly a one-time sale. Finally, the required return on receivables is R per month, and the variable cost is v per unit.

The analysis here is straightforward. If the firm refuses credit, then the incremental cash flow is zero. If it grants credit, then it spends v (the variable cost) this month and expects to collect $(1 - \pi)P$ next month. The NPV of granting credit is:

NPV $= -v + (1 - \pi)P/(1 + R)$

For Locust Software, this NPV is:

NPV $= -\$20 + (1 - \pi) \times \$49/1.02$

With, say, a 20 percent rate of default, this works out to be:

NPV $= -\$20 + .80 \times \$49/1.02 = \$18.43$

Therefore, credit should be granted. Notice that we have divided by $(1 + R)$ here instead of by R because we now assume that this is a one-time transaction.

Our example illustrates an important point. In granting credit to a new customer, a firm risks its variable cost (v). It stands to gain the full price (P). For a new customer, then, credit may be granted even if the default probability is high. The break-even probability in this case can be determined by setting the NPV equal to zero and solving for π:

NPV $= 0 = -\$20 + (1 - \pi) \times \$49/1.02$
$1 - \pi = \$20/\$49 \times 1.02$
$\pi = .584$, or 58.4%

Locust should extend credit as long as there is a $1 - .584 = .416$, or 41.6% chance or better of collecting. This explains why firms with higher markups tend to have looser credit terms.

This percentage (58.4%) is the maximum acceptable default probability for a *new* customer. If a returning, cash-paying customer wanted to switch to a credit basis, the analysis would be different, and the maximum acceptable default probability would be much lower.

The important difference is that if we extend credit to a returning customer, then we risk the total sales price (P), because this is what we collect if we don't extend credit. If we extend credit to a new customer, then we risk only our variable cost.

Repeat Business   A second, very important factor to keep in mind is the possibility of repeat business. We can illustrate this by extending our one-time sale example. We make one important assumption: A new customer who does not default the first time around will remain a customer forever and never default.

If the firm grants credit, it spends v this month. Next month, it gets nothing if the customer defaults, or it gets P if the customer pays. If the customer pays, then the customer will buy another unit on credit and the firm will spend v again. The net cash inflow for the month is $P - v$. In every subsequent month, this same $P - v$ will occur as the customer pays for the previous month's order and places a new one.

It follows from our discussion that, in one month, the firm will receive $0 with probability π. With probability $(1 - \pi)$ the firm will have a permanent new customer. The value of a new customer is equal to the present value of $(P - v)$ every month forever:

PV $= (P - v)/R$

The NPV of extending credit is:

NPV $= -v + (1 - \pi)(P - v)/R$

For Locust, this is:

NPV $= -\$20 + (1 - \pi) \times (\$49 - 20)/.02$
$= -\$20 + (1 - \pi) \times \$1,450$

Even if the probability of default is 90 percent, the NPV is:

$$\text{NPV} = -\$20 + .10 \times \$1,450 = \$125$$

Locust should extend credit unless default is a virtual certainty. The reason is that it costs only $20 to find out who is a good customer and who is not. A good customer is worth $1,450, so Locust can afford quite a few defaults.

Our repeat business example probably exaggerates the acceptable default probability, but it does illustrate that it will often turn out that the best way to do credit analysis is to extend credit to almost anyone. It also points out that the possibility of repeat business is a crucial consideration. In such cases, the important thing is to control the amount of credit initially offered to any one customer so that the possible loss is limited. The amount can be increased with time. Most often, the best predictor of whether or not someone will pay in the future is whether or not they have paid in the past.

CREDIT INFORMATION

If a firm wants credit information about customers, there are a number of sources. Information sources commonly used to assess creditworthiness include the following:

Web-surfing students should peruse the Dun & Bradstreet home page. This major supplier of credit information can be found at **www.dnb.com**.

1. *Financial statements*: A firm can ask a customer to supply financial statements such as balance sheets and income statements. Minimum standards and rules of thumb based on financial ratios like the ones we discussed in Chapter 3 can then be used as a basis for extending or refusing credit.

2. *Credit reports about the customer's payment history with other firms*: Quite a few organizations sell information about the credit strength and credit history of business firms. The best-known and largest firm of this type is Dun & Bradstreet, which provides subscribers with credit reports on individual firms. Experian is another well-known credit-reporting firm. Ratings and information are available for a huge number of firms, including very small ones. Equifax, TransUnion, and Experian are the major suppliers of consumer credit information.

3. *Banks*: Banks will generally provide some assistance to their business customers in acquiring information about the creditworthiness of other firms.

4. *The customer's payment history with the firm*: The most obvious way to obtain information about the likelihood of customers not paying is to examine whether they have settled past obligations (and how quickly).

CREDIT EVALUATION AND SCORING

There are no magical formulas for assessing the probability that a customer will not pay. In very general terms, the classic **five Cs of credit** are the basic factors to be evaluated:

five Cs of credit
The five basic credit factors to be evaluated: Character, capacity, capital, collateral, and conditions.

1. *Character*: The customer's willingness to meet credit obligations.
2. *Capacity*: The customer's ability to meet credit obligations out of operating cash flows.
3. *Capital*: The customer's financial reserves.
4. *Collateral*: An asset pledged in the case of default.
5. *Conditions*: General economic conditions in the customer's line of business.

credit scoring
The process of quantifying the probability of default when granting consumer credit.

Credit scoring is the process of calculating a numerical rating for a customer based on information collected; credit is then granted or refused based on the result. A firm might rate a customer on a scale of 1 (very poor) to 10 (very good) on each of the five Cs of credit using all the information available about the customer. A credit score could then be calculated by totaling these ratings. Based on experience, a firm might choose to grant credit only to customers with a score above, say, 30.

Firms such as credit card issuers have developed statistical models for credit scoring. Usually, all of the legally relevant and observable characteristics of a large pool of customers are studied to find their historic relation to defaults. Based on the results, it is possible to determine the variables that best predict whether a customer will pay and then calculate a credit score based on those variables.

Because credit-scoring models and procedures determine who is and who is not creditworthy, it is not surprising that they have been the subject of government regulation. In particular, the kinds of background and demographic information that can be used in the credit decision are limited.

Concept Questions

20.5a What is credit analysis?

20.5b What are the five Cs of credit?

Collection Policy

20.6

Collection policy, the final element in credit policy, involves monitoring receivables to spot trouble and obtaining payment on past-due accounts.

MONITORING RECEIVABLES

To keep track of payments by customers, most firms will monitor outstanding accounts. First of all, a firm will normally keep track of its ACP through time. If a firm is in a seasonal business, the ACP will fluctuate during the year; but unexpected increases in the ACP are a cause for concern. Either customers in general are taking longer to pay, or some percentage of accounts receivable are seriously overdue.

The **aging schedule** is a second basic tool for monitoring receivables. To prepare one, the credit department classifies accounts by age.[2] Suppose a firm has $100,000 in receivables. Some of these accounts are only a few days old, but others have been outstanding for quite some time. The following is an example of an aging schedule:

aging schedule
A compilation of accounts receivable by the age of each account.

Aging Schedule		
Age of Account	Amount	Percentage of Total Value of Accounts Receivable
0–10 days	$ 50,000	50%
11–60 days	25,000	25
61–80 days	20,000	20
Over 80 days	5,000	5
	$100,000	100%

If this firm has a credit period of 60 days, then 25 percent of its accounts are late. Whether or not this is serious depends on the nature of the firm's collections and customers. It is often the case that accounts beyond a certain age are almost never collected. Monitoring the age of accounts is very important in such cases.

---

[2]Aging schedules are also used elsewhere in business, such as inventory tracking.

For firms with seasonal sales, the percentages on the aging schedule will change during the year. If sales in the current month are very high, then total receivables will also increase sharply. This means that the older accounts, as a percentage of total receivables, become smaller and might appear less important. Some firms have refined the aging schedule so that they have an idea of how it should change in relation to the peaks and valleys in their sales.

COLLECTION EFFORT

A firm usually goes through the following sequence of procedures for customers whose payments are overdue:

1. It sends out a delinquency letter informing the customer of the past-due status of the account.
2. It makes a telephone call to the customer.
3. It employs a collection agency.
4. It takes legal action against the customer.

At times, a firm may refuse to grant additional credit to customers until arrearages are cleared up. This may antagonize a normally good customer, which points to a potential conflict between the collections department and the sales department.

In probably the worst case, the customer files for bankruptcy. When this happens, the credit-granting firm is just another unsecured creditor. The firm can wait, or it can sell its receivable. For example, when retailer Sports Authority filed for bankruptcy in 2016, it had more than $1 billion in debt, with less than $50,000 in assets listed. Two of its larger suppliers were Nike and Under Armour, to which it owed $48 million and $23 million, respectively.

Concept Questions

20.6a What tools can a manager use to monitor receivables?
20.6b What is an aging schedule?

20.7 Inventory Management

Like receivables, inventories represent a significant investment for many firms. For a typical manufacturing operation, inventories will often exceed 15 percent of assets. For a retailer, inventories could represent more than 25 percent of assets. From our discussion in Chapter 18, we know that a firm's operating cycle is made up of its inventory period and its receivables period. This is one reason for considering credit and inventory policy in the same chapter. Beyond this, both credit policy and inventory policy are used to drive sales, and the two must be coordinated to ensure that the process of acquiring inventory, selling it, and collecting on the sale all proceed smoothly. Changes in credit policy designed to stimulate sales must be accompanied by planning for adequate inventory.

THE FINANCIAL MANAGER AND INVENTORY POLICY

Despite the size of a typical firm's investment in inventories, the financial manager of a firm will not normally have primary control over inventory management. Instead, other functional areas such as purchasing, production, and marketing will usually share decision-making authority regarding inventory. Inventory management has become an increasingly important specialty in its own right, and financial management will often only have input into the decision. For this reason, we will survey some basics of inventory and inventory policy.

Visit the Society for Inventory Management Benchmarking Analysis at **www.simba.org**.

INVENTORY TYPES

For a manufacturer, inventory is normally classified into one of three categories. The first category is *raw material*. This is whatever the firm uses as a starting point in its production process. Raw materials might be something as basic as iron ore for a steel manufacturer or something as sophisticated as disk drives for a computer manufacturer.

The second type of inventory is *work-in-progress*, which is what the name suggests—unfinished product. How big this portion of inventory is depends in large part on the length of the production process. For an airframe manufacturer, work-in-progress can be substantial. The third and final type of inventory is *finished goods*—that is, products ready to ship or sell.

Keep in mind three things concerning inventory types. First, the names for the different types of inventory can be a little misleading because one company's raw materials can be another's finished goods. Going back to our steel manufacturer, iron ore would be a raw material, and steel would be the final product. An auto body panel stamping operation will have steel as its raw material and auto body panels as its finished goods, and an automobile assembler will have auto body panels as raw materials and automobiles as finished products.

The second thing to keep in mind is that the various types of inventory can be quite different in terms of their liquidity. Raw materials that are commodity-like or relatively standardized can be easy to convert to cash. Work-in-progress, on the other hand, can be quite illiquid and have little more than scrap value. As always, the liquidity of finished goods depends on the nature of the product.

Finally, a very important distinction between finished goods and other types of inventories is that the demand for an inventory item that becomes a part of another item is usually termed *derived* or *dependent demand* because the firm's need for these inventory types depends on its need for finished items. In contrast, the firm's demand for finished goods is not derived from demand for other inventory items, so it is sometimes said to be *independent*.

INVENTORY COSTS

As we discussed in Chapter 18, two basic types of costs are associated with current assets in general and with inventory in particular. The first of these is *carrying costs*. Here, carrying costs represent all of the direct and opportunity costs of keeping inventory on hand. These include:

1. Storage and tracking costs.
2. Insurance and taxes.
3. Losses due to obsolescence, deterioration, or theft.
4. The opportunity cost of capital on the invested amount.

The sum of these costs can be substantial, ranging roughly from 20 to 40 percent of inventory value per year.

The second type of cost associated with inventory is *shortage costs*. Shortage costs are costs associated with having inadequate inventory on hand. The two components of shortage costs are restocking costs and costs related to safety reserves. Depending on the firm's business, restocking or order costs are either the costs of placing an order with suppliers or the costs of setting up a production run. The costs related to safety reserves are opportunity costs such as lost sales and loss of customer goodwill that result from having inadequate inventory.

A basic trade-off exists in inventory management because carrying costs increase with inventory levels, whereas shortage or restocking costs decline with inventory levels. The basic goal of inventory management is to minimize the sum of these two costs. We consider ways to reach this goal in the next section.

To give you an idea of how important it is to balance carrying costs with shortage costs, consider the delay in deliveries for a wide variety of companies that we discussed at the beginning of the chapter. The companies all faced shortages and either lost sales or were forced to resort to more expensive shipping methods.

Concept Questions

20.7a   What are the different types of inventory?
20.7b   What are three things to remember when examining inventory types?
20.7c   What is the basic goal of inventory management?

20.8 Inventory Management Techniques

As we described earlier, the goal of inventory management is usually framed as cost minimization. Three techniques are discussed in this section, ranging from the relatively simple to the very complex.

THE ABC APPROACH

The ABC approach is a simple approach to inventory management in which the basic idea is to divide inventory into three (or more) groups. The underlying rationale is that a small portion of inventory in terms of quantity might represent a large portion in terms of inventory value. This situation would exist for a manufacturer that uses some relatively expensive, high-tech components and some relatively inexpensive basic materials in producing its products.

Figure 20.2 illustrates an ABC comparison of items in terms of the percentage of inventory value represented by each group versus the percentage of items represented. As Figure 20.2 shows, the A Group comprises only 10 percent of inventory by item count, but it represents over half of the value of inventory. The A Group items are monitored closely, and inventory levels are kept relatively low. At the other end, basic inventory items, such as nuts and bolts, also exist; because these are crucial and inexpensive, large quantities are ordered and kept on hand. These would be C Group items. The B Group is made up of in-between items.

THE ECONOMIC ORDER QUANTITY MODEL

The economic order quantity (EOQ) model is the best-known approach for explicitly establishing an optimal inventory level. The basic idea is illustrated in Figure 20.3, which plots the various costs associated with holding inventory (on the vertical axis) against inventory levels (on the horizontal axis). As shown, inventory carrying costs rise and restocking costs decrease as inventory levels increase. From our general discussion in Chapter 18 and our

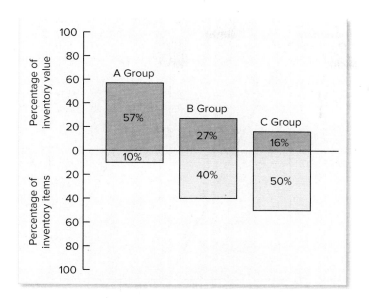

FIGURE 20.2

ABC Inventory Analysis

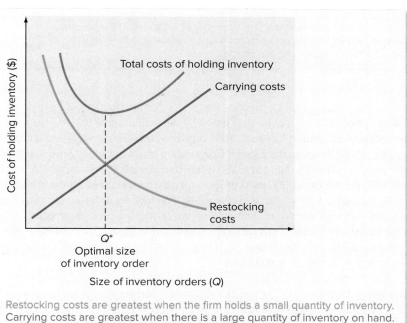

Restocking costs are greatest when the firm holds a small quantity of inventory. Carrying costs are greatest when there is a large quantity of inventory on hand. Total costs are the sum of the carrying and restocking costs.

FIGURE 20.3

Costs of Holding Inventory

discussion of the total credit cost curve in this chapter, the general shape of the total inventory cost curve is familiar. With the EOQ model, we will attempt to specifically locate the minimum total cost point, Q^*.

In our discussion that follows, an important point to keep in mind is that the actual cost of the inventory itself is not included. The reason is that the *total* amount of inventory the firm needs in a given year is dictated by sales. What we are analyzing here is how much the firm should have on hand at any particular time. More precisely, we are trying to determine what order size the firm should use when it restocks its inventory.

FIGURE 20.4

**Inventory Holdings for
the Eyssell Corporation**

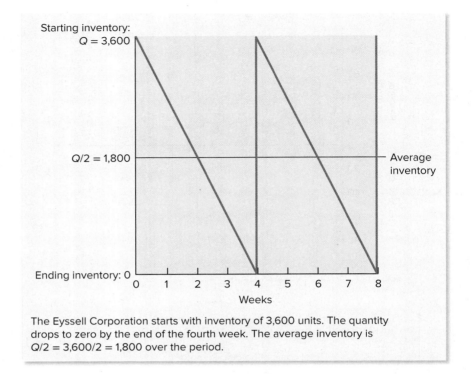

The Eyssell Corporation starts with inventory of 3,600 units. The quantity
drops to zero by the end of the fourth week. The average inventory is
Q/2 = 3,600/2 = 1,800 over the period.

Inventory Depletion   To develop the EOQ, we will assume that the firm's inventory
is sold at a steady rate until it hits zero. At that point, the firm restocks its inventory back to
some optimal level. Suppose the Eyssell Corporation starts out today with 3,600 units of a
particular item in inventory. Annual sales of this item are 46,800 units, which is about 900
per week. If Eyssell sells off 900 units of inventory each week, then all the available inventory will be sold after four weeks, and Eyssell will restock by ordering (or manufacturing)
another 3,600 units and start over. This selling and restocking process produces a sawtooth
pattern for inventory holdings; this pattern is illustrated in Figure 20.4. As the figure shows,
Eyssell always starts with 3,600 units in inventory and ends up at zero. On average, then,
inventory is half of 3,600, or 1,800 units.

The Carrying Costs   As Figure 20.3 illustrates, carrying costs are normally assumed
to be directly proportional to inventory levels. Suppose we let Q be the quantity of inventory that Eyssell orders each time (3,600 units); we will call this the *restocking quantity*.
Average inventory would then be $Q/2$, or 1,800 units. If we let CC be the carrying cost per
unit per year, Eyssell's total carrying costs will be:

> **Total carrying costs = Average inventory × Carrying cost per unit**
> **= (Q/2) × CC**

In Eyssell's case, if carrying costs were $.75 per unit per year, total carrying costs would be
the average inventory of 1,800 units multiplied by $.75, or $1,350 per year.

The Restocking Costs   For now, we will focus only on the restocking costs. In
essence, we will assume that the firm never actually runs short on inventory, so that costs
relating to safety reserves are unimportant. We will return to this issue later.

Restocking costs are normally assumed to be fixed. In other words, every time we place an order, fixed costs are associated with that order (remember that the cost of the inventory itself is not considered here). Suppose we let T be the firm's total unit sales per year. If the firm orders Q units each time, then it will need to place a total of T/Q orders. For Eyssell, annual sales are 46,800, and the order size is 3,600. Eyssel places a total of $46,800/3,600 = 13$ orders per year. If the fixed cost per order is F, the total restocking cost for the year would be:

Total restocking cost = Fixed cost per order × Number of orders   20.11

$$= F \times (T/Q)$$

For Eyssell, order costs might be $50 per order, so the total restocking cost for 13 orders would be $50 \times 13 = \$650$ per year.

The Total Costs   The total costs associated with holding inventory are the sum of the carrying costs and the restocking costs:

Total costs = Carrying costs + Restocking costs   20.12

$$= (Q/2) \times CC + F \times (T/Q)$$

Our goal is to find the value of Q, the restocking quantity, that minimizes this cost. To see how we might go about this, we can calculate total costs for some different values of Q. For the Eyssell Corporation, we had carrying costs (CC) of $.75 per unit per year, fixed costs (F) of $50 per order, and total unit sales (T) of 46,800 units. With these numbers, here are some possible total costs (check some of these for practice):

Restocking Quantity (Q)	Carrying Costs (Q/2 × CC)	+	Restocking Costs (F × T/Q)	=	Total Costs
500	$ 187.5		$4,680.0		$4,867.5
1,000	375.0		2,340.0		2,715.0
1,500	562.5		1,560.0		2,122.5
2,000	750.0		1,170.0		1,920.0
2,500	937.5		936.0		1,873.5
3,000	1,125.0		780.0		1,905.0
3,500	1,312.5		668.6		1,981.1

Inspecting the numbers, we see that total costs start out at almost $5,000 and decline to just under $1,900. The cost-minimizing quantity is about 2,500.

To find the exact cost-minimizing quantity, we can look back at Figure 20.3. What we notice is that the minimum point occurs right where the two lines cross. At this point, carrying costs and restocking costs are the same. For the particular types of costs we have assumed here, this will always be true; so we can find the minimum point by setting these costs equal to each other and solving for Q^*:

Carrying costs = Restocking costs   20.13

$$(Q^*/2) \times CC = F \times (T/Q^*)$$

With a little algebra, we get:

$$Q^{*2} = \frac{2T \times F}{CC}$$

To solve for Q^*, we take the square root of both sides to find:

$$Q^* = \sqrt{\frac{2T \times F}{CC}}$$

[20.14]

economic order
quantity (EOQ)
The restocking quantity that
minimizes the total inventory
costs.

This reorder quantity, which minimizes the total inventory cost, is called the **economic order quantity (EOQ)**. For the Eyssell Corporation, the EOQ is:

$$
\begin{aligned}
Q^* &= \sqrt{\frac{2T \times F}{CC}} \\
&= \sqrt{\frac{(2 \times 46{,}800) \times \$50}{\$.75}} \\
&= \sqrt{6{,}240{,}000} \\
&= 2{,}498 \text{ units}
\end{aligned}
$$

For Eyssell, the economic order quantity is 2,498 units. At this level, verify that the restocking costs and carrying costs are both $936.75.

EXAMPLE 20.2   Carrying Costs

Thiewes Shoes begins each period with 100 pairs of hiking boots in stock. This stock is depleted each period and reordered. If the carrying cost per pair of boots per year is $3, what are the total carrying costs for the hiking boots?

Inventories always start at 100 items and end up at zero, so average inventory is 50 items. At an annual cost of $3 per item, total carrying costs are $150.

EXAMPLE 20.3   Restocking Costs

In Example 20.2, suppose Thiewes sells a total of 600 pairs of boots in a year. How many times per year does Thiewes restock? Suppose the restocking cost is $20 per order. What are total restocking costs?

Thiewes orders 100 items each time. Total sales are 600 items per year, so Thiewes restocks six times per year, or about once every two months. The restocking costs would be 6 orders × $20 per order = $120.

EXAMPLE 20.4   The EOQ

Based on our previous two examples, what size orders should Thiewes place to minimize costs? How often will Thiewes restock? What are the total carrying and restocking costs? The total costs?

We know that the total number of pairs of boots ordered for the year (T) is 600. The restocking cost (F) is $20 per order, and the carrying cost (CC) is $3. We can calculate the EOQ for Thiewes as follows:

$$
\begin{aligned}
EOQ &= \sqrt{\frac{2T \times F}{CC}} \\
&= \sqrt{\frac{(2 \times 600) \times \$20}{\$3}} \\
&= \sqrt{8{,}000} \\
&= 89.44 \text{ units}
\end{aligned}
$$

Because Thiewes sells 600 pairs per year, it will restock $600/89.44 = 6.71$ times. The total restocking costs will be $\$20 \times 6.71 = \$134.16$. Average inventory will be $89.44/2 = 44.72$. The carrying costs will be $\$3 \times 44.72 = \$134.16$, the same as the restocking costs. The total costs are $\$268.33$.

EXTENSIONS TO THE EOQ MODEL

Thus far, we have assumed that a company will let its inventory run down to zero and then reorder. In reality, a company will wish to reorder before its inventory goes to zero for two reasons. First, by always having at least some inventory on hand, the firm minimizes the risk of a stockout and the resulting losses of sales and customers. Second, when a firm does reorder, there will be some time lag before the inventory arrives. To finish our discussion of the EOQ, we consider two extensions: Safety stocks and reordering points.

Safety Stocks   A *safety stock* is the minimum level of inventory that a firm keeps on hand. Inventories are reordered whenever the level of inventory falls to the safety stock level. The top of Figure 20.5 (Part A) illustrates how a safety stock can be incorporated into an EOQ model. Notice that adding a safety stock means that the firm does not run its inventory all the way down to zero. Other than this, the situation here is identical to that described in our earlier discussion of the EOQ.

Reorder Points   To allow for delivery time, a firm will place orders before inventories reach a critical level. The *reorder points* are the times at which the firm will actually place its inventory orders. These points are illustrated in the middle of Figure 20.5 (Part B). As shown, the reorder points occur some fixed number of days (or weeks or months) before inventories are projected to reach zero.

One of the reasons that a firm will keep a safety stock is to allow for uncertain delivery times. We can combine our reorder point and safety stock discussions in the bottom part of Figure 20.5 (Part C). The result is a generalized EOQ model in which the firm orders in advance of anticipated needs and also keeps a safety stock of inventory.

MANAGING DERIVED-DEMAND INVENTORIES

The third type of inventory management technique is used to manage derived-demand inventories. As we described earlier, demand for some inventory types is derived from or dependent on other inventory needs. A good example is the auto manufacturing industry, in which the demand for finished products depends on consumer demand, marketing programs, and other factors related to projected unit sales. The demand for inventory items such as tires, batteries, headlights, and other components is then completely determined by the number of autos planned. Materials requirements planning and just-in-time inventory management are two methods for managing demand-dependent inventories.

Materials Requirements Planning   Production and inventory specialists have developed computer-based systems for ordering and/or scheduling production of demand-dependent types of inventories. These systems fall under the general heading of **materials requirements planning (MRP)**. The basic idea behind MRP is that, once finished goods inventory levels are set, it is possible to determine what levels of work-in-progress inventories must exist to meet the need for finished goods. From there, it is possible to calculate the quantity of raw materials that must be on hand. This ability to schedule backward from finished goods inventories stems from the dependent nature of work-in-progress and raw

materials requirements planning (MRP)
A set of procedures used to determine inventory levels for demand-dependent inventory types such as work-in-progress and raw materials.

FIGURE 20.5

**Safety Stocks and
Reorder Points**

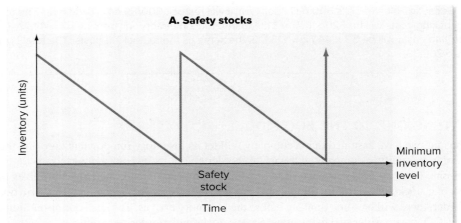

A. Safety stocks

With a safety stock, the firm reorders when inventory reaches a minimum level.

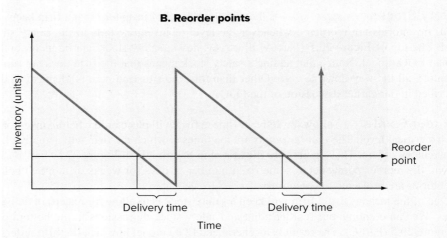

B. Reorder points

When there are lags in delivery or production times, the firm reorders when inventory reaches the reorder point.

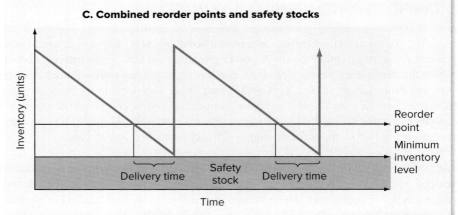

C. Combined reorder points and safety stocks

By combining safety stocks and reorder points, the firm maintains a buffer against unforeseen events.

materials inventories. MRP is particularly important for complicated products for which a variety of components are needed to create the finished product.

Just-in-Time Inventory   **Just-in-time (JIT) inventory** is a modern approach to managing dependent inventories. The goal of JIT is to minimize such inventories, thereby maximizing turnover. The approach began in Japan, and it is a fundamental part of Japanese manufacturing philosophy. As the name suggests, the basic goal of JIT is to have only enough inventory on hand to meet immediate production needs.

The result of the JIT system is that inventories are reordered and restocked frequently. Making such a system work and avoiding shortages requires a high degree of cooperation among suppliers. Japanese manufacturers often have a relatively small, tightly integrated group of suppliers with whom they work closely to achieve the needed coordination. These suppliers are a part of a large manufacturer's (such as Toyota's) industrial group, or *keiretsu*. Each large manufacturer tends to have its own *keiretsu*. It also helps to have suppliers located nearby, a situation that is common in Japan.

The *kanban* is an integral part of a JIT inventory system, and JIT systems are sometimes called *kanban systems*. The literal meaning of *kanban* is "card" or "sign"; but, broadly speaking, a kanban is a signal to a supplier to send more inventory. A kanban can literally be a card attached to a bin of parts. When a worker pulls that bin, the card is detached and routed back to the supplier, who then supplies a replacement bin.

A JIT inventory system is an important part of a larger production planning process. A full discussion of it would necessarily shift our focus away from finance to production and operations management, so we will leave it here.

> **just-in-time (JIT) inventory**
> A system for managing demand-dependent inventories that minimizes inventory holdings.

Concept Questions

20.8a What does the EOQ model determine for the firm?

20.8b Which cost component of the EOQ model does the JIT inventory system minimize?

Summary and Conclusions   20.9

This chapter has covered the basics of credit and inventory policy. The major topics we discussed include these:

1. *The components of credit policy*: We discussed the terms of sale, credit analysis, and collection policy. Under the general subject of terms of sale, the credit period, the cash discount and discount period, and the credit instrument were described.

2. *Credit policy analysis*: We developed the cash flows from the decision to grant credit and showed how the credit decision can be analyzed in an NPV setting. The NPV of granting credit depends on five factors: Revenue effects, cost effects, the cost of debt, the probability of nonpayment, and the cash discount.

3. *Optimal credit policy*: The optimal amount of credit the firm should offer depends on the competitive conditions under which the firm operates. These conditions will determine the carrying costs associated with granting credit and the opportunity costs of the lost sales resulting from the refusal to offer credit. The optimal credit policy minimizes the sum of these two costs.

4. *Credit analysis*: We looked at the decision to grant credit to a particular customer. We saw that two considerations are very important: The cost relative to the selling price and the possibility of repeat business.

5. *Collection policy*: Collection policy determines the method of monitoring the age of accounts receivable and dealing with past-due accounts. We described how an aging schedule can be prepared and the procedures a firm might use to collect on past-due accounts.

6. *Inventory types*: We described the different inventory types and how they differ in terms of liquidity and demand.

7. *Inventory costs*: The two basic inventory costs are carrying and restocking costs; we discussed how inventory management involves a trade-off between these two costs.

8. *Inventory management techniques*: We described the ABC approach and the EOQ model approach to inventory management. We also briefly touched on materials requirements planning (MRP) and just-in-time (JIT) inventory management.

CONNECT TO FINANCE

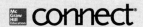 *Connect Finance* offers plenty of opportunities to practice mastering these concepts. Log on to connect.mheducation.com to learn more. If you like what you see, ask your professor about using *Connect Finance*!

Can you answer the following *Connect* Quiz questions?

Section 20.1 What is the difference between the accounts receivable period and the cash collection period?

Section 20.2 Marsha can purchase goods for her store on credit terms of 2/10, net 25. What is the effective annual rate that Marsha will pay if she forgoes the discount on a purchase of $8,700?

Section 20.7 If Rosie's Formal Attire has too low an inventory, the firm is most apt to _____.

CHAPTER REVIEW AND SELF-TEST PROBLEMS

20.1 Credit Policy The Cold Fusion Corp. (manufacturer of the Mr. Fusion home power plant) is considering a new credit policy. The current policy is cash only. The new policy would involve extending credit for one period. Based on the following information, determine if a switch is advisable. The interest rate is 2 percent per period:

	Current Policy	New Policy
Price per unit	$ 175	$ 175
Cost per unit	$ 130	$ 130
Sales per period in units	1,000	1,100

20.2 Credit Where Credit Is Due You are trying to decide whether or not to extend credit to a particular customer. Your variable cost is $15 per unit; the selling price is $22. This customer wants to buy 1,000 units today and pay in 30 days. You think there is a 15 percent chance of default. The required return is 3 percent per 30 days. Should you extend credit? Assume that this is a one-time sale and that the customer will not buy if credit is not extended.

20.3 The EOQ Annondale Manufacturing starts each period with 10,000 "Long John" golf clubs in stock. This stock is depleted each month and reordered. If the carrying cost per golf club is $1, and the fixed order cost is $5, is Annondale following an economically advisable strategy?

ANSWERS TO CHAPTER REVIEW AND SELF-TEST PROBLEMS

20.1 If the switch is made, an extra 100 units per period will be sold at a gross profit of $175 − 130 = $45 each. The total benefit is thus $45 × 100 = $4,500 per period. At 2 percent per period forever, the PV is $4,500/.02 = $225,000.

   The cost of the switch is equal to this period's revenue of $175 × 1,000 units = $175,000 plus the cost of producing the extra 100 units: 100 × $130 = $13,000. The total cost is thus $188,000, and the NPV is $225,000 − 188,000 = $37,000. The switch should be made.

20.2 If the customer pays in 30 days, then you will collect $22 × 1,000 = $22,000. There's only an 85 percent chance of collecting this; so you expect to get $22,000 × .85 = $18,700 in 30 days. The present value of this is $18,700 /1.03 = $18,155.34. Your cost is $15 × 1,000 = $15,000; so the NPV is $18,155.34 − 15,000 = $3,155.34. Credit should be extended.

20.3 We can answer by first calculating Annondale's carrying and restocking costs. The average inventory is 5,000 clubs, and, because the carrying costs are $1 per club, total carrying costs are $5,000. Annondale restocks every month at a fixed order cost of $5, so the total restocking costs are $60. What we see is that carrying costs are large relative to reorder costs, so Annondale is carrying too much inventory.

   To determine the optimal inventory policy, we can use the EOQ model. Because Annondale orders 10,000 golf clubs 12 times per year, total needs (*T*) are 120,000 golf clubs. The fixed order cost is $5, and the carrying cost per unit (CC) is $1. The EOQ is therefore:

$$\text{EOQ} = \sqrt{\frac{2T \times F}{CC}}$$
$$= \sqrt{\frac{(2 \times 120,000) \times \$5}{\$1}}$$
$$= \sqrt{1,200,000}$$
$$= 1,095.45 \text{ units}$$

We can check this by noting that the average inventory is about 550 clubs, so the carrying cost is $550. Annondale will have to reorder 120,000/1,095.45 = 109.54 ≈ 110 times. The fixed order cost is $5, so the total restocking cost is also about $550.

CONCEPTS REVIEW AND CRITICAL THINKING QUESTIONS

1. **Credit Instruments [LO1]** Describe each of the following:
   a. Sight draft.
   b. Time draft.
   c. Banker's acceptance.
   d. Promissory note.
   e. Trade acceptance.

2. **Trade Credit Forms [LO1]** In what form is trade credit most commonly offered? What is the credit instrument in this case?

3. **Receivables Costs [LO1]** What costs are associated with carrying receivables? What costs are associated with not granting credit? What do we call the sum of the costs for different levels of receivables?

4. **Five *C*s of Credit [LO1]** What are the five *C*s of credit? Explain why each is important.

5. **Credit Period Length [LO1]** What are some of the factors that determine the length of the credit period? Why is the length of the buyer's operating cycle often considered an upper bound on the length of the credit period?

6. **Credit Period Length [LO1]** In each of the following pairings, indicate which firm would probably have a longer credit period and explain your reasoning.
   a. Firm A sells a miracle cure for baldness; Firm B sells toupees.
   b. Firm A specializes in products for landlords; Firm B specializes in products for renters.
   c. Firm A sells to customers with an inventory turnover of 10 times; Firm B sells to customers with an inventory turnover of 20 times.
   d. Firm A sells fresh fruit; Firm B sells canned fruit.
   e. Firm A sells and installs carpeting; Firm B sells rugs.

7. **Inventory Types [LO3]** What are the different inventory types? How do the types differ? Why are some types said to have dependent demand whereas other types are said to have independent demand?

8. **Just-in-Time Inventory [LO3]** If a company moves to a JIT inventory management system, what will happen to inventory turnover? What will happen to total asset turnover? What will happen to return on equity (ROE)? *Hint*: Remember the DuPont equation from Chapter 3.

9. **Inventory Costs [LO3]** If a company's inventory carrying costs are $5 million per year and its fixed order costs are $8 million per year, do you think the firm keeps too much inventory on hand or too little? Why?

10. **Inventory Period [LO3]** At least part of Dell's corporate profits can be traced to its inventory management. Using just-in-time inventory, Dell typically maintains an inventory of three to four days' sales. Competitors such as Hewlett-Packard and IBM have attempted to match Dell's inventory policies, but they lag far behind. In an industry where the price of PC components continues to decline, Dell clearly has a competitive advantage. Why would you say that it is to Dell's advantage to have such a short inventory period? If doing this is valuable, why don't all other PC manufacturers switch to Dell's approach?

QUESTIONS AND PROBLEMS

BASIC
(Questions 1–12)

1. **Cash Discounts [LO1]** You place an order for 300 units of inventory at a unit price of $140. The supplier offers terms of 1/10, net 30.
   a. How long do you have to pay before the account is overdue? If you take the full period, how much should you remit?
   b. What is the discount being offered? How quickly must you pay to get the discount? If you do take the discount, how much should you remit?

c. If you don't take the discount, how much interest are you paying implicitly? How many days' credit are you receiving?

2. **Size of Accounts Receivable [LO1]** The Red Zeppelin Corporation has annual sales of $34 million. The average collection period is 28 days. What is the average investment in accounts receivable as shown on the balance sheet? Assume 365 days per year.

3. **ACP and Accounts Receivable [LO1]** Kyoto Joe, Inc., sells earnings forecasts for Japanese securities. Its credit terms are 2/10, net 30. Based on experience, 70 percent of all customers will take the discount.

   a. What is the average collection period for the company?

   b. If the company sells 1,120 forecasts every month at a price of $1,580 each, what is its average balance sheet amount in accounts receivable?

4. **Size of Accounts Receivable [LO1]** Skye Flyer, Inc., has weekly credit sales of $21,900, and the average collection period is 33 days. What is the average accounts receivable figure?

5. **Terms of Sale [LO1]** A firm offers terms of 1/10, net 30. What effective annual interest rate does the firm earn when a customer does not take the discount? Without doing any calculations, explain what will happen to this effective rate if:

   a. The discount is changed to 2 percent.

   b. The credit period is increased to 45 days.

   c. The discount period is increased to 14 days.

6. **ACP and Receivables Turnover [LO1]** Starset, Inc., has an average collection period of 27 days. Its average daily investment in receivables is $46,300. What are annual credit sales? What is the receivables turnover? Assume 365 days per year.

7. **Size of Accounts Receivable [LO1]** Essence of Skunk Fragrances, Ltd., sells 7,900 units of its perfume collection each year at a price per unit of $385. All sales are on credit with terms of 1/10, net 40. The discount is taken by 65 percent of the customers. What is the amount of the company's accounts receivable? In reaction to sales by its main competitor, Sewage Spray, Essence of Skunk is considering a change in its credit policy to terms of 2/10, net 30 to preserve its market share. How will this change in policy affect accounts receivable?

8. **Size of Accounts Receivable [LO1]** The Arizona Bay Corporation sells on credit terms of net 30. Its accounts are, on average, five days past due. If annual credit sales are $8.35 million, what is the company's balance sheet amount in accounts receivable?

9. **Evaluating Credit Policy [LO2]** Air Spares is a wholesaler that stocks engine components and test equipment for the commercial aircraft industry. A new customer has placed an order for eight high-bypass turbine engines, which increase fuel economy. The variable cost is $1.25 million per unit, and the credit price is $1.63 million each. Credit is extended for one period, and based on historical experience, payment for about 1 out of every 200 such orders is never collected. The required return is 1.8 percent per period.

   a. Assuming that this is a one-time order, should it be filled? The customer will not buy if credit is not extended.

   b. What is the break-even probability of default in part (a)?

   c. Suppose that customers who don't default become repeat customers and place the same order every period forever. Further assume that repeat customers never default. Should the order be filled? What is the break-even probability of default?

   d. Describe in general terms why credit terms will be more liberal when repeat orders are a possibility.

10. **Credit Policy Evaluation [LO2]** Sanchez, Inc., is considering a change in its cash-only sales policy. The new terms of sale would be net one month. Based on the following information, determine if the company should proceed or not. Describe the buildup of receivables in this case. The required return is .95 percent per month.

	Current Policy	New Policy
Price per unit	$ 540	$ 540
Cost per unit	$ 395	$ 395
Unit sales per month	1,080	1,130

11. **EOQ [LO4]** Provenza Manufacturing uses 3,400 switch assemblies per week and then reorders another 3,400. If the relevant carrying cost per switch assembly is $7.45, and the fixed order cost is $1,100, is the company's inventory policy optimal? Why or why not?

12. **EOQ [LO4]** The Trektronics store begins each week with 450 phasers in stock. This stock is depleted each week and reordered. If the carrying cost per phaser is $34 per year and the fixed order cost is $130, what is the total carrying cost? What is the restocking cost? Should the company increase or decrease its order size? Describe an optimal inventory policy for the company in terms of order size and order frequency.

INTERMEDIATE
(Questions 13–16)

13. **EOQ Derivation [LO4]** Prove that when carrying costs and restocking costs are as described in the chapter, the EOQ must occur at the point where the carrying costs and restocking costs are equal.

14. **Credit Policy Evaluation [LO2]** The Snedecker Corporation is considering a change in its cash-only policy. The new terms would be net one period. Based on the following information, determine if the company should proceed or not. The required return is 2.3 percent per period.

	Current Policy	New Policy
Price per unit	$ 81	$ 84
Cost per unit	$ 47	$ 47
Unit sales per month	3,280	3,390

15. **Credit Policy Evaluation [LO2]** Veni, Inc., currently has an all-cash credit policy. It is considering making a change in the credit policy by going to terms of net 30 days. Based on the following information, what do you recommend? The required return is .85 percent per month.

	Current Policy	New Policy
Price per unit	$ 131	$ 133
Cost per unit	$ 96	$ 98
Unit sales per month	1,320	1,340

16. **Credit Policy [LO2]** The Silver Spokes Bicycle Shop has decided to offer credit to its customers during the spring selling season. Sales are expected to be 125 bicycles. The average cost to the shop of a bicycle is $750. The owner knows that only 96 percent of the customers will be able to make their payments. To identify the remaining 4 percent, the company is considering subscribing to a credit agency. The initial charge for this service is $1,000, with an additional charge of $8.95 per individual report. Should she subscribe to the agency?

CHALLENGE
(Questions 17–22)

17. **Break-Even Quantity [LO2]** In Problem 14, what is the break-even quantity for the new credit policy?

18. **Credit Markup** [LO2] In Problem 14, what is the break-even price per unit that should be charged under the new credit policy? Assume that the sales figure under the new policy is 3,310 units and all other values remain the same.

19. **Credit Markup** [LO2] In Problem 15, what is the break-even price per unit under the new credit policy? Assume all other values remain the same.

20. **Safety Stocks and Order Points** [LO4] Saché, Inc., expects to sell 700 of its designer suits every week. The store is open seven days a week and expects to sell the same number of suits every day. The company has an EOQ of 500 suits and a safety stock of 100 suits. Once an order is placed, it takes three days for Saché to get the suits in. How many orders does the company place per year? Assume that it is Monday morning before the store opens, and a shipment of suits has just arrived. When will Saché place its next order?

21. **Evaluating Credit Policy** [LO2] Solar Engines manufactures solar engines for tractor-trailers. Given the fuel savings available, new orders for 125 units have been made by customers requesting credit. The variable cost is $6,900 per unit, and the credit price is $7,600 each. Credit is extended for one period. The required return is 1.9 percent per period. If Solar Engines extends credit, it expects that 30 percent of the customers will be repeat customers and place the same order every period forever and the remaining customers will be one-time orders. Should credit be extended?

22. **Evaluating Credit Policy** [LO2] In Problem 21, assume that the probability of default is 15 percent. Should the orders be filled now? Assume the number of repeat customers is affected by the defaults. In other words, 30 percent of the customers who do not default are expected to be repeat customers.

MINICASE

Credit Policy at Howlett Industries

Sterling Wyatt, the president of Howlett Industries, has been exploring ways of improving the company's financial performance. Howlett manufactures and sells office equipment to retailers. The company's growth has been relatively slow in recent years, but with an expansion in the economy, it appears that sales may increase more rapidly in the future. Sterling has asked Evan Bradds, the company's treasurer, to examine Howlett's credit policy to see if a change can help increase profitability.

The company currently has a policy of net 30. As with any credit sales, default rates are always of concern. Because of Howlett's screening and collection process, the default rate on credit is currently only 1.6 percent. Evan has examined the company's credit policy in relation to other vendors, and he has found three available options.

The first option is to relax the company's decision on when to grant credit. The second option is to increase the credit period to net 45, and the third option is a combination of the relaxed credit policy and the extension of the credit period to net 45. On the positive side, each of the three policies under consideration would increase sales. The three policies have the drawbacks that default rates would increase, the administrative costs of managing the firm's receivables would increase, and the receivables period would increase. The effect of the credit policy change would impact all four of these variables to different degrees. Evan has prepared the following table outlining the effect on each of these variables:

	Annual Sales (millions)	Default Rate (% of sales)	Administrative Costs (% of sales)	Receivables Period
Current Policy	$134	1.6%	2.2%	37 days
Option 1	158	2.5	3.2	40 days
Option 2	155	1.8	2.4	50 days
Option 3	170	2.2	3.0	48 days

Howlett's variable costs of production are 45 percent of sales, and the relevant interest rate is a 6 percent effective annual rate.

QUESTIONS

1. Which credit policy should the company use?
2. Notice that in Option 3, the default rate and the administrative costs both exceed those in Option 2. Is this plausible? Why or why not?

20.A More about Credit Policy Analysis

This appendix takes a closer look at credit policy analysis by investigating some alternative approaches and by examining the effect of cash discounts and the possibility of nonpayment.

TWO ALTERNATIVE APPROACHES

From our chapter discussion, we know how to analyze the NPV of a proposed credit policy switch. We now discuss two alternative approaches: The one-shot approach and the accounts receivable approach. These are common means of analysis; our goal is to show that these two approaches and our NPV approach are all the same. Afterward, we will use whichever of the three is most convenient.

The One-Shot Approach   Looking back at our example for Locust Software (in Section 20.3), we see that if the switch is not made, Locust will have a net cash flow this month of $(P - v)Q = \$29 \times 100 = \$2,900$. If the switch is made, Locust will invest $vQ' = \$20 \times 110 = \$2,200$ this month and will receive $PQ' = \$49 \times 110 = \$5,390$ next month. Suppose we ignore all other months and cash flows and view this as a one-shot investment. Is Locust better off with $2,900 in cash this month, or should Locust invest the $2,200 to get $5,390 next month?

The present value of the $5,390 to be received next month is $\$5,390/1.02 = \$5,284.31$; the cost is $2,200, so the net benefit is $\$5,284.31 - 2,200 = \$3,084.31$. If we compare this to the net cash flow of $2,900 under the current policy, then we see that Locust should switch. The NPV is $\$3,084.31 - 2,900 = \$184.31$.

In effect, Locust can repeat this one-shot investment every month and thereby generate an NPV of $184.31 every month (including the current one). The PV of this series of NPVs is:

Present value = $\$184.31 + \$184.31/.02 = \$9,400$

This PV is the same as our answer in Section 20.3.

The Accounts Receivable Approach   Our second approach is the one that is most commonly discussed and is very useful. By extending credit, the firm increases its cash flow through increased gross profits. The firm must increase its investment in receivables and bear the carrying cost of doing so. The accounts receivable approach focuses on the expense of the incremental investment in receivables as compared to the increased gross profit.

As we have seen, the monthly benefit from extending credit is given by the gross profit per unit $(P - v)$ multiplied by the increase in quantity sold $(Q' - Q)$. For Locust, this benefit is $(\$49 - 20) \times (110 - 100) = \$290$ per month.

If Locust makes the switch, then receivables will rise from zero (because there are currently no credit sales) to PQ', so Locust must invest in receivables. The necessary investment has two components. The first part is what Locust would have collected under the old policy (PQ). Locust must carry this amount in receivables each month because collections are delayed by 30 days.

The second part is related to the increase in receivables that results from the increase in sales. Because unit sales increase from Q to Q', Locust must produce the latter quantity today even though it won't collect payment for 30 days. The actual cost to Locust of producing the extra quantity is equal to v per unit, so the investment necessary to provide the extra quantity sold is $v(Q' - Q)$.

In sum, if Locust switches, its investment in receivables will be equal to the $P \times Q$ in revenues plus an additional $v(Q' - Q)$ in production costs:

Incremental investment in receivables $= PQ + v(Q' - Q)$

The required return on this investment (the carrying cost of the receivables) is R per month; so, for Locust, the accounts receivable carrying cost is:

$$
\begin{aligned}
\text{Carrying cost} &= [PQ + v(Q' - Q)] \times R \\
&= (\$4{,}900 + 200) \times .02 \\
&= \$102 \text{ per month}
\end{aligned}
$$

Because the monthly benefit is $290 and the cost per month is only $102, the net benefit is $290 - 102 = \$188$ per month. Locust earns this $188 every month, so the PV of the switch is:

$$
\begin{aligned}
\text{Present value} &= \$188/.02 \\
&= \$9{,}400
\end{aligned}
$$

Again, this is the same figure we previously calculated.

One of the advantages of looking at the accounts receivable approach is that it helps us interpret our earlier NPV calculation. As we have seen, the investment in receivables necessary to make the switch is $PQ + v(Q' - Q)$. If you take a look back at our original NPV calculation, you'll see that this is precisely what we had as the cost to Locust of making the switch. Our earlier NPV calculation amounts to a comparison of the incremental investment in receivables to the PV of the increased future cash flows.

Notice one final thing. The increase in accounts receivable is PQ', and this amount corresponds to the amount of receivables shown on the balance sheet. The incremental investment in receivables is $PQ + v(Q' - Q)$. It is straightforward to verify that this second quantity is smaller by $(P - v)(Q' - Q)$. This difference is the gross profit on the new sales, which Locust does not actually have to put up in order to switch credit policies.

Put another way, whenever we extend credit to a new customer who would not otherwise buy, all we risk is our cost, not the full sales price. This is the same issue that we discussed in Section 20.5.

Extra Credit   EXAMPLE 20A.1

Looking back at Locust Software, determine the NPV of the switch if the quantity sold is projected to increase by only 5 units instead of 10. What will be the investment in receivables? What is the carrying cost? What is the monthly net benefit from switching?

If the switch is made, Locust gives up $P \times Q = \$4{,}900$ today. An extra five units have to be produced at a cost of $20 each, so the cost of switching is $\$4{,}900 + 5 \times \$20 = \$5{,}000$. The benefit each month of selling the extra five units is $5 \times (\$49 - 20) = \$145$. The NPV of the switch is $-\$5{,}000 + \$145/.02 = \$2{,}250$, so the switch is still profitable.

The $5,000 cost of switching can be interpreted as the investment in receivables. At 2 percent per month, the carrying cost is $.02 \times \$5{,}000 = \$100$. Because the benefit each month is $145, the net benefit from switching is $45 per month (= $\$145 - 100$). Notice that the PV of $45 per month forever at 2 percent is $\$45/.02 = \$2{,}250$, as we calculated above.

DISCOUNTS AND DEFAULT RISK

We now take a look at cash discounts, default risk, and the relationship between the two. To get started, we define the following:

π = Percentage of credit sales that go uncollected

d = Percentage discount allowed for cash customers

P' = Credit price (the no-discount price)

Notice that the cash price, P, is equal to the credit price, P', multiplied by $(1 - d)$: $P = P' (1 - d)$, or, equivalently, $P' = P/(1 - d)$.

The situation at Locust is now a little more complicated. If a switch is made from the current policy of no credit, then the benefit from the switch will come from both the higher price (P') and, potentially, the increased quantity sold (Q').

Furthermore, in our previous case, it was reasonable to assume that all customers took the credit because it was free. Now, not all customers will take the credit because a discount is offered. In addition, of the customers who do take the credit offered, a certain percentage (π) will not pay.

To simplify the discussion that follows, we will assume that the quantity sold (Q) is unaffected by the switch. This assumption isn't crucial, but it does cut down on the work (see Problem 5 at the end of the appendix). We will also assume that all customers take the credit terms. This assumption isn't crucial either. It actually doesn't matter what percentage of the customers take the offered credit.[3]

NPV of the Credit Decision   Currently, Locust sells Q units at a price of $P = \$49$. Locust is considering a new policy that involves 30 days' credit and an increase in price to $P' = \$50$ on credit sales. The cash price will remain at $49, so Locust is effectively allowing a discount of $(\$50 - 49)/\$50 = .02$, or 2% for cash.

What is the NPV to Locust of extending credit? To answer, note that Locust is already receiving $(P - v)Q$ every month. With the new higher price, this will rise to $(P' - v)Q$, assuming that everybody pays. Because π percent of sales will not be collected, Locust will collect on only $(1 - \pi) \times P'Q$; so net receipts will be $[(1 - \pi)P' - v] \times Q$.

The net effect of the switch for Locust is the difference between the cash flows under the new policy and those under the old policy:

Net incremental cash flow = $[(1 - \pi)P' - v] \times Q - (P - v) \times Q$

Because $P = P' \times (1 - d)$, this simplifies to:[4]

Net incremental cash flow = $P'Q \times (d - \pi)$ **20A.1**

---

[3]The reason is that all customers are offered the same terms. If the NPV of offering credit is $100, assuming that all customers switch, then it will be $50 if only 50 percent of our customers switch. The hidden assumption is that the default rate is a constant percentage of credit sales.

[4]To see this, note that the net incremental cash flow is:

Net incremental cash flow = $[(1 - \pi)P' - v] \times Q - (P - v) \times Q$

$= [(1 - \pi)P' - P] \times Q$

Because $P = P' \times (1 - d)$, this can be written as:

Net incremental cash flow = $[(1 - \pi)P' - (1 - d)P'] \times Q$

$= P'Q \times (d - \pi)$

If Locust makes the switch, the cost in terms of the investment in receivables is $P \times Q$ because $Q = Q'$. The NPV of the switch is:

$$\text{NPV} = -PQ + P'Q \times (d - \pi)/R \qquad \text{20A.2}$$

Suppose that, based on industry experience, the percentage of "deadbeats" (π) is expected to be 1 percent. What is the NPV of changing credit terms for Locust? We can plug in the relevant numbers as follows:

$$
\begin{aligned}
\text{NPV} &= -PQ + P'Q \times (d - \pi)/R \\
&= -\$49 \times 100 + \$50 \times 100 \times (.02 - .01)/.02 \\
&= -\$2,400
\end{aligned}
$$

Because the NPV of the change is negative, Locust shouldn't switch.

In our expression for NPV, the key elements are the cash discount percentage (d) and the default rate (π). One thing we see immediately is that, if the percentage of sales that goes uncollected exceeds the discount percentage, then $d - \pi$ is negative. Obviously, the NPV of the switch would then be negative as well. More generally, our result tells us that the decision to grant credit here is a trade-off between getting a higher price, thereby increasing sales revenues, and not collecting on some fraction of those sales.

With this in mind, note that $P'Q \times (d - \pi)$ is the increase in sales less the portion of that increase that won't be collected. This is the incremental cash inflow from the switch in credit policy. If d is 5 percent and π is 2 percent, then, loosely speaking, revenues are increasing by 5 percent because of the higher price, but collections rise by only 3 percent because the default rate is 2 percent. Unless $d > \pi$, we will actually have a decrease in cash inflows from the switch.

A Break-Even Application

Because the discount percentage (d) is controlled by the firm, the key unknown in this case is the default rate (π). What is the break-even default rate for Locust Software?

We can answer by finding the default rate that makes the NPV equal to zero:

$$\text{NPV} = 0 = -PQ + P'Q \times (d - \pi)/R$$

Rearranging things a bit, we have:

$$
\begin{aligned}
PR &= P'(d - \pi) \\
\pi &= d - R \times (1 - d)
\end{aligned}
$$

For Locust, the break-even default rate works out to be:

$$
\begin{aligned}
\pi &= .02 - .02 \times (.98) \\
&= .0004, \text{ or } .04\%
\end{aligned}
$$

This is quite small because the implicit interest rate Locust will be charging its credit customers (2 percent discount interest per month, or about $.02/.98 = .020408$, or 2.0408%) is only slightly greater than the required return of 2 percent per month. As a result, there's not much room for defaults if the switch is going to make sense.

Concept Questions

20A.1a What is the incremental investment that a firm must make in receivables if credit is extended?

20A.1b Describe the trade-off between the default rate and the cash discount.

APPENDIX REVIEW AND SELF-TEST PROBLEMS

20A.1   **Credit Policy** Rework Chapter Review and Self-Test Problem 20.1 using the one-shot and accounts receivable approaches. As before, the required return is 2 percent per period, and there will be no defaults. Here is the basic information:

	Current Policy	New Policy
Price per unit	$ 175	$ 175
Cost per unit	$ 130	$ 130
Sales per period in units	1,000	1,100

20A.2   **Discounts and Default Risk** The De Long Corporation is considering a change in credit policy. The current policy is cash only, and sales per period are 2,000 units at a price of $110. If credit is offered, the new price will be $120 per unit, and the credit will be extended for one period. Unit sales are not expected to change, and all customers are expected to take the credit. De Long anticipates that 4 percent of its customers will default. If the required return is 2 percent per period, is the change a good idea? What if only half the customers take the offered credit?

ANSWERS TO APPENDIX REVIEW AND SELF-TEST PROBLEMS

20A.1   As we saw earlier, if the switch is made, an extra 100 units per period will be sold at a gross profit of $175 − 130 = $45 each. The total benefit is thus $45 × 100 = $4,500 per period. At 2 percent per period forever, the PV is $4,500/.02 = $225,000.

The cost of the switch is equal to this period's revenue of $175 × 1,000 units = $175,000 plus the cost of producing the extra 100 units, 100 × $130 = $13,000. The total cost is thus $188,000, and the NPV is $225,000 − 188,000 = $37,000. The switch should be made.

For the accounts receivable approach, we interpret the $188,000 cost as the investment in receivables. At 2 percent per period, the carrying cost is $188,000 × .02 = $3,760 per period. The benefit per period we calculated as $4,500; so the net gain per period is $4,500 − 3,760 = $740. At 2 percent per period, the PV of this is $740/.02 = $37,000.

Finally, for the one-shot approach, if credit is not granted, the firm will generate ($175 − 130) × 1,000 = $45,000 this period. If credit is extended, the firm will invest $130 × 1,100 = $143,000 today and receive $175 × 1,100 = $192,500 in one period. The NPV of this second option is $192,500/1.02 − $143,000 = $45,725.49. The firm is $45,725.49 − 45,000 = $725.49 better off today and in each future period because of granting credit. The PV of this stream is $725.49 + $725.49/.02 = $37,000 (allowing for a rounding error).

20A.2   The costs per period are the same whether or not credit is offered; so we can ignore the production costs. The firm currently has sales of, and collects, $110 × 2,000 = $220,000 per period. If credit is offered, sales will rise to $120 × 2,000 = $240,000.

Defaults will be 4 percent of sales, so the cash inflow under the new policy will be .96 × $240,000 = $230,400. This amounts to an extra $10,400 every period.

At 2 percent per period, the PV is $10,400/.02 = $520,000. If the switch is made, De Long will give up this month's revenues of $220,000; so the NPV of the switch is $300,000. If only half of the customers take the credit, then the NPV is half as large: $150,000. So, regardless of what percentage of customers take the credit, the NPV is positive. Thus, the change is a good idea.

QUESTIONS AND PROBLEMS

1. **Evaluating Credit Policy [LO2]** Bismark Co. is in the process of considering a change in its terms of sale. The current policy is cash only; the new policy will involve one period's credit. Sales are 25,000 units per period at a price of $350 per unit. If credit is offered, the new price will be $368. Unit sales are not expected to change, and all customers are expected to take the credit. Bismark estimates that 3 percent of credit sales will be uncollectible. If the required return is 2.5 percent per period, is the change a good idea?

2. **Credit Policy Evaluation [LO2]** The Johnson Company sells 2,400 pairs of running shoes per month at a cash price of $99 per pair. The firm is considering a new policy that involves 30 days' credit and an increase in price to $100 per pair on credit sales. The cash price will remain at $99, and the new policy is not expected to affect the quantity sold. The discount period will be 20 days. The required return is .75 percent per month.

   a. How would the new credit terms be quoted?

   b. What investment in receivables is required under the new policy?

   c. Explain why the variable cost of manufacturing the shoes is not relevant here.

   d. If the default rate is anticipated to be 8 percent, should the switch be made? What is the break-even credit price? The break-even cash discount?

3. **Credit Analysis [LO2]** Silicon Wafers, Inc. (SWI), is debating whether or not to extend credit to a particular customer. SWI's products, primarily used in the manufacture of semiconductors, currently sell for $975 per unit. The variable cost is $540 per unit. The order under consideration is for 15 units today; payment is promised in 30 days.

   a. If there is a 20 percent chance of default, should SWI fill the order? The required return is 2 percent per month. This is a one-time sale, and the customer will not buy if credit is not extended.

   b. What is the break-even probability in part (a)?

   c. This part is a little harder. In general terms, how do you think your answer to part (a) will be affected if the customer will purchase the merchandise for cash if the credit is refused? The cash price is $910 per unit.

4. **Credit Analysis [LO2]** Consider the following information about two alternative credit strategies:

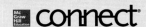

BASIC
(Questions 1–5)

	Refuse Credit	Grant Credit
Price per unit	$ 64	$ 69
Cost per unit	$ 32	$ 33
Quantity sold per quarter	5,800	6,400
Probability of payment	1.0	.90

The higher cost per unit reflects the expense associated with credit orders, and the higher price per unit reflects the existence of a cash discount. The credit period will be 90 days, and the cost of debt is .75 percent per month.

a. Based on this information, should credit be granted?

b. In part (a), what does the credit price per unit have to be to break even?

c. In part (a), suppose we can obtain a credit report for $1.50 per customer. Assuming that each customer buys one unit and that the credit report correctly identifies all customers who will not pay, should credit be extended?

5. **NPV of Credit Policy Switch [LO2]** Suppose a corporation currently sells Q units per month for a cash-only price of P. Under a new credit policy that allows one month's credit, the quantity sold will be Q' and the price per unit will be P'. Defaults will be π percent of credit sales. The variable cost is v per unit and is not expected to change. The percentage of customers who will take the credit is α, and the required return is R per month. What is the NPV of the decision to switch? Interpret the various parts of your answer.

International Corporate Finance

21 | Chapter

IN 2018, CASH BALANCES held overseas by companies based in the United States were in the news. Apple led the way with over $250 billion, followed by such companies as Microsoft ($130 billion), and Google-parent Alphabet ($94 billion). Before 2018, companies like Apple had a strong tax incentive to keep huge cash hoards outside the U.S. All of that changed with the signing of the Tax Cuts and Jobs Act of 2017, which ushered in big changes in the way U.S. corporations are taxed on their overseas operations. In this chapter, we discuss this topic, along with the important roles played by currencies, exchange rates, and other features of the international finance landscape.

Learning Objectives

After studying this chapter, you should be able to:

LO1 Define how exchange rates are quoted, what they mean, and the difference between spot and forward exchange rates.

LO2 Explain purchasing power parity, interest rate parity, unbiased forward rates, uncovered interest rate parity, and the international Fisher effect and

their implications for exchange rate changes.

LO3 Illustrate the different types of exchange rate risk and ways firms manage exchange rate risk.

LO4 Show the impact of political risk on international business investing.

©by_adri/iStockPhotoGettyImages

For updates on the latest happenings in finance, visit fundamentalsofcorporatefinance.blogspot.com.

Corporations with significant foreign operations are often called *international corporations* or *multinationals*. Such corporations must consider many financial factors that do not directly affect purely domestic firms. These include foreign exchange rates, differing interest rates from country to country, complex accounting methods for foreign operations, foreign tax rates, and foreign government intervention.

The basic principles of corporate finance still apply to international corporations; like domestic companies, these firms seek to invest in projects that create more value for the shareholders than they cost and to arrange financing that raises cash at the lowest possible cost. In other words, the net present value principle holds for both foreign and domestic operations, although it is usually more complicated to apply the NPV rule to foreign investments.

711

One of the most significant complications of international finance is foreign exchange. The foreign exchange markets provide important information and opportunities for an international corporation when it undertakes capital budgeting and financing decisions. As we will discuss, international exchange rates, interest rates, and inflation rates are closely related. We will spend much of this chapter exploring the connection between these financial variables.

We won't have much to say here about the role of cultural and social differences in international business. Neither will we be discussing the implications of differing political and economic systems. These factors are of great importance to international businesses, but it would take another book to do them justice. Consequently, we will focus only on some purely financial considerations in international finance and some key aspects of foreign exchange markets.

21.1 Terminology

A common buzzword for the student of business finance is *globalization*. The first step in learning about the globalization of financial markets is to conquer the new vocabulary. As with any specialty, international finance is rich in jargon. Accordingly, we get started on the subject with a highly eclectic vocabulary exercise.

The terms that follow are presented alphabetically, and they are not all of equal importance. We choose these particular ones because they appear frequently in the financial press or because they illustrate the colorful nature of the language of international finance.

See **www.adr.com** for more.

American Depositary Receipt (ADR)
A security issued in the United States representing shares of a foreign stock and allowing that stock to be traded in the United States.

cross-rate
The implicit exchange rate between two currencies (usually non-U.S.) quoted in some third currency (usually the U.S. dollar).

Eurobonds
International bonds issued in multiple countries but denominated in a single currency (usually the issuer's currency).

Eurocurrency
Money deposited in a financial center outside of the country whose currency is involved.

foreign bonds
International bonds issued in a single country, usually denominated in that country's currency.

gilts
British and Irish government securities.

1. An **American Depositary Receipt (ADR)** is a security issued in the United States that represents shares of a foreign stock, allowing that stock to be traded in the United States. Foreign companies use ADRs, which are issued in U.S. dollars, to expand the pool of potential U.S. investors. ADRs are available in two forms for a large and growing number of foreign companies: Company sponsored, which are listed on an exchange, and unsponsored, which usually are held by the investment bank that makes a market in the ADR. Both forms are available to individual investors, but only company-sponsored issues are quoted daily in newspapers.

2. The **cross-rate** is the implicit exchange rate between two currencies (usually non-U.S.) when both are quoted in some third currency, usually the U.S. dollar.

3. A **Eurobond** is a bond issued in multiple countries, but denominated in a single currency, usually the issuer's home currency. Such bonds have become an important way to raise capital for many international companies and governments. Eurobonds are issued outside the restrictions that apply to domestic offerings and are syndicated and traded mostly from London. However, trading takes place anywhere there is a buyer and a seller.

4. **Eurocurrency** is money deposited in a financial center outside of the country whose currency is involved. For instance, Eurodollars—the most widely used Eurocurrency— are U.S. dollars deposited in banks outside the U.S. banking system.

5. **Foreign bonds**, unlike Eurobonds, are issued in a single country and are usually denominated in that country's currency. Often, the country in which these bonds are issued will draw distinctions between them and bonds issued by domestic issuers, including different tax laws, restrictions on the amount issued, and tougher disclosure rules.

   Foreign bonds often are nicknamed for the country where they are issued: Yankee bonds (United States), Samurai bonds (Japan), Rembrandt bonds (the Netherlands), Bulldog bonds (Britain), and dim sum bonds (Chinese yuan-denominated bonds issued in Hong Kong). Partly because of tougher regulations and disclosure requirements, the foreign bond market hasn't grown in past years with the vigor of the Eurobond market.

6. **Gilts**, technically, are British and Irish government securities, although the term also includes issues of local British authorities and some overseas public sector offerings.

7. The **London Interbank Offered Rate (LIBOR)** is the rate that most international banks charge one another for loans of Eurodollars overnight in the London market. LIBOR is a cornerstone in the pricing of money market issues and other short-term debt issues by both government and corporate borrowers. Interest rates are frequently quoted as some spread over LIBOR, and they then float with the LIBOR rate.

8. There are two basic kinds of **swaps:** Interest rate and currency. An interest rate swap occurs when two parties exchange a floating-rate payment for a fixed-rate payment, or vice versa. Currency swaps are agreements to deliver one currency in exchange for another. Often, both types of swaps are used in the same transaction when debt denominated in different currencies is swapped.

London Interbank Offered Rate (LIBOR)
The rate most international banks charge one another for overnight Eurodollar loans.

swaps
Agreements to exchange two securities or currencies.

Concept Questions

21.1a   What are the differences between a Eurobond and a foreign bond?
21.1b   What are Eurodollars?

For current LIBOR rates, see
www.bloomberg.com.

Foreign Exchange Markets and Exchange Rates

21.2

Excel Master It!
Excel Master coverage online

The **foreign exchange market** (also called the forex or FX market) is undoubtedly the world's largest financial market. It is the market where one country's currency is traded for another country's currency. Most of the trading takes place in a few currencies: The U.S. dollar ($), the British pound sterling (£), the Japanese yen (¥), and the euro (€). Table 21.1 lists some of the more common currencies and their symbols.

Country	Currency	Symbol
Australia	Dollar	A$
Canada	Dollar	Can$
China	Yuan (Renminbi)	元
Denmark	Krone	DKr
EMU (Eurozone)	Euro	€
India	Rupee	Rs
Iran	Rial	Rl
Japan	Yen	¥
Kuwait	Dinar	KD
Mexico	Peso	Ps
Norway	Krone	NKr
Saudi Arabia	Riyal	SR
Singapore	Dollar	S$
South Africa	Rand	R
Sweden	Krona	SKr
Switzerland	Franc	SF
United Kingdom	Pound	£
United States	Dollar	$

TABLE 21.1

International Currency Symbols

foreign exchange market
The market in which one country's currency is traded for another country's currency.

The foreign exchange market is an over-the-counter market, so there is no single location where traders get together. Instead, market participants are located in the major commercial and investment banks around the world. They communicate using computer terminals, telephones, and other telecommunications devices. One communications network for foreign transactions is maintained by the Society for Worldwide Interbank Financial Telecommunication (SWIFT), a Belgian not-for-profit cooperative. Using data transmission lines, a bank in New York can send messages to a bank in London via SWIFT regional processing centers.

The many different types of participants in the foreign exchange market include the following:

1. Importers who pay for goods using foreign currencies.
2. Exporters who receive foreign currency and may want to convert to the domestic currency.
3. Portfolio managers who buy or sell foreign stocks and bonds.
4. Foreign exchange brokers who match buy and sell orders.
5. Traders who "make a market" in foreign currencies.
6. Speculators who try to profit from changes in exchange rates.

Visit SWIFT at **www.swift.com**.

EXCHANGE RATES

exchange rate
The price of one country's currency expressed in terms of another country's currency.

An **exchange rate** is the price of one country's currency expressed in terms of another country's currency. In practice, almost all trading of currencies takes place in terms of the U.S. dollar. For example, both the Swiss franc and the Japanese yen are traded with their prices quoted in U.S. dollars. Exchange rates are constantly changing. Our nearby *Work the Web* box shows you how to get up-to-the-minute rates.

WORK THE WEB

You just returned from your dream vacation to Jamaica and feel rich because you have 10,000 Jamaican dollars left over. You now need to convert this to U.S. dollars. How much will you have? You can look up the current exchange rate and do the conversion yourself, or work the web. We went to www.xe.com and used the currency converter on the site to find out. This is what we found:

10,000 JMD =
78.6411 USD

Jamaican Dollar ↔ US Dollar
1 JMD = 0.00786411 USD   1 USD = 127.160 JMD

Live mid-market rate 2017-02-05 23:12 UTC

Looks like you left Jamaica just before you ran out of money.

Questions
1. Using this currency converter, what is the current US$/Jamaican$ exchange rate?
2. The website www.xe.com also lists cross-rates. What is the current ¥/€ cross-rate?

Currencies

U.S.-dollar foreign-exchange rates in late New York trading

FIGURE 21.1
Exchange Rate
Quotations

SOURCE: *The Wall Street
Journal,* 2014.

Country/currency	in US$	per US$	US$ vs, YTD chg (%)	Country/currency	in US$	per US$	US$ vs, YTD chg (%)
Americas				**Europe**			
Argentina peso	.1250	8.0001	**22.7**	**Czech Rep.** koruna	.05050	19.800	**−0.4**
Brazil real	.4476	2.2339	**−5.4**	**Denmark** krone	.1858	5.3816	**−0.8**
Canada dollar	.9126	1.0958	**3.2**	**Euro area** euro	1.3869	.7210	**−0.9**
Chile peso	.001773	564.00	**7.3**	**Hungary** forint	.004524	221.06	**2.2**
Colombia peso	.0005169	1934.50	**0.2**	**Norway** krone	.1683	5.9433	**−2.1**
Ecuador US dollor	1	1	**unch**	**Poland** zloty	.3306	3.0246	**0.1**
Mexico peso	.0767	13.0434	**unch**	**Russia** ruble	.02807	35.620	**8.2**
Peru new sol	.3561	2.808	**0.2**	**Sweden** krona	.1537	6.5068	**1.1**
Uruguay peso	.04379	22.8355	**7.8**	**Switzerland** franc	1.1373	.8793	**−1.5**
Venezuela b. fuerte	.157480	6.3500	**unch**	1-mos forward	1.1376	.8791	**−1.6**
				3-mos forward	1.1381	.8786	**−1.6**
Asia-Pacific				6-mos forward	1.1391	.8779	**−1.6**
Australian dollar	.9274	1.0783	**−3.9**	**Turkey** lira	.4749	2.1057	**−2.0**
1-mos forward	.9255	1.0805	**−4.0**	**UK pound**	1.6893	.5920	**−2.0**
3-mos forward	.9216	1.0851	**−4.0**	1-mos forward	1.6889	.5921	**−2.0**
6-mos forward	.9157	1.0920	**−3.9**	3-mos forward	1.6881	.5924	**−2.0**
China yuan	.1598	6.2590	**3.4**	6-mos forward	1.6867	.5929	**−2.0**
Hong Kong dollar	.1290	7.7528	**unch**				
India rupee	.01663	60.150	**−2.8**	**Middle East/Africa**			
Indonesia rupiah	.0000865	11555	**−5.0**	**Bahrain** dinar	2.6527	.3770	**unch**
Japan yen	.009773	102.32	**−2.8**	**Egypt** pound	.1427	7.0081	**0.8**
1-mos forward	.009775	102.31	**−2.9**	**Israel** shekel	.2896	3.4528	**−0.5**
3-mos forward	.009778	102.27	**−2.9**	**Jordan** dinar	1.4123	.7081	**0.1**
6-mos forward	.009784	102.21	**−2.9**	**Kuwait** dinar	3.5606	.2809	**−0.6**
Malaysia ringgit	.3062	3.2659	**−0.5**	**Lebanon** pound	.0006596	1516.10	**0.7**
New Zealand dollar	.8633	1.1584	**−4.8**	**Saudi Arabia** riyal	.2666	3.7507	**unch**
Pakistan rupee	.01014	98.645	**−6.4**	**South Africa** rand	.0953	10.4879	**unch**
Philippines peso	.0224	44.610	**0.5**	**UAE** dirham	.2723	3.6731	**unch**
Singapore dollar	.7982	1.2528	**−0.8**				
South Korea won	.0009682	1032.80	**−2.2**		Close	Net Chg	% ChgYTD% Chg
Taiwan dollar	.03305	30.256	**1.1**	**WSJ Dollar Index**	72.85 −0.01 −0.01 **−1.31**		
Thailand baht	.03090	32.367	**−1.1**				
Vietnam dong	.00004742	21090	**−0.2**	Sources: ICAP plc., WSJ Market Data Group			

Exchange Rate Quotations

Figure 21.1 reproduces exchange rate quotations as they appeared in *The Wall Street Journal* in 2014. The second column (labeled "in US$") gives the number of dollars it takes to buy one unit of foreign currency. Because this is the price in dollars of a foreign currency, it is called a *direct* or *American quote* (remember that "Americans are direct"). For example, the Australian dollar is quoted at .9274, which means you can buy one Australian dollar with U.S. $.9274.

The third column shows the *indirect*, or European, exchange rate (even though the currency may not be European). This is the amount of foreign currency per U.S. dollar. The Australian dollar is quoted here at 1.0783, so you can get 1.0783 Australian dollars for one U.S. dollar. Naturally, this second exchange rate is the reciprocal of the first one (possibly with a small rounding error), 1/.9274 = 1.0783.

Get up-to-the-minute exchange rates at **www.xe.com** and **www.exchangerate.com**.

Cross-Rates and Triangle Arbitrage

Using the U.S. dollar as the common denominator in quoting exchange rates greatly reduces the number of possible cross-currency quotes. With five major currencies, there would potentially be 10 exchange rates instead of four.[1]

---

[1]There are four exchange rates instead of five because one exchange rate would involve the exchange of a currency for itself. More generally, it might seem that there should be 25 exchange rates with five currencies. There are 25 different combinations, but, of these, five involve the exchange of a currency for itself. Of the remaining 20, half are redundant because they are just the reciprocals of another exchange rate. Of the remaining 10, six can be eliminated by using a common denominator.

Also, the fact that the dollar is used throughout decreases inconsistencies in the exchange rate quotations.

| EXAMPLE 21.1 | A Yen for Euros |

Suppose you have $1,000. Based on the rates in Figure 21.1, how many Japanese yen can you get? Alternatively, if a Porsche costs €100,000 (recall that € is the symbol for the euro), how many dollars will you need to buy it?

The exchange rate in terms of yen per dollar (third column) is 102.32. Your $1,000 will thus get you:

$1,000 × 102.32 yen per $1 = 102,320 yen

To buy the Porsche, because the exchange rate in terms of dollars per euro (second column) is 1.3869, you will need:

€100,000 × $1.3869 per € = $138,690

Earlier, we defined the cross-rate as the exchange rate for a non-U.S. currency expressed in terms of another non-U.S. currency. Suppose we observe the following for the euro (€) and the Swiss franc (SF):

€ per $1 = 1.00
SF per $1 = 2.00

Suppose the cross-rate is quoted as:

€ per SF = .40

What do you think?

The cross-rate here is inconsistent with the exchange rates. To see this, suppose you have $100. If you convert this to Swiss francs, you will receive:

$100 × SF 2 per $1 = SF 200

If you convert this to euros at the cross-rate, you will have:

SF 200 × €.4 per SF 1 = €80

However, if you convert your dollars to euros without going through Swiss francs, you will have:

$100 × €1 per $1 = €100

What we see is that the euro has two prices, €1 per $1 and €.80 per $1, with the price we pay depending on how we get the euros.

To make money, we want to buy low and sell high. The important thing to note is that euros are cheaper if you buy them with dollars because you get 1 euro instead of just .8. You should proceed as follows:

1. Buy 100 euros for $100.
2. Use the 100 euros to buy Swiss francs at the cross-rate. Because it takes .4 euros to buy a Swiss franc, you will receive €100/.4 = SF 250.
3. Use the SF 250 to buy dollars. Because the exchange rate is SF 2 per dollar, you receive SF 250/2 = $125, for a round-trip profit of $25.
4. Repeat Steps 1 through 3.

This particular activity is called *triangle arbitrage* because the arbitrage involves moving through three different exchange rates:

To prevent such opportunities, it is not difficult to see that because a dollar will buy you either 1 euro or 2 Swiss francs, the cross-rate must be:

(€1/$1)/(SF 2/$1) = €1/SF 2

That is, the cross-rate must be 1 euro per 2 Swiss francs. If it were anything else, there would be a triangle arbitrage opportunity.

Shedding Some Pounds	**EXAMPLE 21.2**

Suppose the exchange rates for the British pound and Swiss franc are:

> Pounds per $1 = .60
> SF per $1 = 2.00

The cross-rate is three francs per pound. Is this consistent? Explain how to make some money.

The cross-rate should be SF 2.00/£.60 = SF 3.33 per pound. You can buy a pound for SF 3 in one market, and you can sell a pound for SF 3.33 in another. So, we want to first get some francs, then use the francs to buy some pounds, and then sell the pounds. Assuming you have $100, you could:

1. Exchange dollars for francs: $100 × 2 = SF 200.
2. Exchange francs for pounds: SF 200/3 = £66.67.
3. Exchange pounds for dollars: £66.67/.60 = $111.11.

This would result in an $11.11 round-trip profit.

Types of Transactions   There are two basic types of trades in the foreign exchange market: Spot trades and forward trades. A **spot trade** is an agreement to exchange currency "on the spot," which actually means that the transaction will be completed or settled within two business days. The exchange rate on a spot trade is called the **spot exchange rate**. Implicitly, all of the exchange rates and transactions we have discussed so far have referred to the spot market.

A **forward trade** is an agreement to exchange currency at some time in the future. The exchange rate that will be used is agreed upon today and is called the **forward exchange rate**. A forward trade will normally be settled sometime in the next 12 months.

If you look back at Figure 21.1, you will see forward exchange rates quoted for some of the major currencies. Suppose the spot exchange rate for the Swiss franc is SF 1 = $1.1373. The 180-day (6-month) forward exchange rate is SF 1 = $1.1391. This means you can buy a Swiss franc today for $1.1373, or you can agree to take delivery of a Swiss franc in 180 days and pay $1.1391 at that time.

Notice that the Swiss franc is more expensive in the forward market ($1.1391 versus $1.1373). Because the Swiss franc is more expensive in the future than it is today, it is said

For international news and events, visit **www.ft.com**.

spot trade
An agreement to trade currencies based on the exchange rate today for settlement within two business days.

spot exchange rate
The exchange rate on a spot trade.

forward trade
An agreement to exchange currency at some time in the future.

forward exchange rate
The agreed-upon exchange rate to be used in a forward trade.

to be selling at a *premium* relative to the dollar. For the same reason, the dollar is said to be selling at a *discount* relative to the Swiss franc.

Why does the forward market exist? One answer is that it allows businesses and individuals to lock in a future exchange rate today, thereby eliminating any risk from unfavorable shifts in the exchange rate.

EXAMPLE 21.3   **Looking Forward**

Suppose you are expecting to receive a million British pounds in six months, and you agree to a forward trade to exchange your pounds for dollars. Based on Figure 21.1, how many dollars will you get in six months? Is the pound selling at a discount or a premium relative to the dollar?

In Figure 21.1, the spot exchange rate and the 180-day forward rate in terms of dollars per pound are $1.6893 = £1 and $1.6867 = £1, respectively. If you expect £1 million in 180 days, you will get £1 million × $1.6867 per pound = $1.6867 million. Because it is less expensive to buy a pound in the forward market than in the spot market ($1.6867 versus $1.6893), the pound is said to be selling at a discount relative to the dollar.

As we mentioned earlier, it is standard practice around the world (with a few exceptions) to quote exchange rates in terms of the U.S. dollar. This means rates are quoted as the amount of currency per U.S. dollar. For the remainder of this chapter, we will stick with this form. Things can get extremely confusing if you forget this point. When we say things like "the exchange rate is expected to rise," it is important to remember that we are talking about the exchange rate quoted as units of foreign currency per dollar.

Concept Questions

21.2a   What is triangle arbitrage?
21.2b   What do we mean by the 90-day forward exchange rate?
21.2c   If we say that the exchange rate is SF 1.90, what do we mean?

21.3 Purchasing Power Parity

Now that we have discussed what exchange rate quotations mean, we can address an obvious question: What determines the level of the spot exchange rate? In addition, because we know that exchange rates change through time, we can ask the related question: What determines the rate of change in exchange rates? At least part of the answer in both cases goes by the name of **purchasing power parity (PPP)**: The idea that the exchange rate adjusts to keep purchasing power constant among currencies. As we discuss next, there are two forms of PPP, *absolute* and *relative*.

purchasing power parity (PPP)
The idea that the exchange rate adjusts to keep purchasing power constant among currencies.

ABSOLUTE PURCHASING POWER PARITY

The basic idea behind *absolute purchasing power parity* is that a commodity costs the same regardless of what currency is used to purchase it or where it is selling. This is a straightforward concept. If a beer costs £2 in London, and the exchange rate is £.60 per dollar, then a beer costs £2/.60 = $3.33 in New York. In other words, absolute PPP says that $1 will buy you the same number of, say, cheeseburgers any-where in the world.

More formally, let S_0 be the spot exchange rate between the British pound and the U.S. dollar today (Time 0), and remember that we are quoting exchange rates as the amount of foreign currency per dollar. Let P_{US} and P_{UK} be the current U.S. and British prices, respec-tively, on a particular commodity like apples. Absolute PPP says that:

$$P_{UK} = S_0 \times P_{US}$$

This tells us that the British price for something is equal to the U.S. price for that same thing multiplied by the exchange rate.

The rationale behind PPP is similar to that behind triangle arbitrage. If PPP did not hold, arbitrage would be possible (in principle) if apples were moved from one country to another. Suppose apples are selling in New York for $4 per bushel, whereas in London the price is £2.40 per bushel. Absolute PPP implies that:

$$P_{UK} = S_0 \times P_{US}$$
$$£2.40 = S_0 \times \$4$$
$$S_0 = £2.40/\$4 = £.60$$

That is, the implied spot exchange rate is £.60 per dollar. Equivalently, a pound is worth $1/£.60 = $1.67.

Suppose that, instead, the actual exchange rate is £.50. Starting with $4, a trader could buy a bushel of apples in New York, ship it to London, and sell it there for £2.40. Our trader could then convert the £2.40 into dollars at the prevailing exchange rate, $S_0 = £.50$, yielding a total of £2.40/.50 = $4.80. The round-trip gain would be 80 cents.

Because of this profit potential, forces are set in motion to change the exchange rate and/or the price of apples. In our example, apples would begin moving from New York to London. The reduced supply of apples in New York would raise the price of apples there, and the increased supply in Britain would lower the price of apples in London.

In addition to moving apples around, apple traders would be busily converting pounds back into dollars to buy more apples. This activity would increase the supply of pounds and simultaneously increase the demand for dollars. We would expect the value of a pound to fall. This means that the dollar would be getting more valuable, so it would take more pounds to buy one dollar. Because the exchange rate is quoted as pounds per dollar, we would expect the exchange rate to rise from £.50.

For absolute PPP to hold absolutely, several things must be true:

1. The transactions costs of trading apples—shipping, insurance, spoilage, and so on—must be zero.

2. There must be no barriers to trading apples—no tariffs, taxes, or other political barriers.

3. Finally, an apple in New York must be identical to an apple in London. It won't do for you to send red apples to London if the English eat only green apples.

Given the fact that the transactions costs are not zero and that the other conditions are rarely exactly met, it is not surprising that absolute PPP is really applicable only to traded goods, and then only to very uniform ones.

For this reason, absolute PPP does not imply that a Mercedes costs the same as a Ford or that a nuclear power plant in France costs the same as one in New York. In the case of the cars, they are not identical. In the case of the power plants, even if they were identical, they are expensive and would be very difficult to ship. On the other hand, we would be surprised to see a significant violation of absolute PPP for gold.

Check out the most recent Big Mac Index at **www.economist .com/content/big-mac-index**.

The Economist publishes the Big Mac Index, which shows whether a currency is overvalued or undervalued relative to the U.S. dollar based on the price of a McDonald's Big Mac. In the January 2017 index, two of the 43 currencies in the index were overvalued by more than 10 percent, and 39 currencies were undervalued by more than 10 percent.

RELATIVE PURCHASING POWER PARITY

As a practical matter, a relative version of purchasing power parity has evolved. *Relative purchasing power parity* does not tell us what determines the absolute level of the exchange rate. Instead, it tells what determines the *change* in the exchange rate over time.

The Basic Idea   Suppose the British pound–U.S. dollar exchange rate is currently $S_0 =$ £.50. Further suppose that the inflation rate in Britain is predicted to be 10 percent over the coming year, and (for the moment) the inflation rate in the United States is predicted to be zero. What do you think the exchange rate will be in a year?

If you think about it, you see that a dollar currently costs .50 pounds in Britain. With 10 percent inflation, we expect prices in Britain to generally rise by 10 percent. So we expect that the price of a dollar will go up by 10 percent, and the exchange rate should rise to £.50 × 1.1 = £.55.

If the inflation rate in the United States is not zero, then we need to worry about the *relative* inflation rates in the two countries. Suppose the U.S. inflation rate is predicted to be 4 percent. Relative to prices in the United States, prices in Britain are rising at a rate of 10% − 4% = 6% per year. So we expect the price of the dollar to rise by 6 percent, and the predicted exchange rate is £.50 × 1.06 = £.53.

The Result   In general, relative PPP says that the change in the exchange rate is determined by the difference in the inflation rates of the two countries. To be more specific, we will use the following notation:

S_0 = Current (Time 0) spot exchange rate (foreign currency per dollar)

$E(S_t)$ = Expected exchange rate in t periods

h_{US} = Inflation rate in the United States

h_{FC} = Foreign country inflation rate

Based on our preceding discussion, relative PPP says that the expected percentage change in the exchange rate over the next year, $[E(S_1) − S_0]/S_0$, is:

$$[E(S_1) − S_0]/S_0 = h_{FC} − h_{US}$$ **21.1**

In words, relative PPP says that the expected percentage change in the exchange rate is equal to the difference in inflation rates. If we rearrange this slightly, we get:

$$E(S_1) = S_0 × [1 + (h_{FC} − h_{US})]$$ **21.2**

This result makes a certain amount of sense, but care must be used in quoting the exchange rate.

In our example involving Britain and the United States, relative PPP tells us that the exchange rate will rise by $h_{FC} − h_{US} = 10\% − 4\% = 6\%$ per year. Assuming the difference in inflation rates doesn't change, the expected exchange rate in two years, $E(S_2)$, will be:

$$
\begin{aligned}
E(S_2) &= E(S_1) × (1 + .06) \\
&= .53 × 1.06 \\
&= .562
\end{aligned}
$$

Notice that we could have written this as:

$$E(S_2) = .53 \times 1.06$$
$$= .50 \times (1.06 \times 1.06)$$
$$= .50 \times 1.06^2$$

In general, relative PPP says that the expected exchange rate at some time in the future, $E(S_t)$, is:

$$E(S_t) = S_0 \times [1 + (h_{FC} - h_{US})]^t \qquad \text{21.3}$$

As we will see, this is a very useful relationship.

Because we don't really expect absolute PPP to hold for most goods, we will focus on relative PPP in our following discussion. Henceforth, when we refer to PPP without further qualification, we mean relative PPP.

It's All Relative

EXAMPLE 21.4

Suppose the Japanese exchange rate is currently 105 yen per dollar. The inflation rate in Japan over the next three years will run, say, 2 percent per year, whereas the U.S. inflation rate will be 6 percent. Based on relative PPP, what will the exchange rate be in three years?

Because the U.S. inflation rate is higher, we expect that a dollar will become less valuable. The exchange rate change will be 2% − 6% = −4% per year. Over three years, the exchange rate will fall to:

$$E(S_3) = S_0 \times [1 + (h_{FC} - h_{US})]^3$$
$$= 105 \times [1 + (-.04)]^3$$
$$= 92.90$$

Currency Appreciation and Depreciation   We frequently hear things like "the dollar strengthened (or weakened) in financial markets today" or "the dollar is expected to appreciate (or depreciate) relative to the pound." When we say that the dollar strengthens or appreciates, we mean that the value of a dollar rises, so it takes more foreign currency to buy a dollar.

What happens to the exchange rates as currencies fluctuate in value depends on how exchange rates are quoted. Because we are quoting them as units of foreign currency per dollar, the exchange rate moves in the same direction as the value of the dollar: It rises as the dollar strengthens, and falls as the dollar weakens.

Relative PPP tells us that the exchange rate will rise if the U.S. inflation rate is lower than the foreign country's inflation rate. This happens because the foreign currency depreciates in value and weakens relative to the dollar.

Concept Questions

21.3a   What does absolute PPP say? Why might it not hold for many types of goods?

21.3b   According to relative PPP, what determines the change in exchange rates?

21.4 Interest Rate Parity, Unbiased Forward Rates, and the International Fisher Effect

The next issue we need to address is the relationship between spot exchange rates, forward exchange rates, and interest rates. To get started, we need some additional notation:

F_t = Forward exchange rate for settlement at Time t

R_{US} = U.S. nominal risk-free interest rate

R_{FC} = Foreign country nominal risk-free interest rate

As before, we will use S_0 to stand for the spot exchange rate. You can take the U.S. nominal risk-free rate, R_{US}, to be the T-bill rate.

COVERED INTEREST ARBITRAGE

Suppose we observe the following information about U.S. and Swiss currency in the market:

$$S_0 = \text{SF } 2.00$$
$$F_1 = \text{SF } 1.90$$
$$R_{US} = 10\%$$
$$R_S = 5\%$$

where R_S is the nominal risk-free rate in Switzerland. The period is one year, so F_1 is the 360-day forward rate.

Do you see an arbitrage opportunity here? There is one. Suppose you have $1 to invest, and you want a riskless investment. One option you have is to invest the $1 in a riskless U.S. investment such as a 360-day T-bill. If you do this, then, in one period, your $1 will be worth:

$$\$ \text{ value in 1 period} = \$1 \times (1 + R_{US})$$
$$= \$1.10$$

Alternatively, you can invest in the Swiss risk-free investment. To do this, you need to convert your $1 to Swiss francs and simultaneously execute a forward trade to convert francs back to dollars in one year. The necessary steps would be as follows:

1. Convert your $1 to $1 × S_0 = SF 2.00.
2. At the same time, enter into a forward agreement to convert Swiss francs back to dollars in one year. Because the forward rate is SF 1.90, you will get $1 for every SF 1.90 that you have in one year.
3. Invest your SF 2.00 in Switzerland at R_S. In one year, you will have:

$$\text{SF value in 1 year} = \text{SF } 2.00 \times (1 + R_S)$$
$$= \text{SF } 2.00 \times 1.05$$
$$= \text{SF } 2.10$$

4. Convert your SF 2.10 back to dollars at the agreed-upon rate of SF 1.90 = $1. You end up with:

$$\$ \text{ value in 1 year} = \text{SF } 2.10/1.90$$
$$= \$1.1053$$

For exchange rates and even pictures of non-U.S. currencies, see **www.travlang.com/ money**.

Notice that the value in one year resulting from this strategy can be written as:

$$\$ \text{ value in 1 year} = \$1 \times S_0 \times (1 + R_S)/F_1$$
$$= \$1 \times 2 \times 1.05/1.90$$
$$= \$1.1053$$

The return on this investment is apparently 10.53 percent. This is higher than the 10 percent we get from investing in the United States. Because both investments are risk-free, there is an arbitrage opportunity.

To exploit the difference in interest rates, you need to borrow, say, $5 million at the lower U.S. rate and invest it at the higher Swiss rate. What is the round-trip profit from doing this? To find out, we can work through the steps outlined previously:

1. Convert the $5 million at SF 2 = $1 to get SF 10 million.
2. Agree to exchange Swiss francs for dollars in one year at SF 1.90 to the dollar.
3. Invest the SF 10 million for one year at $R_S = 5\%$. You end up with SF 10.5 million.
4. Convert the SF 10.5 million back to dollars to fulfill the forward contract. You receive SF 10.5 million/1.90 = $5,526,316.
5. Repay the loan with interest. You owe $5 million plus 10 percent interest, for a total of $5.5 million. You have $5,526,316, so your round-trip profit is a risk-free $26,316.

The activity that we have illustrated here goes by the name of *covered interest arbitrage*. The term *covered* refers to the fact that we are covered in the event of a change in the exchange rate because we lock in the forward exchange rate today.

INTEREST RATE PARITY

If we assume that significant covered interest arbitrage opportunities do not exist, then there must be some relationship between spot exchange rates, forward exchange rates, and relative interest rates. To see this relationship, we can look at the general implications from the two strategies in the previous discussion. Strategy 1, investing in a riskless U.S. investment, gives us $1 + R_{US}$ for every dollar we invest. Strategy 2, investing in a foreign risk-free investment, gives us $S_0 \times (1 + R_{FC})/F_1$ for every dollar we invest. Because these have to be equal to prevent arbitrage, it must be the case that:

interest rate parity (IRP)
The condition stating that the interest rate differential between two countries is equal to the percentage difference between the forward exchange rate and the spot exchange rate.

$$1 + R_{US} = S_0 \times (1 + R_{FC})/F_1$$

Rearranging this a bit gets us the famous **interest rate parity (IRP)** condition:

$$\boldsymbol{F_1/S_0 = (1 + R_{FC})/(1 + R_{US})}$$

 21.4

There is a very useful approximation for IRP that illustrates very clearly what is going on and is not difficult to remember. If we define the percentage forward premium or discount as $(F_1 - S_0)/S_0$, then IRP says that this percentage premium or discount is *approximately* equal to the difference in interest rates:

$$\boldsymbol{(F_1 - S_0)/S_0 = R_{FC} - R_{US}}$$

 21.5

Very loosely, what IRP says is that any difference in interest rates between two countries for some period is just offset by the change in the relative value of the currencies, thereby eliminating any arbitrage possibilities. Notice that we could also write:

$$\boldsymbol{F_1 = S_0 \times [1 + (R_{FC} - R_{US})]}$$

 21.6

In general, if we have t periods instead of just one, the IRP approximation is written as:

$$F_t = S_0 \times [1 + (R_{FC} - R_{US})]^t$$

EXAMPLE 21.5 | **Parity Check**

Suppose the exchange rate for Japanese yen, S_0, is currently ¥120 = \$1. If the interest rate in the United States is R_{US} = 10% and the interest rate in Japan is R_J = 5%, then what must the forward rate be to prevent covered interest arbitrage?

From IRP, we have:

$$F_1 = S_0 \times [1 + (R_J - R_{US})]$$
$$= ¥120 \times [1 + (.05 - .10)]$$
$$= ¥120 \times .95$$
$$= ¥114$$

Notice that the yen will sell at a premium relative to the dollar (why?).

FORWARD RATES AND FUTURE SPOT RATES

In addition to PPP and IRP, we need to discuss one more basic relationship. What is the connection between the forward rate and the expected future spot rate? The **unbiased forward rates (UFR)** condition says that the forward rate, F_1, is equal to the *expected* future spot rate, $E(S_1)$:

$$F_1 = E(S_1)$$

With t periods, UFR would be written as:

$$F_t = E(S_t)$$

Loosely, the UFR condition says that, on average, the forward exchange rate is equal to the future spot exchange rate.

If we ignore risk, then the UFR condition should hold. Suppose the forward rate for the Japanese yen is consistently lower than the future spot rate by, say, 10 yen. This means that anyone who wanted to convert dollars to yen in the future would consistently get more yen by not agreeing to a forward exchange. The forward rate would have to rise to interest anyone in a forward exchange.

Similarly, if the forward rate were consistently higher than the future spot rate, then anyone who wanted to convert yen to dollars would get more dollars per yen by not agreeing to a forward trade. The forward exchange rate would have to fall to attract such traders.

For these reasons, the forward and actual future spot rates should be equal to each other, on average. What the future spot rate will actually be is uncertain, of course. The UFR condition may not hold if traders are willing to pay a premium to avoid this uncertainty. If the condition does hold, then the 180-day forward rate that we see today should be an unbiased predictor of what the exchange rate will actually be in 180 days.

PUTTING IT ALL TOGETHER

We have developed three relationships, PPP, IRP, and UFR, that describe the interaction between key financial variables such as interest rates, exchange rates, and inflation rates. We now explore the implications of these relationships as a group.

unbiased forward rates (UFR)
The condition stating that the current forward rate is an unbiased predictor of the future spot exchange rate.

How are the international markets doing? Find out at **www.marketwatch.com**.

Uncovered Interest Parity   To start, it is useful to collect our international financial market relationships in one place:

$$\text{PPP: } E(S_1) = S_0 \times [1 + (h_{FC} - h_{US})]$$
$$\text{IRP: } F_1 = S_0 \times [1 + (R_{FC} - R_{US})]$$
$$\text{UFR: } F_1 = E(S_1)$$

We begin by combining UFR and IRP. Because we know that $F_1 = E(S_1)$ from the UFR condition, we can substitute $E(S_1)$ for F_1 in IRP. The result is:

$$\text{UIP: } E(S_1) = S_0 \times [1 + (R_{FC} - R_{US})]$$

This important relationship is called **uncovered interest parity (UIP)**, and it will play a key role in our international capital budgeting discussion that follows. With t periods, UIP becomes:

$$E(S_t) = S_0 \times [1 + (R_{FC} - R_{US})]^t$$

uncovered interest parity (UIP)
The condition stating that the expected percentage change in the exchange rate is equal to the difference in interest rates.

The International Fisher Effect   Next, we compare PPP and UIP. Both of them have $E(S_1)$ on the left-hand side, so their right-hand sides must be equal. We have that:

$$S_0 \times [1 + (h_{FC} - h_{US})] = S_0 \times [1 + (R_{FC} - R_{US})]$$
$$h_{FC} - h_{US} = R_{FC} - R_{US}$$

international Fisher effect (IFE)
The theory that real interest rates are equal across countries.

This tells us that the difference in returns between the United States and a foreign country is equal to the difference in inflation rates. Rearranging this slightly gives us the **international Fisher effect (IFE)**:

$$\boldsymbol{R_{US} - h_{US} = R_{FC} - h_{FC}}$$

21.7

The IFE says that *real* rates are equal across countries.[2]

The conclusion that real returns are equal across countries is really basic economics. If real returns were higher in Brazil than in the United States, money would flow out of U.S. financial markets and into Brazilian markets. Asset prices in Brazil would rise and their returns would fall. At the same time, asset prices in the United States would fall and their returns would rise. This process acts to equalize real returns.

Having said all this, we need to note a couple of things. First of all, we really haven't explicitly dealt with risk in our discussion. We might reach a different conclusion about real returns once we do, particularly if people in different countries have different tastes and attitudes toward risk. Second, there are many barriers to the movement of money and capital around the world. Real returns might be different in two different countries for long periods of time if money can't move freely between them.

Despite these problems, we expect that capital markets will become increasingly internationalized. As this occurs, any differences in real rates that do exist will probably diminish. The laws of economics have very little respect for national boundaries.

Concept Questions

21.4a   What is covered interest arbitrage?
21.4b   What is the international Fisher effect?

---

[2]Notice that our result here is in terms of the approximate real rate, $R - h$ (see Chapter 7), because we used approximations for PPP and IRP. For the exact result, see Problem 18 at the end of the chapter.

21.5 International Capital Budgeting

Kihlstrom Equipment, a U.S.-based international company, is evaluating an overseas investment. Kihlstrom's exports of drill bits have increased to such a degree that it is considering building a distribution center in France. The project will cost €2 million to launch. The cash flows are expected to be €.9 million per year for the next three years.

The current spot exchange rate for euros is €.5. Recall that this is euros per dollar, so a euro is worth $1/€.5 = $2. The risk-free rate in the United States is 5 percent, and the risk-free rate in "Euroland" is 7 percent. Note that the exchange rate and the two interest rates are observed in financial markets, not estimated.[3] Kihlstrom's required return on dollar investments of this sort is 10 percent.

Should Kihlstrom take this investment? As always, the answer depends on the NPV; but how do we calculate the net present value of this project in U.S. dollars? There are two basic methods:

1. *The home currency approach*: Convert all the euro cash flows into dollars, and then discount at 10 percent to find the NPV in dollars. Notice that for this approach, we have to come up with the future exchange rates to convert the future projected euro cash flows into dollars.

2. *The foreign currency approach*: Determine the required return on euro investments, and discount the euro cash flows to find the NPV in euros. Then convert this euro NPV to a dollar NPV. This approach requires us to somehow convert the 10 percent dollar required return to the equivalent euro required return.

The difference between these two approaches is primarily a matter of when we convert from euros to dollars. In the first case, we convert before estimating the NPV. In the second case, we convert after estimating NPV.

It might appear that the second approach is superior because we have to come up with only one number, the euro discount rate. Furthermore, because the first approach requires us to forecast future exchange rates, it probably seems that there is greater room for error with this approach. As we illustrate next, based on our previous results, the two approaches are really the same.

METHOD 1: THE HOME CURRENCY APPROACH

To convert the project's future cash flows into dollars, we will invoke the uncovered interest parity, or UIP, relationship to come up with the projected exchange rates. Based on our earlier discussion, the expected exchange rate at Time t, $E(S_t)$, is:

$$E(S_t) = S_0 \times [1 + (R_\epsilon - R_{US})]^t$$

where R_ϵ stands for the nominal risk-free rate in Euroland. Because R_ϵ is 7 percent, R_{US} is 5 percent, and the current exchange rate (S_0) is €.5:

$$E(S_t) = .5 \times [1 + (.07 - .05)]^t$$
$$= .5 \times 1.02^t$$

---

[3]For example, the interest rates might be the short-term Eurodollar and euro deposit rates offered by large money center banks.

The projected exchange rates for the drill bit project are:

Year	Expected Exchange Rate
1	€.5 × 1.02^1 = €.5100
2	€.5 × 1.02^2 = €.5202
3	€.5 × 1.02^3 = €.5306

Using these exchange rates, along with the current exchange rate, we can convert all of the euro cash flows to dollars:

Year	(1) Cash Flow in €mil	(2) Expected Exchange Rate	(3) Cash Flow in $mil (1)/(2)
0	−€2.0	€.5000	−$4.00
1	.9	.5100	1.76
2	.9	.5202	1.73
3	.9	.5306	1.70

To finish, we calculate the NPV in the usual way:

$$\text{NPV}_\$ = -\$4 + \$1.76/1.10 + \$1.73/1.10^2 + \$1.70/1.10^3$$
$$= \$.3 \text{ million}$$

So, the project appears to be profitable.

METHOD 2: THE FOREIGN CURRENCY APPROACH

Kihlstrom requires a nominal return of 10 percent on the dollar-denominated cash flows. We need to convert this to a rate suitable for euro-denominated cash flows. Based on the international Fisher effect, we know that the difference in the nominal rates is:

$$R_\epsilon - R_{US} = h_\epsilon - h_{US}$$
$$= 7\% - 5\% = 2\%$$

The appropriate discount rate for estimating the euro cash flows from the drill bit project is approximately equal to 10 percent plus an extra 2 percent to compensate for the greater euro inflation rate.

If we calculate the NPV of the euro cash flows at this rate, we get:

$$\text{NPV}_\epsilon = -€2 + €.9/1.12 + €.9/1.12^2 + €.9/1.12^3$$
$$= €.16 \text{ million}$$

The NPV of this project is €.16 million. Taking this project makes us €.16 million richer today. What is this in dollars? Because the exchange rate today is €.5, the dollar NPV of the project is:

$$\text{NPV}_\$ = \text{NPV}_\epsilon/S_0 = €.16/.5 = \$.3 \text{ million}$$

This is the same dollar NPV that we previously calculated.

The important thing to recognize from our example is that the two capital budgeting procedures are actually the same and will always give the same answer.[4] In this second

---

[4]Actually, there will be a slight difference because we are using the approximate relationships. If we calculate the required return as $1.10 \times (1 + .02) - 1 = 12.2\%$, then we get exactly the same NPV. See Problem 18 for more detail.

approach, the fact that we are implicitly forecasting exchange rates is hidden. Even so, the foreign currency approach is computationally a little easier.

UNREMITTED CASH FLOWS

The previous example assumed that all aftertax cash flows from the foreign investment could be remitted to (paid out to) the parent firm. Actually, substantial differences can exist between the cash flows generated by a foreign project and the amount that can actually be remitted, or "repatriated," to the parent firm.

A foreign subsidiary can remit funds to a parent in many forms, including the following:

1. Dividends.
2. Management fees for central services.
3. Royalties on the use of trade names and patents.

However cash flows are repatriated, international firms must pay special attention to remittances because there may be current and future controls on remittances. Many governments are sensitive to being exploited by foreign national firms. In such cases, governments are tempted to limit the ability of international firms to remit cash flows. Funds that cannot currently be remitted are sometimes said to be *blocked*.

Concept Questions

21.5a What financial complications arise in international capital budgeting? Describe two procedures for estimating NPV in the case of an international project.

21.5b What are blocked funds?

21.6 Exchange Rate Risk

exchange rate risk
The risk related to having international operations in a world where relative currency values vary.

Exchange rate risk is the natural consequence of international operations in a world where relative currency values move up and down. Managing exchange rate risk is an important part of international finance. As we discuss next, there are three different types of exchange rate risk, or exposure: Short-run exposure, long-run exposure, and translation exposure. Chapter 23 contains a more detailed discussion of the issues raised in this section.

SHORT-RUN EXPOSURE

The day-to-day fluctuations in exchange rates create short-run risks for international firms. Most such firms have contractual agreements to buy and sell goods in the near future at set prices. When different currencies are involved, such transactions have an extra element of risk.

Imagine that you are importing imitation pasta from Italy and reselling it in the United States under the Impasta brand name. Your largest customer has ordered 10,000 cases of Impasta. You place the order with your supplier today, but you won't pay until the goods arrive in 60 days. Your selling price is $6 per case. Your cost is 8.4 euros per case, and the exchange rate is currently €1.50; so it takes 1.50 euros to buy $1.

At the current exchange rate, your cost in dollars of filling the order is €8.4/1.5 = $5.60 per case, so your pretax profit on the order is $10,000 \times (\$6 - 5.60) = \$4,000$. The exchange rate in 60 days will probably be different, so your actual profit will depend on what the future exchange rate turns out to be.

If the rate goes to €1.6, your cost is €8.4/1.6 = $5.25 per case. Your profit goes to $7,500. If the exchange rate goes to €1.4, then your cost is €8.4/1.4 = $6, and your profit is zero.

The short-run exposure in our example can be reduced or eliminated in several ways. The most obvious way is by entering into a forward exchange agreement to lock in an exchange rate. Suppose the 60-day forward rate is €1.58. What will your profit be if you hedge? What profit should you expect if you don't hedge?

If you hedge, you lock in an exchange rate of €1.58. Your cost in dollars will be €8.4/1.58 = $5.32 per case, so your profit will be 10,000 × ($6 − 5.32) = $6,835. If you don't hedge, then, assuming that the forward rate is an unbiased predictor (in other words, assuming the UFR condition holds), you should expect that the exchange rate will actually be €1.58 in 60 days. You should expect to make $6,835.

Alternatively, if this strategy is unfeasible, you could borrow the dollars today, convert them into euros, and invest the euros for 60 days to earn some interest. Based on IRP, this amounts to entering into a forward contract.

LONG-RUN EXPOSURE

In the long run, the value of a foreign operation can fluctuate because of unanticipated changes in relative economic conditions. Imagine that we own a labor-intensive assembly operation located in another country to take advantage of lower wages. Through time, unexpected changes in economic conditions can raise the foreign wage levels to the point where the cost advantage is eliminated or even becomes negative.

The impact of changes in exchange rate levels can be substantial. During early 2017, the U.S. dollar continued to strengthen against other currencies. This meant domestic manufacturers took home more for each dollar's worth of sales they made, which can lead to big profit swings. For example, during 2016, IBM estimated that it lost almost $140 million due to currency swings, which is a lot, but way less than the $1.7 billion it lost in 2015. The dramatic effect of exchange rate movements on profitability is also shown by the analysis done by Iluka Resources, Ltd., an Australian mining company, which stated that a one-cent movement in the Australian dollar–U.S. dollar exchange rate would change its net income by $5 million.

Hedging long-run exposure is more difficult than hedging short-term risks. For one thing, organized forward markets don't exist for such long-term needs. Instead, the primary option that firms have is to try to match up foreign currency inflows and outflows. The same thing goes for matching foreign currency–denominated assets and liabilities. A firm that sells in a foreign country might try to concentrate its raw material purchases and labor expense in that country. That way, the dollar values of its revenues and costs will move up and down together. Probably the best examples of this type of hedging are the so-called transplant auto manufacturers such as BMW, Honda, Mercedes, and Toyota, which now build a substantial portion of the cars they sell in the United States, thereby obtaining some degree of immunization against exchange rate movements.

For example, BMW produces 400,000 cars in South Carolina and exports about 280,000 of them. The costs of manufacturing the cars are paid mostly in dollars; when BMW exports the cars to Europe, it receives euros. When the dollar weakens, these vehicles become more profitable for BMW. At the same time, BMW exports about 200,000 cars to the United States each year. The costs of manufacturing these cars imported into the U.S. are mostly in euros, so they become less profitable when the dollar weakens. Taken together, these gains and losses tend to offset each other and provide BMW with a natural hedge. In fact, according to the German Association of the Automotive Industry, about 60 percent of German-owned company autos manufactured in the U.S. are exported.

Similarly, a firm can reduce its long-run exchange rate risk by borrowing in the foreign country. Fluctuations in the value of the foreign subsidiary's assets will then be at least partially offset by changes in the value of the liabilities.

TRANSLATION EXPOSURE

When a U.S. company calculates its accounting net income and EPS for some period, it must "translate" everything into dollars. This can create some problems for the accountants when there are significant foreign operations. In particular, two issues arise:

1. What is the appropriate exchange rate to use for translating each balance sheet account?
2. How should balance sheet accounting gains and losses from foreign currency translation be handled?

To illustrate the accounting problem, suppose we started a small foreign subsidiary in Lilliputia a year ago. The local currency is the gulliver, abbreviated GL. At the beginning of the year, the exchange rate was GL 2 = $1, and the balance sheet in gullivers looked like this:

Assets	GL 1,000	Liabilities	GL 500
		Equity	500

At two gullivers to the dollar, the beginning balance sheet in dollars was as follows:

Assets	$500	Liabilities	$250
		Equity	250

Lilliputia is a quiet place, and nothing at all actually happened during the year. As a result, net income was zero (before consideration of exchange rate changes). However, the exchange rate did change to 4 gullivers = $1, purely because the Lilliputian inflation rate is much higher than the U.S. inflation rate.

Because nothing happened, the accounting ending balance sheet in gullivers is the same as the beginning one. If we convert it to dollars at the new exchange rate, we get:

Assets	$250	Liabilities	$125
		Equity	125

Notice that the value of the equity has gone down by $125, even though net income was exactly zero. Despite the fact that nothing really happened, there is a $125 accounting loss. How to handle this $125 loss has been a controversial accounting question.

One obvious and consistent way to handle this loss is to report the loss on the parent's income statement. During periods of volatile exchange rates, this kind of treatment can dramatically impact an international company's reported EPS. This is purely an accounting phenomenon; even so, such fluctuations are disliked by some financial managers.

The current approach to handling translation gains and losses is based on rules set out in the Financial Accounting Standards Board (FASB) *Statement of Financial Accounting Standards No. 52* (FASB 52), issued in December 1981. For the most part, FASB 52 requires that all assets and liabilities be translated from the subsidiary's currency into the parent's currency using the exchange rate that currently prevails.

Any translation gains and losses that occur are accumulated in a special account within the shareholders' equity section of the balance sheet. This account might be labeled something like "unrealized foreign exchange gains (losses)." The amounts involved can be substantial, at least from an accounting standpoint. For example, IBM's December 31, 2016, fiscal year-end balance sheet shows an increase in equity in the amount of $5.4 billion for translation adjustments related to assets and liabilities of non-U.S. subsidiaries. These gains and losses are not reported on the income statement. As a result, the impact of translation gains and losses will not be recognized explicitly in net income until the underlying assets and liabilities are sold or otherwise liquidated.

MANAGING EXCHANGE RATE RISK

For a large multinational firm, the management of exchange rate risk is complicated by the fact that there can be many different currencies involved in many different subsidiaries. A change in an exchange rate will likely benefit some subsidiaries and hurt others. The net effect on the overall firm depends on its net exposure.

Suppose a firm has two divisions. Division A buys goods in the United States for dollars and sells them in Britain for pounds. Division B buys goods in Britain for pounds and sells them in the United States for dollars. If these two divisions are of roughly equal size in terms of their inflows and outflows, then the overall firm obviously has little exchange rate risk.

In our example, the firm's net position in pounds (the amount coming in less the amount going out) is small, so the exchange rate risk is small. However, if one division, acting on its own, were to start hedging its exchange rate risk, then the overall firm's exchange rate risk would go up. The moral of the story is that multinational firms have to be conscious of their overall positions in a foreign currency. For this reason, management of exchange rate risk is probably best handled on a centralized basis.

Concept Questions

21.6a What are the different types of exchange rate risk?

21.6b How can a firm hedge short-run exchange rate risk? Long-run exchange rate risk?

Political Risk

21.7

One final element of risk in international investing is **political risk**. Political risk refers to changes in value that arise as a consequence of political actions. For example, in June 2016, British voters shocked the rest of Europe when they voted in favor of "Brexit," the U.K. exit from the European Union. Although the treaty that tied the U.K. to the rest of Europe required a two-year process to complete the withdrawal, financial markets didn't take that long to react. The British pound dropped 11 percent against the U.S. dollar on the day, and London's FTSE and Stoxx Europe 600 stock market indexes dropped about 8 percent. Preeminent British banks Barclays and Lloyds Banking Group were both hit even harder, as they saw stock price drops of more than 30 percent on the day. Unfortunately (or fortunately, depending on your view), the drop in the British pound wasn't finished. It continued to fall against the U.S. dollar, reaching its lowest level since 1985.

political risk
Risk related to changes in value that arise because of political actions.

THE TAX CUTS AND JOBS ACT OF 2017

In our chapter opener, we described the large cash balances held "overseas" by U.S. corporations. As we noted, the reason Apple and other large U.S. corporations held such large balances overseas has to do with U.S. tax law. Tax laws are a form of political risk faced by multinational firms.

Specifically, before the signing of the Tax Cuts and Jobs Act of 2017, the U.S. had corporate tax rates that were among the highest in the developed world. At the same time, the U.S. was somewhat unique in that it taxed corporate profits wherever they were earned, but only after the profits were brought back, or "repatriated," to the U.S. But what does this mean, exactly?

To answer, let's go back to Lilliputia, which has a 20 percent corporate tax rate, compared to what would have been 35 percent in the U.S. If we earned a profit in our Lilliputian subsidiary, that subsidiary would pay taxes to Lilliputia at the 20 percent rate. If we had left the profits in Lilliputia, then no additional taxes were owed. But, if we had brought the profits back to the U.S., we would have owed additional taxes of 15 percent, the difference between the U.S. and Lilliputian tax rates. Avoiding this extra tax gave U.S. companies a strong incentive *not* to repatriate profits.

Here is where it gets confusing. In the media, companies like Apple are depicted as having huge piles of cash sitting outside the borders of the U.S, but that's not what is really going on. Apple's cash is actually mostly in dollars, and it is mostly invested in various U.S. financial assets. So, the money isn't really "outside" the U.S.

Instead, because Apple has chosen not to pay the extra tax on its overseas profits, it is prohibited from using that cash inside the U.S. to do things like pay dividends or build new facilities. Note that Apple can easily get around this limitation by, for example, borrowing against its cash and securities portfolio if it chooses to do so.

The Tax Cuts and Jobs Act of 2017 changed things in a number of ways. First, the new flat 21 percent tax rate (down from a maximum of 35 percent) reduced the incentive to leave cash overseas. Second, the law imposed a one-time tax of 15.5 percent on cash, securities, and receivables, and a one-time tax of 8 percent on other, less liquid assets (e.g., plant, property, and equipment) purchased with untaxed overseas dollars . Finally, broadly speaking, new repatriated earnings are no longer subject to additional U.S. taxes, thereby eliminating the repatriation issue.

MANAGING POLITICAL RISK

Some countries have more political risk than others, of course. When firms operate in these riskier countries, the extra political risk may lead the firms to require higher returns on overseas investments to compensate for the possibility that funds may be blocked, critical operations interrupted, and contracts abrogated. In the most extreme case, the possibility of outright confiscation may be a concern in countries with relatively unstable political environments.

Political risk also depends on the nature of the business; some businesses are less likely to be confiscated because they are not particularly valuable in the hands of a different owner. An assembly operation supplying subcomponents that only the parent company uses would not be an attractive "takeover" target, for example. Similarly, a manufacturing operation that requires the use of specialized components from the parent is of little value without the parent company's cooperation.

Natural resource developments, such as copper mining or oil drilling, are just the opposite. Once the operation is in place, much of the value is in the commodity. The political risk for such investments is much higher for this reason. Also, the issue of exploitation is more pronounced with such investments, again increasing the political risk.

Political risk can be hedged in several ways, particularly when confiscation or nationalization is a concern. The use of local financing, perhaps from the government of the foreign country in question, reduces the possible loss because the company can refuse to pay the debt in the event of unfavorable political activities. Based on our discussion in this section, structuring the operation in such a way that it requires significant parent company involvement to function is another way to reduce political risk.

A great site for evaluating the political risk of a country is **www.cia.gov/library/ publications/the-world-factbook/index.html.**

Concept Questions

21.7a   What is political risk?

21.7b   What are some ways of hedging political risk?

Summary and Conclusions   21.8

The international firm has a more complicated life than the purely domestic firm. Management must understand the connection between interest rates, foreign currency exchange rates, and inflation, and it must become aware of many different financial market regulations and tax systems. This chapter is intended to be a concise introduction to some of the financial issues that come up in international investing.

Our coverage has been necessarily brief. The main topics we discussed are the following:

1. *Some basic vocabulary*: We briefly defined some exotic terms such as *LIBOR* and *Eurocurrency*.

2. *The basic mechanics of exchange rate quotations*: We discussed the spot and forward markets and how exchange rates are interpreted.

3. *The fundamental relationships between international financial variables*:
   a. Absolute and relative purchasing power parity, PPP.
   b. Interest rate parity, IRP.
   c. Unbiased forward rates, UFR.

   Absolute purchasing power parity states that $1 should have the same purchasing power in each country. This means that an orange costs the same whether you buy it in New York or in Tokyo.

   Relative purchasing power parity means that the expected percentage change in exchange rates between the currencies of two countries is equal to the difference in their inflation rates.

   Interest rate parity implies that the percentage difference between the forward exchange rate and the spot exchange rate is equal to the interest rate differential. We showed how covered interest arbitrage forces this relationship to hold.

   The unbiased forward rates condition indicates that the current forward rate is a good predictor of the future spot exchange rate.

4. *International capital budgeting*: We showed that the basic foreign exchange relationships imply two other conditions:
   a. Uncovered interest parity.
   b. The international Fisher effect.

   By invoking these two conditions, we learned how to estimate NPVs in foreign currencies and how to convert foreign currencies into dollars to estimate NPV in the usual way.

5. *Exchange rate and political risk*: We described the various types of exchange rate risk and discussed some commonly used approaches to managing the effect of fluctuating exchange rates on the cash flows and value of the international firm. We also discussed political risk and some ways of managing exposure to it.

6. *The Tax Cuts and Jobs Act of 2017:* We explained the much-discussed "repatriation" issue and how the Act changed a number of tax-related incentives for multinational corporations.

CONNECT TO FINANCE

For more practice, you should be using *Connect Finance*. Log on to connect.mheducation.com to get started!

Can you answer the following *Connect* Quiz questions?

Section 21.1 United Travel is exchanging a fixed-rate payment for Foreign Travel's variable-rate payment. This exchange is called a(n)_____.

Section 21.3 Roger purchased a cell phone in Canada for Can$189. The exchange rate is $1 = Can$1.08. If absolute purchasing power parity exists, what is the price of this same phone in the United States?

Section 21.6 When will a U.S. firm recognize, for income statement purposes, any accounting gain or loss the firm has from converting a firm's foreign balance sheet into U.S. dollars?

CHAPTER REVIEW AND SELF-TEST PROBLEMS

21.1 **Relative Purchasing Power Parity** The inflation rate in the United States is projected at 3 percent per year for the next several years. The New Zealand inflation rate is projected to be 5 percent during that time. The exchange rate is currently NZ$1.66. Based on relative PPP, what is the expected exchange rate in two years?

21.2 **Covered Interest Arbitrage** The spot and 360-day forward rates on the Swiss franc are SF 2.1 and SF 1.9, respectively. The risk-free interest rate in the United States is 6 percent, and the risk-free rate in Switzerland is 4 percent. Is there an arbitrage opportunity here? How would you exploit it?

ANSWERS TO CHAPTER REVIEW AND SELF-TEST PROBLEMS

21.1 Based on relative PPP, the expected exchange rate in two years, $E(S_2)$, is:

$$E(S_2) = S_0 \times [1 + (h_{NZ} - h_{US})]^2$$

where h_{NZ} is the New Zealand inflation rate. The current exchange rate is NZ$1.66, so the expected exchange rate is:

$$E(S_2) = \text{NZ\$}1.66 \times [1 + (.05 - .03)]^2$$
$$= \text{NZ\$}1.66 \times 1.02^2$$
$$= \text{NZ\$}1.73$$

21.2 Based on interest rate parity, the forward rate should be (approximately):

$$F_1 = S_0 \times [1 + (R_{SF} - R_{US})]$$
$$= \text{SF } 2.1 \times [1 + (.04 - .06)]$$
$$= \text{SF } 2.06$$

Because the forward rate is actually SF 1.9, there is an arbitrage opportunity.

To exploit the arbitrage opportunity, you first note that dollars are selling for SF 1.9 each in the forward market. Based on IRP, this is too cheap because they should be selling for SF 2.06. So you want to arrange to buy dollars with Swiss francs in the forward market. To do this, you can:

1. *Today*: Borrow, say, $1 million for 360 days. Convert it to SF 2.1 million in the spot market, and buy a forward contract at SF 1.9 to convert it back to dollars in 360 days. Invest the SF 2.1 million at 4 percent.

2. *In one year*: Your investment has grown to SF 2.1 million × 1.04 = SF 2.184 million. Convert this to dollars at the rate of SF 1.9 = $1. You will have SF 2.184 million/1.9 = $1,149,474. Pay off your loan with 6 percent interest at a cost of $1 million × 1.06 = $1,060,000 and pocket the difference of $89,474.

CONCEPTS REVIEW AND CRITICAL THINKING QUESTIONS

1. **Spot and Forward Rates** [LO1] Suppose the exchange rate for the Swiss franc is quoted as SF 1.50 in the spot market and SF 1.53 in the 90-day forward market.

    a. Is the dollar selling at a premium or a discount relative to the franc?
    b. Does the financial market expect the franc to strengthen relative to the dollar? Explain.
    c. What do you suspect is true about relative economic conditions in the United States and Switzerland?

2. **Purchasing Power Parity** [LO2] Suppose the rate of inflation in Mexico will run about 3 percent higher than the U.S. inflation rate over the next several years. All other things being the same, what will happen to the Mexican peso-U.S. dollar exchange rate? What relationship are you relying on in answering?

3. **Exchange Rates** [LO1] The exchange rate for the Australian dollar is currently A$1.40. This exchange rate is expected to rise by 10 percent over the next year.

    a. Is the Australian dollar expected to get stronger or weaker?
    b. What do you think about the relative inflation rates in the United States and Australia?
    c. What do you think about the relative nominal interest rates in the United States and Australia? Relative real rates?

4. **Yankee Bonds** [LO3] Which of the following most accurately describes a Yankee bond?

    a. A bond issued by General Motors in Japan with the interest payable in U.S. dollars.
    b. A bond issued by General Motors in Japan with the interest payable in yen.
    c. A bond issued by Toyota in the United States with the interest payable in yen.
    d. A bond issued by Toyota in the United States with the interest payable in dollars.
    e. A bond issued by Toyota worldwide with the interest payable in dollars.

5. **Exchange Rates** [LO3] Are exchange rate changes necessarily good or bad for a particular company?

6. **International Risks** [LO4] At one point, Duracell International confirmed that it was planning to open battery-manufacturing plants in China and India. Manufacturing in these countries allows Duracell to avoid import duties of between 30 and 35 percent that have made alkaline batteries prohibitively expensive for some consumers. What additional advantages might Duracell see in this proposal? What are some of the risks to Duracell?

7. **Multinational Corporations** [LO3] Given that many multinationals based in many countries have much greater sales outside their domestic markets than within them, what is the particular relevance of their domestic currency?

8. **Exchange Rate Movements** [LO3] Are the following statements true or false? Explain why.

    a. If the general price index in Great Britain rises faster than that in the United States, we would expect the pound to appreciate relative to the dollar.
    b. Suppose you are a German machine tool exporter, and you invoice all of your sales in foreign currency. Further suppose that the Euroland monetary authorities begin to undertake an expansionary monetary policy. If it is certain that the easy money policy will result in higher inflation rates in Euroland relative to those in other countries, you should use the forward markets to protect yourself against future losses resulting from the deterioration in the value of the euro.
    c. If you could accurately estimate differences in the relative inflation rates of two countries over a long period while other market participants were unable to do so, you could successfully speculate in spot currency markets.

9. **Exchange Rate Movements** [LO3] Some countries encourage movements in their exchange rate relative to those of some other country as a short-term means of addressing foreign trade imbalances. For each of the following scenarios, evaluate the impact the announcement would have on an American importer and an American exporter doing business with the foreign country:

   a. Officials in the administration of the U.S. government announce that they are comfortable with a rising euro relative to the dollar.

   b. British monetary authorities announce that they feel the pound has been driven too low by currency speculators relative to the dollar.

   c. The Brazilian government announces that it will print billions of new reals and inject them into the economy in an effort to reduce the country's unemployment rate.

10. **International Capital Market Relationships** [LO2] We discussed five international capital market relationships: relative PPP, IRP, UFR, UIP, and the international Fisher effect. Which of these would you expect to hold most closely?

QUESTIONS AND PROBLEMS

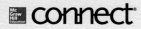

BASIC
(Questions 1–13)

1. **Using Exchange Rates** [LO1] Take a look back at Figure 21.1 to answer the following questions:

   a. If you have $100, how many euros can you get?

   b. How much is one euro worth?

   c. If you have 5 million euros, how many dollars do you have?

   d. Which is worth more, a New Zealand dollar or a Singapore dollar?

   e. Which is worth more, a Mexican peso or a Chilean peso?

   f. How many Mexican pesos can you get for a euro? What do you call this rate?

   g. Per unit, what is the most valuable currency of those listed? The least valuable?

2. **Using the Cross-Rate** [LO1] Use the information in Figure 21.1 to answer the following questions:

   a. Which would you rather have, $100 or £100? Why?

   b. Which would you rather have, 100 Swiss francs (SF) or £100? Why?

   c. What is the cross-rate for Swiss francs in terms of British pounds? For British pounds in terms of Swiss francs?

3. **Forward Exchange Rates** [LO1] Use the information in Figure 21.1 to answer the following questions:

   a. What is the six-month forward rate for the Japanese yen in yen per U.S. dollar? Is the yen selling at a premium or a discount? Explain.

   b. What is the three-month forward rate for Australian dollars in U.S. dollars per Australian dollar? Is the dollar selling at a premium or a discount? Explain.

   c. What do you think will happen to the value of the dollar relative to the yen and the Australian dollar, based on the information in the figure? Explain.

4. **Using Spot and Forward Exchange Rates** [LO1] Suppose the spot exchange rate for the Canadian dollar is Can$1.29 and the six-month forward rate is Can$1.31.

   a. Which is worth more, a U.S. dollar or a Canadian dollar?

   b. Assuming absolute PPP holds, what is the cost in the United States of an Elkhead beer if the price in Canada is Can$2.50? Why might the beer actually sell at a different price in the United States?

c. Is the U.S. dollar selling at a premium or a discount relative to the Canadian dollar?

d. Which currency is expected to appreciate in value?

e. Which country do you think has higher interest rates—the United States or Canada? Explain.

5. **Cross-Rates and Arbitrage [LO1]** Suppose the Japanese yen exchange rate is ¥114 = $1, and the British pound exchange rate is £1 = $1.26.

   a. What is the cross-rate in terms of yen per pound?

   b. Suppose the cross-rate is ¥147 = £1. Is there an arbitrage opportunity here? If there is, explain how to take advantage of the mispricing and the potential arbitrage profit. What is your arbitrage profit per dollar used?

6. **Interest Rate Parity [LO2]** Use Figure 21.1 to answer the following questions: Suppose interest rate parity holds, and the current six-month risk-free rate in the United States is 1.3 percent. What must the six-month risk-free rate be in Great Britain? In Japan? In Switzerland?

7. **Interest Rates and Arbitrage [LO2]** The treasurer of a major U.S. firm has $30 million to invest for three months. The interest rate in the United States is .28 percent per month. The interest rate in Great Britain is .31 percent per month. The spot exchange rate is £.791, and the three-month forward rate is £.803. Ignoring transaction costs, in which country would the treasurer want to invest the company's funds? Why?

8. **Inflation and Exchange Rates [LO2]** Suppose the current exchange rate for the Polish zloty is Z 4.04. The expected exchange rate in three years is Z 4.13. What is the difference in the annual inflation rates for the United States and Poland over this period? Assume that the anticipated rate is constant for both countries. What relationship are you relying on in answering?

9. **Exchange Rate Risk [LO3]** Suppose your company imports computer motherboards from Singapore. The exchange rate is given in Figure 21.1. You have just placed an order for 30,000 motherboards at a cost to you of 218.50 Singapore dollars each. You will pay for the shipment when it arrives in 90 days. You can sell the motherboards for $185 each. Calculate your profit if the exchange rate goes up or down by 10 percent over the next 90 days. What is the break-even exchange rate? What percentage rise or fall does this represent in terms of the Singapore dollar versus the U.S. dollar?

10. **Exchange Rates and Arbitrage [LO2]** Suppose the spot and six-month forward rates on the Norwegian krone are Kr 8.39 and Kr 8.48, respectively. The annual risk-free rate in the United States is 3.8 percent, and the annual risk-free rate in Norway is 5.7 percent.

    a. Is there an arbitrage opportunity here? If so, how would you exploit it?

    b. What must the six-month forward rate be to prevent arbitrage?

11. **The International Fisher Effect [LO2]** You observe that the inflation rate in the United States is 3.5 percent per year and that T-bills currently yield 4.1 percent annually. Using the approximate international Fisher effect, what do you estimate the inflation rate to be in:

    a. Australia, if short-term Australian government securities yield 4 percent per year?

    b. Canada, if short-term Canadian government securities yield 7 percent per year?

    c. Taiwan, if short-term Taiwanese government securities yield 9 percent per year?

12. **Spot versus Forward Rates [LO1]** Suppose the spot and three-month forward rates for the yen are ¥113.65 and ¥113.18, respectively.

    a. Is the yen expected to get stronger or weaker?

b. What would you estimate is the difference between the annual inflation rates of the United States and Japan?

13. **Expected Spot Rates** [LO2] Suppose the spot exchange rate for the Hungarian forint is HUF 289.97. The inflation rate in the United States will be 2.9 percent per year. It will be 4.5 percent in Hungary. What do you predict the exchange rate will be in one year? In two years? In five years? What relationship are you using?

14. **Capital Budgeting** [LO2] Lakonishok Equipment has an investment opportunity in Europe. The project costs €10.5 million and is expected to produce cash flows of €1.7 million in Year 1, €2.4 million in Year 2, and €3.3 million in Year 3. The current spot exchange rate is €.94/$ and the current risk-free rate in the United States is 2.3 percent, compared to that in Europe of 1.8 percent. The appropriate discount rate for the project is estimated to be 13 percent, the U.S. cost of capital for the company. In addition, the subsidiary can be sold at the end of three years for an estimated €7.9 million. What is the NPV of the project?

15. **Capital Budgeting** [LO2] You are evaluating a proposed expansion of an existing subsidiary located in Switzerland. The cost of the expansion would be SF 13.8 million. The cash flows from the project would be SF 3.9 million per year for the next five years. The dollar required return is 12 percent per year, and the current exchange rate is SF 1.09. The going rate on Eurodollars is 5 percent per year. It is 4 percent per year on Euroswiss.

    a. What do you project will happen to exchange rates over the next four years?

    b. Based on your answer in (a), convert the projected franc flows into dollar flows and calculate the NPV.

    c. What is the required return on franc flows? Based on your answer, calculate the NPV in francs and then convert to dollars.

16. **Translation Exposure** [LO3] Atreides International has operations in Arrakis. The balance sheet for this division in Arrakeen solaris shows assets of 38,000 solaris, debt in the amount of 12,000 solaris, and equity of 26,000 solaris.

    a. If the current exchange ratio is 1.50 solaris per dollar, what does the balance sheet look like in dollars?

    b. Assume that one year from now the balance sheet in solaris is exactly the same as at the beginning of the year. If the exchange rate is 1.60 solaris per dollar, what does the balance sheet look like in dollars now?

    c. Rework part (b) assuming the exchange rate is 1.41 solaris per dollar.

17. **Translation Exposure** [LO3] In Problem 16, assume the equity increases by 1,250 solaris due to retained earnings. If the exchange rate at the end of the year is 1.54 solaris per dollar, what does the balance sheet look like?

18. **Using the Exact International Fisher Effect** [LO2] From our discussion of the Fisher effect in Chapter 7, we know that the actual relationship between a nominal rate, R, a real rate, r, and an inflation rate, h, can be written as:

    $$1 + r = (1 + R)/(1 + h)$$

    This is the *domestic* Fisher effect.

    a. What is the nonapproximate form of the international Fisher effect?

    b. Based on your answer in (a), what is the exact form for UIP? (*Hint*: Recall the exact form of IRP and use UFR.)

    c. What is the exact form for relative PPP? (*Hint*: Combine your previous two answers.)

    d. Recalculate the NPV for the Kihlstrom drill bit project (discussed in Section 21.5) using the exact forms for UIP and the international Fisher effect. Verify that you get precisely the same answer either way.

EXCEL MASTER IT! PROBLEM

The St. Louis Federal Reserve has historical exchange rates on its website, www.stlouisfed.org. On the website, look for the FRED® data. Download the exchange rate with U.S. dollars over the past five years for the following currencies: Brazilian reals, Canadian dollars, Hong Kong dollars, Japanese yen, Mexican pesos, South Korean won, Indian rupees, Swiss francs, Australian dollars, and the euro. Graph the exchange rate for each of these currencies in a dashboard that can be printed on one page.

MINICASE

S&S Air Goes International

Mark Sexton and Todd Story, the owners of S&S Air, have been in discussions with a light aircraft dealer in Monaco about selling the company's planes in Europe. Jarek Jacho-wicz, the dealer, wants to add S&S Air to his current retail line. Jarek has told Mark and Todd that he feels the retail sales will be approximately €5.7 million per month. All sales will be made in euros, and Jarek will retain 5 percent of retail sales as a commission, which will be paid in euros. Because the planes will be customized to order, the first sales will take place in one month. Jarek will pay S&S Air for the order 90 days after it is filled. This payment schedule will continue for the length of the contract between the two companies.

Mark and Todd are confident the company can handle the extra volume with its existing facilities, but they are unsure about the potential financial risks of selling their planes in Europe. In their discussion with Jarek, they found that the current exchange rate is $1.09/€. At the current exchange rate, the company would spend 80 percent of the sales on production costs. This number does not reflect the sales commission paid to Jarek.

Mark and Todd have decided to ask Chris Guthrie, the company's financial analyst, to prepare an analysis of the proposed international sales. Specifically, they ask Chris to answer the following questions.

QUESTIONS

1. What are the pros and cons of the international sales? What additional risks will the company face?

2. What happens to the company's profits if the dollar strengthens? What if the dollar weakens?

3. Ignoring taxes, what are S&S Air's projected gains or losses from this proposed arrangement at the current exchange rate of $1.09/€? What happens to profits if the exchange rate changes to $1.03/€? At what exchange rate will the company break even?

4. How could the company hedge its exchange rate risk? What are the implications for this approach?

5. Taking all factors into account, should the company pursue the international sales further? Why or why not?

22 | Behavioral Finance: Implications for Financial Management

THE NASDAQ STOCK MARKET WAS RAGING in the late 1990s, gaining about 23 percent in 1996, 14 percent in 1997, 35 percent in 1998, and 87 percent in 1999. Of course, that spectacular run came to a jarring halt, and the NASDAQ lost about 40 percent in 2000, followed by another 30 percent in 2001. The ISDEX, an index of Internet-related stocks, rose from 100 in January 1996 to 1,100 in February 2000, a gain of 1,000 percent! It then fell like a rock to 600 by May 2000. A bubble can exist on a single asset, as well. For example, many investors saw a tech bubble echo in Tesla Motors, which increased more than 590 percent from March 22, 2013, to February 26, 2014. In fact, one analysis of the company's valuation indicated that the stock could be overvalued by about 150 percent. Tesla's stock evidently ran out of juice as it gained only about 12 percent over the next three years.

The performance of the NASDAQ over this period, and particularly the rise and fall of Internet stocks, has been described by many as one of the greatest market "bubbles" in history. The argument is that prices were inflated to economically ridiculous levels before investors came to their senses, which then caused the bubble to pop and prices to plunge. Debate over whether the stock market of the late 1990s really was a bubble has generated much controversy. In this chapter, we introduce the subject of behavioral finance, which deals with questions such as how bubbles can come to exist. Some of the issues we discuss are quite controversial and unsettled. We will describe competing ideas, present some evidence on both sides, and examine the implications for financial managers.

Learning Objectives

After studying this chapter, you should be able to:

LO1 Describe how behaviors such as overconfidence, overoptimism, and confirmation bias can affect decision making.

LO2 Demonstrate how framing effects can result in inconsistent and/or incorrect decisions.

LO3 Show how the use of heuristics can lead to suboptimal financial decisions.

LO4 Define the shortcomings and limitations to market efficiency from the behavioral finance view.

For updates on the latest happenings in finance, visit fundamentalsofcorporatefinance.blogspot.com.

Be honest: Do you think of yourself as a better-than-average driver? If you do, then you are not alone. About 80 percent of the people who are asked this question will say yes. Evidently, we tend to overestimate our abilities behind the wheel. Is the same true when it comes to making financial management decisions?

It will probably not surprise you when we say that human beings sometimes make errors in judgment. How these errors, and other aspects of human behavior, affect financial managers falls under the general heading of "behavioral finance." In this chapter, our goal is to acquaint you with some common types of mistakes and their financial implications. As you will see, researchers have identified a wide variety of potentially damaging behaviors. By learning to recognize situations in which mistakes are common, you will become a better decision maker, both in the context of financial management and elsewhere.

Introduction to Behavioral Finance   22.1

Sooner or later, you are going to make a financial decision that winds up costing you (and possibly your employer and/or stockholders) a lot of money. Why is this going to happen? You already know the answer. Sometimes, you make sound decisions, but you get unlucky in the sense that something happens that you could not have reasonably anticipated. Other times (however painful to admit), you just make a bad decision, one that could have (and should have) been avoided. The beginning of business wisdom is to recognize the circumstances that lead to poor decisions and thereby cut down on the damage done by financial blunders.

As we have previously noted, the area of research known as **behavioral finance** attempts to understand and explain how reasoning errors influence financial decisions. Much of the research done in the behavioral finance area stems from work in cognitive psychology, which is the study of how people, including financial managers, think, reason, and make decisions. Errors in reasoning are often called *cognitive* errors. In the next several subsections, we will review three main categories of such errors: (1) Biases, (2) framing effects, and (3) heuristics.

behavioral finance
The area of finance dealing with the implications of reasoning errors on financial decisions.

Biases   22.2

If your decisions exhibit systematic biases, then you will make systematic errors in judgment. The type of error depends on the type of bias. In this section, we discuss three particularly relevant biases: (1) Overconfidence, (2) overoptimism, and (3) confirmation bias.

OVERCONFIDENCE

Serious errors in judgment occur in the business world due to **overconfidence**. We are all overconfident about our abilities in at least some areas (recall our earlier question about driving ability). Here is another example that we see a lot: Ask yourself what grade you will receive in this course (in spite of the arbitrary and capricious nature of the professor). In our experience, almost everyone will either say "A" or, at worst, "B." Sadly, when this happens, we are always confident (but not overconfident) that at least some of our students are going to be disappointed.

In general, you are overconfident when you overestimate your ability to make the correct choice or decision. Most business decisions require judgments about the unknown future. The belief that you can forecast the future with precision is a common form of overconfidence.

overconfidence
The belief that your abilities are better than they really are.

Another good example of overconfidence comes from studies of stock investors. Researchers have examined large numbers of actual brokerage accounts to see how investors fare when they choose stocks. Overconfidence by investors would cause them to overestimate their ability to pick the best stocks, leading to excessive trading. The evidence supports this view. First, investors hurt themselves by trading. The accounts that have the most trading significantly underperform the accounts with the least trading, primarily because of the costs associated with trades.

A second finding is equally interesting. Accounts registered to men underperform those registered to women. The reason is that men trade more on average. This extra trading is consistent with evidence from psychology that men have greater degrees of overconfidence than women.

OVEROPTIMISM

overoptimism
Taking an overly optimistic view of potential outcomes.

Overoptimism leads to overestimating the likelihood of a good outcome and underestimating the likelihood of a bad outcome. Overoptimism and overconfidence are related, but they are not the same thing. An overconfident individual could (overconfidently) forecast a bad outcome, for example.

Optimism is usually thought of as a good thing. Optimistic people have "upbeat personalities" and "sunny dispositions." However, excessive optimism leads to bad decisions. In a capital budgeting context, overly optimistic analysts will consistently overestimate cash flows and underestimate the probability of failure. Doing so leads to upward-biased estimates of project NPVs, a common occurrence in the business world.

CONFIRMATION BIAS

confirmation bias
Searching for (and giving more weight to) information and opinions that confirm what you believe rather than information and opinions to the contrary.

When you are evaluating a decision, you collect information and opinions. A common bias in this regard is to focus more on information that agrees with your opinion and to downplay or ignore information that doesn't agree with or support your position. This phenomenon is known as **confirmation bias**, and people who suffer from it tend to spend too much time trying to prove themselves correct rather than searching for information that might prove them wrong.

Here is a classic example from psychology. Below are four cards. Notice that the cards are labeled a, b, 2, and 3. You are asked to evaluate the following statement: "Any card with a vowel on one side has an even number on the other." You are asked which of the four cards has to be turned over to decide if the statement is true or false. It costs $100 to turn over a card, so you want to be as economical as possible. What do you do?

| a | b | 2 | 3 |

You would probably begin by turning over the card with an "a" on it, which is correct. If we find an odd number, then we are done because the statement is incorrect.

Suppose we find an even number. What next? Most people will turn over the card with a 2. Is that the right choice? If we find a vowel, then we confirm the statement, but if we find a consonant, we don't learn anything. In other words, this card can't prove that the statement is wrong; it can only confirm it, so selecting this card is an example of confirmation bias.

Continuing, there is no point in turning over the card labeled "b" because the statement doesn't say anything about consonants, which leaves us with the last card. Do we have to turn it over? The answer is yes because it might have a vowel on the other side, which would disprove the statement, but most people will choose the 2 card over the 3 card.

Framing Effects

22.3

You are susceptible to framing effects if your decisions depend on how a problem or question is framed. Consider the following example: A disaster has occurred, 600 people are at risk, and you are in charge. You must choose between the two following rescue operations:

SCENARIO 1

Option A: Exactly 200 people will be saved.

Option B: There is a 1/3 chance that all 600 people will be saved and a 2/3 chance that no people will be saved.

Which would you choose? There is no necessarily right answer, but most people will choose Option A. Now suppose your choices are as follows:

SCENARIO 2

Option C: Exactly 400 people will die.

Option D: There is a 1/3 chance that nobody will die and a 2/3 chance that all 600 will die.

Now which do you pick? Again, there is no right answer, but most people will choose Option D.

Although most people will choose Options A and D in our hypothetical scenarios, you probably see that doing so is inconsistent because Options A and C are identical, as are Options B and D. Why do people make inconsistent choices? It's because the options are framed differently. The first scenario is positive because it emphasizes the number that will be saved. The second is negative because it focuses on losses, and people react differently to positive versus negative framing, which is a form of **frame dependence**.

frame dependence
The tendency of individuals to make different (and potentially inconsistent) decisions depending on how a question or problem is framed.

LOSS AVERSION

Here is another example that illustrates a particular type of frame dependence:

SCENARIO 1: Suppose we give you $1,000. You have the following choices:

Option A: You can receive another $500 for sure.

Option B: You can flip a fair coin. If the coin flip comes up heads, you get another $1,000, but if it comes up tails, you get nothing.

SCENARIO 2: Suppose we give you $2,000. You have the following choices:

Option C: You can lose $500 for sure.

Option D: You can flip a fair coin. If the coin flip comes up heads, you lose $1,000, but if it comes up tails, you lose nothing.

What were your answers? Did you choose Option A in the first scenario and Option D in the second? If that's what you did, you are guilty of just focusing on gains and losses, and not paying attention to what really matters, namely, the impact on your wealth. However, you are not alone. About 85 percent of the people who are presented with the first scenario choose Option A, and about 70 percent of the people who are presented with the second scenario choose Option D.

If you look closely at the two scenarios, you will see that they are actually identical. You end up with $1,500 for sure if you pick Option A or C, or else you end up with a 50–50 chance of either $1,000 or $2,000 if you pick Option B or D. So, you should pick the same option in both scenarios. Which option you prefer is up to you, but the point is that you should never pick Option A in our first scenario and Option D in our second one.

This example illustrates an important aspect of financial decision making. Focusing on gains and losses instead of overall wealth is an example of *narrow framing*, and it leads to a phenomenon known as *loss aversion*. In fact, the reason that most people avoid Option C in Scenario 2 in our example is that it is expressed as a sure loss of $500. In general, researchers have found that individuals are reluctant to realize losses and will gamble at unfavorable odds to avoid doing so.

Loss aversion is also known as *get-evenitus* or the *break-even effect* because it frequently shows up as individuals and companies hang on to bad investments and projects (and perhaps even invest more) hoping that something will happen that will allow them to break even and thereby escape without a loss. For example, we discussed the irrelevance of sunk costs in the context of capital budgeting, and the idea of a sunk cost seems clear. Nonetheless, we constantly see companies (and individuals) throw good money after bad rather than just recognize a loss in the face of sunk costs.

How destructive is get-evenitus? Perhaps the most famous case occurred in 1995, when 28-year-old Nicholas Leeson caused the collapse of his employer, the 233-year-old Barings Bank. At the end of 1992, Mr. Leeson had lost about £2 million, which he hid in a secret account. By the end of 1993, his losses were about £23 million, and they mushroomed to £208 million at the end of 1994 (at the time, this was about $300 million).

Instead of admitting to these losses, Mr. Leeson gambled more of the bank's money in an attempt to "double-up and catch-up." On February 23, 1995, Mr. Leeson's losses were about £827 million ($1.3 billion), and his trading irregularities were uncovered. Although he attempted to flee from prosecution, he was caught, arrested, tried, convicted, and imprisoned. Also, his wife divorced him.

Do you suffer from get-evenitus? Maybe so. Consider the following scenario: You just lost $78 somehow. You can just live with the loss, or you can make a bet. If you make the bet, there is an 80 percent chance that your loss will grow to $100 (from $78) and a 20 percent chance that your loss will be nothing. Do you take the loss or take the bet? We bet you choose the bet. If you do, you have get-evenitus because the bet is a bad one. Instead of a sure loss of $78, your expected loss from the bet is $(.80 \times \$100) + (.20 \times \$0) = \$80$.

In corporate finance, loss aversion can be quite damaging. We already mentioned the pursuit of sunk costs. We also might see managers bypassing positive NPV projects because they have the possibility of large losses (perhaps with low probability). Another phenomenon that we see is debt avoidance. As we discuss in our coverage of capital structure, debt financing generates valuable tax shields for profitable companies. Even so, there are hundreds of profitable companies listed on major stock exchanges that completely (or almost completely) avoid debt financing. Because debt financing increases the likelihood of losses and even bankruptcy, this potentially costly behavior could be due to loss aversion.

HOUSE MONEY

Las Vegas casinos know all about a concept called *playing with house money*. The casinos have found that gamblers are far more likely to take big risks with money that they have won from the casino (i.e., house money). Also, casinos have found that gamblers are not as upset about losing house money as they are about losing the money they brought with them to gamble.

It may seem natural for you to feel that some money is precious because you earned it through hard work, sweat, and sacrifice, while other money is less precious because it came to you as a windfall. But these feelings are plainly irrational because any dollar you have buys the same amount of goods and services no matter how you obtained that dollar.

Let's consider another common situation to illustrate several of the ideas we have explored thus far. Consider the following two investments:

Investment 1: You bought 100 shares in Moore Enterprises for $35 per share. The shares immediately fell to $20 each.

Investment 2: At the same time, you bought 100 shares in Miller Co. for $5 per share. The shares immediately jumped to $20 each.

How would you feel about your investments?

You would probably feel pretty good about your Miller investment and be unhappy with your Moore investment. Here are some other things that might occur:

1. You might tell yourself that your Miller investment was a great idea on your part; you're a stock-picking genius. The drop in value on the Moore shares wasn't your fault—it was just bad luck. This is a form a confirmation bias, and it also illustrates *self-attribution bias*, which is taking credit for good outcomes that occur for reasons beyond your control, while attributing bad outcomes to bad luck or misfortune.

2. You might be unhappy that your big winner was essentially nullified by your loser, but notice in our example that your overall wealth did not change. Suppose instead that shares in both companies didn't change in price at all, so that your overall wealth was unchanged. Would you feel the same way?

3. You might be inclined to sell your Miller stock to "realize" the gain, but hold on to your Moore stock in hopes of avoiding the loss (which is, of course, loss aversion). The tendency to sell winners and hold losers is known as the *disposition effect*. Plainly, the rational thing to do is to decide if the stocks are attractive investments at their new prices and react accordingly.

Suppose you decide to keep both stocks a little longer. Once you do, both decline to $15. You might now feel very differently about the decline depending on which stock you looked at. With Moore, the decline makes a bad situation even worse. Now you are down $20 per share on your investment. On the other hand, with Miller you only "give back" some of your "paper profit." You are still way ahead. This kind of thinking is playing with house money. Whether you lose from your original investment or from your investment gains is irrelevant.

Our Moore and Miller example illustrates what can happen when you become emotionally invested in decisions such as stock purchases. When you add a new stock to your portfolio, it is human nature for you to associate the stock with its purchase price. As the price of the stock changes through time, you will have unrealized gains or losses when you compare the current price to the purchase price. Through time, you will mentally account for these gains and losses, and how you feel about the investment depends on whether you are ahead or behind. This behavior is known as *mental accounting*.

When you engage in mental accounting, you unknowingly have a personal relationship with each of your stocks. As a result, it becomes harder to sell one of them. It is as if you have to "break up" with a stock or "fire" it from your portfolio. As with personal relationships, these stock relationships can be complicated and, believe it or not, make selling stocks difficult at times. What can you do about mental accounting? Legendary investor Warren Buffett offers the following advice: "The stock doesn't know you own it. You have feelings about it, but it has no feelings about you. The stock doesn't know what you paid. People shouldn't get emotionally involved with their stocks."

Loss aversion, mental accounting, and the house money effect are important examples of how narrow framing leads to poor decisions. Other, related types of judgment errors have been documented. Here are a few examples:

Myopic loss aversion. This behavior is the tendency to focus on avoiding short-term losses, even at the expense of long-term gains. For example, you might fail to invest in stocks for long-term retirement purposes because you have a fear of loss in the near term.

Regret aversion. This aversion is the tendency to avoid making a decision because you fear that, in hindsight, the decision would have been less than optimal. Regret aversion relates to myopic loss aversion.

Endowment effect. This effect is the tendency to consider something that you own to be worth more than it would be if you did not own it. Because of the endowment effect, people sometimes demand more money to give up something than they would be willing to pay to acquire it.

Money illusion. If you suffer from a money illusion, you are confused between real buying power and nominal buying power (i.e., you do not account for the effects of inflation).

Concept Questions

22.3a   What is frame dependence? How is it likely to be costly?
22.3b   What is loss aversion? How is it likely to be costly?
22.3c   What is the house money effect? Why is it irrational?

22.4 Heuristics

heuristics
Shortcuts or rules of thumb used to make decisions.

Financial managers (and managers in general) often rely on rules of thumb, or **heuristics**, in making decisions. For example, a manager might decide that any project with a payback period less than two years is acceptable and therefore not bother with additional analysis. As a practical matter, this mental shortcut might be just fine for most circumstances, but we know that sooner or later, it will lead to the acceptance of a negative NPV project.

THE AFFECT HEURISTIC

We frequently hear business and political leaders talk about following their gut instinct. In essence, such people are making decisions based on whether the chosen outcome or path feels "right" emotionally. Psychologists use the term *affect* (as in *affection*) to refer to emotional feelings, and the reliance on gut instinct is called the **affect heuristic**.

affect heuristic
The reliance on instinct instead of analysis in making decisions.

Reliance on instinct is closely related to reliance on intuition and/or experience. Both intuition and experience are important and, used properly, help decision makers identify potential risks and rewards. However, instinct, intuition, and experience should be viewed as complements to formal analysis, not substitutes. Overreliance on emotions in making decisions will almost surely lead (at least on occasion) to costly outcomes that could have been avoided with careful, structured thinking. An obvious example would be making capital budgeting decisions based on instinct rather than on market research and discounted cash flow analysis.

THE REPRESENTATIVENESS HEURISTIC

People often assume that a particular person, object, or outcome is broadly representative of a larger class. Suppose an employer hired a graduate of your high-quality educational institution and, in fact, is quite pleased with that person. The employer might be inclined to look to your school again for future employees because the students are so good. Of course, in doing so, the employer is assuming that the recent hire is representative of all the students, which is an example of the **representativeness heuristic**. A little more generally, the representativeness heuristic is the reliance on stereotypes, analogies, or limited samples to form opinions about an entire class.

representativeness heuristic
The reliance on stereotypes, analogies, or limited samples to form opinions about an entire class.

REPRESENTATIVENESS AND RANDOMNESS

Another implication of the representativeness heuristic has to do with perceiving patterns or causes where none exist. For example, basketball fans generally believe that success breeds success. Suppose we look at the recent performance of two basketball players named LeBron and Shaquille. Both of these players make half of their shots. But, LeBron has just made two shots in a row, while Shaquille has just missed two in a row. Researchers have found that if they ask 100 basketball fans which player has the better chance of making the next shot, 91 of them will say LeBron, because he has a "hot hand." Further, 84 of these fans believe that it is important for teammates to pass the ball to LeBron after he has made two or three shots in a row.

But, and the sports fans among you will have a hard time with this, researchers have found that the hot hand is an illusion. That is, players really do not deviate much from their long-run shooting averages—although fans, players, announcers, and coaches think they do. In one study, cognitive psychologists actually analyzed the shooting percentage of one professional basketball team for a season. Here is what they found:

| Shooting Percentages and the History of Previous Attempts ||
Shooting Percentage on Next Shot	History of Previous Attempts
46%	Has made 3 in a row
50	Has made 2 in a row
51	Has made 1 in a row
52	First shot of the game
54	Has missed 1 in a row
53	Has missed 2 in a row
56	Has missed 3 in a row

Detailed analysis of shooting data failed to show that players make or miss shots more or less frequently than what would be expected by chance. That is, statistically speaking, all the shooting percentages listed here are the same.

From the shooting percentages, it may appear that teams will try harder to stop a shooter who has made the last two or three shots. To take this into account, researchers also studied free-throw percentages. Researchers told fans that a certain player was a 70 percent free-throw shooter and was shooting two foul shots. They asked fans to predict what would happen on the second shot if the player:

1. Made the first free throw.
2. Missed the first free throw.

Fans thought that this 70 percent free-throw shooter would make 74 percent of the second free throws after making the first free throw but would only make 66 percent of the second free throws after missing the first free throw. Researchers studied free-throw data from a professional basketball team over two seasons. They found that the result of the first free throw does not matter when it comes to making or missing the second free throw. On average, the shooting percentage on the second free throw was 75 percent when the player made the first free throw. On average, the shooting percentage on the second free throw was also 75 percent when the player missed the first free throw.

It is true that basketball players shoot in streaks. But these streaks are within the bounds of long-run shooting percentages. So, it is an illusion that players are either "hot" or "cold." If you are a believer in the hot hand you are likely to reject these facts because you "know better" from watching your favorite teams over the years. If you do, you are being fooled by randomness.

The *clustering illusion* is our human belief that random events that occur in clusters are not really random. For example, it strikes most people as very unusual if heads comes up four times in a row during a series of coin flips. However, if a fair coin is flipped 20 times, there is about a 50 percent chance of getting four heads in a row. Ask yourself, if you flip four heads in a row, do you think you have a "hot hand" at coin flipping?

THE GAMBLER'S FALLACY

People commit the *gambler's fallacy* when they assume that a departure from what occurs on average, or in the long run, will be corrected in the short run. Interestingly, some people suffer from both the hot-hand illusion (which predicts continuation in the short run) and the gambler's fallacy (which predicts reversal in the short run)! The idea is that because an event has not happened recently, it has become overdue and is more likely to occur. People sometimes refer (wrongly) to the law of averages in such cases.

Roulette is a random gambling game where gamblers can make various bets on the spin of the wheel. There are 38 numbers on an American roulette table, 2 green ones, 18 red ones, and 18 black ones. One possibility is to bet whether the spin will result in a red number or a black number. Suppose a red number has appeared five times in a row. Gamblers will often become (over) confident that the next spin will be black, when the true chance remains at about 50 percent (of course, it is exactly 18 in 38).

The misconception arises from the human intuition that the overall odds of the wheel must be reflected in a small number of spins. That is, gamblers often become convinced that the wheel is "due" to hit a black number after a series of red numbers. Gamblers do know that the odds of a black number appearing are always unchanged: 18 in 38. But, gamblers cannot help but feel that after a long series of red numbers, a black one must appear to restore the balance between red and black numbers over time.

Of course, there are many other related errors and biases due to heuristics. Here is a partial list:

Law of small numbers. If you believe in the law of small numbers, you believe that a small sample of outcomes always resembles the long-run distribution of outcomes. If your investment guru has been right five out of seven times recently, you might believe that his long-run average of being correct is also five out of seven. The law of small numbers is related to recency bias (see our next item) and to the gambler's fallacy.

Recency bias. Humans tend to give recent events more importance than less recent events. For example, during the great bull market that occurred from 1995 to 1999, many investors thought the market would continue its big gains for a long time—forgetting that bear markets also occur (which happened from 2008 to early 2009). Recency bias is related to the law of small numbers.

Anchoring and adjustment. People have an anchoring bias when they are unable to account for new information in a correct way. That is, they become "anchored" to a previous price or other value and fail to adjust their thinking. If you have an anchoring bias, you will tend to be overly conservative in the face of fresh news.

Aversion to ambiguity. This bias results when people shy away from the unknown. Consider the following choice: You get $1,000 for sure, or you can draw a ball out of a big bin containing 100 balls. If the ball is blue, you win $2,000. If it is red, you win nothing. When people are told that there are 50 blue balls and 50 red balls in the bin, about 40 percent choose to draw a ball. When they are told nothing about how many balls in the bin are blue, most choose to take the $1,000—ignoring the possibility that the odds might really be in their favor. That is, there could be more than 50 blue balls in the bin.

False consensus. This is the tendency to think that other people are thinking the same thing you are thinking (with no real evidence). False consensus relates to overconfidence and confirmation bias.

Availability bias. You suffer from availability bias when you put too much weight on information that is easily available and place too little weight on information that is hard to obtain. Your financial decisions will suffer if you only consider information that is easy to obtain.

Visit **www.behaviouralfinance.net**. for many other terms and concepts of behavioral finance.

Concept Questions

22.4a What is the affect heuristic? How is it likely to be costly?
22.4b What is the representativeness heuristic? How is it likely to be costly?
22.4c What is the gambler's fallacy?

Behavioral Finance and Market Efficiency   22.5

Our discussion thus far has focused on how cognitive errors by individuals can lead to poor business decisions. It seems both clear and noncontroversial that such errors are real and financially important. We now venture into a much less clear area—the implications of behavioral finance for stock prices.

In Chapter 12, we introduced the notion of market efficiency. The key idea is that, in an efficient market, prices fully reflect available information. Put differently, prices are correct in the sense that a stock purchase or sale is a zero NPV investment. In a well-organized, liquid market such as the NYSE, the argument is that competition among profit-motivated, economically rational traders ensures that prices can never drift far from their zero-NPV level.

In this chapter, we have already seen a few examples of how cognitive errors, such as overconfidence, can lead to damaging decisions in the context of stock ownership. If many traders behave in ways that are economically irrational, then is there still reason to think that markets are efficient?

First off, it is important to realize that the efficient markets hypothesis does not require every investor to be rational. Instead, all that is required for a market to be efficient is at least some rational and well-financed investors. These investors are prepared to buy and sell to take advantage of any mispricing in the marketplace. This activity is what keeps markets efficient. It is sometimes said that market efficiency doesn't require that *everyone* be rational, just that *someone* be rational.

LIMITS TO ARBITRAGE

Investors who buy and sell to exploit mispricings are engaging in a form of *arbitrage* and are known as *arbitrageurs* (or *arbs* for short). Sometimes a problem arises in this context. The term **limits to arbitrage** refers to the notion that, under certain circumstances, it may not be possible for rational, well-capitalized traders to correct a mispricing, at least not quickly. The reason is that strategies designed to eliminate mispricings are often risky, costly, or somehow restricted. Three important such problems are:

limits to arbitrage
The notion that the price of an asset may not equal its correct value because of barriers to arbitrage.

1. **Firm-specific risk.** This issue is the most obvious risk facing a would-be arbitrageur. Suppose that you believe that the observed price on General Motors stock is too low, so you purchase many, many shares. Then, there is some unanticipated negative news that drives the price of General Motors stock even lower. Of course, you could try to hedge some of the firm-specific risk, but any hedge you create is likely to be either imperfect and/or costly.

noise trader
A trader whose trades are not based on information or meaningful financial analysis.

2. **Noise trader risk.** A **noise trader** is someone whose trades are not based on information or financially meaningful analysis. Noise traders could, in principle, act together to worsen a mispricing in the short run. Noise trader risk is important because the worsening of a mispricing could force the arbitrageur to liquidate early and sustain steep losses. As Keynes once famously observed, "Markets can remain irrational longer than you can remain solvent."[1]

sentiment-based risk
A source of risk to investors above and beyond firm-specific risk and overall market risk.

   Noise trader risk is also called **sentiment-based risk**, meaning the risk that an asset's price is being influenced by sentiment (or irrational belief) rather than fact-based financial analysis. If sentiment-based risk exists, then it is another source of risk beyond the systematic and unsystematic risks we discussed in an earlier chapter.

3. **Implementation costs.** All trades cost money. In some cases, the cost of correcting a mispricing may exceed the potential gains. Suppose you believe a small, thinly-traded stock is significantly undervalued. You want to buy a large quantity. The problem is that as soon as you try to place a huge order, the price jumps because the stock isn't heavily traded.

When these or other risks and costs are present, a mispricing may persist because arbitrage is too risky or too costly. Collectively, these risks and costs create barriers or limits to arbitrage. How important these limits are is difficult to say, but we do know that mispricings occur, at least on occasion. To illustrate, we next consider two well-known examples.

The 3Com/Palm Mispricing   On March 2, 2000, 3Com, a profitable provider of computer networking products and services, sold 5 percent of its Palm subsidiary to the public via an initial public offering (IPO). 3Com planned to distribute the remaining Palm shares to 3Com shareholders at a later date.[2] Under the plan, if you owned one share of 3Com, you would receive 1.5 shares of Palm. So, after 3Com sold part of Palm via the IPO, investors could buy Palm shares directly, or they could buy them indirectly by purchasing shares of 3Com.

What makes this case interesting is what happened in the days that followed the Palm IPO. If you owned one 3Com share, you would be entitled, eventually, to 1.5 shares of Palm. Therefore, each 3Com share should be worth *at least* 1.5 times the value of each Palm share. We say *at least* because the other parts of 3Com were profitable. As a result, each 3Com share should have been worth much more than 1.5 times the value of one Palm share. But, as you might guess, things did not work out this way.

---

[1]This remark is generally attributed to Keynes, but whether he actually said it is not known.

[2]In other words, as we discuss in our chapter on mergers and acquisitions, 3Com did an equity carve-out and planned to subsequently spin off the remaining shares.

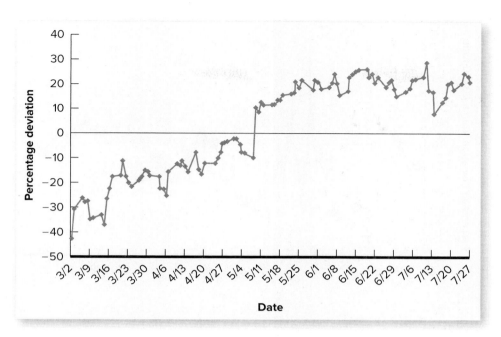

FIGURE 22.1

The Percentage Deviation between 1 Share of 3Com and 1.5 Shares of Palm, March 2, 2000, to July 27, 2000

The day before the Palm IPO, shares in 3Com sold for $104.13. After the first day of trading, Palm closed at $95.06 per share. Multiplying $95.06 by 1.5 results in $142.59, which is the minimum value one would expect to pay for 3Com. But the day Palm closed at $95.06, 3Com shares closed at $81.81, more than $60 lower than the price implied by Palm. It gets stranger.

A 3Com price of $81.81 when Palm is selling for $95.06 implies that the market values the rest of 3Com's businesses (per share) at: $81.81 − 142.59 = −$60.78. Given the number of 3Com shares outstanding at the time, this means the market placed a *negative* value of about −$22 billion on the rest of 3Com's businesses. Of course, a stock price cannot be negative. This means, then, that the price of Palm relative to 3Com was much too high, and investors should have bought and sold such that the negative value was instantly eliminated.

What happened? As you can see in Figure 22.1, the market valued 3Com and Palm shares in such a way that the non-Palm part of 3Com had a negative value for about two months, from March 2, 2000, until May 8, 2000. Even then, it took approval by the IRS for 3Com to proceed with the planned distribution of Palm shares before the non-Palm part of 3Com once again had a positive value.

The Royal Dutch/Shell Price Ratio   Another fairly well-known example of an apparent mispricing involves two large oil companies. In 1907, Royal Dutch of the Netherlands and Shell of the U.K. agreed to merge their business enterprises and split operating profits on a 60–40 basis. So, whenever the stock prices of Royal Dutch and Shell were not in a 60–40 ratio, there was a potential opportunity to make an arbitrage profit.

Figure 22.2 contains a plot of the daily deviations from the 60–40 ratio of the Royal Dutch price to the Shell price. If the prices of Royal Dutch and Shell are in a 60–40 ratio, there is a zero percentage deviation. If the price of Royal Dutch is too high compared to the Shell price, there is a positive deviation. If the price of Royal Dutch is too low compared to the price of Shell, there is a negative deviation. As you can see in Figure 22.2, there have been large and persistent deviations from the 60–40 ratio. In fact, the ratio is seldom at 60–40 for most of the time from 1962 through mid-2005 (when the companies merged).

FIGURE 22.2

Royal Dutch and Shell 60–40 Price Ratio Deviations, 1962 to 2005

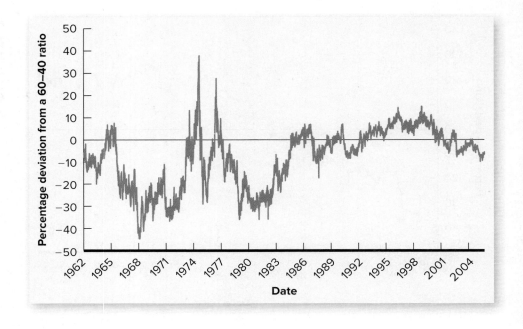

BUBBLES AND CRASHES

To paraphrase a famous song, history has shown, over and again, the many follies of men. Nowhere is this statement seemingly more appropriate in finance than in a discussion of bubbles and crashes.

bubble
A situation where observed prices soar far higher than fundamentals and rational analysis would suggest.

A **bubble** occurs when market prices soar far in excess of what normal and rational analysis would suggest. Investment bubbles eventually pop because they are not based on fundamental values. When a bubble does pop, investors find themselves holding assets with plummeting values.

A **crash** is a significant and sudden drop in marketwide values. Crashes are generally associated with a bubble. Typically, a bubble lasts much longer than a crash. A bubble can form over weeks, months, or even years. Crashes, on the other hand, are sudden, generally lasting less than a week. However, the disastrous financial aftermath of a crash can last for years.

crash
A situation where market prices collapse significantly and suddenly.

The Crash of 1929 During the Roaring Twenties, the stock market was supposed to be the place where everyone could get rich. The market was widely believed to be a no-risk situation. Many people invested their life savings without learning about the potential pitfalls of investing. At the time, investors could purchase stocks by putting up 10 percent of the purchase price and borrowing the remainder from a broker. This level of leverage was one factor that led to the sudden market downdraft in October 1929.

As you can see in Figure 22.3, on Friday, October 25, the Dow Jones Industrial Average closed up about a point, at 301.22. On Monday, October 28, it closed at 260.64, down 13.5 percent. On Tuesday, October 29, the Dow closed at 230.07, with an intraday low of 212.33, which was about 30 percent lower than the closing level on the previous Friday. On this day, known as "Black Tuesday," NYSE volume of 16.4 million shares was more than four times normal levels.

Although the Crash of 1929 was a large decline, it pales with respect to the ensuing bear market. As shown in Figure 22.4, the DJIA rebounded about 20 percent following the October 1929 crash. However, the DJIA then began a protracted fall, reaching the bottom at 40.56 on July 8, 1932. This level represents about a 90 percent decline from the record high

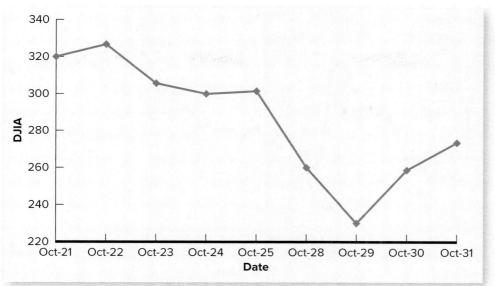

FIGURE 22.3

Dow Jones Industrial Average, October 21, 1929, to October 31, 1929

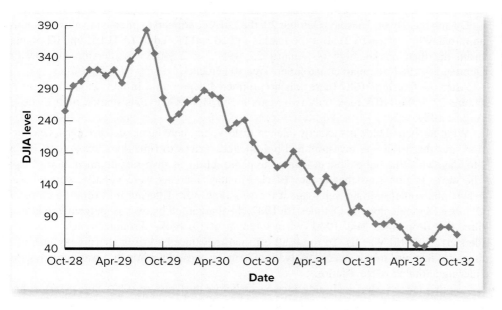

FIGURE 22.4

Dow Jones Industrial Average, October 1928 to October 1932

level of 386.10 on September 3, 1929. By the way, the DJIA did not surpass its previous high level until November 24, 1954, more than 25 years later.

The Crash of October 1987   Once, when we spoke of *the* Crash, we meant October 29, 1929. That was until October 1987. The Crash of 1987 began on Friday, October 16. On huge volume (at the time) of about 338 million shares, the DJIA fell 108 points to close at 2,246.73. It was the first time in history that the DJIA fell by more than 100 points in one day.

October 19, 1987, now wears the mantle of "Black Monday," and this day was indeed a dark and stormy one on Wall Street; the market lost about 22.6 percent of its value on a new record volume of about 600 million shares traded. The DJIA plummeted 508.32 points to close at 1,738.74.

FIGURE 22.5

Dow Jones Industrial Average, October 1986 to October 1990

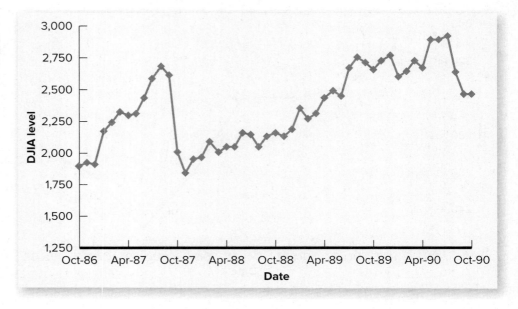

During the day on Tuesday, October 20, the DJIA continued to plunge in value, reaching an intraday low of 1,616.21. But the market rallied and closed at 1,841.01, up 102 points. From the then market high on August 25, 1987, of 2,746.65 to the intraday low on October 20, 1987, the market had fallen over 40 percent.

After the Crash of 1987 there was no protracted depression. In fact, as you can see in Figure 22.5, the DJIA took only two years to surpass its previous market high made in August 1987.

What happened? It's not exactly ancient history, but, here again, debate rages. One faction says that irrational investors had bid up stock prices to ridiculous levels until Black Monday, when the bubble burst, leading to panic selling as investors dumped their stocks. The other faction says that before Black Monday, markets were volatile, volume was heavy, and some ominous signs about the economy were filtering in. From the close on October 13 to the close on October 16, 1987, the market fell by over 10 percent, the largest three-day drop since May 1940 (when German troops broke through French lines near the start of World War II). To top it all off, market values had risen sharply because of a dramatic increase in takeover activity, but Congress was in session and was actively considering antitakeover legislation.

Another factor is that beginning a few years before the Crash of 1987, large investors had developed techniques known as *program trading* designed for very rapid selling of enormous quantities of shares of stock following a market decline. These techniques were still largely untested because the market had been strong for years. Following the huge sell-off on October 16, 1987, sell orders came pouring in on Monday at a pace never before seen. In fact, these program trades were (and are) blamed by some for much of what happened.

One of the few things we know for certain about the Crash of 1987 is that the stock exchanges suffered a meltdown. The NYSE could not handle the volume. Posting of prices was delayed by hours, so investors had no idea what their positions were worth. The specialists couldn't handle the flow of orders, and some specialists actually began selling. NASDAQ went off-line when it became impossible to get through to market makers.

On the two days following the crash, prices *rose* by about 14 percent, one of the biggest short-term gains ever. Prices remained volatile for some time, but as antitakeover talk in Congress died down, the market recovered.

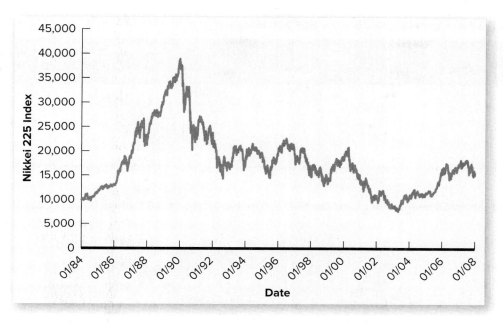

FIGURE 22.6

Nikkei 225 Index, January 1984 to December 2007

The Nikkei Crash   The crash of the Nikkei Index, which began in 1990, lengthened into a particularly long bear market. It is quite like the Crash of 1929 in that respect.

The Asian crash started with a booming bull market in the 1980s. Japan and emerging Asian economies seemed to be forming a powerful economic force. The "Asian economy" became an investor outlet for those wary of the U.S. market after the Crash of 1987.

To give you some idea of the bubble that was forming in Japan between 1955 and 1989, real estate prices in Japan increased by 70 times, and stock prices increased 100 times over. In 1989, price-earnings ratios of Japanese stocks climbed to unheard-of levels as the Nikkei Index soared past 39,000. In retrospect, there were numerous warning signals about the Japanese market. At the time, however, optimism about the continued growth in the Japanese market remained high. Crashes never seem to occur when the outlook is poor, so, as with other crashes, many people did not foresee the impending Nikkei crash.

As you can see in Figure 22.6, in three years from December 1986 to the peak in December 1989, the Nikkei 225 Index rose 115 percent. Over the next three years, the index lost 57 percent of its value. In early 2018, the Nikkei Index stood at a level that was about 60 percent off its peak in December 1989.

The "Dot-Com" Bubble and Crash   How many websites do you think existed at the end of 1994? Would you believe only about 10,000? By the end of 1999, the number of active websites stood at about 9.5 million, and by early 2018, there were about 1.3 billion active websites.

By the mid-1990s, the rise in Internet use and its international growth potential fueled widespread excitement over the "new economy." Investors did not seem to care about solid business plans—only big ideas. Investor euphoria led to a surge in Internet IPOs, which were commonly referred to as "dot-coms" because so many of their names ended in ".com". Of course, the lack of solid business models doomed many of the newly formed companies. Many of them suffered huge losses, and some folded relatively shortly after their IPOs.

The extent of the dot-com bubble and subsequent crash is presented in Table 22.1 and Figure 22.7, which compare the Amex Internet Index and the S&P 500 index. As shown

The growth of the World Wide Web is documented at **www.zakon.org/robert/internet/timeline**.

TABLE 22.1   Values of the Amex Internet Index and the S&P 500 Index

Date	Amex Internet Index Value	Gain to Peak from Oct. 1, 1998 (%)	Loss from Peak to Trough (%)	S&P 500 Index Value	Gain to Peak from Oct. 1, 1998 (%)	Loss from Peak to Trough (%)
October 1, 1998	114.68			986.39		
Late March 2000 (Internet index peak)	688.52	500%		1,293.72	31%	
Early October 2002 (Internet index trough)	58.59		−91%	776.76		−40%

SOURCE: Author calculations.

FIGURE 22.7   Values of the AMEX Internet Index and the S&P 500 Index, October 1995 through October 2007

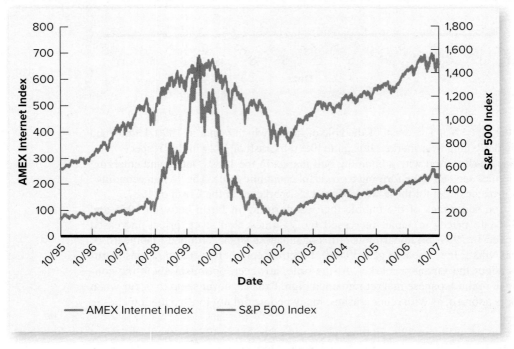

in Table 22.1, the Amex Internet Index soared from a level of 114.68 on October 1, 1998, to its peak of 688.52 in late March 2000, an increase of 500 percent. The Amex Internet Index then fell to a level of 58.59 in early October 2002, a drop of 91 percent. By contrast, the S&P 500 index rallied about 31 percent in the same 1998–2000 time period and fell 40 percent during the 2000–2002 time period.

By now, you're probably wondering how anyone could sensibly think that financial markets are in any way efficient. Before you make up your mind, be sure to carefully read our next section. As you will see, there is a powerful argument in favor of market efficiency.

Concept Questions

22.5a What is meant by the term *limits to arbitrage*?
22.5b What is noise trader risk?

Market Efficiency and the Performance of Professional Money Managers

22.6

You probably know what a mutual fund is. Investors pool their money and pay a professional to manage the portfolio. There are many types of mutual funds. We will focus here on funds that only buy stocks, and we will refer to such funds as *general equity funds* (GEFs). There are thousands of GEFs in the United States, and the performance of these professionally managed funds has been extensively studied.

Most GEFs are actively managed, meaning that the fund manager actively buys and sells stocks in an attempt to improve the fund's performance. However, one type of mutual fund, known as an *index fund*, is passively managed. Such funds try to replicate the performance of stock market indexes, so there is no trading (unless the index changes, which happens from time to time). The most common type of index fund mimics the S&P 500 index, which we studied in Chapter 12. The Vanguard 500 Index Fund is a well-known example. As of early 2018, this fund was one of the largest mutual funds in the United States, with about $400 billion in assets.

If markets are inefficient because investors behave irrationally, then stock prices will deviate from their zero-NPV levels, and it should be possible to devise profitable trading strategies to take advantage of these mispricings. As a result, professional money managers in actively managed mutual funds should be able to systematically outperform index funds. In fact, that is what money managers are paid large sums to do.

The number of GEFs has grown substantially during the past 20 years. Figure 22.8 shows the growth in the number of GEFs from 1986 through 2014. The solid green line shows the

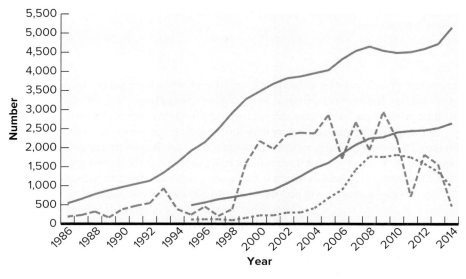

FIGURE 22.8

The Growth of Actively Managed Equity Funds, 1986–2014

— Total funds
- - - Funds beating Vanguard 500 over past one year
— Funds existing for 10 years
---- Funds beating Vanguard 500 over past 10 years

SOURCE: Author calculations.

Most of the chief financial officers (CFOs) I know admit that there is a gap between what they learned about corporate finance in business schools and what they put into practice as executives. A major reason for this gap is the material you are studying in this chapter.

It really is true that financial managers do not practice textbook corporate finance. In the 1990s, I became convinced that this was the case after I joined the organization Financial Executives International (FEI), which gave me an opportunity to meet many CFOs on a regular basis and discuss with them how they practice corporate finance. In doing so, I gained a great deal of information that led me to conclude that behavioral finance was highly applicable to corporate life.

Behavioral corporate finance is important for at least three reasons. First, being human, financial managers are susceptible to the behavioral phenomena you are reading about in this chapter. Textbook corporate finance offers many valuable concepts, tools, and techniques. My point is not that the material in traditional corporate finance textbooks lacks value, but that psychological obstacles often stand in the way of this material being implemented correctly. Behavioral costs can be very expensive. For example, I would argue that psychological pitfalls were central to the financial decisions that led to the global financial crisis that erupted in 2008. I would also argue that psychological pitfalls were central to the decisions that led to the worst environmental disaster in U.S. history, associated with the explosion of BP's well, Deepwater Horizon, in the Gulf of Mexico during 2010.

Second, the people with whom financial managers interact are also susceptible to mistakes. Expecting other people to be immune to mistakes is itself an error that can lead managers to make bad decisions.

Third, investors' mistakes can sometimes lead prices to be inefficient. In this respect, managers can make one of two different mistakes. They might believe that prices are efficient when they are actually inefficient. Or they might believe that prices are inefficient when they are actually efficient. Managers need to know how to think about the vulnerability to both types of errors, and how to deal with each.

The material in this chapter is a wonderful start to learning about behavioral finance. However, for this material to really make a difference, you need to integrate the material with what you are learning about traditional topics such as capital budgeting, capital structure, valuation, payout policy, market efficiency, corporate governance, and mergers and acquisition. You need to study behavioral cases about real people making real decisions and see how psychology impacts those decisions. You need to learn from their mistakes in an effort to make better decisions yourself. This is how behavioral corporate finance will generate value for you.

Hersh Shefrin holds the Mario L. Belotti Chair at the Leavey School of Business at Santa Clara University and is the author of Behavioral Corporate Finance: Decisions that Create Value.

total number of funds that have existed for at least 1 year, while the solid orange line shows the number of funds that have existed for at least 10 years. From Figure 22.8, you can see that it is difficult for professional money managers to keep their funds in existence for 10 years (if it were easy, there would not be much difference between the solid green line and the solid orange line).

Figure 22.8 also shows the number of these funds that beat the performance of the Vanguard 500 Index Fund. You can see that there is much more variation in the dashed green line than in the dashed orange line. What this means is that in any given year, it is hard to predict how many professional money managers will beat the Vanguard 500 Index Fund. But the low level and low variation of the dashed orange line means that the percentage of professional money managers who can beat the Vanguard 500 Index Fund over a 10-year investment period is low and stable.

Figures 22.9 and 22.10 are bar charts that show the percentage of managed equity funds that beat the Vanguard 500 Index Fund. Figure 22.9 uses return data for the previous year only, while Figure 22.10 uses return data for the previous 10 years. As you can see from Figure 22.9, in only 9 of the 29 years spanning 1986 through 2014 did more than half the professional money managers beat the Vanguard 500 Index Fund. The performance is worse when it comes to 10-year investment periods (1986–1995 through 2005–2014). As shown in Figure 22.10, in only 7 of these 17 investment periods did more than half the professional money managers beat the Vanguard 500 Index Fund.

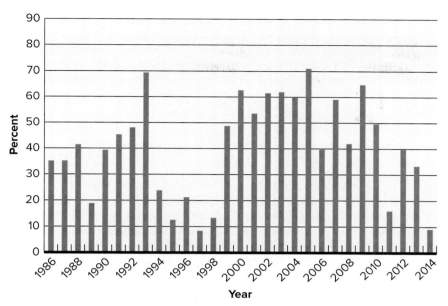

SOURCE: Author calculations.

FIGURE 22.9

Percentage of Managed Equity Funds Beating the Vanguard 500 Index Fund, One-Year Returns

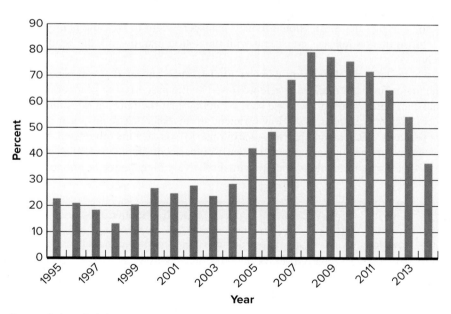

SOURCE: Author calculations.

FIGURE 22.10

Percentage of Managed Equity Funds Beating the Vanguard 500 Index Fund, 10-Year Returns

Table 22.2 presents more evidence concerning the performance of professional money managers. Using data from 1980 through 2014, we divide this time period into 1-year investment periods, rolling 3-year investment periods, rolling 5-year investment periods, and rolling 10-year investment periods. Then, after we calculate the number of investment periods, we ask two questions: (1) What percentage of the time did half the professionally managed funds beat the Vanguard 500 Index Fund? and (2) What percentage of the time did three-fourths of the professionally managed funds beat the Vanguard 500 Index Fund?

TABLE 22.2   **The Performance of Professional Money Managers versus the Vanguard 500 Index Fund**

Length of Each Investment Period (Years)	Span	Number of Investment Periods	Number of Investment Periods Half the Funds Beat Vanguard	Percent	Number of Investment Periods Three-Fourths of the Funds Beat Vanguard	Percent
1	1986–2014	29	9	31.0%	0	0.0%
3	1988–2014	27	11	40.7	0	0.0
5	1990–2014	25	10	40.0	1	4.0
10	1995–2014	20	7	35.0	3	15.0

SOURCE: Author calculations.

As you see in Table 22.2, the performance of professional money managers is generally quite poor relative to the Vanguard 500 Index Fund. In addition, the performance of professional money managers declines the longer the investment period.

The figures and table in this section raise some difficult and uncomfortable questions for security analysts and other investment professionals. If markets are inefficient, and tools like fundamental analysis are valuable, why don't mutual fund managers do better? Why can't mutual fund managers even beat a broad market index?

The performance of professional money managers is especially troublesome when we consider the enormous resources at their disposal and the substantial survivorship bias that exists. The survivorship bias comes into being because managers and funds that do especially poorly disappear. If beating the market were possible, then this Darwinian process of elimination should lead to a situation in which the survivors, as a group, are capable of doing so. The fact that professional money managers seem to lack the ability to outperform a broad market index is consistent with the notion that, overall, the equity market is efficient.

So where does our discussion of behavioral finance and market efficiency leave us? Are the major financial markets efficient? Based on the past 40 or so years of research, we can make an observation or two. We start by noting that the relevant question isn't, "Are markets efficient?" Instead, it's "How efficient are markets?" It seems clear that markets are not perfectly efficient, and barriers to arbitrage do exist. On the other hand, the inability of professional money managers to consistently outperform simple market indexes strongly suggests that the major markets operate with a relatively high degree of efficiency.

Concept Questions

22.6a   How does an index fund differ from an actively managed mutual fund?

22.6b   What do we learn from studying the historical performance of actively managed general equity funds?

22.7 Summary and Conclusions

In this chapter, we examined some of the implications of research in cognitive psychology and behavioral finance. In the first part of the chapter, we learned that a key to becoming a better financial decision maker is to be aware of, and avoid, certain types of behaviors. By studying behavioral finance, you can see the potential damage from errors due to biases, frame dependence, and heuristics.

Biases can lead to bad decisions because they lead to unnecessarily poor estimates of future outcomes. Overoptimism, for example, leads to overly favorable estimates and opinions. Frame dependence leads to narrow framing, which is focusing on the smaller picture instead of the bigger one. The use of heuristics as shortcuts ignores potentially valuable insights that more detailed analysis would reveal.

In the second part of the chapter, we turned to a much more difficult question, and one where the evidence is not at all clear. Do errors in judgment by investors influence market prices and lead to market inefficiencies? This question is the subject of raging debate among researchers and practitioners, and we are not going to take sides. Instead, our goal is to introduce you to the ideas and issues.

We saw that market inefficiencies can be difficult for arbitrageurs to exploit because of firm-specific risk, noise trader (or sentiment-based) risk, and implementation costs. We called these difficulties *limits to arbitrage*, and the implication is that some inefficiencies may only gradually disappear, and smaller inefficiencies can persist if they cannot be profitably exploited.

Looking back at market history, we saw some examples of evident mispricing, such as the Palm IPO. We also saw that markets appear to be susceptible to bubbles and crashes, suggesting significant inefficiency. However, our examination of the performance of professional money managers revealed clear and striking evidence to the contrary. The pros can't consistently outperform broad market indexes, which is strong evidence in favor of market efficiency.

CONNECT TO FINANCE

 If you are using *Connect Finance* in your course, get online to take a Practice Test, check out study tools, and find out where you need additional practice.

Can you answer the following *Connect* Quiz questions?

Section 22.1   Cognitive errors are best explained as errors in _____.

Section 22.2   Darren is the type of manager who is constantly looking for affirmation that his decisions are correct. Darren most likely suffers most from which bias?

Section 22.5   The Asian crisis caused the Japanese market, as measured by the Nikkei Index, to lose approximately what percentage of its value?

CONCEPTS REVIEW AND CRITICAL THINKING QUESTIONS

1. **Limits to Arbitrage** [LO4] In the chapter, we discussed the 3Com/Palm and Royal Dutch/Shell mispricings. Which of the limits to arbitrage would least likely be the main reason for these mispricings? Explain.

2. **Overconfidence** [LO1] How could overconfidence affect the financial manager of the firm and the firm's shareholders?

3. **Frame Dependence** [LO2] How can frame dependence lead to irrational investment decisions?

4. **Noise Trader Risk** [LO4] What is noise trader risk? How can noise trader risk lead to market inefficiencies?

5. **Probabilities** [LO3] Suppose you are flipping a fair coin in a coin-flipping contest and have flipped eight heads in a row. What is the probability of flipping a head on

your next coin flip? Suppose you flipped a head on your ninth toss. What is the probability of flipping a head on your tenth toss?

6. **Performance of the Pros [LO4]** In the mid- to late-1990s, the performance of the pros was unusually poor—on the order of 90 percent of all equity mutual funds underperformed a passively managed index fund. How does this fact bear on the issue of market efficiency?

7. **Efficient Markets Hypothesis [LO4]** The efficient markets hypothesis implies that all mutual funds should obtain the same expected risk-adjusted returns. Therefore, we can pick mutual funds at random. Is this statement true or false? Explain.

8. **Evidence on Market Efficiency [LO4]** Some people argue that the efficient markets hypothesis cannot explain the 1987 market crash or the high price-to-earnings ratio of Internet stocks during the late 1990s. What alternative hypothesis is currently used for these two phenomena?

9. **Behavioral Finance and Efficient Markets [LO4]** Proponents of behavioral finance use three concepts to argue that markets are not efficient. What are these arguments?

10. **Frame Dependence [LO2]** In the chapter, we presented an example where you have lost $78 and are given the opportunity to make a wager in which you have an 80 percent chance that your loss will increase to $100 and a 20 percent chance that your loss will decrease to $0. Using the stand-alone principle from capital budgeting, explain how your decision to accept or reject the proposal could have been affected by frame dependence. In other words, reframe the question in a way in which most people are likely to analyze the proposal correctly.

MINICASE

Your 401(k) Account at S&S Air

You have been at your job with S&S Air for a week now and have decided you need to sign up for the company's 401(k) plan. Even after your discussion with Audrey Sanborn, the Bledsoe Financial Services representative, you are still unsure as to which investment option you should choose. Recall that the options available to you are stock in S&S Air, the Bledsoe S&P 500 Index Fund, the Bledsoe Small-Cap Fund, the Bledsoe Large-Company Stock Fund, the Bledsoe Bond Fund, and the Bledsoe Money Market Fund. You have decided that you should invest in a diversified portfolio, with 70 percent of your investment in equities, 25 percent in bonds, and 5 percent in the money market fund.

You have also decided to focus your equity investment on large-cap stocks, but you are debating whether to select the S&P 500 Index Fund or the Large-Company Stock Fund. In thinking it over, you understand the basic difference in the two funds. One is a purely passive fund that replicates a widely followed large-cap index, the S&P 500, and has low fees. The other is actively managed with the intention that the skill of the portfolio manager will result in improved performance relative to an index. Fees are higher in the latter fund. You're just not

certain which way to go, so you ask Chris Guthrie, who works in the company's finance area, for advice.

After discussing your concerns, Chris gives you some information comparing the performance of equity mutual funds and the Vanguard 500 Index Fund. The Vanguard 500 is the world's largest equity index mutual fund. It replicates the S&P 500, and its return is only negligibly different from the S&P 500. Fees are very low. As a result, the Vanguard 500 is essentially identical to the Bledsoe S&P 500 Index Fund offered in the 401(k) plan, but it has been in existence for much longer, so you can study its track record for over two decades. Chris suggests that you study Figure 22.10 and answer the following questions.

QUESTIONS

1. What implications do you draw from the graph for mutual fund investors?

2. Is the graph consistent or inconsistent with market efficiency? Explain carefully.

3. What investment decision would you make for the equity portion of your 401(k) account? Why?

Enterprise Risk Management

23 | Chapter

NATURAL DISASTERS ARE A MAJOR RISK for property and casualty insurance companies. For example, the 2011 tsunami in Japan was estimated to have cost $235 billion, and Hurricane Katrina caused over $80 billion in damages in 2005. So how do insurance and reinsurance companies handle this risk? One way is to use catastrophe, or "cat," bonds. With a cat bond, the issuer pays the coupon like any other bond; however, if a "trigger" is hit, the issuer does not have to repay the principal. During 2017, companies issued a little more than $12.5 billion in cat bonds, the largest amount issued during a single year. By the end of 2017, a total of $29.6 billion worth of cat bonds was outstanding. As we will see in this chapter, there are a variety of sophisticated financial tools available to deal with risks, including futures, options, and swaps.

Learning Objectives

After studying this chapter, you should be able to:

LO1 Outline the exposures to risk in a company's business and how a company could choose to hedge these risks.

LO2 Describe the similarities and differences between futures and forward contracts and how these contracts are used to hedge risk.

LO3 Define the basics of swap contracts and how they are used to hedge interest rates.

LO4 Explain the payoffs of option contracts and how they are used to hedge risk.

©by_adri/iStockPhoto/GettyImages

For updates on the latest happenings in finance, visit fundamentalsofcorporatefinance.blogspot.com.

All businesses face risks of many types. Some, such as unexpected cost increases, may be obvious, while others, such as disasters caused by human error, are not. **Enterprise risk management (ERM)** is the process of identifying and assessing risks and, where financially sensible, seeking to mitigate potential damage. Companies have always taken steps to manage risks. The change in recent years has been to view risk management more as a holistic, integrated exercise rather than as something to be done on a piecewise basis. There is much greater awareness of the variety, complexity, and interactions of risks at the companywide level. In fact, as the benefits from ERM have become increasingly clear, many companies have created a new "c-level" executive position, the chief risk officer (CRO).

Broadly speaking, risks fall into four types. First, *hazard risks* involve damage done by outside forces such as natural disasters, theft, and lawsuits. Second, *financial risks* arise from such things as adverse exchange rate changes, commodity price fluctuations, and

enterprise risk management (ERM)
The process of identifying and assessing risks and seeking to mitigate potential damage.

Check out the International
Financial Risk Institute for more
on risk management at **ifci.ch**.

interest rate movements. Third, *operational risks* encompass impairments or disruptions in operations from a wide variety of business-related sources, including human resources; product development, distribution, and marketing; and supply chain management. Finally, *strategic risks* include large-scale issues such as competition, changing customer needs, social and demographic changes, regulatory and political trends, and technological innovation. Another important strategic risk is damage done to a company's reputation as a result of product problems, fraud, or other unfavorable publicity.

One important aspect of ERM is to view risks in the context of the entire company. A risk that damages one division of a company might benefit another such that they more or less offset each other. In this case, mitigating the risk in one division makes the overall company worse off. Consider a vertically integrated oil company in which one division drills for oil and another refines it. An increase in oil prices benefits the driller and harms the refiner, but taken together, there may be little or no overall impact on the company's cash flows. Similarly, for a multinational with operations in many countries, exchange rate fluctuations may have limited impact at the overall company level. Another thing to recognize is that not all risks are worth eliminating. It is important to prioritize and identify risks that have the greatest potential for economic and social harm.

For all firms, risk management begins with prevention. Taking steps to promote things like product safety and accident avoidance is obviously very important, but these issues are likely to be very company-specific and thus hard to discuss in general terms. Prevention also is more of an operating activity than a financial activity. However, certain types of financial instruments are used by companies of all types to manage and mitigate risk, particularly financial and hazard risk, and these will be the primary focus of our chapter.

23.1 Insurance

Insurance is the most widely used risk management tool. It is generally used to protect against hazard risks. Insurance can be used to provide protection against losses due to damage to a firm's property and any associated loss of income. It also protects against liabilities that may arise as a result of interactions with third parties. For example, like individuals, companies will usually carry property insurance to protect against large-scale losses due to hazards ranging from fire to storm damage. Other types of insurance commonly purchased include:

- *Commercial liability insurance:* Protects against costs that can occur because of damages to others caused by the company's products, operations, or employees.
- *Business interruption insurance:* Protects against the loss of earnings if business operations are interrupted by an insured event such as fire or natural disaster.
- *Key personnel insurance:* Protects against losses due to loss of critical employees.
- *Workers' compensation and employer's liability insurance:* Protects against costs a firm is required to pay in connection with work-related injuries sustained by its employees.

It is important that companies and their risk managers fully understand the policy limits, policy conditions, and perils covered by the insurance policies they purchase. Losses due to earthquakes, flooding, and terrorism are typically excluded from standard commercial property policies. Firms wishing coverage for these perils must make special arrangements with their insurers. Firms must also abide by policy conditions; for instance, policies often require the insurer to be notified of any loss in a timely manner. A risk manager does not want to become familiar with a firm's insurance policy exclusions after a loss occurs. Whether to purchase insurance is, at least in principle, a straightforward NPV question. The insurance premium is the cost. The benefit is the present value of the expected payout by the insurance company to the firm. Imagine a firm has a key production facility. There is a small chance, say 1-in-10,000 (or .01 percent) that the facility will be destroyed by fire or natural disaster in the next year. The cost to the firm to rebuild plus any lost profits would be $200 million if that occurs. Thus, the firm either loses $0 or $200 million. Its expected loss is:

$$\text{Expected loss} = (.9999 \times \$0) + (.0001 \times \$200 \text{ million}) = \$20,000$$

Of course, if the firm could eliminate the possibility of loss for the present value of $20,000 (or less), it would do so. But assuming that the cost of completely eliminating the risk (if that is even technologically possible) is greater than the present value of $20,000, then the firm can purchase insurance.

The firm's decision to purchase insurance, or what types of insurance a firm decides to purchase, depends on the nature of the firm's business, the size of the firm, and the firm's risk aversion, as well as legal and third-party requirements that may demand proof of insurance. Large firms will often forgo insurance against less costly events, opting to "self-insure." When looking across all of the smaller risks faced by a big firm, it can be less expensive to sustain a certain loss rate than to pay the insurance premiums. Alternatively, firms may opt to purchase insurance with large deductibles, meaning the firm will cover losses up to some level before the insurance kicks in. This approach protects the firm from truly catastrophic losses.

Concept Questions

23.1a What are some basic types of insurance purchased by companies?

23.1b What does it mean for a company to self-insure?

Managing Financial Risk   ## 23.2

Purchasing insurance is one way to manage risk, particularly hazard risks. Managing financial risks is often handled by firms without the assistance of insurance companies. In the remainder of this chapter, we discuss ways firms reduce their exposure to price and rate fluctuations, a process known as **hedging**. The term *immunization* is sometimes used as well. As we will discuss, there are many different types of hedging and many different techniques. Frequently, when a firm desires to hedge a particular risk, there will be no direct way of doing so. The financial manager's job in such cases is to create a way by using available financial instruments to create new ones. This process has come to be called *financial engineering*.

hedging
Reducing a firm's exposure to price or rate fluctuations. Also called *immunization*.

Financial risk management often involves the buying and selling of **derivative securities**. A derivative security is a financial asset that represents a claim to another asset. For example, a stock option gives the owner the right to buy or sell stock, a financial asset; so stock options are derivative securities. Financial engineering frequently involves creating new derivative securities, or else combining existing derivatives to accomplish specific hedging goals.

derivative security
A financial asset that represents a claim to another financial asset.

To effectively manage financial risk, financial managers need to identify the types of price fluctuations that have the greatest impact on the value of the firm. Sometimes these will be obvious, but other times they will not. Consider a forest products company. If

FIGURE 23.1

Risk Profile for a Wheat Grower

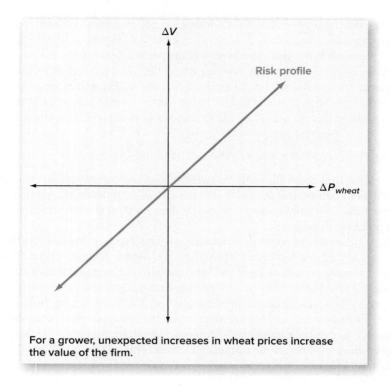

For a grower, unexpected increases in wheat prices increase the value of the firm.

interest rates increase, then its borrowing costs will clearly rise. Beyond this, however, the demand for housing typically declines as interest rates rise. As housing demand falls, so does demand for lumber. An increase in interest rates thus leads to increased financing costs and, at the same time, decreased revenues.

THE RISK PROFILE

risk profile

A plot showing how the value of the firm is affected by changes in prices or rates.

The basic tool for identifying and measuring a firm's exposure to financial risk is the **risk profile**. The risk profile is a plot showing the relationship between changes in the price of some good, service, or rate and changes in the value of the firm. Constructing a risk profile is conceptually very similar to performing a sensitivity analysis (described in Chapter 11).

To illustrate, consider an agricultural products company that has a large-scale wheat farming operation. Because wheat prices can be very volatile, we might wish to investigate the firm's exposure to wheat price fluctuations—that is, its risk profile with regard to wheat prices. To do this, we plot changes in the value of the firm (ΔV) versus unexpected changes in wheat prices (ΔP_{wheat}). Figure 23.1 shows the result.

The risk profile in Figure 23.1 tells us two things. First, because the line slopes up, increases in wheat prices will increase the value of the firm. Because wheat is an output, this comes as no surprise. Second, because the line has a fairly steep slope, this firm has a significant exposure to wheat price fluctuations, and it may wish to take steps to reduce that exposure.

REDUCING RISK EXPOSURE

Fluctuations in the price of any particular good or service can have very different effects on different types of firms. Going back to wheat prices, we now consider the case of a food processing operation. The food processor buys large quantities of wheat and has a risk profile like that illustrated in Figure 23.2. As with the agricultural products firm, the value

FIGURE 23.2

Risk Profile for a Wheat Buyer

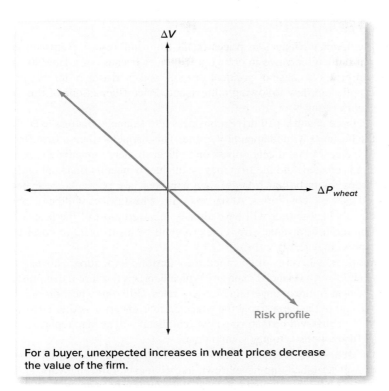

Risk profile

For a buyer, unexpected increases in wheat prices decrease the value of the firm.

of this firm is sensitive to wheat prices; but because wheat is an input, increases in wheat prices lead to decreases in firm value.

Both the agricultural products firm and the food processor are exposed to wheat price fluctuations, but such fluctuations have opposite effects for the two firms. If these two firms get together, then much of the risk can be eliminated. The grower and the processor can agree that, at set dates in the future, the grower will deliver a certain quantity of wheat, and the processor will pay a set price. Once the agreement is signed, both firms will have locked in the price of wheat for as long as the contract is in effect, and both of their risk profiles with regard to wheat prices will be completely flat during that time.

We should note that, in reality, a firm that hedges financial risk usually won't be able to create a completely flat risk profile. For example, our wheat grower doesn't actually know what the size of the crop will be ahead of time. If the crop is larger than expected, then some portion of the crop will be unhedged. If the crop is small, then the grower will have to buy more to fulfill the contract and will thereby be exposed to the risk of price changes. Either way, there is some exposure to wheat price fluctuations; but hedging sharply reduces that exposure.

There are a number of other reasons why perfect hedging is usually impossible, but this is not really a problem. With most financial risk management, the goal is to reduce the risk to more bearable levels and thereby flatten out the risk profile, not necessarily to eliminate the risk altogether.

In thinking about financial risk, there is an important distinction to be made. Price fluctuations have two components. Short-run, essentially temporary changes are the first component. The second component has to do with more long-run, essentially permanent changes. As we discuss next, these two types of changes have very different implications for the firm.

HEDGING SHORT-RUN EXPOSURE

Short-run, temporary changes in prices result from unforeseen events or shocks. Some examples are sudden increases in orange juice prices because of a late Florida freeze, increases in oil prices because of political turmoil, and increases in lumber prices because available supplies are low following a hurricane. Price fluctuations of this sort are often called *transitory* changes.

Short-run price changes can drive a business into financial distress even though, in the long run, the business is fundamentally sound. This happens when a firm finds itself with sudden cost increases that it cannot pass on to its customers immediately. A negative cash flow position is created, and the firm may be unable to meet its financial obligations.

Wheat crops might be much larger than expected in a particular year because of unusually good growing conditions. At harvest time, wheat prices will be unexpectedly low. By that time, a wheat farmer will have already incurred most of the costs of production. If prices drop too low, revenues from the crop will be insufficient to cover the costs, and financial distress may result.

**transactions
exposure**
Short-run financial risk arising
from the need to buy or sell at
uncertain prices or rates in the
near future.

Short-run financial risk is often called **transactions exposure**. This name stems from the fact that short-term financial exposure typically arises because a firm must make transactions in the near future at uncertain prices or rates. With our wheat farmer the crop must be sold at the end of the harvest, but the wheat price is uncertain. Alternatively, a firm may have a bond issue that will be maturing next year that it will need to replace, but the interest rate that the firm will have to pay is unknown.

As we will see, short-run financial risk can be managed in a variety of ways. The opportunities for short-term hedging have grown tremendously in recent years, and firms in the United States are increasingly hedging away transitory price changes.

CASH FLOW HEDGING: A CAUTIONARY NOTE

One thing to notice is that, in our discussion thus far, we have talked conceptually about hedging the value of the firm. In our example concerning wheat prices, what is really hedged is the firm's near-term cash flow. In fact, at the risk of ignoring some subtleties, we will say that hedging short-term financial exposure, hedging transactions exposure, and hedging near-term cash flows amount to much the same thing.

It will usually be the case that directly hedging the value of the firm is not really feasible; instead, the firm will try to reduce the uncertainty of its near-term cash flows. If the firm is thereby able to avoid expensive disruptions, then cash flow hedging will act to hedge the value of the firm, but the linkage is indirect. In such cases, care must be taken to ensure that the cash flow hedging does have the desired effect.

Imagine a vertically integrated firm with an oil-producing division and a gasoline-retailing division. Both divisions are affected by fluctuations in oil prices. However, it may well be that the firm as a whole has very little transactions exposure because any transitory shifts in oil prices benefit one division and cost the other. The overall firm's risk profile with regard to oil prices is essentially flat. Put another way, the firm's net exposure is small. If one division, acting on its own, were to begin hedging its cash flows, then the firm as a whole would suddenly be exposed to financial risk. The point is that cash flow hedging should not be done in isolation. Instead, a firm needs to worry about its net exposure. As a result, any hedging activities should probably be done on a centralized, or at least cooperative, basis.

HEDGING LONG-TERM EXPOSURE

Price fluctuations can also be longer-run, more permanent changes. These result from fundamental shifts in the underlying economics of a business. If improvements in agricultural technology come about, then wheat prices will permanently decline (in the absence of agricultural price subsidies!). If a firm is unable to adapt to the new technology, then it will not be economically viable over the long run.

A firm's exposure to long-run financial risks is often called its **economic exposure**. Because long-term exposure is rooted in fundamental economic forces, it is much more difficult, if not impossible, to hedge on a permanent basis. Is it possible that a wheat farmer and a food processor could permanently eliminate exposure to wheat price fluctuations by agreeing on a fixed price forever?

The answer is no; in fact, the effect of such an agreement might even be the opposite of the one desired. The reason is that if, over the long run, wheat prices were to change on a permanent basis, one party to this agreement would ultimately be unable to honor it. Either the buyer would be paying too much, or the seller would be receiving too little. In either case, the loser would become uncompetitive and fail. Something of the sort happened in the 1970s when public utilities and other energy consumers entered into long-run contracts with natural gas producers. Natural gas prices plummeted in later years, and a great deal of turmoil followed.

economic exposure
Long-term financial risk arising from permanent changes in prices or other economic fundamentals.

CONCLUSION

In the long run, either a business is economically viable or it will fail. No amount of hedging can change this simple fact. Nonetheless, by hedging over the near term, a firm gives itself time to adjust its operations and thereby adapt to new conditions without expensive disruptions. So, drawing our discussion in this section together, we can say that, by managing financial risks, the firm can accomplish two important things. The first is that the firm insulates itself from otherwise troublesome transitory price fluctuations. The second is that the firm gives itself a little breathing room to adapt to fundamental changes in market conditions.

Concept Questions

23.2a What is a risk profile? Describe the risk profiles with regard to oil prices for an oil producer and a gasoline retailer.
23.2b What can a firm accomplish by hedging financial risk?

Hedging with Forward Contracts   23.3

Forward contracts are among the oldest and most basic tools for managing financial risk. Our goal in this section is to describe forward contracts and discuss how they are used to hedge financial risk.

FORWARD CONTRACTS: THE BASICS

A **forward contract** is a legally binding agreement between two parties calling for the sale of an asset or product in the future at a price agreed on today. The terms of the contract call for one party to deliver the goods to the other on a certain date in the future, called the *settlement date*. The other party pays the previously agreed *forward price* and takes the goods. Looking back, note that the agreement we discussed between the wheat grower and the food processor was, in fact, a forward contract.

Forward contracts can be bought and sold. The *buyer* of a forward contract has the obligation to take delivery and pay for the goods; the *seller* has the obligation to make delivery

forward contract
A legally binding agreement between two parties calling for the sale of an asset or product in the future at a price agreed on today.

FIGURE 23.3 **Payoff Profiles for a Forward Contract**

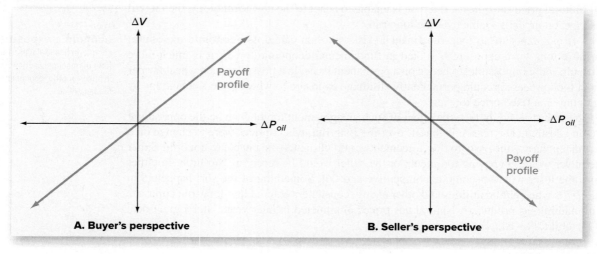

and accept payment. The buyer of a forward contract benefits if prices increase because the buyer will have locked in a lower price. Similarly, the seller wins if prices fall because a higher selling price has been locked in. Note that one party to a forward contract can win only at the expense of the other, so a forward contract is a zero-sum game.

THE PAYOFF PROFILE

payoff profile
A plot showing the gains and losses that will occur on a contract as the result of unexpected price changes.

The **payoff profile** is the key to understanding how forward contracts (and other contracts we discuss later) are used to hedge financial risks. In general, a payoff profile is a plot showing the gains and losses on a contract that result from unexpected price changes. Suppose we were examining a forward contract on oil. Based on our discussion, the buyer of the forward contract is obligated to accept delivery of a specified quantity of oil at a future date and pay a set price. Part A of Figure 23.3 shows the resulting payoff profile on the forward contract from the buyer's perspective.

What Part A of Figure 23.3 shows is that, as oil prices increase, the buyer of the forward contract benefits by having locked in a lower-than-market price. If oil prices decrease, then the buyer loses because that buyer ends up paying a higher-than-market price. For the seller of the forward contract, things are reversed. The payoff profile of the seller is illustrated in Part B of Figure 23.3.

HEDGING WITH FORWARDS

To illustrate how forward contracts can be used to hedge, we consider the case of a public utility that uses oil to generate power. The prices that our utility can charge are regulated and cannot be changed rapidly. As a result, sudden increases in oil prices are a source of financial risk.[1] The utility's risk profile is illustrated in Figure 23.4.

If we compare the risk profile in Figure 23.4 to the buyer's payoff profile on a forward contract shown in Part A of Figure 23.3, we see what the utility needs to do. The payoff profile for the buyer of a forward contract on oil is exactly the opposite of the utility's risk profile with respect to oil. If the utility buys a forward contract, its exposure to unexpected changes in oil prices will be eliminated. This result is shown in Figure 23.5.

---

[1] Actually, many utilities are allowed to automatically pass on oil price increases.

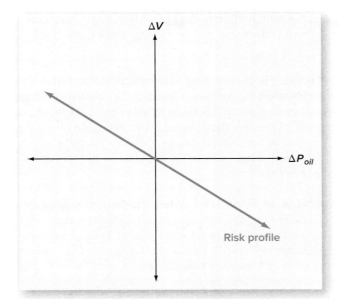

FIGURE 23.4

Risk Profile for an Oil Buyer

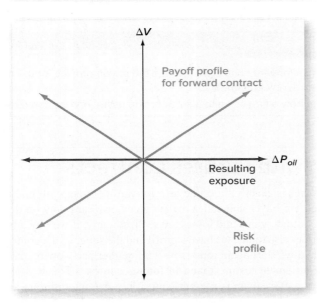

FIGURE 23.5

Hedging with Forward Contracts

Our public utility example illustrates the fundamental approach to managing financial risk. We first identify the firm's exposure to financial risk using a risk profile. We then try to find a financial arrangement, such as a forward contract, that has an offsetting payoff profile.

A Caveat Figure 23.5 shows that the utility's net exposure to oil price fluctuations is zero. If oil prices rise, then the gains on the forward contract will offset the damage from increased costs. However, if oil prices decline, the benefit from lower costs will be offset by losses on the forward contract.

An important thing to remember about hedging with forward contracts is that price fluctuations can be good or bad, depending on which way they go. If we hedge with forward contracts, we eliminate the risk associated with an adverse price change. However, we also eliminate the potential gain from a favorable move. You might wonder if we couldn't somehow just hedge against unfavorable moves. We can, and we describe how in a subsequent section.

Credit Risk   Another important thing to remember is that with a forward contract, no money changes hands when the contract is initiated. The contract is an agreement to transact in the future, so there is no up-front cost to the contract. However, because a forward contract is a financial obligation, there is credit risk. When the settlement date arrives, the party on the losing end of the contract has a significant incentive to default on the agreement. As we discuss in the next section, a variation on the forward contract exists that greatly diminishes this risk.

Forward Contracts in Practice   Where are forward contracts commonly used to hedge? Because exchange rate fluctuations can have disastrous consequences for firms that have significant import or export operations, forward contracts are routinely used by such firms to hedge exchange rate risk. For example, Jaguar, the U.K. auto manufacturer (and former subsidiary of Ford Motor Co.), historically hedged the U.S. dollar–British pound exchange rate for six months into the future. (The subject of exchange rate hedging with forward contracts is discussed in greater detail in Chapter 21.)

Concept Questions

23.3a   What is a forward contract? Describe the payoff profiles for the buyer and the seller of a forward contract.

23.3b   Explain how a firm can alter its risk profile using forward contracts.

23.4 Hedging with Futures Contracts

futures contract
A forward contract with the feature that gains and losses are realized each day rather than only on the settlement date.

A **futures contract** is exactly the same as a forward contract with one exception. With a forward contract, the buyer and seller realize gains or losses only on the settlement date. With a futures contract, gains and losses are realized daily. If we buy a futures contract on oil, then if oil prices rise today, we have a profit and the seller of the contract has a loss. The seller pays up, and we start again tomorrow with neither party owing the other.

The daily resettlement feature found in futures contracts is called *marking-to-market*. As we mentioned earlier, there is a significant risk of default with forward contracts. With daily marking-to-market, this risk is greatly reduced. This is probably why organized trading is much more common in futures contracts than in forward contracts (outside of international trade).

TRADING IN FUTURES

In the United States and elsewhere around the world, futures contracts for a remarkable variety of items are routinely bought and sold. The types of contracts available are traditionally divided into two groups: Commodity futures and financial futures. With a financial future, the underlying goods are financial assets such as stocks, bonds, or currencies. With a commodity future, the underlying goods can be just about anything other than a financial asset.

There are commodity futures contracts on a wide variety of agricultural products such as corn, orange juice, and, yes, pork bellies. There is even a contract on fertilizer. There are commodity contracts on precious metals such as gold and silver, and there are contracts on basic goods such as copper and lumber. There are contracts on various petroleum products such as crude oil, heating oil, and gasoline. Wherever there is price volatility, there may be a demand for a futures contract, and new futures contracts are introduced on a fairly regular basis.

FUTURES EXCHANGES

There are a number of futures exchanges in the United States and elsewhere, and more are being established. The Chicago Board of Trade (CBT) is among the largest. Other notable exchanges include the Chicago Mercantile Exchange (CME), the London International Financial Futures and Options Exchange (LIFFE), and the New York Mercantile Exchange (NYMEX).

Table 23.1 gives a partial *Wall Street Journal* listing for selected futures contracts. Taking a look at the corn contracts in the left portion of the table (under the Agriculture Futures heading), note that the contracts trade on the CBT, one contract calls for the delivery of 5,000 bushels of corn, and prices are quoted in cents per bushel. The months in which the contracts mature are given in the first column.

For the corn contract with a March maturity, the first number in the row is the opening price (369.50 cents per bushel), the next number is the high price for the day (372.75), and the following number is the low price for the day (367.50). The *settlement price* is the fourth number (369.50), and it is essentially the closing price for the day. For purposes of marking-to-market, this is the figure used. The change listed next is the movement in the settlement price since the previous trading session. Finally, the *open interest* (500,405), the number of contracts outstanding at the end of the day, is shown.

To see how large futures trading can be, take a look at the CBT Treasury note contracts (under the Interest Rate Futures heading). One contract is for Treasury notes with a face, or par, value of $100,000. The total open interest for all months is about 3.17 million contracts. The total face value outstanding is therefore $317 billion for this one type of contract!

HEDGING WITH FUTURES

Hedging with futures contracts is conceptually identical to hedging with forward contracts, and the payoff profile on a futures contract is drawn just like the profile for a forward contract. The only difference in hedging with futures is that the firm will have to maintain an account with a broker so that gains and losses can be credited or debited each day as a part of the marking-to-market process.

Even though many types of futures contracts exist, it is unlikely that a particular firm will be able to find the precise hedging instrument it needs. We might produce a particular grade or variety of oil but find that no contract exists for exactly that grade. However, all oil prices tend to move together, so we could hedge our output using futures contracts on other grades of oil. Airlines hedge jet fuel costs using heating oil contracts. Using a contract on a related, but not identical, asset as a means of hedging is called **cross-hedging**.

When a firm does cross-hedge, it does not actually want to buy or sell the underlying asset. This presents no problem because the firm can reverse its futures position at some point before maturity. This means that if the firm sells a futures contract to hedge something, then it will buy the same contract at a later date, thereby eliminating its futures position. In fact, futures contracts are rarely held to maturity by anyone (despite horror stories of individuals waking up to find mountains of soybeans in their front yards); as a result, actual physical delivery very rarely takes place.

Surf over to the home pages of two of these exchanges at **www.cmegroup.com** and **derivatives.euronext.com**. These websites provide a great deal of information about the services and financial products found on the respective exchanges.

To get some real-world experience at very low cost, visit the fascinating futures exchange at the University of Iowa: **tippie.biz.uiowa.edu/iem**.

cross-hedging
Hedging an asset with contracts written on a closely related, but not identical, asset.

TABLE 23.1   Sample *Wall Street Journal* Futures Price Quotations

Metal & Petroleum Futures

	Open	High	hi lo Low	Settle	Chg	Open interest
Copper-High (CMX)-25,000 lbs; $ per lb.						
Feb	2.6735	2.6735	2.6715	**2.6480**	−0.0125	672
March	2.6660	2.6765	2.6410	**2.6535**	−0.0130	120,434
Gold (CMX)-100 troy oz; $ per troy oz.						
Feb	1239.40	1243.50	1226.90	**1235.10**	−2.50	1,387
April	1242.70	1246.20	1226.10	**1236.80**	−2.70	288,888
June	1246.10	1249.00	1230.00	**1240.00**	−2.70	63,531
Aug	1250.10	1252.00	1235.10	**1243.10**	−2.80	18,296
Dec	1254.00	1256.90	1239.00	**1249.20**	−2.70	29,516
June'18	1266.00	1266.00	1254.80	**1259.00**	−2.50	4,419
Palladium (NYM)-50 troy oz; $ per troy oz.						
Feb	732.85	732.85	732.85	**772.60**	2.80	1
March	770.60	778.80	768.00	**772.55**	2.80	22,948
June	771.00	780.00	770.40	**774.00**	2.85	6,503
Sept	775.30	777.00	775.10	**775.00**	3.60	17
Platinum (NYM)-50 troy oz; $ per troy oz						
Feb	978.80	979.10	978.80	**1019.20**	2.80	42
April	1019.60	1032.10 ▲	1016.20	**1022.20**	2.80	59,479
Silver (CMX)-5,000 troy oz.; $ per troy oz.						
Feb	17.750	17.815 ▲	17.750	**17.720**	0.037	179
March	17.780	17.845	17.615	**17.741**	0.036	113,427
Crude Oil, Light Sweet (NYM)-1,000 bbls; $ per bbl.						
March	52.37	53.21	52.37	**53.00**	0.66	385,634
April	52.98	53.70	52.95	**53.46**	0.55	280,780
May	53.42	54.10	53.41	**53.88**	0.51	192,554
June	53.90	54.45	53.90	**54.25**	0.49	264,679
Dec	54.79	55.35	54.79	**55.21**	0.49	229,809
Dec'18	55.10	55.50	55.04	**55.32**	0.37	111,505
NY Harbor ULSD (NYM)-42,000 gal; $ per gal.						
March	1.6360	1.6624	1.6345	**1.6415**	.0055	111,133
April	1.6443	1.6693	1.6435	**1.6500**	.0059	72,273
Gasoline-NY RBOB (NYM)-42,000 gal; $ per gal.						
March	1.5510	1.5811	1.5471	**1.5702**	.0175	112,099
April	1.7600	1.7800	1.7575	**1.7741**	.0122	85,512
Natural Gas (NYM)-10,000 MMBtu; $ per MMBtu.						
March	3.143	3.189	3.110	**3.141**	.015	197,215
April	3.212	3.253	3.179	**3.209**	.013	146,224
May	3.269	3.311	3.240	**3.272**	.017	137,143
June	3.339	3.365	3.298	**3.330**	.019	79,485
July	3.385	3.413	3.350	**3.380**	.020	79,570
Oct	3.385	3.423	3.358	**3.392**	.020	93,442

Agriculture Futures

	Open	High	Low	Settle	Chg	Open interest
Corn(CBT)-5,000 bu; cents per bu.						
March	369.50	372.75 ▲	367.50	**369.50**	−1.25	500,405
May	377.25	380.25 ▲	375.25	**377.25**	−1.25	346,739
Oats(CBT)-5,000 bu; cents per bu.						
March	256.00	257.50	250.00	**254.50**	.50	4,155
May	248.25	254.00	246.00	**253.00**	3.00	3,027
Soybeans (CBT)-5,000 bu; cents per bu.						

Metal & Petroleum Futures

	Open	High	hi lo Low	Settle	Chg	Open interest
March	1057.00	1061.50	1045.00	**1050.50**	−8.25	248,998
May	1067.25	1071.50	1055.50	**1061.50**	−7.75	210,368
Soybean Meal (CBT)-100 tons; $ per ton.						
March	340.70	341.60	335.90	**338.40**	−2.80	126,399
May	344.80	345.80	340.10	**342.60**	−2.70	122,484
Soybean Oil (CBT)-60,000 lbs; cents per lb.						
March	34.67	34.98	34.47	**34.67**	−.02	123,991
May	34.96	35.26	34.76	**34.95**	−.03	118,319
Rough Rice (CBT)-2,000 cwt; $ per cwt.						
March	953.00	960.50	942.00	**947.50**	−8.00	9,388
May	978.50	984.50	968.00	**972.50**	−8.50	2,516
Wheat (CBT)-5,000 bu.; cents per bu.						
March	430.50	444.00 ▲	429.50	**443.50**	11.00	179,982
May	442.00	455.50 ▲	440.75	**455.25**	11.75	137,497
Wheat (KC)-5,000 bu; cents per bu.						
March	440.25	451.75	438.25	**451.25**	9.25	71,740
July	465.25	475.25	462.75	**475.00**	8.50	69,377
Wheat (MPLS)-5,000 bu; cents per bu.						
March	557.50	569.50	556.00	**568.50**	11.00	24,788
May	556.75	567.00	555.50	**566.50**	9.25	29,537
Cattle-Feeder (CME)-50,000 lbs.; cents per lb.						
March	122.525	123.800	121.900	**123.625**	1.325	19,575
April	123.250	124.200	122.450	**124.050**	1.075	10,511
Cattle-Live (CME)-40,000 lbs; cents per lb.						
Feb	117.250	117.750	116.775	**117.650**	.875	17,410
April	115.000	115.175	114.125	**114.825**	.075	144,593
Hogs-Lean (CME)-40,000 lbs; cents per lb.						
Feb	73.900	74.500 ▲	73.550	**74.225**	.875	14,671
April	72.125	72.250	70.625	**70.775**	−.950	104,603
Lumber (CME)-110.000 bd. ft., $ per 1,000 bd. ft.						
March	381.70	381.70 ▲	373.80	**375.40**	3.50	2,698
May	379.60	381.70 ▲	375.90	**378.40**	2.60	1,541
Milk (CME)-200,000 lbs.; cents per lb.						
Feb	16.87	16.89	16.79	**16.85**	...	4,180
March	16.91	17.03	16.73	**16.97**	.03	4,392
Cocoa (ICE-US)-10 metric tons; $ per ton.						
March	1,993	2,018 ▼	1,969	**1,974**	−19	35,455
May	2,008	2,038 ▼	1,988	**1,996**	−15	105,293
Coffee (ICE-US)-37,500 lbs; cents per lb.						
March	143.40	145.70	142.85	**145.20**	2.30	43,558
May	145.95	148.05	145.25	**147.60**	2.30	73,254
Sugar-World (ICE-US)-112,000 lbs; cents per lb.						
March	20.74	21.03	20.62	**20.65**	−.11	220,619
May	20.72	20.97	20.61	**20.65**	−.08	224,526
Sugar-Domestic (ICE-US)-112,000 lbs; cents per lb.						
May	30.40	30.40	30.40	**30.32**	.07	946
July	30.40	30.40	30.39	**30.40**	...	1,768
Cotton (ICE-US)-50,000 lbs; cents per lb.						
March	75.43	76.13	75.25	**75.58**	.33	104,332

TABLE 23.1   (*continued*)

Metal & Petroleum Futures

	Open	High	hi lo	Low	Settle	Chg	Open interest
May	76.40	77.30		76.40	**76.65**	.22	97,772

Orange Juice (ICE-US)-15,000 lbs; cents per lb.

	Open	High	hi lo	Low	Settle	Chg	Open interest
March	172.65	175.00		171.55	**174.00**	1.00	7,438
May	167.80	169.75		166.80	**168.75**	.60	3,434

Interest Rate Futures

Treasury Bonds(CBT)-$100,000; pts 32nds of 100%

	Open	High	hi lo	Low	Settle	Chg	Open interest
March	153–160	153–170		151–310	**152–060**	−1–030	622,929
June	152–060	152–060		150–240	**150–300**	−1–030	2,310

Treasury Notes (CBT)-$100,000; pts 32nds of 100%

	Open	High	hi lo	Low	Settle	Chg	Open interest
March	125–155	125–155		124–270	**124–295**	−14.0	3,169,794
June	124–265	124–270		124–105	**124–120**	−14.5	68,648

5 Yr. Treasury Notes (CBT)-$100,000; pts 32nds of 100%

	Open	High	hi lo	Low	Settle	Chg	Open interest
March	118–132	118–132		118–012	**118–025**	−8.5	3,119,541
June	118–015	118–015		117–230	**117–235**	−9.0	137,090

2 Yr. Treasury Notes (CBT)-$200,000; pts 32nds of 100%

	Open	High	hi lo	Low	Settle	Chg	Open interest
March	108–170	108–172		108–142	**108–147**	−2.0	1,349,070
June	108–060	108–060		108–060	**108–055**	−2.5	8,979

30 Day Federal Funds (CBT)-$5,000,000; 100-daily avg.

	Open	High	hi lo	Low	Settle	Chg	Open interest
Feb	99.343	99.345		99.343	**99.342**	−.001	100,104
April	99.315	99.320	▲	99.305	**99.310**	−.005	373,852

10 Yr. Del. Int. Rate Swaps (CBT)-$100,000; pts 32nds of 100%

	Open	High	hi lo	Low	Settle	Chg	Open interest
March	94.703	94.766		94.359	**94.438**	−.438	31,717

1 Month Libor (CME)-$3,000,000; pts of 100%

	Open	High	hi lo	Low	Settle	Chg	Open interest
Feb	...	...	▲	...	**99.2275**	...	4,896

Eurodollar (CME)-$1,000,000; pts of 100%

	Open	High	hi lo	Low	Settle	Chg	Open interest
Feb	98.9650	98.9650		98.9625	**98.9625**	−.0025	83,716
March	98.9450	98.9450		98.9300	**98.9350**	−.0100	1,455,611
June	98.8000	98.8000		98.7750	**98.7800**	−.0200	1,434,355
Dec	98.5400	98.5450		98.5000	**98.5050**	−.0300	1,350,776

Currency Futures

Japanese Yen (CME)-¥12,500,000; $ per 100¥

	Open	High	hi lo	Low	Settle	Chg	Open interest
March	.8948	.8949		.8829	**.8834**	−.0097	191,960
June	.8982	.8986		.8868	**.8872**	−.0096	9,846

Canadian Dollar (CME)-CAD 100.000; $ per CAD

	Open	High	hi lo	Low	Settle	Chg	Open interest
March	.7610	.7639		.7596	**.7614**	.0011	115,305
June	.7619	.7646		.7604	**.7622**	.0011	2,625

British Pound (CME)-£62,500; $ per £

	Open	High	hi lo	Low	Settle	Chg	Open interest
March	1.2544	1.2589		1.2497	**1.2502**	−.0031	208,495

Metal & Petroleum Futures

	Open	High	hi lo	Low	Settle	Chg	Open interest
June	1.2563	1.2616		1.2527	**1.2531**	−.0032	1,661

Swiss Franc (CME)-CHF 125,000; $ per CHF

	Open	High	hi lo	Low	Settle	Chg	Open interest
March	1.0066	1.0079		.9995	**.9999**	−.0064	47,842
June	1.0100	1.0136		1.0055	**1.0058**	−.0064	180

Australian Dollar (CME)-AUD 100,000; $ per AUD

	Open	High	hi lo	Low	Settle	Chg	Open interest
March	.7636	.7659		.7605	**.7622**	−.0004	115,779
June	.7617	.7641		.7589	**.7605**	−.0004	1,205
Sept	.7576	.7611		.7576	**.7593**	−.0004	688

Mexican Peso (CME)-MXN 500,000; $ per MXN

	Open	High	hi lo	Low	Settle	Chg	Open interest
March	.04861	.04904		.04847	**.04879**	.00018	142,828
June	.04791	.04837		.04782	**.04811**	.00018	47,992

Euro (CME)-€125,000; $ per €

	Open	High	hi lo	Low	Settle	Chg	Open interest
March	1.0706	1.0721		1.0662	**1.0670**	−.0029	391,573
June	1.0746	1.0770		1.0712	**1.0720**	−.0029	10,473

Index Futures

Mini DJ Industrial Average (CBT)-$5 x index

	Open	High	hi lo	Low	Settle	Chg	Open interest
March	20010	20158	▲	19982	**20136**	134	126,519
June	19921	20093	▲	19921	**20073**	136	893

S&P 500 Index (CME)-$250 x index

	Open	High	hi lo	Low	Settle	Chg	Open interest
March	2290.70	2307.50	▲	2288.30	**2304.30**	14.10	68,270
June	2295.50	2302.90	▲	2295.50	**2299.10**	14.20	1,259

Mini S&P 500(CME)-$50 x index

	Open	High	hi lo	Low	Settle	Chg	Open interest
March	2290.50	2307.75	▲	2287.75	**2304.25**	14.00	2,882,114
June	2285.00	2302.75	▲	2282.50	**2299.00**	14.00	36,548

Mini S&P Midcap 400 (CME)-$100 x index

	Open	High	hi lo	Low	Settle	Chg	Open interest
March	1694.30	1712.80		1691.70	**1709.70**	16.30	94,526

Mini Nasdaq 100 (CME)-$20 x index

	Open	High	hi lo	Low	Settle	Chg	Open interest
March	5189.8	5219.3	▲	5186.3	**5212.3**	21.0	233,819
June	5193.3	5217.8	▲	5186.0	**5211.3**	21.0	621

Mini Russell 2000 (ICE-US)-$100 x index

	Open	High	hi lo	Low	Settle	Chg	Open interest
March	1356.50	1380.10		1354.60	**1377.00**	21.00	613,166
June	1357.30	1375.70		1357.30	**1374.30**	21.00	540

Mini Russell 1000 (ICE-US)-$100 x index

	Open	High	hi lo	Low	Settle	Chg	Open interest
March	1275.10	1282.10	▲	1274.60	**1280.60**	8.50	7,872

U.S. Dollar Index (ICE-US)-$1,000 x index

	Open	High	hi lo	Low	Settle	Chg	Open interest
March	100.24	100.67		100.08	**100.65**	.38	69,426
June	100.22	100.58		100.05	**100.56**	.36	2,792

SOURCES: SIX Financial Information; *The Wall Street Journal*, February 10, 2017.

A related issue has to do with contract maturity. A firm might wish to hedge over a relatively long period of time, but the available contracts might have shorter maturities. A firm could therefore decide to roll over short-term contracts, but this entails some risks. For example, Metallgesellschaft AG, a German firm, nearly went bankrupt in 1993 after losing more than $1 billion in the oil markets, mainly through derivatives. The trouble began in 1992 when MG Corp., a U.S. subsidiary, began marketing gasoline, heating oil, and diesel fuel. It entered into contracts to supply products for fixed prices for up to 10 years. Thus, if the price of oil rose, then the firm stood to lose money. MG protected itself by, among other things, buying short-term oil futures that fluctuated with near-term energy prices. Under

For information about the regulation of futures contracts, go to the Commodity Futures Trading Commission at **www.cftc.gov**.

these contracts, if the price of oil rose, the derivatives gained in value. Unfortunately for MG, oil prices dropped, and the firm incurred huge losses on its short-term derivatives positions without an immediate, offsetting benefit on its long-term contracts. Its primary problem was that it was hedging a long-term contract with short-term contracts, a less than ideal approach.

Concept Questions

23.4a   What is a futures contract? How does it differ from a forward contract?

23.4b   What is cross-hedging? Why is it important?

23.5 Hedging with Swap Contracts

swap contract
An agreement by two parties to exchange, or swap, specified cash flows at specified intervals in the future.

As the name suggests, a **swap contract** is an agreement by two parties to exchange, or swap, specified cash flows at specified intervals. Swaps are a recent innovation; they were first introduced to the public in 1981 when IBM and the World Bank entered into a swap agreement. The market for swaps has grown tremendously since that time.

A swap contract is really just a portfolio, or series, of forward contracts. Recall that with a forward contract, one party promises to exchange an asset (such as bushels of wheat) for another asset (cash) on a specific future date. With a swap, the only difference is that there are multiple exchanges instead of just one. In principle, a swap contract could be tailored to exchange just about anything. In practice, most swap contracts fall into one of three basic categories: Currency swaps, interest rate swaps, and commodity swaps. Other types will surely develop, but we will concentrate on just these three.

CURRENCY SWAPS

With a *currency swap*, two parties agree to exchange a specific amount of one currency for a specific amount of another at specific dates in the future. Suppose a U.S. firm has a German subsidiary and wishes to obtain debt financing for an expansion of the subsidiary's operations. Because most of the subsidiary's cash flows are in euros, the company would like the subsidiary to borrow and make payments in euros, thereby hedging against changes in the euro–dollar exchange rate. Unfortunately, the company has good access to U.S. debt markets but not to German debt markets.

A great place to get information about swaps is the International Swaps and Derivatives Association website at **www.isda.org**.

At the same time, a German firm would like to obtain U.S. dollar financing. It can borrow cheaply in euros, but not in dollars. Both firms face a similar problem. They can borrow at favorable rates—but not in the desired currency. A currency swap is a solution. These two firms agree to exchange dollars for euros at a fixed rate at specific future dates (the payment dates on the loans). Each firm obtains the best possible rate and then arranges to eliminate exposure to exchange rate changes by agreeing to exchange currencies, a neat solution.

INTEREST RATE SWAPS

Imagine the following scenario: A firm wishes to obtain a fixed-rate loan but can get a good deal on only a floating-rate loan—that is, a loan for which the payments are adjusted periodically to reflect changes in interest rates. Another firm can obtain a fixed-rate loan, but wishes to obtain the lowest possible interest rate; it is willing to take a floating-rate loan. (Rates on floating-rate loans are generally lower than rates on fixed-rate loans; why?) Both firms could accomplish their objectives by agreeing to exchange loan payments; in other words, the two firms could agree to make each other's loan payments. This is an example of an *interest rate swap*; what is really being exchanged is a floating interest rate for a fixed one.

Interest rate swaps and currency swaps are often combined. One firm obtains floating-rate financing in a particular currency and swaps it for fixed-rate financing in another currency. Also, note that payments on floating-rate loans are always based on some index, such as the one-year Treasury rate. An interest rate swap might involve exchanging one floating-rate loan for another as a way of changing the underlying index.

COMMODITY SWAPS

As the name suggests, a *commodity swap* is an agreement to exchange a fixed quantity of a commodity at fixed times in the future. Commodity swaps are the newest type of swap, and the market for them is small relative to that for other types. The potential for growth is enormous, however.

Swap contracts for oil have been engineered. Say that an oil user has a need for 20,000 barrels every quarter. The oil user could enter into a swap contract with an oil producer to supply the needed oil. What price would they agree on? As we mentioned previously, they can't fix a price forever. Instead, they could agree that the price would be equal to the *average* daily oil price from the previous 90 days. As a result of using an average price, the impact of the relatively large daily price fluctuations in the oil market would be reduced, and both firms would benefit from a reduction in transactions exposure.

THE SWAP DEALER

Unlike futures contracts, swap contracts are not traded on organized exchanges. The main reason is that they are not sufficiently standardized. Instead, the *swap dealer* plays a key role in the swaps market. In the absence of a swap dealer, a firm that wished to enter into a swap would have to track down another firm that wanted the opposite end of the deal. This search would probably be expensive and time-consuming.

Instead, a firm wishing to enter into a swap agreement contacts a swap dealer, and the swap dealer takes the other side of the agreement. The swap dealer will then try to find an offsetting transaction with some other party or parties (perhaps another firm or another dealer). Failing this, a swap dealer will hedge its exposure using futures contracts.

Commercial banks are the dominant swap dealers in the United States. As a large swap dealer, a bank would be involved in a variety of contracts. It would be swapping fixed-rate loans for floating-rate loans with some parties and doing just the opposite with other participants. The total collection of contracts in which a dealer is involved is called the *swap book*. The dealer will try to keep a balanced book to limit its net exposure. A balanced book is often called a *matched* book.

INTEREST RATE SWAPS: AN EXAMPLE

To get a better understanding of swap contracts and the role of the swap dealer, we consider a floating-for-fixed interest rate swap. Suppose Company A can borrow at a floating rate equal to prime plus 1 percent or at a fixed rate of 10 percent. Company B can borrow at a floating rate of prime plus 2 percent or at a fixed rate of 9.5 percent. Company A desires a fixed-rate loan, whereas Company B desires a floating-rate loan. Clearly, a swap is in order.

Company A contacts a swap dealer, and a deal is struck. Company A borrows the money at a rate of prime plus 1 percent. The swap dealer agrees to cover the loan payments; in exchange, the company agrees to make fixed-rate payments to the swap dealer at a rate of, say, 9.75 percent. Notice that the swap dealer is making floating-rate payments and receiving fixed-rate payments. The company is making fixed-rate payments, so it has swapped a floating payment for a fixed one.

Company B also contacts a swap dealer. The deal here calls for Company B to borrow the money at a fixed rate of 9.5 percent. The swap dealer agrees to cover the fixed loan

FIGURE 23.6

Illustration of an Interest Rate Swap

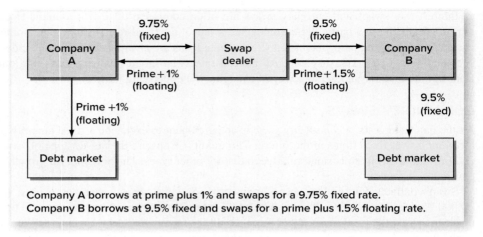

Company A borrows at prime plus 1% and swaps for a 9.75% fixed rate.
Company B borrows at 9.5% fixed and swaps for a prime plus 1.5% floating rate.

payments, and the company agrees to make floating-rate payments to the swap dealer at a rate of prime plus, say, 1.5 percent. In this second arrangement, the swap dealer is making fixed-rate payments and receiving floating-rate payments.

What's the net effect of these machinations? First, Company A gets a fixed-rate loan at a rate of 9.75 percent, which is cheaper than the 10 percent rate it can obtain on its own. Second, Company B gets a floating-rate loan at prime plus 1.5 percent instead of prime plus 2 percent. The swap benefits both companies.

The swap dealer also wins. When all the dust settles, the swap dealer receives (from Company A) fixed-rate payments at a rate of 9.75 percent and makes fixed-rate payments (for Company B) at a rate of 9.5 percent. At the same time, it makes floating-rate payments (for Company A) at a rate of prime plus 1 percent and receives floating-rate payments at a rate of prime plus 1.5 percent (from Company B). Notice that the swap dealer's book is perfectly balanced in terms of risk, and it has no exposure to interest rate volatility.

Figure 23.6 illustrates the transactions in our interest rate swap. Notice that the essence of the swap transactions is that one company swaps a fixed payment for a floating payment, while the other exchanges a floating payment for a fixed one. The swap dealer acts as an intermediary and profits from the spread between the rates it charges and the rates it receives.

Concept Questions

23.5a What is a swap contract? Describe three types.

23.5b Describe the role of the swap dealer.

23.5c Explain the cash flows in Figure 23.6.

23.6 Hedging with Option Contracts

The contracts we have discussed thus far—forwards, futures, and swaps—are conceptually similar. In each case, two parties agree to transact on a future date or dates. The key is that both parties are obligated to complete the transaction.

option contract

An agreement that gives the owner the right, but not the obligation, to buy or sell a specific asset at a specific price for a set period of time.

In contrast, an **option contract** is an agreement that gives the owner the right, but not the obligation, to buy or sell (depending on the option type) some asset at a specified price for a specified time. Options are covered in detail elsewhere in our book. Here we will quickly discuss some option basics and then focus on using options to hedge volatility in commodity prices, interest rates, and exchange rates. In doing so, we will sidestep a wealth of detail concerning option terminology, option trading strategies, and option valuation.

OPTION TERMINOLOGY

Options come in two flavors: Puts and calls. The owner of a **call option** has the right, but not the obligation, to buy an underlying asset at a fixed price, called the *strike price* or *exercise price*, for a specified time. The owner of a **put option** has the right, but not the obligation, to sell an underlying asset at a fixed price for a specified time.

The act of buying or selling the underlying asset using the option contract is called *exercising* the option. Some options ("American" options) can be exercised anytime up to and including the *expiration date* (the last day); other options ("European" options) can be exercised only on the expiration date. Most options are American.

Because the buyer of a call option has the right to buy the underlying asset by paying the strike price, the seller of a call option is obligated to deliver the asset and accept the strike price if the option is exercised. Similarly, the buyer of the put option has the right to sell the underlying asset and receive the strike price. In this case, the seller of the put option must accept the asset and pay the strike price.

call option
The right to buy an asset at a fixed price during a particular period.

put option
The right to sell an asset at a fixed price during a particular period of time. The opposite of a call option.

OPTIONS VERSUS FORWARDS

There are two key differences between an option contract and a forward contract. The first is obvious. With a forward contract, both parties are obligated to transact; one party delivers the asset, and the other party pays for it. With an option, the transaction occurs only if the owner of the option chooses to exercise it.

The second difference between an option and a forward contract is that no money changes hands when a forward contract is created, but the buyer of an option contract gains a valuable right and must pay the seller for that right. The price of the option is frequently called the *option premium*.

The Chicago Board Options Exchange (CBOE) is the world's largest options exchange. Make a virtual visit at **www.cboe.com**.

OPTION PAYOFF PROFILES

Figure 23.7 shows the general payoff profile for a call option from the owner's viewpoint. The horizontal axis shows the difference between the asset's value and the strike price on the

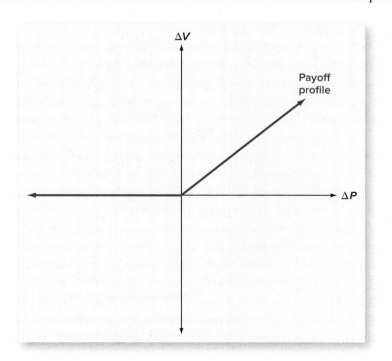

FIGURE 23.7

Call Option Payoff Profile for an Option Buyer

FIGURE 23.8   **Option Payoff Profiles**

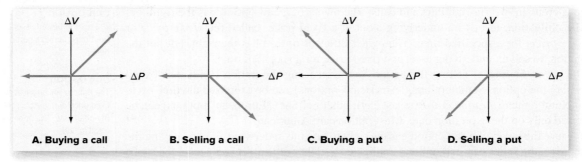

A. Buying a call   B. Selling a call   C. Buying a put   D. Selling a put

A good introduction to the
options markets is available at
www.optionseducation.org.

option (ΔP). As illustrated, if the price of the underlying asset rises above the strike price, then the owner of the option will exercise the option and enjoy a profit (ΔV). If the value of the asset falls below the strike price, the owner of the option will not exercise it. Notice that this payoff profile does not consider the premium that the buyer paid for the option.

The payoff profile that results from buying a call is repeated in Part A of Figure 23.8. Part B shows the payoff profile on a call option from the seller's side. A call option is a zero-sum game, so the seller's payoff profile is exactly the opposite of the buyer's.

Part C of Figure 23.8 shows the payoff profile for the buyer of a put option. In this case, if the asset's value falls below the strike price, then the buyer profits because the seller of the put must pay the strike price. Part D shows that the seller of the put option loses out when the price falls below the strike price.

OPTION HEDGING

Suppose a firm has a risk profile that looks like the one in Part A of Figure 23.9. If the firm wishes to hedge against adverse price movements using options, what should it do? Examining the different payoff profiles in Figure 23.8, we see that the one that has the desirable shape is C, buying a put. If the firm buys a put, then its net exposure is as illustrated in Part B of Figure 23.9.

FIGURE 23.9   **Hedging with Options**

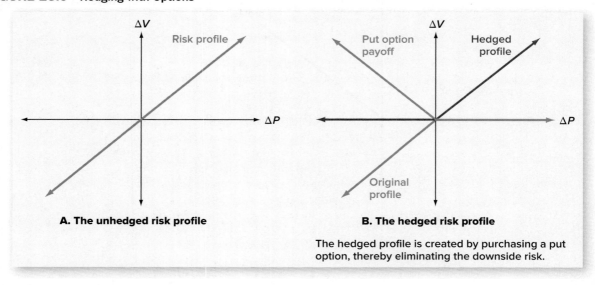

A. The unhedged risk profile   B. The hedged risk profile

The hedged profile is created by purchasing a put option, thereby eliminating the downside risk.

In this case, by buying a put option, the firm has eliminated the downside risk—that is, the risk of an adverse price movement. However, the firm has retained the upside potential. In other words, the put option acts as a kind of insurance policy. Remember that this desirable insurance is not free: The firm pays for it when it buys the put option.

HEDGING COMMODITY PRICE RISK WITH OPTIONS

We saw earlier that futures contracts are available for a variety of basic commodities. In addition, an increasing number of options are available on these same commodities. In fact, the options that are typically traded on commodities are actually options on futures contracts; for this reason, they are called *futures options*.

These work as follows: When a futures call option on wheat is exercised, the owner of the option receives two things. The first is a futures contract on wheat at the current futures price. This contract can be immediately closed at no cost. The second thing the owner of the option receives is the difference between the strike price on the option and the current futures price. The difference is paid in cash.

Table 23.2 gives corn futures options quotations from the CME Group website with a May 2017 expiration. Note that the middle column of numbers tells us the different strike prices that are available.[2] The "High" and "Low" columns are the high and low price of the day, the "Prior Settle" column is essentially the closing price yesterday, and the "Last" column is the price of the most recent trade. In the quote, you will notice the apostrophe. These contracts are traded in eighths. The last trade on the May 375 put was 17'1, which is 17 1/8 cents, or $.17125.

Suppose you buy the May 395 corn futures call option. You will pay $.08375 per bushel for the option (they're actually sold in multiples of 5,000, but we'll ignore this). If you exercise your option, you will receive a futures contract on corn and a cash payment for the difference between the current futures price and the strike price of $3.95.

HEDGING EXCHANGE RATE RISK WITH OPTIONS

Futures options are available on foreign currencies as well as on commodities. These work in exactly the same way as commodities futures options. In addition, there are other traded options for which the underlying asset is currency rather than a futures contract on a currency. Firms with significant exposure to exchange rate risk frequently purchase put options to protect against adverse exchange rate changes.

HEDGING INTEREST RATE RISK WITH OPTIONS

The use of options to hedge against interest rate risk is a very common practice, and there are a variety of options available to serve this purpose. Some are futures options like the ones we have been discussing, and these trade on organized exchanges. For example, we mentioned the Treasury note contract in our discussion of futures. There are options available on this contract and a number of other financial futures as well. Beyond this, there is a thriving over-the-counter market in interest rate options. We will describe some of these options in this section.

A Preliminary Note   Some interest rate options are actually options on interest-bearing assets such as bonds (or on futures contracts for bonds). Most of the options that are traded on exchanges fall into this category. As we will discuss in a moment, some others are actually options on interest rates. The distinction is important if we are thinking about using one type or the other to hedge. To illustrate, suppose we want to protect ourselves against an increase in interest rates using options; what should we do?

We need to buy an option that increases in value as interest rates go up. One thing we can do is buy a *put* option on a bond. Why a put? Remember that when interest rates go up,

The Association of Corporate Treasurers (**www.treasurers .org**) has lots of information about a variety of subjects, including risk management.

---

[2]Notice that the strike prices are all quoted in cents; for example, the first entry is 360.0, meaning $3.60 per bushel.

TABLE 23.2

Sample CME Group Futures Options Price Quotations

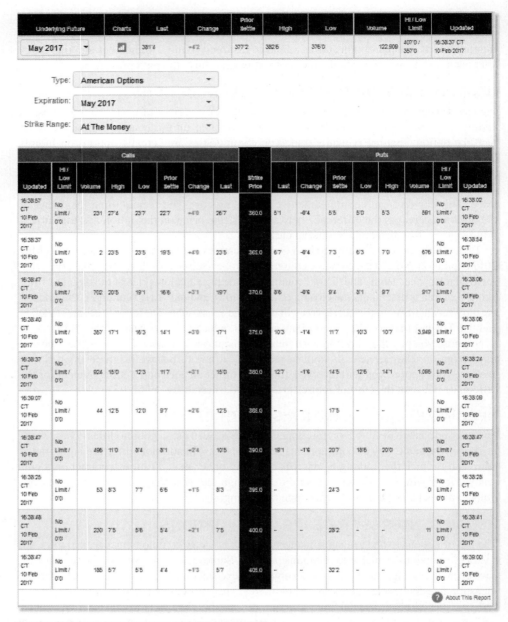

SOURCE: CME Group (www.cmegroup.com), February 10, 2017.

bond values go down; so one way to hedge against interest rate increases is to buy put options on bonds. The other way to hedge is to buy a *call* option on interest rates. We discuss this alternative in more detail in the next section.

We actually saw interest rate options in Chapter 7 when we discussed the call feature on a bond. Remember that the call provision gives the issuer the right to buy back the bond at a set price, known as the *call price*. What happens is that if interest rates fall, the bond's price will rise. If it rises above the call price, the issuer will exercise the option and acquire the bond at a bargain price. The call provision can be viewed as either a call option on a bond or a put option on interest rates.

Interest Rate Caps   An *interest rate cap* is a call option on an interest rate. Suppose a firm has a floating-rate loan. It is concerned that interest rates will rise sharply and the firm will experience financial distress because of the increased loan payment. To guard against this, the firm can purchase an interest rate cap from a bank (there are banks that specialize in such products). What will happen is that if the loan payment ever rises above an agreed-upon limit (the "ceiling"), the bank will pay the difference between the actual payment and the ceiling to the firm in cash.

A *floor* is a put option on an interest rate. If a firm buys a cap and sells a floor, the result is a *collar*. By selling the put and buying the call, the firm protects itself against increases in interest rates beyond the ceiling by the cap. However, if interest rates drop below the floor, the put will be exercised against the firm. The result is that the rate the firm pays will not drop below the floor rate. In other words, the rate the firm pays will always be between the floor and the ceiling.

Other Interest Rate Options   We will close out our chapter by briefly mentioning two relatively new types of interest rate options. Suppose a firm has a floating-rate loan. The firm is comfortable with its floating-rate loan, but it would like to have the right to convert it to a fixed-rate loan in the future.

What can the firm do? What it wants is the right, but not the obligation, to swap its floating-rate loan for a fixed-rate loan. In other words, the firm needs to buy an option on a swap. Swap options exist, and they have the charming name *swaptions*.

We've seen that there are options on futures contracts and options on swap contracts, but what about options on options? Such options are called *compound* options. As we have just discussed, a cap is a call option on interest rates. Suppose a firm thinks that, depending on interest rates, it might like to buy a cap in the future. As you can probably guess, in this case, what the firm might want to do today is buy an option on a cap. Inevitably, it seems, an option on a cap is called a *caption*, and there is a large market for these instruments.

ACTUAL USE OF DERIVATIVES

Because derivatives do not usually appear in financial statements, it is much more difficult to observe the use of derivatives by firms compared to, say, bank debt. Much of our knowledge of corporate derivative use comes from academic surveys. Most surveys report that the use of derivatives appears to vary widely among large publicly traded firms. Large firms are far more likely to use derivatives than are small firms. Table 23.3 shows that for firms that use derivatives, foreign currency and interest rate derivatives are the most frequently used types.

The prevailing view is that derivatives can be very helpful in reducing the variability of firm cash flows, which, in turn, reduces the various costs associated with financial distress. It is somewhat puzzling that large firms use derivatives more often than small firms— because large firms tend to have less cash flow variability than small firms. Also, some surveys report that firms occasionally use derivatives when they want to speculate about future prices and not just hedge risks.

However, most of the evidence is consistent with the theory that derivatives are most frequently used by firms where financial distress costs are high and access to the capital markets is constrained.

Concept Questions

23.6a   Suppose that the unhedged risk profile (Part A) in Figure 23.9 sloped down instead of up. What option-based hedging strategy would be suitable in this case?

23.6b   What is a futures option?

23.6c   What is a caption? Who might want to buy one?

TABLE 23.3
Derivative Usage:
Survey Results

Percent of Companies Using Derivatives	
2010	71%
2009	79

In Which Asset Classes Do You Use Derivatives?		
	2010	2009
Interest rates	65%	68%
Currencies	62	58
Credit	13	13
Energy	19	13
Commodities	23	22
Equities	13	9

Do You Expect Your Use of Derivatives to Change?				
	2010		2009	
	Increase	Decrease	Increase	Decrease
Interest rates	19%	15%	13%	20%
Currencies	20	8	31	6
Credit	4	4	2	13
Energy	11	7	5	9
Commodities	16	6	12	10
Equities	6	7	7	6

Do You Use an Integrated Risk Management Strategy or Do You Hedge Transactions or Specific Currency Exposures?		
	2010	2009
Hedge total risk	31.8%	21.1%
Hedge transactions	34.1	47.4
Hedge specific currency exposures	34.1	31.6

SOURCE: Adapted from *Treasury & Risk Management* (March 2010 and March 2012).

23.7 Summary and Conclusions

This chapter introduced some of the basic principles of financial risk management and financial engineering. The motivation for risk management and financial engineering stems from the fact that a firm will frequently have an undesirable exposure to some type of risk. This is particularly true today because of the increased volatility in key financial variables such as interest rates, exchange rates, and commodity prices.

We describe a firm's exposure to a particular risk with a risk profile. The goal of financial risk management is to alter the firm's risk profile through buying and selling derivative assets such as futures contracts, swap contracts, and option contracts. By finding instruments with appropriate payoff profiles, a firm can reduce or even eliminate its exposure to many types of risk.

Hedging cannot change the fundamental economic reality of a business. What it can do is allow a firm to avoid expensive and troublesome disruptions that might otherwise result from short-run, temporary price fluctuations. Hedging also gives a firm time to react and adapt to changing market conditions. Because of the price volatility and rapid economic change that characterize modern business, intelligently dealing with volatility has become an increasingly important task for financial managers.

Many other option types are available in addition to those we have discussed, and more are created every day. One very important aspect of financial risk management that we have not discussed is that options, forwards, futures, and swaps can be combined in a wide variety of ways to create new instruments. These basic contract types are really just the building blocks used by financial engineers to create new and innovative products for corporate risk management.

CONNECT TO FINANCE

connect *Connect Finance* offers you plenty of opportunities to practice mastering these concepts. Log on to connect.mheducation.com to learn more. If you like what you see, ask your professor about using *Connect Finance*!

Can you answer the following *Connect* Quiz questions?

Section 23.2   Keith is preparing a graph that compares the value of his firm to various prices for his firm's services. This graph is called a _____.

Section 23.3   A cereal maker needs a large quantity of wheat for its production processes. If the firm manages to completely hedge its risk exposure to wheat prices, then its risk profile for wheat will be _____.

Section 23.6   What is an interest rate cap?

CHAPTER REVIEW AND SELF-TEST PROBLEMS

23.1 Futures Contracts Suppose Golden Grain Farms (GGF) expects to harvest 50,000 bushels of wheat in September. GGF is concerned about the possibility of price fluctuations between now and September. The futures price for September wheat is $2 per bushel, and the relevant contract calls for 5,000 bushels. What action should GGF take to lock in the $2 price? Suppose the price of wheat actually turns out to be $3. Evaluate GGF's gains and losses. Do the same for a price of $1. Ignore marking to market.

23.2 Options Contracts In the previous question, suppose that September futures put options with a strike price of $2 per bushel cost $.15 per bushel. Assuming that GGF hedges using put options, evaluate its gains and losses for wheat prices of $1, $2, and $3.

ANSWERS TO CHAPTER REVIEW AND SELF-TEST PROBLEMS

23.1 GGF wants to deliver wheat and receive a fixed price, so it needs to *sell* futures contracts. Each contract calls for delivery of 5,000 bushels, so GGF needs to sell 10 contracts. No money changes hands today.

   If wheat prices actually turn out to be $3, then GGF will receive $150,000 for its crop; but it will have a loss of $50,000 on its futures position when it closes that position because the contracts require it to sell 50,000 bushels of wheat at $2, when the going price is $3. It thus nets $100,000 overall.

If wheat prices turn out to be $1 per bushel, then the crop will be worth only $50,000. However, GGF will have a profit of $50,000 on its futures position, so GGF again nets $100,000.

23.2 If GGF wants to insure against a price decline only, it can buy 10 put contracts. Each contract is for 5,000 bushels, so the cost per contract is 5,000 × $.15 = $750. For 10 contracts, the cost will be $7,500.

If wheat prices turn out to be $3, then GGF will not exercise the put options (why not?). Its crop is worth $150,000, but it is out the $7,500 cost of the options, so it nets $142,500.

If wheat prices fall to $1, the crop is worth $50,000. GGF will exercise its puts (why?) and thereby force the seller of the puts to pay $2 per bushel. GGF receives a total of $100,000. If we subtract the cost of the puts, we see that GGF's net is $92,500. In fact, verify that its net at any price of $2 or lower is $92,500.

CONCEPTS REVIEW AND CRITICAL THINKING QUESTIONS

1. **Hedging Strategies** [LO1] If a firm is selling futures contracts on lumber as a hedging strategy, what must be true about the firm's exposure to lumber prices?

2. **Hedging Strategies** [LO1] If a firm is buying call options on pork belly futures as a hedging strategy, what must be true about the firm's exposure to pork belly prices?

3. **Forwards and Futures** [LO2] What is the difference between a forward contract and a futures contract? Why do you think that futures contracts are much more common? Are there any circumstances under which you might prefer to use forwards instead of futures? Explain.

4. **Hedging Commodities** [LO1] Bubbling Crude Corporation, a large Texas oil producer, would like to hedge against adverse movements in the price of oil because this is the firm's primary source of revenue. What should the firm do? Provide at least two reasons why it probably will not be possible to achieve a completely flat risk profile with respect to oil prices.

5. **Sources of Risk** [LO1] A company produces an energy-intensive product and uses natural gas as the energy source. The competition primarily uses oil. Explain why this company is exposed to fluctuations in both oil and natural gas prices.

6. **Hedging Commodities** [LO1] If a textile manufacturer wanted to hedge against adverse movements in cotton prices, it could buy cotton futures contracts or buy call options on cotton futures contracts. What would be the pros and cons of the two approaches?

7. **Options** [LO4] Explain why a put option on a bond is conceptually the same as a call option on interest rates.

8. **Hedging Interest Rates** [LO1] A company has a large bond issue maturing in one year. When it matures, the company will float a new issue. Current interest rates are attractive, and the company is concerned that rates next year will be higher. What are some hedging strategies that the company might use in this case?

9. **Swaps** [LO3] Explain why a swap is effectively a series of forward contracts. Suppose a firm enters into a swap agreement with a swap dealer. Describe the nature of the default risk faced by both parties.

10. **Swaps** [LO3] Suppose a firm enters into a fixed-for-floating interest rate swap with a swap dealer. Describe the cash flows that will occur as a result of the swap.

11. **Transactions versus Economic Exposure** [LO1] What is the difference between transactions and economic exposure? Which can be hedged more easily? Why?

12. **Hedging Exchange Rate Risk** [LO2] If a U.S. company exports its goods to Japan, how would it use a futures contract on Japanese yen to hedge its exchange rate risk? Would it buy or sell yen futures? In answering, assume that the exchange rate quoted in the futures contract is quoted as dollars per yen.

13. **Hedging Strategies** [LO1] For the following scenarios, describe a hedging strategy using futures contracts that might be considered. If you think that a crosshedge would be appropriate, discuss the reasons for your choice of contract.

    a. A public utility is concerned about rising costs.

    b. A candy manufacturer is concerned about rising costs.

    c. A corn farmer fears that this year's harvest will be at record high levels across the country.

    d. A manufacturer of photographic film is concerned about rising costs.

    e. A natural gas producer believes there will be excess supply in the market this year.

    f. A bank derives all its income from long-term, fixed-rate residential mortgages.

    g. A stock mutual fund invests in large-company blue-chip stocks and is concerned about a decline in the stock market.

    h. A U.S. importer of Swiss Army knives will pay for its order in six months in Swiss francs.

    i. A U.S. exporter of construction equipment has agreed to sell some cranes to a German construction firm. The U.S. firm will be paid in euros in three months.

14. **Swaps** [LO3] In 2009 and 2010, investment banks were under fire for interest rate swaps sold to municipalities and nonprofits. For example, California's water resource authority paid about $305 million, North Carolina paid about $60 million, and Harvard University paid about $923 million to unwind swaps agreements. To unwind a swaps position, you make a reverse trade. For example, if you had agreed to a fixed-for-variable swap, you would enter a variable-for-fixed swap. The controversy was caused because many people felt that investment banks had taken advantage of municipalities and nonprofits. Is this argument correct? Why or why not?

15. **Insurance** [LO4] Suppose you own a home that costs $200,000 and you buy homeowner's insurance to cover your house against fire, wind, tornados, and other disasters. One way to view your insurance is that you purchased an option. What type of option is the homeowner's policy? As the homeowner, are you buying or selling this option?

16. **Insurance** [LO4] With some insurance policies, the value of the asset to be replaced is the current market value. For example, if you bought a couch five years ago for $1,000, and the current value of the couch is $300, you would only get $300 if the couch were destroyed. However, many insurance companies offer a "rider" that gives full replacement. In this case, if a comparable new couch were now $1,200, you would get the full $1,200 if your couch were destroyed. How would you view this rider in option terms?

QUESTIONS AND PROBLEMS

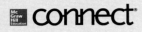

BASIC   ✗
(Questions 1–5)

1. **Futures Quotes [LO2]** Refer to Table 23.1 in the text to answer this question. Suppose you purchase a March 2017 cocoa futures contract this day at the last price of the day. What will your profit or loss be if cocoa prices turn out to be $1,965 per metric ton at expiration?

2. **Futures Quotes [LO2]** Refer to Table 23.1 in the text to answer this question. Suppose you sell five March 2017 silver futures contracts this day at the last price of the day. What will your profit or loss be if silver prices turn out to be $17.81 per ounce at expiration? What if silver prices are $17.64 per ounce at expiration?

3. **Futures Options Quotes [LO4]** Refer to Table 23.2 in the text to answer this question. Suppose you purchase the May 2017 call option on corn futures with a strike price of $3.85. Assume you purchased the option at the last price. How much does your option cost per bushel of corn? What is the total cost? Suppose the price of corn futures is $3.74 per bushel at expiration of the option contract. What is your net profit or loss from this position? What if corn futures prices are $4.13 per bushel at expiration?

4. **Put and Call Payoffs [LO4]** Suppose a financial manager buys call options on 50,000 barrels of oil with an exercise price of $57 per barrel. She simultaneously sells a put option on 50,000 barrels of oil with the same exercise price of $57 per barrel. Consider her gains and losses if oil prices are $52, $55, $57, $59, and $62. What do you notice about the payoff profile?

5. **Futures Options Quotes [LO4]** Refer to Table 23.2 in the text to answer this question. Suppose you purchase the May 2017 put option on corn futures with a strike price of $3.80. Assume your purchase was at the last price. What is the total cost? Suppose the price of corn futures is $3.61 per bushel at expiration of the option contract. What is your net profit or loss from this position? What if corn futures prices are $3.97 per bushel at expiration?

INTERMEDIATE
(Questions 6–7)

6. **Insurance [LO1]** Suppose your company has a building worth $165 million. Because it is located in a high-risk area for natural disasters, the probability of a total loss in any particular year is 1.15 percent. What is your company's expected loss per year on this building?

7. **Hedging with Futures [LO2]** Refer to Table 23.1 in the text to answer this question. Suppose today is February 10, 2017, and your firm produces breakfast cereal and needs 145,000 bushels of corn in May 2017 for an upcoming promotion. You would like to lock in your costs today because you are concerned that corn prices might rise between now and May.

   a. How could you use corn futures contracts to hedge your risk exposure? What price would you effectively be locking in based on the closing price of the day?

   b. Suppose corn prices are $3.69 per bushel in May. What is the profit or loss on your futures position? Explain how your futures position has eliminated your exposure to price risk in the corn market.

CHALLENGE
(Questions 8–10)

8. **Interest Rate Swaps [LO3]** ABC Company and XYZ Company need to raise funds to pay for capital improvements at their manufacturing plants. ABC Company is a well-established firm with an excellent credit rating in the debt market; it can borrow funds either at an 11 percent fixed rate or at LIBOR + 1 percent floating rate. XYZ Company is a fledgling start-up firm without a strong credit history. It can borrow funds either at a 10 percent fixed rate or at LIBOR + 3 percent floating rate.

a. Is there an opportunity here for ABC and XYZ to benefit by means of an interest rate swap?

b. Suppose you've just been hired at a bank that acts as a dealer in the swaps market, and your boss has shown you the borrowing rate information for your clients ABC and XYZ. Describe how you could bring these two companies together in an interest rate swap that would make both firms better off while netting your bank a 2.0 percent profit.

9. **Financial Engineering** [LO2, 4] Suppose there were call options and forward contracts available on coal, but no put options. Show how a financial engineer could synthesize a put option using the available contracts. What does your answer tell you about the general relationship among puts, calls, and forwards?

10. **Insurance** [LO4] In calculating insurance premiums, the actuarially fair insurance premium is the premium that results in a zero NPV for both the insured and the insurer. As such, the present value of the expected loss is the actuarially fair insurance premium. Suppose your company wants to insure a building worth $245 million. The probability of loss is 1.25 percent in one year, and the relevant discount rate is 4 percent.

a. What is the actuarially fair insurance premium?

b. Suppose that you can make modifications to the building that will reduce the probability of a loss to .90 percent. How much would you be willing to pay for these modifications?

MINICASE

Chatman Mortgage, Inc.

Joi Chatman recently received her finance degree and has decided to enter the mortgage broker business. Rather than working for someone else, she will open her own shop. Her cousin Mike has approached her about a mortgage for a house he is building. The house will be completed in three months, and he will need the mortgage at that time. Mike wants a 25-year, fixed-rate mortgage in the amount of $400,000 with monthly payments.

Joi has agreed to lend Mike the money in three months at the current market rate of 6 percent. Because Joi is just starting out, she does not have $400,000 available for the loan; she approaches Ian Turnbell, the president of IT Insurance Corporation, about purchasing the mortgage from her in three months. Ian has agreed to purchase the mortgage in three months, but he is unwilling to set a price on the mortgage. Instead, he has agreed in writing to purchase the mortgage at the market rate in three months. There are Treasury bond futures contracts available for delivery in three months. A Treasury bond contract is for $100,000 in face value of Treasury bonds.

QUESTIONS

1. What is the monthly mortgage payment on Mike's mortgage?

2. What is the most significant risk Joi faces in this deal?

3. How can Joi hedge this risk?

4. Suppose that in the next three months the market rate of interest rises to 7 percent.

   a. How much will Ian be willing to pay for the mortgage?

   b. What will happen to the value of Treasury bond futures contracts? Will a long or short position increase in value?

5. Suppose that in the next three months the market rate of interest falls to 5 percent.

   a. How much will Ian be willing to pay for the mortgage?

   b. What will happen to the value of T-bond futures contracts? Will a long or short position increase in value?

6. Are there any possible risks Joi faces in using Treasury bond futures contracts to hedge her interest rate risk?

Chapter

24 | Options and Corporate Finance

YOU INVEST $5,000 IN YAHOO! COMMON STOCK and just months later sell the shares for $7,500, realizing a 50 percent return. Not bad! At the same time, your neighbor invests $5,000 in Yahoo! stock options, which are worth $25,000 at expiration—a 400 percent return. Yahoo! Alternatively, your shares fall in value to $2,500, and you realize a 50 percent loss. Too bad! But at the same time, your neighbor's Yahoo! stock options are now worthless. Clearly, there is a big difference between stock shares and stock options.

In this chapter, we will explore the basics of options and option valuation. As you will see, options show up in many places in corporate finance. In fact, once you know what to look for, you can find them just about everywhere, so understanding how they work is essential.

Learning Objectives

After studying this chapter, you should be able to:

LO1 Lay out the basics of call and put options and explain how to calculate their payoffs and profits.

LO2 List the factors that affect option values and show how to price call and put options using no arbitrage conditions.

LO3 Explain the basics of employee stock options and their benefits and disadvantages.

LO4 Value a firm's equity as an option on the firm's assets.

LO5 Value options in capital budgeting projects, including timing options, the option to expand, the option to abandon, and the option to contract.

LO6 Define the basics of convertible bonds and warrants and how to value them.

©by_adri/iStockPhotoGettyImages

For updates on the latest happenings in finance, visit fundamentalsofcorporatefinance.blogspot.com.

option
A contract that gives its owner the right to buy or sell some asset at a fixed price on or before a given date.

Options are a part of everyday life. "Keep your options open" is sound business advice, and "We're out of options" is a sure sign of trouble. In finance, an **option** is an arrangement that gives its owner the right to buy or sell an asset at a fixed price anytime on or before a given date. The most familiar options are stock options. These are options to buy and sell shares of common stock, and we will discuss them in some detail in the following sections.

Of course, stock options are not the only options. In fact, at the root of it, many different kinds of financial decisions amount to the evaluation of options. We will show how understanding options adds several important details to the NPV analysis we have discussed in earlier chapters.

Also, virtually all corporate securities have implicit or explicit option features, and the use of such features is growing. As a result, understanding securities that possess option features requires general knowledge of the factors that determine an option's value.

This chapter starts with a description of different types of options. We identify and discuss the general factors that determine option values and show how ordinary debt and equity have optionlike characteristics. We then examine employee stock options and the important role of options in capital budgeting. We conclude by illustrating how option features are incorporated into corporate securities by discussing warrants, convertible bonds, and other optionlike securities.

Options: The Basics

24.1

An option is a contract that gives its owner the right to buy or sell some asset at a fixed price on or before a given date. An option on a building might give the holder of the option the right to buy the building for $1 million anytime on or before the Saturday prior to the third Wednesday of January 2021.

Options are a unique type of financial contract because they give the buyer the right, but not the obligation, to do something. The buyer uses the option only if it is profitable to do so; otherwise, the option can be thrown away.

There is a special vocabulary associated with options. Here are some important definitions:

1. **Exercising the option**: The act of buying or selling the underlying asset via the option contract is called *exercising the option*.
2. **Strike price**, or exercise price: The fixed price specified in the option contract at which the holder can buy or sell the underlying asset is called the *strike price* or *exercise price*. The strike price is often called the *striking price*.
3. **Expiration date**: An option usually has a limited life. The option is said to expire at the end of its life. The last day on which the option may be exercised is called the *expiration date*.
4. **American** and **European options**: An American option may be exercised anytime up to and including the expiration date. A European option may be exercised only on the expiration date.

exercising the option
The act of buying or selling the underlying asset via the option contract.

strike price
The fixed price in the option contract at which the holder can buy or sell the underlying asset. Also, the *exercise price* or *striking price*.

expiration date
The last day on which an option may be exercised.

American option
An option that may be exercised at any time until its expiration date.

European option
An option that may be exercised only on the expiration date.

PUTS AND CALLS

Options come in two basic types: Puts and calls. A **call option** gives the owner the right to *buy* an asset at a fixed price during a particular time period. It may help you to remember that a call option gives you the right to "call in" an asset.

A **put option** is essentially the opposite of a call option. Instead of giving the holder the right to buy some asset, it gives the holder the right to *sell* that asset for a fixed exercise price. If you buy a put option, you can force the seller of the option to buy the asset from you for a fixed price and thereby "put it to them."

What about an investor who *sells* a call option? The seller receives money up front and has the *obligation* to sell the asset at the exercise price if the option holder wants it.

call option
The right to buy an asset at a fixed price during a particular period.

put option
The right to sell an asset at a fixed price during a particular period of time. The opposite of a call option.

Similarly, an investor who *sells* a put option receives cash up front and is then obligated to buy the asset at the exercise price if the option holder demands it.[1]

The asset involved in an option can be anything. The options that are most widely bought and sold are stock options. These are options to buy and sell shares of stock. Because these are the best-known types of options, we will study them first. As we discuss stock options, keep in mind that the general principles apply to options involving any asset, not just shares of stock.

STOCK OPTION QUOTATIONS

On April 26, 1973, the Chicago Board Options Exchange (CBOE) opened and began organized trading in stock options. Put and call options involving stock in some of the best-known corporations in the United States are traded there. The CBOE is still the largest organized options market, but options are traded in a number of other places today, including the NYSE and NASDAQ. Almost all such options are American (as opposed to European).

A simplified quotation for a CBOE option might look something like this:

Prices at Close June 15, 2017							
RWJ (RWJ)					**Underlying Stock Price: $100.00**		
		Call			**Put**		
Expiration	**Strike**	**Last**	**Volume**	**Open Interest**	**Last**	**Volume**	**Open Interest**
Jun	95	6	120	400	2	80	1,000
July	95	6.50	40	200	2.80	100	4,600
Aug	95	8	70	600	4	20	800

The first thing to notice here is the company identifier, RWJ. This tells us that these options involve the right to buy or sell shares of stock in the RWJ Corporation. To the right of the company identifier is the closing price on the stock. As of the close of business on the day before this quotation, RWJ was selling for $100 per share.

The first column in the table shows the expiration months (June, July, and August). All CBOE options expire following the third Friday of the expiration month. The next column shows the strike price. The RWJ options listed here have an exercise price of $95.

The next three columns give us information about call options. The first thing given is the most recent price (Last). Next, we have volume, which tells us the number of option *contracts* that were traded that day. One option contract involves the right to buy (for a call option) or sell (for a put option) 100 shares of stock, and all trading actually takes place in contracts. Option prices are quoted on a per-share basis.

The last piece of information given for the call options is the open interest. This is the number of contracts of each type currently outstanding. The three columns of information for call options (price, volume, and open interest) are followed by the same three columns for put options.

The first option listed would be described as the "RWJ June 95 call." The price for this option is $6. If you pay the $6, then you have the right anytime between now and the third Friday of June to buy one share of RWJ stock for $95. Because trading takes place in round lots (multiples of 100 shares), one option contract costs you $6 × 100 = $600.

Check out these options exchanges: **www.cboe.com** and **www.euronext.com**

---

[1]An investor who sells an option is often said to have "written" the option.

January, 2018

Expires January 19, 2018

In the Money

Calls						Strike	Puts					
Last	Change	Bid	Ask	Volume	Open Int.		Last	Change	Bid	Ask	Volume	Open Int.
17.15	-0.10	18.00	19.80	24	29	13.00	0.07	-0.02	0.06	0.07	5	2480
16.10	+1.10	17.20	17.40	1	212	15.00	0.11	-0.02	0.10	0.13	10	3559
13.26	+1.06	13.00	14.80	10	389	18.00	0.21	-0.03	0.19	0.23	338	7331
12.00	+0.50	11.40	12.60	5	937	20.00	0.31	-0.01	0.30	0.32	25	11970
9.25	+0.25	8.70	9.50	50	3253	23.00	0.52		0.48	0.52	656	21567
7.28	+0.51	6.85	7.70	111	6443	25.00	0.76	-0.01	0.72	0.76	664	19264
5.45	-0.12	5.80	5.95	55	6553	27.00	1.12	-0.02	1.09	1.11	491	41442
3.60	+0.20	3.60	3.70	565	19847	30.00	1.96	-0.10	1.93	1.97	918	21101
2.46	+0.19	2.44	2.53	860	25952	32.00	2.93	-0.02	2.76	2.82	147	3104
					Last Trade	32.31	as of 02/14/17 4:00 PM ET					
1.20	+0.10	1.21	1.29	488	42290	35.00	5.40	-0.40	4.55	4.65	16	1743
0.70	+0.06	0.70	0.77	176	6791	37.00	7.00	-0.85	6.00	6.25	10	76
0.29	+0.04	0.29	0.33	15	6122	40.00	9.35	+0.10	8.55	9.50	24	38

SOURCE: *The Wall Street Journal* online, February 14, 2017.

The other quotations are similar. The July 95 put option costs $2.80. If you pay $2.80 × 100 = $280, then you have the right to sell 100 shares of RWJ stock anytime between now and the third Friday in July at a price of $95 per share.

Table 24.1 contains a more detailed CBOE quote reproduced from *The Wall Street Journal* (online). The company is Cisco Systems (CSCO). Looking near the center of the table, we see that CSCO is selling for $32.31 per share. Notice that there are multiple strike prices quoted. As shown, puts and calls with strike prices ranging from 13.00 up to 40.00 are available.

To check your understanding of option quotes, suppose you want the right to sell 100 shares of CSCO for $30 anytime up until the third Friday in January. What should you do and how much will it cost you?

Because you want the right to sell the stock for $30, you need to buy a *put* option with a $30 exercise price. So you go online and place an order for one CSCO January 30 put contract. Because the January 30 put is quoted at $1.97, you will have to pay $1.97 per share, or $197 in all (plus commission).

Of course, you can look up option prices many places on the web. Our nearby *Work the Web* box gives one example. Notice how much more complicated the ticker symbols are for the options compared to the stock.

OPTION PAYOFFS

Looking at Table 24.1, suppose you buy 50 January 30 call contracts. The option is quoted at $3.70, so the contracts cost $370 each. You spend a total of 50 × $370 = $18,500. You wait awhile, and the expiration date rolls around.

Now what? You have the right to buy CSCO stock for $30 per share. If CSCO is selling for less than $30 a share, then this option isn't worth anything and you throw it away. In this case, we say that the option has finished "out of the money" because the stock price is less than the exercise price. Your $18,500 is, alas, a complete loss.

If CSCO is selling for more than $30 per share, then you need to exercise your option. In this case, the option is "in the money" because the stock price exceeds the exercise price. Suppose CSCO has risen to, say, $35 per share. Because you have the right to buy CSCO at $30, you make a $5 profit on each share upon exercise. Each contract involves 100 shares, so you make $5 per share × 100 shares per contract = $500 per contract. Finally, you own

WORK THE WEB

How do you find option prices for options that are currently traded? To illustrate, we went to finance .yahoo.com, got a stock quote for Southwest Airlines (LUV), and followed the Options link. As you can see below, there were 17 call option contracts trading for Southwest with a January 2019 expiration date.

Calls For January 18, 2019

∧ Strike	Contract Name	Last Price	Bid	Ask	Change	% Change	Volume	Open Interest	Implied Volatility
23.00	LUV190118C00023000	25.82	26.60	28.90	0.00	0.00%	2	105	0.00%
25.00	LUV190118C00025000	24.28	23.10	26.00	0.00	0.00%	20	0	0.00%
30.00	LUV190118C00030000	18.80	24.30	28.60	0.00	0.00%	2	2	53.06%
33.00	LUV190118C00033000	22.10	22.70	24.00	0.00	0.00%	16	17	36.35%
35.00	LUV190118C00035000	15.15	14.50	16.00	0.00	0.00%	2	2	0.00%
38.00	LUV190118C00038000	16.60	15.40	17.30	0.00	0.00%	5	5	0.00%
40.00	LUV190118C00040000	16.48	17.40	18.60	0.00	0.00%	1	19	34.44%
42.00	LUV190118C00042000	11.13	12.10	15.10	0.00	0.00%	1	1	23.76%
45.00	LUV190118C00045000	15.20	14.10	15.60	0.00	0.00%	3	37	34.90%
47.00	LUV190118C00047000	12.14	12.80	13.60	0.00	0.00%	10	35	31.45%
50.00	LUV190118C00050000	11.48	11.10	11.80	1.18	11.46%	18	68	30.73%
55.00	LUV190118C00055000	8.88	8.60	9.10	0.56	6.73%	26	157	29.46%
60.00	LUV190118C00060000	7.32	6.30	7.60	0.08	1.10%	1	71	30.81%
65.00	LUV190118C00065000	5.29	4.90	5.80	-0.08	-1.49%	14	33	29.97%
70.00	LUV190118C00070000	3.86	3.30	4.30	0.26	7.22%	14	145	29.04%
75.00	LUV190118C00075000	3.10	2.70	3.20	0.00	0.00%	12	0	28.50%
80.00	LUV190118C00080000	1.95	1.60	2.35	0.00	0.00%	50	0	28.02%

The Chicago Board Options Exchange sets the strike prices for traded options. The strike prices are centered around the current stock price, and the number of strike prices depends in part on the trading volume in the stock. One thing you should notice after reading our section on option price boundaries is that a couple of the options appear to be mispriced. For example, the last sale on the $30 call option was for $18.80, and the $33 call's last trade was $22.10. A call is always more valuable when the strike price decreases, so you would expect the $30 call to sell for more than the $33 call. The reason the last prices for the $30 call and $33 put appear to be incorrect is because they never occurred at the same time. Options can be very illiquid, and what is happening is that the last price on the $30 call option is "stale," meaning that it did not occur recently. You may even encounter bid and ask prices on options that don't make sense because the options are so illiquid that none of the market makers have even bothered to update their prices.

Questions

1. *Look up the options that are currently available for Southwest. What is the expiration date of the longest-term options available? Compare the prices of these long-term options to shorter-term options with the same strike price. What do you find?*
2. *Find the IBM options with the shortest maturity. How many strike prices for IBM options are available? Are there more strike prices available for IBM than Southwest? Why do you think this is?*

50 contracts, so the value of your options is a handsome $25,000. Notice that because you invested $18,500, your net profit is $6,500.

As our example indicates, the gains and losses from buying call options can be quite large. To illustrate further, suppose you purchase the stock with the $18,500 instead of buying call options. In this case, you will have about $18,500/$32.31 = 572.58 shares. We can now compare what you have when the option expires for different stock prices:

Ending Stock Price	Option Value (50 contracts)	Net Profit or Loss (50 contracts)	Stock Value (572.58 shares)	Net Profit or Loss (572.58 shares)
$20	$ 0	-$18,500	$ 11,452	-$7,048
25	0	-18,500	14,314	-4,186
28	0	-18,500	16,032	-2,468
32	10,000	-8,500	18,323	-177
35	25,000	6,500	20,040	1,540
40	50,000	31,500	22,903	4,403

The option position clearly magnifies the gains and losses on the stock by a substantial amount. The reason is that the payoff on your 50 option contracts is based on $50 \times 100 = 5,000$ shares of stock instead of 572.58.

In our example, notice that, if the stock price ends up below the exercise price, then you lose all $18,500 with the option. With the stock, you still have some portion of your investment as long as the stock price doesn't drop to zero. Also notice that the option can never be worth less than zero because you can always throw it away. As a result, you can never lose more than your original investment (the $18,500 in our example).

It is important to recognize that stock options are a zero-sum game. By this we mean that whatever the buyer of a stock option makes, the seller loses, and vice versa. To illustrate, suppose, in our preceding example, you *sell* 50 option contracts. You receive $18,500 up front, and you will be obligated to sell the stock for $30 if the buyer of the option wishes to exercise it. In this situation, if the stock price ends up below $30, you will be $18,500 ahead. If the stock price ends up above $30, you will have to sell something for less than it is worth, so you will lose the difference. If the stock price is $35, you will have to sell $50 \times 100 = 5,000$ shares at $30 per share, so you will be out $35 - 30 = $5 per share, or $25,000 total. Because you received $18,500 up front, your net loss is $6,500. We can summarize some other possibilities as follows:

Ending Stock Price	Net Profit to Option Seller
$20	$18,500
25	18,500
28	18,500
32	8,500
35	-6,500
40	-31,500

Notice that the net profits to the option buyer (calculated previously) are just the opposites of these amounts.

EXAMPLE 24.1   **Put Payoffs**

Looking at Table 24.1, suppose you buy 10 CSCO January 25 put contracts. How much does this cost (ignoring commissions)? Just before the option expires, CSCO is selling for $21.50 per share. Is this good news or bad news? What is your net profit?

The option is quoted at $.76, so one contract costs 100 × $.76 = $76. Your 10 contracts total $760. You now have the right to sell 1,000 shares of CSCO for $25 per share. If the stock is currently selling for $21.50 per share, then this is most definitely good news. You can buy 1,000 shares at $21.50 and sell them for $25. Your puts are worth $25 − 21.50 = $3.50 per share, or $3.50 × 1,000 = $3,500 in all. Because you paid $760, your net profit is $3,500 −760 = $2,740.

Concept Questions

24.1a   What is a call option? A put option?

24.1b   If you thought that a stock was going to drop sharply in value, how might you use stock options to profit from the decline?

24.2 Fundamentals of Option Valuation

Now that we understand the basics of puts and calls, we can discuss what determines their values. We will focus on call options in the discussion that follows, but the same type of analysis can be applied to put options.

VALUE OF A CALL OPTION AT EXPIRATION

We have already described the payoffs from call options for different stock prices. In continuing this discussion, the following notation will be useful:

S_1 = Stock price at expiration (in one period)
S_0 = Stock price today
C_1 = Value of the call option on the expiration date (in one period)
C_0 = Value of the call option today
E = Exercise price on the option

From our previous discussion, remember that, if the stock price (S_1) ends up below the exercise price (E) on the expiration date, then the call option (C_1) is worth zero. In other words:

$$C_1 = 0 \quad \text{if } S_1 \leq E$$

Or, equivalently:

$$\mathbf{C_1 = 0 \quad if\ S_1 - E \leq 0}$$ **[24.1]**

This is the case in which the option is out of the money when it expires.

If the option finishes in the money, then $S_1 > E$, and the value of the option at expiration is equal to the difference:

$$C_1 = S_1 - E \quad \text{if } S_1 > E$$

Or, equivalently:

$$\mathbf{C_1 = S_1 - E \quad if\ S_1 - E > 0}$$ **[24.2]**

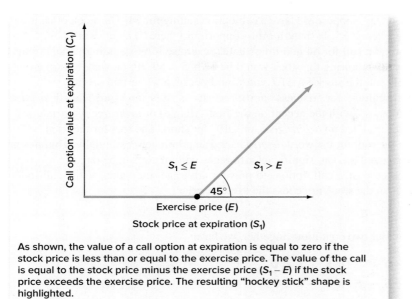

FIGURE 24.1

Value of a Call Option at Expiration for Different Stock Prices

As shown, the value of a call option at expiration is equal to zero if the stock price is less than or equal to the exercise price. The value of the call is equal to the stock price minus the exercise price ($S_1 - E$) if the stock price exceeds the exercise price. The resulting "hockey stick" shape is highlighted.

Suppose we have a call option with an exercise price of $10. The option is about to expire. If the stock is selling for $8, then we have the right to pay $10 for something worth only $8. Our option is worth exactly zero because the stock price is less than the exercise price on the option ($S_1 \leq E$). If the stock is selling for $12, then the option has value. Because we can buy the stock for $10, the option is worth $S_1 - E = \$12 - 10 = \$2$.

Figure 24.1 plots the value of a call option at expiration against the stock price. The result looks something like a hockey stick. Notice that for every stock price less than E, the value of the option is zero. For every stock price greater than E, the value of the call option is $S_1 - E$. Also, once the stock price exceeds the exercise price, the option's value goes up dollar for dollar with the stock price.

THE UPPER AND LOWER BOUNDS ON A CALL OPTION'S VALUE

Now that we know how to determine C_1, the value of the call at expiration, we turn to a somewhat more challenging question: How can we determine C_0, the value sometime *before* expiration? We will be discussing this in the next several sections. For now, we will establish the upper and lower bounds for the value of a call option.

The Upper Bound   What is the most a call option can sell for? If you think about it, the answer is obvious. A call option gives you the right to buy a share of stock, so it can never be worth more than the stock itself. This tells us the upper bound on a call's value: A call option will always sell for no more than the underlying asset. So, in our notation, the upper bound is:

$$C_0 \leq S_0$$

The Lower Bound   What is the least a call option can sell for? The answer here is a little less obvious. First of all, the call can't sell for less than zero, so $C_0 \geq 0$. Furthermore, if the stock price is greater than the exercise price, the call option is worth at least $S_0 - E$.

To see why, suppose we have a call option selling for $4. The stock price is $10, and the exercise price is $5. Is there a profit opportunity here? The answer is "yes" because you could buy the call for $4 and immediately exercise it by spending an additional $5. Your total cost of acquiring the stock would be $4 + 5 = $9. If you were to turn around and immediately sell the stock for $10, you would pocket a $1 certain profit.

Opportunities for riskless profits such as this one are called *arbitrages* (say "are-bitrazhes," with the accent on the first syllable) or *arbitrage opportunities*. One who arbitrages is called an *arbitrageur*, or "arb" for short. The root for the term *arbitrage* is the same as the root for the word *arbitrate*, and an arbitrageur essentially arbitrates prices. In a well-organized market, significant arbitrages will, of course, be rare.

In the case of a call option, to prevent arbitrage, the value of the call today must be greater than the stock price less the exercise price:

$$C_0 \geq S_0 - E$$

If we put our two conditions together, we have:

$$C_0 \geq 0 \qquad \text{if } S_0 - E < 0$$
$$C_0 \geq S_0 - E \quad \text{if } S_0 - E \geq 0$$

24.4

These conditions say that the lower bound on the call's value is either zero or $S_0 - E$, whichever is bigger.

intrinsic value
The lower bound of an option's value, or what the option would be worth if it were about to expire.

Our lower bound is called the **intrinsic value** of the option, and it is what the option would be worth if it were about to expire. With this definition, our discussion thus far can be restated as follows: At expiration, an option is worth its intrinsic value; it will generally be worth more than that anytime before expiration.

Figure 24.2 displays the upper and lower bounds on the value of a call option. Also plotted is a curve representing typical call option values for different stock prices prior to maturity. The exact shape and location of this curve depend on a number of factors. We begin our discussion of these factors in the next section.

FIGURE 24.2

Value of a Call Option before Expiration for Different Stock Prices

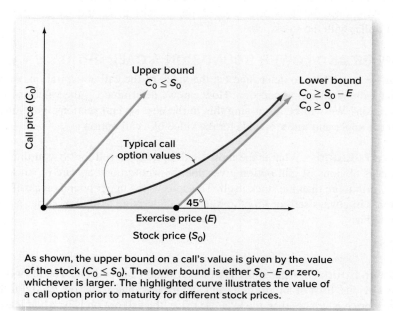

As shown, the upper bound on a call's value is given by the value of the stock ($C_0 \leq S_0$). The lower bound is either $S_0 - E$ or zero, whichever is larger. The highlighted curve illustrates the value of a call option prior to maturity for different stock prices.

A SIMPLE MODEL: PART I

Option pricing can be a complex subject, and we defer a detailed discussion to a later chapter. Fortunately, as is often the case, many of the key insights can be illustrated with a simple example. Suppose we are looking at a call option with one year to expiration and an exercise price of $105. The stock currently sells for $100, and the risk-free rate, R_f, is 20 percent.

The value of the stock in one year is uncertain, of course. To keep things simple, suppose we know that the stock price will be either $110 or $130. It is important to note that we *don't* know the odds associated with these two prices. In other words, we know the possible values for the stock, but not the probabilities associated with those values.

Because the exercise price on the option is $105, we know that the option will be worth either $110 − 105 = $5 or $130 − 105 = $25; but, once again, we don't know which. We do know one thing, however: Our call option is certain to finish in the money.

The Basic Approach   Here is the crucial observation: It is possible to exactly duplicate the payoffs on the stock using a combination of the option and the risk-free asset. How? Do the following: Buy one call option and invest $87.50 in a risk-free asset (such as a T-bill).

What will you have in a year? Your risk-free asset will earn 20 percent, so it will be worth $87.50 × 1.20 = $105. Your option will be worth $5 or $25, so the total value will be either $110 or $130, the same as the value of the stock:

Stock Value	vs.	Risk-Free Asset Value	+	Call Value	=	Total Value
$110		$105		$ 5		$110
130		105		25		130

As illustrated, these two strategies—buying a share of stock or buying a call and investing in the risk-free asset—have exactly the same payoffs in the future.

Because these two strategies have the same future payoffs, they must have the same value today or else there would be an arbitrage opportunity. The stock sells for $100 today, so the value of the call option today, C_0, is:

$$\$100 = \$87.50 + C_0$$
$$C_0 = \$12.50$$

Where did we get the $87.50? This is the present value of the exercise price on the option, calculated at the risk-free rate:

$$E/(1 + R_f) = \$105/1.20 = \$87.50$$

Given this, our example shows that the value of a call option in this simple case is given by:

$$S_0 = C_0 + E/(1 + R_f)$$
$$C_0 = S_0 - E/(1 + R_f)$$

24.5

In words, the value of the call option is equal to the stock price minus the present value of the exercise price.

A More Complicated Case   Obviously, our assumption that the stock price in one year will be either $110 or $130 is a vast oversimplification. We can now develop a more realistic model by assuming that the stock price in one year can be *anything* greater than or equal to the exercise price. Once again, we don't know how likely the different possibilities are, but we are certain that the option will finish somewhere in the money.

We again let S_1 stand for the stock price in one year. Now consider our strategy of investing $87.50 in a riskless asset and buying one call option. The riskless asset will again be worth $105 in one year, and the option will be worth $S_1 - \$105$, the value of which will depend on the stock price.

When we investigate the combined value of the option and the riskless asset, we observe something very interesting:

$$\text{Combined value} = \text{Riskless asset value} + \text{Option value}$$
$$= \$105 + (S_1 - \$105)$$
$$= S_1$$

As we had before, buying a share of stock has exactly the same payoff as buying a call option and investing the present value of the exercise price in the riskless asset.

Once again, to prevent arbitrage, these two strategies must have the same cost, so the value of the call option is equal to the stock price less the present value of the exercise price:[2]

$$C_0 = S_0 - E/(1 + R_f)$$

Our conclusion from this discussion is that determining the value of a call option is not difficult as long as we are certain that the option will finish somewhere in the money.

FOUR FACTORS DETERMINING OPTION VALUES

If we continue to suppose that our option is certain to finish in the money, then we can readily identify four factors that determine an option's value. There is a fifth factor that comes into play if the option can finish out of the money. We will discuss this last factor in the next section.

For now, if we assume that the option expires in t periods, then the present value of the exercise price is $E/(1 + R_f)^t$, and the value of the call is:

Call option value = Stock value − Present value of the exercise price
$$C_0 = S_0 - E/(1 + R_f)^t$$

24.6

If we take a look at this expression, we see that the value of the call obviously depends on four factors:

1. *The stock price*: The higher the stock price (S_0) is, the more the call is worth. This comes as no surprise because the option gives us the right to buy the stock at a fixed price.

---

[2]You're probably wondering what would happen if the stock price were less than the present value of the exercise price, which would result in a negative value for the call option. This can't happen because we are certain that the stock price will be at least E in one year because we know the option will finish in the money. If the current price of the stock is less than $E/(1 + R_f)$, then the return on the stock is certain to be greater than the risk-free rate, which creates an arbitrage opportunity. For example, if the stock is currently selling for $80, then the minimum return will be $(\$105 - 80)/\$80 = .3125$, or 31.25%. Because we can borrow at 20 percent, we can earn a certain minimum return of 11.25 percent per dollar borrowed. This, of course, is an arbitrage opportunity.

2. *The exercise price*: The higher the exercise price (E) is, the less the call is worth. This is also not a surprise because the exercise price is what we have to pay to get the stock.

3. *The time to expiration*: The longer the time to expiration (t) is, the more the option is worth. Once again, this is obvious. Because the option gives us the right to buy for a fixed length of time, its value goes up as the length of time increases.

4. *The risk-free rate*: The higher the risk-free rate (R_f) is, the more the call is worth. This result is a little less obvious. Normally, we think of asset values as going down as rates rise. In this case, the exercise price is a cash *outflow*, a liability. The current value of the liability goes down as the discount rate goes up.

Concept Questions

24.2a What is the value of a call option at expiration?

24.2b What are the upper and lower bounds on the value of a call option anytime before expiration?

24.2c Assuming that the stock price is certain to be greater than the exercise price on a call option, what is the value of the call? Why?

Valuing a Call Option   24.3

We now investigate the value of a call option when there is the possibility that the option will finish out of the money. We will again examine the simple case of two possible future stock prices. This case will let us identify the remaining factor that determines an option's value.

A SIMPLE MODEL: PART II

From our previous example, we have a stock that currently sells for $100. It will be worth either $110 or $130 in a year, and we don't know which. The risk-free rate is 20 percent. We are now looking at a different call option, however. This one has an exercise price of $120 instead of $105. What is the value of this call option?

This case is a little harder. If the stock ends up at $110, the option is out of the money and worth nothing. If the stock ends up at $130, the option is worth $130 − 120 = $10.

Our basic approach to determining the value of the call option will be the same. We will show once again that it is possible to combine the call option and a risk-free investment in a way that exactly duplicates the payoff from holding the stock. The only complication is that it's a little harder to determine how to do it.

Suppose we bought one call and invested the present value of the exercise price in a riskless asset as we did before. In one year, we would have $120 from the riskless investment plus an option worth either zero or $10. The total value would be either $120 or $130. This is not the same as the value of the stock ($110 or $130), so the two strategies are not comparable.

Instead, consider investing the present value of $110 (the lower stock price) in a riskless asset. This guarantees us a $110 payoff. If the stock price is $110, then any call options we own are worthless, and we have exactly $110 as desired.

When the stock is worth \$130, the call option is worth \$10. Our risk-free investment is worth \$110, so we are \$130 − 110 = \$20 short. Because each call option is worth \$10, we need to buy two of them to replicate the value of the stock.

In this case, investing the present value of the lower stock price in a riskless asset and buying two call options exactly duplicates owning the stock. When the stock is worth \$110, we have \$110 from our risk-free investment. When the stock is worth \$130, we have \$110 from the risk-free investment plus two call options worth \$10 each.

Because these two strategies have exactly the same value in the future, they must have the same value today, or arbitrage would be possible:

$$S_0 = \$100 = 2 \times C_0 + \$110/(1 + R_f)$$
$$2 \times C_0 = \$100 - \$110/1.20$$
$$C_0 = \$4.17$$

Each call option is worth \$4.17.

EXAMPLE 24.2 | **Don't Call Us, We'll Call You**

We are looking at two call options on the same stock, one with an exercise price of \$20 and one with an exercise price of \$30. The stock currently sells for \$35. Its future price will be either \$25 or \$50. If the risk-free rate is 10 percent, what are the values of these call options?

The first case (with the \$20 exercise price) is not difficult because the option is sure to finish in the money. We know that the value is equal to the stock price less the present value of the exercise price:

$$C_0 = S_0 - E/(1 + R_f)$$
$$= \$35 - \$20/1.1$$
$$= \$16.82$$

In the second case, the exercise price is \$30, so the option can finish out of the money. At expiration, the option is worth \$0 if the stock is worth \$25. The option is worth \$50 − 30 = \$20 if it finishes in the money.

As before, we start by investing the present value of the lowest stock price in the risk-free asset. This costs \$25/1.1 = \$22.73. At expiration, we have \$25 from this investment.

If the stock price is \$50, then we need an additional \$25 to duplicate the stock payoff. Because each option is worth \$20 in this case, we need \$25/\$20 = 1.25 options. So, to prevent arbitrage, investing the present value of \$25 in a risk-free asset and buying 1.25 call options must have the same value as the stock:

$$S_0 = 1.25 \times C_0 + \$25/(1 + R_f)$$
$$\$35 = 1.25 \times C_0 + \$25/(1 + .10)$$
$$C_0 = \$9.82$$

Notice that this second option had to be worth less because it has the higher exercise price.

THE FIFTH FACTOR

We now illustrate the fifth (and last) factor that determines an option's value. Suppose everything in our example is the same as before except that the stock price can be \$105 or \$135 instead of \$110 or \$130. Notice that the effect of this change is to make the stock's future price more volatile than before.

We investigate the same strategy that we used previously: Invest the present value of the lowest stock price ($105 in this case) in the risk-free asset and buy two call options. If the stock price is $105, then, as before, the call options have no value and we have $105 in all.

If the stock price is $135, then each option is worth $S_1 - E = \$135 - 120 = \$15$. We have two calls, so our portfolio is worth $\$105 + 2 \times \$15 = \$135$. Once again, we have exactly replicated the value of the stock.

What has happened to the option's value? More to the point, the variance of the return on the stock has increased. Does the option's value go up or down? To find out, we need to solve for the value of the call just as we did before:

$$S_0 = \$100 = 2 \times C_0 + \$105/(1 + R_f)$$
$$2 \times C_0 = \$100 - \$105/1.20$$
$$C_0 = \$6.25$$

The value of the call option has gone up from $4.17 to $6.25.

Based on our example, the fifth and final factor that determines an option's value is the variance of the return on the underlying asset. Furthermore, the *greater* that variance is, the *more* the option is worth. This result appears a little odd at first, and it may be somewhat surprising to learn that increasing the risk (as measured by return variance) on the underlying asset increases the value of the option.

The reason that increasing the variance on the underlying asset increases the value of the option isn't hard to see in our example. Changing the lower stock price to $105 from $110 doesn't hurt a bit because the option is worth zero in either case. However, moving the upper possible price to $135 from $130 makes the option worth more when it is in the money.

More generally, increasing the variance of the possible future prices on the underlying asset doesn't affect the option's value when the option finishes out of the money. The value is always zero in this case. On the other hand, increasing the variance increases the possible payoffs when the option is in the money, so the net effect is to increase the option's value. Put another way, because the downside risk is always limited, the only effect is to increase the upside potential.

In a later discussion, we will use the usual symbol, σ^2, to stand for the variance of the return on the underlying asset.

A CLOSER LOOK

Before moving on, it will be useful to consider one last example. Suppose the stock price is $100, and it will move either up or down by 20 percent. The risk-free rate is 5 percent. What is the value of a call option with a $90 exercise price?

The stock price will be either $80 or $120. The option is worth zero when the stock is worth $80, and it's worth $120 - 90 = \$30$ when the stock is worth $120. We will invest the present value of $80 in the risk-free asset and buy some call options.

When the stock finishes at $120, our risk-free asset pays $80, leaving us $40 short. Each option is worth $30 in this case, so we need $40/$30 = 4/3 options to match the payoff on the stock. The option's value must be given by:

$$S_0 = \$100 = 4/3 \times C_0 + \$80/1.05$$
$$C_0 = (3/4) \times (\$100 - 76.19)$$
$$= \$17.86$$

TABLE 24.2

Five Factors That Determine Option Values

Factor	Direction of Influence	
	Calls	Puts
Current value of the underlying asset	(+)	(−)
Exercise price on the option	(−)	(+)
Time to expiration on the option	(+)	(+)
Risk-free rate	(+)	(−)
Variance of return on the underlying asset	(+)	(+)

To make our result a little bit more general, notice that the number of options that you need to buy to replicate the value of the stock is always equal to $\Delta S/\Delta C$, where ΔS is the difference in the possible stock prices and ΔC is the difference in the possible option values. In our current case, ΔS would be $120 − 80 = \$40$ and ΔC would be $30 − 0 = \$30$, so $\Delta S/\Delta C$ would be $\$40/\$30 = 4/3$, as we calculated.

Notice also that when the stock is certain to finish in the money, $\Delta S/\Delta C$ is always exactly equal to 1, so one call option is always needed. Otherwise, $\Delta S/\Delta C$ is greater than 1, so more than one call option is needed.

This concludes our discussion of option valuation. The most important thing to remember is that the value of an option depends on five factors. Table 24.2 summarizes these factors and the direction of their influence for both puts and calls. In Table 24.2, the sign in parentheses indicates the direction of the influence.[3] In other words, the sign tells us whether the value of the option goes up or down when the value of a factor increases. Notice that increasing the exercise price reduces the value of a call option. Increasing any of the other four factors increases the value of the call. Notice also that the time to expiration and the variance of return act the same for puts and calls. The other three factors have opposite signs in the two cases.

We have not considered how to value a call option when the option can finish out of the money and the stock price can take on more than two values. A very famous result, the Black-Scholes option pricing model, is needed in this case. We cover this subject in detail in Chapter 25.

Concept Questions

24.3a What are the five factors that determine an option's value?

24.3b What is the effect of an increase in each of the five factors on the value of a call option? Give an intuitive explanation for your answer.

24.3c What is the effect of an increase in each of the five factors on the value of a put option? Give an intuitive explanation for your answer.

24.4 Employee Stock Options

employee stock option (ESO)

An option granted to an employee by a company giving the employee the right to buy shares of stock in the company at a fixed price for a fixed time.

Options are important in corporate finance in a lot of different ways. In this section, we begin to examine some of these by taking a look at **employee stock options**, or ESOs. An ESO is, in essence, a call option that a firm grants to employees giving them the right to buy shares of stock in the company. The practice of granting options to employees has become widespread. It is almost universal for upper management; but some companies, like

---

[3] The signs in Table 24.2 are for American options. For a European put option, the effect of increasing the time to expiration is ambiguous, and the direction of the influence can be positive or negative.

The Gap and Starbucks, grant options to almost every employee. Thus, an understanding of ESOs is important. Why? Because you may soon be an ESO holder!

ESO FEATURES

Because ESOs are basically call options, we have already covered most of the important aspects. However, ESOs have a few features that make them different from regular stock options. The details differ from company to company, but a typical ESO has a 10-year life, which is much longer than most ordinary options. Unlike traded options, ESOs cannot be sold. They also have what is known as a "vesting" period: Often, for up to three years or so, an ESO cannot be exercised and also must be forfeited if an employee leaves the company. After this period, the options "vest," which means they can be exercised. Sometimes, employees who resign with vested options are given a limited time to exercise their options.

Why are ESOs granted? There are basically two reasons. First, going back to Chapter 1, the owners of a corporation (the shareholders) face the basic problem of aligning shareholder and management interests and also of providing incentives for employees to focus on corporate goals. ESOs are a powerful motivator because, as we have seen, the payoffs on options can be very large. High-level executives in particular stand to gain enormous wealth if they are successful in creating value for stockholders.

The second reason some companies rely heavily on ESOs is that an ESO has no immediate, up-front, out-of-pocket cost to the corporation. In smaller, possibly cash-strapped companies, ESOs are a substitute for ordinary wages. Employees are willing to accept them instead of cash, hoping for big payoffs in the future. In fact, ESOs are a major recruiting tool, allowing businesses to attract talent that they otherwise could not afford.

See **www.esopassociation.org** for a site devoted to employee stock options.

ESO REPRICING

ESOs are almost always "at-the-money" when they are issued, meaning that the stock price is equal to the strike price. Notice that, in this case, the intrinsic value is zero, so there is no value from immediate exercise. Of course, even though the intrinsic value is zero, an ESO is still quite valuable because of, among other things, its very long life.

If the stock falls significantly after an ESO is granted, then the option is said to be "underwater." On occasion, a company will decide to lower the strike price on underwater options. Such options are said to be "restruck" or "repriced."

The practice of repricing ESOs is controversial. Companies that do it argue that once an ESO becomes deeply out of the money, it loses its incentive value because employees recognize there is only a small chance that the option will finish in the money. In fact, employees may leave and join other companies where they receive a fresh options grant.

Critics of repricing point out that a lowered strike price is, in essence, a reward for failing. They also point out that if employees know that options will be repriced, then much of the incentive effect is lost. Because of this controversy, many companies do not reprice options or have voted against repricing. For example, pharmaceutical giant Bristol-Myers Squibb's explicit policy prohibiting option repricing states, "It is the board of directors' policy that the company will not, without stockholder approval, amend any employee or nonemployee director stock option to reduce the exercise price (except for appropriate adjustment in the case of a stock split or similar change in capitalization)." However, other equally well-known companies have no such policy, and some have been labeled "serial repricers." The accusation is that such companies routinely drop strike prices following stock price declines.

For more information about ESOs, try the National Center for Employee Ownership at **www.nceo.org**.

An option exchange is a variation on a repricing. What typically happens is that underwater ESOs are exchanged for a smaller number of new ESOs with a lower exercise price, although this is not always the case. For example, in 2016, content processing solutions company Top Image Systems exchanged 377,275 options held by employees for new options at

Stock options can be granted to executive and other employees as an incentive device. They strengthen the relation between compensation and a firm's stock price performance, thus boosting effort and improving decision making within the firm. Further, to the extent that decision makers are risk averse (as most of us are), options induce more risk taking, which can benefit shareholders. However, options also have a dark side. They can be used to (i) conceal true compensation expenses in financial reports, (ii) evade corporate taxes, and (iii) siphon money from corporations to executives. One example that illustrates all three of these aspects is that of option backdating.

To understand the virtue of option backdating, it is first important to realize that for accounting, tax, and incentive reasons, most options are granted at-the-money, meaning that their exercise price equals the stock price on the grant date. Option backdating is the practice of selecting a past date (e.g., from the past month) when the stock price was particularly low to be the official grant date. This raises the value of the options, because they are effectively granted in-the-money. Unless this is properly disclosed and accounted for (which it rarely is), the practice of backdating can cause an array of problems. First, granting options that are effectively in-the-money violates many corporate option plans or other securities filings stating that the exercise price equals the fair market value on the grant day. Second, camouflaging in-the-money options as at-the-money options understates compensation expenses in the financial statements. In fact, under the old accounting rule APB 25 that was phased out in 2005, companies could expense options according to their intrinsic value, such that at-the-money options were not expensed at all. Third, at-the-money option grants qualify for certain tax breaks that in-the-money option grants do not qualify for, such that backdating can result in underpaid taxes.

Empirical evidence shows that the practice of backdating was prevalent from the early 1990s to 2005, especially among tech firms. As this came to the attention of the media and regulators in 2006, a scandal erupted. More than 100 companies were investigated for manipulation of option grant dates. As a result, numerous executives were fired, old financial statements were restated, additional taxes became due, and countless lawsuits were filed against companies and their directors. With new disclosure rules, stricter enforcement of the requirement that took effect as part of the Sarbanes-Oxley Act in 2002 that grants have to be filed within two business days, and greater scrutiny by regulators and the investment community, we likely have put the practice of backdating options behind us.

Erik Lie is a Henry B. Tippie Research Professor of Finance at the University of Iowa. His research focuses on corporate financial policy, M&A, and executive compensation.

a lower strike price of $2.11. Interestingly, the company stated that options for 79,166 shares held by the CEO and two board members would not be repriced unless the repricing was approved by shareholders. Frequently, option exchanges are structured such that the value of the new options is approximately equal to that of the old ones. In essence, a large number of underwater options are exchanged for a smaller number of at-the-money options.

Today, many companies award options on a regular basis, perhaps annually or even quarterly. That way, an employee will always have at least some options that are near the money even if others are underwater. Also, regular grants ensure that employees always have unvested options, which gives them an added incentive to stay with their current employer rather than forfeit the potentially valuable options.

ESO BACKDATING

A scandal erupted in 2006 over the backdating of ESOs. Recall that ESOs are almost always at the money on the grant date, meaning that the strike price is set equal to the stock price on the grant date. Financial researchers discovered that many companies had a practice of looking backward in time to select the grant date. Why did they do this? The answer is that they would pick a date on which the stock price (looking back) was low, thereby leading to option grants with low strike prices relative to the current stock price.

Backdating ESOs is not necessarily illegal or unethical as long as there is full disclosure and various tax and accounting issues are handled properly. Before the Sarbanes-Oxley Act of 2002 (which we discussed in Chapter 1), companies had up to 45 days after the end of their fiscal years to report options grants, so there was ample leeway for backdating. Because of Sarbanes-Oxley, companies are now required to report option grants within two business days of the grant dates, thereby limiting the gains from any backdating.

Concept Questions

24.4a What are the key differences between a traded stock option and an ESO?

24.4b What is ESO repricing? Why is it controversial?

Equity as a Call Option on the Firm's Assets   24.5

Now that we understand the basic determinants of an option's value, we turn to examining some of the many ways that options appear in corporate finance. One of the most important insights we gain from studying options is that the common stock in a leveraged firm (one that has issued debt) is effectively a call option on the assets of the firm. This is a remarkable observation, and we explore it next.

Looking at an example is the easiest way to get started. Suppose a firm has a single debt issue outstanding. The face value is $1,000, and the debt is coming due in a year. There are no coupon payments between now and then, so the debt is effectively a pure discount bond. In addition, the current market value of the firm's assets is $980, and the risk-free rate is 12.5 percent.

In a year, the stockholders will have a choice. They can pay off the debt for $1,000 and thereby acquire the assets of the firm free and clear, or they can default on the debt. If they default, the bondholders will own the assets of the firm.

In this situation, the stockholders essentially have a call option on the assets of the firm with an exercise price of $1,000. They can exercise the option by paying the $1,000, or they can choose not to exercise the option by defaulting. Whether or not they will choose to exercise obviously depends on the value of the firm's assets when the debt becomes due.

If the value of the firm's assets exceeds $1,000, then the option is in the money, and the stockholders will exercise by paying off the debt. If the value of the firm's assets is less than $1,000, then the option is out of the money, and the stockholders will optimally choose to default. What we now illustrate is that we can determine the values of the debt and equity using our option pricing results.

CASE I: THE DEBT IS RISK-FREE

Suppose that in one year the firm's assets will be worth either $1,100 or $1,200. What is the value today of the equity in the firm? The value of the debt? What is the interest rate on the debt?

To answer these questions, we first recognize that the option (the equity in the firm) is certain to finish in the money because the value of the firm's assets ($1,100 or $1,200) will always exceed the face value of the debt. In this case, from our discussion in previous sections, we know that the option value is the difference between the value of the underlying asset and the present value of the exercise price (calculated at the risk-free rate). The present value of $1,000 in one year at 12.5 percent is $888.89. The current value of the firm is $980, so the option (the firm's equity) is worth $980 − 888.89 = $91.11.

What we see is that the equity, which is effectively an option to purchase the firm's assets, must be worth $91.11. The debt must actually be worth $888.89. In fact, we really didn't need to know about options to handle this example because the debt is risk-free. The reason is that the bondholders are certain to receive $1,000. Because the debt is risk-free, the appropriate discount rate (and the interest rate on the debt) is the risk-free rate, and we know immediately that the current value of the debt is $1,000/1.125 = $888.89. The equity is worth $980 − 888.89 = $91.11, as we calculated.

CASE II: THE DEBT IS RISKY

Suppose now that the value of the firm's assets in one year will be either $800 or $1,200. This case is a little more difficult because the debt is no longer risk-free. If the value of the assets turns out to be $800, then the stockholders will not exercise their option and will thereby default. The stock is worth nothing in this case. If the assets are worth $1,200, then the stockholders will exercise their option to pay off the debt and will enjoy a profit of $1,200 − 1,000 = $200.

What we see is that the option (the equity in the firm) will be worth either zero or $200. The assets will be worth either $1,200 or $800. Based on our discussion in previous sections, a portfolio that has the present value of $800 invested in a risk-free asset and ($1,200 − 800)/($200 − 0) = 2 call options exactly replicates the value of the assets of the firm.

The present value of $800 at the risk-free rate of 12.5 percent is $800/1.125 = $711.11. This amount, plus the value of the two call options, is equal to $980, the current value of the firm:

$$\$980 = 2 \times C_0 + \$711.11$$
$$C_0 = \$134.44$$

Because the call option in this case is actually the firm's equity, the value of the equity is $134.44. The value of the debt is $980 − 134.44 = $845.56.

Finally, because the debt has a $1,000 face value and a current value of $845.56, the interest rate is ($1,000/$845.56) − 1 = .1827, or 18.27%. This exceeds the risk-free rate, of course, because the debt is now risky.

Equity as a Call Option

EXAMPLE 24.3

Swenson Software has a pure discount debt issue with a face value of $100. The issue is due in one year. At that time, the assets of the firm will be worth either $55 or $160, depending on the sales success of Swenson's latest product. The assets of the firm are currently worth $110. If the risk-free rate is 10 percent, what is the value of the equity in Swenson? The value of the debt? The interest rate on the debt?

To replicate the value of the assets of the firm, we first need to invest the present value of $55 in the risk-free asset. This costs $55/1.10 = $50. If the assets turn out to be worth $160, then the option is worth $160 − 100 = $60. Our risk-free asset will be worth $55, so we need ($160 − 55)/$60 = 1.75 call options. Because the firm is currently worth $110, we have:

$$\$110 = 1.75 \times C_0 + \$50$$
$$C_0 = \$34.29$$

The equity is worth $34.29; the debt is worth $110 − 34.29 = $75.71. The interest rate on the debt is about ($100/$75.71) − 1 = .321, or 32.1%.

Concept Questions

24.5a Why do we say that the equity in a leveraged firm is effectively a call option on the firm's assets?

24.5b All other things being the same, would the stockholders of a firm prefer to increase or decrease the volatility of the firm's return on assets? Why? What about the bondholders? Give an intuitive explanation.

Options and Capital Budgeting

24.6

Most of the options we have discussed so far are financial options because they involve the right to buy or sell financial assets such as shares of stock. In contrast, **real options** involve real assets. As we will discuss in this section, our understanding of capital budgeting can be greatly enhanced by recognizing that many corporate investment decisions really amount to the evaluation of real options.

real option
An option that involves real assets as opposed to financial assets such as shares of stock.

To give a simple example of a real option, imagine that you are shopping for a used car. You find one that you like for $4,000, but you are not completely sure. So, you give the owner of the car $150 to hold the car for you for one week, meaning that you have one week to buy the car or else you forfeit your $150. As you probably recognize, what you have done here is to purchase a call option, giving you the right to buy the car at a fixed price for a fixed time. It's a real option because the underlying asset (the car) is a real asset.

The use of options such as the one in our car example is common in the business world. For example, real estate developers frequently need to purchase several smaller tracts of land from different owners to assemble a single larger tract. The development can't go forward unless all of the smaller properties are obtained. In this case, the developer will often buy options on the individual properties but will exercise those options only if all of the necessary pieces can be obtained.

These examples involve explicit options. As it turns out, almost all capital budgeting decisions contain numerous *implicit* options. We discuss the most important types of these next.

THE INVESTMENT TIMING DECISION

Consider a business that is examining a new project of some sort. What this normally means is management must decide whether to make an investment outlay to acquire the new assets needed for the project. If you think about it, what management has is the right, but not the obligation, to pay some fixed amount (the initial investment) and thereby acquire a real asset (the project). In other words, essentially all proposed projects are real options!

Based on our discussion in previous chapters, you already know how to analyze proposed business investments. You would identify and analyze the relevant cash flows and assess the net present value (NPV) of the proposal. If the NPV is positive, you would recommend taking the project, where taking the project amounts to exercising the option.

There is a very important qualification to this discussion that involves mutually exclusive investments. Remember that two (or more) investments are said to be mutually exclusive if we can take only one of them. A standard example is a situation in which we own a piece of land that we wish to build on. We are considering building either a gasoline station or an apartment building. We further think that both projects have positive NPVs, but, of course, we can take only one. Which one do we take? The obvious answer is that we take the one with the larger NPV.

Here is the key point: Just because an investment has a positive NPV doesn't mean we should take it today. That sounds like a complete contradiction of what we have said all along, but it isn't. The reason is that if we take a project today, we can't take it later. Put differently, almost all projects compete with themselves in time. We can take a project now, a month from now, a year from now, and so on. We therefore have to compare the NPV of taking the project now versus the NPV of taking it later. Deciding when to take a project is called the **investment timing decision**.

investment timing decision
The evaluation of the optimal time to begin a project.

A simple example is useful to illustrate the investment timing decision. A project costs $100 and has a single future cash flow. If we take it today, the cash flow will be $120 in one year. If we wait one year, the project will still cost $100, but the cash flow the following year (two years from now) will be $130 because the potential market is bigger. If these are the only two options, and the relevant discount rate is 10 percent, what should we do?

To answer this question, we need to compute the two NPVs. If we take it today, the NPV is:

$$NPV = -\$100 + \$120/1.1 = \$9.09$$

If we wait one year, the NPV at that time will be:

$$NPV = -\$100 + \$130/1.1 = \$18.18$$

This $18.18 is the NPV one year from now. We need the value today, so we discount back one period:

$$NPV = \$18.18/1.1 = \$16.53$$

So, the choice is clear. If we wait, the NPV is $16.53 today compared to $9.09 if we start immediately, so the optimal time to begin the project is one year from now.

The fact that we do not have to take a project immediately is often called the "option to wait." In our simple example, the value of the option to wait is the difference in NPVs: $16.53 − 9.09 = $7.44. This $7.44 is the extra value created by deferring the start of the project as opposed to taking it today.

As our example illustrates, the option to wait can be valuable. How valuable depends on the type of project. If we were thinking about a consumer product intended to capitalize on a current fashion or trend, then the option to wait is probably not very valuable because the window of opportunity is probably short. In contrast, suppose the project in question is a proposal to replace an existing production facility with a new, higher-efficiency one. This type of investment can be made now or later. In this case, the option to wait may be valuable.

The Investment Timing Decision   EXAMPLE 24.4

A project costs $200 and has a future cash flow of $42 per year forever. If we wait one year, the project will cost $240 because of inflation, but the cash flows will be $48 per year forever. If these are the only two options, and the relevant discount rate is 12 percent, what should we do? What is the value of the option to wait?

In this case, the project is a simple perpetuity. If we take it today, the NPV is:

NPV = −$200 + $42/.12 = $150

If we wait one year, the NPV at that time will be:

NPV = −$240 + $48/.12 = $160

So, $160 is the NPV one year from now, but we need to know the value today. Discounting back one period, we get:

NPV = $160/1.12 = $142.86

If we wait, the NPV is $142.86 today compared to $150 if we start immediately, so the optimal time to begin the project is now.

What's the value of the option to wait? It is tempting to say that it is $142.86 − 150 = −$7.14, but that's wrong. Why? Because, as we discussed earlier, an option can never have a negative value. In this case, the option to wait has a zero value.

There is another important aspect regarding the option to wait. Just because a project has a negative NPV today doesn't mean that we should permanently reject it. Suppose an investment costs $120 and has a perpetual cash flow of $10 per year. If the discount rate is 10 percent, then the NPV is $10/.10 − $120 = −$20, so the project should not be taken now.

We should not just forget about this project forever, though. Suppose that next year, for some reason, the relevant discount rate falls to 5 percent. Then the NPV would be $10/.05 − $120 = $80, and we would take the project (assuming that further waiting isn't even more valuable). More generally, as long as there is some possible future scenario under which a project has a positive NPV, then the option to wait is valuable, and we should just shelve the project proposal for now.

MANAGERIAL OPTIONS

Once we decide the optimal time to launch a project, other real options come into play. In our capital budgeting analysis thus far, we have more or less ignored the impact of managerial actions that might take place *after* a project is launched. In effect, we assumed that, once a project is launched, its basic features cannot be changed.

In reality, depending on what actually happens in the future, there will always be opportunities to modify a project. These opportunities, which are an important type of real option, are often called **managerial options**. There are a great number of these options. The ways in which a product is priced, manufactured, advertised, and produced can all be changed, and these are just a few of the possibilities.

For example, in 2008, faced with dramatically higher fuel costs, US Airways announced major changes in its operations. First, the company decided to cut domestic capacity by

managerial options
Opportunities that managers can exploit if certain things happen in the future.

6 to 8 percent in the fourth quarter of 2008 and an additional 7 to 9 percent in 2009. It also planned to return 10 jetliners to lessors by 2009, and it canceled the leases on two wide-body jets originally scheduled for its fleet in 2009. Further fleet reductions were to occur in 2010.

US Airways also planned to eliminate 1,700 jobs through attrition, voluntary leaves of absence, and furloughs. The biggest job cuts would be in Las Vegas, where 600 jobs would be lost. The company's intention was to cut the number of destinations served from Las Vegas from 55 to 31 and to reduce the number of daily flights to that city from 141 to 81.

Finally, US Airways announced increases in fees. It would begin charging $15 for a passenger's first checked bag, which was later raised to $25 for the first bag and $35 for the second bag. There would be a $2 charge for nonalcoholic beverages on domestic flights, and the cost of alcoholic beverages would rise from $5 to $7. The company also planned to charge $25 for mileage-award tickets and to increase fees for tickets purchased through its reservations line.

Contingency Planning　The various what-if procedures, particularly the break-even measures we discussed in an earlier chapter, have a use beyond that of evaluating cash flow and NPV estimates. We can also view these procedures and measures as primitive ways of exploring the dynamics of a project and investigating managerial options. What we think about in this case are some of the possible futures that could come about and what actions we might take if they do.

We might find that a project fails to break even when sales drop below 10,000 units. This is a fact that is interesting to know; but the more important thing is to then go on and ask: What actions are we going to take if this actually occurs? This is called **contingency planning**, and it amounts to an investigation of some of the managerial options implicit in a project.

There is no limit to the number of possible futures or contingencies we could investigate. However, there are some broad classes, and we consider these next.

contingency planning
Taking into account the managerial options implicit in a project.

The Option to Expand　One particularly important option we have not explicitly addressed is the option to expand. If we truly find a positive NPV project, then there is an obvious consideration. Can we expand the project or repeat it to get an even larger NPV? Our static analysis implicitly assumes that the scale of the project is fixed.

If the sales demand for a particular product were to greatly exceed expectations, then we might investigate increasing production. If this is not feasible for some reason, then we could always increase cash flow by raising the price. Either way, the potential cash flow is higher than we have indicated because we have implicitly assumed that no expansion or price increase is possible. Overall, because we ignore the option to expand in our analysis, we *underestimate* NPV (all other things being equal).

The Option to Abandon　At the other extreme, the option to scale back or even abandon a project is also quite valuable. If a project does not break even on a cash flow basis, then it can't even cover its own expenses. We would be better off if we just abandoned it. Our discounted cash flow (DCF) analysis implicitly assumes that we would keep operating even in this case.

Sometimes, the best thing to do is punt. For example, in 2016, Adidas and Nike admitted to a shank when they announced that they were exiting the golf equipment business. Also in 2016, golf retailer Golfsmith announced that it was selling off Golf Town, its Canadian operations. Later in the year, Golfsmith sold off the remaining U.S. assets to Dick's Sporting Goods and a group of liquidators.

More generally, if sales demand is significantly below expectations, we might be able to sell off some capacity or put it to another use. Maybe the product or service could be re-designed or otherwise improved. Regardless of the specifics, we once again *underestimate* NPV if we assume that the project must last for some fixed number of years, no matter what happens in the future.

The Option to Suspend or Contract Operations   An option that is closely related to the option to abandon is the option to suspend operations. Frequently, we see companies choosing to temporarily shut down an activity of some sort. For example, automobile man-ufacturers sometimes find themselves with too many vehicles of a particular type. In this case, production is often halted until the excess supply is sold. At some point in the future, production resumes.

The option to suspend operations is particularly valuable in natural resource extraction. Suppose you own a gold mine. If gold prices fall dramatically, then your analysis might show that it costs more to extract an ounce of gold than you can sell the gold for, so you quit mining. The gold just stays in the ground and you can always resume operations if the price rises sufficiently. In fact, operations might be suspended and restarted many times over the life of the mine.

Companies also sometimes choose to permanently scale back an activity. If a new prod-uct does not sell as well as planned, production might be cut back and the excess capacity put to some other use. This case is really just the opposite of the option to expand, so we will label it the option to contract.

For example, in 2013, Ford faced tremendous pressure from political and union leaders in Belgium when the company closed its plant in Genk. Ford planned to move production to other plants in Europe. Some estimate that plants in Europe can produce seven to eight million more cars and light trucks than the market can absorb.

Options in Capital Budgeting: An Example   Suppose we are examining a new project. To keep things relatively simple, let's say that we expect to sell 100 units per year at $1 net cash flow apiece into perpetuity. Thus, we expect that the cash flow will be $100 per year.

In one year, we will know more about the project. In particular, we will have a better idea of whether it is successful. If it looks like a long-term success, the expected sales will be revised upward to 150 units per year. If it does not, the expected sales will be revised downward to 50 units per year. Success and failure are equally likely. Notice that because there is an even chance of selling 50 or 150 units, the expected sales are still 100 units, as we originally projected. The cost is $550, and the discount rate is 20 percent. The project can be dismantled and sold in one year for $400 if we decide to abandon it. Should we take it?

A standard DCF analysis is not difficult. The expected cash flow is $100 per year for-ever, and the discount rate is 20 percent. The PV of the cash flows is $100/.20 = $500, so the NPV is $500 − 550 = −$50. We shouldn't take the project.

This analysis ignores valuable options. In one year, we can sell for $400. How can we account for this? We have to decide what we are going to do one year from now. In this sim-ple case, we need to evaluate only two contingencies, an upward revision and a downward revision, so not much extra work is needed.

In one year, if the expected cash flows are revised to $50, then the PV of the cash flows is revised downward to $50/.20 = $250. We get $400 by abandoning the project, so that is what we will do (in one year, the NPV of keeping the project is $250 − 400 = −$150).

If the demand is revised upward, then the PV of the future cash flows at Year 1 is $150/.20 = $750. This exceeds the $400 abandonment value, so we will keep the project.

We have a project that costs $550 today. In one year, we expect a cash flow of $100 from the project. In addition, this project will be worth either $400 (if we abandon it because it is a failure) or $750 (if we keep it because it succeeds). These outcomes are equally likely, so we expect the project to be worth ($400 + 750)/2, or $575.

Summing up, in one year, we expect to have $100 in cash plus a project worth $575, or $675 total. At a 20 percent discount rate, this $675 is worth $562.50 today, so the NPV is $562.50 − 550 = $12.50. We should take the project.

The NPV of our project has increased by $62.50. Where did this come from? Our original analysis implicitly assumed we would keep the project even if it was a failure. At Year 1, however, we saw that we were $150 better off ($400 versus $250) if we abandoned. There was a 50 percent chance of this happening, so the expected gain from abandoning is $75. The PV of this amount is the value of the option to abandon: $75/1.20 = $62.50.

Strategic Options   Companies sometimes undertake new projects just to explore possibilities and evaluate potential future business strategies. This is a little like testing the water by sticking a toe in before diving. Such projects are difficult to analyze using conventional DCF methods because most of the benefits come in the form of **strategic options**—that is, options for future, related business moves. Projects that create such options may be very valuable, but that value is difficult to measure. Research and development is an example of a strategic option that is an important and valuable activity for many firms, precisely because it creates options for new products and procedures.

strategic options
Options for future, related business products or strategies.

To give another example, a large manufacturer might decide to open a retail outlet as a pilot study. The primary goal is to gain some market insight. Because of the high start-up costs, this one operation won't break even. However, using the sales experience gained from the pilot, the firm can then evaluate whether to open more outlets, to change the product mix, to enter new markets, and so on. The information gained and the resulting options for actions are all valuable, but coming up with a reliable dollar figure is probably infeasible.

Conclusion   We have seen that incorporating options into capital budgeting analysis is not easy. What can we do about them in practice? The answer is that we need to keep them in mind as we work with the projected cash flows. We will tend to underestimate NPV by ignoring options. The damage might be small for a highly structured, very specific proposal, but it might be great for an exploratory one.

> **Concept Questions**
>
> **24.6a** Why do we say that almost every capital budgeting proposal involves mutually exclusive alternatives?
> **24.6b** What are the options to expand, abandon, and suspend operations?
> **24.6c** What are strategic options?

24.7 Options and Corporate Securities

In this section, we return to financial assets by considering some of the most common ways options appear in corporate securities and other financial assets. We begin by examining warrants and convertible bonds.

WARRANTS

A **warrant** is a corporate security that looks a lot like a call option. It gives the holder the right, but not the obligation, to buy shares of common stock directly from a company at a fixed price for a given time period. Each warrant specifies the number of shares of stock the holder can buy, the exercise price, and the expiration date.

warrant
A security that gives the holder the right to purchase shares of stock at a fixed price over a given period of time.

The differences in contractual features between the call options that trade on the Chicago Board Options Exchange and warrants are relatively minor. Warrants usually have much longer maturity periods. In fact, some warrants are actually perpetual and have no fixed expiration date.

Warrants are sometimes called *sweeteners* or *equity kickers* because they are often issued in combination with privately placed loans or bonds. Throwing in some warrants is a way of making the deal a little more attractive to the lender, and it is a common practice. Warrants have been listed and traded on the NYSE since April 13, 1970. In early 2017, there were only 20 warrants listed on the NYSE. In Europe, warrants are still popular. Also in early 2017, Euronext listed about 57,000 of them.

In many cases, warrants are attached to bonds when issued. The loan agreement will state whether the warrants are detachable from the bond. Usually, the warrant can be detached immediately and sold by the holder as a separate security.

The Difference between Warrants and Call Options   As we have explained, from the holder's point of view, warrants are similar to call options on common stock. A warrant, like a call option, gives its holder the right to buy common stock at a specified price. From the firm's point of view, a warrant is different from a call option sold on the company's common stock.

The most important difference between call options and warrants is that call options are issued by individuals and warrants are issued by firms. When a call option is exercised, one investor buys stock from another investor. The company is not involved. When a warrant is exercised, the firm must issue new shares of stock. Each time a warrant is exercised, then, the firm receives some cash and the number of shares outstanding increases. Notice that the employee stock options we discussed earlier in the chapter are issued by corporations; so, strictly speaking, they are warrants rather than options.

To illustrate, suppose the Endrun Company issues a warrant giving holders the right to buy one share of common stock at $25. Further suppose the warrant is exercised. Endrun must print one new stock certificate. In exchange for the stock certificate, it receives $25 from the holder.

In contrast, when a call option is exercised, there is no change in the number of shares outstanding. Suppose Ms. Enger purchases a call option on the common stock of the Endrun Company from Mr. Swift. The call option gives Ms. Enger the right to buy (from Mr. Swift) one share of common stock of the Endrun Company for $25.

If Ms. Enger chooses to exercise the call option, then Mr. Swift is obligated to give her one share of Endrun's common stock in exchange for $25. If Mr. Swift does not already own a share, he must go into the stock market and buy one.

The call option amounts to a side bet between Ms. Enger and Mr. Swift on the value of the Endrun Company's common stock. When a call option is exercised, one investor gains and the other loses. The total number of shares outstanding of the Endrun Company remains constant, and no new funds are made available to the company.

Earnings Dilution   Warrants (and convertible bonds, as we will see) frequently cause the number of shares to increase. This happens (1) when the warrants are exercised and (2) when the bonds are converted, causing the firm's net income to be spread over a larger number of shares. Earnings per share therefore decrease.

Firms with significant numbers of warrants and convertible issues outstanding will generally calculate and report earnings per share on a *diluted basis*. This means that the calculation is based on the number of shares that would be outstanding if all the warrants were exercised and all the convertibles were converted. Because this increases the number of shares, diluted EPS will be lower than "basic" EPS, which is calculated only on the basis of shares actually outstanding.

CONVERTIBLE BONDS

convertible bond
A bond that can be exchanged for a fixed number of shares of stock for a specified amount of time.

A **convertible bond** is similar to a bond with warrants. The most important difference is that a bond with warrants can be separated into distinct securities (a bond and some warrants), but a convertible bond cannot. A convertible bond gives the holder the right to exchange the bond for a fixed number of shares of stock anytime up to and including the maturity date of the bond.

Preferred stock can frequently be converted into common stock. A convertible preferred stock is the same as a convertible bond except that it has an infinite maturity date.[4]

Features of a Convertible Bond   We can illustrate the basic features of a convertible bond by examining a particular issue. In March 2014, electric car manufacturer Tesla issued $1.2 billion in convertible bonds. The bonds have a 1.25 percent coupon rate, mature in 2021, and can be converted into Tesla common stock at a **conversion price** of $359.87. Because each bond has a face value of $1,000, the owner can receive $1,000/$359.87 = 2.7788 shares of Tesla's stock. The number of shares per bond, 2.7788 in this case, is called the **conversion ratio**.

conversion price
The dollar amount of a bond's par value that is exchangeable for one share of stock.

conversion ratio
The number of shares per bond received for conversion into stock.

When Tesla issued its convertible bonds, its common stock was trading at $252.54 per share. The conversion price was ($359.87 − 252.54)/$252.54 = .425, or 42.5 percent higher than its actual stock price. This 42.5 percent is called the **conversion premium**. It reflects the fact that the conversion option in Tesla's bonds was out of the money at the time of issuance; this is usually the case.

conversion premium
The difference between the conversion price and the current stock price, divided by the current stock price.

Value of a Convertible Bond   Even though the conversion feature of the convertible bond cannot be detached like a warrant, the value of the bond can still be decomposed into the bond value and the value of the conversion feature. We discuss how this is done next.

The easiest way to illustrate convertible bond valuation is with an example. Suppose a company called Micron Origami (MO) has an outstanding convertible bond issue. The coupon rate is 7 percent and the conversion ratio is 15. There are 12 remaining coupons, and the stock is trading for $68.

straight bond value
The value a convertible bond would have if it could not be converted into common stock.

Straight Bond Value   The **straight bond value** is what the convertible bond would sell for if it could not be converted into common stock. This value will depend on the general level of interest rates on debentures and on the default risk of the issuer.

Suppose straight debentures issued by MO are rated B, and B-rated bonds are priced to yield 8 percent. We can determine the straight bond value of MO convertible bonds by discounting the $35 semiannual coupon payments and maturity value at 8 percent, just as we did in Chapter 7:

$$\text{Straight bond value} = \$35 \times (1 - 1/1.04^{12})/.04 + \$1,000/1.04^{12}$$
$$= \$328.48 + 624.60$$
$$= \$953.07$$

---

[4] Any dividends paid are, of course, not tax deductible for the corporation. Interest paid on a convertible bond is tax deductible.

The straight bond value of a convertible bond is a minimum value in the sense that the bond is always worth at least this amount. As we discuss next, it will usually be worth more.

Conversion Value   The **conversion value** of a convertible bond is what the bond would be worth if it were immediately converted into common stock. We compare this value by multiplying the current price of the stock by the number of shares that will be received when the bond is converted.

Each MO convertible bond can be converted into 15 shares of MO common stock. MO common was selling for $68. The conversion value was $15 \times \$68 = \$1,020$.

A convertible cannot sell for less than its conversion value, or an arbitrage opportunity exists. If MO's convertible had sold for less than $1,020, investors would have bought the bonds, converted them into common stock, and sold the stock. The arbitrage profit would have been the difference between the value of the stock and the bond's conversion value.

Floor Value   As we have seen, convertible bonds have two *floor values*: the straight bond value and the conversion value. The minimum value of a convertible bond is given by the greater of these two values. For the MO issue, the conversion value is $1,020 and the straight bond value is $953.07. At a minimum, this bond is worth $1,020.

Figure 24.3 plots the minimum value of a convertible bond against the value of the stock. The conversion value is determined by the value of the firm's underlying common stock. As the value of the common stock rises and falls, the conversion value rises and falls with it. If the value of MO's common stock increases by $1, the conversion value of its convertible bonds will increase by $15.

In Figure 24.3, we have implicitly assumed that the convertible bond is default-free. In this case, the straight bond value does not depend on the stock price, so it is plotted as a horizontal line. Given the straight bond value, the minimum value of the convertible depends on the value of the stock. When the stock price is low, the minimum value of a convertible is most significantly influenced by the underlying value as straight debt. When

conversion value
The value a convertible bond would have if it were to be immediately converted into common stock.

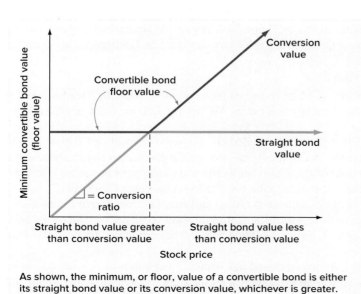

FIGURE 24.3

Minimum Value of a Convertible Bond versus the Value of the Stock for a Given Interest Rate

As shown, the minimum, or floor, value of a convertible bond is either its straight bond value or its conversion value, whichever is greater.

FIGURE 24.4

Value of a Convertible Bond versus the Value of the Stock for a Given Interest Rate

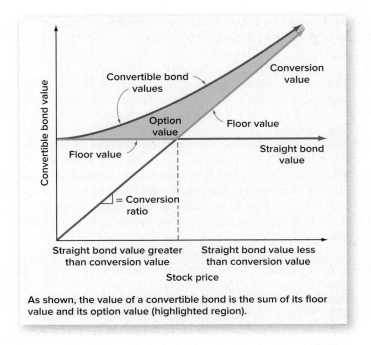

As shown, the value of a convertible bond is the sum of its floor value and its option value (highlighted region).

the value of the firm is very high, the value of a convertible bond is mostly determined by the underlying conversion value. This is also illustrated in Figure 24.3.

Option Value   The value of a convertible bond will always exceed the straight bond value and the conversion value unless the firm is in default or the bondholders are forced to convert. The reason is that holders of convertibles do not have to convert immediately. Instead, by waiting, they can take advantage of whichever is greater in the future, the straight bond value or the conversion value.

This option to wait has value, and it raises the value of the convertible bond over its floor value. The total value of the convertible is equal to the sum of the floor value and the option value. This is illustrated in Figure 24.4. Notice the similarity between this picture and the representation of the value of a call option in Figure 24.2, referenced in our earlier discussion.

OTHER OPTIONS

We've discussed two of the more common optionlike securities: warrants and convertibles. Options appear in many other places. We briefly describe a few in this section.

The Call Provision on a Bond   As we discussed in Chapter 7, most corporate bonds are callable. A call provision allows a corporation to buy the bonds at a fixed price for a fixed period of time. In other words, the corporation has a call option on the bonds. The cost of the call feature to the corporation is the cost of the option.

Convertible bonds are almost always callable. This means that a convertible bond is really a package of three securities: A straight bond, a call option held by the bondholder (the conversion feature), and a call option held by the corporation (the call provision).

Put Bonds   As we discussed in Chapter 7, put bonds are a relatively new innovation. Recall that such a bond gives the owner the right to force the issuer to buy the bond back at a fixed price for a fixed time. We now recognize that such a bond is a combination of a straight bond and a put option—hence the name.

A given bond can have a number of embedded options. One popular type of bond is a LYON, which stands for "liquid yield option note." A LYON is a callable, putable, convertible, pure discount bond. It is a package of a pure discount bond, two call options, and a put option.

Insurance and Loan Guarantees   Insurance of one kind or another is a financial feature of everyday life. Most of the time, having insurance is like having a put option. Suppose you have $1 million in fire insurance on an office building. One night your building burns down, which reduces its value to nothing. In this case, you will effectively exercise your put option and force the insurer to pay you $1 million for something worth very little.

Loan guarantees are a form of insurance. If you lend money to someone and they default, then, with a guaranteed loan, you can collect from someone else, often the government. When you lend money to a commercial bank (by making a deposit), your loan is guaranteed (up to $250,000) by the government.

In two particularly well-known cases of loan guarantees, Lockheed (now Lockheed Martin) Corporation (in 1971) and Chrysler Corporation (in 1980) were saved from impending financial doom when the U.S. government came to the rescue by agreeing to guarantee new loans. Under the guarantees, if Lockheed or Chrysler had defaulted, the lenders could have obtained the full value of their claims from the U.S. government. From the lenders' point of view, the loans were as risk-free as Treasury bonds. These guarantees enabled Lockheed and Chrysler to borrow large amounts of cash and get through difficult times.

Loan guarantees are not cost-free. The U.S. government, with a loan guarantee, has provided a put option to the holders of risky bonds. The value of the put option is the cost of the loan guarantee. This point was made clear by the collapse of the U.S. savings and loan industry in the early 1980s. The final cost to U.S. taxpayers of making good on the guaranteed deposits in these institutions was a staggering $150 billion.

In more recent times, following the September 11, 2001, terrorist attacks, Congress established the Air Transportation Stabilization Board (ATSB). The ATSB was authorized to issue up to $10 billion in loan guarantees to U.S. air carriers that suffered losses as a result of the attacks. By mid-2004, $1.56 billion in guarantees had been issued to six borrowers. Interestingly, recipients of loan guarantees were required to compensate the government for the risk being borne by the taxpayers. This compensation came in the form of cash fees and warrants to buy stock. These warrants represented between 10 and 33 percent of each company's equity. Because of recoveries (and subsequent stock price increases) at some borrowers, the ATSB's warrant portfolio became quite valuable. According to the U.S. Treasury Department, the government earned just under $350 million from fees and stock sales.

Concept Questions

24.7a   How are warrants and call options different?
24.7b   What is the minimum value of a convertible bond?
24.7c   Explain how car insurance acts like a put option.
24.7d   Explain why U.S. government loan guarantees are not free.

24.8 Summary and Conclusions

This chapter has described the basics of option valuation and discussed optionlike corporate securities:

1. Options are contracts giving the right, but not the obligation, to buy and sell underlying assets at a fixed price during a specified period. The most familiar options are puts and calls involving shares of stock. These options give the holder the right, but not the obligation, to sell (the put option) or buy (the call option) shares of common stock at a given price.

    As we discussed, the value of any option depends on only five factors:

    a. The price of the underlying asset.

    b. The exercise price.

    c. The expiration date.

    d. The interest rate on risk-free bonds.

    e. The volatility of the underlying asset's value.

2. Companies have begun to use employee stock options (ESOs) in rapidly growing numbers. Such options are similar to call options and serve to motivate employees to boost stock prices. ESOs are also an important form of compensation for many workers, particularly at more senior management levels.

3. Almost all capital budgeting proposals can be viewed as real options. Also, projects and operations contain implicit options, such as the option to expand, the option to abandon, and the option to suspend or contract operations.

4. A warrant gives the holder the right to buy shares of common stock directly from the company at a fixed exercise price for a given period of time. Typically, warrants are issued in a package with bonds. Afterwards, they often can be detached and traded separately.

5. A convertible bond is a combination of a straight bond and a call option. The holder can give up the bond in exchange for a fixed number of shares of stock. The minimum value of a convertible bond is given by its straight bond value or its conversion value, whichever is greater.

6. Many other corporate securities have option features. Bonds with call provisions, bonds with put provisions, and bonds backed by a loan guarantee are just a few examples.

CONNECT TO FINANCE

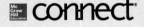 Do you use *Connect Finance* to practice what you have learned? If you don't, you should—we can help you master the topics presented in this material. Log on to connect.mheducation.com to learn more!

Can you answer the following *Connect* Quiz questions?

Section 24.1 Steve sold a put option when the option premium was $1.20. What is Steve's total profit if the exercise price was $15 and the option was never exercised?

Section 24.2 The value of a call option is equal to the _____.

Section 24.4 What is a "restruck" employee stock option?

CHAPTER REVIEW AND SELF-TEST PROBLEMS

24.1   Value of a Call Option   Stock in the Nantucket Corporation is currently selling for $25 per share. In one year, the price will be either $20 or $30. T-bills with one year to maturity are paying 10 percent. What is the value of a call option with a $20 exercise price? A $26 exercise price?

24.2   Convertible Bonds   Old Cycle Corporation (OCC), publisher of *Ancient Iron* magazine, has a $1,000 par value convertible bond issue that is currently selling in the market for $950. Each bond can be exchanged for 100 shares of stock at the holder's option.

The bond has a 7 percent coupon, payable annually, and it will mature in 10 years. OCC's debt is BBB-rated. Debt with this rating is priced to yield 12 percent. Stock in OCC is trading at $7 per share.

What is the conversion ratio on this bond? The conversion price? The conversion premium? What is the floor value of the bond? What is its option value?

ANSWERS TO CHAPTER REVIEW AND SELF-TEST PROBLEMS

24.1   With a $20 exercise price, the option can't finish out of the money (it can finish "at the money" if the stock price is $20). We can replicate the value of the stock by investing the present value of $20 in T-bills and buying one call option. Buying the T-bill will cost $20/1.1 = $18.18.

If the stock ends up at $20, the call option will be worth zero and the T-bill will pay $20. If the stock ends up at $30, the T-bill will again pay $20, and the option will be worth $30 − 20 = $10, so the package will be worth $30. Because the T-bill–call option combination exactly duplicates the payoff on the stock, it has to be worth $25 or arbitrage is possible. Using the notation from the chapter, we can calculate the value of the call option:

$$S_0 = C_0 + E/(1 + R_f)$$
$$\$25 = C_0 + \$18.18$$
$$C_0 = \$6.82$$

With the $26 exercise price, we start by investing the present value of the lower stock price in T-bills. This guarantees us $20 when the stock price is $20. If the stock price is $30, then the option is worth $30 − 26 = $4. We have $20 from our T-bill, so we need $10 from the options to match the stock. Because each option is worth $4 in this case, we need to buy $10/$4 = 2.5 call options. Notice that the difference in the possible stock prices (ΔS) is $10 and the difference in the possible option prices (ΔC) is $4, so $\Delta S/\Delta C = 2.5$.

To complete the calculation, we note that the present value of the $20 plus 2.5 call options has to be $25 to prevent arbitrage, so:

$$\$25 = 2.5 \times C_0 + \$20/1.1$$
$$C_0 = \$6.82/2.5$$
$$= \$2.73$$

24.2   Because each bond can be exchanged for 100 shares, the conversion ratio is 100. The conversion price is the face value of the bond ($1,000) divided by the conversion ratio, or $1,000/100 = $10. The conversion premium is the percentage difference between the current price and the conversion price, or ($10 − 7)/ $7 = .43, or 43%.

The floor value of the bond is the greater of its straight bond value or its conversion value. Its conversion value is what the bond is worth if it is immediately converted: $100 \times \$7 = \$700$. The straight bond value is what the bond would be worth if it were not convertible. The annual coupon is $70, and the bond matures in 10 years. At a 12 percent required return, the straight bond value is:

$$\text{Straight bond value} = \$70 \times (1 - 1/1.12^{10})/.12 + \$1,000/1.12^{10}$$
$$= \$395.52 + 321.97$$
$$= \$717.49$$

This exceeds the conversion value, so the floor value of the bond is $717.49. Finally, the option value is the value of the convertible in excess of its floor value. Because the bond is selling for $950, the option value is:

$$\text{Option value} = \$950 - 717.49$$
$$= \$232.51$$

CONCEPTS REVIEW AND CRITICAL THINKING QUESTIONS

1. **Options [LO1]** What is a call option? A put option? Under what circumstances might you want to buy each? Which one has greater *potential* profit? Why?

2. **Options [LO1]** Complete the following sentence for each of these investors:
    a. A buyer of call options.
    b. A buyer of put options.
    c. A seller (writer) of call options.
    d. A seller (writer) of put options.
    "The (buyer/seller) of a (put/call) option (pays/receives) money for the (right/obligation) to (buy/sell) a specified asset at a fixed price for a fixed length of time."

3. **Intrinsic Value [LO2]** What is the intrinsic value of a call option? How do we interpret this value?

4. **Put Options [LO2]** What is the value of a put option at maturity? Based on your answer, what is the intrinsic value of a put option?

5. **Option Pricing [LO2]** You notice that shares of stock in the Patel Corporation are going for $50 per share. Call options with an exercise price of $35 per share are selling for $10. What's wrong here? Describe how you can take advantage of this mispricing if the option expires today.

6. **Options and Stock Risk [LO2]** If the risk of a stock increases, what is likely to happen to the price of call options on the stock? To the price of put options? Why?

7. **Option Rise [LO2]** True or false: The unsystematic risk of a share of stock is irrelevant in valuing the stock because it can be diversified away; therefore, it is also irrelevant for valuing a call option on the stock. Explain.

8. **Option Pricing [LO2]** Suppose a certain stock currently sells for $30 per share. If a put option and a call option are available with $30 exercise prices, which do you think will sell for more, the put or the call? Explain.

9. **Option Price and Interest Rates [LO2]** Suppose the interest rate on T-bills suddenly and unexpectedly rises. All other things being the same, what is the impact on call option values? On put option values?

10. **Contingent Liabilities** [LO4] When you take out an ordinary student loan, it is usually the case that whoever holds that loan is given a guarantee by the U.S. government, meaning that the government will make up any payments you skip. This is one example of the many loan guarantees made by the U.S. government. Such guarantees don't show up in calculations of government spending or in official deficit figures. Why not? Should they show up?

11. **Option to Abandon** [LO5] What is the option to abandon? Explain why we underestimate NPV if we ignore this option.

12. **Option to Expand** [LO5] What is the option to expand? Explain why we underestimate NPV if we ignore this option.

13. **Capital Budgeting Options** [LO5] In Chapter 10, we discussed Porsche's launch of its new Cayenne. Suppose sales of the Cayenne go extremely well and Porsche is forced to expand output to meet demand. Porsche's action in this case would be an example of exploiting what kind of option?

14. **Option to Suspend** [LO5] Natural resource extraction facilities (such as oil wells or gold mines) provide a good example of the value of the option to suspend operations. Why?

15. **Employee Stock Options** [LO3] You own stock in the Hendrix Guitar Company. The company has implemented a plan to award employee stock options. As a shareholder, does the plan benefit you? If so, what are the benefits?

QUESTIONS AND PROBLEMS

1. **Calculating Option Values** [LO2] T-bills currently yield 3.4 percent. Stock in Deadwood Manufacturing is currently selling for $58 per share. There is no possibility that the stock will be worth less than $50 per share in one year.

   BASIC
   (Questions 1–13)

   a. What is the value of a call option with a $45 exercise price? What is the intrinsic value?

   b. What is the value of a call option with a $35 exercise price? What is the intrinsic value?

   c. What is the value of a put option with a $45 exercise price? What is the intrinsic value?

2. **Understanding Option Quotes** [LO1] Use the option quote information shown here to answer the questions that follow. The stock is currently selling for $85.

Option	Expiration	Strike Price	Calls Vol.	Calls Last	Puts Vol.	Puts Last
RWJ	Mar	80	230	2.80	160	.80
	Apr	80	170	6.00	127	1.40
	Jul	80	139	8.50	43	3.90
	Oct	80	60	10.20	11	3.65

   a. Are the call options in the money? What is the intrinsic value of an RWJ Corp. call option?

   b. Are the put options in the money? What is the intrinsic value of an RWJ Corp. put option?

   c. Two of the options are clearly mispriced. Which ones? At a minimum, what should the mispriced options sell for? Explain how you could profit from the mispricing in each case.

3. **Calculating Payoffs [LO1]** Use the option quote information shown here to answer the questions that follow. The stock is currently selling for $40.

Option	Expiration	Strike Price	Calls		Puts	
			Vol.	Last	Vol.	Last
Macrosoft	Feb	38	85	2.35	37	.24
	Mar	38	61	3.15	22	.93
	May	38	22	4.87	11	2.44
	Aug	38	3	6.15	3	3.56

   a. Suppose you buy 10 contracts of the February 38 call option. How much will you pay, ignoring commissions?

   b. In part (a), suppose that Macrosoft stock is selling for $43 per share on the expiration date. How much is your options investment worth? What if the terminal stock price is $39? Explain.

   c. Suppose you buy 10 contracts of the August 38 put option. What is your maximum gain? On the expiration date, Macrosoft is selling for $32 per share. How much is your options investment worth? What is your net gain?

   d. In part (c), suppose you *sell* 10 of the August 38 put contracts. What is your net gain or loss if Macrosoft is selling for $34 at expiration? For $41? What is the break-even price—that is, the terminal stock price that results in a zero profit?

4. **Calculating Option Values [LO2]** The price of Chive Corp. stock will be either $67 or $91 at the end of the year. Call options are available with one year to expiration. T-bills currently yield 4 percent.

   a. Suppose the current price of the company's stock is $75. What is the value of the call option if the exercise price is $70 per share?

   b. Suppose the exercise price is $80 in part (a). What is the value of the call option now?

5. **Calculating Option Values [LO2]** The price of Cilantro, Inc., stock will be either $70 or $90 at the end of the year. Call options are available with one year to expiration. T-bills currently yield 6 percent.

   a. Suppose the current price of the company's stock is $80. What is the value of the call option if the exercise price is $60 per share?

   b. Suppose the exercise price is $65 in part (a). What is the value of the call option now?

6. **Using the Pricing Equation [LO2]** A one-year call option contract on Cheesy Poofs Co. stock sells for $845. In one year, the stock will be worth $64 or $81 per share. The exercise price on the call option is $70. What is the current value of the stock if the risk-free rate is 3 percent?

7. **Equity as an Option [LO4]** Rackin Pinion Corporation's assets are currently worth $1,065. In one year, they will be worth either $1,000 or $1,340. The risk-free interest rate is 3.9 percent. Suppose the company has an outstanding debt issue with a face value of $1,000.

   a. What is the value of the equity?

   b. What is the value of the debt? The interest rate on the debt?

   c. Would the value of the equity go up or down if the risk-free rate were 20 percent? Why? What does your answer illustrate?

8. **Equity as an Option** [LO4] Buckeye Industries has a bond issue with a face value of $1,000 that is coming due in one year. The value of the company's assets is currently $1,040. Urban Meyer, the CEO, believes that the assets in the company will be worth either $940 or $1,270 in a year. The going rate on one-year T-bills is 4.8 percent.

   a. What is the value of the company's equity? The value of the debt?

   b. Suppose the company can reconfigure its existing assets in such a way that the value in a year will be $850 or $1,750. If the current value of the assets is unchanged, will the stockholders favor such a move? Why or why not?

9. **Calculating Conversion Value** [LO6] A $1,000 par convertible debenture has a conversion price for common stock of $27 per share. With the common stock selling at $31, what is the conversion value of the bond?

10. **Convertible Bonds** [LO6] The following facts apply to a convertible bond making semiannual payments:

Conversion price	$37/share
Coupon rate	2.6%
Par value	$1,000
Yield on nonconvertible debentures of same quality	5%
Maturity	25 years
Market price of stock	$34/share

   a. What is the minimum price at which the convertible should sell?

   b. What accounts for the premium of the market price of a convertible bond over the total market value of the common stock into which it can be converted?

11. **Calculating Values for Convertibles** [LO6] You have been hired to value a new 30-year callable, convertible bond. The bond has a coupon rate of 2.7 percent, payable semiannually, and its face value is $1,000. The conversion price is $54, and the stock currently sells for $38.

   a. What is the minimum value of the bond? Comparable nonconvertible bonds are priced to yield 4.9 percent.

   b. What is the conversion premium for this bond?

12. **Calculating Warrant Values** [LO6] A bond with 20 detachable warrants has just been offered for sale at $1,000. The bond matures in 20 years and has an annual coupon of $24. Each warrant gives the owner the right to purchase two shares of stock in the company at $45 per share. Ordinary bonds (with no warrants) of similar quality are priced to yield 6 percent. What is the value of one warrant?

13. **Option to Wait** [LO5] Your company is deciding whether to invest in a new machine. The new machine will increase cash flow by $275,000 per year. You believe the technology used in the machine has a 10-year life; in other words, no matter when you purchase the machine, it will be obsolete 10 years from today. The machine is currently priced at $1.8 million. The cost of the machine will decline by $140,000 per year until it reaches $1.1 million, where it will remain. If your required return is 8 percent, should you purchase the machine? If so, when should you purchase it?

14. **Abandonment Value** [LO5] We are examining a new project. We expect to sell 7,100 units per year at $56 net cash flow apiece for the next 10 years. In other words,

INTERMEDIATE (Questions 14–20)

the annual cash flow is projected to be $56 \times 7,100 = \$397,600$. The relevant discount rate is 14 percent, and the initial investment required is $1,800,000.

a. What is the base-case NPV?

b. After the first year, the project can be dismantled and sold for $1,200,000. If expected sales are revised based on the first year's performance, when would it make sense to abandon the investment? In other words, at what level of expected sales would it make sense to abandon the project?

c. Explain how the $1,200,000 abandonment value can be viewed as the opportunity cost of keeping the project in one year.

15. **Abandonment** [LO5] In Problem 14, suppose you think it is likely that expected sales will be revised upward to 10,800 units if the first year is a success and revised downward to 3,900 units if the first year is not a success.

a. If success and failure are equally likely, what is the NPV of the project? Consider the possibility of abandonment in answering.

b. What is the value of the option to abandon?

16. **Abandonment and Expansion** [LO5] In Problem 15, suppose the scale of the project can be doubled in one year in the sense that twice as many units can be produced and sold. Naturally, expansion would be desirable only if the project is a success. This implies that if the project is a success, projected sales after expansion will be 21,600. Again assuming that success and failure are equally likely, what is the NPV of the project? Note that abandonment is still an option if the project is a failure. What is the value of the option to expand?

17. **Intuition and Option Value** [LO2] Suppose a share of stock sells for $63. The risk-free rate is 5 percent, and the stock price in one year will be either $70 or $80.

a. What is the value of a call option with an exercise price of $70?

b. What's wrong here? What would you do?

18. **Intuition and Convertibles** [LO6] Which of the following two sets of relationships, at time of issuance for convertible bonds, is more typical? Why?

	A	B
Offering price of bond	$ 800	$1,000
Bond value (straight debt)	800	950
Conversion value	1,000	900

19. **Convertible Calculations** [LO6] Campbell, Inc., has a $1,000 face value convertible bond issue that is currently selling in the market for $960. Each bond is exchangeable at any time for 18 shares of the company's stock. The convertible bond has a 4.9 percent coupon, payable semiannually. Similar nonconvertible bonds are priced to yield 7.4 percent. The bond matures in 20 years. Stock in the company sells for $45 per share.

a. What are the conversion ratio, conversion price, and conversion premium?

b. What is the straight bond value? The conversion value?

c. In part (b), what would the stock price have to be for the conversion value and the straight bond value to be equal?

d. What is the option value of the bond?

20. **Abandonment Decisions** [LO5] Liberty Products, Inc., is considering a new product launch. The firm expects to have annual operating cash flow of $5.3 million for the next eight years. The company uses a discount rate of 11 percent for new product

launches. The initial investment is $23 million. Assume that the project has no salvage value at the end of its economic life.

a. What is the NPV of the new product?

b. After the first year, the project can be dismantled and sold for $18 million after taxes. If the estimates of remaining cash flows are revised based on the first year's experience, at what level of expected cash flows does it make sense to abandon the project?

21. **Pricing Convertibles** [LO6] You have been hired to value a new 25-year callable, convertible bond. The bond has a coupon rate of 2.3 percent, payable annually. The conversion price is $68, and the stock currently sells for $27.83. The stock price is expected to grow at 11 percent per year. The bond is callable at $1,200, but, based on prior experience, it won't be called unless the conversion value is $1,300. The required return on this bond is 8 percent. What value would you assign?

CHALLENGE
(Questions 21–22)

22. **Abandonment Decisions** [LO5] Consider the following project of Hand Clapper, Inc. The company is considering a four-year project to manufacture clap-command garage door openers. This project requires an initial investment of $14 million that will be depreciated straight-line to zero over the project's life. An initial investment in net working capital of $900,000 is required to support spare parts inventory; this cost is fully recoverable whenever the project ends. The company believes it can generate $10.1 million in pretax revenues with $3.8 million in total pretax operating costs. The tax rate is 38 percent and the discount rate is 13 percent. The market value of the equipment over the life of the project is as follows:

Year	Market Value (millions)
1	$8.90
2	7.70
3	5.30
4	.00

a. Assuming the company operates this project for four years, what is the NPV?

b. Now compute the project NPV assuming the project is abandoned after only one year, after two years, and after three years. What economic life for this project maximizes its value to the firm? What does this problem tell you about not considering abandonment possibilities when evaluating projects?

MINICASE

S&S Air's Convertible Bond

S&S Air is preparing its first public securities offering. In consultation with Renata Harper of underwriter Raines and Warren, Chris Guthrie decided that a convertible bond with a 20-year maturity was the way to go. He met the owners, Mark and Todd, and presented his analysis of the convertible bond issue. Because the company is not publicly traded, Chris looked at comparable publicly traded companies and determined that the average PE ratio for the industry is 14.5. Earnings per share for the company are $1.30. With this in mind, Chris has suggested a conversion price of $25 per share.

Several days later, Todd, Mark, and Chris met again to discuss the potential bond issue. Both Todd and Mark had researched convertible bonds and they had some questions for Chris. Todd began by asking Chris if the convertible bond issue would have a lower coupon rate than a comparable bond without a conversion feature. Chris informed him that a par value convertible bond issue would require a 4 percent coupon rate with a conversion value of $800, while a plain vanilla bond would have a 7 percent coupon rate. Todd nodded in agreement and explained that the convertible bonds are a win-win form of financing. He further explained that if the value of the company stock did not rise above the conversion price, the company would be issuing debt at a cost below the market rate (4 percent instead of 7 percent). If the company's stock did rise to the conversion value, on the other hand, the company would be effectively issuing stock at a price above the current value.

Mark immediately disagreed, saying that convertible bonds are a no-win form of financing. He argued that if the value of the company stock were to rise to more than $25, the company would be forced to sell stock at the conversion price. This means the new shareholders—in other words, those who bought the convertible bonds—would benefit from a bargain price. Put another way, if the company prospers, it would have been better to have issued straight debt so that the gains would not be shared.

Chris has gone back to Renata for help. As Renata's assistant, you've been asked to prepare another memo answering the following questions.

QUESTIONS

1. Why do you think Chris is suggesting a conversion price of $25? Given that the company is not publicly traded, does it even make sense to talk about a conversion price?

2. Is there anything wrong with Todd's argument that it is cheaper to issue a bond with a convertible feature because the required coupon is lower?

3. Is there anything wrong with Mark's argument that a convertible bond is a bad idea because it allows new shareholders to participate in gains made by the company?

4. How can you reconcile the arguments made by Todd and Mark?

5. In the course of the debate, a question comes up concerning whether or not the bonds should have an ordinary (not make-whole) call feature. Chris confuses everybody by stating, "The call feature lets S&S Air force conversion, thereby minimizing the problem that Mark has identified." What is he talking about? Is he making sense?

Option Valuation

ON FEBRUARY 20, 2017, the closing stock prices for Walmart, rural retail store Tractor Supply Company, and medical technology company Inogen were $71.74, $71.32, and $69.11, respectively. Each company had a call option trading on the Chicago Board Options Exchange with a $70 strike price and an expiration date of April 21, 2017, 60 days away. You might expect that the prices on these call options would be similar, but they weren't. The Walmart options sold for $1.39, Tractor Supply options traded at $2.20, and Inogen options traded at $5.00. Why would options on these three similarly priced stocks be priced so differently when the strike prices and the time to expiration were exactly the same? If you go back to our earlier chapter about options, the volatility of the underlying stock is an important determinant of an option's value, and, in fact, these three stocks have very different volatilities. In this chapter, we explore this issue—and many others—in much greater depth using the Nobel Prize–winning Black-Scholes option pricing model.

Learning Objectives

After studying this chapter, you should be able to:

LO1 Describe the relationship between stock prices, call prices, and put prices using put-call parity.

LO2 Describe the famous Black-Scholes option pricing model and its uses.

LO3 Explain how the five factors in the Black-Scholes formula affect the value of an option.

LO4 Demonstrate how the Black-Scholes model can be used to value the debt and equity of a firm.

LO5 Show how option valuation can result in some surprising conclusions regarding mergers and capital budgeting decisions.

©by_adril/iStockPhotoGettyImages

For updates on the latest happenings in finance, visit fundamentalsofcorporatefinance.blogspot.com.

In an earlier chapter, we explored the basics of options, but we didn't discuss how to value them in much detail. Our goal in this chapter is to take this next step and examine how to actually estimate what an option is worth. To do this, we will explore two very famous results: The put-call parity condition and the Black-Scholes option pricing model.

An understanding of option valuation lets us illustrate and explore some very important ideas in corporate finance. We will show why certain types of mergers are a bad idea. We will also examine some conflicts between bondholder and stockholder interests. We will even provide some examples under which companies have an incentive to take negative NPV projects. In each case, option-related effects underlie the issue.

25.1 Put-Call Parity

From our earlier discussions, recall that the purchaser of a call option pays for the right, but not the obligation, to buy an asset for a fixed time at a fixed price. The purchaser of a put option pays for the right to sell an asset for a fixed time at a fixed price. The fixed price is called the *exercise* or *strike* price.

PROTECTIVE PUTS

The Options Industry Council has a web page featuring a lot of educational materials. See **www.optionseducation.org**.

protective put
The purchase of stock and a put option on the stock to limit the downside risk associated with the stock.

Consider the following investment strategy. Today, you buy one share of Microsoft for $110. At the same time, you also buy one put option with a $105 strike price. The put option has a life of one year, and the premium is $5. Your total investment is $115, and your plan is to hold this investment for one year and then sell out.[1]

What have you accomplished here? To answer, we created Table 25.1, which shows your gains and losses one year from now for different stock prices. In the table, notice that the worst thing that ever happens to you is that the value of your investment falls to $105. The reason is that if Microsoft's stock price is below $105 per share one year from now, you will exercise your put option and sell your stock for the strike price of $105; so that is the least you can possibly receive.

By purchasing the put option, you have limited your downside risk to a maximum potential loss of $10 (= $115 − 105). This particular strategy of buying a stock and also buying a put on the stock is called a **protective put** strategy because it protects you against losses beyond a certain point. Notice that the put option acts as a kind of insurance policy that pays off in the event that an asset you own (the stock) declines in value.

In our example, we picked a strike price of $105. You could have picked a higher strike price and limited your downside risk to even less. Of course, a higher strike price would mean that you would have to pay more for the put option; so there is a trade-off between the amount of protection and the cost of that protection.

AN ALTERNATIVE STRATEGY

Now consider a different strategy. You take your $115 and purchase a one-year *call* option on Microsoft with a strike price of $105. The premium is $15. That leaves you with

TABLE 25.1

Gains and Losses in One Year. Original investment: Purchase one share at $110 plus a one-year put option with a strike price of $105 for $5. Total cost is $115.

Stock Price in One Year	Value of Put Option (Strike Price = $105)	Combined Value	Total Gain or Loss (Combined Value Less $115)
$125	$ 0	$125	$ 10
120	0	120	5
115	0	115	0
110	0	110	−5
105	0	105	−10
100	5	105	−10
95	10	105	−10
90	15	105	−10

[1] Of course, in reality, you can't buy an option on one share, so you would need to buy 100 shares of Microsoft and one put contract (at a minimum) to actually implement this strategy. We're explaining the calculations on a per-share basis.

Stock Price in One Year	Value of Call Option (Strike Price = $105)	Value of Risk-Free Asset	Combined Value	Total Gain or Loss (Combined Value Less $115)
$125	$ 20	$105	$125	$ 10
120	15	105	120	5
115	10	105	115	0
110	5	105	110	−5
105	0	105	105	−10
100	0	105	105	−10
95	0	105	105	−10
90	0	105	105	−10

TABLE 25.2

Gains and Losses in One Year. Original investment: Purchase a one-year call option with a strike price of $105 for $15. Invest $100 in a risk-free asset paying 5 percent. Total cost is $115.

$100, which you decide to invest in a riskless asset such as a T-bill. The risk-free rate is 5 percent.

What does this strategy accomplish? Once again, we will create a table to illustrate your gains and losses. Notice that in Table 25.2 your $100 grows to $105 based on a 5 percent interest rate. If you compare Table 25.2 to Table 25.1, you will make an interesting discovery. No matter what the stock price is one year from now, the two strategies *always* have the same value in one year!

The fact that the two strategies always have exactly the same value in one year explains why they have the same cost today. If one of these strategies were cheaper than the other today, there would be an arbitrage opportunity involving buying the one that's cheaper and simultaneously selling the one that's more expensive.

THE RESULT

Our example illustrates a very important pricing relationship. What it shows is that a protective put strategy can be exactly duplicated by a combination of a call option (with the same strike price as the put option) and a riskless investment. In our example, notice that the investment in the riskless asset, $100, is exactly equal to the present value of the strike price on the option calculated at the risk-free rate: $105/1.05 = $100.

Putting it all together, what we have discovered is the **put-call parity (PCP)** condition. It says that:

put-call parity (PCP)
The relationship between the prices of the underlying stock, a call option, a put option, and a riskless asset.

Share of stock + put option = Present value of strike price + call option

In symbols, we can write:

$S + P = PV(E) + C$

where S and P are stock and put values, respectively, and $PV(E)$ and C are the present value of the exercise price and the value of the call option, respectively.

Because the present value of the exercise price is calculated using the risk-free rate, you can think of it as the price of a risk-free, pure discount instrument (such as a T-bill) with a face value equal to the strike price. In our experience, the easiest way to remember the PCP condition is to remember that "stock plus put equals T-bill plus call."

The PCP condition is an algebraic expression, meaning that it can be rearranged. Suppose we know that the risk-free rate is .5 percent per month. A call with a strike price of

$40 sells for $4, and a put with the same strike price sells for $3. Both have a three-month maturity. What's the stock price?

To answer, we use the PCP condition to solve for the stock price:

$$S = PV(E) + C - P$$
$$= \$40/1.005^3 + \$4 - \$3$$
$$= \$40.41$$

25.3

The PCP condition really says that between a riskless asset (like a T-bill), a call option, a put option, and a share of stock, we can always figure out the price of any one of the four given the prices of the other three.

EXAMPLE 25.1   **Put-Call Parity**

Suppose a share of stock sells for $60. A six-month call option with a $70 strike price sells for $2. The risk-free rate is .4 percent per month. What's the price of a six-month put option with a $70 strike?

Using the PCP condition to solve for the put price, we get:

$$P = PV(E) + C - S$$
$$= \$70/1.004^6 + \$2 - \$60$$
$$= \$10.34$$

Notice that, in this example, the put option is worth a lot more than the call. Why?

EXAMPLE 25.2   **More Parity**

Suppose a share of stock sells for $110. A one-year, at-the-money call option sells for $15. An at-the-money put with the same maturity sells for $5. Can you create a risk-free investment by combining these three instruments? How? What's the risk-free rate?

Here, we can use the PCP condition to solve for the present value of the strike price:

$$PV(E) = S + P - C$$
$$= \$110 + 5 - 15$$
$$= \$100$$

The present value of the strike price is $100. Notice that because the options are at the money, the strike is the same as the stock price, $110. So, if you put $100 in a riskless investment today and receive $110 in one year, the implied risk-free rate is obviously 10 percent.

CONTINUOUS COMPOUNDING: A REFRESHER COURSE

Back in Chapter 6, we saw that the effective annual interest rate (EAR) on an investment depends on compounding frequency. We also saw that, in the extreme, compounding can occur every instant, or continuously. So, as a quick refresher, suppose you invest $100 at a rate of 6 percent per year compounded continuously. How much will you have in one year? How about in two years?

In Chapter 6, we saw that the EAR with continuous compounding is:

$$EAR = e^q - 1$$

where q is the quoted rate (6 percent, or .06, in this case) and e is the number 2.71828 …, the base of the natural logarithms. Plugging in the numbers, we get:

$$\begin{aligned} \text{EAR} &= e^q - 1 \\ &= 2.71828^{.06} - 1 \\ &= .06184 \end{aligned}$$

or about 6.2 percent. Notice that most calculators have a key labeled "e^x," so doing this calculation is a matter of entering .06 and then pressing this key. With an EAR of 6.184 percent, your $100 investment will grow to $106.18 in one year. In two years, it will grow to:

$$\begin{aligned} \text{Future value} &= \$100 \times 1.06184^2 \\ &= \$100 \times 1.1275 \\ &= \$112.75 \end{aligned}$$

When we move into option valuation, continuous compounding shows up quite a bit, and it helps to have some shortcuts. In our examples here, we first converted the continuously compounded rate to an EAR and then did our calculations. It turns out that we don't need to do the conversion at all. Instead, we can calculate present and future values directly. In particular, the future value of $1 for t periods at a continuously compounded rate of R per period is:

$$\text{Future value} = \$1 \times e^{Rt}$$

Looking back at the problem we just solved, the future value of $100 in two years at a continuously compounded rate of 6 percent is:

$$\begin{aligned} \text{Future value} &= \$100 \times e^{.06(2)} \\ &= \$100 \times 2.71828^{.12} \\ &= \$100 \times 1.1275 \\ &= \$112.75 \end{aligned}$$

which is exactly what we had before.

Similarly, we can calculate the present value of $1 to be received in t periods at a continuously compounded rate of R per period as follows:

$$\text{Present value} = \$1 \times e^{-Rt}$$

So, if we want the present value of $15,000 to be received in five years at 8 percent compounded continuously, we would calculate:

$$\begin{aligned} \text{Present value} &= \$15,000 \times e^{-.08(5)} \\ &= \$15,000 \times 2.71828^{-.4} \\ &= \$15,000 \times .67032 \\ &= \$10,054.80 \end{aligned}$$

Continuous Compounding   EXAMPLE 25.3

What is the present value of $500 to be received in six months if the discount rate is 9 percent per year, compounded continuously?

In this case, notice that the number of periods is equal to one-half because six months is half of a year. The present value is:

$$\begin{aligned} \text{Present value} &= \$500 \times e^{-.09(1/2)} \\ &= \$500 \times 2.71828^{-.045} \\ &= \$500 \times .956 \\ &= \$478 \end{aligned}$$

Looking back at our PCP condition, we wrote:

$$S + P = PV(E) + C$$

If we assume that R is the continuously compounded risk-free rate per year, then we could write this as:

$$\mathbf{S + P = E \times e^{-Rt} + C}$$ **25.4**

where t is the time to maturity (in years) on the options.

Finally, suppose we are given an EAR and we need to convert it to a continuously compounded rate. If the risk-free rate is 8 percent per year compounded annually, what's the continuously compounded risk-free rate?

Going back to our first formula, we had:

$$EAR = e^q - 1$$

Now, we need to solve for q, the continuously compounded rate. Plugging in the numbers, we have:

$$.08 = e^q - 1$$
$$e^q = 1.08$$

Taking the natural logarithm (ln) of both sides to solve for q, we get:

$$\ln(e^q) = \ln(1.08)$$
$$q = .07696$$

or about 7.7 percent. Notice that most calculators have a button labeled "ln", so doing this calculation involves entering 1.08 and then pressing this key.

EXAMPLE 25.4 | **Even More Parity**

Suppose a share of stock sells for $30. A three-month call option with a $25 strike sells for $7. A three-month put with the same strike price sells for $1. What's the continuously compounded risk-free rate?

We need to plug the relevant numbers into the PCP condition:

$$S + P = E \times e^{-Rt} + C$$
$$\$30 + 1 = \$25 \times e^{-R(1/4)} + \$7$$

Notice that we used one-fourth for the number of years because three months is a quarter of a year. We now need to solve for R:

$$\$24 = \$25 \times e^{-R(1/4)}$$
$$.96 = e^{-R(1/4)}$$
$$\ln(.96) = \ln(e^{-R(1/4)})$$
$$-.0408 = -R(1/4)$$
$$R = .1633, \text{ or } 16.33\%$$

This is about 16.33 percent, which is a very high risk-free rate!

Concept Questions

25.1a   What is a protective put strategy?

25.1b   What strategy exactly duplicates a protective put?

The Black-Scholes Option Pricing Model   **25.2**

We're now in a position to discuss one of the most celebrated results in modern finance, the Black-Scholes option pricing model (OPM). The OPM was an important discovery and the basis for the Nobel Prize in Economics in 1997. The underlying development of the Black-Scholes OPM is fairly complex, so we will focus only on the main result and how to use it.

THE CALL OPTION PRICING FORMULA

Black and Scholes showed that the value of a European-style call option on a non-dividend-paying stock, C, can be written as follows:

$$C = S \times N(d_1) - E \times e^{-Rt} \times N(d_2)$$

25.5

where S, E, and e^{-Rt} are as we previously defined them and $N(d_1)$ and $N(d_2)$ are probabilities that must be calculated. More specifically, $N(d_1)$ is the probability that a standardized, normally distributed random variable (widely known as a "z" variable) is less than or equal to d_1, and $N(d_2)$ is the probability of a value less than or equal to d_2. Determining these probabilities requires a table such as Table 25.3.

To illustrate, suppose we are given the following information:

$S = \$100$
$E = \$90$
$R = 4\%$ per year, continuously compounded
$d_1 = .60$
$d_2 = .30$
$t = 9$ months

Based on this information, what is the value of the call option, C?

To answer, we need to determine $N(d_1)$ and $N(d_2)$. In Table 25.3, we first find the row corresponding to a d of .60. The corresponding probability $N(d)$ is .7257, so this is $N(d_1)$. For d_2, the associated probability $N(d_2)$ is .6179. Using the Black-Scholes OPM, we calculate that the value of the call option is:

$$
\begin{aligned}
C &= S \times N(d_1) - E \times e^{-Rt} \times N(d_2) \\
&= \$100 \times .7257 - \$90 \times e^{-.04(3/4)} \times .6179 \\
&= \$18.60
\end{aligned}
$$

Notice that t, the time to expiration, is 9 months, which is 9/12, or 3/4 of one year.

As this example illustrates, if we are given values for d_1 and d_2 (and the table), then using the Black-Scholes model is not difficult. Generally, we would not be given the values of d_1 and d_2, and we would need to calculate them. This requires a little extra effort. The values for d_1 and d_2 for the Black-Scholes OPM are given by:

$$d_1 = [\ln(S/E) + (R + \sigma^2/2) \times t]/(\sigma \times \sqrt{t})$$
$$d_2 = d_1 - \sigma \times \sqrt{t}$$

25.6

In these expressions, σ is the standard deviation of the rate of return on the underlying asset. Also, $\ln(S/E)$ is the natural logarithm of the current stock price divided by the exercise price.

TABLE 25.3   Cumulative Normal Distribution

d	N(d)	d	N(d)	d	N(d)	d	N(d)	d	N(d)	d	N(d)
−3.00	.0013	−1.58	.0571	−.76	.2236	.06	.5239	.86	.8051	1.66	.9515
−2.95	.0016	−1.56	.0594	−.74	.2297	.08	.5319	.88	.8106	1.68	.9535
−2.90	.0019	−1.54	.0618	−.72	.2358	.10	.5398	.90	.8159	1.70	.9554
−2.85	.0022	−1.52	.0643	−.70	.2420	.12	.5478	.92	.8212	1.72	.9573
−2.80	.0026	−1.50	.0668	−.68	.2483	.14	.5557	.94	.8264	1.74	.9591
−2.75	.0030	−1.48	.0694	−.66	.2546	.16	.5636	.96	.8315	1.76	.9608
−2.70	.0035	−1.46	.0721	−.64	.2611	.18	.5714	.98	.8365	1.78	.9625
−2.65	.0040	−1.44	.0749	−.62	.2676	.20	.5793	1.00	.8413	1.80	.9641
−2.60	.0047	−1.42	.0778	−.60	.2743	.22	.5871	1.02	.8461	1.82	.9656
−2.55	.0054	−1.40	.0808	−.58	.2810	.24	.5948	1.04	.8508	1.84	.9671
−2.50	.0062	−1.38	.0838	−.56	.2877	.26	.6026	1.06	.8554	1.86	.9686
−2.45	.0071	−1.36	.0869	−.54	.2946	.28	.6103	1.08	.8599	1.88	.9699
−2.40	.0082	−1.34	.0901	−.52	.3015	.30	.6179	1.10	.8643	1.90	.9713
−2.35	.0094	−1.32	.0934	−.50	.3085	.32	.6255	1.12	.8686	1.92	.9726
−2.30	.0107	−1.30	.0968	−.48	.3156	.34	.6331	1.14	.8729	1.94	.9738
−2.25	.0122	−1.28	.1003	−.46	.3228	.36	.6406	1.16	.8770	1.96	.9750
−2.20	.0139	−1.26	.1038	−.44	.3300	.38	.6480	1.18	.8810	1.98	.9761
−2.15	.0158	−1.24	.1075	−.42	.3372	.40	.6554	1.20	.8849	2.00	.9772
−2.10	.0179	−1.22	.1112	−.40	.3446	.42	.6628	1.22	.8888	2.05	.9798
−2.05	.0202	−1.20	.1151	−.38	.3520	.44	.6700	1.24	.8925	2.10	.9821
−2.00	.0228	−1.18	.1190	−.36	.3594	.46	.6772	1.26	.8962	2.15	.9842
−1.98	.0239	−1.16	.1230	−.34	.3669	.48	.6844	1.28	.8997	2.20	.9861
−1.96	.0250	−1.14	.1271	−.32	.3745	.50	.6915	1.30	.9032	2.25	.9878
−1.94	.0262	−1.12	.1314	−.30	.3821	.52	.6985	1.32	.9066	2.30	.9893
−1.92	.0274	−1.10	.1357	−.28	.3897	.54	.7054	1.34	.9099	2.35	.9906
−1.90	.0287	−1.08	.1401	−.26	.3974	.56	.7123	1.36	.9131	2.40	.9918
−1.88	.0301	−1.06	.1446	−.24	.4052	.58	.7190	1.38	.9162	2.45	.9929
−1.86	.0314	−1.04	.1492	−.22	.4129	.60	.7257	1.40	.9192	2.50	.9938
−1.84	.0329	−1.02	.1539	−.20	.4207	.62	.7324	1.42	.9222	2.55	.9946
−1.82	.0344	−1.00	.1587	−.18	.4286	.64	.7389	1.44	.9251	2.60	.9953
−1.80	.0359	−.98	.1635	−.16	.4364	.66	.7454	1.46	.9279	2.65	.9960
−1.78	.0375	−.96	.1685	−.14	.4443	.68	.7518	1.48	.9306	2.70	.9965
−1.76	.0392	−.94	.1736	−.12	.4522	.70	.7580	1.50	.9332	2.75	.9970
−1.74	.0409	−.92	.1788	−.10	.4602	.72	.7642	1.52	.9357	2.80	.9974
−1.72	.0427	−.90	.1841	−.08	.4681	.74	.7704	1.54	.9382	2.85	.9978
−1.70	.0446	−.88	.1894	−.06	.4761	.76	.7764	1.56	.9406	2.90	.9981
−1.68	.0465	−.86	.1949	−.04	.4840	.78	.7823	1.58	.9429	2.95	.9984
−1.66	.0485	−.84	.2005	−.02	.4920	.80	.7881	1.60	.9452	3.00	.9987
−1.64	.0505	−.82	.2061	.00	.5000	.82	.7939	1.62	.9474	3.05	.9989
−1.62	.0526	−.80	.2119	.02	.5080	.84	.7995	1.64	.9495		
−1.60	.0548	−.78	.2177	.04	.5160						

This table shows the probability [N(d)] of observing a value less than or equal to d. For example, as illustrated, if d is −.24, then N(d) is .4052.

The formula for d_1 looks a little intimidating, but it is mostly a matter of plug and chug with a calculator. Suppose we have the following:

$S = \$70$
$E = \$80$
$R = 4\%$ per year, continuously compounded
$\sigma = 60\%$ per year
$t = 3$ months

With these numbers, d_1 is:

$$d_1 = [\ln(S/E) + (R + \sigma^2/2) \times t]/(\sigma \times \sqrt{t})$$
$$= [\ln(\$70/\$80) + (.04 + .6^2/2) \times \tfrac{1}{4}]/(.6 \times \sqrt{\tfrac{1}{4}})$$
$$= -.26$$
$$d_2 = d_1 - \sigma \times \sqrt{t}$$
$$= -.26 - .6 \times \sqrt{\tfrac{1}{4}}$$
$$= -.56$$

Referring to Table 25.3, the values of $N(d_1)$ and $N(d_2)$ are .3974 and .2877, respectively. Plugging all the numbers in, we get:

$$C = S \times N(d_1) - E \times e^{-Rt} \times N(d_2)$$
$$= \$70 \times .3974 - \$80 \times e^{-.04(1/4)} \times .2877$$
$$= \$5.03$$

If you take a look at the Black-Scholes formula and our examples, you will see that the price of a call option depends on five, and only five, factors. These are the same factors that we identified earlier: Namely, the stock price, the strike price, the time to maturity, the risk-free rate, and the standard deviation of the return on the stock.

Call Option Pricing	EXAMPLE 25.5

Suppose you are given the following:

$S = \$40$
$E = \$36$
$R = 4\%$ per year, continuously compounded
$\sigma = 70\%$ per year
$t = 3$ months

What's the value of a call option on the stock?
We need to use the Black-Scholes OPM. So, we first need to calculate d_1 and d_2:

$$d_1 = [\ln(S/E) + (R + \sigma^2/2) \times t]/(\sigma \times \sqrt{t})$$
$$= [\ln(\$40/\$36) + (.04 + .7^2/2) \times \tfrac{1}{4}]/(.7 \times \sqrt{\tfrac{1}{4}})$$
$$= .50$$
$$d_2 = d_1 - \sigma \times \sqrt{t}$$
$$= .50 - .7 \times \sqrt{\tfrac{1}{4}}$$
$$= .15$$

Referring to Table 25.3, the values of $N(d_1)$ and $N(d_2)$ are .6915 and .5597, respectively. To get the second of these, we averaged the two numbers on each side $(.5557 + .5636)/2 = .5597$. Plugging all the numbers in, we get the following:

$$C = S \times N(d_1) - E \times e^{-Rt} \times N(d_2)$$
$$= \$40 \times .6915 - \$36 \times e^{-.04(1/4)} \times .5597$$
$$= \$7.71$$

A question that sometimes comes up concerns the probabilities $N(d_1)$ and $N(d_2)$. What are they the probabilities of? In other words, how do we interpret them? The answer is that they don't really correspond to anything in the real world. We mention this because there is a common misconception about $N(d_2)$ in particular. It is frequently thought to be the probability that the stock price will exceed the strike price on the expiration day, which is also the probability that a call option will finish in the money. Unfortunately, that's incorrect—at least not unless the expected return on the stock equals the risk-free rate.

Tables such as Table 25.3 are the traditional means of looking up z values, but they have been mostly replaced by computers. Tables are not as accurate because of rounding, and they also have only a limited number of values. Our nearby *Spreadsheet Strategies* box shows how to calculate Black-Scholes option prices using a spreadsheet. Because this is so much easier and more accurate, we will do all the calculations in the rest of this chapter using computers instead of tables.

SPREADSHEET STRATEGIES

	A	B	C	D	E	F	G	H	I	J	K
1											
2			Using a spreadsheet to calculate Black-Scholes option prices								
3											
4	XYZ stock has a price of $65 and an annual return standard deviation of 50%. The riskless										
5	interest rate is 5%. Calculate call and put option prices with a strike of $60 and a 3-month										
6	time to expiration.										
7											
8		Stock =	65		d1 =	.4952		N(d1) =	.6898		
9		Strike =	60								
10		Sigma =	.5		d2 =	.2452		N(d2) =	.5968		
11		Time =	.25								
12		Rate =	.05								
13											
14			Call = Stock x N(d1) − Strike x exp(− Rate x Time) x N(d2) =								$9.47
15											
16			Put = Strike x exp(− Rate x Time) + Call − Stock					=			$3.72
17											
18	Formula entered in E8 is =(LN(B8/B9)+(B12+.5*B10^2)*B11)/(B10*SQRT(B11))										
19	Formula entered in E10 is =E8−B10*SQRT(B11)										
20	Formula entered in H8 is =NORMSDIST(E8)										
21	Formula entered in H10 is =NORMSDIST(E10)										
22	Formula entered in K14 is =B8*H8−B9*EXP(−B12*B11)*H10										
23	Formula entered in K16 is =B9*EXP(−B12*B11)+K14−B8										

PUT OPTION VALUATION

Our examples thus far have focused only on call options. A little extra work is needed to value put options. Basically, we pretend that a put option is a call option and use the

Black-Scholes formula to value it. We then use the put-call parity (PCP) condition to solve for the put value. To see how this works, suppose we have the following:

$S = \$40$

$E = \$40$

$R = 4\%$ per year, continuously compounded

$\sigma = 80\%$ per year

$t = 4$ months

What's the value of a *put* option on the stock?

For practice, calculate the Black-Scholes call option price and see if you agree that a call option would be worth about $7.53. Now, recall the PCP condition:

$$S + P = E \times e^{-Rt} + C$$

which we can rearrange to solve for the put price:

$$P = E \times e^{-Rt} + C - S$$

Plugging in the relevant numbers, we get:

$$P = \$40 \times e^{-.04(1/3)} + \$7.53 - \$40$$
$$= \$7.00$$

The value of a put option is $7.00. So, once we know how to value call options, we also know how to value put options.

A CAUTIONARY NOTE

For practice, let's consider another put option value. Suppose we have the following:

$S = \$70$

$E = \$90$

$R = 8\%$ per year, continuously compounded

$\sigma = 20\%$ per year

$t = 12$ months

What's the value of a put option on the stock?

For practice, calculate the call option's value and see if you get $1.65. Once again, we use PCP to solve for the put price:

$$P = E \times e^{-Rt} + C - S$$

The put value we get is:

$$P = \$90 \times e^{-.08(1)} + \$1.65 - \$70$$
$$= \$14.73$$

Does something about our put option value seem odd? The answer is yes. Because the stock price is $70 and the strike price is $90, you could get $20 by exercising the put immediately; so it looks like we have an arbitrage opportunity. Unfortunately, we don't. This example illustrates that we have to be careful with assumptions. The Black-Scholes formula is for *European*-style options (remember that European-style options can be exercised only on the final day, whereas American-style options can be exercised anytime). In fact, our PCP condition holds only for European-style options.

What our example shows is that an American-style put option is worth more than a European-style put. The reason is not hard to understand. Suppose you buy a put with a strike price of $80. The very best thing that can happen is for the stock price to fall to zero.

If the stock price falls to zero, no further gain on your option is possible, so you will want to exercise it immediately rather than wait. If the option is American style, you can, but if it is European style, you cannot. More generally, it often pays to exercise a put option once it is well into the money because any additional potential gains are limited; exercising an American-style option is valuable.

What about call options? Here the answer is a little more encouraging. As long as we stick to non-dividend-paying stocks, it will never be optimal to exercise a call option early. Again, the reason is not complicated. A call option is worth more alive than dead, meaning you would always be better off selling the option than exercising it. In other words, for a call option, the exercise style is irrelevant.

Here is a challenge for the more mathematically inclined among you. We have a formula for a European-style put option. What about for an American-style put? Despite a great deal of effort, this problem has never been solved, so no formula is known. To be clear, we have numerical procedures for valuing put options, but no explicit formula. Call us if you figure one out.

Concept Questions

25.2a   What are the five factors that determine an option's value?

25.2b   Which is worth more, an American-style put or a European-style put? Why?

25.3   More about Black-Scholes

Excel Master It!

Excel Master coverage online

In this section, we take a closer look at the inputs into the option pricing formula and their effects on option values. Table 25.4 summarizes the inputs and their impacts (positive or negative) on option values. In the table, a plus sign means that increasing the input increases the option's value and vice versa.

Table 25.4 also indicates that four of the five effects have common names. For fairly obvious reasons given their names, these effects are collectively called the *greeks*. We discuss them in the next several sections. In some cases, the calculations can be fairly involved; but the good news is that options calculators are widely available on the web. See our nearby *Work the Web* box for one example.

VARYING THE STOCK PRICE

The effect that the stock price has on put and call values is pretty obvious. Increasing the stock price increases call values and decreases put values. However, the strength of

TABLE 25.4

Five Inputs Determining the Value of an American Option on a Non-Dividend-Paying Stock

Input	Impact on Option Price from an Increase in Input		
	Call Options	Put Options	Common Name
Stock price (S)	+	−	Delta
Strike price (E)	−	+	
Time to expiration (t)	+	+	Theta
Standard deviation of return on stock (σ)	+	+	Vega
Risk-free rate (R)	+	−	Rho

NOTE: The effect of increasing the time to maturity is positive for an American put option, but the impact is ambiguous for a European put.

WORK THE WEB

The Black-Scholes OPM is a wonderful tool; but as we have seen, the calculations can get somewhat tedious. One way to find the price of an option without the effort is to work the web. We went to the options calculator at www.ivolatility.com and entered "MSFT," the ticker symbol for Microsoft. As shown, the current stock price is $64.62, the standard deviation of the stock's return is 17.88 percent per year, and the risk-free rate is .8019 percent. Here is what we found:

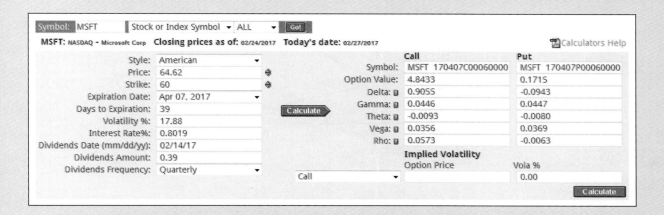

As you can see, a call option on MSFT with a strike price of $60 should sell for $4.8433 and a put option should sell for $.1715. Now that's easy! Notice that the "greeks" are also calculated. What does "gamma" tell you? Visit the site to learn more.

Questions

1. Go to www.ivolatility.com and find current option prices for Microsoft. Compare the prices of calls and puts with the same strike prices for the closest maturities and the most distant maturities. What relationship do you see in comparing these prices?

2. Go to www.ivolatility.com and find current option prices for eBay with strike prices closest to the current stock price. Compare the deltas of the calls and puts with the closest maturities and the most distant maturities. What relationship do you see in the deltas?

the effect varies depending on the "moneyness" of the option (how far in or out of the money it is).

For a given set of input values, we illustrate the relationship between call and put option prices and the underlying stock price in Figure 25.1. In the figure, stock prices are measured on the horizontal axis and option prices are measured on the vertical axis. Notice that the lines for put and call values are bowed. The reason is that the value of an option that is far out of the money is not as sensitive to a change in the underlying stock price as an in-the-money option.

Another good options calculator can be found at **www.fintools .com/resources/online -calculators/options-calcs /options-calculator/**.

FIGURE 25.1   Put and Call Option Prices

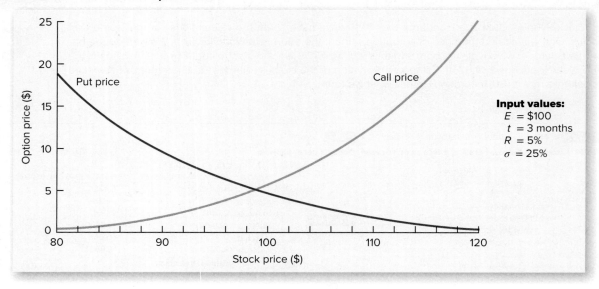

delta

Measures the effect on an option's value of a small change in the value of the underlying stock.

The sensitivity of an option's value to small changes in the price of the underlying stock is called the option's **delta**. For European options, we can directly measure the deltas as follows:

Call option delta = $N(d_1)$

Put option delta = $N(d_1) - 1$

The "$N(d_1)$" that we need to calculate these deltas is the same one we used to calculate option values, so we already know how to do it. Remember that $N(d_1)$ is a probability, so its value ranges somewhere between 0 and 1.

For a small change in the stock price, the change in an option's price is approximately equal to its delta multiplied by the change in the stock price:

Change in option value ≈ Delta × Change in stock value

To illustrate this, suppose we are given the following:

$S = \$120$
$E = \$100$
$R = 8\%$ per year, continuously compounded
$\sigma = 80\%$ per year
$t = 6$ months

Using the Black-Scholes formula, the value of a call option is $37.80. The delta [$N(d_1)$] is .75, which tells us that if the stock price changes by, say, $1, the option's value will change in the same direction by $.75.

We can check this directly by changing the stock price to $121 and recalculating the option value. If we do this, the new value of the call is $38.55, an increase of $.75; so the approximation is pretty accurate (it is off in the third decimal point).

If we price a put option using these same inputs, the value is $13.88. The delta is .75 − 1, or −.25. If we increase the stock price to $121, the new put value is $13.63, a change of −.25; so, again, the approximation is fairly accurate as long as we stick to relatively small changes.

Looking back at our graph in Figure 25.1, we now see why the lines get progressively steeper as the stock price rises for calls and falls for puts. The delta for a deeply in-the-money option is close to 1, whereas the delta for a deeply out-of-the-money option is close to 0.

| **Delta** | **EXAMPLE 25.6** |

Suppose you are given the following:

$S = \$40$
$E = \$30$
$R = 6\%$ per year, continuously compounded
$\sigma = 90\%$ per year
$t = 3$ months

What's the delta for a call option? A put option? Which one is more sensitive to a change in the stock price? Why?

We need to calculate $N(d_1)$. See if you agree that it's .815, which is the delta for the call. The delta for the put is $.815 - 1 = -.185$, which is much smaller (in absolute value). The reason is that the call option is well in the money and the put is out of the money.

VARYING THE TIME TO EXPIRATION

The impact of changing the time to maturity on American-style options is also fairly obvious. Because an American-style option can be exercised anytime, increasing the option's time to expiration can't possibly hurt and (especially for out-of-the-money options) might help. For both puts and calls, increasing the time to expiration has a positive effect.

For a European-style call option, increasing the time to expiration also never hurts because, as we discussed earlier, the option is always worth more alive than dead, and any extra time to expiration only adds to its "alive" value. With a European-style put, increasing the time to expiration may or may not increase the value of the option. As we have discussed, for a deep in-the-money put, immediate exercise is often desirable, so increasing the time to expiration only reduces the value of the option. If a put is out of the money, then increasing the time to expiration will probably increase its value.

Figure 25.2 shows the effect of increasing the time to expiration on a put and a call. The options are exactly at the money. In the figure, notice that once time to maturity reaches about six months, further increases have little impact on the put's value. The call's value, in contrast, keeps rising.

The sensitivity of an option's value to the passage of time is called its **theta**. There is a formula for theta, but it is fairly complicated, so we will not present it. The important thing to realize is that option values are sensitive to the passage of time (especially call option values). To see why this is important, imagine that you buy an option today and hold it for a month. During the month, the stock price never changes. What happens to the value of your option?

theta
Measures the sensitivity of an option's value to a change in the time to expiration.

The value of your option declines because time to expiration has gotten shorter even though the underlying asset has not changed in value. We sometimes say that an option is a *wasting* asset, meaning that its value declines as time goes by, all else held constant. The tendency of an option's value to decline as time passes is also called *time decay*. An option's theta is a measure of the rate of time decay.

Recall from our earlier chapter about options that the intrinsic value of an option is:

Call intrinsic value $= \text{Max}[S - E, 0]$

Put intrinsic value $= \text{Max}[E - S, 0]$

FIGURE 25.2   **Option Prices and Time to Expiration**

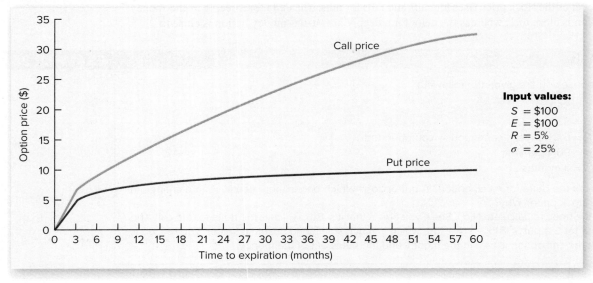

where "Max[$S - E$, 0]" means $S - E$ or 0, whichever is higher. American-style options can never sell for less than their intrinsic value because, if one did, there would be an arbitrage opportunity. Suppose a stock sells for $60. A three-month call option with a $50 strike price sells for $8. What do you think?

You think you are going to be rich because you can buy the option for $8, exercise it for $50, then sell the stock for $60 for a $2 riskless profit. To prevent this type of simple arbitrage, the option has to sell for at least its intrinsic value of $60 − 50 = $10. In reality, the option might sell for $11. The extra $1 in value over the intrinsic value is called the *time premium*. In other words, an option's value can be written as:

Option value = Intrinsic value + Time premium

It is the time premium that wastes away or decays as time goes by. The reason is that the day an option expires, it is worth exactly its intrinsic value: On that day, it must be exercised or torn up. The existence of the time premium also explains our earlier observation that a call option is always worth more alive than dead. If you exercise an option, you receive the intrinsic value. If you sell it, you get the intrinsic value plus any remaining time premium.

EXAMPLE 25.7   **Time Premiums**

In February 2017, shares in Tesla Motors were going for about $246.32. A call option expiring in November 2017 with a $250 strike was quoted at $27.28. A put with the same strike was quoted at $35.98. For both options, what are the intrinsic value and time premium?

Beginning with the call option, we see that it is out of the money because the $250 strike price is higher than the $246.32 stock price. The intrinsic value is zero, and the entire $27.28 is therefore time premium. The put is in the money, and its intrinsic value is $250 − 246.32 = $3.68. The put's value is $35.98, so the time premium is $35.98 − 3.68 = $32.30.

VARYING THE STANDARD DEVIATION

Figure 25.3 illustrates the impact on option values of varying the standard deviation of the return on the underlying asset. As shown, the effect is positive and pronounced for both puts and calls. In fact, increasing the standard deviation has an almost identical effect on them.

FIGURE 25.3   **Option Prices and Sigma**

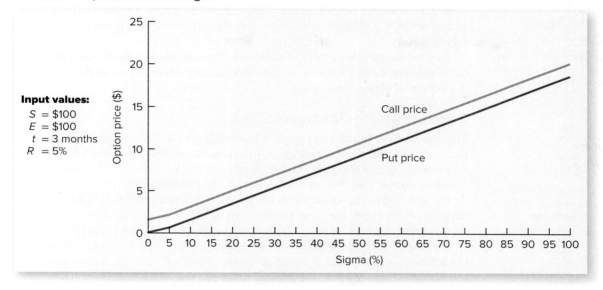

Input values:
S = $100
E = $100
t = 3 months
R = 5%

FIGURE 25.4   **Options Prices and Interest Rates**

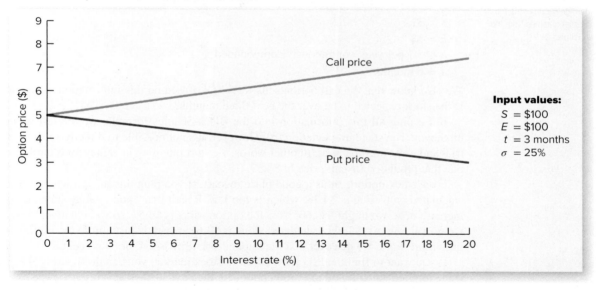

Input values:
S = $100
E = $100
t = 3 months
σ = 25%

The sensitivity of an option's value to the volatility of the underlying asset is called its **vega**.[2] Once again, the formula is somewhat complicated, so we will omit it. The main thing to understand from Figure 25.3 is that option values are very sensitive to standard deviations, and changes in the volatility of the underlying asset's return can have a strong impact on option values.

vega
Measures the sensitivity of an option's value to a change in the standard deviation of the return on the underlying asset.

VARYING THE RISK-FREE RATE

We illustrate the effect of changing the risk-free rate on option values in Figure 25.4. As shown, increasing the risk-free rate has a positive impact on call values and a negative

[2]The Greek scholars among you will recognize that vega is not a Greek letter. (It is a star in the constellation Lyra and also a particularly forgettable automobile manufactured by Chevrolet in the 1960s and 1970s.)

impact on put values. Notice, for realistic changes in interest rates, option values don't change a lot. In other words, option values are not as sensitive to changes in interest rates as they are to, say, changes in volatilities. An option's sensitivity to interest rate changes is called its **rho**.

rho
Measures the sensitivity of an option's value to a change in the risk-free rate.

There are a few other greeks in addition to the ones we have discussed, but we will end our Greek lesson here. What we now discuss is a very important use of Black-Scholes: The calculation of implied volatilities.

IMPLIED STANDARD DEVIATIONS

Thus far, we have focused on using the Black-Scholes OPM to calculate option values; but there is another very important use. Of the five factors that determine an option's value, four can be directly observed: The stock price, the strike price, the risk-free rate, and the life of the option. Only the standard deviation must be estimated.

For an option-oriented website focusing on volatilities, visit **www.ivolatility.com**.

The standard deviation we use in the OPM is actually a prediction of what the standard deviation of the underlying asset's return is going to be over the life of the option. Often, we already know the value of an option because we observe its price in the financial markets. In such cases, we can use the value of the option, along with the four observable inputs, to back out a value for the standard deviation. When we solve for the standard deviation this way, the result is called the **implied standard deviation** or ISD (which some people pronounce as "iz-dee"), also known as the *implied volatility*.

implied standard deviation
An estimate of the future standard deviation of the return on an asset obtained from the Black-Scholes OPM.

To illustrate this calculation, suppose we are given the following:

$S = \$12$
$E = \$8$
$R = 5\%$ per year, continuously compounded
$t = 6$ months

We also know that the call option sells for $4.59. Based on this information, how volatile is the stock expected to be over the next three months?

If we plug all this information into the Black-Scholes formula, we are left with one unknown: The standard deviation (σ). However, it's not possible to directly solve for σ, so trial and error must be used. In other words, we start plugging in values for σ until we find one that produces the call price of $4.59.

For a stock option, .50 is a good place to start. If you plug this in, you will see that the calculated call value is $4.38, which is too low. Recall that option values increase as we increase σ, so we might try .60. Now the option value is $4.53, so we're getting close, but we're still low. At .65, the calculated value is $4.61, which is just a little too high. After a little more work, we discover that the implied volatility is .64, or 64 percent.

If you want to find the ISD for the overall stock market, you can do so easily. The VIX is the implied volatility of S&P 500 options for the next 30 days. It is often viewed as a fear gauge because a higher VIX implies that the market expects a higher volatility in the next 30 days. Historically, the VIX has been 15 to 20, although it climbed into the 80s during the market turmoil of 2008. In order to allow investors to trade on volatility, exchange-traded futures and options are available on the VIX index. Here is a question for you: Suppose you were to calculate the ISD of a VIX option. What would this number mean?

EXAMPLE 25.8 — ISD

On February 28, 2017, common stock in social network company Facebook closed at $135.45. A call option expiring on September 15, 2017, with a strike price of $140 traded for $8.25. Treasury bills maturing on September 15, 2017, were paying 1.077 percent. Based on this information, how volatile is the return on Facebook predicted to be?

To summarize, the relevant numbers we have are:

$S = \$135.45$
$E = \$140$
$R = 1.077\%$ per year, compounded annually
$\sigma = ?$
$t = 199$ days
$C = \$8.25$

From here, it's plug and chug. As you have probably figured out by now, it's easier to use an options calculator to solve this problem. That's what we did; the implied standard deviation is about 25 percent. Our nearby *Work the Web* box shows you how to do this.

In principle, to solve this problem, we need to convert the interest rate of 1.077 percent to a continuously compounded rate. If we do this, we get 1.0828 percent. However, we've seen that option values are not very sensitive to small changes in interest rates; and in this case, it actually makes almost no difference. For this reason, in practice, the continuous compounding issue is often ignored, especially when rates are low.

WORK THE WEB

From our discussion of implied standard deviation, you can see that solving for ISD when you know the option price is done by trial and error. Fortunately, most options calculators will do the work for you. To illustrate, we found the ISD for the Facebook call option we discussed in Example 25.8. To refresh your memory, Facebook stock closed at $135.45. A call option with a strike price of $140 and a maturity of 199 days was selling for $8.25. Treasury bills with the same maturity had a yield of 1.0828 percent. What is the ISD of Facebook stock? We went to www.vindeep.com and used the options calculator at the site. After entering all the information, this is what we found:

Option Type	Call Option ▼	
Spot Price	135.45	
Strike Price	140	
Risk Free Rate	1.0828	%
Time To Expiry	199	Days
Market Price	8.25	
Implied Volatility	24.77	%

So, Facebook stock has an ISD of 24.77 percent per year.

Questions

1. Go to finance.yahoo.com and find option quotes for IBM. Pick a maturity and find the lowest strike price call, the call with a strike price nearest the current stock price, and the call with the highest strike price. Calculate the implied standard deviation for each using the calculator at www.vindeep.com. What do you observe?

2. Go to finance.yahoo.com and find option quotes for Pfizer. Pick three call options with a strike price near the current stock price with different expiration months. Calculate the implied standard deviations using the calculator at www.vindeep.com. What do you observe?

Concept Questions

25.3a What are an option's delta, rho, theta, and vega?

25.3b What is an ISD?

25.4 Valuation of Equity and Debt in a Leveraged Firm

In our earlier chapter about options, we pointed out that the equity in a leveraged corporation (a corporation that has borrowed money) can be viewed as a call option on the assets of the business. The reason is that when a debt comes due, the stockholders have the option to pay off the debt, and thereby acquire the assets free and clear, or else default. The act of paying off the debt amounts to exercising an in-the-money call option to acquire the assets. Defaulting amounts to letting an out-of-the-money call option expire. In this section, we expand on the idea of equity as a call option in several ways.

VALUING THE EQUITY IN A LEVERAGED FIRM

Consider a firm that has a single zero coupon bond issue outstanding with a face value of $10 million. It matures in six years. The firm's assets have a current *market* value of $12 million. The volatility (standard deviation) of the return on the firm's assets is 40 percent per year. The continuously compounded risk-free rate is 6 percent. What is the current market value of the firm's equity? Its debt? What is its continuously compounded cost of debt?

What this case amounts to is that the stockholders have the right, but not the obligation, to pay $10 million in six years. If they do, they get the assets of the firm. If they don't, they default and get nothing. So, the equity in the firm is a call option with a strike price of $10 million.

Using the Black-Scholes formula in this case can be a little confusing because now we are solving for the stock price. The symbol "C" is the value of the stock, and the symbol "S" is the value of the firm's assets. With this in mind, we can value the equity of the firm by plugging the numbers into the Black-Scholes OPM with $S = \$12$ million and $E = \$10$ million. When we do so, we get $6.554 million as the value of the equity, with a delta of .852.

Now that we know the value of the equity, we can calculate the value of the debt using the standard balance sheet identity. The firm's assets are worth $12 million and the equity is worth $6.554 million, so the debt is worth $12 − 6.554 = \$5.446$ million.

To calculate the firm's continuously compounded cost of debt, we observe that the present value is $5.446 million and the future value in six years is the $10 million face value. We need to solve for a continuously compounded rate, R_D, as follows:

$$\$5.446 = \$10 \times e^{-R_D(6)}$$
$$.5446 = e^{-R_D(6)}$$
$$R_D = -1/6 \times \ln(.5446)$$
$$= .10$$

So, the firm's cost of debt is 10 percent, compared to a risk-free rate of 6 percent. The extra 4 percent is the default risk premium—that is, the extra compensation the bondholders demand because of the risk that the firm will default and bondholders will receive assets worth less than $10 million.

We also know that the delta of the option here is .852. How do we interpret this? In the context of valuing equity as a call option, the delta tells us what happens to the value of the equity when the value of the firm's assets changes. This is an important consideration. Suppose the firm undertakes a project with an NPV of $100,000, meaning that the value of the firm's assets will rise by $100,000. We now see that the value of the stock will rise (approximately) by only .852 × $100,000 = $85,162.[3] Why?

The reason is that the firm has made its assets more valuable, which means default is less likely to occur in the future. As a result, the bonds gain value, too. How much do they gain? The answer is $100,000 − 85,162 = $14,838—in other words, whatever value the stockholders don't get.

Equity as a Call Option   EXAMPLE 25.9

Consider a firm that has a single zero coupon bond issue outstanding with a face value of $40 million. It matures in five years. The risk-free rate is 4 percent. The firm's assets have a current market value of $35 million, and the firm's equity is worth $15 million. If the firm takes a project with a $200,000 NPV, approximately how much will the stockholders gain?

To answer this question, we need to know the delta, so we need to calculate $N(d_1)$. To do this, we need to know the relevant standard deviation, which we don't have. We do have the value of the option ($15 million), though, so we can calculate the ISD. If we use C = $15 million, S = $35 million, and E = $40 million along with the risk-free rate of 4 percent and time to expiration of five years, we find that the ISD is 48.1 percent. With this value, the delta is .725; so, if $200,000 in value is created, the stockholders will get 72.5 percent of it, or about $145,000.

OPTIONS AND THE VALUATION OF RISKY BONDS

Let's continue with the case we just examined of a firm with $12 million in assets and a six-year, zero coupon bond with a face value of $10 million. Given the other numbers, we showed that the bonds were worth $5.446 million. Suppose that the holders of these bonds wish to eliminate the risk of default. In other words, the holders want to turn their risky bonds into risk-free bonds. How can they do this?

The answer is that the bondholders can do a protective put along the lines we described earlier in the chapter. In this case, the bondholders want to make sure their bonds will never

---

[3]Delta is used to evaluate the effect of a small change in the underlying asset's value, so it might look like we shouldn't use it to evaluate a shift of $100,000. "Small" is relative, however, and $100,000 is small relative to the $12 million total asset value.

be worth less than the face value of $10 million, so the bondholders need to purchase a put option with a six-year life and a $10 million face value. The put option is an option to sell the assets of the firm for $10 million.

Remember that if the assets of the firm are worth more than $10 million in six years, the shareholders will pay the $10 million. If the assets are worth less than $10 million, the stockholders will default, and the bondholders will receive the assets of the firm. At that point, however, the bondholders will exercise their put and sell the assets for $10 million. Either way, the bondholders get $10 million.

What we have discovered is that a risk-free bond is the same thing as a combination of a risky bond and a put option on the assets of the firm with a matching maturity and a strike price equal to the face value of the bond:

Value of risky bond + Put option = Value of risk-free bond   [25.7]

In our example, the face value of the debt is $10 million, and the risk-free rate is 6 percent, so the value of the bonds if they were risk-free would be:

$$\text{Value of risk-free bonds} = \$10 \text{ million} \times e^{-.06(6)}$$
$$= \$6.977 \text{ million}$$

If we compare this to the value of the risky bonds, $5.446 million, we see that the put option is worth $6.977 − 5.446 = $1.531 million. Notice that the value of the risk-free bonds is also the present value of the strike price at the risk-free rate.

We can check that this put value is correct. We know the value of the underlying assets is $12 million, the value of the call option (the stock) is $6.554 million, and the present value of the strike price is $6.977 million. Using the PCP condition:

$$P = \$6.977 + 6.554 - 12$$
$$= \$1.531 \text{ million}$$

which is exactly what we calculated.

We can restate our result here as follows:

Value of risky bond = Value of risk-free bond − Put option   [25.8]
$$= E \times e^{-Rt} - P$$

This shows us that anything that increases the value of the put option *decreases* the value of the firm's bonds. With this in mind, we can use the PCP condition to bring together and unite a lot of our discussion in this chapter (and this book!).

Using the PCP condition, we can write:

$$S = C + E \times e^{-Rt} - P$$

Remember that, in this case, the stock is the underlying asset. Now, if we are thinking of the stock in a firm as being a call option on the assets of the firm, here is how we would interpret this:

Value of assets (S) = Value of stock (C) + (E × e⁻ᴿᵗ − P)   [25.9]

where E, the strike price, is the face value of the firm's debt. Notice that, as we have just seen, the term in parentheses is the value of the firm's risky bonds, so this expression is really the balance sheet identity:

Value of assets (S) = Value of stock (C) + Value of bonds (E × e⁻ᴿᵗ − P)   [25.10]

The PCP condition and the balance sheet identity say the same thing, but recognizing the nature of the optionlike features of the equity and debt in a leveraged firm leads to a far richer understanding of corporate finance. We illustrate some important examples in the next section.

25.4a Why do we say that the equity in a leveraged firm is a call option? What does the delta of the call option tell us in this context?

25.4b What is the connection between the standard balance sheet identity and the put-call parity (PCP) condition?

Options and Corporate Decisions: Some Applications

25.5

In this section, we explore the implications of options analysis in two key areas: Capital budgeting and mergers. We start with mergers and show a very surprising result. We then go on to show that the net present value rule has some important wrinkles in a leveraged firm.

MERGERS AND DIVERSIFICATION

Elsewhere in our book, we discuss mergers and acquisitions. There we mention that diversification is frequently cited as a reason for two firms to merge. Is diversification a good reason to merge? It might seem so. After all, in an earlier chapter, we spent a lot of time explaining why diversification is very valuable for investors in their own portfolios because of the elimination of unsystematic risk.

To investigate this issue, let's consider two companies, Sunshine Swimwear (SS) and Polar Winterwear (PW). For obvious reasons, both companies have seasonal cash flows; in their respective off-seasons, both companies worry about cash flow. If the two companies were to merge, the combined company would have a much more stable cash flow. In other words, a merger would diversify away some of the seasonal variation and, in fact, would make bankruptcy much less likely.

Notice that the operations of the two firms are very different, so the proposed merger is a purely "financial" merger. This means there are no "synergies" or other value-creating possibilities except possible gains from risk reduction. Here is some premerger information:

	Sunshine Swimwear	Polar Winterwear
Market value of assets	$30 million	$10 million
Face value of pure discount debt	$12 million	$ 4 million
Debt maturity	3 years	3 years
Asset return standard deviation	50 percent	60 percent

The risk-free rate, continuously compounded, is 5 percent. Given this, we can calculate the following (check these for practice):

	Sunshine Swimwear	Polar Winterwear
Market value of equity	$20.424 million	$7.001 million
Market value of debt	$9.576 million	$2.999 million

If you check these, you may get slightly different answers if you use Table 25.3 (we used an options calculator).

After the merger, the combined firm's assets will be the sum of the premerger values, $30 + 10 = $40, because no value was created or destroyed. Similarly, the total face value of the debt is now $16 million. However, we will assume that the combined firm's asset return standard deviation is 40 percent. This is lower than for either of the two individual firms because of the diversification effect.

So, what is the impact of this merger? To find out, we compute the postmerger value of the equity. Based on our discussion, here is the relevant information:

	Combined Firm
Market value of assets	$40 million
Face value of pure discount debt	$16 million
Debt maturity	3 years
Asset return standard deviation	40 percent

Once again, we can calculate equity and debt values:

	Combined Firm
Market value of equity	$26.646 million
Market value of debt	$13.354 million

What we notice is that this merger is a terrible idea, at least for the stockholders! Before the merger, the stock in the two separate firms was worth a total of $20.424 + 7.001 = $27.425 million, compared to only $26.646 million postmerger, so the merger vaporized $27.425 − 26.646 = $.779 million, or almost $1 million, in equity.

Where did nearly $1 million in equity go? It went to the bondholders. Their bonds were worth $9.576 + 2.999 = $12.575 million before the merger and $13.354 million after, a gain of exactly $.779 million. This merger neither created nor destroyed value, but it shifted it from the stockholders to the bondholders.

Our example shows that pure financial mergers are a bad idea, and it also shows why. The diversification works in the sense that it reduces the volatility of the firm's return on assets. This risk reduction benefits the bondholders by making default less likely. This is sometimes called the *coinsurance effect*. Essentially, by merging, the firms insure each other's bonds. The bonds are less risky, and they rise in value. If the bonds increase in value, and there is no net increase in asset values, then the equity must decrease in value. So, pure financial mergers are good for creditors, but not stockholders.

Another way to see this is that because the equity is a call option, a reduction in return variance on the underlying asset has to reduce its value. The reduction in value in the case of a purely financial merger has an interesting interpretation. The merger makes default (and bankruptcy) *less* likely to happen. That is obviously a good thing from a bondholder's perspective, but why is it a bad thing from a stockholder's perspective? The answer is simple: The right to go bankrupt is a valuable stockholder option. A purely financial merger reduces the value of that option.

OPTIONS AND CAPITAL BUDGETING

In our earlier chapter about options, we discussed the many options embedded in capital budgeting decisions, including the option to wait, the option to abandon, and others. To add to these option-related issues, we now consider two additional issues. What we show is that, for a leveraged firm, the shareholders might prefer a lower NPV project to a higher one. We then show that they might even prefer a *negative* NPV project to a positive NPV project.

As usual, we will illustrate these points first with an example. Here is the basic background information for the firm:

Market value of assets	$20 million
Face value of pure discount debt	$40 million
Debt maturity	5 years
Asset return standard deviation	50 percent

The risk-free rate is 4 percent. As we have now done many times, we can calculate equity and debt values:

Market value of equity	$5.744
Market value of debt	$14.256

This firm has a fairly high degree of leverage; the debt-equity ratio based on market values is $14.256/$5.744 = 2.48, or 248 percent. This is high, but not unheard of. Notice also that the option here is out of the money; as a result, the delta is .547.

The firm has two mutually exclusive investments under consideration. They both must be taken now or never, so there is no timing issue. The projects affect both the market value of the firm's assets and the firm's asset return standard deviation as follows:

	Project A	Project B
NPV (millions)	$4	$2
Market value of firm's assets ($20 + NPV)	$24	$22
Firm's asset return standard deviation	40 percent	60 percent

Which project is better? It is obvious that Project A has the higher NPV, but by now you are wary of the change in the firm's asset return standard deviation. One project reduces it; the other increases it. To see which project the stockholders like better, we have to go through our (by now) very familiar calculations:

	Project A	Project B
Market value of equity	$5.965	$8.751
Market value of debt	$18.035	$13.249

There is a dramatic difference between the two projects. Project A benefits both the stockholders and the bondholders, but most of the gain goes to the bondholders. Project B has a huge impact on the value of the equity, plus it reduces the value of the debt. Clearly, the stockholders prefer B.

What are the implications of our analysis? We have discovered two things. First, when the equity has a delta significantly smaller than 1.0, any value created will go partially to bondholders. Second, stockholders have a strong incentive to increase the variance of the return on the firm's assets. More specifically, stockholders will have a strong preference for variance-increasing projects as opposed to variance-decreasing ones, even if that means a lower NPV.

Let's do one final example. Here is a different set of numbers:

Market value of assets	$20 million
Face value of pure discount debt	$100 million
Debt maturity	5 years
Asset return standard deviation	50 percent

The risk-free rate is 4 percent, so the equity and debt values are:

Market value of equity	$2.012 million
Market value of debt	$17.988 million

Notice that the change from our previous example is that the face value of the debt is now $100 million, so the option is far out of the money. The delta is only .241, so most of any value created will go to the bondholders.

The firm has an investment under consideration that must be taken now or never. The project affects both the market value of the firm's assets and the firm's asset return standard deviation as follows:

Project NPV	−$1 million
Market value of firm's assets ($20 million + NPV)	$19 million
Firm's asset return standard deviation	70 percent

The project has a negative NPV, but it increases the standard deviation of the firm's return on assets. If the firm takes the project, here is the result:

Market value of equity	$4.834 million
Market value of debt	$14.166 million

This project more than doubles the value of the equity! Once again, what we are seeing is that stockholders have a strong incentive to increase volatility, particularly when the option is far out of the money. What is happening is that the shareholders have relatively little to lose because bankruptcy is the likely outcome. As a result, there is a strong incentive to go for a long shot, even if that long shot has a negative NPV. It's a bit like using your very last dollar on a lottery ticket. It's a bad investment, but there aren't a lot of other options!

Concept Questions

25.5a What is a pure financial merger?

25.5b Why might stockholders in a leveraged firm prefer a low NPV project over a higher NPV project?

25.6 Summary and Conclusions

This chapter introduced the wide world of option valuation and some of its more important implications for corporate finance:

1. The put-call parity (PCP) condition tells us that among a call option, a put option, a risk-free investment like a T-bill, and an underlying asset such as shares of stock, we can replicate any one using the other three.

2. The Black-Scholes option pricing model (OPM) lets us explicitly value call options given values for the five relevant inputs, which are the price of the underlying asset, the strike price, the time to expiration, the risk-free rate, and the standard deviation of the return on the underlying asset.

3. The effect of changing the inputs into the Black-Scholes OPM varies. Some changes have positive effects; some have negative effects. The magnitude also varies; relatively small changes in the risk-free rate don't have much of an effect, but changes in the standard deviation can have a very large effect. These various effects are known as the *greeks* because of the Greek (and quasi-Greek) letters used to identify them.

4. The equity in a leveraged corporation can be viewed as a call option on the assets of the firm. This gives the stockholders a strong incentive to increase the volatility of the return on the firm's assets, even if that means accepting projects with lower NPVs.

CONNECT TO FINANCE

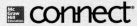 For more practice, you should be in *Connect Finance*. Log on to connect .mheducation.com to get started!

Can you answer the following *Connect* Quiz questions?

Section 25.1   What is the effective annual rate of 7.6 percent, compounded continuously?

Section 25.3   A call option has a value of $8.40. $N(d_1)$ is .32. Assume that the underlying stock increases in value by $.50. What is the approximate amount of the resulting change in the call option value?

Section 25.4   When using the put-call parity formula to compute the value of equity in a firm, the equity in the firm is represented by which one of the variables in the put-call parity formula?

CONCEPTS REVIEW AND CRITICAL THINKING QUESTIONS

1. **Options and Expiration Dates** [LO3] What is the impact of lengthening the time to expiration on an option's value? Explain.

2. **Options and Stock Price Volatility** [LO3] What impact does an increase in the volatility of the underlying stock's return have on an option's value? Explain.

3. **Options and Interest Rates** [LO3] How do interest rates affect option prices? Explain.

4. **Protective Puts** [LO1] The protective put strategy we discussed in the chapter is sometimes referred to as *stock price insurance*. Why?

5. **Intrinsic Value** [LO2] What is the intrinsic value of a call option? Of a put option? How do we interpret this value?

6. **Time Value** [LO2] What is the time value of a call option? Of a put option? What happens to the time value of a call option as the maturity increases? What about a put option?

7. **Option Valuation and NPV** [LO5] You are CEO of Titan Industries and have just been awarded a large number of employee stock options. The company has two mutually exclusive projects available. The first project has a large NPV and will reduce the total risk of the company. The second project has a small NPV and will increase the total risk of the company. You have decided to accept the first project when you remember your employee stock options. How might this affect your decision?

8. **Put-Call Parity [LO1]** You find a put and a call with the same exercise price and maturity. What do you know about the relative prices of the put and call? Prove your answer and provide an intuitive explanation.

9. **Put-Call Parity [LO1]** A put and a call have the same maturity and strike price. If they have the same price, which one is in the money? Prove your answer and provide an intuitive explanation.

10. **Put-Call Parity [LO1]** One thing put-call parity tells us is that given any three of a stock, a call, a put, and a T-bill, the fourth can be synthesized or replicated using the other three. For example, how can we replicate a share of stock using a call, a put, and a T-bill?

QUESTIONS AND PROBLEMS

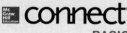

BASIC
(Questions 1–12)

1. **Continuous Compounding [LO2]** If you have $1,275 today, how much will it be worth in six years at 8 percent per year compounded continuously?

2. **Continuous Compounding [LO2]** If you need $20,000 in 12 years, how much will you need to deposit today if you can earn 9 percent per year compounded continuously?

3. **Put-Call Parity [LO1]** A stock is currently selling for $67 per share. A call option with an exercise price of $70 sells for $3.21 and expires in three months. If the risk-free rate of interest is 2.6 percent per year, compounded continuously, what is the price of a put option with the same exercise price?

4. **Put-Call Parity [LO1]** A put option that expires in six months with an exercise price of $45 sells for $2.34. The stock is currently priced at $48, and the risk-free rate is 3.5 percent per year, compounded continuously. What is the price of a call option with the same exercise price?

5. **Put-Call Parity [LO1]** A put option and a call option with an exercise price of $70 and three months to expiration sell for $1.30 and $6.25, respectively. If the risk-free rate is 3.1 percent per year, compounded continuously, what is the current stock price?

6. **Put-Call Parity [LO1]** A put option and call option with an exercise price of $50 expire in four months and sell for $5.99 and $8.64, respectively. If the stock is currently priced at $52.27, what is the annual continuously compounded rate of interest?

7. **Black-Scholes [LO2]** What are the prices of a call option and a put option with the following characteristics?

> Stock price = $64
> Exercise price = $60
> Risk-free rate = 2.7% per year, compounded continuously
> Maturity = 4 months
> Standard deviation = 62% per year

8. **Delta [LO2]** What are the deltas of a call option and a put option with the following characteristics? What does the delta of the option tell you?

> Stock price = $87
> Exercise price = $85
> Risk-free rate = 4.3% per year, compounded continuously
> Maturity = 9 months
> Standard deviation = 46% per year

9. **Black-Scholes and Asset Value [LO4]** You own a lot in Key West, Florida, that is   ✂
    currently unused. Similar lots have recently sold for $1,250,000. Over the past five
    years, the price of land in the area has increased 7 percent per year, with an annual
    standard deviation of 30 percent. A buyer has recently approached you and wants
    an option to buy the land in the next 12 months for $1,500,000. The risk-free rate
    of interest is 5 percent per year, compounded continuously. How much should you
    charge for the option?

10. **Black-Scholes and Asset Value [LO4]** In Problem 9, suppose you wanted the op-
    tion to sell the land to the buyer in one year. Assuming all the facts are the same,
    describe the transaction that would occur today. What is the price of the transaction
    today?

11. **Time Value of Options [LO2]** You are given the following information concerning
    options on a particular stock:

    > Stock price = $59
    > Exercise price = $55
    > Risk-free rate = 2% per year, compounded continuously
    > Maturity = 6 months
    > Standard deviation = 54% per year

    a. What is the intrinsic value of the call option? Of the put option?

    b. What is the time value of the call option? Of the put option?

    c. Does the call or the put have the larger time value component? Would you expect
        this to be true in general?

12. **Put-Call Parity [LO1]** A call option with an exercise price of $25 and four months
    to expiration has a price of $2.75. The stock is currently priced at $23.80, and the
    risk-free rate is 2.5 percent per year, compounded continuously. What is the price of
    a put option with the same exercise price?

13. **Black-Scholes [LO2]** A call option matures in six months. The underlying stock   **INTERMEDIATE**
    price is $75, and the stock's return has a standard deviation of 20 percent per year.   (Questions 13–20)
    The risk-free rate is 4 percent per year, compounded continuously. If the exercise
    price is $0, what is the price of the call option?

14. **Black-Scholes [LO2]** A call option has an exercise price of $60 and matures in six
    months. The current stock price is $64, and the risk-free rate is 5 percent per year,
    compounded continuously. What is the price of the call if the standard deviation of
    the stock is 0 percent per year?

15. **Black-Scholes [LO2]** A stock is currently priced at $47. A call option with an ex-
    piration of one year has an exercise price of $50. The risk-free rate is 12 percent per
    year, compounded continuously, and the standard deviation of the stock's return is
    infinitely large. What is the price of the call option?

16. **Equity as an Option [LO4]** Sunburn Sunscreen has a zero coupon bond issue out-
    standing with a $15,000 face value that matures in one year. The current market value
    of the firm's assets is $16,200. The standard deviation of the return on the firm's
    assets is 34 percent per year, and the annual risk-free rate is 6 percent per year, com-
    pounded continuously. Based on the Black-Scholes model, what is the market value
    of the firm's equity and debt?

17. **Equity as an Option and NPV [LO4]** Suppose the firm in Problem 16 is consider-
    ing two mutually exclusive investments. Project A has an NPV of $1,900, and Project B

has an NPV of $2,800. As the result of taking Project A, the standard deviation of the return on the firm's assets will increase to 46 percent per year. If Project B is taken, the standard deviation will fall to 29 percent per year.

a. What is the value of the firm's equity and debt if Project A is undertaken? If Project B is undertaken?

b. Which project would the stockholders prefer? Can you reconcile your answer with the NPV rule?

c. Suppose the stockholders and bondholders are in fact the same group of investors. Would this affect your answer to (b)?

d. What does this problem suggest to you about stockholder incentives?

✗ 18. **Equity as an Option [LO4]** Frostbite Thermalwear has a zero coupon bond issue outstanding with a face value of $23,000 that matures in one year. The current market value of the firm's assets is $26,200. The standard deviation of the return on the firm's assets is 38 percent per year, and the annual risk-free rate is 6 percent per year, compounded continuously. Based on the Black-Scholes model, what is the market value of the firm's equity and debt? What is the firm's continuously compounded cost of debt?

19. **Mergers and Equity as an Option [LO5]** Suppose Sunburn Sunscreen and Frostbite Thermalwear in the previous problems have decided to merge. Because the two companies have seasonal sales, the combined firm's return on assets will have a standard deviation of 21 percent per year.

a. What is the combined value of equity in the two existing companies? Value of debt?

b. What is the value of the new firm's equity? Value of debt?

c. What was the gain or loss for shareholders? For bondholders?

d. What happened to shareholder value here?

✗ 20. **Equity as an Option and NPV [LO4, 5]** A company has a single zero coupon bond outstanding that matures in five years with a face value of $17.5 million. The current value of the company's assets is $15.9 million, and the standard deviation of the return on the firm's assets is 41 percent per year. The risk-free rate is 6 percent per year, compounded continuously.

a. What is the current market value of the company's equity?

b. What is the current market value of the company's debt?

c. What is the company's continuously compounded cost of debt?

d. The company has a new project available. The project has an NPV of $2.2 million. If the company undertakes the project, what will be the new market value of equity? Assume volatility is unchanged.

e. Assuming the company undertakes the new project and does not borrow any additional funds, what is the new continuously compounded cost of debt? What is happening here?

CHALLENGE
(Questions 21–28)

21. **Debt Valuation and Time to Maturity [LO4]** Zevon Industries has a zero coupon bond issue that matures in two years with a face value of $40,000. The current value of the company's assets is $26,700, and the standard deviation of the return on assets is 60 percent per year.

a. Assume the risk-free rate is 5 percent per year, compounded continuously. What is the value of a risk-free bond with the same face value and maturity as the company's bond?

b. What price would the bondholders have to pay for a put option on the firm's assets with a strike price equal to the face value of the debt?

c. Using the answers from (a) and (b), what is the value of the firm's debt? What is the continuously compounded yield on the company's debt?

d. From an examination of the value of the assets of the company, and the fact that the debt must be repaid in two years, it seems likely that the company will default on its debt. Management has approached bondholders and proposed a plan whereby the company would repay the same face value of debt, but the repayment would not occur for five years. What is the value of the debt under the proposed plan? What is the new continuously compounded yield on the debt? Explain why this occurs.

22. **Debt Valuation and Asset Variance [LO4]** Colosseum Corp. has a zero coupon bond that matures in five years with a face value of $65,000. The current value of the company's assets is $62,000, and the standard deviation of its return on assets is 34 percent per year. The risk-free rate is 7 percent per year, compounded continuously.

a. What is the value of a risk-free bond with the same face value and maturity as the current bond?

b. What is the value of a put option on the firm's assets with a strike price equal to the face value of the debt?

c. Using the answers from (a) and (b), what is the value of the firm's debt? What is the continuously compounded yield on the company's debt?

d. Assume the company can restructure its assets so that the standard deviation of its return on assets increases to 43 percent per year. What happens to the value of the debt? What is the new continuously compounded yield on the debt? Reconcile your answers in (c) and (d).

e. What happens to bondholders if the company restructures its assets? What happens to shareholders? How does this create an agency problem?

23. **Black-Scholes and Dividends [LO2]** In addition to the five factors discussed in the chapter, dividends also affect the price of an option. The Black-Scholes option pricing model with dividends is:

$$C = S \times e^{-dt} \times N(d_1) - E \times e^{-Rt} \times N(d_2)$$
$$d_1 = [\ln(S/E) + (R - d + \sigma^2/2) \times t]/(\sigma \times \sqrt{t})$$
$$d_2 = d_1 - \sigma \times \sqrt{t}$$

All of the variables are the same as the Black-Scholes model without dividends except for the variable d, which is the continuously compounded dividend yield on the stock.

a. What effect do you think the dividend yield will have on the price of a call option? Explain.

b. A stock is currently priced at $87 per share, the standard deviation of its return is 50 percent per year, and the risk-free rate is 4 percent per year, compounded continuously. What is the price of a call option with a strike price of $85 and a maturity of six months if the stock has a dividend yield of 2 percent per year?

24. **Put-Call Parity and Dividends [LO1]** The put-call parity condition is altered when dividends are paid. The dividend-adjusted put-call parity formula is:

$$S \times e^{-dt} + P = E \times e^{-Rt} + C$$

where d is again the continuously compounded dividend yield.

a. What effect do you think the dividend yield will have on the price of a put option? Explain.

b. From Problem 23, what is the price of a put option with the same strike and time to expiration as the call option?

25. **Put Delta [LO2]** In the chapter, we noted that the delta for a put option is $N(d_1) - 1$. Is this the same thing as $-N(-d_1)$? (*Hint:* Yes, but why?)

26. **Black-Scholes Put Pricing Model [LO2]** Use the Black-Scholes model for pricing a call, put-call parity, and Problem 25 to show that the Black-Scholes model for directly pricing a put can be written as:

$$P = E \times e^{-Rt} \times N(-d_2) - S \times N(-d_1)$$

27. **Black-Scholes [LO2]** A stock is currently priced at $50. The stock will never pay a dividend. The risk-free rate is 12 percent per year, compounded continuously, and the standard deviation of the stock's return is 60 percent. A European call option on the stock has a strike price of $100 and no expiration date, meaning that it has an infinite life. Based on Black-Scholes, what is the value of the call option? Do you see a paradox here? Do you see a way out of the paradox?

28. **Delta [LO2]** You purchase one call and sell one put with the same strike price and expiration date. What is the delta of your portfolio? Why?

EXCEL MASTER IT! PROBLEM

In addition to spinners and scroll bars, there are numerous other Controls in Excel. You need to build a Black-Scholes Option Pricing Model spreadsheet using several of these controls.

a. Buttons are always used in sets. Using buttons permits you to check an option and the spreadsheet will use that input. In this case, you need to create two buttons, one for a call option and one for a put option. When using the spreadsheet, if you click the call option, the spreadsheet will calculate a call price and if you click the put option it will calculate the price of a put. Notice on the next spreadsheet that cell B20 is blank. This cell should change names. The names should be "Call option price" and "Put option price." In the price cell, only the price for the call option or put option is displayed depending on which button is selected. For the button, use the button under Form Controls.

b. A Combo Box uses a drop down menu with values entered by the spreadsheet developer. One advantage of a Combo Box is that the user can either choose values from the drop down menu or enter another value. In this case, you want to create a Combo Box for the stock price and a separate Combo Box for the strike price. In the right-hand side of the spreadsheet, we have values for the drop down menu. The values for the drop down menu should be created in an array before the Combo Box is inserted. To create an ActiveX Combo Box, go to Developer, Insert, and select Combo Box from the ActiveX Controls menu. After you draw the Combo Box, right click on the box, select Properties, and enter the LinkedCell, which is the cell where you want the output displayed, and the ListFillRange, which is the range that contains the list of values you want displayed in the drop down menu.

c. In contrast to a Combo Box, a List Box permits the user to scroll through a list of possible values that is predetermined by the spreadsheet developer. No other values can be entered. You need to create a List Box for the interest rate using the interest rate array on the right-hand side of the spreadsheet. To insert a List Box, go to Developer, Insert, and choose the List Box from the ActiveX Controls. To enter the linked cell and array of values, you will need to go to the Properties for the List Box. To do this, right click on the List Box and select Properties from the menu. We should note here that to edit both the Combo Box and List box you need to make sure that Design Mode is checked on the Developer tab.

MINICASE

Exotic Cuisines Employee Stock Options

As a new graduate, you've taken a management position with Exotic Cuisines, Inc., a restaurant chain that just went public last year. The company's restaurants specialize in exotic main dishes, using ingredients such as alligator, bison, and ostrich. A concern you had going in was that the restaurant business is very risky. However, after some due diligence, you discovered a common misperception about the restaurant industry. It is widely thought that 90 percent of new restaurants close within three years; however, recent evidence suggests the failure rate is closer to 60 percent over three years. So, it is a risky business, although not as risky as you originally thought.

During your interview process, one of the benefits mentioned was employee stock options.

Upon signing your employment contract, you received options with a strike price of $55 for 10,000 shares of company stock. As is fairly common, your stock options have a three-year vesting period and a 10-year expiration, meaning that you cannot exercise the options for a period of three years, and you lose them if you leave before they vest. After the three-year vesting period, you can exercise the options at any time. Thus, the employee stock options are European (and subject to forfeit) for the first three years and American afterward. Of course, you cannot sell the options, nor can you enter into any sort of hedging agreement. If you leave the company after the options vest, you must exercise within 90 days or forfeit any options that are not exercised.

Exotic Cuisines stock is currently trading at $26.32 per share, a slight increase from the initial offering price last year. There are no market-traded options on the company's stock. Because the company has been traded for only about a year, you are reluctant to use the historical returns to estimate the standard deviation of the stock's return. However, you have estimated that the average annual standard deviation for restaurant company stocks is about 55 percent. Because Exotic Cuisines is a newer restaurant chain, you decide to use a 60 percent standard deviation in your calculations. The company is relatively young, and you expect that all earnings will be reinvested back into the company for the near future. Therefore, you expect no dividends will be paid for

at least the next 10 years. A 3-year Treasury note currently has a yield of 2.4 percent, and a 10-year Treasury note has a yield of 3.1 percent.

QUESTIONS

1. You're trying to value your options. What minimum value would you assign? What is the maximum value you would assign?

2. Suppose that, in three years, the company's stock is trading at $60. At that time, should you keep the options or exercise them immediately? What are some important determinants in making such a decision?

3. Your options, like most employee stock options, are not transferable or tradable. Does this have a significant effect on the value of the options? Why?

4. Why do you suppose employee stock options usually have a vesting provision? Why must they be exercised shortly after you depart the company even after they vest?

5. A controversial practice with employee stock options is repricing. What happens is that a company experiences a stock price decrease, which leaves employee stock options far out of the money or "underwater." In such cases, many companies have "repriced" or "restruck" the options, meaning that the company leaves the original terms of the option intact, but lowers the strike price. Proponents of repricing argue that because the option is very unlikely to end in the money due to the stock price decline, the motivational force is lost. Opponents argue that repricing is in essence a reward for failure. How do you evaluate this argument? How does the possibility of repricing affect the value of an employee stock option at the time it is granted?

6. As we have seen, much of the volatility in a company's stock price is due to systematic or marketwide risks. Such risks are beyond the control of a company and its employees. What are the implications for employee stock options? In light of your answer, can you recommend an improvement over traditional employee stock options?

26 | Mergers and Acquisitions

IN JUNE 2016, Microsoft made a splash in business social media when it announced plans to acquire LinkedIn for $26.2 billion in cash. Microsoft CEO Satya Nadella stated that the combined companies could accelerate LinkedIn's growth. Microsoft also felt that LinkedIn could be incorporated into Office 365 and Dynamics, Microsoft's new platform to support accounting and financial applications.

So how do companies like Microsoft determine whether such acquisitions are worthwhile? This chapter explores the reasons why mergers and acquisitions take place and—equally important—the reasons why they should not.

Learning Objectives

After studying this chapter, you should be able to:

LO1 Discuss the different types of mergers and acquisitions, why they should (or shouldn't) take place, and the terminology associated with them.

LO2 Describe how accountants construct the combined balance sheet of the new company.

LO3 Define the gains from a merger or acquisition and how to value the transaction.

For updates on the latest happenings in finance, visit fundamentalsofcorporatefinance.blogspot.com.

There is no more dramatic or controversial activity in corporate finance than the acquisition of one firm by another or the merger of two firms. It is the stuff of headlines in the financial press, and it is occasionally an embarrassing source of scandal. And there are a lot of mergers. During 2016, U.S. companies announced mergers and acquisitions valued at about $642 billion, an 18 percent decline from the $786 billion announced during 2015.

The acquisition of one firm by another is, of course, an investment made under uncertainty, and the basic principles of valuation apply. One firm should acquire another only if doing so generates a positive net present value for the shareholders of the acquiring firm. Because the NPV of an acquisition candidate can be difficult to determine, mergers and acquisitions, or M&A activities, are interesting topics in their own right.

Some of the special problems that come up in this area of finance include the following:

1. The benefits from acquisitions can depend on such things as strategic fits. Strategic fits are difficult to define precisely, and it is not easy to estimate the value of strategic fits using discounted cash flow techniques.

2. There can be complex accounting, tax, and legal effects that must be taken into account when one firm is acquired by another.

3. Acquisitions are an important control device for shareholders. Some acquisitions are a consequence of an underlying conflict between the interests of existing managers and those of shareholders. Agreeing to be acquired by another firm is one way that shareholders can remove existing managers.

4. Mergers and acquisitions sometimes involve "unfriendly" transactions. In such cases, when one firm attempts to acquire another, the activity does not always confine itself to quiet, genteel negotiations. The sought-after firm often resists takeover and may resort to defensive tactics with exotic names such as poison pills, greenmail, and white knights.

We discuss these and other issues associated with mergers in the sections that follow. We begin by introducing the basic legal, accounting, and tax aspects of acquisitions.

The Legal Forms of Acquisitions   26.1

There are three basic legal procedures that one firm can use to acquire another firm:

1. Merger or consolidation.
2. Acquisition of stock.
3. Acquisition of assets.

Although these forms are different from a legal standpoint, the financial press frequently does not distinguish between them. The term *merger* is often used regardless of the actual form of the acquisition.

In our discussion, we will frequently refer to the acquiring firm as the *bidder*. This is the company that offers to distribute cash or securities to obtain the stock or assets of another company. The firm that is sought (and perhaps acquired) is often called the *target firm*. The cash or securities offered to the target firm are the *consideration* in the acquisition.

MERGER OR CONSOLIDATION

A **merger** is the complete absorption of one firm by another. The acquiring firm retains its name and its identity, and it acquires all the assets and liabilities of the acquired firm. After a merger, the acquired firm ceases to exist as a separate business entity.

A **consolidation** is the same as a merger except that an entirely new firm is created. In a consolidation, both the acquiring firm and the acquired firm terminate their previous legal existence and become part of a new firm. For this reason, the distinction between the acquiring and the acquired firm is not as important in a consolidation as it is in a merger.

The rules for mergers and consolidations are basically the same. Acquisition by merger or consolidation results in a combination of the assets and liabilities of acquired and acquiring firms; the only difference lies in whether or not a new firm is created. We will henceforth use the term *merger* to refer generically to both mergers and consolidations.

There are some advantages and some disadvantages to using a merger to acquire a firm:

1. A primary advantage is that a merger is legally simple and does not cost as much as other forms of acquisition. The reason is that the firms agree to combine their entire

merger
The complete absorption of one company by another, wherein the acquiring firm retains its identity and the acquired firm ceases to exist as a separate entity.

consolidation
A merger in which an entirely new firm is created and both the acquired firm and the acquiring firm cease to exist.

operations. There is no need to transfer title to individual assets of the acquired firm to the acquiring firm.

2. A primary disadvantage is that a merger must be approved by a vote of the stockholders of each firm.[1] Typically, two-thirds (or even more) of the share votes are required for approval. Obtaining the necessary votes can be time-consuming and difficult. Furthermore, as we discuss in greater detail a bit later, the cooperation of the target firm's existing management is almost a necessity for a merger. This cooperation may not be easily or cheaply obtained.

ACQUISITION OF STOCK

A second way to acquire another firm is to purchase the firm's voting stock with an exchange of cash, shares of stock, or other securities. This process will often start as a private offer from the management of one firm to that of another.

Regardless of how it starts, at some point the offer is taken directly to the target firm's stockholders. This can be accomplished by a tender offer. A **tender offer** is a public offer to buy shares. It is made by one firm directly to the shareholders of another firm.

tender offer
A public offer by one firm to directly buy the shares of another firm.

Those shareholders who choose to accept the offer tender their shares by exchanging them for cash or securities (or both), depending on the offer. A tender offer is frequently contingent on the bidder's obtaining some percentage of the total voting shares. If not enough shares are tendered, then the offer might be withdrawn or reformulated.

The tender offer is communicated to the target firm's shareholders by public announcements such as those made in newspaper advertisements. Sometimes, a general mailing is used in a tender offer. This is uncommon because a general mailing requires the names and addresses of the stockholders of record. Obtaining such a list without the target firm's cooperation is not easy.

The following are some factors involved in choosing between an acquisition by stock and a merger:

For up-to-date information about happenings in the world of M&A, go to **www.marketwatch.com**, then type "merger" into its search option.

1. In an acquisition by stock, no shareholder meetings have to be held and no vote is required. If the shareholders of the target firm don't like the offer, they are not required to accept it and need not tender their shares.

2. In an acquisition by stock, the bidding firm can deal directly with the shareholders of the target firm by using a tender offer. The target firm's management and board of directors can be bypassed.

3. Acquisition is occasionally unfriendly. In such cases, a stock acquisition is used in an effort to circumvent the target firm's management, which is usually actively resisting acquisition. Resistance by the target firm's management often makes the cost of acquisition by stock higher than the cost of a merger.

4. Frequently, a significant minority of shareholders will hold out in a tender offer. The target firm cannot be completely absorbed when this happens, and this may delay realization of the merger benefits or may be costly in some other way. For example, if the bidder ends up with less than 80 percent of the target firm's shares, it must pay tax on 20 to 30 percent of any dividends paid by the target firm to the bidder.

5. Complete absorption of one firm by another requires a merger. Many acquisitions by stock are followed up with a formal merger later.

ACQUISITION OF ASSETS

A firm can effectively acquire another firm by buying most or all of its assets. This accomplishes the same thing as buying the company. In this case, the target firm will not

---

[1]Mergers between corporations require compliance with state laws. In virtually all states, the shareholders of each corporation must give their assent.

necessarily cease to exist; it will have just sold off its assets. The "shell" will still exist unless its stockholders choose to dissolve it.

This type of acquisition requires a formal vote of the shareholders of the selling firm. One advantage to this approach is that there is no problem with minority shareholders holding out. However, the acquisition of assets may involve transferring titles to individual assets. The legal process of transferring assets can be costly.

ACQUISITION CLASSIFICATIONS

Financial analysts typically classify acquisitions into three types:

1. *Horizontal acquisition:* This is an acquisition of a firm in the same industry as the bidder. For example, in March 2016, Marriott International announced that it was acquiring competitor Starwood. And in January 2016, pharmaceutical company Shire announced that it was purchasing rival pharmaceutical company Baxalta.

2. *Vertical acquisition:* A vertical acquisition involves firms at different steps of the production process. For example, the Microsoft acquisition of LinkedIn, discussed at the beginning of the chapter, is a vertical acquisition, since Microsoft plans to integrate LinkedIn into its Office 365 platform. And in May 2016, chemical delivery systems maker Ichor Systems announced it was acquiring Ajax Custom Manufacturing, which makes plastic components used by Ichor.

Got the urge to merge? See **www.firstlist.com** and **www.dealstream.com** for ideas.

3. *Conglomerate acquisition:* When the bidder and the target firm are in unrelated lines of business, the merger is called a conglomerate acquisition. Conglomerate acquisitions are popular in the technology area. For example, by 2016, Alphabet (formerly Google) had acquired more than 200 companies since 2003. So, while you may be familiar with Google's Android operating system for cell phones, you may not be aware that Google acquired Android in 2005.

A NOTE ABOUT TAKEOVERS

Takeover is a general and imprecise term referring to the transfer of control of a firm from one group of shareholders to another. A takeover occurs whenever one group takes control from another.[2] This can occur through any one of three means: Acquisitions, proxy contests, and going-private transactions. Thus, takeovers encompass a broader set of activities than just acquisitions. These activities can be depicted as follows:

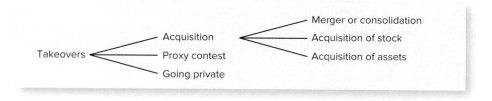

As we have mentioned before, a takeover achieved by acquisition will occur by merger, tender offer, or purchase of assets. In mergers and tender offers, the bidder buys the voting common stock of the target firm.

Takeovers can also occur with proxy contests. **Proxy contests** occur when a group attempts to gain controlling seats on the board of directors by voting in new directors. A *proxy* is the right to cast someone else's votes. In a proxy contest, proxies are solicited by an unhappy group of shareholders from the rest of the shareholders.

proxy contest
An attempt to gain control of a firm by soliciting a sufficient number of stockholder votes to replace existing management.

---

[2]Having *control* may be defined as having a majority vote on the board of directors.

going-private transactions
Transactions in which all publicly owned stock in a firm is replaced with complete equity ownership by a private group.

leveraged buyouts (LBOs)
Going-private transactions in which a large percentage of the money used to buy the stock is borrowed. Often incumbent management is involved.

In **going-private transactions**, all of the equity shares of a public firm are purchased by a small group of investors. Usually, the group includes members of incumbent management and some outside investors. Such transactions have come to be known generically as **leveraged buyouts (LBOs)** because a large percentage of the money needed to buy up the stock is usually borrowed. Such transactions are also termed *management buyouts* (MBOs) when existing management is heavily involved. The shares of the firm are delisted from stock exchanges and can no longer be purchased in the open market.

LBOs have become increasingly common, and some recent ones have been quite large. One of the largest cash acquisitions in history (and possibly the single largest private transaction ever of any kind) was the 2007 LBO of TXU Corp., the energy giant. The acquisition price in that buyout was an astonishing $45 billion. In that LBO, as with most of the large ones, much of the financing came from junk bond sales (see Chapter 7 for a discussion of junk bonds).

ALTERNATIVES TO MERGER

Firms don't have to merge to combine their efforts. At a minimum, two (or more) firms can agree to work together. They can sell each other's products, perhaps under different brand names, or jointly develop a new product or technology. Firms will frequently establish a **strategic alliance**, which is usually a formal agreement to cooperate in pursuit of a joint goal. An even more formal arrangement is a **joint venture**, which commonly involves two firms putting up the money to establish a new firm. Verizon Wireless was originally a joint venture between Verizon Communications and Vodafone.

strategic alliance
Agreement between firms to cooperate in pursuit of a joint goal.

joint venture
Typically an agreement between firms to create a separate, co-owned entity established to pursue a joint goal.

Concept Questions

26.1a   What is a merger? How does a merger differ from other acquisition forms?
26.1b   What is a takeover?

26.2   Taxes and Acquisitions

If one firm buys another firm, the transaction may be taxable or tax-free. In a *taxable acquisition*, the shareholders of the target firm are considered to have sold their shares, and they will have capital gains or losses that will be taxed. In a *tax-free acquisition*, the acquisition is considered an exchange instead of a sale, so no capital gain or loss occurs at the time of the transaction.

DETERMINANTS OF TAX STATUS

The general requirements for tax-free status are that the acquisition be for a business purpose, and not to avoid taxes, and that there be a continuity of equity interest. In other words, the stockholders in the target firm must retain an equity interest in the bidder.

The specific requirements for a tax-free acquisition depend on the legal form of the acquisition; but, in general, if the buying firm offers the selling firm cash for its equity, it will be a taxable acquisition. If shares of stock are offered, the transaction will generally be a tax-free acquisition.

In a tax-free acquisition, the selling shareholders are considered to have exchanged their old shares for new ones of equal value, so that no capital gains or losses are experienced.

TAXABLE VERSUS TAX-FREE ACQUISITIONS

There are two factors to consider when comparing a tax-free acquisition and a taxable acquisition: The capital gains effect and the write-up effect. The *capital gains effect* refers to the fact that the target firm's shareholders may have to pay capital gains taxes in a taxable acquisition. They may demand a higher price as compensation, thereby increasing the cost of the merger. This is a cost of a taxable acquisition.

The tax status of an acquisition also affects the appraised value of the assets of the selling firm. In a taxable acquisition, the assets of the selling firm are revalued or "written up" from their historic book value to their estimated current market value. This is the *write-up effect*, and it is important because it means that the depreciation expense on the acquired firm's assets can be increased in taxable acquisitions. Remember that an increase in depreciation is a noncash expense, but it has the desirable effect of reducing taxes.

The benefit from the write-up effect was sharply curtailed by the Tax Reform Act of 1986. The reason is that the increase in value from writing up the assets is now considered a taxable gain. Before this change, taxable mergers were much more attractive because the write-up was not taxed.

Concept Questions

26.2a   What factors influence the choice between a taxable and a tax-free acquisition?

26.2b   Under current tax law, why are taxable acquisitions less attractive than they once were?

Accounting for Acquisitions

26.3

In 2001, the Federal Accounting Standards Board (FASB) determined that the buyer had to treat all acquisitions under the *purchase accounting method*. Prior to 2001, firms were allowed to choose from more than one method. In all of this, keep in mind that we are examining purely accounting-related issues. How a merger is treated for financial reporting purposes has no cash flow consequences.

THE PURCHASE METHOD

The *purchase accounting method* of reporting acquisitions requires that the assets of the target firm be reported at their fair market value on the books of the bidder. With this method, an asset called *goodwill* is created for accounting purposes. Goodwill is the difference between the purchase price and the estimated fair market value of the net assets (assets less liabilities) acquired.

To illustrate, suppose Firm A acquires Firm B, thereby creating a new firm, AB. The balance sheets for the two firms on the date of the acquisition are shown in Table 26.1. Suppose Firm A pays $18 million in cash for Firm B. The money is raised by borrowing the full amount. The net fixed assets of Firm B, which are carried on the books at $8 million, are appraised at $14 million fair market value. Because the working capital is $2 million, the balance sheet assets are worth $16 million. Firm A pays **$2 million** in excess of the estimated market value of these net assets. This amount is the goodwill.[3]

---

[3]Remember, there are assets such as employee talents, good customers, growth opportunities, and other intangibles that don't show up on the balance sheet. The $2 million excess pays for these.

TABLE 26.1

Accounting for Acquisitions: Purchase (in Millions)

Firm A				Firm B			
Working capital	$ 4	Equity	$20	Working capital	$ 2	Equity	$10
Fixed assets	16			Fixed assets	8		
Total	$20	Total	$20	Total	$10	Total	$10

Firm AB			
Working capital	$ 6	Debt	$18
Fixed assets	30	Equity	20
Goodwill	2		
Total	$38	Total	$38

The market value of the fixed assets of Firm B is $14 million. Firm A pays $18 million for Firm B by issuing debt.

The last balance sheet in Table 26.1 shows what the new firm looks like under purchase accounting. Notice that:

1. The total assets of Firm AB increase to **$38 million**. The fixed assets increase to **$30 million**. This is the sum of the fixed assets of Firm A and the revalued fixed assets of Firm B ($16 million + 14 million = **$30 million**).
2. The **$2 million** excess of the purchase price over the fair market value is reported as goodwill on the balance sheet.[4]

MORE ABOUT GOODWILL

As we just discussed, the purchase method generally leads to the creation of an intangible asset called goodwill. Pre-2001 guidelines required firms to amortize this goodwill, meaning that a portion of it was deducted as an expense every year over some period of time. In essence, the goodwill, like any asset, had to be depreciated until it was completely written off.

Despite the cash flow irrelevance of goodwill amortization, FASB's decision to require purchase accounting caused a great deal of protest, much of it due to the treatment of goodwill and its impact on reported earnings. As a compromise, in 2001 FASB eliminated the requirement that goodwill be amortized and put in place a new rule. In essence, the new rule says that each year firms must assess the value of the goodwill on their balance sheets. If the value has gone down (or become "impaired" in accounting-speak), the firm must deduct the decrease; otherwise, no amortization is required.

Concept Questions

26.3a What is "goodwill"?
26.3b What happens to goodwill if the value of the acquisition declines over time?

---

[4]You might wonder what would happen if the purchase price were less than the estimated fair market value. Amusingly, to be consistent, it seems that the accountants would need to create a liability called *ill will*! Instead, the fair market value is revised downward to equal the purchase price.

Gains from Acquisitions

26.4

To determine the gains from an acquisition, we need to first identify the relevant incremental cash flows, or, more generally, the source of value. In the broadest sense, acquiring another firm makes sense only if there is some concrete reason to believe that the target firm will somehow be worth more in our hands than it is worth by itself. As we will see, there are a number of reasons why this might be so.

SYNERGY

Suppose Firm A is contemplating acquiring Firm B. The acquisition will be beneficial if the combined firm will have greater value than the sum of the values of the separate firms. If we let V_{AB} stand for the value of the merged firm, then the merger makes sense only if:

$$V_{AB} > V_A + V_B$$

Visit **www.thedeal.com** for current news about mergers.

where V_A and V_B are the separate values. A successful merger requires that the value of the whole exceed the sum of the parts.

The difference between the value of the combined firm and the sum of the values of the firms as separate entities is the incremental net gain from the acquisition, ΔV:

$$\Delta V = V_{AB} - (V_A + V_B)$$

When ΔV is positive, the acquisition is said to generate **synergy**. For example, when Comcast announced its intention to acquire Time Warner Cable in early 2014, the company estimated that the savings in operating expenses would be $750 million the first year and would eventually reach $1.5 billion.

If Firm A buys Firm B, it gets a company worth V_B plus the incremental gain, ΔV. The value of Firm B to Firm A (V_B^*) is:

synergy
The positive incremental net gain associated with the combination of two firms through a merger or acquisition.

Value of Firm B to Firm A $= V_B^* = \Delta V + V_B$

We place an * on V_B^* to emphasize that we are referring to the value of Firm B to Firm A, not the value of Firm B as a separate entity.

V_B^* can be determined in two steps: (1) Estimating V_B and (2) estimating ΔV. If B is a public company, then its market value as an independent firm under existing management (V_B) can be observed directly. If Firm B is not publicly owned, then its value will have to be estimated based on similar companies that are publicly owned. Either way, the problem of determining a value for V_B^* requires determining a value for ΔV.

To determine the incremental value of an acquisition, we need to know the incremental cash flows. These are the cash flows for the combined firm less what A and B could generate separately. In other words, the incremental cash flow for evaluating a merger is the difference between the cash flow of the combined company and the sum of the cash flows for the two companies considered separately. We will label this incremental cash flow as ΔCF.

Synergy	**EXAMPLE 26.1**

Firms A and B are competitors with very similar assets and business risks. Both are all-equity firms with aftertax cash flows of $10 per year forever, and both have an overall cost of capital of 10 percent. Firm A is thinking of buying Firm B. The aftertax cash flow from the merged firm would be $21 per year. Does the merger generate synergy? What is V_B^*? What is ΔV?

> The merger does generate synergy because the cash flow from the merged firm is $\Delta CF = \$1$ greater than the sum of the individual cash flows ($21 versus $20). Assuming the risks stay the same, the value of the merged firm is $\$21/.10 = \$210$. Firms A and B are each worth $\$10/.10 = \$100$, for a total of $200. The incremental gain from the merger, ΔV, is $\$210 - 200 = \$10$. The total value of Firm B to Firm A, V_B^*, is $100 (the value of B as a separate company) plus $10 (the incremental gain), or $110.

From our discussions in earlier chapters, we know that the incremental cash flow, ΔCF, can be broken down into four parts:

$$\Delta CF = \Delta EBIT + \Delta Depreciation + \Delta Tax - \Delta Capital\ requirements$$
$$= \Delta Revenue - \Delta Cost - \Delta Tax - \Delta Capital\ requirements$$

where $\Delta Revenue$ is the difference in revenues, $\Delta Cost$ is the difference in costs, ΔTax is the difference in taxes, and $\Delta Capital\ requirements$ is the change in new fixed assets and net working capital.

Based on this breakdown, the merger will make sense only if one or more of these cash flow components are beneficially affected by the merger. The possible cash flow benefits of mergers and acquisitions fall into four basic categories: Revenue enhancement, cost reductions, lower taxes, and reductions in capital needs.

REVENUE ENHANCEMENT

One important reason for an acquisition is that the combined firm may generate greater revenues than two separate firms. Increases in revenue may come from marketing gains, strategic benefits, and increases in market power.

Marketing Gains   It is frequently claimed that mergers and acquisitions can produce greater operating revenues from improved marketing. Improvements might be made in the following areas:

1. Previously ineffective media programming and advertising efforts.
2. A weak existing distribution network.
3. An unbalanced product mix.

For example, in March 2016, paint-maker Sherwin-Williams announced a bid for competitor Valspar. Sherwin-Williams stated that it expected to save $280 million per year within two years from lower sourcing costs; lower selling, general, and administrative costs; and process and efficiency savings. The long-term goal was to achieve synergies of $320 million per year.

Strategic Benefits   Some acquisitions promise a strategic advantage. This is an opportunity to take advantage of the competitive environment if certain things occur or, more generally, to enhance management flexibility with regard to the company's future operations. In this latter sense, a strategic benefit is more like an option than a standard investment opportunity.

Suppose a computer manufacturer can use its technology to enter other businesses. The electronics and software technology from the original business can provide opportunities to begin manufacturing consumer electronics (think Apple).

The word *beachhead* has been used to describe the process of entering a new industry to exploit perceived opportunities. The beachhead is used to spawn new opportunities based on "intangible" relationships. One example is Procter & Gamble's initial acquisition of the Charmin Paper Company as a beachhead, which allowed P&G to develop a highly interrelated cluster of paper products—disposable diapers, paper towels, feminine hygiene products, and bathroom tissue.[5]

Increases in Market Power   One firm may acquire another to increase its market share and market power. In such mergers, profits can be enhanced through higher prices and reduced competition for customers. Of course, mergers that substantially reduce competition in the market may be challenged by the U.S. Department of Justice or the Federal Trade Commission on antitrust grounds.

COST REDUCTIONS

One of the most basic reasons to merge is that a combined firm may operate more efficiently than two separate firms. A firm can achieve greater operating efficiency in several different ways through a merger or an acquisition.

Economies of Scale   Economies of scale relate to the average cost per unit of producing goods and services. As illustrated below, if the per-unit cost of production falls as the level of production increases, then an economy of scale exists.

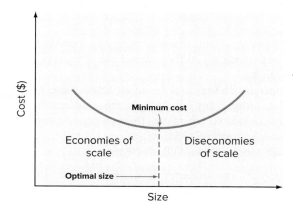

Frequently, the phrase *spreading overhead* is used in connection with economies of scale. This expression refers to the sharing of central facilities such as corporate headquarters, top management, and computer services. For example, in April 2008, when Delta Air Lines and Northwest Airlines announced a merger agreement, the companies issued a statement that they expected to generate cost synergies from more effective aircraft utilization, a more comprehensive and diversified route system, and savings from reduced overhead and improved operational efficiency.

Economies of Vertical Integration   Operating economies can be gained from vertical combinations as well as from horizontal combinations. The main purpose of vertical acquisitions is to make it easier to coordinate closely related operating activities. Benefits from vertical integration are probably why most forest product firms that cut timber also own sawmills and hauling equipment. Economies of vertical integration may explain why some airline companies have purchased hotels and car rental companies.

---

[5]This example comes from Michael Porter, *Competitive Advantage* (New York: Free Press, 1985).

Technology transfers are another reason for vertical integration. Very frequently, a company will decide that the cheapest—and fastest—way to acquire another firm's technological skills is to buy the firm. For obvious reasons, this rationale is particularly common in high-tech industries.

Complementary Resources   Some firms acquire others to make better use of existing resources or to provide the missing ingredient for success. Think of a ski equipment store that could merge with a tennis equipment store to produce more even sales over both the winter and summer seasons, thereby better using store capacity.

LOWER TAXES

Tax gains are a powerful incentive for some acquisitions. The possible tax gains from an acquisition include the following:

1. The use of tax losses.
2. The use of unused debt capacity.
3. The use of surplus funds.
4. The ability to write up the value of depreciable assets.

Net Operating Losses   Firms that lose money on a pretax basis will not pay taxes. Such firms can end up with tax losses they cannot use. These tax losses are referred to as *net operating losses* (NOL).

A firm with net operating losses may be an attractive merger partner for a firm with significant tax liabilities. Absent any other effects, the combined firm will have a lower tax bill than the two firms considered separately. This is a good example of how a firm can be more valuable merged than standing alone.

There are two qualifications to our NOL discussion:

1. Federal tax laws permit firms that experience periods of profit and loss to even things out through loss carryforward provisions (carrybacks were eliminated by the Tax Cuts and Jobs Act of 2017). Thus, a merger to exploit unused tax shields must offer tax savings over and above what can be accomplished by firms via carryforwards.
2. The IRS may disallow an acquisition if the principal purpose of the acquisition is to avoid federal tax by acquiring a deduction or credit that would not otherwise be available.

Unused Debt Capacity   Some firms do not use as much debt as they are able. This makes them potential acquisition candidates. Adding debt can provide important tax savings, and many acquisitions are financed with debt. The acquiring company can deduct interest payments on the newly created debt and reduce taxes (subject to limits created by the Tax Cuts and Jobs Act of 2017, which we discussed elsewhere).

Surplus Funds   Another quirk in the tax laws involves surplus funds. Consider a firm that has free cash flow—cash flow available after all taxes have been paid and after all positive net present value projects have been financed. In such a situation, aside from purchasing fixed-income securities, the firm has several ways to spend the free cash flow, including:

1. Paying dividends.
2. Buying back its own shares.
3. Acquiring shares in another firm.

We discussed the first two options in an earlier chapter. We saw that an extra dividend will increase the income tax paid by some investors. A share repurchase will reduce the taxes paid by shareholders as compared to paying dividends, but this is not a legal option if the sole purpose is to avoid taxes that otherwise would have been paid by shareholders.

To avoid these problems, the firm can buy another firm. By doing this, the firm avoids the tax problem associated with paying a dividend. Also, the dividends received from the purchased firm are not taxed in a merger.

Asset Write-Ups   We have previously observed that, in a taxable acquisition, the assets of the acquired firm can be revalued. If the value of the assets increases, the tax deductions for depreciation will be a benefit; but this benefit will usually be more than offset by taxes due on the write-up.

REDUCTIONS IN CAPITAL NEEDS

All firms must invest in working capital and fixed assets to sustain an efficient level of operating activity. A merger may reduce the combined investments needed by the two firms. For example, Firm A may need to expand its manufacturing facilities, whereas Firm B may have significant excess capacity. It may be much cheaper for Firm A to buy Firm B than to build from scratch.

In addition, acquiring firms may see ways of more effectively managing existing assets. This can occur with a reduction in working capital resulting from more efficient handling of cash, accounts receivable, and inventory. Finally, the acquiring firm may also sell off certain assets that are not needed in the combined firm.

Firms will often cite many reasons for merging. Typically, when firms agree to merge, they generate a list of the economic benefits that shareholders can expect from the merger. For example, the U.S. Steel and Marathon Oil agreement stated (emphasis added):

> U.S. Steel believes that the acquisition of Marathon provides U.S. Steel with an attractive opportunity to *diversify* into the energy business. Reasons for the merger include, but are not limited to, the facts that consummation of the merger will allow U.S. Steel to consolidate Marathon in U.S. Steel's federal *income tax return*, will also contribute to *greater efficiency*, and will enhance the *ability to manage capital* by permitting movements of cash between U.S. Steel and Marathon. Additionally, the merger will *eliminate the possibility of conflicts of interest* between the interests of minority and majority shareholders and will *enhance management flexibility*. The acquisition will provide Marathon shareholders with a substantial premium over historic market prices for their shares. However, [Marathon] shareholders will no longer continue to share in the future prospects of the company.

The more recent merger of satellite radio providers XM and Sirius is another good example. In the middle of 2008, the market capitalization of Sirius was about $3.2 billion and the market capitalization of XM was about $2.5 billion. Analysts estimated that the merger could result in cost savings with a present value of between $3 to $7 billion, potentially more than the combined market cap of the two companies! Why were the estimated savings so large? The companies gave a lot of reasons:

1. Operating cost savings across the board:
    a. General and administrative costs.
    b. Sales and marketing costs.
    c. Subscriber acquisition costs.
    d. Research and development costs.
    e. Product development, manufacturing, and inventory costs.
    f. Programming operating infrastructure.
2. Additional shareholder value in the longer term due to savings on satellite fleet, terrestrial infrastructure, and other capital cost redundancies.
3. Greater appeal to large national advertisers that have a significant number of media alternatives.
4. Advertising sales expense savings.
5. Enhanced operating leverage resulting in accelerated free cash flow generation.

AVOIDING MISTAKES

Evaluating the benefit of a potential acquisition is more difficult than a standard capital budgeting analysis because so much of the value can come from intangible, or otherwise difficult to quantify, benefits. Consequently, there is a great deal of room for error. Here are some general rules that should be remembered:

1. *Do not ignore market values:* There is no point to, and little gain from, estimating the value of a publicly traded firm when that value can be directly observed. The current market value represents a consensus opinion of investors concerning the firm's value (under existing management). Use this value as a starting point. If the firm is not publicly held, then the place to start is with similar firms that are publicly held.
2. *Estimate only incremental cash flows:* It is important to estimate the incremental cash flows that will result from the acquisition. Only incremental cash flows from an acquisition will add value to the acquiring firm. Acquisition analysis should focus only on the newly created, incremental cash flows from the proposed acquisition.
3. *Use the correct discount rate:* The discount rate should be the required rate of return for the incremental cash flows associated with the acquisition. It should reflect the risk associated with the use of funds, not the source. In particular, if Firm A is acquiring Firm B, then Firm A's cost of capital is not particularly relevant. Firm B's cost of capital is a much more appropriate discount rate because it reflects the risk of Firm B's cash flows.
4. *Be aware of transactions costs:* An acquisition may involve substantial (and sometimes astounding) transactions costs. These will include fees to investment bankers, legal fees, and disclosure requirements.

A NOTE ABOUT INEFFICIENT MANAGEMENT

There are firms whose value could be increased with a change in management. These are firms that are poorly run or otherwise do not efficiently use their assets to create shareholder value. Mergers are a means of replacing management in such cases.

The fact that a firm might benefit from a change in management does not necessarily mean that existing management is dishonest, incompetent, or negligent. Instead, as some athletes are better than others, so might some management teams be better at running a business. This can be particularly true during times of technological change or other periods when innovations in business practice are occurring. In any case, to the extent that corporate "raiders" can identify poorly run firms or firms that, for other reasons, will benefit from a change in management, these raiders provide a valuable service to target firm shareholders and society in general.

> **Concept Questions**
>
> **26.4a** What are the relevant incremental cash flows for evaluating a merger candidate?
> **26.4b** What are some different sources of gains from acquisitions?

Some Financial Side Effects of Acquisitions   **26.5**

In addition to the various possibilities we have discussed thus far, mergers can have some purely financial side effects—that is, things that occur regardless of whether the merger makes economic sense or not. Two such effects are particularly worth mentioning: EPS growth and diversification.

EPS GROWTH

An acquisition can create the appearance of growth in earnings per share, or EPS. This may fool investors into thinking that the firm is doing better than it really is. What happens is easiest to see with an example.

Suppose Global Resources, Ltd., acquires Regional Enterprises. The financial positions of Global and Regional before the acquisition are shown in Table 26.2. We assume that the merger creates no additional value, so the combined firm (Global Resources after acquiring Regional) has a value that is equal to the sum of the values of the two firms before the merger.

Before the merger, both Global and Regional have 100 shares outstanding. However, Global sells for $25 per share, versus a price of $10 per share for Regional. Global acquires Regional by exchanging 1 of its shares for every 2.5 shares in Regional. Because there are 100 shares in Regional, this will take 100/2.5 = 40 shares in all.

After the merger, Global will have 140 shares outstanding, and several things will happen (see the third column of Table 26.2):

1. The market value of the combined firm is **$3,500**. This is equal to the sum of the values of the separate firms before the merger. If the market is "smart," it will realize that the combined firm is worth the sum of the values of the separate firms.

	Global Resources before Merger	Regional Enterprises before Merger	Global Resources after Merger The Market Is Smart	The Market Is Fooled
Earnings per share	$1	$1	$1.43	$1.43
Price per share	$25	$10	$25	$35.71
Price-earnings ratio	25	10	17.5	25
Number of shares	100	100	140	140
Total earnings	$100	$100	$200	$200
Total value	$2,500	$1,000	$3,500	$5,000

TABLE 26.2

Financial Positions of Global Resources and Regional Enterprises

Exchange ratio: 1 share in Global for 2.5 shares in Regional.

2. The earnings per share of the merged firm are **$1.43**. The acquisition enables Global to increase its earnings per share from $1 to $1.43, an increase of 43 percent.

3. Because the stock price of Global after the merger is the same as before the merger, the price-earnings ratio must fall. This is true as long as the market is smart and recognizes that the total market value has not been altered by the merger.

If the market is "fooled," it might mistake the 43 percent increase in earnings per share for true growth. In this case, the price-earnings ratio of Global may not fall after the merger. Suppose the price-earnings ratio of Global remains equal to 25. Because the combined firm has earnings of **$200**, the total value of the combined firm will increase to **$5,000** (**= 25 × $200**). The per-share value for Global will increase to **$35.71 (= $5,000/140)**.

This is earnings growth magic. Like all good magic, it is illusion. For it to work, the shareholders of Global and Regional must receive something for nothing. This, of course, is unlikely with so simple a trick.

DIVERSIFICATION

Diversification is commonly mentioned as a benefit of a merger. We previously noted that U.S. Steel included diversification as a benefit in describing its acquisition of Marathon Oil. The problem is that diversification per se probably does not create value.

Going back to Chapter 13, recall that diversification reduces unsystematic risk. We also saw that the value of an asset depends on its systematic risk, and systematic risk is not directly affected by diversification. Because the unsystematic risk is not especially important, there is no particular benefit from reducing it.

An easy way to see why diversification isn't an important benefit of a merger is to consider someone who owned stock in U.S. Steel and Marathon Oil. Such a stockholder was already diversified between these two investments. The merger didn't do anything the stockholders couldn't do for themselves.

More generally, stockholders can get all the diversification they want by buying stock in different companies. As a result, they won't pay a premium for a merged company for the benefit of diversification.

By the way, we are not saying that U.S. Steel made a mistake. At the time of the merger, U.S. Steel was a cash-rich company (over 20 percent of its assets were in the form of cash and marketable securities). It is not uncommon to see firms with surplus cash articulating a "need" for diversification.

Concept Questions

26.5a Why can a merger create the appearance of earnings growth?
26.5b Why is diversification by itself not a good reason for a merger?

26.6 The Cost of an Acquisition

We've discussed some of the benefits of acquisition. We now need to discuss the cost of a merger.[6] We learned earlier that the net incremental gain from a merger is:

$$\Delta V = V_{AB} - (V_A + V_B)$$

---

[6]For a more complete discussion of the costs of a merger and the NPV approach, see S. C. Myers, "A Framework for Evaluating Mergers," in *Modern Developments in Financial Management*, ed. S. C. Myers (New York: Praeger Publishers, 1976).

Also, the total value of Firm B to Firm A, V_B^*, is:

$$V_B^* = V_B + \Delta V$$

The net present value (NPV) of the merger is:

NPV = V_B^* − Cost to Firm A of the acquisition   (26.1)

To illustrate, suppose we have the following premerger information for Firm A and Firm B:

	Firm A	Firm B
Price per share	$ 20	$ 10
Number of shares	25	10
Total market value	**$500**	**$100**

Both of these firms are 100 percent equity. You estimate that the incremental value of the acquisition, ΔV, is $100.

The board of Firm B has indicated that it will agree to a sale if the price is $150, payable in cash or stock. This price for Firm B has two parts. Firm B is worth $100 as a stand-alone, so this is the minimum value that we could assign to Firm B. The second part, $50, is called the merger premium, and it represents the amount paid above the stand-alone value.

Should Firm A acquire Firm B? Should it pay in cash or stock? To answer, we need to determine the NPV of the acquisition under both alternatives. We can start by noting that the value of Firm B to Firm A is:

$$V_B^* = \Delta V + V_B$$
$$= \$100 + 100 = \$200$$

The total value received by A as a result of buying Firm B is $200. The question then is: How much does Firm A have to give up? The answer depends on whether cash or stock is used as the means of payment.

CASE I: CASH ACQUISITION

The cost of an acquisition when cash is used is the cash itself. So, if Firm A pays $150 in cash to purchase all of the shares of Firm B, the cost of acquiring Firm B is $150. The NPV of a cash acquisition is:

$$NPV = V_B^* - \text{Cost}$$
$$= \$200 - 150 = \$50$$

The acquisition is profitable.

After the merger, Firm AB will still have 25 shares outstanding. The value of Firm A after the merger is:

$$V_{AB} = V_A + \left(V_B^* - \text{Cost} \right)$$
$$= \$500 + 200 - 150$$
$$= \$550$$

This is the premerger value of $500 plus the $50 NPV. The price per share after the merger is $550/25 = $22, representing a gain of $2 per share.

CASE II: STOCK ACQUISITION

Things are somewhat more complicated when stock is the means of payment. In a cash merger, the shareholders in B receive cash for their stock; and, as in the U.S. Steel-Marathon

Oil example, they no longer participate in the company. As we have seen, the cost of the acquisition in this case is the amount of cash needed to pay off B's stockholders.

In a stock merger, no cash actually changes hands. Instead, the shareholders of Firm B come in as new shareholders in the merged firm. The value of the merged firm in this case will be equal to the premerger values of Firms A and B plus the incremental gain from the merger, ΔV:

$$
\begin{aligned}
V_{AB} &= V_A + V_B + \Delta V \\
&= \$500 + 100 + 100 \\
&= \$700
\end{aligned}
$$

To give \$150 worth of stock for Firm B, Firm A will have to give up \$150/\$20 = 7.5 shares. After the merger, there will be 25 + 7.5 = 32.5 shares outstanding, and the per-share value will be \$700/32.5 = \$21.54.

Notice that the per-share price after the merger is lower under the stock purchase option. The reason has to do with the fact that B's shareholders own stock in the new firm.

It appears that Firm A paid \$150 for Firm B. However, it actually paid more than that. When all is said and done, B's stockholders own 7.5 shares of stock in the merged firm. After the merger, each of these shares is worth \$21.54. The total value of the consideration received by B's stockholders is 7.5 × \$21.54 = \$161.54.

This \$161.54 is the true cost of the acquisition because it is what the sellers actually end up receiving. The NPV of the merger to Firm A is:

$$
\begin{aligned}
NPV &= V_B^* - \text{Cost} \\
&= \$200 - 161.54 = \$38.46
\end{aligned}
$$

We can check this by noting that Firm A started with 25 shares worth \$20 each. The gain to Firm A of \$38.46 works out to be \$38.46/25 = \$1.54 per share. The value of the stock has increased to \$21.54, as we calculated.

When we compare the cash acquisition to the stock acquisition, we see that the cash acquisition is better in this case, because Firm A gets to keep all of the NPV if it pays in cash. If it pays in stock, Firm B's stockholders share in the NPV by becoming new stockholders in Firm A.

CASH VERSUS COMMON STOCK

The distinction between cash and common stock financing in a merger is an important one. If cash is used, the cost of an acquisition is not dependent on the acquisition gains. All other things being the same, if common stock is used, the cost is higher because Firm A's shareholders must share the acquisition gains with the shareholders of Firm B. However, if the NPV of the acquisition is negative, then the loss will be shared between the two firms.

Whether a firm should finance an acquisition with cash or with shares of stock depends on several factors, including the following:

1. *Sharing gains:* If cash is used to finance an acquisition, the selling firm's shareholders will not participate in the potential gains from the merger. Of course, if the acquisition is not a success, the losses will not be shared, and shareholders of the acquiring firm will be worse off than if stock had been used.
2. *Taxes:* Acquisition by paying cash usually results in a taxable transaction. Acquisition by exchanging stock is generally tax-free.
3. *Control:* Acquisition by paying cash does not affect the control of the acquiring firm. Acquisition with voting shares may have implications for control of the merged firm.

In a typical year, in terms of the total number of deals, cash financing is much more common than stock financing. The same is usually true based on the total dollar values, though the difference is smaller. The reason is that stock financing becomes more common if we look at very large deals.

Concept Questions

26.6a Why does the true cost of a stock acquisition depend on the gain from the merger?

26.6b What are some important factors in deciding whether to use stock or cash in an acquisition?

Defensive Tactics

26.7

Target firm managers frequently resist takeover attempts. Resistance usually starts with press releases and mailings to shareholders that present management's viewpoint. It can eventually lead to legal action and solicitation of competing bids. Managerial action to defeat a takeover attempt may make target firm shareholders better off if it elicits a higher offer premium from the bidding firm or another firm.

Of course, management resistance may reflect pursuit of self-interest at the expense of shareholders. This is a controversial subject. At times, management resistance has greatly increased the amount ultimately received by shareholders. At other times, management resistance appears to have defeated all takeover attempts to the detriment of shareholders.

In this section, we describe various defensive tactics that have been used by target firms' management to resist unfriendly attempts. The law surrounding these defenses is not settled, and some of these maneuvers may ultimately be deemed illegal or otherwise unsuitable.

THE CORPORATE CHARTER

The *corporate charter* consists of the articles of incorporation and corporate bylaws that establish the governance rules of the firm. The corporate charter establishes the conditions that allow for a takeover. Firms frequently amend corporate charters to make acquisitions more difficult. For example, usually two-thirds (67 percent) of the shareholders of record must approve a merger. Firms can make it more difficult to be acquired by changing this required percentage to 80 percent or so. Such a change is called a *supermajority amendment*.

Another device is to stagger the election of the board members. This makes it more difficult to elect a new board of directors quickly. Such a board is sometimes called a *classified board*. We discussed staggered elections in Chapter 8.

REPURCHASE AND STANDSTILL AGREEMENTS

Managers of target firms may attempt to negotiate *standstill agreements*. Standstill agreements are contracts wherein the bidding firm agrees to limit its holdings in the target firm. These agreements usually lead to the end of a takeover attempt.

Standstill agreements often occur at the same time that a *targeted repurchase* is arranged. In a targeted repurchase, a firm buys a certain amount of its own stock from an individual investor, usually at a substantial premium. These premiums can be thought of as payments to potential bidders to eliminate unfriendly takeover attempts. Critics of such payments view them as bribes and label them **greenmail**.

greenmail
In a targeted stock repurchase, payments made to potential bidders to eliminate unfriendly takeover attempts.

POISON PILLS AND SHARE RIGHTS PLANS

poison pill
A financial device designed to make unfriendly takeover attempts unappealing, if not impossible.

A **poison pill** is a tactic designed to repel would-be suitors. The term comes from the world of espionage. Agents are supposed to bite a pill of cyanide rather than permit capture. Presumably, this prevents enemy interrogators from learning important secrets.

In the equally colorful world of corporate finance, a poison pill is a financial device designed to make it impossible for a firm to be acquired without management's consent—unless the buyer is willing to commit financial suicide.

A majority of the largest firms in the United States have adopted poison pill provisions of one form or another, often calling them **share rights plans** (SRPs) or something similar. SRPs differ quite a bit in detail from company to company; we will describe a kind of generic approach here. In general, when a company adopts an SRP, it distributes share rights to its existing stockholders.[7] These rights allow shareholders to buy shares of stock (or preferred stock) at some fixed price.

share rights plans
Provisions allowing existing stockholders to purchase stock at some fixed price should an outside takeover bid come up, discouraging hostile takeover attempts.

The rights issued with an SRP have a number of unusual features. First, the exercise, or subscription, price on the right is usually set high enough so that the rights are well out of the money, meaning that the purchase price is much higher than the current stock price. The rights will often be good for 10 years, and the purchase, or exercise, price is usually a reasonable estimate of what the stock will be worth at the end of that time.

In addition, unlike ordinary stock rights, these rights can't be exercised immediately, and they can't be bought and sold separately from the stock. Also, they can essentially be canceled by management at any time; often, they can be redeemed (bought back) for a penny apiece, or some similarly trivial amount.

Things get interesting when, under certain circumstances, the rights are "triggered." This means that the rights become exercisable, they can be bought and sold separately from the stock, and they are not easily canceled or redeemed. Typically, the rights will be triggered when someone acquires 20 percent of the common stock or announces a tender offer.

When the rights are triggered, they can be exercised. Because they are out of the money, this fact is not especially important. Certain other features come into play, however. The most important is the *flip-in provision*.

The flip-in provision is the "poison" in the pill. In the event of an unfriendly takeover attempt, the holder of a right can pay the exercise price and receive common stock in the target firm worth twice the exercise price. In other words, holders of the rights can buy stock in the target firm at half price. Simultaneously, the rights owned by the raider (the acquirer) are voided. The goal of the flip-in provision is to massively dilute the raider's ownership position.[8] Doing so greatly increases the cost of the merger to the bidder because the target firm's shareholders end up with a much larger percentage of the merged firm.

Notice that the flip-in provision doesn't prevent someone from acquiring control of a firm by purchasing a majority interest. It just acts to vastly increase the cost of doing so.

The intention of a poison pill is to force a bidder to negotiate with management. Frequently, merger offers are made with the contingency that the rights will be canceled by the target firm.

---

[7] We discussed ordinary share rights in Chapter 15.

[8] Some plans also contain "flip-over" provisions. These allow the holders to buy stock in the merged company at half price.

Some new varieties of poison pills have appeared on the scene in recent years. For example, a "chewable" pill, common in Canada but not in the United States, is a pill that is installed by shareholder vote and can be redeemed by shareholder vote. Then there's the "deadhand pill," which explicitly gives the directors who installed the pill, or their handpicked successors, the authority to remove the pill. This type of pill is controversial because it makes it virtually impossible for new directors elected by stockholders to remove an existing poison pill.

Recently, a method of circumventing poison pills has grown in popularity. Hedge funds or other large investors, all of whom have the same agenda, such as removing the company's management or changing the way the company operates, band together and purchase a large block of stock. They then vote to remove the board of directors and company management without triggering the poison pill provision.

GOING PRIVATE AND LEVERAGED BUYOUTS

As we have previously discussed, going private is what happens when the publicly owned stock in a firm is replaced with complete equity ownership by a private group, which may include elements of existing management. As a consequence, the firm's stock is taken off the market (if it is an exchange-traded stock, it is delisted) and no longer traded.

One result of going private is that takeovers via tender offer can no longer occur because there are no publicly held shares. In this sense, a leveraged buyout (or more specifically, a management buyout, or MBO) can be a takeover defense. However, it's a defense only for management. From the stockholders' point of view, an LBO is a takeover because they are bought out.

OTHER DEVICES AND JARGON OF CORPORATE TAKEOVERS

As corporate takeovers have become more common, a new vocabulary has developed. The terms are colorful, and, in no particular order, some of them are listed here:

1. *Golden parachute:* Some target firms provide compensation to top-level managers if a takeover occurs. For example, when Verizon agreed to acquire Yahoo! in 2016, it was reported that Yahoo! CEO Marissa Mayer would receive a $57 million severance package if she left the company. The opposite of a golden parachute is a "golden handcuff," which is an incentive package designed to get executives to stay on board once the acquisition is completed.

   Depending on your perspective and the amounts involved, golden parachutes can be viewed as a payment to management to make it less concerned for its own welfare and more interested in stockholders when considering a takeover bid.

2. *Poison put:* A poison put is a variation on the poison pill we described earlier. A poison put forces the firm to buy securities back at some set price.

3. *Crown jewel:* Firms often sell or threaten to sell major assets—crown jewels—when faced with a takeover threat. This is sometimes referred to as the *scorched earth* strategy. This tactic often involves a lockup, which we discuss shortly.

4. *White knight:* A firm facing an unfriendly merger offer might arrange to be acquired by a different, friendly firm. The firm is thereby rescued by a "white knight." Alternatively, the firm may arrange for a friendly entity to acquire a large block of stock. White knights can often increase the amount offered for the target firm. For example, in 2016, *Los Angeles Times* and *Chicago Tribune* publisher Tribune Publishing received a bid of $12.25 per share from *USA Today* publisher Gannett Company. In response, Tribune Publishing found a white knight in Nant Capital, which invested $70.5 million in new equity to help fight off the bid. Although Gannett increased its offer to $15 per share, it eventually withdrew all offers and stopped its acquisition efforts.

So-called white squires or big brothers are individuals, firms, or even mutual funds involved in friendly transactions of these types. Sometimes white knights or others are granted exceptional terms or otherwise compensated. Inevitably, it seems, this has been called *whitemail.*

5. *Lockup:* A lockup is an option granted to a friendly suitor (a white knight, perhaps) giving it the right to purchase stock or some of the assets (the crown jewels, possibly) of a target firm at a fixed price in the event of an unfriendly takeover.

6. *Shark repellent:* A shark repellent is any tactic (a poison pill, for example) designed to discourage unwanted merger offers.

7. *Bear hug:* A bear hug is an unfriendly takeover offer designed to be so attractive that the target firm's management has little choice but to accept it. For example, in May 2016, Bayer made a $62 billion bear hug offer for Monsanto. Evidently this bear hug wasn't tight enough because, in December 2016, Monsanto stockholders eventually agreed to a sale at $66 billion.

8. *Fair price provision:* A fair price provision is a requirement that all selling shareholders receive the same price from a bidder. The provision prevents a "two-tier" offer. In such a deal, a bidder offers a premium price only for a percentage of the shares large enough to gain control. It offers a lower price for the remaining shares. Such an offer can set off a stampede among shareholders as they rush to get the better price.

9. *Dual class capitalization:* In an earlier chapter, we noted that some firms such as Alphabet have more than one class of common stock and that voting power is typically concentrated in a class of stock not held by the public. Such a capital structure means that an unfriendly bidder will not succeed in gaining control.

10. *Countertender offer:* Better known as the "Pac-Man" defense, the target responds to an unfriendly overture by offering to buy the bidder! This tactic is rarely used, in part because target firms are usually too small to realistically purchase the bidder. However, such a countertender offer occurred in 2013. Jos. A. Bank made an offer to acquire Men's Wearhouse, which turned down the offer. When Jos. A. Bank pulled the offer, Men's Wearhouse responded with a $1.5 billion bid for Jos. A. Bank. Finally, after it was raised to $2.3 billion, Jos. A. Bank accepted the offer in March 2014.

Concept Questions

26.7a   What can a firm do to make a takeover less likely?

26.7b   What is a share rights plan? Explain how the rights work.

26.8 Some Evidence on Acquisitions: Does M&A Pay?

One of the most controversial issues surrounding our subject is whether mergers and acquisitions benefit shareholders. A very large number of studies have attempted to estimate the effect of mergers and takeovers on stock prices of the bidding and target firms. These studies have examined the gains and losses in stock value around the time of merger announcements.

One conclusion that clearly emerges is that M&A pays for target firm shareholders. There is no mystery here. The premium typically paid by bidders represents an immediate, relatively large gain, often on the order of 20 percent or more.

Matters become much murkier when we look at bidders, and different studies reach different conclusions. One thing is clear: Shareholders in bidder firms seem to neither win nor lose very much, at least on average. This finding is a bit of a puzzle, and there are a variety of explanations:

1. Anticipated merger gains may not be completely achieved, and shareholders experience losses. This can happen if managers of bidding firms tend to overestimate the gains from acquisition.
2. The bidding firms are usually much larger than the target firms. Even though the dollar gains to the bidder may be similar to the dollar gains earned by shareholders of the target firm, the percentage gains will be much lower.
3. Another possible explanation for the low returns to the shareholders of bidding firms in takeovers is that management may not be acting in the interest of shareholders when it attempts to acquire other firms. Perhaps it is attempting to increase the size of the firm, even if this reduces its value per share.
4. The market for takeovers may be sufficiently competitive that the NPV of acquiring is zero because the prices paid in acquisitions fully reflect the value of the acquired firms. In other words, the sellers capture all of the gain.
5. Finally, the announcement of a takeover may not convey much new information to the market about the bidding firm. This can occur because firms frequently announce intentions to engage in merger "programs" long before they announce specific acquisitions. In this case, the stock price for the bidding firm may already reflect anticipated gains from mergers.

Concept Questions

26.8a What does the evidence say about the benefits of mergers and acquisitions to target company shareholders?

26.8b What does the evidence say about the benefits of mergers and acquisitions to acquiring company shareholders?

Divestitures and Restructurings

26.9

In contrast to a merger or acquisition, a **divestiture** occurs when a firm sells assets, operations, divisions, and/or segments to a third party. Note that divestitures are an important part of M&A activity. After all, one company's acquisition is usually another's divestiture. Also, following a merger, it is very common for certain assets or divisions to be sold. Such sales may be required by antitrust regulations; they may be needed to raise cash to help pay for a deal; or the divested units may be unwanted by the acquirer.

Divestitures also occur when a company decides to sell off a part of itself for reasons unrelated to mergers and acquisitions. This can happen when a particular unit is unprofitable or not a good strategic fit. Or, a firm may decide to cash out of a very profitable operation. Finally, a cash-strapped firm may have to sell assets to raise capital (this commonly occurs in bankruptcy).

A divestiture usually occurs like any other sale. A company lets it be known that it has assets for sale and seeks offers. If a suitable offer is forthcoming, a sale occurs.

In some cases, particularly when the desired divestiture is a relatively large operating unit, companies will elect to do an **equity carve-out**. To do a carve-out, a parent company

divestiture
The sale of assets, operations, divisions, and/or segments of a business to a third party.

equity carve-out
The sale of stock in a wholly owned subsidiary via an IPO.

first creates a completely separate company of which the parent is the sole shareholder. Next, the parent company arranges an initial public offering (IPO) in which a fraction, perhaps 20 percent or so, of the parent's stock is sold to the public, creating a publicly held company.

spin-off
The distribution of shares in a subsidiary to existing parent company stockholders.

Instead of a carve-out, a company can elect to do a **spin-off**. In a spin-off, the company distributes shares in the subsidiary to its existing stockholders on a pro rata basis. Shareholders can keep the shares or sell them as they see fit. Very commonly, a company will first do an equity carve-out to create an active market for the shares and then subsequently do a spin-off of the remaining shares at a later date. Many well-known companies were created by this route. For example, insurance giant Allstate was spun off by Sears; Agilent Technologies was a Hewlett-Packard spin-off; and Conoco was once a part of DuPont.

split-up
The splitting up of a company into two or more companies.

In a less common, but more drastic move, a company can elect to do (or be forced to do) a **split-up**. A split-up is exactly what the name suggests: A company splits itself into two or more new companies. Shareholders have their shares in the old company swapped for shares in the new companies. Probably the most famous split-up occurred in the 1980s. As the result of an antitrust suit by the Justice Department, AT&T was forced to split up through the creation of seven regional phone companies (the so-called Baby Bells). Today, the Baby Bells survive as companies such as Verizon. In an unusual turn of events, in 2005, SBC Communications acquired its former parent company, AT&T. In a nod to AT&T's history and name brand recognition, the new company kept the AT&T name even though SBC was the acquirer.

Split-ups are often touted as a way of "unlocking" value, meaning a situation where the whole is worth less than the sum of the parts. For example, in November 2016, Conoco-Phillips announced that it planned to spin off $5 to $8 billion of its assets related to natural gas production in the United States. Also in 2016, aluminum producer Alcoa announced that it would split into two companies. After the split, the name would be retained by the company that focused on smelting and refining, and the other company would be known as Arconic, Inc., and would focus on engineering products for the aerospace and automotive industries.

Concept Questions

26.9a What is an equity carve-out? Why might a firm wish to do one?
26.9b What is a split-up? Why might a firm choose to do one?

26.10 Summary and Conclusions

This chapter has introduced you to the extensive literature on mergers and acquisitions. We mentioned a number of issues:

1. *Forms of merger:* One firm can acquire another in several different ways. The three legal forms of acquisition are merger or consolidation, acquisition of stock, and acquisition of assets.

2. *Tax issues:* Mergers and acquisitions can be taxable or tax-free transactions. The primary issue is whether the target firm's stockholders sell or exchange their shares. Generally, a cash purchase will be a taxable merger, whereas a stock exchange will not be

taxable. In a taxable merger, there are capital gains effects and asset write-up effects to consider. In a stock exchange, the target firm's shareholders become shareholders in the merged firm.

3. *Accounting issues:* In 2001, FASB determined that all acquisitions must be treated under the purchase accounting method. As a result, a merger or acquisition will generally result in the creation of goodwill; but under the new guidelines, goodwill does not have to be amortized.

4. *Merger valuation:* If Firm A is acquiring Firm B, the benefits (ΔV) from the acquisition are defined as the value of the combined firm (V_{AB}) less the value of the firms as separate entities (V_A and V_B):

$$\Delta V = V_{AB} - (V_A + V_B)$$

The gain to Firm A from acquiring Firm B is the increased value of the acquired firm, ΔV, plus the value of Firm B as a separate firm, V_B. The total value of Firm B to Firm A, V_B^*, is:

$$V_B^* = \Delta V + V_B$$

An acquisition will benefit the shareholders of the acquiring firm if this value is greater than the cost of the acquisition.

The cost of an acquisition can be defined in general terms as the price paid to the shareholders of the acquired firm. The cost frequently includes a merger premium paid to the shareholders of the acquired firm. Moreover, the cost depends on the form of payment—that is, the choice between paying with cash or paying with common stock.

5. *Benefits*: The possible benefits of an acquisition come from several sources, including the following:

   a. Revenue enhancement.

   b. Cost reductions.

   c. Lower taxes.

   d. Reductions in capital needs.

6. *Defensive tactics*: Some of the most colorful language of finance comes from defensive tactics used in acquisition battles. *Poison pills*, *golden parachutes*, *crown jewels*, and *greenmail* are some of the terms that describe various antitakeover tactics.

7. *Effect on shareholders*: Mergers and acquisitions have been extensively studied. The basic conclusions are that, on average, the shareholders of target firms do well, whereas the shareholders of bidding firms do not appear to gain much.

8. *Divestitures*: For a variety of reasons, companies often wish to sell assets or operating units. For relatively large divestitures involving operating units, firms sometimes elect to do carve-outs, spin-offs, or split-ups.

CONNECT TO FINANCE

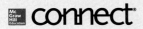 If you are using *Connect Finance* in your course, get online to take a Practice Test, check out study tools, and find out where you need additional practice.

Can you answer the following *Connect* Quiz questions?

Section 26.2 What is one result of the Tax Reform Act of 1986?

Section 26.3 When accounting for an acquisition, goodwill is the difference between what two things?

Section 26.6 What factors should be considered when deciding whether an acquisition should be financed with cash or with shares of stock?

CHAPTER REVIEW AND SELF-TEST PROBLEMS

26.1 Merger Value and Cost Consider the following information for two all-equity firms, Firm A and Firm B:

	Firm A	Firm B
Shares outstanding	2,000	6,000
Price per share	$ 40	$ 30

Firm A estimates that the value of the synergistic benefit from acquiring Firm B is $6,000. Firm B has indicated that it would accept a cash purchase offer of $35 per share. Should Firm A proceed?

26.2 Stock Mergers and EPS Consider the following information for two all-equity firms, Firm A and Firm B:

	Firm A	Firm B
Total earnings	$3,000	$1,100
Shares outstanding	600	400
Price per share	$ 70	$ 15

Firm A is acquiring Firm B by exchanging 100 of its shares for all the shares in Firm B. What is the cost of the merger if the merged firm is worth $63,000? What will happen to Firm A's EPS? Its PE ratio?

ANSWERS TO CHAPTER REVIEW AND SELF-TEST PROBLEMS

26.1 The total value of Firm B to Firm A is the premerger value of Firm B plus the $6,000 gain from the merger. The premerger value of Firm B is $30 × 6,000 = $180,000, so the total value is $186,000. At $35 per share, Firm A is paying $35 × 6,000 = $210,000; the merger therefore has a negative NPV of $186,000 − 210,000 = −$24,000. At $35 per share, Firm B is not an attractive merger partner.

26.2 After the merger, the firm will have 700 shares outstanding. Because the total value is $63,000, the price per share is $63,000/700 = $90, up from $70. Because Firm B's stockholders end up with 100 shares in the merged firm, the cost of the merger is 100 × $90 = $9,000, not 100 × $70 = $7,000.

Also, the combined firm will have $3,000 + 1,100 = $4,100 in earnings, so EPS will be $4,100/700 = $5.86, up from $3,000/600 = $5. The old PE ratio was $70/$5 = 14.00. The new one is $90/$5.86 = 15.37.

CONCEPTS REVIEW AND CRITICAL THINKING QUESTIONS

1. **Merger Types** [LO1] In 2014, Japanese liquor company Suntory Holdings Ltd. acquired U.S. bourbon maker Beam Inc., for $14 billion. Is this a horizontal or vertical acquisition? How do you suppose Beam's nationality affected Suntory's decision?

2. **Merger Terms** [LO1] Define each of the following terms:
    a. Greenmail
    b. White knight
    c. Golden parachute
    d. Crown jewels
    e. Shark repellent
    f. Corporate raider
    g. Poison pill
    h. Tender offer
    i. Leveraged buyout (LBO)

3. **Merger Rationale** [LO1] Explain why diversification per se is probably not a good reason for a merger.

4. **Corporate Split** [LO3] In 2016, activist investor Elliott Management was pressuring Marathon Petroleum to split up the company. Elliott felt that Marathon should sell off its Speedway gas and retail stores. Why might investors prefer that a company split into multiple companies? Is there a possibility of reverse synergy?

5. **Poison Pills** [LO1] Are poison pills good or bad for stockholders? How do you think acquiring firms are able to get around poison pills?

6. **Mergers and Taxes** [LO2] Describe the advantages and disadvantages of a taxable merger as opposed to a tax-free exchange. What is the basic determinant of tax status in a merger? Would an LBO be taxable or nontaxable? Explain.

7. **Economies of Scale** [LO3] What does it mean to say that a proposed merger will take advantage of available economies of scale? Suppose Eastern Power Co. and Western Power Co. are located in different time zones. Both of them operate at 60 percent of capacity except for peak periods, when they operate at 100 percent of capacity. The peak periods begin at 9:00 a.m. and 5:00 p.m. local time and last about 45 minutes. Explain why a merger between Eastern and Western might make sense.

8. **Hostile Takeovers** [LO1] What types of actions might the management of a firm take to fight a hostile acquisition bid from an unwanted suitor? How do the target firm shareholders benefit from the defensive tactics of their management team? How are the target firm shareholders harmed by such actions? Explain.

9. **Merger Offers** [LO1] Suppose a company in which you own stock has attracted two takeover offers. Would it ever make sense for your company's management to favor the lower offer? Does the form of payment affect your answer at all?

10. **Merger Profit** [LO2] Acquiring firm stockholders seem to benefit very little from takeovers. Why is this finding a puzzle? What are some of the reasons offered in explanation?

QUESTIONS AND PROBLEMS

BASIC
(Questions 1–8)

1. **Calculating Synergy [LO3]** Pearl, Inc., has offered $228 million cash for all of the common stock in Jam Corporation. Based on recent market information, Jam is worth $214 million as an independent operation. If the merger makes economic sense for Pearl, what is the minimum estimated value of the synergistic benefits from the merger?

✗ 2. **Balance Sheets for Mergers [LO2]** Consider the following premerger information about Firm X and Firm Y:

	Firm X	Firm Y
Total earnings	$85,000	$11,000
Shares outstanding	30,000	8,000
Per-share values:		
Market	$ 58	$ 13
Book	$ 6	$ 2

Assume that Firm X acquires Firm Y by issuing new long-term debt for all the shares outstanding at a merger premium of $6 per share. Assuming that neither firm has any debt before the merger, construct the postmerger balance sheet for Firm X under the purchase accounting method.

3. **Balance Sheets for Mergers [LO2]** Assume that the following balance sheets are stated at book value. Suppose that Meat Co. purchases Loaf, Inc.

Meat Co.			
Current assets	$18,000	Current liabilities	$ 6,100
Net fixed assets	43,000	Long-term debt	13,700
		Equity	41,200
Total	$61,000	Total	$61,000

Loaf, Inc.			
Current assets	$ 3,900	Current liabilities	$ 1,500
Net fixed assets	6,900	Long-term debt	2,600
		Equity	6,700
Total	$10,800	Total	$10,800

The fair market value of Loaf's fixed assets is $9,800 versus the $6,900 book value shown. Meat pays $17,800 for Loaf and raises the needed funds through an issue of long-term debt. Construct the postmerger balance sheet under the purchase accounting method.

✗ 4. **Balance Sheets for Mergers [LO2]** Silver Enterprises has acquired All Gold Mining in a merger transaction. Construct the balance sheet for the new corporation if the merger is treated as a purchase of interests for accounting purposes. The following balance sheets represent the premerger book values for both firms:

Silver Enterprises			
Current assets	$ 5,700	Current liabilities	$ 3,100
Other assets	1,600	Long-term debt	8,150
Net fixed assets	18,400	Equity	14,450
Total	$25,700	Total	$25,700

All Gold Mining			
Current assets	$1,600	Current liabilities	$1,590
Other assets	680	Long-term debt	0
Net fixed assets	7,400	Equity	8,090
Total	$9,680	Total	$9,680

The market value of All Gold Mining's fixed assets is $9,300; the market values for current and other assets are the same as the book values. Assume that Silver Enterprises issues $16,000 in new long-term debt to finance the acquisition.

5. **Cash versus Stock Payment** [LO3] Penn Corp. is analyzing the possible acquisition of Teller Company. Both firms have no debt. Penn believes the acquisition will increase its total aftertax annual cash flows by $1.6 million indefinitely. The current market value of Teller is $38 million, and that of Penn is $65 million. The appropriate discount rate for the incremental cash flows is 10 percent. Penn is trying to decide whether it should offer 40 percent of its stock or $51.5 million in cash to Teller's shareholders.
   a. What is the cost of each alternative?
   b. What is the NPV of each alternative?
   c. Which alternative should Penn choose?

6. **Calculating Synergy** [LO3] Three Guys Burgers, Inc., has offered $16.5 million for all of the common stock in Two Guys Fries, Corp. The current market capitalization of Two Guys as an independent company is $13.4 million. Assume the required return on the acquisition is 9 percent and the synergy from the acquisition is a perpetuity. What is the minimum annual synergy that Three Guys feels it will gain from the acquisition?

7. **EPS, PE, and Mergers** [LO3] The shareholders of Bread Company have voted in favor of a buyout offer from Butter Corporation. Information about each firm is given here:

	Bread	Butter
Price-earnings ratio	6.35	12.7
Shares outstanding	73,000	146,000
Earnings	$230,000	$690,000

Bread's shareholders will receive one share of Butter stock for every three shares they hold in Bread.
   a. What will the EPS of Butter be after the merger? What will the PE ratio be if the NPV of the acquisition is zero?
   b. What must Butter feel is the value of the synergy between these two firms? Explain how your answer can be reconciled with the decision to go ahead with the takeover.

8. **Cash versus Stock as Payment** [LO3] Consider the following premerger information about a bidding firm (Firm B) and a target firm (Firm T). Assume that both firms have no debt outstanding.

	Firm B	Firm T
Shares outstanding	5,300	1,200
Price per share	$ 44	$ 16

Firm B has estimated that the value of the synergistic benefits from acquiring Firm T is $9,300.

    a. If Firm T is willing to be acquired for $19 per share in cash, what is the NPV of the merger?

    b. What will the price per share of the merged firm be assuming the conditions in (a)?

    c. In part (a), what is the merger premium?

    d. Suppose Firm T is agreeable to a merger by an exchange of stock. If B offers one of its shares for every two of T's shares, what will the price per share of the merged firm be?

    e. What is the NPV of the merger assuming the conditions in (d)?

INTERMEDIATE
(Questions 9–13)

9. **Cash versus Stock as Payment** [LO3] In Problem 8, are the shareholders of Firm T better off with the cash offer or the stock offer? At what exchange ratio of B shares to T shares would the shareholders in T be indifferent between the two offers?

10. **Effects of a Stock Exchange** [LO3] Consider the following premerger information about Firm A and Firm B:

	Firm A	Firm B
Total earnings	$4,350	$1,300
Shares outstanding	1,600	400
Price per share	$ 43	$ 47

Assume that Firm A acquires Firm B via an exchange of stock at a price of $49 for each share of B's stock. Both Firm A and Firm B have no debt outstanding.

    a. What will the earnings per share (EPS) of Firm A be after the merger?

    b. What will Firm A's price per share be after the merger if the market incorrectly analyzes this reported earnings growth (that is, the price-earnings ratio does not change)?

    c. What will the price-earnings ratio of the postmerger firm be if the market correctly analyzes the transaction?

    d. If there are no synergy gains, what will the share price of Firm A be after the merger? What will the price-earnings ratio be? What does your answer for the share price tell you about the amount Firm A bid for Firm B? Was it too high? Too low? Explain.

11. **Merger NPV** [LO3] Show that the NPV of a merger can be expressed as the value of the synergistic benefits, ΔV, less the merger premium.

12. **Merger NPV** [LO3] Fly-By-Night Couriers is analyzing the possible acquisition of Flash-in-the-Pan Restaurants. Neither firm has debt. The forecasts of Fly-By-Night show that the purchase would increase its annual aftertax cash flow by $375,000 indefinitely. The current market value of Flash-in-the-Pan is $8.7 million. The current market value of Fly-By-Night is $21 million. The appropriate discount rate for the incremental cash flows is 8 percent. Fly-By-Night is trying to decide whether it should offer 35 percent of its stock or $12 million in cash to Flash-in-the-Pan.

    a. What is the synergy from the merger?

    b. What is the value of Flash-in-the-Pan to Fly-By-Night?

    c. What is the cost to Fly-By-Night of each alternative?

    d. What is the NPV to Fly-By-Night of each alternative?

    e. Which alternative should Fly-By-Night use?

13. **Merger NPV [LO3]** Harrods PLC has a market value of £95 million and 4.5 million shares outstanding. Selfridge Department Store has a market value of £32 million and 1.8 million shares outstanding. Harrods is contemplating acquiring Selfridge. Harrods's CFO concludes that the combined firm with synergy will be worth £145 million, and Selfridge can be acquired at a premium of £3.3 million.

    a. If Harrods offers 1.1 million shares of its stock in exchange for the 1.8 million shares of Selfridge, what will the stock price of Harrods be after the acquisition?

    b. What exchange ratio between the two stocks would make the value of a stock offer equivalent to a cash offer of £35.3 million?

14. **Calculating NPV [LO3]** BQ, Inc., is considering making an offer to purchase iReport Publications. The vice president of finance has collected the following information:

CHALLENGE
(Question 14)

	BQ	iReport
Price-earnings ratio	14.5	9.2
Shares outstanding	1,400,000	195,000
Earnings	$4,300,000	$705,000
Dividends	$1,075,000	$375,000

    BQ also knows that securities analysts expect the earnings and dividends of iReport to grow at a constant rate of 5 percent each year. BQ management believes that the acquisition of iReport will provide the firm with some economies of scale that will increase this growth rate to 7 percent per year.

    a. What is the value of iReport to BQ?

    b. What would BQ's gain be from this acquisition?

    c. If BQ were to offer $38 in cash for each share of iReport, what would the NPV of the acquisition be?

    d. What's the most BQ should be willing to pay in cash per share for the stock of iReport?

    e. If BQ were to offer 205,000 of its shares in exchange for the outstanding stock of iReport, what would the NPV be?

    f. Should the acquisition be attempted? If so, should it be as in (c) or as in (e)?

    g. BQ's outside financial consultants think that the 7 percent growth rate is too optimistic and a 6 percent rate is more realistic. How does this change your previous answers?

MINICASE

The Birdie Golf–Hybrid Golf Merger

Birdie Golf, Inc., has been in merger talks with Hybrid Golf Company for the past six months. After several rounds of negotiations, the offer under discussion is a cash offer of $185 million for Hybrid Golf. Both companies have niche markets in the golf club industry, and both believe that a merger will result in synergies due to economies of scale in manufacturing and marketing, as well as significant savings in general and administrative expenses.

Bryce Bichon, the financial officer for Birdie, has been instrumental in the merger negotiations. Bryce has prepared the following pro forma financial statements for Hybrid Golf assuming the merger takes place. The financial statements include all synergistic benefits from the merger.

	2019	2020	2021	2022	2023
Sales	$330,000,000	$375,000,000	$415,000,000	$445,000,000	$495,000,000
Production costs	231,000,000	262,500,000	290,500,000	311,500,000	346,500,000
Other expenses	33,000,000	38,000,000	41,000,000	45,000,000	49,000,000
Depreciation	27,000,000	31,000,000	33,000,000	36,000,000	36,000,000
EBIT	$ 39,000,000	$ 43,500,000	$ 50,500,000	$ 52,500,000	$ 63,500,000
Interest	7,500,000	9,000,000	10,000,000	10,500,000	11,000,000
Taxable income	$ 31,500,000	$ 34,500,000	$ 40,500,000	$ 42,000,000	$ 52,500,000
Taxes (21%)	6.615,000	7,245,000	8,505,000	8,820,000	11,025,000
Net income	$ 24,885,000	$ 27,255,000	$ 31,995,000	$ 33,180,000	$ 41,475,000
Additions to retained earnings	0	$ 16,000,000	$ 19,000,000	$ 21,000,000	$ 25,000,000

If Birdie Golf buys Hybrid Golf, an immediate dividend of $55 million would be paid from Hybrid Golf to Birdie. Stock in Birdie Golf currently sells for $87 per share, and the company has 18 million shares of stock outstanding. Hybrid Golf has 8 million shares of stock outstanding. Both companies can borrow at an 8 percent interest rate. Bryce believes the current cost of capital for Birdie Golf is 11 percent. The cost of capital for Hybrid Golf is 12.4 percent, and the cost of equity is 16.9 percent. In five years, the value of Hybrid Golf is expected to be $235 million.

Bryce has asked you to analyze the financial aspects of the potential merger. Specifically, he has asked you to answer the following questions.

QUESTIONS

1. Suppose Hybrid shareholders will agree to a merger price of $23.13 per share. Should Birdie proceed with the merger?

2. What is the highest price per share that Birdie should be willing to pay for Hybrid?

3. Suppose Birdie is unwilling to pay cash for the merger but will consider a stock exchange. What exchange ratio would make the merger terms equivalent to the original merger price of $23.13 per share?

4. What is the highest exchange ratio Birdie should be willing to pay and still undertake the merger?

Leasing

HAVE YOU EVER FLOWN on GE Airlines? Probably not; but with about 2,000 aircraft, GE Capital Aviation Services (GECAS), part of GE, owns one of the largest aircraft fleets in the world. In fact, this arm of GE owns about $40 billion in assets and generated about $6.1 billion in profits during 2016. Overall, about 40 percent of all commercial jetliners worldwide are leased. So why is GECAS in the business of buying assets, only to lease them out? And why don't the companies that lease from GECAS purchase the assets themselves? This chapter answers these and other questions associated with leasing.

Learning Objectives

After studying this chapter, you should be able to:

LO1 Define the types of leases and how the IRS qualifies leases.

LO2 Explain the reasons for leasing and the reasons for not leasing.

LO3 Show how to calculate the net advantage of leasing and related issues.

For updates on the latest happenings in finance, visit fundamentalsofcorporatefinance.blogspot.com.

Leasing is a way businesses finance plant, property, and equipment.[1] Just about any asset that can be purchased can be leased, and there are many good reasons for leasing. For example, when we take vacations or business trips, renting a car for a few days is a convenient thing to do. After all, buying a car and selling it a week later would be a great nuisance. We discuss additional reasons for leasing in the sections that follow.

Although corporations engage in both short-term and long-term leasing, this chapter is primarily concerned with long-term leasing, where *long-term* typically means more than five years. As we will discuss in greater detail shortly, leasing an asset on a long-term basis is much like borrowing the needed funds and buying the asset. Thus, long-term leasing is a form of financing much like long-term debt. When is leasing preferable to long-term borrowing? This is a question we seek to answer in this chapter.

Up-to-date news and articles on the leasing industry are available at **www.monitordaily.com**.

---

[1] We are indebted to James Johnson of Northern Illinois University for helpful comments and suggestions about this chapter.

27.1 Leases and Lease Types

lessee
The user of an asset in a leasing agreement. The lessee makes payments to the lessor.

lessor
The owner of an asset in a leasing agreement. The lessor receives payments from the lessee.

A *lease* is a contractual agreement between two parties: The **lessee** and the **lessor**. The lessee is the user of the equipment; the lessor is the owner. In the example we used to open the chapter, GE Capital Aviation Services is the lessor.

Typically, a company first decides what asset it needs. It then negotiates a lease contract with a lessor for use of that asset. The lease agreement establishes that the lessee has the right to use the asset and, in return, must make periodic payments to the lessor, the owner of the asset. The lessor is usually either the asset's manufacturer or an independent leasing company. If the lessor is an independent leasing company, it must buy the asset from a manufacturer. The lessor then delivers the asset to the lessee, and the lease goes into effect.

There are some giant lessors in the United States. For example, IBM Global Financing leases billions in equipment annually. Other major lessors include General Electric, International Lease Finance, and AirFleet Capital.

Should you lease or buy that next car? Visit MarketWatch at **www.marketwatch.com** for a calculator to help you decide.

LEASING VERSUS BUYING

As far as the lessee is concerned, it is the use of the asset that is important, not necessarily who has title to it. One way to obtain the use of an asset is to lease it. Another way is to obtain outside financing and buy it. The decision to lease or buy amounts to a comparison of alternative financing arrangements for the use of an asset.

Figure 27.1 compares leasing and buying. The lessee, Sass Company, might be a hospital, a law firm, or any other firm that uses computers. The lessor is an independent leasing company that purchased the computer from a manufacturer such as Hewlett-Packard (HP). Leases of this type, in which the leasing company purchases the asset from the manufacturer, are called *direct leases*. Of course, HP might choose to lease its own computers; and

FIGURE 27.1   Leasing versus Buying

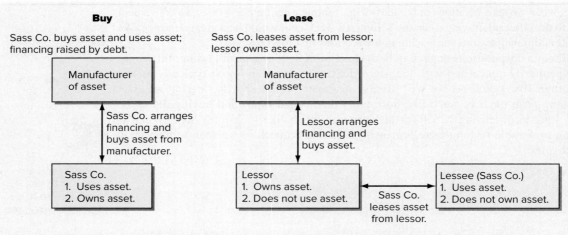

many companies have set up wholly owned subsidiaries called *captive finance companies* to lease out their products.[2]

As shown in Figure 27.1, whether it leases or buys, Sass Company ends up using the asset. The key difference is that in one case (buy), Sass arranges the financing, purchases the asset, and holds title to the asset. In the other case (lease), the leasing company arranges the financing, purchases the asset, and holds title to the asset.

OPERATING LEASES

Years ago, a lease in which the lessee received an equipment operator along with the equipment was called an **operating lease**. Today, an operating lease (or *service lease*) is difficult to define precisely, but this form of leasing has several important characteristics.

First of all, with an operating lease, the payments received by the lessor are usually not enough to allow the lessor to fully recover the cost of the asset. A primary reason is that operating leases are often relatively short-term. Therefore, the life of the lease may be much shorter than the economic life of the asset. For example, if you lease a car for two years, the car will have a substantial residual value at the end of the lease, and the lease payments you make will pay off only a fraction of the original cost of the car. The lessor in an operating lease expects to either lease the asset again or sell it when the lease terminates.

A second characteristic of an operating lease is that it frequently requires that the lessor maintain the asset. The lessor also may be responsible for any taxes or insurance. Of course, these costs will be passed on, at least in part, to the lessee in the form of higher lease payments.

The third, and perhaps most interesting, feature of an operating lease is the cancellation option. This option can give the lessee the right to cancel the lease before the expiration date. If the option to cancel is exercised, the lessee returns the equipment to the lessor and ceases to make payments. The value of a cancellation clause depends on whether technological or economic conditions are likely to make the value of the asset to the lessee less than the present value of the future lease payments.

To leasing practitioners, these three characteristics define an operating lease. As we will see shortly, accountants use the term in a somewhat different way.

operating lease
Usually a shorter-term lease under which the lessor is responsible for insurance, taxes, and upkeep. May be cancelable by the lessee on short notice.

One websites for equipment leasing is **www.keystoneleasing.com**.

FINANCIAL LEASES

A **financial lease** is the other major type of lease. In contrast to the situation with an operating lease, the payments made under a financial lease (plus the anticipated residual, or salvage, value) are usually sufficient to fully cover the lessor's cost of purchasing the asset and pay the lessor a return on the investment. For this reason, a financial lease is sometimes said to be a fully amortized or full-payout lease, whereas an operating lease is said to be partially amortized. Financial leases are often called *capital leases* by accountants.

With a financial lease, the lessee (not the lessor) is usually responsible for insurance, maintenance, and taxes; for that reason, financial leases are often called *triple net leases*. A financial lease generally cannot be canceled, at least not without a significant penalty. In other words, the lessee must make the lease payments or face possible legal action.

The characteristics of a financial lease, particularly the fact that it is fully amortized, make it very similar to debt financing, so the name is a sensible one. There are three types of financial leases that are of particular interest: *Tax-oriented leases*, *leveraged leases*, and *sale and leaseback agreements*. We consider these next.

financial lease
Typically a longer-term, fully amortized lease under which the lessee is responsible for maintenance, taxes, and insurance. Usually not cancelable by the lessee without penalty.

---

[2] In addition to arranging financing for asset users, captive finance companies (or subsidiaries) may purchase their parent company's products and provide debt or lease financing to the users. Ford Credit and Caterpillar Financial Services Corp. are examples of captive finance companies.

tax-oriented lease
A financial lease in which the lessor is the owner for tax purposes. Also called a *true lease* or a *tax lease*.

Tax-Oriented Leases   A lease in which the lessor is the owner of the leased asset for tax purposes is called a **tax-oriented lease**. Such leases are also called *tax leases* or *true leases*. In contrast, a *conditional sales agreement lease* is not a true lease. Here the lessee is the owner for tax purposes. Conditional sales agreement leases are really just secured loans. The financial leases we discuss in this chapter are all tax leases.

Tax-oriented leases make the most sense when the lessee is not in a position to efficiently use tax credits or depreciation deductions that come with owning the asset. By arranging for someone else to hold title, a tax lease passes these benefits on. The lessee can benefit because the lessor may return a portion of the tax benefits to the lessee in the form of lower lease payments.

leveraged lease
A financial lease in which the lessor borrows a substantial fraction of the cost of the leased asset on a nonrecourse basis.

Leveraged Leases   A **leveraged lease** is a tax-oriented lease in which the lessor borrows a substantial portion of the purchase price of the leased asset on a *nonrecourse* basis, meaning that if the lessee defaults on the lease payments, the lessor does not have to keep making the loan payments. Instead, the lender must proceed against the lessee to recover its investment. In contrast, with a *single-investor lease*, if the lessor borrows to purchase the asset, the lessor remains responsible for the loan payments whether or not the lessee makes the lease payments. Leveraged leases can be quite complicated and are primarily used for big-ticket transactions.

sale and leaseback
A financial lease in which the lessee sells an asset to the lessor and then leases it back.

Sale and Leaseback Agreements   A **sale and leaseback** occurs when a company sells an asset it owns to another party and simultaneously leases it back. In a sale and leaseback, two things happen:

1. The lessee receives cash from the sale of the asset.
2. The lessee continues to use the asset.

Often, with a sale and leaseback, the lessee may have the option to repurchase the leased asset at the end of the lease.

Sale and leaseback arrangements have multiplied during recent years. For example, in October 2017, Albertsons posted a $720 million gain from the sale and leaseback of 71 company owned stores. In June of that year, Finnish rental equipment company Ramirent executed the sale and leaseback of the company's operating facility for €15 million.

Concept Questions

27.1a   What are the differences between an operating lease and a financial lease?
27.1b   What is a tax-oriented lease?
27.1c   What is a sale and leaseback agreement?

27.2 Accounting and Leasing

Before November 1976, leasing was frequently called *off-balance-sheet financing*. As the name implies, a firm could arrange to use an asset through a lease and not necessarily disclose the existence of the lease contract on the balance sheet. Lessees had to report information about leasing activity only in the footnotes to their financial statements.

In November 1976, the Financial Accounting Standards Board (FASB) issued its *Statement of Financial Accounting Standards No. 13* (FASB 13), "Accounting for Leases." The basic idea of FASB 13 is that certain financial leases must be "capitalized." Essentially,

A. Balance Sheet with Purchase (The company finances a $100,000 truck with debt.)			
Truck	$100,000	Debt	$100,000
Other assets	100,000	Equity	100,000
Total assets	$200,000	Total debt plus equity	$200,000
B. Balance Sheet with Operating Lease (The company finances the truck with an operating lease.)			
Truck	$ 0	Debt	$ 0
Other assets	100,000	Equity	100,000
Total assets	$100,000	Total debt plus equity	$100,000
C. Balance Sheet with Capital Lease (The company finances the truck with a capital lease.)			
Assets under capital lease	$100,000	Obligations under capital lease	$100,000
Other assets	100,000	Equity	100,000
Total assets	$200,000	Total debt plus equity	$200,000

TABLE 27.1

Leasing and the Balance Sheet

In the first case, a $100,000 truck is purchased with debt. In the second case, an operating lease is used; no balance sheet entries are created. In the third case, a capital (financial) lease is used; the lease payments are capitalized as a liability, and the leased truck appears as an asset.

this requirement means that the present value of the lease payments must be calculated and reported along with debt and other liabilities on the right-hand side of the lessee's balance sheet. The same amount must be shown as the capitalized value of leased assets on the left-hand side of the balance sheet. Operating leases are not disclosed on the balance sheet except in the footnotes. Exactly what constitutes a financial or operating lease for accounting purposes will be discussed in just a moment.

Beginning in 2019, companies will be required to disclose operating leases on their balance sheets, which is a major change. The implication is that most leases will be reported on the balance sheet, so off-balance-sheet financing will be largely eliminated (at least from leasing activities).

To illustrate why the issue of off-balance-sheet financing is important, take a look at Table 27.1. The firm has $100,000 in assets and no debt, which implies that the equity is also $100,000. The firm needs a truck costing $100,000, which it can lease or buy. The top of the table (Part A) shows the balance sheet assuming that the firm borrows the money and buys the truck.

If the firm leases the truck, then one of two things will happen. If the lease is an operating lease, then the balance sheet under the current rules will look like the one in Part B of the table. In this case, neither the asset (the truck) nor the liability (the present value of the lease payments) appears. If the lease is a capital lease, then the balance sheet will look more like the one in Part C of the table, where the truck is shown as an asset and the present value of the lease payments is shown as a liability.[3]

Beginning in 2019, whether the lease is classified as operating or financial will become less important. In both cases, the balance sheet will look like Part C of the table (with some minor differences due to accounting nitty-gritty).

---

[3]In Part C, we have made the simplifying assumption that the present value of the lease payments under the capital lease is equal to the cost of the truck. In general, the lessee must report the lesser of the present value of the lease payment stream or the cost of the equipment under lease.

For accounting purposes, a lease is declared to be a capital lease if at least one of the following criteria is met:

1. The lease transfers ownership of the property to the lessee by the end of the term of the lease.
2. The lessee has an option to purchase the asset that is relatively certain to be used.
3. The lease term is for a major part of the economic life of the asset.
4. The present value of the lease payments plus any other residual value equals or exceeds the value of the asset.
5. The asset is so specialized that it is expected to have no alternative use to the lessor at the end of the lease.

If one or more of the five criteria are met, the lease is a capital lease; otherwise, it is an operating lease for accounting purposes.

Concept Questions

27.2a What is meant by the term "off-balance-sheet" financing?
27.2b For accounting purposes, what constitutes a capital lease?

27.3 Taxes, the IRS, and Leases

The lessee can deduct lease payments for income tax purposes if the lease is deemed to be a true lease by the Internal Revenue Service (IRS). The tax shields associated with lease payments are critical to the economic viability of a lease, so IRS guidelines are an important consideration. Essentially, the IRS requires that a lease be primarily for business purposes and not merely for purposes of tax avoidance.

In broad terms, a lease is a contract that gives the lessee the right to control the use of a specific asset for a set period of time in exchange for payments made to the lessor. The lessee has the "right to control" if, during the lease, the lessee:

1. Has the right to essentially all the economic benefits from the use of the asset, and
2. Has the right to direct the use of the asset.

The IRS is concerned about lease contracts because leases sometimes appear to be set up solely to defer taxes. To see how this could happen, suppose that a firm plans to purchase a $1 million bus that has a five-year life for depreciation purposes. Assume that straight-line depreciation to a zero salvage value is used. The depreciation expense would be $200,000 per year. Now, suppose the firm can lease the bus for $500,000 per year for two years and buy the bus for $1 at the end of the two-year term. The present value of the tax benefits is clearly less if the bus is bought than if the bus is leased. The speedup of lease payments greatly benefits the firm and basically gives it a form of accelerated depreciation. In this case, the IRS might decide that the primary purpose of the lease is to defer taxes and disallow the tax treatment.

Concept Questions

27.3a Why is the IRS concerned about leasing?
27.3b What are some standards the IRS uses in evaluating a lease?

The Cash Flows from Leasing

27.4

To begin our analysis of the leasing decision, we need to identify the relevant cash flows. The first part of this section illustrates how this is done. A key point, and one to watch for, is that taxes are a very important consideration in a lease analysis. Also, while the changes to lease accounting coming in 2019 impact both the balance sheet and (potentially) income statement for reporting purposes, they do not generally affect leasing cash flows.

THE INCREMENTAL CASH FLOWS

Consider the decision confronting the Tasha Corporation, which manufactures pipe. Business has been expanding, and Tasha currently has a five-year backlog of pipe orders for the Trans-Missouri Pipeline.

The International Boring Machine Corporation (IBMC) makes a pipe-boring machine that can be purchased for $10,000. Tasha has determined that it needs a new machine, and the IBMC model will save Tasha $6,000 per year in reduced electricity bills for the next five years.

Tasha has a corporate tax rate of 21 percent. For simplicity, we assume that five-year straight-line depreciation will be used for the pipe-boring machine; after five years, the machine will be worthless. Johnson Leasing Corporation has offered to lease the same pipe-boring machine to Tasha for lease payments of $2,500 paid at the end of each of the next five years. With the lease, Tasha would remain responsible for maintenance, insurance, and operating expenses.[4]

Susan Smart has been asked to compare the direct incremental cash flows from leasing the IBMC machine to the cash flows associated with buying it. The first thing she realizes is that, because Tasha will get the machine either way, the $6,000 savings will be realized whether the machine is leased or purchased. Thus, this cost savings, and any other operating costs or revenues, can be ignored in the analysis.

Upon reflection, Ms. Smart concludes that there are only three important cash flow differences between leasing and buying:[5]

1. If the machine is leased, Tasha must make a lease payment of $2,500 each year. However, lease payments are fully tax deductible, so the aftertax lease payment would be $2,500 × (1 − .21) = $1,975. This is a cost of leasing instead of buying.

2. If the machine is leased, Tasha does not own it and cannot depreciate it for tax purposes. The depreciation would be $10,000/5 = $2,000 per year. A $2,000 depreciation deduction generates a tax shield of $2,000 × .21 = $420 per year. Tasha loses this valuable tax shield if it leases, so this is a cost of leasing.

3. If the machine is leased, Tasha does not have to spend $10,000 today to buy it. This is a benefit from leasing.

The cash flows from leasing instead of buying are summarized in Table 27.2. Notice that the cost of the machine shows up with a positive sign in Year 0. This is a reflection of the fact that Tasha *saves* the initial $10,000 equipment cost by leasing instead of buying.

---

[4]We have assumed that all lease payments are made in arrears—that is, at the end of the year. Actually, many leases require payments to be made at the beginning of the year.

[5]There is a fourth consequence of leasing that we do not discuss here. If the machine has a nontrivial residual value, then, if we lease, we give up that residual value. This is another cost of leasing instead of buying.

TABLE 27.2

Incremental Cash Flows for Tasha Corp. from Leasing Instead of Buying

Lease versus Buy	Year 0	Year 1	Year 2	Year 3	Year 4	Year 5
Aftertax lease payment		−$1,975	−$1,975	−$1,975	−$1,975	−$1,975
Lost depreciation tax shield		− 420	− 420	− 420	− 420	− 420
Cost of machine	+$10,000					
Total cash flow	+$10,000	−$2,395	−$2,395	−$2,395	−$2,395	−$2,395

A NOTE ABOUT TAXES

Susan Smart has assumed that Tasha can use the tax benefits of the depreciation allowances and the lease payments. This may not always be the case. If Tasha were losing money, it would not pay taxes, and the tax shelters would be worthless (unless they could be shifted to someone else). As we mentioned before, this is one circumstance under which leasing may make a great deal of sense. If this were the case, the relevant entries in Table 27.2 would have to be changed to reflect a zero tax rate. We will return to this point later.

Concept Questions

27.4a What are the cash flow consequences of leasing instead of buying?

27.4b Explain why the $10,000 in Table 27.2 has a positive sign.

27.5 Lease or Buy?

Based on our discussion thus far, Ms. Smart's analysis comes down to this: If Tasha Corp. decides to lease instead of buy, it saves $10,000 today because it avoids having to pay for the machine, but it must give up $2,395 per year for the next five years in exchange. We now must decide whether getting $10,000 today and then paying back $2,395 per year for five years is a good idea.

A PRELIMINARY ANALYSIS

Suppose Tasha were to borrow $10,000 today and promise to make aftertax payments of $2,395 per year for the next five years. This is essentially what Tasha will be doing if it leases instead of buying. What interest rate would Tasha be paying on this "loan"? Going back to Chapter 6, note that we need to find the unknown rate for a five-year annuity with payments of $2,395 per year and a present value of $10,000. It is easy to verify that the rate is 6.325 percent.

The cash flows for our hypothetical loan are identical to the cash flows from leasing instead of buying, and what we have illustrated is that when Tasha leases the machine, it effectively arranges financing at an aftertax rate of 6.325 percent. Whether this is a good deal or not depends on what rate Tasha would pay if it borrowed the money. Suppose Tasha can arrange a five-year loan with its bank at a rate of 7.1 percent. Should Tasha sign the lease or should it go with the bank?

Because Tasha is in a 21 percent tax bracket, the aftertax interest rate would be 7.1 × (1 − .21) = 5.609 percent. This is less than the 6.325 percent aftertax rate on the lease. In this particular case, Tasha would be better off borrowing the money because it would get a better rate.

There's an online lease-versus-buy calculator at (where else?) **www.lease-vs-buy.com**.

Based on this analysis, Tasha should buy rather than lease. The steps in our analysis can be summarized as follows:

1. Calculate the incremental aftertax cash flows from leasing instead of buying.
2. Use these cash flows to calculate the aftertax interest rate on the lease.
3. Compare this rate to the company's *aftertax* borrowing cost and choose the cheaper source of financing.

The most important thing to note from our discussion thus far is that in evaluating a lease, the relevant rate for the comparison is the company's *aftertax* borrowing rate. The fundamental reason is that the alternative to leasing is long-term borrowing, so the aftertax interest rate on such borrowing is the relevant benchmark.

THREE POTENTIAL PITFALLS

There are three potential problems with the interest rate that we calculated on the lease. First of all, we can interpret this rate as the internal rate of return, or IRR, on the decision to lease rather than buy; but doing so can be confusing. To see why, notice that the IRR from leasing is 6.325 percent, which is greater than Tasha's aftertax borrowing cost of 5.609 percent. Normally, the higher the IRR, the better; but we decided that leasing was a bad idea here. The reason is that the cash flows are not conventional; the first cash flow is positive and the rest are negative, which is the opposite of the conventional case (see Chapter 9 for a discussion). With this cash flow pattern, the IRR represents the rate we pay, not the rate we get—so the *lower* the IRR, the better.

A second, and related, potential pitfall has to do with the fact that we calculated the advantage of leasing instead of buying. We could have done the opposite and come up with the advantage of buying instead of leasing. If we did this, the cash flows would be the same, but the signs would be reversed. The IRR would be the same. Now, the cash flows would be conventional, so we could interpret the 6.325 percent IRR as saying that borrowing and buying is better.

The third potential problem is that our interest rate is based on the net cash flows of leasing instead of buying. There is another rate that is sometimes calculated based solely on the lease payments. If we wanted to, we could note that the lease provides $10,000 in financing and requires five payments of $2,500 each. It would be tempting to then determine a rate based on these numbers; but the resulting rate would not be meaningful for making lease-versus-buy decisions, and it should not be confused with the return on leasing instead of borrowing and buying.

Perhaps because of these potential sources of confusion, the IRR approach we have outlined thus far is not as widely used as the NPV-based approach that we describe next.

NPV ANALYSIS

Now that we know that the relevant rate for evaluating a lease-versus-buy decision is the firm's aftertax borrowing cost, an NPV analysis is straightforward. We discount the cash flows back to the present at Tasha's aftertax borrowing rate of 5.609 percent as follows:

$$\text{NPV} = \$10,000 - \$2,395 \times (1 - 1/1.05609^5)/.05609$$
$$= -\$196.83$$

The NPV from leasing instead of buying is −$196.83, verifying our earlier conclusion that leasing is a bad idea. Once again, notice the signs of the cash flows; the first is positive, and the rest are negative. The NPV we have computed here is often called the **net advantage to leasing (NAL)**. Surveys indicate that the NAL approach is the most popular means of lease analysis in the real world. Our nearby *Work the Web* box illustrates the use of lease-versus-buy analysis of automobiles.

net advantage to leasing (NAL)
The NPV that is calculated when deciding whether to lease an asset or to buy it.

WORK THE WEB

A major financial decision that you will likely encounter at some point is whether to buy or lease a car. We went to www.financialmentor.com to find a lease-versus-buy calculator. We analyzed a new car purchase for $40,500 with a 48-month loan and a $4,300 down payment. The loan rate would be 3.2 percent, and the car has a residual value of $27,500 in four years. To lease the car for three years requires a down payment of $4,300; the interest rate would be 3.1 percent; and the car would have a residual value of $27,500 in three years. Both options require $850 in fees when you take possession of the car and have a 7 percent tax rate. Based on this information, here is the lease-versus-buy analysis:

Description	(A) Lease:	(B) Buy:
14. Monthly payment:	$346.62	$804.47
15. Total of payments:	$12,478.39	$38,614.39
16. Total interest expense:		$2,414.39
17. Net up-front expenses:	$1,151.00	$3,685.00
18. Depreciation expense:		$16,000.00
19. Forgone Interest earnings:	$0.00	$0.00
20. Total cost:	$13,629.39	$22,099.39
21. Average cost per year:	$4,543.13	$5,524.85

According to www.financialmentor.com, leasing the car is the better financial decision because it will cost $4,543.13 per year versus $5,524.85.

Questions

1. Go to www.financialmentor.com and complete the same analysis, but change the term of the loan for purchasing the car to 60 months instead of the 48 months shown above. Which option is better now? Do you see a flaw in this analysis?

2. Go to the website for your favorite car manufacturer and find the price for your favorite new car. Complete the lease-versus-buy analysis for this car. Should you lease or buy your car?

A MISCONCEPTION

In our lease-versus-buy analysis, it looks as though we ignored the fact that if Tasha borrows the $10,000 to buy the machine, it will have to repay the money with interest. In fact, we reasoned that if Tasha leased the machine, it would be better off by $10,000 today because it wouldn't have to pay for the machine. It is tempting to argue that if Tasha borrowed the money, it wouldn't have to come up with the $10,000. Instead, Tasha would make a series of principal and interest payments over the next five years. This observation is true, but not particularly relevant. The reason is that if Tasha borrows $10,000 at an aftertax cost of 5.609 percent, the present value of the aftertax loan payments is $10,000, no matter what the repayment schedule is (assuming that the loan is fully amortized). We could write down the aftertax loan repayments and work with these, but it would be extra work for no gain, assuming the lessee is currently paying taxes (see Problem 12 at the end of the chapter for an example).

Lease Evaluation　　　　　　　　　　　　　　　　　**EXAMPLE 27.1**

In our Tasha Corp. example, suppose Tasha is able to negotiate a lease payment of $2,000 per year. What would be the NPV of the lease in this case?

With this new lease payment, the aftertax lease payment would be $2,000 × (1 − .21) = $1,580, which is $1,975 − 1,580 = $395 less than before. Referring back to Table 27.2, note that the aftertax cash flows would be −$2,000 instead of −$2,395. At 5.609 percent, the NPV would be:

NPV = $10,000 − $2,000 × (1 − 1/1.05609⁵)/.05609

　　= $1,484.90

The lease is very attractive.

Concept Questions

27.5a What is the relevant discount rate for evaluating whether or not to lease an asset? Why?

27.5b Explain how to go about a lease-versus-buy analysis.

A Leasing Paradox　　　　　　　　　　　　　　**27.6**

We previously looked at the lease-versus-buy decision from the perspective of the potential lessee, Tasha. We now turn things around and look at the lease from the perspective of the lessor, Johnson Leasing. The cash flows associated with the lease from Johnson's perspective are shown in Table 27.3. First, Johnson must buy the machine for $10,000, so there is a $10,000 outflow today. Next, Johnson depreciates the machine at a rate of $10,000/5 = $2,000 per year, so the depreciation tax shield is $2,000 × .21 = $420 each year. Finally, Johnson receives a lease payment of $2,500 each year, on which it pays taxes. The aftertax lease payment received is $1,975, and the total cash flow to Johnson is $2,395 per year.

What we see is that the cash flows to Johnson are exactly the opposite of the cash flows to Tasha. This makes perfect sense because Johnson and Tasha are the only parties to the transaction, and the lease is a zero-sum game. In other words, if the lease has a positive

TABLE 27.3

Incremental Cash Flows for Johnson Leasing

	Year 0	Year 1	Year 2	Year 3	Year 4	Year 5
Aftertax lease payment		+$1,975	+$1,975	+$1,975	+$1,975	+$1,975
Depreciation tax shield		+ 420	+ 420	+ 420	+ 420	+ 420
Cost of machine	−$10,000					
Total cash flow	−$10,000	+$2,395	+$2,395	+$2,395	+$2,395	+$2,395

NPV to one party, it must have a negative NPV to the other. In our case, Johnson hopes that Tasha will do the deal because the NPV for Johnson would be +$196.83, the amount Tasha would lose.

We seem to have a paradox. In any leasing arrangement, one party must inevitably lose (or both parties exactly break even). Why, then, would leasing take place? We know that leasing is very important in the real world, so the next section describes some factors that we have omitted from our analysis thus far. These factors can make a lease attractive to both parties.

EXAMPLE 27.2   **It's the Lease We Can Do**

In our Tasha example, a lease payment of $2,500 makes the lease unattractive to Tasha, and a lease payment of $2,000 makes the lease very attractive. What payment would leave Tasha indifferent between leasing and buying?

Tasha will be indifferent when the NPV from leasing is zero. For this to happen, the present value of the cash flows from leasing instead of buying will have to be −$10,000. From our previous efforts, we know that the lease payment must be somewhere between $2,500 and $2,000. To find the exact payment, we note that there are five payments and the relevant rate is 5.609 percent per year, so the cash flow from leasing instead of borrowing must be −$2,348.77 per year.

Now that we have the cash flow from leasing instead of borrowing, we have to work backward to find the lease payment that produces this cash flow. Suppose we let LP stand for the lease payment. Referring back to Table 27.2, we see that we must have −LP × (1 − .21) − $420 = −$2,348.77. With a little algebra, we see that the zero NPV lease payment is $2,441.48.

Concept Questions

27.6a   Why do we say that leasing is a zero-sum game?

27.6b   What paradox does the previous question create?

27.7 Reasons for Leasing

Proponents of leasing make many claims about why firms should lease assets rather than buy them. Some of the reasons given to support leasing are good, and some are not. Here, we evaluate some of these reasons.

GOOD REASONS FOR LEASING

If leasing is a good choice, one or more of the following will probably be true:

1. Taxes may be reduced by leasing.
2. The lease contract may reduce certain types of uncertainty that might otherwise decrease the value of the firm.
3. Transactions costs may be lower for a lease contract than for buying the asset.
4. Leasing may require fewer (if any) restrictive covenants than secured borrowing.
5. Leasing may encumber fewer assets than secured borrowing.

Tax Advantages   As we have hinted in various places, by far the most economically justifiable reason for long-term leasing is tax deferral. If the corporate income tax were repealed, long-term leasing would become much less important. The tax advantages of leasing exist because firms are in different tax positions. A potential tax shield that cannot be used as efficiently by one firm can be transferred to another by leasing.

Any tax benefits from leasing can be split between the two firms by setting the lease payments at the appropriate level, and the shareholders of both firms will benefit from this tax transfer arrangement. The loser will be the IRS. A firm in a high tax bracket will want to act as the lessor. Low tax bracket firms will be lessees, because they will not be able to use the tax advantages of ownership, such as depreciation and debt financing, as efficiently.

Recall the example from Section 27.6 and the situation of Johnson Leasing. The value of the lease it proposed to Tasha was $369.10. However, the value of the lease to Tasha was exactly the opposite (−$369.10). Because the lessor's gains came at the expense of the lessee, no mutually beneficial deal could be arranged. If Tasha paid no taxes and the lease payments were reduced to $2,475 from $2,500, both Johnson and Tasha would find a positive NPV in their leasing arrangement.

To see this, we can rework Table 27.2 with a zero tax rate and a $2,475 lease payment. In this case, notice that the cash flows from leasing are the lease payments of $2,475 because no depreciation tax shield is lost and the lease payment is not tax deductible. The cash flows from leasing are:

The biggest lessor by dollar value is **www.aercap.com**.

Lease versus Buy	Year 0	Year 1	Year 2	Year 3	Year 4	Year 5
Lease payment		−$2,475	−$2,475	−$2,475	−$2,475	−$2,475
Cost of machine	+$10,000					
Total cash flow	+$10,000	−$2,475	−$2,475	−$2,475	−$2,475	−$2,475

Given this scenario, the value of the lease for Tasha is:

$$NPV = \$10,000 - \$2,475 \times (1 - 1/1.0757575^5)/.0757575$$
$$= \$6.55$$

which is positive. Notice that the discount rate here is 7.57575 percent because Tasha pays no taxes; in other words, this is both the pretax and the aftertax rate.

Using Table 27.3, the value of the lease to Johnson can be worked out. With a lease payment of $2,475, verify that the cash flows to Johnson will be $2,375.25. The value of the lease to Johnson is:

$$NPV = -\$10,000 + \$2,375.25 \times (1 - 1/1.05^5)/.05$$
$$= \$283.59$$

which is also positive.

As a consequence of different tax rates, the lessee (Tasha) gains $6.55 and the lessor (Johnson) gains $283.59. The IRS loses. What this example shows is that the lessor and the lessee can gain if their tax rates are different. The lease contract allows the lessor to take advantage of the depreciation and interest tax shields that cannot be used by the lessee. The IRS will experience a net loss of tax revenue, and some of the tax gains to the lessor can be passed on to the lessee in the form of lower lease payments.

A Reduction of Uncertainty   We have noted that the lessee does not own the property when the lease expires. The value of the property at this time is called the *residual value* (or *salvage value*). When the lease contract is signed, there may be substantial uncertainty about what the residual value of the asset will be. A lease contract is a method of transferring this uncertainty from the lessee to the lessor.

Transferring the uncertainty about the residual value of an asset to the lessor makes sense when the lessor is better able to bear the risk. If the lessor is the manufacturer, then the lessor may be better able to assess and manage the risk associated with the residual value. The transfer of uncertainty to the lessor amounts to a form of insurance for the lessee. A lease therefore provides something besides long-term financing. Of course, the lessee pays for this insurance implicitly, but the lessee may view the insurance as a relative bargain.

Reduction of uncertainty is the motive for leasing most cited by corporations. For example, computers have a way of becoming technologically outdated very quickly, and computers are very commonly leased instead of purchased. In one survey, 82 percent of the responding firms cited the risk of obsolescence as an important reason for leasing, whereas only 57 percent cited the potential for cheaper financing.

Lower Transactions Costs   The costs of changing ownership of an asset many times over its useful life will frequently be greater than the costs of writing a lease agreement. Consider the choice that confronts a person who lives in Los Angeles but must do business in New York for two days. Obviously, it would be cheaper to rent a hotel room for two nights than it would be to buy a condominium for two days and then sell it. Thus, lower transactions costs may be the major reason for short-term leases (operating leases). However, it is probably not the major reason for long-term leases.

Fewer Restrictions and Security Requirements   As we discussed in Chapter 7, with a secured loan, the borrower will generally agree to a set of restrictive covenants, spelled out in the indenture, or loan agreement. Such restrictions are not generally found in lease agreements. Also, with a secured loan, the borrower may have to pledge other assets as security. With a lease, only the leased asset is so encumbered.

DUBIOUS REASONS FOR LEASING

Other claims provided in favor of leasing are not so good. We take a look at some of these reasons, and why they are dubious, next.

Leasing and Accounting Income   Leasing can have a significant effect on the appearance of the firm's financial statements. If a firm is successful at keeping its leases off the books, the balance sheet and, potentially, the income statement can be made to look better. As a consequence, accounting-based performance measures such as return on assets, or ROA, can appear to be higher. As we have mentioned, changes in lease accounting coming in 2019 will make keeping leases off the books much more difficult.

Because an operating lease does not appear on the balance sheet under current (2017) rules, total assets (and total liabilities) will be lower with an operating lease than they would be if the firm were to borrow the money and purchase the asset. From Chapter 3, we know that ROA is computed as net income divided by total assets. With an operating lease, net income is usually bigger and total assets are smaller, so ROA will be larger. In addition, debt covenants often do not consider operating leases as debt, which may allow a firm to obtain debtlike financing without a covenant violation.

100 Percent Financing   It is often claimed that an advantage to leasing is that it provides 100 percent financing, whereas secured equipment loans require an initial down payment. Of course, a firm can borrow the down payment from another source that provides unsecured credit. Moreover, leases do usually involve a down payment in the form of an advance lease payment (or security deposit). Even when they do not involve a down payment, leases may be implicitly secured by assets of the firm other than those being leased (leasing may give the appearance of 100 percent financing, but not the substance).

Having said this, we should add that it may be the case that a firm (particularly a small one) cannot obtain debt financing because additional debt would violate a loan agreement. Operating leases frequently don't count as debt, so they may be the only source of financing available. In such cases, it isn't lease or buy—it's lease or die!

Low Cost   Unscrupulous lessors can encourage lessees to base leasing decisions on the "interest rate" implied by the lease payments, which is often called the *implicit* or *effective rate*. As we discussed earlier under potential pitfalls, this rate is not meaningful in leasing decisions, and it also has no legal meaning.

OTHER REASONS FOR LEASING

There are, of course, many special reasons for some companies to find advantages in leasing. In one celebrated case, the U.S. Navy leased a fleet of tankers instead of asking Congress for appropriations. Thus, leasing may be used to circumvent capital expenditure control systems set up by bureaucratic firms. This is alleged to be a relatively common occurrence in hospitals. Likewise, many school districts lease buses and modular classrooms and pay for them out of their operating budgets when they are unable to gain approval for a bond issue to raise funds.

Concept Questions

27.7a   Explain why the existence of differential tax rates may be a good reason for leasing.

27.7b   If leasing is tax motivated, who will have the higher tax bracket, the lessee or the lessor?

Summary and Conclusions   27.8

A large fraction of America's equipment is leased rather than purchased. This chapter has described different lease types, the accounting and tax implications of leasing, and how to evaluate financial leases.

1. Leases can be separated into two types: Financial and operating. Financial leases are generally longer term, fully amortized, and not cancelable without a hefty termination payment. Operating leases are usually shorter term, partially amortized, and cancelable.

2. The distinction between financial and operating leases is important in financial accounting. Financial (capital) leases must be reported on a firm's balance sheet; operating leases are not. We discussed the specific accounting criteria for classifying leases as either capital or operating.

3. Taxes are an important consideration in leasing, and the IRS has some specific rules about what constitutes a valid lease for tax purposes.

4. A long-term financial lease is a source of financing much like long-term borrowing. We showed how to perform an NPV analysis of leasing to decide whether leasing is cheaper than borrowing. A key insight was that the appropriate discount rate is the firm's aftertax borrowing rate.

5. We saw that the existence of differential tax rates can make leasing an attractive proposition for all parties. We also mentioned that a lease decreases the uncertainty surrounding the residual value of the leased asset. This is a primary reason for leasing cited by corporations.

CONNECT TO FINANCE

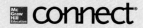 *Connect Finance* offers you plenty of opportunities to practice mastering these concepts. Log on to connect.mheducation.com to learn more. If you like what you see, ask your professor about using *Connect Finance*!

Can you answer the following *Connect* Quiz question?

Section 27.4 Winston, Inc., is computing the net advantage to leasing for a new food processing machine. How should the estimated $46,000 of salvage value be handled? The lease is for four years, the tax rate is 21 percent, and the aftertax discount rate is 5.2 percent.

CHAPTER REVIEW AND SELF-TEST PROBLEMS

27.1 Lease or Buy Your company wants to purchase a new network file server for its wide-area computer network. The server costs $75,000. It will be completely obsolete in three years. Your options are to borrow the money at 10 percent or to lease the machine. If you lease, the payments will be $27,000 per year, payable at the end of each of the next three years. If you buy the server, you can depreciate it straight-line to zero over three years. The tax rate is 21 percent. Should you lease or buy?

27.2 NPV of Leasing In the previous question, what is the NPV of the lease to the lessor? At what lease payment will the lessee and the lessor both break even?

ANSWERS TO CHAPTER REVIEW AND SELF-TEST PROBLEMS

27.1 If you buy the server, the depreciation will be $25,000 per year. This generates a tax shield of $25,000 × .21 = $5,250 per year, which is lost if the server is leased. The aftertax lease payment would be $27,000 × (1 − .21) = $21,330.

Looking back at Table 27.2, you can lay out the cash flows from leasing as follows:

Lease versus Buy	Year 0	Year 1	Year 2	Year 3
Aftertax lease payment		−$21,330	−$21,330	−$21,330
Lost depreciation tax shield		− 5,250	− 5,250	− 5,250
Cost of machine	+$75,000			
Total cash flow	+$75,000	−$26,580	−$26,580	−$26,580

The appropriate discount rate is the aftertax borrowing rate of $.10 \times (1 - .21) = .079$, or 7.9 percent. The NPV of leasing instead of borrowing and buying is:

$$NPV = \$75,000 - \$26,580 \times (1 - 1/1.079^3)/.079$$
$$= \$6,376.97$$

so leasing is cheaper.

27.2 Assuming that the lessor is in the same tax situation as the lessee, the NPV to the lessor is −$6,376.97. In other words, the lessor loses precisely what the lessee makes.

    For both parties to break even, the NPV of the lease must be $0. With a 7.9 percent rate for three years, a cash flow of −$29,050.02 per year has a present value of −$75,000. The lost depreciation tax shield is still −$5,250, so the aftertax lease payment must be $23,800.02. The lease payment that produces a zero NPV is therefore $23,800.02/.79 = $30,126.60 per year.

CONCEPTS REVIEW AND CRITICAL THINKING QUESTIONS

1. **Leasing versus Borrowing [LO2]** What are the key differences between leasing and borrowing? Are they perfect substitutes?

2. **Leasing and Taxes [LO3]** Taxes are an important consideration in the leasing decision. Who is more likely to lease, a profitable corporation in a high tax bracket or a less profitable one in a low tax bracket? Why?

3. **Leasing and IRR [LO3]** What are some of the potential problems with looking at IRRs in evaluating a leasing decision?

4. **Leasing [LO2]** Comment on the following remarks:
    a. Leasing reduces risk and can reduce a firm's cost of capital.
    b. Leasing provides 100 percent financing.
    c. If the tax advantages of leasing were eliminated, leasing would disappear.

5. **Accounting for Leases [LO1]** Discuss the accounting criteria for determining whether or not a lease must be reported on the balance sheet using the accounting rules in place before 2019. In each case, give a rationale for the criterion.

6. **IRS Criteria [LO1]** Discuss the IRS criteria for determining whether or not a lease is tax deductible. In each case, give a rationale for the criterion.

7. **Off-Balance-Sheet Financing [LO1]** What is meant by the term *off-balance-sheet financing*? When do leases provide such financing, and what are the accounting and economic consequences of such activity?

8. **Sale and Leaseback [LO1]** Why might a firm choose to engage in a sale and leaseback transaction? Give two reasons.

9. **Leasing Cost [LO3]** Explain why the aftertax borrowing rate is the appropriate discount rate to use in lease evaluation.

Refer to the following example for Questions 10 through 12:

In February 2017, Air Lease Corporation (ALC) announced a deal to lease five new Boeing 787-9 passenger aircraft to China Southern Airlines. ALC had the aircraft on purchase order from Boeing and planned to deliver three of the planes to China Southern in 2019 and the other two planes in 2020.

10. **Lease versus Purchase [LO2]** Why wouldn't China Southern purchase the planes if they were obviously needed for the company's operations?

11. **Reasons to Lease** [LO2] Why would ALC be willing to buy planes from Boeing and then lease them to China Southern? How is this different from lending money to China Southern to buy planes?

12. **Leasing** [LO2] What do you suppose happens to the planes at the end of the lease period?

QUESTIONS AND PROBLEMS

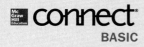

BASIC
(Questions 1–6)

Use the following information to work Problems 1 through 6:

You work for a nuclear research laboratory that is contemplating leasing a diagnostic scanner (leasing is a very common practice with expensive, high-tech equipment). The scanner costs $4,800,000, and it would be depreciated straight-line to zero over four years. Because of radiation contamination, it actually will be completely valueless in four years. You can lease it for $1,430,000 per year for four years.

1. **Lease or Buy** [LO3] Assume that the tax rate is 21 percent. You can borrow at 8 percent before taxes. Should you lease or buy?

2. **Leasing Cash Flows** [LO3] What is the NAL of the lease from the lessor's viewpoint? Assume a 21 percent tax rate.

3. **Finding the Break-Even Payment** [LO3] What would the lease payment have to be for both lessor and lessee to be indifferent about the lease?

4. **Taxes and Leasing Cash Flows** [LO3] Assume that your company does not anticipate paying taxes for the next several years. What are the cash flows from leasing in this case?

5. **Setting the Lease Payment** [LO3] In Problem 4, over what range of lease payments will the lease be profitable for both parties?

6. **MACRS Depreciation and Leasing** [LO3] Rework Problem 1 assuming that the scanner will be depreciated as three-year property under MACRS (see Chapter 10 for the depreciation allowances).

Use the following information to work Problems 7 through 9:

INTERMEDIATE
(Questions 7–11)

The Wildcat Oil Company is trying to decide whether to lease or buy a new computer-assisted drilling system for its oil exploration business. Management has decided that it must use the system to stay competitive; it will provide $2.3 million in annual pretax cost savings. The system costs $7.3 million and will be depreciated straight-line to zero over five years. Wildcat's tax rate is 21 percent, and the firm can borrow at 7 percent. Lambert Leasing Company has offered to lease the drilling equipment to Wildcat for payments of $1.625 million per year. Lambert's policy is to require its lessees to make payments at the start of the year.

7. **Lease or Buy** [LO3] What is the NAL for Wildcat? What is the maximum lease payment that would be acceptable to the company?

8. **Leasing and Salvage Value** [LO3] Suppose it is estimated that the equipment will have an aftertax residual value of $900,000 at the end of the lease. What is the maximum lease payment acceptable to Wildcat now?

9. **Deposits in Leasing** [LO3] Many lessors require a security deposit in the form of a cash payment or other pledged collateral. Suppose Lambert requires Wildcat to pay a $600,000 security deposit at the inception of the lease. If the lease payment is still $1.625 million, is it advantageous for Wildcat to lease the equipment now?

10. **Setting the Lease Price** [LO3] An asset costs $630,000 and will be depreciated in a straight-line manner over its three-year life. It will have no salvage value. The lessor

can borrow at 6 percent and the lessee can borrow at 9 percent. The corporate tax rate is 21 percent for both companies.

   a. How does the fact that the lessor and lessee have different borrowing rates affect the calculation of the NAL?

   b. What set of lease payments will make the lessee and the lessor equally well off?

   c. Assume that the lessee pays no taxes and the lessor is in the 21 percent tax bracket. For what range of lease payments does the lease have a positive NPV for both parties?

11. **Automobile Lease Payments [LO3]** Automobiles are often leased, and several terms are unique to auto leases. Suppose you are considering leasing a car. The price you and the dealer agree on for the car is $41,900. This is the base capitalized cost. Other costs added to the capitalized cost price include the acquisition (bank) fee, insurance, or extended warranty. Assume these costs are $850. Capitalization cost reductions include any down payment, credit for trade-in, or dealer rebate. Assume you make a down payment of $4,300, and there is no trade-in or rebate. If you drive 10,000 miles per year, the lease-end residual value for this car will be $30,500 after three years. The lease or "money" factor, which is the interest rate on the loan, is the APR of the loan divided by 2,400.[6] The lease factor the dealer quotes you is .00195. The monthly lease payment consists of three parts: A depreciation fee, a finance fee, and sales tax. The depreciation fee is the net capitalization cost minus the residual value, divided by the term of the lease. The net capitalization cost is the cost of the car minus any cost reductions plus any additional costs. The finance fee is the net capitalization cost plus the residual, times the money factor, and the monthly sales tax is the depreciation payment plus the finance fee, times the tax rate. What APR is the dealer quoting you? What is your monthly lease payment for a 36-month lease if the sales tax is 7 percent?

12. **Lease versus Borrow [LO3]** Return to the case of the diagnostic scanner used in Problems 1 through 6. Suppose the entire $4,800,000 purchase price of the scanner is borrowed. The rate on the loan is 8 percent, and the loan will be repaid in equal installments. Create a lease-versus-buy analysis that explicitly incorporates the loan payments. Show that the NPV of leasing instead of buying is not changed from what it was in Problem 1. Why is this so?

        CHALLENGE
        (Question 12)

---

[6] The money factor of 2,400 is the product of three numbers: 2, 12, and 100. The 100 is used to convert the APR, expressed as a percentage, to a decimal number. The 12 converts this rate to a monthly rate. Finally, the monthly rate is applied to the sum of the net capitalization cost plus the residual. If we divide this sum by 2, the result is the average anticipated book value. Thus, the end result of the calculation using the money factor is to multiply a monthly rate by the average book value to get a monthly payment.

MINICASE

The Decision to Lease or Buy at Warf Computers

Warf Computers has decided to proceed with the manufacture and distribution of the virtual keyboard (VK) the company has developed. To undertake this venture, the company needs to obtain equipment for the production of the microphone for the keyboard. Because of the required sensitivity of the microphone and its small size, the company needs specialized equipment for production.

Nick Warf, the company president, has found a vendor for the equipment. Clapton Acoustical Equipment has offered to sell Warf Computers the necessary equipment at a price of $6.1 million. Because of the rapid development of new technology, the equipment falls in the three-year MACRS depreciation class. At the end of four years, the market value of the equipment is expected to be $780,000.

Alternatively, the company can lease the equipment from Hendrix Leasing. The lease contract calls for four annual payments of $1.48 million due at the beginning of the year. Additionally, Warf Computers must make a security deposit of $400,000 that will be returned when the lease expires. Warf Computers can issue bonds with a yield of 11 percent, and the company has a marginal tax rate of 21 percent.

QUESTIONS

1. Should Warf buy or lease the equipment?
2. Nick mentions to James Hendrix, the president of Hendrix Leasing, that although the company will need the equipment for four years, he would like a lease contract for two years instead. At the end of the two years, the lease could be renewed. Nick would also like to eliminate the security deposit, but he would be willing to increase the lease payments to $1.775 million for each of the two years. When the lease is renewed in two years, Hendrix would consider the increased lease payments in the first two years when calculating the terms of the renewal. The equipment is expected to have a market value of $3.2 million in two years. What is the NAL of the lease contract under these terms? Why might Nick prefer this lease? What are the potential ethical issues concerning the new lease terms?

3. In the leasing discussion, James informs Nick that the contract could include a purchase option for the equipment at the end of the lease. Hendrix Leasing offers three purchase options:
   a. An option to purchase the equipment at the fair market value.
   b. An option to purchase the equipment at a fixed price. The price will be negotiated before the lease is signed.
   c. An option to purchase the equipment at a price of $250,000.

   How would the inclusion of a purchase option affect the value of the lease?

4. James also informs Nick that the lease contract can include a cancellation option. The cancellation option would allow Warf Computers to cancel the lease on any anniversary date of the contract. To cancel the lease, Warf Computers would be required to give 30 days' notice prior to the anniversary date. How would the inclusion of a cancellation option affect the value of the lease?

MATHEMATICAL TABLES

TABLE A.1
Future value of $1 at the end of t periods $= (1 + r)^t$

TABLE A.2
Present value of $1 to be received after t periods $= 1/(1 + r)^t$

TABLE A.3
Present value of an annuity of $1 per period for t periods $= [1 - 1/(1 + r)^t]/r$

TABLE A.4
Future value of an annuity of $1 per period for t periods $= [(1 + r)^t - 1]/r$

TABLE A.5
Cumulative normal distribution

TABLE A.1   Future value of $1 at the end of *t* periods = $(1 + r)^t$

Period	1%	2%	3%	4%	5%	6%	7%	8%	9%
					Interest Rate				
1	1.0100	1.0200	1.0300	1.0400	1.0500	1.0600	1.0700	1.0800	1.0900
2	1.0201	1.0404	1.0609	1.0816	1.1025	1.1236	1.1449	1.1664	1.1881
3	1.0303	1.0612	1.0927	1.1249	1.1576	1.1910	1.2250	1.2597	1.2950
4	1.0406	1.0824	1.1255	1.1699	1.2155	1.2625	1.3108	1.3605	1.4116
5	1.0510	1.1041	1.1593	1.2167	1.2763	1.3382	1.4026	1.4693	1.5386
6	1.0615	1.1262	1.1941	1.2653	1.3401	1.4185	1.5007	1.5869	1.6771
7	1.0721	1.1487	1.2299	1.3159	1.4071	1.5036	1.6058	1.7138	1.8280
8	1.0829	1.1717	1.2668	1.3686	1.4775	1.5938	1.7182	1.8509	1.9926
9	1.0937	1.1951	1.3048	1.4233	1.5513	1.6895	1.8385	1.9990	2.1719
10	1.1046	1.2190	1.3439	1.4802	1.6289	1.7908	1.9672	2.1589	2.3674
11	1.1157	1.2434	1.3842	1.5395	1.7103	1.8983	2.1049	2.3316	2.5804
12	1.1268	1.2682	1.4258	1.6010	1.7959	2.0122	2.2522	2.5182	2.8127
13	1.1381	1.2936	1.4685	1.6651	1.8856	2.1329	2.4098	2.7196	3.0658
14	1.1495	1.3195	1.5126	1.7317	1.9799	2.2609	2.5785	2.9372	3.3417
15	1.1610	1.3459	1.5580	1.8009	2.0789	2.3966	2.7590	3.1722	3.6425
16	1.1726	1.3728	1.6047	1.8730	2.1829	2.5404	2.9522	3.4259	3.9703
17	1.1843	1.4002	1.6528	1.9479	2.2920	2.6928	3.1588	3.7000	4.3276
18	1.1961	1.4282	1.7024	2.0258	2.4066	2.8543	3.3799	3.9960	4.7171
19	1.2081	1.4568	1.7535	2.1068	2.5270	3.0256	3.6165	4.3157	5.1417
20	1.2202	1.4859	1.8061	2.1911	2.6533	3.2071	3.8697	4.6610	5.6044
21	1.2324	1.5157	1.8603	2.2788	2.7860	3.3996	4.1406	5.0338	6.1088
22	1.2447	1.5460	1.9161	2.3699	2.9253	3.6035	4.4304	5.4365	6.6586
23	1.2572	1.5769	1.9736	2.4647	3.0715	3.8197	4.7405	5.8715	7.2579
24	1.2697	1.6084	2.0328	2.5633	3.2251	4.0489	5.0724	6.3412	7.9111
25	1.2824	1.6406	2.0938	2.6658	3.3864	4.2919	5.4274	6.8485	8.6231
30	1.3478	1.8114	2.4273	3.2434	4.3219	5.7435	7.6123	10.063	13.268
40	1.4889	2.2080	3.2620	4.8010	7.0400	10.286	14.974	21.725	31.409
50	1.6446	2.6916	4.3839	7.1067	11.467	18.420	29.457	46.902	74.358
60	1.8167	3.2810	5.8916	10.520	18.679	32.988	57.946	101.26	176.03

continued on next page

10%	12%	14%	15%	16%	18%	20%	24%	28%	32%	36%
1.1000	1.1200	1.1400	1.1500	1.1600	1.1800	1.2000	1.2400	1.2800	1.3200	1.3600
1.2100	1.2544	1.2996	1.3225	1.3456	1.3924	1.4400	1.5376	1.6384	1.7424	1.8496
1.3310	1.4049	1.4815	1.5209	1.5609	1.6430	1.7280	1.9066	2.0972	2.3000	2.5155
1.4641	1.5735	1.6890	1.7490	1.8106	1.9388	2.0736	2.3642	2.6844	3.0360	3.4210
1.6105	1.7623	1.9254	2.0114	2.1003	2.2878	2.4883	2.9316	3.4360	4.0075	4.6526
1.7716	1.9738	2.1950	2.3131	2.4364	2.6996	2.9860	3.6352	4.3980	5.2899	6.3275
1.9487	2.2107	2.5023	2.6600	2.8262	3.1855	3.5832	4.5077	5.6295	6.9826	8.6054
2.1436	2.4760	2.8526	3.0590	3.2784	3.7589	4.2998	5.5895	7.2058	9.2170	11.703
2.3579	2.7731	3.2519	3.5179	3.8030	4.4355	5.1598	6.9310	9.2234	12.166	15.917
2.5937	3.1058	3.7072	4.0456	4.4114	5.2338	6.1917	8.5944	11.806	16.060	21.647
2.8531	3.4785	4.2262	4.6524	5.1173	6.1759	7.4301	10.657	15.112	21.199	29.439
3.1384	3.8960	4.8179	5.3503	5.9360	7.2876	8.9161	13.215	19.343	27.983	40.037
3.4523	4.3635	5.4924	6.1528	6.8858	8.5994	10.699	16.386	24.759	36.937	54.451
3.7975	4.8871	6.2613	7.0757	7.9875	10.147	12.839	20.319	31.691	48.757	74.053
4.1772	5.4736	7.1379	8.1371	9.2655	11.974	15.407	25.196	40.565	64.359	100.71
4.5950	6.1304	8.1372	9.3576	10.748	14.129	18.488	31.243	51.923	84.954	136.97
5.0545	6.8660	9.2765	10.761	12.468	16.672	22.186	38.741	66.461	112.14	186.28
5.5599	7.6900	10.575	12.375	14.463	19.673	26.623	48.039	85.071	148.02	253.34
6.1159	8.6128	12.056	14.232	16.777	23.214	31.948	59.568	108.89	195.39	344.54
6.7275	9.6463	13.743	16.367	19.461	27.393	38.338	73.864	139.38	257.92	468.57
7.4002	10.804	15.668	18.822	22.574	32.324	46.005	91.592	178.41	340.45	637.26
8.1403	12.100	17.861	21.645	26.186	38.142	55.206	113.57	228.36	449.39	866.67
8.9543	13.552	20.362	24.891	30.376	45.008	66.247	140.83	292.30	593.20	1178.7
9.8497	15.179	23.212	28.625	35.236	53.109	79.497	174.63	374.14	783.02	1603.0
10.835	17.000	26.462	32.919	40.874	62.669	95.396	216.54	478.90	1033.6	2180.1
17.449	29.960	50.950	66.212	85.850	143.37	237.38	634.82	1645.5	4142.1	10143.0
45.259	93.051	188.88	267.86	378.72	750.38	1469.8	5455.9	19426.7	66520.8	*
117.39	289.00	700.23	1083.7	1670.7	3927.4	9100.4	46890.4	*	*	*
304.48	897.60	2595.9	4384.0	7370.2	20555.1	56347.5	*	*	*	*

*The factor is greater than 99,999.

A-4   **APPENDIX A**   Mathematical Tables

TABLE A.2   **Present value of $1 to be received after t periods $= 1/(1 + r)^t$**

Period	1%	2%	3%	4%	5%	6%	7%	8%	9%
				Interest Rate					
1	.9901	.9804	.9709	.9615	.9524	.9434	.9346	.9259	.9174
2	.9803	.9612	.9426	.9246	.9070	.8900	.8734	.8573	.8417
3	.9706	.9423	.9151	.8890	.8638	.8396	.8163	.7938	.7722
4	.9610	.9238	.8885	.8548	.8227	.7921	.7629	.7350	.7084
5	.9515	.9057	.8626	.8219	.7835	.7473	.7130	.6806	.6499
6	.9420	.8880	.8375	.7903	.7462	.7050	.6663	.6302	.5963
7	.9327	.8706	.8131	.7599	.7107	.6651	.6227	.5835	.5470
8	.9235	.8535	.7894	.7307	.6768	.6274	.5820	.5403	.5019
9	.9143	.8368	.7664	.7026	.6446	.5919	.5439	.5002	.4604
10	.9053	.8203	.7441	.6756	.6139	.5584	.5083	.4632	.4224
11	.8963	.8043	.7224	.6496	.5847	.5268	.4751	.4289	.3875
12	.8874	.7885	.7014	.6246	.5568	.4970	.4440	.3971	.3555
13	.8787	.7730	.6810	.6006	.5303	.4688	.4150	.3677	.3262
14	.8700	.7579	.6611	.5775	.5051	.4423	.3878	.3405	.2992
15	.8613	.7430	.6419	.5553	.4810	.4173	.3624	.3152	.2745
16	.8528	.7284	.6232	.5339	.4581	.3936	.3387	.2919	.2519
17	.8444	.7142	.6050	.5134	.4363	.3714	.3166	.2703	.2311
18	.8360	.7002	.5874	.4936	.4155	.3503	.2959	.2502	.2120
19	.8277	.6864	.5703	.4746	.3957	.3305	.2765	.2317	.1945
20	.8195	.6730	.5537	.4564	.3769	.3118	.2584	.2145	.1784
21	.8114	.6598	.5375	.4388	.3589	.2942	.2415	.1987	.1637
22	.8034	.6468	.5219	.4220	.3418	.2775	.2257	.1839	.1502
23	.7954	.6342	.5067	.4057	.3256	.2618	.2109	.1703	.1378
24	.7876	.6217	.4919	.3901	.3101	.2470	.1971	.1577	.1264
25	.7798	.6095	.4776	.3751	.2953	.2330	.1842	.1460	.1160
30	.7419	.5521	.4120	.3083	.2314	.1741	.1314	.0994	.0754
40	.6717	.4529	.3066	.2083	.1420	.0972	.0668	.0460	.0318
50	.6080	.3715	.2281	.1407	.0872	.0543	.0339	.0213	.0134

continued on next page

10%	12%	14%	15%	16%	18%	20%	24%	28%	32%	36%
.9091	.8929	.8772	.8696	.8621	.8475	.8333	.8065	.7813	.7576	.7353
.8264	.7972	.7695	.7561	.7432	.7182	.6944	.6504	.6104	.5739	.5407
.7513	.7118	.6750	.6575	.6407	.6086	.5787	.5245	.4768	.4348	.3975
.6830	.6355	.5921	.5718	.5523	.5158	.4823	.4230	.3725	.3294	.2923
.6209	.5674	.5194	.4972	.4761	.4371	.4019	.3411	.2910	.2495	.2149
.5645	.5066	.4556	.4323	.4104	.3704	.3349	.2751	.2274	.1890	.1580
.5132	.4523	.3996	.3759	.3538	.3139	.2791	.2218	.1776	.1432	.1162
.4665	.4039	.3506	.3269	.3050	.2660	.2326	.1789	.1388	.1085	.0854
.4241	.3606	.3075	.2843	.2630	.2255	.1938	.1443	.1084	.0822	.0628
.3855	.3220	.2697	.2472	.2267	.1911	.1615	.1164	.0847	.0623	.0462
.3505	.2875	.2366	.2149	.1954	.1619	.1346	.0938	.0662	.0472	.0340
.3186	.2567	.2076	.1869	.1685	.1372	.1122	.0757	.0517	.0357	.0250
.2897	.2292	.1821	.1625	.1452	.1163	.0935	.0610	.0404	.0271	.0184
.2633	.2046	.1597	.1413	.1252	.0985	.0779	.0492	.0316	.0205	.0135
.2394	.1827	.1401	.1229	.1079	.0835	.0649	.0397	.0247	.0155	.0099
.2176	.1631	.1229	.1069	.0930	.0708	.0541	.0320	.0193	.0118	.0073
.1978	.1456	.1078	.0929	.0802	.0600	.0451	.0258	.0150	.0089	.0054
.1799	.1300	.0946	.0808	.0691	.0508	.0376	.0208	.0118	.0068	.0039
.1635	.1161	.0829	.0703	.0596	.0431	.0313	.0168	.0092	.0051	.0029
.1486	.1037	.0728	.0611	.0514	.0365	.0261	.0135	.0072	.0039	.0021
.1351	.0926	.0638	.0531	.0443	.0309	.0217	.0109	.0056	.0029	.0016
.1228	.0826	.0560	.0462	.0382	.0262	.0181	.0088	.0044	.0022	.0012
.1117	.0738	.0491	.0402	.0329	.0222	.0151	.0071	.0034	.0017	.0008
.1015	.0659	.0431	.0349	.0284	.0188	.0126	.0057	.0027	.0013	.0006
.0923	.0588	.0378	.0304	.0245	.0160	.0105	.0046	.0021	.0010	.0005
.0573	.0334	.0196	.0151	.0116	.0070	.0042	.0016	.0006	.0002	.0001
.0221	.0107	.0053	.0037	.0026	.0013	.0007	.0002	.0001	*	*
.0085	.0035	.0014	.0009	.0006	.0003	.0001	*	*	*	*

*The factor is zero to four decimal places.

TABLE A.3 Present value of an annuity of $1 per period for t periods $= [1 - 1/(1 + r)^t]/r$

Number of Periods	Interest Rate								
	1%	2%	3%	4%	5%	6%	7%	8%	9%
1	.9901	.9804	.9709	.9615	.9524	.9434	.9346	.9259	.9174
2	1.9704	1.9416	1.9135	1.8861	1.8594	1.8334	1.8080	1.7833	1.7591
3	2.9410	2.8839	2.8286	2.7751	2.7232	2.6730	2.6243	2.5771	2.5313
4	3.9020	3.8077	3.7171	3.6299	3.5460	3.4651	3.3872	3.3121	3.2397
5	4.8534	4.7135	4.5797	4.4518	4.3295	4.2124	4.1002	3.9927	3.8897
6	5.7955	5.6014	5.4172	5.2421	5.0757	4.9173	4.7665	4.6229	4.4859
7	6.7282	6.4720	6.2303	6.0021	5.7864	5.5824	5.3893	5.2064	5.0330
8	7.6517	7.3255	7.0197	6.7327	6.4632	6.2098	5.9713	5.7466	5.5348
9	8.5660	8.1622	7.7861	7.4353	7.1078	6.8017	6.5152	6.2469	5.9952
10	9.4713	8.9826	8.5302	8.1109	7.7217	7.3601	7.0236	6.7101	6.4177
11	10.3676	9.7868	9.2526	8.7605	8.3064	7.8869	7.4987	7.1390	6.8052
12	11.2551	10.5753	9.9540	9.3851	8.8633	8.3838	7.9427	7.5361	7.1607
13	12.1337	11.3484	10.6350	9.9856	9.3936	8.8527	8.3577	7.9038	7.4869
14	13.0037	12.1062	11.2961	10.5631	9.8986	9.2950	8.7455	8.2442	7.7862
15	13.8651	12.8493	11.9379	11.1184	10.3797	9.7122	9.1079	8.5595	8.0607
16	14.7179	13.5777	12.5611	11.6523	10.8378	10.1059	9.4466	8.8514	8.3126
17	15.5623	14.2919	13.1661	12.1657	11.2741	10.4773	9.7632	9.1216	8.5436
18	16.3983	14.9920	13.7535	12.6593	11.6896	10.8276	10.0591	9.3719	8.7556
19	17.2260	15.6785	14.3238	13.1339	12.0853	11.1581	10.3356	9.6036	8.9501
20	18.0456	16.3514	14.8775	13.5903	12.4622	11.4699	10.5940	9.8181	9.1285
21	18.8570	17.0112	15.4150	14.0292	12.8212	11.7641	10.8355	10.0168	9.2922
22	19.6604	17.6580	15.9369	14.4511	13.1630	12.0416	11.0612	10.2007	9.4424
23	20.4558	18.2922	16.4436	14.8568	13.4886	12.3034	11.2722	10.3741	9.5802
24	21.2434	18.9139	16.9355	15.2470	13.7986	12.5504	11.4693	10.5288	9.7066
25	22.0232	19.5235	17.4131	15.6221	14.0939	12.7834	11.6536	10.6748	9.8226
30	25.8077	22.3965	19.6004	17.2920	15.3725	13.7648	12.4090	11.2578	10.2737
40	32.8347	27.3555	23.1148	19.7928	17.1591	15.0463	13.3317	11.9246	10.7574
50	39.1961	31.4236	25.7298	21.4822	18.2559	15.7619	13.8007	12.2335	10.9617

continued on next page

10%	12%	14%	15%	16%	18%	20%	24%	28%	32%	36%
.9091	.8929	.8772	.8696	.8621	.8475	.8333	.8065	.7813	.7576	.7353
1.7355	1.6901	1.6467	1.6257	1.6052	1.5656	1.5278	1.4568	1.3916	1.3315	1.2760
2.4869	2.4018	2.3216	2.2832	2.2459	2.1743	2.1065	1.9813	1.8684	1.7663	1.6735
3.1699	3.0373	2.9137	2.8550	2.7982	2.6901	2.5887	2.4043	2.2410	2.0957	1.9658
3.7908	3.6048	3.4331	3.3522	3.2743	3.1272	2.9906	2.7454	2.5320	2.3452	2.1807
4.3553	4.1114	3.8887	3.7845	3.6847	3.4976	3.3255	3.0205	2.7594	2.5342	2.3388
4.8684	4.5638	4.2883	4.1604	4.0386	3.8115	3.6046	3.2423	2.9370	2.6775	2.4550
5.3349	4.9676	4.6389	4.4873	4.3436	4.0776	3.8372	3.4212	3.0758	2.7860	2.5404
5.7590	5.3282	4.9464	4.7716	4.6065	4.3030	4.0310	3.5655	3.1842	2.8681	2.6033
6.1446	5.6502	5.2161	5.0188	4.8332	4.4941	4.1925	3.6819	3.2689	2.9304	2.6495
6.4951	5.9377	5.4527	5.2337	5.0286	4.6560	4.3271	3.7757	3.3351	2.9776	2.6834
6.8137	6.1944	5.6603	5.4206	5.1971	4.7932	4.4392	3.8514	3.3868	3.0133	2.7084
7.1034	6.4235	5.8424	5.5831	5.3423	4.9095	4.5327	3.9124	3.4272	3.0404	2.7268
7.3667	6.6282	6.0021	5.7245	5.4675	5.0081	4.6106	3.9616	3.4587	3.0609	2.7403
7.6061	6.8109	6.1422	5.8474	5.5755	5.0916	4.6755	4.0013	3.4834	3.0764	2.7502
7.8237	6.9740	6.2651	5.9542	5.6685	5.1624	4.7296	4.0333	3.5026	3.0882	2.7575
8.0216	7.1196	6.3729	6.0472	5.7487	5.2223	4.7746	4.0591	3.5177	3.0971	2.7629
8.2014	7.2497	6.4674	6.1280	5.8178	5.2732	4.8122	4.0799	3.5294	3.1039	2.7668
8.3649	7.3658	6.5504	6.1982	5.8775	5.3162	4.8435	4.0967	3.5386	3.1090	2.7697
8.5136	7.4694	6.6231	6.2593	5.9288	5.3527	4.8696	4.1103	3.5458	3.1129	2.7718
8.6487	7.5620	6.6870	6.3125	5.9731	5.3837	4.8913	4.1212	3.5514	3.1158	2.7734
8.7715	7.6446	6.7429	6.3587	6.0113	5.4099	4.9094	4.1300	3.5558	3.1180	2.7746
8.8832	7.7184	6.7921	6.3988	6.0442	5.4321	4.9245	4.1371	3.5592	3.1197	2.7754
8.9847	7.7843	6.8351	6.4338	6.0726	5.4509	4.9371	4.1428	3.5619	3.1210	2.7760
9.0770	7.8431	6.8729	6.4641	6.0971	5.4669	4.9476	4.1474	3.5640	3.1220	2.7765
9.4269	8.0552	7.0027	6.5660	6.1772	5.5168	4.9789	4.1601	3.5693	3.1242	2.7775
9.7791	8.2438	7.1050	6.6418	6.2335	5.5482	4.9966	4.1659	3.5712	3.1250	2.7778
9.9148	8.3045	7.1327	6.6605	6.2463	5.5541	4.9995	4.1666	3.5714	3.1250	2.7778

TABLE A.4 Future value of an annuity of $1 per period for t periods $= [(1 + r)^t - 1]/r$

Number of Periods	Interest Rate								
	1%	2%	3%	4%	5%	6%	7%	8%	9%
1	1.0000	1.0000	1.0000	1.0000	1.0000	1.0000	1.0000	1.0000	1.0000
2	2.0100	2.0200	2.0300	2.0400	2.0500	2.0600	2.0700	2.0800	2.0900
3	3.0301	3.0604	3.0909	3.1216	3.1525	3.1836	3.2149	3.2464	3.2781
4	4.0604	4.1216	4.1836	4.2465	4.3101	4.3746	4.4399	4.5061	4.5731
5	5.1010	5.2040	5.3091	5.4163	5.5256	5.6371	5.7507	5.8666	5.9847
6	6.1520	6.3081	6.4684	6.6330	6.8019	6.9753	7.1533	7.3359	7.5233
7	7.2135	7.4343	7.6625	7.8983	8.1420	8.3938	8.6540	8.9228	9.2004
8	8.2857	8.5830	8.8932	9.2142	9.5491	9.8975	10.260	10.637	11.028
9	9.3685	9.7546	10.159	10.583	11.027	11.491	11.978	12.488	13.021
10	10.462	10.950	11.464	12.006	12.578	13.181	13.816	14.487	15.193
11	11.567	12.169	12.808	13.486	14.207	14.972	15.784	16.645	17.560
12	12.683	13.412	14.192	15.026	15.917	16.870	17.888	18.977	20.141
13	13.809	14.680	15.618	16.627	17.713	18.882	20.141	21.495	22.953
14	14.947	15.974	17.086	18.292	19.599	21.015	22.550	24.215	26.019
15	16.097	17.293	18.599	20.024	21.579	23.276	25.129	27.152	29.361
16	17.258	18.639	20.157	21.825	23.657	25.673	27.888	30.324	33.003
17	18.430	20.012	21.762	23.698	25.840	28.213	30.840	33.750	36.974
18	19.615	21.412	23.414	25.645	28.132	30.906	33.999	37.450	41.301
19	20.811	22.841	25.117	27.671	30.539	33.760	37.379	41.446	46.018
20	22.019	24.297	26.870	29.778	33.066	36.786	40.995	45.762	51.160
21	23.239	25.783	28.676	31.969	35.719	39.993	44.865	50.423	56.765
22	24.472	27.299	30.537	34.248	38.505	43.392	49.006	55.457	62.873
23	25.716	28.845	32.453	36.618	41.430	46.996	53.436	60.893	69.532
24	26.973	30.422	34.426	39.083	44.502	50.816	58.177	66.765	76.790
25	28.243	32.030	36.459	41.646	47.727	54.865	63.249	73.106	84.701
30	34.785	40.568	47.575	56.085	66.439	79.058	94.461	113.28	136.31
40	48.886	60.402	75.401	95.026	120.80	154.76	199.64	259.06	337.88
50	64.463	84.579	112.80	152.67	209.35	290.34	406.53	573.77	815.08
60	81.670	114.05	163.05	237.99	353.58	533.13	813.52	1253.2	1944.8

continued on next page

10%	12%	14%	15%	16%	18%	20%	24%	28%	32%	36%
1.0000	1.0000	1.0000	1.0000	1.0000	1.0000	1.0000	1.0000	1.0000	1.0000	1.0000
2.1000	2.1200	2.1400	2.1500	2.1600	2.1800	2.2000	2.2400	2.2800	2.3200	2.3600
3.3100	3.3744	3.4396	3.4725	3.5056	3.5724	3.6400	3.7776	3.9184	4.0624	4.2096
4.6410	4.7793	4.9211	4.9934	5.0665	5.2154	5.3680	5.6842	6.0156	6.3624	6.7251
6.1051	6.3528	6.6101	6.7424	6.8771	7.1542	7.4416	8.0484	8.6999	9.3983	10.146
7.7156	8.1152	8.5355	8.7537	8.9775	9.4420	9.9299	10.980	12.136	13.406	14.799
9.4872	10.089	10.730	11.067	11.414	12.142	12.916	14.615	16.534	18.696	21.126
11.436	12.300	13.233	13.727	14.240	15.327	16.499	19.123	22.163	25.678	29.732
13.579	14.776	16.085	16.786	17.519	19.086	20.799	24.712	29.369	34.895	41.435
15.937	17.549	19.337	20.304	21.321	23.521	25.959	31.643	38.593	47.062	57.352
18.531	20.655	23.045	24.349	25.733	28.755	32.150	40.238	50.398	63.122	78.998
21.384	24.133	27.271	29.002	30.850	34.931	39.581	50.895	65.510	84.320	108.44
24.523	28.029	32.089	34.352	36.786	42.219	48.497	64.110	84.853	112.30	148.47
27.975	32.393	37.581	40.505	43.672	50.818	59.196	80.496	109.61	149.24	202.93
31.772	37.280	43.842	47.580	51.660	60.965	72.035	100.82	141.30	198.00	276.98
35.950	42.753	50.980	55.717	60.925	72.939	87.442	126.01	181.87	262.36	377.69
40.545	48.884	59.118	65.075	71.673	87.068	105.93	157.25	233.79	347.31	514.66
45.599	55.750	68.394	75.836	84.141	103.74	128.12	195.99	300.25	459.45	700.94
51.159	63.440	78.969	88.212	98.603	123.41	154.74	244.03	385.32	607.47	954.28
57.275	72.052	91.025	102.44	115.38	146.63	186.69	303.60	494.21	802.86	1298.8
64.002	81.699	104.77	118.81	134.84	174.02	225.03	377.46	633.59	1060.8	1767.4
71.403	92.503	120.44	137.63	157.41	206.34	271.03	469.06	812.00	1401.2	2404.7
79.543	104.60	138.30	159.28	183.60	244.49	326.24	582.63	1040.4	1850.6	3271.3
88.497	118.16	158.66	184.17	213.98	289.49	392.48	723.46	1332.7	2443.8	4450.0
98.347	133.33	181.87	212.79	249.21	342.60	471.98	898.09	1706.8	3226.8	6053.0
164.49	241.33	356.79	434.75	530.31	790.95	1181.9	2640.9	5873.2	12940.9	28172.3
442.59	767.09	1342.0	1779.1	2360.8	4163.2	7343.9	22728.8	69377.5	*	*
1163.9	2400.0	4994.5	7217.7	10435.7	21813.1	45497.2	*	*	*	*
3043.8	7471.6	18535.1	29220.0	46057.5	*	*	*	*	*	*

*The factor is greater than 99,999.

TABLE A.5   Cumulative normal distribution

d	N(d)	d	N(d)	d	N(d)	d	N(d)	d	N(d)	d	N(d)	d	N(d)
-3.00	.0013	-1.58	.0571	-.76	.2236	.06	.5239	.86	.8051	1.66	.9515		
-2.95	.0016	-1.56	.0594	-.74	.2297	.08	.5319	.88	.8106	1.68	.9535		
-2.90	.0019	-1.54	.0618	-.72	.2358	.10	.5398	.90	.8159	1.70	.9554		
-2.85	.0022	-1.52	.0643	-.70	.2420	.12	.5478	.92	.8212	1.72	.9573		
-2.80	.0026	-1.50	.0668	-.68	.2483	.14	.5557	.94	.8264	1.74	.9591		
-2.75	.0030	-1.48	.0694	-.66	.2546	.16	.5636	.96	.8315	1.76	.9608		
-2.70	.0035	-1.46	.0721	-.64	.2611	.18	.5714	.98	.8365	1.78	.9625		
-2.65	.0040	-1.44	.0749	-.62	.2676	.20	.5793	1.00	.8413	1.80	.9641		
-2.60	.0047	-1.42	.0778	-.60	.2743	.22	.5871	1.02	.8461	1.82	.9656		
-2.55	.0054	-1.40	.0808	-.58	.2810	.24	.5948	1.04	.8508	1.84	.9671		
-2.50	.0062	-1.38	.0838	-.56	.2877	.26	.6026	1.06	.8554	1.86	.9686		
-2.45	.0071	-1.36	.0869	-.54	.2946	.28	.6103	1.08	.8599	1.88	.9699		
-2.40	.0082	-1.34	.0901	-.52	.3015	.30	.6179	1.10	.8643	1.90	.9713		
-2.35	.0094	-1.32	.0934	-.50	.3085	.32	.6255	1.12	.8686	1.92	.9726		
-2.30	.0107	-1.30	.0968	-.48	.3156	.34	.6331	1.14	.8729	1.94	.9738		
-2.25	.0122	-1.28	.1003	-.46	.3228	.36	.6406	1.16	.8770	1.96	.9750		
-2.20	.0139	-1.26	.1038	-.44	.3300	.38	.6480	1.18	.8810	1.98	.9761		
-2.15	.0158	-1.24	.1075	-.42	.3372	.40	.6554	1.20	.8849	2.00	.9772		
-2.10	.0179	-1.22	.1112	-.40	.3446	.42	.6628	1.22	.8888	2.05	.9798		
-2.05	.0202	-1.20	.1151	-.38	.3520	.44	.6700	1.24	.8925	2.10	.9821		
-2.00	.0228	-1.18	.1190	-.36	.3594	.46	.6772	1.26	.8962	2.15	.9842		
-1.98	.0239	-1.16	.1230	-.34	.3669	.48	.6844	1.28	.8997	2.20	.9861		
-1.96	.0250	-1.14	.1271	-.32	.3745	.50	.6915	1.30	.9032	2.25	.9878		
-1.94	.0262	-1.12	.1314	-.30	.3821	.52	.6985	1.32	.9066	2.30	.9893		
-1.92	.0274	-1.10	.1357	-.28	.3897	.54	.7054	1.34	.9099	2.35	.9906		
-1.90	.0287	-1.08	.1401	-.26	.3974	.56	.7123	1.36	.9131	2.40	.9918		
-1.88	.0301	-1.06	.1446	-.24	.4052	.58	.7190	1.38	.9162	2.45	.9929		
-1.86	.0314	-1.04	.1492	-.22	.4129	.60	.7257	1.40	.9192	2.50	.9938		
-1.84	.0329	-1.02	.1539	-.20	.4207	.62	.7324	1.42	.9222	2.55	.9946		
-1.82	.0344	-1.00	.1587	-.18	.4286	.64	.7389	1.44	.9251	2.60	.9953		
-1.80	.0359	-.98	.1635	-.16	.4364	.66	.7454	1.46	.9279	2.65	.9960		
-1.78	.0375	-.96	.1685	-.14	.4443	.68	.7518	1.48	.9306	2.70	.9965		
-1.76	.0392	-.94	.1736	-.12	.4522	.70	.7580	1.50	.9332	2.75	.9970		
-1.74	.0409	-.92	.1788	-.10	.4602	.72	.7642	1.52	.9357	2.80	.9974		
-1.72	.0427	-.90	.1841	-.08	.4681	.74	.7704	1.54	.9382	2.85	.9978		
-1.70	.0446	-.88	.1894	-.06	.4761	.76	.7764	1.56	.9406	2.90	.9981		
-1.68	.0465	-.86	.1949	-.04	.4840	.78	.7823	1.58	.9429	2.95	.9984		
-1.66	.0485	-.84	.2005	-.02	.4920	.80	.7881	1.60	.9452	3.00	.9987		
-1.64	.0505	-.82	.2061	.00	.5000	.82	.7939	1.62	.9474	3.05	.9989		
-1.62	.0526	-.80	.2119	.02	.5080	.84	.7995	1.64	.9495				
-1.60	.0548	-.78	.2177	.04	.5160								

This table shows the probability [N(d)] of observing a value less than or equal to d. For example, as illustrated, if d is -.24, then N(d) is .4052.

KEY EQUATIONS

B

CHAPTER 2

1. The balance sheet identity or equation:

Assets = Liabilities + Shareholders' equity **[2.1]**

2. The income statement equation:

Revenues − Expenses = Income   **[2.2]**

3. The cash flow identity:

Cash flow from assets =
Cash flow to creditors +
Cash flow to stockholders   **[2.3]**

where:

  a. Cash flow from assets = Operating cash flow (OCF) − Net capital spending − Change in net working capital (NWC)
    (1) Operating cash flow = Earnings before interest and taxes (EBIT) + Depreciation − Taxes
    (2) Net capital spending = Ending net fixed assets − Beginning net fixed assets + Depreciation
    (3) Change in net working capital = Ending NWC − Beginning NWC
  b. Cash flow to creditors = Interest paid − Net new borrowing
  c. Cash flow to stockholders = Dividends paid − Net new equity raised

CHAPTER 3

1. The current ratio:

$$\text{Current ratio} = \frac{\text{Current assets}}{\text{Current liabilities}} \quad \textbf{[3.1]}$$

2. The quick or acid-test ratio:

$$\text{Quick ratio} = \frac{\text{Current assets} - \text{Inventory}}{\text{Current liabilities}} \quad \textbf{[3.2]}$$

3. The cash ratio:

$$\text{Cash ratio} = \frac{\text{Cash}}{\text{Current liabilities}} \quad \textbf{[3.3]}$$

4. The ratio of net working capital to total assets:

Net working capital to total assets

$$= \frac{\text{Net working capital}}{\text{Total assets}} \quad \textbf{[3.4]}$$

5. The interval measure:

Interval measure

$$= \frac{\text{Current assets}}{\text{Average daily operating costs}} \quad \textbf{[3.5]}$$

6. The total debt ratio:

Total debt ratio

$$= \frac{\text{Total assets} - \text{Total equity}}{\text{Total assets}} \quad \textbf{[3.6]}$$

7. The debt-equity ratio:

Debt-equity ratio

$$= \frac{\text{Total debt}}{\text{Total equity}} \quad \textbf{[3.7]}$$

8. The equity multiplier:

Equity multiplier

$$= \frac{\text{Total assets}}{\text{Total equity}} \quad \textbf{[3.8]}$$

9. The long-term debt ratio:

Long-term debt ratio

$$= \frac{\text{Long-term debt}}{\text{Long-term debt} + \text{Total equity}} \quad \textbf{[3.9]}$$

10. The times interest earned (TIE) ratio:

$$\text{Times interest earned ratio} = \frac{\text{EBIT}}{\text{Interest}} \quad \textbf{[3.10]}$$

11. The cash coverage ratio:

Cash coverage ratio

$$= \frac{\text{EBIT} + \text{Depreciation}}{\text{Interest}} \quad \textbf{[3.11]}$$

12. The inventory turnover ratio:

Inventory turnover

$$= \frac{\text{Cost of goods sold}}{\text{Inventory}} \quad \textbf{[3.12]}$$

13. The average days' sales in inventory:

Days' sales in inventory

$$= \frac{365 \text{ days}}{\text{Inventory turnover}} \quad \textbf{[3.13]}$$

14. The receivables turnover ratio:
Receivables turnover
$$= \frac{\text{Sales}}{\text{Accounts receivable}} \quad [3.14]$$

15. The days' sales in receivables:
Days' sales in receivables
$$= \frac{365 \text{ days}}{\text{Receivables turnover}} \quad [3.15]$$

16. The net working capital (NWC) turnover ratio:
$$\text{NWC turnover} = \frac{\text{Sales}}{\text{NWC}} \quad [3.16]$$

17. The fixed asset turnover ratio:
$$\text{Fixed asset turnover} = \frac{\text{Sales}}{\text{Net fixed assets}} \quad [3.17]$$

18. The total asset turnover ratio:
$$\text{Total asset turnover} = \frac{\text{Sales}}{\text{Total assets}} \quad [3.18]$$

19. Profit margin:
$$\text{Profit margin} = \frac{\text{Net income}}{\text{Sales}} \quad [3.19]$$

20. Return on assets (ROA):
$$\text{Return on assets} = \frac{\text{Net income}}{\text{Total assets}} \quad [3.20]$$

21. Return on equity (ROE):
$$\text{Return on equity} = \frac{\text{Net income}}{\text{Total equity}} \quad [3.21]$$

22. The price-earnings (PE) ratio:
$$\text{PE ratio} = \frac{\text{Price per share}}{\text{Earnings per share}} \quad [3.22]$$

23. The market-to-book ratio:
$$\text{Market-to-book ratio} = \frac{\text{Market value per share}}{\text{Book value per share}} \quad [3.23]$$

24. Enterprise value:
Enterprise value = Total market value of the stock +
Book value of all liabilities −
Cash   [3.24]

25. The EBITDA (earnings before interest, tax, depreciation, and amortization) ratio:
$$\text{EBITDA ratio} = \frac{\text{Enterprise value}}{\text{EBITDA}} \quad [3.25]$$

26. The DuPont identity:
$$\text{ROE} = \underbrace{\frac{\text{Net income}}{\text{Sales}} \times \frac{\text{Sales}}{\text{Assets}}}_{\text{Return on assets}} \times \frac{\text{Assets}}{\text{Equity}} \quad [3.26]$$
= Profit margin
× Total asset turnover
× Equity multiplier

CHAPTER 4

1. The dividend payout ratio:
Dividend payout ratio
$$= \frac{\text{Cash dividends}}{\text{Net income}} \quad [4.1]$$

2. The internal growth rate:
$$\text{Internal growth rate} = \frac{\text{ROA} \times b}{1 - \text{ROA} \times b} \quad [4.2]$$

3. The sustainable growth rate:
$$\text{Sustainable growth rate} = \frac{\text{ROE} \times b}{1 - \text{ROE} \times b} \quad [4.3]$$

CHAPTER 5

1. The future value of $1 invested for t periods at a rate of r per period:
$$\text{Future value} = \$1 \times (1 + r)^t \quad [5.1]$$

2. The present value of $1 to be received t periods into the future at a discount rate of r:
$$\text{PV} = \$1 \times [1/(1 + r)^t] = \$1/(1 + r)^t \quad [5.2]$$

3. The relationship between future value and present value (the basic present value equation):
$$\text{PV} \times (1 + r)^t = \text{FV}_t$$
$$\text{PV} = \text{FV}_t /(1 + r)^t = \text{FV}_t \times [1/(1 + r)^t] \quad [5.3]$$

CHAPTER 6

1. The present value of an annuity of C dollars per period for t periods when the rate of return or interest rate is r:
Annuity present value
$$= C \times \left(\frac{1 - \text{Present value factor}}{r} \right)$$
$$= C \times \left\{ \frac{1 - [1/(1 + r)^t]}{r} \right\} \quad [6.1]$$

2. The future value factor for an annuity:
Annuity FV factor
$$= (\text{Future value factor} - 1)/r \quad [6.2]$$
$$= [(1 + r)^t - 1]/r$$

3. Annuity due value = Ordinary annuity value
$$\times (1 + r) \quad [6.3]$$

4. Present value of a perpetuity:
$$\text{PV for a perpetuity} = C/r \quad [6.4]$$

5. Growing annuity present value
$$= C \times \left[\frac{1 - \left(\frac{1 + g}{1 + r}\right)^t}{r - g} \right] \quad [6.5]$$

6. Growing perpetuity present value
$$= \frac{C}{r - g} \quad [6.6]$$

7. Effective annual rate (EAR), where m is the number of times the interest is compounded during the year:
$$\text{EAR} = [1 + (\text{Quoted rate}/m)]^m - 1 \quad [6.7]$$

8. Effective annual rate (EAR), where q stands for the continuously compounded quoted rate:
$$\text{EAR} = e^q - 1 \quad [6.8]$$

CHAPTER 7

1. Bond value if bond has (1) a face value of F paid at maturity, (2) a coupon of C paid per period, (3) t periods to maturity, and (4) a yield of r per period:

$$\begin{aligned}\text{Bond value} &= C \times [1 - 1/(1 + r)^t]/r + F/(1 + r)^t \\ &= \begin{array}{c}\text{Present value} \\ \text{of the coupons}\end{array} + \begin{array}{c}\text{Present value} \\ \text{of the face amount}\end{array}\end{aligned} \quad \text{[7.1]}$$

2. The Fisher effect:

$$1 + R = (1 + r) \times (1 + h) \quad \text{[7.2]}$$
$$R = r + h + r \times h \quad \text{[7.3]}$$
$$R \approx r + h \quad \text{[7.4]}$$

CHAPTER 8

1. Per-share present value of common stock, where D_1 is the cash dividend paid at the end of the period, and R is the required return:

$$P_0 = (D_1 + P_1)/(1 + R) \quad \text{[8.1]}$$

2. Per-share present value of common stock with zero growth, where the dividend is constant and R is the required return:

$$P_0 = D/R \quad \text{[8.2]}$$

3. The dividend growth model:

$$P_0 = \frac{D_0 \times (1 + g)}{R - g} = \frac{D_1}{R - g} \quad \text{[8.3]}$$

4. The dividend growth model can be modified slightly to give the price of a stock as of Time t:

$$P_t = \frac{D_t \times (1 + g)}{R - g} = \frac{D_{t+1}}{R - g} \quad \text{[8.4]}$$

5. Two-stage growth model:

$$P_0 = \frac{D_1}{R - g_1} \times \left[1 - \left(\frac{1 + g_1}{1 + R}\right)^t\right] + \frac{P_t}{(1 + R)^t} \quad \text{[8.5]}$$

6. The two-stage growth model can be modified to give the price of a stock at Time t:

$$P_t = \frac{D_{t+1}}{R - g_2} = \frac{D_0 \times (1 + g_1)^t \times (1 + g_2)}{R - g_2} \quad \text{[8.6]}$$

7. Required return:

$$R = D_1/P_0 + g \quad \text{[8.7]}$$

8. Stock valuation using benchmark PE evaluation:

Price at Time $t = P_t = $ Benchmark PE ratio $\times EPS_t$ **[8.8]**

CHAPTER 9

1. Net present value (NPV):

NPV = Present value of future cash flows − Investment cost

2. Payback period:

Payback period = Number of years that pass before the sum of an investment's cash flows equals the cost of the investment

3. Discounted payback period:

Discounted payback period = Number of years that pass before the sum of an investment's *discounted* cash flows equals the cost of the investment

4. The average accounting return (AAR):

$$\text{AAR} = \frac{\text{Average net income}}{\text{Average book value}}$$

5. Internal rate of return (IRR):

IRR = Discount rate or required return such that the net present value of an investment is zero

6. Profitability index:

$$\text{Profitability index} = \frac{\text{PV of cash flows}}{\text{Cost of investment}}$$

CHAPTER 10

1. Bottom-up approach to operating cash flow (OCF):

OCF = Net income + Depreciation **[10.1]**

2. Top-down approach to operating cash flow (OCF):

OCF = Sales − Costs − Taxes **[10.2]**

3. Tax shield approach to operating cash flow (OCF):

OCF = (Sales − Costs) $\times (1 - T_c)$ + Depreciation $\times T_c$ **[10.3]**

CHAPTER 11

1. Accounting break-even point:

$$Q = (\text{FC} + D)/(P - v) \quad \text{[11.1]}$$

2. Project operating cash flow (OCF), ignoring taxes:

$$\text{OCF} = (P - v) \times Q - \text{FC} \quad \text{[11.2]}$$

3. Relationship between operating cash flow (OCF) and sales volume, ignoring taxes:

$$Q = (\text{FC} + \text{OCF})/(P - v) \quad \text{[11.3]}$$

4. Cash break-even point:

$$Q = \text{FC}/(P - v)$$

5. Cash break-even point:

$$Q = (\text{FC} + \text{OCF}^*)/(P - v)$$

where
OCF* = Zero NPV cash flow

6. Degree of operating leverage (DOL):

$$\text{DOL} = 1 + \text{FC}/\text{OCF} \quad \text{[11.4]}$$

CHAPTER 12

1. Total dollar return on an investment:

Total dollar return = Dividend income + Capital gain (or loss) **[12.1]**

2. Total cash if stock is sold = Initial investment + Total return **[12.2]**

3. Standard deviation of returns, SD(R) or σ:

$$\text{SD}(R) = \sqrt{\text{Var}(R)}$$

4. Variance of returns, Var(R) or σ^2:

$$\text{Var}(R) = \frac{1}{T-1}[(R_1 - \overline{R})^2 + \cdots + (R_T - \overline{R})^2] \quad \textbf{[12.3]}$$

5. Geometric average return:

$$\text{Geometric average return} = [(1 + R_1) \times$$
$$(1 + R_2) \times \ldots \times$$
$$(1 + R_T)]^{1/T} - 1 \quad \textbf{[12.4]}$$

6. Blume's formula:

$$R(T) = \frac{T-1}{N-1} \times \text{Geometric average} +$$
$$\frac{N-T}{N-1} \times \text{Arithmetic average} \quad \textbf{[12.5]}$$

CHAPTER 13

1. Risk premium:

$$\text{Risk premium} = \text{Expected return} -$$
$$\text{Risk-free rate} \quad \textbf{[13.1]}$$

2. Expected return on a portfolio:

$$E(R_P) = x_1 \times E(R_1) + x_2 \times E(R_2) + \cdots$$
$$+ x_n \times E(R_n) \quad \textbf{[13.2]}$$

3. Risk and return:

$$\text{Total return} = \text{Expected return} +$$
$$\text{Unexpected return} \quad \textbf{[13.3]}$$
$$R = E(R) + U$$

4. Components of an announcement:

$$\text{Announcement} = \text{Expected part} + \text{Surprise} \quad \textbf{[13.4]}$$

5. Systematic and unsystematic components of return:

$$R = E(R) + \text{Systematic portion} +$$
$$\text{Unsystematic portion} \quad \textbf{[13.5]}$$

6. Total risk:

$$\text{Total risk} = \text{Systematic risk} + \text{Unsystematic risk} \quad \textbf{[13.6]}$$

7. The reward-to-risk ratio:

$$\text{Reward-to-risk ratio} = \frac{E(R_i) - R_f}{\beta_i}$$

8. The market risk premium:

$$\text{SML slope} = E(R_M) - R_f$$

9. The capital asset pricing model (CAPM):

$$E(R_i) = R_f + [E(R_M) - R_f] \times \beta_i \quad \textbf{[13.7]}$$

CHAPTER 14

1. Required return on equity, R_E (dividend growth model):

$$R_E = D_1/P_0 + g \quad \textbf{[14.1]}$$

2. Required return on equity, R_E:

$$R_E = R_f + \beta_E \times (R_M - R_f) \quad \textbf{[14.2]}$$

3. The cost of preferred stock, R_P:

$$R_P = D/P_0 \quad \textbf{[14.3]}$$

4. The market value of a firm's debt and equity:

$$V = E + D \quad \textbf{[14.4]}$$

5. The percentages of a firm's capital represented by debt and equity:

$$100\% = E/V + D/V \quad \textbf{[14.5]}$$

6. The weighted average cost of capital (WACC):

$$\text{WACC} = (E/V) \times R_E + (D/V) \times$$
$$R_D \times (1 - T_C) \quad \textbf{[14.6]}$$

7. The weighted average cost of capital (WACC) with preferred stock:

$$\text{WACC} = (E/V) \times R_E + (P/V) \times R_P +$$
$$(D/V) \times R_D \times (1 - T_C) \quad \textbf{[14.7]}$$

8. Calculating a firm's "adjusted" taxes:

$$\text{Taxes}^* = \text{EBIT} \times T_C \quad \textbf{[14.8]}$$

9. Adjusted cash flow from assets (CFA):

$$\text{CFA}^* = \text{EBIT} + \text{Depreciation} - \text{Taxes}^* -$$
$$\text{Change in NWC} - \text{Capital spending}$$
$$= \text{EBIT} + \text{Depreciation} - \text{EBIT} \times T_C -$$
$$\text{Change in NWC} - \text{Capital spending} \quad \textbf{[14.9]}$$

10. Simplified adjusted cash flow from assets (CFA):

$$\text{CFA}^* = \text{EBIT} \times (1 - T_C) + \text{Depreciation} -$$
$$\text{Change in NWC} - \text{Capital spending} \quad \textbf{[14.10]}$$

11. The value of a firm today is:

$$V_0 = \frac{\text{CFA}^*_1}{1 + \text{WACC}} + \frac{\text{CFA}^*_2}{(1 + \text{WACC})^2} +$$
$$\frac{\text{CFA}^*_3}{(1 + \text{WACC})^3} + \cdots + \frac{\text{CFA}^*_t + V_t}{(1 + \text{WACC})^t} \quad \textbf{[14.11]}$$

12. Firm value, using the growing perpetuity formula:

$$V_t = \frac{\text{CFA}^*_{t+1}}{\text{WACC} - g} \quad \textbf{[14.12]}$$

13. Weighted average flotation cost, f_A:

$$f_A = (E/V) \times f_E + (D/V) \times f_D \quad \textbf{[14.13]}$$

CHAPTER 15

1. Rights offerings:

a. Number of new shares:

$$\text{Number of new shares} = \frac{\text{Funds to be raised}}{\text{Subscription price}} \quad \textbf{[15.1]}$$

b. Number of rights needed:

$$\text{Number of rights needed to buy a share of stock} = \frac{\text{Old shares}}{\text{New shares}} \quad \textbf{[15.2]}$$

c. Value of a right:

$$\text{Value of a right} = \text{Rights-on price} -$$
$$\text{Ex-rights price}$$

CHAPTER 16

1. Modigliani-Miller propositions (no taxes):
    a. Proposition I:
$$V_L = V_U$$
    b. Proposition II:
$$R_E = R_A + (R_A - R_D) \times (D/E) \qquad \textbf{[16.1]}$$

2. Modigliani-Miller propositions (with taxes):
    a. Value of the interest tax shield:
Present value of the interest tax shield
$$= T_C \times D \qquad \textbf{[16.2]}$$
    b. Proposition I:
$$V_L = V_U + T_C \times D \qquad \textbf{[16.3]}$$
    c. Proposition II:
$$R_E = R_U + (R_U - R_D) \times (D/E) \times (1 - T_C) \qquad \textbf{[16.4]}$$

CHAPTER 18

1. Basic balance sheet identity:
Net working capital + Fixed assets
$$= \text{Long-term debt} + \text{Equity} \qquad \textbf{[18.1]}$$

2. Net working capital:
Net working capital = (Cash + Other current assets)
$$- \text{Current liabilities} \qquad \textbf{[18.2]}$$

3. Cash identity:
Cash = Long-term debt + Equity +
    Current liabilities −
    Current assets other than cash −
$$\text{Fixed assets} \qquad \textbf{[18.3]}$$

4. The operating cycle:
Operating cycle = Inventory period +
$$\text{Accounts receivable period} \qquad \textbf{[18.4]}$$

5. The cash cycle:
Cash cycle = Operating cycle −
$$\text{Accounts payable period} \qquad \textbf{[18.5]}$$

6. Total cash collections:
Cash collections = Beginning accounts receivable +
$$1/2 \times \text{Sales} \qquad \textbf{[18.6]}$$

CHAPTER 19

1. Float measurement:
    a. Average daily float:
$$\text{Average daily float} = \frac{\text{Total float}}{\text{Total days}} \qquad \textbf{[19.1]}$$
    b. Average daily float:
Average daily float
$$= \text{Average daily receipts} \times \text{Weighted average delay} \qquad \textbf{[19.2]}$$

2. The Baumol-Allais-Tobin (BAT) model:
    a. Opportunity costs:
$$\text{Opportunity costs} = (C/2) \times R \qquad \textbf{[19A.1]}$$
    b. Trading costs:
$$\text{Trading costs} = (T/C) \times F \qquad \textbf{[19A.2]}$$
    c. Total cost:
Total cost = Opportunity costs +
$$\text{Trading costs} \qquad \textbf{[19A.3]}$$
    d. The optimal initial cash balance:
$$C^* = \sqrt{(2T \times F)/R} \qquad \textbf{[19A.4]}$$

3. The Miller-Orr model:
    a. The optimal cash balance:
$$C^* = L + (3/4 \times F \times \sigma^2/R)^{(1/3)} \qquad \textbf{[19A.5]}$$
    b. The upper limit:
$$U^* = 3 \times C^* - 2 \times L \qquad \textbf{[19A.6]}$$
    c. The average cash balance:
$$\text{Average cash balance} = (4 \times C^* - L)/3 \qquad \textbf{[19A.7]}$$

CHAPTER 20

1. The size of receivables:
Accounts receivable = Average daily sales ×
$$\text{ACP} \qquad \textbf{[20.1]}$$

2. NPV of switching credit terms:
    a. Cash flow with old policy $= (P - v)Q$ **[20.2]**
    b. Cash flow with new policy $= (P - v)Q'$ **[20.3]**
    c. Present value of switching:
$$PV = [(P - v)(Q' - Q)]/R \qquad \textbf{[20.4]}$$
    d. Cost of switching:
$$\text{Cost of switching} = PQ + v(Q' - Q) \qquad \textbf{[20.5]}$$
    e. NPV of switching:
NPV of switching $= -[PQ + v(Q' - Q)] +$
$$[(P - v)(Q' - Q)]/R \qquad \textbf{[20.6]}$$
    f. Break-even point of switching:
$$Q' - Q = PQ/[(P - v)/R - v] \qquad \textbf{[20.7]}$$

3. NPV of granting credit:
    a. With no repeat business:
$$\text{NPV} = -v + (1 - \pi)P/(1 + R) \qquad \textbf{[20.8]}$$
    b. With repeat business:
$$\text{NPV} = -v + (1 - \pi)(P - v)/R \qquad \textbf{[20.9]}$$

4. The economic order quantity (EOQ) model:
    a. Total carrying costs:
Total carrying costs
$$= \text{Average inventory} \times \text{Carrying cost per unit}$$
$$= (Q/2) \times \text{CC} \qquad \textbf{[20.10]}$$

b. Total restocking cost:

Total restocking cost
$$= \text{Fixed cost per order}$$
$$\times \text{Number of orders}$$
$$= F \times (T/Q) \qquad [20.11]$$

c. Total costs:

Total costs = Carrying costs
$$+ \text{Restocking costs}$$
$$= (Q/2) \times CC + F \times (T/Q) \qquad [20.12]$$

d. Q^*:

Carrying costs = Restocking costs
$$(Q^*/2) \times CC = F \times (T/Q^*) \qquad [20.13]$$

e. The optimal order size Q^*:
$$Q^* = \sqrt{\frac{2T \times F}{CC}} \qquad [20.14]$$

5. Net incremental cash flow $= P'Q \times (d - \pi)$ [20A.1]

6. $\text{NPV} = -PQ + P'Q \times (d - \pi)/R$ [20A.2]

CHAPTER 21

1. Expected percentage change in the exchange rate:

a. $[E(S_1) - S_0]/S_0 = h_{FC} - h_{US}$ [21.1]

b. $E(S_1) = S_0 \times [1 + (h_{FC} - h_{US})]$ [21.2]

2. Purchasing power parity (PPP):

$E(S_t) = S_0 \times [1 + (h_{FC} - h_{US})]^t$ [21.3]

3. Interest rate parity (IRP) condition:

a. Exact, single period:

$F_1/S_0 = (1 + R_{FC})/(1 + R_{US})$ [21.4]

b. Approximate, single period:

$(F_1 - S_0)/S_0 = R_{FC} - R_{US}$ [21.5]

c. $F_1 = S_0 \times [1 + (R_{FC} - R_{US})]$ [21.6]

4. International Fisher effect (IFE):

$R_{US} - h_{US} = R_{FC} - h_{FC}$ [21.7]

CHAPTER 24

1. Value of a call option at maturity:

a. $C_1 = 0$ if $S_1 - E \leq 0$ [24.1]

b. $C_1 = S_1 - E$ if $S_1 - E > 0$ [24.2]

2. Bounds on the value of a call option:

a. Upper bound:

$C_0 \leq S_0$ [24.3]

b. Lower bound:

$C_0 \geq 0$ if $S_0 - E < 0$ [24.4]

$C_0 \geq S_0 - E$ if $S_0 - E \geq 0$

3. Value of a call option (simple case):

$S_0 = C_0 + E/(1 + R_f)$
$C_0 = S_0 - E/(1 + R_f)$ [24.5]

4. Value of a call that is certain to finish in the money:

Call option value
$$= \text{Stock value}$$
$$- \text{Present value of the exercise price}$$
$$C_0 = S_0 - E/(1 + R_f)^t \qquad [24.6]$$

CHAPTER 25

1. Put-call parity condition (PCP):

a. Share of stock + A put option
$$= \text{Present value of strike price} + \text{A call option} \quad [25.1]$$

b. $S + P = PV(E) + C$ [25.2]

c. Stock price:

$S = PV(E) + C - P$ [25.3]

d. $S + P = E \times e^{-Rt} + C$ [25.4]

2. The Black-Scholes call option formula:

$C = S \times N(d_1) - E \times e^{-Rt} \times N(d_2)$ [25.5]

PCP and the balance sheet identity:

$d_1 = [\ln(S/E) + (R + \sigma^2/2) \times t]/(\sigma \times \sqrt{t})$

$d_2 = d_1 - \sigma \times \sqrt{t}$ [25.6]

3. PCP and the balance sheet identity:

a. Value of risky bond + Put option
$$= \text{Value of risk-free bond} \qquad [25.7]$$

b. Value of risky bond = Value of risk-free bond
$$- \text{Put option}$$
$$= E \times e^{-Rt} - P \qquad [25.8]$$

c. Value of assets (S) = Value of stock (C)
$$+ (E \times e^{-Rt} - P) \qquad [25.9]$$

d. Value of assets (S)
$$= \text{Value of stock } (C)$$
$$+ \text{Value of bonds } (E \times e^{-Rt} - P) \qquad [25.10]$$

CHAPTER 26

4. The NPV of a merger:

$\text{NPV} = V_B^* - \text{Cost to Firm A of}$
$$\text{the acquisition} \qquad [26.1]$$

ANSWERS TO SELECTED END-OF-CHAPTER PROBLEMS

C

CHAPTER 2

2. $255,450
6. Average rate = 32.48%
Marginal rate = 39%
10. −$85,000
14. a. $97,575
   b. $17,800
   c. $13,100
   d. $1,975
18. a. $18,340; $3,009,000
   b. $3,400; $3,400
22. a. 2017: $3,069
      2018: $3,959
   b. $42
   c. Fixed assets sold = $118
      Cash flow from assets = $3,501
   d. Cash flow to creditors = $221
      Debt retired = $337

CHAPTER 3

2. Net income = $835,000
ROA = 6.47%
ROE = 11.60%
6. EPS = $3.74
DPS = $1.29
BVPS = $32.94
Market-to-book ratio = 1.97 times
PE ratio = 17.40 times
P/S ratio = 1.48 times
10. 82.74 days
18. $208.37
22. Firm A: 14.29%
Firm B: 16.36%
26. a. 1.17 times; 1.30 times
   b. .69 times; .79 times
   c. .45 times; .45 times
   d. .81 times
   e. 8.19 times
   f. 18.24 times
   g. .34 times; .36 times
   h. .53 times; .57 times
   i. 1.53 times; 1.57 times
   j. 5.72 times

k. 7.98 times
l. 11.94%
m. 9.66%
n. 15.20%

CHAPTER 4

2. $990
5. $467.04
12. 6.04%
16. 9.89%
19. 1.36 times
21. Sustainable growth rate = 15.46%
New borrowing = $11,904.11
Internal growth rate = 6.17%

CHAPTER 5

2. $8,929.88; $13,734.06; $363,508.30; $487,874.54
6. 9.01%
10. $150,568,214.49
14. −4.46%
18. $400,897.66; $154,563.40

CHAPTER 6

2. @ 5%: $PV_X = \$27,145.49$
       $PV_Y = \$26,409.81$
   @ 15%: $PV_X = \$18,846.75$
        $PV_Y = \$20,448.15$
6. $252,415.91
10. $744,680.85
14. First National EAR = 13.92%
First United EAR = 13.85%
18. $32,529.18
22. APR = 1,733.33%
EAR = 313,916,515.69%
26. $38,126.53
30. 5.64% semiannual
2.78% quarterly
.92% monthly
38. $3,058,897.35
42. $343,996.22
46. Profit = $3,815.99
Break-even rate = 12.14%

50. $84,121.21
54. $1,103.54
58. PV of lease payments = $20,899.86
PV of purchase = $19,601.94
Break-even resale price = $26,446.80
60. 17.51%
64. 3.033 points
70. Value of payments at 65 = $328,996.36
74. $178,442.82; $144,645.85

CHAPTER 7

4. 2.97%
8. 5.75%
12. Approximate real rate = 2.50%
Exact real rate = 2.45%
26. YTM = 4.89%; Current yield = 5.23%
28. a. $298.13
  b. First year = $14.79; Last year = $47.26
  c. $28.07

CHAPTER 8

2. 10.82%
6. $3.72
10. $13,975,043
14. $33.22
18. $68.64
20. $69.69

CHAPTER 9

4. 1.89 years; 2.23 years; 3.40 years
8. $2,816.58; −$4,028.70
12. a. 19.71%; 18.76%
  b. $6,330.67; $8,138.59
  c. 16.48%
16. a. 1.141; 1.267
  b. $8,870.02; $4,146.13
22. a. $C = I/N$
  b. $C > I/\text{PVIFA}_{R\%,N}$
  c. $C = 2.0 * I/\text{PVIFA}_{R\%,N}$

CHAPTER 10

2. $703,400,000
8. $1,348,448
12. $CF_0 = -\$2,570,000$
  $CF_1 = \$1,034,389.60$
  $CF_2 = \$1,124,684.00$
  $CF_3 = \$1,311,176.40$
  NPV = $183,422.80
16. −$122,979.65
22. $.03126

CHAPTER 11

2. Total costs = $10,093,300
Marginal cost = $57.54
Average cost = $69.61
Minimum revenue = $287,700
8. $D = \$311,624$
  $P = \$46.97$
  VC = $74.94
12. OCF = $85,642
  DOL = 3.043
18. DOL = 1.59
  $DOL_A = 2.63$
22. $\Delta NPV/\Delta P = \$175,263.08$
  $\Delta NPV/\Delta Q = \$1,285.26$
30. DOL = 1.20
  $\Delta OCF = +4.00\%$

CHAPTER 12

2. $R_D = 2.23\%$
  $R_C = 9.23\%$
6. $r_G = 2.91\%$
  $r_C = 3.20\%$
16. $R_A = 10.89\%$
  $R_G = 10.62\%$
20. 11.02%; 10.78%; 10.32%

CHAPTER 13

2. 10.04%
6. 10.80%
10. a. 10.51%
  b. $\sigma_P^2 = .01378$
    $\sigma_P = 11.74\%$
14. .88
16. 3.32%
24. $C = \$383,070.87$
  $R_F = \$101,929.13$
26. $\beta_I = 1.74$
  $\sigma_I = 6.78\%$
  $\beta_{II} = .83$
  $\sigma_{II} = 18.08\%$

CHAPTER 14

2. 10.46%
4. $R_A = 11.89\%$
  $R_G = 11.88\%$
8. Book value = $135,000,000
  Market value = $115,150,000
  Aftertax cost = 4.04%
12. a. $E/V = .3373$
    $D/V = .6627$
  b. $E/V = .8108$
    $D/V = .1892$

16. a. $D/V = .2684$
$P/V = .0461$
$E/V = .6854$
  b. 8.52%
20. $25,626,741

CHAPTER 15

2. a. $53; anything greater than $0
  b. 744,681; 5.24
  c. $52.04; $.96
6. 3,133,641
12. $22.05
14. $29,904.31

CHAPTER 16

2. a. $1.53; $2.55; $3.31
  b. $1.74; $3.31; $4.49
6. a. $5.36; $5.54; $5.27
  b. $71,250; $71,250
  c. $71,250
  d. $3.22; $3.32; $3.16
  e. $71,250; $71,250; $71,250
10. $1,369,200
12. a. 14.53%
  b. 10.30%
  c. 17.07%; 13.69%; 10.30%
16. $389,412.50

CHAPTER 17

2. a. 5,000 new shares
  b. 12,500 new shares
4. a. $40.80
  b. $59.13
  c. $47.72
  d. $119.00
  e. 883,333; 609,500; 755,250; 302,857
8. Shares outstanding = 281,750
Capital surplus = $2,529,000
10. $P_0 = 45.84
$D = 28.20

CHAPTER 18

2. Cash = $1,385
Current assets = $6,160
4. a. *I,I*
  b. *I,N*
  c. *D,D*
  d. *D,D*
  e. *D,N*
  f. *I,I*

8. a. $264.00; $252.00; $279.00; $279.45
  b. $243.00; $264.00; $252.00; $279.00
  c. $250.00; $260.00; $261.00; $279.15
14. a. 3.03%
  b. 6.87%
  c. 6.77%
18. 9.51%

CHAPTER 19

2. a. $68,000
    $-$44,000
    $24,000
  b. $68,000
    $-$22,000
    $46,000
6. a. $26,712
  b. 2.53 days
  c. $26,712
  d. $4.95
  e. $10,865
10. NPV = $4,450,000
Net savings = $111,250

APPENDIX 19A

A.2 $3,366.50
A.4 a. Opportunity cost = $30
    Trading cost = $350
  b. $5,123.48
A.10 2.38%

CHAPTER 20

2. $2,608,219.18
6. Sales = $625,907.41
Accounts receivable turnover = 13.5185 times
10. NPV = $160,207.89
12. Carrying cost = $7,650
Order cost = $6,760
EOQ = 423.01
Orders = 55.32 per year
16. Net savings = $1,631.25

APPENDIX 20A

A.2 a. 1/20, net 30
  b. $240,000
  d. NPV = $-$2,477,600
    Break-even price = $108.42
    Break-even discount = 8.68%
A.4 b. $70.45
  c. NPV = $151,131.30

CHAPTER 21

6. Great Britain: 1.45%
Japan: 1.19%
Switzerland: 1.14%
10. b. Krone 8.4693
12. b. U.S. 1.64% greater

CHAPTER 23

2. Price = $17.81: Loss = $1,725
Price = $17.64: Gain = $2,525

CHAPTER 24

4. a. $7.69
  b. $4.85
8. a. $E_0 = \$117.04$
    $D_0 = \$922.96$
  b. $E_0 = \$190.78$
14. a. $273,927.58
   b. Abandon if $Q < 4{,}332$
20. a. $4,274,450.63
   b. $3,819,874.85

CHAPTER 25

2. $6,791.91
6. 2.29%

10. $263,144.11
14. $5.48
16. Equity = $3,245.62
   Debt = $12,954.38
22. a. $45,804.73
   b. $9,044.63
   c. $36,760.10; 11.40%
   d. $33,098.68; 13.50%
   e. Bondholders lose $3,661.42
      Stockholders gain $3,661.42

CHAPTER 26

7. a. EPS = $5.40
    PE = 11.11
9. .4215
13. a. £25.89
   b. .8045

CHAPTER 27

2. −$36,887.87
6. −$3,078.69

USING THE HP 10B AND TI BA II PLUS FINANCIAL CALCULATORS

This appendix is intended to help you use your Hewlett-Packard HP 10B or Texas Instruments TI BA II Plus financial calculator to solve problems encountered in an introductory finance course. It describes the various calculator settings and provides keystroke solutions for nine selected problems from this book. Please see your owner's manual for more complete instructions. For more examples and problem-solving techniques, please see *Financial Analysis with an Electronic Calculator,* 7th edition, by Mark A. White (New York: McGraw-Hill, 2007).

CALCULATOR SETTINGS

Most calculator errors in introductory finance courses are the result of inappropriate settings. Before beginning a calculation, you should ask yourself the following questions:

1. Did I clear the financial registers?
2. Is the compounding frequency set to once per period?
3. Is the calculator in END mode?
4. Did I enter negative numbers using the +/- key?

Clearing the Registers

All calculators have areas of memory, called registers, where variables and intermediate results are stored. There are two sets of financial registers, the time value of money (TVM) registers and the cash flow (CF) registers. These must be cleared before beginning a new calculation. On the Hewlett-Packard HP 10B, pressing ▓ {CLEAR ALL} clears both the TVM and the CF registers.[1] To clear the TVM registers on the TI BA II Plus, press **2nd** {CLR TVM}. Press **2nd** {CLR Work} from within the cash flow worksheet to clear the CF registers.

Compounding Frequency

Both the HP 10B and the TI BA II Plus are hardwired to assume monthly compounding, that is, compounding 12 times per period. Because very few problems in introductory finance courses make this assumption, you should change this default setting to once per period. On the HP 10B, press 1 ▓ {P/YR}. To verify that the default has been changed, press the ▓ key, then press and briefly hold the **INPUT** key.[2] The display should read "1P_Yr".

On the TI BA II Plus, you can specify both payment frequency and compounding frequency, although they should normally be set to the same number. To set both to once per period, press the key sequence **2nd** {P/Y} 1 **ENTER**, then press ↓ 1 **ENTER**. Pressing **2nd** {QUIT} returns you to standard calculator mode.

END Mode and Annuities Due

In most problems, payment is made at the end of a period, and this is the default setting (end mode) for both the HP 10B and the TI BA II Plus. *Annuities due* assume payments are made at the *beginning* of each period (begin mode). On the HP 10B, pressing ▓ {BEG/END} toggles between begin and end mode. Press the key sequence **2nd** {BGN} **2nd** [SET] **2nd** {QUIT} to accomplish the same task on the TI BA II Plus. Both calculators will indicate on the display that your calculator is set for begin mode.

---

[1] The ▓ key is colored orange and serves as a Shift key for the functions in curly brackets.

[2] This is the same keystroke used to clear all registers; pretty handy, eh?

Sign Changes

Sign changes are used to identify the direction of cash inflows and outflows. Generally, cash inflows are entered as positive numbers and cash outflows are entered as negative numbers. To enter a negative number on either the HP 10B or the TI BA II Plus, first press the appropriate digit keys and then press the change sign key, +/– . Do *not* use the minus sign key, – , as its effects are quite unpredictable.

SAMPLE PROBLEMS

This section provides keystroke solutions for selected problems from the text illustrating the nine basic financial calculator skills.

1. Future Value or Present Value of a Single Sum

Compute the future value of $2,250 at a 17 percent annual rate for 30 years.

HP 10B	TI BA II PLUS
-2,250.00 **PV**	-2,250.00 **PV**
30.00 **N**	30.00 **N**
17.00 **I/YR**	17.00 **I/Y**
FV 249,895.46	**CPT FV** 249,895.46

The future value is $249,895.46.

2. Present Value or Future Value of an Ordinary Annuity

Betty's Bank offers you a $20,000, seven-year term loan at 11 percent annual interest. What will your annual loan payment be?

HP 10B	TI BA II PLUS
-20,000.00 **PV**	-20,000.00 **PV**
7.00 **N**	7.00 **N**
11.00 **I/YR**	11.00 **I/Y**
PMT 4,244.31	**CPT PMT** 4,244.31

Your annual loan payment will be $4,244.31.

3. Finding an Unknown Interest Rate

Assume that the total cost of a college education will be $75,000 when your child enters college in 18 years. You presently have $7,000 to invest. What rate of interest must you earn on your investment to cover the cost of your child's college education?

HP 10B	TI BA II PLUS
-7,000.00 **PV**	-7,000.00 **PV**
18.00 **N**	18.00 **N**
75,000.00 **FV**	75,000.00 **FV**
I/YR 14.08	**CPT I/Y** 14.08

You must earn an annual interest rate of at least 14.08 percent to cover the expected future cost of your child's education.

4. Finding an Unknown Number of Periods

One of your customers is delinquent on his accounts payable balance. You've mutually agreed to a repayment schedule of $374 per month. You will charge 1.4 percent per month interest on the overdue balance. If the current balance is $12,000, how long will it take for the account to be paid off?

HP 10B	TI BA II PLUS
-12,000.00 **PV**	-12,000.00 **PV**
1.40 **I/YR**	1.40 **I/Y**
374.00 **PMT**	374.00 **PMT**
N 42.90	**CPT N** 42.90

The loan will be paid off in 42.90 months.

5. Simple Bond Pricing

Mullineaux Co. issued 11-year bonds one year ago at a coupon rate of 8.25 percent. The bonds make semiannual payments. If the YTM on these bonds is 7.10 percent, what is the current bond price?

HP 10B	TI BA II PLUS
41.25 **PMT**	41.25 **PMT**
1,000.00 **FV**	1,000.00 **FV**
20.00 **N**	20.00 **N**
3.55 **I/YR**	3.55 **I/Y**
PV -1,081.35	**CPT PV** -1,081.35

Because the bonds make semiannual payments, we must halve the coupon payment (8.25 ÷ 2 = 4.125 ==>

$41.25), halve the YTM (7.10 ÷ 2 ==> 3.55), and double the number of periods (10 years remaining × 2 = 20 periods). Then, the current bond price is $1,081.35.

6. Simple Bond Yields to Maturity

Vasicek Co. has 12.5 percent coupon bonds on the market with eight years left to maturity. The bonds make annual payments. If one of these bonds currently sells for $1,145.68, what is its YTM?

HP 10B		TI BA II PLUS	
-1,145.68 **PV**		-1,145.68 **PV**	
125.00 **PMT**		125.00 **PMT**	
1,000.00 **FV**		1,000.00 **FV**	
8.00 **N**		8.00 **N**	
I/YR 9.79		**CPT** **I/Y** 9.79	

The bond has a yield to maturity of 9.79 percent.

7. Cash Flow Analysis

What are the IRR and NPV of the following set of cash flows? Assume a discount rate of 10 percent.

YEAR	CASH FLOW
0	−$1,300
1	400
2	300
3	1,200

HP 10B		TI BA II PLUS		
-1,300.00 **CFj**		**CF**		
400.00 **CFj**		**2nd** {CLR Work}		
1.00 ▦ {Nj}		-1,300.00 **ENTER**	↓	
300.00 **CFj**		400.00 **ENTER**	↓	
1.00 ▦ {Nj}		1.00 **ENTER**	↓	
1,200.00 **CFj**		300.00 **ENTER**	↓	
1.00 ▦ {Nj}		1.00 **ENTER**	↓	
▦ {IRR/YR} 17.40		1,200.00 **ENTER**	↓	
10.00 **I/YR**		1.00 **ENTER**	↓	
▦ {NPV} 213.15		**IRR** **CPT** 17.40		
		NPV		
		10.00 **ENTER**		
		↓ **CPT** 213.15		

The project has an IRR of 17.40 percent and an NPV of $213.15.

8. Loan Amortization

Prepare an amortization schedule for a three-year loan of $24,000. The interest rate is 16 percent per year, and the loan calls for equal annual payments. How much interest is paid in the third year? How much total interest is paid over the life of the loan?

To prepare a complete amortization schedule, you must amortize each payment one at a time:

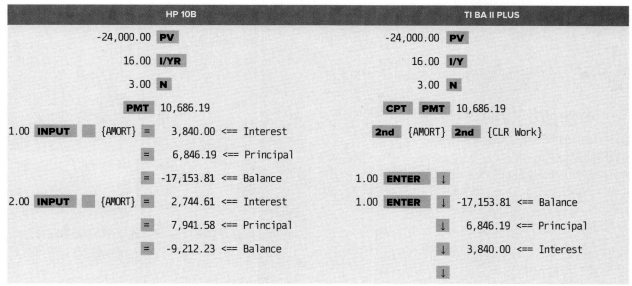

HP 10B		TI BA II PLUS	
-24,000.00 **PV**		-24,000.00 **PV**	
16.00 **I/YR**		16.00 **I/Y**	
3.00 **N**		3.00 **N**	
PMT 10,686.19		**CPT** **PMT** 10,686.19	
1.00 **INPUT** ▦ {AMORT} = 3,840.00 <== Interest		**2nd** {AMORT} **2nd** {CLR Work}	
= 6,846.19 <== Principal			
= -17,153.81 <== Balance		1.00 **ENTER** ↓	
2.00 **INPUT** ▦ {AMORT} = 2,744.61 <== Interest		1.00 **ENTER** ↓ -17,153.81 <== Balance	
= 7,941.58 <== Principal		↓ 6,846.19 <== Principal	
= -9,212.23 <== Balance		↓ 3,840.00 <== Interest	
		↓	

(Continued)

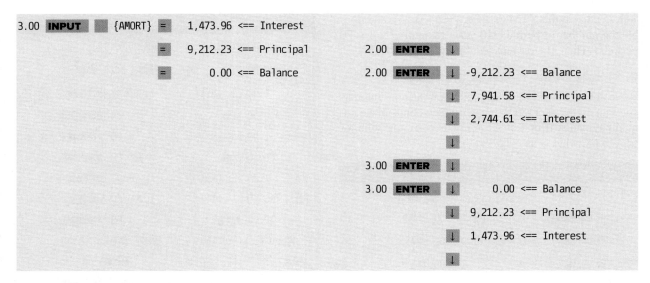

Interest of $1,473.96 is paid in the third year.

Enter both a beginning and an ending period to compute the total amount of interest or principal paid over a particular period of time.

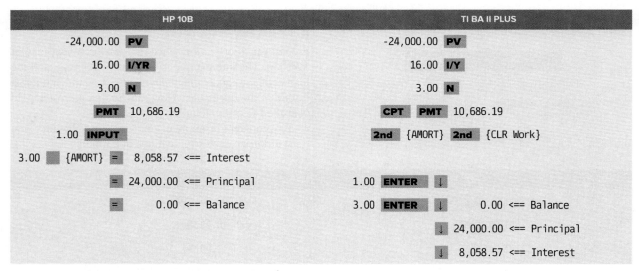

Total interest of $8,058.57 is paid over the life of the loan.

9. Interest Rate Conversions

Find the effective annual rate (EAR) corresponding to a 7 percent annual percentage rate (APR) compounded quarterly.

HP 10B		TI BA II PLUS	
4.00	{P/YR}	**2nd** {IConv}	
7.00	{NOM%}		7.00 **ENTER**
{EFF%} 7.19		↓ ↓	
			4.00 **ENTER**
		↑ **CPT** 7.19	

The effective annual rate equals 7.19 percent.

Name Index

Formulas Index

Subject Index